A STUDY OF HISTORY

A STUDY OF HISTORY

BY

ARNOLD J. TOYNBEE

HON. D.LITT. OXON. AND BIRMINGHAM
HON. LL.D. PRINCETON, F.B.A.

Director of Studies in the Royal Institute of International Affairs
Research Professor of International History in the University of London
(both on the Sir Daniel Stevenson Foundation)

'Except the Lord build the house,
their labour is but lost that build it.
'Except the Lord keep the city,
the watchman waketh but in vain.'

Ps. cxxvii. 1–2

VOLUME IV

Issued under the auspices of the Royal Institute of International Affairs

OXFORD UNIVERSITY PRESS
LONDON NEW YORK TORONTO

Oxford University Press, Amen House, London E.C. 4

EDINBURGH GLASGOW NEW YORK TORONTO MELBOURNE
WELLINGTON BOMBAY CALCUTTA MADRAS CAPE TOWN

Geoffrey Cumberlege, Publisher to the University

FIRST EDITION 1939
SECOND IMPRESSION 1940
THIRD IMPRESSION 1946
FOURTH IMPRESSION 1948

PRINTED IN GREAT BRITAIN
BY JARROLD AND SONS, LTD., THE EMPIRE PRESS
NORWICH

THE PLAN OF THE BOOK

PREFACE

THESE three volumes contain Parts IV and V of the thirteen parts which are set out in the plan of the book on p. v above. The writer hopes to publish the remaining eight parts in one more batch of volumes, as he believes that the five parts contained in the first six volumes will prove to amount, in aggregate length, to rather more than two-thirds of the whole work. Part V, as now published, includes much that, in the first sketch, was left over for treatment in Parts VI–VIII; on the other hand, nothing of what was originally intended to be treated in the first five parts has been omitted from the final version of these.

The index to the volumes now published, like the index to the preceding volumes, has been made by the writer's friend and colleague and co-author of the *Annual Survey of International Affairs*, Miss V. M. Boulter. While the writer cannot let pass this opportunity of expressing his now double gratitude to her on this head, it seems hardly necessary this time to draw attention to the excellence of her contribution, or to its indispensability to the reader, because every reader of volumes i–iii will have found out these facts for himself, and will know, in advance, on learning that the index to vols. iv–vi comes from the same expert hand, that, once again, he will have the same admirable guidance in finding his way through the labyrinth of the text. The writer need only point out that the greater length of the present batch of volumes has made the indexer's task even more difficult—and unfortunately also even more laborious—this time than it was before. Gratitude to colleagues and affection for friends are feelings that mount up with the years; and a lustrum which in retrospect seems as long as a lifetime has now passed since the previous index was compiled.

During the same five years Miss Reddin has typed, with the same patience and accuracy as always, many thousands more sheets of complicated manuscript, not only for the present volumes of this work, but also for the heavily laden current volumes of the *Survey of International Affairs*; and, in again having her aid throughout, both the writer and the printer have been as fortunate as before.

The writer also wishes to thank another colleague, Miss P. F. Beard, for her resourcefulness and good nature in helping him, when the present volumes were being sent to press, to settle a number of outstanding queries.

He is also again deeply indebted to other friends of his who have found time—or made time—to read parts of these volumes in the typescript. And again these kind critics, through the trouble that they have taken for the writer's benefit, have put it in his power to diminish a number of weaknesses in his original draft—though this, of course, without any one beyond the writer himself being in any way responsible for the final result. For this invaluable help the writer wishes to express his most sincere gratitude to Professor Gilbert Murray, Mr. and Mrs. J. L. Hammond, the Librarian of Ampleforth Abbey, Lord Samuel, Professor N. H. Baynes, Dr. W. W. Tarn, Father H. Thurston, S.J., Mr. Geoffrey Barraclough, Mr. G. M. Gathorne-Hardy, Mr. R. N. Carew Hunt, Dr. Edwyn Bevan, Professor A. L. Sadler, Sir George Sansom, Mr. M. P. Charlesworth, Dr. Martin Braun, the writer's sister, Miss J. M. C. Toynbee, and other scholars to whom acknowledgements are made in footnotes to the text.

In addition to these debts to individual scholars the writer is also once again indebted to several learned institutions. The Council of the Royal Institute of International Affairs have continued to make, out of a grant which they have been receiving from the Rockefeller Foundation for research in the field of international studies, an allocation for the purpose of releasing the writer's time and energy for writing the present work, and for the same purpose the trustees of the Leverhulme Fellowship Fund have given him aid for which he takes this opportunity to express in public a gratitude of which the trustees themselves are, he feels sure, long since aware. As for his indebtedness to Chatham House—on the staff of which he has by now had the honour and happiness of serving for more than fifteen years—this would not be fully accounted for even in a complete catalogue of all the acts of help and kindness that have been done him, during these years, by the Council and his colleagues. He also owes more than he can tell, or can repay, to the spirit of Chatham House itself; for he knows that —while he owes his interest in history to his Mother, who died while the present volumes were in the press—he could never have produced this book without also having received a stimulus that is by now perhaps familiar to all scholars who have done any work under the auspices of this great institution.

Though the original sketch of Parts IV and V was worked out, like that of all the parts that precede and follow, in the summers of 1927 and 1928, the actual writing of Part IV was not begun before the summer of 1933, and the last proofs were sent to press, at a moment of public anxiety and private grief, in March 1939. It will be seen from the dates that the contemporary atmosphere in which the present three volumes were produced was painfully appropriate to the themes of 'breakdown' and 'disintegration' which these volumes have for their subjects. There were moments when it almost seemed like tempting Fate and wasting effort to go on writing a book that must be the work of many years, when a catastrophe might overtake the writer's world within the next few weeks or days. At such moments the writer has often fortified his will by calling to mind the dates of writing of another book with which this book is comparable only on the single point of length. Saint Augustine did not begin writing *De Civitate Dei* before the sack of Rome by Alaric in A.D. 410; yet he finished the work within the next twenty years, and, although, at the moment of his death in A.D. 430 in his episcopal see of Hippo, a Vandal war-band was beleaguering the city-walls, the book survived to inform the minds and inspire the souls of Christians from that day to this, in times and places that were far beyond the fifth-century African Father's mundane horizon. Of course the author of this tale of two cities had a supra-mundane range of vision in comparison with which no appreciable difference is made by a few thousand terrestrial miles or years more or less; and a glimpse of this vision is the boon for which the present writer is the most deeply grateful to the writer of *De Civitate Dei*.

ARNOLD J. TOYNBEE

LONDON
31st *March*, 1939

CONTENTS OF VOLUMES IV–VI

VOLUME IV

IV. THE BREAKDOWNS OF CIVILIZATIONS

VOLUME V

V. THE DISINTEGRATIONS OF CIVILIZATIONS

VOLUME VI

V. THE DISINTEGRATIONS OF CIVILIZATIONS (*cont.*)

IV

THE BREAKDOWNS OF CIVILIZATIONS

A. THE PROBLEM OF THE BREAKDOWNS OF CIVILIZATIONS

THE problem of the breakdowns of civilizations is more obvious than the problem of their growths. Indeed, it is almost as obvious as the problem of their geneses. The geneses of civilizations call for explanation in view of the mere fact that this species of societies has come into existence and that we are able to enumerate twenty-six representatives of the species (counting in the five arrested civilizations)[1] that have come to birth up to date, as against four civilizations that have been abortive.[2] We may now go on to observe that while only four civilizations, to our knowledge, have miscarried, as against twenty-six that have been born alive, no less than sixteen out of these twenty-six are by now dead and buried.

These sixteen dead civilizations include all the six representatives of the 'unrelated' class:[3] the Egyptiac, the Andean, the Sinic, the Minoan, the Sumeric, and the Mayan civilizations. Of the fifteen 'related' civilizations, six—namely the Indic, the Hittite, the Syriac, the Hellenic, the Babylonic, and the Mexic—are now dead likewise; and two more of them—the Arabic and the Yucatec—have been swallowed alive by sister civilizations: the Arabic by the Iranic Civilization,[4] and the Yucatec by the Mexic.[5] Of the five arrested civilizations, two—the Spartan and the Ottoman—are also now extinct. We are thus left with no more than ten civilizations out of twenty-six (including three arrested civilizations out of five) that are actually alive to-day. These ten are our own Western Society, the main body of Orthodox Christendom in the Near East, the offshoot of Orthodox Christendom in Russia, the Islamic Society, the Hindu Society, the main body of the Far Eastern Society in China, and the offshoot of the Far Eastern Society in Japan, together with the three arrested civilizations of the Poly-

[1] For the arrested Polynesian, Eskimo, Nomadic, Ottoman, and Spartan civilizations see Part III. A, in vol. iii, above.

[2] For the abortive Far Western Christian, Scandinavian, Far Eastern Christian, and Syriac civilizations see II. D (vii), vol. ii, pp. 322–91, above.

[3] For the distinction between 'related' and 'unrelated' civilizations see I. C (ii), vol. i, pp. 129–30, above. In the same chapter there is a catalogue of the civilizations of both classes that have been identified by an empirical inquiry in I. C (i) (*b*), vol. i, pp. 63–129, above.

[4] See I. C (i) (*b*), vol. i, pp. 70–2, with I. C (i) (*b*), Annex I, above.

[5] See I. C (i) (*b*), vol. i, pp. 123–4, above.

nesians and the Esquimaux and the Nomads. If we look more closely at these ten survivors, we observe that the Polynesian and the Nomadic civilizations are now in their last agonies, and that seven out of the eight others are all, in different degrees, under threat of either annihilation or assimilation by our own Civilization of the West. Moreover, no less than six out of these seven civilizations whose existence is now threatened (that is, all except the Eskimo Civilization, whose growth was arrested in infancy), bear marks of having already broken down and gone into disintegration.

One of the most conspicuous of the marks of disintegration, which we have already noticed in this Study at an earlier point,[1] is a phenomenon of the last stage but one in a decline and fall, when a disintegrating civilization purchases a reprieve by submitting to a forcible political unification within the framework of a 'universal state'. For a Western student of history the classical example of a universal state in this special sense of the term is the Roman Empire, into which the Hellenic Society was forcibly gathered up in the penultimate chapter of its history, immediately before the interregnum in which the Hellenic Society passed out of existence and our own Western Society came to birth. With this clue in our hands, we have succeeded, at the outset of this Study, in identifying a number of other now extinct civilizations by working backwards from their respective universal states, whose memories still stand out as conspicuous features in our mental landscape of the Past.[2] We did not employ the same clue for dealing with any of the living civilizations, because we were able to identify these at once by a direct observation of their existence in the world of to-day. We have noticed incidentally, however, that one of these still living civilizations, namely the main body of Orthodox Christendom, has already been through a universal state in the shape of the Ottoman Empire.[3] We have also noticed that the offshoot of Orthodox Christendom in Russia entered into a universal state towards the turn of the fifteenth and sixteenth centuries of the Christian Era after the political unification, in A.D. 1478, of Muscovy and Novgorod, which were the two principal parochial states in the Russian Orthodox Christian World of the time.[4] We may now observe that at least three more of the civilizations in question have had their universal states likewise: the Hindu Civilization in the shape of the Timurid Mughal Empire and its successor the British Rāj; the

[1] See I. C (i) (*a*), vol. i, pp. 52–5, above.
[2] See I. C (i) (*b*), *passim*, in vol. i, pp. 63–129, above.
[3] See Part III. A, vol. iii, pp. 26–7, above.
[4] See I. C (i) (*b*), Annex I, vol. i, p. 374; II. D (v), vol. ii, p. 175; and III. C (i) (*a*), vol. iii, p. 145, above.

main body of the Far Eastern Civilization in the shape of the Mongol Empire and in the resuscitation of the Mongol Empire—in a less colossal but also less ephemeral form—at the hands of the Manchus; and the Japanese offshoot of the Far Eastern Civilization in the shape of the Tokugawa Shogunate. And when we pass to the Islamic Civilization, we may perhaps discern at least an 'ideological' premonition of a universal state, here too, in the shape of the Pan-Islamic Movement.

If we accept this phenomenon of a universal state as a token of decline, we shall conclude that all the six non-Western civilizations that are alive to-day (leaving the arrested civilization of the Esquimaux out of account) had broken down internally before they were broken in upon by the impact of our Western Civilization from outside. At a later stage of this Study,[1] when we come to investigate the contacts of civilizations with one another, we shall find reason for believing that we have stumbled here upon an example of a general 'law'; and that, whenever we see one civilization intruding upon another successfully, we may infer that the civilization which is suffering the intrusion has already broken down and is no longer in its growth. For our present purpose we have merely to take note of the fact that, among the civilizations which are alive at the present day, every one, apparently, has already broken down and is now in process of disintegration, with the possible exception of our own.

And what of our Western Civilization? In contrast to all its living contemporaries, the Western Civilization has manifestly not yet reached its universal state; and, to outward appearance at least, it is not yet within sight of that historical landmark. The paroxysm of Nationalism by which the Western World was being racked in the year 1938 rather suggested—unless, perhaps, this frenzy was a last desperate bout of kicking against the pricks—that the political unification of our Western World might have to be bought at a heavy price, and that our parochial national states might have to pass through further bouts of internecine fratricidal warfare before they would either bring themselves to enter into an effective social contract or else submit to the terrible alternative of being unified by force.[2] Yet a universal state is not the first stage in the disintegration of a civilization, any more than it is the last. While it is followed by an interregnum, a universal state is preceded, as we have seen,[3] by a 'Time of Troubles' that seems usually to occupy several centuries; and if we in our generation were to permit ourselves to judge by the purely subjective criterion of our own feeling

[1] In Part IX below. [2] See V. C (ii) (*b*), vol. vi, pp. 318–21, below.
[3] In I. C (i) (*a*), vol. i, p. 53, above.

about our own age, the best judges among us would probably declare unanimously that our 'Time of Troubles' has undoubtedly descended upon us in our Western World of to-day—*tanta stat praedita culpa.*[1]

Nor would this subjective judgement be entirely without the support of objective evidence. For, on an empirical test, we have found strong grounds for believing that one of the symptoms of social disintegration is a geographical expansion on the grand scale;[2] and we have already asked ourselves, in this connexion, whether the latter-day expansion of our own Western Civilization over the face of the Earth may not be, perhaps, an intimation of mortality. In our generation, no doubt, we must be content to leave this question unanswered.[3] Yet, if there is happily still no proof that our Western Civilization has already broken down and gone into decline, we are equally without assurance that our year is still in the spring.

Meanwhile, we children of the West are in the posture of the Ancient Mariner after Life-in-Death had won him for her own while Death had gained dominion over his shipmates.

> The many men, so beautiful!
> And they all dead did lie:
> And a thousand thousand slimy things
> Lived on; and so did I.

As we cast our eyes around a world in which the majority of the civilizations known to us are already dead, while the rest of the survivors are all either in decline or *in extremis*, and as we remind ourselves that we have not any means of divining what our own society's expectation of life may be, we may be inclined to read into the panorama of history the same grim *motif* that the poet divined in the stones of Westminster Abbey.

> Mortality, behold and fear!
> What a change of flesh is here!

In truth, the problem of the breakdowns of civilizations stares us in the face.

> Haud igitur leti praeclusa est ianua caelo
> nec soli terraeque neque altis aequoris undis,
> sed patet immane et vasto respectat hiatu.[4]

1 Lucretius: *De Rerum Natura*, Book V, l. 199.

2 See III. C (i) (*a*), vol. iii, pp. 139–54, above.

3 See I. B (iv), vol. i, pp. 36–7, above, and V. C (ii) (*b*), vol. vi, pp. 313–4, below.

4 Lucretius: *De Rerum Natura*, Book V, ll. 373–5. (The passage has been quoted already in vol. ii, p. 9, and in vol. iii, p. 374, above.)

B. THE NATURE OF THE BREAKDOWNS OF CIVILIZATIONS

HAVING recognized that the breakdowns of civilizations present a problem, and having set ourselves to search for a solution, we shall be wise to make certain that we are agreed upon the nature of the phenomenon with which we are concerned, before we attempt to investigate its cause.

As it happens, we have defined the nature of the breakdowns of civilizations already. These breakdowns are failures in an audacious attempt to ascend from the level of a Primitive Humanity, living the life of a social animal, to the height of some superhuman kind of being in a Communion of Saints; and we have described the casualties of this great enterprise in various similes. We have compared them to the drivers of motor-cars whose cars backslide before they have succeeded in passing out through the exit from a one-way street;[1] and we have compared them to climbers who fall to their death, or to an ignominious state of life-in-death, upon the ledge from which they have last started, before they succeed in completing the 'pitch' and reaching a new resting-place on the ledge above.[2]

We have also described the nature of these breakdowns in non-material terms as a loss of creative power in the souls of the creative individuals, or the creative minorities, who have been the leaders of any given civilization at any given stage in the history of its growth;[3] and we have seen that this failure of vitality on the leaders' side divests them of their magic power to influence and attract the uncreative masses. Where there is no creation, there is also no mimesis. The piper who has lost his cunning can no longer conjure the feet of the multitude into a dance; and if, in rage and panic, he now attempts to turn himself into a drill-sergeant or a slave-driver, and to coerce by physical force a people whom he feels that he can no longer lead by his old magnetic charm, then, all the more surely and more swiftly, he defeats his own intention; for the followers who had merely flagged and fallen behind as the heavenly music died away will be stung by a touch of the whip into active rebellion.

We have seen, in fact,[4] that when, in the history of any society, a Creative Minority degenerates into a mere Dominant Minority which

[1] See I. C (iii) (*d*), vol. i, pp. 176–7, above.
[2] See Part II. B, vol. i, pp. 192–5, above.
[3] See I. C (i) (*a*), vol. i, pp. 53–7, and Part II. A, vol. i, pp. 187–8, above.
[4] Ibid. See further IV. C (iii) (*a*), in the present volume, pp. 119–33, and V. C (i) (*a*)–(*c*), *passim*, in vol. v, pp. 35–337, below.

attempts to retain by force a position which it has ceased to merit, this fatal change in the character of the ruling element provokes, on the other side, the secession of a Proletariat which no longer spontaneously admires, or freely imitates, the ruling element, and which revolts against being reduced to the status of an unwilling 'under-dog'. We have also seen that this Proletariat, when it asserts itself, is divided from the outset into two distinct parts. There is an 'Internal Proletariat', prostrate yet recalcitrant, under the Dominant Minority's heel within the disintegrating society's borders, and an 'External Proletariat' of barbarians beyond the pale who now violently resist incorporation. And thus the breakdown of a civilization gives rise to a class-war within the body social of a society which was neither divided against itself by hard-and-fast divisions nor sundered from its neighbours by unbridgeable gulfs so long as it was in growth.

On this showing, the nature of the breakdowns of civilizations can be summed up in three points: a failure of creative power in the minority, an answering withdrawal of mimesis on the part of the majority, and a consequent loss of social unity in the society as a whole. With this picture of the nature of these breakdowns in our minds, we may now proceed to inquire into their cause.

C. THE CAUSE OF THE BREAKDOWNS OF CIVILIZATIONS

I. SAEVA NECESSITAS?

ONE of the perennial infirmities of human beings is to ascribe their own failure to the operation of forces which are entirely beyond their control and immeasurably wider in range than the compass of human action. This mental manœuvre, which promises to convert an importunate sense of humiliation into a new assurance of self-importance—by setting the great engine of the Universe in motion in order to break one human career—is among the most insidious of 'the Consolations of Philosophy'. It is particularly attractive to sensitive minds in periods of decline and fall; and in the decline and fall of the Hellenic Civilization it was a commonplace of different schools of philosophers to explain the social decay which they deplored but could not arrest as the incidental and inevitable effect of an all-pervasive onset of 'cosmic senescence'.

This was the philosophy of an Epicurean poet in the last generation of the Hellenic 'Time of Troubles' before the Hellenic Society obtained the temporary reprieve of the *Pax Augusta*:

> Sic igitur magni quoque circum moenia mundi
> expugnata dabunt labem putrisque ruinas.
> iamque adeo fracta est aetas, effetaque tellus
> vix animalia parva creat quae cuncta creavit
> saecla deditque ferarum ingentia corpora partu.
> haud, ut opinor, enim mortalia saecla superne
> aurea de caelo demisit funis in arva
> nec mare nec fluctus plangentes saxa crearunt,
> sed genuit tellus eadem quae nunc alit ex se.
> praeterea nitidas fruges vinetaque laeta
> sponte sua primum mortalibus ipsa creavit,
> ipsa dedit dulces fetus et pabula laeta;
> quae nunc vix nostro grandescunt aucta labore,
> conterimusque boves et vires agricolarum,
> conficimus ferrum vix arvis suppeditati:
> usque adeo parcunt fetus augentque laborem.
> iamque caput quassans grandis suspirat arator
> crebrius, incassum manuum cecidisse labores,
> et cum tempora temporibus praesentia confert
> praeteritis, laudat fortunas saepe parentis
> et crepat, antiquum genus ut pietate repletum
> perfacile angustis tolerarit finibus aevum,
> cum minor esset agri multo modus ante viritim.

tristis: item vetulae vitis sator atque vietae
temporis incusat momen caelumque fatigat
nec tenet omnia paulatim tabescere et ire
ad capulum spatio aetatis defessa vetusto.[1]

The theme recurs in a work of controversy which was written by one of the Fathers of the Western Christian Church some three hundred years later, under the impression of the stricken Hellenic Society's next relapse into a time of tribulation which had found Thascius Cyprianus a pagan scholar and which saw him become a Christian martyr before the crisis passed:[2]

'You ought to be aware that the age is now senile (*senuisse iam saeculum*). It has not now the stamina that used to make it upstanding, nor the vigour and robustness that used to make it strong. This truth is proclaimed, even if we keep silence . . . , by the World itself, which testifies to its own decline by giving manifold concrete evidences of the process of decay. There is a diminution in the winter rains that give nourishment to the seeds in the earth, and in the summer heats that ripen the harvests. The springs have less freshness and the autumns less fecundity. The mountains, disembowelled and worn out, yield a lower output of marble; the mines, exhausted, furnish a smaller stock of the precious metals: the veins are impoverished, and they shrink daily. There is a decrease and deficiency of farmers in the fields, of sailors on the sea, of soldiers in the barracks, of honesty in the market-place, of justice in court, of concord in friendship, of skill in technique, of strictness in morals. When a thing is growing old, do you suppose that it can still retain, unimpaired, the exuberance of its fresh and lusty youth? Anything that is near its end and is verging towards its decline and fall is bound to dwindle. The Sun, for instance, radiates his beams with a less brilliant and less fiery splendour when he is setting, and the Moon grows thin, with her horns all eaten away, when she is on the wane. The tree which was once so green and so luxuriant turns sterile later on, as its branches wither up, and grows ugly with old age; and old age likewise stops the flow of the spring, until the bounteous outpouring of its welling sources dwindles into a bare trickle. This is the sentence that has been passed upon the World; this is the law of God: that what has been born must die, and what has grown up must grow old, and what has been strong must lose its strength, and what has been great must be diminished; and that this loss of strength and loss of stature must end, at last, in annihilation.'[3]

[1] Lucretius: *De Rerum Natura*, Book II, *ad fin.*, ll. 1144–5 and 1150–74.

[2] The terrible social relapse which swept away the *Pax Augusta* in the third century of the Christian Era may be said to have begun (or at least to have become glaringly manifest) with the murder of Alexander Severus, at the instigation of Maximin, in A.D. 235, and to have been surmounted (or perhaps rather to have been hidden under a veil) after Diocletian had struck down Arrius Aper in A.D. 284. Cyprian was converted to Christianity in the twelfth year of this time of tribulation (i.e. in A.D. 246); he wrote the tract *In Demetrianum* in the eighteenth year (i.e. in A.D. 252); and he suffered martyrdom in the twenty-fourth year (i.e. in A.D. 258).

[3] Thascius Caecilius Cyprianus: *Ad Demetrianum*, chap. 3. Cf. Saint Augustine: *Sermo* lxxxi, chap. 8 (apropos of Psalm ciii. 5).

This implication of death, as the inevitable consummation of an unmistakable senescence, was the argument in the mind of Lucretius when he wrote the lines above quoted as the tail-piece to a canto which is devoted to a demonstration that the Universe is doomed to destruction; and in another passage the pagan poet pronounces his Epicurean sentence upon the World in almost Christian tones of mingled horror and exultation:

> Principio maria ac terras caelumque tuere;
> quorum naturam triplicem, tria corpora, Memmi,
> tris species tam dissimiles, tria talia texta,
> una dies dabit exitio, multosque per annos
> sustentata ruet moles et machina mundi.[1]

This cosmic sentence of death is not unfamiliar to us, since we are accustomed to hearing it pronounced by our own physical scientists in our own generation when they talk of 'matter' being transformed into 'radiation':

'The capacity of Space for radiation is practically infinite when judged by any amount of radiation which can ever be poured into it. It follows that the transformation of matter into radiation is a "one-way" or, as it is technically called, an "irreversible" process. Matter can change into radiation, but under present conditions radiation can never change back into matter. Ultimately a time must come when every atom which is capable of dissolving into radiation will have done so. The Universe is like a clock which is running down: a clock which, so far as Science knows, no one ever winds up, which cannot wind itself up, and so must stop in time. . . . [A state in which] there [will] be neither sunlight nor starlight but only a cool glow of radiation uniformly diffused through Space . . . is indeed, so far as present-day Science can see, the final end towards which all creation moves, and at which it must, at long last, arrive.'[2]

For the latter-day Westerner, who has deliberately reinvested his treasure in This World after taking the most up-to-date professional advice, this sentence upon the Material Cosmos bears with it none of that promise of spiritual liberation—through the extinction of our consciousness or else through its etherialization—which it bore for a Lucretius and a Cyprian. And if we were bidden to believe, as well, that the destiny of our Western Civilization is bound up with the destiny of our Physical Universe, and that the symptoms of social breakdown, which in our day we seem to see on every side, are signs that the final cosmic catastrophe is now upon us, then our neo-pagan spirits would be damped indeed!

1 Lucretius: *De Rerum Natura*, Book V, ll. 92–6.
2 Jeans, Sir James: *Eos, or the Wider Aspects of Cosmogony* (London 1930, Kegan Paul), pp. 52 and 56.

As it happens, however, our Western cosmologists part company from their Hellenic confrères at this point; for they present us with a Time-chart in which human history and cosmic history are plotted on such utterly different scales that, from the practical standpoint, they can be regarded as being quite out of relation with one another.

'Taking a very gloomy view of the future of the Human Race, let us suppose that it can only expect to survive for two thousand million years longer, a period about equal to the past age of the Earth. Then, regarded as a being destined to live for three-score years and ten, Humanity, although it has been born in a house seventy years old, is itself only three days old. . . . Utterly inexperienced beings, we are standing at the first flush of the dawn of Civilization. . . . In time, the glory of the morning must fade into the light of common day; and this, in some far distant age, will give place to evening twilight, presaging the final eternal night. But we children of the dawn need give but little thought to the far-off sunset.'[1]

Indeed, if the expectation-of-life of the *Genus Homo* is (as Sir James Jeans here computes) something in the order of 8517 times the length of its actual life up to date, the expectation-of-life of the species of human societies called civilizations dwarfs the actual span of the existence of this species hitherto by a vastly greater measure. At an earlier point in this Study[2] we have satisfied ourselves that if we accept our cosmologists' time-chart, and if we make the unverifiable but not intrinsically unreasonable assumption that the average life-span of the twenty-one known civilizations which have come to birth and have proceeded to grow gives the general average for all future as well as for all past representatives of the species, then, 'on a conservative estimate', there is time ahead of us for at least 1,743,000,000 civilizations to come into existence and to pass away.[3] On this showing, it is obvious that no light whatever can be thrown upon the problem of the historic breakdowns of civilizations by the alleged inevitability of an ultimate breakdown of the Physical Universe.

Accordingly, our latter-day Western advocates of a predestinarian or deterministic explanation of the breakdowns of civilizations do not attempt to link the destinies of these human institutions up with the ultimate destiny of the Physical Universe as a whole. They appeal, instead, to a law of senescence and death with a shorter wave-length, for which they claim jurisdiction over the whole Kingdom of Life on this planet. Here are the terms in

[1] Jeans, op. cit., pp. 12–13 and 83–4.
[2] See I. C (iii) (*e*), Annex, vol. i, pp. 462–4, above.
[3] This is on the computation that the Human Race has at least 500,000 million years of existence still to look forward to.

which, on this ground, the death-sentence is demanded by our most celebrated post-war exponent of a philosophy of history:

'Every civilization (*Kultur*) passes through the same succession of ages as an individual human being. Every one of them has its childhood, its youth, its manhood and its old age. A young, timid, anxious soul reveals itself in the early dawn of Romanesque and Gothic. . . . One feels here the breath of the breezes of spring. . . . Childhood proclaims itself likewise, and this in kindred accents, in the early Homeric Doric. . . . The nearer a civilization approaches to the midday zenith of its existence, the greater become the manliness, the severity, the discipline and the self-fulfilment of its self-expression (*Formensprache*), which is now at last assured; and there is a corresponding increase of certainty in its feeling of its own strength, and increase of clarity in its features. (In the archaic age, all this is still blurred and confused and tentative—still inspired by childish longing and at the same time by childish fear.) . . . Now, in the full consciousness of a mature formative power, . . . every detail of expression gives evidence of a fastidiousness, a precision, a sense of proportion and an amazing facility and naturalness. This age is all shot through with flashes of a dazzling perfection. . . . Later still, we encounter a tenderness, a brittleness that is near to breaking-point, a painful sweetness like the feel of the last October days, in the Cnidian Aphrodite and in the Caryatid-portico of the Erechtheum, in the arabesques of Saracenic horse-shoe arches, in the Schloss at Dresden, and in the work of Watteau and Mozart. Last of all, in the time of old age . . . , the soul's fire goes out. The society's ebbing strength ventures just once again, and this time with only partial success, to attempt a great act of creation in the shape of the Classicism which is characteristic of every expiring civilization; and then, in a Romantic Movement, the soul casts back its thoughts once more, sorrowfully, to its childhood. Finally the soul turns weary, listless and cold; she loses the appetite for existence; and all her longing is to leave the light in which she has lived for a thousand years and to sink back into the darkness of primitive mysticism, into the womb, into the grave.'[1]

In this passage we may acknowledge a fine appreciation of the successive changes in êthos that can be observed in the course of the histories of certain civilizations which, at some point in their growth, have in fact had the misfortune to break down and to lapse into a decline. But Herr Spengler is here demanding from us much more than a recognition of empirically verifiable facts. He is asking us to induce from this handful of facts a universal and inexorable law; and, with (no doubt, unconscious) jugglery, he is attempting to mask the inadequacy of the evidential basis on which his tremendous induction has to stand, behind the simile in which

[1] Spengler, O.: *Der Untergang des Abendlandes*, vol. i (Munich 1920, Beck), pp. 154–5. Compare Frobenius, L.: *Paideuma* (Frankfort 1928, Frankfurter Societäts-Druckerei), p. 40.

he likens the career of a civilization to the life-history of a human being or other living organism. As an effective artifice of literary expression, this simile might have been allowed to pass; but, when we detect its author in the act of misusing it for the purpose of glozing over a weakness in his chain of argument, we are bound to point out that this simile has no basis in fact.

At an earlier stage in this Study[1] we have noted that societies are not, in fact, living organisms in any sense; and we may be sure that our apparent glimpses of a living and breathing Leviathan will always resolve themselves, under cold scrutiny, into the prosaically inanimate realities of a bunch of gasometers or a pall of smoke on the horizon. In subjective terms, societies are the intelligible fields of historical study.[2] In objective terms, they are the common ground between the respective fields of activity of a number of individual human beings[3] who are themselves living organisms but who cannot conjure up a giant in their own image out of the intersection of their own shadows and then breathe into this unsubstantial body the breath of their own life. The individual energies of all the human beings who constitute the so-called 'members' of a society are the vital forces whose operation works out the history of that society, including its Time-span. And who can decree or forecast what the characters and the interactions of all these actors are to be, or how many of them are to appear upon this particular stage from first to last? To declare dogmatically that every society has a predestined Time-span is as foolish as it would be to declare that every play that is written and produced is bound to consist of just so many acts, or that every film that is photographed and thrown upon the screen is bound to measure just so many yards or metres.

Nor does our historical determinist strengthen his case when he abandons the simile of an individual organism for the simile of a species of organisms or a genus:

'The *habitus* of any group of organisms includes, among other things, a definite life-span and a definite *tempo* of development; and no morphology of history can dispense with these concepts. The musical time of Hellenic life was different from that of Egyptiac or Arabic life. One may legitimately speak of the Graeco-Roman *andante* and of the Faustian[4] *allegro con brio*. The concept of the life-span of a human being, an eagle, a tortoise, an oak or a palm is bound up with a definite numerical value which is quite independent of all the accidental elements in the fate of the individual. In the life of all human beings a decade of years is a Time-section of approximately equal significance, and the metamorphosis of insects is in some cases bound up with a particular number

[1] See III. C (ii) (*a*), vol. iii, pp. 219–23, above.
[2] See Part I. B, in vol. i, above.
[3] See III. C (ii) (*a*), vol. iii, pp. 223–48, above.
[4] i.e. Western.—A.J.T.

of days which is accurately known in advance. The Romans defined their concepts of *pueritia*, *adulescentia*, *iuventus*, *virilitas*, *senectus* with an absolutely mathematical exactitude. The Biology of the future will undoubtedly find the point of departure for an entirely new formulation of its problems in the concept of the pre-ordained life-span of the genera and species. . . . The span of a generation—whatever creature may be in question—is a numerical value of almost mystical significance. And these relations are also valid for all[1] civilizations—and this in a way that has never before been dreamt of. Every civilization, every archaic age, every rise and every downfall, and every inevitable phase of each of these movements, has a definite Time-span which is always the same and which always recurs with symbolic emphasis. What is the significance of the fifty-year period in the rhythm of political, intellectual and artistic life which is prevalent in all civilizations? (The basis of this particular period is the spiritual relation between the grandfather and the grandchild.) What is the significance of the three-hundred-year periods of Gothic, Baroque, Doric, Ionic, of the great mathematical systems, of Attic sculpture, of mosaic, of counterpoint, and of Galileo's system of mechanics? What is the significance of the millennium which is the ideal life-span of all civilizations, considered in proportion to the individual human being's "three-score years and ten"?'[2]

The conclusive answer to these questionings is that a society is not a species or a genus,[3] any more than it is an organism. It is itself an individual representative of some species of the genus 'societies', and the individual human beings who are the 'members' of a society are representatives of a species or a genus likewise. But the genus of which we human beings are the individuals is neither the Western Society (or the Hellenic Society or any other society) in particular nor the genus of societies in general, but the *Genus Homo*; and this simple truth absolves us from any obligation to examine here Herr Spengler's dogma that genera and species have pre-ordained life-spans on the analogy of the individual organisms in which the biological genera and species are represented.

Let us assume, for the moment, without prejudice, that the *Genus Homo* has a mandate of limited duration for reproducing itself on the face of this planet, and that it cannot look forward to

[1] In this word 'all' the watchful reader will observe a sudden alteration in the major premise of Herr Spengler's argument. The 'group of organisms' with which Herr Spengler sets out to deal at the beginning of this passage is a *single* civilization—Hellenic, Egyptiac, or Arabic—in which the organisms are presumably the human beings who are the 'members' of the civilization. From the present point onwards, however, the group becomes the species 'civilizations' of the genus 'societies', and the organisms become the several civilizations in which the species is represented. This change of premise has implicated the philosopher in an unresolved contradiction. At the beginning of the passage he tells us that 'the musical time' of each civilization is unique; at the close he tells us that the rhythm, as well as the Time-span, of all civilizations is uniform.—A.J.T.

[2] Spengler, O.: *Der Untergang des Abendlandes*, vol. i (Munich 1920, Beck), pp. 157–8.

[3] For Herr Spengler's own inconsistency in regard to this premise of his argument see the last footnote but one.

remaining in being as a matter of course until the progress of cosmic radiation eventually makes the Material Universe too chilly a place for human life to continue here. Even on this assumption, a brief consideration of the actual historical duration of biological genera and species on the surface of this planet up to date shows at once that it is just as impossible to link up the breakdown and disintegration of any given civilization with this hypothetical expiry of the mandate of the *Genus Homo* as it is to link it up with the dissolution of the Material Universe into radiation. The *Genus Homo* is supposed to have been in existence, in a recognizably human form, for some 300,000 years already, as against the 6,000 years or less that have elapsed since the first emergence of the species of societies called civilizations.[1] What warrant is there for assuming that the mandate of this genus (if it is really subject to any mandate) is not good for another 300,000 years at least? And, to come to grips again with our immediate problem of the breakdowns of civilizations, what ground is there for suggesting that these breakdowns are accompanied by any symptoms of physical or psychic degeneration in the individual human beings who happen to be the living 'members' of the particular society in question at the moment when the breakdown occurs? Were the Athenians of the generation of Socrates and Euripides and Thucydides and Pheidias and Pericles, who were overtaken by the catastrophe of 431 B.C., intrinsically poorer creatures, in either soul or body, than the generation of the *Μαραθωνομάχαι*, who shone in retrospect in the illusively intensified light of an age which appeared more glorious than it had been in truth by contrast with the tragedy of the age which followed?

An explanation of the breakdowns of civilizations in terms of a supposed science of eugenics does, perhaps, appear to be suggested by Plato in a famous passage of *The Republic*:

'A society with the ideal constitution is not easily thrown out of equilibrium; but, after all, everything that has a genesis is foredoomed to eventual disintegration, and even the ideal constitution will not endure in perpetuity but will break down in the end. The breakdown is connected with the periodic rhythm (with a short wave-length for short-lived creatures and a long wave-length for those at the other end of the scale) which is the rhythm of Life in the Animal as well as in the Vegetable Kingdom, and which is the determinant of both physical and psychic fecundity. The specific laws of human eugenics will baffle both the reason and the intuition of our trained ruling minority, in spite of all their intellectual power. These laws will elude them; and one day they will beget children inopportunely. For superhuman beings that have had a genesis in Time, the numerical value of their wave-length is an

[1] See I. C (iii) (e), Annex, vol. i, p. 462, above.

integer; but for human beings it is the number which is expressed in the following formula:

[A fantastically intricate formula follows.]

'This number is the governing factor in the laws of human eugenics; and when our trustees—acting in ignorance of these laws—happen to mate brides with bridegrooms unseasonably, then the children born of these unions will be neither fine nor fortunate. The best individuals of this generation will be duly installed in office by their elders; but, being below standard, they will misuse the powers bequeathed to them by their fathers and will begin to neglect their trusteeship *vis-à-vis* their fellows, undervaluing first mental and secondly physical culture, with the result that there will be a falling off in the culture of the rising generation. In this next generation, rulers will be installed who will be quite lacking in the trustee's essential faculty of distinguishing between the several 'races'—of gold and silver and bronze and iron—whose existence we have postulated on the venerable authority of Hesiod. And when silver is alloyed with iron, and gold with bronze, this introduces those factors of incongruity and disharmony which invariably generate war and enmity wherever they are introduced. Wherever this happens at any time, one must pronounce that this generation has fallen into social discord.'[1]

When we look into this passage more closely, we see that Plato does not represent the racial degeneration, to which he attributes the social breakdown, as being an automatic or a predetermined event. He traces the degeneration back, in its turn, to a false step of some sort on the part of his ruling minority, and does not ascribe this false step, vice versa, to an antecedent degeneration. The false step, as he describes it half whimsically in terms of a philosophy which interprets moral aberrations as intellectual mistakes, is a failure of technique: in fact, an error in mathematics! But whether it be intellectual or moral, the failure to which the social breakdown of Plato's ideal society is ultimately traced back is not a deterioration in the 'make-up' of the human psyche or the human physique, but a lapse in the sphere of human action: a failure to meet a challenge with the appropriate response.

Nor is there any warrant for following Plato in accepting racial degeneration as even a secondary link in the chain of causation through which a social breakdown leads on to a decline. For although, in times of social decline, the members of the declining society may seem to dwindle into pygmies, or to stiffen into cripples or bedridden invalids, by contrast with the kingly stature and the magnificent activity of their forebears in the age of social growth, to ascribe this malady to degeneration is a false diagnosis. The biological heritage of the epigoni is the same as that of the pioneers,

[1] Plato: *Respublica*, 546 A–547 A.

and all the pioneers' endeavours and achievements are potentially within their descendants' reach. The malady which holds the children of the decadence fast bound in misery and iron[1] for generation after generation is no paralysis of their natural faculties as human beings but a breakdown and disintegration of their social heritage, which debars them from finding scope for their unimpaired faculties in effective and creative social action. The wreck of the social structure cribs and cabins and confines their natures like those hideous strait-waistcoats in which, in Ancient Egypt, well-framed and healthy children were deliberately deformed into artificial dwarfs. The dwarfing of the epigoni is the effect of the social breakdown and not its cause.[2]

This untenable hypothesis that a racial degeneration is the cause of a social breakdown and decline is sometimes supported by the observation that, during the interregnum which intervenes between the final dissolution of a decadent society and the first emergence of a new-born society related to it by 'affiliation', there is frequently a Völkerwanderung in which the population of the identical home of the two successive societies is treated to 'an infusion of new blood'. On the logic of *post hoc propter hoc* it is assumed that the fresh access of creative power which the new-born civilization displays in the course of its growth is the gift of this 'new blood' from 'the pure source' of 'a primitive barbarian race'; and it is then inferred that, conversely, the loss of creative power in the life of the antecedent civilization must have been due to some kind of racial anaemia or pyaemia which nothing but a fresh infusion of healthy blood could cure.

In support of this view an alleged case in point is cited from the history of Italy. It is pointed out that the inhabitants of Italy exhibited a pre-eminent energy and creative power during a period of some four centuries running from about the fourth to the last century B.C.,[3] and again during a period of some six centuries running from the eleventh to the sixteenth century of the Christian Era. During the first of these periods the Italians dealt the Hellenic Civilization its *coup de grâce* and then endowed the prostrate society

[1] Psalm cvii. 10.

[2] This dwarfing effect of unfavourable social conditions upon human souls is noticed by Longinus: *On the Sublime*, chap. 44. Longinus has in mind the conditions in a Hellenic universal state in which, as he saw it, people were now engrossed in the sordid business of making and spending money because they were debarred from the political activities that had stimulated and ennobled the souls of their forebears in the Hellenic Society's age of growth. A modern Western student of history who visited South Wales or North Bohemia in A.D. 1938 might conclude that the same dwarfing effect could be produced by a withdrawal of opportunities for making and spending money in a society in which the traditional idea of the good life was a régime, not of subsidized public service, but of remunerated private labour.

[3] In this computation the achievements of the Greek and Etruscan colonists are, of course, ignored, and only those of the native Italians are taken into account.

with its universal state in the shape of the Roman Empire. During the second period the Italians insulated themselves from the rest of Western Christendom and then worked out a new and higher form of Western culture which inaugurated a fresh chapter in Western history when it was imparted to the Transalpine 'barbarians' in due course.[1] In both of these two great ages of their history the Italians performed feats which have not been outdone by any other people in any other place or time. On the other hand the two ages are separated from one another by a thousand years of decadence, prostration, and convalescence, in which it seemed for a time as though the virtue had gone out of the Italians altogether. This fantastically chequered history would be inexplicable, argue the racialists, if the key were not supplied by Clio herself, who has preserved for our instruction a record of the infusion into Italian veins of the new blood which was brought in, during the post-Hellenic Völkerwanderung, by the advent of the Goths and the Lombards. This fresh barbarian blood was the elixir of life which produced, in the fullness of time, the Italian Renaissance. It was for lack of this fresh blood that Italy languished, during the Imperial Age, after the demonic output of Italian energy in the Age of the Roman Republic. And this energy which burst into action in the last four centuries B.C. was itself, perhaps, the product of an earlier infusion of fresh barbarian blood which Italy had received during the post-Minoan interregnum, when the Oscans and Sabellians were descending upon the peninsula out of Central Europe in the same Völkerwanderung that carried their Achaean and 'Dorian' cousins into Greece.

This racial explanation of Italian history from the fourth century B.C. to the sixteenth century of the Christian Era has a certain plausibility so long as we are careful to cut short our survey of Italian history at this point. But if we allow our thoughts to travel on from the sixteenth century to the present day, we shall see that Italian history has repeated itself in circumstances that rule the racial explanation out.

From the close of the sixteenth century to the close of the eighteenth, Italy suffered a fresh eclipse; and in the nineteenth century this has been followed by a fresh recovery. The Italian *Risorgimento* is, as its name implies, at least as notable a feat of rejuvenation as the Italian Renaissance; and if we are to accept the racialists as our ciceroni, we may fairly ask them to specify the new infusion of blood, at some date between the years 1600 and 1800, which, on their theory, must have been received by Italy in order to make the *Risorgimento* possible. The answer is, of course, that

[1] See III. C (ii) (*b*), vol. iii, pp. 299–300 and 341–50, above.

the racial composition of the Italian people in the nineteenth and twentieth centuries, when they have been displaying this fresh manifestation of creative power, has been precisely what it was in the immediately preceding period of eclipse and precisely what it was, before that, in the great age of the Renaissance. In fact, there has been no substantial change in the racial 'make-up' of the inhabitants of Italy since the peninsula was partially overrun by numerically weak war-bands of Lombards in the sixth century.[1] Since then, the only considerable 'infusions of new blood' have been in Calabria and Sicily; and their role in medieval and modern Italian history has been secondary to the parts that have been played by the Centre and the North.[2]

Accordingly, if we are to account for the decline of Italy after the Renaissance and for her recent recovery after her decline, we must find some explanation which does not depend upon a race-theory; and such an explanation is not really very far to seek. In an earlier passage[3] we have traced the decline of Italy, in and after the sixteenth century, to the failure of Italian statesmanship to achieve that concord and co-operation between the Italian states of the age which had to be achieved in order to counteract the mechanical operation of the Balance of Power to the detriment of the small Italian Powers at the centre of the Italian World and to the advantage of the large 'barbarian' Powers on the periphery. This failure of Italian statesmanship caused Italy to become the battle-field of the Transalpine Powers from 1494 to 1859; and

[1] The Italian territories which escaped being occupied and settled by the Lombards included Venice, the Romagna, the Pentapolis (i.e. a considerable portion of the Marche), Perugia, the Agro Romano, Naples, Amalfi, Calabria, and Sicily. This mere catalogue is enough to show that there is no geographical correspondence between the districts which received an infusion of Lombard blood and the districts which have been pre-eminent in energy and creative power in the history of medieval and modern Italy. Amalfi contests with Venice the honour of having been the pioneer in starting the medieval commerce of Italy with the Levant; and as for the Romagnols, they have the reputation of being the most lively and the most domineering people in Italy. In the Middle Ages Bologna was more pugnacious than any of the city-states of Lombardy; and in the sequel the Romagnols have distinguished themselves repeatedly: first in the Napoleonic period and then in the *Risorgimento* and latterly in the 'post-war' chapter of Italian history, in which the Romagna has provided the Fascist movement with its founder and leader. Has anything comparable come out of Pavia, which was the capital of the Lombard Kingdom, or out of Spoleto and Benevento, which were the seats of the two autonomous Lombard duchies? If any racial conclusions are to be drawn from this geographico-historical evidence, we shall have to pronounce that the best Italian blood has been the blood which has remained free from a Lombard taint!

[2] In Sicily there was an infusion of Arab and Berber blood in the ninth and tenth centuries of the Christian Era, when the island was conquered from the East Roman Empire by the Muslims of Ifriqīyah; and there was an infusion of Apulian and North Italian blood in the twelfth century, after the conquest of Sicily by the Normans. (This last infusion has left a lasting trace of itself in the Romance dialect which has entirely supplanted the previously prevalent Greek, except for one or two places where Greek has been re-introduced by modern Greek immigrants (see III. C (i) (*a*), Annex, vol. iii, pp. 458–9, above).) In Calabria, in the ninth and tenth centuries, there was an infusion of Sicilian blood, introduced by settlements of Sicilian refugees, which temporarily turned the former Magna Graecia into a Greek-speaking country again (see IV. C (iii) (*c*) 2 (*β*), pp. 356–7, below).

[3] In III. C (ii) (*b*), vol. iii, pp. 299–309, above.

during this age of Italian impotence and adversity the Italians fell behind their Transalpine neighbours not only in military power but also in those arts of peace which the French and the Spaniards and the Austrians had originally learnt from Italian masters. This explains the Italian decadence; and the *Risorgimento* is explained, in its turn, by the stimulus which Italy received, at the turn of the eighteenth and nineteenth centuries, from her temporary incorporation into the Napoleonic Empire: a passing political association that effectively carried Italy back into the main current of Western life and gave her a baptism of new ideas and new experiences which was a far more potent influence than any infusion of new blood could ever be.[1]

It is not more difficult to find non-racial explanations for the previous rise of Italy at the beginning of the second millennium of the Christian Era and for her foregoing decline which declared itself in the course of the last two centuries B.C. This last-mentioned decline was manifestly the nemesis of the Roman militarism, which brought upon Roman Italy the scourge of Hannibal and all the appalling social evils that followed in the train of the Hannibalic War.[2] The beginnings of social recovery in Italy, during the post-Hellenic interregnum, can be traced with equal certainty to the work of creative personalities of the old Italian race—a Benedict and a Gregory—who are the fathers, not only of the rejuvenated Italy of the Middle Ages, but of the new Western Civilization of which the medieval Italians were members.[3]

We can even drive the racialists out of their one remaining Italian stronghold by finding an alternative explanation for the rise of the Roman Republic which will dispense us from having to recognize any special virtue in the new blood which had been infused into Italy out of Central Europe during the post-Minoan Völkerwanderung. The rise of the Romans, and of the other pre-Greek and pre-Etruscan inhabitants of Italy, in the course of the last millennium B.C. can be explained as a response to the challenge of Greek and Etruscan colonization. Were the native peoples of the Italian Peninsula to resign themselves to that choice between the alternatives of extermination, subjugation, and assimilation which had been forced upon their cousins in Sicily and in those Umbrian territories that had been transformed into an Etruria?

1 The significance of the Napoleonic Empire in the histories of Italy, Flanders, and Western Germany is discussed further in IV. C (iii) (*c*) 2 (α), pp. 283–9, and in V. C (i) (*d*) 6 (γ), Annex I, vol. v, pp. 619–42, below.

2 See I. B (iv), vol. i, pp. 40–1; II. D (vi), vol. ii, pp. 213–16; and III. C (i) (*b*), vol. iii, pp. 166–7 and 170–1, above, and IV. C (ii) (*a*), in the present volume, pp. 48–9, and IV. C (iii) (*c*) 3 (β), pp. 505–10, below.

3 For the work of SS. Benedict and Gregory see III. C (ii) (*b*), vol. iii, pp. 264–9, above.

Or were they to hold their own against the formidable intruders by adopting the Hellenic Civilization of their own accord and on their own terms, and thereby raising themselves to the Greek and Etruscan level of cultivation and efficiency? The Romans decided to make this latter response, and in taking this decision they became the authors of their own subsequent greatness.[1]

The Italian vicissitudes of renaissance and eclipse and *risorgimento* in the Modern Age of our Western history have an almost exact parallel, in Hellenic history, in the vicissitudes that were experienced by the Greek city-states along the western coast of Anatolia and on the inshore islands.

We have seen that, in the first age of Hellenic history, the Ionians and Aeolians were the creators and the pioneers;[2] but in the sixth century B.C. they fell on evil days. They forfeited their political independence first to the Lydian Empire and afterwards to the greater empire of the Achaemenidae; the mismanaged revolt of 499–494 ended in the disaster of the fall and sack of Miletus; and their 'liberation' from the Achaemenidae by the Athenians in or after 479 B.C. only added to the Ionians' troubles. For the next hundred and fifty years they were bandied about between the Achaemenian Empire and whichever of the Powers of European Greece was momentarily mistress of the Aegean; and as often as not they were bullied and fleeced by their fellow Greeks and by their fellow Asiatics simultaneously. In fact, all through the great age of Athens, Ionia was in eclipse; but she achieved a remarkable revival in the new chapter of Hellenic history which opened with Alexander's passage of the Hellespont. In the third century B.C., when Athens fell out of the ranks of the Great Powers of the Hellenic World after her bitter experience in the Chremonidean War,[3]

'the old Greek cities of Asia, . . . with their ancient traditions, large populations, compact and busy life, growing wealth, magnificent public buildings, and vast walls,[4] scarcely felt themselves inferior to a kingdom. . . . Magnesia on the Maeander could stretch her arms from Ithaca to the Oxus; she helped to defend Delphi against the Gauls, she gave to Bactrian Hellenism its most powerful dynasty and thereby invaded

[1] For this barbarian reaction to Greek and Etruscan pressure in Italy see further V. C (i) (*c*), 1, vol. v, p. 55, with footnote 4, and V. C (i) (*c*) 3, vol. v, pp. 211–2, below. [2] III. C (ii) (*b*), vol. iii, pp. 338–9, above. [3] See III. C (ii) (*b*), vol. iii, pp. 338 and 340, above.

[4] At the time of the Peloponnesian War, when Ionia was at her political nadir, we have explicit testimony that a number of the continental and insular Asiatic Greek cities were unfortified. Perhaps this was one of the unrecorded stipulations of the peace-settlement between Athens and the Achaemenian Empire which had been negotiated by Callias in 446 B.C. The evidence is as follows: for the Ionian cities in general, Thucydides III. 33; for Chios, Erythrae, and Clazomenae, VIII. 14; for Clazomenae again, VIII. 31; for Chios previously, IV. 51; for Cnidus, VIII. 35; for Cos, VIII. 41 and 108; for Camirus, VIII. 44; for Samos, VIII. 51; for Cyzicus VIII. 107; for Lampsacus, VIII. 62, and Xenophon *Hellenica*, I. 2, § 15; for Phocaea, Xenophon, op. cit., I. 5, § 11. Teos had been re-fortified, for reasons unrecorded, not by the Teians themselves but by the Athenians (Thucydides VIII. 16).—A.J.T.

India, and she helped the Seleucid to create Antioch-towards-Pisidia, Antioch-in-Persis, and doubtless, if we knew, other cities; there was not much infanticide in third-century Magnesia.'[1]

As for Ephesus, she succeeded, between the generation of Lysimachus and the generation of Augustus, in extending her commercial hinterland so far eastwards into the interior of Asia Minor that by the beginning of the Christian Era the products of Cappadocia were diverted from Sinope and shipped through Ephesus,[2] though Ephesus was at least twice as far as Sinope was from Mazaca. This second bloom of Ionia lasted throughout the Imperial Age and only wilted with Hellenism itself; and when the Emperor Justinian resolved to build, in Constantinople, a fane which should embody the spirit of the nascent Orthodox Christian Civilization, he sent for the Ionian architects Anthemius of Tralles and Isidorus of Miletus.[3] The last feat of the Ionian genius was to create the never-to-be-transcended masterpiece of a new-fangled architecture which was the very antithesis of the classic style that was enshrined in the Ionian fanes of Apollo at Didyma and of Artemis at Ephesus.

What is the explanation of Ionia's deep eclipse and brilliant reemergence? In the fifth and fourth centuries B.C. the Ionians were a by-word for softness in the mouths of Athenians and Spartans and Thebans and Persians. Had the cancer of racial degeneration sapped the *moral* and ruined the physique of the descendants of those 'brazen men'[4] who had risen out of the sea in the seventh century to sell their swords to an Egyptian Psammetichus? This explanation will only work if we can point to some fresh infusion of new blood which nerved a Magnesian Euthydemus in the third century B.C. to emulate the hardihood of his sixth-century ancestors—who had carved their names on the colossus at Abu Simbel[5]—by carving out a kingdom for himself in Bactria and handing it on to a son who doubled it by his conquests in India. Can our racialists point to any infusion of the kind between 494 and 334 B.C.? If the Ionian cities did receive any fresh blood during this dark period in their history, it must have been

[1] Tarn, W. W.: *Hellenistic Civilization* (London 1927, Arnold), pp. 138–9. Cf. eundem: *The Greeks in Bactria and India* (Cambridge 1938, University Press), p. 6.

[2] 'Cappadocia produces the so-called "Sinopic" red lead, which is the finest in the World. . . . It is called "Sinopic" because the dealers used to bring it to Sinope for shipment before the commercial hinterland of Ephesus expanded into these parts.'—Strabo: *Geographica*, Book XII, chap. 10, p. 540.

[3] Procopius: *De Aedificiis*, Book I, chap. 1, § 24.

[4] Herodotus, Book II, chap. 152.

[5] The oldest extant Greek inscriptions are those carved upon the two southern colossi of the Great Temple at Abu Simbel by Ionian mercenaries in the service of the Egyptian King Psammetichus II (*regnabat* 593–588 B.C.)—a successor of the original Psammetichus who had founded the Twenty-Sixth Dynasty and given Egypt a new lease of political independence with the aid of earlier Ionian 'brazen men'.

supplied by the Asiatic subjects of the Great King in their Continental hinterland—a strain which would be condemned with equal conviction by a contemporary Spartan or Athenian Hellenomaniac and by a latter-day Western racialist. We are driven to conclude that the blood which coursed in a Euthydemus's veins was certainly no racier than that which had throbbed in the pulses of his forebears four centuries back. Ionian history, like Italian history, is impossible to explain on racial lines; and the satisfactory non-racial explanation which we have found for the chequered course of Italian history offers a clue which it is not difficult to follow out.

Ionia fell on evil days because, at the turn of the sixth and fifth centuries B.C., her statesmen failed as signally as Italian statesmanship failed at the turn of the fifteenth and sixteenth centuries of the Christian Era to respond to the challenge of a growing pressure from surrounding Powers by solving the problem of the house divided against itself.[1] Her plight in the fifth and fourth centuries, as a pawn in the political game of the Athenians and Spartans and Thebans and Achaemenidae, is remarkably like the plight of Italy in the sixteenth, seventeenth, and eighteenth centuries, when Lombardy was the battle-field of the French and Spaniards and Austrians, while the Levantine outposts of Genoa and of Venice were being captured by the 'Osmanlis. Ionia, again, was impoverished in the fifth century B.C. by the attraction of the maritime trade of the Aegean to the Peiraeus while simultaneously her overland trade with her Asiatic hinterland was being cut off by the new political frontier between the Athenian and Achaemenian Empires —just as Italy was impoverished in the sixteenth century by the double blow of the Ottoman conquest of the Levant and the diversion of sea-borne commerce from the Mediterranean to the Oceanic routes. If we pursue the analogy, we can discern that the discomfiture of Thebes and Athens and Sparta by Philip of Macedon and the destruction of the Achaemenian Empire by Alexander had substantially the same effect, *mutatis mutandis*, as the overthrow of the *ancien régime* in Europe and the reopening of the Levant to European enterprise by Napoleon. Like Italy *post Napoleonem*, Ionia *post Alexandrum* was drawn back into the main current of the

[1] The keener minds of Ionia, at this crisis in Ionia's fate, were evidently aware that their only hope of salvation lay in achieving the *tour de force* of political consolidation. This is apparent in a legend which is recorded by Herodotus: 'Before Ionia was ruined [by the Achaemenian conquest], an admirable policy was suggested to the Ionians by Thales of Miletus. . . . Thales proposed that the Ionians should have one single Government, and that the seat of this Government should be at Teos (Teos being the geographical centre-point of Ionia). The other Ionian cities were to go on being inhabited just as before, but were to be reduced politically to the status of parishes' (Herodotus, Book I, chap. 170). *Mutatis mutandis*, this is the policy which is advocated in the last chapter of Machiavelli's *Prince*.

life of the society to which she belonged. Politically the Asiatic Greek city-states received a far more gracious and considerate treatment from Alexander and his successors than they had been accustomed to receive either from Athenian tax-collectors or from Spartan residents or from Persian satraps. Economically they benefited by the reopening of the overland route from the east coast of the Aegean to the interior of Asia still more appreciably than Italy has gained by the reopening of the Levantine maritime route to India and China which was heralded by Napoleon's expedition to Egypt and was consummated by the cutting of the Suez Canal.[1]

The histories of the Ionian and Italian *risorgimenti* discredit the hypothesis of racial degeneration by demonstrating that a people which has fallen into social decadence after a period of brilliant achievements is capable of recovering its social health again without any change whatever in its racial composition from first to last.

We have now disposed of three predestinarian explanations of the breakdowns of civilizations: the theory that they are the incidental consequence of a running-down of the clockwork of the Physical Universe; the theory that a civilization, like a living organism, has its own inherent life-span and life-curve which compel it to pass, within a definite number of centuries, from birth through growth and senescence to death; and the theory that the breakdown of any given civilization at any given date is due to the racial degeneration of the particular portion of the Human Race from which this particular civilization happens to have drawn its 'members'. We have still to consider one further predestinarian hypothesis which follows out to its logical conclusion the hypothetical analogy between the lives of civilizations and the lives of the Physical Universe and of the Human Race and of individual human beings. This hypothesis assumes that civilizations succeed one another, by a law of their nature which is the common law of the Cosmos, in a perpetually recurrent cycle of alternating birth and death.

The application of this theory of cycles to the history of Mankind was a natural corollary to the sensational astronomical discovery, which appears to have been made in the Babylonic World some time between the eighth and the sixth centuries B.C., that the three conspicuous and familiar astronomical cycles—the terrestrial cycle of day-and-night and the lunar cycle of the month and the solar cycle of the year—were not the only instances of periodic recurrence in the movements of the heavenly bodies; that there

[1] For the vast and rapid increase of wealth in the Ionian cities *post Alexandrum* see Tarn, *Hellenistic Civilization*, pp. 96–7.

was also a larger co-ordination of stellar movements which embraced all the planets as well as the Earth and the Moon and the Sun; and that 'the music of the spheres', which was made by the harmony of this heavenly chorus, came round full circle, chord for chord, in a cycle of great cosmic months and years which dwarfed the solar year into insignificance. The inference was that the annual birth and death of the terrestrial vegetation, which was manifestly governed by the solar year cycle, had its counterpart in a recurrent birth and death of all things on the Time-scale of the cosmic year cycle; and minds which came under the spell of this idea were apt to project this pattern of periodicity into every object of their thought.[1] The interpretation of Human history in these cyclic terms evidently fascinated Plato.

ATHENIAN STRANGER. Do you feel that the ancient legends have any truth in them?

CLEINIAS OF CRÉTE. Which legends?

STRANGER. The legends of repeated destructions of the Human Race by floods and plagues and many other catastrophes, in which only a tiny remnant of Mankind survived.

CLEINIAS. Why, certainly, the whole of that body of legend carries conviction with everybody.[2]

This brief exposition of the cyclic hypothesis in the *Laws* has its counterpart in the *Timaeus* in a myth which is placed in the mouth of an old Egyptian priest to justify his exclamation to Solon that 'the Hellenes are perpetual children' and that 'such a thing as an old Hellene does not exist'.

'All of you,' proceeds Plato's Egyptian priest in reply to the Platonic Solon's expostulation: 'All of you Hellenes are young in mind. Your minds contain no thoughts handed down from Antiquity by ancient tradition and no knowledge hoary with age. There is a reason for this, which I will explain. A series of catastrophes in a variety of forms has befallen, and will continue to befall, the Human Race—the greatest being the work of fire or water, while the others, which are of less violence, are produced by an infinity of different causes. In Hellas you have a tradition that Phaethon, the child of the Sun, once harnessed his father's chariot but proved incompetent to drive it along his father's course, with the result that he burnt up everything on the face of the

[1] For the consequent invention of the pseudo-science of Astrology see V. C (i) (*c*) 1, vol. v, pp. 56–7, below.

[2] Plato: *Leges*, 677 A; compare *Critias*, 109 D. This Hellenic concept of repetition *ad infinitum* in the Time-dimension was matched, in one school of Hellenic thought, by a corresponding concept of repetition *ad infinitum* in the Space-dimension as well. On this view there was not only an infinite number of successive worlds, but also an infinite number of worlds existing simultaneously at any given moment. Logically the two doctrines hang together; but Plato appears to have adopted the hypothesis of an infinite repetition in Time without admitting that the same hypothesis was applicable to Space on the same showing. (See Cornford, F. M.: 'The Invention of Space' in *Essays in Honour of Gilbert Murray* (London 1936, Allen & Unwin).)

Earth before his own career was cut short for ever by the thunderbolt. Although this tradition has been dressed in a legendary form, it preserves the scientific fact that, at immense intervals of time, there is a declination in the orbit of the heavenly bodies revolving round the Earth and a catastrophe which overtakes life on this planet in the shape of a vast conflagration. At this juncture the inhabitants of regions with a mountainous relief, a high altitude, or an arid climate pay a heavier toll than those of riverain or maritime neighbourhoods; and on these occasions we in Egypt are rescued by the Nile, our unfailing saviour, from a quandary from which he is immune himself. There are other occasions on which the Gods cleanse the Earth with a deluge of water, and in these circumstances the shepherds and herdsmen on the mountains survive, while the inhabitants of your towns in Hellas are swept away by the rivers. In Egypt, however, water never descends upon the fields from above—not even in these pluvial epochs—but rises from below by a law of Nature which never varies. Thus, for the above reasons, the traditions preserved in Egypt are the most ancient in the World. . . . And glorious or important or in any way remarkable events in the history of Hellas or of Egypt itself or of any other region within our field of knowledge are recorded and preserved in our shrines here in Egypt since a remote antiquity. On the other hand, human society in Hellas or elsewhere has always just arrived at the point of equipping itself with written records and the other requisites of Civilization when, after the regular interval, the waters that are above the firmament descend upon you like a recurrent malady and only permit the illiterate and uncultivated members of your society to survive, with the result that you become as little children and start again from the beginning with no knowledge whatever of Ancient History either in Egypt or in your own world. . . . You have only preserved the memory of one deluge which is the most recent in a long series.'[1]

[1] Plato: *Timaeus*, 21 E–23 C. It will be seen that Plato deliberately emphasizes the periodic recurrence of the floods and other natural catastrophes which he represents as perpetually destroying successive human attempts at Civilization in every part of the *Οἰκουμένη* except Egypt. On the other hand the version of the Sumeric flood-myth which the Jews brought back to Syria from their Babylonish captivity is equally emphatic in recording God's promise that the visitation should never be repeated (Gen. viii. 21–2, and ix. 11–17). It is interesting to find the notion of a periodic destruction of the World by natural catastrophes reappearing in the mythology of the Mexic Society. According to an Aztec myth, there were four successive world-ages, each ending in a destruction of the World by jaguars, by hurricane, by a volcanic rain of fire, and by water, respectively (Spinden, H. J.: *Ancient Civilisations of Mexico and Central America* (New York 1922, American Museum of Natural History), p. 191; Joyce, T. A.: *Mexican Archaeology* (London 1914, Lee Warner), pp. 50–1; Spence, L.: *The Civilisation of Ancient Mexico* (Cambridge 1912, University Press), p. 84). This notion of cycles of civilization punctuated by catastrophes may have been inherited by the Mexic Civilization from the antecedent Mayan Civilization (Spinden, op. cit., p. 205; Joyce, op. cit., p. 239). In any case we may safely assume that it arose in the New World independently of the similar notions, once current in the Old World, which we have just been surveying. On the other hand we may postulate an Indic or Babylonic origin for the system of recurrent cycles of 129,600 years—each cycle ending in a catastrophe—which is expounded by the Far Eastern philosopher Chu Hsi (*vivebat* A.D. 1131–1200), though no doubt the ground for the reception of this idea in the Far Eastern World had been prepared by the familiarity of Far Eastern thought with the Sinic conception of the perpetual alternation of Yin and Yang. (For Chu Hsi's theory of cycles see Hackmann, H.: *Chinesische Philosophie* (Munich 1927, Rheinhardt), pp. 337–8.)

The same conception of recurrent alternating catastrophe and rehabilitation is applied to the Cosmos as a whole, instead of just to a portion of the *Οἰκουμένη*, and is at the same time translated into theological terms, in another Platonic myth:

'This Universe is sometime conducted on its path and guided in its orbit by God, while at other times, when the cycles of its appointed time have arrived at their term, it is released from control by God and proceeds to revolve in the opposite direction by itself (which it can do, because it is a living creature endowed with intelligence by the being who originally constructed it). The tendency towards this reverse motion is inevitably innate in the Universe . . . in virtue of the principle that perpetual self-consistency and self-identity are properties confined to a supremely divine order of existence, to which Matter, by its nature, does not belong. That which we call Space and the Cosmos has been endowed with many blessings by its Begetter, but these blessings do not include freedom from a material ingredient. For this reason it is impossible for the Cosmos to be permanently exempt from change, though up to the limits of its capacity it does its utmost to move with a constant and unvarying rhythm in the same locus, and has therefore been allowed (when it changes) to revolve in the reverse direction as involving the slightest possible deviation from its proper motion. Perpetual self-rotation, however, is beyond the capacity of almost every being except that by which all things that move are conducted, and this being is precluded from moving them sometimes in one direction and sometimes in the opposite. From these various premises it follows that the Cosmos, in alternating between the two contrary revolutions to which it is subject, neither rotates itself perpetually nor is entirely and perpetually rotated by God, and again that there are not two gods rotating it with contradictory purposes, but that (as has just been stated and is the only remaining alternative) it is sometimes conducted by a divine cause outside itself, in which phase it receives an access of vitality and a renewal of immortality from its Creator, while at other times it is released from control and moves by itself. . . .

'In the previous period the whole circular motion itself, in the first place, was controlled and superintended by God, and the same superintendence was provided locally by the assignment of all the parts of the Cosmos to other controlling deities. Living creatures too, according to their kinds, were taken in charge, in flocks, by divine spirits, and each of these good shepherds was efficient in every respect to care for the creatures under his particular charge, so that there was no savagery, no preying upon one another, and no war or discord among them at all. . . .

'When, however, the period of this dispensation had been completed and a change was due . . . , at that point the Helmsman of the Universe abandoned control of His rudder and retired to His observation-post, and the Cosmos was set rotating in the reverse direction by Destiny and Innate Desire. Forthwith, all the local gods who shared the authority of the Great Spirit realized what was happening and successively abandoned control of those parts of the Cosmos which were under their immediate charge. Then the Cosmos, as it reversed its motion, experienced the shock of two contrary momenta, which were simultaneously beginning and coming to an end. It quaked to its depths with a terrible convulsion, which worked corresponding havoc among every race of living creatures. Afterwards, with the lapse of time, the Cosmos began to emerge from this tumult and disorder, to obtain relief from the seismic storms, and to settle down into its own habitual rhythm, in which it exercised control and authority over itself and all that was therein, and followed the instructions of its Creator and Father to the best of its recollection.

'At the beginning it performed its functions with comparative precision, and then with growing clumsiness as it approached the final phase. The cause of this degeneration was the material element in its composition, which was one of the original ingredients in its nature and which had been in an utterly chaotic state before the present cosmic order was imposed upon it. By its Constructor the Cosmos has been endowed with all good qualities. On the other hand, from its previous condition it has inherited in itself and reproduces in its living creatures all the evil and unrighteousness that arises in the World of Space. So long as the Cosmos enjoyed the co-operation of the Helmsman in breeding its living creatures, it implanted in them only trifling defects with a predominance of good; and, when it parts company with Him, it always performs its functions best during the phase least far removed from its release. As time goes on, however, and forgetfulness invades it, the malady of its original disharmony begins to gain the upper hand, until in the final phase it breaks out openly. Then the Cosmos recruits its composition with such minute doses of good elements and with so predominant an admixture of the opposite that it comes to be in danger of involving itself and all things in it in a common destruction.

'At this point God, who had originally set it in order, perceives the straits into which the Cosmos has fallen, and—anxious lest it may break up under the tempestuous blows of confusion and may founder in the fathomless gulf where all things are incommensurable—He again assumes control of its rudder, reverses the tendencies towards sickness and dissolution which had asserted themselves in the previous period when the Cosmos had been left to itself, sets it in order, corrects that which was amiss, and thus endows the Cosmos with immortality and eternal youth. . . .'[1]

The same cyclic doctrine, with the same religious imprint, reappears in the second most famous of the poems of Virgil:

> Ultima Cumaei venit iam carminis aetas;
> magnus ab integro saeclorum nascitur ordo.
> iam redit et virgo, redeunt Saturnia regna,
> iam nova progenies caelo demittitur alto.[2] . . .

[1] Plato: *Politicus*, 269 C 4–270 A; 271 D 2–E 2; 272 D 6–273 E 4. See further the Annex to the present chapter on pp. 585–8 below.

[2] This line reads like a deliberate contradiction of Lucretius: *De Rerum Natura*, Book II, ll. 1153–4, which has been quoted on p. 7, above.—A.J.T.

alter erit tum Tiphys, et altera quae vehat Argo
delectos heroas; erunt etiam altera bella,
atque iterum ad Troiam magnus mittetur Achilles.[1]

This philosophy of sheer recurrence, which intrigued, without ever quite captivating, the Hellenic genius,[2] came to dominate con-contemporary Indic minds, including Siddhārtha Gautama's,[3] and it has exercised the same domination over the mental outlook of Hinduism.

'For Hindus the World is endless repetition, not a progress towards

[1] Virgil: *Eclogue* IV, ll. 4–7 and 34–6.

[2] The allusions to this philosophy in Hellenic literature are far too numerous for us to survey in this place; but we may note one characteristic reference in the surviving works of the Roman historian Tacitus, and a group of references in the *Meditations* of the Roman Emperor Marcus Aurelius.

The passage of Tacitus (*Annals*, Book III, chap. 55) occurs, as an incidental reflexion, at the close of a parenthetical note on the variations in the manners and customs of the Roman aristocracy during the first century of the Principate:

'Unless perchance there is, inherent in all things, a kind of cycle which generates a periodicity of manners and customs to match that of times and seasons. This would imply that our predecessors are not, after all, our superiors in everything, but that our age, too, has produced many monuments of an admirable ingenuity for Posterity to copy.'

A doctrine that seems comforting to Tacitus seems desolating, however, to Marcus.

'There is a deadly monotony about the cyclic motion of the Cosmos—up and down, world without end. . . . Soon we shall be buried under the Earth, and next the Earth herself will be transformed, and then whatever has arisen out of her transmutation will undergo the same process again and again to infinity' (Marcus: *Meditations*, Book IX, chap. 28; cf. Book V, chap. 13, and Book VII, chap. 1).

The emperor-philosopher relentlessly pursues this theory of the objective nature of the Universe into its subjective consequences for the Soul:

'He who has once seen the Present has for ever seen all things—all that will be in an infinite Future, as well as all that has been in a Past that is without beginning. All things are homogeneous and uniform' (Marcus: *Meditations*, Book VI, chap. 37).

The logical conclusion is that a man of forty, if he is not positively deficient in intelligence, must know as much about human life as if he had been studying it for 10,000 years (Book VII, chap. 49)—must, in fact, have beheld all things, past and future (Book XI, chap. 1, quoted in this Study in V. C (i) (*d*) 10, vol. vi, p. 137, below).

This philosophy of disenchantment and *ennui* had, of course, been inherited by Marcus from a long line of Hellenic predecessors (compare, for example, Lucretius: *De Rerum Natura*, Book III, ll. 944–9); and from these it had already been transmitted to the children of alien civilizations upon which a post-Alexandrine Hellenism had impinged. This radiation of a Hellenic *Weltanschauung* is no doubt the explanation of a remarkable assonance between the passages just quoted from Marcus's *Meditations* and a passage in a Jewish philosophical treatise which was written before the beginning of the Christian Era.

'The thing that hath been, it is that which shall be; and that which is done is that which shall be done; and there is no new thing under the Sun. Is there any thing whereof it may be said: "See, this is new"? It hath been already of old time, which was before us' (Ecclesiastes i. 9–10).

A place for this Hellenic philosophy of recurrence was found in the Jewish *Weltanschauung* by the ingenuity of Philo of Alexandria.

'The divine plan (λόγος) which is commonly called Chance (τύχην) makes its rhythmic movement in a cyclic course (χορεύει ἐν κύκλῳ)' (Philo: *Quod Deus Immutabilis*, § 176).

But, notwithstanding this Philonic *tour de force*, the whole conception was too profoundly alien from the Syriac outlook and temperament to allow of any effective reconciliation or even compromise. In Saint Augustine's *De Civitate Dei* (Book XII, chaps. 14, 18, 20, and 21) the philosophy of recurrence is mentioned only to be combated. Yet the Christian theologian is hard put to it when he tries to rebut the suggestion that our passage of Ecclesiastes is an exposition of the cyclic theory of the Hellenic philosophers.

[3] One of the surest marks of the Buddha's greatness is his heroic struggle with this dominating and paralysing idea, until at length he conquered it by finding a way of escape out of the Wheel of Existence into *Nirvāna*. The courage required for this spiritual feat of reconnaissance deserves the paean, written by Lucretius in honour of Democritus, which has been quoted above in II. C (ii) (*b*) 1, vol. i, p. 299.

an end. Creation has rarely the sense which it bears for Europeans. An infinite number of times the Universe has collapsed in flaming or watery ruin, aeons of quiescence follow the collapse, and then the Deity (he has done it an infinite number of times) emits again from himself worlds and souls of the same old kind. . . .

'Hindu chronology revels in periods, whose enormous length, though expressed in figures, leaves no real impression on the mind: days and nights of Brahma, Kalpas, Manvantaras, and Yugas, in which gods and worlds are absorbed into the supreme essence and born again. But there is no finality about these catastrophes: the destruction of the whole Universe is as certain as the death of a mouse, and to the philosopher not more important. Everything is periodic: Buddhas, Jinas, and incarnations of all sorts are all members of a series. They all deserve great respect and are of great importance in their own day, but they are none of them final, still less are they able to create a new Heaven and Earth or to rise above the perpetual flux of Samsāra.'[1]

The exuberant Hindu fancy has even expressed itself in figures which come amusingly close to the laborious calculations of our Western astronomers.

'Time, like soul and matter, is a phase of the Supreme Spirit. As Brahmā wakes or sleeps, the Universe wakes or sleeps also. Each day and each night of Brahmā is an "aeon" (*kalpa*) and is equivalent to a thousand "great ages" (*mahāyuga*): that is to say, 1,000×4,320,000 mortal years. During an "aeon" fourteen Manus or "Fathers of Mankind" appear, each presiding over a period of seventy-one "great ages" with a surplus. Each "great age" is further divided into four "ages" (*yuga*) of progressive deterioration like the golden, silver, brazen and iron ages of Greek and Roman mythology.'[2]

Under the influence of Hinduism or of Neoplatonism[3] or of both, the philosophy of recurrence has actually succeeded in insinuating itself, in the mind of at least one Muslim mystic, into the Syriac myth of the First and Last Things: a myth which insists, in the original, upon the uniqueness of the series of divine events which it purports to reveal. According to Ibn Khaldūn,[4] the Sūfī Ibn Abī Watīl taught that history consists of a recurring cycle of three phases—the first phase being the appearance of a prophet or a saint, the second phase a caliphate, and the third phase the temporary rule of 'the Lie' (*Dajal*) under the reign of Antichrist (*Dajjāl*), pending the appearance of the next deliverer of Mankind. According to

[1] Eliot, Sir Charles: *Hinduism and Buddhism* (London 1921, Arnold, 3 vols.), vol. i, pp. lxviii and 46–7. Compare the same work, vol. ii, pp. 298–9, apropos of the Sānkhya philosophy.

[2] Rapson, E. J., in *The Cambridge History of India*, vol. i (Cambridge 1922, University Press), p. 303, apropos of the chronological scheme of the Puranas.

[3] The doctrine of the world-periods is mentioned in passing by Plotinus in *Ennead* V. 7. 2, *ad fin.*

[4] Ibn Khaldūn: *Muqaddamāt*, translation by de Slane, Baron McG. (Paris 1863–8, Imprimerie Impériale, 3 vols), vol. ii, p. 192.

this Sūfī scheme of history, the expected Mahdī was to play the part, in the next age to come, that had been played in the current age by the Prophet Muhammad.

Are these 'vain repetitions of the Gentiles'[1] really the law of the Universe and therefore, incidentally, the law of the histories of civilizations? This question is of immeasurable importance—

> temporis aeterni quoniam, non unius horae
> ambigitur status[2]

—and if we find that the answer is in the affirmative we can hardly escape the conclusion that we are the perpetual victims of an everlasting cosmic practical joke, which condemns us to endure our sufferings and to overcome our difficulties and to purify ourselves of our sins—only to know in advance that the automatic and inevitable lapse of a certain meaningless measure of Time cannot fail to stultify all our human exertions by reproducing the same situation again and again *ad infinitum*, just as though we had never exerted ourselves at all. In an eternally repetitive universe all human endurance becomes the torment of a Tityos or an Ixion, and all human action becomes the ineffective gesture of a Tantalus or else the lost labour of a Sisyphus or a Danaid.[3]

This conclusion may be tolerable to an unusually robust intellect in an unusually sanguine mood. Aristotle, for example, shows no sign of distress when he pricks the bubble of his own philosophy by making the casual observation, in the middle of a treatise on meteorology, that

> 'In human history the recurrence of identical scientific views does not happen just once or twice or a small number of times; it happens *ad infinitum*.'[4]

In another passage, again, Aristotle deals with the problem of periodicity in human affairs, through the concrete example of the implications of a recurrence of the Trojan War, as though these implications were nothing more than an intellectual conundrum.

> 'How are the concepts of priority and posteriority to be taken? Are we to take it that the generation of the Trojan War is prior to ours, and that their predecessors are prior to them, and that those who are previous

[1] Matt. vi. 7.

[2] Lucretius: *De Rerum Natura*, Book III, ll. 1073–4, quoted in I. C (i) (*a*), vol. i, on p. 56, footnote, above.

[3] It is possible (see V. C (ii) (*a*), Annex II, vol. vi, pp. 522–3, below) that the repetition *in aeternum* of the actions and sufferings of these figures of Hellenic mythology, which is of the essence of their myths in the forms in which these have come down to us, was not an original trait but was an adventitious idea that was read into them, in and after the sixth century B.C., under the influence of Orphism.

[4] οὐ γὰρ δὴ φήσομεν ἅπαξ οὐδὲ δὶς οὐδ' ὀλιγάκις τὰς αὐτὰς δόξας ἀνακυκλεῖν γινομένας ἐν τοῖς ἀνθρώποις, ἀλλ' ἀπειράκις—Aristotle: *Meteorologica*, Book I, chap. 3, apropos of Anaxagoras' anticipation of Aristotle's own theory of the ether. A similar illustration of the cyclic theory is used by Saint Augustine in *De Civitate Dei*, Book XII, chap. 14.

are prior *ad infinitum*? Or, if the Universe has a beginning and a middle and an end, and if, when anybody is brought by old age to the terminus, he comes round right back again to the starting-point, then what stands in the way of our being nearer to the starting-point than the generation of the Trojan War were?[1] And if, in virtue of this, we might possess priority, what stands in the way of a correspondence between the process of the genesis and disintegration of things subject to decay and the circular motion that is characteristic of all the heavenly bodies? Why should not their genesis and decay be repetitive, in the sense of the proverb that "Human life is a vicious circle"? It would be silly, of course, to suppose that the same state of human society was reproduced statistically, but a morphological reproduction would not be so difficult to demonstrate. On this showing, we might actually possess priority, and one might conceive the structure of the series as a continuous and uniform process of coming round again full circle to the starting-point. According to Alcmaeon, human beings are subject to death because they do not possess the art of joining their beginning to their end; and it is a brilliant observation if one takes the aphorism symbolically without attempting a literal application. Well, if human history is a circle, and if a circle has no starting-point and no terminus, it follows that the priority which consists in being nearer to the starting-point cannot be possessed either by us over the generation of the Trojan War or by that generation over us.'[2]

Thus Aristotle propounds the problem and feels no pang; but when Virgil plays with the doctrine of recurrence in his Fourth Eclogue, and applies it in his turn to the Trojan War in a passage quoted above, his sensitive imagination apprehends the nightmare vision of human affairs which it is on the point of conjuring up, and his literary dexterity promptly contrives a deft retreat. Virgil grasps at the Platonic conceit of an alternation between two movements in contrary directions, and professes to have caught his glimpse of a recurring Trojan War in a magic rewinding of the film of Hellenic history from the year of Pollio's consulship right back to the blissful reign of Cronos.[3] This reverse-movement is so

[1] In this abstract speculation Aristotle happens to have hit the mark in respect of the particular pair of historical moments which he has taken as his illustrations; for 'the generation of the Trojan War' actually lived at the very terminus of the history of the Minoan Civilization, whereas Aristotle's own generation, which lived more than eight hundred years later on the single-track scale of Astronomical Time, was born into the history of the Hellenic Civilization more than a thousand years before its terminal date. Thus, as a matter of fact, Aristotle was prior to Agamemnon (in the sense in which Aristotle uses the term 'priority' in this passage) by more than 800 years if we find the Hellenic counterpart and 'contemporary' of the Minoan Agamemnon in a Theodoric, and by more than 900 if we find him in a Dagobert. But of course this historical fact is no sufficient ground for a theory of cycles that are all predestined and are each of the same invariable length.—A.J.T.

[2] Aristotle: *Problemata*, xviii. 3.

[3] Here Virgil's ultimate source may well be the passage in Plato's *Politicus* from which quotations have been made in this chapter on pp. 26–7, above; for the notion of a reverse movement, which is applied to the life of the Cosmos as a whole in the portions of the passage that have been quoted, is worked out in the context with particular application to the life of Man and the other animals, and is explicitly made to lead back in this domain to the ἐπὶ τῆς Κρόνου δυνάμεως βίος (Plato: *Politicus*, 270 D–272 D).

miraculously speeded up that the historic events which it has taken twelve centuries to evolve are re-wound, in the poet's fancy, between the birth and the coming of age of the Child of Promise. In this setting the recurrent Trojan War is lightly dismissed by Virgil as a slight and momentary recrudescence of the Old Adam, which simply serves as a foil to the swiftly and securely re-dawning Golden Age, like a patch which brings out the colour of an eighteenth-century beauty's cheek.

Pauca tamen suberunt priscae vestigia fraudis,
quae temptare Thetim ratibus, quae cingere muris
oppida, quae iubeant telluri infindere sulcos.[1]

Yet the poet has not really succeeded, by this *leger de main*, in exorcising the spectre which he has evoked; for in his heart he knows all the time that Life and Action cannot ever really run backwards, and that the Trojan War, whose recurrence he has foreseen, cannot be just an interlude after which the Golden Age will set in again untarnished. When Virgil returns from his day-dream of an Earthly Paradise Regained to resume the spiritual burden of his own tormented generation, he confesses that the heroic warfare of the Achaeans in the pre-Hellenic interregnum has led on, through a continuous chain of *karma*, to the internecine warfare of the Roman war-lords.

Satis iam pridem sanguine nostro
Laomedonteae luimus periuria Troiae . . .
quippe ubi fas versum atque nefas; tot bella per orbem.
tam multae scelerum facies, non ullus aratro
dignus honos, squalent abductis arva colonis,
et curvae rigidum falces conflantur in ensem. . . .
vicinae ruptis inter se legibus urbes
arma ferunt; saevit toto Mars impius orbe;
ut cum carceribus sese effudere quadrigae,
addunt in spatio, et frustra retinacula tendens
fertur equis auriga neque audit currus habenas.[2]

Is the Trojan War to recur innumerable times over, when it is fated each time to precipitate an age-long avalanche of wickedness and woe? This question, which Virgil dares not face, is answered by Shelley in a chorus which begins as a Virgilian reminiscence and ends on a note which is altogether Shelley's own:—

The World's great age begins anew,
The golden years return,
The Earth doth like a snake renew
Her winter weeds outworn:
Heaven smiles, and faiths and empires gleam
Like wrecks of a dissolving dream . . .

[1] Virgil: *Eclogue* IV, ll. 31–3.
[2] Virgil: *Georgic* I, ll. 501–2, 505–8, 510–4.

A loftier Argo cleaves the main,
  Fraught with a later prize;
Another Orpheus sings again,
  And loves, and weeps, and dies;
A new Ulysses leaves once more
Calypso for his native shore.

Oh! write no more the Tale of Troy,
  If Earth Death's scroll must be!
Nor mix with Laian rage the joy
  Which dawns upon the free,
Although a subtler Sphinx renew
Riddles of death Thebes never knew. . . .

Oh cease! Must Hate and Death return?
  Cease! Must men kill and die?
Cease! Drain not to its dregs the urn
  Of bitter prophecy.
The World is weary of the Past:
Oh might it die or rest at last!

If the law of the Universe is really the sardonic law *Plus ça change plus c'est la même chose*,[1] no wonder that the poet cries for the Buddhist release from a Wheel of Existence which may be a thing of beauty so long as it is merely guiding the stars in their courses, but which is an intolerable tread-mill for our human feet.

Does reason constrain us to believe that the cyclic movement of the stars is also the movement of human history? A skilful advocate of the cyclic doctrine might concede that, on the showing of our Western cosmologists, the wave-length of the hypothetical social cycles can have no direct relation to the vastly longer wave-length of the hypothetical cycles of alternate unwinding and re-winding in the clockwork of the material Universe.[2] But, having made this concession, he might then go on to suggest that the occurrence of symptoms of periodicity in the social history of Mankind and in the astronomical history of the Cosmos alike is a coincidence which can hardly be dismissed as just fortuitous. Does it not rather indicate that this periodicity is the very rhythm of Existence; and, in the course of this Study of History, have we not stumbled upon examples of the same rhythm time and again—in fact, whenever we have had any measure of apparent success in digging down to the roots of the Tree of Life and in laying our finger on the springs of human action? What, 'in the last analysis', are those movements of Yin-and-Yang and Challenge-and-Response and Withdrawal-and-Return and Apparentation-and-Affiliation

[1] Karr, Alphonse: *Les Guêpes*, January 1849.
[2] For this consideration see p. 10, above.

which we have taken some intellectual pleasure in discerning and bringing to light? Are not these all just different variations on the periodic rhythm?

Our reply to this dialectical manœuvre will be to concede, in turn, our opponent's point but to contest the inference that he seeks to draw from it.

Certainly, in all these movements of the forces that weave the web of human history, an element of sheer recurrence can be detected. Indeed, it stares us in the face. Yet the shuttle which shoots backwards and forwards across the loom of Time[1] in a perpetual to-and-fro is all this time bringing into existence a tapestry in which there is manifestly 'a progress towards an end' and not just an 'endless repetition' in the likeness of the shuttle's own action. This we know from our empirical study of the outcome of Yin-and-Yang and Challenge-and-Response and Withdrawal-and-Return in the histories of civilizations.

The transition from Yin to Yang, in any given case, is no doubt one repetition of a repetitive action; yet this repetition is neither vain nor stale, since it is the necessary condition for an act of creation which is new and spontaneous and unique.[2] Similarly, the response to a challenge which provokes a further challenge and thereby evokes a further response which is likewise provocative in its turn, no doubt sets up a cyclic movement like the endless repetition of a particular group of figures that follows the appearance of the first recurrent cypher in a recurring decimal. Yet we have seen that it is precisely this kind of response—the response which inaugurates a cyclic movement by providing for its own successor—that releases the Promethean *élan* of social growth.[3] Again, the withdrawal and return of individual personalities, or of minorities, who first leave and afterwards re-enter the common life of the society to which they belong, may look like a monotonous process when the historical examples are set out in a catalogue. Yet we have seen that these are the creative individuals and minorities to whose experiences and actions a growing society owes its growth; and they are able to exercise this creative power upon their return because they have acquired it during their withdrawal. At each repetition the familiar cycle of Withdrawal-and-Return brings about a unique transformation of a personality and enhancement of its powers and ennoblement of its functions.

The simple truth is that, in any analysis of rhythm, we have to distinguish between the movements of the part and of the whole

[1] See Goethe: *Faust*, ll. 501–9, quoted in Part II. B, vol. i, p. 204, above, and again in V. C (iii), vol. vi, p. 324, below.
[2] See II. C (ii) (*b*) 1, *passim*, in vol. i, above.
[3] See Part III. B, *passim*, in vol. iii, above.

and between the natures of the means and of the end. There is no law of pre-established harmony which decrees that the end must have the same nature as the means or the whole the same movement as the part; and this is immediately obvious in the case of the wheel, which is the original simile and the permanent symbol of the whole cyclic philosophy. The movement of the wheel is admittedly repetitive in relation to the wheel's own axle; but the wheel has only been manufactured and fitted to its axle in order to become a part of a vehicle; and the fact that the vehicle can only move in virtue of the wheel's circular movement round the axle does not compel the vehicle itself to travel like a merry-go-round in a circular track. It is true that, without the repetitive circular movement of the wheel, the vehicle could not move on any track at all; but while the wheel is indispensable to the vehicle as a means of locomotion, it is incapable of dictating the course on which the vehicle is to move when once the wheel is working and the vehicle's powers of locomotion are thereby assured. The course depends upon the manipulation of the reins or the steering-gear by the driver. It would be fantastic to suggest that, just because the wheel possesses the power to bring the vehicle to a halt by refusing to go on turning round, it must therefore possess the further power of compelling the vehicle to travel in a circular orbit, in the likeness of the wheel's own orbit round its axle, by some occult art of sympathetic magic![1]

[1] The following comments on this passage have been communicated to the writer by Lord Samuel, who very kindly read the present chapter before it went to press:

'The illustration of the wheel and the wagon is ingenious and illuminating; but does it do more than remove the difficulty from the long range to the short range—or rather the relatively shorter range? For the short range is long enough to include, not only every individual life, but successions of many generations. If we are to distinguish between wheel and wagon, individuals are particles of the wheel, since they are subject to the short range alternation. Although in a thousand years the hub of the wheel, with the rest of the wagon, may be further forward, the individuals, on this theory, must find themselves inexorably moved round the circle. And is not the movement of the wagon itself the consequence of the movement of the wheels? If not, of what is it the consequence? I believe the truth to be that each person, and each society, is indeed the product of causes, and that Necessity prevails, if by Necessity you mean the total sum of all those causes. But the causes in every case are innumerable. If they are traced back even some little way towards their origins, they will soon run into millions, most of them indefinable by us. And their interactions are of infinite complexity. It is impossible, therefore, to predict what will be the outcome of any actual combination of causes, whether in the case of a person or of a society. We may be able to disentangle a few causes here and there, and say that experience shows that such and such effects will follow from them. And we do this in our systems of education and of politics. But we cannot carry this process far enough, or accurately enough, to be able to predict what will happen in each particular case, and that is why life is an art rather than a science—and so, I believe, is politics. An individual acts according to his character, and a society similarly; and, starting as from that character, as it is at any moment, the individual or the society has freedom to act. But the character itself is the product of causes, and therefore is, at that level, the outcome of Necessity.'

In Lord Samuel's argument (which will also be found set out less summarily in his since published book *Belief and Action* (London 1937, Cassell), pp. 194–205) it will be seen that he does not disagree with the present writer's primary proposition that in human affairs there is a net of Necessity as well as a breath of Freedom. Lord Samuel's criticism is directed against the secondary proposition that the texture of cause-and-

Indeed, if the relations between wheel and vehicle or part and whole or means and end are governed by any law at all, it is not a law of identity but a law of diversity, under which a repetitive movement of the wheel or the part or the means brings about a non-repetitive movement of the vehicle or the whole or the end, while conversely the end attains its unique realization and the whole its unique individuality and the vehicle its unique goal through the repetitive employment of similar means and the repetitive juxtaposition of standard parts and the repetitive revolution of a wheel round its axle.

In the mechanism of any mechanical tractor this is true not only of the road-wheels but of every wheel in the engine, including the fly-wheel. To the novice in mechanics the giant fly-wheel, which is the most prominent part of a traction-engine in motion, seems to be spinning round quite aimlessly in the air and using up power which might be better employed; but the mechanician knows that, if the fly-wheel were un-mounted, then the road-wheels of the traction-engine might catch and stick at their dead-points, with the result that the traction-engine itself, with all its train of trucks, would be brought to an abrupt halt instead of moving steadily forward towards its journey's end. Thus, contrary to all appearance, the sheer cyclic movement of the fly-wheel is helping to carry the whole train forward continuously in a straight line, and the train is accomplishing its 'one-way' journey through the agency of wheels that are turning round and round.

This harmony of two diverse movements—a major irreversible movement which is borne on the wings of a minor repetitive movement—is perhaps the essence of what we mean by rhythm; and we can discern this play of forces not only in the mechanized rhythm of our man-made machinery but likewise in the organic rhythm of life. The annual procession of the seasons, which brings with it the annual withdrawal and return of vegetation, has made possible the secular evolution of the Vegetable Kingdom. The sombre cycle of birth and reproduction and death has made possible the evolution of all the higher animals up to Man

effect is woven on a pattern that can be discerned by human minds. This proposition is no doubt speculative and disputable. The empirical method by which we have tried to test it can establish, at best, only a presumption and not a proof. If, however, for the sake of the argument, this presumption may be assumed for the moment to have been established, that conclusion does not, so far as the present writer can see, circumscribe the bounds of human freedom more narrowly than they have been drawn by Lord Samuel. If once it is admitted that there is an element of Necessity—coexisting side by side with an element of Freedom—in human affairs, the scope of this Freedom is surely not affected by our answer to the question whether Saeva Necessitas, in her own acknowledged sphere, dances to a perceptible rhythm or obeys no intelligible law. At any rate the writer heartily agrees with Lord Samuel (*Belief and Action*, p. 205) that for human beings 'everything depends upon their own individual decisions and actions', and that 'there can be no division between State morality and personal morality'.

himself.[1] The goose-step of a pair of legs enables a walker to 'cover the ground'; the pumping-action of the lungs and the heart enables the human being to live out his life; the bars of music and the feet, lines, stanzas and cantos of poetry enable the composer and the poet to expound their themes; the scenes and acts of plays permit the presentation of the plots; the cyclic rotation of the praying-wheel carries the Buddhist towards the goal of *Nirvāna* in the alternative vehicles of the Hīnayāna and the Mahāyāna; and even the Wheel of Existence, from which the Buddhist discipline promises release, produces the abiding and cumulative burden of *karma* which is handed on from one incarnation-cycle to the next and thereby transforms a trivial round into a tragic history. The planetary 'Great Year'[2] itself, which is perhaps the origin of the whole cyclic philosophy, can no longer be mistaken for the ultimate and all-embracing movement of a stellar cosmos in which our local solar system has dwindled into a speck of dust under the mighty magnifying lens of our latter-day Western Astronomy. The repetitive 'music of the spheres' dies down to an undertone in an expanding physical universe of nebulae and star-clusters which are apparently receding from one another with incredible velocity, while the relativity of the Space-Time framework gives to each successive position of the vast astral array the irrevocable historic uniqueness of a dramatic 'situation' in some play in which the actors are living personalities.

Thus the detection of periodic repetitive movements in our analysis of the process of Civilization does not by any means imply that the process itself, to which these contributory movements minister, is of the same cyclic order as they are. On the contrary, if any inference at all can be drawn legitimately from the periodicity of these minor movements, we may rather infer that the major movement which they bear along upon their monotonously rising and falling wings is of the diverse order, or, in other words, that it is not recurrent but is progressive. This tentative conclusion[3] is

[1] For the annual cycle of the corn and the life-cycle of Mankind and for the analogies between the two see III. C (ii) (*b*), vol. iii, pp. 248–63, above.

[2] For the Babylonic discovery of the 'Great Year' see the present chapter, pp. 23–4, above, and V. C (i) (*c*) 1, vol. v, pp. 56–7, below.

[3] In the view that has been put forward above, a Spenglerian belief in an element of recurrence in human affairs has been combined with an Einsteinian belief in an element of uniqueness and irreversibility in the movement of the stars. An eighteenth-century philosopher who combined a belief in human progress with a Newtonian conception of physics saw the Physical Universe as the wheel and Mankind as the vehicle for which this wheel's vain repetitions provide a means of locomotion along a 'one-way' road.

'Les phénomènes de la nature, soumis à des lois constantes, sont renfermés dans un cercle de révolutions toujours les mêmes. Tout renaît, tout périt; et dans ces générations successives, par lesquelles les végétaux et les animaux se reproduisent, le temps ne fait que ramener à chaque instant l'image de ce qu'il a fait disparaître. La succession des hommes, au contraire, offre de siècle en siècle un spectacle toujours varié. La raison, les passions, la liberté, produisent sans cesse de nouveaux événements. Tous les âges

sufficient for our purpose at the moment, since it effectively breaks the spell that was threatening to keep Ixion bound for ever to his wheel and Sisyphus for ever rolling his stone towards the summit of the mountain. We are not condemned to believe in the cyclic version of predestinarianism as the supreme law of our human history; and this was the last form of the necessitarian doctrine with which we had to contend.

This is a message of encouragement for us children of the Western Civilization as we drift to-day alone, on the 'wide wide sea' of human history, with none but dead or stricken civilizations around us. Manifestly 'the door of death is not closed'.[1] *Si monumentum requiris circumspice.* The dead civilizations strew the deck of the ship of human fortunes; and we, and we only, are left.[2] By the Law of Chance the odds are certainly sixteen to ten, and possibly twenty-five to one, that Death the Leveller will lay his icy hand on us likewise; and, as we contemplate these disconcerting figures, we may still be inclined to repine in the elegiac mood of William Dunbar's Lament:

I that in heill was and gladnèss
Am trublit now with great sickness
And feeblit with infirmity:
Timor Mortis conturbat me . . .

That strong unmerciful tyrand
Takis, on the motheris breast sowkand,
The babe full of benignitie:
Timor Mortis conturbat me . . .

He spairis no lord for his piscence,
Na clerk for his intelligence;
His awful straik may no man flee:
Timor Mortis conturbat me . . .

He has done petuously devour
The noble Chaucer, of makaris flour,
The Monk of Bury, and Gower, all three:
Timor Mortis conturbat me . . .

He has tane Rowll of Aberdene,
And gentill Rowll of Corstophine;
Two better fallowis did no man see:
Timor Mortis conturbat me . . .

sont enchaînés . . . et le genre humain, considéré depuis son origine, paraît aux yeux d'un philosophe un tout immense, qui lui-même a, comme chaque individu, son enfance et ses progrès.'—Turgot, A. R. J.: 'Second Discours, sur les Progrès Successifs de l'Esprit Humain, prononcé le 11 Décembre, 1750', in *Œuvres de Turgot* (Paris 1844, Guillaumin, 2 vols.), vol. ii, pp. 597–8.

1 Lucretius: *De Rerum Natura*, Book V, l. 373, quoted in Part IV. A, on p. 4, above.

2 1 Kings xviii. 22, and xix. 10 and 14.

Sen he has all my brothers tane,
He will nocht let me live alane;
Of force I mon his next prey be:
Timor Mortis conturbat me . . .

Yet, even in our forlorn and melancholy plight, our deliverance from the incubus of the predestinarian creed should put us in better heart; for, if this creed is non-proven, then even in Life-in-Death there is still Hope-against-Hope. The Goddess with whom we have to do battle is not Saeva Necessitas[1] with her lethal armoury, but only Probability, whom mortal valour wielding mortal weapons may one day drive ignominiously off the field, as Diomede, with Athena's blessing, once routed Aphrodite.[2] The Mariner's proper watchword, as he keeps his lonely vigil in this haunted ship upon enchanted seas, is not the Scots poet's elegy but the Greek sailor's epitaph:

Ναυηγοῦ τάφος εἰμί· σὺ δὲ πλέε· καὶ γὰρ ὅθ' ἡμεῖς
ὠλόμεθ', αἱ λοιπαὶ νῆες ἐποντοπόρουν.[3]

The dead civilizations are not 'dead by fate'; and therefore a living civilization is not doomed inexorably in advance *migrare ad plures*: to join the majority of its kind that have suffered shipwreck. Though sixteen civilizations may have perished already to our knowledge, and nine others may be now at the point of death, and though Nature, in her wanton prodigality, may be wont to slay the representatives of a species, not by tens or scores, but by thousands and tens of thousands,[4] before she rouses herself to create a new specific mutation, we need fear no evil from the encompassing shadow of Death;[5] for we are not compelled to submit our fate to the blind arbitrament of statistics. The divine spark of creative power is instinct in ourselves; and if we have the grace to kindle it into flame, then the stars in their courses[6] cannot defeat our efforts to attain the goal of human endeavours.

II. LOSS OF COMMAND OVER THE ENVIRONMENT?

(*a*) THE PHYSICAL ENVIRONMENT

If we have proved to our satisfaction that the breakdowns of civilizations are not brought about by the operation, either recurrent or progressive, of cosmic forces which are outside human control, we have still to find the true cause of these human catastrophes; and, in pursuing our search, we shall look now for some fatal miscarriage in the action of the human beings whose overlapping fields

[1] Horace: *Carmina*, Book I, Ode 35, l. 17.
[2] *Iliad*, Book V, ll. 330–54.
[3] Theodorides in *Anthologia Palatina*, No. 282.
[4] 1 Samuel xviii. 7.
[5] Psalm xxiii. 4.
[6] Judges v. 20.

of activity conjure a civilization into existence on their common ground.[1] Are the breakdowns of civilizations due to some loss of command over the environment on the part of their human 'members'? In attempting to answer this question, it will be convenient to abide by our usual distinction between two kinds of environment: the physical and the human.

Do civilizations break down owing to a loss of command over the physical environment? As a measure of the degree of command over the physical environment that is possessed by any given society at any given stage in its history, we may take, as before, the state of its technique; and we have already ascertained, in the course of a previous inquiry into the process by which civilizations grow, that, if we set ourselves to plot out two sets of curves—one set representing the vicissitudes in the histories of civilizations and the other set the contemporary vicissitudes in the state of technique—the two sets not only fail to correspond but display wide and frequent discrepancies.[2] We find cases of technique improving while civilizations remain static or go into decline, as well as examples of the converse situation in which technique remains static while civilizations are in movement—either forward or backward[3] as the case may be.[4] It will be seen that, in the act of proving that an increase of command over the physical environment is not the criterion of the growths of civilizations, we have gone a long way towards proving incidentally that a loss of command over the physical environment is not the criterion of their breakdowns. In order to complete this latter demonstration in this place, we have still to show that, in certain cases in which the breakdown and disintegration of a civilization have been accompanied by a decline in technique, so that the two curves here exceptionally coincide, the coincidence does not mean that the downward movement of technique and the downward movement of the civilization are related to one another as cause and as effect respectively.

An investigation of these cases will make it clear that, in so far as any causal relation at all can be established, it is always the decline of the civilization that is the cause and the decline of technique the consequence or symptom. When a civilization is in

[1] See III. C (ii) (*a*), vol. iii, pp. 223–48, above.

[2] See III. C (i) (*b*), vol. iii, pp. 154–74, above.

[3] 'Pour la vapeur et toutes les découvertes industrielles, je dirai aussi, comme de l'imprimerie, que ce sont de grands moyens; j'ajouterai que l'on a vu quelquefois des procédés nés de découvertes scientifiques se perpétuer a l'état de routine, quand le mouvement intellectuel qui les avait fait naître s'était arrêté pour toujours, et avait laissé perdre le secret théorique d'où ces procédés émanaient. Enfin, je rappellerai que le bien-être matériel n'a jamais été qu'une annexe extérieure de la civilisation, et qu'on n'a jamais entendu dire d'une société qu'elle avait vécu uniquement parce qu'elle connaissait les moyens d'aller vite et de se bien vêtir.'—de Gobineau, le Comte J. A.: *Essai sur l'Inégalité des Races Humaines* (Paris 1853–5, Firmin Didot, 4 vols.), vol. i, pp. 200–1.

[4] See III. C (i) (*b*), vol. iii, p. 159, above.

decline in all its aspects and activities, it sometimes happens that a particular technique which has been both feasible for and profitable to this civilization in the growth-stage now begins to encounter increasing social obstacles and to yield diminishing economic returns; and if, in the end, the technique in question becomes positively and patently unremunerative, it is sometimes deliberately abandoned even before it has become socially impossible to practise. It would obviously be a complete inversion of the true order of cause and effect in such a case to suggest that the abandonment of the technique was neither an act of economic policy nor a confession of social bankruptcy, but was a consequence of a loss of technical command, and that this hypothetical loss of command, in its turn, was the cause of the long antecedent breakdown of the civilization. The cause of this breakdown is not to be found in a retrogression in technique, when this retrogression is no more than a symptom of the decline by which the breakdown is followed.

An obvious case in point is the abandonment of the Roman roads in Western Europe, which was manifestly not the cause but the consequence of the break-up of the Roman Empire and the previous breakdown of a Hellenic Society which was embodied in the Roman Empire in the last stage but one of the Hellenic decline. This social malady was the cause of the abandonment of the roads, and not any loss of the technique of road-building and road-maintenance. These Roman roads became derelict, not through a failure of technical skill, but because in Western Europe, between the fifth century of the Christian Era and the eighteenth, the general state of society was such that a road-system of the Roman standard would not have paid its way and would therefore have been a social incubus instead of a social asset. Since the recent revival of road-building in the Western World, there have been similar examples of the deliberate abandonment, for the same reason, of roads that have been built in non-Western countries which have been under temporary Western occupation. For instance, the roads built by the British authorities in the Ionian Islands during the British protectorate of 1815–64 have been partly abandoned, or at least they have considerably deteriorated, since the termination of the British connexion and the incorporation of the islands into the Kingdom of Greece. And the same fate has overtaken the roads that were built by the Allied Armies in Greek Macedonia in 1916–18, and by a British force in Eastern Persia (to the Persian city of Mashhad from the British-Indian rail-head in Baluchistan) during the same years.

Nor can the decline and fall of the Hellenic Civilization be traced back to a decline in technique simply by extending our vision from the single technique of road-building to embrace the whole technical apparatus of economic life. 'The economic explanation of the decay of the Ancient World must be rejected completely. . . . The economic simplification of ancient life was not the cause of what we call the decline of the Ancient World, but one of the aspects of the more general phenomenon.'[1] This more general phenomenon, to which Professor Rostovtzeff alludes in this passage, is 'the failure of administration and the ruin of the middle class, as revealed by the Theodosian Code', which is described in detail by Professor Dill.[2] This general social breakdown accounts for the abandonment not only of the Roman roads but also of other parts of the technical apparatus of the Roman World which were abandoned at the same time: for instance, the shipping services which had ensured the food-supply of the population of the City of Rome by providing for the maritime transport of corn that had been grown on the African side of the Mediterranean. Without recourse to the unsubstantiated hypothesis of a loss of technical skill, the technical decline is easily deducible from social causes; but, by the same token, this technical decline affords no explanation of the social decline which is the object of our present investigation.

The abandonment of the Roman roads has a contemporary parallel in the partial abandonment of the far older irrigation-system in the alluvial delta of the Tigris–Euphrates Basin.[3] In the seventh century of the Christian Era the reconditioning of these hydro-engineering works was left in default in a large section of South-Western 'Irāq after the works had been put out of action by a flood which had probably done no more serious damage than many floods that had come and gone in the course of the preceding four thousand years. Thereafter, in the thirteenth century, the entire irrigation-system of 'Irāq was allowed to go to ruin. Why, on these occasions, did the inhabitants of 'Irāq abandon the conservation of a system which their predecessors had successfully maintained for some thousands of years without a break—a system, moreover, on which the agricultural productivity of the country depended and, therewith, its capacity for supporting the existing population at its existing standard of living? At first sight, this

1 Rostovtzeff, M.: *The Social and Economic History of the Roman Empire* (Oxford 1926, Clarendon Press), pp. 302–5 and 482–5.

2 Dill, Samuel: *Roman Society in the Last Century of the Western Empire*, 2nd edition London 1905, Macmillan), Book III.

3 See Lestrange, Guy: *The Lands of the Eastern Caliphate* (Cambridge 1905, University Press), pp. 25–9. The great catastrophe, which resulted in a diversion of the main stream of the Tigris in its lower course from a channel approximately coincident with its present bed into the channel now known as the Shatt-al-Hayy, appears to have taken place in the reign of the Sasanian Emperor Khusrū Parwīz (*imperabat* A.D. 590–628). There had been an anticipatory disaster in the reign of Kawādh [Qubādh] I (*imperabat* A.D. 488–531), but this had been partially, though only partially, retrieved in the reign of Khusrū Anūshirwān (*imperabat* A.D. 531–79).

manifestly suicidal neglect looks so perverse that a sheer inability to perform the work, owing to a loss of technique, might appear to be the only plausible explanation. Yet no historical evidence of this hypothetical loss of engineering technique appears to be forthcoming; and the true explanation seems to be that the abandonment of the works was not the cause but was rather the consequence of a decline in population and in prosperity which was itself the result of social causes. The ancient irrigation-system of the Land of Shinar was allowed to fall locally derelict in the seventh century of the Christian Era and to go to ruin altogether in the thirteenth century because, in each of those two ages, the Syriac Civilization was at so low an ebb in ʿIrāq, and the consequent general state of insecurity was so extreme, that nobody at the time had either the means of investing capital, or the motive for employing energy, in river-conservancy and irrigation work. So far from it being a loss of technique that wrecked the irrigation-system of ʿIrāq and thereby contributed to the decline and fall of the Syriac Civilization, it was this social decline and fall that caused the progressive abandonment of the ʿIrāqī irrigation-system by overwhelming the people of ʿIrāq under a succession of social catastrophes: the great Romano-Persian War of A.D. 603–28; the consequent, and immediately subsequent, overrunning of ʿIrāq by the Primitive Muslim Arabs; and the Mongol invasion of A.D. 1258 which dealt the moribund Syriac Civilization its *coup de grâce*.[1] By the same token, our examination of the technical factor leaves the decline and fall of the Syriac Civilization still unexplained.

The conclusion that the decline and fall of the Syriac Civilization is to be regarded not as an effect but rather as the cause of the progressive ruin of the irrigation-system of ʿIrāq in the sixth, seventh, and thirteenth centuries of the Christian Era is supported by an historical precedent; for the Syriac Society was not, of course, the first civilization that had installed itself in the Land of Shinar. In this portion of its eventual domain the Syriac Society was the residuary legatee of the Babylonic (which was itself the successor of a Sumeric Society which had been the original creator of the fields and cities of Sumer and Akkad out of an inhospitable and untenanted jungle-swamp[2]); and the unrepaired ruin of the irrigation-system of the whole of the Land of Shinar in the course of the

[1] In a similar way the anticipatory physical disaster in the reign of Kawādh [Qubādh] I can be explained as the reflexion of an earlier bout of social catastrophes: e.g. the destruction of the Emperor Pīrūz and his army by the Ephthalite Eurasian Nomads in A.D. 484 (see V. C (i) (*c*) 3, vol. v, p. 279, footnote 1, and V. C (i) (*c*) 3, Annex II, vol. v, p. 600, below); the Romano-Persian wars of A.D. 502–5 and 528–32; and the social upheaval, fathered by the Prophet Mazdak, which came to a head *circa* A.D. 528–9 (see V. C (i) (*c*) 2, vol. v, p. 129, below).

[2] See II. C (ii) (*b*) 2, vol. i, pp. 315–18, above.

last eight centuries of Syriac history has an analogue in the unretrieved destruction of the local network of drainage- and irrigation-canals in the territory of the ancient city-state of Ur in an earlier age when the Babylonic Civilization was *in extremis*.

At other points in this Study[1] the disintegration of the Babylonic Civilization is traced through a 'Time of Troubles', which was precipitated by the social disease of Assyrian militarism, into a universal state which was inaugurated by the Neo-Babylonian Empire and was continued in the form of the Achaemenian and Seleucid régimes; and it was under these last two political dispensations that the moribund Babylonic Society was progressively absorbed into the tissues of an encircling Syriac Society until the last vestiges of a distinctive Babylonic culture were obliterated in the last century B.C. It was also in this age that, in the territory of Ur, the local irrigation and agriculture which had been maintained there over a previous period of at least 3,000 years were permanently put out of action by a shift in the course of the Euphrates which worked havoc that was never repaired.[2] Thus, here again, we find a decline of civilization and a decay of irrigation proceeding *pari passu*; but, here again likewise, there is no suggestion that the failure to retrieve the physical disaster was either the consequence of a loss of technique or the cause of the accompanying dissolution of an ancient society. According to the greatest living authority on the subject, it is rather the decrepitude into which the Babylonic Civilization had already sunk, by the time when the physical disaster occurred, that accounts for the failure to bring the waters under human control again.

'To make good the disaster required a co-ordinated effort which the country then was too poor or too ill-organized to attempt. . . . [For] everything depended on hard work and upon system. The boast of a Sumerian king was that he had honoured the gods, had overcome his enemies, had secured equal justice for his people, and had built canals. The last was not the least important function of the Government; but the task did not stop with the building. The cleaning of the channels,

[1] See I. C (i) (*b*), vol. i, pp. 79–81, and II. D (v), vol. ii, pp. 137–8, above, and IV. C (ii) (*b*) 2, in the present volume, pp. 100–103, and IV. C (iii) (*c*) 3 (α), pp. 468–84, below.

[2] The fatal economic effects of this unretrieved physical disaster are forcefully described in the following passage from the pen of Sir Leonard Woolley, the modern Western archaeologist who has rescued Ur from an oblivion under which the famous city lay for more than two thousand years:

'The river Euphrates burst its banks and, flowing across the open plain, made a new bed for itself more or less where it runs now, eleven miles to the east; and with that change the entire system of water-supply was broken up. The old irrigation-canals that had tapped the river further up were left high and dry; the new river-course, not yet confined within artificial banks, was a wide lake whose waters, level with the plain, blocked the ends of the drainage-channels so that these became stagnant back-waters. The surface of the plain was scorched by the tropic sun, the sub-soil was saturated, and the constant process of evaporation left in the earth such quantities of salt that to-day irrigation brings to the surface a white crust like heavy hoar-frost which blights all vegetation at birth' (Woolley, C. L.: *Abraham* (London 1936, Faber), p. 69).

were deliberately sabotaged by invaders as a short cut to tne military objective of bringing their victims to their knees; and a war-worn people had not the heart to go on repairing a damage that had been inflicted so many times over and that was virtually certain to be inflicted many times again.[1] On this showing, the ultimate explanation of the decline and fall of the Indic Civilization in Ceylon has to be sought in a social cause—the social malady of warfare—and this social malady, which is the key to the problem, proves to have been itself the cause and not the consequence of the loss of command over the physical environment which is implied in the ruin of the irrigation-system. Thus, upon investigation, the technical factor dwindles, in this case again, into an incidental and subordinate link in a chain of social cause and effect which has still to be traced back to its social origins.

This chapter in the history of the Indic Civilization in Ceylon has a close parallel in the history of the Hellenic Civilization in the Mediterranean Basin.

Here, too, we find that some of the regions where this now vanished civilization once lived its most brilliant life and put forth its most vital energies have since become malarial swamps that have been reclaimed only within living memory. The Copaic marshes, which have been drained by the enterprise of a British company since 1887, after having been a pestilential wilderness for at least two thousand years, were once the fields that fed the citizens of Orchomenos the Wealthy; and the Pomptine marshes, which have been drained and repopulated and re-cultivated under Signor Mussolini's régime, after as long a period of desolation, once harboured a swarm of Volscian cities and Latin colonies. The high cultivation and dense population of this region filled Molossian Pyrrhus with astonishment and admiration when he penetrated thus far at the farthest point of his vain offensive against the Roman Commonwealth.[2] In Boeotia and in Latium, as in Ceylon, there is reason to believe that the reign of malaria did not begin until, in each of these regions, the Hellenic Civilization had passed its zenith. A modern Western scholar who has examined the extant fragments of the contemporary evidence on the subject has come to the conclusion that in Greece malaria did not become endemic until after the outbreak of the Atheno-Peloponnesian War of 431–

[1] Still, op. cit., pp. 88–90.

[2] For the impression which the Pomptine region made upon Pyrrhus's mind, see Dio Cassius: 'Εκ τῶν πρὸ τοῦ λϛ', fragment 40, § 23, ed. Melber (Leipzig 1890, Teubner). In a passage of words with his Italiot and Italian allies Pyrrhus 'said to them that their inferiority to the Romans leapt to the eye in the very aspect of the countryside. In the territory under Roman sovereignty there were fruit-trees of all kinds and vineyards and arable lands and agricultural improvements of immense capital value, whereas his own friends' territories had been devastated to a degree at which it was impossible to tell even whether they had ever been inhabited'.

404 B.C.;[1] and in Latium the disease does not seem to have gained the upper hand over human physique until after the Hannibalic War of 218–201 B.C.[2] It also seems to be established that in the Mediterranean Basin, as in Ceylon, the malaria-carrying mosquito was enabled to breed because the once healthy and productive fields had been turned into stagnant swamps by the ruin of the engineering works which had formerly regulated the flow of the waters. Are we, then, to pronounce that the Hellenic Civilization was laid low by malaria, and that this malaria was let loose by a failure of engineering technique?

In this case the absurdity of that reconstruction of historical cause and effect is palpable; for the age in which the Pomptine country was passing out of the dominion of Man into the dominion of the Anopheles Mosquito was actually the age in which the Romans were constructing their most imposing public works. To say nothing of the roads which were being made to radiate from Rome to the extremities of the Empire, and the aqueducts which were being made to supply Rome with water from the Alban and the Sabine hills, we may remind ourselves of a notable hydro-engineering work which was carried out, in the neighbourhood of the Pomptine region, by the Emperor Claudius. In A.D. 52 Claudius opened a tunnel through the Marsic Mountains which drained the waters of the Fucine Lake away into the bed of the River Liris and thereby captured the lake-bottom for cultivation.[3] Is it arguable that a government which was able to drain the Fucine Lake in this way was technically incompetent to carry out, if it had chosen, the simpler engineering enterprise of draining the Pomptine marshes, which were separated by no mountain barrier from their natural outlet to the sea?

The real reason, of course, why the Pomptine country was allowed to become derelict, and to remain so, was not technical but social. The social breakdown which had been brought upon the heart of the Hellenic World by the Atheno-Peloponnesian War of 431–404 B.C. had been extended by the Hannibalic War to Italy. The Hannibalic War, and the Roman predatory wars and civil wars which followed in its train during the next two centuries, had a profoundly disintegrating effect upon Italian social life. The peasant culture and economy, which had been the basis of Italy's social well-being in the Pre-Hannibalic Age, was first undermined and finally swept away by the cumulative effect of a number of inimical forces: the devastation of Southern Italy by Hannibal himself; the perpetual

1 Jones, W. H. S.: *Malaria and Greek History* (Manchester 1909, University Press).

2 Greenidge, A. H. J.: *A History of Rome from the Tribunate of Tiberius Gracchus to the End of the Jugurthine War, 133–104 B.C.* (London 1904, Methuen), p. 70.

3 See Tacitus: *Annals*, Book XII, chaps. 56–7.

mobilization of the Italian peasantry for campaigns which carried them ever farther afield for ever longer periods of continuous military service; the agrarian revolution (first accomplished in the devastated areas) which substituted large-scale cash-crop farming and stock breeding with a slave labour-force for small-scale subsistence farming by a free citizen-peasantry;[1] the mass-migration from a no longer self-sufficient countryside into the more and more parasitic cities; and an arbitrary and unequal redistribution of wealth which aroused a revolutionary temper in the masses—a temper for which the state dole of free rations was a sedative but not a cure. This combination of social evils amply accounts for the husbandman's retreat and the Anopheles Mosquito's advance in Italy during the seven centuries that intervened between the generation of Hannibal and the generation of Benedict.[2]

As for Greece, a similar combination of evils, going back not merely to the Hannibalic Age but to the disaster of 431 B.C., some two centuries earlier, had resulted, by the time of Polybius (*vivebat circa* 206–128 B.C.), in a degree of depopulation which was still more extreme than the contemporary depopulation of Italy. In a famous passage Polybius lays his finger upon the practice of restricting the size of families (by abortion or infanticide) as the principal cause of the social and political downfall of Greece in his day;[3] and in another passage, which occurs in his account of the post-Hannibalic war between Rome and the Seleucid Power (192–188 B.C.), he happens to mention that the social disintegration which was apparent in Greece as a whole was particularly flagrant in Boeotia. The special Boeotian symptoms were a twenty-five years' moratorium upon legal proceedings; a public dole distributed to paupers; and a custom, among the well-to-do minority, of bequeathing their property to their clubs—a custom which was not confined to people who died without issue.[4] It will be seen that no hypothesis of retrogression in engineering technique is necessary in order to explain why the Copaic, like the Pomptine, plain was allowed to transform itself from a granary into a nest of mosquitoes.

Our diagnosis of these past chapters in the histories of 'Irāq and Ceylon and Italy and Greece is borne out by an observation of what has been taking place in China, under our eyes, in our own

[1] 'Innumerabilem multitudinem liberorum capitum in eis fuisse locis quae nunc vix seminario exiguo militum relicto servitia Romana ab solitudine vindicant' is one of Livy's alternative answers to his conundrum 'unde totiens victis Volscis et Aequis suffecerint milites' (Book VI, chap. 12).

[2] For the social evils that followed in the train of the Hannibalic War, see I. B (iv), vol. i, pp. 40–2; II. D (vi), vol. ii, pp. 213–6; and III. C (i) (*b*), vol. iii, pp. 170–1, above, and IV. C (iii) (*c*) 3 (β), in the present volume, pp. 505–10, below. For the turn in the tide of Italian agrarian history which was brought about by Saint Benedict, see III. C (ii) (*b*), vol. iii, p. 266, above.

[3] Polybius, Book XXXVI, chap. 17.

[4] Polybius, Book XX, chap. 6, §§ 1–6.

generation. In China, during the second and third decades of the twentieth century of the Christian Era, the railways throughout the country, as well as the river-conservancy works in the basins of the Yellow River and the Hwai River and the Yangtse, were going to rack and ruin; and in this case it is patent that a decline in technical skill cannot have been the cause; for in this generation there have undoubtedly been a far larger number of civil engineers in China, with a far higher standard of technical efficiency, than ever before. Under the impact of our Western Civilization upon the Far Eastern Society, thousands of able young Chinese who, in any other generation during the previous two thousand years, would have studied the Confucian Classics and followed a literary and administrative career, have actually been taking up, instead, the Applied Physical Science of the West: partly on the rational consideration that the Chinese people must make themselves masters of this Western technique if they mean to hold their own in a Westernized World, and partly from a blind and vulgar desire to be 'in the fashion' of the alien civilization which is obviously paramount, in wealth and in power, in the world of the day. If these young Chinese engineers had had a free field for the exercise of their skill, it is evident that they could have begun to equip China with a system of river-conservancy works and irrigation-canals and roads and railways the like of which had never been seen on the face of this land during all the centuries that had elapsed since the Sinic Civilization first arose there. But it was part of the paradox and the tragedy of China in these years that the majority of these young Chinese engineers who had received this expensive technical education in America or in Europe remained unemployed, while under their eyes the existing engineering-works in China—works which, even in repair, were quite inadequate to the country's needs and which these young men might have improved out of recognition[1]—were rapidly going to pieces.

What is the explanation? In this latter-day Chinese case, where we are not driven back upon conjecture but can use our own eyes, we can see at once that the general condition of society in China in our day is the key to the puzzle. The public works that were the

[1] An indication of what the living generation of Chinese Western-trained engineers was capable of achieving, if their technical abilities were freed from prohibitive political and social handicaps, was afforded by the extraordinary rapidity and thoroughness with which the river-conservancy works were restored along the middle course of the Yangtse after the disastrous floods of the summer of 1931. In this great operation not only the labour-force but the engineering staff was Chinese, and the function of the International Flood Relief Commission, under whose auspices the work was carried out, was not technical (as might have been expected *a priori*) so much as diplomatic. The participation of the International Commission made the work possible by giving it a neutral complexion and thereby taking it out of the arena of Chinese civil war and party politics. It was this exceptional release from the political handicap that gave the Chinese engineers a rare opportunity for showing what they could do.

fruits of technical skill were deteriorating in China, at a time when technical skill was actually on the increase there, because the encounter between the Far Eastern Civilization and the West, which had led to this increase of technical skill among the Chinese people in the domain of civil engineering, had also turned the whole life of the Far Eastern Society in China upside down and had produced the political anarchy and the social ferment and the individual spiritual convulsions with which the Chinese people were being tormented ever since the Westernizing Revolution had broken through the traditional crust of Far Eastern life in China in A.D. 1911. The recent dilapidation of public works in China was not the cause but an incidental and paradoxical consequence of the dissolution of the ancient Far Eastern body social; and in order to find the cause of this social dissolution we must study the action of another social force, the corroding Western solvent. In this Chinese case the investigation of the factor of technique is demonstrably a false scent if the dissolution of the old Far Eastern order of society in China is the phenomenon which we are seeking to account for.

We shall arrive at corresponding conclusions if we pass from the practical technique of engineering to the artistic techniques of architecture and sculpture and painting and calligraphy and literature.

Why, for example, did the cuneiform script, which the Babylonic Society had inherited from the Sumeric Society, go out of use in the last century B.C. after having served as a vehicle of culture for more than three thousand years? And why did the Egyptiac hieroglyphic and demotic scripts, and with them the Egyptiac styles of architecture and sculpture, go out of use between the third and the fifth century of the Christian Era after at least as long a span of uninterrupted currency? Why, again, did the Hellenic style of architecture go out of use between the fourth century of the Christian Era and the seventh? We may feel our way towards the answers to these questions by asking why the Ottoman Turks abandoned the Arabic Alphabet in A.D. 1928;[1] why the Japanese and even the Chinese are now meditating the abandonment of the Sinic characters; and why almost every non-Western society in the World is discarding to-day its own traditional dress and architecture and art. And we may bring the problem home to ourselves by asking finally why our own traditional Western styles of music and dancing and painting and sculpture are being abandoned by our own rising generation.

In our own case, is the explanation a loss of artistic technique? Have we forgotten the rules of rhythm and counterpoint and per-

[1] See Toynbee, A. J., and Boulter, V. M.: *Survey of International Affairs, 1928*, III. A (viii), and the present Study, V. C (i) (*d*) 9 (β), vol. vi, pp. 112–13, below.

spective and light and proportion which were discovered, or invented, by that Italian and Flemish creative minority which carried our Western Society out of the second chapter in its history into the third chapter some four or five centuries ago?[1] In this case, in which we happen to be first-hand witnesses, the answer to our question is palpably in the negative. In these days of mass-education our Western World is more amply supplied than ever before with *virtuosi* who are masters of these techniques and who could put them into operation again any day if they felt the impulse in themselves and received the demand from their public. The prevailing tendency to abandon our Western artistic traditions is no involuntary capitulation to a paralytic stroke of technical incompetence; it is the deliberate abandonment of a style of art which is losing its appeal to the rising generation because this generation is ceasing to cultivate its aesthetic sensibilities on the traditional Western lines. We have wilfully cast out of our souls the great masters who have been the familiar spirits of our forefathers; and, while we have been wrapt in self-complacent admiration of the spiritual vacuum which we have discovered how to make, a Tropical African spirit of music and dancing and statuary has made an unholy alliance with a pseudo-Byzantine spirit of painting and bas-relief, and has entered in to dwell in a house that it has found empty and swept and garnished.[2] The decline which betrays itself in this revolutionary change in aesthetic taste is not technical but is spiritual. In repudiating our own native Western tradition of art and thereby reducing our aesthetic faculties to a state of inanition and sterility in which they seize upon the exotic and primitive art of Dahomey and Benin as though this were manna in the wilderness, we are confessing before all men that we have forfeited our spiritual birthright. Our abandonment of our traditional artistic technique is manifestly the consequence of some kind of spiritual breakdown in our Western Civilization; and the cause of this breakdown evidently cannot be found in a phenomenon which is one of the subsequent symptoms.

The recent abandonment of the Arabic Alphabet by the Turks in favour of the Latin Alphabet is to be explained on the same lines, *mutatis mutandis*. The notion that this change has been made because the adult generation of Turks has been finding the Arabic Alphabet hard to read and write and the Latin Alphabet easy cannot possibly be entertained by any alien observer who has had occasion, since 1928, to watch Turks who have been brought up on the Arabic Alphabet attempting to do their business with the Latin

[1] See III. C (ii) (*b*), vol. iii, pp. 299–300 and 341–50, above.
[2] Matt. xii. 43–5; Luke xi. 24–6.

substitute. It is patent that they find the Latin Alphabet not only ugly but clumsy by comparison with their own (and, indeed, the Arabic cursive, in the hands of a master, is so far superior to our Latin cursive in brevity and fluency that a community which employs the Arabic Alphabet finds no need for the use of short-hand).

It has, of course, been one of the official arguments of President Mustafā Kemāl Atatürk that a new generation of Turkish children, starting with a clean slate, will be able to make itself literate in the non-cursive Latin Alphabet with considerably less expenditure of time and energy than is required for the mastering of the Arabic Alphabet with its Protean letters which change their form in accordance with their positions and their ligatures;[1] and the older generation has been exhorted to sacrifice its own convenience for the sake of smoothing the way in Turkey for the advent of universal education. Yet the assumption, underlying this argument, that the key to literacy is the character of the script, and that when the script is simplified there will be a corresponding rise in the percentage of literates in the population, is not borne out by an empirical survey. In Japan, for example, the percentage of illiterates in the population in A.D. 1923 was as low as 0·94, notwithstanding the fact that the script in use was the incomparably complicated Sinic legion of characters—and this in a specially confusing Japanese usage, in which some characters are employed as syllabic phonograms while others are employed concurrently as ideograms in the original Sinic manner. On the other hand, in Portugal the percentage of illiterates in A.D. 1911 was as high as 68·9, and in Mexico in A.D. 1925 as high as 62·0, in spite of the fact that the relatively simple Latin Alphabet was the script in use in both these countries.[2] These facts militate against the argument which was officially put forward in Turkey in A.D. 1928. Yet, in a sense, this is beside the point; for the positive consideration of practical utility for the education of the rising generation of Turkish children was not, perhaps, the strongest motive in the mind of the statesman at whose fiat the change of alphabet was carried out.

The strongest motive for this change in Turkey would appear to have been the negative consideration that the historical Ottoman Turkish literature, and the classical Persian and Arabic literature which was a part of the Ottoman cultural heritage from the latest phase of the 'apparented' Syriac Civilization, were no longer worth

[1] The Arabic Alphabet, of course, differs from the Latin Alphabet in being a cursive script exclusively. If there were a form of the Arabic Alphabet in which the letters were each separate from the other and each of one single unvarying shape, then the Arabic Alphabet would be no more difficult than the Latin; and, conversely, if the sole form of the Latin Alphabet were the cursive in which the present writer is at this moment writing this note on the margin of his sheet, the Latin Alphabet would be just as difficult as the Arabic.

[2] See Toynbee and Boulter, op. cit., p. 219, footnote 3.

preserving, and that it was therefore useless for the Turkish people in these latter days to retain their mastery of the Arabic Alphabet, which was chiefly valuable as a key to this ancient cultural treasure-house.[1] In other words, the old Ottoman Civilization had declined, by the year A.D. 1928, to a point at which, in the eyes of the Turks themselves—or, at any rate, of their active leaders—it had ceased to be worth while to master the script in which the literary heritage of this decadent civilization was preserved. Thus it was the decline in the Ottoman Civilization that led to a deliberate abandonment of its traditional script, and not the loss of skill to read and write the Arabic Alphabet that sped the Ottoman Civilization on its downward course.

This account of the causal relation between the decline of the Ottoman Civilization and the abandonment of the Arabic Alphabet by the Ottoman Turks in A.D. 1928 applies, *mutatis mutandis*, to the contemporary moves in favour of abandoning the Sinic script in Japan and China, and likewise to the historic abandonment of the cuneiform script by the Babylonians in the last century B.C., and of the hieroglyphic and demotic scripts by the Egyptians between the third and the fifth century of the Christian Era.[2] We may take it that there was no loss of technical command over the traditional scripts in the Babylonic or in the Egyptiac World at these respective dates; that the abandonment of those scripts was not involuntary but was deliberate; and that this was a consequence and not a cause of the decline of the civilization in question in either case.

A particularly interesting example of a similar substitution of one technique for another in a different subdivision of the artistic field is the abandonment of the traditional Hellenic style of architecture in favour of the new-fangled Byzantine style in the Hellenic World between the fourth and the seventh century of the Christian Era. For in this case the architects of a society which was by this time *in articulo mortis* were abandoning the unusually simple architectural schema of architrave on column in order to experiment in the unusually difficult problem of crowning a cruciform building with a circular dome. Is it credible that the Ionian architects who triumphantly solved this problem for the Emperor Justinian[3] would have been technically incompetent to build a

[1] For this motive see further V. C (i) (*d*) 9 (*β*), vol. vi, pp. 112–13, below.

[2] The latest known example of the use of the demotic script dates from A.D. 476; but the Coptic script—which was an adaptation of the Greek Alphabet for the purpose of conveying the vernacular language of the age—was already prevalent in the third century of the Christian Era, and in the fourth century the hieroglyphic script was already out of use—if we may make this inference from the fanciful interpretations given to hieroglyphic characters by a fourth-century Egyptian adept in occultism, Hôrapollôn (see Jensen, H.: *Geschichte der Schrift* (Hanover 1925, Lafaire), pp. 48–9).

[3] For Anthemius of Tralles and Isidorus of Miletus see IV. C (i), p. 21, above.

replica of the Parthenon, if that had been the autocrat's will—and theirs?

In this case it is clear that the old architecture was abandoned for a new architecture because the old civilization, of which the old architecture was part and parcel, had declined by this time to so low a degree that it seemed no longer possible, within its traditional framework, to perform any fresh act of creation in any field of activity. In the field of architecture the attractiveness of the new Byzantine style in the eyes of a Justinian and an Anthemius was probably due to the very fact that this Byzantine style presented the greatest contrast to the Hellenic style that was well conceivable. The Hellenic architecture was a structure of straight lines and flat surfaces meeting at right-angles; the Byzantine architecture was a structure of curves and cupolas. The Hellenic temple looked outwards towards an assembly in the open air; the Byzantine church looked inwards towards a congregation in the interior. The Haghia Sophia was the monumental protest of a generation which could no longer find inspiration in the Parthenon or in any of those things for which the Parthenon stood.[1] In building an Haghia Sophia instead of a Parthenon, Anthemius was doing, in essence, what a Synesius or a Sidonius Apollinaris was doing when he became a bishop instead of remaining just a cultivated country gentleman, or an Augustine when he became a bishop instead of remaining just a professor of rhetoric, or an Ambrose or a Gregory the Great when he became a bishop instead of remaining just an Imperial official. In each of these cases a creative personality was breaking his way out of his hereditary social framework, in which his creative powers had been baulked, and was setting himself into a new framework in which these powers were offered an outlet.[2]

No doubt this is also the story of those Egyptian scribes of the third, fourth, and fifth centuries who gave up copying the Book of the Dead in the Egyptiac script and in a traditional form of the Egyptian language, in which their predecessors had been copying the same ritual *vade mecum* for the past two thousand years,[3] in order to copy a vernacular Coptic version of the Christian

[1] The substitution of the Haghia Sophia for the Parthenon was the architectural counterpart of the substitution of the cataphract for the legionary. (For this see III. C (i) (*b*), vol. iii, pp. 162–4, above, and IV. C (iii) (*c*) 2 (γ), in the present volume, pp. 439–45, below.)

[2] For the lives of Synesius and Sidonius see II. D (v), vol. ii, pp. 165–6; for the life of Saint Gregory the Great see III. C (ii) (*b*), vol. iii, pp. 267–9, above.

[3] The elements out of which the Book of the Dead was put together were current as early as the sixteenth century B.C., though there was no canonical redaction before the fourth century B.C. (Breasted, J. H.: *The Development of Religion and Thought in Ancient Egypt* (London 1912, Hodder & Stoughton), p. 293). The Classical Egyptian that was a legacy of the Old Kingdom was ousted by New Egyptian, as a vehicle of polite literature, in the fourteenth century B.C., in and after the reign of Ikhnaton (*imperabat circa* 1370–1352 B.C.) (see V. C (i) (*d*) 6 (γ), vol. v, p. 496, and V. C (i) (*d*), 8 (γ), vol. vi, p. 62, footnote 1, below).

Scriptures in an adaptation of the Greek Alphabet. Certainly this is the story of the Chinese student of our generation who abandons the study of the Confucian Classics among the litterati of Peking or Loyang in order to study the Western technique of civil engineering or the Western theory of economics and politics in Chicago or in London. Is it also the story of this Chinese student's Western contemporary who abandons the rhythms and tones of Bach and Beethoven and the lines and colours of Botticelli and Leonardo for the music of Darkest Africa and for a pseudo-Byzantine depiction of 'Anglo-Saxon attitudes'?

The upshot of our present investigation seems to be that the abandonment of a traditional artistic style, so far from being a possible cause of the breakdown of the particular civilization to which this style belongs, is actually an indication that the breakdown of this civilization has long since passed into a decline and is now culminating in a dissolution.[1] When we see a creative spirit abandoning the traditional style of his society in any field of artistic activity and seizing upon some exotic style instead, we may suspect that the world on which he is turning his back is 'a city of destruction' which is about to suffer the fate of Sodom and Gomorrah or, in Platonic language, to 'founder in the fathomless gulf where all things are incommensurable'.[2] As the foundering ship quivers before her final plunge, the intrepid seaman who has the will to live refuses to stay cowering on board in order to be sucked under with the sinking vessel. Before it is too late, he dives into the water and swims away with all his might from the fast settling gunwale in the hope of finding some drifting spar or cruising catamaran that will bring him—strange passenger on untried craft—alive to his journey's end.

(b) THE HUMAN ENVIRONMENT

1. '*The Triumph of Barbarism and Religion*'?

If loss of command over the physical environment, as measured by the history of technique, proves not to be a cause of the breakdowns of civilizations, we have still to consider whether a loss of command over the human environment may be the cause of which we are in search.

The significance of a command over the human environment has also engaged our attention when we have been studying the growths of civilizations at an earlier point in this work. We have

[1] In III. C (iii), vol. iii, pp. 378–80, above, we have already come to the conclusion that the test afforded by artistic style is the surest as well as the subtlest index of the temporal as well as the spatial extension of a civilization.

[2] See the passage from the *Politicus* which is quoted in IV. C (i), on pp. 26–7, above.

seen that the degree of command over the human environment which is possessed by any given society at any given stage in its history can be measured, for practical purposes, in terms of geographical expansion; and we have found, on an empirical test, that a good case can be made out for a correlation of geographical expansion, not with social growth, but on the contrary with social disintegration.[1] This inductive conclusion is supported by two *a priori* considerations. In the first place, one of the commonest forms in which the breakdown of a civilization declares itself is an outbreak of fratricidal warfare between the states members of the society; and if ever the children of the household pause for a moment from their self-imposed task of self-destruction in order to turn their arms against outsiders, it is likely enough that the improvements in the art of war which they have been making at the price of their own blood will purchase them a wide dominion over their neighbours.[2] The second and more fundamental consideration which makes it probable, *a priori*, that a widely and rapidly expanding society will prove to be also a disintegrating society arises from the fact that the social radiation of a society into the life of alien bodies social attains its greatest penetrative power when the different elements in the radiating society are being radiated separately: the economic elements penetrating in the van, the political elements following in the next wave of attack, and the cultural elements—which are the essence of a civilization—bringing up the rear in order to occupy and organize the captured ground. The diffraction of a civilization's social rays into these separate beams of different quality and different wave-lengths is one of the consequences of a civilization's social breakdown and disintegration. So long as a civilization is in the growth stage, all its elements cohere to constitute an indivisible whole, and the civilization radiates abroad either in its totality or not at all. Since the radiation of a civilization in its totality is hard and rare, any manifestation of violent radiative activity is an indication *prima facie*—though not, of course, a proof—that the civilization in question has broken down and begun to disintegrate already.[3]

If this concordance of *a priori* considerations with empirical evidence gives good ground for the belief that an increase in command over the human environment, as measured in terms of geographical expansion, is a consequence and symptom of breakdown and decline, then it seems extremely improbable that the cause of this self-same breakdown and decline is to be found in the precisely

[1] See III. C (i) (*a*), vol. iii, especially pp. 139–53, above.

[2] For this consideration see III. C (i) (*a*), vol. iii, pp. 150–1, above.

[3] For this consideration see III. C (i) (*a*), vol. iii, pp. 151–2, above, and V. C (i) (*c*) 3, vol. v, pp. 199–201, below.

inverse tendency—a tendency, that is to say, towards a decrease in command over the human environment, as measured by a successful encroachment of alien human forces. Nevertheless the view has been widely held that civilizations, like primitive societies, commonly lose their lives by violence, as the result of successful assaults upon them on the part of external human powers.[1] And a classic exposition of this view, worked out empirically in a particularly celebrated example, is given by Edward Gibbon in *The History of the Decline and Fall of the Roman Empire*. The theme is declared in the single sentence in which Gibbon sums up his story in retrospect: 'I have described the triumph of Barbarism and Religion'.[2] The Hellenic Society, embodied in a Roman Empire which was at its zenith in the Age of the Antonines, is represented as having been overthrown by a simultaneous assault from two alien enemies attacking on two different fronts: the North European barbarians issuing out of the no-man's-land beyond the Imperial frontiers along the Rhine and the Danube, and the Christian Church emerging from the subjugated but never assimilated Oriental provinces.

The key to this interpretation of the Decline and Fall is given in the famous opening passage of Gibbon's work in which he enunciates the plot of his drama by painting a magnificent picture of the Empire in the Antonine Age and then presaging its fall—without yet disclosing the identities of the villains of the piece:

'In the second century of the Christian Aera the empire of Rome comprehended the fairest part of the Earth and the most civilised portion of Mankind. The frontiers of that extensive monarchy were guarded by ancient renown and disciplined valour. The gentle, but powerful, influence of laws and manners had gradually cemented the union of the provinces. Their peaceful inhabitants enjoyed and abused the advantages of wealth and luxury. The image of a free constitution was preserved with decent reverence. The Roman senate appeared to possess the sovereign authority, and devolved on the emperors all the executive powers of government. During a happy period of more than fourscore years the public administration was conducted by the virtue and abilities of Nerva, Trajan, Hadrian and the two Antonines. It is the design of this and of the two succeeding chapters to describe the prosperous condition of their empire; and afterwards, from the death of Marcus Antoninus, to deduce the most important circumstances of its decline and fall: a revolution which will ever be remembered, and is still felt by the nations of the Earth.'[3]

[1] This is, no doubt, the most common way in which primitive societies, in contrast to civilizations, do lose their lives. (On this point see I. C (iii) (*a*), vol. i, pp. 148–9, above.)

[2] Gibbon, op. cit., chap. lxxi (already quoted in this Study in I. B (iv), vol. i, p. 42, above).

[3] Gibbon, E.: *The History of the Decline and Fall of the Roman Empire*, chap. i, *init.*

Whenever the writer of this Study reads this masterpiece of Edward Gibbon's art, there rises up before his mind's eye a vision of the Connecticut Valley as he once saw it, late in the Fall, on a visit to Amherst. As he drove through the woods in the valley bottom, every leaf was still intact in its place, and every leaf had turned pure crimson or pure gold. Nor did the course of his journey prevent him from seeing the wood for the trees; for, as the car began to climb the hills by which the valley is bounded, the widening horizon showed that the beauty of detail was trivial compared with the beauty of the whole. As we paused at the highest point, we looked back over miles and miles of golden and crimson woodland spread out below us. The sky was clear blue, without a cloud; the sun was in power and glory; the air was bathed in golden light; and it seemed to be passing on this gift to the leaves, though these hardly needed any enhancement of their natural brilliance. The whole landscape made an overwhelming impression of tranquil splendour. Here, surely, was 'a thing of beauty' which could not pass but was destined to remain to be 'a joy for ever'.

I do not know whether my New Englander companion had read my thoughts and was breaking in upon them purposely when, at this moment, abruptly, he began to tell me which roads would be left derelict for the winter, and which would be kept open by a service of motor snow-ploughs when the ground would be snow-covered and the boughs all bare some two months hence. To me, who was seeing for the first time what I was seeing that day, and who had never lived in New England through the whole round of the seasons, this prosaic announcement of the imminence of winter was incredible. But my companion's native eyes were not deceived by the beautv that had dazzled mine. He knew that this was not the summer, and not the spring *a fortiori*. It was 'the Indian Summer', whose brief splendour celebrates, not the Promethean *élan* of Life, but the inexorable onset of Mortality. *Morituri te salutamus* was the silent declaration of the leaves which now wore those brilliant colours in place of the living green. Under sentence of death they hung on their boughs but hung by a thread. One breath of wind, one touch of frost, and they would drop, blackened and crumpled, to the ground. With my inexperienced eye I had not understood the true meaning of the spectacle which had taken my breath away and captivated my imagination.

Was not Gibbon the victim of some such illusion as this on that notable evening of the 15th October, 1764, when his magnificent vision of the Age of the Antonines rose up in his mind and inspired him to write as he 'sat musing amidst the ruins of the Capitol while the barefooted fryars were singing Vespers in the Temple of

Jupiter'?[1] For was not the Age of the Antonines 'the Indian Summer' of Hellenic history? To a Western historian who finds himself musing and writing in the fourth decade of the twentieth century of the Christian Era amidst the ruins of the Western World of Gibbon's day,[2] the colour and atmosphere of the Antonine Age, as Gibbon has painted it in his incomparable opening passage, is poignantly suggestive of a long-drawn-out decay and a fast approaching dissolution—like that autumn gold and crimson of the New England woods or like the rainbow hues of spilt petrol or disinterred Roman glass. Thanks to a wider knowledge and a deeper insight that do not spring from any merits of his own, but have been conferred on him by the historical accident of the date of his birth, the twentieth-century Western historian can perhaps read more clearly than the greatest of his eighteenth-century predecessors the signs of the times on the impressive face of that magnificent Antonine landscape. As the New Englander, when confronted once more in due season with the autumn colours of the Connecticut Valley, was insensible to the impressions of an English stranger because his native eyes well knew these intimations of Mortality for what they were, so the twentieth-century Western observer of a second-century Hellenic landscape will not allow himself to be captivated by the hallucination of an eighteenth-century man-of-letters. So far from acquiescing in the judgement of Gibbon, he will be readier to view the World of the Antonines through the penetrating eyes of contemporaries who saw below the surface and staked their lives on their confidence in the truth of their vision. And this true contemporary vision is conjured up in a sermon preached in commemoration of two Christian heroes of that ostensibly golden age by the spiritual pastor of a Rome which, in the meantime, had passed out of a second-century 'Indian Summer' into a sixth-century winter.

'To-day,' Saint Gregory the Great[3] once declared to his flock, 'there is on every side death, on every side grief, on every side desolation; on every side we are being smitten, on every side our cup is being filled with draughts of bitterness. . . . [On the other hand] those saints at

[1] *The Autobiographies of Edward Gibbon*, edited by Murray, J. (London 1896, Murray), p. 302. For Gibbon's inspiration see further Part XIII, below.

[2] Gibbon himself just lived to see the beginning of a chapter of Western history which is perhaps coming to its tragic climax in our day. He had barely completed the last volume of his *magnum opus* when the tranquillity of his retreat at Lausanne was rudely disturbed by the first reverberations of a thunderstorm which broke over France. The outbreak of the French Revolution evidently shook Gibbon to the core. With the intuition of a great historian he seems to have divined the magnitude of the disturbance. What would he have felt if he had lived to see the sequel? For this latter-day relapse of the Western World, after an eighteenth-century lull, into a violence which had been the note of its seventeenth-century and sixteenth-century courses, see IV. C (iii) (*b*) 3 and 4, pp. 141–85, and V. C (ii) (*b*), vol. vi, pp. 315–9, below.

[3] For the life-work of Saint Gregory the Great see III. C (ii) (*b*), vol. iii, pp. 267–9, above.

whose tomb we are now standing lived in a world that was flourishing, yet they trampled upon its material prosperity with their spiritual contempt. In that world life was long, well-being was continuous, there was material wealth, there was a high birth-rate, and there was the tranquillity of a lasting peace; and yet, when that world was still so flourishing in itself, it had already withered (*aruerat*) in the hearts of those saints.'[1]

To the mind of a latter-day Western historian who is living, like Gregory, in a wintry age, the severe verdict of the sixth-century Roman saint on the Age of the Antonines will probably carry greater weight than the indulgent appraisal of the eighteenth-century English philosopher. For the hearts in which the World of the Antonines had withered underneath its brilliant surface were not only those of a Christian minority who had laid up their treasure elsewhere. It had also withered in the hearts of a pagan majority, from a Marcus encumbered by his purple to a Lucius hide-bound in his ass's skin; and these hearts knew a deeper bitterness because they held the key to no other treasure-house than a Hellenism which had wrinkled into a hollow shell.

The degree of Gibbon's hallucination is betrayed by the very title of his great work. *The History of the Decline and Fall of the Roman Empire!* The author of a history that bears this name is surely beginning his narrative at a point which is very near the end of the actual story; for the Roman Empire itself was a monumental symptom of the far-advanced decline of a Hellenic Society of which this empire was the universal state. When the whole story is taken into account, the rapid downfall of the Empire after the Antonine Age is seen to be not at all surprising. On the contrary, it would have been surprising if the Empire had endured; for this empire was already doomed before it was established. It was doomed because its establishment was nothing but a rally[2] which could delay, but not permanently arrest, the already irretrievable ruin of a Hellenic Society which the Roman Empire temporarily embodied.[3]

The breakdown and disintegration of the Hellenic Society itself is the story in which Gibbon would have found a subject altogether

1 Saint Gregory the Great: *Homiliae Quadraginta in Evangelia*, No. xxviii (Migne, J. P.: *Patrologia Latina*, vol. lxxvi, col. 1212).

2 For the movement of Rally-and-Relapse which punctuates the disintegrations of civilizations, see V. C (ii) (*b*), vol. vi, pp. 278–321, below.

3 In defence of Gibbon (if it is not sheer impertinence to offer any defence at all for a historian who is so great a master of his art) it may be mentioned that Gibbon's interpretation of the Age of the Antonines was anticipated by at least one distinguished observer who lived and wrote in that age itself. The passage from Gibbon's pen which has been quoted above may be compared with the Introduction to the *Studies in Roman History* of Appian of Alexandria (*vivebat circa* A.D. 90–160). Yet Gibbon—had his eyes been opened by the spectacle of a Western World in its Post-Gibbonian Age—might have taken another cue from an Apuleius or a Lucian. On the pages of these two Antonine writers the brilliant colours of 'the Indian Summer' unmistakably reveal themselves—for those who have eyes to see—as the hectic flush on the cheeks of a patient who is dying of a galloping consumption.

worthy of his genius; and if he had set himself to tell this longer tale from the beginning, he would have found that 'the triumph of Barbarism and Religion' was not the plot of the play, but only an epilogue—not a cause of the breakdown, but only an inevitable accompaniment of the dissolution in which the long process of disintegration was bound to end. More than that, he would have found that the triumphant Church and Barbarians were not, after all, external powers, but were really children of the Hellenic household who had been morally alienated from the dominant minority of the Hellenic Society in the course of a 'Time of Troubles' which had intervened between a Periclean breakdown and an Augustan rally.[1] In fact, if Gibbon had carried his inquest back to the true beginning of the tragedy, he would have had to return a different verdict. He would have had to report that the Hellenic Society was a suicide who had attempted to undo the fatal results of his own self-immolation when his life was already past saving, and who eventually received a *coup de grâce* from his own mishandled and alienated children at a time when the Augustan rally had already given way to a third-century relapse and the patient was manifestly dying from the after-effects of his old self-inflicted wounds.[2]

In these circumstances the historian-coroner would certainly not concentrate his attention upon the epilogue, but would employ all his mental energy and acumen in attempting to determine exactly when and how and why the suicide had first laid violent hands upon himself. In prospecting for the date, he would probably lay his finger upon the outbreak of the Atheno-Peloponnesian War in 431 B.C.—a social catastrophe which was anathematized at the time, by one of the actors in the exordium of the tragedy, as 'a beginning of great evils for Hellas'.[3] In reporting upon how the members of the Hellenic Society perpetrated their monstrous crime—a crime against the cause for which they, and their civilization with them, had come into the World[4]—the coroner would probably lay equal emphasis upon the twin abominations of inter-state war and inter-class war which, doubtless unintentionally but none the less effectively, set up a process of 'inverse selection': 'die Ausrottung der Besten', in the terrible but unanswerable and unforgettable phrase of one of Gibbon's successors who has

[1] For the roles of the Church and the Barbarians as 'the internal proletariat' and 'the external proletariat' of the disintegrating society see I. B (iv), vol. i, pp. 40–1, and I. C (i) (*a*), vol. i, pp. 53–62, above, as well as V. C (i) (*c*) 2 and 3, *passim*, in vol. v, pp. 58–337, below.

[2] On this point see I. C (i) (*a*), vol. i, pp. 53 and 62, above.

[3] Melesippus, Diacritus's son, the Spartan, as reported by Thucydides in Book II, chap. 12.

[4] John xviii. 37.

ventured to re-open the case and to probe more deeply into its origins.[1]

Though the twenty-seven years' war of 431–404 B.C. was only the first chapter in a 'Time of Troubles' which lasted for four hundred years before it was brought to a close by the establishment of a two-hundred-years-long *Pax Augusta*, the two terrible social evils that were let loose in this social breakdown were already out of hand, and already producing their fatal fruits, before this first chapter was over. The new spirit of atrocity which was inspiring inter-state warfare is exemplified in the treatment of the Melians by the Athenians in 416 B.C. and in the treatment of the survivors of the Athenian expeditionary force by the Syracusans in 413 B.C. and in the cold-blooded massacre of the Athenian prisoners-of-war after the Battle of Aegospotami in 404 B.C. The advent of the same evil spirit in the relations between social classes is exemplified in the murderous faction-fights by which the Corcyraeans disgraced themselves in 427–425 B.C.[2] On this showing, there is really no need to pursue the argument that the Hellenic Society did not receive its mortal blow in the Post-Antonine Age at the hands of the Christians and the Barbarians. The mortal blow was delivered at least six hundred years earlier, and the hand that dealt it was the victim's own.[3] We are still confronted with the question why the victim was overtaken by a suicidal mania of this kind at this time; and the positive answer still eludes us; but we have at least arrived at the negative conclusion that the verdict must be one of suicide and not one of murder.

If we now extend our inquest from the case of the Hellenic Society to the cases of the other undoubtedly dead or apparently moribund civilizations, we shall find that the same verdict has manifestly to be returned in a number of other instances.

For example, in the decline and fall of the Sumeric Society, 'the Golden Age of Hammurabi'[4] represents an even later phase of 'the Indian Summer' than we see in the Age of the Antonines; for

[1] 'Die Ausrottung der Besten' is the title of Part II, chap. 2, in vol. i of Otto Seeck's *Geschichte des Untergangs der Antiken Welt* (4th edition, Stuttgart 1921, Metzler, 6 vols. with supplements).

[2] See Thucydides, Book III, chaps. 70–85, and Book IV, chaps. 46–8.

[3] The long-drawn-out self-destruction of the Hellenic Society during the four centuries that intervened between the year 431 B.C. and the year 31 B.C. might well be described in the language of Herodotus's gruesome account of the suicide of the first King Cleomenes of Sparta, a man of genius who went out of his mind. Having obtained possession of a knife, 'Cleomenes began to mutilate himself from the calves of his legs upwards. He slit up his flesh lengthwise; and, beginning with his calves, he went on to his thighs, and then from his thighs to his hips and flanks, until finally he reached his stomach and found his death in slashing his stomach into ribbons' (Herodotus, Book VI, chap. 75). There is no redeeming feature in this protracted form of hara-kiri.

[4] This is the title of chapter xiv of volume i of *The Cambridge Ancient History*. It may be conjectured that the title of the chapter was chosen, and that the exposition of the subject was determined, under the influence of Gibbon's presentation of the Age of the Antonines.

Hammurabi is not the Trajan nor even the Marcus Aurelius of Sumeric history, but its Diocletian or its Constantine; and in this age the decadent society is like the New England forest after the first of the winter storms has come and gone without shaking down all the brilliant leaves at one fell swoop or leaving yet a permanent pall of snow upon the ground. Accordingly we shall not identify the slayers of the Sumeric Civilization with the trans-frontier barbarians who descended upon 'the Kingdom of the Four Quarters' in the eighteenth century B.C.: the Aryas who swept across the Land of Shinar into Syria, or the Hittites who sacked Babylon in a transitory raid,[1] or the Kassites who crawled upon the carrion. We shall detect the fatal strokes in certain events that had occurred some nine hundred years earlier: the class-war between Urukagina of Lagash and the local priesthood, and the militarism of Urukagina's destroyer Lugalzaggisi of Erech (Uruk) and Umma; for these far-off catastrophes were the authentic beginning of the Sumeric 'Time of Troubles'.[2]

Similarly, in the decline and fall of the Minoan Society, we seem to detect the material evidence of an Antonine 'Indian Summer' in 'the Palace Style' of the age which our archaeologists have labelled 'Late Minoan II';[3] and we shall not lay the destruction of the Minoan Civilization to the charge of the Central European barbarians who swept over the Aegean in the immediately subsequent age which bears the archaeological label 'Late Minoan III'.[4] In attempting to reconstruct the history of the Minoan Civilization out of our archaeological materials, we shall conjecture that 'the thalassocracy of Minos', which was the Minoan universal state, corresponds to the archaeological strata called 'Middle Minoan III' and 'Late Minoan I' and 'Late Minoan II'; that this universal state, like others, was the outward and visible sign of a social rally after a 'Time of Troubles'; and that the culmination of this 'Time of Troubles' is marked by the archaeologically attested destruction of the first palaces at Cnossos and Phaestus at the end of 'Middle Minoan II', a catastrophe which we may tentatively ascribe to the

[1] In I. C (i) (*b*), vol. i, p. 111, above, the Hittite war-lord Mursil I's raid on Babylon has been dated *circa* 1750 B.C. on the strength of Meyer, E.: *Die Aeltere Chronologie Babyloniens, Assyriens und Aegyptens* (Stuttgart and Berlin 1925, Cotta), pp. 5 and 25. On the other hand Delaporte, L.: *Les Hittites* (Paris 1936, Renaissance du Livre), p. 64, dates the raid *circa* 1806 B.C.

[2] See I. C (i) (*b*), vol. i, p. 109, above.

[3] This suggestion may perhaps offer a means of reconciling the at first sight incompatible interpretations of the archaeological evidence of L.M. II which are given by G. Glotz in *La Civilisation Egéenne* (Paris 1923, Renaissance du Livre), p. 53, and by M. P. Nilsson in *Minoan-Mycenaean Religion and its Survival in Greek Religion* (London 1927, Milford), p. 27. For this discrepancy of interpretation see I. C (i) (*b*), vol. i, p. 93, footnote 4, above.

[4] In the chronology on pp. 28–31 of Glotz, op. cit., L.M. II is dated 1450–1400 B.C. and L.M. III 1400–1200 B.C.

evil spirit of a fratricidal inter-state warfare.[1] It will be seen that the breakdown of the Minoan Civilization must be dated at least 500 years, and probably a longer span of years than that, before the Achaeans and the 'Dorians' appeared upon the scene.

In the decline and fall of the Sinic Society 'the triumph of Barbarism and Religion' is represented by the foundation of Eurasian Nomad barbarian 'successor-states'[2] of the Sinic universal state[3] in the basin of the Yellow River at the turn of the third and fourth centuries of the Christian Era, and by the simultaneous invasion of the interior of the Sinic World by the Mahayanian form of Buddhism, which was one of the religions of the internal proletariat of the Sinic Society in the outlying western provinces which it had conquered from the Indic World in the Tarim Basin.[4] But these victories, like those of the North European barbarians and the Christian Church at the Hellenic Society's expense, were only the victories of the moribund society's own external and internal proletariats. There was no conquest of the Sinic World by any wholly alien forces at any stage in the Sinic decline and fall; and the victories of the Sinic proletariat over the dominant minority by whom the universal state had been founded and preserved were the last chapter in the whole story. The Sinic universal state itself was the institutional embodiment of a social rally after a 'Time of Troubles' in which the Sinic body social had been torn in pieces by an internecine fratricidal warfare between the parochial states into which the society had once been articulated; and 'the Period of the Contending States' (*Chan Kuo*), which ended with Ts'in She Hwang-ti's knock-out blow in 221 B.C., unquestionably began long before 479 B.C., which has been taken as the conventional opening date for this period of Sinic history simply because it is the traditional date of the death of Confucius. This fratricidal warfare must already have inflicted cruel wounds upon the Sinic body social by

1 See I. C (i) (*b*), vol. i, p. 92, footnote 3, above, and V. C (i) (*c*) 3, vol. v, p. 236, and V. C (ii) (*b*), vol. vi, p. 312, below.

2 See V. C (i) (*c*) 3, vol. v, pp. 272–3, V. C (i) (*c*) 4, vol. v, p. 356, and V. C (i) (*d*) 6 (α), vol. v, p. 465, below.

3 The Sinic universal state was the empire which was founded in 221 B.C. by Ts'in She Hwang-ti, which was carried on by the Prior and Posterior Han, and which was ephemerally restored by the Western or United Tsin (*imperabant* A.D. 280–317), after having fallen apart into the indigenous 'successor-states' called 'the Three Kingdoms'.

4 The Mahāyāna is said to have made its first lodgement in the Sinic World in the seventh decade of the first century of the Christian Era—the traditional date of the foundation of the first Buddhist monastery at Loyang—but it did not begin to gain a hold upon the people until the third century. In this connexion it may be observed that the Sinic reconquest of the Tarim Basin was begun by Pan Chao, the general of the Posterior Han, in A.D. 73, almost simultaneously with the conquest of NW. India by the Kushan Power from the Oxus-Jaxartes Basin. Thereafter there was constant intercourse, sometimes hostile but also sometimes friendly, between the Empire of the Han and the Empire of the Kushan for about a hundred years; and this helps to explain the subsequent religious development in the Far East; for the Kushan Empire seems to have been the political crucible in which the Mahayanian form of Buddhism was precipitated. The rise and spread of the Mahāyāna are examined further in V. C (i) (*c*) 2, vol. v, pp. 133–46, below.

the time when fourteen states held a disarmament conference in 546 B.C. and sought to ensure the maintenance of peace by arranging for a joint hegemony of the two Great Powers of Tsin and Ch'u over the league of the central *Kleinstaaten* which was the heart of the Sinic World.[1] Perhaps the beginning of the Sinic 'Time of Troubles' may be dated from the outbreak of the first great war for hegemony between Tsin and Ch'u in 634 B.C.[2]—and this was more than 900 years before 'the triumph of Barbarism and Religion' was consummated.

In the decline and fall of the Indic Society 'the Indian Summer' was manifestly 'the Golden Age of the Guptas' (*imperabant circa* A.D. 375–475),[3] which was followed immediately by the devastating triumph of the Eurasian Nomad barbarian Hun and Gurjara invaders. But in this case the religion of the Indic internal proletariat, which shared the barbarians' triumph, was not an alien power at all, but was the wholly indigenous religion of Hinduism,[4] while the Hun invasion of India in the fifth century of the Christian Era was separated in time from the original breakdown of the Indic Civilization not only by the whole duration of the Indic universal state and of the foregoing 'Time of Troubles', but also by the Time-span of the Hellenic intrusion upon the Indic World—an intrusion which intervened between the establishment of the Gupta Empire *circa* A.D. 375 and the fall of the Maurya Empire (which had been the first avatar of the Indic universal state) in 185 B.C.[5] The fratricidal warfare between parochial states which preceded the foundation of the Maurya Empire was already in full swing by the time at which we catch our first rare glimpses of Indic history in the seventh century B.C.[6] The event which marks the original break-

[1] See Cordier, H.: *Histoire Générale de la Chine* (Paris 1920–1, Geuthner, 3 vols.), vol. i, p. 135; Maspéro, H.: *La Chine Antique* (Paris 1927, Boccard), pp. 347–8; and Franke, O.: *Geschichte des Chinesischen Reiches*, vol. i (Berlin and Leipzig 1930, de Gruyter), pp. 170–2. The covenant of 546 B.C. was broken by Ch'u in 538 B.C. (For the Sinic 'Time of Troubles' see further V. C (ii) (*b*), vol. vi, pp. 291–5, below).

[2] In this round of the struggle for hegemony between these two Powers, Tsin inflicted a heavy defeat on Ch'u in 632 B.C. For this catastrophe see Hirth, F.: *The Ancient History of China* (New York 1908, Columbia University Press), pp. 210 and 216; Franke, O.: *Geschichte des Chinesischen Reiches*, vol. i (Berlin and Leipzig 1930, de Gruyter), p. 165. This war lasted from 634 to 628 B.C. In the next round Ch'u took its revenge for the reverse of 632 B.C. by inflicting a comparable defeat on Tsin in 597 B.C.

[3] See I. C (i) (*b*), vol. i, p. 85, above.

[4] See Part IX below for the social 'law' that the universal church which is created by the internal proletariat of a disintegrating society is apt to draw its inspiration exclusively from sources that are indigenous to that society if the normal process of decline and fall has been interrupted, during the universal state phase, by the intrusion of an alien society (as the decline and fall of the Indic Society was in fact interrupted by the intrusion of the Hellenic Society).

[5] See I. C (i) (*b*), vol. i, p. 86, above. The Hellenic intrusion upon the Indic World is to be dated, not from Alexander's raid in 326–325 B.C., but from Demetrius's invasion *circa* 190 B.C. (more precisely, *circa* 183–182 B.C., according to Tarn, W. W.: *The Greeks in Bactria and India* (Cambridge 1938, University Press), p. 133).

[6] See Smith, V. A.: *The Early History of India*, 3rd edition (Oxford 1914, Clarendon Press), pp. 28–30.

down of the Indic Civilization may prove, if ever we identify it, to date from before the year 700 B.C.—that is to say, from a time more than 1,100 years earlier than the advent of the Huns.

As for the Syriac Society, which enjoyed its 'Indian Summer' under the 'Abbasid Caliphate of Baghdad, and which saw 'the triumph of Barbarism and Religion' in the invasions of the Eurasian Nomad barbarian Turks and Mongols and in the captivation of these savage conquerors by the indigenous religion of Islam—we may observe that the Syriac, like the Indic, decline and fall was drawn out to an exceptional length by a Hellenic intrusion which lasted, in this case, little short of a thousand years (if we reckon up the span of time that intervened between the conquests of Alexander the Great and the counter-conquests of the Caliph 'Umar).[1] To arrive at the date of the breakdown of the Syriac Civilization, we have to cast our thoughts back, behind the first incarnation of the Syriac universal state in the Achaemenian Empire, into a Syriac 'Time of Troubles' that preceded the establishment of a *Pax Achaemenia* by Cyrus.

What caused the breakdown of a civilization which, during its brief foregoing age of growth, had proved its genius and displayed its vitality in the three immense discoveries of Monotheism and the Alphabet and the Atlantic? At first glance it may seem as though we have stumbled here, at last, upon an authentic instance of a civilization being struck down by the impact of an external human force. Did not the Syriac Civilization break down under the hail of blows with which it was belaboured by an Assyrian militarism in the ninth and eighth and seventh centuries B.C.? This is, no doubt, the first obvious diagnosis; but closer inspection proves it to be mistaken; for, by the time when 'the Assyrian came down like a wolf on the fold', Syria was no longer 'one fold' with 'one shepherd'.[2] The tenth-century attempt to unite politically, under an Israelite hegemony, the galaxy of Hebrew and Phoenician and Aramaean and Hittite cantons and city-states which lay in the fairway between the Babylonic and the Egyptiac World had lamentably failed, and it was the resulting outbreak of Syriac fratricidal warfare that offered the Assyrians their opportunity and tempted them to take it. The ignominious defeat of King Shalmaneser III by a partial and ephemeral combination of Syriac forces at the Battle of Qarqar in 853 B.C.[3] shows that the Syriac World could have kept this Assyrian militarism at arm's length if the Syriac statesmanship of the age had taken to heart 'how good and pleasant

1 For the structure of Syriac history see I. C (i) (*b*), vol. i, pp. 72–84, above.

2 John x. 16.

3 See IV. C (iii) (*c*) 3 (α), pp. 468, 473, and 475, and V. C (ii) (*b*), vol. vi, p. 303, below.

a thing it is for brethren to dwell together in unity'.[1] The breakdown of the Syriac Civilization, like the breakdown of its Hellenic sister, turns out, after all, to have been a case of suicide and not a case of murder. The Syriac peoples had begun their deadly gladiatorial contest among themselves before the Assyrian giant strode into their arena. The breakdown of the Syriac Civilization is to be dated, not from the first crossing of the Euphrates by Asshurnazirpal II in 876 B.C., but from the evaporation of Solomon's hegemony after that Syriac prince's death *circa* 937 B.C.

If we turn to the history of the decline and fall of Orthodox Christendom, and accept the view that in Orthodox Christian history the role of universal state has been played by the Ottoman Empire,[2] we shall find rudiments of a post-Ottoman 'triumph of Barbarism' in the abortive attempts of Albanian and Serb and Maniot and Kurdish and Arab tribesmen from the fringes of the Empire to carve out 'successor-states' in the heart of the Empire during the last quarter of the eighteenth century and the first quarter of the nineteenth century of the Christian Era. Perceptible, though even slighter, rudiments of a corresponding 'triumph of Religion' are discernible in certain abortive attempts to supplant both the Sunnī Islam of the Ottoman founders of the Empire and the Orthodox Christianity of their subject *ra'īyeh* by revised or resuscitated versions of Islam which might purport to achieve a synthesis between the two faiths and so to offer a basis of reconciliation on which the deep religious cleavage between Orthodoxy and the Sunnah might perhaps be transcended. The first of these abortive attempts was the militant movement of Sheykh Bedr-ed-Dīn of Simāv, which came to a head in A.D. 1416.[3] The second was the propagation of a resuscitated Imāmī Shi'ism by the Safawīs at the turn of the fifteenth and sixteenth centuries of the Christian Era.[4] The third was the propagation of various alternative revised versions of Islam which were ostensibly Sunnī but esoterically heterodox. The most successful of these was the doctrine and discipline of the Bektāshī Order of Dervishes, which had become so prevalent among the Janissaries by the latter part of the seven-

[1] Psalm cxxxiii. 1. (This poem was written, of course, at least seven hundred years after the time in the ninth century B.C. when the Syriac World, for want of unity, had fallen a prey to the Assyrians.)

[2] For an exposition of this view see Part III. A, vol. iii, pp. 26–7, above, and V. C (ii) (*b*), vol. vi, pp. 298–300, below.

[3] See I. C (i) (*b*), Annex I, in vol. i, p. 364, above, and V. C (i) (*c*) 2, vol. v, p. 111, below. A deeper examination of Sheykh Bedr-ed-Dīn's movement and its affiliations has been made by Babinger, Fr., in *Der Islam*, vols. xi and xii. A reconciliation and fraternization between Muslims and Christians was one of the principal planks in the Sheykh's platform according to the contemporary Orthodox Christian historian Michael Ducas, chap. 21 (pp. 111–15 in I. Bekker's edition (Bonn 1834, Weber)).

[4] For the history of this propaganda, and for an explanation of its failure, see I. C (i) (*b*), Annex I, in vol. i, above.

teenth century of the Christian Era that it seems at this time to have been regarded almost as the established regimental religion, while the attraction which it once exerted upon the impressionable barbarians on the fringes of the Empire is attested by its survival in the present Albanian 'successor-state' of the Ottoman Empire as a relatively large and well-organized sect.[1]

In the case in point, of course, nobody will think of suggesting that the propaganda of Hājj Bektāsh and his spiritual successors between the fourteenth and the seventeenth century of the Christian Era, or the Völkerwanderung in which the Albanians overran the Morea during the great Russo-Turkish war of A.D. 1768–74, are to be regarded as the causes of the breakdown of the Orthodox Christian Civilization! And this fantastic hypothetical diagnosis of the Orthodox Christian decline and fall may be taken as a *reductio ad absurdum* of the whole Gibbonian schema of 'the triumph of Barbarism and Religion', since the stirrings of Bektāshī faith and of Albanian barbarism in the Ottoman body politic are morphologically true

[1] See Rycaut, Sir Paul: *The Present State of the Ottoman Empire* (first edition; London 1668), Book II, chaps. 12–20, for the religious ferment in the Ottoman Empire in Rycaut's time. The Bektāshī Movement is described in chaps. 12 and 19. These abortive universal churches which attempted to establish themselves within, and on the margin of, the framework of the Ottoman Empire are examined further in V. C (i) (*c*) 2, vol. v, pp. 110–11, and V. C (i) (*c*) 3, vol. v, pp. 295–6, below. See also Gibb, H. A. R., and Bowen, H.: *Islamic Society and the West* (Oxford 1939, University Press), vol. i, chaps. 13 and 14:—

'The heterodox Sufism professed by the Bātinī propagandists of earlier centuries had appealed to the Turkish tribesmen, as they first immigrated into the lands of Islam, on account of its latitudinarianism. But the Janissary corps was manned by men in a similar case of more or less compulsory conversion; so the same doctrine, preached now by the Bektāshīs, was admirably framed to appeal to them. The Janissaries, as long as they remained a slave corps, were, almost to a man, of Christian origin. It is not surprising, therefore, to find that Bektashism has several features of a quasi-Christian character, such as the belief in a Trinity—Allah, Muhammad, and 'Alī—and a belief in the efficacy of confession and absolution. It was a tenet of the whole ultra-Bātinī-Sūfī movement that all religions are equally valid, so that the adoption of such beliefs and practices did not involve any compromise of its original character. Indeed, some of the Christian-like features that Bektashism displayed were common to other branches of the movement. And in the later centuries of Ottoman rule over what had formerly been the Orthodox Christian World, the prevalence of a more or less disguised heterodoxy of this type—outside the actual sphere of Bektashism—among all the lower classes of the Muslim population led to a curious development. The veneration of saints and a belief in the magical efficacy of sites and objects connected with them was perhaps the most marked feature both of Orthodox Christianity and [of] this heterodox Muhammadanism in their more popular forms. It came to pass, consequently, that throughout the Balkans and Asia Minor many saints and shrines were venerated and visited in common by the adherents of both religions. . . .

'It is not surprising to find, therefore, that the relations subsisting between Muslims and Christians during the early centuries of Ottoman rule were much more cordial than they had been under earlier orthodox [Muslim] dynasties, or were to be later, after the Sultans had turned to [Islamic] orthodoxy. Thus in the Ottomans' earliest campaigns they were supported by many Christian allies; and several of the earlier Sultans took Christian princesses to wife. During the invasion of the Balkans, moreover, large numbers of Christians turned Muslim; and though this may not seem to be evidence of good Muslim-Christian relations, it is to some extent so in fact, since it shows that the transition—if we are to judge by the frequency with which it was performed—was less painful at this period than it became later, when Muslim orthodoxy forbade any compromise in belief. Indeed, if this return to, or adoption of, [Islamic] orthodoxy had never occurred, it seems possible that the veneration of shrines in common by the adherents of the two religions might have ended in their sinking their differences and evolving a syncretic faith—a Sufistic Christianity.'

equivalents of the triumphant conquest of the Roman body politic by the North European barbarians and by the Christian Church.

In the Orthodox Christian case those inquirers who are not prevented by religious or cultural prejudice from perceiving that the Ottoman Empire is the Orthodox Christian universal state will justifiably take it for granted that the Orthodox Christian Civilization must not only have broken down but have also travelled very far along the path of disintegration before it became so weak as to succumb to an Ottoman domination and so sick as to derive social benefit from the bitter medicine of a *Pax Ottomanica.* The unprejudiced student of Orthodox Christian history will recognize, nevertheless, that the *Pax Ottomanica* did perform for Orthodox Christendom the same positive and indispensable social service that was performed for the Hellenic Society by the *Pax Romana* and has been performed for the Hindu Society by the *Pax Britannica.* But this, of course, is not the popular view among the Orthodox Christian peoples and their sentimental Western patrons at the present day. The popular view is that all the historic misfortunes of Orthodox Christendom derive from the Turkish conquest; and this diagnosis has been implicitly accepted by our latter-day Ottoman Turks of the school of President Mustafā Kemāl Atatürk, who have made it their doctrine that the old Ottoman Empire—bound up, as it was, with the old Ottoman Slave-Household—has been an even greater curse to the ʿOsmanlis themselves than it has been to their *ci-devant* subjects![1] As for the descendants of the Ottoman *raʿīyeh,* however violently they may differ on almost every other question of current politics or past history, our latter-day Greeks and Bulgars (echoed by their attendant Philhellenes and Bulgarophils) will protest with one voice that their common Orthodox Christian Civilization, in which they each claim the leading role for their own respective forebears, was going from strength to strength,[2] on a flood tide of life and growth, until the moment when it fell a victim to the brutally aggressive force of Turkish militarism, which is represented as having burst without warning upon the Orthodox Christian World out of some Islamic inferno below the Asiatic horizon.[3]

[1] For President Mustafā Kemāl's Atatürk's revolutionary breach with the old Ottoman order see Part III. A, vol. iii, pp. 48–9, above, and V. C (i) (*d*) 9 (*β*), vol. vi, pp. 102 and 112–13, below.

[2] Psalm lxxxiv. 7.

[3] The view that Orthodox Christendom suffered injury from a Turkish militarism in one chapter of its history is not, of course, irreconcilable with the view that, in the next chapter, the stricken society received benefit from a *Pax Ottomanica.* In the Hellenic case, for example, nobody disputes that the Hellenic Society received benefit from the *Pax Romana* during the span of 200 years extending from the principate of Augustus to the principate of Marcus Aurelius inclusive. At the same time, nobody can deny that during the preceding two hundred years, between the outbreak of the Hannibalic War and the Battle of Actium, the role of the Romans in Hellenic history was as destruc-

The modern Greek national historian will probably ascribe the ruin of the Orthodox Christian Civilization to an earlier wave of Turkish aggression than will come within the ken of his Bulgar contemporary and confrère. The Greek will find 'the beginning of evils' for Orthodox Christendom in the invasion of the Anatolian territories of the East Roman Empire by the Saljūq Turks in the third quarter of the eleventh century of the Christian Era. More than that, if our imaginary Greek savant happens to be still inspired by a reminiscence of the old-fashioned Orthodox sentiment that the Pope's tiara is at least as objectionable as the Prophet's turban,[1] and if he has not altogether succumbed to the latter-day Greek vanity of self-identification with 'the enlightened West', he may decide to place the Latins as well as the Turks in the dock. And it is unquestionably true that the first Norman raid upon the East Roman Empire's dominions in Italy in A.D. 1017 preceded the first Saljūq raid upon the Empire's dominions in Anatolia in A.D. 1037 by twenty years, and that the Latin conquest of Constantinople in A.D. 1204 was a greater disaster for the Orthodox Christian Civilization than the Turkish conquest in A.D. 1453. If it were to be taken for granted that the Orthodox Christian Civilization met its death at foreign hands, and that it is merely a question of determining the respective responsibilities of the Turkish and the Latin prisoner at the bar, then a candid Western inquirer might be constrained to admit that his own Latin forebears not only delivered the first blow but were also ahead of their Turkish competitors in striking at their victim's heart. But when we have made the fullest allowance for the Latin share, as well as for the Turkish share, in the murderous assaults of which Orthodox Christendom was the victim from the eleventh century of the Christian Era onwards, are we sure that we have ascertained the true cause of the victim's death? If we pursue our post-mortem examination farther, we shall find unmistakable evidence that the Orthodox Christian Society, like the Syriac Society in a different time and place, had laid violent hands upon itself before either of its reputed assassins appeared upon the scene. The criminal intent of both the Latins and the Turks may have been fully as heinous as is commonly alleged; but there is reason to doubt the effectiveness of their criminal action; for there is reason to believe that the alien body social into which they plunged and replunged their swords was the body of a suicide whose life-blood was already ebbing away through a self-inflicted wound.

tive as that of the Turks in Orthodox Christian history at their worst. It is not only possible, but common, to find the same people or the same individual playing contrary roles in successive acts of the same play.

1 For the prevalence of this sentiment among the Orthodox in Constantinople on the eve of the capture of the city by the 'Osmanlis in A.D. 1453 see Gibbon, E.: *The History of the Decline and Fall of the Roman Empire*, chap. lxviii.

The true date of the breakdown of the Orthodox Christian Civilization is marked by a domestic event in Orthodox Christian history which occurred before either the Normans or the Saljūqs had come within range of Orthodox Christendom. The beginning of the Orthodox Christian 'Time of Troubles' dates from the outbreak, in A.D. 977, of the great Bulgaro-Roman War of A.D. 977–1019.[1] This internecine struggle between the two Great Powers of the Orthodox Christian World did not come to an end until one of the two belligerents had not only suffered defeat but had been deprived of its political existence. From A.D. 1019 onwards for more than a century and a half, until A.D. 1186, Bulgaria was effaced from the political map by being incorporated completely into the body politic of the East Roman Empire. This enormous political disaster in the life of the second most important state in the Orthodox Christian World was bound to administer a profound shock to the whole Orthodox Christian body social; and the Bulgarian Empire's total loss was not counterbalanced by any gain on the credit side of the East Roman Empire's account; for, in a war so long drawn out between belligerents who were so closely matched, the ostensible victor emerged from the struggle in little better condition than his prostrated opponent.

On the political map the East Roman Empire vastly increased its territorial possessions as a result of the 'knock-out blow' of A.D. 1019. From that year until the successful Bulgarian revolt of A.D. 1186 the domain of the East Roman Empire in the Balkan Peninsula was as extensive as the Roman Empire's domain in the same quarter in the reign of Justinian; but an eye which knew how to read the social and economic map below the ostentatious political surface could have discerned that the military triumph in the Balkans had been purchased by the East Roman Power at the price of a prohibitive sacrifice in Anatolia. The strain of the great Bulgaro-Roman War of A.D. 977–1019 exacerbated a social malady in Central and Eastern Anatolia[2] which had first become noticeable (to judge by the testimony of East Roman agrarian legislation) during the preceding Bulgaro-Roman War of A.D. 913–27. In this Anatolian region an increasing inequality in the distribution of the ownership and the product of the land was keeping pace with an increasing impoverishment of the whole country-side, with the result that the peasantry and the big landowners were becoming increasingly alienated both from one another and from the East Roman Government at Constantinople, at whose door they not unfairly laid the responsibility for their local distress. The military

[1] See Part III. A, vol. iii, p. 26, above, and IV. C (iii) (*c*) 2 (*β*), in the present volume, pp. 388–93, below.

[2] For this see further IV. C (iii) (*c*) 2 (*β*), pp. 395–9, below.

glory which the Emperor Basil the Bulgar-killer (ὁ Βουλγαροκτόνος) was winning by his successful war of attrition against the Empire's formidable sister and adversary in Europe was marred by a succession of insurrections headed by representatives of the East Roman landed aristocracy in Asia.

These outbreaks occurred too frequently, and lasted too long, to be dismissed as the work of unruly or ambitious individuals. They were expressions of the Anatolians' profound economic distress and political discontent, and this exhaustion and disaffection of Eastern and Central Anatolia was a loss which could not be made good by the most extensive conquests in Europe; for the military strength of the Eastern and Central Anatolian army-corps districts was the rock on which the East Roman Empire had been founded by Leo the Syrian three hundred years earlier.[1] In A.D. 1019, at the close of the great Bulgaro-Roman War, the whole of this region in the interior of Anatolia, which had once been the Empire's solid core, was so rotten with social decay that it was ready to fall away at a touch, while the newly acquired provinces in the interior of the Balkan Peninsula, which were socially sound in so far as they had not been devastated by the recent warfare, were being held down only by sheer force.[2] Thus in A.D. 1019, when the East Roman Empire stretched to the Euphrates in one direction and to the Danube in the other, it was inwardly weaker than it had been in A.D. 716, when its European domain was almost confined to the bridge-head of Constantinople and the enclave of Salonica and when the Arabs were marching across Anatolia to put Constantinople under siege. For in A.D. 716 Leo the Syrian had achieved the master-stroke of East Roman statesmanship which Basil the Bulgar-killer was never able to emulate. Leo had united under his leadership the forces of the Anatolic and Armeniac army-corps; and, with the military strength of Anatolia intact, he could await with equanimity the Arabs' assault upon the Empire's European capital.

This estimate of the difference in the East Roman Empire's inward strength at these respective dates is borne out by the respective sequels to the Arab assault at the one date and the Saljūq assault at the other. When the Arabs were repulsed from the walls of Constantinople in A.D. 717, they ebbed right back from the Bosphorus to the south-eastern foot of the Taurus; and although, for two more centuries, they continued to harry the Anatolian

[1] For Leo's life-work see I. C (i) (*b*), vol. i, p. 64, footnote 3, and III. C (ii) (*b*), vol. iii, pp. 274–6, above, and IV. C (iii) (*c*) 2 (β), in the present volume, pp. 341–2, below.

[2] For the eventual transference of the social centre of gravity of the main body of Orthodox Christendom from the Anatolian Peninsula to the Balkan Peninsula see I. C (i) (*b*), vol. i, p. 65, footnote 2; II. D (iii), vol. ii, p. 79; and Part III. A, vol. iii, p. 27, above.

marches of the Empire in annual raids, they never secured a permanent foot-hold upon the Anatolian Plateau. On the other hand, when the Saljūqs were driven out of their advanced post at Nicaea in A.D. 1097 by the combined forces of the East Romans and the Latin Crusaders, they retired no farther than to Qōnīyah; and they continued to hold their ground in Central Anatolia for a full hundred years during which their principality of Rūm was almost completely encircled by Orthodox or Latin Christian Powers: a temporarily reinvigorated East Roman Empire on the west and north; an Armenian Kingdom in Cilicia; and the Latin Crusader principalities in Syria. In fact, the Turks successfully stood on the defensive in Central Anatolia until, at the close of the twelfth century of the Christian Era, the next relapse in the decline of Orthodox Christendom opened the way for the 'successor-states' of the Anatolian Saljūq Sultanate to make themselves masters of almost all the rest of the Anatolian Peninsula at the turn of the thirteenth and fourteenth centuries, when the Greeks and Latins had exhausted themselves in a long and bitter struggle for the more spectacular prizes of Constantinople and Salonica. And thus the feat of statesmanship by which one of these 'successor-states'—the Ottoman Turkish principality of Sultān Önü—transformed itself, in the fourteenth century of the Christian Era, into the universal state of the Orthodox Christian World, was made possible by the feat of endurance through which, in the twelfth century, the Saljūq Turks had held their ground at Qōnīyah.[1]

How was it that the Saljūqs were able to hold out in Central Anatolia when they were so easily driven out of Nicaea and Smyrna? An explanation is suggested by the fact that the area which the East Roman Power failed to recapture from the Saljūqs in the twelfth century substantially coincides with the area which had been afflicted with the malady of economic distress and social discontent during the tenth and eleventh centuries, before the Saljūqs arrived on the scene. Though the social history of this region from the twelfth to the fifteenth century is exceedingly obscure, and has to be reconstructed—in the almost total absence of contemporary evidence—by a comparison of the previous with the subsequent conditions, we may conjecture, with some assurance, that the strength of the Saljūqs in Central Anatolia lay in the support, or at least the passive acquiescence, of the local peasantry. In this region the social effect of the Saljūq conquest had been to release the peasantry from the grievous service of the local landlords and the heavy yoke of the Government at Constantinople as repre-

[1] For the direct action of Challenge-and-Response in the history of the rise of the 'Osmanlis see II. D (v), vol. ii, pp. 150–4, above.

sented by the recruiting-sergeant and the tax-collector. How could they pray for the restoration of an Orthodox Emperor whose little finger would be thicker than the loins of the Turkish unbeliever?[1] And why, now that they were relieved of the incubus of the landlords and the officials and the bishops, should they continue to practise the Orthodox rite or to cultivate the Greek language? From the twelfth century of the Christian Era onwards the Orthodox Christian peasantry of Central Anatolia turned Muslim *en masse*; and even the minority that remained true to their hereditary faith turned Turk in language.

The descendants of these Central Anatolian Orthodox Christians who survived in their native region, under the name of Qāramānlī, until the wholesale compulsory exchange of minorities between Greece and Turkey that followed the Anatolian War of 1919–22, had not only come to speak the Turkish of their Muslim neighbours as their own mother tongue; they had so utterly forgotten their ancestral Greek that they had even found it necessary to translate the Liturgy of the Orthodox Church into Turkish,[2] though liturgies are notoriously the last refuges of dead languages. On the eve of the Anatolian War of 1919–22, which gave the last lingering survival of Orthodox Christendom in Anatolia its *coup de grâce*, the Greek language, which had enjoyed exclusive currency throughout Anatolia from the extinction of the last of the pre-Greek vernaculars in the sixth century of the Christian Era down to the advent of the Turkish language in the eleventh century, was only alive in half a dozen remote villages in the fastnesses of Anti-Taurus and on the extreme southern and south-eastern edges of the Plateau at a distance from the main lines of communication.[3] At the opening of the twentieth century these fast dwindling islets of Greek in the heart of a *ci-devant* Greek-speaking region were a happy hunting-ground for the philologist and phonetician, who was able here to catch in the act, and study in the life, the metamorphosis of one living language into another.[4]

We have now perhaps convincingly demonstrated that the original breakdown of the Orthodox Christian Civilization was caused by

[1] 1 Kings xii. 10.

[2] The Turkish version of the Orthodox Liturgy which was used by the Qāramānlīs, and the Turkish version of the Gregorian Liturgy which was used by the Armenian 'Diasporà' in Anatolia, were conveyed respectively in the Greek and the Armenian Alphabet and not in the Arabic Alphabet which was employed by the Turkish-speaking Muslims.

[3] There was, of course, a much more numerous Greek-speaking Orthodox Christian population at Smyrna and Aydyn and Ayvalyq and Bergama and other places on or near the west coast of Anatolia; but these communities appear to have been the recent products of immigration from the Aegean islands and from the Morea.

[4] See Dawkins, R. M.: *Modern Greek in Asia Minor* (Cambridge 1916, University Press), and the present Study, IV. C (iii) (*c*) 2 (*β*), in the present volume, pp. 398–9, below.

a domestic conflict in the tenth century of the Christian Era and not by Latin and Turkish assaults which only began in the course of the eleventh century. *A fortiori* we may dismiss the idea that the breakdown could have been caused by the rudimentary and abortive religious propaganda and barbarian Völkerwanderung which we have detected, where we should expect *a priori* to find them, in the last agonies of an Ottoman Empire which was the Orthodox Christian universal state.

2. *The Triumph of an Alien Civilization?*

We may next ask ourselves why these movements were abortive in the Ottoman Empire, in contrast to the historic 'triumph of Barbarism and Religion' in the Roman Empire and in the Empire of Sumer and Akkad and in the Minoan Thalassocracy and in the Sinic universal state. The answer to this question is not far to seek.

If the Orthodox Christian World had been breaking up *in vacuo*, out of touch with any other living civilization of superior vitality, there can be little doubt that, in the course of the nineteenth century of the Christian Era, the former territories of the Ottoman Empire would all have been parcelled out into 'successor-states' established by war-bands of barbarian intruders from the fringes. In the first stages of the break-up of the Roman Empire, at the turn of the fourth and fifth centuries of the Christian Era, there were incidents which are exactly analogous to the occupation of the Morea, from A.D. 1769 to A.D. 1779, by Albanian *foederati* who had been called in by the Ottoman Government to drive out the Russians, and to the embarrassing eagerness of the Muslim Slavs of Old Serbia and the Geghs of the North Albanian highlands to serve in Khurshīd Pasha's expedition against 'Alī of Yánnina in A.D. 1821 and to take direct action against the Orthodox Christian *ra'īyeh* within their reach in reprisal for the insurrection of the Maniots against the Pādishāh in the same year.[1] If we pursue the analogy, we may discern in the Kurds the counterparts of the Isaurians and in the Wahhābīs the counterparts of the Primitive Muslims; and we may see in an 'Alī of Yánnina and in a Mehmed 'Alī of Kavala a Clovis and a Theodoric manqué.

Why was it that war-lords such as these did not make the Alba-

[1] For these incidents in the break-up of the Ottoman Empire see Vlakhogiánnis, G: *Κλέφτες τοῦ Μοριᾶ* (Athens 1935, no imprint of publisher's name), pp. 85–109; Finlay, George: *A History of Greece from its Conquest by the Romans to the Present Time* (Oxford 1877, Clarendon Press, 7 vols.), vol. v, pp. 255–64; vol. vi, pp. 89 and 205. With the former we may compare Alaric's occupation of the Morea in A.D. 395–6; with the latter, Atawulf's ready acceptance, in A.D. 412, of Honorius's invitation to him to employ the Visigothic war-band which he had inherited in Italy from Alaric on the lucrative task of extirpating the nascent 'successor-states'—indigenous as well as barbarian—that were in process of supplanting the Roman Imperial Government in the Transalpine provinces.

nians masters of Rumili and Egypt and the Kurds masters of Anatolia and the Wahhābīs masters of Syria and 'Irāq? The answer is that the mighty march of an irresistibly expanding Western Civilization was treading hard upon these ephemeral barbarians' heels. 'The triumph of Westernization',[1] and not 'the triumph of Barbarism and Religion', was the process to which the break-up of the Ottoman Empire actually ministered. Instead of taking their natural form of barbarian principalities of 'the Heroic Age', the 'successor-states' of the Ottoman Empire were moulded, by Western pressure, as fast as they emerged, into the exotic shape of national states members of a comity of Western states which was in the act of reorganizing itself on a basis of nationalism at this time.

In some cases an incipient barbarian 'successor-state' transformed itself directly (though not without painful and dangerous convulsions) into one of these new-fangled national states on a Western model. For example, the national state of Serbia was the final product of the insurrection of the barbarian Serb backwoodsmen of the Shumadiya in A.D. 1804, and the national state of Greece arose likewise out of the insurrection of the barbarian Greek highlanders of the Mani in A.D. 1821.[2] On the other hand the barbarians who were still so little affected at this time by the radiation of the Western Civilization that they were incapable of turning their political activities into a Western nationalistic channel paid the penalty of missing their opportunity. The Albanians forfeited the Ottoman heritage in the Balkan Peninsula to the Greeks and Serbs and Bulgars in the nineteenth century in order to enter the Western comity of nations in the twentieth century with a patrimony so grievously diminished that it now constitutes the smallest and least populous and weakest, as well as the most backward, of the national states of Europe.[3] As for the Kurds and the Wahhābīs, the Kurds were reduced to order by Sultan Mahmūd II, and the Wahhābīs were temporarily subjected and were permanently confined to their deserts by Mahmūd's viceroy in Egypt, Mehmed 'Alī,[4] through

[1] For the Westernization of the 'Osmanlis' Christian *ra'īyeh* see II. D (v), vol. ii, pp. 181–6, and II. D (vi), vol. ii, pp. 226–7, above, and V. C (i) (*c*) 3, vol. v, pp. 299–302, below. For the Westernization of the 'Osmanlis themselves see II. D (vi), vol. ii, pp. 227–8, and Part III. A, vol. iii, pp. 48–50, above, and V. C (i) (*d*) 9 (β), vol. vi, pp. 102 and 112–13, below.

[2] For the contrast between the Moreot and the Phanariot currents in the Greek *Epanastasis* see II. D (vi), vol. ii, pp. 226–8, above.

[3] Even the miniature Albanian national state that made its belated appearance on the political map in 1913 was not the product of native Albanian initiative. The whole of the territory inhabited by Albanians would undoubtedly have been partitioned between Serbia and Greece after their joint victory in the First Balkan War of 1912, if the Hapsburg Monarchy and Italy had not then insisted, in their own interests, upon the establishment of a sovereign independent Albania which the Albanians could never have established for themselves.

[4] See V. C (ii) (*a*), vol. vi, p. 233, with footnote 5, below.

the timely employment of a new-fangled military equipment and organization and method which these two great Ottoman 'Westernizers' had borrowed at the eleventh hour from Napoleonic France and from post-Napoleonic Prussia. To-day, when a hundred years have passed since Mahmūd and Mehmed 'Alī completed their work of 'pacification', there is once more a Wahhābī Empire in the Arabian Peninsula;[1] but the Wahhābī King of the Najd and the Hijāz has no apparent prospect of acquiring the crowns of 'Irāq and Syria. In the meantime the Kurds have fared still worse than the Albanians; for to-day the whole of Kurdistan is partitioned between the three national states of Turkey and 'Irāq and Persia; and the barbarians who were potential successors of the 'Osmanlis in the mastery of Asia Minor a century ago are now not even the masters in their own house.[2]

Thus, in the history of the Orthodox Christian Civilization, in which the *Pax Ottomanica* was the last act but one, the last act of all has been, not 'the triumph of Barbarism and Religion,' but the triumph of an alien civilization which has been swallowing the moribund society whole and has been incorporating its fabric into its own social tissue.

We have stumbled, here, upon an alternative way in which a moribund civilization may finally lose its identity. 'The triumph of Barbarism and Religion' means that the moribund civilization has been thrown upon the scrap-heap by an iconoclastic revolt on the part of its own external and internal proletariat, in order that one or other of these insurgents may obtain a free field for bringing a new civilization to birth. In this event, the older society duly passes away—

> cedit enim rerum novitate extrusa vetustas
> semper[3]—

yet in a sense it still lives on vicariously, in the younger civilization's life, through the relation which we have learnt to call 'Apparentation-and-Affiliation'. In the alternative event, when the moribund civilization is not thrown upon the scrap-heap to make way for a new representative of the species that stands in a special relation to it, but is swallowed and assimilated by some living civilization which is one of its own contemporaries,[4] the loss of identity is manifestly more complete in one sense though less complete in another. The communities into which the moribund society is

[1] For the policy and achievements of King 'Abd-al-'Azīz Āl Sa'ūd see V. C (i) (*c*) 3, vol. v, pp. 333–4, and V. C (ii) (*a*), vol. vi, p. 234, below.

[2] See IV. C (iii) (*b*) 5, pp. 189–90, below.

[3] Lucretius: *De Rerum Natura*, Book III, ll. 964–5

[4] This contact between civilizations in the Space-dimension is examined further in Part IX, below.

articulated may be spared the extreme agonies of social dissolution; they may be extricated from the body social of the one society and incorporated into that of the other without any absolute break of historic continuity (as the Greek people, for example, has refashioned itself into one of the nations of a Westernized World after having lived for four centuries the life of an Ottoman *millet*). From another point of view, however, the loss of identity in this event will be more complete and not less; for the society that passes away through incorporation into another society, and not through apparentation and dissolution, preserves—if it does succeed in preserving—some continuity in its material fabric at the price of forfeiting altogether the power of creation which, in the alternative event, it may still exercise vicariously. And creation, after all, is a civilization's *raison d'être*.

The instance in which this process of extinction through assimilation has come to our attention is the last chapter in the history of the main body of the Orthodox Christian Society, which has been incorporated into the body social of our own Western Civilization since the beginning of the break-up of the old Ottoman Empire in the last quarter of the eighteenth century of the Christian Era, after a preliminary exposure, since about the last quarter of the seventeenth century, to the radiation of the Western culture. We can see at once that, at the present moment, all the other extant civilizations are in course of travelling along the same road. This is the current history of the offshoot of Orthodox Christendom in Russia;[1] of the Islamic and Hindu societies; and of the far Eastern Society, both in its main body in China and in its offshoot in Korea and Japan. It is also the history of the three extant arrested societies of the Esquimaux and the Nomads and the Polynesians, which are all apparently in process of being incorporated into the Western body social in so far as the social radiation of the Western Civilization is not destroying them outright.

We can see, too, that a number of the civilizations that are now extinct have lost their identity, in the last chapter of their history, in the same way. The process of 'Westernization', which began to overtake Orthodox Christendom in the last quarter of the seventeenth century of the Christian Era, and the other living non-Western civilizations about a hundred years later, was brought to bear upon the Central American Civilization and the Andean Civilization in the first and second quarters of the sixteenth century; and in both these cases the process now appears to be virtually

[1] For a discussion of the possible alternative interpretations of the Russian Communist Movement as a development in the relations between Russian Orthodox Christendom and the Western World see III. C (i) (*d*), vol. iii, pp. 200–2, and III. C (ii) (*b*), vol. iii, pp. 363–5, above.

complete.[1] The peoples which were once the creators and propagators of these two civilizations have not been exterminated or evicted, like the barbarians and the savages who once occupied the present domains of the United States and Canada. But the physical survival of the descendants of the Mayas and the Toltecs and the Collas and the Incas attests the fact that they have lost the cultural birthright which was bequeathed to them by their forebears in order to become members of an intrusive alien society in whose history they have not so far succeeded in playing any creative part.

In the present Latin-American republics of Peru and Bolivia and Ecuador, which are the 'successor-states' of the Spanish Viceroyalty of Peru and are therefore, at one remove, the 'successor-states' of the Empire of the Incas, the 'Indians', whatever may be their status in constitutional theory, have been so far in fact a submerged social stratum—an inferior caste which has played only a passive part in the social life of its own Andean homeland since this land has been annexed to the domain of Western Christendom. In Mexico the 'Indians' have been more self-assertive. Since the severance of the political connexion between Mexico and Spain in A.D. 1821, individual Mexican 'Indians' have repeatedly risen to the highest positions of political power in the turbulent republican 'successor-state' of New Spain, as the Spanish Viceroyalty in Mexico was officially styled; and since the Revolution of A.D. 1910 there has been a general ferment and upheaval among the Mexican 'Indian' masses. In Mexico, however, still more than in China (where the contemporary revolution displays the same general character), the movement of revolt has been not a reaction against the Civilization of the West but an offensive movement towards it. The Mexicans have not been seeking to extricate themselves from the Western toils in which the civilization of their forebears was caught and bound, four hundred years ago, by Cortes and his fellow *conquistadores*. On the contrary, the Mexicans have been seeking in our generation to take a fabulous Western Kingdom of Heaven by storm. In their campaigns against the latifundia and

[1] The latest perceptible expression of an Andean social consciousness was the rebellion of Tupac Amaru against the Spanish régime in Peru in A.D. 1780–3 (see I. C (i) (*b*), vol. i, p. 120, footnote 1, above). As for the M[illegible]ic social consciousness, it is reported to be alive down to this day among certain of the 'Indians' of New Mexico, a state of the North American Union which was once the northernmost outpost of the Mexic World. 'I was told not long ago,' writes Mr. Edwyn Bevan (in *The Hellenistic Age* (Cambridge 1923, University Press), p. 103) 'by some one who knew intimately the native peoples of New Mexico, that they cherished still, by a secret tradition, the unconquerable belief that Montezuma was not really dead, that one day he would come back and drive out the White Man and restore the world as it was before. In some villages it was the custom for a man to climb every day before daybreak to the top of a neighbouring hill and all alone watch the dawn, because that might be the day on which Montezuma might return.' This is a remarkable parallel to the daily visit of the Imāmī Shi'is of Hillah to the sanctuary of the Master of the Age (see III. C (ii) (*b*), Annex I, in vol. iii, p. 464, above).

against the oil-interests and against the Catholic Church the Mexican revolutionaries have been attacking the privileges or monopolies of native Mexicans of Spanish descent, and of foreign prelates and capitalists, with the object of securing for the 'Indian'-descended masses of the Mexican people that mastery in their own national house which has been proclaimed as the inherent right of every people in our latter-day Western political gospel of Democracy.

On this showing, we may pronounce that the *ci-devant* Central American Civilization, as well as the *ci-devant* Andean Civilization, has now been completely incorporated into our Western body social; and we can point to other *ci-devant* civilizations which have been incorporated into other bodies social with comparable completeness in other times and places. The Babylonic Society, for example, merged its identity in the Syriac body social in the last century B.C., after its hold upon its own cultural tradition had been weakened by the attraction of Hellenism; and the disintegrating effect of the radiation of the Hellenic culture likewise prepared the way for the absorption of the Egyptiac Society into the same Syriac body social in the course of the third, fourth, and fifth centuries of the Christian Era. This Syriac assimilation of the Egyptiac Society—the longest lived and most firmly compacted and most organically unified and most individually accentuated civilization that has ever yet been seen—is perhaps the most extraordinary feat of social assimilation that has been achieved to our knowledge so far.

If we now glance again at the group of living civilizations that are in process of being assimilated by our own Western Civilization at the present time, we shall observe that the process is proceeding at different paces on different planes.

On the economic plane every one of these societies has been caught in the network of relations which our modern Western Industrialism has cast over all the habitable lands and navigable seas on the face of the planet.[1] On the political plane, again, the children of all these apparently moribund civilizations have been seeking admission to membership in the Western comity of states through various doors. In the main body of Orthodox Christendom the 'successor-states' of the Ottoman Empire have been transforming themselves, as we have seen, into national states on our latter-day Western pattern; and the peoples of the Islamic World seem now to be inclined likewise to part company with one another on their way towards the Western political fold, and to pursue their identical objective, in the prevalent Western manner, along separate national paths. The Pan-Islamic dream of a restoration of the

[1] On this point see I. B (iii), vol. i, p. 30, above.

pristine political unity of the Islamic World[1] has been shattered by the conversion of the Arabic-speaking Muslim peoples to Nationalism[2]—a conversion which was proclaimed in a sensational manner in A.D. 1916 when the Hāshimī Sharīf of Mecca rose in insurrection against the Ottoman Sultan-Caliph and joined forces with Christian states against whom the Caliph was then engaged in a life-and-death struggle for the preservation of the empire which was the basis of his temporal power.[3] Thus both the Islamic World and the main body of Orthodox Christendom are entering the Western fold with politically divided forces. On the other hand the offshoot of Orthodox Christendom in Russia and the offshoot of the Far Eastern Civilization in Japan have each succeeded in gaining admittance into the Western comity of nations—Russia before the close of the seventeenth century and Japan before the close of the nineteenth—without losing the political unity of which

[1] See Part IV. A in the present volume, p. 3, above.

[2] For the Arabic 'successor-states' of the Ottoman Empire which have entered, or are on their way to entering, the comity of national states which is the political structure of a Westernized 'Great Society', see the present chapter, p. 107, below. For the relation of the *ci-devant* Arabic Society to an Islamic Society which was constituted by the Ottoman conquest of the Arabic World in the first quarter of the sixteenth century of the Christian Era, see the present chapter, pp. 112–14, below.

[3] The apparent triumph of our Western Political Nationalism in the Islamic World since the beginning of the twentieth century of our era—and, conspicuously, since the outbreak of the general war of A.D. 1914–18—is a remarkable testimony to the assimilative power of our Western Civilization and to the inability of the Islamic Civilization to hold its own against it. For the Pan-Islamic Movement, which was set in motion under the patronage of the Ottoman Sultan-Caliph 'Abd-al-Hamīd (*imperabat* A.D. 1876–1909) as an attempt to enable the Islamic World to repel the Western offensive, was not only good strategy on its merits (on the principle that 'union is strength'); it was also in the true line of the Islamic tradition; for, from the time of the Hijrah, which was the crucial event in the career of Muhammad and in the history of the institution that he founded, Islam had been a unitary society which embraced both the two Western social fields of Church and State; and, after the founder's death, the unity of Islam in its political aspect had been incarnated in the Arab Caliphate (see III. C (ii) (*b*), Annex II, in vol. iii, above). Thus the Pan-Islamic attempt to restore the political unity of Islam, under the historic aegis of a Caliphate, in face of a formidable external menace to the Islamic Society's very existence, might have seemed a promising stroke of statesmanship; and the rapid rout of Pan-Islamism by an irresistible outbreak of Nationalism in the Muslim ranks is a surprising denouement.

On the other hand there is nothing to be wondered at in the triumph of Nationalism in Orthodox Christendom; for, in the main body of the Orthodox Christian World, the course of events which, in the West, has culminated in Nationalism, was anticipated by some eight hundred years. In the Western World as a whole it was not until the sixteenth century of the Christian Era that the parochial national states gained the upper hand over an oecumenical church, whereas this happened as early as the eighth century in Orthodox Christendom. (This chapter of Orthodox Christian history is examined further in IV. C (iii) (*c*) 2 (β), pp. 320–408, with Annex II, pp. 592–623, below.) In fitting the 'successor-states' which they have carved out of the Ottoman Empire into the framework of our modern Western Nationalism, the Orthodox Christian peoples have merely been reverting, upon their extrication from the Ottoman Empire, to an indigenous tradition of their own. It is one of the ironies of history that this precocious Orthodox Christian Nationalism of the Middle Ages, to which these peoples have reverted now that the *Pax Ottomanica* has broken down, was the principal cause of the medieval decline and fall that led to the Ottoman conquest. This eager revival of a pernicious tradition is a bad omen for the Orthodox Christian peoples' new start in life as naturalized members of our Society of the West. And, conversely, the history of Orthodox Christian Nationalism in the Middle Ages, of which we know the whole story, is a bad omen for the prospects of our Western Society in its own belated Nationalistic Era, from which it has not yet emerged.

they were each in possession (Russia under the Muscovite Tsardom and Japan under the Tokugawa Shogunate) at the time when they each first began to feel the impact of the West. Finally, the Hindu Society, which now enjoys a precarious political unity under the British Rāj, and the main body of the Far Eastern Society, which is clinging to a vestige of political unity under the flag of the Chinese Republic, are both trying to emulate the feat, which Japan and Russia have accomplished under more favourable conditions, of becoming full-fledged members of the Western comity of states without paying the price of political disruption.

It will be seen that, while there is perhaps a greater diversity in the process of Westernization on the political plane than on the economic plane, the political as well as the economic Westernization of all the living non-Western civilizations is now in full swing. On the cultural plane, on the other hand, there is no uniform corresponding tendency. In the main body of Orthodox Christendom the former *ra'īyeh* of the Ottoman Empire—Greeks, Serbs, Rumans, and Bulgars—appear to have welcomed the prospect of cultural as well as political and economic Westernization with open arms; and the epigoni of their former lords and masters the Ottoman Turks have latterly followed their example. But these cases seem to be exceptional. The Arabs and Persians and Hindus and Chinese, and even the Japanese, are accepting our Western culture with conscious mental and moral reservations as far as they are accepting it at all; and they are all manifestly on the look-out for some form of social compromise which will allow them to participate in the economic and political systems of the West without ceasing to possess their own non-Western souls.[1] As for the Russians, they have passed right out of the phase of cultural Westernization, through which the Balkan peoples are passing to-day, and have now moved on into a cultural reaction against the West, of which an early symptom can be detected in one aspect of the Slavophil Movement and a later manifestation in one aspect of Communism.[2]

On this showing, the present tendency towards the Westernization of the World may prove to be neither so far advanced nor so well assured of ultimate success as it would appear to be at first sight. On the other hand the four cases of the Central American and Andean and Egyptiac and Babylonic civilizations are sufficient to show that the loss of identity through assimilation can be just as complete and just as definitive as the alternative process of Apparentation-and-Dissolution in which the Hellenic and Indic and Sinic and Minoan and Sumeric societies have met their ends.

1 This point has been touched upon already in I. B (iii), vol. i, pp. 35–6, above.
2 See III. C (i) (*d*), vol. iii, pp. 200–2, and III. C (ii) (*b*), vol. iii, pp. 363–5, above.

We have next to observe that when we find the last chapter in the decline and fall of a broken-down civilization taking the form of the triumph of an alien civilization, we are no nearer to having discovered the cause of the original breakdown than in the alternative case, which we have examined already, where the last chapter takes the form of 'the triumph of Barbarism and Religion'. In this case, as in that, the loss of identity is the final outcome of a long decline; and this decline has to be traced back to its distant beginning in order to arrive at the original breakdown which it is our object to explain.

We have seen, for example, that the main body of Orthodox Christendom did not lose its identity through absorption into the body social of the Western Civilization until the Orthodox Christian universal state had run out into an interregnum. The peoples of the Ottoman Empire did not succumb completely to Westernization until after they had experienced the rudiments of a barbarian Völkerwanderung; and even the beginnings of the Westernization of the Greeks and Serbs only date from the last quarter of the seventeenth century, while the Westernization of the Ottoman Turks did not begin until about a hundred years later. These dates are very late in the history of a decline which goes back, as we have observed, to the great Bulgaro-Roman War of A.D. 977–1019.

There are still longer intervals between the original breakdowns of the Egyptiac Civilization, and of the main body of the Far Eastern Civilization in China, and the respective dates at which the Egyptiac Society lost its identity through conversion to Christianity and at which the Far Eastern Society began to be penetrated by our Western social radiation. For both these civilizations not only broke down and passed through a 'Time of Troubles' and entered into a universal state before the alien influence began to work upon them; in both cases, the universal state phase was drawn out to unusual lengths.

The breakdown of the Egyptiac Civilization may be equated approximately with the transition from the Fifth Dynasty to the Sixth Dynasty, *circa* 2424 B.C.,[1] when the sins of the Pyramid-Builders were visited upon their successors and the top-heavy political structure of 'the Old Kingdom' collapsed.[2] The Egyptiac 'Time of Troubles' may be equated with the following 'Feudal Age', when the Egyptiac World broke up into a multiplicity of decadent local principalities which reproduced (with the melancholy difference between autumn and spring) the situation that had existed in

[1] For this date see further V. C (i) (*c*) 3, vol. v, p. 267, footnote 2, below.

[2] For an account of the breakdown of the Egyptiac Civilization see III. C (i) (*d*), vol. iii, pp. 213–16, above, and IV. C (ii) (*b*) 3, pp. 116–17, and IV. C (iii) (*c*) 2 (*β*), pp. 408–14, below.

the Egyptiac World a thousand years earlier, before the establishment of the United Kingdom. The Egyptiac universal state was founded *circa* 2070/2060 B.C. under that sovereign of the Eleventh Dynasty who commemorated his achievement by styling himself 'the Uniter of the Two Lands';[1] and this 'Middle Empire', after giving the Egyptiac Society the 'Indian Summer' of the Twelfth Dynasty, eventually passed out into an interregnum in which 'the triumph of Barbarism' was celebrated by the invasion of the Hyksos. At this stage, however, Egyptiac history took a peculiar turn; for, instead of going into dissolution and thereby making way for a new society to come to birth, the Egyptiac Society obstinately refused to give up the ghost. It was the Hyksos who had to make way for a resurrection of the defunct Egyptiac Society in the mummy-case of a restored universal state, the so-called 'New Empire'.[2] And even then, when 'the New Empire' had run its course like 'the Middle Empire' before it, the dried and withered mummy of the Egyptiac body social still grimly held together. 'The New Empire' expended its last ounce of strength on the *tour de force* of frustrating 'the triumph of Barbarism' for a second time when the Egyptiac World was in danger of being overwhelmed by the back-wash of the post-Minoan Völkerwanderung at the turn of the thirteenth and twelfth centuries B.C.[3] Thereafter the Egyptiac Society lingered on for some fifteen centuries longer in a state of low but tenacious vitality. Successive alien conquerors—Assyrians and Achaemenidae—were evicted in turn, like the Hyksos before them, by the sudden uncanny uprising of a prostrate body which the intruders had taken for a corpse; and the same ignominious fate would unquestionably have overtaken the Ptolemies[4] if the Roman Emperors had not stepped into their shoes and held Egypt down with an iron hand until the powerful solvent of Hellenism had had time to do its disintegrating work. It was only after this that the Egyptiac Society lost its identity through the mass-conversion of the Egyptian people, in the course of the third, fourth, and fifth centuries of the Christian Era, to the Helleno-Syriac syncretistic religion of Christianity[5]—from which, in Egypt, the Hellenic

[1] See I. C (ii), vol. i, p. 137 and p. 140, footnote 2, and II. D (v), vol. ii, p. 112, above, and V. C (i) (*c*) 3, vol. v, p. 267, and V. C (ii) (*a*), vol. vi, p. 190, below.

[2] For these chapters of Egyptiac history see I. C (ii), vol. i, pp. 136–46, above.

[3] See I. C (i) (*b*), vol. i, pp. 93 and 101, above, and IV. C (iii) (*c*) 2 (*β*), in the present volume, p. 422, V. C (i) (*c*) 3, vol. v, p. 269, and V. C (ii) (*a*), vol. vi, p. 207, below.

[4] For the series of Egyptian insurrections against the Ptolemaic régime which began before the close of the third century B.C., see V. C (i) (*c*) 2, vol. v, p. 68, below.

[5] It will be seen that the conversion of Egypt to Christianity, which marks the disappearance of the distinctive tradition of the Egyptiac culture, did not take place until some two thousand years after the date at which 'the Middle Empire', which was the Egyptiac universal state, passed over into the abortive interregnum which was marked by the ephemeral triumph of the Hyksos. Thus the Egyptiac Civilization cheated Destiny, in the manner of King Mycerinus in the fairy-story, by contriving to double

alloy was progressively purged away by the reconversion of the Egyptians, first from Primitive Christianity to Monophysitism, and eventually from Monophysitism to Islam (save for a residual Coptic minority). This last stage in the purge was only completed in the course of the post-Syriac interregnum *circa* A.D. 975–1275; and thus the final absorption of the Egyptiac Society into the Syriac body social was separated in time from the original breakdown of the Egyptiac Civilization by an interval of more than three thousand years.

The interval between the breakdown of the Far Eastern Civilization in China and the beginning of the present intensive process of Westernization is not of the same order of magnitude; but the intervening course of Far Eastern history in China is not unlike the period of Egyptiac history which we have just surveyed. The breakdown of the Far Eastern Civilization in China may be equated with the decay of the T'ang Dynasty in the last quarter of the ninth century of the Christian Era; and the subsequent 'Time of Troubles'—which was occupied, but not caused, by the progressive encroachments of the Khitan Nomad and the Kin highlander Power upon Chinese soil[1]—was brought to an end in A.D. 1280.

its proper term of life—and this on the scale of two millennia. Moreover, even *in articulo mortis*, the indomitable mummy of a long-dead society took a sardonic revenge upon its audacious destroyers; for, if it was the forcible incorporation of Egypt into the Roman Empire that enabled the solvent of Hellenism to corrode the tough Egyptiac social fabric at last into a featureless mass of debris, it was also the influence of the Egyptiac tradition—imposing even in the final state of its decay—that set the characteristic Egyptiac stamp of 'the servile state' upon a reconstructed Roman Empire—the Empire of Aurelian and Diocletian and Constantine—which was the Hellenic Civilization's last avatar. 'The tradition of the Great State maintained itself in Egypt through all the . . . periods of dissolution and foreign invasion down to the Christian Era, and, as Professor Rostovtzeff has shown' [see Rostowzew, M.: *Studien zur Geschichte des Römischen Kolonates* (Leipzig and Berlin 1910, Teubner), *passim*; and Rostovtzeff, M.: *A History of the Ancient World* (Oxford 1926, University Press, 2 vols.), vol. ii, pp. 325–33—A.J.T.], 'it exercised a formative influence on the tradition of European state administration through its inheritance by the Hellenistic monarchies and the Roman Empire. The Empire of the fourth century, above all, with its régime of fixed hereditary occupations and forced services, its official hierarchy centring in the Sacred Palace, and its vast organization of state ownership and fiscal exploitation, may be regarded as nothing less than an adaptation to the Mediterranean World in general of a system that had been inherited by the Caesars in Egypt as the successors of the Ptolemies and the Pharaohs. . . . It is remarkable that in the Roman Empire also, from the reign of Aurelian to that of Constantine, a solar monotheism' [the worship of Sol Invictus: see V. C (i) (*c*) 2, vol. v, p. 82, footnote 4, and V. C (i) (*d*) 6 (δ), Annex, vol. v, pp. 649–50 and 691–4, below—A.J.T.] 'was becoming the official religion' (Dawson, Christopher: *The Age of the Gods* (reissue: London 1933, Sheed & Ward), pp. 161–2). In Professor Rostovtzeff's own words, 'the main business of every social and economic centre in the realm was now to serve the state and work for the state. This conception was no novelty to the Ancient World: the public life of Egypt in the Hellenistic Age was largely based upon it; and now Diocletian introduced it throughout the Empire. . . . The state was entirely organized on the principles of an Eastern despotism: an autocratic ruler controlled an omnipotent bureaucracy, which suppressed every trace of self-government while professing to retain it, and a population of serfs, living and working principally for the purposes of the Government. What a departure from the Graeco-Roman ideals of freedom and self-government!' (Rostovtzeff, op. cit., vol. ii, pp. 327 and 331; see also the present Study, IV. C (iii) (*c*) 2 (β), in the present volume, p. 414, below).

[1] See II. D (v), vol. ii, p. 121, above, and V. C (i) (*c*) 3, vol. v, p. 308, and V. C (ii) (*b*), vol. vi, p. 307, below.

when the Mongol supplanters and successors of the Kin completed the barbarian conquest of China and thereby brought her some tardy alleviation of the sufferings which the Mongols' predecessors had inflicted and which the Mongols themselves had aggravated in bringing them to a climax.[1] The *Pax Mongolica* which was effectively imposed upon China by Qubilay Khan promised to endow China with her universal state; but the Chinese were unwilling to receive even this benefit at barbarian hands. Within less than a hundred years the Mongols were evicted by the Ming[2] as, in a comparable chapter of Egyptiac history, the Hyksos were evicted by the founders of 'the New Empire'. The Ming in China, like the Eighteenth Dynasty in Egypt, stood for a purist reaction against the indignity of barbarian domination and the taint of barbarian manners; but their strength was insufficient for their task; and the *Pax Mongolica*, which the Ming had managed to destroy but never quite effectively to replace, was eventually restored by the Mongols' fellow barbarians the Manchus, who conquered the whole of China in the course of the seventeenth century of the Christian Era, as the Mongols had conquered it four hundred years earlier. This was the long history, in China, of the Far Eastern decline and fall. On the other hand it was only in the sixteenth century of the Christian Era, in the later days of the Ming, that the contact of China with the modern Western World began;[3] and it was only in the nineteenth century, in the later days of the Manchus, that the present Western pressure upon China began to be seriously felt. The Sino-British 'Opium War' of A.D. 1840–2, in which 'the South Sea Barbarians' brutally battered down the Middle Kingdom's long-closed gates, was separated by a span of 962 years from the sack of the great port of Khānfū[4]—by Chinese hands—in A.D. 878;

[1] It will be seen that the local succession of Eurasian Nomads—Khitan and Mongols—played the same part in the decline and fall of the Far Eastern Civilization in China as was played in the decline and fall of Orthodox Christendom by the Saljūqs and the 'Osmanlis. In both cases the first wave of the Nomad invaders was purely destructive, while the last wave eventually performed the constructive work of compulsorily endowing the disintegrating society with a universal state. It is to be emphasized that the Nomads were not the authors of the breakdown in either case. They appeared on the scene after the breakdown had taken place; and then they merely rode through a breach which their victims had already blown in their own defences in the course of a fratricidal struggle which had gone to extremes before the Nomads' arrival.

[2] See II. D (v), vol. ii, p. 121, above, and Part V. A, vol. v, pp. 3–4, V. C (i) (*c*) 1, vol. v, p. 54, V. C (i) (*c*) 3, vol v, p. 309, V. C (i) (*c*) 4, vol. v, p. 348, V. C (ii) (*a*), vol. vi, p. 193, and V. C (ii) (*b*), vol. vi, p. 305, below.

[3] The contact of China with the medieval Western Christendom during the brief period when the Mongol universal state extended continuously from the coasts of China to the coasts of the Black Sea and the Baltic was a curiosity of history which, like Alexander's raid on India, had no lasting effect.

[4] There is some disagreement among scholars as to whether the port which is called by this name in the Arabic records was Canton or Kanpu—the latter being the port of Hangchow. Khānfū would be the closest possible Arabic transliteration of Kanpu, since there is no letter 'P' in the original version of the Arabic Alphabet which is used for conveying the Arabic language. The letter has only been added in the version used for conveying Persian and Turkish.

and that great disaster, which put an end to the China trade of the Arab and Persian subjects of the ʿAbbasid Caliphate, had been one of the outstanding events in the suicidal Chinese civil war which had accompanied the collapse of the T'ang Dynasty and had inaugurated the decline and fall, in China, of the Far Eastern Civilization.[1]

In the histories of the decline of the Far Eastern Civilization in Japan and the decline of the Orthodox Christian Civilization in Russia the current of Westernization gained the mastery at an earlier stage; for the Tokugawa Shogunate and the Romanov Tsardom, which the Japanese authors of the Meiji Revolution and the Russian Tsar Peter the Great set themselves, respectively, to transform into national states members of the Western comity of nations, were both of them universal states which had not yet passed over into interregna and had not been drawn out to unusual lengths, but were still well within the normal term. The foundation of the universal state in Japan, which was the cumulative achievement of Nobunaga and Hideyoshi and Ieyasu, may be dated at about the turn of the sixteenth and seventeenth centuries of the Christian Era. The foundation of the universal state in Russia may be equated with the union between Muscovy and Novgorod—the two principal members of the previous plurality of parochial Russian states—in A.D. 1478. It will be seen that the Japanese universal state had been in existence for rather less than 300, and the Russian for rather more than 200, years by the respective dates at which the great Japanese and the great Russian 'Westernizers' performed their *tours de force*.

In these two cases there will perhaps be little inclination to suggest that the incorporation of Russia and of Japan into the Society of the West, which was achieved by Peter and by his Japanese counterparts, is to be regarded as the cause of the breakdown of the Orthodox Christian Civilization in Russia and of the Far Eastern Civilization in Japan. So far from that, these achievements of Russian and Japanese statesmanship were so remarkably successful—at least on a short view—that many observers may be inclined rather to take them as evidence that the societies which deliberately put themselves through this radical metamorphosis, and which came through it—at any rate, for the moment—without mishap, must still have been in the full *élan* of life and growth. The Russian reaction in the seventeenth century and the Japanese reaction in the nineteenth century to the impact of the West cer-

[1] An English translation of an account of this sack of Kanpu or Canton from the pen of Abu Zayd al-Hasan of Siraf will be found in Renaudot, E.: *Ancient Accounts of India and China by two Mohammedan Travellers* (London 1733, Harding), pp. 40–5. The passage also gives a graphic description of the whole political and social breakdown in which the sack of Khānfū was an incident.

tainly appear to display a command of the situation and a mastery over events which stand out in contrast to the ineffectiveness of the 'Osmanlis and the Hindus and the Chinese and the Aztecs and the Incas in dealing with an identical challenge.

Instead of waiting heedlessly and passively for an expanding and aggressive West to breach their walls and stave in their doors and take possession of their house and refurnish it throughout according to a Western taste without consulting the native owners and occupiers, the Russians and the Japanese not only divined, at an early stage, the seriousness of the Western challenge and the severity of the penalties which they would incur if they failed to respond to it; they also took action in good time in order to meet the trouble half-way; and this combination of prescience with resoluteness won conspicuous rewards. Instead of undergoing a process of compulsory 'Westernization' at the hands of Swedish or German or Spanish or American intruders, the Russians and the Japanese were able to carry their social metamorphosis through with their own hands because they submitted themselves to it voluntarily and deliberately; and, instead of being socially submerged like the Central American and Andean peoples, or being politically subjected to the rule of a Western Power like the Hindus and Muslims in India, or being forced to pay for their political 'Westernization' by the sacrifice of their political unity like the Muslim and Orthodox peoples of the Ottoman Empire, they succeeded in preserving their existing unitary commonwealth. Without any break of political continuity they respectively transformed the Romanov Tsardom and the Tokugawa Shogunate from 'hermit kingdoms' which each embraced the whole of its 'short and narrow-vergèd' universe into members of a Western comity of states with the calibre and the standing of Great Powers which were able at once to play an active part in the international life of the Great Society of the day.

No doubt the later history of Russia, who entered upon the path of 'Westernization' some two hundred years earlier than Japan and who has therefore had that much time longer to experience the consequence, will make cautious observers chary of pronouncing prematurely that the Russian experiment of 'Westernization' has justified Peter's policy in the long run; and in Japan, likewise, the turn of events in our generation suggests that the second phase in the history of the Japanese experiment may pass less smoothly than the first. The Solonian maxim *respice finem*[1] is eminently applicable to both the Russian and the Japanese enterprises; and, if these enterprises do come to grief unmistakably in the end, there will assuredly be some apologists who will maintain that all was well with Japan

[1] Herodotus, Book I, chap. 33.

and with Russia until our Western Society crossed their paths, and that, in spite of their gallant first attempts to hold their own against the formidable Western intruder by borrowing his weapons and paying him in his own coin, the encounter has been fatal to both these non-Western societies after all.

This hypothetical future apologia, however, can be refuted in advance, here and now. by an examination of Russian and Japanese history in the periods preceding the voluntary 'self-Westernization' of Russia and of Japan respectively.

At this earlier stage, again, we shall admire the handling of 'the Western Question' by Russian and Japanese statesmanship; for, before either the Russians or the Japanese were able to secure leisure and elbow-room for 'Westernizing' their life on their own initiative, they each had to meet and repulse a Western attempt to bring them under Western domination—as the Central Americans and Andeans and Hindus and Chinese have actually been dominated by divers Western aggressors in divers degrees. For the first establishment of relations with the modern Western World, which occurred in Russian and in Japanese history almost contemporaneously, about the middle of the sixteenth century of the Christian Era, was followed in both cases—again almost contemporaneously, in the early years of the seventeenth century—by a serious threat of Western conquest.

In the Russian case the impact of the West took the crude form of a regular military invasion of Russia, and a temporary occupation of Moscow, which was at that time the capital of the Russian universal state, by the forces of Russia's Western next-door neighbour, the United Kingdom of Poland-Lithuania, on the pretext of supporting a pretender to the Russian Imperial throne, the notorious 'False Dmitri'.[1] In the Japanese case the impact took the more ethereal form of the conversion of several hundreds of thousands of Japanese souls to Catholicism by Portuguese and Spanish missionaries. Yet this peaceful conquest of Japanese hearts and minds by a Western religious propaganda was fraught with potential dangers for the Japanese body social and even for the Japanese body politic; for although these converts were numerically an inconsiderable minority of the total population of Japan, they were strong in enthusiasm and in organization and in the social vitality of the alien way of life which they had adopted; and it would not have been a forlorn hope if this minority had attempted to make itself master of Japan with the military backing of the temporarily united kingdoms of Spain and Portugal.[2] Thus Japan as well as

[1] See II. D (v), vol. ii, pp. 157 and 176, above.

[2] The union of the Spanish and Portuguese crowns lasted *de facto* from A.D. 1581 to A.D. 1640.

Russia was seriously threatened with being overtaken in the seventeenth century by the fate which had actually overtaken Mexico and Peru at Spanish hands in the sixteenth century and which was subsequently to overtake India in the nineteenth century at the hands of the English. But both Japanese and Russian history was given a different turn by the effective action of the Russians and the Japanese themselves. The Russians drove out the Poles by a spontaneous national uprising,[1] while the Japanese exorcized 'the White Peril' by expelling all resident Western missionaries and merchants, forbidding Westerners to set foot on Japanese soil in future under pain of death,[2] and exterminating the native Japanese Catholic community by a ruthless persecution. Having thus rid themselves momentarily of 'the Western Question', both the Japanese and the Russians imagined at first that they had merely to retire into their own shells in order to 'live happily ever after'. Time showed, however, that, after all, they had not finally disposed of 'the Western Question' by these tactics of self-isolation; and it was this subsequent discovery that eventually led the Russians and the Japanese in turn to continue the pursuit of their perpetual aim by a complete reversal of their policy, and to hold their own still, against a renewed and redoubled pressure from the West, by transforming their polities deliberately from archaistic 'hermit kingdoms' into 'Westernized' Great Powers.

Thus the Russians and the Japanese prove to have handled 'the Western Question' as ably in the late sixteenth and early seventeenth centuries of our Era as they have handled it since, under altered conditions, down to the beginning of the chapter which is now in progress. And yet there are unmistakable indications that, before ever the first Portuguese ship sailed into Nagasaki, or the first English ship into Archangel, both the Far Eastern Civilization in Japan and the Orthodox Christian Civilization in Russia had already broken down.

In Russian history the true 'Time of Troubles', in the sense in which that term is used in this Study, is not the bout of anarchy in the early years of the seventeenth century for which the term has been coined by the Russians themselves. The so-called Russian 'Time of Troubles' in the early seventeenth century was an interlude between the first and the second phase of the Russian universal state, corresponding to the bout of anarchy in the Hellenic World, in the middle of the third century, which intervened

1 See V. C (ii) (*a*), vol. vi, p. 207, below.

2 The sole exception was the licensed establishment of Dutch traders who were allowed to reside, as pariahs, on the islet of Deshima (see II. D (vi), vol. ii, pp. 232–3, above).

between the *Pax Augusta* and the *Pax Diocletiana*.[1] The chapter of Russian history which corresponds to the chapter of Hellenic history between the outbreak of the Atheno-Peloponnesian War and the Battle of Actium, and which therefore represents the Russian 'Time of Troubles' in our sense, is the time of adversity which preceded the foundation of the Russian universal state through the union of Novgorod with Muscovy in A.D. 1478.[2] On the same showing, the true 'Time of Troubles' in Japanese history is represented by the so-called Kamakura and Ashikaga periods of feudal anarchy and civil war which preceded the disciplinary and unificatory and pacificatory work of Nobunaga and Hideyoshi and Ieyasu; and the combined span of these two periods extends, according to the conventional dates, from A.D. 1184 to A.D. 1597.[3]

If these identifications of the true Japanese and the true Russian 'Time of Troubles' are accepted, we have to lay our fingers on their respective origins and to trace each of them to some pre-Western cause; and a Russian apologist for the decline and fall of the Russian Orthodox Christian Civilization will have his explanation on the tip of his tongue. He will remind us that, in our 'philosophy of history', the foundation of a universal state represents a social rally, in which the process of social disintegration is temporarily arrested, and then he will point out that the union of Novgorod with Muscovy in A.D. 1478, which we have taken as the foundation of the Russian universal state, was accompanied by the final liberation of Russia from the alien yoke of the Eurasian Nomad horde whose head-quarters were at the Saray on the Lower Volga. Is not the Russian rally in the last quarter of the fifteenth century to be attributed to the liberation of the Russian Orthodox Christendom from 'the Tatars' rather than to the mere union of Russian forces which made this liberation possible? And, if so, then is not the breakdown of the Russian Orthodox Christendom, which precipitated the 'Time of Troubles', to be identified with the devastating invasion of Russia by Chingis Khan's grandson Batu in A.D. 1238—the catastrophe which originally fastened the 'Tatar' yoke upon Russia's neck? Have we not found the cause of the breakdown here, and found it in a blow which was delivered by an external human force?

This is certainly a commonly accepted explanation of the breakdown of the Russian Orthodox Christian Civilization in 'the Middle Ages'; but before we concur in condemning the Mongols

[1] See I. C (i) (*a*), vol. i, p. 53, footnote 2, above, and V. C (ii) (*b*), vol. vi, p. 311, below.

[2] For the structure of the Russian 'Time of Troubles' see further V. C (ii) (*b*), vol. vi, pp. 308–10, below.

[3] For the structure of the Japanese 'Time of Troubles' see further V. C (ii) (*b*), vol. vi, pp. 303–5, below.

to be the villains of the piece in a Russian historical melodrama, we must be sure that we are not assigning them a more important as well as a more criminal role than they deserve. These Mongols, after all, were the brothers of the Mongols whom we have already encountered in the history of the Far Eastern Civilization in China; and they were the cousins of the Khitan and Kin who were the Mongols' forerunners on Chinese soil, and of the Saljūqs and 'Osmanlis who played corresponding parts in the history of the main body of Orthodox Christendom. In each of these other cases we have had to deal with determined attempts to turn the Eurasian Nomad invaders into scapegoats, and in each case we have come to the conclusion that these attempts are unjustified. Our verdict has been that the Orthodox Christian Society in Anatolia and the Balkans dealt itself a suicidal blow in the great Bulgaro-Roman War of A.D. 977–1019, before ever the Saljūqs made their first raid across the Asiatic frontiers of the East Roman Empire, and that the Far Eastern Society in China did itself an equally mortal injury in the great anarchy of A.D. 875–960, before ever the Khitan crossed the Great Wall.[1] Is it not possible that in Russia, likewise, the Orthodox Christian Society may have already brought about its own breakdown by its own act, before ever the Mongols crossed the Volga in A.D. 1238?

To put this last question aside for a moment, we can pronounce at once that the eruption of the Mongols was not the cause of the breakdown of the Far Eastern Civilization in Japan; for the great Mongol invasion of Japan in A.D. 1281[2] was such an ignominious failure that it was never repeated; and the Japanese feat of driving into the sea the hitherto invincible conquerors of the Continent must have been as stimulating a triumph as the Athenians' victory over the Persians at Marathon.

To what are we to attribute this Japanese triumph over a Power which shattered every other adversary that it encountered, with the single exception of the Egyptian Mamlūks? No doubt the Japanese benefited by their insularity; for the Mongols were as much out of their element on the sea as they were at home on the Steppe; and they cannot have been at their best in a fiercely contested landing operation in which their wonderful light cavalry had to fight as an awkward squad of horse-marines. In this amphibious warfare the Japanese long-bowmen were at a still greater advantage over their opponents than the English bowmen were at Crécy or Poictiers.

[1] See the preceding chapter, pp. 72–6, and the present chapter, pp. 87–8, above.

[2] In this invasion Japan was attacked by a converging movement of Mongol armadas from Korea and from China, and the Mongols were able to throw into the enterprise the forces which had been liberated by the completion of their conquest of South China in the preceding year. Hence the Mongol invasion of Japan in A.D. 1281 was a more formidable affair than the previous reconnaissance in A.D. 1274.

Yet when we have allowed for these points of military technique, we shall have to admit that they must have been of less importance than the psychological forces. For the Mongol horsemen who had penetrated the Russian forests and had stormed the strongholds of 'the Old Man of the Mountain' in the fastnesses of the Elbrūz might have subdued the Japanese Archipelago by the sheer terror of their name if they had not met their military match in their Japanese opponents.

The fundamental reason why the Japanese beat the Mongols in A.D. 1281 was that, in the thirteenth century of the Christian Era, the Japanese were as fine soldiers as the Mongols themselves; and the school in which these Japanese warriors had been trained was the school of fratricidal warfare. It was in the course of a hundred years of suicidal struggles with one another on their native soil that the Japanese had acquired the prowess to which the Mongol invaders now succumbed; and it follows that even if, in A.D. 1281, the fortune of war had inclined the other way and if Japan had then been added to the tale of Mongol conquests, the breakdown of the Far Eastern Society in Japan would still have to be traced back to some earlier event of a domestic order. As a matter of fact, we have already had occasion to notice, in another connexion,[1] what was the origin of this Japanese fratricidal warfare which had been rife for the best part of a century before the Mongols challenged the Japanese to combat, and which was to continue for more than three centuries longer after that, until it attained its culmination in the time of Hideyoshi and its close in the time of Ieyasu. The fratricidal warfare which marked the Japanese 'Time of Troubles' began towards the end of the twelfth century of the Christian Era when the Japanese feudal nobility which had come into existence in the backwoods, in the slow and arduous process of enlarging the borders of the Far Eastern Society in Japan at the expense of the barbarian Ainu, eventually faced about towards the home front and asserted the ascendency of this new military Japanese Society in the Kwanto over the old civil Japanese Society in Yamato. The disaster which accounts for the breakdown of the Far Eastern Civilization in Japan is the protracted military revolution which overthrew the régime of 'the Cloistered Emperors' and inaugurated the beginning of the feudal anarchy between A.D. 1156 and A.D. 1185;[2] and these fatal strokes were not the work of any foreign hand.

[1] In II. D (v), vol. ii, on pp. 158–9, above.

[2] This revolution worked itself out in three successive bouts, of which the respective dates were A.D. 1156, A.D. 1160, and A.D. 1183–5. But this rapid succession of explosions was fired by a train of gunpowder which had been smouldering and spluttering for a long time before it blew the Far Eastern Society in Japan into fragments. The militarization of the marches in the North-East had begun as early as A.D. 940 (Murdoch, J.: *History of Japan*, vol. i (London 1910, Kegan Paul), pp. 252 and 257). The first known

This reading of Japanese history suggests an answer to our question concerning the cause and the date of the breakdown of the Orthodox Christian Civilization in Russia; for in this chapter, as in others, the histories of Russia and Japan are analogous, as we have noticed in the earlier passage of this Study which has just been referred to.[1] It is true that the thirteenth-century Russians, unlike the contemporary Japanese, were no match for the Mongol invaders. They went down before them in as lamentable a débâcle as the Khwarizmians or the Hungarians. Yet, notwithstanding this difference of outcome, the antecedent history of Russia had been following a Japanese course. For more than a hundred years before the Mongols' advent the Orthodox Christendom in Russia had been partitioned politically into a plurality of contending states; and the militarism which the parochial Russian princes had learnt to exercise against each other had been acquired in the backwoods of the north-east, where the frontier warfare in which the Russian pioneers were gradually enlarging the borders of the Russian World at the expense of the forest Finns effaced the social effects of the exotic Orthodox Christian culture from Constantinople which had been transplanted, at the close of the tenth century, to the original centre of the Russian Power at Kiev. In this chapter of Russian history Kiev in the Dniepr Basin corresponds, as we have seen, to Kyoto in Yamato, while Vladímir and the other new outposts of the Russian Society in the basins of the Volga and the Arctic Dvina correspond to the new frontier fiefs of the Japanese Empire in the Kwanto. In Russian history, as in Japanese, a time came at which the political supremacy passed to the warlike and barbaric marches from the relatively urbané and pacific interior; and in Russian history, again, this shift of the centre of gravity was

case of a Mahayanian Buddhist monastery in Japan taking to arms dates from A.D. 961 (Murdoch, op. cit., vol. i, p. 266; compare the present Study, V. C (ii) (*b*), vol. vi, p. 304, footnote 4, below). The minting of coins in Japan ceased in A.D. 958 and was not resumed until A.D. 1587 (Murdoch, op. cit., pp. 191 and 496). One result of the military revolution at Kyoto in A.D. 1156 was the infliction of the death penalty at the Imperial Court for the first time in 346 years (Murdoch, op. cit., vol. i, p. 299). The first recorded case of the practice of hara-kiri dates from A.D. 1170 (Murdoch, op. cit., vol. i, p. 312). In fact, the overt breakdown of the Far Eastern Civilization in the twelfth century B.C. was heralded by a relapse into barbarism which began as early as the ninth century (Murdoch, op. cit., vol. i, p. 265). The modern Western student of Japanese history whom we are here following sums up this relapse in the formula that in the ninth century Japan reverted to the condition in which she had been before the establishment of a political constitution of the Far Eastern pattern, *à la* T'ang, in A.D. 645 (Murdoch, op. cit., vol. i, p. 263). In terms of a later chapter of the present Part of this Study (IV. C (iii) (*b*) 1, pp. 133–7, below) we might describe the Japanese *coup d'état* of A.D. 645 as a revolutionary effect of the impact of the new forces of the Far Eastern Civilization on the old institutions of a Japanese barbarism; and on the same showing the *coups* of A.D. 1156 and 1160 and 1183–5 might be described as a counter-revolutionary reaction of this barbarism against a civilization which had not, in the event, proved strong enough to overcome it in its new domain in the north-eastern marches. For the religious consequences of the breakdown of the Far Eastern Civilization in Japan in the latter part of the twelfth century of the Christian Era see V. C (i) (*c*) 2, vol. v, pp. 96–103, below.

[1] See loc. cit. on p. 94, footnote 1, above.

accompanied by a breakdown of the transplanted civilization, which was unable to stand the aggravation of an alien social climate that was distinctly adverse even at its mildest. In the Russian case there is no definite event, like the Japanese revolutions of A.D. 1156–85, to mark the breakdown; but the change in the Russian situation which brought the breakdown with it was taking place approximately at, or towards, the turn of the eleventh and twelfth centuries of the Christian Era,[1] and its completion was openly recognized in A.D. 1157, when Vladímir, in the Volga Basin, supplanted Kiev as the seat of the (now no more than titular) prince-suzerain of All the Russias.[2] The Russian 'Time of 'Troubles', in our sense of the term, was thus in full swing by the time when Batu appeared on the scene to take advantage of it; and 'the beginning of evils' in Russia was the work, not of Mongol, but of Russian hands.

In the histories of the declines and falls of the Hindu and Andean and Babylonic civilizations the process of assimilation into the tissues of an alien body social supervened, as in the cases of Japan and Russia, when the declining societies were in their universal states and before these universal states had reached the normal term of their existence. In these other three cases, however, the process took a more catastrophic turn; for the statesmen of the declining societies did not remain masters of the situation even to the extent of being able to accomplish their own social metamorphosis on their own initiative; and they did not succeed in preserving their universal states, as the Russians preserved the Romanov Empire and the Japanese preserved the Tokugawa Shogunate, by transforming them into states members of an alien political comity. In all three cases the declining society suffered an alien military conquest, and the universal state in which it had previously been embodied was superseded by a new polity which was imposed by the conquerors.

In Hindu history one such alien polity, imposed by conquest, has been the British Rāj; and the brief century of this British Rāj may still shine in retrospect with the serene beauty of an 'Indian Summer'—and this perhaps even in Indian eyes. For the British

[1] This is the date suggested by Kliutschewski, W. [Kluchevski, V.]: *Geschichte Russlands*, vol. i (Berlin 1925, Obelisk-Verlag), p. 166, and by Mirsky, Prince D. S., in *The Cambridge Medieval History*, vol. vii (Cambridge 1932, University Press), p. 609. In the words of the latter of these two authorities,

'The decisive turning-point in the history of Kiev is the last third of the eleventh century, when the Cumans, favoured by the feuds of the princes, some of whom led them as allies into Russia, secured their control over the Steppe. It was then that the Lower Dniepr ceased to be an avenue to Greece. . . . The sack of Kiev [in A.D. 1169] and the refusal of Andreii to fix his residence there is only a dramatic moment in a long process of degradation.'

[2] See II. D (v), vol. ii, pp. 154 and 158–9, above.

Rāj was only founded after the antecedent universal state of the Hindu World had broken down into an anarchy which has made the eighteenth century of the Christian Era as evil a memory in Hindu history as the third century was in the history of the Roman Empire. It was this post-Mughal anarchy, and not the *Pax Mogulica* which preceded it, that the British conquest of India swept away by force. The *Pax Britannica*, which the British conquerors then imposed, has been more effective, more pervasive, and, in Western eyes at any rate, more beneficent than the peace which had been imposed, two centuries earlier, by Akbar (*imperabat* A.D. 1556–1605); and if the British and the Mughal régimes in India are to be compared, it cannot be argued that, even if the British régime is superior in practical achievement, the Mughal régime is morally more admirable in virtue of being a native product; for the founders of the Mughal Rāj were as utterly alien as the founders of the British Rāj were from the native social order of Hinduism; and a Bābur, cast away in Hindustan through the fortunes of war in Central Asia, was just as homesick for the temperate clime of his native Farghānā as any English sojourner in India has ever been for Kentish hop-fields or for Yorkshire moors.[1] On this point the Mughal Rāj can have no greater sentimental appeal than the British Rāj to an unprejudiced Hindu mind; and although, nevertheless, a favourable verdict upon the British Rāj may be almost impossible for a Hindu of our generation to accept —particularly when it proceeds from a Western observer's mouth —the British Rāj, as it passes, may be content to await the verdict of History; for the future consensus of enlightened and disinterested opinion seems unlikely to convict the British Rāj of responsibility for the breakdown of the Hindu Civilization. The future historian seems more likely to pronounce that, at a time when the Hindu Society was already far advanced in its decline, and when the Mughal attempt to provide the Hindu World with a universal state had miscarried, the British Rāj gave India a political unity and efficiency and stability which neither Mughal nor Hindu had ever succeeded in giving her; and that, when the assimilation of the Hindu Society into the body social of the West was already inevitable, and when the only question left open was the way in which the metamorphosis was to take place, the existence of the British Rāj gave India an opportunity of entering the Great Society on the relatively favourable terms which had been secured—by

[1] In the Indian chapters of Bābur's memoirs there are repeated expressions of the author's dislike for the Hindu World upon which he had forcibly inflicted himself; and, if these querulous passages were quoted anonymously, in isolation from their context, they might easily be taken for the indiscretions of some disgruntled twentieth-century English lieutenant-governor of an Indian province

native and not by alien initiative—for Russia and Japan, instead of having to undergo the tribulation which the Greeks and the Turks and the Chinese had undergone on their thorny paths towards the goal of Westernization.

The acquittal of the British Rāj, however, would not necessarily imply that the responsibility for the breakdown of the Hindu Civilization lies on the Hindus' own heads; for if the overseas British invader of India cannot be made to serve as the scapegoat, it may still be possible to conscript the overland Turkish invader and to cast him, in the Englishman's place, for the scapegoat's part. Turkish Akbar, who has perhaps deserved well of Hinduism in endowing the Hindu World with a first attempt at a universal state, was after all the grandson of Turkish Bābur; and Bābur was the last of a long line of Turkish invaders from Central Asia who had made havoc in India from the last quarter of the tenth to the first quarter of the sixteenth century of the Christian Era.[1] Is this series of Turkish invasions the cause to which the breakdown of the Hindu Civilization is to be ascribed? There can be little doubt that, if the English had never made their appearance on the Indian stage or were not playing a prominent part on it to-day, the twentieth-century Hindu apologist for the decline and fall of Hinduism would be as vociferous as the twentieth-century Greek apologist for the decline and fall of Orthodox Christendom in denouncing 'the unspeakable Turk' as the guilty party.

Manifestly the series of Turkish intruders upon India which begins with Mahmūd the destroyer and culminates in Akbar the preserver does correspond historically to the series of Turkish intruders upon Orthodox Christendom which begins with the Saljūq raiders in Anatolia and culminates in the Ottoman founders of an Orthodox Christian universal state; and both series correspond to the succession of Khitan and Kin and Mongols in the history of the decline and fall of the Far Eastern Civilization in China. But, in the light of our previous findings in regard to these other cases, the very admission of the legitimacy of the historical parallel establishes an *a priori* presumption against the legitimacy of the indictment of the Turks as the assassins of the Hindu Civilization. We have ascertained that the Far Eastern Civilization in China and the Orthodox Christian Civilization in Anatolia and in the Balkan Peninsula were the victims, not of their respective Eurasian Nomad invaders, but of their own fratricidal violence; and we have been able to bring foward good evidence of the fatal blows which they

[1] Sebuktegīn, the Turkish predecessor of the great Turkish raider Mahmūd of Ghaznah, conquered Kābul in A.D. 975 and began to raid the Panjab in A.D. 986–7 (see II. D (iii), vol. ii, p. 78, above). Bābur descended upon Hindustan from Afghanistan in A.D. 1519 (see II. D (v), vol. ii, p. 149, above).

had each inflicted upon themselves with their own hands before the invaders arrived. If we now turn back to Hindu history with these analogies in our minds, we shall find that the plot of the Hindu tragedy has followed the same pattern.

The effective conquest of the heart of the Hindu World by the Turks did not take place until the turn of the twelfth and thirteenth centuries of the Christian Era (A.D. 1191–1204), when the Turkish aggressors broke through the Hindu marches along the line of the Jumna and swept right down the Ganges Valley to the coast of Bengal.[1] It is this far-reaching and long-enduring Turkish occupation of Hindustan that corresponds to the Hellenic conquest of the same region by the Greek princes of Bactria during the first half of the second century B.C. The raids of Sebuktegīn and Mahmūd of Ghaznah and their successors during the two centuries preceding the great Turkish 'break through' cut no deeper into the flesh of the contemporary Indian body social, and had no greater effect upon the course of contemporary Indian history, than Alexander's raid in 326–325 B.C. In the Turkish intrusion upon Hindu soil the great 'break through' of A.D. 1191 was the decisive event; and when we examine the immediate antecedents of this Hindu disaster on the Hindu side of the previous borderline between the Hindu and the Syriac World, we observe that, about the middle of the twelfth century of the Christian Era, the Hindu Powers in the marches (that is to say, in the territories now comprised in the United Provinces of the British Indian Empire) had fallen into an internecine warfare with one another.[2]

It was this fatal division of the House of Hinduism against itself that made it possible for the Turkish highwaymen to force an entry. The earlier onslaught of an alien aggressor in the shape of the Primitive Muslim Arabs, who had assailed the Hindu World in the eighth century of the Christian Era, had been effectively repulsed in the ninth century by a union of Hindu forces, from Gujerat to Oude, under the leadership of the Prātihāra Rājputs;[3] and this successful self-defence of the Hindu Society at this earlier date

[1] See II. D (v), vol. ii, p. 131, above. In strict accuracy it must be observed that the leaders of this victorious Turkish offensive against the Hindu World were not Turks but Ghūrīs: i.e. Iranian mountaineers from the highlands between Ghaznah and Herāt and Qandahār. These Ghūrīs, however, were followed as well as preceded by Turkish war-lords (e.g. the Turkish 'Slave-Kings' at Delhi: see Part III. A, vol. iii, p. 30 and p. 31, footnote 1, above); and from first to last it was the impetus of the Turkish eruption out of the Eurasian Steppe that gave the whole movement its driving power.

[2] See Smith, V. A.: *The Early History of India*, 3rd edition (Oxford 1914, Clarendon Press), pp. 384–7. If we wish to identify the breakdown of the Hindu Civilization with some particular event, we may perhaps equate it with the abduction, *circa* A.D. 1175, of the daughter of Rāja Jaichand, the King of Kanauj and Benares, by the King of Ajmīr and Delhi, Rāja Prithīrāj. If we do not choose to see in this lady a Hindu Helen of Troy, an alternative date would be A.D. 1182—a year which was signalized by Prithīrāj's victory over Rāja Chandel, the King of Bundelcund.

[3] See II. D (v), vol. ii, pp. 130–1, above.

stands out in instructive contrast to the débâcle in which the descendants of the Rājputs went down before the Turkish successors of the Arabs some four hundred years later; for the latent strength of the Hindu Society cannot have been so great in A.D. 800, when this society was still in its infancy, as it must have been in A.D. 1200, when the society was in the spring of its youth, while on the other side the religious enthusiasm of Primitive Islam and the material resources of the Umayyad Caliphate made the Arab invaders who were baffled in the ninth century a far more formidable military power in themselves than the Turks who were able, in the twelfth century, to carry all before them. Even as late as A.D. 991, when the first warning trickle of the imminent Turkish flood had just begun to spill over the watershed of the Hindu Kush and to run down into the Kābul Valley, a coalition of Rājput princes was able, in the strength of its united forces, to push its way up the Kurram Valley against the current of the descending Turkish stream.[1] These historical facts may be taken as presumptive evidence that if in the twelfth century the Rājputs had not turned their swords suicidally upon themselves, the Hindu World might have continued, without any undue drain upon its energies, to keep the Turks at bay and to work out its own destinies under its own control. And thus the verdict proves, on appeal, to be suicide instead of assassination in this case also.

In Babylonic history the indigenous universal state was 'the Neo-Babylonian Empire' of Nabopolassar and Nebuchadnezzar and Nabonidus, which united in a single body politic all that remained of the Babylonic Society after the downfall of the Assyrian Power at the close of the seventh century B.C.[2] In this case the alien polity imposed by conquest was the Achaemenian Empire, which engulfed the Neo-Babylonian Empire when Cyrus took Babylon in 539 B.C. Under the Achaemenian régime and under the régime of the Seleucidae, who were the Achaemenids' Hellenic successors in Asia, the Babylonic Society was gradually absorbed into the tissues of the Syriac body social; for the Achaemenian Empire served as an instrument for the propagation of the Syriac and not of the Babylonic culture;[3] and the solvent of Hellenism, which was introduced into a decaying Babylonic World by the instrumentality of Alexander and his successors, worked, contrary to Hellenic intention,[4] for the profit of the Syriac culture by accelera-

[1] See, Smith, V. A.: *The Early History of India*, 3rd edition (Oxford 1914, Clarendon Press), p. 382.

[2] For this Neo-Babylonian Empire see II. D (v), vol. ii, p. 138, above.

[3] This perhaps explains why it was that the Babylonians never became reconciled to the Achaemenian régime (see V. C (i) (*c*) 2, vol. v, p. 94 and p. 123, with footnote 2; V. C (i) (*c*) 4, vol. v, pp. 347–8; and V. C (ii) (*a*), Annex II, vol. vi, p. 442, below).

[4] Alexander appears to have presented himself to the Babylonians, and to have been

ting the process of Babylonic disintegration. In consequence the Babylonic culture became almost entirely extinct in the last century B.C., and thereafter the Syriac culture occupied all but one patch of the ground that had once borne a Babylonic crop.[1] On this showing, the conquest of Babylon by Cyrus in 539 B.C. started a train of historical events which ended in the Babylonic Society's finally losing its identity some five hundred years later. Yet no historian will be tempted to equate this last chapter in the decline and fall of the Babylonic Civilization with its original breakdown, or to ascribe to the comparatively mild and conservative—albeit alien and unpopular—Achaemenian régime the destruction which was manifestly brought upon the Babylonic World, at a time when the Achaemenidae had not vet been heard of, by the native militarism of the Assyrians.

The manifest cause of the breakdown of the Babylonic Civilization was the secular conflict between Babylonia and Assyria, which were the two principal Powers of the Babylonic World; and the perennial sources of this fatal domestic strife were the perpetual aggressiveness of the militarily superior Assyrian Power and the perpetual recalcitrance of the culturally superior Babylonia against the forcible imposition of an Assyrian yoke.[2] This domestic

accepted by them, in the guise of a liberator from the Achaemenian yoke; and thereafter there was a genuine fraternization—mainly on scientific and religious grounds—between the Hellenic and the Babylonic societies (see V.C (i) (*c*) 2, vol. v, p. 94 and p. 123, footnote 2; V. C (i) (*c*) 4, vol. v, pp. 347–8; and V. C (ii) (*a*), Annex II, vol. vi, p. 442, below).

[1] As a curiosity of history, we may notice that, for nearly a thousand years after the extinction of the Babylonic Civilization elsewhere, a fossilized remnant of it survived in the outlying but ancient Babylonic city of Harran in North-Western Mesopotamia on the River Balīkh, a Sumerian foundation whose patron divinity was the Moon-God Sin. At Harran the worship of the pantheon which the Babylonic Society had inherited from its Sumeric predecessors (see I. C (i) (*b*), vol. i, p. 115, above) was kept up, without a break, until the Age of the ʿAbbasid Caliphate; and the ʿAbbasid Caliphs were captivated by the mathematical and philosophical learning which these strange survivors of a vanished culture had partly inherited from their own forebears and partly acquired from their prolonged contact with Hellenism. In consequence these undisguised 'idolaters' were treated by the Commanders of the Faithful with an indulgence which they were not always so ready to show to the officially tolerated Jewish and Christian 'People of the Book'. It is remarkable that this fossil of the Babylonic culture should have been preserved at a point which had been perilously exposed to the impact of the Syriac Civilization from first to last. The neighbourhood of Harran lay right in the track of the Aramaean assaults upon Assyria in the eleventh and tenth centuries B.C. (see II. D (v), vol. ii, pp. 134–5, above), while the next city above Harran on the bank of the River Balīkh was Edessa, the cradle of Syriac Christianity and the base of operations from which the Nestorian branch of this Syriac Christendom propagated itself to the Yaman in one direction and to China in the other. It is extraordinary that this Edessan missionary movement should have been still kept at bay by the walls of Harran after it had succeeded in making a lodgement within the walls of Najrān and of Si Ngan, and that the Babylonic culture should have lingered on by the waters of the Balīkh for nearly a thousand years after it had died out by the waters of Babylon. Yet Harran is doubly distinguished in Babylonic history as the last stronghold both of the Assyrian Army and of the Babylonic Civilization.

[2] Psychologically the feud between Babylonia and Assyria, which tore the Babylonic World in two from the ninth to the seventh century B.C., may be compared with the feud between the East Roman Empire and the Bulgarian Empire which devastated Orthodox Christendom in the tenth and eleventh centuries of the Christian Era (see IV. C (iii) (*c*) 2 (β), pp. 382–93, below).

struggle in the Babylonic World became serious about the middle of the eighth century B.C., when the Assyrians seem deliberately to have set themselves the superhuman military task of conquering Babylonia with one hand and Syria simultaneously with the other.[1] The Assyro-Babylonian feud became suicidally destructive when the Chaldaean tribesmen who had drifted into Babylonia out of the North Arabian Steppe took up the cudgels on their adopted country's behalf. When the Chaldaean chieftain Merodach-Baladan made himself master of Babylon in 721 B.C. and set Assyria at defiance, he started a hundred years' war which only ended with the destruction of the Assyrian state and the extermination of the Assyrian people.[2]

Thus the Assyrian militarism brought ruin upon the whole Babylonic World before it annihilated Assyria herself; and there was no compensation for the Babylonic Civilization in the military conquests that Assyria made incidentally at the Syriac Society's expense; for we have noticed already that the Syriac Civilization actually gained in the long run by the treatment which it suffered at the Assyrians' hands.[3] The Assyrians' policy of securing their conquests by uprooting the conquered peoples and deporting them to the opposite extremities of the Assyrian *Machtgebiet* had the unintended effect of inoculating the Medes and Persians with germs of Syriac culture; and these Medes and Persians were to be the lords and masters of South-Western Asia. In the last round of the Assyro-Babylonian fratricidal conflict the Babylonians were constrained to take the Medes for their allies and to leave the lion's share of the Assyrian spoils in Median hands; and the Persian neighbours and cousins and supplanters of the Medes rounded off the Median Empire by adding the Neo-Babylonian Empire to it. This rise of the Medes and Persians to political supremacy in South-Western Asia naturally made the fortune of the Syriac Civilization to which these Iranian barbarians had been converted by the Assyrian militarists' deportees; and in these circumstances the capture of Babylon by Cyrus in 539 B.C. spelled not only the immediate disappearance of the Babylonic universal state but also the ultimate extinction of the Babylonic Civilization itself.

This crowning misfortune, however, had been brought upon the Babylonic Society by no other hands than its own; and the enormities of the Assyrian militarism were the suicidal acts.[4] If the

[1] See IV. C (iii) (*c*) 3 (α), p. 476, below.

[2] See II. D (v), vol. ii, pp. 135–6, above, and IV. C (iii) (*c*) 3 (α), in the present volume, pp. 477–84, below.

[3] On this point see I. C (i) (*b*), vol. i, pp. 79–82; II. D (v), vol. ii, pp. 137–8; and III. C (i) (*a*), vol. iii, p. 141, above.

[4] It is true that these suicidal acts were manifestations and consequences of the militaristic spirit that inspired them, and that we have not found the ultimate explanation of the

Assyrians had not outraged the Babylonians and carried the Syrians away captive in the eighth century B.C., it is improbable that Cyrus would have entered Babylon as a conqueror in 539 B.C., and it is certain that, even if history had followed its actual course to that extent, the cultural consequences of Cyrus's military triumph would have been utterly different from what they actually were. For if no Syrian deportees had ever been planted by Assyrian militarists on the Iranian Plateau, then the Iranian barbarians would eventually have descended upon Babylon, if at all, as converts not to the Syriac but to the Babylonic Civilization, and in the metropolis of their adopted culture they would have made it their mission not to destroy but to fulfil.

In Andean history the indigenous universal state was the Empire of the Incas, under which the whole domain of the Andean Society both on the Coast and on the Plateau (save for the country of the Chibchas in the territory of the present Latin-American republic of Colombia) had been united in a single body politic before the advent of the Spanish *conquistadores*. The sudden, violent, and complete overthrow of the Inca Empire by the Spaniards is often cited as an undoubted instance—and, in fact, as the classic example—of the destruction of a civilization through the impact of an external human force.

It is, of course, manifestly true that the Inca Empire was destroyed by the impact of the Spaniards; and it is probable that, if the peoples of our Western World had never found their way across the Atlantic, the Inca Empire would have lasted several centuries longer; for at the moment in the second quarter of the sixteenth century of our era when the Spaniards destroyed it the Inca Empire was at the maximum of its territorial extent; it was only just beginning to show signs of having passed the zenith of its power; and it had only been fulfilling its political mission as an Andean universal state for about a century, if we equate the establishment of the Andean universal state with the Inca conquest of Chimu in the reign of the Inca Pachacutec (*imperabat circa* A.D. 1400–48).[1] The destruction of this majestic and efficient and beneficent Andean political institution does undoubtedly lie at the Spaniards' door; but the crime of having destroyed the Andean universal

breakdown of the Babylonic Civilization until we have traced this Assyrian militarism back to its origins. In an earlier passage of this Study (see II. D (v), vol. ii, pp. 134–5, above) we have found the genesis of Assyrian militarism in the long struggle of Assyria against her Aramaean invaders in the eleventh and tenth centuries B.C.; and these Aramaeans were, of course, the north-eastern vanguard of the then nascent Syriac Civilization; but it would not be admissible to argue from these premisses that the ultimate responsibility for the breakdown of the Babylonic Civilization lies at the Syriac Civilization's door; for the Aramaeans merely presented the Assyrians with a challenge, and the Assyrians themselves must bear the responsibility for their own response.

[1] See I. C (i) (*b*), vol. i, pp. 121–2, above.

state is not the same crime as the destruction of the Andean Civilization itself. This second and more heinous crime is attributed to the Spaniards by a confusion of thought; and this confusion is an uncritically repeated commonplace which dates from the period, before the days of archaeological research in the Andean area, when the Empire of the Incas was the only phase in which the Andean Civilization was known to the scholars of our Western World.

This error is less excusable to-day, when our knowledge of Andean history has been vastly extended and illuminated by the progress of archaeological discovery. For we know now that the military and political rise of the Incas, so far from being identical with the cultural rise of the Andean Civilization, was actually a late incident in that civilization's decline and fall. Even on the Plateau the work of the Incas was merely an imperfect revival, after centuries of decadence, of an earlier highland culture which has left its unsurpassed monument in Tiahuanaco; and this earlier highland culture, which was never rivalled by any later achievements in the same region, was itself no original manifestation of creative power, but was derived from a still earlier culture on the Coast. The creative responses to challenges, which brought the Andean Civilization to birth in its two coastal cradles of Chimu and Nasca, date at least from the beginning of the Christian Era, some fifteen hundred years before the Spaniards' arrival.[1] In this historical perspective, which the enterprise of our latest Western archaeologists has recently opened up before our eyes, it becomes evident that the century of the Incas' undisputed supremacy in the Andean World was not the 'Golden Age' which it appeared to be in the eyes of the Spanish chroniclers who followed the Spanish *conquistadores*.

The chroniclers salved their private consciences and flattered their national pride by building a magnificent sepulchre for the mighty empire which the *conquistadores* had killed; but to the eye of a Western historian of our later generation, who can view the century of Inca supremacy, from a farther distance, with less sentiment and with more knowledge, the *Pax Incaica* reveals the unmistakable tokens of an 'Indian Summer' in which the landscape is already wintry and the sunlight pale. We can be certain that the true summer of Andean history had turned to autumn in the earlier age, some five hundred years back, when our archaeological evidence tells us that the highland culture of Tiahuanaco and the contemporary culture on the Coast went into simultaneous decline. It is true that Archaeology, which in some matters tells us so much, is apt to be tantalizingly silent on the questions which happen to be

[1] For an outline of the lineaments of Andean history, as these have been brought to light by our archaeologists, see I. C (i) (*b*), vol. i, pp. 119–23, above.

of capital importance for an understanding of history; and the positive acts which caused the breakdown of the Andean Civilization in that age still remain beyond our knowledge. Yet Archaeology does afford us the important negative information that, before the arrival of the Spaniards, the Andean World was a social universe in itself which had no direct intercourse with other civilizations and knew no neighbours beyond its own external proletariat of Amazonian and Araucanian barbarians. We may fairly infer that the Andean Civilization, like so many of its sisters, received its mortal wound from its own hands; and we may go so far as to conjecture that the 'beginning of evils' here was a fratricidal conflict between the People of the Mountain and the People of the Shore.

When we turn to the histories of the Central American and the Islamic Civilization, we observe that the process of assimilation by an alien civilization has overtaken both these societies while they have still been in their 'Time of Troubles', before they have entered upon a universal state at all.

In the history of the Central American decline and fall Cortez found the Central American 'Time of Troubles' in its final paroxysm and an indigenous universal state on the point of being established by the Aztec Power which had already completed the society's ruin through a worse-than-Assyrian Aztec militarism.[1] At the moment of Cortez' arrival Tlaxcala was the only important Central American Power that was left for the Aztecs to subdue. Yet Cortez was in time to overthrow the Aztecs by joining forces with the Tlaxcalecs; and he forestalled the establishment of an indigenous Central American universal state by turning the domain of the Central American Civilization, at one all-conquering stroke, into the Spanish Viceroyalty of New Spain.[2] In the history of the Islamic decline and fall the intrusive Western Civilization gained the upper hand, and forestalled the natural course of Islamic events by giving it a Western turn, at a rather earlier stage in the declining society's 'Time of Troubles'. If we equate the date of the breakdown of both the Mexic and the Yucatec Society with the establishment of the Toltec mercenaries' domination over Yucatan —and the consequent unification of the Yucatec with the Mexic World into a single Central American Society—at the close of the twelfth century of the Christian Era,[3] we must reckon that the

[1] This Aztec militarism seems to have become rampant *circa* A.D. 1376 (Spinden, H. J.: *The Ancient Civilisations of Mexico and Central America* (New York 1922, American Museum of Natural History), p. 183). The Aztec military ascendancy over the Mexican Lakes Basin had been established by A.D. 1428 (Spence, L.: *The Civilisation of Ancient Mexico* (Cambridge 1912, University Press), p. 38) or A.D. 1430 (Joyce, T. A.: *Mexican Archaeology* (London 1914, Lee Warner), p. 21).

[2] See I. C (i) (*b*), vol. i, p. 120, above.

[3] See I. C (i) (*b*), vol. i, pp. 123–4, above.

Central American 'Time of Troubles' had already entered upon its fourth century before it was cut short by the Spanish conquest, while the last quarter of the eighteenth century of the Christian Era, which was the epoch at which the pressure of the West became the governing factor in Islamic history, was separated by a span of less than three centuries from the schism in the Iranic World and the establishment of the Ottoman domination over the Arabic countries at the beginning of the sixteenth century: the two historic events which we have taken as the tokens of the Iranic breakdown.[1]

This difference in the stage at which the decisive Western intrusion took place may partly account for the difference in the subsequent histories of the Central American and the Islamic Society. In the Central American World the abortive—but only just abortive—indigenous Aztec universal state was not simply ruled out by the Spanish conquest but was given an alien substitute in the shape of the Spanish Viceroyalty of New Spain which the conquerors established on the ruins of Montezuma's imperial ambitions; and, thanks to this consummation and consolidation, by Spanish hands, of the work of political unification which had been carried so far towards completion, before the Spaniards arrived, by the force of Aztec arms, the Central American World was enabled to enter the political comity of Western states as a single political unit when, just three centuries after Cortez' conquest of Tenochtitlan, the Spanish Empire in this quarter was replaced by its present 'successor-state', the Mexican Republic.[2] On the other hand in the Islamic World, where the process of 'Westernization' gained the upper hand before the establishment of any indigenous Islamic universal state was even within sight, there has been no Western substitute for an indigenous universal state, and no practical possibility of the Islamic Society entering the political comity of Western states as a single body politic. The political Pan-Islamism which was mooted at the turn of the nineteenth and twentieth

[1] For the schism in the Iranic World at this epoch, and for the simultaneous incorporation of the Arabic Society into the Iranic Society, see I. C (i) (*b*), Annex I, in vol. i, above.

[2] The Mexican Republic has always included within its frontiers the former domain of the Yucatec Civilization in the Peninsula of Yucatan, as well as the former domain of the Mexic Civilization on the Mexican Plateau. The territories of the British colony of Honduras and of the six Latin-American republics that now occupy the rest of the isthmus between Mexico and Colombia all lie outside the borders of the *ci-devant* Yucatec and Mexic worlds, though the domain of the Mayan Civilization, to which both the Yucatec and the Mexic Society were 'affiliated', is now comprised in the territories of Guatemala and the two Hondurases. It is noteworthy that although the Mexic and Yucatec societies coalesced into a single Central American Society more than seven hundred years ago, and though Mexico and Yucatan have been also politically united now for some 400 years, first under Spanish and latterly under Mexican rule, they still remain geographically two worlds apart, with no practicable lines of communication between them except by sea across the Mexican Gulf.

centuries of the Christian Era has been a shortlived dream;[1] and the Islamic countries have pushed their way into the ranks of the Great Society each for themselves, in a scramble in which the Devil of Western or Russian Imperialism has successfully overtaken the hindermost in the Maghrib and the Caucasus and Transcaspia and Transoxania. The Arabic 'successor-states' of the Ottoman Empire, which have evaded or shaken off the political toils of the protectorates or mandates which British or French policy has sought to impose upon them, have emerged as the parochial kingdoms of Egypt and 'Irāq and Sa'ūdī Arabia and San'ā;[2] and the Persian Empire, which has been the parochial outcome of Shah Ismā'īl's abortive attempt to found an oecumenical Shī'ī Power, has succeeded in these latter days in making its own entry into the Great Society almost intact[3] as a Persian national state.[4]

Thus, in both Islamic and Central American history, the process of assimilation has supervened—under rather different conditions and with rather different results in the two cases—at a distinctly earlier stage of the decline and fall than in the histories of any of the other civilizations whose ultimate fate it has likewise been to lose their identity in that of our omnivorous Civilization of the West. Yet in these two histories also it is manifest that the process of 'Westernization' has been the end of the decline and not its beginning. In both cases we can trace the beginning of the 'Time of Troubles' to internal catastrophes which occurred—at the close of the twelfth century in Central America and at the opening of the sixteenth century in the Islamic World—several centuries before the pressure of the West became overwhelming. In the Iranic and Arabic worlds in the generation of Ismā'īl Shāh Safawī and the Ottoman Pādishāh Selīm I the Western factor was a negligible quantity; while in the Mexic and Yucatec worlds at the close of the twelfth century the very existence of another world beyond the Atlantic was quite unknown. On this showing, the Mexic and Iranic societies are to be added to our already long list of suicides; and it is clear that the Yucatec Society falls within the same category; for it was the outbreak of a fratricidal conflict between the

[1] See the present chapter, pp. 81–2, above.

[2] By the time when this chapter was being revised for the press in A.D. 1938 the number of Arabic parochial states-members of a Great Society on a Western basis was in prospect of being increased by the addition of a Syrian and a Lebanese Republic and a Palestinian State in which the major part of Cisjordanian Palestine was to be united with the existing Principality of Transjordan.

[3] The most serious territorial diminution which the Persian Empire has suffered since the definitive Ottoman conquest of 'Irāq has been the loss of the Transcaucasian territory which was conquered by Russia in the early nineteenth century and which now constitutes a Republic of Azerbaijan which is one of the constituent states-members of the U.S.S.R.

[4] See II. D (vi), vol. ii, pp. 254–5, above, for the predisposition of the Persians towards our modern Western Nationalism as a result of their own history since the time of Shah Ismā'īl.

Yucatec city-states that opened the way for the Toltec domination in Yucatan.[1]

We have now dealt with seventeen cases, and we are left with thirteen still to consider: the five arrested civilizations; the four abortive civilizations; the Arabic, Hittite, and Mayan civilizations; and our own Civilization of the West.

The Western Civilization may fairly be left out of account; for we cannot tell, in our generation, whether this civilization has already broken down or whether it is still in growth;[2] and in these circumstances it would be premature to discuss the cause of a breakdown that is still an unproven possibility and not an established fact.

As for the Mayan Civilization, we do not know the cause of the break-up of 'the First Empire' of the Mayas in Guatemala, which was the Mayan universal state. *A fortiori* we are ignorant of the cause of the foregoing breakdown of the Mayan Civilization.[3] We do know, however, that the broken-down Mayan Civilization did not eventually lose its identity through assimilation into the social tissues of an alien society. It found its end in the alternative way by becoming 'apparented' to two new societies, the Yucatec Society and the Mexic. In this last chapter of Mayan history, in so far as Archaeology has revealed it to us, we can perceive no trace of any alien society's intervention; and indeed the whole history of the Mayan Civilization, in so far as it is known to us at all, is markedly pacific. It is only on the north-western fringes of the Mayan World that there is any archaeological evidence for the practice of the art of war; and here it seems merely to have been a border warfare against outer barbarians. There is no evidence either of fratricidal warfare between the Mayan city-states themselves or of military collisions with any alien society of the Mayan Society's own calibre. And thus, while we have to confess that the cause of the breakdown of the Mayan Civilization is still unknown to us, we may guess with some confidence that this cause will not prove, if it one day comes to light, to have been the impact of an alien human force.

On the other hand, violent collisions with alien human forces play as prominent a part in the last chapter of Hittite history as in the latter ends of the Central American and Andean civilizations. The Empire of Khatti, which exercised not merely a hegemony but at least a suzerainty and perhaps even an outright sovereignty

[1] See I. C (i) (*b*), vol. i, p. 124, above.

[2] We do know that our Western Civilization has not yet entered into a universal state, but we do not know whether it is or is not already in a 'Time of Troubles'. On this question see further I. B (iv), vol. i, pp. 36–7, above, and V. C (ii) (*b*), vol. vi, pp. 313–5, as well as Part XII, below.

[3] See I. C (i) (*b*), vol. i, pp. 125–6, and II. D (vii), Annex I, in vol. ii, above.

over the greater part of the Hittite World throughout the fifteenth, fourteenth, and thirteenth centuries B.C., was violently and suddenly overthrown, in the early years of the twelfth century B.C., by a back-wash of the last and greatest wave of the post-Minoan Völkerwanderung in the Levant;[1] and the fate of the Hittite Society itself was involved in this overthrow of the Khatti State. From the twelfth century onwards this society only survived in a few refugee communities in Cilicia and Northern Syria; and even this local survival only prolonged the Hittite Society's existence for about five hundred years; for the Hittite fossils on the Asiatic Continent were absorbed into the Syriac body social during or after the age of the Assyrian militarism, while their overseas colonies in Italy—if we are right in attributing this Hittite origin to the Etruscans[2]—were drawn into the current of the Hellenic Civilization at about the same date.

Thus the Hittite Society undoubtedly received its *coup de grâce* from an alien sword; and if we now trace Hittite history backwards from the time of the crushing blow which felled the Empire of Khatti *circa* 1200/1190 B.C., we shall find a convincing explanation for the utter collapse of the Khatti Power under the impact of the post-Minoan Völkerwanderung in the intense exhaustion of the Hittite body social after a long-drawn-out conflict with another,

[1] See I. C (i) (*b*), vol. i, pp. 93, 101, and 113–14, above. In the opinion of Monsieur Eugène Cavaignac (*Le Problème Hittite* (Paris 1936, Leroux), pp. 128–9) the war-bands which sacked and devastated the Khatti capital Khattusas (Boghazköi) and overthrew the Khatti State were not identical with those that travelled, partly by ship and partly by ox-waggon, along the Levantine coasts from the south-east corner of the Aegean to the north-east frontier of Egypt. Cavaignac points out (in op. cit., p. 2) that Khattusas lay, not at the heart of the Hittite World, but at its north-western extremity, where it served as a shield and buckler for the interior against the barbarians beyond the pale; and on this showing the Khatti capital ought to have been cited, in an earlier passage of this Study (II. D (v), vol. ii, pp. 112–208), as an illustration of the stimulus of pressures, side by side with Thebes, Peking, Babylon, Samarqand, Mycenae, Constantinople, Vienna, London, Paris, Tenochtitlan, and Cuzco. Cavaignac suggests (op. cit., p. 130) that Khattusas was eventually overwhelmed by the Anatolian barbarians whom the fortress-capital had so long and so strenuously held at bay, when these local barbarians were reinforced, from the farther side of the Straits, by European recruits. 'Ce qu'il est permis de supposer, c'est que derrière les deux invasions — invasion maritime, invasion continentale — il y a eu un mouvement plus ou moins ample venu des profondeurs de la péninsule balkanique. L'analogie de l'invasion galate du iiie siècle, inondant d'un côté la Grèce, de l'autre l'Asie-Mineure, se présente d'elle-même à l'esprit.' An acceptance of Cavaignac's view does not imply an abandonment of the supposition that the overthrow of Khatti was an incidental consequence of the dissolution of the Minoan World; for the continental no less than the maritime stream of invasion is to be explained as a part of the post-Minoan Völkerwanderung.

[2] On the question of the origin of the Etruscans see I. C (i) (*b*), vol. i, pp. 114–15, with Annex II, 2, above. See also the very interesting discussion of the problem by Mr. Christopher Dawson in *The Age of the Gods* (reissue: London 1933, Sheed & Ward), pp. 365–84. Mr. Dawson suggests that not only the Etruscans but the Veneti and the Liburni may have been of Anatolian origin, and that the Central Italian Iron-Age culture of Villanova and Novilara may have been introduced by these peoples. On this theory the Etruscans would have arrived in Italy not in the eighth century B.C., as contemporaries and rivals of the Phoenician and Greek colonists in the Western Mediterranean, but in the twelfth century, as contemporaries and companions in misfortune of the North Syrian Hittite refugees from the wreck of the Khatti Empire.

and a far more formidable, alien force. The Khatti Power had courted the destruction which duly overtook it at the north-western barbarians' hands at the beginning of the twelfth century B.C. by fighting a hundred years' war with 'the New Empire' of Egypt for the possession of Syria. This military struggle, which ended inconclusively in the partition of Syria between the two belligerents in the peace settlement of 1278 B.C.,[1] was evidently more exhausting for the young and immature Hittite Society than it was for the veteran Egyptiac Society with its greater reserves of economic strength; and the difference between the respective conditions in which the Hittite and the Egyptiac Great Power emerged from their protracted conflict was demonstrated in a sensational way by the difference in their fortunes, three-quarters of a century later, when they both had to face the same ordeal of a human deluge from the north-west; for while the Empire of Khatti went down to destruction with a facility which was strangely out of keeping with its military tradition, 'the New Empire' of Egypt just succeeded in stemming the barbarian tide by mobilizing[2] and expending the last dregs of its social resources.[3] Thus the Hittite Society ultimately paid with its very existence for its trial of strength with its Egyptiac neighbour; and this trial was not forced upon the Hittite Society but was wantonly incurred by it through its own temerity; for the hundred years' war was set in train by the aggression of the Khatti King Subbilulyuma against the Egyptian dominions in Asia.

Subbilulyuma reigned between about 1380 and 1346 B.C.; and this was only about two hundred years after the first emergence of the nascent Hittite Civilization out of the post-Sumeric social interregnum.[4] If we are to regard Subbilulyuma's reckless act of aggression against an older and tougher alien Power as 'the beginning of evils' in Hittite history, then this history seems to confront us with one instance in which a collision with the human environment, in the shape of an alien society, has been the cause of the original breakdown of a civilization and not merely the occasion of its ultimate extinction at the end of the last chapter in its decline and fall; for the hundred years' war between Khatti and Egypt,

[1] See I. C (i) (*b*), vol. i, p. 114, above. *Circa* 1278 is Eduard Meyer's date for the treaty (see *Geschichte des Altertums*, vol. ii, part (1), second edition (Stuttgart and Berlin 1928, Cotta), p. 479). On the other hand *The Cambridge Ancient History* (vol. ii, p. 149) dates the treaty 1272 B.C.

[2] For the fighting Pharaohs under whose leadership the Egyptiac Society stood at bay in this crisis, see V. C (ii) (*a*), vol. vi, p. 207, below.

[3] Compare the respective fortunes of the Roman Empire and the Sasanian Empire when these two Powers were smitten simultaneously, by the impact of the Primitive Muslim Arab eruption, on the morrow of the great Romano-Persian Wars of A.D. 572–91 and A.D. 603–28. In this ordeal the Sasanian Empire collapsed completely, while the Roman Empire preserved its existence at the price of losing half its provinces and all its vitality.

[4] See I. C (i) (*b*), vol. i, pp. 110–13, above.

which Subbilulyuma precipitated when the Hittite Society was just entering upon the third century of its history, led on, through the chain of cause-and-effect which has been traced above, to the annihilation of the Hittite Society at the beginning of the fifth century of its history by the Sea-Raiders.

At first sight this interpretation of Hittite history may appear to hold the field, since it may seem improbable *a priori* that the breakdown of the Hittite Civilization can have been brought about by some earlier event, before Subbilulyuma's time, when the civilization itself was less than two hundred years old. Yet this possibility cannot be ruled out of account in our present state of almost complete ignorance in regard to the history of the Hittite World in its earliest age; and, in the fragmentary information which we do possess, two facts stand out which suggest, when read together, that the disastrous collision of the Hittite World with the Egyptiac World in Subbilulyuma's reign may actually have been preceded by an even more disastrous domestic conflict within the bosom of the Hittite Society. The first of these two outstanding facts is the extreme local diversity of the nascent Hittite World: the wealth of local languages and the multiplicity of local states. In this respect the Hittite World stands at the opposite pole to the Egyptiac World, while it bears a striking resemblance to our own Western World at all stages of our Western history. The second outstanding fact in the first chapter of Hittite history is the precocious political unification of this polyglot and polycratic society under the sceptre of a single predominant military power, the Empire of Khatti.

This political predominance of Khatti in the Hittite World is already an accomplished fact by the time when the veil which shrouds the beginnings of Hittite history is lifted by the masterful hand of the Egyptian militarist Thothmes III (*imperabat solus circa* 1480–1450 B.C.);[1] and we do not know how Khatti's greatness was achieved. Yet, considering the manifest inclination of the Hittite Society towards local diversity and parochial autonomy, it seems unlikely that the political supremacy of Khatti can have been accepted by the other parochial Hittite states without a struggle; and, if we pursue our parallel between the Hittite World and Western Christendom, we shall find a suggestive counterpart of the precocious Empire of Khatti in the precocious empire which was established by Charlemagne. Charlemagne, as we know for a fact, met with resistance from the Lombards, and with still more strenuous resistance from the Saxons, in carrying out his policy of unification by force; and the effort of overcoming this resistance

[1] See I. C (i) (*b*), vol. i, p. 111, above.

subjected the nascent Western Society to so severe a strain that the whole Carolingian structure quickly collapsed. Let us imagine for a moment that, in the ninth century of the Christian Era, Western Christendom had not been thus happily relieved of the Carolingian incubus by the collapse of the top-heavy building under its own weight. Let us imagine that the Carolingian Empire had lasted on as 'a going concern', and that a dynastic appetite for military conquest, which had been whetted by Charlemagne's own relatively easy victory over the Lombards, had tempted Charlemagne's successors to take advantage of the recrudescence of the Iconoclastic Conflict at Constantinople in order to lay their covetous Frankish hands upon the outlying provinces of the East Roman Empire in Calabria and Sicily and Sardinia. Supposing that this hypothetical act of Carolingian aggression had unexpectedly precipitated a Franco-Roman hundred years' war: in this imaginary reconstruction of our Western history in the ninth century of our Era we may conceivably have found a parallel to the unknown events in Hittite history which preceded the establishment of the Empire of Khatti and led on to the hundred years' war between Khatti and Egypt.

At any rate we cannot be sure that the Hittite Society had not already ruined itself in its infancy, during this obscure first phase of its history, before ever it ran its head against the massive masonry of 'the New Empire' of Egypt, and consequently fell a victim to the onslaught of the north-western barbarians. On the other hand, when we turn to the corresponding chapter in Arabic history, between the emergence of the Arabic Society out of the post-Syriac interregnum and its cataclysmic submergence under the wave of Ottoman conquest, we cannot so readily give the reputed alien assassins the benefit of a corresponding doubt; for the course of events in the Arabic World from the last quarter of the thirteenth century of the Christian Era to the first quarter of the sixteenth century is adequately recorded; and there is nothing in the record to suggest that, within this span of some 250 years, the Arabic peoples had prepared the way for the Ottoman aggressor by doing themselves any fatal injury with their own hands. It is true that this Arabic Society had not shown any marked signs of promise before the time when it was submerged by the Ottoman flood; for the loneliness of Ibn Khaldūn's star is as striking as its brilliance. Yet the apparently aimless turbulence of Ifriqīyah under the Hafsids, as well as the apparently lifeless torpidity of Egypt under the Mamlūks, may have masked the vigorous and purposeful progress of a healthily growing society from infancy through childhood towards adolescence; and we have no valid warrant, in the Arabic history of that age, for pronouncing dogmatically that the Arabic Society would never in any event have burst into flower if the Ottoman conquest had not blighted it.

Thus in Arabic history we might seem to have one case in which the breakdown of a civilization can be traced to the destructive effects of an alien society's impact; and the most that can be said is that the Iranic Society, as represented by the ʿOsmanlis, simply submerged the Arabic Society without assimilating it. It is certainly true that in Ifriqīyah the Ottoman ascendancy never extended far beyond the outworks of a few strongholds along the coast, and that in Egypt the state of society was not essentially altered by the Ottoman conquest. In Egypt the conquest simply added a new alien military caste, in the shape of the Janissaries, to the old alien military caste with which Egypt had been saddled ever since the Mamlūks had been introduced by the Ayyubids.[1] And, underneath this exotic military crust, the indigenous Arabic Society of Egypt still continued to lead its separate and self-sufficient life, in which the peasantry and the ʿulamā and the urban guilds of merchants and artisans each played their interdependent parts, and all recognized one another's respective functions in the corporate life of their common body social.[2] Indeed, the forcible unification of the Arabic Society with the Sunnī fraction of the sister Iranic Society through the external act of the Ottoman conquest did not ever pass over into an inward social fusion; and the unitary Islamic Society which has confronted the modern Western World, and which has made such an imposing impression of unity on our Western minds, has always been something of an illusion. At heart the Arabs and the ʿOsmanlis have remained strangers to one another; and, in so far as there has been any genuine cultural give-and-take, it has been the conquered Arab that has taken the Ottoman conqueror captive.[3]

Thus, within the last hundred and fifty years, as the old Ottoman superstructure has gradually crumbled into dust, and this dust has been blown away by the wild West Wind that has been sweeping over the World, the Arabic peoples have re-emerged[4]—as Jonah

1 See IV. C (iii) (*c*) 2 (γ), pp. 452–3, below.

2 The êthos of this self-sufficient Arabic Society which went on living its own life, under the Ottoman surface, throughout the four centuries of the Ottoman régime, is mirrored in Shaykh ʿAbd-ar-Rahmān al-Jabartī's *ʿAjā'ib-al-Āthār fi't-Tarājim wa'l-Ahbār* (French translation: Paris 1888–96, Leroux, 9 vols.), which carries the history of the Arabic Society in Egypt in the author's own times down to the eve of the author's own death in A.D. 1821. See further Gibb, H. A. R., and Bowen, H.: *Islamic Society and the West*, vol. i (Oxford 1939, University Press), chaps. 4–7.

3 For the cultural consequences of the Ottoman conquest of the Arabic countries see I. C (i) (*b*), Annex I, in vol. i, pp. 395–6, above, and Gibb and Bowen, op. cit., vol. i.

4 For this re-emergence of the Arabic peoples in the guise of nations in the Western sense of the term see the present chapter, pp. 82 and 107, above.

once emerged, in the legend, from the belly of the whale, or as, in prosaic 'real life', a string of toads sometimes crawls, half-dazed, out of the stiffening jaws of a newly killed snake which has swallowed the toads alive and has not succeeded in digesting them before its own life has been cut short by Fate. This re-emergence of the Arabic Society is still so recent that it seems scarcely possible for an observer in this generation to make a clear diagnosis of the society's condition. Is the Arabic Society in our day really in disintegration, as the outward symptoms suggest? Or is it simply displaying the effects of a temporary shock on the morrow of a harrowing experience which, after all, has not proved fatal? For the present it seems so hazardous to choose between these alternative explanations that it may be wiser in this case, too, to return a provisional verdict of non-proven, and to leave the Arabic Civilization—as we have decided to leave the Hittite Civilization—in suspense.

We have now reviewed the declines and falls of all the broken-down civilizations that have enjoyed a period—however short a period—of growth before their breakdowns; and we need not linger long over the cases of the four abortive civilizations that have failed to come to birth[1] and the five arrested civilizations that have failed to pass beyond the threshold of life.[2] The arrested civilizations have experienced neither growth nor breakdown; and, when once they have fallen into the impasse of their irretrievably exact and intolerably exacting equilibrium with their environment, it is of little interest or importance if they eventually collapse at the touch of an alien hand, since, even if they are left to themselves, their ultimate collapse from sheer exhaustion is only a matter of time. As for the abortive civilizations, the question of whether they are to be or not to be has turned, in each case, upon their response to a challenge which has proved to be of prohibitive severity; and it is true that, in each of the four cases that have come within our view, this intractable challenge has been delivered by some human neighbour or rival or adversary. Yet the detection of this human agency, in the qualifying test which these abortive civilizations have tried and failed to pass, does not entitle us to pronounce that the abortive civilizations have been deprived of their prospect of life by an external act of violence. The truth may be that these miscarriages have been due to some inherent weakness in the embryos, and that the pre-natal shocks by which the miscarriages have been precipitated have simply brought this existing weakness out.

[1] For these see II. D (vii), in vol. ii, above.
[2] For these see Part III. A, in vol. iii, above.

3. *A Negative Verdict*

We can now sum up the results at which we have arrived in the two preceding chapters.

Leaving the abortive and the arrested civilizations out of account for the reasons that have just been given, and suspending judgement on the Western and on the Mayan Civilization for the reasons that have been suggested above, we find that, out of the nineteen remaining civilizations, no less than sixteen prove to have broken down through their own acts, before ever any alien human force succeeded in dealing them a potentially mortal blow. In all these cases the most that the alien enemy has achieved has been to give the expiring suicide his *coup de grâce* or to devour his carcass after it has already become carrion. The breakdown of the Minoan Civilization seems likewise to have been self-inflicted, so far as we can tell from the archaeological evidence, which is all that we have to go upon. The histories of the Arabic and the Hittite Civilization are the only two cases out of the nineteen in which the original breakdown, as well as the last act in the decline and fall, wears the appearance of being the work of an alien hand; and even in these two cases this finding is only tentative and not conclusive; for in the Hittite case the stricken society may have already laid violent hands upon itself in an antecedent chapter of its history of which no record survives, while in the Arabic case it is not yet certain that the successive shocks of 'Ottomanization' and 'Westernization' have deprived the victim of all chance of living out his life, and have thereby saved him from all possibility of committing suicide.

On this showing, we may fairly conclude that the cause of the breakdowns of civilizations is not to be found in a loss of command over the human environment, as measured by the successful encroachment of alien human forces upon the life of any given society whose breakdown we may be attempting to investigate. Indeed, where the encroachment takes the radical form of a violent attack, the normal effect upon the life of the assaulted party would appear, on an empirical survey of the evidence, to be not destructive but positively stimulating.

For example, the Hellenic Society in Continental Greece was stimulated by Xerxes' attack in 480 B.C. to the highest manifestations of its literary and artistic, as well as its military, capacity;[1] and

[1] See II. D (iv), vol. ii, p. 109, above. For the stresses and strains in the internal structure of the Hellenic body social which arose incidentally out of the victorious Hellenic response to the Achaemenian challenge of 480 B.C., and for the failure of the Hellenic Society to respond successfully to the new challenge which these internal stresses and strains eventually presented, see III. C (i) (*d*), vol. iii, pp. 198–9, above, and IV. C (iii) (*b*) 10, in the present volume, p. 210, as well as Part IX, below.

Western Christendom was stimulated by the Norse and Magyar attacks in the ninth century of the Christian Era into performing those feats of valour and statesmanship which resulted in the foundation of the kingdoms of England and France and in the reconstruction of the Holy Roman Empire by the Saxons.[1] At a later stage of our Western history the city-state worlds-within-a-world, which differentiated themselves in Northern Italy and in Flanders out of the body social of Western Christendom, were stimulated into a triumphant vindication of their *de facto* independence by the respective attempts of the Hohenstaufen Emperors and the French Crown to reassert their *de jure* authority by force of arms. In a still later chapter of Western history the Dutch and the English were stimulated, by the Spanish Crown's attempts to suppress these insurgents and interlopers, into breaking the Spanish and Portuguese monopoly of the New World and building up out of the spoils a more efficient commercial system and a more durable colonial empire than the Spaniards had been able to build when they had the field to themselves; and these Dutch and English feats of military prowess and business enterprise were accompanied by a flowering of art and letters which showed that the stimulus of the Spanish attack had fructified the whole of the assaulted peoples' social life. The infant Hindu Society, likewise, was stimulated by the Primitive Muslim Arab onslaught in the eighth century of the Christian Era;[2] and the Assyrian frontiersmen of the Babylonic World were stimulated by the Aramaean pressure in the eleventh and tenth centuries B.C.[3]

The foregoing examples are all cases in which the assaulted party was still in growth at the time when the alien assault upon it was made; but we can cite at least as many cases in which an alien assault has given a temporary stimulus to a society after this society has already broken down through its own mishandling of itself; and in this second set of cases the intrinsically stimulating effect of external blows and pressures is demonstrated with still greater force.[4]

The classic instance is the repeated reaction of the Egyptiac

[1] See II. D (v), vol. ii, pp. 168 and 196–202, above.

[2] See II. D (v), vol. ii, p. 130, above.

[3] See II. D (v), vol. ii, pp. 134–5, above. For the malady of Militarism to which the Assyrians succumbed, under the strain which their successful resistance to the Aramaean onslaught had imposed upon them, see II. D (v), vol. ii, pp. 135–6, and IV. C (ii) (*b*) 2, in the present volume, pp. 101–2, above, and IV. C (iii) (*c*) 3 (α), pp. 468–84, below.

[4] The outcome of the assaulted society's reaction to the stimulus of the assault is no doubt different in the two different situations. When the assaulted society is still in growth, it is stimulated to perform some fresh act of creation. On the other hand, when it is already in decline, it is stimulated into an archaistic reaction towards some phase of its own past. (For Archaism as one of the psychological symptoms of social disintegration see V. C (i) (*d*) 8, vol. vi, pp. 49–97, below.) Yet, though the outcome may be different, the stimulus itself is the same, and it is this fact that concerns us here.

Society to this stimulus; for this Egyptiac reaction was evoked and re-evoked over a span of some two thousand years; and this long epilogue to Egyptiac history was inaugurated at a moment when the Egyptiac Society had already passed out of its universal state ('the Middle Empire') and had entered upon a subsequent interregnum in which it might have been expected finally to pass out of existence. At this moment the apparently defunct society was recalled to life and action by an overwhelming impulse to chastise the Hyksos trespassers who had ventured to desecrate a swept and garnished house by their unclean presence. The stimulus was so powerful that it raised the Egyptiac Society not just from its death-bed but actually from the bier on which it was being carried to the grave;[1] and in this demonic xenophobia the society seemed to have discovered, at the thirteenth hour, the long-sought elixir of immortality; for the same stimulus worked the same miracle time and again. The *tour de force* of the expulsion of the Hyksos was repeated in the repulse of the Sea-Raiders[2] and in the eviction of the Assyrians[3] and in the series of insurrections in which the Egyptian people shook off the yoke of the Achaemenidae[4] and stubbornly resisted the process of Hellenization to which they were afterwards subjected under the régime of the Ptolemies.[5]

There has been an analogous series of reactions to external blows and pressures in the history of the decline and fall of the Far Eastern Civilization in China. The expulsion of the Mongols by the Ming[6] is reminiscent, both in temper and in circumstance, of the expulsion of the Hyksos by the Theban founders of 'the New Empire'. The Manchu yoke has been shaken off through the same indomitable resurgence of an implacable xenophobia that likewise proved too strong for Achaemenian imperialism in Egypt. And the militant resistance of the Egyptiac Society to the process of Hellenization under the Ptolemies has its analogue in a Chinese anti-Western movement which attempted, in A.D. 1925–7, to fight out its losing battle to the bitter end by borrowing the exotic weapons of Russian Communism[7] after its native weapons had

[1] See I. C (ii), vol. i, p. 139, footnote 1, and pp. 144–5, and IV. C (ii) (*b*) 2, in the present volume, p. 85, above, and IV. C (iii) (*c*) 2 (*β*), in the present volume, p. 412; Part V. A, vol. v, pp. 2–3; V. C (i) (*c*) 2, vol. v, p. 152; and V. C (i) (*c*) 4, vol. v, pp. 351–2, below.

[2] See I. C (i) (*b*), vol. i, pp. 93 and 101, and IV. C (ii) (*b*) 2, in the present volume, pp. 85 and 110, above, and V. C (i) (*c*) 3, vol. v, p. 269, below.

[3] See II. D (v), vol. ii, p. 114, above, and IV. C (iii) (*c*) 3 (α), in the present volume, p. 476, below.

[4] See V. C (ii) (*b*), vol. vi, p. 302, below.

[5] See IV. C (ii) (*b*) 2, in the present volume, p. 85, above, and V. C (i) (*c*) 2, vol. v, p. 68, below.

[6] See II. D (v), vol. ii, pp. 121–2, above, and V. C (i) (*c*) 4, vol. v, pp. 348–51, below.

[7] See Toynbee, A. J.: *Survey of International Affairs, 1926* (Oxford 1928, University Press), pp. 283–5 and 333–41.

been discredited by the failure of the Boxer Rising of A.D. 1900. Logically, no doubt, this forlorn attempt to repel one alien influence by surrendering to another is the *reductio ad absurdum* of Chinese xenophobia, and it is true that the desperate expedient soon ended in an acrimonious quarrel between such ill-assorted allies;[1] but, psychologically, the willingness of the Left Wing of the Kuomintang to place itself in Borodin's hands in order to combat Western Imperialism gives the measure of the violence of the Chinese reaction to Western pressure; and, by the same token, it reveals the strength of the stimulus which this Western pressure has administered.

In a similar way the strength of the stimulus which the intrusion of Hellenism administered to the decadent Syriac and Indic civilizations is revealed in the respective series of religious reactions which, in both cases, were eventually successful in driving the intrusive culture out: the Nestorian and Monophysite reactions which culminated in the triumph of Islam, and the Tantric Mahayanian Buddhist reaction which was followed by the triumph of Hinduism. In the history of the Hellenic Society itself the overrunning of the western provinces of the Roman Empire by the North European barbarians in the fifth century of the Christian Era evoked the Justinianean *revanche*, in the sixth century, against the Vandals and the Ostrogoths.[2] In the history of Orthodox Christendom the Latin and Turkish assaults upon the East Roman Empire in the eleventh century of the Christian Era evoked the ephemeral yet unmistakable Comnenian revival in the century following.[3]

We can see, finally, that an alien assault has sometimes administered part of the stimulus in the strength of which a disintegrating society has pulled itself together so far as to rally its forces for a moment in the formation of a universal state. The overrunning of the Egyptiac World by Asiatic barbarians during 'the Feudal Age' that followed the collapse of 'the Old Kingdom' was evidently one of the stimuli that evoked 'the Middle Empire';[4] the overrunning of the Sumeric World by the Gutaeans more patently evoked the Empire of Sumer and Akkad;[5] and the desire to throw off the yoke of the Mongols was probably the master-motive which reconciled Novgorod and the other parochial states of Russia to their incorporation into the Empire of Muscovy.[6] On

[1] See Toynbee, A. J.: *Survey of International Affairs, 1927* (Oxford 1929, University Press), pp. 331–65.

[2] For the recoil of this *revanche* see IV. C (iii) (*c*) 2 (*β*), pp. 326–8; and V. C (ii) (*a*), vol. vi, p. 209, footnote 2, and p. 223, below.

[3] For this revival see V. C (ii) (*b*), vol. vi, p. 298, below.

[4] See I. C (ii), vol. i, p. 137, above.

[5] See I. C (i) (*b*), vol. i, p. 109, above.

[6] See the present chapter, pp. 92–3, above. On this showing, the popular conception of the causal relation between the breaking of the Tatar yoke and the contemporary rally

these analogies we may conjecture that the way was smoothed for Chandragupta's political venture by the sensational raid of Alexander the Great, which must have revealed in a flash to Indian minds the imminence of the Hellenic menace and have reconciled them to accepting the Maurya Empire as a safeguard.[1] On the same showing, the work of Augustus may have been facilitated by the anxiety of the Hellenic Society to preserve itself from being overwhelmed by the North European barbarians and the Orientals;[2] and the anxiety of the Sinic Society to keep at bay the rising power of the Eurasian Nomad Hiongnu may have played into the hands of Ts'in She Hwang-ti.[3]

These illustrations perhaps sufficiently support our thesis that the normal effect of blows or pressures from outside is stimulating and not destructive; and, if this thesis is accepted, it confirms our conclusion that a loss of command over the human environment is not the cause of the breakdowns of civilizations.

III. FAILURE OF SELF-DETERMINATION

(a) THE MECHANICALNESS OF MIMESIS

Our inquiry into the cause of the breakdowns of civilizations has led us, so far, to a succession of negative conclusions. We have found that these breakdowns are not acts of God. They are neither the inexorable operations of a Saeva Necessitas nor the sadistic sport of a Kali snatching another bead for her necklace of skulls. Nor are they the vain repetitions of senseless laws of Nature, like the monotonous revolutions of the Earth round its own axis and of the Planets round the Sun, or like the mechanical churning of the arms of the windmill which lifted Don Quixote out of his saddle and hoisted him sky-high and threatened to dash out his brains because the amiable knight had mistaken this inanimate monster for a creature 'of a reasonable soul and human flesh subsisting'. We have found, again, that we cannot legitimately attribute these breakdowns to a loss of command over the environment, either physical or human. The breakdowns of civilizations are not catastrophes of the same order as famines and floods and tornadoes and

of the Russian Orthodox Christendom is the exact inverse of the truth. So far from the rally having been the result of the liberation, it was the liberation that was the result of the rally.

[1] If this was really one of the considerations which induced the Indic Society to acquiesce in Chandragupta's tyranny, it was justified by the event; for the Hellenic intrusion upon the Indic World, which had been presaged in Alexander's raid, did not come to pass until after the Maurya Empire had fallen.

[2] 'Hinc movet Euphrates, illinc Germania bellum'.—Virgil, *Georgic* I, l. 509.

[3] At any rate, Ts'in She Hwang-ti's work in completing and consolidating the Great Wall is the only one of his works for which this tyrant is remembered for good and not for evil in the Sinic tradition; and it seems not unreasonable to assume that this tradition reflects the light in which Ts'in She Hwang-ti was regarded by his contemporaries.

fires and shipwrecks and railway-accidents; and they are not the equivalent, in the experiences of bodies social, of mortal injuries inflicted in homicidal assaults.

In successively rejecting all these untenable explanations we have not arrived at the object of our search; but the last of the fallacies that we have just cited has incidentally given us a clue. In demonstrating that the broken-down civilizations have not met their death from an assassin's hand, we have found no reason to dispute the allegation that they have been the victims of violence, and in almost every instance we have been led, by the logical process of exhaustion, to return a verdict of suicide. Our best hope of making some positive progress in our inquiry is to follow this single clue up; and there is one hopeful feature of our verdict which we can observe at once. There is no originality about it!

The conclusion at which we have arrived at the end of a rather laborious search has been divined with a sure intuition by a modern Western poet.

> In tragic life, God wot,
> No villain need be! Passions spin the plot:
> We are betrayed by what is false within.[1]

And Meredith's flash of insight is not a new discovery of nineteenth-century Western wisdom, like the Origin of Species or the Law of the Conservation of Energy. A century earlier the genius of Volney had casually exploded the eighteenth-century doctrine of the natural goodness and automatic improvement of Human Nature by testifying that 'la source de ses calamités . . . réside dans l'homme même; il la porte dans son cœur'.[2] And the same truth is declared in a fragment of Menander, which almost anticipates the English poet's words,[3] and in a passage of the Gospel according to Saint Matthew:

'Whatsoever entereth in at the mouth goeth into the belly, and is cast out into the draught. But those things which proceed out of the mouth come forth from the heart; and they defile the man. For out of the heart proceed evil thoughts, murders, adulteries, fornications, thefts, false witness, blasphemies. These are the things which defile a man.'[4]

This truth about the lives of human beings is equally true of the lives of societies. A Hellenic philosopher, Dicaearchus, is reported to have maintained—in a lost work called *How Men go to Destruc-*

[1] George Meredith: *Love's Grave.*

[2] Volney, C. F.: 'Les Ruines' in *Œuvres Complètes* (Paris 1876, Didot), pp. 12–13.

[3] Menander, fragment 540:

> *ὑπὸ τῆς ἰδίας ἕκαστα κακίας σήπεται,*
> *καὶ πᾶν τὸ λυμαινόμενόν ἐστιν ἔνδοθεν.*
>
> Things rot through evils native to their selves,
> And all that injures issues from within.

[4] Matt. xv. 18–20.

tion[1]—that the greatest danger to Man is Man. And Volney offers this explanation of the destruction of bodies politic in lieu of the untenable hypothesis that the lives of communities, like those of individuals, have a limited life-span and a formulated life-curve.[2]

'On s'aperçoit qu'il existe dans la marche, et, si j'ose dire, dans la vie des corps politiques, un mécanisme qui indique l'existence de lois plus générales et plus constantes qu'on ne le croit vulgairement. Ce n'est pas que cette pensée n'ait déjà été exprimée par la comparaison que l'on a faite de cette vie des corps politiques à la vie des individus, en prétendant trouver les phases de la jeunesse, de la maturité et de la vieillesse dans les périodes d'accroissement, de splendeur et de décadence des empires; mais cette comparaison, vicieuse à tous égards, a jeté dans une erreur d'autant plus fâcheuse, qu'elle a fait considérer comme une nécessité naturelle la destruction des corps politiques, de quelque manière qu'ils fussent organisés; tandis que cette destruction n'est que l'effet d'un vice radical des législations.'[3]

This application to politics of Volney's intuition that 'la source de ses calamités réside dans l'homme même' is anticipated in a passage of Saint Cyprian, in which the African Father applies the same truth to the entire field of social life.[4]

'You complain of the aggression of foreign enemies; yet, if the foreign enemy were to cease from troubling, would Roman really be able to live at peace with Roman (*esse pax inter ipsas togas possit*)? If the external danger of invasion by armed barbarians were to be stamped out, should we not be exposed to a fiercer and a heavier civil bombardment, on the home front, in the shape of calumnies and injuries inflicted by the powerful upon their weaker fellow citizens? You complain of crop-failures and famine; yet the greatest famines are made not by drought but by rapacity, and the most flagrant distress springs from profiteering and price-raising in the corn-trade. You complain that the clouds do not disgorge their rain in the sky, and you ignore the barns that fail to disgorge their grain on terra firma. You complain of the fall in production, and ignore the failure to distribute what is actually produced to those who are in need of it. You denounce plague and pestilence, while really the effect of these scourges is to bring to light, or bring to a head, the crimes of

[1] Dicaearchus: Περὶ Φθορᾶς Ἀνθρώπων.

[2] For an examination of this doctrine see IV. C (i), pp. 10–13, above.

[3] Volney, C. F.: 'Leçons d'Histoire' in *Œuvres Complètes* (Paris 1876, Didot), p. 587.

[4] The two passages are also analogous inasmuch as they both fly in the face of the prevailing philosophy of the day. Volney's intuition, as we have observed, gives the lie to the fundamental doctrine of eighteenth-century Western philosophy, while the passage here quoted from Cyprian contradicts another passage from Cyprian's own pen which occurs in the same tract *Ad Demetrianum*. In this other passage (which has been quoted above in IV. C (i) on p. 8) Cyprian advocates the view that the Hellenic Society of the age is suffering from an automatic process of senile decay. A judicious admirer of Cyprian will not attempt to explain this manifest contradiction away. He will be content to observe that in chapter 3 of the tract the author is simply reproducing one of the commonplaces of Hellenic philosophy, while in chapter 10 he is expounding a Christian doctrine which has become a living part of Cyprian's own thought.

human beings: the callousness that shows no pity for the sick, and the covetousness and rapine that are in full cry after the property of the dead.'[1]

In this passage a man of penetrating insight and deep feeling, who was an heir to the tradition of the Hellenic culture before he became a convert to Christianity, has given the true explanation of the breakdown which had cut the growth of the Hellenic Civilization short some six or seven hundred years before, and which had brought the broken-down society to all but the last stage of its decline and fall in Cyprian's own day. The Hellenic Civilization had broken down because, in the internal economy of this society in its growth stage, at some point something had gone wrong with that interaction between individuals through which the growth of every growing civilization is achieved.

What is the weakness that exposes a growing civilization to this risk of stumbling and falling in mid-career and losing its Promethean *élan*? The weakness must be radical; for, although the catastrophe of breakdown is a risk and not a certainty, the risk is evidently high. To leave the abortive and the arrested civilizations out of account, and to consider only those twenty-one civilizations that have been born alive and have proceeded to grow, we are faced with the fact that thirteen out of the twenty-one are dead and buried already; that seven out of the eight living civilizations are apparently in decline; and that the eighth, which is our own Civilization of the West, may also have passed its zenith for all that we know. On an empirical test the career of a growing civilization would appear to be a dangerous activity; and, if we now recall our analysis of Growth in a previous part of this Study,[2] we shall realize that, on our own showing, the danger is constant and acute because it lies in the very nature of the course which a growing civilization is constrained to take.

This course is not the narrow way 'which leadeth unto life—and few there be that find it';[3] for, although the few that do find this way are precisely those creative personalities who set a civilization in motion and carry it forward, they cannot simply lay aside every weight and run the race that is set before them[4] on that infallible road to the goal of human endeavours which is visible to eyes that have seen salvation.[5] They cannot take this simple course, because, being 'social animals', they cannot go on moving forward themselves unless they can contrive to carry their fellows with them in their advance; and the uncreative rank-and-file of Mankind, which in every known society hitherto has always been in an overwhelm-

[1] Thascius Caecilius Cyprianus: *Ad Demetrianum*, chap. 10.
[2] See III. C (ii), in vol. iii, above.
[3] Matt. vii. 14.
[4] Hebrews xii. 1.
[5] Luke ii. 30.

ıg majority, cannot be transfigured *en masse* in the twinkling of an ye. In these conditions, which are inherent in the very nature of ɔcial life, the higher personalities, who arise here and there and ow and then by a mutation of ordinary Human Nature, are hallenged to attempt a *tour de force*: 'to convert a species, which ; essentially a created thing, into creative effort; to make a moveıent out of something which, by definition, is a halt.'[1]

This *tour de force* is not impossible to achieve; and indeed there a perfect way: the 'strenuous . . . communion and intimate . . . ıtercourse' that impart the divine fire from one soul to another ike light caught from a leaping flame'.[2] This is the perfect way ecause the receptive soul, 'once alight, feeds its own flame thenceɔrward'.[3] Yet it is an unpractical counsel of perfection to enjoin his way, as Plato enjoins it, to the exclusion of all others; for the ıward spiritual grace through which an unillumined soul is fired y communion with a saint is almost as rare as the miracle that has rought the saint himself into the World. The world in which the reative personality finds himself, and in which he has to work, is society in which his fellows are ordinary human beings. His task Plato concedes)[4] is to make his fellows into his followers; and Mankind in the mass can only be set in motion towards a goal eyond itself by enlisting the primitive and universal faculty of nimesis.[5] For this mimesis is a kind of social drill;[6] and the dull ars that are deaf to the unearthly music of Orpheus' lyre are well ttuned to the drill-sergeant's raucous word of command.[7] When

[1] Bergson, Henri: *Les Deux Sources de la Morale et de la Religion* (Paris 1932, Alcan), . 251 (quoted in III. C (ii) (*a*), in vol. iii, on p. 235, above).

[2] Plato's Letters, No. 7, 341 B–E, quoted in III. C (ii) (*a*), in vol. iii, p. 245, above.

[3] Plato, op. cit., loc. cit. The same counsel was given by Confucius in political terms ı his maxim that a ruler ought to obtain his results by eliciting co-operation and not by ssuing commands (Forke, A.: *Die Gedankenwelt des Chinesischen Kulturkreises* (Munich nd Berlin 1927, Oldenbourg), p. 187).

[4] Plato's attitude on this point is examined by Archer-Hind, R. D., in *The Phaedo of 'lato*, second edition (London 1894, Macmillan), Appendix I: *Δημοτικὴ καὶ Πολιτικὴ ἀρετή*:

'While all *δημοτικὴ ἀρετή* is radically distinguished from philosophical morality by he fact that it is *ἄνευ φρονήσεως*, we may . . . discern two well-marked varieties of it, epresented by [*Respublica* 554 C] and [*Respublica* 500 D]. . . . The first is an ethical code ɔrmed (1) by the multitude for themselves, (2) on utilitarian principles, (3) without nowledge of the good; the second is (1) formed by the philosopher for the multitude, 2) not on utilitarian principles, (3) with knowledge of the good, but (4) accepted by the nultitude on utilitarian principles, and without knowledge of the good. The first Plato egards with unmixed contempt; the second he recognizes as the best which the great ıajority of Mankind can attain, and by it he hopes to supersede the other: nay, so much mportance does he attach to this that his philosophers must take it in turns to desist rom their own meditations and give their minds to instructing their fellow citizens' op. cit., p. 154).

[5] See III. C (ii) (*a*), vol. iii, p. 245, above.

[6] See the quotation, in loc. cit., from Bergson, op. cit., p. 99; and compare Frobenius, ..: *Paideuma* (Frankfurt 1928, Frankfurter Societäts-Druckerei), p. 234.

[7] Compare Bacon, Francis: *Of the Proficience and Advancement of Learning, Divine ınd Humane*, Book I, chap. 8, § 3.

'We see the dignity of the commandment is according to the dignity of the commanded: o have commandment over beasts, as herdmen have, is a thing contemptible: to have

the Piper of Hamelin assumes King Frederick William's Prussian voice, the rank-and-file, who have stood stolid hitherto, mechanically break into movement in obedience to the martinet's orders, and the evolution which he causes them to execute brings them duly to heel; but they can only catch him up by taking a short cut,[1] and they can only find room to march in formation by deploying into the broad way that leadeth to destruction.[2] When the road to destruction has perforce to be trodden on the quest of Life, it is perhaps no wonder that the quest should sometimes end in disaster.

Moreover there is a weakness in the actual exercise of mimesis, quite apart from the way in which the faculty may be exploited. For, if it is true that mimesis is a kind of drill, it is also true that drill is a kind of mechanization of human movement and life; and our concept of a 'machine' has an ambiguous connotation.

When we talk of 'a delicate mechanism' or 'an ingenious mechanism' or 'mechanical ingenuity' or 'a skilled mechanic', the words call up the general idea of a triumph of Life over Matter and the particular idea of the triumph of human will and thought over the physical environment of a human society. And the same ideas are suggested by concrete examples of machinery when we come across them—from a twentieth-century Western gramophone or wireless-set or aeroplane-engine back to the first wheel and the first earthenware crock and the first dug-out canoe and the first flaked flint instrument, which are the most wonderful inventions in the whole series.[3] The sight of these machines which human hands have made gives us a thrill of pride and self-confidence; and this feeling has its justification; for the invention of machinery immensely extends Man's power over Man's environment by so manipulating inanimate objects that they are made to carry out human purposes, as the drill-sergeant's commands are executed by his platoon of mechanized human beings. In drilling his platoon the drill-sergeant expands himself into a giant Briarieus whose hundred adventitious legs and arms obey his will almost as promptly and exactly as though

commandment over children, as schoolmasters have, is a matter of small honour: to have commandment over galley-slaves is a disparagement rather than an honour. Neither is the commandment of tyrants much better, over people which have put off the generosity of their minds: and therefore it was ever holden that honours in free monarchies and commonwealths had a sweetness more than in tyrannies, because the commandment extendeth more over the wills of men, and not only over their deeds and services. And therefore, when Virgil putteth himself forth to attribute to Augustus Caesar the best of human honours, he doth it in these words:

Victorque volentes
Per populos dat jura, viamque affectat Olympo.'

[1] See III. C (ii) (*a*), vol. iii, pp. 247–8, above.

[2] Matt. vii. 13.

[3] For the superiority of the human ingenuity which went to the making of these primary machines over the ingenuity that has gone to the making of their myriad derivatives, see III. C (i) (*b*), vol. iii, pp. 158–9, above.

they had been originally his own. And similarly the telescope is an extension and enhancement of the human eye, and the trumpet of the human voice, and the stilt of the human leg, and the sword of the human hand.

Nature herself has implicitly complimented Man upon his mechanical ingenuity by anticipating him in the use of mechanical devices. She has made an audaciously extensive use of them in the piece of natural mechanism with which we are most familiar: her *chef d'œuvre*, the human body. In the heart and the lungs she has constructed two self-regulating machines which are models of their kind; and we, her creatures, owe her gratitude for this beneficent triumph of mechanization in the medium of our flesh and blood. By adjusting our heart and our lungs to the performance of their appointed tasks with such perfection that they 'work automatically', Nature has released a margin of our muscular and nervous and psychic energies from the monotonously repetitive Danaids' task of making breath follow breath and heart-beat follow heart-beat, and has set these marginal energies free to do the 'original work' of locomotion and sensation and thought. This is the trick by which, in the evolution of organic life, she has succeeded in building up ever more and more elaborate organisms. At every stage in this advance she has acted as Orpheus acts when he resorts to the methods of the drill-sergeant. In each successive organism in her ascending series she has introduced the maximum possible amount of drill or, in other words, of mechanization. Her aim has been to arrange that, say, ninety per cent. of the functions which any given organism has to perform shall be performed automatically and therefore with a minimum expenditure of energy, in order that a maximum amount of energy may be concentrated upon the remaining ten per cent. of this organism's activities, in which Nature is feeling her way towards a fresh advance in organization. In fact, a natural organism is made up, like a human society, of a creative minority and an uncreative majority of 'members'; and in a growing organism, as in a growing society, the majority is drilled into following the minority's lead mechanically.

When we have lost ourselves in admiration of these natural and human mechanical triumphs, it is disconcerting to be reminded that there are other phrases—'machine-made goods', 'machine-like movements', 'mechanical behaviour', 'the party machine'—in which the connotation of the word 'machine' is exactly the reverse. Yet there is no doubt about it: in each of the phrases in this second group the idea that is suggested is not the triumph of Life over Matter but the mastery of Matter over Life; and, instead of the thrill of self-confidence and pride, we feel a shock of humiliation and misgiving as we realize that the master-tool of Life and Mind, which promises to give them a boundless dominion over the Material Universe, may actually turn in their hands into an instrument for their own subjugation to the Kingdom of Ancient Night. 'Cette matière est instrument et elle est aussi obstacle.'[1] 'Le corps est bien pour nous un moyen d'agir, mais c'est aussi un empêchement de percevoir.'[2] 'La mécanique, en se développant, pourra se retourner contre la mystique.'[3] The powers which, one moment ago, seemed to have discovered the secret of setting the Universe on fire, now suddenly turn out to have quenched their own flame and put out their own light by rashly smothering the spark under its potential fuel.

This Janus-like quality in the nature of Machinery is disconcerting because at first sight it seems like a betrayal; but on second thoughts it becomes apparent that it is 'all in the game'. For the mechanic to denounce his machine because it has 'caught him out' is as irrational as it would be for the losing team in a tug-of-war to blame the rope for their defeat when they have gone out of their way to challenge the other team to a trial of strength and have woven the rope with their own hands in order to make the match playable. Or we may compare the losing party to a wrestler who has slyly challenged a lay-figure and has congratulated himself, in closing with this adversary of his choice, upon getting the better grip—only to find, to his amazement and horror, that his own muscles go slack at the touch of the dummy's flabby frame. The discomfited competitor's error has lain in taking it for granted that when once the battle was joined he could not fail to win. Yet the tug-of-war team's rope or the wrestler's grip do not, of course, in themselves guarantee a victory to either side. They are merely neutral ways and means for a trial of strength in which the issue is not a foregone conclusion. And, in the cosmic tug-of-war between Life and Matter, this neutral function is fulfilled by everything that comes under the category of Machinery. Machines are ambiguous in their essence, and to call this ambiguity a betrayal is to convict oneself of being the bad workman who complains of his tools. *Homo Faber* has apprenticed himself to a dangerous trade; and any one who sets out to act on the principle of 'Nothing venture nothing win' is manifestly exposing himself to the risk of losses as the price of putting himself in the running for the victor's crown.

If this risk is involved in Man's use of machinery for dealing with his physical environment, it must be incurred, *a fortiori*, when he resorts to the device of mechanization in his relations with

[1] Bergson, op. cit., p. 119. [2] Ibid., p. 340. [3] Ibid., p. 252.

himself and his fellow men.[1] For an expedient which is dangerous to Life when it is employed, as Nature has intended it to be employed, in the struggle between Life and Matter, becomes a sheer *tour de force* when Life attempts to exploit it against Life itself. In the realm of Thought we have put ourselves on our guard, at an early stage of this Study,[2] against 'the apathetic fallacy' of treating living creatures as though they were inanimate. The mechanization of Life, either in the inner workings of a soul or in the external relations between a number of human beings in a society, is a translation of this 'apathetic fallacy' into practical action; and if the human 'social animal' is constrained to act on so false a premiss as this, the action may be expected to have catastrophic consequences.

Thus a risk of catastrophe proves to be inherent in the use of the faculty of mimesis, which is the vehicle of mechanization in the medium of Human Nature; and it is evident that this inherent risk will be greater in degree when the faculty of mimesis is called into play in a society which is in dynamic movement than when the same faculty is given rein in a society which is in a state of rest. The weakness of mimesis lies in its being a mechanical response to a suggestion from some alien source, so that the action that is performed through mimesis is, *ex hypothesi*, an action that would never have been performed by its performer upon his own initiative. Thus all action that proceeds from mimesis is essentially precarious because it is not self-determined; and the best practical safeguard against the danger of its breaking down is for the exercise of the faculty of mimesis to become crystallized in the form of habit or custom[3]—as it actually is in primitive societies in the Yin-state, which is the only stage of their history in which we know them.[4] In 'the cake of custom' the double-edged blade of mimesis is comfortably padded. But the breaking of 'the cake of custom' is of the essence of the change through which the state of rest that is the

1 Two pertinent examples of the practice—one taken from the sophisticated life of societies in process of civilization, and the other from the life of primitive societies in their latter-day static condition (see I. C (iii) (*e*), vol. i, pp. 179–80, and Part II. B, vol. i, pp. 192–4, above)—are given in Bergson, H.: *Les Deux Sources de la Morale et de la Religion* (Paris 1932, Alcan), pp. 177–8:

'L'acteur qui étudie son rôle se donne pour tout de bon l'émotion qu'il doit exprimer; il note les gestes et les intonations qui sortent d'elle: plus tard, devant le public, il ne reproduira que l'intonation et le geste, il pourra faire l'économie de l'émotion. Ainsi pour la magie. Les "lois" qu'on lui a trouvées ne nous disent rien de l'élan naturel d'où elle est sortie. Elles ne sont que la formule des procédés que la paresse a suggérés à cette magie originelle pour s'imiter elle-même.'

2 See Part I. A, vol. i, pp. 7–8, above.

3 This consideration was presumably in Plato's mind when he suggested (*Phaedo* 82 B) that the life of a bee or an ant would be the appropriate next incarnation for a soul which, in a life as a human being, had behaved as a good social animal 'from habit and practice, without philosophy or conscious intelligence (ἐξ ἔθους τε καὶ μελέτης ἄνευ φιλοσοφίας τε καὶ νοῦ)'.

4 See Part II. B, vol. i, pp. 191–5, above.

last phase in the history of a primitive society gives place to the fresh dynamic movement that we call a civilization.[1] The mimesis which has been directed towards the older generation of the living members of the society, as incarnations of an accumulated social heritage, is now reoriented towards creative personalities whose eyes have seen on the horizon a further goal of human endeavours, and whose wills have become bent upon leading their fellows with them towards this promised land. In this new movement the edged tool of mimesis is not discarded, but is employed with enhanced effect now that the breaking of 'the cake of custom' has laid its cutting edges bare. This baring of a blade means the removal of a safeguard; and the necessity of using the tool of mimesis without the protection of a customary régime—a necessity which is the price of growth—condemns a growing civilization to live dangerously. More than that, the danger is perpetually imminent, since the condition which is required for the maintenance of the Promethean *élan* of growth is a condition of unstable equilibrium in which 'the cake of custom' is never allowed to set hard before it is broken up again.[2] The *tour de force* of the exploit of Civilization lies in this necessity of resorting to mimesis without a possibility of taking precautions at any stage. In this hazardous pursuit of the goal of human endeavours there can never be such a thing as a provisional insurance against the perils which mimesis entails. There can only be an ultimate and radical solution of the problem through the complete elimination of mimesis in a society which has transformed itself into a communion of saints; and this consummation, which is nothing less than the attainment of the goal, has never been even distantly approached by any known civilization hitherto.

In the meantime—and, on the scale of human lives, the time is long-drawn-out—the mechanized column of route is perpetually in danger of coming to a halt or of falling out of formation on the march if ever the rank-and-file are left to act without a lead in some situation without a precedent. A classic example of this mischance is the history of the mutineers of *The Bounty*, who relapsed from the level of our Western Civilization in the Modern Age to the level of Primitive Humanity after they had marooned themselves on Pitcairn Island. The abyss which always yawns open before the feet of human beings who are taking the broad road towards Civilization is continually revealed in abnormal accidents like shipwrecks or fires, which usually evoke exhibitions of astonishing demoralization as well as astonishing heroism; and the depth of this moral abyss is still deeper where the abnormal ordeal is not a natural accident but a social malady like a war or a revolution. In the his-

[1] See Part II. B, loc. cit., above.

[2] See Part III. B, in vol. iii, above.

tory of Man's attempt at Civilization hitherto there has never been any society whose progress in Civilization has gone so far that, in times of revolution or war, its members could be relied upon not to commit atrocities. To confine ourselves to the history of our own society in our own generation, we can cite the behaviour of the German Army in Belgium in 1914 and the British 'Black-and-Tans' in Ireland in 1920 and the French Army in Syria in 1925–6 and the German National-Socialist 'Storm Troops' at home in 1933 and the Italian Blackshirts at Addis Ababa in February 1937 as proof positive that, in certain conditions of abnormality and under a certain degree of strain, atrocities will be committed by most members of the least uncivilized societies that have yet existed—

> quo magis in dubiis hominem spectare periclis
> convenit adversisque in rebus noscere qui sit;
> nam verae voces tum demum pectore ab imo
> eliciuntur et eripitur persona, manet res.[1]

In times of stress the mask of Civilization is torn away from the primitive countenance of raw Humanity in the rank-and-file; but the moral responsibility for the breakdowns of civilizations lies upon the heads of the leaders.

> 'Woe unto the World because of offences! For it must needs be that offences come; but woe to that man by whom the offence cometh!'[2]

The creative personalities in the vanguard of a civilization who have had recourse to the mechanism of mimesis are exposing themselves to the risk of failure in two degrees, one negative and the other positive.

The possible negative failure is that, undesignedly and perhaps unconsciously, these leaders may infect themselves with the hypnotism which they have deliberately induced in their followers; and in that event the docility of the rank-and-file will have been purchased at the disastrous price of a loss of initiative in the officers. 'If the blind lead the blind, both shall fall into the ditch';[3] and 'if the salt have lost his savour, wherewith shall it be salted?'[4] There is an equivalent failure which may be the nemesis of Nature's device of resorting to mechanization in her construction of bodily organisms. The ingenuity of mechanizing 90 per cent. of the functions of an organism in order to concentrate the maximum amount of energy upon a creative evolution of the rest is an ingenuity which will have utterly defeated its own ends if the energy which has thus been released for a creative activity is converted, by force of

[1] Lucretius: *De Rerum Natura*, Book III, ll. 55–8.
[2] Matt. xviii. 7. [3] Matt. xv. 14. [4] Matt. v. 13.

suggestion, into the mechanical rhythm of its surroundings. In the former of these two states, in which the mechanization is subservient to a creative purpose, the organism is 'a marvel of mechanical ingenuity' in the appreciative sense; but the extension of the mechanical rhythm from 90 per cent. of the organism's activity to the whole degrades the organism into the monstrosity of 'a machine-like automaton'. The difference between 90 per cent. and 100 per cent. of mechanization is all the difference in the world; and there is just this kind of difference between a civilization that is in growth and a civilization that has become arrested.

We have seen what is wrong with the arrested civilizations in the empirical survey of five civilizations of this class which we have made in an earlier part of this Study.[1] The arrested civilizations have achieved so close an adaptation to their environment that they have taken its shape and colour and rhythm instead of impressing the environment with a stamp which is their own. The equilibrium of forces in their life is so exact that all their energies are absorbed in the effort of maintaining the position which they have attained already, and there is no margin of energy left over for reconnoitring the course of the road ahead, or the face of the cliff above them, with a view to a further advance. The effort by which they barely succeed in holding their own is so strenuous that it compels our admiration; yet when we view the life of the Esquimaux or the Nomads or the 'Osmanlis or the Spartans dispassionately and comprehensively, we feel the same contradictory combination of respect and contempt that is aroused in us by the contemplation of machinery. The apparently superhuman qualities which the Spartiate 'Peer' can be counted upon to display so long as he is on active service under the Lycurgean *agôgê* have to be discounted in the lurid light of the demoralization and inefficiency which invariably come over the self-same Spartiate if ever he finds himself out of his own element. And a discipline which looks at first sight like a transcending of Human Nature looks, on closer inspection, like a reversion to animality.[2] In the arrested civilizations we have a classic illustration of the negative failure in which the leaders them-

[1] In Part III. A, in vol. iii, above.

[2] See Part III. A, in vol. iii, above, especially pp. 79–81. Tolstoy has a story of a little boy who, on being taken for the first time in his life to see a military review, was drawn by curiosity to venture close up to the troops and then came running back to his mother crying, 'Mummy! Mummy! What do you think I have found out? These soldiers were once men.' Such *robots* wear the same appearance in Hindu as in Russian eyes. 'In the West the national machinery of commerce and politics turns out neatly compressed bales of humanity which have their use and high market value; but they are bound in iron hoops, labelled and separated off with scientific care and precision. Obviously God made Men to be human; but this modern product has such marvellous square-cut finish, savouring of gigantic manufacture, that the Creator will find it difficult to recognise it as a thing of spirit and a creature made in His own divine image.'—Tagore, Sir R.: *Nationalism* (London 1917, Macmillan), p. 6.

selves become hypnotized by the drill which they have inculcated into the rank-and-file. In this predicament the column comes to a dead halt, at whatever point on its route it may happen to find itself at the moment, simply because there is nobody left at the head of the column to give fresh orders. The ten thousand Greek troops whose moral paralysis on the night after the loss of their senior officers has been so graphically depicted by Xenophon's pencil were the same ten thousand who, only a few weeks before, had gladdened the heart of Cyrus and had given the queen of Cilicia the fright of her life by the precision of their discipline on the parade-ground.[1]

This negative failure, however, is seldom the end of the story; for the salt that has lost his savour 'is thenceforth good for nothing but to be cast out and to be trodden under foot of men'.[2] In abandoning Orpheus' music for the drill-sergeant's word of command, the leaders have played upon the faculty of mimesis in the rank-and-file by an exertion of power—as a substitute for the radiation of the magic charm of genius that is only attractive to kindred spirits. In the interaction between leaders and led, mimesis and power are correlatives; and power is a force which is perhaps rarely brought into play without being abused.[3] In any event the tenure of power is an abuse in itself if those who hold the power have lost the faculty of leadership; and this abuse is flagrant. Accordingly the halt of the column of route, which we have pictured in our military simile, is apt to be followed by mutiny on the part of the rank-and-file and by 'frightfulness' on the part of the officers—who make a desperate attempt to retain by brute force, against overwhelming numerical odds, an authority which they have ceased to merit by any signal contribution to the common weal. An Orpheus who has cast away his lyre now lays about him with Xerxes' whip; and the result is a hideous pandemonium, in which the military formation breaks up into an Ishmaelitish anarchy. This is the positive failure which is the nemesis of the resort to mimesis in the life of a growing civilization;

[1] Compare Xenophon: *Anabasis*, Book III, chap. 1, §§ 1–12, with the same work, Book I, chap. 2, §§ 14–18. The story of the practical joke which Clearchus played upon the august spectators of the military review at Tarsus has been put into modern dress—with the British Viceroy of India playing Cyrus's part and the Amir of Afghanistan Queen Epyaxa's—by Rudyard Kipling in *The Jungle Book* ('Her Majesty's Servants'). In similar circumstances in a different time and place a queen of Abyssinia was likewise impressed by the drill, *à la suisse*, of the Portuguese matchlockmen of Christovão da Gama's expeditionary force (Castanhoso, M. de, and Bermudez, J.: *The Portuguese Expedition to Abyssinia in 1541*, English translation (=Hakluyt Society, second series, vol. x, 1902), pp. 20–1).

[2] Matt. v. 13.

[3] The sinister importance of the abuse of power as a factor in social life has been appreciated by Ibn Khaldūn. See the chapter entitled 'Dans un empire, le souverain est naturellement porté à réserver toute l'autorité; on s'y abandonne au luxe, à l'indolence et au repos' (*Muqaddamāt*, translated by de Slane, Baron McG. (Paris 1863–8, Imprimerie Impériale, 3 vols.), vol. i, pp. 340–3. Compare vol. ii, pp. 114–16.). See also the present Study, V. C (ii) (*a*), vol. vi, pp. 178–213, below: 'The Saviour with the Sword.'

and in the language of another simile this failure is familiar to us already. It is that 'disintegration' of a broken-down civilization which declares itself in 'the Secession of the Proletariat' from a *ci-devant* band of leaders which has degenerated into a 'Dominant Minority'.[1] The successive transformations of the prophet into the drill-sergeant and of this martinet into a terrorist explain the declines and falls of civilizations in terms of leadership.

In terms of relation or interaction the failure of the Promethean *élan* declares itself in a loss of harmony.

The significance of this symptom is perhaps most obvious in the concrete case of the bodily organism of a galloping horse:

'During continued movement any addition to speed obtained by increased instability of equilibrium necessitates increased muscular effort in maintaining the centre of gravity of the body at a suitable height.... The faster the pace, the greater will be the muscular expenditure of the fore limbs, as compared to the speed. Consequently, when a horse gallops fast, the muscles of his fore-hand tire much more quickly than those of his hind limbs.... When a horse begins to tire in a long-distance race . . . , his ordinary "level" style of "going" generally becomes changed more or less into an up-and-down motion, which is caused by the muscles of his fore-hand being too fatigued to work in unison with those of his hind-quarters.'[2]

A corresponding loss of harmony attends the flagging of the Promethean *élan* in a personality, which is a whole whose parts are spiritual faculties, and in a society, which is a whole whose parts are institutions. In the movement of Life a change in any one part of a whole ought to be accompanied by sympathetic adjustments of the other parts if all is to go well; but when Life is mechanized one part may be altered while others are left as they have been, and a loss of harmony is the result.

In any whole of parts a loss of harmony between the parts is paid for by the whole in a corresponding loss of self-determination; and the fate of a declining civilization is described in Jesus's prophecy to Peter:

'When thou wast young, thou girdedst thyself, and walkedst whither thou wouldest; but when thou shalt be old . . . another shall gird thee and carry thee whither thou wouldest not.'[3]

A loss of self-determination is the ultimate criterion of breakdown; and this conclusion is what we should expect, since it is the inverse of the conclusion, which we have reached in an earlier

[1] For an explanation of these terms see I. B (iv), vol. i, p. 41, and I. C (i) (*a*), vol. i, pp. 53–62, above.

[2] Hayes, Captain M. H.: *Points of the Horse*, 5th edition (London 1930, Hurst and Blackett), pp. 53–4.

[3] John xxi. 18.

part of this Study, that a progress towards self-determination is the criterion of growth.[1] In the rest of this Part we shall examine some of the forms in which this loss of self-determination through loss of harmony is manifested.

(*b*) THE INTRACTABILITY OF INSTITUTIONS

1. *New Wine in Old Bottles*

In the last chapter we came to the conclusion that a society breaks down through a loss of harmony between its parts which is paid for by the society as a whole in a loss of self-determination. One source of disharmony between the institutions of which a society is composed is the introduction into the life of the society of new social forces—aptitudes or emotions or ideas[2]—which the existing set of institutions was not originally designed to carry.

The destructive effect of this incongruous juxtaposition of 'things new and old'[3] has been pointed out in one of the most famous of the sayings that are attributed to Jesus:

> 'No man putteth a piece of new cloth unto an old garment, for that which is put in to fill it up taketh from the garment, and the rent is made worse. Neither do men put new wine into old bottles—else the bottles break and the wine runneth out and the bottles perish; but they put new wine into new bottles, and both are preserved.'[4]

In the domestic economy from which this simile is taken the precept can, of course, be carried out to the letter, because the cloth and the garment and the wine and the bottles are material chattels over which the householder has an absolute power of disposal. But in the economy of social life men's power to order their affairs at will on a rational plan is narrowly restricted, since a society is not the chattel of any owner, but is the common ground of many men's fields of action; and for this reason a precept which is common sense in the economy of the household and practical wisdom in the life of the spirit is a counsel of perfection in social affairs.

Ideally, no doubt, the introduction of any new dynamic forces or creative movements into the life of a society ought to be accompanied by a reconstruction of the whole existing set of institutions if a healthy social harmony is to be preserved; and, in the actual history of any growing civilization, there is in fact a constant remodelling or readjustment of the most flagrantly anachronistic institutions *ex hypothesi*, at least to the minimum extent that is necessary in order to save the civilization from breaking down. At

[1] See III. C (i) (*d*), vol. iii, p. 216, above.
[2] See Part II. B, vol. i, p. 191, above.
[3] Matt. xiii. 52.
[4] Matt. ix. 16–17.

the same time, sheer *vis inertiae* tends at all times to keep most parts of the social structure as they are, in spite of their frequent incongruity with the new social forces that are constantly being brought into action by the creative energies of the growing society as its growth proceeds;[1] and in this situation the new forces are apt to operate in two diametrically opposite ways simultaneously. On the one hand they perform the creative work which it is their business to perform by finding vent either in new institutions which they have established for themselves or in old institutions which they have successfully adapted to serve their purposes; and, in pouring themselves into these harmonious channels, they promote the welfare of the civilization by giving fresh impetus to its *élan*. At the same time they also enter, indiscriminately, into any institutions which happen to lie in their path—as some immensely powerful head of steam which had forced its way into an engine-house might rush into the works of any old engine that happened to be installed there.

In such an event one or other of two alternative disasters is apt to occur. Either the pressure of the new head of steam is so very much higher than the maximum pressure which the old-fashioned engine was originally built to bear that the works simply explode and are blown to pieces when the steam has entered into them; or else the antique plates and castings do 'stand the racket', and then the disaster takes an even more destructive and a far more monstrous turn. The unprecedentedly powerful 'drive' of the new motive-force then sets the old machinery to work in a way which was never contemplated by its makers. If it was a rather unsatisfactory machine, the tolerably bad results which it originally produced are now magnified to an intolerable degree; and even if it was a fairly satisfactory machine, the tolerably good performance that was originally obtained from it may have amazing and appalling effects now that the machine has been so powerfully 'keyed up'. The dentist's implement which delicately files away the decayed tip of a tooth when it is operated with the proper power may perhaps pierce the palate to the brain, and cause the patient's death instead of giving him a salutary relief, if the strength of the electric

[1] It was in this aspect, as obstacles to progress, that institutions were envisaged by the eighteenth-century French Encyclopaedists, and in particular by Condorcet (Bury, J. B.: *The Idea of Progress* (London 1924, Macmillan), pp. 210–11). The same point is made by Walter Bagehot in his *Physics and Politics*, 10th edition (London 1894, Kegan Paul), p. 149: 'The very institutions which most aid at step number one are precisely those which most impede at step number two.' Bagehot illustrates this thesis by the case of the institution of Caste. After pointing out (op. cit., p. 148) that Caste is of value to primitive societies in helping them to reconcile the two desiderata of social rigidity and social variety, he goes on (op. cit., p. 149) to point out that 'several non-caste nations have continued to progress, but all caste nations have stopped early, though some have lasted long'. In fact, 'progress would not have been the rarity it is if the early food had not been the late poison' (op. cit., p. 74).

current is suddenly increased out of all measure. Similarly, a drug which acts as a potent stimulant when it is taken in a minute quantity may work with equal potency as a poison if the dose is largely increased.

To translate these parables into terms of social life, the explosions of the old engines which cannot stand the new steam-pressure—or the burstings of the old bottles which cannot stand the fermentation of the new wine—are the revolutions which sometimes overtake institutions that have become anachronisms.[1] On the other hand the baneful performances of the old engines which have successfully stood the strain of being 'keyed up' are the social enormities which a 'die-hard' institutional anachronism sometimes engenders.

Revolutions may be defined as retarded, and proportionately violent, acts of mimesis. The mimetic element is of their essence; for every revolution always has reference to something that has happened already elsewhere—at an earlier moment and on a different spot from the place and the time at which the revolutionary outbreak of violence occurs—and it is always manifest, when the revolution is studied in its historical setting, that this outbreak would never have occurred of itself if it had not been thus evoked by a previous play of external forces.[2] The element of retardation is likewise of the essence of revolutions; and it is this that accounts for the violence which is their most prominent feature. Revolutions are violent because they are the belated triumphs of powerful new social forces over tenacious old institutions which have been temporarily thwarting and cramping these new expressions of life. The longer the obstruction holds out, the greater becomes the pressure of the force whose outlet is being obstructed;

[1] For this theory of the nature of revolutions see Teggart, F. J.: *The Processes of History* (New Haven 1918, Yale University Press), p. 130, following Walter Bagehot's *Physics and Politics*.

[2] This external factor in the geneses of revolutions is impossible to ignore in those cases where a revolution in the social structure of one society is evoked by the impact of social forces that emanate from a different society (this class of cases is dealt with in Parts IX and X below). But the operation of the external factor can always be detected, on close inspection, in the history of any revolution, even when the whole movement works itself out within one single society's bosom. For instance, 'the confluence of French theory with American example caused the [French] Revolution to break out' when it did (Lord Acton, quoted by Bury, J. B.: *The Idea of Progress* (London 1924, Macmillan), p. 203). In both these varieties of a substantially identical experience the social structure of the passive party to the encounter is apt to oppose so obstinate a resistance to the impinging force that, when this force does eventually break through, the resolution of forces takes a revolutionary form. 'The great events of history that strike the eye are generally the sequel to a long process of preparation, and most of them constitute the conclusion and climax of some process that is less conspicuous than they are. It is only when the Hellenic idea has quietly and silently permeated the East that Alexander—following the direction thereby given to him—goes on the war-path and founds his empire. It is only when the French idea has pushed its way right across Germany and on beyond into Russia that Napoleon goes on the war-path and seeks to extend the realm of French glory by force of arms' (Frobenius, L.: *Paideuma* (Frankfurt 1928, Frankfurter Societäts-Druckerei), p. 276).

and the greater this pressure, the more violent the explosion in which the imprisoned force ultimately breaks through.[1]

As for the social enormities that are the alternatives to revolutions, these may be defined as the penalties that a society has to pay when the act of mimesis which ought to have brought an old institution into harmony with a new social force has been, not simply retarded, but frustrated altogether.

It will be seen that, whenever some new aptitude or emotion or idea arises in the life of any society, this new force is likely, in proportion to its strength and its range and its importance, to come into collision with a greater or a lesser number of the society's existing institutions, and each of these collisions may have any one of three alternative outcomes. The obstructive institution may either be brought into harmony with the new force promptly and peaceably through some constructive social adjustment; or it may be eliminated tardily and violently through a revolution; or it may succeed in defying both adjustment and elimination, and in this last event some social enormity will result from the unnatural 'drive' which will now be put into the intractable institution automatically by the new force that has failed to master it. It is evident that, whenever the existing institutional structure of a society is challenged by the impact of a new social force, each and all of these three possible alternative outcomes of the collision may actually be realized simultaneously in respect of different parts of the structure; and it is further evident that the ratio in which the three outcomes are represented in the total result of this particular round of Challenge-and-Response will be a matter of momentous importance in the working out of the society's destiny.

If the adjustments predominate over the revolutions and the enormities, then the well-being of the society will be maintained and the continuation of its growth will be assured during the current chapter of its history. If the predominant outcomes are revolutionary, then the fortunes of the society in this chapter will be 'on the razor's edge'. It is possible that the revolutions may save the society's life by blasting away a number of anachronistic institutions which have not proved amenable to pacific adjustment and which would have rankled into enormities if they had proved altogether intractable; it is equally possible that the havoc made

[1] This explains, for example, the violence of the revolution through which a Catholic France caught up with a Protestant England at the close of the eighteenth century. The reason why there was no explosion of that violence in England at that time was that in England, in contrast to France, the medieval institutional obstructions to the modern social forces had already been partially broken down by stages in previous centuries—in a sixteenth-century religious reformation and in a seventeenth-century political upheaval. On this point see Masaryk, T. G.: *The Spirit of Russia*, English translation (London 1919, Allen & Unwin, 2 vols.), vol. ii, pp. 495 and 517–23.

by the revolutionary outbreaks may be so great (and, in every revolution, there is always a heavy bill of social damages to pay) that no amount of social liberation can compensate for it, and then the society may suffer almost as severely as if the predominant outcomes in this instance had been not revolutions but enormities. Finally, if the perversion of anachronistic institutions into enormities predominates over the elimination of them through violent revolutions or the conversion of them, through pacific and constructive adjustments, into satisfactory vents for the new social forces, then the dislocation of the whole social structure may be so serious that a breakdown may be virtually impossible to avoid.[1]

In the historic breakdowns of civilizations this working out of the principle of Challenge-and-Response in the medium of institutions has indeed played an important part; and now that we have formulated it *a priori* in the imagery of a parable, we shall perhaps do well to study it in the life by resorting once more to our well-tried method of an empirical survey.

2. *The Impact of Industrialism upon Slavery*

Let us begin our survey with a familiar instance from the modern history of our own Western World which happens to be a particularly clear illustration of the possible diversity in the outcome when new social forces collide with an old institution.

In the recent chapter of our Western history in which the protagonists were an English creative minority[2]—a chapter that came to its close towards the end of the nineteenth century[3]—the two great new dynamic social forces which were conjured up and set in motion were Industrialism and Democracy,[4] and one of the old institutions upon which these new forces impinged was Slavery.

Since the institution of Slavery has been recognized to be intrinsically evil by a consensus of all men in all times and places who have been in a position to study it at first hand objectively, it must be regarded as one of the merits, or at least as one of the

[1] 'Catastrophes are necessary to free the World from the monstrosities that periodically torment it. Powerful as he is, Man is an imperfect and unbalanced creature, and he always ends by exaggerating the principles, aspirations and needs most in keeping with his nature to such a monstrous pitch that they become unbearable afflictions. The most splendid civilisations have perished either directly through the action of these insufferable miscreations or indirectly through Man's desperate efforts to get rid of them' (Ferrero, G.: *Peace and War*, English translation (London 1933, Macmillan), pp. 92–3). This tendency in human nature is discussed further in this Study in IV. C (iii) (*c*) 2 (γ), Annex, pp. 635–9, below.

[2] For the role of England in the third chapter of the growth of our Western Society see III. C (ii) (*b*), vol. iii, pp. 350–63, above.

[3] See Part I. A, vol. i, p. 1, footnote 2, above.

[4] See Part I. A, vol. i, *init.* The impact of these two new forces in our Western life upon a number of old Western institutions, which is the main subject of the present chapter, has been touched upon already, by anticipation, in III. C (i) (*d*), vol. iii, p. 212, and III. C (ii) (*a*), vol. iii, p. 241, above.

advantages, of the Western Civilization that, in its history down to the advent of the democratic and industrial régime, this pernicious institution had never played at all a dominant part. Fortunately for the Western Society the system of plantation-slavery, which had contributed so largely to the decline and fall of the 'apparented' Hellenic Society, had broken down in the breakdown of the Hellenic Society itself[1] and had therefore not entered into the 'affiliated' Western Society's original social heritage; and although this social evil had afterwards established itself in the Western body social likewise at the turn of the fifteenth and sixteenth centuries of the Christian Era, when Western Christendom had expanded out of Europe overseas, this modern Western recrudescence of plantation-slavery had not at first shown itself very formidable. At the moment when, some three hundred years later, at the turn of the eighteenth and nineteenth centuries, the new forces of Democracy and Industrialism began to radiate out of Great Britain into the rest of the Western World, the institution of Slavery was still practically confined to the colonial fringes of Western Christendom; it had made no serious lodgements in the European homelands;[2] and, even overseas, the geographical range of the institution was contracting. For example, in the course of the eighteenth century Slavery died a natural death in the English colonies along the Atlantic seaboard of North America to the north of the Mason and Dixon Line; and if the Industrial Revolution had not broken out, or had only broken out a hundred years later than the actual date of its outbreak, it is possible that Slavery would have disappeared successively in one after another of the overseas communities of English, Dutch, French, Spanish, and Portuguese origin until it might have become completely extinct throughout the Western World without any social upheaval or even any realization that an important advance had been made in the progress of our Western Civilization. This possibility, however, was ruled out by the outbreak of the Industrial Revolution in Great Britain, since the market for the produce of the overseas plantations was immensely stimulated by the demand for raw materials to feed the new industries which were called into existence by the new European technique, and for food-stuffs to feed the new urban populations which were called into existence by the new industries. The impact of Industrialism thus gave the languishing institution of Slavery a new lease of life; and there could not any longer be any question of the evil institution gradually

1 See III. C (i) (*b*), vol. iii, pp. 169–71, above.

2 The exception which proves the rule in this case is Portugal; for the spread of the institution of Negro plantation-slavery from Brazil into the European dominions of the Portuguese Crown was contemporaneous with the eclipse of Portugal as a Great Power (see Phillips, U. B.: *American Negro Slavery* (New York 1918, Appleton), p. 13).

dying out of itself. The Western Society was now faced with a choice between taking active steps to put an end to Slavery immediately, or else seeing this ancient social evil converted, by the driving-force of the new power of Industrialism, into a mortal danger to the society's very life.

In this situation an anti-slavery movement came into action, and this movement achieved some very great pacific successes. It succeeded pacifically in abolishing the international slave-trade altogether, and also in abolishing the institution of Slavery itself over vast areas: in most of the Latin-American countries whose White inhabitants liberated themselves in the early decades of the nineteenth century from the dominion of the Spanish and Portuguese Crowns; and then again in the British and French colonial empires, where Slavery was finally extinguished in A.D. 1833 and in A.D. 1848. To this extent the new social problem arising from the impact of Industrialism upon Slavery was solved by a timely and a pacific adjustment; but there was one great region in which the anti-slavery movement failed to make peaceful headway, and this was 'the cotton-belt' in the Southern States of the North American Union.

'The cotton-belt' was the crux; for the greatest technical and financial triumph of the Industrial System in the first phase of its development was the set of brilliant inventions which made it profitable now to clean and spin and weave cotton on the grand scale; and this gave an immense impetus to the production of cotton in the Southern States of the North American Union, south of the Mason and Dixon line, where Slavery was still a going concern and where cotton was cultivated by slave labour. Accordingly, in the Southern States of the Union, Slavery remained in force for one generation longer; and in this short interval of thirty years between A.D. 1833 (the date at which Slavery was abolished in the British Empire) and A.D. 1863 (the date at which it was abolished in the United States) the 'Peculiar Institution' of the Southern States, with the whole driving-force of Industrialism now behind it, swelled into a monstrous growth which threatened to overshadow the North American Continent.[1] After that, the monster was brought

[1] An apologist for the obstinacy which was shown by the slave-owners in 'the cotton-belt' of the United States in clinging to Slavery after it had admittedly become their 'Peculiar Institution' can fairly point out that, at the very time when the profitableness of cotton-cultivation was being vastly increased by the rise of the new cotton textile industry in Lancashire and New England, the profitableness of sugar-cultivation in the British and French possessions in the West Indies was being diminished by the new invention of extracting sugar from beet-root—a discovery which promised to render Europe independent of the West Indian sugar crop. No doubt these economic facts do partly account for the relative ease, and the relatively early date, of the abolition of Slavery in the West Indian 'sugar-belt'; but this consideration does not affect our present argument; for it is not our purpose here to pass a comparative ethical judgement upon the difference in the handling of the Slavery problem in the British Empire and in the

to bay and was destroyed; but this belated eradication of Slavery in the United States had to be paid for at the price of a shattering revolution which began with the Civil War of A.D. 1861–5 and continued to work itself out in the sordid tragedy of the post-bellum years, when the defeated South went through the agonies of an economic and social collapse, while the victorious North tarnished its victory by countenancing the scandals of 'Reconstruction'.[1] Indeed, the devastating effects of this revolution are still visible in American life at the present day; for the manner in which the *ci-devant* slaves were liberated and enfranchised has done lasting mischief to the social relations between the White and Black races in the United States. So heavy has been the penalty for a thirty years' delay.

Still, our Western Society may congratulate itself that, even at this price, the social evil of Slavery has eventually been destroyed root and branch in its last Western stronghold, and has not anywhere survived to become the intolerable enormity which it was bound to become if it had continued to exist in an industrialized world. For this mercy we have to thank the new force of Democracy, which came into our Western World a little in advance of Industrialism. Since Democracy is the political expression of Humanitarianism, and since Humanitarianism and Slavery are obviously mortal foes, the new democratic spirit put 'drive' into the anti-slavery movement at the very time when Industrialism was putting 'drive' into 'the Peculiar Institution'.[2] It was this inspiration that enabled the anti-slavery movement to achieve so large a measure of success in driving Slavery off the map pacifically in time to avoid a revolution; and it is safe to say that if, in the struggle over Slavery, the working of the force of Industrialism had not been neutralized to a large extent by the counter-operation of the force of Democracy, our Western World would not have rid itself of Slavery at the cheap price of a single revolutionary catastrophe.

This judgement is supported by two pertinent considerations. On the one hand we have taken note already[3] of the devastating

United States. We are concerned with this difference here because it is a signal illustration of the contrast between an adjustment and a revolution; and in this aspect the difference is simply a matter of historical fact.

1 See III. C (i) (*b*), vol. iii, pp. 171–2, above.

2 The anti-slavery movement received its original initiative and its main permanent impetus from a school of humanitarians in Great Britain, which was the place where the new force of Democracy had first emerged in the modern Western World. In this connexion it may be noted that Great Britain was also the cradle of the Industrialism which was threatening to put fresh 'drive' into Slavery. Is it possible that the conscious humanitarian motive of the English originators of the anti-slavery movement was reinforced by an unconscious intuitive apprehension of the enormity into which the old institution of Slavery would grow if the new force of Industrialism, which was emerging in England under their eyes, were allowed to put its 'drive' into it?

3 In III. C (i) (*b*), vol. iii, pp. 169–71, above.

effect, in Hellenic history, of the system of plantation-slavery which came into operation in the Hellenic World in the fifth century B.C. and which was not neutralized by the fifth-century Hellenic movement towards Democracy. On the other hand we are well aware that, in these latter days of our own Western history, the success of our efforts to eradicate Slavery has not yet been matched by any corresponding success in our efforts to eradicate War; and if we take a comparative view of these two modern Western problems we shall notice at once that one outstanding difference between the two situations is this: in the struggle against Slavery the two new master-forces of Industrialism and Democracy were ranged on opposite sides, whereas the movement to banish War has had to contend with both forces simultaneously. For the 'drive' of Democracy, as well as the 'drive' of Industrialism, has entered into the institution of War; and this double reinforcement has intensified the evil of War enormously.

3. *The Impact of Democracy and Industrialism upon War*

The point may be illustrated from the American Civil War of A.D. 1861–5, which has just engaged our attention apropos of Slavery. In fact, though not in theory, this was a war to end Slavery, and this aim was substantially achieved by it. But the American Civil War was not a war to end War; and its significance in the history of modern Western Warfare was as ominous for the future of our Western Civilization as its role in the history of Slavery was decisive and beneficent. In putting an end to Slavery, the victory of the North in the American Civil War rid the Western World, as we have seen, of an ancient evil into which the new force of Industrialism had been breathing fresh vigour. But when we examine the means by which the North won this military victory, of which the final abolition of Slavery was the first-fruits, we observe that the North not only brought into action against Slavery the very force of Industrialism which had given Slavery itself new power; the North mobilized Democracy against Slavery as well, and it won the Civil War by employing, in combination, a number of potent new weapons which Industrialism and Democracy, between them, had placed in a belligerent's hands by the beginning of the seventh decade of the nineteenth century. The Northerners fought the Slave Power with railways and with heavy artillery; but these weapons forged by Industrialism would not have decided the issue by themselves if they had not been combined with the weapon of conscription; and conscription is a weapon that has been placed in a belligerent Government's hands by Democracy. The compulsory recruitment of man-power for 'cannon-fodder', which autocracies do not lightly attempt, becomes practicable in a democratic community when it is fighting a national war in a popular cause. The American Civil War of A.D. 1861–5 marks an epoch in the history of War because it saw the application of both the two new driving-forces—Democracy as well as Industrialism—to an ancient social evil.[1] In consequence of the introduction of the formidable new weapons which Democracy and Industrialism had forged, War had become a more terrible thing by the year 1865, when the American Civil War stopped, than it had been in 1861, when the Civil War began.[2] And so, while it is true that the abolition of Slavery was the first-fruits of the American Civil War and that this result was good, it is also true that the American Civil War had an effect in the military sphere which was profoundly evil. It carried our Western Society a long step forward in the process of 'keying up' War and thus making War a more terrible scourge than it had been in the past.

If we now cast our minds back to the state of our Western World on the eve of the emergence of Industrialism and Democracy, we shall notice that at this time, about the middle of the eighteenth century, War was in much the same condition as Slavery: it was an ancient social evil which was manifestly on the wane.

Our forebears in the eighteenth century looked back with distaste to a recent past in which War had been keyed up to an atrocious intensity by the 'drive' of sectarian Religious Fanaticism; but they also looked back with a self-complacent relief to the divorce between War and Religion which had been achieved before the end of the seventeenth century by the fathers of the Enlightenment.[3] The 'drive' of sectarian Religious Fanaticism had first entered into Western Warfare upon the break-up of the religious unity of Western Christendom in the early part of the sixteenth century;[4] and from the outbreak of the Reformation down to the end of the Thirty

[1] On the same grounds the Austro-Prussian War of A.D. 1866 is taken as a turning-point in the history of modern Western warfare in Europe by Woodward, E. L.: *War and Peace in Europe, 1815–1870* (London 1931, Constable), p. 19.

[2] One reason why the American Civil War was so perversely fruitful in the improvement of military technique was because it was mainly a war of amateurs, who were fairly representative of all the talent that the community could muster, and who were not inhibited from applying their wits to military affairs by the cramping effect of a hide-bound military tradition. The majority of our great Western wars in the Modern Age have been fought under the command of professional officers; and some instinct of self-preservation has inspired our modern Western Society to recruit its military officers from among its less able members, and then to cripple the abilities which they possess by a rigid routine. The exception which proves this rule is the school of professional officers in Prussia who won the European wars of 1864–71.

[3] For the spirit of this modern Western Enlightenment see IV. C (iii) (*b*) 12, pp. 227–8; V. C (i) (*d*) 6 (δ), Annex, vol. v, pp. 669–71; and V. C (ii) (*b*), vol. vi, pp. 316–18, below.

[4] For the remarkable similarity in êthos between the Protestant Reformation in Western Christendom and the nearly contemporary revival of Shiʿism in the Iranic World see I. C (i) (*b*), Annex I, vol. i, pp. 393–4, above.

Years' War in A.D. 1648 on the Continent—and in England down to the Restoration of the Monarchy in A.D. 1660—this demonic force had inspired most of the wars in Western Christendom and had magnified the evil of War into an unprecedented enormity. In the latter part of the seventeenth century, however, the devil of sectarian Religious Fanaticism was successfully cast out; and, although it was exorcized in a spirit of cynical disillusionment and not through the grace of a deeper religious insight, the immediate effect was to reduce the evil of War in the eighteenth century to a minimum which has never been approached in any other chapter of our Western history, either before or after, up to date.

This age of relatively 'civilized' warfare, which began when the institution of War was disconnected from the driving-force of sectarian Religious Fanaticism at the close of the seventeenth century, came to an end at the close of the eighteenth century when War began to be keyed up to an atrocious intensity once again by the new driving forces of Industrialism and Democracy which we have seen at work, two generations later, in the American Civil War. If we ask ourselves which of these two new forces has played the greater part in the intensification of War during the last hundred and fifty years, we may be inclined to attribute the more important role to Industrialism; for the mechanization of Warfare during our so-called 'machine age' has been spectacular, and the 'progress' in the Art of War since the close of the eighteenth century is popularly estimated in terms of rifles and steamships and railways and armour-plate and mammoth guns and submarines and bombing-planes and tanks. But our second thoughts remind us that the Wars of Religion in the sixteenth and seventeenth centuries came very near to wrecking our Western Civilization without any of these mechanical aids, and that a number of other civilizations—the Babylonic, the Hellenic, the Central American—have been completely successful in committing suicide through indulgence in a destructive militarism, though their technical equipment for the purpose would have seemed rudimentary even to a sixteenth-century Portuguese matchlockman. In all these cases the force which put the lethal 'drive' into War was not material but was spiritual; and in our own modern case in the Western World, where the material force of Industrialism and the spiritual force of Democracy have both been engaged in keying up our modern Western Warfare, we shall see that Democracy has been the dominant factor.

The fundamental reason why, in our world, War was less atrocious in the eighteenth century than it has been in the nineteenth and twentieth centuries is that, in the eighteenth century, when War was no longer being used as an instrument of ecclesiastical policy and had not yet begun to be used as an instrument of national policy, there was an interval during which War was merely 'the sport of kings'.

'Restricted by small numbers, poverty and the laws of honour, war became a kind of game between sovereigns. A war was a game with its rules and its stakes—a territory, an inheritance, a throne, a treaty. The loser paid,[1] but a just proportion was always kept between the value of the stake and the risks to be taken, and the parties were always on guard against the kind of obstinacy which makes a player lose his head. They tried to keep the game in hand and to know when to stop. It was for this reason that the great eighteenth-century theorists of warfare urged that neither justice, nor right, nor any of the great passions that move a people should ever be mixed up with war.'[2]

Morally, of course, the waging of War from this motive and in this spirit is profoundly shocking; for the intrinsic and inevitable waste and wickedness and misery of War, in any circumstances, are so terrible that human consciences can only condone a resort to War either in sheer self-defence or else in pursuit of some aim which is recognized to be of transcendent moral worth and social value. In most times and places this common view of the ethics of War has received lip-service, at any rate, from the statesmen by whom the wars have been made; and they have not gone to war without taking the trouble to find specious pretexts of necessity or altruism under which they could mask their underlying war-aims. Our eighteenth-century princes in the West were exceptional in the frankness with which they waged their wars as a private sport; yet it was no more possible for them than for other war-makers to ride rough-shod over the consciences of their fellow human beings; and just because, in this age, the ancient crime was openly being perpetrated as the recreation of a small number of highly privileged individuals, the players of this eighteenth-century war-game found themselves constrained to be as moderate in the conduct of their wars as they were cynical about the motives for which they made them. So long as people are persuaded that a war is being fought for the sake of religious truth or for the sake of national survival, they will throw themselves into the struggle in deadly earnest, and then there is almost no sacrifice that they will not make and almost no atrocity that they will not commit. But when War is not the absorbing business of whole churches or whole nations, but a form

1 'I have lost a battle; I will pay with a province' said the Emperor Francis Joseph (an eighteenth-century sovereign born out of due time) on the day after the Battle of Solferino in 1859 (cited by Ferrero in the work here quoted, p. 59).—A.J.T.

2 Ferrero, G.: *Peace and War*, English translation (London 1933, Macmillan), 'War: then and now', p. 7.

of recreation—and this for the entertainment of the few and not of the many—then there are fairly definite limits beyond which the privileged sportsmen cannot push their war-game with impunity. The royal players know quite well the degree of licence that their subjects will readily allow them—how much treasure they can safely squander and how much blood they can safely spill—and since they do not intend to lose their crowns for the sake of a royal pastime, they are usually careful not to exceed their measure. Hence the saving graces of eighteenth-century warfare; and though these were merely negative virtues which were based on no more solid or enduring psychological foundations than an 'enlightened self-interest' and a studied imperviousness to 'enthusiasm' (a twentieth-century virtue which was an eighteenth-century vice),[1] they did produce considerable practical benefits while they lasted.

A list of the most obvious of these saving graces makes an imposing catalogue. For example, eighteenth-century armies were not recruited by conscription; eighteenth-century armies did not live off the country like their predecessors in the Wars of Religion,[2] nor did they wipe the country out of existence like the armies in the War of A.D. 1914–18; eighteenth-century commanders observed the rules of the military game;[3] eighteenth-century Governments set themselves moderate objectives and did not impose crushing peace terms upon defeated opponents.

On the capital question of conscription it will be sufficient to cite the opinion of the most eminent of the royal players of the eighteenth-century war-game, Frederick the Great. In describing the

[1] The monarchs and aristocracies who ruled the states of the Western World before the outbreak of the French Revolution 'could fight each other without excessive animosity. . . . A nation at war must . . . *hate* the enemy, which means that it must be convinced that it is defending the most righteous of causes against the most infamous aggression.' After the Revolution, 'in the non-professional soldier, passion replaced professional training; myths became weapons as necessary as cannon and muskets' (Ferrero, G.: *Peace and War*, English translation (London 1933, Macmillan), 'War: then and now', pp. 57–8 and p. 9).

[2] On this point see Ferrero, G.: op. cit., p. 5. The author points out (p. 4) that in the Thirty Years' War, when the armies were still living off the peasantry in the German theatre of operations, they were already living on a commissariat in Flanders and Catalonia.

[3] The 'complicated and cunning rules' of eighteenth-century warfare, 'which it is so hard for us to understand to-day, form one of those peaks of human evolution which Man painfully attains from time to time, and on which he stays but for a moment, to slide back once more into imperfection' (Ferrero, op. cit., p. 54). The Italian historian's point is borne out by the following words of a contemporary French soldier who was the greatest authority of his own age on the Art of War: 'La vieille escrime, les méthodes surannées, pour nous, à cette époque-ci de l'histoire, au milieu de l'Europe qui nous entoure, c'est cette guerre sans solution décisive, à but restreint, guerre de manœuvres sans combat' (Foch, Marshal F.: *Des Principes de la Guerre*, fourth edition (Paris–Nancy 1917, Berger-Levrault), p. 26). Marshal Foch proceeds (op. cit., p. 27) to quote the Maréchal de Saxe: 'Je ne suis point pour les batailles, surtout au début d'une guerre. Je suis persuadé même qu'un habile général pourra la faire toute sa vie sans s'y voir obligé.' It will be noticed that the British Museum copy of Marshal Foch's book, from which these quotations were taken, was printed under fire of German guns.

reign of his own father and predecessor, King Frederick William I of Prussia, Frederick the Great remarks that

'This régime was wholly military. The size of the Army was increased; and, in the ardour of the first enrolments, some artisans were taken for soldiers. This spread terror among the rest, and a number of them ran away, and this unforeseen accident did considerable damage to our manufactures. The King stepped in to remedy this abuse, and he devoted himself with particular care to the re-establishment and the progress of Industry.'[1]

It will be seen that even such notorious eighteenth-century militarists as Frederick William I and Frederick the Great regarded the conscription of artisans as an abuse which no monarch in his senses would countenance.[2]

The eighteenth-century punctiliousness over fine points of the military game may be illustrated by the famous legend of the encounter between the English Guards and the French Guards at the Battle of Fontenoy in the War of the Austrian Succession. When the Red Line and the White Line had approached one another to within point-blank range, an English officer is said to have stepped forward from the ranks, made his bow to the enemy, and cried: 'Gentlemen of the French Guards, fire first!' Obviously the Guards could not have afforded to indulge in these courtesies if a precocious Industrial Revolution had enabled King George and King Louis to equip their toy-soldiers with Bren guns instead of muzzle-loading smooth-bore muskets; but it is equally obvious that, even if the French and English troops had been armed, in A.D. 1745, with weapons that were no more formidable than those of Cortez's Aztec adversaries, and could thus have exchanged their courtesies with almost complete material impunity, they would not have exchanged them, even so, if they had not been acting as 'living chessmen' but had been fighting in deadly earnest for causes which they personally had at heart.

[1] Frederick the Great: *Des Mœurs, des Coutumes, de l'Industrie, des Progrès de l'Esprit Humain dans les Arts et dans les Sciences sous la Dynastie des Hohenzollern.*

[2] Like so many of the eighteenth-century virtues, this self-restraint that was practised by an eighteenth-century Prussian militarism was inspired, not by goodness, but by common sense. The reason why the Prussian artisan was exempted from a conscription to which the Prussian serf was subject was because the King of Prussia wanted to play the militarist efficiently and had the intelligence to realize that, for the waging of war in semi-civilized societies, man-power is of no avail without money-power to back it. This hard fact had set a problem to Prussian statesmanship in an age when Prussia was still poor while warfare was already expensive; and the predecessors of Frederick William I had sought to solve this problem on lines which, in the Hellenic World of the sixth century B.C., had been followed by the Athenian statesman Solon with a view to remedying the natural poverty of Attica. Like Solon, the Prussian Government had encouraged the immigration of skilled artisans from abroad, on the calculation that their labours would increase the income of the community and that there would be a proportionate increase in the yield of taxation (see Bruford, W. H.: *Germany in the Eighteenth Century* (Cambridge 1935, University Press), pp. 157, 173, and 174).

The punctiliousness of these eighteenth-century soldiers towards one another was matched by the consideration which they usually displayed towards the civilian population, and by the care which they usually took to avoid inflicting serious injury upon the permanent capital equipment of social life in the war-zone. In this they were animated by that blend of discretion and good feeling and sheer delight in *expertise* which moves the sportsman riding to hounds to enjoy the pleasure of a cross-country gallop at the least possible cost in damage to the farmers' gates and fences. The attitude of eighteenth-century war-makers on this point comes to light in the almost unanimous and unmistakably genuine indignation to which they were moved by the few flagrant breaches of the rule: for example, by the devastation of the Palatinate by Louis XIV in A.D. 1674 and 1689 and the devastation of the Neumark and burning of Cüstrin by the Russian Army in A.D. 1758. The latter of these atrocities was written off as a not incomprehensible lapse in the manners of barbarians who had only recently been admitted into the polite society of the West. The misconduct of the *Roi Soleil*, who had more or less established his pretension to be the luminary of the Western social universe, gave the lesser lights a greater moral shock.[1]

The moderateness of the objects for which the eighteenth-

[1] It is interesting to find evidence of a similar considerateness towards the civilian population in the conduct of War in the Hellenic World in a period of Hellenic history when War was for a time 'the sport of kings' instead of being the serious business of the citizens of city-states. This evidence is furnished, retrospectively and incidentally, by Polybius in a passage (Book XVIII, ch. 3) describing a conference—held in Malis before the decisive campaign in the Second Romano-Macedonian War (200–197 B.C.)—which was attended by King Philip V of Macedon on the one side and the Roman commander T. Quinctius Flamininus, accompanied by representatives of the Greek allies of Rome, on the other:

'When Phaenias, the General of the Aetolian Confederacy, had finished speaking, he was followed by Alexander surnamed Isius, who enjoyed a reputation as an able speaker and man of affairs. Alexander complained that Philip was neither making peace sincerely now nor in the habit of making war honourably when war was the order of the day. Just as his method in conferences and conversations was to lay ambushes and watch for opportunities and behave exactly like a belligerent, so in war itself he followed an immoral and extremely dishonourable line of conduct. He abandoned any attempt to face his opponents in the field, but signalised his flight by burning and plundering the towns—a policy of avenging defeat by ruining the prizes of the victors. What an utter contrast to the standards observed by his predecessors on the throne of Macedon! These sovereigns had fought one another continuously in the open country but had rarely destroyed and wrecked the towns. This was a fact of general knowledge, established by the war which Alexander the Great waged against Darius for the empire of Asia and again by the struggle of Alexander's successors over his inheritance, when they fought Antigonus in coalition for the possession of Asia. Moreover, the policy of the successors in the second generation, down to Pyrrhus, had been the same. They were ready enough to stake their fortunes in battle in the open country and they left nothing undone in their efforts to overcome one another by force of arms, but they used to spare the towns in order that the victors might enjoy the dominion over them and might receive due honours at the hands of their subjects. On the other hand, to destroy the objects of contention in the war while leaving the war itself in existence was the act of a madman and of one far gone in the malady; yet that was precisely what Philip was doing now. In the course of his forced march from the pass in Epirus Philip had wrecked in Thessaly more towns whose friend and ally he professed to be than had ever been wrecked by any Power with whom the Thessalians were at war.'

century wars were waged may be illustrated by an incidental remark of a great eighteenth-century historian, Edward Gibbon.

'In War', Gibbon observes in a famous passage of *The History of the Decline and Fall of the Roman Empire*,[1] 'the European forces are exercised by temperate and undecisive contests. The Balance of Power will continue to fluctuate, and the prosperity of our own or the neighbouring kingdoms may be alternately exalted or depressed; but these partial events cannot essentially injure our general state of happiness, the system of arts and laws and manners, which so advantageously distinguish, above the rest of Mankind, the Europeans and their colonists.'

In quoting this passage at an earlier point in this Study[2] we have noticed already that Gibbon appears to have passed these words for publication some time during the first quarter of the year 1781,[3]

1 Chap. xxxviii, *ad finem*: 'General Observations on the Fall of the Roman Empire in the West.'

2 In III. C (ii) (*b*), vol. iii, p. 311, above. It is quoted again in IV. C. (iii) (*b*) 5, in the present volume, p. 189, in IV. C (iii) (*c*) 2 (α), p. 283, and in V. C (i) (*d*) 6 (γ), Annex I, vol. v, p. 625, footnote 1, below.

3 In this other context it has been suggested that the passage was not merely passed for publication some time during the first quarter of the year 1781, but was actually written at that date. That the passage was passed for publication in the first quarter of 1781 would seem to be a legitimate inference from the preface to volumes ii and iii of *The Decline and Fall*, since this is dated Bentinck Street, the 1st March, 1781. On the other hand the assumption that the 'General Observations on the Fall of the Roman Empire in the West' were written later than the rest of volumes ii and iii, and only just before the writing of the preface, rested on the supposition that the different parts of *The Decline and Fall* were originally drafted in the order in which they were eventually published; and this supposition is not only unproven; it is definitely in conflict with such evidence as there is for the original date of composition of the 'Observations', at any rate.

In the opinion of one of the chief living authorities on the subject, Mr. G. M. Young, 'the conclusion of the third volume was in draft before the first volume was written' (Young, G. M.: *Gibbon* (London 1932, Davies), p. 93); and Mr. Young has been kind enough to communicate to the writer of this Study, in a letter of the 13th July, 1937, the evidence on which his opinion is based.

'(i) Gibbon began *The Decline and Fall* in the winter of 1772–3 (Gibbon, E.: *The Memoirs of the Life of Edward Gibbon, with Various Observations and Excursions by Himself*, edited by Hill, G. B. (London 1900, Methuen), p. 187); (ii) he made very slow progress at first (op. cit., p. 189); (iii) Louis XVI acceded to the French throne on the 10th May, 1774; (iv) the first volume of *The Decline and Fall* was finished in the winter of 1775–6 and was published in February 1776 (op. cit., p. 195); therefore the first volume was not written by the 10th May, 1774; but (v) the Arcadius and Honorius passage in the "Observations", which Louis XVI was supposed to have resented, was "written before his accession to the throne" (Gibbon's Memoir of the 2nd March, 1791); (vi) this passage is really integral to the whole reasoning of the "General Observations" (the federation of modern Europe and the variety within the fabric); *ergo*: the concluding observations were *drafted* before the first volume was *written*. For a closer date, what do you say to the partition of Poland in 1772 between Julian and Semiramis?'

In the inquiry to which this letter was a reply, the writer of the present Study had called attention to one passage in the 'Observations' which wears the appearance of having been written after the outbreak of the American Revolutionary War:

'Whatever may be the changes of their political situation, they [i.e. the European settlers in America] must preserve the manners of Europe; and we may reflect with some pleasure that the English language will probably be diffused over an immense and populous continent.'

On this Mr. Young comments, in the letter above quoted:

'Enough had happened [by the year 1772] to make a thoughtful man wonder what the future of the American colonies might be—though of course Gibbon may well have put in that *caveat* as an afterthought when he revised his draft observations in 1782 [*sic*: ? for 1781]. This seems the more likely as it occurs in a footnote. Gibbon always

when the author's own country happened to be engaged in fighting a losing battle. At that moment the American Revolutionary War was approaching its crisis. His Britannic Majesty was at war with France and Spain and Holland, as well as with the thirteen insurgent American colonies; the Northern Powers of Europe were maintaining an unfriendly 'armed neutrality'; and the decisive campaign of the war, which was to end at Yorktown so disastrously for British arms, was about to open! And yet Gibbon's confidence was justified in the event by the peace settlement of A.D. 1783. In the American Revolutionary War Great Britain was eventually defeated by an overwhelming coalition of opposing forces; but her opponents did not think of crushing her. They had been fighting for the limited and precise objective of establishing the insurgent colonies' independence of the British Crown—the colonists because, for them, this independence was an end in itself, and the colonists' French allies because, in the estimation of a refined French statesmanship, the secession of the thirteen American colonies from the British Empire would just suffice to restore a Balance of Power which had been unduly inclined in Great Britain's favour by the cumulative effect of successive British victories in three previous wars. In A.D. 1783, when the victory was once more with the French for the first time in nearly a hundred years, French statesmanship was content to attain a minimum objective with a maximum economy of means. No rancorous memory of previous reverses tempted the French Government to seize this opportunity for paying off old scores. They were not even tempted to fight on for the dis-annexation of Canada, the principal American dominion of the French Crown, which had been conquered by the British Crown during the Seven Years' War and had been officially ceded by King Louis to King George in the peace settlement of A.D. 1763, only twenty years back. In the peace settlement of A.D. 1783 Canada was left in the British Crown's possession by a victorious France; and Great Britain, let off with the loss of her thirteen colonies, could congratulate herself, in Gibbonian language, upon having survived, without shipwreck, a fluctuation in the Balance of Power in which her turn had come to see her prosperity depressed, but in which no essential injury had been done to the general state of happiness of a polite society which was the common spiritual home of the subjects of King George and the subjects of King Louis.

thought in paragraphs and used the footnote as a sort of tool-shed for odds and ends which would have spoiled their shape.'

For the reminiscence, in this particular footnote, of an observation in a private letter which Gibbon had received in 1767 from Hume, see V. C (i) (*d*) 6 (γ), Annex II, in vol. v, p. 644, below.

These illustrations may suffice to display the saving graces of eighteenth-century warfare;[1] and at the same time they reveal the precariousness of this temporary alleviation of an ancient social evil.[2] The unenthusiastically enlightened soul of *Homo Tricornifer* remained smugly content with having bowed the unclean spirit of Ecclesiastical Fanaticism out of the house; and so, when the new-born spirits of Democracy and Industrialism presented themselves at the door a hundred years later, they found the house empty, swept, and garnished, and it was the easiest thing in the world for them to enter in and dwell there. The society which had sought to minimize the evil of War by the cynical expedient of treating it as 'the sport of kings' was incapable of preserving it from the intrusion of two new social forces which re-imported into War the deadly earnestness of an earlier age. And so the last state of this society has been worse than the first.[3] In the nineteenth and twentieth centuries of the Christian Era the new double 'drive' of Democracy and Industrialism has been keying up the scourge of War towards the pitch of enormity which it attained in the sixteenth and seventeenth centuries through the impetus of Ecclesiastical Fanaticism.

In A.D. 1790 the French National Assembly was warned by the prophetic voice of Mirabeau that a representative parliamentary body was likely to prove more bellicose than a monarch.[4] In A.D.

[1] 'Une humanité nouvelle qu'on a introduite dans le fléau de la guerre, et qui en adoucit les horreurs, a contribué . . . à sauver les peuples de la destruction qui semble les menacer à chaque instant. C'est un mal, à la vérité, très-déplorable, que cette multitude de soldats entretenus continuellement par tous les princes; mais aussi . . . ce mal produit un bien: les peuples ne se mêlent point de la guerre que font leurs maîtres; les citoyens des villes assiégées passent souvent d'une domination à une autre, sans qu'il en ait coûté la vie à un seul habitant; ils sont seulement le prix de celui qui a eu le plus de soldats, de canons et d'argent' (Voltaire: *Essai sur les Mœurs, ad fin.*).

[2] 'Happy eighteenth century, which had only humane weapons, small forces and limited funds at its command in warfare. . . . Restricted warfare was one of the loftiest achievements of the eighteenth century. It belongs to the class of hot-house plants which can only thrive in an aristocratic and qualitative civilization. We are no longer capable of it. It is one of the fine things which we have lost as a result of the French Revolution' (Ferrero, op. cit., pp. 63–4).

[3] Matt. xii. 43–5.

[4] 'Je vous demande à vous-mêmes: sera-t-on mieux assuré de n'avoir que des guerres justes, équitables, si l'on délègue exclusivement à une assemblée de 700 personnes l'exercice du droit de faire la guerre? Avez-vous prévu jusqu'où les mouvemens passionnés, jusqu'où l'exaltation du courage et d'une fausse dignité pourroient porter et justifier l'imprudence. . .? Pendant qu'un des membres proposera de délibérer, on demandera la guerre à grands cris; vous verrez autour de vous une armée de citoyens. Vous ne serez pas trompés par des ministres; ne le serez-vous jamais par vous-mêmes? . . . Voyez les peuples libres; c'est par des guerres plus ambitieuses, plus barbares qu'ils se sont toujours distingués. Voyez les assemblées politiques; c'est toujours sous le charme de la passion qu'elles ont décrété la guerre' (Mirabeau in the French National Assembly on the 20th May, 1790).

In this matter the statesman Mirabeau showed a clearer vision than the philosopher Volney, whose eighteenth-century complacency on the subject of War was apparently still unshaken in 1791, to judge by the following passage of *Les Ruines*, which was published in that year:

'Si les guerres sont devenues plus vastes dans leurs masses, elles ont été moins meurtrières dans leurs détails; si les peuples y ont porté moins de personnalité, moins

1792, less than ten years after the statesmanlike peace settlement of 1783, the menacing accents of a Democracy conscripted for War were heard by Goethe's sensitive ears in the cannonade at Valmy;[1] and the *levée en masse* of a Revolutionary France[2] swept away the eighteenth-century régime in Germany, to clear the arena for the German riposte of the *Befreiungskrieg*.[3] By the seventh decade of the nineteenth century,[4] which saw the new note of the Revolu-

d'énergie, leur lutte a été moins sanguinaire, moins acharnée. Ils ont été moins libres, mais moins turbulents; plus amollis, mais plus pacifiques.'

Considering the time and place of publication, we must pronounce the writer singularly blind to the signs of the times. For evidence of Volney's subsequent awakening see IV. C (iii) (*b*) 4, p. 161, footnote 2, below.

[1] 'So war der Tag hingegangen; unbeweglich standen die Franzosen, Kellermann hatte auch einen bequemeren Platz genommen; unsere Leute zog man aus dem Feuer zurück, und es war eben als wenn nichts gewesen wäre. Die grösste Bestürzung verbreitete sich über die Armee. Noch am Morgen hatte man nicht anders gedacht als die sämmtlichen Franzosen anzuspiessen und aufzuspeisen, ja mich selbst hatte das unbedingte Vertrauen auf ein solches Heer, auf den Herzog von Braunschweig, zu Theilnahme an dieser gefährlichen Expedition gelockt; nun aber ging jeder vor sich hin, man sah sich nicht an, oder wenn es geschah, so war es um zu fluchen oder zu verwünschen. Wir hatten, eben als es Nacht werden wollte, zufällig einen Kreis geschlossen, in dessen Mitte nicht einmal wie gewöhnlich ein Feuer konnte angezündet werden; die meisten schwiegen, einige sprachen, und es fehlte doch eigentlich einem jeden Besinnung und Urtheil. Endlich rief man mich auf was ich dazu denke — denn ich hatte die Schaar gewöhnlich mit kurzen Sprüchen erheitert und erquickt. Diessmal sagte ich: "Von hier und heute geht eine neue Epoche der Weltgeschichte aus, und ihr könnt sagen ihr seyd dabei gewesen"' (Goethe: *Campagne in Frankreich*, Den 19 bis 22 September 1792).

[2] In this French *levée en masse* we can perceive the emergence of the 'totalitarian' conception of the modern Western state.

'Que voulez-vous?' asks Barère in his *Rapport fait au nom du Comité de Salut Publique sur la réquisition civique de tous les Français pour la défense de la Patrie* (Séance du 23 août 1793): 'Un contingent . . .? Le contingent de la France pour sa liberté comprend toute sa population, toute son industrie, tous ses travaux, tout son génie. . . . Publions une grande vérité: la liberté est devenue créancière de tous les citoyens; les uns lui doivent leur industrie, les autres leur fortune, ceux-ci leurs conseils, ceux-là leurs bras; tous lui doivent le sang qui coule dans leurs veines.'

Thus, at one stroke of baleful magic, the French state is transformed from a public utility into a goddess. The first article of the draft law which was introduced by Barrère's report runs as follows:

'Dès ce moment jusqu'à celui où les ennemis auront été chassés du territoire de la République, tous les Français sont en réquisition permanente pour le service des armées. Les jeunes gens iront au combat; les hommes mariés forgeront les armes et transporteront les subsistances; les femmes feront des tentes, des habits, et serviront dans les hôpitaux; les enfans mettront le vieux linge en charpie; les vieillards se feront porter sur les places publiques pour exciter le courage des guerriers, prêcher la haine des rois et l'unité de la République.'

This article so deeply thrilled the deputies that they begged the rapporteur to recite it twice over; and each time it was cheered to the echo by men who sincerely believed that they were liberating themselves from Tyranny! For the fallacy of the view that a state is a 'whole' of which the parts are human beings see III. C (ii) (*a*), vol. iii, pp. 219–23, above. A twentieth-century French master of the Art of War remarks that the French Revolution 'osa . . . opposer victorieusement aux armées minutieusement et rigidement instruites de la vieille Europe, les bandes inexpérimentées de la levée en masse qu'animaient par contre de violentes passions' (Foch, Marshal F.: *Des Principes de la Guerre*, 4th edition (Paris–Nancy 1917, Berger-Levrault), p. 25).

[3] In the nineteenth century it was the Prussian and not the French General Staff that took to heart and systematically applied the lesson of the French *levée en masse* which had been improvised in A.D. 1793 by the Committee of Public Safety (see footnote 4, below).

[4] Ferrero points out (op. cit., p. 11) that, except in Prussia, the 'totalitarian' system of warfare which had been substituted for the restricted eighteenth-century system in the French *levée en masse* was not applied completely in any country—not even in its mother-country France—during the years 1815–70. During that period all the

tionary and Napoleonic Wars raised to a still higher pitch in the American Civil War and in Bismarck's three Prussian wars of aggrandizement, the terrible consequences that were latent in the application to War of the new driving-power which Industrialism and Democracy had imported into human affairs might already have been discerned by an acute observer. As we can see now in retrospect, the issue which stares our own generation in the face was actually confronting our grandfathers. They could not afford to rest content any longer with the negative eighteenth-century policy of leaving War to die gradually of inanition after turning it into a triviality; for by A.D. 1871 War was not 'the sport of kings' any longer. It had become the serious business of peoples who were inspired with all the enthusiasm that Democracy could excite and were armed with all the weapons that Industrialism could forge;[1] and in these circumstances there was a choice between taking active steps to put an end to War altogether, or else seeing it rankle into an enormity without precedent in our Western history.

If the experience of the wars of 1861–71 had evoked an anti-war movement of anything like the same intensity and persistence as

Continental European countries except Prussia applied a system, devised in France, which was a compromise between the Revolutionary innovation and the eighteenth-century tradition. Under this transitional system the obligation to perform compulsory military service was universal, but less than one-fifth of the total annual contingent of potential conscripts was actually levied; this fraction was taken by lot; any one on whom the lot fell was allowed to contract out of his obligation if he could afford to pay for a satisfactory substitute; and the men who were finally enrolled were kept with the colours for seven years—a term of service which was long enough to allow them to be formed into semi-professional soldiers. On the other hand, Prussia (op. cit., p. 13) was already applying a system of universal compulsory military service on a three years' term during this post-Waterloo period—thus anticipating by half a century the adoption of an unmitigatedly 'totalitarian' system in other states.

1 Marshal Foch (op. cit., pp. 29–30) formulates 'l'antithèse des deux époques' in the following terms:

'D'un côté, exploitation à l'extrême des masses humaines, animées de passions ardentes, absorbant toutes les activités de la société. . . . De l'autre côté, au contraire (XVIIIe siècle), exploitation régulière et méthodique de ces parties matérielles qui deviennent les bases de systèmes différents . . . tendant toujours . . . à régir l'emploi des troupes, en vue de ménager l'armée, capital du souverain, indifférente d'ailleurs à la cause pour laquelle elle se bat, mais non dépourvue de vertus professionnelles, d'esprit et d'honneur militaires en particulier.'

The French soldier's antithesis between eignteenth-century and twentieth-century warfare has been translated into general terms by a French philosopher:

'On peut . . . voir des exercices préparatoires ou des jeux dans la plupart des guerres enregistrées par l'histoire. . . . En revanche, si l'on place à côté des querelles accidentelles les guerres décisives, qui aboutirent à l'anéantissement d'un peuple, on comprend que celles-ci furent la raison d'être de celles-là. . . . De ce nombre sont les guerres d'aujourd'hui. . . . Plus de délégation à un nombre restreint de soldats chargés de représenter la nation. Plus rien qui ressemble à un duel. Il faut que tous se battent contre tous, comme firent les hordes des premiers temps. Seulement on se bat avec les armes forgées par notre civilisation' (Bergson, H.: *Les Deux Sources de la Morale et de la Religion* (Paris 1932, Alcan), pp. 307–8 and 309–10).

The Italian historian whom we have quoted above points out that, after the change inaugurated by the French Revolution, the Art of War in the West discarded both its two characteristic eighteenth-century elegances: 'The aim of manœuvres was no longer to avoid battles, but to provoke them so as to hasten the decisive result. . . . Once again, as in the sixteenth century, armies lived by pillage or requisition' (Ferrero, op. cit., p. 9).

the anti-slavery movement which had been set on foot before the end of the eighteenth century, then our position to-day might perhaps have been more favourable than it actually is. It happened, however, that the crop of wars in the seventh decade of the nineteenth century was followed, like the General War of 1792–1815, by half a century of general peace, which was only broken by a few local wars of a semi-colonial character: the Russo-Turkish War of 1877–8; the Spanish-American War of 1898; the South African War of 1899–1902; the Russo-Japanese War of 1904–5. These latter wars at the turn of the nineteenth and twentieth centuries did not afford much new insight into the general tendency of warfare in the Western World in this age, because they were fought between not more than two belligerents in each case, and not in any instance in regions lying near the heart of the Western World. Hence the terrible transformation in the character of War which had been brought about by the introduction of the new driving-power of Industrialism and Democracy took our generation by surprise in 1914. This time the shock has been so profound that an eager and active movement for the abolition of War has followed the Armistice of 1918. But this movement is gravely handicapped by its belated birth on the morrow of the World War, when it should have been born in 1871 or, better still, in 1815.[1]

Our contemporary effort to abolish War by the organization of an international system of 'collective security' will be so familiar to readers of this Study that it would be superfluous to give any account of it here. It need only be pointed out that the aim of the system—an aim which inspires both the Covenant of the League of Nations and the Kellogg-Briand Pact (or Multilateral Treaty of Paris for the Renunciation of War as an Instrument of National Policy)—is the pacific, even though belated, abolition of War through a free agreement and voluntary co-operation between all the fully self-governing states in the contemporary world. Whether this movement will succeed in its purpose is a question which lies to-day on the knees of the Gods. At this stage we can only be sure that, in our Western World, War will now be abolished sooner or later by one means or another. If it is not abolished in the near future by the method of pacific adjustment, then it is certain to be abolished—and this in a future which may not be much more remote—by the alternative method of 'the knock-out blow', in which a war—or a series of wars—of attrition will end in the decisive and

[1] Our twentieth-century movement for the abolition of War is an outgrowth of one of the two antithetical reactions against the eighteenth-century conception of War as 'the sport of kings' (see IV. C (iii) (c) 3 (α), Annex, pp. 643–7, below); but it has been markedly slower in coming to maturity than the rival movement, which has set itself, not to abolish war, but to salvage it by re-converting it into the serious business of peoples.

definitive victory of one single Power through the annihilation of all the rest.

The picture of this war of attrition as it will be fought—if it should be fought—to-morrow is so vividly present in all living minds that there is no need in this place to dwell on the hideous details of mechanical warfare and chemical warfare and submarine warfare and aerial warfare and their probable combined result: that is to say, the wholesale annihilation, by starvation and by high explosives and poison gas, of the civilian populations which the eighteenth-century militarists took pains to spare. To indicate the consummation which the Art of War is rapidly approaching in our time, it is sufficient to remind ourselves of a piece of legislation which has been passed in France; for the French, with characteristic clear-sightedness, have envisaged the character of future warfare and have taken what steps they can in order to be prepared for it. They have realized that another war, if it comes, will engulf everything and everybody; and so they have passed legislation for the general organization of French national resources and French national life in war-time.

On the 7th March, 1927, a drastic bill for this purpose, which was sponsored by the Socialist statesman Monsieur Paul-Boncour, was voted by the Chamber of Deputies unanimously, with the sole exception of the Communist members. At this stage the bill provided for the conscription of wealth and the conscription of intellect as well as the conscription of man-power; and though some of these provisions were pruned away before the bill passed the Senate on the 17th February, 1928, the essence of the bill survived and duly passed into law, while the pre-suppositions on which it was based were elucidated and endorsed by the Senate's rapporteur on the bill, Monsieur Klotz, in the report in which he recommended his colleagues to accept the bill in the modified form in which it was eventually enacted.

'The conception of *la guerre totale*, which is the formula that we have to envisage in the future and the formula to which the organization that we contemplate must respond (and on this point your Army Commission is in complete agreement with the authors of the bill)—this conception condemns the peoples who to-morrow may find themselves engaged in a fresh conflict to find that their efforts can no longer be limited to the action of armed masses, but that they must be ready to throw into the battle, in order to snatch victory out of it, the totality of their forces and their resources. Their duty is to attain superiority in means of warfare up to the maximum degree; and, in pursuing this aim, they will never be able to allow themselves to relax, since none can feel sure that he is strong enough so long as he has the possibility of being still stronger than he is already.'

This is the enormity into which the not altogether intolerable evil of eighteenth-century warfare has been fatally transformed by the combined impact of Democracy and Industrialism. Democracy has turned 'the sport of kings' into the deadly earnest of peoples who now throw themselves into the wars of Nationality as passionately as their sixteenth- and seventeenth-century forebears once threw themselves into the wars of Religion.[1] Industrialism has converted the entire material wealth of a belligerent community into *matériel de guerre*, and has at the same time enabled and compelled a belligerent Government to mobilize the entire working population of the belligerent country. The men and women who produce the supplies and munitions in the interior are as indispensable for the waging of the war, and as strongly imbued with the spirit of it, as the soldiers at the front. Both technically and morally, they have ceased to be non-combatants and have therefore become fair targets for enemy attack. And at the moment when the carefully guarded eighteenth-century distinction between civilians and *militaires* has thus broken down, the economic unification of the World and the practical application of Physical Science to the Art of War have placed in an enemy's hands two potent weapons—the economic blockade and the aerial bombing raid—for developing the old-fashioned 'war of fronts', in which belligerency was a limited liability, into a new-fangled 'war of areas', in which the whole territory, equipment, and population of an enemy country becomes a direct object of hostile operations.

This 'totalitarian' kind of warfare, which is the antithesis of the eighteenth-century 'sport of kings' both in its spirit and in its social consequences,[2] is the only kind of warfare that it is open to us any longer to wage now that the ancient institution of War has received a fresh and unprecedentedly powerful impetus from the impact of the new social forces of Democracy and Industrialism. In this situation we have the single choice between abolishing War through peaceful agreement or allowing War to abolish itself through a 'knock-out blow'; and the destiny of our Western Civilization depends upon which of these two alternatives we in our generation choose.

1 'Une ère nouvelle s'était ouverte, celle des guerres nationales aux allures déchaînées, parce qu'elles allaient consacrer à la lutte toutes les ressources de la nation . . . parce qu'elles allaient ainsi mettre en jeu l'intérêt et les moyens de chacun des soldats, par suite, des sentiments, des passions, c'est-à-dire des éléments de force, jusqu'alors inexploités. . . . La nouvelle guerre est partie; on va désormais se battre avec les cœurs des soldats' (Foch, op. cit., pp. 28–9). In a footnote to this passage the author recalls that 'dans le passé déjà, c'étaient les guerres de religion, guerres pour les idées, qui avaient amené les luttes les plus violentes'.

2 'When it took on its new pace and pressure, War increased the effectiveness of the means at its disposal, but at the same time lost the power to achieve its proper purpose, which is peace' (Ferrero, op. cit., p. 126).

4. *The Impact of Democracy and Industrialism upon Parochial Sovereignty*

We have now looked at the effects of the impact of the two dominant social forces of the last age of Western history upon two ancient institutions—War and Slavery—and our inquiry has brought to light the fact that, while the effect of Industrialism upon both these institutions has been the same, the effect of Democracy has been apparently inconsistent—and indeed contradictory—in the two cases. Whereas the advent of Industrialism has intensified the evil of War and the evil of Slavery alike, Democracy appears to have worked as a mitigating influence upon Slavery and as an aggravating influence upon War. What is the explanation of this apparent inconsistency? And how is it possible, *a priori*, for Democracy to act as an anti-social force? For Democracy 'breathes the spirit of the Gospels . . . and its motive-force is Love'.[1]

One possible explanation might be found in the well-known faculty of the human spirit for 'departmentalizing' its field of action and for acting, thinking, and feeling quite inconsistently in regard to different parts of this arbitrarily and artificially divided whole. In the case of Slavery and Democracy, for example, an extreme inconsistency was exhibited, in entire good faith, by the Virginian slave-owners who were moved to a genuine democratic indignation at the tyranny of a George III or an Abraham Lincoln,[2] and by the Attic slave-owners who gave their lives to vindicate the liberty of all free Hellenes against the tyrannous ambitions of the Achaemenidae.[3] It did not occur to the Virginian patriots—'Bible

[1] Bergson, Henri: *Les Deux Sources de la Morale et de la Religion* (Paris 1932, Alcan), pp. 304–5, quoted in this Study already in Part I. A, vol. i, p. 9, above.

[2] *Sic Semper Tyrannis* was the official motto of the State of Virginia; and the words were declaimed by Lincoln's Southern murderer from the stage of the theatre at Washington on to which the criminal leapt after having inflicted a mortal wound upon the liberator of the Southern slaves.

[3] In fairness to the Athenians it must be noted that at Athens, in the great age of the Athenian democracy in the fifth century B.C., the domestic slaves who were in direct personal relations with their masters, and with their masters' fellow freemen, were very much more humanely treated than the Helots in contemporary Laconia (for the treatment of the Helots by their Spartan masters see II. D (vi), vol. ii, p. 233, footnote 4, and III. A, vol. iii, pp. 65–6, above). For this contrast between the two treatments we have the convincing testimony of a contemporary Athenian witness—the anonymous author of the pseudo-Xenophontic *Institutions of Athens* (chap. i, quoted in V. C (i) (*d*) 6 (α), vol. v, pp. 451–2, below)—who was no admirer of the Athenian democracy either in this respect or in any other.

'Slaves . . . and permanently domiciled aliens enjoy an extreme degree of licence at Athens, where it is illegal to assault them and where the slave will not make way for you. The reason why this is the local custom shall be explained. If it were legal for the slave—or the alien or the freedman—to be struck by the free citizen, your Athenian citizen himself would always have been getting hit through being mistaken for a slave. The free proletariat at Athens are no better dressed than the slaves and aliens, and no more respectable in appearance. If any reader is surprised at the further fact that at Athens they allow the slaves to live in luxury and in some instances to keep up an imposing establishment, it would not be difficult to demonstrate the good sense of their policy in this point as well. The fact is that, in any country that maintains a naval establishment

Christians' though they might be—to take to heart the Parable of the Unmerciful Servant; and it is unlikely that any Athenian patriot who gave his life for freedom at Marathon or Salamis ever saw himself, *vis-à-vis* his own slaves, in the light of a petty-Darius or petty-Xerxes.[1] A similar psychological 'departmentalism' might possibly explain how the spirit of Democracy could come into our modern Western World without ranging itself against War as it has actually ranged itself against Slavery. Yet this negative explanation cannot account for the fact that, in our case, as we have noticed above, Democracy has not merely failed to work against War, but has positively put its 'drive' into War and has done still more than the sister force of Industrialism has done to key our Western warfare up from the low tension of the eighteenth-century 'sport of kings' to the enormity of 'la guerre totale'. In thus aggravating the evils of War, Democracy has been working in direct opposition to its own spirit, and it is hardly conceivable that it would have thus reversed its natural action if it had collided with War, as it collided

[and where the rich are therefore heavily taxed to foot the bill—A.J.T.], it is essential for slaves to bring in money by their services, in order that I [the master] may receive at least the royalties on the profits of my slave's labour; and this involves [eventual] manumission. In a country, however, in which wealthy slaves exist, it is no longer desirable that my slave should be afraid of you—as he is, for example, in Lacedaemon. If your slave is afraid of me, that fact will keep him under a perpetual threat of having to stand and deliver his own money [to me as blackmail]. This is the reason why we have put our slaves on a social equality with our freemen.'

Here we see in embryo the pert and pampered domestic slaves of fourth-century and third-century Athens whose Roman successors learnt to manage an Emperor's household, and thereby to rule the Hellenic *Orbis Terrarum*, in the names of a Claudius and a Nero. This unseemly practical reversal of the juridical relations between slave and master was the nemesis of a democratic humanitarianism when this right attitude towards human relations, having failed to sweep Slavery away, was imported into a traditional institution which was essentially wrong in itself. A more healthy outcome of Athenian equalitarianism was the parity in the wages paid to slaves and freemen who were employed on the same work (a parity which is strikingly apparent in the inscribed monetary accounts for certain Athenian public works which our modern Western archaeologists have brought to light). It is true that the freeman's wage which was earned by the Athenian slave-artisan went into the pocket of the slave's master and not into the pocket of the slave-worker himself. But this inequitable economic discrimination against skilled slave-labour must have counted psychologically for less than the fact that, in Athenian public works, slaves and freemen of equal skill worked side by side and were reckoned as being of equal value. On the other hand, in the Attic silver-mines at Laurium, which were worked with unskilled slave-labour that was hired out by contractors in the mass, as though it were a material commodity, there is no reason to suppose that the inhumanity of the treatment was any less than was customary in mines and quarries in other parts of the Hellenic World; and, in general, the conditions in the Hellenic mining industry in all ages seem to have rivalled the horrors which our own eighteenth-century Western forebears tolerated in 'the Middle Passage'. The conditions in the Attic silver-mines at Laurium, after the discovery of the rich vein of ore in 483 B.C., are described, with citations from the original authorities, by A. E. Zimmern in *The Greek Commonwealth* (Oxford 1911, Clarendon Press), chapter 16. These fifth-century conditions of life and work in the mines of Attica were bad enough; but they appear to have been surpassed in later ages of Hellenic history in more outlying parts of the Hellenic World. See, for example, the description given by Strabo (Book XII, chap. 40, p. 562) of the mortality in some mines in the Pontic district of Pimolisene which were worked with convict-labour.

[1] The Cretan slave-owner does, however, compare himself, with brutal self-complacency, to 'the Great King' in the Song of Hybrias which has been quoted in III. A, vol. iii, p. 87, footnote 1, above.

with Slavery, in a direct encounter, face to face. As it has happened, however, the history of the impact of Democracy upon War in our Western World has been less simple than this. Before colliding with the institution of War, our modern Western Democracy has collided with the institution of Parochial Sovereignty in a society that has been broken up politically into a plurality of parochial states; and the importation of the new driving-forces of Democracy and Industrialism into the old machine of the Parochial State has generated the twin enormities of Political and Economic Nationalism. It is in this gross derivative form, in which the etherial spirit of Democracy has emerged from its passage through an alien medium, that Democracy has put its 'drive' into War instead of working against it.[1]

Here, again, our Western Society was in a happier posture in the pre-nationalistic and post-sectarian eighteenth century than in either the previous age or this subsequent age into which our own generation has been born. In the eighteenth century, when War was 'the sport of kings' and not the serious business of peoples, the parochial sovereign states of our modern Western World were not, as a rule, the instruments of the 'general wills' of 'citizen bodies', but were virtually the private estates of dynasties: dynastic properties which might pass from one royal owner to another by being hazarded as the stakes in the royal war-game when they did not pass by the more respectable and more normal processes of inheritance or marriage-settlement. It is true that there were certain states on the eighteenth-century political map whose rulers, at any rate *de facto*, were not monarchs but oligarchies which professed to shape their policies in the interests of the people and which effectively consulted their own narrower interests at all events. Eighteenth-century Venice and Hamburg, for example, were relics of the abortive cosmos of city-states which had failed to replace the feudal monarchies of medieval Western Christendom,[2] while eighteenth-century Holland and Great Britain were precocious examples of the national states into which almost the whole of our latter-day Great Society is partitioned at the present moment.[3] The Dynastic State, however, was the typical state of the eighteenth century; and royal marriages and royal wars were the two main

[1] This sinister perversion of a noble spiritual force has been noticed, by anticipation, in Part I. A, vol. i, p. 9, above.

[2] See III. C (ii) (*b*), vol. iii, pp. 343–50, above.

[3] A third type of oligarchically governed eighteenth-century state is represented by eighteenth-century Poland and Hungary; but these East European oligarchies were of relatively small importance, partly because of the general social backwardness of the countries in which they were established and partly because of certain special political circumstances. In Poland the oligarchy had paralysed itself by exaggerating the liberties of parliamentary government into the licence of the *Liberum Veto*. In Hungary, where the local oligarchy was much more efficient in itself, it was held in check during the eighteenth century by the monarchical power of the Hapsburg Dynasty.

agencies through which the changes in the eighteenth-century political map of the Western World were brought about.

This transfer of sovereignty as though it were private property to be traded or gambled away is as shocking intrinsically as the waging of war for the recreation of crowned heads; and to twentieth-century consciences which reconcile themselves to acts of conquest by taking posthumous plebiscites, it seems peculiarly outrageous that, in the eighteenth century, provinces should have been conveyanced like fields and their human inhabitants transferred from one royal owner to another, like so much live stock, on a profit-and-loss account which was reckoned in millions of souls. Yet in this matter, again, it would be rash for us, in our generation, to adopt a pharisaical attitude towards our forebears without ascertaining how a comparison between our ways and their ways works out.

Eighteenth-century statesmanship has at least this to be said in its favour, that, in finding its ways and means for changing the political map, it always preferred royal marriages to royal wars, if the matrimonial method could be managed. It considered, very rightly, that the matrimonial method was the cheaper and the more elegant way; and this point of view is summed up in a famous Latin epigram on the fortunes of the House of Austria, which built up and retained a great empire through a series of successful dynastic marriages, though it was notoriously apt to come out on the losing side in any wars in which it took part.

'Bella gerant alii; tu, felix Austria, nube.'[1] The very names of eighteenth-century wars tell the same tale: 'the War of the Spanish Succession'; 'the War of the Polish Succession'; 'the War of the Austrian Succession'. The understanding was that, as a rule, these conveyances of royal estates would be peacefully arranged between the diplomatic match-makers, with due consideration for the interests of third parties. They only gave occasion for 'the sport of kings' in exceptional cases, when the royal chafferers found themselves totally unable to agree.

This tendency, which was prevalent in the eighteenth century, to treat international politics as the private family affairs of dynasties, and not as the public business of peoples, undoubtedly turned international politics into something rather petty and rather sordid; but at least it performed one socially beneficial negative service. It 'took the shine out of' patriotism; and, with 'the shine', it took the sting.[2]

[1] The epigram is applicable to eighteenth-century Austria, though its authorship is attributed to a fifteenth-century king of Hungary, Matthias Corvinus (*regnabat* A.D. 1458–90).

[2] 'Dans ces derniers temps la générosité, les vertus, les affections douces s'étendant toujours, du moins en Europe, diminuent l'empire de la vengeance et des haines nationales' (Turgot, A. R. J.: 'Plan de Deux Discours sur l'Histoire Universelle' in *Œuvres de Turgot* (Paris 1844, Guillaumin, 2 vols.), vol. ii, pp. 632–3).

In damping down patriotic enthusiasm the eighteenth-century system of international politics dissipated the mists of patriotic prejudice in some degree. It lifted, for a moment, the veil which usually prevents 'the man in the street' from perceiving that all other human beings—foreigners and compatriots alike—are 'men of like passions with' himself.[1] Aristotle has nicknamed Man 'the political animal'; and the nickname is well deserved. Ordinarily this primitive political parochialism dominates the outlook and the action of the rank-and-file of Mankind in civilizations as well as in primitive societies. In the eighteenth century an abnormal and temporary system of politics which was not admirable in itself did nevertheless have the socially beneficial effect of making it rather less difficult than usual for men and women to shake themselves free from their political animality.

There is a classic expression of this negatively oecumenical eighteenth-century êthos in a well-known passage of Laurence Sterne's *Sentimental Journey through France and Italy*. Sterne has got as far as Paris, and has been in Paris some days, when, on coming back one evening to his hotel, he is told that he has been inquired after by the police.

' "The deuce take it!" said I: "I know the reason.". . . . I had left London with so much precipitation that it never enter'd my mind that we were at war with France; and had reached Dover, and looked through my glass at the hills beyond Boulogne, before the idea presented itself; and, with this in train, that there was no getting there without a passport. . . . So, hearing the Count de —— had hired the packet, I begged he would take me in his suite. The Count had some little knowledge of me, so made little or no difficulty—only said, his inclination to serve me could reach no farther than Calais, as he was to return by way of Brussels to Paris; however, when I had once pass'd there, I might get to Paris without interruption; but that in Paris I must make friends and shift for myself—"Let me get to Paris, Monsieur le Count", said I, "and I shall do very well." So I embark'd, and never thought more of the matter.'

According to Sterne's own story—which may not be true in the letter but is none the less true in the spirit—this eighteenth-century traveller in an 'enemy country' did in fact shift for himself quite successfully. After the visit from the French police in Paris, he took a cab to Versailles, called on an unknown French nobleman there on the strength of being a compatriot of Shakespeare, found no difficulty in inducing the nobleman to procure him a passport from the French authorities, and continued his journey across France without further inconvenience. To us, in our generation, this eighteenth-century anecdote reads like a fairy-story. England

[1] Acts xiv. 15.

and France are at war; yet a private nobleman can hire the packet-boat to convey him from Dover to Boulogne; he can take any other private person whom he chooses in his suite; all that is required, in order to travel in an enemy country in war-time, is a passport; our traveller does not even comply with that requirement; yet he is able to reach Paris and stay there some days before the police begin to bother him; whereupon an unknown French nobleman, out of sheer politeness, procures the necessary passport for him! And, with this formality accomplished, our eighteenth-century 'enemy alien's' troubles are over!

In this matter our forebears in the eighteenth century lived up to a standard of civilization from which their descendants in the twentieth century have fallen away far indeed. A state of war exists, but it only affects the fighting forces. Civilians are immune, because War is simply 'the sport of kings' and international politics are no concern—for weal or for woe—of these kings' subjects. The author of the *Sentimental Journey* is still living in a pre-nationalistic as well as pre-industrial age. But very soon after Sterne's unmolested passage through France at the tail-end of the Seven Years' War the spirit of international relations begins to change.[1] Warfare now is no longer just a *jeu de paume* among a party of kings; it is a serious conflict between peoples. The peoples themselves are once more at enmity, as they were in the age of sectarian Religious Fanaticism;[2] and every civilian, every non-combatant, has to bear the consequences.

This great evil has come to pass, yet the humane eighteenth-century spirit has died hard. Even after the French Revolution, even after the advent of Napoleon, it was regarded as an outrage

[1] Sterne's exploit was, however, emulated, half a century later, by a distinguished British traveller who visited the United States in peace and comfort during the Anglo-American War of A.D. 1812–15. In 1813 the Scottish law lord, Lord Jeffrey, sailed from Liverpool for the United States; and he walked and talked, unmolested, on 'enemy' soil from the 4th October, 1813, to the 2nd January, 1814. During those three months the 'enemy' visitor not only achieved his private object—which was to persuade a fellow countrywoman, who was at that time living as an 'enemy alien' in the United States, to marry him; the successful suitor also spent two days in discussing the perennial question of Neutral Rights with the Secretary of State, Mr. Monroe, and on the second day he went over the same ground again with President Madison, who had invited him to dinner. Jeffrey's business with the Secretary of State was the same as Sterne's with the unknown French nobleman. He wanted a passport ('cartel'); and this was granted to him so promptly that he was able to thank the President for it when he dined with him the day after his first application (see Cockburn, Lord: *Life of Lord Jeffrey* (Edinburgh 1852, Black, 2 vols.), vol. i, pp. 214–30).

[2] Volney, who was still living in his eighteenth-century fool's paradise in A.D. 1791 (see IV. C (iii) (*b*) 3, p. 150, footnote 4, above), was writing in a very different strain a few years later:

'Après nous être affranchis du fanatisme juif, repoussons ce fanatisme vandale ou romain, qui, sous des dénominations politiques, nous retrace les fureurs du monde religieux; repoussons cette doctrine sauvage, qui, par la résurrection des haines nationales, ramène dans l'Europe policée les mœurs des hordes barbares.'

This passage of Volney's *Leçons d'Histoire* was written by a philosopher who had witnessed the *levée en masse* and the Terror.

when, upon the breakdown of the Peace of Amiens and the consequent resumption of war between England and France, Napoleon decreed, on the 22nd May, 1803, that all British civilians between the ages of eighteen and sixty who happened to be travelling in France should be interned. Napoleon defended his action not, as any Government would defend the same action at the present day, on the simple ground that war had broken out. He admitted that the internment of enemy citizens in war-time was a breach of the rules of the game; and he defended his action as reprisals for the alleged seizure of two French merchantmen by the British Navy before war had been declared. Yet Napoleon did not 'get away with it'. His action was condemned not only by contemporary public opinion but also by posterity. It is still described as 'his unheard-of action, which condemned some 10,000 Britons to detention', in a book published as recently as A.D. 1904[1]—only ten years before 'enemy aliens' were being interned wholesale, as a matter of course, by all belligerent Governments, upon the outbreak of the Great War of our generation in 1914.

During the century and a half that separates the year 1914 from the date of the *Sentimental Journey*, it is evident that the eighteenth-century standard for the treatment of civilians in war-time has been attacked and undermined with increasing energy by some potent new moral—or immoral—force until at last the old standard has been completely overthrown and swept away. This triumphant antinomian force is, of course, Political Nationalism; and, if we analyse our modern Western Political Nationalism into its constituent elements, we shall find that it is the monstrous outcome of the impact of our modern Western Democracy upon the Parochial State. In origin and essence, Democracy is not parochial but universal, not militant but humanitarian. Its essence is a spirit of fraternity which knows no bounds but those of Life itself; and, in virtue of this quality, Democracy exercises a compelling power over human souls—a power of evoking loyalty and devotion and enthusiasm—which the dynastic political dispensation of the eighteenth-century Western World could not ever have expected, and perhaps did not ever even desire, to possess. Our eighteenth-century dynasties were content, as we have seen, to employ their feeble spiritual energies in operating the modern Western political system of parochial states at low tension. But this field of activity, in which the application of the dynastic principle was comparatively innocuous, was invaded before the close of the eighteenth century by the new force of Democracy, which was as pervasive socially as it was spiritually

[1] Rose, John Holland: *The Life of Napoleon I* (London 1904, Bell, 2 vols.), vol. i, p. 426.

dynamic; and, in this diversion from its natural outlet into an alien channel, the new force was perverted. The natural field of action for Democracy is a field that embraces all Mankind; and it is on this range that its spiritual potency is beneficent. But when this potent spiritual driving-force is diverted into the mechanism of a parochial state, it not only ceases to be beneficent but becomes malignantly subversive. *Corruptio optimi pessima.* Democracy imprisoned in parochial states degenerates into Nationalism.

If we pursue our empirical method of study, we can watch this disastrous corruption poisoning the political life of our modern Western Society.

In examining the impact of Democracy upon War in our modern Western history, we have seen that Gibbon's characterization of the American Revolutionary War as a 'temperate contest' was vindicated by the moderation of the subsequent peace settlement; and that one of the most striking exhibitions of this moderation was the victorious French Crown's willingness to leave the former French dominion of Canada under the sovereignty of the discomfited British Crown, instead of fighting on to recover a possession which had been ceded to King George by King Louis only twenty years before, at the end of a previous 'temperate contest' in which the fortunes of war had happened to go the other way. If the French Crown had insisted upon the recovery of Canada in 1783, the American Revolutionary War might have been inflamed from a 'temperate contest' into a war *à outrance;* but the credit for the moderation which saved the Western World from that disaster does not belong to the French Government alone. The honours are divided between French and British statesmanship; for if, in 1783, the French Government felt no temptation to fight on for the recovery of Canada, this was largely because the Canadians were substantially contented with their experience of British rule, and they were contented because the British Crown had been as good as its word in giving the Canadians, in the Quebec Act of 1774, the liberal treatment to which it had pledged itself in the peace-settlement of 1763,[1] when the sovereignty over Canada had been transferred. In 1783 the Canadians were duly living under their customary French laws and enjoying liberty of worship according to their hereditary Roman Catholic religion; and the British Government's proof of good faith made it morally possible for the French Government to show moderation. Conversely, if the Canadians

[1] 'His Britannic Majesty . . . agrees to grant the liberty of the Catholic religion to the inhabitants of Canada; he will consequently give the most precise and most effectual orders that his new Roman Catholic subjects may profess the worship of their religion according to the rites of the Romish Church, as far as the laws of Great Britain permit.'—Peace Treaty of the 10th February, 1763, between the Crowns of Great Britain, France, Spain, and Portugal, Article 4.

under British rule had been oppressed, or if they had been evicted from their homes to make way for British colonists, then, in 1783, it would have been morally almost impossible for the French Government not to continue the war until Canada, as well as the Thirteen Colonies, had been liberated from British rule.

The British Crown had not been tempted to break its word to the French Government over the treatment of the Canadians because, in this eighteenth-century interlude of common sense between the two frenzies of Sectarian and National Fanaticism, the parochial Governments of the Western World were both secular and cosmopolitan in their outlook and therefore did not feel it their duty to coerce their subjects into either a uniformity of faith or a uniformity of law and language. So far from that, eighteenth-century statesmanship was rather sensitively scrupulous in such matters because it had unpleasant memories—dating from a recent past—of barbarities which we have been witnessing again in our World in our day: the penalization or oppression or eviction or massacre of alien minorities and other subject populations. All these barbarities had been inflicted and suffered by our eighteenth-century forebears' immediate predecessors during an age of sectarian Religious Fanaticism in the sixteenth and seventeenth centuries. The last case of the kind had been the expulsion of the Protestants from the Catholic Bishopric of Salzburg by the Prince-Bishop in 1731–2; but this Salzburg barbarity had raised an outcry; for by that time religious persecution had ceased to be countenanced by Western public opinion. The last serious cases before that had been Claverhouse's campaigns against the Covenanters and Louis XIV's persecution of the Huguenots: the dragonnades and the revocation of the Edict of Nantes.

The exception which proves the rule of eighteenth-century conduct in this matter is the case of the Acadians, the original French settlers in the North American province which has since become Nova Scotia. After having been transferred from French to British sovereignty by the Peace Treaty of Utrecht in A.D. 1713, the Acadians were eventually deported from their homes by the British authorities in A.D. 1755. The British Government were moved to take this action because Acadia was a border-province between the British and French dominions in North America as they then were; the French authorities in Canada were inciting the French settlers under British rule in Acadia to rise against the British Government; and the Seven Years' War was on the point of breaking out. In these circumstances the British authorities reluctantly deported the Acadians as a last resort; and not more than 8,000 persons were involved. Yet the British Government were apologetic over their action, and it was decidedly condemned by the public opinion of the contemporary Western World. If the eviction of the Protestant Salzburgers in A.D. 1731–2 has an historic interest as a last belated case of religious persecution, the deportation of the Acadians in A.D. 1755 has also an historic interest of its own as a harbinger of the latter-day persecutions which were to be inflicted upon alien minorities and other subject populations in our modern Western World—this time in the name, not of Religion, but of Nationality. Less than thirty years later there was a fresh and more flagrant case of this new social evil on the same continent.

While the peace settlement of A.D. 1783 was moderate indeed from the standpoint of the British Crown—which was allowed to retain Canada and was only mulcted of the Thirteen Colonies as the price of its defeat—there was one set of people involved in the American Revolutionary War to whom the settlement appeared in a very different light, and these were the so-called United Empire Loyalists: the people in the Thirteen Colonies who had taken the side of the Crown against the insurgents. Unlike the French colonists in Canada after the previous war, these partisans of the British Crown in the Thirteen Colonies had to leave their homes, bag and baggage, after the American Revolutionary War, when their country came under the new flag. Under the Stars and Stripes the Loyalists found life impossible, and the Canadian provinces of Nova Scotia and New Brunswick and Ontario are peopled with their descendants down to this day; whereas only twenty years earlier the Canadians, who had shown an equal loyalty to the French Crown during the Seven Years' War, had found it not impossible, after the transfer of sovereignty in Canada, to lead a tolerable life under the Union Jack, with the result that they have remained at home, as contented subjects of the British Crown, from that day to this.

In the new rancour and new harshness with which the Loyalists were treated by the North American victors in the war of A.D. 1775–83, we see the Nationalism that we know by bitter experience to-day already showing its familiar face and bringing forth its familiar fruits. And the dragon's-tooth seed was sown all over Europe in the Revolutionary and Napoleonic Wars. We see a national consciousness—and, with it, a national passion and fanaticism and ruthlessness—flaring up first in France and then in Spain and Germany and Russia and then in Belgium and Italy: in the French Revolutionary *levée en masse*; in the Spanish guerrilla war; in the burning of Moscow; in the German *Befreiungskrieg*; in the Belgian Revolution of 1830; in the Italian *Risorgimento*. And, as international politics became infected with these mutually hostile national enthusiasms, the moderation which had been the virtue of eighteenth-century statesmanship ceased to govern the conduct of international affairs. The last moderate peace terms in our modern Western history were those which Bismarck imposed on the Hapsburg Monarchy in 1866. In 1871, when he had to make peace with a defeated France, Bismarck was confronted with a German Nationalism that had gained such strength under his fostering hand that it had become his master instead of his servant; and, against his better judgement, he was compelled by this masterfully recalcitrant anti-social force to inflict a rankling wound on the French national consciousness by tearing away Alsace-Lorraine from the French body politic. In our generation we have reaped the cruel harvest of this nineteenth-century sowing, in the legion of internecine national conflicts that have been devastating the World since 1914.

If we ask ourselves how this disastrous change for the worse in the spirit of international relations has come about, the fate of the Loyalists in the American Revolutionary War will give us our answer. For the people who made the Loyalists' lives impossible to live any longer in their old homes were the victorious insurgents in the Thirteen Colonies; and that reminds us that, although this war was still on the whole a 'temperate contest' in Gibbon's sense, it was not entirely fought as 'the sport of kings'. In this American war, King George and King Louis, with their moderate war-aims and their lukewarm feelings, were not the only belligerents. The protagonist, this time, was no crowned head but a new-born nation —the American nation—and this American nation was fighting for its national aim of political independence in deadly earnest. The measure of its earnestness was the harshness of the treatment which it meted out, in the hour of its own victory, to the defeated Loyalists; for, in the eyes of American patriots, these adherents of the British Crown were traitors who had committed the unforgivable sin of striving to prevent the new nation from coming to birth. The democratic movement which had welled up in A.D. 1775 out of a North American spring had lost none of its pristine dynamic force in A.D. 1783; but in the short intervening span of eight years the welling waters which had promised to bring fresh life to all Mankind had been transformed from a life-giving fountain into a devastating torrent by being forced into the ancient channel of political parochialism. The movement which had begun with a proclamation of the Rights of Man in the Declaration of Independence[1] simply resulted in the establishment of one more parochial state; and the fixation, upon this idol, of a new democratic enthusiasm which ought to have been bestowed upon Humanity at large en-

[1] 'We hold these truths to be self-evident: that all men are created equal; that they are endowed by their Creator with certain unalienable rights; that among these are life, liberty and the pursuit of happiness.'

gendered a ruthless Nationalism which demanded the sacrifice of the Loyalists upon its altar.

This Political Nationalism which confronts us at the birth of the United States, and which has since taken possession of most other parochial states throughout the World,[1] is the outcome of the impact of Democracy upon a society in which a plurality of states has been the reigning political dispensation; and it is in this perverted form that our modern Western Democracy has put fresh driving-force into modern Western Warfare. The Economic Nationalism which has grown into as great a social evil as our Political Nationalism in our day has been engendered by a corresponding perversion of Industrialism under the same social conditions.

Economic motives and ambitions and rivalries were not, of course, unknown in the international politics of the Western World in the Pre-Industrial Age. Far from that, the intellectual and moral outlook which is expressed in the Economic Nationalism of our day received its classical expression in the 'Mercantilism' of the eighteenth century; and the prizes of eighteenth-century diplomacy and war included markets, like the market for African negro slaves in Spanish America, and sources of supply, like the sugar islands of the Antilles, as well as provinces, like Canada or Silesia, and the 'souls' that were transferred from sovereignty to sovereignty, with the provinces in which they lived, as though they were so much live stock. Moreover, in so far as the eighteenth-century Western Governments contended with one another for economic prizes, their contests tended to become more serious; for merchants are a less frivolous class than kings; and, when they exert themselves, it is for profit and not for sport. In eighteenth-century Great Britain, where the agrarian land-owning oligarchy, which was the real governing power, was in political alliance with the merchants of London and Bristol and Glasgow, the motive of mercantile profit quite overshadowed the motive of royal or aristocratic sport in the conduct of foreign policy; and the steadiness of aim and persistence of effort by which the conduct of British foreign policy was consequently distinguished go far to account for the successes which were continually being gained in the international arena by eighteenth-century Great Britain at the expense of eighteenth-century France. The predominance of the economic factor which can be observed in eighteenth-century British foreign policy was not, however, characteristic of Western international politics in that age. It was a notable exception; and even in eighteenth-century British policy

[1] For the idolization of the institution of the Sovereign National State in our latter-day Western, or Westernized, World see further IV. C (iii) (*c*) 2 (β), pp. 317–20 and 405–8, below.

it would be easy to exaggerate the importance of the part which was played by economic considerations. For one thing, the merchants in whose interests foreign policy was largely conducted were a small minority of the population of the country—even though they might seem numerous by comparison with their aristocratic compatriots and confederates or with the French and Spanish monarchs who were their adversaries. And, for another thing, these eighteenth-century economic rivalries, though they were something rather less frivolous than a royal sport, were also something vastly less serious than a matter of national life or death. The economic prizes of eighteenth-century diplomacy and war were not the staple food-stuffs without which whole peoples would starve, and they were not the staple markets and sources of supply without which whole trades and industries would be unable to earn their livelihood. They were lucrative superfluities in which the fortunes of individual merchants might be made or lost but which hardly touched the daily lives of the people at large;[1] and in this respect the stakes of the merchants resembled the stakes of the kings in the eighteenth-century game of international politics. They were not of such values as to introduce any element of overstrain or ruthlessness into the 'temperate and undecisive' eighteenth-century contests.

Indeed, these economic competitions were still more remote from ordinary private life in the eighteenth-century Western World than the contests for territorial sovereignty; for even in the eighteenth century it did make a certain difference to the lives of the inhabitants of Canada whether they were subjects of King Louis or of King George, and to the lives of the inhabitants of Silesia whether they were subjects of the Hapsburg or of the Hohenzollern. On the other hand, the Canadian or Silesian peasant, and the English yeoman or farmer or agricultural labourer, delved and span and ate and drank and clothed and housed themselves in the same traditional fashion, whatever ring of merchants was monopolizing the international trade in slaves or sugar or tea. For the agricultural population of the eighteenth-century Western World the economic horizon seldom or never extended beyond the political frontiers; and it generally fell far short of these, since, in an age when land-transport was only beginning to shift from the backs of pack-animals on to wheeled vehicles, the range of profitable transport for agricultural produce was extremely short. Considering that,

[1] For the contrary assumption that the livelihood of the people at large was dependent upon foreign trade it might be difficult to find chapter and verse that was older than the nineteenth century. An early instance is cited by J. L. and Barbara Hammond in *The Rise of Modern Industry*, 5th edition (London 1937, Methuen), p. 203: 'When Fox destroyed the [slave] trade in 1806 even Sir Robert Peel complained that we were philosophizing when our looms were idle, and George Rose, that Americans would take up the trade, and that Manchester, Stockport, and Paisley would starve.'

in this age, the agricultural population accounted for an overwhelmingly large proportion of the whole, it may be said, with little exaggeration, that the normal field of self-contained and autonomous economic activity in the eighteenth-century Western World was the Lilliputian area of the village community. For the majority of Mankind at that time the bounds of the social universe were as narrow, for practical purposes, as those which are sketched in the picture of rural life in Gray's *Elegy*.

This general state of economic equilibrium at low tension on a minute scale was violently disturbed by the advent of Industrialism; for this new economic force, like the sister political force of Democracy, is intrinsically universal in its operation. We have seen that the essence of Democracy is a spirit of fraternity which embraces all Mankind; and if we now ask ourselves what is the essence of Industrialism, we shall find that the answer runs on parallel lines. Industrialism is a co-operative system of work which demands the unification of all the habitable lands and navigable seas on the face of the planet as a common home for the entire living generation of Mankind. Industrialism will not work freely or effectively or beneficently except in so far as the World is organized into one single field of economic activity—a single world-field in which everybody is at liberty to live and work and produce and consume and collect and distribute and sell and buy and travel and transact business without let or hindrance. The social dispensation which Industrialism demands was truly declared by the eighteenth-century pioneers of the new economic technique in their famous watchword 'Laissez faire! Laissez passer!'

This ideal condition of economic world unity, which Industrialism postulates, was far indeed from being realized in the state of our Western Society when Industrialism first impinged upon it. This eighteenth-century Western World was divided up, as we have just seen, into hundreds of petty economic units, and each of these petty units was isolated from all the others by economic barriers which were very difficult to pass. That was the state of the World in which Industrialism had to make its way. Yet one of the presuppositions of Industrialism is the eventual attainment of economic world unity. This is the necessary condition for a permanent organization of the economic life of the World on our modern industrial lines; and if Industrialism cannot secure this necessary condition of world unity—or, at least, come within a measurable distance of securing it—it seems doomed to die of asphyxiation. At this very moment we are watching how Industrialism, caught in the trammels of the Parochial State, is struggling desperately to save itself from ruin by striving to achieve its oecumenical destiny instead of being perverted into Economic Nationalism. And this struggle has really been going on all the time (though not, of course, always at its present pitch of desperation) ever since our modern Industrialism made its first appearance. Finding the World divided into small economic units fenced off from one another by high economic barriers, Industrialism has been working, for the last hundred and fifty years, to re-shape the economic structure of the World in two ways, both leading in the direction of world unity. It has been trying to make the local economic units fewer and bigger; and at the same time it has been trying to lower the barriers between them.

If we glance now at the history of these efforts that Industrialism has been making along these two lines, we shall find that this history has a turning point round about the 'sixties' and the 'seventies' of the nineteenth century.[1] Down to the 'eighteen-sixties' and the 'eighteen-seventies' Industrialism was supported and assisted by Democracy in its efforts to diminish the number of the local economic units in the World and to increase their average size and to lower the barriers dividing them; and during the century or so, ending in those decades, during which Democracy was working together with Industrialism in this direction, some substantial progress towards economic world unity was achieved. On the other hand, for the last sixty years or more—reckoning down to the year 1938—the whole rhythm of the world movement has been in the opposite sense. During the last half-century the driving-force of Industrialism, like the driving-force of Democracy, has been diverted from building a world order into fortifying the political parochialism of our Western Society. And, by thus giving this parochialism an immense accession of strength, the two great new forces in the World have actually been raising up, by their own action, the most formidable obstacles to that unification of the World which it is their nature to bring about. This will be apparent if we take these two chapters of modern Western economic history in their chronological order, looking first at the century which ended in the 'eighteen-seventies' and then at the couple of generations which brings us down to 1938.

The intimacy of the connexion between industrialization and unification is illustrated by the modern history of Great Britain; for in the eighteenth century, after the union of England and Scotland in A.D. 1707, Great Britain was the largest single free-trade area in the World; and undoubtedly this was one of the principal reasons why Great Britain forged ahead of all her neighbours in her economic development before the eighteenth century was over.

[1] This has been noticed, by anticipation, in Part I. A, vol. i, p. 14, above.

Great Britain was the birth-place of modern Industrialism; and she was also the birth-place of modern Democracy. And, as Democracy and Industrialism spread simultaneously out of Great Britain over the rest of the World from the last quarter of the eighteenth century onwards, we can watch these two forces working together, for the next hundred years, to increase the size of economic units and to reduce the barriers between them.

In this connexion we may recur to the effects of the American Revolutionary War of 1775–83. American independence was the result of British Democracy. The Thirteen Colonies in North America wanted to enjoy the same measure of self-government that was enjoyed by Great Britain herself. In the Revolutionary War the colonists got their way; and it looked at first sight as if this outcome of the war, which was the first victory gained, beyond the shores of Britain, by the new political force of Democracy, was at the same time a set-back for the other new force, the economic force of Industrialism. Industrialism demands big units; and in the peace settlement of 1783 the unity of the eighteenth-century British Empire was broken up. But in the immediate sequel the disruptive effects of this political schism were more than outbalanced by new tendencies towards consolidation. The Thirteen Colonies had no sooner secured their political and economic independence from Great Britain than they followed the example of England and Scotland by forming among themselves a North American Union which was not only a political union but an economic union likewise. Moreover the United States had no sooner come into existence than it began to expand; and this expansion was so rapid and on so vast a scale that, within sixty-four years[1] of the establishment of the Union, the Continental United States had grown to its present gigantic size. A string of thirteen states along the Atlantic sea-board of North America had expanded into a country stretching right across the continent from Atlantic to Pacific. And in this, its final, extent the United States supplanted and entirely dwarfed the United Kingdom in the role of being the largest free-trade area in the Western World.[2]

Thus, in the early history of the United States, we see an example of an unprecedentedly large economic unit being built up by the agency of Democracy in co-operation with Industrialism. We see

[1] Reckoning from the coming into force of the Federal Constitution in 1789 to the date of the Gadsden Purchase, which was transacted in 1853.

[2] The United States is not, of course, the largest free-trade area in the Great Society into which our Western Society has latterly expanded, for it is far surpassed in extent by the free-trade area of the Russian Empire and its successor the U.S.S.R.—the *ci-devant* universal state of the Russian Orthodox Christendom which has obtained admission into the comity of Western states without forfeiting its own unity. (See IV. C (ii) (*b*) 2, pp. 88–9, above.)

another example of the same co-operation towards the same end in the French Revolution. The French, like the preceding American, Revolution was primarily a political movement inspired by the idea of Democracy. But one of the first acts of the revolutionaries was to convert the territory of France into one single economic unit by sweeping away all the internal customs-barriers which had formerly divided one French province or group of provinces from another.

Two still more striking examples of the same tendency are offered by the unification of Germany and the unification of Italy—unions which were both achieved between 1815 and 1871. On their political side these German and Italian movements were both nationalistic. They were assertions of German and Italian nationhood against French and Austrian imperialism, as the establishment of the United States of America had been an assertion of American nationhood against British imperialism. At the same time, both the German and the Italian national movement resulted in the substitution of one large territorial unit for a number of small units. The German and Italian petty states of the eighteenth century had been at the mercy of France and Austria as the Thirteen Colonies had been at the mercy of Great Britain, and for the same reason. Their weakness had lain in their disunity; and, when they found the remedy for this former weakness by achieving national unification, the union which they established included economic as well as political unity. In Germany a customs union—the German Zollverein—actually anticipated, and prepared the ground for, the establishment of a political union, the German Reich. In Italy economic union went hand in hand with political union as a matter of course.

Thus, during the century ending in A.D. 1871, we see the number of large-scale units in the Western World notably increasing. In 1771 the only economically unified area on a large scale had been Great Britain. By 1871 the British economic unit was equalled in scale by the three new units of France, Germany, and Italy, and was altogether dwarfed by the gigantic new unit of the United States.

Moreover, while the average size of the local economic units was increasing, the barriers dividing them were tending to diminish. After the former American colonies of Great Britain had become an independent country, the trade between the United States and Britain, instead of falling off, became greater than it had ever been when the two countries were under one sovereignty. Thereafter, in the early years of the nineteenth century, the political separation of the former Spanish colonies in Central and South America from Spain led to the removal of the economic barriers by which the Spanish Government had formerly preserved a monopoly of the Spanish colonial trade for Spain herself. With the achievement of political independence the new republics of Latin America all came into the field of international trade. In the fifth decade of the nineteenth century the United Kingdom abolished its own economic barriers against the rest of the World altogether; and it looked as though this adoption of a system of Free Trade by the country which was the fountain-head of Industrialism might inaugurate an entirely new epoch in the history of international economic relations. The middle decades of the nineteenth century did, in fact, see a great extension of the network of economic treaties. The German Zollverein, again, pursued a policy of keeping tariffs low during the first chapter of its history; and this chapter did not come to an end until after the foundation of the German Reich in 1871. The French Government, too, pursued a low-tariff policy during the reign of Napoleon III, which lasted from the *coup d'état* of A.D. 1852 until after the outbreak of the Franco-Prussian War in 1870. As for American tariff policy, it went through many fluctuations in its early stages; but the United States did not commit itself definitely to high tariffs until the time of the Civil War of 1861–5.

It will be seen that the British Free Trade movement of the 'eighteen-forties' was in accordance with the general spirit of the times. The United Kingdom did, no doubt, take the lead in the Free Trade movement and put the principle of Free Trade into practice more thoroughly than any other country; and at a later stage she also clung to Free Trade more tenaciously than most other countries—right down, in fact, to the year 1932. At the same time it will be seen that, during the twenty years or so ending about 1870, the British example was followed to a large extent by a number of economically important countries which at this time made great reductions in their tariffs, short of abolishing them completely. Moreover, tariff barriers were not the only economic barriers that were tending to diminish during the century which began with the American Revolutionary War and ended with the Franco-Prussian War. Those hundred years saw the removal of impediments not only to the free flow of goods, but also to the free flow of capital and the free flow of population. The era of British investment all over the World—in Continental Europe, in the United States and in Latin America—began after the end of the Napoleonic Wars in A.D. 1815. The era of mass-immigration into the United States began in the 'eighteen-forties' with the Irish Famine and the Continental European Revolutions of 1848.

This, in outline, is the economic picture of the hundred years ending in the 'eighteen-seventies', and it presents a striking contrast to the picture of the last half-century; for since the 'eighteen-seventies' the main tendencies of the previous hundred years have been exactly reversed. Down to A.D. 1871 the number of economic units in the World was becoming fewer, the average size of these units was becoming greater, and the barriers between them were diminishing in height. Since 1871, on the contrary, the barriers have been growing higher while the average size of the units has been diminishing and their number has been increasing. This change of trend is only what was to be expected as a result of the sinister success of the old institution of the Parochial State in dominating the new forces that had made their appearance in the field of Western life; for, *a priori*, it would be paradoxical if a unification of Mankind and of the Habitable World were ultimately brought nearer by the imprisonment of the oecumenical forces of Democracy and Industrialism within the strait-waistcoats of parochial states.

As regards the absolute number and the average size of economic units, the course of events since A.D. 1871 makes it clear, in retrospect, that the aggregative movement which is exemplified in the unification of the United States and the French Republic and the Kingdom of Italy and the German Reich has been temporary and exceptional, and that the normal secular movement is represented by the disruption of the eighteenth-century British Empire to which the establishment of the United States was the sequel. It is true that, since the 'sixties' and 'seventies' of the nineteenth century, the aggregative movement has not altogether ceased. In the 'sixties', for example, the unity of the United States was preserved and re-established by the victory of the North in the American Civil War; and in the same decade it was emulated by the federation of all but one of the British provinces in North America into the Dominion of Canada. Even since the turn of the century the same process of aggregation has been exemplified in the federation of the British colonies in Australia into the Commonwealth and the federation of the British territories and the *ci-devant* independent republics in South Africa into the Union. On the whole, however, it is not aggregation but disruption that has been the prevalent tendency in these latter days—above all in Central and Eastern Europe and in South-Western Asia, where the same decade which saw the union of Italy and the union of Germany completed in 1871 saw the disruption of the Ottoman, Hapsburg, Romanov, and Hohenzollern Empires inaugurated by the partition of Turkey-in-Europe into the nuclei of new national 'successor-states' in 1878. In this great region the disruptive process has worked itself out to its conclusion in the series of catastrophes which began with the outbreak of the Italo-

Turkish War in Tripoli in the autumn of 1911 and which ended with the termination of the Graeco-Turkish War-after-the-War in Anatolia in the autumn of 1922. In these eleven years the zone of 'Balkanization' has been extended from the Balkan Peninsula itself to the eastern frontiers of Italy and Germany on one side and to the western frontiers of Persia and the U.S.S.R. on the other. This considerable portion of the surface of the Earth which, little more than half a century ago, was almost all comprehended in the dominions of four great empires,[1] is now divided among a bevy of not less than twenty 'successor-states' ranging from Finland to Egypt and from Czechoslovakia to 'Irāq. And these states are now not only politically independent of one another. They have made use of their new parochial sovereign independence in order to isolate themselves economically as well by setting up round their fresh-cut frontiers a zariba of economic *chevaux de frise*: tariffs and quotas and migration-restrictions and embargoes on the movement of capital. In fact, almost every one of these 'successor-states' is now in a mood of violent Economic Nationalism; and this temper has greatly aggravated the economic dislocation which an increase in the absolute number and a decrease in the average size of the economic units was bound, in any case, to inflict upon an industrialized world. In the violence of their post-war Economic Nationalism, however, the new-born 'successor-states' are simply displaying 'the zeal of the convert'. For Economic Nationalism did not make its first appearance in our Western World after the War of 1914–18 in post-war Poland or Czechoslovakia; it was born in the United States during the Civil War of 1861–5 and in Germany after the foundation of the Reich in 1871.

Economic Nationalism may be defined as an exploitation of the apparatus of a parochial state for the purpose of promoting the economic interests of the population of that state at the expense of the rest of Mankind. On the moral plane such a policy is indefensible in any circumstances; and in an industrialized world it is also economically disastrous for all parties, since it is attempting the impossible in trying to harness the intrinsically oecumenical force of Industrialism to a parochial aim. At the same time it is manifest in retrospect that an epidemic of Economic Nationalism was the inevitable nemesis of letting this new oecumenical force of Industrialism loose in a world in which parochial states were the

[1] The only completely independent *Kleinstaaten* in this area between the years 1871 and 1878 were Greece and Montenegro, and the Greece of that date was very far from including the whole national home of the Greek people, while Montenegro was no more than a minute fraction of the national home of the Serbs—and *a fortiori* of the Jugoslavs (a nationality which, as a matter of fact, had not, at that date, yet been invented (see Part I. A, vol. i, p. 13, above)).

reigning political institution. For a community which keys up its economic life to the tension and the rhythm of Industrialism is consciously or unconsciously setting itself the ambition of making its country into a 'Workshop of the World'; and as one local community after another undergoes the Industrial Revolution there is bound to be a competition between a number of local industrial Powers for the same world-market. Owing to the frailty of human nature, such competition usually provokes conflict before it promotes co-operation; the conflict tempts the combatants to resort to whatever weapons may come to hand; and a whole armoury of weapons for an economic conflict between local industrial Powers is offered, ready made, in the apparatus for economic warfare which the parochial states of our latter-day Western World have inherited from the age of 'Mercantilism',[1] when privileged commercial oligarchies were joining in 'the sport of kings' by using states as instruments for capturing from one another the international trade in superfluities.

This pernicious outcome of the impact of Industrialism upon the Parochial State was not foreseen by the British pioneers of Industrialism who were the first people to entertain the industrial ambition of taking the whole World for the field of their economic activities. For the very reason that they happened to be the first in this field, British industrialists were able for the most part—at least down to the 'seventies' of the nineteenth century—to secure free play for British industrial ability and enterprise by a 'peaceful penetration' which was private and haphazard, without need of intervention by the British Government on British Industry's behalf.[2] Indeed, the whole tendency of British social development in that age was for the Government to renounce whatever intervention in the course of private business it had previously been accustomed to undertake. The great landmark in the rise of the new industrial Great Britain in the nineteenth century was, of course, the establishment of Free Trade in the 'eighteen-forties'; and this meant the withdrawal of the Government from the field of economic action altogether. 'The Manchester School' of British statesmanship looked forward, at the time, to seeing this British lead towards Free Trade followed by the rest of the World; and we have observed[3]

[1] See pp. 167–8, above.

[2] This statement requires the qualification—'for the most part'—with which it is put forward here; for while it holds good in respect of the expansion of British trade during this period in the Western World—and this not only in Europe but also overseas—it does not apply to the contemporary British conquests of Oriental markets and sources of supply. These conquests were not metaphorical but literal. It was the armed forces of the East India Company and the Crown that opened up the sub-continent of India to British trade through the wars of 1799–1849, and it was the Royal Navy that opened up the sub-continent of China to British trade through the War of 1840–2.

[3] On pp. 172–3, above.

that this expectation was in fact realized to some extent. In both French and German economic history, for instance, the 'fifties' and 'sixties' of the nineteenth century were, as we have seen, a period of low tariffs. We have also noticed, however, that, outside Britain itself, this mid-nineteenth-century tendency towards Free Trade was neither very far-reaching nor very long-lived. The United States, for example, adopted, during the Civil War of 1861–5, a high tariff policy from which it has never again departed. And both Germany and France turned their faces in the same direction in the 'seventies' and 'eighties'.

In this connexion it must be borne in mind that both Germany and the United States went through the Industrial Revolution a full generation or even half a century later than Great Britain; so that in the 'sixties' and 'seventies' and 'eighties', when first the Americans and then the Germans turned decidedly protectionist, the United States and Germany were more or less in the same phase of Industrialism in which Great Britain had been in the 'forties'. The 'forties', as we have seen, were just the time when the British people turned away from Protection to Free Trade; and this comparison of relative dates raises a question and at the same time suggests the answer to it. Why was it that the same process of industrialization, at the same stage, inspired one fiscal policy in Great Britain and exactly the opposite policy in these other countries? The answer to this question is given by the mere fact of the difference in the dates. The Americans and the Germans, when they went through the Industrial Revolution, conceived just the same economic ambition that the British had conceived when they had been going through the same experience at an earlier date. The Americans and the Germans each aspired, just like the British, to make their country into a 'Workshop of the World'. In fact, they actually caught this idea from the British, who had been the first people to think of it and to put it into practice. But evidently the problem of making one's country into a 'Workshop of the World' is one thing if one is in the position of the British people in the 'eighteen-forties', making the attempt with no predecessors and no rivals; it is quite another thing if one is in the position of the American people or the German people, embarking on the same enterprise a generation or half a century later, with the British not only already in the field but established there in a predominant position of advantage. The problem is the same; the goal is the same; but the circumstances are so different that the late comers are led into seeking their solution of the common problem along just the opposite lines from those which were followed by the first comer. The late comers approach the identical goal from an entirely different angle. The British people, seeking to make Britain into a 'Workshop of the World' at a time when Britain has no rival to fear, proceed to throw Britain open to free trade. The American and the German peoples, seeking to follow the British people into a world-market in which the British are already dominant, proceed to protect their infant industries against the high blast of British competition behind the shelter of an artificial tariff-wall.

Thus, in the course of the nineteenth century, two mutually incompatible prescriptions for turning one's country into a 'Workshop of the World' came into the field one after the other. In the 'eighteen-forties' British statesmen and economists prescribed Free Trade; in the 'sixties' and 'seventies' and 'eighties' American and German statesmen and economists prescribed high protection. And, ever since then, there has been a vigorous controversy over the respective merits of these two fiscal policies which are both in the field and which are wholly irreconcilable with each other. The argument has gone on, and is going on still to-day; and so far neither party—neither the Protectionists nor the Free Traders—have been reduced to admitting that their opponents are right and that they themselves are in error. The argument has remained open; but the balance of power has not remained stationary. Looking back from the year 1938 over the last sixty or seventy years, one can see that in the realm of fact, as distinct from the realm of thought, Free Trade has decidedly been losing and Protection gaining ground. The British practice of Free Trade has remained the exception; the American and German practice of high protection has become the rule. Of the sixty or seventy fully self-governing states that exist in the World to-day, the vast majority have modelled their fiscal policy on the German-American pattern rather than on the British pattern; and this majority includes all the self-governing Dominions of the British Crown outside the United Kingdom. In the United Kingdom itself the traditional British policy of Free Trade has been challenged more and more energetically since the turn of the century until at last, in the year 1932, we have seen the British people abandon their own distinctive traditional practice and fall into line with the German-American practice which has become the rule in the contemporary world. This abandonment, by the British pioneers of Industrialism, of a Free Trade policy which had been adopted by British statesmanship a hundred years back, and which had become one of the most cherished institutions of the United Kingdom, is an unmistakable token that the policy and temper of Economic Nationalism have won the day.

Our survey of the impacts of Democracy and Industrialism upon the institution of Parochial Sovereignty in the Western World during the last hundred and fifty years of our Western history seems to show that we are confronted, in our generation, with an unescapable choice between overhauling the old institution or allowing it to wreck our civilization through the enhanced and misdirected 'drive' which it has acquired from the new forces. The triumph of Political and Economic Nationalism means that the inactive innocuous parochial state of the eighteenth century has disappeared for ever from the Western social landscape; and we can already perceive the enormity which Nationalism is enthroning in its place.

If, in the new world which Democracy and Industrialism have called into existence, the Parochial State survives without any abatement of its traditional claim to exercise an absolute Parochial Sovereignty, it will no longer be a state which leaves the greater part of the lives of the majority of its subjects unaffected by its existence for good or for evil. It will be the new-fangled 'Totalitarian State', which has shown its face, since the War of 1914–18, in a Communist Union of Soviet Socialist Republics and in a Fascist Italy and in a National-Socialist Germany. This Totalitarian Parochial State is an enormity because it is an attempt to confine new social forces which are intrinsically oecumenical in their spirit and operation within the prison-house of a parochial institution which was originally established under quite different social conditions in order to meet quite different human needs. The social friction that is produced by this institutional enormity is so violent that it can hardly fail to make life intolerable for any human beings on whom it is imposed; and, though the violence of the friction can also hardly fail to bring the monstrous institution itself to grief, this prospect offers little consolation to its victims. A plurality of parochial totalitarian states will assuredly give place, sooner or later, to a single oecumenical totalitarian state in which the forces of Democracy and Industrialism will at any rate secure, at last, their natural world-wide field of operation, even if they are still condemned to put their 'drive' into a political mechanism;[1] but, if once our society succumbs to a totalitarian political dispensation, it is virtually inconceivable that the ultimately inevitable change from plural to singular—from a multiplicity of local states to one state embracing all the World—can still be achieved by peaceful means. Under these conditions the change will come, when it does come, through the delivery of a 'knock-out blow' in a 'totalitarian war', or series of 'totalitarian wars', of the kind envisaged in the French Law of A.D. 1928.[2] And even if those days are shortened

[1] For this prospect see further Part V. A, vol. v, pp. 9–10, below.
[2] See IV. C (iii) (*b*) 3, p. 154, above.

so far as to reprieve Mankind from the doom of physical extermination, the tribulation will be so great that our present Western Civilization will have little hope of recovering from the shock.[1]

The truth seems to be that in both Democracy and Industrialism the impetus towards universality is so strong that these forces are bound to work their way through to a world-wide field of operation sooner or later, in one way or another. If their titanic energies are caught in the toils of Parochial Sovereignty, they will eventually burst their bonds by destroying the institution that is cramping them; and if we are to escape this catastrophic revolutionary denouement, we must take active and timely steps to adjust the old institution to the working of the new forces in such a way as to give these a peaceful entry into the world-wide field of operation which they demand, before they take their oecumenical kingdom by storm. Now that Democracy and Industrialism are at large in our Western World, we cannot afford simply to leave the sixty or seventy fully self-governing states on the 'post-war' political map to exercise, unmodified, their traditional prerogative of absolute sovereign independence. We have to modify the theory and practice of Parochial Sovereignty to whatever extent this may be necessary in order to build our parochial states into some kind of world order. For a world order is the necessary institutional framework for the new oecumenical forces.

In our generation, in the light of the World War of 1914–18, it is manifest that a world order cannot come into existence without some considerable modification of Parochial Sovereignty and that this cannot be expected to happen automatically. Our world order must be brought into existence by a deliberate effort of statesmanship; and it must not be limited to any single plane of social life, but must prevail on all planes alike. Unfortunately we have learnt these lessons late in the day, when the Nationalism that has been generated by a perversion of Democracy and Industrialism has already made great headway. The prospect of solving the problem by peaceful adjustment would have been more promising if the task with which we are grappling now had been taken in hand a hundred years earlier.

It is true that, within the last hundred years, a rudimentary economic world order has grown up, mainly through the work of British hands, with the London money-market as its centre. The intricacy of this *de facto* oecumenical economic system, and the importance of the role which British bankers and shippers and merchants and manufacturers have played in it, have become apparent since the system—now patently threatened with destruction—has

[1] Matt. xxiv. 21–2.

ceased to be taken for granted. This nineteenth-century British economic world order, however, has grown up without any corresponding political framework and indeed without any design at all. For there was no conscious philosophy behind the activities of the British men of business who played the leading part in building it up. The bankers who lent money for the opening-up of the United States and Latin America and the British Dominions overseas, the engineers who built gas-works in Berlin and railways in Argentina and China and Turkey and cotton-mills in Russia, and the industrialists who provided raw materials like coal or manufactured articles like iron girders, never thought of themselves as building up an economic world order, and *a fortiori* they never reflected that this economic order which they were nevertheless undesignedly constructing could not be developed or maintained unless certain political conditions were realized in the new world which had been called into being by the economic enterprise of a new industrial age.

This truth was not interesting or indeed apparent to the majority of the 'practical' men of affairs who built the new system up by 'a fortuitous concourse of efforts', as coral reefs are built by marine animalculae. And although there was one school of thought in Early Victorian England—'the Manchester School' of philosophic statesmen and statesmanlike philosophers—who did realize that the advent of Democracy and Industrialism was a turning point in history and that a world order was a necessity in this new world, these English thinkers almost made a virtue of the thoughtlessness of the contemporary English men of action through a mistakenly thorough application of their own Liberal principle of *laisser faire*.

Cobden and his companions looked forward to seeing the peoples and the states of the World drawn into a social unity by the new and unprecedentedly close-knit web of world-wide economic relations which was being woven blindly, from a British node, by the youthful energies of Industrialism; and they exerted themselves to help this process on its way by converting their own countrymen, and any foreigners who would give ear, to the policy of Free Trade. It would be an injustice both to the Cobdenites themselves and to their contemporaries who carried out their precepts to dismiss the Victorian British Free Trade movement as nothing more than a masterpiece of 'enlightened self-interest'. The movement was also the expression of a moral idea and of a constructive international policy. At a time when the British were the leading commercial and industrial people in the World, they threw open their empire to the commerce of all other peoples; and by this step they hoped to achieve something more than their self-interested economic aim of making Great Britain 'the Workshop of the World' and the mistress of the world market. They also hoped to promote the gradual evolution of a political world order in which the new economic world order could thrive: to create a political atmosphere in which a world-wide exchange of goods and services could be carried on in peace and security—ever increasing in activity and bringing with it, at each stage, a rise in the standard of living for the whole of Mankind.

Cobden's policy failed because he failed to reckon with the effect of the impact of Industrialism and Democracy upon a bevy of parochial states. The Cobdenites assumed that these giants could be trusted to go on lying torpid in the nineteenth century, as they had lain in the eighteenth century, until the human spiders who were spinning the new world-wide industrial web had had time to enmesh all the states of the World in their gossamer bonds, as the Lilliputians tied down Gulliver while he slept. They did not realize that, so far from rendering Gulliver incapable of ever again doing any mischief, the new forces were actually galvanizing him into fresh activity and stimulating him to run amok. And so the Cobdenites complacently encouraged their countrymen to give hostages to Fortune. They believed in such good faith that the World was destined to become a social unity, with Great Britain serving as this unified World's workshop, that they actually carried through the transformation of their country into a workshop for the World when the world unity, upon which they confidently counted, was still utterly precarious. They looked on while the population of their island increased to a size at which little more than one-fifth of the inhabitants could be maintained out of the island's own insular resources, while the remaining four-fifths had become dependent for their livelihood upon importing foreign food-stuffs and raw materials in exchange for exports of British manufactures. This new British method of earning a living required the uninterrupted maintenance of a world trade in staple commodities, and this economic requisite required, in its turn, the uninterrupted maintenance of World Peace. It is no exaggeration to say that the early nineteenth-century British pioneers of Industrialism staked their daily bread, and the daily bread of future generations in Great Britain, upon the quite unwarrantable expectation of a world order which was to be equally secure on the economic plane and on the political. That the 'practical' men of business should have taken this risk without realizing what they were doing is not so surprising; but it is less easy to understand the apparent blindness of the statesmen and the philosophers. Perhaps they were at fault in an interpretation of human nature and of Western history which overlooked some significant qualities of the first and some significant truths of the second.

In their reading of history 'the Manchester School' appear to have assumed that the Revolutionary and Napoleonic Wars which had come to an end in 1815 were destined to be the last bout of general warfare in the annals of the Western Civilization. If they had not implicitly made this assumption, they would presumably have dreaded, instead of welcoming, the new economic régime which had made the livelihood of the British people dependent on international trade, since it was evident from the history of the Napoleonic Wars that international trade might be dislocated and even destroyed by warfare on the grand scale. In making this assumption the Cobdenites were presumably counting upon the unifying and pacifying and constructive effects which it was manifestly in the nature of Democracy and Industrialism to produce. They did not reckon with the possibility that these self-same forces, at the very same time, might be producing disruptive and subversive and destructive effects by putting new 'drive' into old institutions like the Parochial State. They did not pause to consider that 'the shot heard round the World', which had been fired at Concord by 'the embattled farmers' in 1775, had been a signal, not for peace on Earth among men of goodwill,[1] but for nation to rise against nation and kingdom against kingdom.[2] Nor did they reflect that the good tidings of fraternity which had been proclaimed to all peoples by the prophets of Revolutionary France had been followed immediately by the Napoleonic conquest of Europe.

Still stranger was 'the Manchester School's' assumption that, in a world which remained politically divided against itself, the triumph of Peace would infallibly be assured by the advent of Industrialism. This fundamental tenet of the Cobdenite faith finds a characteristic expression in the following sentences:

'The past history of our race proclaims the supremacy of force, the selfishness of empire, and the subjugation of Mankind, as the prevailing aspect of Society. But the rise and progress of the industrial arts, and the extension of beneficent commerce, indicate, in terms too plain to be misunderstood, the real destiny of Society and the existence of a new epoch which shall substitute the ploughshare for the sword and the loom for the battery. The cause of Industry is the cause of Humanity.'[3]

To a twentieth-century reader of these lines, in his wisdom after the event, it will seem obvious that if the parochial states of the

[1] Luke ii. 14. [2] Matt. xxiv. 7.

[3] These sentences occur in an introduction (pp. viii–ix) prefixed by an anonymous member of the Manchester Athenaeum to his translation into English of a French observer's work—Faucher, L.: *Manchester in 1844* (London 1844, Simpkin, Marshall). The passage is quoted by J. L. and Barbara Hammond in *The Age of the Chartists* (London 1930, Longmans, Green), p. 39, footnote 4.

pre-industrial eighteenth-century Western World waged wars for the sake of snatching from one another the profits of an international commerce in superfluities, then *a fortiori* the same parochial states would fight one another *à outrance* for economic objects in an age when the Industrial Revolution had transformed the function of international commerce from an exchange of luxuries into an exchange of the necessities of life.

This consideration brings to light the mistake which 'the Manchester School' made in their interpretation of human nature. They did not apprehend that even a merely economic world order cannot be built upon merely economic foundations, and that such were not the foundations of their own belief or the mainspring of their own action. The Cobdenites themselves, as we have seen, were inspired, not by an 'enlightened self-interest', but by a moral idealism; and this idealism was religious in character and in origin. The nineteenth-century English Free Trade movement was a secularized moral and emotional substitute for eighteenth-century and seventeenth-century Methodist and Puritan religious enthusiasm. The prophets of Free Trade had still before their eyes 'the vision splendid' of an Other World, and they would not have succeeded in converting their countrymen if they had not come 'trailing clouds of glory' from a spiritual home which was not that of *Homo Economicus*. They were doing less than justice to themselves when they omitted from their official creed their own personal and traditional belief that 'Man shall not live by bread alone';[1] and at the same time they were dooming their cause to defeat; for to offer bread alone is almost as uninviting as to offer stones for bread.[2]

This fatal mistake had not been made by Gregory the Great and the other founders of Western Christendom from whom the religious inspiration of Victorian England was ultimately derived. These men, who were whole-heartedly dedicated to a supra-mundane cause, had not consciously attempted to found a world order. Their worldly aim had been limited to the more modest material ambition of keeping the survivors of a shipwrecked society alive; and in acquitting themselves of this burdensome and thankless task they were forced, against the grain, to undertake economic responsibilities. Gregory himself had to spend the best years of his life in 'serving tables' in order to save the urban proletariat of a derelict imperial city from starvation.[3] The economic edifice that was raised by Gregory and his peers was avowedly extempore and makeshift; yet, in raising it, they took care to build upon a religious rock and not upon economic sands; and, thanks to their labours,

[1] Matt. iv. 4.
[2] Matt. vii. 9.
[3] See III. C (ii) (*b*), vol. iii, pp. 267–9, above.

the structure of our Western Christendom rested on solid religious foundations in the early days when it was still only a tiny society in an out-of-the-way corner of the World. On this religious soil our Western Civilization has grown like the grain of mustard seed until it has become a tree in whose branches all the other living societies have come to lodge.[1] In less than fourteen centuries the narrow-verged Western Christendom of Gregory's generation has grown into the ubiquitous Great Society of our day. If a religious basis was required for Gregory's unpretentious economic building, and if it is this basis that has enabled our civilization to grow on the material plane until it has overshadowed the Earth, it seems unlikely, on this showing, that the vaster structure of a world order, which it is our task to build in our day, can ever be securely based upon the rubble foundation of sordid economic interests.

Perhaps these considerations may explain why the attempt of 'the Manchester School' to endow our Great Society with a world order has failed; and, if our explanation is right, it may perhaps also serve as a warning to us who, in our generation, are challenged to repeat the attempt at the eleventh hour.

5. *The Impact of Nationalism upon the Historic Political Map*

We have seen that the Nationalism which is making such havoc of our world is the outcome of a perversion of Industrialism and Democracy through the impact of these new forces upon the old institution of Parochial Sovereignty; but this does not mean that each particular national movement always sets itself in the framework of some particular parochial sovereign state which it finds waiting ready for it on the political map. If national movements did all duly conform to the pre-existent pattern of state territories and inter-state frontiers, then the havoc wrought by Nationalism would be much less extensive than it has actually been.

There are, of course, cases in which this harmony is achieved. A conspicuous example is the case of France, where the national consciousness which flared up in the French Revolution was acquired by all the inhabitants of all the territories which, in the course of previous centuries, had been brought together under the sovereignty of the French Crown, whether their mother-tongue happened to be French or Flemish or Breton or Basque or German, while the French-speaking inhabitants of Geneva and Savoy and the Swiss Confederation and the Austrian Netherlands, who happened not to be embraced within the fortuitous boundaries of France as these stood in A.D. 1789, did not come to feel themselves Frenchmen in virtue of their community of speech with their

[1] Matt. xiii. 31–2.

neighbours on the French side of the frontiers. In this case the geographical limits of a national consciousness were manifestly determined by the boundaries of a particular parochial state which was 'a going concern' before the new national consciousness was awakened within its borders. The case of France, however, is the exception rather than the rule in the history of our Western Nationalism during the last hundred and fifty years. More frequently, a national movement that has been generated by the encounter between the spirit of Democracy and the institution of Parochial Sovereignty has striven to secure for itself a new political framework of its own, either by making a schism in the body politic of some pre-existent state or by merging the identities of a number of pre-existent states in a body politic embracing them all. Both these methods of manufacturing a body politic *ad hoc* in order to incorporate a nascent nationality are exemplified in the history of the foundation of the United States, which began with the secession of the Thirteen Colonies from the British Empire and was completed by their permanent federation with one another into a new political union. There has been a similar combination of a centripetal with a centrifugal movement in the foundation of the United States of Brazil and in the creation of the Dominion of Canada and the Commonwealth of Australia and the Union of South Africa. The formation of a new national state through the purely centripetal process of a unification of a bevy of *Kleinstaaten* is exemplified in the foundations of the Kingdom of Italy and of the German Reich. The purely centrifugal process of schism is exemplified in the emergence of eighteen 'successor-states' out of the carcase of the former Spanish Empire in the New World, and twenty 'successor-states' out of the carcases of the former Ottoman, Hapsburg, Hohenzollern, and Romanov empires in Central and Eastern Europe and South-Western Asia.

Thus, on the whole, our modern Western Nationalism has been inclined to demand a drastic revision of the political map instead of being content to leave the map as it stands and to seek self-expression within an existing political framework; and this revisionary tendency in the development of national movements has confronted statesmen with a choice between two alternatives. They may either make a voluntary adjustment of the political map to a sufficient extent, and at a sufficiently early stage, to satisfy the particular national movement with which they have to settle accounts in any particular case, or else they may bend all their efforts to keeping the map as it is and defying the waves of Nationalism that are beating upon their frontiers, from outside or from within, to do their worst. In this latter event there are again two possible outcomes. Either the recalcitrant state will be shattered, sooner or later, by the national movements to which it has refused to adjust itself; and then the old map will be re-drawn on new national lines in a revolutionary way; or else the old political order may prevail and the new Nationalism may kick against the pricks in vain. In the last hundred and fifty years of Western history the revolutionary development has been the most frequent, while there have been comparatively few cases in which a national movement has been either successfully repressed or voluntarily granted a right of way.

The voluntary grant of an outright political divorce in satisfaction of a national aspiration has been rare indeed; but there are at least two examples that can be cited from our modern Western history. In A.D. 1864 the British Empire renounced its protectorate over the Ionian Islands and allowed the islanders to unite themselves with their fellow Greeks in the Kingdom of Greece.[1] In 1905 the Kingdom of Sweden waived whatever juridical right it might have claimed for insisting upon the maintenance of the existing political union between Sweden and Norway,[2] and allowed the Norwegians to assume complete sovereign independence.[3]

A less uncommon method of voluntary adjustment between national aspirations and the existing political régime has been the method of devolution in some degree short of an absolute separation of sovereignties. The classic example of this method at one end of the scale is the British device of Dominion Status, through which the people of this or that portion of the British Empire are enabled to find political expression for a local national consciousness, as it arises, by securing full self-government for themselves within the framework of a new-built parochial state which is released from all formal political ties with the rest of the British Empire except the bond of a common citizenship under a single crown.[4] At the other end of the scale we may cite the post-war treaties for the protection of alien minorities in certain of the national 'successor-states' of the old dynastic empires of Central and Eastern Europe and South-Western Asia; for the intention of these treaties is to secure to such alien minorities the minimum charter of special political rights that will just suffice to make life not intolerable for them within the frontiers of a national state which is not their own.

If we take the status granted to alien minorities under these minorities-protection treaties and the status of the fully self-govern-

1 See Cruttwell, C. R. M. F.: *A History of Peaceful Change in the Modern World* (London 1937, Milford), pp. 52–5.

2 This union was a legacy of the peace settlement of A.D. 1814–15.

3 See Cruttwell, op. cit., pp. 91–5.

4 The grant of complete national self-government to Iceland by Denmark in 1918 without breaking the link of a common crown is an example of the application of this British device outside the British Empire (see Cruttwell, op. cit., p. 95).

ing Dominions of the British Crown as the two extreme poles in the field of adjustment through devolution, we can see that the gulf between these two poles, broad though it is in itself, is spanned to-day by a gradation of statuses that lie betwixt and between the two extremes. In Switzerland, for instance, the German-speaking, French-speaking, Italian-speaking, and Ladin-speaking citizens of the Confederation have adjusted their common citizenship to their several desires for self-expression in their respective mother-tongues on a footing of perfect equality with one another. In the U.S.S.R. the British experiment of adjusting the common citizenship of a great empire to the aspirations of a hydra-headed Nationalism through the device of progressive devolution has been emulated in a complex system of autonomies within autonomies; and, although the Soviet Union has withheld, even from the constituent states of the highest category, that exercise of self-government in economic and social affairs which has always been the first instalment of autonomy to be granted to the self-governing states-members of the British Commonwealth, in other departments of administration the Soviet Union has gone farther than the British Commonwealth in almost thrusting national autonomy upon backward peoples before they have begun to demand it for themselves.

The reward which statesmanship may hope to reap from these concessions to Nationalism in these various degrees is the avoidance of a catastrophic denouement through some violent process of revolution—which is, as we have observed, the method by which, in our modern Western World, a national movement most frequently succeeds in incorporating itself into a national state. The American nation thus incorporated itself into the United States at the expense of the British Empire in the Revolutionary War of A.D. 1775–83 and at the expense of 'States' Rights' in the Civil War of A.D. 1861–5. The Italian and German nations incorporated themselves respectively into the Kingdom of Italy and into the German Reich, at the expense of the Danubian Hapsburg Monarchy on the one hand and of the Italian and German *Kleinstaaten* on the other, in the crop of European revolutions and wars which was reaped between A.D. 1848 and A.D. 1871. The Belgian nation incorporated itself into the Kingdom of Belgium at the expense of the Kingdom of the Netherlands in the revolution of A.D. 1830 and sixteen out of the eighteen Spanish-speaking nations of the New World established their separate republics at the expense of the Spanish Empire in the revolutionary struggles of the early nineteenth century.[1] Most of the European nationalities that were

[1] The seventeenth Spanish-American republic—the Republic of Cuba—had to wait for its establishment until the War of A.D. 1898 between Spain and the United States. The eighteenth—Panamá—seceded from Colombia in 1903.

formerly subject to the Romanov, Hapsburg, and Hohenzollern Empires achieved statehood in the General War of A.D. 1914–18; and the same war carried to completion a corresponding process in the Ottoman Empire which had begun more than a hundred years back.

When these instances of a revolutionary satisfaction of national aspirations in a modern Western, or Westernized, World are ranged in their chronological sequence, they offer a particularly striking illustration of the social 'law', which we have formulated in the first section of this chapter,[1] that, if old institutions obstruct the action of new social forces without ultimate success, the degree of violence of the eventual revolution is proportionate to the Time-span of its retardation. The American Revolutionary War, which is the earliest of the nationalistic upheavals in our series, was still justly reckoned, by the sagacious contemporary judgement of Gibbon, among those 'temperate and undecisive contests' of the eighteenth century which could inflict no essential injury upon the general state of happiness.[2] The nineteenth-century wars which were the price of satisfying national aspirations in Latin America, Belgium, Italy, and Germany took a toll from the spiritual and material well-being of our Western Society which was possibly not an excessive price to pay for such considerable results. On the other hand, those national aspirations in Eastern Europe and South-Western Asia which still remained unsatisfied at the opening of the twentieth century have only been able to secure their tardy satisfaction in our day at the cost of a war which has shattered two great empires into fragments; mutilated, prostrated, and inwardly distracted two others; and carried the whole of our society, without distinction between the nominal victors and their officially vanquished adversaries, to the verge of breakdown or, for all that we yet know, beyond it.

While certain national aspirations have thus found vent at a cost which has risen as time has passed, there are several national movements in the World to-day whose efforts to secure political expression have been more or less frustrated. The political map of the year 1938 displayed a Catalonia still fighting for statehood;[3] a Basqueland whose momentarily re-asserted statehood had been at least momentarily suppressed once again in favour of Castilian imperialism; and no sovereign independent state at all of the Ukraine or Armenia or Assyria or Kurdistan. It is true that, inside the Soviet

1 See IV. C (iii) (*b*) 1, pp. 135–6, above.

2 See the passage quoted in III. C (ii) (*b*), vol. iii, p. 311, and in IV. C (iii) (*b*) 3, in the present volume, p. 148, above, and in IV. C (iii) (*c*) 2 (α), p. 283, and in V. C (i) (*d*) 6 (γ), Annex I, vol. v, p. 625, footnote 1, below.

3 For the previous history of Catalan nationalism see II. D (v), vol. ii, p. 205, footnote 1, above.

Union, there were an Ukrainian and an Armenian Soviet Socialist Republic among the eleven then existing constituent states of the U.S.S.R. But the autonomy of these states within the framework of the Union was imperfect, and, even on these terms, the political unification of both the Armenians and the Ukrainians was incomplete. The large Ukrainian populations in Galicia and Volhynia were living an unhappy life under Polish rule with little comfort from a minorities-protection treaty that had been signed in A.D. 1919 and repudiated in A.D. 1934 by the Polish Government; the survivors of the pre-war Armenian community in Turkey were living as refugees under a French mandate in Syria. As for the Kurds, they were politically partitioned in 1938 between the four sovereignties of Syria, Turkey, Persia, and 'Irāq; and the measure of cultural and administrative autonomy which had been guaranteed to the Kurdish population under 'Irāqī rule was more than counterbalanced by the policy of systematic and forcible denationalization which was being pursued against their brethren in Turkey.[1] Finally, the Assyrian Nestorian Christians of Hakkīyārī and Urumīyah,[2] who had been evicted from their ancestral homes during the War of 1914–18, and who had since found life impossible to live in their post-war asylum in 'Irāq, were a tragic instance of a nationality which had 'found no rest for the sole of her foot'.[3] The same might be said of those Macedonians (and they appeared to be a large majority) who were Bulgarian in their national sentiment; for the Jugoslav Government had refused to recognize them as an alien minority which was entitled to benefit by the minorities-protection treaty which Jugoslavia had signed; and, in consequence, the Macedonians could only find freedom for their Bulgarian national self-expression at the price of leaving their ancestral homes, which were now under Jugoslav rule, and seeking asylum as refugees within the narrowly circumscribed post-war frontiers of the Kingdom of Bulgaria. These are all cases in which the impact of Nationalism upon the political map has resulted neither in an adjustment nor in a revolution but in an enormity—if it is to be regarded as a greater enormity that a national movement should be denied the self-expression which Nationalism claims as its 'sacred right' than that it should succeed in fulfilling its own sectional ambitions at the cost of an oecumenical catastrophe like the Great War of 1914–18.

[1] See IV. C (ii) (*b*) 2, p. 78, above.

[2] Spelt 'Hakkiari' and 'Urmia' in vol. ii, pp. 257–8.

[3] Gen. viii. 9. For the respective histories of the Assyrians and the Kurds in 'Irāq, during and since the emancipation of the kingdom of 'Irāq from the mandatory régime, see Toynbee, A. J., and Boulter, V. M.: *Survey of International Affairs, 1934* (Oxford 1935, University Press), pp. 109–74.

6. *The Impact of Industrialism upon Private Property*

Private Property is an institution which is apt to establish itself in societies in which the single family or household is the normal unit of economic activity—whether the family business be agriculture or stock-breeding or shop-keeping or handicraft. In societies whose economic life is organized on this family basis, Private Property is probably the least unsatisfactory system of governing the distribution of material wealth; and, if the Family is to be regarded as a social institution which is of absolute and permanent value in itself, it may be desirable to maintain the corresponding system of ownership on this account and to constrain the economic life of Society to remain in conformity with it. This question, however, has become rather academic in the Western Society of our day, when the Industrial System of economic operations has not only asserted itself but has successfully pushed its way to the acquisition of an ascendancy over our Western economic life; for, as we have seen,[1] the natural unit of activity in an industrialized society is neither the single family nor the single village community or national state, but the entire living generation of Mankind. Since the advent of Industrialism our modern Western economy has transcended the family unit *de facto* and has therefore logically transcended the family institution of Private Property. Yet in practice the old institution has remained in force; and in these circumstances Industrialism has put its formidable social 'drive' into Private Property and has gone far towards making nonsense of it by enhancing the man-of-property's social power while at the same time diminishing his social responsibility, until an institution which may have been socially beneficent in the Pre-Industrial Age has been half transformed into a social evil.

In these circumstances our society to-day is confronted with the task of adjusting the old institution of Private Property to the workings of the new force of Industrialism—under penalty, in case of failure, of seeing the old institution either swept away altogether by revolution or else swollen into an enormity which may become a deadly danger to the social health of our civilization. The method of pacific adjustment is to counteract the maldistribution of Private Property which the impact of Industrialism automatically brings about by arranging for a deliberate, rational, and equitable re-distribution through the agency of the State. The State can mitigate the ill effects of extreme individual poverty by providing public social services, and it can find ways and means for making this provision by a high taxation of extreme individual wealth. At the

[1] In IV. C (iii) (*b*) 4, pp. 169–70, above.

present time it is impossible to predict whether our current attempts to achieve an adjustment on these lines will succeed or fail; but at least it can be said that there is no inherent reason why they should not be successful—and they have the incidental social advantage that they tend to promote the transformation of the State from the killing-machine which it has been in the past into an agency for social welfare. In any case we may be fairly sure that, if we do fail in our attempt, the revolutionary alternative will overtake us in the shape of a system of State Communism which will either abolish Private Property outright or at least reduce it to vanishing-point. This seems to be the only practical alternative to an adjustment, because the maldistribution of Private Property through the operation of Industrialism would be too great a social evil to be borne if it were not effectively mitigated by some form of state intervention. Yet, as the Russian experiment indicates, the revolutionary remedy of state intervention in the form of Communism might prove to be little less deadly than the disease itself; for, in every society that exists in the World to-day, the institution of Private Property, which the impact of Industrialism is threatening to make intolerable, is at the same time so intimately bound up with what is best in a pre-industrial social heritage that its complete and abrupt abolition could hardly fail to produce a disastrous break in the social tradition.

7. *The Impact of Democracy upon Education*

One of the greatest social changes that has been brought about by the advent of Democracy in our modern Western World has been the spread of Education. In the progressive countries a system of universal compulsory gratuitous public instruction has made Education the birthright of every child in the community—in contrast to the role of Education in the Pre-Democratic Age, when it was the monopoly of a privileged minority. And this new educational system which the progressive states of the Western World have already put into effective practice has become one of the principal social ideals and aims of every state that aspires to hold an honourable place in the comity of our latter-day Great Society. When Universal Education was first inaugurated under the inspiration of Democracy, it was greeted by the Liberal opinion of the day as one of those things which many prophets and righteous men had desired to see, and had not seen,[1] through all the ages: a triumph of justice and enlightenment which might be expected to usher in a new era of happiness and well-being for our Western Society, and perhaps for the whole of Mankind. In retrospect

[1] Matt. xiii. 17.

these expectations can be seen to have left out of account the presence of several stumbling-blocks on this broad road towards the Millennium; and in this matter, as so often happens in human affairs, it has been the unforeseen factors that have proved to be of paramount importance.

One unforeseen stumbling-block has been the inevitable impoverishment in the intellectual results of Education when the process is reduced to its elements and is divorced from its traditional social and cultural background in order to make it 'available' for 'the masses'. The good intentions of Democracy have no magic power to perform the miracle of the Loaves and Fishes; and the draught which, in its benevolent ministrations, it may succeed in bringing to the lips of every child in the community will be at best a weak dilution of the elixir of intellectual life. A second stumbling-block has been the utilitarian spirit in which the fruits of Education are apt to be turned to account when they are placed within everybody's reach. Under a social régime in which Education is confined to a few members of the community who have either inherited the right to receive it as a social privilege or have earned the right by an industrious cultivation of natural intellectual gifts, Education is either a pearl cast before swine which is trampled under foot,[1] or else it is a pearl of great price which the finder buys at the cost of all that he has.[2] In neither case is it a means to an end: an instrument of worldly ambition or of frivolous amusement. The possibility of turning Education to account as a means of amusement for the masses—and of profit for the *entrepreneurs* by whom the amusement is purveyed—has only arisen since the introduction of Universal Education of an elementary kind; and this new possibility has conjured up a third stumbling-block which is the greatest of all; for it is this that has cheated our educationists, when they have cast their bread upon the waters, of their expectation of finding it after many days.[3] The bread of Universal Education is no sooner cast upon the waters of social life than a shoal of sharks rises from the depths and devours the children's bread[4] under the philanthropists' eyes. In the educational history of England, for example, the dates speak for themselves. Universal compulsory gratuitous public instruction was inaugurated in this country in A.D. 1870;[5] the Yellow Press was invented some twenty years later—as soon as the first generation of children from the national schools had come into the labour market and acquired some purchasing power —by a stroke of irresponsible genius which had divined that the

[1] Matt. vii. 6.
[2] Matt. xiii. 45–6.
[3] Ecclesiastes xi. 1.
[4] Matt. xv. 26.
[5] The system of universal direct compulsion was not made complete until 1880, and the practical establishment of free education not until 1891.

educational philanthropist's labour of love could be made to yield the newspaper-king a royal profit.[1]

A genius of a very different order, who was one of the intellectual lights of our Western World in the eighteenth century, apprehended the social 'law' that learning is apt to be sterilized by diffusion from a study of the educational history of the Hellenic World under the Roman Empire; and he predicted by analogy the truth, which we have now learnt by experience, that in our own society a like development would produce a like effect.

'All the sciences and liberal arts have been imported to us from the South; and it is easy to imagine that, in the first order of application, when excited by emulation and by glory, the few who were addicted to them would carry them to the greatest height and stretch every nerve and every faculty to reach the pinnacle of perfection. Such illustrious examples spread knowledge everywhere and beget an universal esteem for the sciences: after which, it is no wonder that industry relaxes while men meet not with suitable encouragements nor arrive at such distinction by their attainments. The universal diffusion of learning among a people and the entire banishment of gross ignorance and rusticity is therefore seldom attended with any remarkable perfection in particular persons. It seems to be taken for granted in the dialogue *De Oratoribus* that knowledge was much more common in Vespasian's age than in that of Cicero and Augustus. Quintilian also complains of the profanation of learning by its becoming too common. "Formerly", says Juvenal, "science was confined to Greece and Italy. Now the whole World emulates Athens and Rome. Eloquent Gaul has taught Britain, knowing in the laws. Even Thule entertains thoughts of hiring rhetoricians for its instruction."[2] This state of learning is remarkable because Juvenal is himself the last of the Roman writers that possessed any degree of genius. Those who succeeded are valued for nothing but the matter of fact of which they give us information. I hope the late conversion of

[1] This point has been touched upon already, by anticipation, in III. C (ii) (*a*), vol. iii, p. 241, above. There is a brilliant thumb-nail sketch of Lord Northcliffe's career in the first volume of Mr. H. G. Wells' *Experiment in Autobiography* (London, 1934, Gollancz), pp. 325–33. 'The Harmsworth brothers . . . sailed into this business of producing saleable letterpress for the coppers of the new public, with an entire disregard for good taste, good value, educational influence, social consequences or political responsibility. They were as blind as young kittens to all those aspects of life. That is the most remarkable fact about them from my present point of view, and I think Posterity will find it even more astonishing. In pristine innocence, naked of any sense of responsibility, with immense native energy, they set about pouring millions of printed sheets, of any sort of trash that sold, into the awakening mind of the British masses.' Mr. Wells also brings out the still stranger fact that the business instinct which prompted these irresponsible activities was equally blind, notwithstanding the unerringness with which it aimed at, and hit, its mark. 'Neither Newnes nor Harmsworth, when they launched these ventures, had the slightest idea of the scale of the new forces they were tapping. They thought they were going to sell to a public of at most a few score thousands, and they found they were publishing for the million. They did not so much climb to success; they were rather caught by success and blown sky-high,' without having 'had the faintest suspicion of' this 'preposterous thrust of opportunity'.

[2] Juvenal: *Satires*, No. xv, ll. 110–12.

Muscovy to the study of the sciences will not prove a like prognostic to the present period of learning.'[1]

Hume's belief that there was a progressive diffusion of learning under the Roman Imperial régime has been borne out by the discoveries of our latter-day archaeologists—from among whom we will cite, as a witness, a particularly distinguished living scholar who happens to be one of Hume's 'converted Muscovites'.

'The third century represents the climax in the spread of primary education all over the Empire. To the schools in the small villages of Egypt, which were probably connected with the temples, we owe most of the recently discovered literary papyri, which served as text-books for the pupils; and it is in the third century, in the time of Alexander Severus, that we first hear of village elementary schoolmasters as a class. In the third book of his *Opiniones* Ulpian speaks of these schoolmasters and emphasizes the fact that they were to be found both in the cities and in the villages.'[2]

In Hellenic history this climax in the spread of primary education portended, as we know from the event, not merely the extinction of an intellectual life which had maintained its vitality for a thousand years, but the downfall of a civilization; for the enlightened and benevolent Emperor Alexander Severus was the Roman counterpart of Louis XVI: the innocent victim of a deluge which had been eluded by his less reputable predecessors. The assassination of Alexander Severus in A.D. 235 was the signal, as we have seen,[3] for the overthrow of the *Pax Augusta* and for 'the Triumph of Barbarism and Religion' in the fifty years' anarchy that followed. And if we had a more intimate knowledge of the spiritual history of those times of tribulation, we might conceivably find that the educationists of the Antonine and Severan Age had been tragically defeating their own ends by placing the masses at the mercy of a propaganda which was discharged in the fullness of time, with subversive social effects, by the abler of 'the Thirty Tyrants'.

In our own world in our own generation we have had a taste of the enormity which the impact of Democracy upon Education can produce. We have suffered under the tyranny which was exercised by the press-lords in the democratic belligerent countries during the General War of A.D. 1914–18. It is perhaps true that this tyranny was partly dependent for its effectiveness upon the distraction of men's minds through the agony of an ordeal for which they had not been prepared either intellectually or morally; and it is certain that with the restoration of peace the press-lords' power

[1] Hume, David: Essay *Of National Characters*.

[2] Rostovtzeff, M.: *The Social and Economic History of the Roman Empire* (Oxford. 1926, Clarendon Press), p. 375.

[3] In IV. C (i), on p. 8, footnote 2, above.

over public affairs waned as noticeably as the profits of the other war-profiteers. Yet our experience of this temporary press-tyranny in a time of exceptional stress has given us an inkling of a social enormity which might become a permanent feature of our social life if a social stress which was exceptional in 1914–18 were to become the normal condition of life in later decades of the twentieth century, or if the minds of the masses were to become so thoroughly debauched by the corrupting influences to which their imperfect education exposes them that they learnt to respond docilely to the press-lord's suggestion even in times when the corrupter did not have a public calamity to assist him in his devil's work. Indeed, even in the relatively tranquil post-war years the enormity of the Yellow Press—and of the other instruments, like the Cinema, that have since been invented for the same lucrative business of making a profit out of the entertainment of the masses—has been still so gross that it has provoked attempts to sweep it away through revolution.

These revolutionary reactions to the impact of Democracy upon Education, like the revolutionary reactions to the impact of Industrialism upon Private Property, have found their weapon in 'the totalitarian state'; and in Communist Russia and Fascist Italy and National-Socialist Germany the press-lord and the cinema-lord have been the first members of the Capitalist tribe to be deprived of their ill-gotten and ill-used power by revolutionary violence. Yet, here again, the revolutionary remedy may prove still worse than the monstrous disease; for, in all these 'totalitarian' states, the means by which the masses have been delivered from the curse of mental exploitation for private profit has been the confiscation and manipulation of the Press and the Cinema by the Government. The elaborate and ingenious machinery for the mass-enslavement of elementarily educated minds, which was invented in the nineteenth century for the sake of private commercial profit under a régime of *laisser faire*, has here simply been taken over *in toto* by the rulers of states who have decided to employ these mental appliances for their own factious political purposes; and, though their intellectual tyranny may be less sordid in its aims, it is more crushing and more pervasive in its incidence than the tyranny of the private *entrepreneurs* into whose shoes the propaganda departments of the 'totalitarian' Governments have stepped.

Thus, in countries where the system of Universal Education has been introduced, the people are in danger of falling under an intellectual tyranny of one kind or the other, whether it be exercised by private capitalists or by public authorities; and, if they are to be saved from both of these two almost equally lamentable fates, the only third alternative is to raise the standard of mass-cultivation to a degree at which the minds of the children who are put through the educational mill are rendered immune against at least the grosser forms of either private or public propaganda. This is no easy task; for the corrupting intellectual influences to which these minds become exposed when they have been educated in an elementary way all militate against the achievement of any further intellectual advance in any mind which has been caught in the toils. In fact, the play of propaganda upon elementarily educated minds is apt to establish a vicious circle which it is hard to break; and, if it is not broken, we cannot hope even to maintain the intellectual cultivation of the masses at its present miserable level, but must face the prospect of an intellectual retrogression which will be a moral retrogression as well, and which will leave these masses of latter-day Western men and women at a considerably lower spiritual level than that at which their ancestors stood at the moment when the new social engine of Universal Elementary Education was first applied to them.[1] Happily, there are certain disinterested and effective educational agencies in the Western World of our day—such agencies as the Workers' Educational Association and the British Broadcasting Corporation in the United Kingdom and the High Schools for agricultural labourers in Denmark and the extra-

[1] If it is true, as has been argued in a previous Part of this Study (in III. C (ii) (*a*), vol. iii, pp. 239–44), that in the most progressive civilizations at the height of their achievement, as well as in the primitive societies, the vast majority of the members have so far always remained at the primitive level, then the introduction of a system of compulsory Universal Education may be described not inaptly as an intellectual offensive against the barbarism which persists—in a 'solid core of paganism and savagery'—below the surface of even the most highly polished civilization hitherto known. If this simile is legitimate, then we may remind ourselves of the fact that, when a civilization launches a military offensive against a barbarian society which is external to its own body social, it cannot allow its advance to stop short of complete victory without provoking a violent counter-offensive and courting a signal disaster. We have seen that the Celtic Völkerwanderung is attributable to the failure of the Etruscans to press home their ambitious offensive in the Po Basin (II. D (vii), vol. ii, pp. 276 and 280), and the Scandinavian Völkerwanderung to the similar failure of Charlemagne in his onslaught upon his barbarian neighbours in Northern Europe (II D (vii), vol. ii, pp. 344–6). On these analogies we cannot afford, in our age and in our world, to halt at the present inconclusive position in our educational campaign against the barbarism of our nascent Western proletariat.

The reality of the present danger of retrogression may be illustrated, *ad hominem*, by the present writer from his personal acquaintance in a village in Yorkshire. In this village, in A.D. 1935, there was still living an old agricultural labourer who had not only never been to school but had never learnt to read or write, yet was unquestionably a cultivated man in virtue of knowing a large part of the Bible by heart, constantly turning it over in his mind, savouring its beauty of language, and feeling its spiritual power. In the same village, in the same year, there was a boy who was the clever child in his family (to the point of having prospects of being selected for promotion from the primary to the secondary school), and who showed his cleverness chiefly by being an omnivorous reader. A well-meant word of congratulation to his mother drew the unexpected reply: 'Yes, he does read anything he can lay hands on, but I am going to take good care that he gets no more of that!' In this countrywoman's mind (and she was a person of character) the printed word meant mental garbage in the style of the Yellow Press, and a facility in reading, in a child, spelt exposure to moral corruption. This woman's view was a tragic commentary upon the social effects of our present half-baked system of Universal Education.

mural extensions of many universities in many countries—which are actually grappling with this problem of giving elementary education an additional impetus of sufficient force to carry the minds of the masses beyond the intellectual danger-zone where they are at the mercy of propaganda from whatever source. If these attempts to adjust the system of Education to the impact of Democracy achieve some degree of success within some measurable time, then our Western Society may still succeed in steering its hazardous educational course through the narrow fairway between a Northcliffian Scylla and a Hitlerian Charybdis; but at the present moment the fortunes of our perilous voyage are still in doubt.

8. *The Impact of Italian Efficiency upon Transalpine Government*

We have now examined six formidable disharmonies that have been produced in the institutional structure of our Western Society, directly or indirectly, by the impact of the two new forces of Democracy and Industrialism within the last hundred and fifty years. We may glance next at one or two similar events in earlier chapters of our Western history and in the histories of certain other civilizations, and we may close the inquiry upon which we are here engaged by observing the same play of forces in several situations which are apt to arise in the histories of all civilizations alike.

One example from an earlier chapter of our own Western history is the disharmony that was produced, in the transition between our 'Medieval' and our 'Modern' Age, by the impact of Italian Efficiency upon Transalpine Government.

We have observed already, at an earlier point in this Study, that in the medieval Italian cosmos of city-states Efficiency impinged upon Government, and was perverted into Autocracy, from the opening of the fourteenth century of the Christian Era onwards;[1] and that, when the medieval Italian culture radiated out into the Transalpine parts of Western Christendom, one of the effects, in the political sphere, was to transform the medieval Transalpine feudal monarchies into autocracies on a supra-Italian scale but on the efficient Italian pattern—with the result that, in every Transalpine country except England, the indigenous Transalpine parliamentary institutions wilted away. This introduction, into the Transalpine World, of an Italian political absolutism which was alien to the Transalpine genius threatened to produce a political enormity which might provoke, in turn, a revolutionary reaction. The response

[1] See III. C (ii) (*b*), vol. iii, pp. 354–7, above.

which was demanded by this challenge to the political abilities of the Transalpine peoples was manifestly an avoidance of the autocratic short cut through some adjustment of the old indigenous parliamentary institutions to the new standard of administrative efficiency; and in England this response was duly made because in England, by the time of the Italian impact, the parliamentary system had already been developed to a higher degree of efficiency than in France or in Aragon or in Castile.[1] In England the attempt of the Crown in the sixteenth century to impose the Italian standard of administrative efficiency upon the country at the price of Autocracy was victoriously resisted in the seventeenth century by the Parliament, which demonstrated its ability to govern at least as efficiently as the Crown without the sacrifice of the country's traditional institutions. In its victory over the English Crown the English Parliament found a path for the peoples of other Transalpine countries to follow; but this path was not easy.

Even in England itself the parliamentary solution of the problem did not prevail over the autocratic solution without a certain delay and therefore not altogether without a revolutionary struggle. From the accession of King Henry VII to the accession of King Charles I it looked—at any rate on a superficial view—as though in England, as in other Transalpine countries, Autocracy on the Italian pattern was to sweep the medieval system of government away; and this English trend towards Autocracy persisted for about a hundred and fifty years before it was violently reversed during the momentous half-century that began with the outbreak of the Civil War in A.D. 1642 and ended with 'the Glorious Revolution' of A.D. 1688. Indeed, if the abortive revival of Autocracy in the early years of King George III is taken into the reckoning, it may even be argued that it required the American Revolutionary War in the New World to make English parliamentary government finally secure at home.

A fortiori it required revolutions to overthrow an Autocracy which had secured a tighter grip, over a longer period, upon the political life of the Continental Transalpine countries and of the British colonies in North America—towards which the Parliament at Westminster showed the countenance of a Strafford and not of a Hampden. Accordingly, in the Thirteen Colonies, the overthrow of Autocracy exacted the price of the Revolutionary War of A.D. 1775–83, and, in France, the price of the series of political eruptions which began in 1789 and continued until 1871. The French in the nineteenth century and the Americans in the eighteenth century had to pay a heavier price than the British in the seventeenth

[1] See III. C (ii) (*b*), vol. iii, pp. 357–62, above.

century in order to purchase the same political benefits;[1] but the nemesis of delay is demonstrated still more forcibly by the case of Germany. Alone among the leading peoples of the Western World, the Germans retained an element of Autocracy in their government after A.D. 1871; and, although there was a large infusion of Parliamentarism in the constitution of the Bismarckian Reich, the survival into the twentieth century of even a remnant of a sixteenth-century autocratic régime in the government of one of the Great Powers of the Western World was sufficient to involve not only Germany herself, but all the other countries that were members of the Great Society of the day, in the catastrophe of A.D. 1914.

9. *The Impact of the Solonian Economic Revolution upon the Domestic Politics of the Hellenic City-States*

The Italian political efficiency which made its impact upon the government of the Transalpine countries of the Western World at the time of transition from the second to the third chapter of our Western history has a counterpart, in Hellenic history, in the economic efficiency which was achieved, under the pressure of the Malthusian problem, in certain city-states of the Hellenic World in the course of the seventh and sixth centuries B.C. For this new economic efficiency did not remain confined to the communities in which it had originated, but radiated out over Hellas and, in

[1] This retardation in the replacement of Autocracy by Parliamentarism in the Governments of the United States and France—a delay which condemned these two countries to purchase their constitutional transformation at the cost of a more destructive political and social upheaval than England had to undergo in passing through the same process at an earlier date—had the posthumous effect of making the derivative forms which this Parliamentarism took, in its belated acclimatization on French and American soil, more convenient models for mimesis by the rest of the World than the English original. In general the latter-day parliamentary institutions of the Central and East European countries have been inspired less by English Parliamentarism than by French, and those of the Latin-American countries, again, less by the English model than by the Constitution of the United States. This fact, and the explanation of it, have already been noticed above (in III. C (ii) (*b*), vol. iii, pp. 370–1). The explanation is that the English original has been virtually impossible to transplant because it is a spontaneous and peculiar outcrop from the English soil, whereas the American and French derivatives, being the successful products of a deliberate and artificial transplantation, lend themselves much more readily to a repetition of the same process. The unwritten constitution of the Kingdom of England, and of the United Kingdom into which it incorporated itself in A.D. 1707, has evolved, in and since the seventeenth century, quite empirically, as a direct embodiment of political practice, without either a prelude or an aftermath of political theory. On the other hand, in the history of both the American and the French Parliamentarism, the effect of the retardation in achievement has been to make theory (based on a study of English practice and not on first-hand American and French experience) come first, so that in these two cases theory, instead of being anticipated and elbowed out by practice, has had time to establish itself in its own right as a recognized political authority to which subsequent political experience must bow. It is this course of historical events that has given the French and American Parliamentarism that doctrinaire or academic touch which distinguishes them both from our British Parliamentarism; and it is precisely this academic quality—the mellow fruit of a belated development—that has made the French and American constitutions more convenient than the British to imitate.

radiating, made impacts upon both the domestic and the international politics of the whole Hellenic city-state cosmos.

In other parts of this book[1] we have come across this Hellenic achievement of economic efficiency in response to a Malthusian challenge in the classic instance of the Solonian economic revolution at Athens,[2] and we have noticed the nature of the economic change in which the achievement consisted. It was a change from 'subsistence farming' to 'cash-crop farming' accompanied by a development of commerce and industry; and this specialization in production with a view to exchange did duly secure, for a community which carried it through, an effective increase in productivity. This solution of an old economic problem, however, called two new political problems into existence; for, in changing the character of their economic activity, the peasantry of Attica—or any other country which went through this Hellenic economic revolution—inevitably implicated itself in new social relations: on one side with a new-born class of urban commercial and industrial workers whom the economic revolution had conjured into existence in the home country; and, on another side, with the peoples of neighbouring city-states, with whom the community which had now undergone the economic revolution had previously been living side by side for generations without being drawn into social intercourse with them. This customary isolation of one city-state from another was bound to give way to an interdependence on the economic plane as soon as the new economic system of production for exchange came to transcend the narrow boundaries of a single city-state territory; and when once two or more city-states had become economically interdependent, it was thenceforth impossible that they should remain, without disaster, in their pristine state of isolation on the plane of politics.

The impact of the Solonian economic revolution upon Hellenic political life will be easier to observe if we examine the effect on domestic politics and the effect on international politics separately.

In the domestic political life of the Hellenic city-states the economic revolution brought with it the problem of enfranchising the new urban class; and this new class could not be taken into the

[1] In II. D (ii), vol. ii, pp. 37–42, anticipated in I. B (i), vol. i, pp. 24–5, above.

[2] This Attic example is the classic case in two senses: on the one hand, we happen to have much more information about the Solonian economic revolution in Attica than about the corresponding revolutions in Miletus or Chalcis or Corinth or Aegina; and, on the other hand, the Solonian revolution was actually of much greater historical importance than the others, because in Attica the problem was solved with such outstanding success that a post-Solonian Athens became 'the Education of Hellas': that is to say, the triumphant pioneer in whose footsteps the rank-and-file of Hellenic city-states now deliberately set themselves to follow. In point of date, however, the Athenians were possibly the latest, besides being certainly the most successful, of the several pioneers in this Hellenic social venture.

bosom of the body politic without a radical change in the basis of political association. The traditional kinship-basis, which had served well enough in an old-fashioned agrarian society, had to be replaced, in order to enfranchise the new artisanry and bourgeoisie, by a new-fangled franchise based on property;[1] and, here again, if the tension arising from the encounter between the old political institution and the new economic force were not relieved by a timely adjustment, it was likely to produce either a revolution or an enormity.

The salutary method of adjustment was a change-over from the birth-franchise to the property-franchise at an early date, by free consent and in a moderate measure; and all these three conditions were more or less effectively fulfilled in the domestic political history of Athens within a period extending from the generation of Solon to the generation of Pericles. At Athens the adjustment was unquestionably made in good time, since it was inaugurated by the same statesman as the economic revolution of which it was the political corollary. It was made by free consent, since Solon, in so far as he exercised dictatorial powers, was invested with these powers through an agreement between the contending parties, and not through the forcible self-assertion of any single class or party over the rest. In the third place the political adjustment in Attica was distinguished by its moderation in almost all its stages. The Solonian constitutional reconstruction itself, while radical in principle, was conservative in its application, since the new-fangled property-franchise which it introduced was limited in scope by being graded in four degrees; and although, within the next century and a half, the property-qualification for the exercise of the highest political rights was reduced to zero[2] by the successive reforms of Cleisthenes and Ephialtes,[3] this eventual translation of political radicalism from principle into practice was not a mere indulgence of doctrinaire 'extremism', but was rather a statesmanlike recognition of the social fact that, since the prosperity and power of Athens had come to depend upon her industry and commerce and shipping, the industrial population of the City and the seafaring population of the Peiraeus had become at least as important politically as the agrarian interests in the countryside.

The form of political revolution which was the penalty for undue delay in making this political adjustment on the Athenian pattern

[1] See III. C (ii) (*b*), vol. iii, pp. 342–3, with footnote 1 on p. 343, above.
[2] See III. C (ii) (*b*), vol. iii, p. 343, footnote 1, above.
[3] Ephialtes appears to have been the initiator of the Attic political reform movement in the fourth decade of the fifth century B.C. which was eventually carried to completion by the younger statesman Pericles after Ephialtes' career had been cut short by assassination.

was a temporary political dictatorship (*tyrannis*), in which some individual man of action was allowed to seize despotic political power by force in order to accomplish, by the same rough and ready method, those social changes which had to be made somehow, but which the contending classes and parties were failing to accomplish by voluntary agreement. The preferable method of voluntary and timely adjustment seems to have been found so difficult in the Hellenic Society of that age that even the Athenians—who practised adjustment with greater success than any of their neighbours—proved unable to dispense with the dictatorial 'short cut' altogether. The Solonian adjustment so far failed to do its work that, in the next generation, the Athenians had to submit to the dictatorship of Peisistratus, and to allow the dictator to achieve the necessary redistribution of wealth and power within the citizen-body through the revolutionary method of confiscation which Solon had striven to avoid. At Athens, however, the Peisistratean tyranny was only an interlude between the Solonian and the Cleisthenean reform. Peisistratus himself did not effectively consolidate his power at Athens until the third attempt, and his sons did not succeed in retaining their father's political legacy for more than a few years after his death. The classic field of the seventh-century and sixth-century Hellenic *tyrannis* was not in Athens but in Miletus and Samos and Corinth and Sicyon. In these other city-states the dictatorship was not only of considerably longer duration; it was also the chief, if not the sole, instrument by which, in these communities, social changes corresponding to the contemporary changes in Attica were carried through.

At the price of a prolonged dictatorship Corinth eventually secured a stable 'oligarchic' constitution, on a conservative property-franchise, which did not differ in principle from the 'democratic' constitution of Periclean Athens. But Athens and Corinth had neighbours who did not succeed in carrying through, either by voluntary adjustment or by dictatorial revolution, the domestic political changes which the economic revolution demanded, and these communities condemned themselves, by their double political failure, to be victims of the political enormity of chronic internal strife: the dreaded, and dreadful, Hellenic political malady of *stasis*.

For example, in Corinth's daughter-city Syracuse the overthrow of the dictatorship of the Deinomenidae *circa* 466 B.C. was followed by alternate bouts of *stasis* and recurrences of dictatorship in a fatal chain which proved stronger than the idealism of a Dion or the statesmanship of a Timoleon. This chain was only broken after more than two and a half centuries had passed, and then only by the Roman sack of the city in 212 B.C., which was the end of Syracusan political history.[1] In another Corinthian foundation, Corcyra, the evil of *stasis*, inflamed by the heat of war, attained a pitch of atrocity, till then unknown in Hellenic history, in the massacres of 427–425 B.C. which have been immortalized by Thucydides.[2] At Argos, which seems to have fallen into a state of internal political torpor after the precocious dictatorship of King Pheidon, a belated attempt to catch up, at one bound, with the long political development of Athens was made in the third decade of the fifth century B.C., when the prestige of Athenian political institutions was at a premium in Hellas owing to the brilliance of the part which Athens had played in the winning of the recent Pan-Hellenic victory over Xerxes.[3] In the tardiness of this Argive attempt at adjustment we may perhaps detect one of the causes of a subsequent internal discord which signalized itself, a hundred years later, in the notorious 'clubbing incident' (ῥοπαλισμός) of 371 B.C. At Sparta, where the process of reform was arrested, the remedy of dictatorship rejected, and an endeavour made to cheat Destiny by falling out of the general Hellenic line of march in order to follow a lone Laconian trail, the natural penalty of *stasis* was only averted by being transformed into the grimmer penance of a repression which bore as heavily upon the agents of it as upon their victims, and which fatally blighted the Spartan community's growth.[4] And, even at this price, the enormity of *stasis* was not completely exorcised from Spartan life; for the agitated 'post-war' years of Hellenic history which followed the discomfiture of Xerxes witnessed, in the Peloponnese, not only the democratic revolution at Argos, but also the great insurrection of the Messenian Helots and Perioeci against their Spartan masters.

Finally, we may cite the case of Rome, a non-Greek community which was not an original member of the Hellenic Society but was a convert brought into the fold as a result of the geographical expansion of the Hellenic Civilization *circa* 725–525 B.C.[5] It was not till after this conversion that Rome entered upon the course of economic and political development which was the normal career of a Hellenic or Hellenized city-state in this second chapter of Hellenic history;

[1] The Syracusan dictatorship of the Deinomenidae (*circa* 485–466 B.C.) was followed at intervals by those of the Dionysii (405–344 B.C.), Agathocles (316–289 B.C.), and Hiero with his grandson Hieronymus (266–214 B.C.). For the function of the Sicilian despotisms in the field of international affairs see III. C (ii) (*b*), vol. iii, p. 357, footnote 1, above.

[2] Thucydides, Book III, chaps. 70–85, and Book IV, chaps. 46–8, cited in IV. C (ii) (*b*) 1, on p. 63, above, and quoted in V. C (i) (*c*) 2, vol. v, pp. 58–60, below.

[3] On this point see III. C (ii) (*b*), Annex IV, vol. iii, p. 477, footnote 2, above.

[4] See Part III. A, vol. iii, pp. 50–79, above.

[5] For this expansion see II. D (ii), vol. ii, pp. 42–5; Part III. A, vol. iii, p. 51; Part III. B, vol. iii, pp. 121–2; III. C (i) (*a*), vol. iii, pp. 148–9, above, and V. C (i) (*c*) 3, vol. v, pp. 210–12, below.

and the consequence was that in this chapter Rome passed through every stage with a Time-lag of some 140 or 150 years behind the date when the corresponding stage was traversed by Athens.[1] It is noteworthy that, for this extreme political retardation, Rome paid an extreme penalty in the shape of a long and bitter *stasis* (following upon an abortive *tyrannis* set up by sophisticated Etruscan intruders) between the Patrician monopolists of power by right of birth and the Plebeian claimants to power by right of wealth and numbers. This Roman *stasis*, which seems to have broken out early in the fifth century B.C. and which lasted on into the third, went to such lengths that the Plebs, on several occasions, seceded from the Populus by a physical act of geographical withdrawal, while it permanently established a Plebeian anti-state—complete with its own institutions, assemblies, and officers—within the bosom of the legitimate commonwealth. It was only thanks to a temporary external pressure and a subsequent domestic relief arising from a series of hard-fought wars of conquest that Roman statesmanship found it possible, in 287 B.C., to cope with this constitutional enormity by bringing state and anti-state into a working political unity; and when, in the second century B.C., the imperialism which had temporarily simplified the domestic problem revenged itself upon Rome, in due course, by exposing her to a new internal political strain, the makeshift character of the settlement of 287 B.C. was rapidly revealed. The unannealed amalgam of Patrician and Plebeian institutions, which the Romans had been content to accept as the ultimate constitution of their ramshackle republic, proved so inept a political instrument for attempting to achieve a new social adjustment that, after a respite of little more than a hundred and fifty years' duration, Rome fell into a second bout of *stasis* (*flagrabat* 133–31 B.C.); and this bout was far more terrible than the first because of the formidable increase, in the interval, in the scale of Roman life and in the driving-power of Roman social forces. This time, after a century of self-laceration, the Roman body politic submitted itself to a permanent dictatorship; and since, by this date, Roman arms had completed their conquest of the Hellenic World, the Roman *tyrannis* of Augustus and his successors incidentally provided the Hellenic Society with its universal state.[2]

This stupendous persistent ineptitude of the Romans in fumbling with their domestic political problems presents an extreme, and at first sight extraordinary, contrast to their unfailing and unrivalled ability in making, retaining, and organizing their foreign

[1] For this Time-lag in Roman social evolution in this chapter of Hellenic history see further V. C (ii) (*b*), vol. vi, p. 288, and Part XI, below.

[2] For the Roman Empire's historical role as a Hellenic universal state see I. C (i) (*a*), vol. i, pp. 52–3, above.

conquests. The explanation of this apparent paradox may be that the militarism and imperialism of the Romans were the expression of their native abilities, while their domestic political institutions were an imitation—and a belated imitation—of Hellenic models which were hardly calculated to work smoothly except in the hands that had originally fashioned them. At any rate it is noticeable that the Athenians—who failed signally, in the fifth century B.C., to create that urgently needed Hellenic international order which the Romans succeeded in establishing in a fashion some four hundred years later—were unrivalled, for their part, in the success with which they exorcised *stasis* from their domestic political life. During the 189 years running from 507 to 318 B.C.—a period which saw Athens accomplish her greatest achievements in every field of activity—the city enjoyed an almost unbroken régime of domestic political tranquillity under a moderate constitution.[1] The only serious breaks were the tyrannies of the Four Hundred in 411 B.C. and the Thirty in 404–403 B.C.; and these are exceptions of the kind that prove a rule; for these Attic recurrences of dictatorship were direct effects of the abnormal strain to which the Athenians were subjected by the Great War of 431–404 B.C., with its disastrous outcome; and, considering the magnitude of this Athenian political disaster in the international field, we can only marvel at the transitoriness of the inevitably untoward domestic political effects.

10. *The Impact of the Solonian Economic Revolution upon the International Politics of the Hellenic World*

The contrast, which we have just touched upon, between the political histories of Athens and Rome has brought out the fact that the comparative success of Athens in her domestic politics was offset by a signal Athenian political failure in the field of international affairs; and this may serve to remind us that we have still

1 This 'Golden Age' of Athenian democracy, which began *circa* 507 B.C. with the Cleisthenean reforms, is comparable to the 'Golden Age' of British parliamentarism, which began in A.D. 1688 with 'the Glorious Revolution'. In the terms used in a previous part of this Study (in III. C (ii) (*b*), vol. iii, pp. 366–8, above) these two comparable Athenian and British 'Golden Ages' were each of them a 'constructive phase'—distinguished by substantial achievements in many spheres of activity—in a movement of Withdrawal-and-Return. Moreover the combination of timeliness with moderation, which was the note of Athenian constitutional development during these 189 years, is equally characteristic of British constitutional history during the corresponding period. The contrast between the timely and moderate English Revolution of A.D. 1688 and the violent course taken by the French Revolution, the outbreak of which was delayed until 1789, is analogous to the contrast between the Cleisthenean Reform of 507 B.C. and the Argive and Laconian political upheavals in the third and fourth decades of the fifth century B.C. At a later stage again the British Reform of A.D. 1832 was more moderate (in spite of being delayed for 40 years owing to the General War of A.D. 1792–1815), than the French upheavals of 1830 and 1848 and 1870–1.

to examine the effect, in this field, of the impact of the Solonian economic revolution upon Hellenic political life.

In a previous age, when exceptionally favourable opportunities for sheer extensive geographical expansion had made it possible for the Hellenic Society to provide for a growing population without departing from the old-fashioned economic system of subsistence farming, the self-sufficiency (*αὐτάρκεια*) of each single Hellenic city-state, on every plane of social activity, was a simple matter of fact. The Solonian economic revolution was needed in order to solve the new economic problem of continuing to provide for a population which had not ceased to grow, yet finding this provision within the limits of a Hellenic World whose expansion had been cut short by the successfully organized resistance of its Syriac and barbarian neighbours. The solution lay, as we have seen,[1] in changing over from subsistence farming to a specialized production—industrial as well as agrarian—with a view to exchange; but this solution involved the abandonment of economic self-sufficiency, since the new economic system of specialization and exchange could not be made to yield the enhanced productivity which was its object, so long as its field of action was confined within the narrow limits of the standard-size city-state domain.

In order to produce its fruits, the new economy must burst the bounds of the single city-state and operate freely over a vastly larger area, embracing not only the entire Hellenic World but also Egypt in one direction and Scythia in another and the African and European hinterlands of the West Mediterranean Basin in a third. In fact, the Solonian economic revolution could not be carried out without enlarging the ordinary working unit of Hellenic economic life from a city-state scale to an oecumenical scale; and the historical fact that this economic revolution did take place means that this great enlargement of the field of economic operations was actually achieved. By the beginning of the fifth century B.C. the immense area whose range has just been indicated had actually come to be the normal field of economic activity for the wine-growers and olive-oil producers and potters and merchants and sailors of economically progressive Hellenic city-states like Miletus and Corinth and Aegina and Athens. But this expansion of the range of economic activity from a parochial to an oecumenical scale solved an economic problem only to create a political problem; and the solution of the economic problem remained precarious so long as the consequent political problem had not been solved with equal success along its own lines.

The Milesians and Aeginetans could never count, for certain,

[1] In IV. C (iii) (*b*) 9, p. 201, above.

on the livelihood which they had learnt to gain through an oecumenical economic activity, unless their freedom of economic action in this oecumenical field were guaranteed by the establishment of some kind of political order on the same oecumenical scale. So long as the ordinary working unit of Hellenic political life continued to be the city-state whose limits had now been so far transcended on the economic plane, it was possible that a political conflict between city-states, in the shape of war or privateering or piracy, might at any moment arbitrarily cut short those oecumenical economic activities which had now become indispensable for the maintenance of the increased and increasing population of Aegina or Miletus individually and of Hellas as a whole. In short, in the international field the Solonian economic revolution confronted the Hellenic Society with the necessity for establishing a political world order. The accomplished fact of the abolition of city-state self-sufficiency on the economic plane now called for its abolition on the political plane as well; and when the transition from a parochial to an oecumenical range had just been successfully achieved on the one plane, there was no apparent reason, *a priori*, why it should not be achieved on the other plane in due course.

The obstacle in the way was the inherited political institution of City-State Sovereignty; and the removal of this obstacle to political solidarity was the task which was set by Fate to Hellas when the fifth century B.C. opened. The obstacle, however, became more formidable in the act of being grappled with; for this City-State Sovereignty which had previously been taken for granted began to draw attention and inspire affection as soon as it became evident that its existence was threatened. From the opening of the fifth century B.C. onwards the whole of the rest of Hellenic political history can be formulated in terms of an endeavour to transcend City-State Sovereignty and of the resistance which this endeavour evoked.[1] Before the fifth century closed, the obstinacy of the resistance to the accomplishment of this urgent political task had brought the Hellenic Civilization to its breakdown; and though the problem which had baffled an Athenian first attempt to solve it was eventually solved in a fashion by Rome, it was not solved in time to prevent the disintegration of the Hellenic Society from running its course to its final dissolution.[2] In this outcome of the impact of the Solonian economic revolution upon the international

[1] For the idolization, in the Hellenic World, of the institution of the Sovereign City-State see IV. C (iii) (*c*) 2 (*β*), pp. 303–20, below.

[2] This explanation of the breakdown and disintegration of the Hellenic Civilization has been touched upon, by anticipation, in Part III. B, vol. iii, p. 122, footnote 3, and in III. C (ii) (*b*), vol. iii, p. 340, footnote 1, above. See also V. C (ii) (*b*), vol. vi, pp. 287–91, below.

politics of the Hellenic World the alternatives of adjustment, revolution, and enormity present themselves once again.

In this case the solution of the problem through adjustment lay in a permanent limitation of City-State Sovereignty by voluntary agreement between the city-states themselves for the sake of providing the necessary political security for a now indispensable economic intercourse.

A treaty apparently dating from about the middle of the fifth century B.C., and embodying an agreement to such effect between two city-states on the western shore of the Crisaean Gulf, has come into the hands of the modern Western historian through the accident of archaeological discovery;[1] and since the two high contracting parties were, both of them, small and obscure communities, while the district in which they were situated—the Ozolian or 'colonial' Locris—is included by Thucydides in a region of North-Western Continental Greece which he takes as a 'living museum' of the elsewhere obsolete Hellenic Society of the Dark Age,[2] we may reasonably conjecture that a practice which had spread to this backward part of Hellas by about the year 440 B.C. had become general throughout the Hellenic World in the course of the first half of the fifth century. The type of treaty of which this surviving treaty between Oeanthea and Chaleum may be taken as a late and unimportant example, is a bilateral agreement between two city-states for the enactment between them, *ad hoc*, of a rudimentary code of international law to govern their economic relations with each other; and no doubt this expedient for dealing with the new problem of international politics was useful as far as it went. At the same time it is manifest that the results must have fallen far short of what was needed. For instance, the treaty between Oeanthea and Chaleum, by itself, can hardly have contributed appreciably to the security of international trade and seafaring even in the waters of the Crisaean Gulf; for there were several other equally small and obscure, but also equally sovereign, city-states which were likewise 'riverain Powers'; and all the 'riverain Powers', between them,

[1] The bronze tablet on which the text is inscribed was found at Galaxídhi (the latter-day equivalent of the Hellenic Oeanthea) and is now in the British Museum. The text is printed, with a translation and commentary, by E. L. Hicks and G. F. Hill in *A Manual of Greek Historical Inscriptions*, 2nd edition (Oxford 1901, Clarendon Press), pp. 73–6. The treaty provides that 'no Oeanthean, if he make a seizure, shall carry off a foreign merchant from Chalean soil, nor a Chalean a merchant from Oeanthean soil; nor shall either Oeanthean or Chalean seize a merchant's cargo within the territory of the other city. If any one breaks this rule, it shall be lawful to seize him with impunity. ...' On the same tablet there is also inscribed, in a different hand, the text of regulations made in one of the two contracting states (presumably in Oeanthea, where the tablet was found) for assuring to resident aliens the enjoyment of their treaty-made legal rights.

[2] Thucydides, Book I, chap. 5. For this social backwardness of North-Western and Northern Greece in the second chapter of the history of the growth of the Hellenic Civilization see III. C (ii) (*b*), Annex IV, vol. iii, pp. 478–9, above.

would only have accounted for a small fraction of the shipping which plied within sight of their shores; for this waterway was one of the main approaches to the Pan-Hellenic shrine at Delphi, and in the fifth century B.C. Delphi was in communication with almost every community in the Hellenic World, as far afield as Cyrene and Trebizond and Marseilles. In order to provide effectively, by means of bilateral treaties, for the security of all ships and merchandise that had occasion to traverse the Crisaean Gulf, the single bilateral treaty between Oeanthea and Chaleum would have to be supplemented by a vast network of such treaties, not only binding the local riverain Powers among themselves, but also binding each of them to almost every other state-member of the Hellenic Society.[1] When we consider further that the Crisaean Gulf, though an important sea-route in itself, was only a minute fraction of the total surface of the Mediterranean and its annexes, and that almost the whole of this area was embraced, at this date, in the field of Hellenic maritime trade,[2] we can see at once that the creation of anything like a comprehensive and uniform system of oecumenical law-and-order in the Hellenic World on a basis of voluntary bilateral treaties was a Psyche's task.

As a matter of historical fact, we find that, in those attempts at establishing a Hellenic world order which came the nearest to success, a network of voluntary bilateral treaties was only one of several bases on which the structure was reared. In these relatively successful experiments a local enterprise in treaty-making was reinforced by the stimulus of a general emergency and by the leadership of a single predominant Power. The Delian League (*vivebat* 478–454 B.C.) was established under the stimulus of the Pan-Hellenic war of defence and liberation (*gerebatur* 480–478 B.C.) against the Achaemenian Power, and under the leadership of Athens, whose naval strength had made her the saviour of Hellas and left her the mistress of the Eastern Mediterranean. The Roman Empire was established under the stimulus of a paroxysm of war and revolution which threatened the Hellenic Society with imminent dissolution in the last century B.C., and under the leadership of Rome, who had already (between 220 and 168 B.C.) delivered 'the knock-out blow'

[1] It is significant that the bilateral Chaleo-Oeanthean treaty, above quoted, goes on to say that 'the property of a foreigner [i.e. a citizen of any third state] may be seized on the sea without incurring the penalty, except in the actual harbour of the city'.

[2] The only Mediterranean waters that were a *mare clausum* to the Hellenes at this time were those bounded by the north coast of North Africa west of a point just north by west of Carthage, by the south-east coast of Spain as far as a point at some unknown distance north-east of (the future site of) Cartagena, and by the Carthaginian insular possessions in the Balearic Islands, Sardinia, and the western tip of Sicily. For the light thrown upon the limits of this Carthaginian preserve by the terms of successive commercial treaties between Carthage and Rome see Strachan-Davidson, J. L.: *Selections from Polybius* (Oxford 1888, Clarendon Press), pp. 65–70.

to all other Great Powers in the Hellenic World of that age.[1] The circumstances show that, in Hellenic history, the establishment of a political world order by process of adjustment was never even approached without a potent admixture of the untoward elements of revolution and enormity. The revolutionary way of constructing an oecumenical political framework for an oecumenical field of economic activity was to abrogate the institution of City-State Sovereignty altogether, by *force majeure*, and to bring the whole of the ground, when it had been cleared of previous obstructions by this high-handed method, under the common roof of a single universal state. The enormity which was the penalty of failure to achieve a world order by either adjustment or revolution was an agglomeration of city-states in which a certain measure of city-state autonomy was preserved, but in which the association between the participating communities was neither on a voluntary basis nor on an equal footing, but was maintained by a forcible and selfish domination of some single city-state over all the rest. This inequitable system of association was evidently the line of least resistance for arriving at a compromise between an old parochial tradition and the new necessity of transcending it; but it was none the less an enormity inasmuch as it only transcended the old parochialism in a material sense, while morally it capitulated to it by allowing one strong parochial community to indulge its egotism to an unprecedented degree at its weaker neighbours' expense. The moral condemnation which this enormity evoked in Hellenic consciences was not averted by the euphemistic title of 'hegemony' (*das Führerprinzip*), by which a 'tyrant-city' preferred to describe its twofold exploitation of its own superiority in military power and of the World's need for political unity.

If we let our minds run over the course of Hellenic history, we shall observe that this enormity of 'hegemony', as well as the revolutionary alternative of the *Gleichschaltung* of City-State Sovereignty by a merger into a universal state, was already a familiar phenomenon in the Hellenic World before the foundation of the Delian League; and we shall also observe that in the Roman Empire—which belatedly and partially succeeded, where the Delian League had failed, in establishing a Hellenic world order through an association of city-states—the vicious element of 'hegemony' far outweighed the salutary element of freedom, and was only eliminated, in the course of the Empire's history, by a gradual process of *Gleichschaltung* which destroyed the autonomy of all Rome's subject cities *pari passu* with the ascendancy of Rome herself.

If we examine rather more in detail the circumstances in which

[1] See the quotation from Polybius in III. C (ii) (*b*), vol. iii, pp. 312–13, above.

the Delian League was founded in 478 B.C., we shall find, as we might expect, that its organizer, the Athenian statesman Aristeides, was working, not in a political vacuum, but in an atmosphere of political precedents of which his work distinctly bears the marks.

It would have been strange if Aristeides had borrowed nothing from the institution of 'hegemony', when Athens herself had been living under the 'hegemony' of Sparta, off and on and in varying degrees, ever since the Spartan King Cleomenes had expelled the Peisistratidae from Athens in 511 B.C.[1] Indeed, the very occasion which had called for the establishment of the Delian League was the renunciation of this Spartan hegemony in 478 B.C. in respect of Athens and those Asiatic Greek communities which had just been liberated from Achaemenian rule; and if the Lacedaemonian Government had not made this deliberate withdrawal[2] it is safe to say that the Delian League would never have been called into existence at all. In the circumstances it was natural that the Athenians should step into the Spartans' shoes and should include an element of Athenian 'hegemony' in the structure of an Athenian-made experiment in a Hellenic world order.

It was equally natural that, in framing a new international régime for a constellation of Hellenic city-states which had been incorporated, for some sixty or seventy years past, in the Achaemenian Empire, Aristeides should borrow certain convenient institutions to which these communities had grown accustomed under the Achaemenian régime from which they had just been liberated. The Achaemenian precedent is unmistakably accountable for an arrangement so alien from the indigenous Hellenic tradition of city-state sovereignty as the imposition of a money-contribution to a federal war-chest at Delos upon states-members of the League which were unable, or disinclined, to contribute an effective contingent of war-ships to the federal navy;[3] and the same alien tendency towards *Gleichschaltung*, in the characteristic vein of the Achaemenian Empire and of every other universal state,[4] may perhaps be discerned

[1] See III. C (ii) (*b*), vol. iii, p. 336, footnote 3, above.

[2] For the motives which inspired this Spartan policy see Part III. A, vol. iii, pp. 70–1, above.

[3] The majority of the city-states which acquiesced in the payment of a money-tribute as their contribution to the League, and which accepted the assessment that was made by Aristeides, were 'liberated' communities which had previously belonged to the Achaemenian Empire; and for these the tribute was something to which they had long since been broken in. It made little difference to them that the money previously payable to a treasury at Sardis or Dascylium should now be made payable, instead, to a treasury at Delos. It is perhaps significant that Scyros and Carystus, which were the only two city-states that were brought into the Delian League at the beginning by coercion instead of by consent, had neither of them ever lost their independence to the Achaemenian Empire; and it may also be noted that Naxos and Thasos, which were the first two members of the League that endeavoured to secede, had neither of them had more than a brief taste of Achaemenian domination—Thasos for only thirteen years, and Naxos for only eleven years, ending in 479 B.C.

[4] For the character and genius of universal states see further Part VI, below.

likewise in the progressive centralization, in the courts at Athens, of private litigation in suits to which citizens of the 'allied' cities were parties: an infringement of local sovereignty which was perhaps more bitterly resented than the exaction of the monetary tribute. This Athenian attempt to establish a Pan-Hellenic common law and a Pan-Hellenic jurisdiction on an Athenian basis would have been impossible if the Athenians had not possessed, and employed, the means of coercion; this coercion was only thinly veiled by the network of treaties, between Athens and her associates in the Delian League, on which the process of judicial centralization was formally grounded; and this expedient of conjuring into existence an oecumenical system of law-and-order by compelling the city-states to enter into a network of treaties, wholesale, was demonstrably borrowed by the Athenians from their Achaemenian predecessors in the dominion over the Asiatic Greeks. It is recorded that, after the Achaemenian Government had succeeded in suppressing the great Asiatic Greek revolt of 499–494 B.C., Darius's brother 'Artaphernes, the Statthalter at Sardis, summoned delegates from the [re-subjugated] city-states to his presence, and compelled the Asiatic Greeks to enter into treaties with one another for the regulation, by judicial procedure, of disputes [between their respective *ressortissants*], in substitution for their [traditional] practice of seeking satisfaction, in such cases, by [methods of barbarism like] piracy and brigandage'.[1]

It will be seen that if the Delian League was, in one aspect, an endeavour to provide the Hellenic Society with a political world order by a process of voluntary adjustment, it was also partly inspired by the precedents of a Spartan 'hegemony' and an Achaemenian *Gleichschaltung*; and in this light the disastrous failure of this endeavour, and of all its successors, no longer appears surprising. Every one of these successive Hellenic attempts at a world order was morally a hybrid product; and the healthy ingredient in the social compound was always eventually overcome by the poisonous ingredients with which it had been contaminated from the outset. Within the brief Time-span of the 'Pentecontaetia' (478–431 B.C.) the Delian League degenerated into the international tyranny of the Athenian Empire; the chastisement with whips, which this Athenian imperialism inflicted upon the Hellenic World during the half-century ending in 404 B.C., was renewed and outdone by the chastisement with scorpions which a Roman imperialism inflicted, in its turn, during the two centuries that followed the outbreak of the Hannibalic War; and even when, at last, the long Roman oppression was transmuted into a belated Hellenic world

[1] Herodotus: Book VI, chap. 42.

order by the genius of Caesar and the remorse of Augustus, this magnified reflexion—or travesty—of the Delian League did not escape in the long run the untoward metamorphosis which had so swiftly overtaken its original. The ultimate fate of the Hellenic cosmos of city-states under the aegis of the Caesars was a *Gleichschaltung* of the kind to which the Asiatic Greek communities had been subjected already both after the foundation of the Delian League, under the aegis of Athens, and before the foundation of the Delian League, under the aegis of the Achaemenidae. In short, the history of Hellenic endeavours to create a political world order is a tragedy whose gloom is hardly relieved by one brief gleam of sunshine in a Periclean spring and another in an Antonine 'Indian Summer'.[1]

II. *The Impact of Parochialism upon the Western Christian Church*

While the Hellenic Society broke down and went into disintegration through a failure to transcend a traditional Parochialism, our Western Society has failed—with consequences that are still hidden in the future—to maintain a social solidarity which was perhaps the most precious part of its original endowment.

In the time of transition from the so-called 'medieval' second chapter of our Western history to the so-called 'modern' third chapter, one of the most prominent symptoms and significant expressions of the current social change was the rise of a new Parochialism in contrast and opposition to the Oecumenicalism of the outgoing age. In our generation it is not altogether easy for us to regard this Parochialism dispassionately and objectively, even in studying its origins, on account of the vast evils which it has since brought, and is still bringing, upon our World owing to its anachronistic and incongruous survival in the radically altered circumstances of our day. Yet we can still perceive that there was much to be said in favour of the change from a medieval Oecumenicalism to this modern Parochialism at the time when this change took place some four or five centuries ago. Our medieval Western Oecumenicalism, for all its moral grandeur, was a ghost from the past—a cherished legacy from the last chapter in the history of the antecedent Hellenic Society[2]—and on the medieval stage of Western social life there was always an unseemly discrepancy between the theoretical supremacy and ubiquity of this inherited oecumenical idea and the *de facto* anarchy which played so large a part in actual

[1] For the Age of the Antonines as 'the Indian Summer' of the Hellenic decline and fall see IV. C (ii) (*b*) 1, pp. 58–61, above.

[2] On this point see further Part X, below.

medieval practice. By comparison the new Parochialism which boldly usurped the stage at the dawn of the Modern Age was more honest in its account of itself, and more effective in enforcing its pretensions, though at the same time it might be more cynical intellectually and on a lower level morally. In any case the new force won the day; and its victory affected every aspect and every institution of our Western life, since this modern Parochialism had just as many facets as there were activities in the society which gave it birth. In politics it displayed itself in the form of a plurality of new parochial sovereign states, in letters in the form of a plurality of new vernacular literatures, and in the field of religion it collided violently with the medieval Western Church.

The violence of this collision was due partly to the fundamental fact that the Church, now elaborately and powerfully organized under the Papal 'hierocracy', was the master institution of the medieval oecumenical régime,[1] and partly to the incidental fact that Italy, which happened for historical reasons to contain the local seat of the Papacy, was also the place where the new Parochialism first worked itself out experimentally in the seed-bed of the North and Central Italian constellation of medieval city-states.[2] Through the combined effect of these two facts the rise of the modern Parochialism confronted the Papal Church with a grave and urgent problem.

This problem was probably open to a solution by adjustment along lines which the Papacy had already reconnoitred while it was still at the height of its power. For example, in encountering the parochial impulse to make use of local vernacular languages as vehicles for cultural expression side by side with, or even in substitution for, Latin, the Roman Church had already made at least one notable concession—namely, the permission to have the Roman Liturgy translated into the Croatian language and conveyed in Glagolitic characters—in a frontier zone where it found itself in direct competition with a rival, the Orthodox Church, whose policy in

[1] This position of unrivalled dominance in Western Christendom, to which the Papacy finally attained through its victory in its war to the knife with the Hohenstaufen Dynasty, of course placed on the Papacy's shoulders a unique responsibility for worthily and successfully upholding the oecumenical principle of which it had deliberately made itself the exclusive exponent when it insisted upon delivering a 'knock-out blow' to its already discomfited adversary, the Holy Roman Empire. In so far as it failed to live up to this self-imposed responsibility, the Papacy was in part the cause of the subsequent outbreak of Parochialism, of which it was also the most eminent victim; and its share in the disastrous work of bringing the new spirit of Parochialism to a head was undoubtedly very large. The ὕβρις with which the Papacy exploited its victory over the Empire—in first trampling on a prostrate foe and then attempting to exercise on its own account the oecumenical despotism which it had refused to tolerate in the hands of a Barbarossa or a Frederick II—quickly turned the public opinion of Western Christendom, not only against the Papacy itself, but against the whole principle of oecumenicalism which was now embodied in the Papacy alone. On this see further IV. C (iii) (*c*) 3 (β), pp. 512–84, below.

[2] See I. B (i), vol. i, p. 19, and III. C (ii) (*b*), vol. iii, pp. 341–6, above.

regard to the ecclesiastical use of vernacular languages was much more liberal than the ordinary Roman practice.[1] At more recent dates the Papacy had gone still farther in the terms on which it accepted the allegiance of renegades from the Orthodox Church and from the Monotheletes, Monophysites, and Nestorians. So long as these Uniates were willing to acknowledge the Roman supremacy and to subscribe to the Roman doctrine, they were granted a wide licence to persist in the liturgical use not only of their vernacular languages but even of their traditional rites.

Again, in dealing with the medieval precursors of the modern parochial sovereign states, the Popes who had been intransigent in maintaining their 'hierocratic' claims against the secular pretensions of the Holy Roman Emperors had been more accommodating in their policy towards temporal rulers in England and Castile and other kingdoms on the fringes of the medieval Western World, whose pretensions to local sovereignty had no bearing on the status of the Pope in his own Roman See, while their goodwill and loyalty to the Roman Church seemed worth purchasing at a certain price owing to the importance of the services which it was in the power of these outlying local sovereigns to render or withhold for the propagation of the Catholic Faith and the Roman connexion *in partibus infidelium et schismaticorum.*

Thus the Holy See was not altogether unschooled in rendering unto Caesar[2] the things that are Caesar's by the time when a full-fledged neo-Caesarism asserted itself—first in the persons of the despots who made themselves masters of a majority of the Italian city-states, and later in the persons of their Transalpine emulators: a Spanish Ferdinand and Isabella, a French Louis XI, and an English Henry VII. In this political field a possible line of adjustment to the new situation had already revealed itself; and, in the event, the Vatican learnt to follow this line to considerable lengths in the various concordats which it ultimately made with a number of parochial sovereign Powers whose assertion of their sovereignty

[1] For the use of a Slavonic version of the Liturgy in certain Roman Catholic dioceses of Croatia, Istria, and Dalmatia see *The Cambridge Medieval History*, vol. iv (Cambridge 1923, University Press), p. 229. For the survival of the original Slavonic Alphabet, i.e. the so-called Glagolitic Alphabet, here, after it had been superseded by the so-called Cyrillic Alphabet among the Slavonic adherents of the Orthodox Christian Church, see Jensen, H.: *Geschichte der Schrift* (Hanover 1925, Lafaire), pp. 189–90; Bury, J. B., in his edition of Gibbon's *The History of the Decline and Fall of the Roman Empire* (*editio minor*, London 1900–2, Methuen, 7 vols.), vol. vi, p. 550; and Runciman, S.: *A History of the First Bulgarian Empire* (London 1930, Bell), Appendix IX. For the part played by the Slavonic Liturgy in the relations between the Western and the Orthodox Church in South-Eastern Europe in the latter part of the ninth century see IV. C (iii) (*c*) 2 (*β*), pp. 375–7 and 381–2, and IV. C (iii) (*c*) 2 (*β*), Annex II, pp. 608–10, below.

[2] Caesar, that is, in the metaphorical sense; for the Holy Roman Emperors, who laid claim to the title of Caesar *de jure*, were notably less successful in coaxing or wringing concessions from the Holy See than were the medieval kings of England and Castile.

in the teeth of the Roman 'hierocracy' had not gone the length of a repudiation of their ecclesiastical allegiance. The lengths to which the Vatican—schooled, at the thirteenth hour, by overwhelming adversity—has eventually learnt to go, on its own part, in deferring to parochial secular Powers, are exemplified in the terms of the concordats which it has concluded respectively in A.D. 1929 and in A.D. 1933 with two 'post-modern' apostles of a 'totalitarian' Parochial Sovereignty, Signor Mussolini and Herr Hitler. These two latest instances, however, in which the policy of concession has been carried to extremes, perhaps indicate that the form of compromise which is represented by the conclusion of a concordat between the Papacy and the sovereign government of a parochial state may be not so much a genuine adjustment as a 'face-saving' method of acquiescence in a revolutionary *fait accompli*.

The modern system of concordats between the Holy See and the parochial secular sovereigns of Catholic populations is the Dead Sea Fruit of abortive oecumenical councils; and it is arguable that the Papacy missed the opportunity of making a genuine adjustment between the oecumenical tradition of Western Christendom and the new spirit of Parochialism when it set itself in opposition to the Conciliar Movement which was mooted at the turn of the fourteenth and fifteenth centuries and was brought into action in the successive councils of Pisa (*sedebat* A.D. 1409), Constance (*sedebat* A.D. 1414–18), and Basel (*sedebat* A.D. 1431–49).

The Conciliar Movement was a constructive effort, on lines of constitutional development which were well known and well tried in Western Christendom by that date, to provide a remedy for the unchecked and unbalanced power which the Papacy had acquired through the overthrow, in the thirteenth century, of the Imperial authority. So long as the Holy Roman Empire had been something more than a shadow, the autocratic oecumenical power of the Papacy had been at least partially balanced by the salutary counterweight of a second oecumenical power of the same autocratic order. The downfall and demoralization of the Papacy, which had swiftly followed the ruin of the Hohenstaufen, and which had been shamefully exposed in 'the Babylonish Captivity' (A.D. 1305–77) and in the Great Schism (A.D. 1378–1417),[1] had made it abundantly clear that an uncontrolled Papal autocracy in the Western *Respublica Christiana* was even more disastrous for the Papacy itself than it was pernicious for the society in which the Papacy was the leading institution. The Conciliar Movement offered a golden opportunity for Papal statesmanship because it aimed at remedying flagrant

[1] For the history of the medieval Papacy as an example of the tragedy of κόρος-ὕβρις-ἄτη see IV. C (iii) (*c*) 3 (β), pp. 512–84, below.

abuses by moderate measures. Though it was in one aspect an expression of the new Parochialism, it was ready to be content with a measure of devolution within the framework of an undismembered *Respublica Christiana*, and it repudiated the Hussite anticipation of those radical forms of Parochialism which triumphed eventually, a hundred years later. Again, though the stimulus by which the Conciliar Movement was evoked was the scandal of persistent Papal misconduct, the moderate majority of its supporters were ready to see the Christian Republic endowed with a parliamentary constitution without demanding that the Pope should cease to be its executive head.

The settlement which was here proffered to, and refused by, the one surviving oecumenical authority in Western Christendom was in essence the same as that which, in the parochial kingdom of England, had already been accepted by the Crown after a few discouraging experiments in kicking against the pricks. In the course of the thirteenth and fourteenth centuries the English Crown had come to realize that, on a long view, it would be strengthening and not weakening its own position by taking Parliament into partnership; and by the opening of the fifteenth century the Papacy—which had lately been experiencing as great disasters and humiliations as an English King Richard II—might have learnt the same lesson as the English Crown through the wisdom that is born of suffering.[1] Instead, the popes who encountered the Conciliar Movement chose, one after another, to harden their hearts; and this Papal intransigence was disastrously successful. It succeeded in its purpose of bringing the Conciliar Movement to naught; and for this barren success it paid the disastrous price of throwing away a last opportunity for adjustment[2] and thereby condemning Western Christendom to be rent by a violent internal discord between its ancient oecumenical heritage and its new parochial proclivities.

This discord has had issue in a melancholy crop of revolutions and enormities.

The revolutionary solution of the conflict between Parochialism and an Oecumenical Church is not only to be seen in that overt revolution by which, in the Protestant parts of the Western Chris-

[1] Aeschylus: *Agamemnon*, ll. 177–8, quoted in I. C (iii) (*b*), vol. i, p. 169, footnote 1, and II. C (ii) (*b*) 1, vol. i, p. 298, above, and IV. C (iii) (*c*) 3 (*β*), in the present volume, p. 584, V. C (i) (*c*) 2, vol. v, p. 78, V. C (i) (*d*) 4, vol. v, p. 416, footnote 3, and V. C (ii) (*a*), vol. vi, p. 275, below.

[2] If the Papacy had sincerely welcomed the Conciliar Movement and had loyally co-operated with it, then Western Christendom in the Modern Age might perhaps have succeeded in reconciling a traditional unity with a new parochial consciousness by transforming the Papal imperium, without any revolutionary break, into something like that historic 'amphictyony' which succeeded in some degree in holding together the parochially minded city-states of Hellas by keeping alive their common feeling of attachment to the two oecumenical religious centres at Delphi and Thermopylae.

tian World, the authority of the Papacy has been officially replaced by that of the individual conscience privately interpreting the Scriptures. The power which has been taken from the Papacy in Protestant countries, in order to be transferred in theory to this new authority, has in practice passed in large measure into the hands of the Parochial State, and, in passing, has helped to create the modern Western institution of Parochial Sovereignty. In the modern Western World, however, Parochial Sovereignty has never been a monopoly of the Protestant countries. One source of it, as we have seen,[1] has been the constellation of Italian city-states which arose, before Protestantism was heard of, in a part of Western Christendom in which Protestantism has never gained a footing. And, in the Transalpine World at the beginning of the Modern Age, Parochial Sovereignty raised its head in the Protestant and the Catholic countries simultaneously. This fact points to the truth that the revolutionary solution of the conflict between Parochialism and an Oecumenical Church is not only to be seen in the drastic revolution of Protestantism, but is also to be detected in the less sensational changes which have come over the relations between Church and State in countries that have remained within the Catholic fold. In the modern Catholic World these changes have been carried through sometimes amicably, under the mask of concordats, and sometimes acrimoniously, as in France and Italy between the outbreak of the French Revolution and the outbreak of the General War of 1914–18, or (belatedly) in Mexico since the outbreak of the revolution of 1910; but in some form and in some degree they have taken place in a majority of the leading Catholic countries. 'Libera Chiesa in Libero Stato'[2] and 'État Laique' are the characteristic formulae of the neo-pagan nationalists *in partibus Catholicorum* who have taken the offensive in carrying this revolution out; and some of the most high-handedly revolutionary apostles of 'the totalitarian state'—from a Hapsburg Joseph II and a Corsican Napoleon I to a Romagnol Mussolini and an Upper Austrian Hitler—are the nurslings of purely Catholic environments.

The enormities which have arisen out of the conflict, in so far as it has not been resolved either violently through revolution or

[1] See p. 215, footnote 2, with references, above.

[2] This formula was employed by Cavour in his speech on the Roman Question before the Italian Chamber of Deputies on the 27th March, 1861, but it was not invented on this occasion nor, apparently, by Cavour himself. It already occurs in a letter of the 20th November, 1860, which was written to Cavour from Rome by Pantaleoni enclosing a list of conditions to be offered as the basis for an arrangement between the Holy See and the Kingdom of Italy. The first point on this list is: 'Si proclamerà il principio di Libera Chiesa in Libero Stato.' Against this point Cavour wrote 'Approvo' before returning the draft to Pantaleoni on the 28th November. These texts are to be found in *La Questione Romana negli Anni 1860–1866: Carteggio del Conte di Cavour con D. Pantaleoni, C. Passaglia, O. Vimercati* (Bologna 1929, a cura della Commissione Reale Editrice).

peacefully through adjustment, have been of two kinds. On the one hand, in a number of countries which broke away altogether from the Roman ecclesiastical connexion by turning Protestant, the modern Parochial Sovereign Power was not content with emancipating itself from the Papal domination in the political sphere, but attempted, at the same time, to substitute itself for the Papacy in the ecclesiastical sphere by usurping, within its own narrow frontiers, the 'hierocratic' authority which the medieval Papacy had claimed—and had more or less effectively exercised—on an oecumenical range which had extended over the whole of Western Christendom. On the other hand the Roman See itself, as well as a number of bishoprics within the Transalpine domain of the Holy Roman Empire—e.g. Mainz and Trier and Köln and Liége and Salzburg and Münster—stooped to the level of their secular adversaries by entering the political arena and assuming the prerogatives of the modern Parochial Sovereign State on a petty scale.

The incongruity of these petty ecclesiastical principalities with the oecumenical imperium of the Roman Catholic Church, and the incompatibility of their mundane preoccupations with the Church's 'other-worldly' mission, are so flagrant that, in the eyes of a non-Catholic observer, this temporal power wears the appearance of a grievous incubus; and, whatever may be the official view of the Roman Church herself, the non-Catholic will be inclined to regard it as a signal gain for her that the Transalpine prince-bishoprics have been extinguished once for all through being sacrificed to the territorial greed of the secular Powers in the transactions that took place between the secular states of the Holy Roman Empire and the envoys of the French Republic during the Congress of Rastadt between A.D. 1797 and A.D. 1799, and that the Papal State in Central Italy temporarily suffered the same fate, first when it was partitioned between the Napoleonic French Empire and the Napoleonic Kingdom of Italy, and secondly when it was annexed to the present Kingdom of Italy in successive stages between A.D. 1860 and A.D. 1870. On the same showing, the rehabilitation of the parochial secular sovereignty of the Pope, within the minute domain of the State of the Vatican City, in virtue of the Lateran Treaty of A.D. 1929,[1] can only be regarded as having been, in itself and in principle, an error of Papal statesmanship, however sincerely the non-Catholic observer may admire the courage and perseverance and ingenuity which were displayed by Pope Pius XI and by Signor Mussolini alike in carrying their negotiations through to a successful conclusion, and however heartily

[1] See Toynbee, A. J., and Boulter, V. M.: *Survey of International Affairs, 1929* (Oxford 1930, University Press), pp. 422–78.

he may rejoice at the consequent suspension of a feud between the Holy See and the Kingdom of Italy which, for three generations, had tormented the consciences of millions of Italians who happened to be both devout Catholics and patriotic citizens. Nevertheless the non-Catholic must regret that, at a time when, to all appearance, the Parochial Sovereign State has become the chief obstacle to human welfare and indeed the arch-enemy of the Human Race, the Pope should have ranged himself, even if only formally,[1] on the side of this pernicious institutional anachronism by successfully reasserting his own title to Parochial Sovereignty, instead of being content to remain on the side of the angels in virtue of the fortunate misfortune which had deprived him of an invidious earthly kingdom and had thrust upon him, instead, the *beau rôle* of 'the prisoner of the Vatican'.

As for the usurpation of the medieval Papacy's 'hierocratic' authority by Protestant parochial sovereigns, it has produced the fantastic doctrine of 'the Divine Right of Kings' which is still working havoc in the Western World in the grim shape of the pagan worship of sovereign national states. This doctrine found its corollary in the field of international affairs in the monstrously cynical formula '*Cujus Regio Ejus Religio*', upon which the first truce in the long-drawn-out and ever more inclusive Western Wars of Religion was based in A.D. 1555.[2] The practical outcome of the doctrine and the corollary, taken together, in the Protestant countries has been the replacement of the repudiated oecumenical Catholic Church, one and indivisible, by a plurality of parochial 'Churches', each of which is borne upon the establishment of some particular parochial sovereign state, is subject *de facto*, in matters spiritual as well as temporal, to the sovereign power in the state to which it belongs, and is confined in its membership to such Christians as happen to live within this particular state's frontiers. In

[1] Pope Pius XI's own point of view in regard to the reassertion of the Pope's territorial sovereignty is set forth in an address which he delivered to the parish priests of Rome on the 11th February, 1929, at the moment when the Lateran agreements were being signed:

'A true and proper and real territorial sovereignty (there being no such thing in the World, at least down to the present, as a true and proper sovereignty which is not embodied in a definitely territorial form) [is] a status which is self-evidently necessary and due to One who, in virtue of the divine mandate and the divine representation with which He is invested, is unable to be the subject of any sovereignty on Earth. . . . We must have that quantum of territory that just suffices as a support for the attribute of sovereignty itself, that quantum of territory without which sovereignty could not exist because it would not have a place where to rest the sole of its foot.'

This view of the indispensability of territorial sovereignty for the Papacy seems to have been derived by Pope Pius XI from a passage in the memoirs of Talleyrand which is quoted in Toynbee and Boulter, op. cit., p. 446.

[2] This formula, which was adopted in A.D. 1555 at Augsburg, was already implicit in the Recess of the Diet of Speier which had laid down in A.D. 1526 that in matters of faith each Prince should so conduct himself as he could answer for his behaviour to God and the Emperor.

the freest flight of imagination it would be difficult to conceive of a sharper contradiction of the essence of Christianity—and the essence of all the other historic 'higher religions' as well[1]—than is embodied in this monstrous product of the impact of Parochialism upon the Western Christian Church in the Modern Age of our Western history.[2]

12. *The Impact of the Sense of Unity upon Religion*

The 'higher religions' with a mission to all Mankind are relatively recent arrivals on the mundane scene of human history. They are not only unknown in primitive societies; they have not arisen even among societies in process of civilization until after certain civilizations have broken down and have travelled far along the path of disintegration. It is in response to the challenge presented by the disintegrations of civilizations that these 'higher religions' have made their appearance on Earth.[3] The religious institutions of civilizations of the unrelated class,[4] like those of primitive socie-

1 For the 'higher religions' and their embodiment in would-be universal churches see V. C (i) (*c*) 2, *passim*, vol. v, and Part VII, below.

2 It may be noted that this Protestant enormity of 'established' parochial churches has, in most Protestant countries, been mitigated by a subsequent revolution whereby part, or even the whole, of the local Protestant community has shaken itself free from the local state's control. In the United States—which did not acquire its sovereign independence until a hundred years after the beginning of the modern Western Age of Toleration in matters of religious allegiance, practice, and belief—there has never been an established church; and a complete separation of Church and State has been the régime under which both Protestant and Catholic American citizens have lived from the beginning. In older Protestant states, like England and Scotland, the original established Protestant Church has been maintained, but its membership has been depleted by the foundation of a number of local free Protestant Churches side by side with it; and at the time of revising this chapter for the press in A.D. 1938 it looked as though similar effects were likely to be produced by similar causes in Germany as a result of the pressure to which the German Protestants were being subjected by the rulers of the Third Reich. In regaining their freedom from the control of a parochial secular government, these Protestant Nonconformists have recaptured one of the two great advantages which the Catholics have never lost. Yet these free Protestant Churches still remain at a disadvantage on the whole, for, while they have escaped from the political servitude which is part of the enormity of the 'established' Protestant Churches, they have bought this liberation at the price of carrying Parochialism to a still farther extreme. The classic example of the fissiparous tendency which has been the bane of the free Protestant churches is afforded by the history of Methodism during the sixty-six years immediately following the death of the originator of the movement, John Wesley, in A.D. 1791. It is noteworthy, however, that, during the eighty-two years ending in 1938, the history of Methodism was made happier by a persistent tendency towards re-union which presents a striking and encouraging contrast to the prevalence of the opposite tendency during the preceding chapter. Among the Methodists of Great Britain the reunion was achieved by stages in 1857, 1907, and 1932; among those of the United States it was achieved in 1938–9; among those of Canada it was achieved in 1883. More significant still was the merger, in 1925, of the Canadian Methodists with the Canadian Presbyterians and Congregationalists in a new 'United Church of Canada'. (For all these events see Piette, M.: *John Wesley in the Evolution of Protestantism* (English translation, London 1937, Sheed & Ward), pp. 393–408.) If in the twentieth century the free Protestant churches were truly on the road towards reconciling freedom with unity, their prospects were bright.

3 See I. C (i) (*a*), vol. i, pp. 53–7, above, and V. C (i) (*c*) 2, *passim*, vol. v, pp. 58–194, together with Part VII, below.

4 For the classification of civilizations into an 'unrelated' and a 'related' class see I. C (ii), vol. i, pp. 129–33, above.

ties, resemble the 'established churches' of our modern Western Protestant countries (which are, in fact, reversions to a primitive type) in being bound up with the secular institutions of parochial communities. Through these parochial associations Primitive Religion is bounded by the narrow vision, and implicated in the tribal feuds, which are characteristic of parochial communities in all times and places. But these positive limitations and blemishes of Primitive Religion have one important offsetting negative advantage: they foster a spirit of 'Live and let live' in the relations between one primitive tribal worship and another. Under primitive social conditions the plurality of mutually independent parochial communities is taken for granted as a permanent state of affairs; the possibility of their consolidation into a universal state by one or other of the two alternative methods of voluntary pacific co-operation or violent conquest remains undreamt-of; and since the gods of each and every primitive parochial community are regarded as members of its social circle on much the same footing as its human and animal members, the moral acceptance of a social situation in which a number of separate parochial communities are living together side by side carries with it the moral acceptance of a plurality of parochial gods—each independent of his or her neighbour and locally master or mistress of his or her own domain in perpetuity.

In this social condition human souls are blind to the unity and ubiquity and omnipotence of the Godhead; but, precisely on that account, they are immune from the temptation of succumbing to the sin of intolerance in their relations with other human beings who happen to worship this Godhead under different forms and titles. It is one of the keenest ironies of human history that the very illumination of human souls which has brought into Religion a perception of the Unity of God and of the consequent brotherhood of Mankind[1] should at the same time have made these souls prone to fall into the deadly sins of intolerance and persecution for Religion's sake. The explanation is, of course, that the idea of Unity in its application to Religion impresses the spiritual pioneers who first stumble upon it in this context with so overwhelming a conviction of its transcendent importance that they are apt to plunge into any short cut which promises to hasten the translation of their idea into reality by enabling them to impose it upon their fellow men.[2]

[1] For the sense of unity which is one of the fruits of the harrowing experience of living in a disintegrating society, see V. C (i) (*d*) 7, vol. vi, pp. 1–49, below.

[2] The imperious impulse which commands the pioneers to lead their fellow men along the trail that they have blazed by their individual enterprise, and the expedients to which they are apt to resort in their attempts to obey this 'categorical imperative', have been discussed in III. C (ii) (*a*), vol. iii, pp. 234–48, above.

This enormity of intolerance and persecution in the cause of Unity has shown its hideous countenance, almost without fail, wherever and whenever a 'higher religion' has been discovered and formulated and preached; and the manifestation of this spirit in the souls of religious innovators arouses it, by a sure contagion, in the souls of their opponents. The lists are set for conflict by the tension which arises, in the nature of the relation, between a creative personality and the uncreative mass of Mankind;[1] and the conflict is most bitter when it is fought on the field of Religion, because this is the most important field of any in the whole range of human life.[2]

This fanatical temper flared up in the abortive attempt of the Emperor Ikhnaton (*imperabat circa* 1370–1352 B.C.) to impose his vision of Monotheism upon the Egyptiac World.[3] The high-handedness of the Imperial prophet and the rancour of the organized priesthood of the old school which successfully frustrated his efforts are both apparent even in the fragmentary record of the encounter that has been recovered by our modern Western archaeologists; and the venom of this conflict has proved so potent that, since the record was unearthed the other day, after having been totally forgotten for at least 1,500 years,[4] the taint that clings to it has infected the souls of a generation which has no personal stake in the issue. Through this virulent infection dry-minded Western Egyptologists of the twentieth century of the Christian Era have been transfigured into passionate champions or critics of a controversial Egyptiac personality of the fourteenth century B.C.

An equally ardent fanaticism casts its lurid light over the rise and development of Judaism. A savage denunciation of any participation in the worships of the kindred Syriac communities round about is the reverse side of that 'etherialization' of the local worship of Yahweh into a monotheistic religion which was the positive, and immense, spiritual achievement of the Prophets of

[1] See loc. cit.

[2] The sound of this conflict can be heard echoing even in some of the sayings that are attributed in the Gospels to Jesus: e.g. Matt. x. 34–7 and Luke xii. 49–53; but this militant tone and temper is not, of course, characteristic of the founders of the 'higher religions' and the philosophies. The political career of Muhammad (see III. C (ii) (*b*), Annex II, vol. iii, pp. 466–72, above) is the exception which proves a rule that the Kingdom of the Prophets is not of This World (John xviii. 36). The contrast which a religious Transfiguration and a philosophic Detachment both alike present to a mundane Futurism and Archaism is examined in V. C (i) (*d*) 8–11, vol. vi, pp. 49–168, below. The corresponding contrast between different conceptions of the Saviour is examined in V. C (ii) (*a*), vol. vi, pp. 175–278, below.

[3] For Ikhnaton's enterprise and its failure see I. C (ii), vol. i, pp. 145–6, above, and V. C (i) (*d*) (6) (δ), Annex, vol. v, pp. 695–6, below.

[4] Reckoning from the extinction of the Egyptiac cultural tradition, which fell into oblivion between the third and the fifth century of the Christian Era. The question whether Ikhnaton and Alexander may not both have derived their vision of Unity—Alexander independently of Ikhnaton—from the teaching of the priesthood of Amon-Re is raised in V. C (ii) (*a*), vol. vi, p. 246, footnote 5, below.

Israel and Judah; and this violent spirit passed over from speech into action in the militant *émeute* of the Maccabees against the Seleucidae and in the war to the knife between Judaism and Hellenism which was carried on thereafter intermittently—perpetually breaking out again in ever more violent bouts—for the next three centuries, until finally Judaism received 'the knock-out blow' from the Roman military arm of a Hellenic universal state under the auspices of Vespasian and Hadrian.[1] So persistently did Judaism turn this forbidding face of its Janus-head towards its Hellenic neighbours that it was possible for a Roman satirist who was a child of the last generation of this secular conflict (Decimus Junius Iuvenalis *scribebat circa* A.D. 100–27) to cite the Jew as a sheer embodiment of anti-sociality and superstition[2]—in an apparently genuine ignorance of the moral and intellectual sublimity of the religion which had betrayed its Jewish champions into their notorious militancy. In the history of Christianity likewise—both in its internal schisms and in its encounters with alien faiths—we observe the same evil spirit of fanaticism breaking out again and again.

On this showing, the impact of the Sense of Unity upon Religion is apt to beget a spiritual enormity, in the shape of religious intolerance and religious persecution, which may provoke revolution if it is not exorcized by adjustment.

The moral adjustment which meets the case is the recognition and practice of the virtue of Toleration. The right motive for Toleration[3] is an intuition that all religions alike, from the highest to the lowest, are quests in search of a single common spiritual goal, so that they do not differ in their aim but merely in the extent of the progress which they are able respectively to make with the aid of their varying lights. This intuition makes it apparent that the propagation of one religion at the expense of other religions through the employment of methods of barbarism, on the ground that the religion in whose name the persecution is carried on is a religion of a higher order, is a moral contradiction in terms, since oppression and injustice and cruelty are negations of the very essence of spiritual sublimity.

In at least one noteworthy historical case such tolerance has been

[1] For the lapse of Judaism into militancy see further V. C (i) (*c*) 2, vol. v, pp. 68–9; V. C (i) (*d*) 6 (δ), Annex, vol. v, pp. 657–9; and V. C (i) (*d*) 9 (γ), vol. vi, pp. 120–3, below.

[2] See Juvenal: *Satires*, No. xiv, ll. 96–104. Cf. Horace: *Satires*, Book I, Satire v, ll. 100–1.

[3] For the other and less worthy motives which have inspired, in our modern Western World, a toleration which asserted itself before the end of the seventeenth century and has been losing ground since the beginning of the nineteenth, see the present chapter, pp. 227–8, as well as IV. C (iii) (*b*) 3, pp. 142–3 and 150, and IV. C (iii) (*b*) 4, pp. 184–5, above, and V. C (i) (*d*) 6 (δ), Annex, vol. v, pp. 669–72, and V. C (ii) (*b*), vol. vi, pp. 316–18, below.

enjoined by a prophet upon his followers on this highest ground. The Prophet Muhammad prescribed the religious toleration of Jews and Christians who had made their political submission to the secular arm of Islam, and he gave this ruling expressly on the ground that these two non-Muslim religious communities, like the Muslims themselves, were 'People of the Book'. It is significant of the relatively tolerant spirit which animated a Primitive Islam that, when the Arab conquests brought the Zoroastrians of Iran, as well as the Christians of Syria and Egypt and Mesopotamia and 'Irāq, under Islamic domination, the privilege originally reserved for the Jews and Christians was tacitly extended to the Zoroastrians—though these were not 'People of the Book' in the strict technical sense of believers in the inspiration of the Jewish or Judaistic Scriptures.[1] In tolerating the religion of their Zoroastrian subjects the Primitive Muslim conquerors stretched a point of theological exegesis because they recognized that in fact Zoroastrianism was a 'higher religion' of the same order as Judaism and Christianity and Islam itself, and that therefore any attempt on their part to stamp Zoroastrianism out by force would result, in proportion to the extent of its material success, in debasing and defaming the Islam in whose name the persecution would be conducted.

Less worthy motives than Muhammad's—though perhaps not less worthy than those of his Umayyad successors[2]— appear to have been mainly responsible for the interludes of toleration which punctuate the annals of intolerance in the history of Christianity.

The temporary toleration of the surviving non-Christian religions of the Hellenic World within the boundaries of the Roman Empire, side by side with Christianity, under the rule of Christian Emperors between A.D. 311/13 and A.D. 382/92, and the corresponding toleration of Christianity, side by side with an abortively reorganized Paganism, from A.D. 361 to A.D. 363, under the rule of the Emperor Julian,[3] was manifestly not so much inspired by conviction as dictated by policy. This mutual forbearance was, indeed, little more than a political recognition of the social fact that, during those years, the material strength of the Christians and the non-Christians in the Roman Empire was approximately equal, so that, for the time being, neither party could attempt to suppress the other with any hope of success. The Christians abandoned the policy of

[1] The solitary reference to the Zoroastrians in the Qur'ān is quoted in V. C (i) (*d*) 6 (δ), Annex, vol. v, p. 674, footnote 2, below.

[2] For the fiscal motive that seems to have moved Muhammad's sceptical-minded Umayyad successors to abide, in the matter of tolerating the non-Muslim 'People of the Book', by the precept of a prophet in whose divine inspiration they perhaps had little or no belief in their heart of hearts, see IV. C (iii) (*c*) 2 (β), Annex III, p. 630, and V. C (i) (*d*) 6 (δ), Annex, vol. v, pp. 674–7, below.

[3] For Julian's abortive Neoplatonic Church see V. C (i) (*d*) 6 (δ), Annex, vol. v, pp. 681–3, and V. C (ii) (*a*), vol. vi, pp. 222–3, below.

toleration with alacrity as soon as they became conscious that, in material strength, they had acquired a decisive superiority[1]—just as, in the preceding bout of the struggle, the anti-Christians, on their part, had persisted in a policy of persecution until it had become plain, even to the headstrong and obstinate soul of a Galerius, that the Christian Church was now powerful enough to hold its own against any degree of material pressure which the Imperial Government could apply.[2]

The intolerance to which the Christians abandoned themselves before the end of the fourth century of the Christian Era persisted in Western Christendom for thirteen hundred years; and it did not loose its grip upon Western souls until the iniquity of the fathers had been visited upon the children. The atrocities which were inflicted in the name of the Western Church, during the long centuries of its unity and omnipotence, upon Cathars in Languedoc[3] and Jews and Muslims in Castile[4] and Pagans in the Balticum,[5] were more than avenged within the span of 150 years which followed the first collision between the Western Christian Church and the modern Western spirit of Parochialism.[6] Overtaken by this disruptive movement within its own bosom, with the old spirit of intolerance still reigning in its heart, Western Christendom proceeded to inflict upon its own body social the treatment which it had been wont to mete out to non-Christian minorities. Internecine Wars of Religion between Catholic and Protestant Christians ravaged the Western World from the outbreak of the Reformation until the latter part of the seventeenth century; and these wars were conducted with the ferocity that is peculiar to fratricidal conflicts.[7] This great blot upon our Western Civilization in the early Modern Age presents (like our latter-day Wars of Democracy and Industrialism) an extraordinary contrast to the rapid yet sure-footed contemporary progress of the same society in other directions; and the fact that religious intolerance, in this time and place, was not merely an absolute evil in itself but was also a glaring anachronism no doubt accounts in part for the unprecedented excesses to which it ran in this latest chapter of its history in the West.

The period of religious toleration upon which our modern Western Christendom entered about the third quarter of the seven-

[1] See V. C (i) (*d*) 8 (δ), vol. vi, p. 89, below.

[2] See V. C (i) (*d*) 3, vol. v, pp. 407–9, and V. C (i) (*d*) 6 (δ), Annex, vol. v, p. 650, below.

[3] See IV. C (iii) (*c*) 3 (β), p. 369, and IV. C (iii) (*c*) 3 (β), Annex, pp. 652–6, below.

[4] For the treatment of the Jews under Christian rule in the Iberian Peninsula see II. D (vi), vol. ii, pp. 243–8, above.

[5] See II. D (v), vol. ii, pp. 172–4, above.

[6] See IV. C (iii) (*b*) 11, pp. 218–22, above.

[7] See IV. C (iii) (*b*) 3, pp. 142–3, above, and V. C (i) (*d*) 6 (δ), Annex, vol. v, pp. 668–71, and V. C (ii) (*b*), vol. vi, pp. 315 and 318–19, below.

teenth century of the Christian Era came unpardonably late, and, when it did come at last, it seems to have been inaugurated in a still more cynical mood[1] than the religious toleration in the fourth-century Roman Empire. In that quarter of the seventeenth century the Catholic and Protestant factions in the Western Church, which had been carrying on an embittered religious warfare all over the face of the Western World for the past century and a half, rather suddenly abandoned the struggle (and this almost simultaneously in every province of Western Christendom)—not, apparently, because they had become convicted of sin and convinced that the propagation of a religion by force of arms was a crime against the spiritual cause which they were seeking thus perversely to serve, but rather on the impulse of an overwhelming fit of disillusionment. The warring religious factions seem to have realized at last, at this date, that their forces were so evenly matched, and that the prospect of any substantial change in their balance of power was so slight, that neither of them had the remotest prospect of gaining a decisive victory over the other even if the conflict were to be prolonged *in saecula saeculorum*; and at the same time they seem to have become aware that they no longer cared sufficiently for the questions of theological doctrine and ecclesiastical government which were at issue to be willing to contemplate any further sacrifices of their own personal comfort for the sake of making their own particular views on these subjects prevail. The régime of religious toleration which our immediate forebears enjoyed for some two centuries and a half, and which we begin to see slipping away from us to-day[2], was originally established upon no more solid a moral basis than an enlightened repudiation of 'enthusiasm' (a seventeenth-century and twentieth-century virtue which was an eighteenth-century and nineteenth-century vice).[3]

Nevertheless Toleration, from whatever motive it may derive, is the sovereign and essential antidote to a fanaticism which the impact of the Sense of Unity upon Religion is apt to breed; and, when this prosaic safeguard is lacking or is lost, the nemesis is a choice between a revolutionary revulsion against Religion itself and a hideous triumph of the fanatical spirit. The revolutionary alternative is exemplified in Lucretius's 'Tantum religio potuit suadere malorum',[4] in Voltaire's 'Écrasez l'infâme',[5] and in Gambetta's 'Le cléricalisme, voilà l'ennemi'.[6] The triumph of fanaticism is exemplified in the exploits of the Jewish Sicarii—the 'gangsters'

1 For this mood see also the other passages cited on p. 225, footnote 3, above.
2 See V. C (ii) (*b*), vol. vi, pp. 316–21, below.
3 See IV. C (iii) (*b*) 3, p. 145, above.
4 Lucretius: *De Rerum Natura*, Book I, l. 101.
5 A frequent colophon in Voltaire's letters.
6 Speech in the Chamber of Deputies at Paris on the 4th May, 1877.

of the Zealot persuasion who bear the principal responsibility for the horrors of the great Romano-Jewish War of A.D. 66–70—and in the history of the Spanish Inquisition.

13. *The Impact of Religiosity upon Caste*

The Lucretian and Voltairean view that Religion in itself is an evil—and perhaps the fundamental evil in human life—might be supported by citing, from the annals of Indic and Hindu history, the sinister influence which Religion has ascertainably and incontestably exercised, in the lives of two civilizations, upon the institution of Caste.

This institution, which consists in the social segregation of two or more geographically intermingled groups of human beings or social insects, is apt to establish itself wherever and whenever one community makes itself master of another community without being able or willing either on the one hand to exterminate the subject community or on the other hand to assimilate it into the tissues of its own body social.[1] In the recent history of our own Western World a caste-division has arisen in the United States between the dominant element of White race and European origin and the subject Negro element (whom, *ex hypothesi*, their masters had no desire to exterminate, since they deliberately imported them from Africa as slaves). A similar caste-division has arisen between the two corresponding elements in the population of the Union of South Africa (where the White intruders would find it impossible to exterminate the native African Negroes even if they wished to commit the crime, since, even within the narrow borders of the Union, the Negroes now outnumber the Whites in the proportion of more than three to one, with the whole of Black Africa ranged behind them from the Kalahari Desert to the Sahara and from the Limpopo to the White Nile). In the sub-continent of India the institution of Caste seems to have arisen out of the irruption of the Eurasian Nomad Aryas into the former domain of the so-called 'Indus Culture' in the course of the first half of the second millennium B.C.;[2] and in this Indian case the resulting situation has been still more unhappy than it is in the two cases just cited; for in India there was not only an original diversity of race between the dominant caste and the subject caste—a diversity which has continued to produce its estranging effect socially and morally, long after it has been physically obliterated—but the relative material power of

[1] For an examination of this institution of Caste see II. D (vi), vol. ii, pp. 216–20, and Part III A, vol. iii, pp. 22–107, above.

[2] For the Aryas and the part which they played in the post-Sumeric Völkerwanderung, see I. C (i) (*b*), vol. i, pp. 104–6, and II. D (vii), vol. ii, pp. 388–91, above. For the Indus Culture and its relation to the Sumeric Civilization see I. C (i) (*b*), vol. i, pp. 107–8, with Annex III, above.

the two castes was in inverse ratio to their relative civilization. The Aryan conquerors of the Indus Basin in the second millennium B.C. were barbarians, like the 'Dorian' conquerors of Crete and the Lombard conquerors of Italy,[1] while their victims, like the Minoans and the Romans, were the heirs of a once great civilization.

It will be seen that this institution of Caste has no essential connexion with Religion. In the United States and the Union of South Africa, where the Negroes have abandoned their ancestral religions and have adopted the Christianity of the culturally superior Whites, the divisions between churches cut right across the divisions between races (though it is true that the Black and White members of each church are segregated from each other in their public worship as in all their other social activities). In the Indian case, on the other hand, we may conjecture that from the beginning the castes were distinguished by certain differences of religious practice, since the Aryan intruders who constituted the dominant caste were presumably still in the primitive social stage at which the religious and the secular side of life are not yet distinguished from one another, and at which the possession of a distinct and separate life as a community consequently implies the practice of a distinct and separate religion as well. It is evident, however, that this hypothetical religious ingredient in the original form of the local Indian version of the institution of Caste must have been accentuated when the Indic Civilization developed the religious bent which it has bequeathed to a Hindu Society that is related to it by 'affiliation'.[2] It is further evident that this impact of Religiosity upon the institution of Caste in India must have aggravated the banefulness of the institution very seriously. Caste is always on the verge of being a social enormity; but when Caste is 'keyed up' by receiving a religious interpretation and a religious sanction in a society which is hag-ridden by Religiosity, then the latent enormity of the institution is bound to rankle into a morbid social growth of poisonous tissue and monstrous proportions.

In the actual event the impact of Religiosity upon Caste in India has begotten the unparalleled social abuse of 'Untouchability'; and since there has never been any effective move to abolish or even mitigate 'Untouchability' on the part of the Brahmans—the hieratic caste which has become master of the ceremonies of the whole caste-system and has assigned to itself the highest place in it—the enormity survives, except in so far as it has been assailed by revolution.

[1] For the social effect of the 'Dorian' conquest of Crete and the Lombard conquest of Italy see II. D (iii), Annex, vol. ii, pp. 396–8, above.

[2] For the religious bent of the Indic and Hindu civilizations see III. C (iii), vol. iii, pp. 384–5 and 388, above.

The earliest known revolts against Caste are those of Mahavira the founder of Jainism (*occubuit prae* 500 B.C.) and Siddhārtha Gautama, the founder of Buddhism (*vivebat circa* 567–487 B.C.): two creative personalities who were non-Brahmans themselves and who ignored the established barriers of Caste in recruiting the bands of disciples whom they gathered round them to wrestle with the moral problems of the Indic 'Time of Troubles'.[1] If either Buddhism or Jainism had succeeded in captivating the Indic World, then conceivably the institution of Caste might have been sloughed off with the rest of the social debris of a disintegrating Indic Society, and an affiliated Hindu Civilization might have started life free from this incubus. As it turned out, however, the role of universal church in the last chapter of the Indic decline and fall was played not by Buddhism but by Hinduism—a parvenu archaistic syncretism of things new and old;[2] and one of the old things which Hinduism resuscitated was Caste. Not content with resuscitating this old abuse, it embroidered upon it. The Hindu Civilization has been handicapped from the outset by a considerably heavier burden of Caste (a veritable load of *karma*) than the burden that once weighed upon its predecessor; and accordingly the series of revolts against Caste has run over from Indic into Hindu history.

In the Hindu Age these revolts have no longer taken the form of creative philosophical movements of indigenous origin like Buddhism or Jainism, but have expressed themselves in definite secessions from Hinduism under the attraction of some alien religious system. Some of these secessions have been led by Hindu reformers who have founded new churches in order to combine an expurgated version of Hinduism with certain elements borrowed from alien sources. Thus, for example, Kabīr (*vivebat saeculo quinto decimo aevi Christiani*) and the founder of Sikhism, Nanak (*vivebat* A.D. 1469–1538), created their syncretisms out of a combination between Hinduism and Islam, while Ram Mohan Roy (*vivebat* A.D. 1772–1833) created the Brahmō Samāj out of a combination between Hinduism and Christianity.[3] It is noteworthy that, in all these three syncretisms alike, the institution of Caste is one of the features of Hinduism that have been rejected. In other cases the secessionists have not stopped at any half-way house but have shaken the dust of Hinduism off their feet altogether and have entered outright into the Islamic or the Christian fold; and such conversions have taken place on the largest scale in districts in which

[1] See I. C (i) (*b*), vol. i, p. 87, above, and V. C (i) (*c*) 2, vol. v, p. 131, below.

[2] See I. C (i) (*b*), vol. i, pp. 84–7, above, and V. (i) (*c*) 2, vol. v, pp. 137–8, below.

[3] For these syncretisms between Hinduism and certain non-Hindu religions which have impinged upon the Hindu World, see V. C (i) (*c*) 2, vol. v, p. 106, and V. C (i) (*d*) 6 (δ), vol. v, p. 537, below.

there had previously been a high proportion of members of low castes or depressed classes in the local Hindu population. The classic instance is the latter-day religious history of Eastern Bengal, where the descendants of former barbarians who had been admitted just within the pale of Hinduism on sufferance, with an extremely low status, have become converts to Islam *en masse*.

This is the revolutionary retort to the enormity of 'Untouchability' which has been evoked by the impact of Religiosity upon Caste; and, as the masses of the population of India are progressively stirred by the economic and intellectual and moral ferment of Westernization, the trickle of conversions among the outcasts seems likely to swell into a flood, unless the abolition of the stigma of 'Untouchability' is achieved at the eleventh hour by the non-Brahman majority of the Caste-Hindus themselves, in the teeth of Brahman opposition, under the leadership of the Banya Mahatma Gandhi.

14. *The Impact of Civilization upon the Division of Labour*

We have observed[1] that the institution of the Division of Labour, like the faculty of mimesis, is a common feature of all human societies, so that its presence or absence is not one of the distinguishing marks between primitive societies and civilizations. At the same time the mutation of a primitive society into a civilization must tend to alter the social effect of the Division of Labour in this society's life, because, as we have also observed already,[2] this mutation consists very largely in a reorientation of the faculty of mimesis away from the elders who embody the society's traditional social heritage towards creative personalities whose mission is not to conserve but to innovate. It will be seen that in a primitive society in the Yin-state, in which mimesis acts as a standardizing agency, mimesis and the Division of Labour serve as correctives to one another, whereas in a society which has embarked upon the enterprise of Civilization this same faculty of mimesis, which is now reoriented towards the social pioneers, becomes in its turn a differentiating agency which reinforces the differentiating effect of the Division of Labour instead of mitigating it.

Thus the impact of Civilization upon the Division of Labour tends in a general way to accentuate the division to a degree at which it threatens not merely to bring in diminishing social returns but actually to become anti-social in its working; and this effect is produced in the lives of the creative minority and the uncreative majority alike.[3] The creators are tempted into esotericism, while

[1] In Part II. B, vol. i, pp. 189–91, above.

[2] See Part II. B, vol. i, pp. 191–2, and IV. C (iii) (*a*), in the present volume, pp. 127–8, above.

[3] For this classification of the members of a growing civilization see III. C (ii) (*a*), vol. iii, pp. 234–48, above.

the rank-and-file are pushed into lop-sidedness; and both these misdevelopments lead to the cultural impoverishment—and, at extreme lengths, to the cultural atrophy—of the society as a whole.[1]

Esotericism is a symptom of failure in the careers of creative individuals or creative minorities which we have encountered a number of times already in the course of this Study. It is an accentuation and perversion and perpetuation of the preliminary movement of withdrawal in the creative rhythm of Withdrawal-and-Return. The effect of this is to check the flow of the rhythm before it has entered upon the final movement which is its whole purpose and its only true fulfilment; and this stultification of a would-be creative act revenges itself both upon the withdrawing individual or minority that fails to return and upon the majority that never reaps the harvest of a return to compensate for the cost of a withdrawal. The penalty which overtakes the truant individual or minority that fails to re-enter into communion with the mass is the forfeiture of the field of action which is an indispensable condition for activity and therefore for life itself,[2] so that esotericism is equivalent to a self-imposed sentence of Life-in-Death; and this penalty is equally inexorable whether the esotericism be conscious and deliberate, in the spirit of the Egyptiac Pyramid-Builders[3] and the Hindu Brahmans;[4] or unconscious and unintentional, in the spirit of the free male citizens of the city-states of the Hellenic World in the fifth century B.C.;[5] or conscious but unintentional, in the spirit of the pioneers of Democracy and Industrialism in our modern Western World;[6] or conscious but contrary to intention, in the spirit of Peter the Great.[7] As for the penalty which is imposed upon the mass when a minority succumbs to esotericism, it is a permanent depression of status and standards[8] under the incubus of an aloof minority which weighs upon the rest of Society without giving it any active return for its passive support. This is the condition of the Egyptiac peasantry in and after the Age of the Pyramid-Builders;[9] the condition of the Orthodox Christian peasantry in Eastern and

[1] On this point see Schweitzer, A.: *The Decay and Restoration of Civilization* (London 1923, Black), p. 20.

[2] For the conception of 'fields' see III. C (ii) (*a*), vol. iii, pp. 223–30, above.

[3] See III. C (i) (*d*), vol. iii, pp. 212–15, above, and IV. C (iii) (*c*) 2 (β), in the present volume, pp. 408–9, below.

[4] See III. C (ii) (*a*), vol. iii, p. 240, and IV. C (iii) (*b*) 13, in the present volume, pp. 230–2, above, and IV. C (iii) (*c*) 2 (β), p. 421, footnote 3, below.

[5] See III. C (ii) (*a*), vol. iii, pp. 239–40, above.

[6] See III. C (ii) (*a*), vol. iii, pp. 241–2, above.

[7] See III. C (ii) (*b*), vol. iii, pp. 278–83, above.

[8] 'The Nation has thriven long upon mutilated humanity. Men, the fairest creations of God, came out of the National manufactory in huge numbers as war-making and money-making puppets' (Tagore, Sir R.: *Nationalism* (London 1917, Macmillan), p. 44).

[9] See III. C (i) (*d*), vol. iii, pp. 213–15, above, and IV. C (iii) (*c*) 2 (β), in the present volume, pp. 408–10 and 418–23, below.

Central Anatolia after the successful evocation of an 'East Roman' ghost of the Roman Empire in Orthodox Christendom in the eighth century of the Christian Era;[1] the condition of the Orthodox Christian peasantry in Russia after the imposition of a Westernized superstructure upon Russian Orthodox Christendom by Peter the Great;[2] the condition of the slaves and the women in the Hellenic Society of the fifth century B.C.;[3] the condition of the low castes and the outcasts in the Hindu World;[4] and the partial condition (at the least unfavourable estimate) of the rank-and-file of our own Western Society to-day.[5] This situation is a social danger-signal; for it has only to persist and to deteriorate in order to turn the esoteric minority into a dominant minority and the depressed majority into a morally alienated proletariat in a mood to secede; and we have seen that the secession of a proletariat from a dominant minority is the surest symptom of social disintegration.[6]

These are the penalties which esotericism entails; but there is also a risk that the creative individual or minority, in an anxious determination to steer clear of Scylla, may fall unawares into Charybdis; for, in their efforts to bring the uncreative rank-and-file into line with them by resorting to the primitive social drill of mimesis,[7] they may succeed in regimenting their fellow men, yet produce this effect upon them only at the cost of distorting their natural harmonious development and deforming them into lop-sidedness.

The social problem that awaits the creator when he duly returns from his temporary withdrawal into a renewed communion with the mass of his fellows is the problem of raising a number of ordinary human souls to the higher level that has been attained by the creator himself; and, as soon as he grapples with this task, he is confronted with the apparent fact that many, and perhaps most, of the rank-and-file of his own society in his own generation are individually incapable of living on this higher level with all their heart and with all their soul and with all their strength. In this situation he may be tempted to try a short cut and to resort to the device of raising some single faculty in these ordinary souls to the higher level, without bothering about the whole personality. This means, *ex hypothesi*, the forcing of a human being into a lop-sided development;

[1] See IV. C (ii) (*b*) 1, pp. 72–3, above, and IV. C (iii) (*c*) 2 (β), pp. 395–9, and Part X, below.

[2] See III. C (i) (*d*), vol. iii, pp. 200–2, and III. C (ii) (*b*), vol. iii, pp. 278–83, above.

[3] See III. C (ii) (*a*), vol. iii, pp. 239–40, above.

[4] See III. C (ii) (*a*), vol. iii, p. 240, and IV. C (iii) (*b*) 13, in the present volume, pp. 229–32, above.

[5] See III. C (ii) (*a*), vol. iii, pp. 241–2, above.

[6] On this point see I. B (iv), vol. i, pp. 40–2; I. C (i) (*a*), vol. i, pp. 53–62; and IV. C (iii) (*a*), in the present volume, pp. 119–33, above; and Part V. B, vol. v, pp. 11–14, below.

[7] See III. C (ii) (*a*), vol. iii, pp. 245–8, and IV. C (iii) (*a*), in the present volume, pp. 119–33, above.

and in practice the lop-sidedness is apt to be extreme because, unhappily, the more trivial the faculty selected for hypertrophy, the less difficult it is to produce a superficially impressive material result.

Such results are most readily obtainable on the plane of mechanical technique, since, of all the elements in any given culture, its mechanical aptitudes are the easiest to isolate and to detach and to communicate.[1] On this plane it is not so difficult to train human beings whose souls are on the primitive level to perform activities—or to contribute their mite to a mechanical co-ordination of activities—by the trick of mimesis, even though they could never have created these techniques out of their own unaided resources. In this fashion a primitive Negro, taken out of a Tropical African forest, can be made into an effective engine-driver or machine-gunner, though he and his fellows would never have invented a gun or a locomotive, or even have dreamt of the possibility of such machines, if their life had not been turned upside down by White intruders with a mastery of the modern apparatus of the Western Civilization. And if this is true of the outsiders who have been swept into the meshes of the expanding network of our Western economic system, it is also true of the vast majority of the indigenous workers of the Western World; for in the present 'fool-proof' stage of our Machine Age our workers are being reduced in ever-increasing numbers to the role of mere mechanical executants[2]—when they are lucky enough to escape being replaced altogether by some totally inanimate machine and being thrown out upon the human scrap-heap of unemployment. More than that, we must recognize, on a candid view, that this type of a deformedly lop-sided primitive human creature who is the victim of a summary and superficial method of bringing the rank-and-file into line is not specially characteristic of the masses; it is also to be found far up the social hierarchy of our modern Western Society in classes which are conventionally regarded, and which unquestioningly regard themselves, not at all as victims of the rhythm of social growth but rather as its presiding geniuses and its deserving beneficiaries. Not a few of the prophets of our modern Western Democracy and the inventors of our modern Western Industrialism, and certainly a large number of the politicians and the business men who have appropriated and exploited the genuine pioneers' achievements, have been actually eminent in letters or in science

[1] See III. C (i) (*a*), vol. iii, pp. 151–3, above, and V. C (i) (*c*) 3, vol. v, pp. 199–201, below.

[2] 'The West has been systematically petrifying her moral nature in order to lay a solid foundation for her gigantic abstractions of efficiency. She has all along been starving the life of the personal man into that of the professional' (Tagore, Sir R.: *Nationalism* (London 1917, Macmillan), p. 33).

or in politics or in business alone, while they have shown themselves vulgarly puny in their faculty for faith and love and the other spiritual expressions of Human Nature at its highest.

We have come across this kind of lop-sidedness in this Study already at an earlier point, in our examination of the response to the challenge of penalization which is made by penalized minorities.[1] We have observed that the tyrannical and malignant exclusion of these minorities, by *force majeure*, from certain walks of life is apt to stimulate them—in mockery of the intentions of their oppressors—to prosper and excel in other fields which have still been left open to them out of contempt or oversight; and we have marvelled at and admired a whole gallery of heroic *tours de force* in which these minorities stand out as very incarnations of the invincibility of Human Nature. At the same time we cannot ignore the fact that some of the most conspicuous of these minorities—for example, the Levantines and the Phanariots and the Armenians and, above all, the Jews—have a reputation for being 'not as other men are' for worse as well as for better; and this ill repute, which clings to them in a strange unresolved contradiction with their notorious virtues and accomplishments, is too persistent and too widely spread to be dismissed altogether as a libellous expression of their discomfited oppressors' chagrin. In the unhappy relation between Jews and Gentiles, which is the classic case, the Gentile who is disgusted and ashamed at the behaviour of his Anti-Semite fellow Goyyim is also embarrassed at finding himself constrained to admit that there is some grain of truth in the caricature of the Jewish character which the Jew-baiter draws as a justification for his own bestiality. The heart of the tragedy lies in the fact that a penalization which truly stimulates the penalized minority to a heroic response is as truly apt to warp their human nature as well. They rise to superhuman heights in one dimension at the risk of shrivelling to a sub-human level in another dimension. And what is true of these socially penalized minorities is evidently likewise true of those technologically specialized majorities with which we are now concerned.

The point may be illustrated by the English tale of a legendary Irishman and his blanket. A poor Irishman found that his blanket was not long enough to cover his shoulders when he went to bed, so he cut off a strip from the bottom end of the blanket and sewed it on to the top end—only to find, to his bewilderment, that the bedevilled blanket had now become too short to cover his feet. In truth, of course, the blanket had been shortened instead of lengthened by being cut to pieces and sewn together again—at

[1] See II. D (v), vol. ii, pp. 208–59, above.

least, if we may assume that our Irishman knew enough about needlework to turn over the edges in making his suture. Our poor friend has actually made things worse for himself by his naïve attempt to make them better; and so has the anthropoid ape who has naïvely replied to the challenge 'Which of you by taking thought can add one cubit unto his stature?'[1] by incontinently rising on his hind legs. In this case the riddle is actually solved in the immediate and the literal sense; but the challenge, of course, implies that the addition to the stature is to be permanent and that the creature that achieves it is not to do this at a sacrifice of the health and harmony of its whole bodily organism. It is on this point that the guilelessly presumptuous monkey is eventually caught out; for the physical strain of the unnatural two-legged posture that has enabled him to hold his head so high makes itself felt progressively throughout his system. First the change of posture upsets his digestion by displacing his internal organs; and then his two hind legs—thus unreasonably starved of nourishment when they are being compelled to do the work of four—succumb to rickets and finally double up under him. In this ignominious fashion the ape relapses on to all fours again; but he is not now the ape that he was before he started to play his monkey-trick. The healthy quadruped of yore has been transformed, as a result of his disastrous prank, into a rickety quadruped whose constitution has been permanently undermined.[2]

These fables are applicable to an ordinary uncreative human being who has had one of his human faculties—and this perhaps one of rather trivial value—abnormally and disproportionately developed in the hope of thereby bringing the crown of his head to a level with the height of a creative genius who is a cubit taller by nature than the ordinary run of his fellow men. Such a partial increase in spiritual stature is usually paid for by a general decrease in spiritual stamina. A primitive soul which has been unnaturally developed to a higher capacity in some single line of growth is apt, in all other lines, to shrivel to a lower capacity than that of the natural primitive soul which has not had any liberties taken with its spiritual health.

This malady of spiritual deformation, which is the nemesis of a perverse method of attempting to bring the uncreative rank-and-

[1] Matt. vi. 27.

[2] A more picturesque version of the same fable will be found in Sir Rabindranath Tagore's *Nationalism* (London 1917, Macmillan), pp. 35–6:

'Man, with his mental and material power far outgrowing his moral strength, is like an exaggerated giraffe whose head has suddenly shot up miles away from the rest of him, making normal communication difficult to establish. This greedy head, with its huge dental organisation, has been munching all the topmost foliage of the World, but the nourishment is too late in reaching his digestive organs, and his heart is suffering from want of blood.'

file into line with the creative minority, is as great a social enormity as the antithetical malady of esotericism which is the nemesis that lies in wait for a creator when he ignores the truth that 'none of us liveth to himself and no man dieth to himself'[1] and seeks to repudiate his ineluctable obligation to be his brother's keeper.[2] And these are the two alternative possible enormities that may be produced by the impact of Civilization upon the Division of Labour.

The crime of Procrustes is castigated by Jesus in his denunciation of the Scribes and the Pharisees who

'bind heavy burdens and grievous to be borne, and lay them on men's shoulders; but they themselves will not move them with one of their fingers'.[3]

And it is the same enormity that is in the mind of the Arabic philosopher Ibn Khaldūn when he argues that 'too much severity in a sovereign usually does harm to his realm'.[4]

'Benevolent government is rarely associated with a ruler whose mind is over-alert and intelligence over-developed. Benevolence is most commonly found in rulers who are easy-going or who behave as if they were. The worst defect in the alert-minded ruler is that he lays burdens upon his subjects which are greater than they can bear; and he does this because his mental vision outranges theirs and because his insight penetrates to the ends of things at the beginnings—with disastrous consequences for them. The Prophet says: "Go the pace of the weakest among you"; and in this context the exponent of the Divine Law prescribes in the case of rulers that excess of intelligence should be avoided . . . because it produces oppression and bad government and makes demands upon the people which are contrary to their nature. . . . It is evident from this that intellectuality and intelligence is a fault in an administrator, because this is an excess of mental activity—just as dull-wittedness is an excess of mental torpidity. The two extremes are to be deprecated in every attribute of human nature. The ideal is the Golden Mean . . . and for this reason a man who is over-intellectual has Satanic attributes attributed to him and is called "Satan", "possessed by Satan", and so on.'

In an extreme case the pioneer who racks the laggards' limbs in order to key them up to his own pace may be as great a monster as the fiend who tortures a bird by over-nourishing its liver in order to make *pâté de foie gras*.

The social havoc that is wrought on the one hand by esotericism on the part of a creative minority and on the other hand by a spiritual deformation of the souls of the rank-and-file of the un-

[1] Romans xiv. 7. [2] Gen. iv. 9. [3] Matt. xxiii. 4; cf. Luke xi. 46.

[4] Ibn Khaldūn: *Muqaddamāt*, translated by de Slane, Baron McG. (Paris 1863–8, Imprimerie Impériale, 3 vols.), vol. i, pp. 383–4.

creative mass is so manifestly serious that, where and when it shows itself, there is apt to be a powerful counter-movement to check it by adjustment or, failing that, by revolution. And the more vigorous and vital the growth of a growing civilization, the greater, as a rule, will be its members' sensitiveness to this particular social danger.

Such sensitiveness is a characteristic mark of the Hellenic Civilization at the time when it was rising towards its highest achievements in the fifth century B.C.; and the feeling declared itself in Hellenic language in an uncompromising condemnation of the *ἰδιώτης* at the one extreme and of the *βάναυσος* at the other.

The *ἰδιώτης*, in the fifth-century Greek usage of the word, was a superior personality who committed the social offence of 'living to himself' instead of putting his personal gifts at the service of the common weal; and the light in which such behaviour was regarded in the classical Hellenic World is illustrated by the fact that, in our modern Western vernacular languages, a derivative of this Greek word *ἰδιώτης* has acquired the meaning of 'mental imbecile'. This far-fetched meaning has been imported into the word 'idiot' on the strength of its moral connotation in Hellenic minds. The connotation has been so strong that the meaning has been changed by it out of all recognition. It is amusing to reflect that, if we had managed to forget the original connotation and to carry the original meaning over into the un-Hellenic moral environment of our own code of social ethics, then the English word 'idiot' would presumably be used to-day as a laudatory term; for it would then still signify a man of parts who has devoted his abilities to the acquisition of a personal fortune through private business enterprise; and this classical Hellenic *bête noire* is our latter-day Western hero.

In the Hellenic Society of the fifth century B.C. the free male citizens, who alone lived to the full the intense social life of the city-state, were virtually behaving as *ἰδιῶται* towards the women and the slaves, who had been left behind in the advance of the Hellenic Civilization from the Homeric to the Attic stage. The women and the slaves found themselves virtually outside the social pale of the master institution in which the results of the free male citizens' advance had been embodied.[1] From this point of view it is significant that one of the promptest constructive reactions to the breakdown of the Hellenic Civilization in 431 B.C. was a movement to bring the women and the slaves back into social partnership with the free male citizens as recognized and active members of the commonwealth. This movement declared itself in Athens,

[1] See III. C (ii) (*a*), vol. iii, pp. 239–40, above.

'the Education of Hellas',[1] while the Atheno-Peloponnesian War, which was the beginning of the Hellenic 'Time of Troubles', was still being fought—as witness the war-plays of Aristophanes; and the emancipation of these two great classes in the Hellenic body social may be judged to have reached its apogee during the first century of the third chapter of Hellenic history: a century that began with Alexander's passage of the Dardanelles in 334 B.C. and closed with the outbreak of the Hannibalic War in 218 B.C.[2]

At the opposite extreme to the *ἰδιώτης* stood the *βάναυσος*, who was the other bugbear of fifth-century Hellas. The *βάναυσος* meant a person whose activity was specialized, through a concentration of his energies upon some particular technique, at the expense of his all-round development as a 'social animal'. The kind of technique which was usually in people's minds when they used this term of abuse was some manual or mechanical trade which was practised for private profit. Making money out of industry was as ill looked upon in fifth-century Hellas as it has been well looked upon in the English-speaking communities of a nineteenth-century Western Society; and in the old-fashioned aristocratic Boeotian community of Thebes the social stigma was so severe that it carried a political disqualification with it.[3] The Hellenic horror of *βαναυσία*, however, went farther than this. It implanted in Hellenic minds a deep distrust of all professionalism, even when the medium was something finer than stone or iron or wood or leather and the motive something nobler than money-making.

For example, under the Lycurgean *agôgê*[4] or 'way of life' at Sparta, the Spartiate 'Peers' were forbidden not only to master and practise any lucrative manual trade,[5] but even to train for and take part in any of the international athletic competitions which were

[1] The phrase put into the mouth of the Athenian statesman Pericles by the Athenian historian Thucydides (in Book II, chap. 41).

[2] Though Athens was the scene of the first move in Hellas towards the re-enfranchisement of both the women and the slaves, it was only the emancipation of the slaves that was a native Attic movement (see IV. C (iii) (*b*) 4, p. 156, footnote 3, above). The credit for the emancipation of the women of Hellas belongs not to Athens but to Sparta and to Macedon; for in both these two other Hellenic communities the position of women in the so-called 'Classical Age' of Hellenic history was more favourable than it was at Athens—at Sparta as an undesigned consequence of the depressing effect of the Lycurgean *agôgê* upon the men (see Part III. A, vol. iii, p. 75, above) and in Macedon because she was still in the Homeric stage of development (see III. C (ii) (*b*), Annex IV, vol. iii, pp. 278–9, above)—and in the course of the century beginning in the year 431 B.C. the institutions of Sparta and Macedon successively gained prestige in Hellas through the victories of Spartan and Macedonian over Athenian arms (see Part III. A, vol. iii, pp. 90–3, above). In Aristophanes' feminist comedy *Lysistrata*, which was played in 411 B.C., one of the principal characters is Lampito, who is the leader of a delegation of Spartan women.

[3] According to Aristotle, *Politics*, Book III, chap. 5, p. 1278A (cf. op. cit., Book VI, chap. 7, p. 1321A), 'there was a law at Thebes that any one who had not been out of business for ten years should be ineligible for public office.'

[4] See Part III. A, vol. iii, pp. 54–68, above.

[5] See the story quoted above in Part III. A, vol. iii, on pp. 80–1.

held periodically in the Hellenic World—notwithstanding the two facts that, at the four great Pan-Hellenic festivals, the prizes were not objects of material value but were simple wreaths of green-stuff, and that, in all other Hellenic communities, the winning of one of these wreaths was regarded as the highest honour which a man could possibly gain for himself and for his country.[1] The Spartans, of course, defeated their own ends—and discredited their parochial policy of diverging from the main channel of Hellenic Civilization into a peculiar backwater—by specializing professionally in the Art of War, with disastrous social, and in the end even disastrous military, consequences. It was the paradox and the irony of Spartan history that Spartan militarism, at its height, became *βαναυσία* incarnate. On the other hand the subtler Athenians did not allow themselves to fall into this insidious pitfall. They were on their guard against *βαναυσία* even in the cultivation of those abilities and activities and arts which they were most prone to admire; and they did not hesitate to criticize the professionalism of a countryman of their own who was the most brilliant political genius that Attica had produced and who had used his specialized ability, with dazzling success, to save his country from destruction and to make her great.

'In refined and cultivated society Themistocles used to be girded at by people of so-called liberal education [for his lack of accomplishments] and used to be driven into making the rather cheap defence that he certainly could do nothing with a musical instrument, but that, if you were to put into his hands a country that was small and obscure, he knew how to turn it into a great country and a famous one.'[2]

This sensitiveness to the dangers of *βαναυσία*, which comes out so strongly in Hellenic social life, can also be observed in the institutions of other societies. For example, the social function of the Jewish Sabbath—and of the sabbatarian Sunday of Scotland, England, and the Transmarine English-speaking countries of our modern Western World—is to insure that, for one whole day out of every seven, a creature who has been specializing for six successive days in the week in sordid business for private gain shall

1 These two facts were, of course, connected by a reciprocal relation of cause and effect. The materially valuable prizes which had been offered originally could not have been abolished if these four once merely local festivals had not already attained to so well-established an oecumenical prestige in the Hellenic World that their stewards could feel confident of being able to book an abundance of entries for the sake of the honour and glory which the victories at these particular festivals had come to carry with them. (At other local athletic festivals in Hellas which failed to acquire oecumenical prestige it never proved possible to dispense with the lure of prizes of material value.) Conversely, the prestige of the four Pan-Hellenic festivals was immensely enhanced by the fact that the competitors now competed for the sake of the honour and glory alone, without any vestige of a profit-making motive.

2 Plutarch: *Life of Themistocles*, chap. 2.

remember his Creator and shall live, for a recurrent twenty-four hours, the life of an integral human soul instead of quite uninterruptedly performing the vain repetitions of a money-making machine. Again, it is no accident that in England mountaineering and 'organized games' and other sports should have come into fashion simultaneously with the rise of Industrialism at the turn of the eighteenth and nineteenth centuries; and that this new passion for Sport should since have spread, *pari passu* with Industrialism, from England over the World. For Sport, in this latter-day sense of the term, is a conscious attempt at 'recreation' from the soul-destroying exaggeration of the Division of Labour which the Industrial System of economy entails.

In our latter-day Western World, however, this attempt to adjust Life to Industrialism through Sport has been partially defeated because the spirit and the rhythm of Industrialism have become so insistent and so pervasive that they have invaded and infected Sport itself—just as the *βαναυσία* which the Spartans sought so earnestly to keep at bay eluded their vigilance after all by capturing their own peculiar profession of arms. In the Western World of to-day professional athletes—more narrowly specialized and more extravagantly paid than the most consummate industrial technicians—now vie with the professional entertainers in providing us with horrifying examples of *βαναυσία* at its acme.

In the mind of the writer of this Study this disconcerting industrialization of Sport is summed up in the pictures of three football-fields that are all printed sharply upon his visual memory. One was an English field at Sheffield which he happened once to see out of the railway-carriage window *en route* from York to Oxford. At the parched latter end of summer, when the football season was about to reopen, the grass on this plot of ground was being kept artificially green by hydrants which tapped the municipal water-supply and so made the local groundsman independent of the rain from heaven. And all around this manufactured greensward rose tiers upon tiers of seats, on which thousands of human beings would presently 'take their recreation' in an even closer congestion—with still more pounds of human flesh to the cubic yard of urban space—than during their working hours in shop or office or factory. The other two football-grounds in the writer's mental picture-gallery are to be found on the campuses of two colleges in the United States. One of them was floodlighted, by an ingenious lighting-system which was said to reproduce the exact effect of sunshine, in order that football-players might be manufactured there by night as well as by day, in continuous shifts, as motor-cars or gramophones are produced in factories which run without a break throughout the twenty-four hours. The other American football-ground was roofed over in order that practice might go on whatever the weather. The roof was supported on four immense girders which sprang from the four corners and met above the centre without any interior support. It was said to be the largest span of roof in existence at that moment in the World, and its erection had cost a fabulous sum. Round the sides were ranged beds for the reception of exhausted or wounded warriors. On both these American grounds I found on inquiry that the actual players in any given year were never more in number than an infinitesimal fraction of the total student body; and I was also told that these boys looked forward to the ordeal of playing a match with much the same grim apprehension as their elder brothers had felt when they went into the trenches in 1918. In truth this Anglo-Saxon football was not a game at all. It was the Industrial System celebrating a triumph over its vanquished antidote, Sport, by masquerading in its guise.

A corresponding development can be discerned in the history of the Hellenic World, where the aristocratic amateurs whose victories are immortalized in Pindar's odes were eventually replaced by the professional boxers of the amphitheatre and professional charioteers of the circus, while the shows that were purveyed, *post Alexandrum*, from Parthia to Spain by the *Διονύσου Τεχνῖται* ('United Artists, Ltd.') were as different from the fifth-century celebrations in Dionysus's own theatre, in its hallowed precinct under the shadow of the Acropolis at Athens, as a music-hall revue in Chicago or Shanghai or Buenos Aires is different from a medieval mystery play.[1]

It is no wonder that, when social enormities defy adjustment in this baffling fashion, philosophers should dream of revolutionary plans for sweeping the enormities away. Plato seeks to cut the root of *βαναυσία*, as he sees it rising rankly all around him in the Athens of his day, by planting his Utopia in an inland region with no facilities for maritime trade and with little inducement towards any economic activity beyond 'subsistence farming'.[2] Samuel Butler imagines his Utopians deliberately and systematically destroying all machines and placing a rigid ban upon their construction and operation for the future, for fear that Mankind might cease to be the masters of machines through becoming, instead,

[1] This difference is one of the effects of the phenomenon of social diffraction, which has been touched upon in I. B (iii), vol. i, pp. 26–33, above, and is examined further in V. C (i) (*c*) 3, vol. v, pp. 199–203, as well as in Parts VIII and IX, below.

[2] See the passage quoted from Plato, *Leges*, 704–5, in Part III. A, vol. iii, on p. 91, above.

their domesticated animals.[1] Since a machine is nothing but an artificial extension of the range or 'drive' of some human organ or faculty,[2] the fantasy of a reversal in the relations between machines and human beings is an apt parable of what happens readily enough 'in real life' when the harmony of some commonplace human soul is upset, and its nature is warped and deformed, by the hypertrophe of some single faculty, at the expense of all the rest, in a vain attempt to raise this ordinary creature to an equality with the rarer representative of its kind that has been endowed by their common Creator with a larger spiritual stature.

15. *The Impact of Civilization upon Mimesis.*

A reorientation of the faculty of mimesis away from the elders and towards the pioneers is, as we have seen,[3] the change in the direction of this faculty that accompanies the mutation of a primitive society into a civilization; and the aim in view is the raising of the uncreative mass to a new level that has been reached by a new creative minority. But, because this resort to mimesis is a short cut,[4] the attainment of the goal along this road is apt to be illusory.

Where a genuine transmission of the divine fire from soul to soul would have transformed the inner man and have admitted him, in transforming him, into the Communion of Saints, the glib response of mimesis is apt to do no more than transmogrify the Natural Man, *Homo Integer Antiquae Virtutis*, into the shoddy 'Man in the Street': a *Homo Vulgaris Northcliffii* or a *Homo Demoticus Cleonis*. In that event the impact of Civilization upon mimesis begets the enormity of a pseudo-sophisticated urban crowd, living for its *panem et circenses*,[5] which, on any spiritual criterion, is as signally inferior to the Natural Man in a primitive society as are 'the beasts that perish'.[6] This vulgar social enormity is not so inevitable that it cannot be avoided by an adjustment. In fifth-century Athens, for example, the Dêmos which was exposed to the corrupting influence of the demagogue Cleon's travesty of 'the Education of Hellas' was at the same time being offered pure draughts of the milk of the word[7] in the celebrations at the Dionysiac theatre.

[1] See Butler, Samuel: *Erewhon* (London 1872, Trübner), chap. 20 *ad fin.* and chaps. 21, 22, 23. Compare the chapter entitled 'Der Mensch als Sklave der Maschine' in Spengler, O.: *Der Untergang des Abendlandes*, vol. ii: 'Welthistorische Perspektiven', 1st–15th edition (Munich 1922, Beck), pp. 624–35.

[2] For the perilously ambiguous nature of machinery see IV. C (iii) (*a*), pp. 124–7, above.

[3] In Part II. B, vol. i, pp. 191–5, and IV. C (iii) (*a*), in the present volume, p. 128, above.

[4] See III. C (ii) (*a*), vol. iii, pp. 245–8; and IV. C (iii) (*a*), in the present volume, pp. 119–33, above.

[5] Juvenal, *Satires*, No. x, l. 81, quoted already in II. D (vi), vol. ii, p. 214, above.

[6] 'Man that is in honour and understandeth not is like the beasts that perish' (Psalm xlix. 20).

[7] 1 Peter ii. 2.

Here was a traditional institution which was part of the common people's birthright and in which they remained thoroughly at home while the most daring aesthetic and moral and intellectual pioneers of the age were now using the folk-drama, without ever breaking its traditional mould, as a vehicle for the expression of their own creative ideas. In the fifth-century Attic drama the happy accident that had converted a primitive institution into a mouthpiece for men of genius gave men of goodwill a fleeting opportunity of competing for the guidance of the souls of the Dêmos against men of Cleon's stamp. But a survey of History seems to show that such opportunities are few and far between; and, even in this Attic case, the opportunity was not successfully taken. Cleon won; and the social enormity which he evoked by stamping the Dêmos with his own image had to be exorcized in the end, not by adjustment, but by revolution. The Cleonian 'Man in the Street', whose entry upon the stage of Hellenic history before the close of the fifth century B.C. is one of the unmistakable symptoms of social decline, eventually redeemed his soul by repudiating, outright, a culture which had failed to satisfy his spiritual hunger because he had only succeeded in filling his belly with the husks.[1] As the spiritually awakened child of a dissident proletariat, he worked out his own salvation through the discovery of a higher religion.[2]

Perhaps these examples may suffice to illustrate the part that is played in the breakdowns of civilizations by the intractability of old institutions to the touch of new social forces.

(c) THE NEMESIS OF CREATIVITY

1. *The Problem of Περιπέτεια*

We have now made some study of two aspects of that failure of self-determination to which the breakdowns of civilizations appear to be due. We have considered the mechanicalness of mimesis and the intractability of institutions. We may conclude this part of our inquiry with a consideration of the apparent nemesis of creativity.

It looks as though it were uncommon for the creative responses to two or more successive challenges in the history of a given society to be achieved by one and the same minority or individual. So far from this being the rule, the party that has distinguished itself in dealing with one challenge is apt to fail conspicuously in attempting to deal with the next. This ironical and disconcerting

[1] Luke xv. 16.

[2] For the secession of the internal proletariat from the dominant minority of the Hellenic Society see I. B (iv), vol. i, pp. 40–2, and I. C (i) (*a*), vol. i, pp. 53–62, above, and Part V. C (i) (*c*) 2, vol. v, pp. 58–82, below.

yet apparently normal inconstancy of human fortunes is one of the dominant *motifs* of the Attic drama, and it is noticed and discussed by Aristotle, in his critique of Hellenic poetry, under the name of περιπέτεια or 'the reversal of roles'.[1] This is also one of the principal themes of the New Testament.[2]

In the drama of the New Testament a Christ whose epiphany on Earth in the person of Jesus is, in Christian belief, the true fulfilment of Jewry's long cherished Messianic Hope, is nevertheless rejected by a school of Scribes and Pharisees which, only a few generations back, has come to the front by taking the lead in a heroic Jewish revolt against the triumphal progress of Hellenization.[3] The insight and the uprightness that have brought the Scribes and Pharisees to the fore in that previous crisis of Jewish history desert them now in a crisis of greater import for the destinies of Jewry and of Mankind, and the Jews that comprehend and accept the authentic Jewish Messiah's message are the publicans and harlots.[4] The Messiah himself comes from 'Galilee of the Gentiles';[5] and the greatest of his executors is a Hellenized Jew from Tarsus, a city beyond the traditional horizon of the Promised Land, who carries the preaching of his Galilaean master into the heart of a Hellenized World.

In this Christian rendering of the theme of περιπέτεια the roles that are reversed are sometimes played by the Pharisaic *élite* of Jewry and by the outcasts from the Jewish fold:

'I say unto you that the publicans and the harlots go into the Kingdom of God before you.'[6]

Sometimes, again, the Pharisees' role is assigned to Jewry as a whole, and the publicans' role to the Gentiles—as in the sermon

[1] See Aristotle: *Poetics*, chap. 11, § 1, *et alibi*. See further the interesting note on the word in Butcher, S. H.: *Aristotle's Theory of Poetry and Fine Art*, 3rd edition (London 1902, Macmillan), pp. 329–30. According to Butcher, the word περιπέτεια, as used by Aristotle, has a subjective connotation. Unlike the word μετάβασις, περιπέτεια means not merely a 'change of fortune' but a change in the form of a 'reversal of intention', when an act or a policy produces the opposite result from that which the agent has expected and desired.

[2] See V. C (ii) (*a*), Annex II, vol. vi, pp. 380–1, below.

[3] For this collision between Judaism and Hellenism in the second century B.C. see further V. C (i) (*d*) 9 (β), vol. vi, pp. 103–5, below.

[4] Luke iii. 12–13, and vii. 29–30; Matt. xxi. 31–2.

[5] Isaiah ix. 1; Matt. iv. 15. For the stimulus that was derived by a Christian outgrowth of Judaism from its new ground in Galilee and in the great Gentile World beyond, see II. D (iii), vol. ii, pp. 73–4, above. For the contributions to Christian doctrine and legend which may have been made by a submerged Gentile culture in Galilee and by a dominant Gentile culture in Tarsus, see V. C (ii) (*a*), Annex II, vol. vi, pp. 465, 477–8, and 499–500, below. In this context it may be noted that Galilee was not the only submerged Gentile annex to Judaea that presented Jewry with a saviour in the post-Maccabaean age. While Galilee gave birth, in Jesus, to a Messiah whose message of salvation was that His kingdom was not of This World (see V. C (i) (*d*) 9 (γ), vol. vi, pp. 130–2, below), Idumaea gave birth, in Herod, to a mundane saviour whose humbler mission was to teach the Jews, not how to transcend This World, but how to live in it, and not how to convert a Hellenized Οἰκουμένη, but how to come to terms with it. In the event the Jews rejected their Idumaean as well as their Galilaean saviour's message; and this twofold rejection provoked a crushing nemesis.

[6] Matt. xxi. 31.

in the synagogue at Nazareth in which Jesus reminds his fellow countrymen that the widow to whose aid Elijah was sent in time of famine was not an Israelite but a Sidonian, and that the leper whom Elisha was sent to heal was not an Israelite but a Damascene.[1]

'I say unto you that God is able of these stones to raise up children unto Abraham.'[2]—'The men of Nineveh shall rise in judgment with this generation and shall condemn it, because they repented at the preaching of Jonas, and, behold, a greater than Jonas is here. The Queen of the South shall rise up in the judgment with this generation and shall condemn it; for she came from the uttermost parts of the Earth to hear the wisdom of Solomon, and, behold, a greater than Solomon is here.'[3]—'I say unto you, I have not found so great faith, no, not in Israel. And I say unto you that many shall come from the east and west and shall sit down with Abraham and Isaac and Jacob in the Kingdom of Heaven. But the children of the Kingdom shall be cast out into outer darkness: there shall be weeping and gnashing of teeth.'[4]—'I say unto you, the Kingdom of God shall be taken from you and given to a nation bringing forth the fruits thereof.'[5]—'It was necessary that the word of God should first have been spoken to you; but seeing ye put it from you and judge yourselves unworthy of everlasting life, lo, we turn to the Gentiles.'[6]

The moral that is pointed in the parables of the Labourers in the Vineyard[7] and the Wicked Husbandmen[8] is likewise the moral of the parables of the Prodigal Son[9] and Dives and Lazarus[10] and the Pharisee and the Publican[11] and the Good Samaritan[12] and the guests who rebuff or evade the invitation to the feast and whose places are filled with the poor and the maimed and the halt and the blind from the streets and lanes and highways and hedges.[13] The encounter of Jesus with the Roman centurion[14] has its parallels in his encounter with the Syrophoenician woman beyond the borders of Jewry[15] and with the Greeks at Jerusalem.[16] In the Gospel according to Saint John, in which the last-mentioned incident is narrated, this overture to the Jewish Messiah on the Gentiles' part is made the occasion for Jesus's prophecy of the fructification of his work on Earth.[17]

In the historical setting in which these sayings and parables and incidents in the New Testament are placed, the Christian

1 Luke iv. 16–32. 2 Matt. iii. 9. 3 Matt. xii. 41–2.
4 Matt. viii. 10–12; cf. Luke vii. 9, and xiii. 27–9.
5 Matt. xxi. 43. 6 Acts xiii. 46. 7 Matt. xx. 1–16.
8 Matt. xxi. 33–44 = Mark xii. 1–11 = Luke xx. 9–18. 9 Luke xv. 11–32.
10 Luke xvi. 19–31. 11 Luke xviii. 9–14. 12 Luke x. 25–37.
13 Luke xiv. 15–24 = Matt. xxii. 1–14.
14 Matt. viii. 5–13 = Luke vii. 1–10. This encounter between Jesus and the anonymous Roman centurion at Capernaum has a pendant in the subsequent encounter (Acts x–xi) between Peter and the Roman centurion Cornelius at Joppa (see V. C (i) (*d*) 1, vol. v, p. 393, below).
15 Matt. xv. 21–8 = Mark vii. 24–30. 16 John xii. 20–2. 17 John xii. 23–4.

rendering of the theme of περιπέτεια is a variation on an ancient rendering in the Jewish Scriptures. The New Testament and the Old Testament are, both alike, regarded as instruments through which God has bequeathed a supernatural heritage to human beneficiaries; and the common plot of a twice-played tragedy is a reversal of roles through a transfer of God's priceless gift from human hands that might have had it for the taking to other human hands that, at the opening of the play, do not appear to have any prospect of attaining the prize. In the original performance of the play it is Esau, the first-born, who sells his birthright to his younger brother Jacob. In the second performance the same two players appear on the stage again; but in making their reappearance they exchange their parts; for this time it is Jacob who forfeits his heirloom to Esau. Thus the action of the Christian version of the plot presents a double περιπέτεια—a reversal of a reversal—when the scenes in which this action works itself out in the drama of the New Testament are taken literally in their historical sense. This literal meaning, however, is not the only meaning and not the deepest; for 'Alles Vergängliche ist nur ein Gleichniss',[1] and an historical tragedy which is momentous in itself has at the same time a deeper significance as an allegory of a mystery which is illustrated in the passage of History because it lies at the heart of Life. On this plane the operation of the principle of περιπέτεια is proclaimed in the New Testament in terms that transcend the historical limits of a particular time and place:

'If any man desire to be first, the same shall be last of all and servant of all.'[2]—'And whosoever shall exalt himself shall be abased; and he that shall humble himself shall be exalted.'[3]—'The last shall be first, and the first last.'[4]—'He that is least among you all, the same shall be great.'[5]—'The stone which the builders rejected, the same is become the head of the corner.'[6]

In this timeless and placeless presentation of the play the characters between whom the reversal of roles is transacted are neither Pharisees-and-Publicans nor Jews-and-Gentiles, but are Adults-and-Children.

'I say unto you: Except ye be converted and become as little children, ye shall not enter into the Kingdom of Heaven. Whosoever, therefore, shall humble himself as this little child, the same is greatest in the King-

[1] Goethe: *Faust*, ll. 12104–5.
[2] Mark ix. 35 = Matt. xxiii. 11 (cf. Mark. x. 43–4 = Matt. xx. 26–7).
[3] Matt. xxiii. 12 = Luke xiv. 11, and xviii. 14.
[4] Matt. xx. 16, as the moral of the Parable of the Labourers in the Vineyard. Compare Matt. xix. 30 = Mark x. 31, and Luke xiii. 30.
[5] Luke ix. 48.
[6] Matt. xxi. 42 (quoting Psalm cxviii. 22), as the moral of the Parable of the Wicked Husbandmen. Cf. Mark xii. 10; Luke xx. 17; Acts iv. 11; Eph. ii. 20; 1 Peter ii. 7.

dom of Heaven. And whoso receiveth one such little child in my name, receiveth me.'[1]—'Of such is the Kingdom of Heaven.'[2]

Why did Jesus take the children up in his arms and put his hands upon them and bless them?[3] In another context he is said to have answered this question by quoting a passage of the Jewish Scriptures:

'Out of the mouth of babes and sucklings thou hast perfected praise.'[4]

And the paradox of a περιπέτεια between Sophistication and Simplicity, which is thus revealed as the mystery symbolized in the reversal of roles between Children and Adults in the Gospels, flashes out of its sheath of allegory in the exultant phrases of Saint Paul:

'God hath chosen the foolish things of the World to confound the wise; and God hath chosen the weak things of the World to confound the things which are mighty; and base things of the World, and things which are despised, hath God chosen—yea, and things which are not, to bring to nought things that are: that no flesh should glory in his presence.'[5]

What is the explanation of a principle which plays so prominent a part both in the New Testament and in the Attic drama? This question has received a cynical answer from primitive minds; but this primitive cynicism has not been left unchallenged by a Posterity which has gained deeper insight through sharper suffering.

Primitive human minds are fain to explain the downfalls of pre-eminent human beings as acts of external powers that are human in êthos but superhuman in potency. The overthrowers of great men must be gods; and the motive which primitive minds presuppose, to account for these hypothetical divine interventions, is commonly envy. 'The Envy of the Gods' as an agency in human affairs is one of the *Leitmotivs* of primitive Mythology and one of the principal concerns of primitive superstition in all times and places; and the same subject has both fascinated and exercised Hellenic thought, which, in the religious and the moral sphere, is

[1] Math. xviii. 3–5 (Matt. xviii. 3 is reminiscent of Mark x. 15 = Luke xviii. 17; Matt. xviii. 5 = Matt. x. 40 (where the saying refers, not to children, but to the Twelve Disciples) = Mark ix. 37 = Luke ix. 48).

[2] Matt. xix. 14 = Mark x. 14 = Luke xviii. 16.

[3] Mark x. 16.

[4] Matt. xxi. 16, quoting Psalm viii. 2.

[5] 1 Cor. i. 27–9. Verse 27 is quoted again below, in association with verses 22–3, in V. C (i) (*d*) 11, vol. vi, p. 150. The theme is enlarged upon in 1 Cor. ii; and in 1 Cor. iii. 18–21 the περιπέτεια between 'Wisdom' and 'Foolishness', which is the first of the four antitheses in i. 27–8, is taken up again and carried farther. Compare Col. ii. 8. Some of the changes that have been rung upon this Pauline theme by Saints Ambrose and Augustine are quoted in V. C (i) (*d*) 6 (δ), vol. v, p. 564, footnote 4, below, with reference to the historic περιπέτεια that, in the disintegration of civilizations, is apt to come over the relations between the philosophy of the Dominant Minority and the religion of the Internal Proletariat (see cap. cit., vol. cit., pp. 552–68, and the passage of Eduard Meyer that is quoted in V. C (i) (*d*) 9 (β), vol. vi, pp. 114–5, below).

remarkable for its conservatism in clinging to primitive conceptions as well as for its ingenuity in refining upon them.[1]

A Hellenic view of 'the Envy of the Gods' which is inimitable in its blend of *naïveté* with sophistication is given in the following passage of Herodotus:

'You observe how God blasts with His thunderbolt the animals that overtop their fellows, and how He cannot bear them to show off, while the little animals never irritate Him (οὐδέν μιν κνίζει);[2] and you also observe how He invariably directs these shafts of His upon the highest houses and the tallest trees. God loves to cut short everything that overtops its kind. In this way a great army is destroyed by a small army in certain circumstances—as, for instance, when God in His envy sends down panic upon them, or thunder. Then they perish, and their last state is unworthy of their first. God suffers no one to be proud except Himself.'[3]

The thesis here enunciated with a studied affectation of simplicity that heightens a desired effect of blasphemy is the overture to the Herodotean tragedy of the greatness and fall of the Achaemenian emperor Xerxes. The passage occurs in a fictitious speech from the mouth of Xerxes' uncle Artabanus at a meeting of the Achaemenian Privy Council in which Xerxes has announced his project of conquering Hellas, and has commended it on the ground that its accomplishment will 'make the Persian Empire conterminous with the stratosphere (Διὸς αἰθέρι ὁμορέουσαν), since there will be no *pays limitrophe* to ours for the Sun to set eyes on when I, with your aid, have turned all countries into one country as a result of my triumphal progress through Europe'.[4] In the course of the same speech Herodotus makes Xerxes incur the envy of no fewer than three great gods: Poseidon, through his announcement of his intention to bridge the Hellespont; Zeus, through his boast that he will divide with him the lordship of the Universe; and Helios, through his declared intention of extending the range of his own dominions from sunrise to sunset.[5] In this Herodotean tragedy of Xerxes' greatness and fall the protagonist irrevocably seals his own doom when, on the eve of his passage of the Hellespont, on the road to defeat, the spectacle of his grand army and armada tempts him to declare himself divinely happy (ἑαυτὸν ἐμακάρισε). The moment after uttering this blasphemy, Xerxes

[1] For a study of the history of this idea in Hellenic thought and life see Ranulf, S.: *The Jealousy of the Gods and Criminal Law of Athens: a Contribution to the Sociology of Moral Indignation* (London 1933, Williams & Norgate, 2 vols.).

[2] For some examples of the working of the principle of περιπέτεια in the natural history of the non-human fauna of the planet see IV. C (iii) (*c*) 2 (γ), pp. 423–8, below.—A.J.T.

[3] Herodotus, Book VII, chap. 10.

[4] Herodotus, Book VII, chap. 8.

[5] Compare the latter-day British boast of possessing an empire 'on which the Sun never sets'.

recollects himself and bursts into tears at the poignant thought that not one man of this host will be alive a hundred years hence; but it is too late now for repentance; and this incident only leads to a further colloquy between the Emperor and Artabanus, in which Xerxes hardens his heart and finally sends Artabanus home to Susa in disgrace. This colloquy is opened by Artabanus with the observation that the inevitability of Death is less poignant than the sufferings of Life.

'Human Life is so wretched that Death becomes a blessed escape from it. The tantalizing taste of sweetness, which is all that God gives in the three score years and ten, is proof of the enviousness of God's nature.'[1]

In a more serious vein the same thesis is propounded by Herodotus in the parables of Croesus and Polycrates.[2]

Croesus airs his prosperity, like a peacock's tail, before the eyes of Solon in the hope that the Athenian sage will pronounce him the happiest of Mankind; but a leading question fails to elicit the expected answer; and when the king loses his temper and confesses what is in his mind, he merely gives Solon an opportunity to pass from the particular to the general in his exposition of his philosophy.

'I know for a fact that the Godhead is invariably envious and destructive; and then, Sire, you question me regarding Human Life! . . . Out of all the days which go to make up the seventy years . . . , not one day brings forth anything remotely resembling the offspring of another; and therefore, Sire, Man is nothing but Misfortune. I imagine that you personally are immensely rich and that you have a vast number of subjects; but I cannot yet give you the title which is the object of your question, before I hear that you have been fortunate in your end. . . . Until I see [a man's] end, I must suspend judgement and call him not "happy" but "fortunate.". . . . In order to appraise any phenomenon, the attention must be directed upon the circumstances in which it meets its end. To many people God has given a glimpse of happiness in order to destroy them root and branch.'[3]

Herodotus relates[4] that 'these observations of Solon's did not at all commend themselves to Croesus, who dismissed the philosopher with contempt, as a man of no intelligence whatever, for his principle of discounting present values and appraising every phenomenon by its end. After the departure of Solon, however,

1 Herodotus, Book VII, chaps. 44–53.

2 In the Herodotean schema each of the exalted victims of 'the Envy of the Gods' is warned in advance, but in vain, by a human mentor—Artabanus's role towards Xerxes being played by Solon towards Croesus and by Amasis towards Polycrates. Croesus wins a reprieve from the extremity of Fate by calling upon Solon's name, in order to become, in his turn, the mentor of his conqueror Cyrus, whom he leads, in the end, to destruction by giving him bad advice in good faith (for this Herodotean ending of the story of Croesus and Cyrus see V. C (ii) (*a*), vol. vi, pp. 187–8, below).

3 Herodotus, Book I, chap. 32.

4 Book I, chap. 33.

Croesus was overtaken by a heavy retribution from God—presumably because he had ventured to regard himself as the happiest of all Mankind.' First, Croesus loses his son through the twofold error of failing to see the catch in an oracle and of placing the boy in the care of a man who has been proved desperately unlucky;[1] and then he loses his kingdom through failing to see the catch in an oracle once again, and leaning on the broken reed of an alliance with Sparta.[2] In the end Croesus finds himself standing, shackled, on a lighted pyre, on the point of being burnt alive. It is only in this extremity that he appeases 'the Envy of the Gods' at last by remembering the wisdom of Solon and calling, in contrition, upon the sage's name. The immediate consequence of this religious conversion is to produce a change of heart in Croesus's conqueror Cyrus, who has condemned his vanquished enemy to the flames and is waiting to enjoy the spectacle; and, when the penitent Cyrus orders the fire to be put out and finds that it has caught beyond human power to control it, the God Apollo himself condescends to save Croesus's life by a miracle.[3]

In the parable of Croesus, who is as wantonly presumptuous as Xerxes, yet manages to save his soul alive by a repentance at the eleventh hour, the Herodotean Godhead shows a touch of human kindness. The divine attributes of malignity and implacability reveal themselves, naked and unashamed, in the parable of Polycrates, who seeks, on the advice of his wise ally Amasis, to anticipate the wrecking of his fortunes through 'the Envy of the Gods'[4] by marring his own prosperity through his own act, but is frustrated when his favourite gold-mounted emerald signet-ring, which he has cast ceremoniously into the deep sea, is miraculously restored to him by the implacable Divinities.

'The occurrence struck Polycrates as supernatural, so he wrote all that he had done and all that had come of it in a letter, which he addressed to Egypt. When Amasis read the letter from Polycrates, he realized that it is impossible for one human being to extricate another from the destiny awaiting him, and that no good could be awaiting Polycrates, whose success was so unbroken that he recovered even what he had thrown away. In view of this, he sent a note to Samos denouncing the *entente*. His object in making this *démarche* was to save his own feelings from being harrowed, as they would be for a friend and ally, when Polycrates was overtaken by such a crushing disaster.'

1 See the story in Herodotus, Book I, chaps. 34–45.

2 See the story in Herodotus, Book I, chaps. 46–56 and 69–85.

3 Herodotus, Book I, chaps. 86–7. This legendary *auto da fé* has a better claim to the euphemistic title than the historic holocausts of the Spanish Inquisition.

4 'Your vast successes do not please me', Herodotus makes Amasis write to Polycrates, 'because I know for a fact that the Deity has an envious disposition' (Herodotus, Book III, chap. 40).

And, sure enough, Amasis was right; for 'Polycrates met with a shocking fate, which was quite unworthy of his character and ambitions'. The satrap of Lydia entices Polycrates into his power, tortures him to death, and crucifies his corpse.[1]

This Herodotean note is recaptured by one of the most accomplished Latinizers of Greek verse and Hellenic êthos in the Augustan Age, in a piquant application to Man's greatest material discoveries and inventions:

Nequicquam deus abscidit
prudens Oceano dissociabili
terras, si tamen impiae
non tangenda rates transiliunt vada.
audax omnia perpeti
gens humana ruit per vetitum nefas.
audax Iapeti genus
ignem fraude mala gentibus intulit.
post ignem aetheria domo
subductum macies et nova febrium
terris incubuit cohors,
semotique prius tarda necessitas
leti corripuit gradum.
expertus vacuum Daedalus aëra
pennis non homini datis;
perrupit Acheronta Herculeus labor.
nil mortalibus ardui est;
caelum ipsum petimus stultitia neque
per nostrum patimur scelus
iracunda Iovem ponere fulmina.[2]

The prevalence of this notion of 'the Envy of the Gods' in a disintegrating Hellenic Society is attested perhaps even more impressively by the witness of a Latin philosopher-poet of the last generation of the 'Time of Troubles' who had made it his life-work to preach, with a religious fervour, the illusoriness of the belief that there is any supernatural intervention in human affairs:

Cui non animus formidine divom
contrahitur, cui non correpunt membra pavore,
fulminis horribili cum plaga torrida tellus
contremit et magnum percurrunt murmura caelum?
non populi gentesque tremunt, regesque superbi
corripiunt divom percussi membra timore,
nequid ob admissum foede dictumve superbe
poenarum grave sit solvendi tempus adultum?

[1] Herodotus, Book III, chaps. 39–43 and 122–5. The crucifixion of Polycrates is touched upon further in V. C (ii) (*b*), Annex II, vol. vi, p. 403, footnote 1, below.

[2] Horace: *Carm.* I. 3, ll. 21–40. In a different context the first four lines of the present quotation have been quoted already in II. C (ii) (*b*) 2, vol. i, p. 327. The same note is sounded by Horace's contemporary and friend Virgil in his Fourth Eclogue, ll. 31–3.

summa etiam cum vis violenti per mare venti
induperatorem classis super aequora verrit
cum validis pariter legionibus atque elephantis,
non divom pacem votis adit et prece quaesit
ventorum pavidus paces animasque secundas—
nequiquam, quoniam violento turbine saepe
correptus nilo fertur minus ad vada leti?
usque adeo res humanas vis abdita quaedam
obterit et pulchros fascis saevasque securis
proculcare ac ludibrio sibi habere videtur.[1]

Hellenism is not the only civilization that has inherited this notion of 'the Envy of the Gods' from a primitive past. The same cynical explanation of the working of the Universe is to be found in a book of wisdom which is one of the spiritual fruits of the second and severer bout of a Sinic 'Time of Troubles':[2]

Stretch a bow to the very full,
And you will wish you had stopped in time;
Temper a sword-edge to its very sharpest,
And you will find it soon grows dull.
When bronze and jade fill your hall
It can no longer be guarded.
Wealth and place breed insolence
That brings ruin in its train.

'He who stands on tip-toe, does not stand firm;
He who takes the longest strides, does not walk the fastest.'
He who does his own looking sees little,
He who defines himself is not therefore distinct.
He who boasts of what he will do succeeds in nothing;
He who is proud of his work, achieves nothing that endures.[3]

If we turn from the Sinic World to one which was more remote from the Hellenic World in êthos in spite of its geographical proximity, we shall find in the book of an Israelitish prophet of the eighth century B.C., who was born into the second bout of a Syriac 'Time of Troubles',[4] a curiously close anticipation of the words which Herodotus—writing some three hundred years later than Isaiah—has put into the mouth of Xerxes' mentor Artabanus:[5]

'The day of the Lord of hosts shall be upon every one that is proud and lofty, and upon every one that is lifted up; and he shall be brought low;

[1] Lucretius: *De Rerum Natura*, Book V, ll. 1218–35.
[2] For the two bouts of the Sinic 'Time of Troubles' see V. C (ii) (*b*), vol. vi, pp. 291–5, below.
[3] The *Tao-te King*, chaps. 9 and 24 (translation by Waley, A., in *The Way and its Power* (London 1934, Allen & Unwin)).
[4] For the two bouts of the Syriac 'Time of Troubles' see V. C (ii) (*b*), vol. vi, pp. 302–3, below.
[5] See the present chapter, p. 250, above.

'And upon all the cedars of Lebanon that are high and lifted up, and upon all the oaks of Bashan,

'And upon all the high mountains, and upon all the hills that are lifted up,

'And upon every high tower, and upon every fenced wall,

'And upon all the ships of Tarshish, and upon all pleasant pictures.

'And the loftiness of Man shall be bowed down, and the haughtiness of men shall be made low; and the Lord alone shall be exalted in that day.'[1]

The same philosophy is expounded by a Jewish writer of the second century B.C. who may have been influenced not only by the Prophets of Judah and Israel but also by the Hellenic thought of a post-Herodotean generation that had substituted an impersonal Chance for gods made in human image without having outgrown the naïvely cynical belief in a Divine Envy working havoc with human life.

'I returned and saw under the Sun that the race is not to the swift nor the battle to the strong neither yet bread to the wise nor yet riches to men of understanding nor yet favour to men of skill; but Time and Chance happeneth to them all. For Man also knoweth not his time. As the fishes that are taken in an evil net and as the birds that are caught in the snare, so are the sons of men snared in an evil time, when it falleth suddenly upon them.'[2]

Even some two centuries later, when a prolonged experience of suffering was bringing a tardy enlightenment to Jew and Greek alike, we find, in a passage of lyric poetry in the Gospel according to Saint Luke, that the intervention of God in human affairs is attributed in the first place to a desire to exercise power, and only in the second place to a concern for justice and mercy.

'He hath shewed strength with his arm; he hath scattered the proud in the imagination of their hearts.

'He hath put down the mighty from their seats, and exalted them of low degree. He hath filled the hungry with good things; and the rich He hath sent empty away.'[3]

It was a Greek and not a Jew—and this a Greek older than Herodotus—who first proclaimed the truth that the cause of *περιπέτεια* is not to be found in the intervention of any external power but is an aberration in the soul of the sufferer himself, and that the name of this fatal moral evil is not Envy but Sin.[4]

1 Isaiah ii. 12–17.

2 Ecclesiastes ix. 11–12.

3 The *Magnificat*, in Luke i. 51–3.

4 The spiritual insight of Aeschylus seems to have come to him neither as a congenital endowment nor as a sudden intuition, but as a reward of spiritual travail. At any rate we have evidence, in his surviving literary remains, of a stage in his spiritual history at which he had not yet seen the light. As Ranulf points out in op. cit., vol. i, pp. 69–70, the discomfiture of Xerxes is ascribed to the Envy of the Gods by Aeschylus in *The*

A grey word liveth, from the morn
  Of old time among mortals spoken,
That Man's wealth waxen full shall fall
Not childless, but get sons withal;
And ever of great bliss is born
  A tear unstaunched and a heart broken.

But I hold my thought alone and by others unbeguiled;
'Tis the deed that is unholy shall have issue, child on child,
Sin on sin, like his begetters; and they shall be as they were.
But the man who walketh straight, and the house thereof, tho' Fate
  Exalt him, the children shall be fair.

For Old Sin loves, when comes the hour again,
  To bring forth New,
Which laugheth lusty amid the tears of men;
Yea, and Unruth, his comrade, wherewith none
May plead nor strive, which dareth on and on,
  Knowing not fear nor any holy thing;
Two fires of darkness in a house, born true,
  Like to their ancient spring.

But Justice shineth in a house low-wrought
  With smoke-stained wall,
And honoureth him who filleth his own lot;
But the unclean hand upon the golden stair
With eyes averse she fleeth, seeking where
  Things innocent are; and, recking not the power
Of wealth by men misgloried, guideth all
  To her own destined hour.[1]

The sinner is brought to destruction not by God's act but by his own. His offence lies not in rivalling his Creator—for that is just the opposite of what the sinner does—but in deliberately making himself utterly unlike Him; and God's part in this human tragedy is not active but passive. The sinner's bane is not a Divine Envy; for Man's attribution of this base passion to the Godhead

Persae as positively as it is explained in the same way by Herodotus. Ranulf not only quotes the reference, in terms, to the Envy of the Gods in *The Persae*, l. 362, but also acutely draws attention to the significance of the particle γάρ in line 12. In the history of Hebrew thought we seem to find a counterpart to this Aeschylean evolution in Exodus xx. 3–6, where the jealousy of Yahweh is first mentioned as a deterrent against possible proclivities, on his worshippers' part, to divide their worship between him and other gods, but is then immediately interpreted as an implacability towards them that hate him, which is offset by mercy for them that love him and keep his commandments. This interpretation is a manifest attempt to transfigure the immoral, or at any rate non-moral, quality of envy into a discriminatory treatment of friends and enemies which, in the relation between God and Man, may be taken at a stretch as a manifestation of divine righteousness. This attempt to reconcile old and new conceptions of the divine nature is so strained that it actually emphasizes the breadth of the gulf which divides them, and thereby gives a measure of the spiritual distance which the progress of human thought has traversed. In Exodus xxxiv, where the divine qualities of jealousy and mercy are likewise both mentioned, there is no attempt to relate them to each other.

[1] Aeschylus: *Agamemnon*, ll. 750–81, translated by Gilbert Murray.

is as false as it is blasphemous. The sinner's bane is a divine inability to continue to use as an instrument of creation a creature that has insisted upon alienating itself from the life of its Creator.[1] The sinful soul comes to grief because, so long as it wills to sin, God's grace is unable to inspire and inform it. But if περιπέτεια—'the reversal of roles'—is thus produced by the inward spiritual working of a moral law, and not by the impact of some external agency's immoral envy or unmoral exercise of power, how are we to interpret the plot of this psychological tragedy? If we examine the action of the play, we shall discern two variations on it which are distinguishable in a logical analysis though they are usually blended 'in real life'. In one version the subject errs through an untimely passivity, while in the other he rushes actively to seek his doom.

The passive aberration to which a creative human being is prone on the morrow of an achievement is to 'rest on his oars' in a fool's paradise where he dreams that, by having exerted himself once upon a time, he has won a title to 'live happily ever after'—as though one day's fairly earned wages could be converted, 'in real life', into an interminable and inexhaustible banker's draft upon the Future. Short of this degree of folly, the victor in yesterday's battle is apt to dream that if Time does refuse to stand still—if his successful response to the last challenge does, after all, overbalance into the evocation of a new challenge, and so toss him back into the open sea out of the haven where he has been fain to linger—then the seafarer *malgré lui* has merely to repeat mechanically the motions that served him so well last time in order to be sure of riding any storm which Fate may send down upon him. It is plain that the creative individual who yields to this passive mood is falling into the posture of the arrested individual or the arrested society[2] which has achieved so exact an equilibrium with its environment that it becomes the environment's slave instead of its master. In the case of the arrested civilizations we have seen that this posture is only tenable so long as the environment happens to remain constant, and that it spells disaster so soon as the environment begins to change. The same fate awaits a creative minority which has become infatuated with its own works. According to the Syriac legend of the creation of the Physical Universe, when 'God saw everything that He had made, and, behold, it was very good; and the evening and the morning were the sixth day; . . . and on the seventh day God ended His work which He had made; and He rested on the seventh day from all the work

[1] Ephesians iv. 18.
[2] For a survey of arrested civilizations see Part III. A in vol. iii, above.

which He had made; and God blessed the seventh day and sanctified it, because that in it He had rested from all His work which God had created and made'[1]—the immediate result was a static paradise, and it needed the Serpent's undesignedly beneficent intervention to liberate God's energies for performing a fresh act of creation in spite of Himself.[2] The triumphant creator is carried by his triumph into mortal danger of settling, like Zeus, on to a tyrant's throne[3] or sinking, as Faust feared to sink, on to a sluggard's *Faulbett*.[4] 'Otium et reges prius et beatas perdidit urbes.'[5] In terms of our modern Western Physical Science the nemesis of creativity, when the *ci-devant* creator's aberration takes this passive form, is described by a living biologist in the following language:

'Specialisation—while it leads to temporary prosperity—exposes a species to extinction or at least to very unfavourable conditions when its environment alters. A small change of climate will lead to the disappearance of forests over a wide area, and with them of most of the animals highly adapted to life in them, such as squirrels, woodpeckers, wood-eating beetles, and so forth. A few, like our own ancestors, adapted themselves to a new environment; but the majority, and all the more highly specialised, died out, the new population of the area being recruited from among the less well adapted forms.'[6]

If the moral of this passive aberration that overtakes some creative spirits is 'let him that thinketh he standeth take heed lest he fall',[7] we shall find that 'pride goeth before destruction, and an haughty spirit before a fall'[8] is the epitaph of those others who rush to seek their doom.

This second version of the plot is a tragedy in three acts which are familiar in Greek literature under the titles *κόρος*, *ὕβρις*, *ἄτη*; and in this context these three Greek words all have a subjective as well as an objective connotation. Objectively *κόρος* means 'surfeit', *ὕβρις* 'outrageous behaviour', and *ἄτη* 'disaster'. Subjectively *κόρος* means the psychological condition of being 'spoilt' by success; *ὕβρις* means the consequent loss of mental and moral balance; and *ἄτη* means the blind headstrong ungovernable impulse that sweeps an unbalanced soul into attempting the impos-

1 Gen. i. 31 and ii. 2–3.

2 For the role of the Serpent and Satan and Mephistopheles see II. C (ii) (*b*) 1, vol. i, pp. 271–99, above.

3 See Part III. B, in vol. iii, above.

4 See II. C (ii) (*b*) 1, in vol. i, above.

5 Catullus: *Carmina*, li, ll. 15–16.

6 Haldane, J. B. S.: *Possible Worlds* (London 1927, Chatto & Windus), pp. 42–3.

7 1 Corinthians x. 12.

8 Proverbs xvi. 18. The same truth is expressed in a different idiom by a latter-day Russian Orthodox Christian philosopher:

'Man's self-affirmation leads to his perdition; the free play of human forces unconnected with any higher aim brings about the exhaustion of Man's creative powers. . . . The will to power and "life" destroys the personality' (Berdyaev, N.: *The Meaning of History* (London 1936, Bles), pp. 142 and 215. Cf. pp. 154–5).

sible.[1] This active psychological catastrophe in three acts was the commonest theme—if we may judge by the handful of extant masterpieces—in the fifth-century Athenian tragic drama. It is the story of Agamemnon in Aeschylus's play of that name, and of Xerxes in his *Persae*; the story of Ajax in Sophocles' play of that name, of Oedipus in his *Oedipus Tyrannus*, and of Creon in his *Antigone*; and it is the story of Pentheus in Euripides' *Bacchae*.

'I have said: Ye are gods, and all of you are children of the Most High. But ye shall die like men, and fall like one of the princes.'[2]

In Platonic language,

'If one sins against the laws of proportion and gives something too big to something too small to carry it—too big sails to too small a ship, too big meals to too small a body, too big powers to too small a soul—the result is bound to be a complete upset. In an outburst of ὕβρις the over-fed body will rush into sickness, while the jack-in-office will rush into the unrighteousness that ὕβρις always breeds.'[3]

In these two variant versions of a single plot[4] we can discern and comprehend the nemesis of creativity; and if, 'in real life', this tragedy is really common form—if it is true that the successful creator of one chapter is severely handicapped, by his very success, in endeavouring to resume the creative role in the next chapter, so that the chances are always actually against 'the favourite' and in favour of 'the dark horse'[5]—then it is plain that we have here run

[1] 'Un élan qui peut aller jusqu'à l'emportement à mesure que tombent les obstacles; elle a quelque chose de frénétique.'—Bergson, H.: *Les Deux Sources de la Morale et de la Religion* (Paris 1932, Alcan), p. 320.

[2] Psalm lxxxii. 6–7.

[3] Plato: *Leges*, 691 C.

[4] Plato (*Respublica* 491 E) lays stress on the active kind of moral aberration as a cause of social breakdown:

'Must we not suppose . . . that the souls which have the finest natural endowment are precisely those that tend to go sensationally to the bad under the influence of a bad education? When one looks into the great crimes and the examples of unmitigated wickedness, does one find that these are the fruits of a second-rate character? Are they not apt rather to be the fruits of a vitality that has been corrupted by a wrong upbringing? Is it not the fact that a weak character is never the author of anything great—either for good or for evil?'

[5] The apparently paradoxical, and at the same time fundamentally right and natural, victory of 'the dark horse' is the theme—if this may be said without irreverence—of the Beatitudes in the Sermon on the Mount. 'Blessed are the poor in spirit, for theirs is the Kingdom of Heaven; . . . blessed are the meek, for they shall inherit the Earth' (Matt. v. 3 and 5). The same paradox is the *Leitmotiv* in the 'folk-tale' of the Ugly Duckling which turns into a swan, in the fairy-story of the Cinderella who turns into a princess, and in the romance of the boor who turns into a mighty man of valour like Sir Kay in fiction and Muzio Attendolo 'Sforza' in 'real life'. And, if Sir Leonard Woolley's theory is right, we can see the same principle at work in the first gleam of a revelation of the nature of the One True God which has eventually shone out in Christianity. According to Woolley in his *Abraham* (London 1936, Faber), God revealed himself to the Hebrew patriarch in the shape of the familiar humble tutelary genius of the household, whose worship Abraham carried with him out of Ur into the Wilderness, and not in any of the great deities of a Sumeric Pantheon whose temples the emigrant perforce left behind him in a city of destruction from which he was extricating himself just in time. For the historical relation between the religious enlightenment of Abraham and the disintegration of the Sumeric Civilization see Part VII, below.

to earth a very potent cause of the breakdowns of civilizations. We can see that in the drama of social life this nemesis of creativity would bring on social breakdowns directly in two distinct ways. On the one hand it would seriously diminish the number of possible candidates for playing the creator's role in the face of any given challenge, since it would tend to rule out those who had responded successfully to the last challenge, and these, *ex hypothesi*, were potential creators before their very success in turning promise into achievement threatened to sterilize their creativity in the act of demonstrating it. In the second place this frequent sterilization of the *ci-devant* creators would handicap the society in its next ordeal out of all proportion to the mere numerical ratio between a handful of lost leaders and a host of creative spirits; for, *ex hypothesi* again, the very past achievement which has fatally disqualified these lost souls from achieving anything further has also brought them to the front and has lodged them in key positions where their senile impotence to create is aggravated by their lasting potency *ex officio* to thwart and hinder.[1] When these considerations are taken together, it will be seen that the handicapping or disqualifying or sterilizing of *ci-devant* creators through an inward psychological aberration to which their very achievement makes them prone is the most potent cause of breakdown of any that our survey has revealed.

Can this nemesis of creativity be averted? Clearly it can; for otherwise every civilization that ever came to birth would be arrested inexorably at the threshold of life, whereas we have actually found no more than four instances of civilizations that have succumbed to this fate, as against no less than twenty-one that have succeeded in going on from strength to strength. Yet, though a way of salvation exists, it is a narrow way and it is difficult to find it.[2] The question is, 'How can a man be born when he is old? Can he enter the second time into his mother's womb and be born?'[3] And the answer is that, 'except ye be converted, and become as little children, ye shall not enter into the Kingdom of Heaven'.[4]

How often do the creative minorities which have discovered a successful response to one challenge then qualify themselves, through a spiritual rebirth, to take up the next challenge and the next? And how often do they disqualify themselves by fatuously

[1] This almost malignantly perverse operation of the rhythm of Life is particularly apparent in the disastrous transformation of creative into dominant minorities and the equally disastrous usurpation of the office of peace-makers by statesmen who have risen to power as leaders in war and procurers of military victory. These two illustrations are examined in greater detail in IV. C (iii) (*c*) 2 (α), pp. 297–8 and 298–300, below.

[2] Matt. vii. 14.

[3] John iii. 4.

[4] Matt. xviii. 3, quoted on p. 248, above.

'resting on their oars' or by wilfully rushing down the steep place that leads from κόρος through ὕβρις into ἄτη? Our best hope of finding an answer to this question lies in resorting once more to our trusty and well-beloved method of making an empirical survey.

2. *'Resting on One's Oars'*

(α) *The Idolization of an Ephemeral Self.*

A Definition of Idolatry.

While the attitude of 'resting on one's oars' may be described as the passive way of succumbing to the nemesis of creativity, the negativeness of this mental posture does not certify an absence of moral fault. A fatuous passivity towards the Present springs from an infatuation with the Past; and this infatuation is the sin of idolatry which, in the primitive Hebrew scheme of religion, is the sin most apt to evoke the vengeance of 'a jealous god'. Idolatry may be defined as an intellectually and morally purblind worship of the part instead of the whole, of the creature instead of the Creator, of Time instead of Eternity;[1] and this abuse of the highest faculties of the human spirit, and misdirection of its most potent energies, has a fatal effect upon the object of idolization. It accomplishes the perverse and disastrous miracle of transforming one of 'the ineffably sublime works'[2] of God into an 'abomination of desolation, standing where it ought not'.[3] In practical life this moral aberration may take the comprehensive form of an idolization of the idolator's own personality, or own society, in some ephemeral phase of the never-ceasing movement from challenge through response to further challenge which is the essence of being alive;[4] or, again, it may take the limited form of an idolization of some particular institution, or particular technique, which has once stood the idolator in good stead. It may be convenient to examine these different forms of idolatry separately, and we may start with the idolization of the self, because this will offer us the clearest illustrations of the nature of the sin that we are now setting out to study. If it is indeed the truth

> That men may rise on stepping-stones
> Of their dead selves to higher things,[5]

then the idolator who commits the error of treating one dead self, not as a stepping-stone, but as a pedestal, will be alienating him-

[1] See Part I. A, vol. i, p. 9, with footnote 3, and IV. C (iii) (*b*) 4 and 5, in the present volume, pp. 141–85, above, for the nature of idolatry as exemplified in our modern Western political aberration of Nationalism.

[2] Goethe: *Faust*, l. 249, quoted in II. C (ii) (*b*) 1, vol. i, pp. 276 and 279, above.

[3] Mark xiii. 14 = Matt. xxiv. 15; cf. Luke xxi. 20. These passages in the New Testament are reminiscences of Daniel ix. 27 and xii. 11.

[4] See Part III. B, vol. iii, above.

[5] Tennyson: *In Memoriam*.

self from the life of God[1] as conspicuously as the stylite devotee who maroons himself on the summit of a lonely column dissevers himself from the world of men.

Jewry.

The most notorious historical example of this idolization of an ephemeral self is the error of the Jews which is exposed in the New Testament in a series of passages that we have already quoted[2] as incomparable expressions of the *motif* of περιπέτεια. In a period of their history which began in the infancy of the Syriac Civilization and which culminated in the Age of the Prophets of Israel, the people of Israel and Judah raised themselves head and shoulders above the Syriac peoples round about in responding to the challenge of a 'Time of Troubles' by rising to a higher conception of Religion.[3] Keenly conscious, and rightly proud, of the spiritual treasure which they had thus wrested from an ordeal that had broken the spirit of their Aramaean and Phoenician and Philistine neighbours, the Jews allowed themselves to be 'betrayed, by what' was 'false within',[4] into an idolization of this notable, yet transitory, phase of their own spiritual growth. It was, indeed, a mighty feat of spiritual intuition to perceive in the lineaments of a primitive volcano-demon of the Arabian Wilderness the epiphany of a God who was omnipresent and omnipotent. What the Israelites had come to see in their hereditary tribal divinity Yahweh was never apprehended in Chemosh by the Moabites or in Rimmon by the Damascenes or in Melkart by the Tyrians[5] or in Dagon by the Philistines. In this chapter of their history the Children of Israel had been gifted with an unparalleled spiritual insight. And then, after having divined a truth which was absolute and eternal, they allowed themselves to be captivated by a temporary and relative half-truth. They persuaded themselves that Israel's discovery of the One True God had revealed Israel itself to be God's Chosen People; and this half-truth inveigled them into the fatal error of looking upon a momentary spiritual eminence, which they had attained by labour and travail, as a privilege conferred upon them by God in a covenant which was everlasting.[6] In this delusion—which was a moral as well as an intellectual fault—the Jews 'rested on their oars' when they were called upon to respond to a new challenge which was

1 Ephesians iv. 18.
2 In IV. C (iii) (*c*) 1, on p. 247, above.
3 See III. C (i) (*a*), vol. iii, pp. 140–1, above.
4 Meredith: *Love's Grave*, quoted in IV. C (iii) (*a*), on p. 120, above.
5 The identification of the Tyrian Melkart with the Hellenic Hêraklês, and the possible influence of this act of religious syncretism upon the mythology and theology of Christianity, are discussed in V. C (ii) (*a*), Annex II, vol. vi, pp. 465–76, below.
6 See the passages quoted from the Old Testament in II. C (ii) (*a*) 1, vol. i, p. 246, above.

presented to the Syriac Society *post Alexandrum* by the impact of Hellenism;[1] and, through persisting in this posture, they 'put themselves out of the running' for serving once more as pioneers in the next advance of the Syriac spirit. Brooding over a talent which they had perversely sterilized by hiding it in the earth,[2] they rejected the still greater treasure which God was now offering them. 'A son of man the Son of God? Was a generation in Jewry that was heir to the whole of God's revelation to Abraham and Moses and the Prophets now called upon to betray this magnificent Jewish spiritual heritage by accepting one of those childishly shocking Hellenic *contes* of the amours of Zeus which the wisdom of the Greeks themselves had long ago rejected as being neither intellectually nor morally credible of the Godhead?'[3] The question had only to be framed in order to answer itself in the negative in the mind of an orthodox Jew of the generation of Jesus. And so it came to pass that the Gospel of a Jewish Messiah who was God Himself incarnate was preached by Galilaeans and taken to heart by Gentiles.

Athens.

If Israel succumbed to the nemesis of creativity by idolizing itself in its transitory role of being 'the Chosen People', Athens condemned herself to the same fate by becoming infatuated with her own no less transitory role of being 'the Education of Hellas'.

We have seen how Athens earned a temporary claim to this magnificent title by finding a solution for the Malthusian problem which beset the Hellenic Society in the second chapter of its history,[4] and by going on to solve, with even greater brilliance, the further problems which the very success of the Solonian economic revolution had raised in the two fields of domestic politics[5] and artistic culture. These gifts of Athens to Hellas were indeed immense; yet the Enneacruni were not, any more than Jacob's Well at Samaria, 'a well of water springing up into everlasting life'.[6] This Attic water might momentarily slake the drinker's thirst, but it could not procure him a miraculous release from ever thirsting again;[7] and, indeed, the imperfectness of what Athens had achieved was proclaimed by the very occasion on which her self-conferred title of 'the Education of Hellas' was coined for her by her own son

[1] For this challenge see III. C (ii) (*b*), vol. iii, pp. 263–4, above, and V. C (i) (*d*) 9 (*β*), vol. vi, pp. 103–5, below.

[2] Matt. xxv. 25.

[3] For the points of likeness and difference between the story of the conception and birth of Jesus in the Matthaean and Lucan prologues to the Gospel and the similar stories that are told of certain pagan heroes of Hellenic history see V. C (ii) (*a*), vol. vi, pp. 267–75, and V. C (ii) (*a*), Annex II, vol. vi, pp. 450–1, below.

[4] See I. B (i), vol. i, pp. 24–5, and II. D (ii), vol. ii, pp. 37–42, above.

[5] See IV. C (iii) (*b*) 9, pp. 200–6, above.

[6] John iv. 14.

[7] John iv. 13–14.

Pericles. He coined it in a funeral oration[1] which he delivered in praise of the Athenian dead in the first year of an Atheno-Peloponnesian War which was an outward visible sign of an inward spiritual breakdown in the life of the Hellenic Society. And this fatal war had broken out because one of the problems set by the success of the Solonian economic revolution—the problem of creating a Hellenic political world order—had proved to be beyond the compass of the fifth-century Athenians' moral stature.[2] In the circumstances of the year 431–430 B.C. the orator's proclamation of Athens as 'the Education of Hellas' should therefore not have moved his audience to a thrill of self-adulation, but rather have moved them to 'abhor' themselves 'and repent in dust and ashes'.[3] The military overthrow of Athens in 404 B.C., and the greater moral defeat which the restored Athenian democracy inflicted upon itself in 399 B.C. by the judicial murder of Socrates, did indeed provoke one contemporary Athenian man of genius to repudiate Periclean Athens and almost all her works.[4] Yet Plato's partly petulant and partly affected gesture of fouling his own Attic nest neither profited Plato himself nor impressed his fellow citizens; and the epigoni of those Athenian pioneers who had made their city 'the Education of Hellas' sought to vindicate their claim to a forfeited title by the perverse method of proving themselves unteachable.

Like the French *émigrés* at the turn of the eighteenth and nineteenth centuries of the Christian Era, the restorers of the Athenian democracy at the turn of the fifth and fourth centuries B.C. convicted themselves of having 'forgotten nothing and learnt nothing';[5] and the tone which they set was maintained by their successors to the bitter end of Athenian history. They idolized the dead self of Athens as she had been, for a fleeting moment, in the Periclean Age; and they thereby debarred a post-Periclean Athens from having any part or lot in later Hellenic acts of creation.

On the political plane no cumulation of disasters ever availed to shake Athens out of the 'sacred egoism' which Pericles had taught her to regard as a duty to herself that her past services to Hellas entitled her to cultivate in perpetuity.

In transforming the Delian League into an Athenian Empire, this Attic egoism had not only brought upon Athens the loss of her political primacy in Hellas, but had incidentally brought upon

[1] The phrase, as we have it, occurs in the rendering of Pericles' funeral oration by Thucydides in Book II, chap. 41.

[2] See IV. C (iii) (*b*) 10, p. 213, above.

[3] Job xlii. 6.

[4] For Plato's attitude towards his Attic social heritage see Part III. A, vol. iii, pp. 90–3, above.

[5] 'Personne n'a su ni rien oublier ni rien apprendre.'—Chevalier de Panat in a letter dated London, January 1796, in *Mémoires et Correspondance de Mallet du Pan* (Paris 1851, Amyot & Cherbuliez, 2 vols.), vol. ii, chap. 9, p. 197.

Hellas as a whole the breakdown of the Hellenic Civilization. Yet a post-war Athens learnt so little from the political errors of her pre-war self that the history of the First Athenian Empire was virtually repeated in that of the Second. The disruption of this Second Athenian Empire, owing to Athens' inveterately egoistic proclivities, opened the way for a Philip of Macedon, on the fringes of the fourth-century Hellenic World, to build up a Power of an overwhelmingly superior material calibre.[1] The measure of this superiority was given by the completeness of Athens' defeat at Chaeronea; and, in the next generation, Philip's political achievement in Continental European Greece was emulated by the Romans in Italy and dwarfed by Alexander in Asia. Therewith the whole scale of political life in the Hellenic World was enlarged, and this so vastly and so abruptly that the change opened a new chapter in Hellenic history.[2] Yet it took Athens 76 years—from her overthrow by Philip in 338 B.C. to her overthrow by Antigonus Gonatas in 262—to learn that, in this new world of titans, she could no longer affect with impunity to play her classic role of a Hellenic Great Power.[3]

Even then, the Athenian reading of a Macedonian lesson was fatally negative; for when, in 229–228 B.C., Athens shook herself free again from Macedonian military occupation, she rebuffed an invitation to enter the Achaean League, and withdrew into a selfish isolation[4]—as though she were blind to the patent political truth that, in the international situation of that age of Hellenic history, a policy of solidarity between the little central states was, for each and all of them, the only possible means of salvation from the fate of being overwhelmed by the new Great Powers of titanic calibre on the Hellenic World's expanding periphery.[5] In this posture of an egoism that was bound to defeat itself, Athens looked on passively while Rome delivered 'knock-out blows' to her fellow titans on the periphery and to Athens' neighbours in the centre who had been attempting—without Athenian help—to avert this catastrophe by the expedient of federation; and by this time Athens' egoism had so far stifled both her Hellenic public spirit and her Attic self-respect that she actually stooped to play the part of Greek jackal to the Roman lion. She basely begged for a dole out of Roman spoils and Greek losses—the derelict territory of the neighbouring Boeotian city of Haliartus, which had fallen a victim to Roman

[1] See III. C (ii) (*b*), Annex IV, vol. iii, pp. 485–6, above.

[2] See III. C (i) (*a*), vol. iii, pp. 140 and 150–1, and III. C (i) (*d*), vol. iii, p. 197, above; and IV. C (iii) (*c*) 2 (*β*), in the present volume, pp. 305–6; V. C (i) (*c*) 3, vol. v, p. 214; and V. C (ii) (*b*), vol. vi, pp. 289–90, below.

[3] See III. C (ii) (*b*), vol. iii, p. 338, above.

[4] See III. C (ii) (*b*), vol. iii, pp. 340–1, above.

[5] See loc. cit.

'frightfulness',[1] together with the two islands of Lemnos and Delos—and the insular items in her shameless demand were contemptuously tossed to her.[2]

Yet neither a mercenary gratitude for the lucrative gift of the Delian slave-market, nor a prudent fear of suffering Haliartus's fate, restrained Athens from eventually turning against her Roman patrons and masters. With a supreme inconsequence Athens waited until Rome's world power had been placed on an impregnable basis by the overthrow of all serious competitors, and then she abandoned her latter-day policy of isolation, plunged once again into the maelstrom of the Hellenic 'Time of Troubles' in its final paroxysm, and this time pushed her way into the *mêlée* on the anti-Roman side. In 88 B.C., when King Mithradates of Pontic Cappadocia offered the city-states of Greece a 'liberation' from Roman whips which would merely have exposed them to chastisement with the scorpions of a despotism in the Achaemenian tradition, Athens light-heartedly enlisted under the Oriental war-lord's banner, and paid for her folly two years later when the city was taken by storm by Mithradates' Roman conqueror Sulla. If the price which she paid on this occasion was something less than annihilation, it was because—as Sulla himself explained, in excuse for his unwonted touch of mercy—'he forgave a minority for the sake of a majority: the living for the sake of the dead'.[3] A historian might comment that this posthumous service, which the Athenians of the Solonian and the Periclean Age thus rendered to their degenerate descendants, was, after all, no more than a bare act of justice, considering that the latter-day Athenians' infatuation with their ancestors' withered glory had been so largely instrumental in bringing them to their eventual pass. The extent of the service which Sulla ironically credited to the account of the Athenians of the past must not, however, be overestimated; for, though Athens survived the Sullan sack as a *chef d'œuvre* of architecture and a seat of intellectual life, this last excursion into the arena of international politics was the inglorious end of Athenian political history.

Was it intellectual stupidity or moral aberration that prevented the Athenians from ever learning a lesson which was perpetually being inculcated into them from the days of Lysander to the days of Sulla? Since it can hardly be maintained that the average level, either of native wit or of intellectual cultivation, was lower in Athens than in other parts of the Hellenic World during the last four centuries B.C., the Athenians stand convicted of having brought

1 For the sack of Haliartus and Coronea by the Romans in 171 B.C. see II. D (v), vol. ii, p. 213, and III. C (ii) (*b*), vol. iii, p. 312, above.
2 Polybius, Book XXX, chap. 20 (*olim* 18), and Book XXXII, chap. 7 (*olim* 17).
3 Plutarch's *Life of Sulla*, chap. 14.

their political misfortunes upon themselves through the moral fault of infatuation with their own past; and it is here that we must look for the psychological cause of their inveterate self-stultifying egoism. This explanation will be confirmed if we take a comparative view of the contemporary creative achievements of certain other Hellenic communities which conspicuously lacked the Attic intellectual endowment, but which were also, by the same token, exempt from the incubus of a Periclean halo.

At the moment when, at the turn of the fifth and fourth centuries B.C., the exiled Athenian democrats were preparing for their barren restoration of an Attic *ancien régime*, an Athenian soldier of fortune, who was then seeing service in the Achaemenian pretender Cyrus's famous corps of ten thousand Greek mercenaries, was observing the differences in êthos between the several contingents of troops that composed this variegated force. The Ten Thousand were the human flotsam and jetsam of all the city-states that had been battered by the recent storm of the Atheno-Peloponnesian War; and, since the greater part of the Hellenic World had been involved in the catastrophe,[1] this post-war camp of Greek mercenaries on Achaemenian ground was a fair epitome of the contemporary Hellenic Society. In this miniature Hellas-under-arms the Athenian Xenophon noticed, with a contempt which was half irritable and half condescending, that his Achaean and Arcadian comrades were markedly more wayward, impulsive, improvident, refractory to discipline, and in fact in every way more crude and barbaric, than the representatives of the more sophisticated and progressive Hellenic communities of the day, like his own Athenian self, or his Spartan and Boeotian friends.[2] Xenophon's observation was correct. At the date when he made it, Athens stood on an altogether higher level of culture than Arcadia and Achaia; yet after Xenophon's day the roles were so rapidly reversed that an Arcadian historian of the second century B.C., who was also an Achaean statesman, could pronounce a condemnation which is as convincing as it is severe upon the statesmanship of a fourth-century Athenian politician who was Xenophon's junior by only one generation; and he could drive his verdict home by pointing the contrast between Demosthenes and the author's own forebears who had been Demosthenes' Arcadian contemporaries.

'For Demosthenes the measure of everything was the parochial interest of his Attic fatherland. In his view the whole of Hellas ought to take its cue from Athens as a matter of duty, and any Hellenes who failed

[1] Thucydides, Book I, chap. 1.

[2] For the difference in êthos, and consequent divergence in action, between the Achaeans and Arcadians on the one side and the rest of the Ten Thousand on the other see Xenophon's *Cyri Anabasis, passim*, especially Book VI, chaps. 1–3.

to comply were stigmatized by him as traitors. In this, Demosthenes' policy was, in my opinion, singularly wide of the mark and out of touch with reality; and, as a matter of fact, my opinion is borne out by the verdict of the history of the age, which testified to the political wisdom and foresight, not of Demosthenes, but of [his Arcadian and Messenian contemporaries] Eucampidas and Hieronymus and Cercidas and the sons of Philiadas.'[1]

If this comparative judgement was valid already for the age which saw Athenian statesmanship fail to prevent the new Power of Macedon from imposing its hegemony upon Hellas, it was still more conspicuously valid for the ensuing period which intervened between the Battle of Chaeronea and the date at which Polybius was writing. In the third century B.C. it was unquestionably the wisdom and foresight of Achaean and Arcadian statesmen that liberated the heart of Hellas from Macedonian shackles, and then worked out a constitutional device for safeguarding this recaptured political freedom by making it less difficult for the little states at the centre of a rapidly and widely expanding Hellenic World to hold their own against the Great Powers which were growing up on the periphery. The device was a new system of federating city-states: a form of federation which did not attempt to deprive the individual state-member of its traditional city-state autonomy, yet at the same time took care to confer effective powers upon the common Government of the federal union. The Achaean and Arcadian architects of this new type of Hellenic polity perceived that these were the only terms on which the city-states in the heart of Greece could survive politically at all in a world in which the average unit-size of a sovereign state had already increased, in every other region, to a measure which dwarfed even an Attica or a Lacedaemon, not to speak of the smaller domain of a Sicyon or Megalopolis or Dyme. This truth, of course, was staring all third-century Greek statesmen in the face; but an Aratus and a Lydiadas distinguished themselves by summoning up the strength of mind to act upon their insight,[2] whereas, in this new crisis in Hellenic history, Athens' sole distinction lay in the singular negativeness of her role. Her despised Boeotian neighbours might perhaps find some ground for claiming that the work of Aratus was inspired by Boeotian federal experiments in the past[3]—in so far as it was not a direct reaction to the exigencies of Aratus's own age. Even the Spartans, who incurred a more positive responsibility than the Athenians for the ultimate failure of Aratus's political enterprise,[4] did at least react

1 Polybius, Book XVIII, chap. 14 (*olim* XVII. 14).
2 For their work see III. C (ii) (*b*), vol. iii, pp. 313–14 and 339–41, above.
3 See IV. C (iii) (*c*) 2 (β), pp. 307–8, below.
4 See III. C (ii) (*b*), vol. iii, p. 341, footnote 1, above.

to the Hellenic crisis of the third century B.C. by suddenly and surprisingly shaking off a social catalepsy in which they had lain fast bound for three hundred years;[1] and they did not relapse into lethargy until they had offered two new and notable contributions to the Hellenic commonweal—an experiment in social revolution[2] and a legend of martyr-kings[3]—both of which were harvested in the fullness of time by the Hellenic proletariat, although, at the moment, they brought confusion and not salvation to the dominant minority. At this critical moment when Hellas, in her extremity, was throwing her oldest veterans, as well as her youngest recruits, into her battle with Fate, in a last desperate effort to break through the iron ring, Athens was almost alone in holding coldly aloof.

This negativeness of Athens in her latter days, which we have so far been observing on the political plane, comes out still more strikingly when we turn our attention from politics to culture; for culture, even more than politics, was the sphere of activity in which Athens excelled in the springtime of her history which had opened with her success in solving the Malthusian challenge; and in this field her *floruit* came later and lasted longer. In the souls of a Euripides and a Thucydides and a Socrates and a Plato the very onset of the political adversity that was heralded by the outbreak of the Atheno-Peloponnesian War had the effect of a challenge which evoked the highest moral and intellectual flights of the Attic spirit; and the fourth century B.C., which saw the beginning of the political autumn of Athenian history, marked the height of its cultural summer. Even after the turn of the fourth and third centuries, when the flow of native Attic genius threatened to dwindle, the cultural pre-eminence of Athens seemed to be assured for ever by an established cultural prestige which attracted to her precincts the men of light and learning from ever more distant regions of a continually expanding Hellenic World—an Aristotle of Stageirus and a Zeno of Citium and an Epicurus of Samos—and these eminent Athenians by spiritual adoption left permanent legacies to the city where they had made their home. They reinforced the Platonic Academy with a Peripatus and a Stoa and a Garden. Yet by the time when Polybius of Megalopolis was writing his oecumenical history, Athens could no longer claim to possess a monopoly of the higher Hellenic culture;[4] and even in the field of philosophy,

1 See Part III. A, vol. iii, pp. 53–77, above.

2 See Part III. A, vol. iii, pp. 76–7, above, and V. C (i) (*c*) 2, vol. v, p. 78; V. C (i) (*d*) 1, vol. v, pp. 388–9; and V. C (ii) (*a*), vol. vi, pp. 219–20, below.

3 See V. C (ii) (*a*), Annex II, *passim*, vol. vi, below.

4 Polybius himself records (in Book IV, chaps. 20–1) the deliberate and strenuous and successful efforts which the Arcadians had made, presumably between Xenophon's day and his own, to counteract the barbaric boorish vein which Xenophon had observed in his Arcadian companions-in-arms. Some time before Polybius's day the Arcadians

which she appeared to have made peculiarly and inalienably her own, the conceit of being 'the Education of Hellas' led her into betraying herself when she was visited by a greater than Zeno from a city which was not more outlandish than Citium.

The rejection of Paul by the Athenians[1] is the analogue of his Master's rejection by the Jews. Though Paul disputed—according to the custom of philosophers at Athens—'in the market daily with them that met with him', and though he gave a seasoning of Attic salt to his Areopagitic oration by taking an Attic votive inscription for his text, his preaching of the Resurrection proved an insuperable stumbling-block to an Athenian generation which was infatuated with a Stoic and Epicurean past. Paul's first impression of a 'city wholly given to idolatry' was indeed a true intuition of Athens as she had come to be in the Apostle's day.

'Their idols are silver and gold, the work of men's hands.

'They have mouths, but they speak not; eyes have they, but they see not;

'They have ears, but they hear not; noses have they, but they smell not. . . .

'They that make them are like unto them; so is every one that trusteth in them.'[2]

'So Paul departed from among them . . . and came to Corinth',[3] where his message that God 'now commandeth all men everywhere to repent' found more sensitive ears among the grandchildren of the commercial-minded Roman freedmen who had been settled by Caesar on the derelict site of Athens' annihilated Greek rival.[4] Athens had refused to be charged with a spiritual mission which she might have taken as the crown of her long philosophic preparation; and the function of serving as a seed-bed in which the germs

had subjected themselves to the cultural discipline of a compulsory universal education in community singing; and the effectiveness of this Arcadian institution was demonstrated, towards the close of the third century B.C., by one of those exceptions that prove a rule. At this date the Hellenic World was shocked, and the rest of Arcadia put to shame, by a startling relapse into barbarism in the single Arcadian community of Cynaetha, where the national Arcadian institution of an intensive cultivation of music had been allowed to fall into local neglect.

1 See the account in Acts xvii. 16–34.

2 Psalm cxv. 4–6 and 8.

3 Acts xvii. 33 and xviii. 1.

4 For the commercial-mindedness of Caesar's freedmen-colonists at Corinth see Strabo, *Geographica*, Book VIII, pp. 381–2. After her annihilation in 146 B.C. by the Roman General Mummius, 'Corinth remained derelict for an age, until eventually the eligibility of the site procured the restoration of the city at the hands of Caesar the God. Caesar repopulated Corinth with a large colony of Romans of the freedman class; and these colonists, when they were shifting the ruins and incidentally digging up the graves, came across quantities of *objets de vertu*, both in porcelain and in bronze. This funeral furniture made such an impression on them that they did not leave a single grave unrifled—with the result that they acquired a large stock, disposed of it at a handsome profit, and filled Rome with *necrocorinthia*, as they called the yield of the graves, especially the porcelain. This Corinthian porcelain was highly prized to begin with—quite as highly as the Corinthian bronzes—but afterwards the craze for it subsided (the supply gave out, and, of the pieces already placed on the market, the majority were not a success).'

of Hellenic philosophy and Syriac religion would mingle and blend was fulfilled, not by Attica, but by Asia Minor. The seeds which the Apostle managed to sow among the turbulent Ephesians[1] and the 'foolish' Galatians were ripening, three centuries later, to an Asiatic harvest as far afield as rustic Cappadocia, and were beginning to take root among European barbarians beyond the farthest outposts of the Roman *Orbis Terrarum*, while Athens remained as 'wholly given to idolatry' as ever.

In the fourth century of the Christian Era, when the Cappadocian Fathers of the Church were laying the ecclesiastical foundations of a new social order, Athens was inspiring their Dardanian contemporary Julian with his tragically academic dream of a Paganism re-minted in a Christian image and resuscitated by artificial respiration.[2] The very connotation which the word 'academic' has acquired in our modern Western vernaculars, and the aptness of the word, in its eventual meaning, for describing and explaining the failure of Julian's life-work, bear witness to the fate to which Athens succumbed in the cultural sphere. It was not for nothing that the city which so frivolously rejected the Apostle's religious revelation should have entered with an equal light-heartedness upon the political escapade of the Mithradatic alliance at the instigation of the university professor Aristion.[3] In clinging to her outworn role of being 'the Education of Hellas' in a particular mental groove, Athens fulfilled her ideal of herself in an unfortunately literal way by turning herself into a university town.

In the fifth century of the Christian Era, when she was standing out as a last barren reef of unsubmerged Paganism above the still rising waters of an oecumenical Christian flood, Athens was the scene of a strange cultural alliance between a scholastic intellectualism and an archaistic revival of primitive superstitions[4] which the live genius of Hellenic philosophy had apparently strangled with ease, a thousand years before, in its Ionian infancy.[5] The Athenian

[1] For the re-emergence of Ephesus in particular, and of Ionia and Aeolis in general, from the eclipse under which they had lain from the sixth century B.C. to the fourth, see IV. C (i), pp. 20–3, above.

[2] For Julian's abortive Neoplatonic Church see V. C (i) (*d*) 6 (δ), Annex, vol. v, pp. 680–3, and V. C (ii) (*a*), vol. vi, pp. 222–3, below.

[3] The question whether Aristion was the only professor-dictator who had his day at Athens in this crisis, or whether he had a predecessor of the same profession called Athenion, is discussed in Ferguson, W. S.: *Hellenistic Athens* (London 1911, Macmillan), pp. 446–7, and in *The Cambridge Ancient History*, vol. ix, p. 244, footnote 4.

[4] This infection of the philosophy of the Dominant Minority by the superstition of the Internal Proletariat is examined further in V. C (i) (*d*) 6 (δ), vol. v, pp. 553–68, below.

[5] As early as the sixth century B.C. Superstition had been so effectively sterilized by Rationalism in the more progressive states of Hellas that the native supply of medicine-men and diviners gave out—if we may legitimately draw this inference from a number of cases, recorded by Herodotus, in which the Government of one or other of these states in the heart of the Hellenic World of that age employed the services of a diviner who had been born and bred in one of the backward cantons in the North-West. For example, the Athenian despot Peisistratus employed the Acarnanian Amphilytus (Book I,

professors in the generation of Saint John Chrysostom would pass—with no apparent sense of incongruity—from learnedly commenting on Aristotle in the lecture-room to piously swinging the bull-roarer over Attic fields in the half-affected but also half-serious belief that they were stimulating the crops by the practice of this magic ritual.[1] In this age, when Hellenism was at bay in an Attic fastness, the first and last things in the Hellenic tradition—its lowest and its highest elements—thus entered, at Athens, into a desperate defensive *union sacrée*. Even then the Athenians were being saved, as well as infatuated, by their ancestors; for at Athens this pedantic prolongation of 'the times of ignorance', in defiance of an official veto upon Paganism,[2] was indulgently 'winked at'[3] by the fifth-century Imperial authorities. Yet a mild official indulgence could not save a senile Attic pedantry from being a forlorn hope; and when these latter-day Athenian professorial activities were eventually snuffed out by the Imperial Government's long delayed enforcement of the law in A.D. 529, there was little loss to learning, and none at all to the genius of creative Hellenic thought, whose soul had long since departed from this body academic.

The only practical effect of the Emperor Justinian's vexatiously legal act of closing the University of Athens was to advertise His Christian Majesty's intolerance and to provide a *beau rôle* for His Zoroastrian Majesty Chosroes. The ejected Athenian professors, cut to the heart by this wanton breaking of a nine-centuries-long Platonic 'Golden Chain', and debarred from all activities that gave their own lives any meaning, sought asylum in the East, where, in the springtime of Hellenic philosophy, the Seven Sages had once sought wisdom. The asylum was graciously granted, but the refugees were inevitably disillusioned; for while it was an easy matter for the Sasanian Pādishāh to thwart the purpose, and blacken the face, of his Rūmī rival—the Caesar—by affording protection to the victims of Justinian's tyranny, it was entirely beyond Chosroes' power—and perhaps beyond the range of his imagination—to provide these academic exiles with the cultural atmosphere which they were now no longer allowed to breathe in Attica. Wise men who follow a king's star are unlikely to find their king—be he new-

chap. 62); the Samian despot Polycrates employed an Elean (Book III, chap. 132); the Spartan King Leonidas employed the Acarnanian Megistias (Book VII, chaps. 219, 221, and 228); the Phocians employed the Elean Tellias (Book VIII, chap. 27); the Spartans employed the Elean Tisamenus (Book IX, chaps. 33–6); Mardonius employed the Elean Hegesistratus (Book IX, chap. 37); Mardonius's Greek allies employed the Leucadian Hippomachus (Book IX, chap. 38).

[1] See the passage quoted from Marinus's *Life of Proclus*, chap. 28, in Bidez, J.: *La Vie de l'Empereur Julien* (Paris 1930, Les Belles Lettres), p. 74. The whole of chap. 12 of Bidez's work is worth studying in this connexion.

[2] For the Imperial legislation of A.D. 382–90 for the suppression of Paganism see IV. C (iii) (*b*) 12, pp. 226–7, above, and V. C (i) (*d*) 8 (δ), vol. vi, p. 89, below.

[3] Acts xvii. 30.

born saviour or wizened metaphysician—if they choose to make their pilgrimage widdershins; and the last of the Athenian professors were not vouchsafed, for their own benefit 'in real life', that miraculous reversal of the cosmic rhythm with which they were familiar in a Hellenic legend of Pelops[1] and in a Syriac legend of Joshua.[2] So the stars in their courses duly fought against them;[3] and indeed, in migrating eastward, from Athens to Ctesiphon, they were actually travelling towards the very source of the aggressive Syriac culture whose far-projected radiation had just completed the disintegration of Hellenism in its homeland. If the Syriac spirit was strong enough, even in a Helleno-Syriac syncretism such as Christianity, to make it impossible any longer to lead the life of a Hellenic philosopher at Athens, how could that life conceivably be lived in Ctesiphon under the aegis of a Zoroastrianism which was an undiluted and militantly anti-Hellenic expression of the Syriac genius?[4] It is not surprising to learn that the Athenian refugees in a hospitable 'Irāq soon found themselves painfully and incurably homesick for the inhospitable world of Rūm whose dust they had shaken from off their feet with so antique a gesture; but it is certainly remarkable that their host Khusrū Anūshirwān, so far from taking offence at their apparent ingratitude, showed himself not only sensitive but sympathetic to his odd guests' pitiful despair. He was kind enough to make the professors' interest his royal concern; and, in the peace terms which he negotiated with the Roman Imperial Government in A.D. 533, he insisted upon the inclusion of a special clause which not only secured the readmission of his protégés into Roman territory, but also guaranteed them their liberty to live in the Christian Empire as pagans for the rest of their lives without being molested by the Imperial police.[5]

Thanks to such considerateness on the part of a Persian autocrat, this Athenian tragi-comedy received a happy ending; but the Attic aberration of idolatry did not die with its last professional adepts. In its literal sense of that adoration of graven images which had shocked Saint Paul, this Athenian infatuation with Athens' dead self lived on under the Christian dispensation and even survived the interregnum which intervened between the final disappearance of Hellenism and the incipient emergence of Orthodox

[1] See Euripides: *Electra*, ll. 726–44; *Orestes*, ll. 1001–6; *Iph. Taur.*, l. 816; Plato: *Politicus*, 268 E–269 A.

[2] Joshua x. 12–14.

[3] Judges v. 20.

[4] For Zoroastrianism as a reaction against the intrusion of Hellenism into the Syriac World see I. C (i) (*b*), vol. i, pp. 90–1; II. D (v), vol. ii, p. 203; II. D (vi), vol. ii, pp. 234–6; II. D (vii), vol. ii, pp. 285–6 and p. 374, above, and V. C (i) (*c*) 2, vol. v, pp. 125–6, and V. C (i) (*d*) 6 (δ), Annex, vol. v, pp. 657–61, below.

[5] For the story of King Khusrū Anūshirwān and the Seven Athenian Professors see Agathias of Myrrhina: *A History of His Own Times*, Book II, chap. 30, and Edward Gibbon: *The History of the Decline and Fall of the Roman Empire*, chap. xl.

Christendom. It was assuredly no accident that the East Roman Empress Irene (*imperabat* A.D. 780–802), who restored the images to honour in the Orthodox Christian World after the first outbreak of Iconoclasm,[1] was not Anatolian but Athenian born.

We have now glanced at the part played by Athens in the political history of the Hellenic World after the outbreak of the Atheno-Peloponnesian War, and in its cultural history after the establishment of the four schools of philosophy in their Attic head-quarters; and our cursory survey has brought to light a paradoxical fact. Here is a period of Hellenic history which might aptly be labelled 'the Atticistic Age',[2] in acknowledgement of the truth that in this age the most strongly marked features of Hellenism are the traces of a lasting impress which has been left upon the face of the whole Hellenic Society by the creative work of Athens in the age immediately preceding;[3] and yet, in an age which bears this conspicuous stamp of Attic achievements in the past, Athens makes herself conspicuous—once again, but this time in exactly the opposite way—through the absence of any contemporary Attic contributions to the solution of current Hellenic problems.

Venice

The Attic paradox, for which we have found an explanation in Athens' fatal aberration of idolizing her own dead self, has a [illegible]allel, in our Western World, in the similar contrast between the [illegible]tive roles that Italy has played in the second and in the third [illegible]apter of our Western history.

If the Athens of the fifth and fourth centuries B.C. could fairly claim the title of 'the Education of Hellas', the Italy of the fourteenth and fifteenth centuries of the Christian Era might have called herself 'the Education of Western Christendom' with equal justice. If we scrutinize the countenance of our Western Society in that 'modern' chapter of its history which runs from the latter part of the fifteenth century to the latter part of the nineteenth, we shall find that its 'modern' economic and political efficiency, as well as its 'modern' aesthetic and intellectual culture, is of a distinctively Italian origin. In this chapter of its history our

[1] For the iconoclastic movement in the early life of Orthodox Christendom see IV. C (iii) (*c*) 2 (*β*), pp. 352 and 364, below.

[2] Instead of 'the Hellenistic Age', which is the label commonly used. The word 'Hellenistic' is manifestly out of place in the description of a particular period of Hellenic history. If it is to be used, it ought to be applied, not to any chapter in the history of the civilization which we have called the Hellenic, but to the whole life and activity of the two societies—the Western and the Orthodox Christian—which stand to the Hellenic Society in the relation which we have called 'Affiliation'. The problem of nomenclature in the labelling of periods of history has been touched upon in III. C (ii) (*b*), vol. iii, p. 375, footnote 2, above.

[3] On this point see II. D (ii), vol. ii, p. 42, above.

Western Civilization was launched on a new course by an Italian impetus; and this impetus came from the radiation, into Transalpine Europe, of a special Italian version of the general Western culture of the preceding age.[1] This local Italian culture made its conquests in Transalpine Europe, and thereby opened a new chapter in the history of the Western World as a whole, because it was brilliantly superior, in a number of vital points, to anything that Transalpine Europe had yet succeeded in achieving.[2] The unrivalled creativity of Italy in the fourteenth and fifteenth centuries[3] was thus the original driving-force behind the movement of Western Civilization during a span of four ensuing centuries which, on this account, might aptly be called our 'Italistic Age';[4] and here we find ourselves confronted, once again, by our Attic paradox; for, throughout a period of our common Western history which bore the image and superscription of Italian acts of creation in the past, the contemporary Italian contributions to the general life of the age were conspicuously inferior to those of medieval Italy's modern Transalpine converts.

The comparative cultural sterility of Italy during the four-hundred-years' span of Western history which began *circa* A.D. 1475 was manifest in all the medieval homes of Italian culture—in Florence, in Venice, in Milan, in Siena, in Bologna, in Padua—and a connoisseur of Italian life in this period of eclipse would be able to drive the point home by presenting an eclectic picture com-

[1] For this Italian radiation into Transalpine Europe at the turn of the second ('medieval') and the third ('modern') chapter of our Western history see I. B (i), vol. i, p. 19; III. C (ii) (*b*), vol. iii, pp. 350–63; and IV. C (iii) (*b*) 8, in the present volume, p. 198, above; and V. C (i) (*d*) 6 (γ), Annex I, vol. v, p. 635, footnote 1, and p. 638, below. The effect of the radiation is sometimes popularly described as 'the Renaissance'; but, in application to Transalpine Europe, the expression is misleading. For it was a mimesis of contemporary Italian culture, and not a recapture of some temporarily lost or submerged element in its own Transalpine social heritage, that was the real secret of the sudden advance in civilization that was accomplished by Transalpine Europe at this date. The authentic Renaissance was a re-birth of the defunct Hellenic culture in a new cultural environment through a successful recultivation of Latin and Greek letters; and this was not a Transalpine but an Italian achievement which was a part—though perhaps not the most vital part—of the *Kulturgut* that was transmitted from Italy to the Transalpine provinces of the Western World at the turn of the fifteenth and sixteenth centuries of the Christian Era.

[2] The superiority of Italian over Transalpine culture, which was so striking towards the end of the fifteenth century, is sometimes placed to the credit of the foregoing renaissance in Italy of Latin and Greek letters; but the Italian achievement which is correctly called by that name (see the preceding footnote) was in truth not the cause, but was rather partly an instrument or medium, and partly an incidental consequence, of the special local advance in civilization which Italy made in the course of the fourteenth and fifteenth centuries. The true cause of the advance was not an Italian mimesis of the culture of the 'apparented' Hellenic Society (whether in its local Latin version or in its Greek original), but a series of creative Italian responses to contemporary challenges. For the phenomenon of 'renaissances' in general, and for the Italian example in particular, see further Part X below.

[3] For the phases, and some of the manifestations, of this Italian outburst of creativity see III. C (ii) (*b*), vol. iii, p. 367, above.

[4] For this term, as one of two alternative labels for describing the third chapter of our Western history (*currebat circa* A.D. 1475–1875), see III. C (ii) (*b*), vol. iii, p. 375, footnote 2, above.

posed of features drawn from the life of each and all of these cities.[1] An amateur may content himself with citing the single case of Venice as a particularly poignant illustration of a malady that afflicted every one of these historic Italian communities in this Modern Age.

In a profound change of circumstances which was cruelly adverse to the welfare of the whole Italian city-state cosmos, Venice was superficially more successful than most of her neighbours in holding her own. She did not lose her independence to a Transalpine conqueror (as Milan lost hers after having come within an ace of making herself mistress of all Northern Italy); and she did not lose it to an Italian empire-builder (as Siena lost hers to Florence, and Bologna hers to the Papacy, and Padua hers to Venice herself). Having always previously avoided political commitments on the Italian mainland and concentrated her political energies on acquiring an empire overseas, Venice deliberately reversed her policy in the course of the fourteenth century, and replied to the continental imperialism of the Visconti by embarking on an offensive-defensive movement in the same field which produced more lasting political results than those Milanese conquests which had drawn Venice into the continental arena. When the Visconti had disappeared from the Italian scene, and when Milan herself had become the prize of contending Transalpine Powers—to be bandied about from French hands to Spanish, and from Spanish to Austrian—Venice remained in possession of the largest of the new consolidated dominions which had now replaced the medieval mosaic of North and Central Italian city-states.[2] This latter-day Venetian empire on Italian soil was both more extensive and more dangerously exposed to attack by Transalpine aggressors than the latter-day Florentine empire which became the Grand Duchy of Tuscany;[3] yet, in contrast to Florence, Venice managed both to acquire and to retain her empire without being driven to renounce the luxury of continuing to live under her ancestral republican constitution. This preservation of her medieval domestic liberties was a unique distinction which Venice shared with her maritime rival Genoa; and Genoa—absolved from the necessity of defensive empire-building by her good fortune in enjoying the protection of the

[1] For the general state of Italy in this age see Collison-Morley, L.: *Italy after the Renaissance* (London 1930, Routledge); Belloni, A.: *Il Seicento*, second edition (Milan 1929, Vallardi); Natali, G.: *Il Settecento* (Milan 1930, Vallardi, 2 vols.); eundem: *Cultura e Poesia in Italia nell' Età Napoleonica* (Turin 1932, Società Tipografica), Lee, V.: *Studies of the Eighteenth Century in Italy*, second edition (London 1907, Fisher Unwin).

[2] For this process of territorial consolidation in Italy, and for its ineffectiveness as a means of enabling the Italians to hold their own politically against the rising Transalpine Great Powers, see III. C (ii) (*b*), vol. iii, pp. 355–7, above.

[3] See III. C (ii) (*b*), vol. iii, p. 355, footnote 1, above.

natural rampart of the Maritime Alps—was never called upon to face the fateful question whether an empire can be governed by a republic.[1]

This relative successfulness of Venice in an age of general Italian discomfiture was not a windfall of happy accidents, but was the reward of a clear-headed and unslumbering statesmanship; and the quality of this Venetian statesmanship can be tested by comparing it with Athenian behaviour in corresponding situations. If Venice succeeded in gaining and holding an empire without having to submit herself to a despotism at home, this was because she avoided the strain which Imperialism generally imposes upon communities that indulge in it; and she achieved this negative yet by no means negligible success by making her yoke so easy, and her burden so light,[2] that her Paduan and Brescian subjects were free from any temptation to exchange their present status for that of their Bolognese or Milanese or Pisan contemporaries. In corresponding circumstances Athens made her tyranny so odious to her subject-allies that they soon yearned for a Spartan, or even for an Achaemenian, yoke as a more tolerable alternative servitude. And the inferiority of Athenian to Venetian statesmanship comes out as clearly in its handling of the problem of how a small state at the geographical centre of an international system should keep its footing after it has been dwarfed by the rise of new titans on an expanding periphery. We have seen[3] how Athens was invariably worsted by this problem: how sometimes she recklessly threw down the gauntlet to Powers for whom she was no match, and thereby brought upon herself the disasters of 338 and 262 and 86 B.C., while at other times—as, for instance, in the critical year 228 B.C.—she showed an equal lack of judgement in the unseasonable pursuit of an unaspiring policy of isolation. This persistent ineptitude, which is the main thread of continuity in Athenian foreign policy from the days of Demosthenes to the days of Aristion, affords a remarkable contrast to the masterliness of a Venetian diplomacy which managed to stave off for nearly three hundred years that partition of the Republic's Italian dominions among the Transalpine Powers which was the grand design of the League of Cambrai.

The secret of Venice's success, in certain situations in which Athens failed, was an ability to rise above the vice of self-worship in which those Athenian failures seem to find their explanation. But the success of modern Venice has been only relative and negative; on the whole and in the end, Venice failed to make any fresh creative contribution to the life of a society in which she managed

[1] See III. C (ii) (*b*), vol. iii, p. 356, footnote 1, above.
[2] Matt. xi. 30.
[3] On pp. 264–9, above.

to survive; and this Venetian failure can be explained by the fact that Venice, too, did succumb, in her own way, to the nemesis of creativity.

In the field of domestic politics the infatuation with a dead self which had nerved Venice to maintain her own medieval republican constitution at the same time inhibited her from anticipating or emulating the modern constitutional achievements of Switzerland or the Northern Netherlands by transforming her latter-day Italian empire into a federal state on a republican basis. While Venice was never so wrong-headed as to oppress her subject cities, she was also never so broad-minded as to take them into partnership; and so, in A.D. 1797, the political régime in the Venetian dominions in Italy was still just what it had been in A.D. 1339: that is to say, a mild hegemony under which a number of subject communities had to take their orders from a single privileged sovereign city-state.

Again, in the field of foreign policy, the extraordinary skill with which modern Venetian statesmanship succeeded in maintaining the integrity of the latter-day Venetian dominions in Italy, without involving Venice in efforts beyond her strength, did not find its counterpart in the contemporary policy of Venice in the Levant. In her dealings with the Great Powers of the modern Western World Venice took care not to exhaust herself as Florence exhausted herself in the age of Charles VIII or Holland in the age of Louis XIV. On the other hand Venice devoted herself to the forlorn hope of defending her ancient empire in the Levant against the rising power of the 'Osmanlis with an obstinacy which equalled the Dutch courage of a William of Orange and with a recklessness in facing overwhelming odds which reminds the historian of the spirit in which Athens confronted a Macedonian Philip and Antigonus and a Roman Sulla. In the War of Candia (*gerebatur* A.D. 1645–69) the Venetian Commonwealth—undeterred by the uniformly disastrous outcome of the series of losing battles which it had been fighting against the 'Osmanlis since the time of the War of Negrepont (*gerebatur* A.D.1463–74)—threw the last ounce of its military strength into the prolongation of a struggle which, however long it might last, could have no other ending than the loss of Crete. Through this unseasonable intransigence Venice permanently weakened her stamina without any result beyond the unprofitable satisfaction of knowing that she had compelled the Ottoman Power to pay the same exorbitant price for a Pyrrhic victory.[1]

[1] For the part played by the War of Candia in the disintegration of an Ottoman Slave-Household which had been the secret of the 'Osmanlis' rise to greatness, see III. A, vol. iii, p. 49, footnote 4, above.

The modern Venetian idolization of the medieval Venetian empire in the Levant, which inspired the Venetians to this vain act of self-immolation, drove them on to renew the unequal struggle at the first opportunity. When the tide turned against the 'Osmanlis in a war with the Danubian Hapsburg Power which began with the second Ottoman siege of Vienna in A.D. 1682 and ended in 1699 in the peace of Carlowitz, the Venetians hastened to intervene on the anti-Ottoman side and set out to compensate themselves for the loss of Crete by conquering the Morea. The vehemence with which they prosecuted their revenge was momentarily rewarded by the acquisition of Ottoman territories on the mainland which were greater in area than the aggregate of all the islands which Venice had lost to the Pādishāh between 1463 and 1669. Yet the only enduring effect of this War of the Morea upon Venetian life was to rule out the last faint hope of recovery from the exhausting effects of the War of Candia. The conquest of the Morea itself was ephemeral; for all that Venice had won from the 'Osmanlis on the mainland in 1684–99 she lost to them again in 1715, with the island of Tenos—her last foothold in the Archipelago—into the bargain. In this ill-judged final bid for dominion in the Levant Venice was simply creating a diversion for the benefit of the Hapsburgs and the Romanovs, who duly profited by making permanent acquisitions at the Ottoman Empire's expense in the Danubian Basin and on the Black Sea Steppes.

To serve as the cat's-paw for plucking other people's chestnuts out of the fire was the last role which Venetian statesmanship would have chosen to play; and it was a role which Venice never did fall into playing on the political chessboards of medieval Italy and modern Western Europe. Such political ineptitude ran altogether counter to the Venetian tradition and the Venetian êthos; yet the Venetians succumbed to this folly, and persisted in it to their own undoing, in a sphere where the policy was ruinous from every material standpoint. The cost, in 'blood and treasure', of postponing the loss of Candia for twenty-five years, or obtaining possession of the Morea for twenty-eight, could not be recouped by any commercial profits that were to be drawn from these Levantine dominions; for the territorial possessions which had been effective *points d'appui* for Venetian trade in the Levant in the Pre-Ottoman Age had been rendered, long since, commercially valueless through the mere fact of their being reduced to the position of tiny enclaves in the vast domain of an Ottoman Empire which had engulfed the whole of the hinterland; and this hinterland itself had been impoverished by the diversion of the main stream of international trade from the Mediterranean to the Atlantic. Thus the Levantine stake for which Venice played her ruinous game against Turkey in the Modern Age was nothing more substantial than a passion to 'save' her 'face' by retaining the cumbersome territorial tokens of a past political greatness. The fact that this passion should have mastered the habitually cool and calculating Venetian mind is a striking testimony to the deadliness of the malady of self-idolization.

The spirit in which Venice surrendered herself to this malady is enshrined for Posterity in the material relics of her Levantine empire. The massive fortifications of her original Levantine *places d'armes*—a Negrepont and a Modon and a Coron and a Candia—speak, more eloquently than any words, of the limpet-like tenacity with which, through two hundred years of strenuous defensive warfare, the Venetian Commonwealth clung to every disputed foothold, and incidentally turned these Levantine reefs and crags and islands and peninsulas into a veritable museum of military architecture in which the twentieth-century traveller may watch the transition from medieval tower-and-curtain-wall to modern bastion-and-glacis. The vanity of the ephemeral revenge which Venice took upon the Ottoman victor in her final feat of conquering the Morea is likewise mutely proclaimed in the present state of Monemvasía—'the Little Gibraltar'[1]—where the traveller who cares to scale the rock can still enter the citadel in the footsteps of the Janissaries who made their entry on the 10th September, 1715,[2] and can pick his way over the summit among the carcasses of the dismantled Venetian cannon, whose bronze bodies lie where they fell when their splintered wooden carriages rotted away.

The nemesis of medieval Venetian creativity took a stern material shape in the frowning military works which modern Venice has left as her cenotaph in the Levant; but the same writing on the wall is no less plainly manifest in the melancholy works of art which were being created at home by those latter-day Venetian painters and musicians who were contemporaries of the last of the great Venetian captains, Francesco Morosini, the conqueror of the Morea. At first sight it may seem incredible that the seventeenth- and eighteenth-century Venetians who were living that elegantly frivolous carnival life which the music and the pictures commemorate were the same flesh and blood that fought and died in

[1] Like Gibraltar, Monemvasía is a rock connected with the continent by a low-lying spit of land. The name, in Greek, means 'One Way In'; in English it survives as the label of the 'Malmsey' wine which was exported from the medieval French principality of the Morea to the countries of the West. The missing link between the English Malmsey and the Greek Monemvasía is the French Malvoisie.

[2] For the capitulation of the Venetian garrison of Monemvasía to the Ottoman forces in September 1715 see Brue, B.: *Journal de la Campagne que le Grand Vezir Ali Pacha a faite en 1715 pour la Conquête de la Morée* (Paris 1870, Thorin), pp. 51–7.

the breach at Candia; but second thoughts tell us that the very sharpness of the contrast in êthos proves the two moods complementary. The intolerable strain which modern Venice was incurring in the Levant, in her infatuation with the dead self of her medieval Levantine glory, demanded, and received, in psychological 'compensation', an Epicurean relaxation of Venetian life at home; and this latter-day Venetian cultivation of the pleasures of the passing hour resembled its Hellenic original in being the refined expression of a low vitality. In Canaletto's meticulous portraits of a Venice from whose atmosphere the sunlight has faded away we seem to see the ashes of a holocaust in which the Venetians had burned their energies out since the days when they had savoured the full-blooded colours of a Titian and a Tintoretto; and the same note of 'dust and ashes' struck a nineteenth-century English poet's ear in *A Toccata of Galuppi's*.

Here you come with your old music, and here's all the good it brings.
What, they lived once thus at Venice, where the merchants were the kings,
Where Saint Mark's is, where the Doges used to wed the Sea with rings?

What? Those lesser thirds so plaintive, sixths diminished, sigh on sigh,
Told them something? Those suspensions, those solutions—'Must we die?'
Those commiserating sevenths—'Life might last! we can but try!'

Yes, you, like a ghostly cricket, creaking where a house was burned—
'Dust and ashes, dead and done with, Venice spent what Venice earned!
'The soul, doubtless, is immortal—where a soul can be discerned.'

'Dust and ashes!' So you creak it, and I want the heart to scold.
Dear dead women, with such hair, too—what's become of all the gold
Used to hang and brush their bosoms? I feel chilly and grown old.

The writer of this Study is familiar with a picture of Canaletto's, now hanging in an English house, in which the only patch of colour is the Union Jack which floats from the poop of an English ship riding at anchor among baroque palaces and churches. This blare of English red and blue, which catches and holds the gazer's eye among the muffled Venetian browns and greens and greys, proclaims, in the visual language of Canaletto's brush, that the dominion of the sea has passed into other than Venetian hands.

The truth that Venice is 'dead and done with', and the moral that others, besides 'Venice and its people', may be 'merely born to bloom and drop', have also been impressed upon the present writer's imagination by another visual image which remains as sharply printed on his mind to-day as at the instant when he received it more than twenty-five years ago. Turning the corner of a mountain in a lonely district at the eastern end of Crete, he once suddenly stumbled upon the ruins of a baroque villa which must have been built for the pleasure of a Venetian grandee in the last days of Venetian rule in the island before the 'Osmanlis came to reign there in the Venetians' stead. It was a house which might have been built for a contemporary nobleman in England, and have been lived in—had it stood on English ground—by its builder's descendants down to the tenth generation in the writer's own day; but, having been built, as it happened, by Venetian hands in Crete, this piece of modern Western architecture was as utterly 'dead and done with'—as veritably 'a museum piece'—in A.D. 1912 as the Minoan palaces at Cnossos and Phaestus which the traveller had been looking at a few days before. In the common mortality which had overtaken each of them in turn, at moments more than three thousand years apart, these desolate habitations of vanished thalassocrats bore witness, against their makers, that

in due time, one by one,
Some with lives that came to nothing, some with deeds as well undone,
Death came tacitly and took them where they never see the sun.

As the English traveller recalled the English poet's lines, he reflected that the four and a half centuries for which Venice had been mistress of Crete were a longer span of time than the present age of his own country's rule over the earliest acquired of her overseas dominions; and his ears seemed to catch an echo of Galuppi's music among the Cretan crags.

In you come with your cold music, till I creep in every nerve.

That baroque ruin in Crete, as it stood in A.D. 1912, was a *memento mori* for an England that was then still alive, as well as for a Venice that was then already dead.

This Epimethean chapter of Venetian history, for which Galuppi has written the dirge and Canaletto painted the hatchment, has not turned out, in the event, to be the last phase of Venice's participation in the life of the Western World. For Venice, together with the rest of Italy, has been reprieved from an eighteenth-century life-in-death by undergoing a nineteenth-century *Risorgimento*.[1] At first sight this recent Italian social miracle might seem to testify that, unlike Athens and Sparta, Venice and Florence have eventually triumphed over the nemesis of their previous creativity

[1] The nature of this modern Italian *Risorgimento* has been discussed already in this Study in certain of its aspects (see III. C (ii) (*b*), vol. iii, pp. 311–12, and IV. C (i), in the present volume, pp. 17–19, above, and also V. C (i) (*d*) 6 (γ), Annex I, vol. v, pp. 635–42, below).

by facing it out and living it down; and if this were the truth, it would indicate that the gift of creativity is rather less formidable for its recipient than we have so far taken it to be. On closer inspection, however, we shall find that the modern Italian *Risorgimento* does not bear these implications; for when we look for the creative forces by which the *Risorgimento* was actually achieved, we shall observe that they almost all arose outside the bounds of those historic city-states which were the seed-beds of Italian creativity in the Middle Ages.

In the sixteenth century of the Christian Era, when Italy was confronted with the challenge of Transalpine pressure, these historic Italian communities did not make any attempt at self-redemption that is worthy to be compared with the magnificent failure of the rally in Greece in the third century B.C. For all his intellectual acumen, Machiavelli never achieved the practical effectiveness of an Aratus; and there was no Italian equivalent of the self-sacrifice of a Lydiadas or the martyrdom of an Agis and a Cleomenes. If modern Italy eventually rose again, while third-century Greece fell once for all, this was because, in both these cases, the stage was so set that the outcome did not depend upon the actors' own merits, but was decided by the play of irresistible external forces. The third-century rally in Greece[1] was rendered abortive by the swift destruction of the Balance of Power between the titans on the periphery through a series of 'knock-out blows' that were dealt by Rome to all her rivals; for these blows 'knocked out' Greece as well as all the rest of the contemporary Hellenic World. On the other hand the inveterate inertia of sixteenth- and seventeenth- and eighteenth-century Italy was indulged in with eventual impunity thanks to the moderation of the contemporary Transalpine Powers in exercising their forces 'by temperate and undecisive contests'[2] which neither overthrew the general Balance of Power nor utterly devastated the Italian arena in which so many of these Transalpine contests were fought. And so, by merits not their own, these Italian communities were preserved from destruction until, in the fullness of time, they received an unearned reward for the merits of their ancestors.

Towards the close of the modern chapter of our Western history the Transalpine nations were ready to repay the debt which they owed to medieval Italy. At the beginning of the chapter, in the fifteenth century, Italy had quickened the Transalpine 'barbarians'

[1] For this rally see the present chapter, pp. 268–9, above, and V. C (ii) (*b*), vol. vi, pp. 287–9, below.

[2] This felicitous Gibbonian phrase has been quoted already in III. C (ii) (*b*), vol. iii, p. 311, in IV. C (iii) (*b*) 3, in the present volume, p. 148, and in IV. C (iii) (*b*) 5, p. 189, above. See also V. C (i) (*d*) 6 (γ), Annex I, vol. v, p. 625, below.

into new life by radiating across the Alps her medieval creative achievements. By the beginning of the nineteenth century the *ci-devant* 'barbarians' had laid out their Italian talents to such good effect that they had gained new talents of their own—a modern Transalpine Democracy and a modern Transalpine Industrialism. It thus now lay in the Transalpine peoples' power to make, at last, some return for the benefit which a medieval Italy had freely conferred upon them four hundred years before; and they duly acquitted themselves of this historical obligation by sharing their own new gains with a modern Italy whose turn it had been to play the passive part, and who in consequence had made no modern Italian contribution to this latest enrichment of a common Western culture. The turn of the eighteenth and nineteenth centuries saw the beginning of a new cultural radiation across the Alps in a reverse direction; and this inflow of Transalpine influences into Italy was the first cause of the Italian *Risorgimento.*

The first strong political stimulus was the temporary incorporation of Italy into the Napoleonic Empire,[1] which brought her into association with modern France. The first strong economic stimulus was the reopening of the trade-route through the Mediterranean between Western Europe and India—an eighteenth-century English fancy which was transformed into a reality by the after-effects of Napoleon's invasion of Egypt[2]—since this troubling of Mediterranean waters by the wash of French and English hulls broke in vivifying waves upon Italian shores. These Transalpine stimuli did not, of course, produce their full effect in Italy until they had communicated themselves to Italian agents; but the Italian creative forces by which the *Risorgimento* was brought to harvest did not arise on any Italian ground that had already borne the harvest of a medieval Italian culture.

In the economic field, for example, the first Italian port to win a share for itself in modern Western maritime trade was neither Venice nor Genoa nor Pisa, but Leghorn; and Leghorn was the modern creation of a Tuscan Grand Duke who was concerned to fill the vacuum that had been left by the overthrow of medieval Pisa at the hands of medieval Florence, and who achieved his purpose by planting a settlement of Spanish and Portuguese crypto-Jewish refugees on this promising site in the Tuscan maremma.[3] It was these Hispanic immigrants, and not any

[1] On this point see IV. C (i), p. 19, above, and V. C (i) (*d*) 6 (γ), Annex I, vol. v, pp. 635–42, below.

[2] See V. C (i) (*d*) 6 (γ), Annex I, vol. v, p. 623, below.

[3] For the settlement of this Marrano community at Leghorn in A.D. 1593 see II. D (vi), vol. ii, p. 244, footnote 2, above.

descendants of the medieval Pisans or Genoese, who made the commercial fortunes of Leghorn in the seventeenth and eighteenth centuries.[1]

In the political field the unification of Italy was the achievement of an originally Transalpine principality which had no foothold on the Italian side of the Alps before the eleventh century beyond the French-speaking Val d'Aosta, and which did not lose the last of its Transalpine possessions until 1860. The effective assertion, in Piedmont, of the authority of the House of Savoy was not made good till about four hundred years after the original acquisition of a legal title to the lordship over this sub-Alpine Italian province; and the firm establishment of the Savoyard power on the Italian side of the Alps was thus contemporaneous with the creation of a Venetian empire on the Italian mainland and with the formation of the Grand Duchy of Tuscany; yet this Cisalpine expansion of Savoy was not really part of the general process of political consolidation by which the diminutive domains of some seventy or eighty Italian city-states were welded into ten larger agglomerations of territory at the transition from the Medieval to the Modern Age;[2] for Piedmont was a fringe of Northern Italy into which the city-state dispensation had never effectively spread,[3] and the Savoyard rulers who established themselves in this never wholly conquered fastness of North Italian feudalism were not the despotic heirs of republican liberties, like the Visconti or the Medici. They were legitimate princes of the Holy Roman Empire—genuine peers of the Dukes of Lorraine and the Princes of Orange—who drew their title from a good and ancient feudal source.[4] In fact, this Savoyard principality continued to be a Transalpine state in tradition and in spirit, even after its geographical centre of gravity had shifted to

1 Compare the role, in the modern commercial life of the Levant, of those other Hispanic Jewish refugees who were planted in the sixteenth century at Constantinople and Smyrna and, above all, Salonica by the Ottoman Government. Like their compatriots and contemporaries who settled at Leghorn, these modern Hispanic Jewish settlers in the Levant stepped into the shoes of medieval Italian men of business. (See II. D (vi), vol. ii, p. 246, above.)

2 For this process see III. C (ii) (*b*), vol. iii, pp. 355–6, above.

3 Piedmont was defended from the rising tide of North Italian civic institutions by the Marquessate of Montferrat—another fastness of feudalism, in the mountainous country between the River Po and the River Tanaro, which held out obstinately against the city-state of Asti on the one side and the city-state of Vercelli on the other. In spite of this obstacle the civic movement did succeed in spreading into Piedmont and making itself felt in such Piedmontese towns as Turin and Ivrea; yet on Piedmontese soil it was always exotic and half-hearted.

4 Historically the County of Savoy, which was the nucleus of the dominions of the dynasty to which it gave its name, was a district of Boso's Regnum Provinciae; and this was one of the four fragments (Regnum Lotharii, Regnum Jurense, Regnum Provinciae, Regnum Italicum) into which Lothaire's portion of the Carolingian heritage had split up in the interval between the tripartite division of the Carolingian dominions in A.D. 843 (see I. B (iv), vol. i, pp. 37–40, above) and the reunion of the whole of Lothaire's portion with Ludwig's in the tenth century by the Emperor Otto I (see II. D (v), vol. ii, p. 197, above).

the Italian side of the mountains. No historic Italian city-state was included in the Savoyard dominions till the acquisition of Vercelli in 1427;[1] and it was not till 1748 that the Ticino became the eastern frontier of the Kingdom of Sardinia—as the Savoyard dominions had now come to be styled—along the whole course of the river between its exit from the Lago Maggiore and its confluence with the Po.[2] The House of Savoy did not, in fact, encroach flagrantly upon the patrimony of the medieval Italian city-state cosmos until it swallowed the Genoese Republic in the peace-settlement of 1814–15; and its êthos was at that time still so alien from the city-state tradition that the Genoese chafed under the rule of His Sardinian Majesty until 1848, when the Dynasty won adherents in all parts of the Italian Peninsula by laying aside its parochial dynastic ambitions and putting itself at the head of a national movement for the unification of all Italy.

In 1848 the Austrian régime in Lombardy and Venetia was threatened simultaneously by a Piedmontese invasion and by risings in Venice and Milan and the other Italian cities which were at that time subject to the rule of the Danubian Hapsburg Monarchy; and it is interesting to reflect upon the difference in the historical significance of these two anti-Austrian movements which were both taking place at one and the same moment on Italian soil, and which both figure officially as blows struck in a common cause for the liberation of Italy.

The risings in Venice and Milan were strokes struck for liberty, no doubt; but the vision of liberty which inspired them was the recollection of a medieval past. As the memories of childhood rise up suddenly, unbidden, in old age, and come sharply into focus through a momentary rift in the mental fog of dotage, so, in A.D. 1848, the Lombard insurgents against the Hapsburgs were resuming their twelfth-century and thirteenth-century struggles

[1] Vercelli, which had previously been under the hegemony of Milan, had become a virtual protectorate of the House of Savoy in 1407, twenty years before the formal act of cession. The acquisition of Asti did not follow till more than a hundred years later, in 1531.

[2] Earlier in the eighteenth century the House of Savoy had extended its rule over three more minor Lombard city-states: over Alessandria in the peace settlement of 1712–13 (in execution of a treaty of the 8th November, 1703, with the Emperor), and over Tortona and Novara in the peace settlement of 1735–9. But the chief continental Italian acquisition that was made by the House of Savoy in the eighteenth century was Montferrat (which was acquired, with Alessandria, in 1713); and Montferrat, as we have seen, was feudal soil like Piedmont itself. No historic Lombard city-state was comprised either in the Lomellino and Val di Sesia (which the House of Savoy acquired simultaneously with Montferrat and Alessandria) or in the Vigevinasco, the Transticinane and Traspadane portions of the Pavese, and the sub-Alpine county of Anghiera (which the House of Savoy acquired in 1748, in execution of a treaty of the 13th September, 1743, with the Empress). The details of the House of Savoy's acquisitions in Lombardy in the eighteenth century can be found in the state papers published in vols. ii and iii of *Traités Publics de la Royale Maison de Savoie avec les Puissances Étrangères depuis la Paix de Château-Cambresis jusqu'à Nos Jours* (Turin 1836–44, Imprimerie Royale, 6 vols.).

against the Hohenstaufen, while the Venetians who expelled the Austrian garrison from their city in the same year were repeating their ancestors' feat of expelling a Frankish garrison in A.D. 810. In the heroic failure of 1848 Milan atoned for the tameness with which she had worn a 'barbarian' yoke for more than three centuries, and Venice for the poltroonery with which she had allowed her independence, as well as her empire, to be snuffed out by Napoleon in 1797. The passionate obstinacy with which the Venetians held out to the last against their Austrian besiegers in 1848–9 was worthy of their forebears' conduct in the War of Candia or the War of Chioggia.

Compared with this final feat of Venetian arms, the Piedmontese military performance in 1848–9 was not very creditable; yet the Italian *Risorgimento* was eventually brought to harvest by the Power whose easy march on Milan was followed by an inglorious retreat, and whose irresponsible breach of a prudent armistice was deservedly punished by a shameful defeat at Novara. This Piedmontese disgrace proved more fruitful for Italy than those Milanese and Venetian glories; for the Piedmontese Army lived to take its revenge for Novara, ten years later, at Magenta; and the English-like parliamentary constitution which King Carlo Alberto had granted to his subjects in 1848 survived his abdication to become the basis of the constitution of a United Kingdom of Italy. On the other hand, the glorious feats of Milan and Venice in 1848 were not repeated; and when Milan was liberated from Hapsburg rule once for all in 1859, and Venice in 1866, both of these historic cities played, this time, a passive part and waited for the work of liberation to be performed on their behalf by the Piedmontese Army with the potent assistance of a Transalpine ally.[1]

The explanation is that the Venetian and Milanese exploits in 1848 were virtually foredoomed to failure, however magnificent they might be in their intrinsic worth, because the spiritual driving-force behind them was still that idolization of their own dead selves, as historic medieval city-states, which had been defeating the finest efforts of Italian heroism and Italian statesmanship since the time of Machiavelli. The nineteenth-century Venetians who responded to Manin's call in 1848 were fighting for Venice alone, and not for Piedmont or Milan or even for Padua; they were striving to restore an obsolete Venetian Republic and not to create a new Italian national state; and for this reason their enterprise was a forlorn hope, whereas Piedmont could survive a more shame-

[1] The Transalpine ally of Piedmont was, of course, France in 1859 and Prussia in 1866; and in each case it was this Transalpine adversary of Austria that played the principal part in forcing her to relinquish an Italian province which would probably never have been wrested from her by the unaided force of Piedmontese arms.

ful disaster because the nineteenth-century Piedmontese were not fast bound in the misery and iron of an unforgettable historic past. The Piedmontese were psychologically free to throw themselves into the novel enterprise of creating an Italian national state on the Transalpine pattern; and, in giving them this opportunity, Fortune was placing in their hands a winning card; for this modern Transalpine ideal of Nationalism was the momentarily invincible offspring of the dominant social forces of the age;[1] and the Piedmontese were specially qualified, by the predominance of Transalpine elements in their own social heritage, for serving as the agents who were to translate this Transalpine ideal into an Italian fact.[2]

The difference in êthos between nineteenth-century Piedmont and nineteenth-century Venice is summed up in the contrast between the personalities of Manin and Cavour. Manin was an unmistakable Venetian who would have felt himself quite at home in the Italian city-state cosmos of the fourteenth century if it had been his fate to defend Venice against Genoese instead of Austrian besiegers. Cavour, with his French mother-tongue and his Victorian spirit, would have been as utterly out of his element as his Transalpine contemporaries Bright or Thiers if Fate had happened to make him a citizen of fourteenth-century Alessandria or Tortona, while he could have turned his gifts for international diplomacy and parliamentary politics, and his interest in scientific agriculture and railway-building, to even better use than he did make of them if Fate had chosen to translate him into the seat of some landowner or member of parliament in nineteenth-century England.

On this showing, the role, in the Italian *Risorgimento*, of the outbreak in the year 1848 was essentially negative, and its immediate failure was a precious and, indeed, indispensable factor in the success which crowned the later struggles in the years 1859–70. In 1848 the old idols of a medieval Milan and a medieval Venice were so cruelly battered and defaced that at last they lost their fatal hold upon the idolators' souls; and it was this belated effacement of a medieval Italian past in the seats of its former greatness that cleared the ground for a successful Italian *Risorgimento* under the leadership of the one modern Italian state that

[1] See IV. C (iii) (*b*) 4 and 5, above.

[2] Now that the Piedmontese labours for the creation of an Italian national state on the Transalpine model have been crowned with success, the people of those Italian provinces which were once the patrimony of a medieval Italian city-state cosmos have quickly learnt to play their full part in the new national life and to make their own characteristic contributions to it. We have seen the Piedmontese parliamentarian Giolitti (a caricature of Cavour) brushed aside to make way for the Romagnol dictator Mussolini (in whose countenance we seem to catch a glimpse of a Baldassare Cossa or a Muzio Attendolo 'Sforza'). The nineteenth-century difference in êthos between the Romagnols and the Piedmontese was manifestly a matter of mutable states of mind, and not the reflection of any immutable difference of Race. For the decisive refutation, in Italian history, of the racial theory of social breakdowns see IV. C (i), pp. 16–20, above.

was free from the spiritual incubus of overpoweringly poignant medieval memories.

South Carolina.

If we extend our survey from the Old World to the New, without stepping outside the bounds of our Western Society in the nineteenth century, we shall find a parallel illustration of the nemesis of creativity in the history of the United States; and for our purpose this is an even more noteworthy case, for in twentieth-century North America the dead selves that are still being idolized—with the same blind passion and the same unhappy consequences as in modern Italy down to 1848—do not date from the Middle Ages, but are only two or three centuries old.

If we make a comparative study of the *post-bellum* histories of the several states in 'the Old South' which were members of the Confederacy in the Civil War of 1861–5 and were involved in the Confederacy's defeat, we shall notice a marked difference between them in the extent to which they have since recovered respectively from that common disaster; and we shall also notice that this difference is the exact inverse of an equally well marked difference which had distinguished the same states from one another in the *ante-bellum* period.

A foreign observer who visited 'the Old South' in the seventy-third year after General Lee's capitulation at Appomattox Court House would assuredly pick out Virginia and South Carolina as the two Southern States in which there was least sign, or even promise, of recovery; and he would be astonished to find the effects of even so great a social catastrophe persisting so starkly over so long a period. In these states the memory of the catastrophe of 1861–5 is as green in our generation as if the blow had fallen only yesterday; and 'the War' still means the Civil War on many Virginian and South Carolinian lips, though the United States has twice been at war again in the interval, and one of these two later American wars has been the World War of 1914–18. Again, if there is talk of local politics or family affairs, the stranger will often discover, to his surprise, that the persons and events which are the topics of the conversation are a century or a century and a half old. In fact, twentieth-century Virginia or South Carolina makes the painful and uncanny impression of a country living under a spell, in which Time has been made to stand still. And this impression will be heightened by the contrast of which our traveller will become instantly and acutely aware if he breaks his journey, *en route* from Richmond to Charleston, in the intervening state of North Carolina. In North Carolina he will find new cotton-mills, equipped with the most up-to-date patterns of machinery; mushroom universities; substantial efforts to improve elementary education and local roads; and a 'hustling', 'boosting' spirit which he would rather have expected to find in Oklahoma. He will also find something in North Carolina which Oklahoma cannot match —nor latter-day Virginia or South Carolina either—and that is a crop of distinguished personalities, of the stamp of Walter Page and Woodrow Wilson.

What explains this springlike burgeoning of North Carolina's life while the life of her neighbours still droops in 'the sear, the yellow leaf'?[1] If we turn for enlightenment to the past, we shall find our perplexity momentarily increased when we observe that the present situation is the antithesis of the conditions in the *Ante-Bellum* Age, when North Carolina was socially barren while Virginia and South Carolina were then bursting with social vitality.

During the Time-span of about a hundred years that separates Robert Lee's generation from George Washington's, Virginia and South Carolina were the Southern counterparts of a Northern Massachusetts and Pennsylvania. They were the leading states in their half of the Union in wealth and in intellect and in character; and their fertility in character—the crop of eminent personalities which they continually bred—gave them almost a dominant voice in Federal politics. During these same hundred years North Carolina was seldom heard of; and the cause of her obscurity was not itself obscure. North Carolina was a country with a poor soil and with no ports; and she was therefore settled from the landward side by squatters from Virginia or South Carolina who had failed—perhaps through dullness or poverty or lateness of arrival on the scene—to 'make good' in the first state of their choice. These settlers in North Carolina were not 'bad material' in themselves; the strongest strain among them was a Presbyterian 'Scotch-Irish' element from Ulster whose staying-power has been demonstrated and rewarded in the sequel.[2] But, in the first chapter of their history in their new North-Carolinian home, this population of small farmers—living a hard life in a blind alley—could not vie with the Virginian squires or with the South Carolinian planters.

It will be seen that the *ante-bellum* contrast between North Carolina and her two neighbours was the natural outcome of historical and geographical circumstance. It is the *post-bellum* inversion of this natural situation that has to be explained; and, here again, the explanation is not to be found in any inborn merits

[1] Shakespeare: *Macbeth*, v. iii. 23.

[2] For the more sensational fate of the North Carolinian lowlanders' 'Scotch-Irish' kinsmen who drifted into the highlands of Appalachia and stayed marooned there, see II. D (vii), vol. ii, pp. 309–13, above.

of the community which has achieved an eventual eminence, but rather in its freedom from the incubus that has weighed its fallen neighbours down. The former exaltation of Virginia and South Carolina is the veritable cause of their abasement now. They have failed to rise again from their prostration in the Civil War because they have never succeeded in forgetting the height from which that fearful catastrophe once hurled them, whereas North Carolina, who lost so much less because she had so little to lose, has found it relatively easy to recover from a slighter shock. 'For whosoever exalteth himself shall be abased; and he that humbleth himself shall be exalted.'[1]

Eire.

This hypnotization of a living self by a dead self, which has been the effect of *ante-bellum* upon *post-bellum* Virginia and South Carolina, is also to be seen at work—and this over a far longer span of Time—in the history of Ireland ever since that brilliant flash-in-the-pan which we have glanced at, in an earlier part of this Study, under the name of the Abortive Far Western Christian Civilization.[2]

'One of the most remarkable traits of Gaelic literature is that it deals, so to speak, with a continuous historic present. The same life, the same mode of thought, appear in the eighteenth century as in the eighth. . . . In effect the Gael found a way of life long ago, and a religious faith, that satisfied him then and forever, and seemed to offer all that a man can wring from the World. His literature, therefore, contrasts in a remarkable way with that of such a country as England, where the writings of every generation mirror some philosophic change. Gaelic literature intellectually is a literature of rest, not of change; of intensive cultivation, not of experiment.'[3]

The point that is made in this passage from the pen of an Irish student of Irish literature has also been made independently, with a political application, by a contemporary Welsh statesman who has been in a position to speak from personal experience. During the negotiation of the Anglo-Irish Agreement of 1921 Mr. David Lloyd George is reported to have made the remark that 'in Ireland there is no past; it is all present'.[4] And an English friend of the writer of this Study, who was constantly travelling to and fro between England and Ireland on a private mission of reconciliation during the foregoing months when the warfare between the British

[1] Luke xiv. 11 = xviii. 14 = Matt. xxiii. 12, quoted in IV. C (iii) (*c*) 1, p. 248, above.

[2] See II. D (vii), vol. ii, pp. 322–40, above.

[3] De Blacam, A.: *Gaelic Literature Surveyed*, 2nd edition (Dublin 1933, Talbot Press), pp. xiii–xiv.

[4] See Toynbee, A. J.: *The Conduct of British Empire Foreign Relations since the Peace Settlement* (London 1928, Milford), p. 38.

Government and Sinn Fein was at its height, was once harrowed by receiving from Irish informants the report of a particularly ghastly atrocity which had been committed upon so-and-so, at such-and-such a place, by English hands—only to find that the act had not been done the week before by 'the Black-and-Tans', but in the seventeenth century by the soldiers of Cromwell's army. When the Englishman's Irish interlocutors perceived and corrected his misapprehension, they were benevolently pleased to have relieved his distress, but intellectually at a loss to understand either his peculiar dismay when he supposed that the atrocity had been committed since his last visit to the country, or his intense satisfaction at learning that this particular English disgrace had been staining the honour of England for nearly three centuries and not just for three weeks or three days. In Irish minds, what Cromwell's soldiers had done was an integral part of the current Irish case against England, of precisely the same cogency as the things which were being done at that moment by 'the Black-and-Tans'. When 'the vine of the earth' was once 'cast into the great winepress of the wrath of God',[1] the English notion that the vintage might perhaps lose its potency with the passage of Time was a hard saying for an Irish logician, who would naturally take it for granted that wine improved by keeping. On the other hand, for the English sympathizer with Ireland's sufferings at England's hands it was quite incomprehensible that an atrocity, however sensational, which had been committed not much less than three hundred years ago, should be retailed to-day with the same lively horror and the same indignant zest as if the victim's shrieks were still echoing in the outraged air and his blood still oozing over the desecrated ground of the Ireland of 1921.

This Irish obsession with the Past, which has been the despair of English statesmanship, presents a piquant antithesis to the psychological plasticity which is the characteristic êthos of those 'new countries' in which the same British statesmanship has achieved its signal triumphs.[2] The problem of creating one united community out of a conquered autochthonous population and a 'garrison' of new settlers who have been planted on the conquered soil by the high hand of the conquering Power has confronted British statesmanship in Canada and in South Africa as well as in Ireland; and in these overseas dominions of the British Crown the problem has been handled with a far greater measure of success.

[1] Rev. xiv. 19.

[2] For the way in which this psychological plasticity has worked in favour of the construction of the British Commonwealth of Nations see Toynbee, op. cit., pp. 37–8. The point has also been noticed already in this Study, in III. C (ii) (*b*), vol. iii, p. 303, footnote 1, and in III. C (ii) (*b*), Annex IV, vol. iii, p. 484, above.

While in Ireland the Catholic descendants of the Gael and the Protestant descendants of King James I's and Cromwell's military colonists have behaved towards one another like oil and vinegar in a salad or like Orthodox Christian natives and Turkish Muslim colonists in Rumelia, the original French *habitants* in Canada, and even the original Dutch *boers* in South Africa, have brought themselves to co-operate with the interloping English colonists—whose presence in the country is a living memorial of an English conquest—in the common task of working the political machinery of a fully self-governing Union of South Africa and Dominion of Canada.[1] On the other hand, in the European homeland of our Western Civilization Switzerland is the unique example of a successful multi-national state of the latter-day Canadian and South African type. The Belgian imitation of Switzerland has never achieved the harmony and solidity of its Swiss ensample, while in the Danubian Hapsburg Monarchy the efforts of Austrian statesmanship to make 'a going concern' out of a state composed of diverse national elements have ended in a still greater failure than the corresponding efforts of British statesmanship in Ireland.[2]

If we turn from the domestic to the foreign aspects of the Hapsburg Monarchy's political problem, we shall be no less forcibly struck by the observation that the desperate remedy of cutting

[1] The difference of the psychological atmosphere in Canada and in Ireland has had a doubly potent effect, because in either case the local atmosphere had exercised its influence upon the conquerors as well as the conquered. If the British Government has found the French *habitants* in Canada much easier to deal with as British subjects than the native inhabitants of Ireland, it is also true that the French Canadians have had a much less unpleasant experience than the Irish have had of the English as a ruling power. 'The overseas atmosphere was the more potent for good inasmuch as it produced its effect, not only upon the overseas communities themselves, but upon those statesmen in Great Britain upon whose outlook and action the evolution of relations between the Dominions and the Mother Country in its earlier stages chiefly depended for good or evil. The importance, for the evolution of Dominion Status in its original overseas environment, of this influence of the overseas spirit upon statesmanship in Whitehall can be gauged by the extraordinary contrast between the large-minded generosity of the Quebec Act of 1774—an act which laid the foundations of a friendship between the conquered French settlers in North America and the victorious Empire which was the hereditary enemy of their mother country in Europe—and the ferocity of the anti-Catholic laws which the same British Government kept on the statute book in Ireland until 1829' (Toynbee, A. J.: *The Conduct of British Empire Foreign Relations since the Peace Settlement* (London 1928, Milford), pp. 37–8).

[2] The difference in degree between these two kindred failures of modern Western statesmanship must not be exaggerated; for, although the whole of Ireland has been kept together provisionally under the British Crown in outward constitutional form, the virtual partition of the island between the Free State and the Northern Irish bridgehead of the United Kingdom is in reality as grave a social disaster, and as great a confession of political bankruptcy, as the undisguised partition of the Danubian Monarchy among its 'successor-states'. Moreover it is noteworthy that, if British statesmanship is to be regarded as having scored a point in the avoidance of an outright secession of an Irish Republic from the British Empire, it owes this modest success in its dealings with Ireland to its magnificent success in dealing with the Dominions of the British Crown overseas. The common ground on which the Anglo-Irish Agreement of 1921 is based lies in the acceptance, on both sides, of an analogy between Southern Ireland and Canada. If the principles of 'Dominion Status' had not been worked out in Canada between 1838 and 1921, the Anglo-Irish settlement of the latter year would probably have been impossible to achieve.

the Gordian Knot with the sword, to which Austrian statesmanship, in its dealings with Serbia and Montenegro, resorted with such fatal results in 1914, had been resorted to with impunity by British statesmanship only fifteen years before, in its dealings with the Transvaal Republic and the Orange Free State.

In an age when the political creed of Nationalism was gaining ascendancy throughout the Western World, an identical problem of unusual difficulty presented itself to British imperialism in South Africa and to Austrian imperialism in South-Eastern Europe. In both regions the awakening of the local populations to national consciousness—and to consequent political aspirations towards national unity and independence—found one local nationality partitioned between a great multi-national empire and two small and fragmentary and backward but at the same time independent national states; and in both cases these states came to regard it as their mission to achieve the unity and independence of the whole of their own nation under their own flag, without being deterred by the consideration that the fulfilment of this national ambition on these lines would involve the disruption of the great multi-national empire which now held half their nationals as its more or less unwilling subjects. In both cases the threatened empire made a series of clumsy, but on the whole well-meaning, efforts to safeguard its own integrity against its puny neighbours' preposterous designs without a breach of the peace or a change in the territorial *status quo*; but in both cases the imperial statesmen rather reluctantly came to the conclusion, after a time, that the existing partition of the recalcitrant nationality was not, after all, a possible basis for a permanent settlement, and that therefore their only practical prospect of obtaining a solution that would be satisfactory to themselves lay in taking advantage of their overwhelming superiority in military strength in order to unite the recalcitrant nationality under the imperial flag by putting a forcible end to their puny but aggressive neighbours' independence.

When the Hapsburg Government acted on this policy in 1914 it brought about the exact opposite of the result at which it was aiming; for the ultimatum which it addressed to Serbia precipitated a general war which did not come to an end until the Hapsburg Monarchy itself had been broken in pieces. On the other hand, when the British Government applied the self-same policy in dealing with the Transvaal Republic in 1899, it did successfully achieve its aim by making war. The threat of an anti-British coalition of Continental European Powers never materialized; there was no intervention; the South African War was not enlarged, like the American Revolutionary War of 1775–83 or the Austro-Serbian War of

1914–18, to the dimensions of a general engagement; and so there was no question of its ending disastrously for Great Britain. The two Dutch Republics in South Africa were duly conquered by British arms and annexed by the British Crown; and the problem with which the British Empire had been faced by the rise of the Afrikander Dutch national movement was eventually solved by the creation, within a British political framework, of a Union of South Africa in which the whole of the Afrikander Dutch nation was enabled to enjoy its national self-government in a partnership with the English settlers in its midst. This result of cutting the Gordian Knot in the loosely woven social fabric of South Africa stands out in extreme contrast to the result in South-Eastern Europe, where the indurated texture of historic memories turned the edge of the Austrian sword with such disastrous consequences for the Power that had ventured to draw it. While Dutch nationalism in South Africa has eventually been given satisfaction, at the cost of a minor local war, through a moderate and constructive process of political consolidation, Jugoslav nationalism in South-Eastern Europe has only been satisfied at the cost of a world war which has brought in its train the violent disruption of the whole previous political régime in that quarter of Europe.

The inferiority of the Old World to the New World in psychological plasticity can also be illustrated from the histories of certain modern international frontiers. From the close of the seventeenth century until the end of the Anglo-American War of 1812–15[1] the North American frontier between Canada and the British colonies that subsequently became the United States was the theatre of quite as incessant and at least as rancorous a warfare as the European frontier between France and the German Powers during the same period; yet the subsequent histories of these two frontiers have been remarkably different. Since the close of the particular Franco-German war which had come to an end a few months before the British and American Governments made peace on the 24th December, 1814, there have been three further fierce and bitter Franco-German conflicts,[2] and in the year 1938 the tension on the Franco-German frontier was perhaps as great as it had ever been. On the other hand, after the conclusion of the Peace of Ghent the North American belligerents decided, Red Indian fashion, to 'bury the hatchet'. By common consent the frontier between Canada and the United States was then deliberately demilitarized, and the

1 The Battle of New Orleans was fought on the 8th January, 1815, though peace had been signed at Ghent on the 24th December, 1814.

2 Reckoning the Waterloo campaign as a separate affair from the foregoing conflict, which had lasted, off and on, from 1792 to 1814, but not counting in the Franco-Austrian War of 1859, which was fought in an Italian and not in a Transalpine arena.

moral, as well as physical, disarmament which was thus achieved between the two new nations that were dividing the ownership of the North American Continent was not disturbed thereafter either by the growing length of the frontier or by the increasing disparity in strength between the Powers on either side of it. To-day, when this unfortified frontier stretches over a length of 3,898 miles from Atlantic to Pacific and divides a nation of 122[1] millions from one of ten millions[2] which is physically at its gigantic neighbour's mercy, the achievement is so familiar a fact in North American life that it is simply taken for granted. At the opposite extremity of the Americas the unfortified frontier between Canada and the United States has its counterpart in the pacifically delimited frontier between Chile and Argentina, a Latin-American achievement which is commemorated in the statue of the Christ of the Andes. It is true that certain parallels to these two American frontiers can be found in Europe. For example, the frontier between France and Belgium, which probably saw more fighting than any other frontier in Western Christendom from the beginning of the Modern Age down to the Battle of Waterloo, is now traversed twice a day by thousands of workmen who have their home on one side of the line and earn their living on the other, and who ride across on their bicycles without being asked to show a passport. This present state of the Franco-Belgian frontier in the neighbourhood of Tourcoing and Roubaix will bear comparison satisfactorily with the present state of the Canadian–United States frontier in the neighbourhood of Buffalo or Detroit. Unhappily, however, the Franco-Belgian frontier is less characteristic than the Franco-German frontier is of the prevailing condition of frontiers in twentieth-century Europe.

The Self-Hypnotization of Narcissus.

We have now examined five illustrations of the nemesis of creativity in the particular form of an idolization of some ephemeral self, and, if we pause to take a synoptic retrospective view of our field in this survey, we shall perhaps see in a rather new light a social phenomenon which has occupied our attention in an earlier part of this Study: that is, the tendency for 'new ground' to surpass 'old ground' in social fertility.[3] This phenomenon regularly reappears in our comparative glances at the Jews and Galilaeans and Gentiles in the time of Christ, at Athens and Achaia in the third century B.C., at the *ci-devant* city-state cosmos and Piedmont

[1] The population of the United States came out at 122,775,046 in the census of 1930.
[2] The population of Canada came out at 10,376,786 in the census of 1931.
[3] See II. D (iii), with Annex, in vol. ii, above.

in the Italian *Risorgimento*, at South Carolina and North Carolina after the American Civil War, and finally at Ireland and the Overseas Dominions of the British Crown during the hundred years ending in the year 1938. In every one of these instances the 'new ground'—be it Galilee or the lands of the Goyyim, Achaia or Piedmont, North Carolina or Canada—duly succeeds in making up for the 'old ground's' obstinate sterility by bearing a timely harvest; but we can now see that this superior fertility of the 'new ground' is not invariably or entirely to be accounted for by the stimulus that is inherent in the ordeal of breaking virgin soil. There is a negative as well as a positive reason why 'new ground' is apt to be fruitful; and this negative reason is its intrinsic freedom from the incubus of ineradicable memories with which 'old ground' is, not indeed certain, but at any rate extremely likely, to be burdened. In fact, we have stumbled upon a psychological application of our 'law of compensations'.[1] The law proves to hold good in the Microcosm as well as in the Macrocosm. It not only applies in so far as a challenge is delivered by the physical or by the human environment; it continues to apply when the field of action is transferred from an outer to an inner world, and it can be seen in operation where the challenged individual or community or society receives the challenge from its own self. In this psychological situation the challenge of 'new ground' is presented by the novice's own lack of experience and *expertise*, and this challenge carries with it a compensation in the shape of an immunity from the sinister spell that 'cramps the style' of 'the old hand'. The nemesis of the hero who has performed some creative achievement in the past is to gaze with Narcissus's spell-bound eyes at a reflexion of his own self which would reveal to any seer in his senses the repellent countenance of a wrinkled Tithonus.[2] The privilege of the novice is to stumble upon a hidden treasure because his feet are not bound to a beaten track.

We can also now see the reason for another social phenomenon—the tendency for a creative to degenerate into a merely dominant minority—which we have singled out, at an early stage in this Study, as a prominent symptom of social breakdown and disintegration.[3] While a creative individual or minority is certainly not predestined to undergo this disastrous change for the worse, the creator is at least decidedly pre-disposed in this direction *ex*

[1] For the operation of this law in the action of Challenge-and-Response see II. D (vii), vol. ii, pp. 259–74, above.

[2] This myth of Tithonus is taken in Part VI below as an allegory of a challenge that is apt to present itself to a universal state.

[3] See I. C (i) (*a*), vol. i, pp. 53–5, above.

officio creativitatis. The gift of creativity, which is in origin the reward of a successful response to a challenge, becomes in its turn, in the act of being conferred, a new and uniquely formidable challenge for its devoted recipient.

The War Cabinet.

A flagrant example of the metamorphosis of a creative into a dominant minority is the moral and intellectual blindness which so frequently smites the statesmen of victorious belligerent Powers when they come to impose a peace settlement upon their defeated adversaries. The war-minister who is an 'organizer of victory' is a creative genius of a kind. There are creative gifts of a peculiar sort which his task demands; and he will not win his way to office in war-time, or find himself in the saddle when the armistice is signed, unless he happens to possess these peculiar gifts in a high degree: the intellectual gift of focussing all his attention upon the smallest possible number of clear-cut objectives and obstacles and cynosures and bugbears, and the moral gift of an aptitude for bold experimentation, rapid improvization, and living from hand to mouth in a landscape of short horizons. Just because these qualities are barbarous, they are invaluable in war; and accordingly those statesmen that possess them will come to the top when war breaks out and will develop them further by strenuous exercise before the war comes to an end. But, again just because they are barbarous, these self-same qualities are fatal disqualifications for the task of making peace; for the war-maker's virtues are the peace-maker's vices, and *vice versa.* The task of peace-making demands the intellectual gift of seeing all round a problem, leaving no element out of account, and estimating all the elements in their relative proportions, and the moral gift of an aptitude for cautious conservatism, ripe deliberation, taking long views, and working for distant ends. When the armistice is signed, statesmen endowed with these gifts will no doubt still be in existence; but they will certainly not be appointed to be the plenipotentiaries at the peace conference; for even if they were in office at the moment when war broke out, they will certainly have been deposed and discredited, long before peace has returned, on account of their unwarlike virtues. It is the statesmen who have won the war that will inevitably be entrusted by their grateful and admiring constituents with the task of making the peace settlement; and since they have been chosen for this task by a particularly efficient process of inverse selection, they are almost certain to cancel—and much more than cancel—the benefit which they have conferred upon their constituents in leading them to victory by capping this victory with a peace settlement that will hang like a mill-stone round the victor's necks unto the third and fourth generation.

The perversity of peace settlements is proverbial;[1] and, in the light of the sequel, it is apt to appear so extreme that it becomes difficult to believe that it has not been malignantly deliberate. Yet as a matter of fact we know, from direct contemporary evidence, that the makers of peace settlements are usually well-intentioned. The evil that they do, which so persistently lives after them, is a product, not of a brilliant malignity, but of a deadly blindness; and this blindness has overtaken them because the sounding of 'cease fire' has thrown them, in a trice, entirely out of their element. The good which they have done as the 'organizers of victory' is buried in the grave of the war which they have succeeded in bringing to a victorious conclusion; and the state of mind in which their war-time achievement has left them is the worst possible state for grappling with the utterly different task which is immediately thrust upon their eager hands *ex officio*.

[1] The examples are so notorious that it is hardly necessary to quote them, and a reference to two modern Western peace settlements may suffice.

The makers of the peace settlement of 1814–15, after the General War of 1792–1815, showed their perversity in selecting the dead-and-gone principle of Dynastic Legitimacy as the ideal political foundation for their attempted reconstruction of Society, while they ignored or flouted the rising principle of National Self-Determination, to which the future actually belonged. Similarly, in setting themselves to restore and safeguard the European Balance of Power, they made all their arrangements on the assumption that in the future, as during the past 150 years, the country that would threaten to upset the Balance and subjugate its neighbours would be France, whereas the role which France had been playing in Europe till then was actually to be played thereafter by Prussia. In retrospect it seems extraordinary that this anxiety to build up a barrier against hypothetical future outbreaks of French aggression should have induced so acute a statesman as Metternich to undermine the foundations of his Hapsburg master's re-established hegemony in Germany and Italy by allowing the Hohenzollerns to acquire the Rhineland and the House of Savoy to acquire Genoa. In the event the enlarged Kingdoms of Prussia and Sardinia were never called upon to save Europe from another French attempt at universal dominion; but their gains in territory and strength, through the peace settlement of 1814–15, did enable them, within the next half-century, to establish a new German Reich and a United Kingdom of Italy at the Hapsburg Monarchy's expense. The settlement of 1814–15 contained in itself the warrant of Austria's discomfiture in 1866 for those that had eyes to read the real signs of the times; but even a Metternich was so thoroughly obsessed by the dead facts of the past that he was blind to the vital interests of the Power which he was seeking to serve.

As for the makers of the peace settlement of 1919–20, their blindness, too, has become a by-word in respect of certain of their acts—for example, their handling of the problem of Reparations, and their extortion, from their defeated and momentarily prostrate adversary, of a verbal admission of exclusive guilt for the common sin and calamity of the War. It remains to be seen how the peace settlement of 1919–20 will look after the lapse of half a century! This time the peace-makers have taken, as the ideal political foundation for their attempted reconstruction of Society, the principle of National Self-Determination which their predecessors set at defiance a hundred years before with such disastrous consequences. It is true enough that the obstinate idolization of the anachronistic principle of Dynastic Legitimacy has inflicted incalculable disaster upon Europe between the time of its reaffirmation in 1814–15 and the *coup de grâce* which it received at last in 1918 through the simultaneous downfall of the Hapsburg, Romanov, and Hohenzollern Empires. But the peace-makers have transferred their allegiance from Dynasticism to Nationalism a full century too late; and we may almost take their belated conversion to the younger principle as presumptive evidence that this principle of National Self-Determination has by now become an anachronism in its turn. The consequences of the peace settlement of 1919–20 are touched upon further in V. C (i) (*d*) 6 (γ), Annex I, vol. v, p. 640, footnote 1, below.

This swift metamorphosis of deft winners of victory into clumsy makers of peace is a tragedy for all concerned: for the statesmen themselves, for their compatriots, for their adversaries, and for the whole of the self-lacerated society to which the victors and the vanquished alike belong. And thus the spiritual and material ravages which a war inflicts are far from being confined to the period of belligerency. The original calamity of a barbarous outbreak of violence in a society's life entails the further calamity that the vast issues which the war has opened up have all to be disposed of summarily and simultaneously in a peace settlement, instead of being grappled with one by one and settled in the fullness of Time. *Ex hypothesi* a peace settlement is an almost superhumanly difficult task; the chances of success are slight, even if the business is placed in the ablest hands that can be found; and the penalties of failure are heavy. In such a pass as this the chances of success are diminished almost to vanishing-point and the penalties of failure are increased almost to infinity when this business of making the peace settlement is actually placed in hands peculiarly unfitted for it by being entrusted to the statesmen who have won the foregoing war. It would hardly be an exaggeration to say that the peace-making of the war-winners is the worst of all the calamities that War inflicts on those who perpetrate it.

The Religion of Humanity.

In all the instances of idolization which we have examined in this chapter so far, the idol on to which the adulation of an ephemeral self has been projected has been fashioned out of some fraction of Mankind: a camarilla or a community or a race. We have still to consider the case in which the self is idolized in the shape of Humanity at large with a capital 'H'.

This idolatrous worship of Leviathan has been advocated in all seriousness by one of our modern Western philosophers,[1] Auguste Comte (*vivebat* A.D. 1798–1857).

'The whole of Positive conceptions [is condensed in] the one single idea of an immense and eternal Being, Humanity. . . . Around this real Great Being, the prime mover of each existence, individual or collective, our affections centre by as spontaneous an impulse as do our thoughts and our actions. . . . The growing struggle of Humanity against the sum of the necessities under which it exists[2] offers the heart no less than the

[1] The Hellenic philosopher-king Alexander's gospel of 'the Brotherhood of Man' (ὁμόνοια) appears to have been grounded on a worship, not of Humanity, but of a God who is the common father of all men (see V. C (i) (*d*) 7, vol. vi, pp. 8–10, and V. C (ii) (*a*), vol. vi, p. 246, footnote 5, below).

[2] In this passage, as in many others, Comte frankly admits that his corporate human object of worship is not an absolute or omnipotent godhead (see Caird, E.: *The Social Philosophy and Religion of Comte* (Glasgow 1885, MacLehose), p. 31). Comte maintained

intellect a better object of contemplation than the necessarily capricious omnipotence of its theological predecessor[1]. . . . Humanity definitely substitutes Herself for God, without ever forgetting his provisional services[2]. . . . We adore Her not as the older god, to compliment Her, but in order to serve Her better by bettering ourselves.'[3]

Comte dreamed of embodying his 'Religion of Humanity' in the institution of a universal church; but this dream has not yet come true 'in real life'. Though the atheist French philosopher did his best to animate a lay-figure by dressing it out in garments—at once venerable and familiar—which he ostentatiously plucked from the living body of the Catholic Church, he has not gained the advantage that he expected from his cold-bloodedly pedantic resort to the strategy of Archaism;[4] and in our day, when nearly a hundred years have passed since the *floruit* of the Positivist Prophet, Positivism nowhere survives as a church with a corporate life and a regularly executed order of public worship, except in England, where it has merely added one more to an already long muster-roll of insular sects.[5] It is true that a far wider, as well as more rapid, success has been achieved in our time by a younger and grimmer worship of Humanity which is part and parcel of the creed of Communism.[6] The Communist dogmatically and fanatically rules out a belief in the existence of God which the Positivist merely discards as superfluous. Yet while there is no doubt at all about the sincerity of the

that the new science of Sociology had made it plain that this limited object of worship was a satisfactory one (Caird, op. cit., pp. 28–9). But he might not have found it easy to meet his Scottish critic's objection that 'a relative religion is not a religion at all' (Caird, op. cit., p. 165).—A.J.T.

1 Comte, A.: *The Catechism of Positive Religion*, English translation, second edition (London 1883, Trübner), pp. 45–6.

2 Comte, op. cit., p. 294.

3 Comte, op. cit., p. 61. See further eundem: *Système de Politique*, vol. i (Paris 1851 Matties, Carilian, Goeury et Delmont), Discours Préliminaire, Conclusion Générale: 'Religion de l'Humanité'; vol. ii (1852), chap. 1: 'Théorie Générale de la Religion, ou Théorie Positive de l'Unité Humaine'; vol. iv (1854), 'Conclusion Générale du Tome ivme', p. 524, on the emancipation of the Vrai Grand Être from a fictitious God.

4 For the deliberately imported vein of Archaism in Comte's 'Religion of Humanity' see V. C (i) (*d*) 8 (δ), vol. vi, p. 83, footnote 2, below.

5 After Comte's death his followers in England parted company with those in France over the question whether the apostles of the Positivist Church should, or should not, wait till they had convinced the intellect before they appealed to the emotions. The English Positivists were in favour of going out into the highways and hedges and seeking to convert the women and the proletarians *en masse*; and, in support of this policy of giving the claims of the heart a priority over those of the head, they cited the precedent of the Primitive Christian Church as well as the authority of their own Master, Comte, himself. An account of this controversy in the bosom of the Positivist Church in its Apostolic Age will be found in Caird, E.: *The Social Philosophy and Religion of Comte* (Glasgow 1885, MacLehose), pp. 171–6.

6 On the vexed question whether Communism is to be reckoned as a religion or as a philosophy or merely as a political programme, it will be sufficient—for our present purpose—to point out that Communism at any rate answers to the definition of what constitutes a religion according to Comte. In Comte's view a religion is a comprehensive coherent conception of the Universe which gives us an object upon which we can fix all our affections and an aim to which we can devote all our energies (Caird, op. cit., pp. 24–7; cf. p. 159). The nature and tendency of Communism are examined further in this Study in V. C (i) (*c*) 2, vol. v, pp. 177–88, below.

Communist's rejection of the worship of anything superhuman or divine, there is a distinct and increasing doubt about the constancy of his allegiance to an all-embracing Humanity. At any rate in the Soviet Union, where Communism is to-day the established *idéologie d'état*, there has been showing itself, under the Stalinian régime, a strongly pronounced tendency to withdraw allegiance from Humanity at large in order to concentrate it upon that fraction of the living generation of Mankind that is at present penned within the frontiers of the U.S.S.R.[1] In other words, Soviet Communism seems at this moment to be changing under our eyes from a worship of Humanity into the worship of a tribal divinity of the type of Athene Polias or the Lion of Saint Mark or Kathleen na Hoolihan or Britannia.[2] And this change suggests that Russian Communism, like British Positivism, may be destined to contract to the dimensions of a parochial sect instead of realizing the dream of its founder by growing into a universal church.

Do these apparently unpromising prospects of both Russian Communism and British Positivism portend in their turn a set-back to the worship of the Self in the shape of Humanity at large? This does not necessarily follow; for, while Comte's dream may not yet have been translated into reality, it is nevertheless still in the air.

> 'Il existe, par-dessus les classes et les nations, une volonté de l'espèce de se rendre maîtresse des choses et, quand un être humain s'envole en quelques heures d'un bout de la terre à l'autre, c'est toute la race humaine qui frémit d'orgueil et s'adore comme distincte parmi la création. . . . On peut penser parfois qu'un tel mouvement s'affirmera de plus en plus et que c'est de cette voie que s'éteindront les guerres interhumaines; on arrivera ainsi à une "fraternité universelle", mais qui, loin d'être l'abolition de l'esprit de nation avec ses appétits et ses orgueils, en sera au contraire la forme suprême, la nation s'appelant l'Homme et l'ennemi s'appelant Dieu.'[3]

When a worship of the Self is thus projected on to a human hive or columbarium that has room in it for every human being—dead, living, and unborn—and leaves none but God out in the cold, does the Self cease to be ephemeral and the worship cease to be idolatrous? This question will be answered in the affirmative not only by Communists and Positivists but also by the more numerous adherents of a vaguer, yet perhaps just on that account more representative, school of humanist thinkers and humanitarian men

[1] This change which seems to be coming over the Communism of the Soviet Union is examined further in V. C (i) (*c*) 2, vol. v, pp. 183–6, below.

[2] For the personified political communities that are the idols of a modern Western World, see I. C (iii) (*e*), Annex, vol. i, pp. 442–3, above.

[3] Benda, J.: *La Trahison des Clercs* (Paris 1927, Grasset), pp. 246–7.

of action whose outlook has become the dominant *Weltanschauung* of our Western Society in its Modern Age.[1]

Is this answer the last word? The self-worshipper who has given expression to his heart's desire by substituting an image of Humanity for the presence of a Living God in his panorama of the Universe, can no doubt proclaim

> I am monarch of all I survey;
> My right there is none to dispute.

But is there no bitterness in the boast which Cowper has placed in the mouth of Alexander Selkirk? Is not this monarch a castaway? And must he not pay for his undisputed dominion by living in a spiritual solitude which is an abomination of desolation?

> 'Professing themselves to be wise, they became fools and changed the glory of the uncorruptible God into an image made like to corruptible Man . . . because that, when they knew God, they glorified him not as God, neither were thankful, but became vain in their imaginations, and their foolish heart was darkened.'[2]

(β) *The Idolization of an Ephemeral Institution.*

The Hellenic City-State.

The nemesis of creativity which we have just been studying in the form of an idolization of an ephemeral self may also take the form of an idolatrous worship of some ephemeral institution or technique. Manifestly these idols are of different orders of magnitude in the human hierarchy; for institutions and techniques are no more than the debris of acts of which some human self has been the author. Yet there is also a divine economy in which these human selves and techniques and institutions are, all alike, created things and are therefore, all alike, unworthy and unfit to be made recipients of a worship that is due to none but their Creator; and a moral and intellectual aberration which thus remains in essence the same is not made any less deadly by being indulged in on a narrower human range.[3] The extreme deadli-

[1] At the moment when he was putting these words on paper, the writer of this Study had before him on his desk a letter from an English scholar-statesman who was a humanist and a humanitarian in one; and this letter contained an observation on another passage of the present work (V. C (i) (*c*) 2, vol. v, pp. 160–1, below) which is perhaps even more pertinent to the present passage:

' "Self-worship of the Tribe": very good phrase—yet isn't it only wrong because the "self" is so limited? Once get "humanitarian" and make all Humanity your object—or, better still, if, like the Stoic, you make the Great City of Gods and Man [see V. C (i) (*d*) 7, Annex, vol. vi, pp. 332–8, below—A.J.T.] your object—the self-worship gets pretty right and becomes a "higher religion".'

[2] Romans i. 22–3 and 21.

[3] 'Whoever detaches Race or the Nation or the State or the Form of State or the Government from the temporal scale of values and raises them to be the supreme model and deifies them with idolatrous worship, falsifies the divinely created order of things.'—Papal Encyclical of the 14th March, 1937, addressed primarily to the German Episcopate.

ness of an infatuation with some past institutional or technical achievement has come under our observation, at an earlier point in this Study, in our survey of the arrested civilizations.[1] The effect of idolizing an institution is exemplified in the arrests of the Ottoman Society's growth under the incubus of the Pādishāh's Slave-Household and of the Spartan Society's under the incubus of the Lycurgean *agôgê*; the effect of idolizing a technique is exemplified in the fates of the Nomads and the Esquimaux and the Polynesians. These extreme examples seem to indicate that an idolatry of institutions and an idolatry of techniques are the besetting sins of societies that are confronted with formidable challenges from the human and from the physical environment respectively. With this key in our hands we may now pursue our study of these two varieties of idolatry along our usual lines of an empirical survey. Let us take the idolatry of institutions first, and let us begin with a classic case: the idolization, in the Hellenic World, of the institution of the Sovereign City-State.

In examining the part played by this particular act of idolatry in the breakdown and disintegration of the Hellenic Society, we have to distinguish between two different situations in which the idol of the Sovereign City-State stood as a stumbling-block in the way of the solution of a social problem.

The earlier, and graver, of the two problems was the challenge of being called upon to establish some kind of political world order as a framework for an oecumenical economic system which had become one of the necessities of Hellenic life. This challenge was presented by the impact on Hellenic international politics of the Solonian economic revolution; for Solon at Athens, and the statesmen who were his contemporaries and counterparts at Aegina and Miletus and elsewhere, had solved the Malthusian problem, by which the Hellenic Society had previously been beset, at the price of abandoning the ancient city-state self-sufficiency in economic activities; and in a society whose life had thus become oecumenical—perforce and once for all—on the economic plane, the ancient political luxury of City-State Sovereignty could no longer be indulged in with impunity. We have seen already how the new necessity of transcending this City-State Sovereignty became urgent in the Hellenic World in the fifth century before Christ, and how an Athenian failure to make satisfactory provision for it involved the whole Hellenic Society in the breakdown of 431 B.C.[2] This problem of establishing a world order was the crucial challenge in Hellenic history;[3] and it inexorably persisted in confronting

[1] See Part III. A, in vol. iii, above. [2] See IV. C (iii) (*b*) 10, pp. 211–3, above.
[3] See V. C (ii) (*b*), vol. vi, pp. 287 and 280–91, below.

Hellenic statesmen down to the end of the story; but, while this inescapable and fundamental problem still remained unsolved, a secondary problem, which was of the Hellenic dominant minority's own seeking, came treading upon its heels when Hellenic history passed over from its second chapter into a third towards the turn of the fourth and third centuries B.C.

The chief outward and visible sign of this transition, as we have already observed,[1] was a sudden great increase in the material scale of Hellenic life. A hitherto maritime world which had been confined to the coasts of the Mediterranean Basin from Cyrene and Trebizond to Marseilles, now expanded overland in Asia from the Dardanelles to India and in Europe from Olympus and the Appennines to the Danube and the Rhine. In a society which had swollen to these material dimensions without having solved the spiritual problem of creating law and order between the states into which it was articulated, the Sovereign City-State was so utterly dwarfed that it was no longer a practicable unit of political life. And this incidental political consequence of an increase in material scale was in itself by no means a misfortune for Hellenism in an age in which the always doubtful blessing of City-State Sovereignty had turned into an unmistakable curse. So far from that, the passing of this traditional Hellenic form of Parochial Sovereignty might have been taken as a heaven-sent opportunity for shaking off the incubus of Parochial Sovereignty altogether. And this chance of responding successfully at the eleventh hour to a challenge which was big with the Hellenic Society's fate might perhaps not have been missed if Alexander had lived to join forces with Zeno and Epicurus. Under those joint auspices the Hellenes might have succeeded in stepping straight out of the City-State into the *Cosmopolis*[2]; and in that event the Hellenic Civilization might have been able to take on a new lease of creative life. But Alexander's premature death left the Hellenic World at the mercy of his successors; and these adventurers saw their interest, not in abolishing Parochial Sovereignty, but in preserving it for their own benefit. The personal ambition of each of them was to acquire for himself some portion of their dead master's heritage; and the only purpose for which they knew how to co-operate was to prevent any one of their number from monopolizing the whole of it. Accordingly the abilities of the contending Macedonian war-lords and the wealth of the ransacked Achaemenian Empire were perversely expended on endeavours to

[1] In III. C (i) (*a*), vol. iii, pp. 140 and 150–1; III. C (i) (*d*), vol. iii, p. 197; IV. C (iii) (*c*) 2 (α), in the present volume, p. 265, above. See further V. C (i) (*c*) 3, vol. v, p. 214, and V. C (ii) (*b*), vol. vi, pp. 289–90, below.

[2] For the Hellenic conception of the *Cosmopolis* see V. C (i) (*d*) 7, Annex, vol. vi, pp. 332–8, below.

keep up the institution of Parochial Sovereignty as a going concern in the new era of Hellenic history which Alexander had lived to inaugurate. But on the new material scale of Hellenic life *post Alexandrum* Parochial Sovereignty could only be salvaged on one condition. The traditional sovereignty of the single city-state must be transcended in order to make way—not, after all, for the establishment of an oecumenical world order, but for the forging of new-fangled parochial states of a supra-city-state calibre. This was the secondary problem which the fourth-century expansion of the Hellenic World brought in its train; and it is one of the ironies of Hellenic history that a problem which would have been better left alone should have been successfully solved by statesmen who had wantonly rejected a chance of responding to an unanswered challenge which could not be ignored without inviting disaster. This untoward success of a perverse feat of statesmanship is attested by an historical fact which we have already had occasion to notice in other contexts.[1] In the third century B.C. the new Great Powers of supra-city-state calibre which had been built up, since Alexander's death, on the periphery of an expanding Hellenic World were showing their mettle by exerting a formidable pressure upon the small states at the centre.

These were the two separate and successive problems with which a disintegrating Hellenic Society came to grips in the field of international politics, and, in the event, both problems were disposed of simultaneously by receiving a single solution which was at the same time a supreme calamity. As the result of a series of 'knock-out blows' which Rome delivered, between 220 and 168 B.C., to all the other brand-new Great Powers of the day,[2] the number of sovereign states in the Hellenic World was abruptly reduced from the plural to the singular. The sole surviving Roman Power then embraced the entire Hellenic World in its own dominions; and the establishment of this oecumenical Roman Empire solved the problem of establishing a world order—the crucial challenge that Hellenic statesmanship had hitherto left unanswered—by abolishing Parochial Sovereignty altogether and thereby putting an end to any such thing as international relations in the interior of the Hellenic World. This Roman response to a challenge that had defeated Periclean Athens was as crude as it was drastic, and as drastic as it was belated. Yet, belated and drastic and crude though it might be, it was still a response of a sort; and the point of interest for our present purpose is that both this ultimate Roman response

[1] See III. C (ii) (*b*), vol. iii, pp. 310–13 and 339–41; and IV. C (iii) (*c*) 2 (α), in the present volume, pp. 265–6 and 268–9, above.

[2] See III. C (ii) (*b*), vol. iii, pp. 312–13, and IV. C (iii) (*b*) 10, in the present volume, pp. 210–11, above.

and all the preliminary contributions towards the making of it were the work of members of the Hellenic Society who were not completely infatuated with the idol of City-State Sovereignty.

The very structural principle of the Roman State—the constitutional device which alone made it possible for Rome to grow from a city-state into an oecumenical commonwealth—was something which was quite incompatible with an idolization of City-State Sovereignty *à outrance*; for this cardinal constitutional principle was a 'dual citizenship'; and the psychological basis of this 'dual citizenship' was a harmonious division of the citizen's allegiance between the local city-state into which he was born like his ancestors before him and a wider polity which embraced a number of local city-states within its ambit without grudging them their distinct existence in the capacity of municipalities.[1] This creative compromise was psychologically possible only in those communities in which the idolatrous worship of City-State Sovereignty had not acquired a stranglehold over the citizens' hearts and minds; and the importance of this psychological condition becomes apparent as soon as we remind ourselves of the actual circumstances in which this political invention was gradually evolved in a long historical process which the Roman political genius eventually carried to completion.

The first recorded experiment in constructing a Hellenic commonwealth on a supra-city-state scale through the device of 'dual citizenship' is the establishment of the Boeotian Federation after the liberation of Boeotia from Athenian domination in 447 B.C. In the Boeotian constitution of this date, which has been brought to our knowledge by the enterprise of two modern Western archaeologists,[2] the division of powers between the Federation and its constituent city-states is nicely balanced; yet, though Boeotia was the pioneer in this process of constitutional evolution, she soon fell by the way; for the crux of the problem in Boeotia was the disproportionate size and strength of Thebes by comparison with any other Boeotian city-state; and Boeotian federalism was defeated by Theban egoism. The federal constitution of 447 B.C. had been framed at a moment when Thebes was temporarily humbled by the double disgrace of her 'Medism' in 480 B.C. and her defeat by Athens in 457; and this favourable situation did not recur when the work had to be done all over again after the dissolution of the original Boeotian Federation through a Spartan act of tyranny

[1] For the invention of dual citizenship see III. C (ii) (*b*), Annex IV, vol. iii, p. 481, above.

[2] An account of the Boeotian constitution of 447 B.C. will be found in *Hellenica Oxyrhynchia*, ed. by B. P. Grenfell and A. S. Hunt (Oxford 1909, Clarendon Press), chap. 11.

which the Lacedaemonian Government committed on the strength of the peace-settlement of 383 B.C. ('the Peace of Antalcidas'). This time, when Boeotia's former Lacedaemonian allies were playing the part of her oppressors, Thebes resumed her normal role in Boeotian affairs. In this fourth-century Boeotian struggle against Spartan domination Thebes stood out as the Boeotian protagonist. The critical events of the struggle were the Spartans' seizure of the citadel of Thebes in 382 B.C. and their ejection from it in 378 and their crushing defeat at Leuctra in 371 by the generalship of the Theban commander Epaminondas and the fighting-power of the Theban contingent in the Boeotian army. This liberation of Boeotia by Theban military prowess put the reconstruction of the Boeotian Federation into the hands of Theban statesmen; and Theban statesmanship at once succumbed to the temptation of attempting to swallow the Federation up into a unitary Theban state, in which Thebes would become in Boeotia what Athens was in Attica, while Thespiae and Tanagra and Orchomenos would be reduced to the political nonentity of an Eleusis or a Marathon. This fourth-century Theban policy of *Gleichschaltung* was inimical to the progress of federalism in Boeotia; and though the Boeotian Federation—profiting, perhaps, by the blows which Thebes received at Macedonian hands in 338 and 334 B.C.—protracted its existence until it was finally dissolved by the Romans in 146 B.C.,[1] it missed its 'manifest destiny' of becoming 'the Education of Hellas' in the art of 'dual citizenship'.

This destiny, which was brought within the Boeotians' grasp by the intervention of Sparta—the first time as a friend and the second time as a foe—on the two occasions above mentioned, was snatched out of the Chalcidians' hands by another act of intervention on the part of the same Power.[2] The short political life of half a century (*circa* 432–378 B.C.) which the Chalcidian Federal Commonwealth enjoyed before the Spartans dissolved it in 378 B.C. is of historical interest, not because of any positive effects which it can be seen to have had upon the subsequent course of Hellenic history, but because the Chalcidian constitution was a close anticipation of the Roman. The new feature in both the Chalcidian and the Roman Commonwealth was that the comprehensive body politic, as well as each of its constituent parts, was a

[1] The final and formal dissolution of the Boeotian League by the Romans seems to have taken place in 146 B.C., after Mummius's campaign in Greece, and as the punishment for the Boeotians' folly in throwing in their lot with the Achaeans in their desperate military defiance of the Roman Power. *De facto*, however, the Boeotian League seems to have been broken up by Roman diplomacy as early as 172 B.C., on the eve of the outbreak of the Third Romano-Macedonian War.

[2] For the dissolution of the Chalcidian Commonwealth by Spartan arms in 379 B.C., and for the antecedents and consequences of this high-handed and short-sighted Spartan act, see III. C (ii) (*b*), Annex IV, in vol. iii, above.

city-state. In the third century B.C., when there was a fresh outburst of experimentation in supra-city-state political construction all over the Hellenic World, the experiments at the centre, in Greece, were reversions to the older Boeotian type, in which the constituent parts were city-states but the comprehensive body politic was a national community. This was the essential structure of both the Aetolian and the Achaean Confederacy—though they both took an important step in advance of the Boeotian Federation in incorporating a number of city-states which were outside the pale of the original Aetolian or Achaean national patrimony.[1] These third-century experiments at the centre of the Hellenic World were evoked, however, as we have seen,[2] by pressure from a ring of titanic Powers which had already arisen on the periphery; and while some of these, like Ptolemaic Egypt and, in a looser way, Antigonid Macedonia, were unitary monarchies, the majority were akin to the two new commonwealths in Greece in being constructed on the federal principle out of an agglomeration of constituent city-states. In these third-century Hellenic federal states of the outer circle there were several variations from the Boeotian archetype.

The Carthaginian Power was based on the sheer dominion of a single sovereign city-state over a number of subject communities—an empire of the same kind as that which fifth-century Athens tried, and failed, to make out of the Delian League, and that which modern Venice succeeded in establishing for herself on the Italian mainland. The Roman constitution was a system of 'dual citizenship', on the Chalcidian pattern already described, in which the comprehensive body politic was a city-state as well as each of the constituent parts. The far-flung Seleucid Empire stretched across South-Western Asia, from the Dardanelles to the Iranian Plateau, like a rope of pearls in which each pearl was a city-state, while the thread on which all the pearls were strung was a divine kingship vested in the Seleucid Dynasty.[3] With the single exception of the Roman Commonwealth itself, all the third-century experiments

[1] This capacity for expanding their federal state beyond their own original national limits was an exceedingly important element in the rise of both these confederacies. The Aetolian Confederacy became a Power in the Hellenic World through the incorporation of Phocian Delphi and Trachinian Heraclea, the Achaean Confederacy through the incorporation of Argolic Sicyon and Arcadian Megalopolis; and a Sicyonian Aratus and a Megalopolitan Lydiadas were the two most distinguished statesmen who were ever entrusted with responsibility for Achaean interests. Boeotia followed these examples by incorporating Megara from 224 to 192 B.C. (This was done at the instance of the Achaean Confederacy, to which Megara had previously belonged, when the Megarid was cut off from the rest of the Achaean domain through the Achaean Confederacy's retrocession of Corinth to Macedon.)

[2] In III. C (ii) (*b*), vol. iii, pp. 313–14 and 339–41, and in IV. C. (iii) (*c*) 2 (α), in the present volume, pp. 265 and 268–9, above.

[3] For the structure and function of the Seleucid Empire see Part I. A, vol. i, pp. 5–6, above.

in political construction on a supra-city-state scale were brought to an abrupt and violent end by Roman 'knock-out blows'; but the statesmanship of the victors made use of the political inventions of the Powers annihilated by Roman arms in order to transform the Roman Commonwealth into a Hellenic universal state. In the political architecture of the Augustan Empire the original Roman—and Chalcidian—device of city-states within a city-state was still the main principle of construction; but in so vast a material extension of the building the architect found it wise to supplement the liberal principle of 'dual citizenship' with an effectively tyrannical imperialism of the Carthaginian order, and to brace the whole edifice together with the Seleucid bond of a divine kingship.[1]

If we now glance back at the successive theatres of the cumulative political experiment which reached its term in this Roman culmination, we shall observe one common feature. They were all places in which the subordination of City-State Sovereignty to the requirements of a political structure on a larger scale was psychologically possible, because they were all places in which the idolization of City-State Sovereignty had not won a complete ascendency. Every one of the supra-city-state commonwealths in which the experiment was tried in each of its successive stages will be found to have lain on the outer edge of the Hellenic city-state cosmos of the day, and most of them actually bestrode the border-line between this city-state cosmos, which was the brilliant heart of the Hellenic World, and its pre-city-state penumbra.[2]

Boeotia, close to the heart though it lay, was still, in the fifth century B.C., sufficiently near to the edge (being next door to the old-fashioned countries of Phocis and Locris) to have retained a certain sense of its ancient national unity; and this remnant of Boeotian solidarity was a counterweight to the particularism of the self-conscious city-states—a large self-conscious Thebes or a small self-conscious Plataea—into which the country had come to be articulated. Fourth-century Olynthus and Rome both stood at points on the border-line between the city-state cosmos and its penumbra where the transition was more abrupt and the contrast sharper; and in the third century B.C. the Roman Commonwealth in Italy, the Seleucid Empire in Asia, and the Aetolian and Achaean Confederacies in Greece all alike displayed the common structural feature of uniting city-states with pre-civic communities in a single polity. Aetolia contained ancient city-states like Pleuron and Calydon, as well as 'un-synoecized' cantons like Eurytania, within its

[1] It was characteristic of Roman solidity that the Seleucid thread in a string of pearls was transformed, in Roman hands, into a steel lath in a block of reinforced concrete.

[2] On this point see III. C (ii) (*b*), Annex IV, vol. iii, pp. 484–5, above, apropos of Olynthus and Rome.

own original national limits; and, in expanding, the Aetolian Confederacy incorporated foreign cantons like Aeniania, as well as foreign city-states like Naupactus. Achaia, where the balance of feeling between national solidarity and city-state particularism was perhaps about the same in the third century as it had been in Boeotia in the fifth, now reinforced the pre-civic element in her body politic by incorporating the foreign territory of South-West Arcadia, an exceptional patch of Peloponnesian ground which had gone on living under a pre-civic dispensation until the foundation of Megalopolis in 370 B.C.[1] Rome had incorporated the foreign cantons of the Sabina as well as the foreign city-states in Campania. The Seleucid Monarchy had united a number of ancient Greek city-states on the sea-board of Anatolia with a number of *ci-devant* provinces of the defunct Achaemenian Empire.

If we now look closer, we shall observe that in each of these composite commonwealths the territories in which some kind of pre-civic dispensation was still a living fact, or at any rate a recent memory, were the main scenes of creative political activity. In the Achaean Confederacy, for instance, it was a school of Megalopolitan statesmen that were the best inspired exponents of the Achaean idea;[2] and, when we examine Roman Italy and Seleucid Asia, we find that a majority of the constituent city-states were not merely recent foundations, like Megalopolis in the Peloponnese, but were actually younger than the comprehensive body politic in which they were embraced.

The characteristic means by which the Roman Commonwealth and the Seleucid Monarchy acquired the constituent city-states out of which they fashioned their political fabric was not by the incorporation of existing city-states which had once been sovereign and would therefore still be self-conscious; it was rather by the creation of new city-states on politically virgin soil which had previously lain outside the borders of the Hellenic city-state cosmos. In both Roman Italy and Seleucid Asia these new city-states were generated in a variety of ways. In some cases, as in the *coloniae Latinae* and the *coloniae civium Romanorum*, or in the Asiatic colonies of Greek military veterans which were planted by the Seleucidae,[3] the nucleus of the new civic foundation was created by the physical introduction of new settlers who brought the city-

1 For the constitutional history of South-West Arcadia see III. C (ii) (*b*), Annex IV, vol. iii, pp. 477 and 481, above.

2 See III. C (ii) (*b*), vol. iii, pp. 313–14, above.

3 'The basis of the Seleucid settlement was the military colony and not the Greek city, the *polis*. The first two kings did not . . . fill Asia with Greek cities directly'; at the same time 'the aim of every military colony was to become a full *polis* . . . ; there was a steady upward growth of the colony into the *polis*, and it was this which, before the end of the second century B.C., had filled Asia with "Greek" cities.'—Tarn, W. W.: *The Greeks in Bactria and India* (Cambridge 1938, University Press), pp. 6 and 9.

state tradition with them from their previous homes as part of their social heritage. In other cases the new foundation was called into existence by the 'synoecism' and 'civilization' (in the literal sense) of the indigenous population, as when the Seleucidae created a new city-state out of the domain of some Anatolian or Syrian divinity,[1] or when the Romans organized a Sabine canton into a *praefectura*, or a Picentine village into a *forum* or *conciliabulum*. The most usual method, perhaps, was some combination of conversion with colonization. But, in whichever of these ways any given Roman or Seleucid foundation was started on its career, its citizens could scarcely help taking for granted the supremacy of the Power by whose fiat, and on whose territory, their city had been founded. Often, indeed, they were reminded of the parent Power's *patria potestas* by the very mintage of their city's name, when this recorded the creative act of some Seleucid sovereign, like Seleucia or Apamea,[2] or of some Roman magistrate, like Forum Sempronii or Forum Appii.

Any citizen of an eponymously named city who might be tempted, out of affectation or snobbery, to idolize his Antioch or his Forum Livii as an Athenian idolized Athens or a Praenestine Praeneste, would necessarily be reminded, in the act, that 'it is he that hath made us and not we ourselves',[3] and would probably be pulled up short, by an inward sense of incongruity, before going the length of making any outward gesture of insubordination that would demand the intervention of Roman praetor or Seleucid prince.[4] The normal psychological attitude of the citizens of such city-states towards their sovereign the God Antiochus or the Dea Roma would be the feeling that they were this sovereign's 'people and the sheep of his pasture'.[5] Manifestly, a local community which

[1] For the temple-states in Anatolia and Syria which were part of the social legacy of the Achaemenian Empire, and for the Seleucids' policy towards them, see Tarn, W. W.: *Hellenistic Civilization* (London 1927, Arnold), pp. 114–17. For the genesis of these temple-states see IV. C (iii) (*c*) 3 (α), p. 471, below. The Seleucid city-state of Antioch-towards-Pisidia was founded on territory carved out of a temple-state of the god Mên. For the signal failure of Antiochus IV Epiphanes' attempt to apply the regular Seleucid policy to the temple-state of Yahweh at Jerusalem see V. C (i) (*d*) 9 (β), vol. vi, pp. 103–5, below. There is no record of any military colony or *polis* ever having been founded on land taken from the estate of an Iranian feudal baron (Tarn, *The Greeks in Bactria and India*, p. 32).

[2] 'The only places which were founded directly as *poleis* from the start were *some*, probably the majority, of those which bore the four Seleucid dynastic names: Antioch, Seleuceia, Apamea, Laodicea.'—Tarn, op. cit., p. 12.

[3] Psalm c. 3.

[4] In the Seleucid Empire the obverse of the eponymous cities' (and other royal foundations') loyalty to the Crown was the Crown's tact in dealing with the cities. 'Though in theory the Seleucids were autocrats, they could not afford to ride roughshod over the Greeks, and the popularity of the dynasty shows that they did not do so' (Tarn, op. cit., p. 26). 'The new cities were not, of course, sovereign states. . . . But neither were they municipalities of the Empire, as they were to be of the Roman Empire; they were a sort of half-way house' (Tarn, op. cit., p. 24).

[5] Psalm c, loc. cit.

felt like this would be socially plastic and politically malleable; and the triumphs of Roman and Seleucid political construction were achieved with materials of this kind, just as the triumphs of British political construction have been achieved with dominions of the Crown in 'new countries'.[1]

Any candid Englishman will confess that the British Commonwealth of Nations could never have been built up by English statesmanship if the materials with which it had to work had been all Irelands, with no Canadas or Australias. On this analogy we may reasonably say—without any slighting reflexion upon the Roman or the Seleucid political genius—that Roman Italy could never have been built out of constituent city-states that were all Capuas, with no Aesernias or Venusias, nor Seleucid Asia out of city-states that were all Smyrnas and Lampsacuses, with no Laodiceas or Antiochs. Even as it was, Capua nearly brought the Roman Commonwealth to grief, when the structure of this Roman building was subjected to the supreme test of the Hannibalic War, by seceding on her own account and thereby setting an example which was afterwards followed by Tarentum and other *ci-devant* sovereign city-states which had latterly been incorporated into the Roman body politic. And the demoralization spread so far that a moment came when twelve Latin colonies actually declined to continue their support of the Roman Government in the prosecution of the war by making any further contributions of men or money.[2] As for the Seleucid Empire, its collision with Rome in the war of 192–188 B.C. caused the immediate loss of the Seleucid possessions north-west of Taurus and was the beginning of the end of the Seleucid Power. And the occasion, if not the cause, of this disastrous encounter was an appeal which was addressed to the Roman Government in 193 B.C. by Lampsacus, Smyrna, and other historic Greek city-states on the western seaboard of Asia Minor[3] whose citizens could not forget the City-State Sovereignty which their forebears had lost some four hundred years before, nor reconcile themselves to a suzerainty which the modern Seleucids had inherited from the ancient Mermnad Kings of Lydia through the long chain of a successive Achaemenian and Athenian and Spartan and restored Achaemenian overlordship. These *ci-devant* sovereign Asiatic city-states in the Seleucid Empire had no sooner heard the news that the Romans had restored their sovereignty to the European Greek city-states which had previously been subject to the Kingdom of

[1] On this point see IV. C (iii) (*c*) 2 (α), in the present volume, pp. 292–6, as well as III. C (ii) (*b*), vol. iii, p. 303, footnote 1, above.

[2] For the lapse of these twelve Latin colonies from active into passive belligerency in 209 B.C. see Livy, Book XXVII, chap. 9.

[3] For this appeal and its diplomatic consequences see Livy, Book XXXIV, chaps. 57–9, and Book XXXV, chap. 16.

Macedon[1] than they set their hearts upon obtaining the same boon for themselves from the same puissant Roman hands.[2] They did not pause to consider that there could be little guarantee of genuineness or permanency for a sovereignty that was recaptured by a bevy of city-states at the price of overthrowing the general Balance of Power through the humiliation of two Great Powers and the aggrandizement of one. The idolization of a long-lost status obsessed their minds and determined their policy; and so they played into the Romans' hands. For the destruction of the Seleucid Power carried Rome a long stage farther towards that universal dominion over the Hellenic World in which all other sovereignties but hers were ultimately swallowed up.

Thus, in the fatally long-drawn-out effort to transcend the institution of Parochial City-State Sovereignty—an effort which began with a tragically swift Athenian failure in the fifth century B.C. and ended no less than four hundred years later with a tragically belated Roman success—the historic sovereign city-states of Hellas played, from first to last, a role which was either negatively unconstructive or else positively mischievous. The appeal of Lampsacus and Smyrna to Rome in 193 B.C., which brought the Seleucid Empire to the ground, was inspired by the same perverse spirit that had once led the allies of Athens in the Delian League to rebel against their treaty obligations, and led Athens herself to transform the League into an Athenian tyranny; and the aberration of inward thought and feeling which was responsible for this perversity in outward behaviour was a stiff-necked persistence in idolizing the institution of City-State Sovereignty in an age when this institution had become inimical instead of serviceable to the life of the Hellenic Society. When this idolatry captivated and paralysed the ancient and famous communities which were the original sources of Hellenic light and leadership, the work of political construction, which had to be performed by somebody, was carried out crudely and painfully and slowly by communities which had been lying in obscurity, in the penumbra, in the age when an Athens and a Corinth and a Chalcis and a Miletus had been the brilliant luminaries of the Hellenic firmament. And at the culmination and close of the Hellenic 'Time of Troubles', when this long labour and travail was on the eve of bearing a tardy and savourless fruit, a sudden view of four once magnificent Greek cities lying derelict

[1] In 196 B.C., on the occasion of the Isthmian Games, Titus Quinctius Flamininus, the Roman commander in Greece, proclaimed, in the name of the Roman Government, the liberation of the communities over which the Macedonian Government had been compelled to cede its title to sovereignty after the Battle of Cynoscephalae in 197 B.C. See the accounts of this striking transaction in Livy, Book XXXIII, chaps. 32–3, and in Plutarch's *Life of Titus Quinctius Flamininus*, chap. 10.

[2] On this point see Livy, Book XXXIII, chap. 33, *ad finem*.

within sight of each other, with their brilliance quite extinct, made an overwhelming impression on an experienced Roman statesman of the day.

'On the voyage home from Asia, when my ship was making for Megara from Aegina, I began to take my bearings of the regions round about. Behind me was Aegina, ahead of me Megara, to the right of me Peiraeus, to the left of me Corinth; and all these cities have had their *floruit*—only to lie now prostrate and ruinous for all eyes to see. I began to think to myself: "How monstrous it is for little creatures like ourselves, whose natural term of life is of the shortest, to grow indignant if any of us passes away or has his life taken from him, when the dead bodies of all these cities lie cast out here on this one spot. Servius, pull yourself together and remember that you have been born a son of man."'[1]

In our own Western World in the eighteenth century of the Christian Era a similar train of thought might have arisen in the mind of any philosophic French or English traveller on 'the grand tour' when he had his first sight of the spires of Bruges and Ghent or the towers of Sienna or the domes of Florence and Venice; for these cenotaphs of departed glories testified in that age, like the monuments of Corinth and Athens eighteen centuries earlier, to the deadliness of the idolatrous worship of the sovereignty of a city-state. In our Western World, it is true, the failure of the historic medieval city-states of Italy and Flanders to rise to the occasion, when they were called upon to face the extreme ordeal of transcending themselves, did not bring about the breakdown and disintegration of the whole society of which those city-states were members. As we have noticed in an earlier part of this Study,[2] the Italian and Flemish failure was retrieved, and the situation provisionally saved, by a 'clean cut' with the political tradition of the medieval Western city-state cosmos. The modern school of Western political architecture dispensed with the institution of the city-state altogether, adopted the Transalpine kingdom-state as the standard basis for a new political structure, and managed to combine the old Transalpine scale with the new Italian efficiency by a creative adaptation of the Transalpine feudal institution of Parliament. This English solution of the political problem of the age was the main line of Western political development in the third chapter of our Western history; but, side by side with this new-fangled English work of political creation, there was a simultaneous attempt to solve the same problem of creating an efficient body politic on the supra-civic scale without renouncing the use of city-states as elements in

[1] Letter written by Servius Sulpicius Rufus to Marcus Tullius Cicero from Athens in 45 B.C. (*Ad Familiares*, iv. 5), upon receipt of the news of the death of Cicero's daughter.

[2] In III. C (ii) (*b*), vol. iii, pp. 350–63, above.

the new structure. This was the experiment which was tried in Switzerland and in the Northern Netherlands; and although it has been of less practical importance than the contemporary constitutional developments in England, this Swiss and Dutch experiment is of equal interest to the student of history. Its interest lies in the fact that here, in a secondary line of our modern Western political development, we have a precise parallel to the main line of development in the corresponding chapter of Hellenic history.[1] The Swiss Confederation and the United Netherlands are counterparts of the Aetolian and Achaean Confederacies, inasmuch as they are attempts to produce the same results by a similar use of corresponding materials; and it is profoundly interesting to observe how far the parallel extends.

We observe, for example, that the Swiss and Dutch experiments were not made on the historic soil of Lombardy and Flanders, which was cumbered with the rubbish of obsolete institutions and with the weeds of ineradicable memories; they were made on adjoining ground,[2] in the former penumbra of the medieval Western city-state cosmos, where the city-state was neither an unknown institution nor yet an object of idolatrous worship, and where it was therefore not intractable in the hands of a political architect who wished to try the experiment of using a traditionally sovereign type of polity as a modest brick in a larger and more ambitious political building. We also observe that, in the architecture of both the Swiss and the Dutch federal commonwealth, there was a valuable diversity of type among the constituent parts out of which the whole was constructed. While some of these parts were actual city-states, like Berne and Zürich and Basel and Utrecht, and others were clusters of city-states, like Holland and Seeland, there were also Swiss cantons like the original Forest Cantons or the Graubünden, and Dutch provinces like Friesland or Geldern, which, like the duchy of Cleve and the counties of Mark and Burgundy[3] and

[1] It may be added that the main line of our modern Western political development, as represented by the English system of representative parliamentary government in a limited monarchy on the kingdom-state scale, has likewise its parallel, in the corresponding chapter of Hellenic history, in the temporary and eventually abortive recrudescence of an old-fashioned kingdom-state régime which is represented by the Kingdom of Macedon, and by the Macedonian 'successor-states' of the Achaemenian Empire, from the generation of King Philip II to the generation of King Perseus. During the span of 170 years that intervenes between the dates of the Battle of Chaeronea (338 B.C.) and the Battle of Pydna (168 B.C.), this Macedonian kingdom-state régime occupies the foreground of the Hellenic political stage; and the truth that this was a side-track, and not the main line of development, did not become manifest until the triumph of Rome condemned all the surviving kingdom-states of the Macedonian type to be *peritura regna*. For an examination of the ultimate victory of the city-state over the kingdom-state in the Hellenic World see III. C (ii) (*b*), Annex IV, in vol. iii, above.

[2] This point has been noticed, by anticipation, in III. C (ii) (*b*), vol. iii, p. 351, footnote 1, above.

[3] The Imperial County of Burgundy (*Franche-Comté*), as distinct from the French Duchy of Burgundy, had originally been included, like the Tyrol and Cleve and Mark

the Tyrol, were relics of a pre-civic dispensation in Transalpine Europe. These features in the location, composition, and structure of the Swiss and Dutch commonwealths all have their counterparts in the sketch of the Aetolian and Achaean confederacies that we have given above.

These Swiss and Dutch experiments in political construction have played their part, side by side with English work, in saving the modern Western World from being ruined by a Florentine or Venetian idolatry of the medieval Western city-state. Yet, if we have thus succeeded, in the third chapter of our Western history, in avoiding the fatal false step into which our 'philosophical contemporaries'[1] in the Hellenic World slipped in the corresponding chapter of their history, this provisional avoidance of political shipwreck does not warrant us in 'resting on our oars' in a day-dream of self-congratulation over a fancied superiority. If we are tempted to regard ourselves as the Hellenes' superiors in the game of political construction because we have managed to beat their score by a single point, we shall do well to remind ourselves of the Hellenic wisdom which Herodotus puts into the mouth of Solon.[2] 'In order to appraise any phenomenon, the attention must be directed upon the circumstances in which it meets its end. To many people God has given a glimpse of happiness in order to destroy them root and branch.' Like the Lydian king to whom Solon's observations were addressed, the Hellenic Society has long since met its end, and that end has been tragically disastrous. Yet, in finishing their game in defeat, the Hellenes have at any rate gained the negative advantage that they can no longer take any more false steps or suffer any further losses For them the whole game is over, for good and for ill, while for us, whose civilization is still 'a going concern', the crucial part of this game is probably still to play. Suppose that we were to lose the next point, and after that to go on losing till the end of the set and the match, then the single point to the good, on which our present pretensions to superiority rest, would soon be lost sight of by the spectators of the tournament, and we should be bracketed thenceforth with our Hellenic rivals in the broad and simple category of 'losers'.[3]

and all the constituent provinces of the United Netherlands and cantons of the Swiss Confederation, in the domain of the Holy Roman Empire. (Dutch Flanders, which was carved by Dutch arms out of a Spanish possession that had once been included in the Kingdom of France, was not one of the original constituent provinces of the United Netherlands; it was one of the conquered *Generalitätsländer* which served the Confederation as a kind of military glacis on its anti-Spanish front.)

[1] For the philosophical contemporaneity of all representatives of the species of society which we have called 'civilizations', see I. C (iii) (*c*), vol. i, pp. 172–4, above.

[2] See the passage quoted in IV. C (iii) (*c*) 1, on p. 251, above.

[3] For the philosophical equivalence of all the civilizations that have ever come into existence up to date see I. C (iii) (*d*), vol. i, pp. 175–7, above.

This general consideration should move us to take stock of our own position to-day, and to ask ourselves in what sense and to what extent we have really done better than our Hellenic fellow wanderers in the wilderness. Let us grant that we have been rather more successful in finding a satisfactory political response to the challenge of a sudden large increase in the material scale of our social life. Our Western response to this challenge has been to replace the medieval Sovereign City-State, on the pattern of Florence or Nürnberg, by the modern Sovereign National State, on the pattern of France or Great Britain, as the standard sovereign unit in our political system; and this imposing work of political reconstruction, which is now an accomplished fact, does, no doubt, compare advantageously with the abortive Hellenic efforts to replace a sovereign Athens or a sovereign Tarentum by building up an Aetolian or Achaean Confederacy or a Seleucid Asia or a Roman Italy. But is this judgement the last word? Can we pronounce, with any assurance, that the bold and varied Hellenic experiments of the third century B.C. would not ultimately have resulted in successes comparable to ours if this Hellenic experimentation had not been prematurely cut short by Roman 'knock-out blows'? And, when we inquire how these 'knock-out blows' came to be delivered at this critical moment of Hellenic history, can we pronounce, again, that we ourselves are immune from the possibility of a corresponding disaster in our own world at the present day? As soon as we put the question, we are aware that the answer is not, this time, in our favour; for a 'knock-out blow' which will unify our world by force, and at the same time ruin our civilization, in the Roman manner, is a catastrophe of which we now live in daily dread.[1] As we tremble at this menace which darkens our sky, we long in vain for the assurance with which one Jewish observer was able to confront the vast calamities of the second century B.C.

'Thou shalt not be afraid for the terror by night; nor for the arrow that flieth by day;

'Nor for the pestilence that walketh in darkness; nor for the destruction that wasteth at noonday.

'A thousand shall fall at thy side, and ten thousand at thy right hand, but it shall not come nigh thee.'[2]

The verse that expresses what we actually feel is:

'I am afflicted and ready to die from my youth up; while I suffer thy terrors I am distracted.'[3]

And these terrors beset us because, so far, we have failed, as utterly as the Hellenes failed, to solve the political problem which is

[1] See the present chapter, p. 407, and V. C (ii) (*b*), vol. vi, pp. 314–15 and 319–21, below.

[2] Psalm xci. 5–7.

[3] Psalm lxxxviii. 15.

crucial for our destinies, as it was for theirs—the problem of establishing a political world order.

If we ask ourselves, last of all, why it is that this vital and ever more importunate problem continues to baffle us, we shall find that our reading of Hellenic history supplies us with a key to the riddle. We have seen that the Hellenic Society brought itself to ruin by an inveterate idolization of City-State Sovereignty; and a similar infatuation with the sovereignty of national states is the corresponding aberration that threatens now to bring our ruin upon us.[1] These Western and Hellenic political idolatries are alike destructive, and this through a fundamental vice which is common to them both. They both substitute a part for the whole as the object of devotion; for, however much the national state and the city-state and the federal commonwealth of city-states or nations may differ from one another in size and constitution and structure, they are all akin in being polities of the parochial species, mere fractions or articulations of the society within which, and for which, they exist and to which they owe their being. Without transcending the sovereignty of such parochial states, it is not possible to establish oecumenical law and order; and, so long as this problem remains unsolved, the difficulty of solving it and the penalty of failing are merely increased by enlarging the unit-size of the parochial sovereign body politic from the dimensions of a Plataea to those of a Seleucid Empire, or from the dimensions of a San Marino to those of a British Commonwealth.

This challenge of the conflict between Parochial Sovereignty and world order confronts our world to-day as it confronted the Hellenic World from the fifth to the last century B.C. Are we going to rise to it, or are we, too, going to succumb? The answer to that question still lies to-day 'on the knees of the Gods'—or, more truly, in the hands of ourselves and our children. With what measure of success or failure we shall handle our destiny we cannot yet prophesy; but there are perhaps two things to be said about the Hellenic parallel. On the one hand the fact that the Hellenic Society was worsted by this challenge does not establish any presumption about our future Western fortunes, either one way or the other; the ordeal has no uniform or predestined outcome; the issue lies with us. On the other hand there is a not unimportant point on which the Hellenic parallel does, perhaps, afford a valid analogy and so supply a basis for a cautious prognostication.

[1] In the Vatican City on the 17th July, 1938, Pope Pius XI, in an address delivered to French missionary nuns, denounced 'this curse of exaggerated Nationalism, which hinders the saving of souls, which raises barriers between people and people, which is contrary not only to the Law of God but to the Faith itself, and to the Creed which is said and sung in all churches throughout the World'.

On the showing of Hellenic history, we may expect that our present Western problem of transcending National Sovereignty will receive its solution—in so far as it receives one at all—in some place or places where this institution of National Sovereignty has not been erected into an object of idolatrous worship. We shall not expect to see salvation come from the historic national states of Western Europe—a France or a Spain or a Hungary or a Sweden —where every political thought and feeling and act is bound up with a Parochial Sovereignty which is itself the recognized symbol of a glorious national past. It is not in this Epimethean psychological environment that our society can look forward to making the necessary discovery of some new form of international association which will bring a Parochial Sovereignty under the discipline of a higher law and so forestall the otherwise inevitable calamity of its annihilation by a 'knock-out blow'. If this discovery is ever made, the laboratory of political experimentation where we may expect to see it materialize will be some body politic like the British Commonwealth of Nations, which has mated the experience of one ancient European national state with the plasticity of a number of 'new countries' overseas; or else it will be some body politic like the Soviet Union, which is attempting to organize a number of non-Western communities into an entirely new kind of polity on the basis of a Western revolutionary idea. In the Soviet Union we may perhaps discern the Seleucid Empire of our world, and in the British Empire its Roman Commonwealth. Will these and suchlike bodies politic, on the outskirts of our modern Western cosmos of sovereign nations, eventually produce some form of political structure that will enable us to give more substance, before it is too late, to our inchoate League of Nations? We cannot tell; but we can almost feel sure that, if these pioneers fail, the work will never be done by the petrified devotees of the idol of National Sovereignty.

The East Roman Empire.

A classic case of the idolization of an institution bringing a civilization to grief is the fatal infatuation of Orthodox Christendom with a ghost of the Roman Empire, an ancient institution which had fulfilled its historical function, and completed its natural term of life, in serving as the 'apparented' Hellenic Society's universal state.[1]

At earlier points in this Study[2] we have noticed that the Orthodox

[1] See I. C (i) (*a*), vol. i, pp. 52–3; IV. C (iii) (*b*) 10, in the present volume, pp. 208 and 213–14; and the present chapter, p. 306, above.

[2] In Part III. A, vol. iii, p. 26, and in IV. C (ii) (*b*) 1, in the present volume, p. 72, above.

Christian Civilization broke down in the last quarter of the tenth century of our Era. The most prominent outward symptom of the breakdown was the outbreak of the disastrous Bulgaro-Roman War of A.D. 977–1019. This disaster overtook Orthodox Christendom, and blighted its growth, barely three hundred years after its first emergence out of the chaos of the post-Hellenic interregnum; and this growth-span is miserably short by comparison with the life-history of our Western Christendom—a sister civilization which was coeval with Orthodox Christendom in its birth, while its growth, for all that we know,[1] may still be going forward in our day, nearly a thousand years after the date at which the growth of the twin civilization was unmistakably cut short.

How are we to account for this striking difference between the fortunes of two societies which started life at the same moment and in the same circumstances? The actual outcome, as the passage of a thousand years has unfolded it before our eyes to-day, is the more remarkable considering that it is the exact inverse of what would have been prophesied by any intelligent and impartial observer—an ambassador from Cordova or Baghdad, or a Confucian litteratus from Si Ngan—who might have happened to make a comparative study of Orthodox and Western Christendom in A.D. 938. Such an observer at such a date—or even a hundred years later, before the tardy vitality of the West and the premature senility of the Orthodox Christian Society had become blatantly manifest—would certainly have declared, and that with some confidence, that the Orthodox Christian Civilization's prospects were decidedly brighter than those of this society's Western sister. He would have justified this judgement on the ground that, of the two, the Orthodox Christian Society was manifestly the more effective; and he could have explained what he meant in concrete terms if he had been challenged to give illustrations. He could have recalled, for example, that when the Primitive Muslim Arabs had broken out of the Arabian Peninsula in the seventh century of the Christian Era, they had been brought to a halt on the Orthodox Christian front at the line of the Taurus, almost within sight of the North Arabian Steppe and within easy striking distance of the headquarters of the Umayyad Power at Damascus,[2] whereas they were able, when they broke into Western Christendom out of Egypt, to

[1] It is, of course, impossible for us, in our generation, to be sure that our civilization has not yet broken down, either in our own time or even some time back. The historical beginning of a 'Time of Troubles' can only be recognized, for certain, in retrospect, and we may be far advanced in social disintegration without being aware of it. We can only be sure, in our day, that our society has not yet been gathered up into a universal state! This question of where we stand in the life-history of our own society in our own day has been touched upon in I. B (iv), vol. i, pp. 36–7, above, and is discussed further in V. C (ii) (*b*), vol. vi, pp. 312–21, as well as in Part XII, below.

[2] See II. D (vii), vol. ii, pp. 367–8, above.

overrun the whole of North-West Africa and the whole of the Iberian Peninsula, and to pass the line of the Pyrenees, before they met with any effective resistance.[1] Our hypothetical tenth-century observer could have gone on to point out that the means by which Orthodox Christendom succeeded in stopping the Arab offensive at the line of the Taurus, and thereby retaining possession of the whole of its own Anatolian patrimony, was by rallying and concentrating its own hard-pressed forces through an evocation of a ghost of the Roman Empire. The timeliness and effectiveness and apparent permanence of this great political achievement of the Emperor Leo Syrus[2] would have offered our observer a brilliant foil for showing up the blackness of the failure of the corresponding attempt in the West, when this was made, two generations later, by Charlemagne.[3]

Why was it, then, that the Orthodox Christian Civilization so soon belied its early promise, while, inversely, the Western Civilization has so very much more than made up for an unpromising start? The explanation lies precisely in the contrast, which we have just called to mind, between Charlemagne's failure and Leo's success. Though the Carolingian evocation of a ghost of the Roman Empire was no more than a flash in the pan, its brief flame was enough to burn up the reserves of energy which the infant Western Society had been accumulating for about a hundred years before Charlemagne's accession to power. Charlemagne expended these slender and precious reserves in an unachievably ambitious attempt, first to unify the Western World by force, and then to enlarge its borders by the same means. The fratricidal struggle between the Franks and the Lombards was carried to the extreme conclusion of an outright conquest of one of the two principal surviving Western 'successor-states' of the Roman Empire by the other; and this war of aggression beyond the Alps was capped by another beyond the Rhine—the Thirty Years' War against the Saxons—which was still more exhausting to the official victor.[4] In fact, Charlemagne's long series of Pyrrhic military victories condemned the infant society, whose resources he was burning up, to a crushing social defeat; and this defeat is registered in the ensuing social calamity of 'the post-Carolingian interregnum', which lasted from the morrow of Charlemagne's death until more than half-way

[1] See II. D (vii), vol. ii, pp. 361 and 378–81, with Annex IV, above.

[2] For the work of Leo Syrus see I. C (i) (*b*), vol. i, p. 64, footnote 3; III. C (ii) (*b*), vol. iii, pp. 274–6; and IV. C (ii) (*b*) 1, in the present volume, p. 73, above, and the present chapter, p. 341, below.

[3] For Charlemagne's failure see II. D (v), vol. ii, p. 167, and II. D (vii), vol. ii, pp. 343–5 and 368, above, and IV. C (iii) (*c*) 3 (α), in the present volume, pp. 488–90, below.

[4] See II. D (v), vol. ii, p. 167, and II. D (vii), vol. ii, pp. 345–6, above, and, in the present volume, IV. C (iii) (*c*) 3 (α), pp. 489–90, and IV. C (iii) (*c*) 3 (β), p. 523, below.

through the tenth century, and which was marked by the recurrence, in an acute form, of the grievous social maladies of the foregoing interregnum that had followed the break-up of the Roman Empire, from which the West had so recently and so painfully shaken itself free.[1] If the West managed to survive this second time of tribulation, at the price of seeing its growth checked and retarded for no longer than 150 years, it had to thank the stars that had fought against Charlemagne in their courses. If Charlemagne's evocation of a ghost of the Roman Empire had not proved a fiasco, the infant Western Civilization on whose shoulders he had recklessly imposed this crushing incubus might well have succumbed; and if this diagnosis of our early Western history is correct it will illuminate the history of Orthodox Christendom likewise. If the West was saved by Charlemagne's failure, we may find that the Orthodox Christian Society was ruined by Leo's success.[2]

In fact, we have already observed, at an earlier point in this Study,[3] that Leo's achievement, in effectively resuscitating the institution of the Roman Empire on Orthodox Christian soil, was a response that was over-successful to a challenge that was excessive; and the overstrain of this *tour de force* exacted its penalty in the shape of a malformation. The outward symptom was a premature and excessive aggrandizement of the State in Orthodox Christian social life at the expense of all other institutions. The inward aberration was the idolization of a particular historic polity which had been conjured back from its grave and been decked out in the prestige of an emotionally glorified past in order to save a nascent society from imminent destruction.

This disastrous idolization of a ghost of the Roman Empire in the Orthodox Christian World was, of course, in one sense natural; but in another sense it was perverse; for the region in which the infant Orthodox Christian Society had recently emerged, and the plot of ground on which the East Roman *Imperium Redivivum* was now being erected, were haunted by vivid memories of recent disasters which had been the penalty of an obstinate local idolization of the very polity whose spectre was now being deliberately evoked.

In the last chapter of the history of the Roman Empire, which may be taken, for this purpose, as having begun with the death of

1 For the Völkerwanderung of the Scandinavians, which was one of the conspicuous external manifestations of the post-Carolingian 'heroic age', see II. D (v), vol. ii, pp. 194–202, and II. D (vii), vol. ii, pp. 346–57, above. For the contemporary Magyar Vôlkerwanderung see Part III A, Annex II, vol. iii, pp. 441–3, above.

2 This point has been made, by anticipation, in II. D (vii), vol. ii, p. 368, above.

3 See II. D (vii), vol. ii, pp. 369 and 384–5, above.

the Emperor Theodosius the Great in A.D. 395,[1] there had been, at first, a notable differentiation in the fortunes of the Hellenic universal state in its Latin provinces on the one hand and in its Greek and Oriental provinces on the other. In the Latin provinces there had been an immediate financial, political, and social collapse; the framework of the Empire had broken up and disappeared, and the political vacuum had been occupied by the automatically emancipated proprietors of great agricultural estates and leaders of powerful barbarian war-bands, while the Church had stepped into the social breach. Meanwhile, in an age which thus saw the dissolution of the Empire in the West, the Imperial régime in the Greek and Oriental provinces succeeded in riding one after another of the waves by which its counterpart in the Latin provinces was being broken up.[2]

For example, the successive barbarian war-lords—a Visigothic Alaric and an Ostrogothic Theodoric—who made a motion to carve out 'successor-states' for themselves in the Constantinopolitan Government's domain in the Balkan Peninsula, were adroitly 'passed on', by Constantinopolitan diplomacy, into the derelict dominions of the sister Imperial Government beyond the Adriatic; and the more ambitious barbarian adventurers in the regular Imperial service, who sought to make themselves the masters instead of the servants of the Imperial Government, were courageously crushed before their plans were ripe. Gainas the Goth, who was destroyed in A.D. 400,[3] and Aspar the Alan, who was destroyed in A.D. 471, had been potential Ricimers or Odovacers; but the Imperial authorities at Constantinople were not content simply to nip these attempts at barbarian usurpation in the bud as they threatened to unfold themselves. The statesmanship of Leo the Great (*imperabat* A.D. 457–74) cut the evil at the root by releasing the Empire from its perilous dependence upon barbarian mercenaries from a no-man's-land outside the Imperial frontiers. This breach with a vicious practice which had been growing upon the Empire for the past hundred years was a moral triumph; and Leo made it also

[1] For other purposes the year 378, which saw the overthrow of the Roman infantry by the Gothic cavalry at Adrianople, is perhaps a better conventional date for signalizing the end of the *Pax Romana*. (For the technical military aspect of the defeat of the legionary by the cataphract at the Battle of Adrianople see IV. C (iii) (*c*) 2 (γ), in the present volume, pp. 440–5, below.)

[2] See Bury, J. B.: 'Causes of the Survival of the Roman Empire in the East', reprinted from *The Quarterly Review*, vol. cxcii, No. 383, pp. 146–55, in *Selected Essays of J. B. Bury* (Cambridge 1930, University Press).

[3] The moral, as well as political, crisis that was resolved in this grim way has left an echo in Synesius's *De Regno*, § 14 (p. 1089 B)–§ 18 (p. 1100 D). The Cyrenaean advocate of strong measures at Constantinople lived to practise in his home province what he had once preached in the capital of the Empire. For Synesius's assumption of the double burden of a shepherd of souls and a warden of the marches see II. D (v), vol. ii, pp. 165–6, above.

a material success by finding an alternative recruiting-ground for the Imperial Army in an enclave of recrudescent barbarism in the interior. He relieved the Empire, once for all, of its Gothic and Alan soldiery by substituting his Isaurians;[1] and by this shrewd stroke he killed two birds with one stone; for, in providing a lawful and honourable outlet for the Isaurians' energies, he also relieved the Empire from the ravages of a gang of native brigands in its midst who, in the days of its weakness, had been almost as great a thorn in its flesh as the bands of alien marauders from the north bank of the Danube.[2]

This strong-minded military reform was given the chance to produce its salutary effects by an equally strong-minded breach with another vicious practice. Leo the Great's successor Anastasius (*imperabat* A.D. 491–518) abolished, in the provinces under the Constantinopolitan Government's rule, the morally iniquitous and economically disastrous institution of corporate responsibility for the payment of taxes, and reintroduced the system of direct collection from each individual taxpayer by Imperial officials.[3] Thus, in the course of the fifth century of the Christian Era, an Empire which was going to pieces in the Latin provinces was re-equipped in the Greek and Oriental provinces with a sound army, a sound administration, and a sound financial system. We may add that both Anastasius and his immediate predecessor Zeno (*imperabat* A.D. 474–91) also wrestled, not unsuccessfully, with a particularly difficult problem which was peculiar to their own domain. The threat of a rift between the Greek and the Oriental provinces of the Empire had declared itself, in the fifth century, in the ecclesiastical danger-signal of a Nestorian and a Monophysite reaction against Catholic Christianity;[4] and this danger was provisionally

[1] These so-called 'Isaurians' who made their mark on the history of the later Roman Empire appear to have been the inhabitants of the ancient Cilicia Trachea (which had been a nest of pirates in the last century B.C. as well as in the fourth and fifth centuries of the Christian Era), and not the inhabitants of the cities of Old and New Isaura, which lay, not on the seaward-facing Cilician, but on the landward-facing Lycaonian, slope of the Taurus (see Jones, A. H. M.: *The Cities of the Eastern Roman Provinces* (Oxford 1937, Clarendon Press), pp. 138–40 and 214).

[2] The Roman Emperor Leo I's method of pacifying Isauria may be compared with the policy of Lord Chatham in enlisting the Scottish Highlanders in the British Army after the suppression of the rebellion of A.D. 1745. It must be added that the Isaurians were not converted to law and order in a day, and that the Imperial Government found them almost as difficult to manage as the barbarian soldiery from beyond the frontiers whose place they had taken. Politically, however, the Isaurians were very much less dangerous than the Alans or the Goths, as was proved by the Imperial Government's success in eventually reducing them to obedience, not only at Constantinople, but also in their native highland fastnesses, between A.D. 491 and A.D. 496.

[3] The benefits that were to be expected, *a priori*, from this reform were perhaps diminished by the practice of putting up these new official posts to auction. This vicious system of appointment must have tended to turn officials who were nominally civil servants into something very like the speculative tax-farmers of the last century of the Roman Republic.

[4] For the significance of the Nestorian and Monophysite movements as one stage

parried by the statesmanship of these two Constantinopolitan Emperors.

In fine, the Imperial régime in the Greek and Oriental provinces distinguished itself, throughout the fifth century, by determined efforts to maintain the Empire as 'a going concern' which stand out in striking contrast to the contemporary 'defeatism' of the Imperial régime in the West; and for the moment these efforts seemed to have been rewarded with a triumphant success. The two portions of the divided heritage of Theodosius the Great, which had faced the opening of the fifth century side by side with equally fair—or gloomy—prospects, had apparently drifted poles apart before the same century closed. In the West the Empire had run upon the rocks and suffered total shipwreck; in the Centre and the East the ship of state had not only survived but had actually been overhauled and re-rigged in the course of a stormy passage which had carried it, in the end, into calmer waters. Yet the contrast which the fifth century had brought out was shown by the sixth century to be, after all, superficial and impermanent. For everything that a Leo and a Zeno and an Anastasius had sedulously and cumulatively gathered in was scattered to the winds in the single reign of a Justinian (*imperabat* A.D. 527–65) who was betrayed, by an idolization of the vanished Empire of Constantine and Augustus, into indulging the same prodigious ambition, with the same disastrous results, as his latter-day Austrasian mimic, Charlemagne.[1]

The slender store of social energy which had been so carefully hoarded and so conscientiously bequeathed to him by his predecessors was burnt up by Justinian in his abortive efforts to restore the territorial integrity of the Empire by reincorporating the lost Latin provinces in Africa across the Mediterranean and in Europe beyond the Adriatic.[2] And his death in A.D. 565 was the signal for

in a series of Syriac attempts to expel the intrusive Hellenic culture from the Syriac Society's ancestral domain see I. C (i) (*b*), vol. i, p. 91; II. D (vi), vol. ii, p. 236; II. D (vii), vol. ii, pp. 286–7, above, and V. C (i) (*c*) 2, vol. v, p. 127, below.

[1] The misguidedness and disastrousness of Justinian's ambition have been touched upon, by anticipation, in III. C (i) (*b*), vol. iii, p. 162, above. See further V. C (ii) (*a*), vol. vi, pp. 223–5, below.

[2] There was a minor group of Latin provinces—stretching across the Balkan Peninsula, in a narrow belt, from Praevalitana on the Adriatic to Lower Moesia on the Black Sea—which had remained in the Constantinopolitan Government's hands continuously down to Justinian's own day. The Theodosian partition of the Roman Empire had segregated the Latin from the Greek and Oriental provinces without conscious design, and therefore without precision. The line of partition was consciously determined by considerations that were strategic and administrative, not linguistic or cultural. And on purely geographical grounds Constantinople was a more convenient centre than Milan for the administration of the Latin-speaking districts of the Prefecture of Illyricum and the Diocese of Thrace. These Transadriatic Latin provinces were the nursery of a number of famous Emperors. Diocletian came from Praevalitana, Constantine the Great from Dardania. Dardania was also the home province of Justinian himself; and his native Latinity, of which he was not only conscious but was also vain, was one of the factors which moved him to embark upon a programme of reconquest in the Latin West which had not the same attraction for an Isaurian Zeno or for an Epi-

a collapse of the Empire in the Greek and Oriental provinces which resembled the collapse in the West after the death of Theodosius the Great—except that it came with redoubled swiftness and force in revenge for having been staved off for 170 years longer.

In the relatively short interregnum of a hundred and fifty years that intervened between the death of Justinian and the accession of Leo Syrus, the social fabric of the Roman Empire was more cruelly battered, and more thoroughly destroyed, in the East than it was in the West during an interregnum of more than twice as long a Time-span that separated the date of Leo's accession from the death of Theodosius. The intensity of the tribulation in the Constantinopolitan domain, when the storm broke here at last, may be measured by the length and the intensity of the series of great wars with which this century and a half was filled. The two Romano-Persian Wars of A.D. 572–91 and A.D. 603–28 were followed, without a breathing-space, by a life-and-death struggle with the Primitive Muslim Arabs which began in A.D. 632 and which continued to endanger the very existence of a nascent Orthodox Christian Society until after the failure of the second Arab siege of Constantinople in A.D. 717. In this almost unintermittent warfare on the eastern front all the Oriental provinces of the Empire were shorn away, as well as Justinian's conquests in North-West Africa, which the Arabs took in their stride on their war-path from the Nile to the Loire. Meanwhile the greater part of Justinian's Italian conquests fell a prey to the Lombards, and the greater part of the Balkan provinces to the Slavs.

These Balkan provinces, which were the metropolitan territory of the Constantinopolitan Empire on the European side of the Straits, suffered cruelly in spite of their good fortune in lying outside the Oriental war-zone. In these provinces not merely the Imperial régime but the very fabric of Society, including the physical stock of the local human fauna, was almost entirely wiped out. When the darkness that descends upon the Balkan Peninsula after Justinian's death begins to lighten again in the course of the eighth century, we find that the Slavonic barbarians who have been drifting in have not merely conquered the greater part of the country (as the Lombards have conquered Italy), but have also repopulated this *ci-devant* Roman peninsula[1] (as the English barbarians have repopulated the *ci-devant* Roman island of Britain, and the British

damnian Greek Anastasius (though the latter might conceivably have been glad to recover the Island of Sicily, which was an anomalous Greek enclave in an otherwise Latin Prefecture of Italy).

1 The Slavs appear to have made their first permanent settlement on Roman soil in A.D. 581 (Dvorník, F.: *Les Slaves, Byzance et Rome au ixe Siècle* (Paris 1926, Champion), pp. 4–5).

refugees the peninsula of Armorica).[1] Just as, in eighth-century Britain, the pre-English population only survived in a recognizable shape in the highlands and peninsulas of 'the Celtic Fringe', so, in the eighth-century Balkan Peninsula, the pre-Slavonic Latin-speaking and Greek-speaking inhabitants only retained their mother-tongue and other remnants of their social patrimony in a few isolated fastnesses among the mountains and along the coasts. This annihilation which Justinian brought upon his own kith and kin in his own Illyrian homeland[2] stands out in contrast to the tribulations of Italy and Sicily, which respectively remained a Latin-speaking and a Greek-speaking country after all the Alarics and Genserics and Justinians and Totilas and Alboins had come and gone and successively done their worst to turn their Hesperian battle-ground into a wilderness.

Thus, *de facto*, the Roman Empire perished in its Central and Eastern provinces after the death of Justinian, as, after the death of Theodosius a hundred and seventy years before, it had perished *de facto* in the West.[3]

[1] For the transmarine migrations of the English across the North Sea to Britain and the Bretons across the Channel to Brittany see II. D (iii), vol. ii, pp. 86–100, above.

[2] Justinian's responsibility for the tragedy of Illyricum is touched upon further in the present chapter, pp. 397–8, and in V. C (ii) (*a*), vol. vi, p. 224–5, below.

[3] Among our modern Western historians it is customary to take it for granted that in the eastern portion of the Theodosian heritage the Roman Empire survived until A.D. 1453, and to draw a contrast between its long survival here and its swift disappearance in the West nearly a thousand years earlier, in A.D. 476. This traditional academic antithesis is based on the consideration that the western line of Theodosius's successors, who ruled at Milan or Ravenna, did come to an end in A.D. 476, while the eastern line, whose capital was Constantinople, did officially continue to rule a Roman Empire from A.D. 395 to A.D. 1453 without any formal break (if the Greek princes of Nicaea are accepted as the legal representatives of the Imperial Government of Constantinople during the Latin usurpation of A.D. 1204–61). These facts are not inaccurately stated so far as they go. They are, however, so arbitrarily selected that, in the isolation in which they are usually presented, they become positively misleading. In truth they have as little to do with historical pretensions as they have with historical realities.

If we take our stand on the historical realities, then it seems correct to say, as has been said above, that the Roman Empire began to break up in the western portion of Theodosius's heritage immediately after Theodosius's own death in A.D. 395, and in the eastern portion immediately after the death of his successor Justinian I in A.D. 565. It is true that in Constantinople, between this latter date and the failure of the second Arab siege in A.D. 717, there never ceased to be a Government which claimed to be the Government of the Roman Empire; but, if we ignore claims and take only realities into account, we shall pronounce that, at any rate from the death of Maurice in A.D. 602, the Roman Empire, outside the walls of Constantinople, was as truly non-existent in the *ci-devant* Greek and Oriental provinces as it was in the *ci-devant* Latin provinces in the same age. A so-called Imperial Government in Constantinople which had to look on helplessly while a Slav population supplanted a Latin and Greek population in the Balkan Peninsula, and an improvised system of army-corps districts replaced the Diocletianic provincial system in Anatolia, cannot be regarded as a real Government in any significant sense of the words.

On the other hand, if we amuse ourselves by stepping off the solid ground of reality and following the will-o'-the-wisp of constitutional pretensions, we shall find that, in strict constitutional theory, the two administrative areas into which Theodosius had partitioned the Empire (without prejudice to its remaining constitutionally one and indivisible) were officially re-united in A.D. 476 under the sole authority of the Imperial Government at Constantinople, and so remained (through centuries in which the Constantinopolitan Emperor sometimes had no power, *de facto*, beyond the Bosphorus and the Golden Gate) until the proclamation of Charlemagne as Emperor at Rome on

Indeed, in the seventh century of the Christian Era there was every indication that a nascent society of Orthodox Christendom was entering—tardily yet decidedly—upon a course on which the sister society of Western Christendom was by then already set, and from which Charlemagne subsequently failed to deflect her. When the Empire broke up in the West, it may be said, broadly speaking, that two things happened. In the first place, political authority became plural instead of singular and parochial instead of oecumenical. In the second place—and this second development in the West was a corollary of the first—the political authority of the defunct Empire's parochial 'successor-states' came to be overshadowed by the ecclesiastical authority of an oecumenical Church which, in contrast to the Empire, had succeeded in preserving both its existence and its unity. A symbol for the expression of this unity, and an instrument for the assertion of it, was provided for the Catholic Church in the West by the ancient institution of the Roman Patriarchate or Papacy; and, after the disappearance of the Empire in the provinces which were under the ecclesiastical jurisdiction of the Roman See, the Papacy established a moral hegemony over successive generations of parochial communities in Western Christendom: first over the ephemeral Western 'successor-states' of the Roman Empire itself,[1] and then over the 'successor-states' of the ephemeral Carolingian Empire and of the contemporary English Kingdom of Wessex.[2] Among the successors of this second batch of 'successor-states', from which the living parochial states of our latter-day Western World are lineally descended, the pretension to a plenitude of parochial sovereignty was not overtly asserted against the Papal claim to an oecumenical supremacy until after the opening of the sixteenth century.[3] In the seventh century there were at least two occasions when Orthodox Christendom set its foot tentatively on a parallel path.

the Christmas Day of A.D. 800. From that date until A.D. 811/12 the title to the Empire was in dispute between one Emperor ruling from Constantinople and another ruling from Aachen. After the latter date, at which the rival claimants mutually recognized the legitimacy of one another's titles, there was an East Roman Empire which survived till A.D. 1453, or at any rate till A.D. 1204, and a West Roman Empire ('the Holy Roman Empire') which survived till A.D. 1806 (for this latter constitutional fiction see I. B (iv), Annex, vol. i, pp. 343–4, above), or at any rate until the beginning of 'The Great Interregnum' in A.D. 1254.

It will be seen that the historical realities and the constitutional fictions have little to do with one another, and that in the realm of the realities the Roman Empire broke up in the Greek and Oriental provinces from A.D. 565 onwards, and was virtually non-existent there, as well as in the Latin provinces, after A.D. 602.

1 For the shortness of the lives, and transitoriness of the influence, of these 'successor-states' see I. C (i) (*a*), vol. i, pp. 58–62, above, and Part VIII, below.

2 For the role of the Carolingian Empire in the political history of the Western World see I. B (iii), vol. i, pp. 32–4, and I. B (iv), vol. i, pp. 37–9, above. For the role of the Kingdom of Wessex see I. B (iv), vol. i, p. 37, and II. D (v), vol. ii, pp. 195–6, above.

3 For a discussion of the history of the relations between the Papacy and the parochial states of Western Christendom see IV. C (iii) (*b*) 11, pp. 214–22, above, and IV. C (iii) (*c*) 3 (*β*), pp. 512–84, below.

In A.D. 618,[1] when the Asiatic provinces of the Constantinopolitan Imperial Government were overrun by the Persians, and its European provinces by the Slavs and Avars, the African Emperor Heraclius, who had been summoned as a saviour to Constantinople and been invested with the purple there eight years before, despaired, before the end of the first decennium of his Herculean labours,[2] of saving even a simulacrum of the Imperial authority in a region where the reality had dwindled to a shadow. He accordingly made arrangements for transferring the seat of the nominal Imperial Government to his native Carthage, and he had actually conveyed the Imperial gold reserve on board his ships when his intention was discovered and his plan vetoed by the Oecumenical Patriarch of Constantinople, Sergius, who bound the Emperor over, by a solemn oath, never to abandon the city where the Imperial capital had been established by Constantine. Under this moral compulsion Heraclius renounced his project of evacuation, remained at his post in the East, and crowned a second decennium of labours with the victory of A.D. 628. But this triumph, though complete, was only momentary; for the defeat of the Sasanian Power in a struggle which left both belligerents exhausted simply opened the way for the delivery of a fresh onslaught upon the salvaged wreckage of the Empire by a still more formidable assailant.[3] In A.D. 632 the Arabs took up the offensive which the Persians had just been forced to relinquish; and, after the Heraclian Dynasty had battled against this new attack from the east for thirty years on end, with hardly a breathing-space and no prospect of permanent relief, Heraclius's grandson, Constans II, reverted in A.D. 662 to the family policy of evacuating Constantinople and withdrawing westward to the Dynasty's last line of defence against an Oriental aggressor.

Constans actually succeeded in carrying out the project which his grandfather had been compelled to renounce. This time the clergy and people of Constantinople contented themselves with retaining the truant Emperor's household as hostages,[4] while the

[1] Or perhaps in A.D. 619, if we are to guess that the deciding consideration in Heraclius's mind was the interruption of the corn-supply of the City of Constantinople in consequence of a Persian occupation of Egypt which appears to have taken place not earlier than the latter year (see pp. 40–1 of the proof-sheets of an unpublished paper by Professor N. H. Baynes on 'The Military Operations of the Emperor Heraclius, A.D. 609–30').

[2] For the labours of Heraclius see III. C (ii) (*b*), vol. iii, p. 269, footnote 4, above, and V. C (ii) (*a*), vol. vi, pp. 210–11, below.

[3] See II. D (vii), vol. ii, pp. 287–8, above.

[4] Constans, unlike his grandfather, was a ruler whose will could not be opposed with impunity. He was also—again, unlike his grandfather—a ruler whose subjects might feel satisfaction rather than regret at the prospect of his departure from their midst. Anyhow the Constantinopolitans either could not or would not take steps to prevent Constans from leaving the Imperial City for the West.

truant himself made war on the Lombard intruders in Southern Italy, visited Rome, and established his headquarters in Syracuse—presumably with an eye to organizing the defence of North-West Africa against the next Arab attack.[1] The execution of Constans' policy, however, was cut short within six years of his departure from Constantinople by the assassination of the truant Emperor in his Sicilian fastness in A.D. 668; his son and successor Constantine IV was promptly invested with the purple in Constantinople; and so it came about that the next great Oriental offensive was met and repulsed by the Heraclian Dynasty at the Dynasty's eastern outpost and not, after all, in its western homeland. The Arabs duly compensated themselves for their discomfiture before the walls of Constantinople in A.D. 673–7 by making their definitive conquest of North-West Africa at the turn of the seventh and eighth centuries, and then pressing on across the Straits of Gibraltar and the Pyrenees; but this diversion of Arab energies was made at Western Christendom's expense,[2] while the foregoing Arab reverse at the Bosphorus created the conditions[3] in which a new turn was given to the history of Orthodox Christendom some forty years later by the fatal genius of Leo Syrus.

We may pause to speculate on the alternative course which Orthodox Christian history might have taken if Heraclius had not been prevented from retreating from Constantinople to Carthage, or if Constans had not been assassinated after making good his retreat from Constantinople to Syracuse. We may conjecture that in either of these events the extinction of the Roman Empire in the East in the seventh century would have been followed by results which would have broadly corresponded to the actual results of its extinction in the fifth century in the West.

In the first place we may suppose that the transference of the Imperial Shadow-Government to an apparently more sheltered seat would have had just the opposite consequences from those which Heraclius and Constans intended and expected. Either Carthage or Syracuse would probably have proved on trial to be not a fastness but a trap; and the eastern line of Theodosius's successors would perhaps have been snuffed out here, before the seventh century came to an end, as ingloriously as the western line was actually snuffed out in Italy in A.D. 476.[4]

In the second place we may suppose that, even if the Heraclian Dynasty had succeeded in evacuating Constantinople, an act of

[1] The Arabs had made a first abortive attempt to conquer North-West Africa in A.D. 647.

[2] See II. D (vii), vol ii, pp. 361 and 378–81, with Annex IV, above.

[3] See II. D (vii), vol. ii, pp. 367–8, above.

[4] Grounds for this supposition are given in IV. C (iii) (c) 2 (β), Annex I, below.

desertion which might have proved fatal to the Dynasty itself would not have entailed the annihilation of the nascent society of Orthodox Christendom. When the last paroxysm of the post-Hellenic Völkerwanderung had passed, and the flood of Arab and Slav and Avar and Bulgar barbarian invaders of the eastern portion of the Theodosian heritage had ebbed or subsided, an Orthodox Christian Society would have been still in being and still capable of growth in all probability; but its lineaments would then assuredly have been much more like those of the sister society in the West than like those which were actually imposed upon Orthodox Christendom by Leo Syrus.

In this hypothetical event the now derelict eastern portion of the Theodosian heritage would almost certainly have been partitioned politically for good and all among a number of 'successor-states'. Some of these would have been indigenous growths: we can imagine, for example, that the *ci-devant* Imperial army corps which had withdrawn from Syria and Armenia and Thrace, and had been concentrated and cantoned in Anatolia,[1] would have undergone a gradual metamorphosis into political principalities,[2] while the seafaring population along the seaboards of Anatolia and Greece, and in the Aegean Archipelago, would have fended for itself, like the Venetians and Amalfitans and Neapolitans and Gaetans along the seaboard of Italy, and would have reaped the same reward of *de facto* independence. Contemporaneously the Slav and Bulgar war-bands which fastened upon the Balkan Peninsula would have crystallized into barbarian 'successor-states' corresponding, in a modest way, to those which occupied the greater part of the Western stage during the interregnum that followed the break-up of the Roman Empire in Hesperia.

At the same time we may suppose that this tendency towards

[1] For the parts played bv the Anatolic, Armeniac, and Thracensian army corps in Orthodox Christian history see II. D (iii), vol. ii, pp. 79–81, and II. D (v), vol. ii, pp. 153–4, above.

[2] Indigenous 'successor-states' of a similar origin made a momentary appearance on the stage of Western history immediately after the extinction of the Imperial Government in the western portion of the Theodosian heritage in A.D. 476. Examples are the principality of Nepos in Dalmatia and the principality of Syagrius in the Basin of the Seine. A Nepos and a Syagrius, however, were snuffed out by a Theodoric and a Clovis as easily as a Romulus Augustulus had been snuffed out by an Odovacer; and thereafter the barbarian 'successor-states' had the field almost entirely to themselves in the *ci-devant* Latin provinces of the Roman Empire, save for the passing interlude of the Justinianean reoccupation of North-West Africa and Italy and a fraction of Spain. The only parts of Justinian's Hesperian conquests that did not eventually relapse into barbarian hands were those fragments of Italian territory which were kept out of the hands of the Lombards after having been snatched out of the grasp of the Ostrogoths. This was a paltry net gain to set against the prohibitive costliness of Justinian's conquests. The only notable constructive outcome of the permanent 'de-barbarization' of the Romagna was the communication of the Justinianean *Corpus Juris* to the Western Society, in and after the eleventh century of the Christian Era, thanks to the fact that the *Corpus* had been deposited at Bologna after the Justinianean reconquest and had been subsequently preserved there in cold storage.

political plurality and parochialism, had it declared itself in the Orthodox Christian World, would have been balanced there too, as it actually was in the West, by a simultaneous tendency in the ecclesiastical sphere towards a perpetuation of the Imperial tradition of oecumenical unity in the constitution of the Church. It may be noted that the Patriarch of Constantinople incorporated the word 'Oecumenical' into his title in A.D. 588, on the eve of the political débâcle which was to reduce the Constantinopolitan Imperial Government to a shadow and to make its parade of oecumenical authority ridiculous. Moreover the Constantinopolitan Patriarch John the Faster (*patriarchico munere fungebatur* A.D. 582–95), who thus ventured to claim an Imperial universalism for his ecclesiastical office, was so fortunate as to find in the Patriarch Sergius (*fungebatur* A.D. 610–38) a successor with the vision and the courage to prove in a time of storm and stress that the pretentious-sounding style with which John had decorated the Patriarchal dignity was really something more than an empty phrase.

Sergius showed his strength of character not only in out-willing Heraclius in A.D. 618, but in demonstrating thereafter that his concern to prevent the Emperor from abandoning Constantinople was not due to any misgiving about his own power to take responsibility for the Imperial City in the Emperor's absence. Sergius succeeded so well in restoring Heraclius's *moral* that four years later, in A.D. 622, when a Persian army was still encamped at Calchedon, Heraclius took the audacious step of sailing from Constantinople—this time eastwards and with the Patriarch's sanction—in order to carry the war into the heart of the enemy's country.[1] This bold strategy, pursued through seven successive campaigns, eventually brought King Chosroes to his knees and ended the war in the Christian Empire's favour; but it required two men of action on the Roman side to make this strategy yield a definitive victory instead of an irreparable disaster; and, of these two, Sergius was one. When Heraclius landed in the rear of the Persian advanced-post at Calchedon[2] and plunged into the interior of the Asiatic Continent with the pick of his surviving troops, he would have made his desperate throw in vain if he had had to pay for it by the loss of his capital and base of operations; and it was the Patriarch who rendered possible the Emperor's victory in A.D. 628 by captaining[3] the citizens of Constantinople in A.D. 626 in their magnificent feat of victoriously resisting a concerted siege of the city by the Persians from the

[1] See III. C (ii) (*b*), vol. iii, p. 269, footnote 4, above.

[2] According to Baynes, op. cit., p. 42, the landing-place was somewhere on the shores of the Gulf of Ismid (not the Gulf of Alexandretta), and the date the 5th April, A.D. 622.

[3] The official captain of the garrison of Constantinople was the Magister Militum Bonus, but it was the Oecumenical Patriarch Sergius who was the heart and soul of the defence.

Asiatic and the Avars from the European side of the Bosphorus. It was the Patriarch, again, who enabled the Imperial Government to finance this war of exhaustion by making the Government a loan of all the treasures of the Church;[1] and it was the Patriarch, finally, who faced the problem of safeguarding the fruits of a victory that had been so dearly bought. When the Oriental provinces of the Empire were reunited with the Greek provinces for the last time in the Perso-Roman peace settlement of A.D. 628, Sergius saw that a political unity which had been restored by force of arms could only be maintained by a spiritual pacification; and he therefore immediately set himself to heal the breach between Orthodoxy and Monophysitism, which had been alienating the Oriental provinces from the Empire for the better part of two centuries, by proposing the Monothelete compromise. This theological compromise was abortive—perhaps mainly because the immediate Arab conquest of all the Imperial territories south of Taurus remorselessly cut the political Gordian Knot—but this frustration of Sergius's policy through the sudden overwhelming intervention of an external force does not make the Oecumenical Patriarch's far-sightedness and broad-mindedness any less remarkable.

It will be seen that in Sergius the Oecumenical Patriarchate of Constantinople found an incumbent who can bear comparison with Pope Gregory the Great;[2] and we may feel confident that if, after all, Heraclius had proved a broken reed in Sergius's hands—as Heraclius's predecessors, Maurice and Phocas, had proved in the hands of Gregory—then Sergius would have risen to the occasion in Constantinople as nobly as Gregory actually responded to the challenge of being thrown upon his own resources in Rome. In that event we can imagine the Oecumenical Patriarchate of Constantinople being launched on Sergius's initiative upon the high career to which the Holy See of Rome was dedicated by Gregory the Great. We can see Sergius, like Gregory, taking upon his shoulders the heavy burden of keeping alive the destitute population of a derelict Imperial City; and we can also see him, again like Gregory, making a material achievement bear spiritual fruit by simultaneously transforming the salvaged political capital of a shipwrecked universal state into the central shrine and oracle of a

[1] See Baynes, op. cit., pp. 41–2.

[2] Sergius's courage in allowing Heraclius to embark his expeditionary force for Ismid in A.D. 622, when the Persians were at the gates of Constantinople, may be compared with Gregory's courage in dispatching Augustine to Britain in A.D. 596, when the Lombards were at the gates of Rome (for this comparison see III. C (ii) (*b*), vol. iii, p. 269, footnote 4, above). Sergius's vision in attempting to preserve for Constantinople her reconquered political empire by reconciling the Monophysites with the Calchedonians through the Monothelete compromise may be compared with Gregory's vision in setting out to conquer for Rome an ecclesiastical empire in place of the political empire which she had lost.

new-born society. Under the impetus of Sergius's will and the inspiration of his memory the Oecumenical Patriarchate might have emulated the Holy See in presiding over the growth and expansion of a Christian civilization—giving spiritual harmony and ecclesiastical order to a body social whose political and economic life was turbulent and unco-ordinated, and so leading the turbulence out of a destructive into a creative channel and making out of the disunity a fruitful diversity instead of a barren chaos.

Indeed, if Sergius failed in Orthodox Christendom to lay the foundations of a social structure of the same grandeur as the Western *Respublica Christiana* that was conceived and inaugurated[1] by Gregory, this was largely because Sergius succeeded, and Gregory had no success, in attaining a nearer and narrower objective at which both patriarch and pope were aiming. Sergius did succeed, by an exercise of spiritual power on the shores of the Bosphorus, in evoking a last spasm of life in the shadowy frame of a moribund Imperial Government, as Odysseus, by his blood-offering on the legendary Cimmerian shores of Ocean Stream, was fabled to have reanimated the anaemic shades of the dead.[2] And by this very *tour de force* of transfiguring the Emperor Heraclius into a hero *malgré lui* Sergius ruled out for himself the opportunity of playing Gregory's heroic part. More than that, he secured for Leo Syrus the means of giving Orthodox Christian history a quite un-Western turn a hundred years later. For, by the threefold achievement of salvaging the prestige of the Empire and establishing the prestige of Constantinople[3] and retrieving the Asiatic patrimony of Orthodox Christendom from the clutches of Oriental invaders, Sergius bequeathed to Leo Syrus the indispensable materials for that solid reconstruction of a Roman Empire on Orthodox Christian soil which was Leo's formidable handiwork. And the restoration of the Empire was fatal to the development of the Oecumenical Patriarchate.

In the light of the eventual divergence between the courses of Orthodox Christian and Western history it is interesting to observe that Gregory was no less eager than Sergius to induce the Imperial Government to do its duty in that part of the Imperial dominions in which his own local responsibilities happened to lie. Gregory

1 The actual foundation of the Western *Respublica Christiana* is to be ascribed, not to Gregory the Great, but to Hildebrand, who set himself, some 440 years after Gregory's death, to translate his vision into reality, and who eventually assumed his prototype's name when his own turn came to bear the burden of the Papal office. For Hildebrand's work and its outcome see IV. C (iii) (*c*) 3 (β), pp. 512–84, below.

2 The legend is recounted in the eleventh book of the *Odyssey*.

3 The almost morbidly powerful hold which the City of Constantinople acquired over the sentiment and imagination of Orthodox Christendom was her reward for the heroism with which she defended herself in the successive sieges of A.D. 626 and 673–7 and 717–18 (see II. D (v), Annex II, in vol. ii, p. 400, above).

called upon the Emperor Maurice to stand by Rome as insistently as Sergius called upon Heraclius to stand by Constantinople; and it was only when he lost all hope of seeing the aggression of the Lombards in Italy effectively met by the dispatch of an adequate Imperial expeditionary force from the other side of the Adriatic that Gregory reluctantly stepped into the breach and personally negotiated with the Lombards the peace which the Imperial Government had persistently neglected to impose upon them by force of arms.[1] Gregory was forced into assuming a responsibility from which he shrank, simply because his appeal to the proper quarter had fallen on deaf ears; and his failure to elicit from the Emperor the response which was elicited by Sergius would appear to be accounted for by the obvious handicap of the Roman See's geographical situation. Gregory might perhaps have obtained the Imperial intervention which he implored if his post had happened to lie in the Imperial capital so that he could have appealed to the Emperor in person instead of by correspondence or through the mouth of an apocrisiarius; or he might have been successful again if, in the Imperial strategy of the day, Rome had still been regarded as a central and a vital point which must be defended at all costs, instead of having sunk, as it had, in the Imperial Government's estimation, to the invidious status of an embarrassing outwork, the defence of which could not be held to justify any further dispersion of the heavily committed Imperial forces. If in spite of these obstacles Gregory had succeeded in obtaining for Rome the Imperial consideration which Sergius did obtain for Constantinople, there is no doubt that Gregory would have felt a vast sense of relief. In fine, it might almost be said that Maurice forced Gregory, as Sergius forced Heraclius, to become a hero in spite of himself.

We may add that Gregory's policy of calling upon the Imperial Power to perform its traditional duties was persisted in for at least four hundred years after Gregory's day by Gregory's successors in the Chair of St. Peter.

In the sixth decade of the eighth century, for example, the situation was just what it had been in the last decade of the sixth. In spite of the loss which the prestige of the Constantinopolitan Government must have suffered in Italian eyes through the conquest of Ravenna by the Lombards in 751,[2] we find Pope Stephen II[3] turning immediately thereafter to the East Roman Emperor Constantine V, in the expectation that a prince whose viceroy had

[1] For this achievement of Gregory see III. C (ii) (*b*), vol. iii, p. 269, above.

[2] Up to that time Ravenna had been the seat of the Constantinopolitan exarch or viceroy of the surviving Imperial possessions and dependencies in Italy, including Rome.

[3] Or Stephen III, if account is taken of the three days' reign of his predecessor and namesake.

just been expelled ignominiously from his Italian capital might still save Rome from meeting with Ravenna's fate; and it was only when it became evident that the Emperor could not be prevailed upon to send an expeditionary force to Italy, either for Rome's or for Ravenna's sake, that the Pope, with much heart-searching, made up his mind to address himself to the King of the Franks.

This inveterate Papal habit of looking for assistance to Constantinople is the more remarkable when we remember that in the Roman See's experience the Imperial Government beyond the Adriatic had not only often proved a broken reed, but had quite as often pierced the hand that sought to lean upon it. As far as the Papacy was concerned, the power of the Constantinopolitan Government in Italy, such as it was, had been displayed in acts of tyranny as frequently as in acts of beneficence. Yet Gregory had not been deterred from appealing to Maurice by any memories of the treatment which his predecessors Silverius and Vigilius had received at the hands of Justinian; and Stephen, in his turn, was not deterred from appealing to Constantine V by a longer subsequent series of even more unpleasant incidents: the treatment of Pope Martin I by the Emperor Constans II; the abortive attempt of the Emperor Justinian II to mete out the same measure to Pope Sergius I; the Iconoclasm of the Emperor Leo III, which was anathema to the Western Church; the revenge which Leo had taken for the Papal opposition to his iconoclastic policy (the offended Emperor had forcibly transferred Sicily and Calabria, as well as Illyricum, from the Pope's to the Oecumenical Patriarch's ecclesiastical jurisdiction); and finally the Hyper-Iconoclasm of the Emperor Constantine V himself, to whom Pope Stephen's appeal was addressed!

So strong, even then, was the Papal tradition of dependence on the Imperial Power that, when the Papacy turned away, at last, from these forbidding Iconoclasts and applied for aid in a quarter where aid was readily forthcoming, the Apostolic See did not feel at ease until it had invested its new Frankish friends in need with a semblance of political legitimacy. When Pope Stephen came to Frankland in A.D. 753 and persuaded the Franks to embark on an Italian campaign on his behalf, he was careful, before the Frankish army crossed the Alps, to bestow the Semi-Imperial title of 'Patricians' upon King Pepin and his two sons Carloman and Charles. Half-a-century later, on the historic Christmas Day of the year 800, a successor of Pope Stephen II, Pope Leo III, took the last of these three Frank 'Patricians' by surprise in precipitately crowning him 'Augustus and Emperor of the Romans'; and this Papal precipitation, which embarrassed the recipient of the title in his delicate relations with the Imperial Government at Constantinople, was apparently due to the Pope's anxiety to escape from an embarrassment of his own. So far from relishing the status of sovereign independence which had been conferred upon the Holy See by the sluggishness of Constantine V and the generosity of Pepin, the Papacy had found life intolerable in the open air; and after fifty years of this painful experience the reigning Pope was only eager to escape from the inclemency of the political weather by taking cover under the familiar Imperial roof. His eagerness was actually so great that, when he found the ancient Imperial mansion on the shores of the Bosphorus no longer accessible,[1] he could think of no better recourse than to erect a jerry-built substitute on the banks of the Tiber.

Nor was the Papacy cured of its infatuation with the Imperial idea when the ramshackle Carolingian Empire fell about its ears and involved it in the miseries of the post-Carolingian interregnum which was the nemesis of Charlemagne's megalomania.[2] In A.D. 960 Pope John XII called in Otto the Saxon from beyond the Alps, as Stephen II had called in Pepin the Frank;[3] and in A.D. 962 Otto was crowned Emperor in Rome by John, as Charles had been crowned in 800 by Leo. Less than two years after this second Papal evocation of a ghost of the Roman Empire in the West, Pope John was deposed by an assembly held in St. Peter's under the presidency of the prince on whom he himself had conferred the Imperial title. This informal parliament of the Roman clergy and people[4] appointed in the deposed Pope's place the Emperor's nominee, who ascended the Papal Throne as Leo VIII; and at the same time they acknowledged the Emperor's right of veto over all Papal elections in the future. In 966 this right was formally con-

[1] The last occupant of St. Peter's Chair who addressed himself to the Imperial Government at Constantinople, in the hope of inducing it to act as his *deus ex machina*, appears to have been the 'Antipope' Boniface VII, who fled to Constantinople in A.D. 974, after an abortive attempt to establish himself in the Holy See by violence. In 984 Boniface seized the opportunity offered by a momentary paralysis of the Western Imperial Power upon the death of the Emperor Otto II in order to sail for Rome with an East Roman expeditionary force. Boniface took Rome by storm, ousted the reigning Pope John XIV, and died in the saddle in 985 (see further IV. C (iii) (*c*) 2 (*β*), Annex II, p. 600, below.

[2] For this post-Carolingian interregnum see the references on p. 323, footnote 1, above.

[3] Otto's passage of the Alps in A.D. 961, in response to the call of Pope John XII, was not, of course, his first appearance in Italy, any more than Pepin's passage of the Alps in A.D. 755, in response to the call of Pope Stephen II, was the first occasion on which the Franks had shown themselves under arms on Italian ground. As early as A.D. 951 Otto had already visited Italy on his own initiative in order to establish his suzerainty over the North Italian 'successor-state' of the Carolingian Empire. This was ten years before he himself assumed the Italian Crown at Pavia in A.D. 961, and eleven years before he was crowned Emperor at Rome in 962.

[4] The assembly also included a certain number of prelates—Transalpine as well as Italian—from beyond the frontiers of the Ducatus Romanus (see the list in Liutprand of Cremona: *Historia Ottonis*, chap. 9); and, perhaps on this account, it styled itself a synod.

firmed by Pope Leo VIII himself;[1] and thereafter on one celebrated occasion the Emperor's prerogative was exercised retrospectively in order to annul an accomplished election which proved not to have been carried out according to canonical rules. On the 20th December, 1046, at the Synod of Sutri, Pope Gregory VI abdicated after admitting a charge of simony which was laid against him by the Emperor Henry III; and apparently this synod went so far as to recognize that the Imperial prerogative included not only the right of veto but also the right of nomination.[2]

It was only after this[3] that the indomitable spirit of the Tuscan Ildebrando Aldobrandeschi breathed into the Papacy the courage to aspire deliberately to that painful and perilous eminence which had once been thrust by Necessity upon Gregory the Great. Under Hildebrand's inspiration the Popes nerved themselves for two centuries to brave simultaneously the wrath of the German Imperial Power and the unruliness of rural barons and urban republicans in the Ducatus Romanus—a humiliating local nuisance to which the Holy See now once more laid itself open in pulling down the Imperial roof over its own head. In thus taking its courage in both hands and committing itself to this terrifying venture, the Papacy was acknowledging and embracing, at last, a destiny to which the first Gregory's career had already pointed; and in embracing its own destiny the Roman See at the same time opened a new chapter in the history of Western Christendom.[4] The Epimethean chapter in which a nascent society in the West had been prompted by a Papal oracle at Rome to continue to idolize a past which was symbolized in the Imperial idea, was now followed by a Promethean chapter in which the Papacy deliberately exposed itself to the buffetings of a tempestuous world in order to create a wholly new institution—a Papal *Respublica Christiana*—which was to meet the needs of a growing society and was to give it the strength to find its feet.

The extraordinary feature in the history of the Papacy is that it should have waited so long for a Gregory VII to lead it to its destiny

1 The Pope had then just been appointed by the Emperor to be the Imperial vicegerent in the government of Rome, after the suppression of the third of three Roman insurrections against the Imperial Power with which Otto had had to deal within the space of three years.

2 For the relations of the Papacy with the Western Emperors from Otto I to Henry III inclusive see Bryce, James: *The Holy Roman Empire*, chap. x.

3 The pontificate of Nicholas I (*fungebatur* A.D. 858–67) is an exception which proves our rule, since the reign of this remarkable forerunner of Gregory VII coincides in date with the nadir of the post-Carolingian interregnum.

4 As a conventional date for the transition to the second chapter of Western history from the first we may take the year 1075, in which Hildebrand, now seated in St. Peter's Chair after having served the Holy See for thirty years, proclaimed his own conception of the Papal office by the symbolic act of prohibiting lay investiture. (For a consideration of the rise and fall of the Hildebrandine Church see IV. C (iii) (*c*) 3 (*β*), pp. 512–84, below.)

after a Gregory I had once pointed the way. The explanation lies in the fact that Gregory I's discovery was unintentional, and that a prospect of greatness which one great man's involuntary achievements had opened up remained still uninviting so long as the shelter of an Imperial edifice retained its attractiveness for Papal minds. Nor did the Papacy escape the nemesis of its protracted idolization of the Imperial idea. For the ghost of the Roman Empire, which had been raised by a Papal incantation for the second time in the tenth century, did not submit tamely to be exorcized when the Papacy tardily awoke to the truth that this political anachronism was an incubus and not a shield and buckler. The Papal *Respublica Christiana* was only established at the cost of a life-and-death struggle between the Papal and the Imperial Power which threw the Papacy off its moral balance and betrayed it into replacing a discarded idol by an object of worship which was nobler in its nature and therefore more demoralizing in its effect when it was thus misused. The Papacy escaped from its idolization of the Empire only to fall into an idolization of itself.

This tragic aberration of a Power which had eventually responded to its challenge so well that it had made itself the master-institution of Western Christendom is a classic instance of ὕβρις, and we shall have occasion to examine this tragedy when we come to study the nemesis of creativity in its active form.[1] In this place we have merely to point the contrast between the first and the second phase in the Papacy's career, and to observe that during the first phase the Papacy almost condemned Western Christendom to be overtaken by the passive nemesis to which Orthodox Christendom succumbed.

Orthodox Christendom incurred this fate—through a stroke of tragic irony—by making at the first attempt a substantial success of the *tour de force* which was twice attempted in the West and which there twice ended in a fiasco. The ghost of the Roman Empire which was successfully evoked on Orthodox Christian ground in the eighth century of the Christian Era materialized into a substantial and efficient centralized state with a life-span of nearly five hundred years. In its main features this Eastern *Imperium Redivivum* succeeded in being what it set out to be. It was a recognizable reproduction of the original Roman Empire of Augustus and Diocletian and Constantine and Theodosius and Justinian; and it anticipated the political development of Western Christendom by some seven or eight hundred years;[2] for no state comparable

[1] See IV. C (iii) (*c*) 3 (β), pp. 512–84, below.

[2] 'The eighth century in the East is a portent of the sixteenth in the West. It is the restoration of materialism with its paramour, obsequious art.'—Bell, Clive: *Art* (London 1928, Chatto & Windus: The Phoenix Library), p. 136.

to the eighth-century East Roman Empire ever made its appearance in the Western World until after the radiation of Italian efficiency into the Transalpine kingdoms at the turn of the fifteenth and sixteenth centuries.[1]

How are we to account for this fatally precocious superiority of Orthodox Christendom over the West in political constructiveness? One important factor, no doubt, was the difference in the degree of the pressure which was exerted upon both these Christendoms simultaneously by the aggression of the Primitive Muslim Arabs.[2] In their assault upon the distant West the Arabs shot their bolt in recapturing for the Syriac Society its lost colonial domain in North-West Africa and the Iberian Peninsula. By the time when they had crossed the Pyrenees and were striking at the infant Western Society's heart, the force of their offensive was spent; and when their wild ride round the southern and western rim of the Mediterranean brought them up short at Tours against an Austrasian shield-wall, their nerveless spear-thrusts and sword-cuts glanced off harmlessly from their stolid target. Yet even this passive Austrasian victory over a tired-out Arab assailant was enough to make the fortunes of the Austrasian Power. It was the prestige won at Tours in A.D. 732 that marked Austrasia out as the leader among the rudimentary principalities of Western Christendom; led Pope Gregory III to look beyond the Alps and address himself to the victor Charles Martel in A.D. 739; and thus brought about that *entente* between the Papacy and the Carolingian House which was the genesis of the first Western essay in a revival of the Roman Empire. If the relatively feeble impact of the Arab explosion upon the West was able to ignite the Carolingian flash in the pan,[3] it is not surprising that the solid structure of the East Roman Empire should have been called into existence in Orthodox Christendom as a carapace to withstand the far more violent and far longer sustained bombardment from the same Arab assailant to which Orthodox Christendom was subjected. Another factor which manifestly counted for much in the successful reconstruction of a Roman Empire on Orthodox Christian ground was the personal genius of the Emperors Leo III and Constantine V; and this personal factor had a cumulative effect because the combined reigns of father and son extended continuously over a period of fifty-eight years

[1] For this radiation, and for its political effects, see I. B (i), vol. i, p. 19; III. C (ii) (*b*), vol. iii, pp. 350–63; IV. C (iii) (*b*) 8, in the present volume, pp. 198–200; and IV. C (iii) (*c*) 2 (α), pp. 274–5, above; and V. C (i) (*d*) 6 (γ), Annex I, vol. v, p. 635, footnote 1, and p. 638, below.

[2] See II. D (vii), vol. ii, pp. 360–4 and 367–9, above.

[3] For the local effect of the Arab invasion of Gaul in evoking a Frankish counter-offensive which crossed the Pyrenees in its turn and which did not come to a halt until it had also crossed the Atlantic and created Latin America, see I. B (iv), vol. i, p. 38, and II. D (v), vol. ii, pp. 202–6, above, and V. C (i) (*c*) 3, vol. v, pp. 221–2, below.

(A.D. 717–75).[1] In any case the East Roman Empire was, beyond question, a solid success, whatever the explanation of this success may be.

The new Orthodox Christian Power was founded, to begin with, on a solid territorial basis; for Leo succeeded in reuniting three Orthodox Christian territories—his own army-corps district of the Anatolici, Artavasdus's army-corps district of the Armeniaci, and the incompetent Theodosius's[2] derelict Imperial City of Constantinople—which had been drifting apart into three mutually independent principalities. This act of reunion was confirmed when, on Leo's death, Constantine succeeded in crushing an attempt on Artavasdus's part to reassert his own independence and to put the Imperial City into his pocket (*bellum civile gerebatur* A.D. 741–2). This gave the East Roman Empire a patrimony embracing the whole of Anatolia north-west of the 'natural frontier' of the Taurus, together with a bridge-head on the European side of the Sea of Marmara which was broad enough to cover Constantinople and to secure to the East Roman Government an absolute command over the waterway through the Straits.[3] West of that, the restored Empire gathered under its wing the islands of the Aegean Archipelago and a number of scattered enclaves of continental territory round the coasts of Italy and the Balkan Peninsula—derelict fragments of the Imperial heritage which gravitated automatically towards the solid mass of a state whose torso extended from Adrianople-on-Maritsa to Caesarea-under-Argaeus.

The extent of the territory of this Orthodox Christian Power gave it great material resources; the compactness of its torso offered it the possibility of maintaining these resources intact; and the conservation of the Empire's energy was the cardinal principle of Imperial statesmanship from Leo III's reign onwards for two centuries.

During those two centuries Leo and his successors carefully refrained from indulging in any Justinianean or Carolingian adventures. For example, Constantine V allowed Ravenna to fall to the Lombards and Rome to seek protection from the Franks without making the mistake of sending out another Belisarius or Narses to retrieve the Empire's position in Central and Northern Italy.[4]

[1] For Leo's life-work see I. C (i) (*b*), vol. i, p. 64, footnote 3; III. C (ii) (*b*), vol. iii, pp. 274–6, and IV. C (ii) (*b*) 1, in the present volume, p. 73, above.

[2] This was Theodosius III in the conventional reckoning which treats the Roman and East Roman Emperors as one continuous series from the first Augustus to the last Constantine.

[3] For the geographical function of the East Roman army-corps districts of 'Thrace' and 'Macedonia' as the European bridge-head of an Anatolian Power see Neumann, C.: *Die Weltstellung des Byzantinischen Reiches vor den Kreuzzügen* (Leipzig 1894, Duncker & Humblot), chap. 1, especially pp. 10 and 14.

[4] See the present chapter, p. 337, above.

Again, the same Emperor—finding the aggressive pagan Bulgars as uncomfortably close to the Straits as Charlemagne found the Saxons uncomfortably close to the Rhine—fought a series of strenuous, and necessarily expensive, campaigns in order to push the encroaching barbarians back to a safe distance; but he was content to relax his effort as soon as this minimum objective had been achieved, instead of pressing on, like Charlemagne, to conquer his barbarian neighbours outright at the cost of exhausting his own realm's strength in the process.[1] In the ninth century Constantine V's successors allowed the Bulgars to engulf the stranded Imperial fortresses in the interior of the Balkan Peninsula and to extend their suzerainty over the Balkan Slavs as far south-westward as the hinterland of Salonica.[2] They thus abandoned to Bulgaria the lion's share of the Balkan Slavinias, while for their own part they contented themselves with reducing to obedience the virtually insular Slavs of the Morea and the continental Slavs in the immediate northern hinterland of the Gulf of Corinth. A similar avoidance of unprofitable entanglements was the East Roman Government's policy on the farther side of the Adriatic *a fortiori*. When at the turn of the ninth and tenth centuries they felt themselves compelled to embark on a forward policy in Southern Italy in order to prevent the Muslim conquerors of the Apulian Lombards from establishing a permanent foothold there,[3] they economized their energies by simultaneously abandoning to the Muslims the ancient East Roman province of Sicily. They submitted to the loss of Syracuse in A.D. 878, two years after their entry into Bari; and Tauromenium, which was the last surviving East Roman fortress in Sicily, fell in

1 For Charlemagne's policy of conquest in dealing with the Saxons, and for the disastrous consequences, see the references on p. 322, footnote 4, above.

2 The Romano-Bulgarian peace treaty of A.D. 815–16 left both Philippopolis (Plovdiv) and Sardica (Sofia) under Imperial sovereignty. Both fortresses were engulfed in the course of the ninth century; the interior of Macedonia appears to have been ceded at the moment of Bulgaria's conversion in 865; and after a re-delimitation in A.D. 904 the south-western frontier of Bulgaria came within fifteen miles of Salonica (Runciman, S.: *A History of the First Bulgarian Empire* (London 1930, Bell), pp. 87, 104, and 152).

3 These Muslim conquerors of Lombard territory in Southern Italy came from Ifriqīyah; and a new Muslim Power, ensconced in Bari, might have served as a stepping-stone between Ifriqīyah and Dalmatia, with serious consequences for the East Roman Empire. To begin with, the pagan piratical Narentine Slavs might have become converts to Islam; and after that the Muslim Power in North-West Africa might have felt its way, through a Dalmatian back door, to a contact with Bulgaria. As it was, the Bulgarian Tsar Symeon, when he was planning the grand assault on the East Roman Empire which he made in A.D. 924, sent an embassy to the Fātimid Court at Mahdīyah to propose a collaboration between Bulgaria's land-power and Ifriqīyah's sea-power, and the Bulgarian Embassy was actually returning with a party of Fātimid envoys when their ship was intercepted by an East Roman naval squadron off the Italian coast. Thereupon the East Roman Government promptly made its own terms with the Fātimid Government (Runciman, op. cit., pp. 168–9). This incident in itself was enough to justify the East Roman Government's Transadriatic policy during the preceding fifty years. For the relations between the Muslims of Ifriqīyah and the Dalmatians and Bulgarians see further Gay, J.: *L'Italie Méridionale et l'Empire Byzantin* (Paris 1904, Fontemoing), pp. 91 and 207.

A.D. 902, some thirteen years before the East Romans rounded off their new dominion on the Italian mainland by making their authority effective up to a line drawn from Gaeta to Monte Gargano.

The efficiency of the East Roman Empire in holding together its compact torso, and its statesmanship in economizing its resources and refraining from extravagant adventures, distinguish its history during the two centuries beginning with the elevation of Leo III from the history of any contemporary Western body politic. And both the statesmanship and the efficiency were the fruit of two East Roman institutions—a standing army and a permanent civil service—which were both virtually unknown in the West at any time between the extinction of the western line of Theodosius's successors in the fifth century and the radiation of Italian efficiency into the Transalpine kingdoms in the fifteenth. Those institutions were unknown in the West during those thousand years because the Western World, outside the scattered enclaves of the medieval Western city-state cosmos, did not then command the necessary economic and cultural resources. A professional army and a professional administration cannot exist without a centralized system of public finance and a secular system of higher education; and, unlike the Western Society of that age, the medieval Orthodox Christian Society was able to provide both these indispensable bases for the East Roman Administration and the East Roman Army. In all the metropolitan provinces of the Empire, from Taurus to Rhodope, the revenues were collected by the agents of the Imperial Government and were paid into the Imperial Treasury, which paid out, in its turn, the salaries of the provincial officials and the provincial troops.[1] This financial practice implied, of course, the maintenance of a money economy;[2] and this money economy was embodied in a gold coinage which had a high reputation, and a general currency, throughout the Western World in one direction and the Syriac World in the other on account of its unfailingly sterling standard.[3] As for the secular system of higher

[1] In the fragmentary outlying dominions of the Empire west of Rhodope, in the Balkan Peninsula and Italy, the local revenues were collected by the local authorities, who paid out of them the local costs of administration and defence before remitting a balance to Constantinople. This portion of the Empire in which a system of financial decentralization prevailed was, however, small and unimportant by comparison with the main body throughout which the whole system of public finance was centralized in Constantinople.

[2] A money economy was only maintained in those parts of the Orthodox Christian World that were gathered into the East Roman Empire by Leo Syrus. In the interior of the Balkan Peninsula, which was overrun by the Slavs and Bulgars in the sixth and seventh centuries, and was not incorporated into Orthodox Christendom until the ninth century, the money economy of the Diocletianic Roman Empire broke down, just as it did in the West. After the annexation of West Bulgaria to the East Roman Empire in A.D. 1019 the East Roman Government showed an enlightened common sense in not attempting to introduce the Imperial system of money economy there immediately and *de toutes pièces* (see further p. 394, footnote 1, below).

[3] After the catastrophic depreciation of the Roman Imperial currency during the

education, it was provided for the East Roman military officers in the discipline and technique of the Army itself,[1] and for the East Roman civil servants in an academy which was established in Constantinople, within the precincts of the Imperial Palace,[2] *circa* A.D. 864, by the Caesar Bardas during the reign of the Emperor Michael III (*imperabat* 842–67),[3] *en attendant* the Emperor Constantine IX Monomachus's more ambitious foundation of a University of Constantinople in A.D. 1045.[4]

social convulsions of the third century of the Christian Era the gold coinage, restored by the Roman Emperors Diocletian (*imperabat* A.D. 284–305) and Constantine (*imperabat* A.D. 306–37) was maintained by the Imperial mint at the Constantinian standard, without any fresh depreciation, until the reign of the East Roman Emperor Alexius I Comnenus (*imperabat* A.D. 1081–1118); and throughout this period of some eight centuries the Government at Constantinople never once stopped payments or declared bankruptcy (see Finlay, G.: *A History of Greece from its Conquest by the Romans to the Present Time* (Oxford 1877, Clarendon Press, 7 vols.), vol. i, p. 443; and Gelzer, H.: *Byzantinische Kulturgeschichte* (Tübingen 1909, Mohr), p. 78). This solid and striking fact of monetary history clearly militates, as far as it goes, against one of the theses of the present chapter, in which it has been argued that the official continuity of the East Roman Empire with the Roman Empire was a constitutional fiction which ought not to be taken much more seriously than the pretensions of Charlemagne or Otto I or Frederick I Hohenstaufen to be the legitimate successors of Augustus in the West.

1 The cultivated and scientific character of the East Roman military system is attested by the survival of several treatises on the art of war from East Roman hands (e.g. the *Τακτικά* of the Emperor Leo VI; the *Anonymus Vári*; and the *Περὶ Παραδρομῆς Πολέμου* of an anonymous officer who had seen his service under the Emperor Nicephorus Phocas (*imperabat* A.D. 963–9). The impetus behind this tenth-century East Roman study of the art of war was derived from the *Τακτικά* of the Emperor Maurice (*imperabat* A.D. 582–602), the last effective Roman Emperor in the eastern portion of the Theodosian heritage. The distinguishing feature of this East Roman military science was its principle of adapting its own armaments, tactics, and strategy to the natures of the local *terrain* and the local enemy.

2 In the group of buildings called the Magnaura.

3 The foundation of this academy at Constantinople was the sequel to a renaissance of Hellenic culture in Orthodox Christendom which had, itself, followed the successful evocation of a ghost of the Roman Empire by Leo Syrus; and this work of cultural reconstruction had to start from zero; for the interregnum between the submergence of the 'apparented' Hellenic Civilization and the emergence of the 'affiliated' Orthodox Christian Civilization had been as complete on this as on every other plane of human activity.

'When the Paschal Chronicle deserts us in A.D. 627, we have no contemporary historians or chroniclers for the general course of the Imperial history until we reach the end of the eighth century. There is a gap of more than a century and a half in our series of Byzantine history. The two writers on whom we depend for the reigns of the Heracliad Dynasty and of the early Iconoclast sovereigns lived at the end of the eighth and the beginning of the ninth century: the Patriarch Nicephorus and the monk Theophanes. . . . The endeavours of the Isaurian monarchs to renovate the Empire bore such fruits as were possible at a period when the horizon of the human spirit was determined by a series of ecclesiastical formulae. Whereas at the beginning of the [eighth] century there was no distinguished writer, no man of pre-eminent learning within the limits of the Empire, there was at the close of the century quite a large group of literary men who had studied a great many subjects and could write very good Greek' (Bury, J. B.: Editio Minor of Edward Gibbon's *The History of the Decline and Fall of the Roman Empire*, vol. v (London 1901, Methuen), p. 499; and *A History of the Later Roman Empire* (London 1889, Macmillan, 2 vols.), vol. ii, p. 518).

Dvorník (op. cit., p. 115) points out that the renaissance which thus began before the close of the eighth century and continued during the ninth was twofold. There was a pious cultural movement that radiated from the monastery of Studium, and a secularist movement that radiated from the Imperial Court. According to the same authority (op. cit., pp. 122–3 and 131), one of the conscious purposes of the Caesar Bardas in founding his academy was to take higher education out of the monks' hands.

4 The generation which produced the academy of Bardas was also the generation of Photius (*vivebat circa* A.D. 820–91), who was the most learned and dexterous man-of-letters

These two East Roman institutions of an educated corps of professional military officers and an educated hierarchy of professional lay civil servants were important not merely in themselves but because they made it possible for the resuscitated ghost of the Roman Empire in Orthodox Christendom to achieve its most remarkable and most unfortunate triumph, the effective subordination of the Church to the State. It is in the relations between Church and State that the histories of Orthodox Christendom and Western Christendom show the widest and the most momentous divergence;[1] and here we can locate the parting of the ways that respectively led the Western Society forward along the path of growth and the Orthodox Christian Society away along a path that was to end in destruction.

Leo Syrus and his successors on the East Roman Imperial Throne succeeded in attaining a goal which in the West was never approached by Charlemagne or Otto I or Henry III even with Papal acquiescence, and *a fortiori* not by Henry IV or Henry V or Frederick I or Frederick II in the teeth of Papal resistance. The East Roman Emperors, in their own dominions, turned the Church into a department of state and the Oecumenical Patriarch into a kind of Imperial Under-Secretary of State for Ecclesiastical Affairs,[2] with

in the Orthodox Christian World of his day, though he remained a layman until the moment of his appointment to the Oecumenical Patriarchate in A.D. 858 at an age of perhaps as much as forty. Similarly, in the eleventh century, Michael Psellus (*vivebat* A.D. 1018–78), who was the leading man-of-letters in Orthodox Christendom in that age, obtained his education as a layman and made his reputation and his career as a literary civil servant before he became a monk at the age of thirty-eight; and his tardy entry into the cloister was followed by a quick and permanent return to the world. In medieval Italian history the earliest counterpart of Michael Psellus is Aeneas Sylvius (*vivebat* A.D. 1405–64), while in modern Transalpine Europe we find no counterparts of Photius until we come to the cultivated Erastian clerics of the eighteenth century. Some of the leading lights of lay literature and learning in the history of the Orthodox Christian culture were bred in the Imperial household and were precluded, by their office or by their sex, from ever taking orders: for example, the publicist-emperor Constantine Porphyrogenitus (*vivebat* A.D. 905–59) and the historian-princess Anna Comnena (*vivebat* A.D. 1083–*post* 1148). For the foundation and fortunes of the Monomachian University see Hussey, J. M.: *Church and Learning in the Byzantine Empire, 867–1185* (Oxford 1937, University Press), chap. 3. There was a Faculty of Philosophy (organized by Michael Psellus) and a Faculty of Law (organized by John Xiphilinus). It may be noted that the revival of a secular system of higher education in Orthodox Christendom from the ninth century onwards had a precedent in the previous foundation of a University of Constantinople by the Emperor Theodosius II in A.D. 425 (see the document of the 27th February, A.D. 425, in the *Codex Theodosianus*, xiv. 9. 3). This fifth-century Theodosian University at Constantinople seems to have been as abortive as the sixth-century Justinianean codification of Roman Law, if its effectiveness is to be measured by the immediate local results. In the post-Justinianean interregnum it passed into the hands of the monks, and thereafter it was liquidated by that *malleus monachorum* the Emperor Leo III (see Dvorník, op. cit., p. 116, for the authorities). But it is possible that the record of Theodosius's work may have inspired the educational activities of Bardas and Constantine Monomachus, as the record of Justinian's work certainly did inspire the legislative activities of the Macedonian Dynasty of East Roman Emperors.

[1] See I. C (i) (*b*), vol. i, p. 67, above.

[2] The degradation of the Oecumenical Patriarch to the status of an Imperial civil servant is proclaimed even in the ostensible aggrandizement of his position through the enlargement of the territorial area of his ecclesiastical jurisdiction. When, in

a status that was professional but a tenure that was by no means secure.

In relegating the Church to this position, the East Roman Emperors were simply putting into effect one important part of their programme of making their restoration of the Roman Empire a solid reality; for this relation between Church and State was precisely that which had been contemplated by the Roman Emperor Constantine the Great when he decided to take the Christian Church under his patronage;[1] and this Constantinian conception had been actually realized *de facto* in the history of the later Roman Empire from the reign of Constantine himself to the reign of Justinian inclusive.

This later Roman régime, in which the Christian Church was incorporated into the fabric of the Roman body politic, and was made subject, in the last resort, to the absolute authority of the Emperor as the single sovereign lord of the whole politico-ecclesiastical structure, has been nicknamed 'Caesaro-papism' by modern Western scholars; and this 'hyphenated' term would perhaps also aptly describe the effect of Constantine's work from the standpoint of a Primitive Christian Church which had started life as a private association in a proletarian underworld where it had been out of touch with the political institutions of the Hellenic dominant minority.[2] This insulation of the private life of the Primitive Church from the public life of the pre-Constantinian Roman Empire was defined in the formula 'Render unto Caesar the things

A.D. 732, Calabria and Sicily and the whole of the Imperial Diocese of Illyricum were forcibly transferred from the Pope's to the Oecumenical Patriarch's jurisdiction by the Emperor Leo Syrus, and when again, after the establishment of a definitive frontier between the East Roman Empire and the 'Abbasid Caliphate, the fragment of the Patriarchate of Antioch which still remained under Imperial rule was transferred to the Oecumenical Patriarch's jurisdiction likewise, these deliberate extensions of the Oecumenical Patriarch's jurisdiction up to the territorial limits of the East Roman Emperor's sovereignty were evidence that the Emperor regarded the Oecumenical Patriarch as his creature, in contrast to both the Patriarch of Antioch and the Pope, who could each oppose the Emperor's will with impunity because each of these two sees was now beyond the reach of his arm. It is noteworthy that the East Roman Government's policy of making the Oecumenical Patriarch's jurisdiction co-extensive with the ambit of its own sovereign authority was taken up and followed by the Ottoman Government when it entered into the East Roman Government's heritage and provided the Orthodox Christian World with its universal state. The Ottoman Government gave the Oecumenical Patriarch a measure of civil authority over the entire Millet-i-Rūm; and in Ottoman constitutional law this ecclesiastical community embraced the entire Orthodox Christian population of the Ottoman Empire, whatever their previous ecclesiastical allegiance. The military conquests of the 'Osmanlis thus automatically extended the Oecumenical Patriarch's jurisdiction over the Archbishoprics of Ochrida and Peč, the Patriarchates of Bulgaria and Antioch and Jerusalem and Alexandria, and the autocephalous Church of Cyprus. It was the supreme irony in the history of the Constantinopolitan Patriarchs that they only made good their oecumenical pretensions through becoming the slaves of a Muslim potentate (on this last point see further IV. C (iii) (*c*) 2 (*β*), Annex II, pp. 622–3, below).

1 For Constantine's ecclesiastical policy see further V. C (i) (*d*) 6 (*δ*), Annex, vol. v, pp. 650, 693–4, and 707–9, below.

2 See I. C (i) (*a*), vol. i, pp. 53–7, above, and V. C (i) (*c*) 2, vol. v, pp. 74–80, below.

which are Caesar's and unto God the things that are God's',[1] and it was maintained by the resoluteness of many generations of Christian martyrs who were prepared to sacrifice their lives rather than lend themselves to a formality which signified a recognition of Dea Roma and Divus Augustus as legitimate objects of religious worship. From this Primitive Christian standpoint the 'hyphen-ated' monstrosity of the word 'Caesaro-papism' expressively symbolizes the impious presumption of a human act which joined together what God had put asunder.[2] On the other hand, from the standpoint of the Roman Imperial Government the work of Constantine wore a very different aspect. From this standpoint the act of impious presumption had been the Christians' refusal to recognize the Roman State as an object of religious worship as well as a political institution; for in the minds of a Hellenic dominant minority which was the ruling element in the early Roman Empire the dichotomy of Society into 'Church' and 'State', 'clerical' and 'lay', 'ecclesiastical' and 'civil', 'religious' and 'secular', was a shockingly sacrilegious rending in twain of a seamless robe. From the cosmos of city-states out of which it had sprung the Roman Empire had inherited a conception of Society as something one and indivisible which was always represented in its totality in every one of its activities and its institutions. In the Christians' repudiation of the Hellenic universal state in its religious aspect the Roman governing class correctly divined a moral alienation of the Christian community from the Hellenic culture; and they were genuinely indignant at the pretension of these revolutionary proletarians to treat the undisputed fact of their citizenship in the Empire as a limited liability by interpreting it as a merely political tie which carried no religious associations with it. Their denunciation of the Christians as 'atheists'[3] was made in complete good faith;[4] and they were equally sincere in believing that it was the right and duty of the Imperial authorities to exert the full force of the State—and to employ in the last resort the most extreme methods of 'frightfulness'—in order to stamp this in their view anti-social movement out.

The very sincerity and earnestness of the spirit in which the Imperial Government's persecutions of the Christian Church were carried out explains the deepness of the impression that was made on the mind of the persecuting power by the failure of its utmost endeavours to reduce the Christians to conformity. If the Chris-

[1] Matt. xxii. 15–22 = Mark xii. 13–17 = Luke xx. 19–26.
[2] An inversion of the formula in Matt. xix. 6.
[3] See V. C (i) (*c*) 2, Annex II, vol. v, p. 584; V. C (i) (*d*) 7, vol. vi, p. 40, footnote 2; and V. C (ii) (*a*), Annex II, vol. vi, p. 536, below.
[4] The point has been noticed by Oswald Spengler in *Der Untergang des Abendlandes*, vol. i (Munich 1920, Beck), p. 567.

tians had proved themselves to be more than a match for the Imperial Government, this demonstrated in the eyes of the governing class that the divine powers had deserted their official shrines and had gone to dwell in the strange temples of this invincibly contumacious proletarian sect.

> Excessere omnes, adytis arisque relictis,
> Di quibus imperium hoc steterat . . .[1]

This might be divine wisdom, or it might be just divine caprice. To Hellenic minds the ways of the Godhead were often arbitrary and inscrutable. But, whatever the cause, this secession of the Gods was a patent fact, and it was not a fact which a Hellenic dominant minority with its back to the wall was able to face with equanimity. At the turn of the third and fourth centuries of the Christian Era these epigoni of the ancient Hellenic order remained as fully convinced as they had been before their defeat at the Christians' hands that the Empire could not stand if it were bereft of its indwelling divinity. A godless Empire would be as savourless and sapless as an Athens without her Athena. The secession of the Gods must be retrieved; the divine powers must be enticed back again into the shrines which they had so alarmingly deserted; and, since meanwhile they had insisted upon assuming a Christian guise, the only recourse for the Empire now, in face of the accomplished fact of this metamorphosis, was to reverse its outward policy in order to achieve, in spite of everything, an inward purpose which remained what it had always been. These promptings of Superstition were supported by the counsels of *raison d'état*. If the Christian Church had defeated the Empire's attempt to suppress it and in that way to preserve the ancient unity of religious and political life in the Hellenic universal state, then the broken unity must be restored in another way by the bold diplomatic counterstroke of taking the Christian Church bodily to the Empire's bosom. In the first flush of astonishment and relief at being transformed in a trice from an outlaw into a favourite the Church might be swept off its feet, and its leaders might be induced to accept a converted Empire's terms under the delusion that they were imposing their own. In fact, the Christians might be coaxed into concurring, at the end of the chapter, in a sentence of *Gleichschaltung* which they had resisted to the death so long as a still Pagan Imperial Government had attempted to put this sentence into execution by force.[2]

[1] Virgil, *Aeneid*, Book II, ll. 351–2, quoted already in this connexion in I. C (i) (*a*), vol. i, p. 57, footnote 1, above. When the writer wrote that passage, he was not yet acquainted with Saint Augustine's quotation of the same lines of Virgil in *De Civitate Dei*, Book II, chap. 22. See further the present Study, V. C (ii) (*b*), vol. vi, p. 279, below.

[2] Apropos of this passage Professor N. H. Baynes observes, in a letter to the writer

This, in effect, was the policy of the Emperor Constantine himself and of the line of Christian Emperors who succeeded him; and, just because this policy was neither consciously hypocritical nor deliberately dishonest, it was wonderfully successful. After Constantine had arranged his *entente* with the Church, the Church did fall into the place which he had designed for it. It nestled down promptly and cheerfully into the political shell in which the Imperial authorities now invited it to take up its abode; and it did not make any motion to live its own life in the open again until action was forced upon it by the catastrophe of the shell's breaking into fragments. After the Constantinian settlement Leo the Great (*fungebatur* A.D. 440–61) was the first Pope of Rome, and Sergius (*fungebatur* A.D. 610–38) the first Patriarch of Constantinople, to stand out as a great man of action. It will be seen that the dates of these two great prelates' ministries coincide with the respective dates of the break-up of the Roman Empire in the western and in the eastern portions of the Theodosian heritage. Thereafter, as we have seen,[1] the Popes, as well as the Patriarchs, persisted in lamenting the loss of their comfortable Imperial carapace and in attempting to find their way back into it.

This hankering in the mind of the Church itself for a restoration of the Constantinian settlement is not altogether surprising; for the ruling element in the Roman Empire had been right in regarding the pre-Constantinian relation between Church and Empire as a symptom of a social malady. The Primitive Christians' repudiation of Caesar-worship had been in truth one of the outward expressions of an inward secession of the internal proletariat of the Hellenic Society from the dominant minority, and this schism in the Hellenic body social was a symptom of its being in disintegration.[2] The healthy state of the Hellenic Society had consisted in

of this Study, that 'the Christian is not in general the foe of the State—only of the Paganism with which the State was intimately associated. The significant thing is rather the Christian approximation to the State in the period before the Great Persecution (Tertullian must not be taken to represent the sentiments of the whole Christian body). It was no sacrifice of conviction for the Church to recognize the Christian State. And in this connexion it is important to realize that the Pagan State had already abandoned the *Gottkönigtum* of the Hellenistic period. [On this point see V. C (i) (*d*) 6 (δ), Annex, vol. v, pp. 649–50 and 691–4, below.—A.J.T.] Its theory of monarchy was ready to the Christian's hand; it needed only slight modification, and that modification was effected by Eusebius. What is true is that the change effected by Constantine's conversion was so sudden that the Church was taken by surprise. There is no concordat. Constantine by a unilateral transaction takes the Christian Church into partnership. The Church is given no opportunity of elaborating its own terms.'

[1] See pp. 335–40, above.

[2] The fact that the separation between Church and State is a symptom of a malady in the body social of a civilization does not, of course, necessarily mean that it is a symptom of social retrogression. For a civilization is merely a representative of one particular species of societies; this species is not necessarily the highest possible realization of the potentialities of the genus; and a malady in some creature that is good as far as it goes may incidentally result in the production of something better, as a pearl is produced by a disease in an oyster. The mutation by which the earliest civilizations must have been

that unity and indivisibility of the religious and political aspects of social life which had been a reality during the growth-stage of Hellenic history and which had never ceased to be regarded in Hellenic minds as being the normal state of affairs. Nor was this unity an idiosyncrasy of the Hellenic Civilization. It was one of the regular features of primitive social life;[1] and it had been inherited by the Hellenic Society without a break[2] from primitive European barbarians who had become the fathers of the Hellenic Civilization after having served an apprenticeship in the external proletariat of the antecedent Minoan Civilization.[3] It will be seen that the Constantinian settlement in the last chapter of Hellenic history, and the attempts to re-establish the Constantinian settlement after the post-Hellenic interregnum, had behind them the impetus of a tradition that was of almost universal range and almost immemorial antiquity. In these circumstances the surprising fact is not that Constantine's system should have been successfully re-instituted in Orthodox Christendom by Leo Syrus, but rather that in the West the successive endeavours to do the like that were made first by Charlemagne and Pope Leo III and then by Otto and Pope Leo VIII should have uniformly ended in failure.

Regarded in its 'world-historical' setting, this Western failure seems, indeed, so extraordinary that we can no longer feel much surprise when we see it producing an extraordinary result. In the Papal *Respublica Christiana* 'Church' and 'State' were neither undifferentiated, as they had been in the primitive societies and in the Hellenic city-states; nor, again, were they differentiated without being in relation with each other, as the Primitive Christian Church had been insulated from the early Roman Empire; nor, in the third place, were they reintegrated, *more Hellenico*, through the subordination of the Church to the State, on the pattern of the Christian Roman Empire and of this Empire's East Roman ghost. In the Papal *Respublica Christiana* Church and State were

created out of primitive societies (see Part II. A, vol. ii, p. 188, above) might well have worn the appearance of a malady, when regarded from the primitive societies' standpoint. The possibility that the churches, in their turn, may be a new species of societies of a higher order than civilizations is discussed in Part VII, below.

[1] See V. C (i) (*c*) 2, vol. v, pp. 160–1, below.

[2] In this matter of the unity and indivisibility of social life there is no breach between the religion of an uncontaminated Primitive Mankind and the religion of those primitive societies that have been conscripted into the external proletariat of a disintegrating civilization. In both situations the object of worship is, in effect, the community itself. When a primitive society is conscripted into an external proletariat there is, however, a revolutionary change in the aspect of the community's activity that is singled out to be the focus of religious adoration. A community that has hitherto been worshipped as Vishnu now comes to be worshipped as Shiva. For this religious revolution see V. C (i) (*c*) 3, vol. v, pp. 230–3, below.

[3] For the relation of the Achaeans to the Minoan Society on the one hand and to the Hellenic Society on the other see I. C (i) (*b*), vol. i, pp. 92–100, and II. D (vii), vol. ii, pp. 315–16, above.

reintegrated through the subordination of a multiplicity of local states to a single oecumenical church which was the principle of unity and the source of authority in the Western Christian body social:[1] and this 'hierocratic' constitution of Society was a wholly new creation. Indeed, the Papal *Respublica Christiana* shares with the Italian city-state culture[2] the distinction of being one of the two great creative achievements in the second or 'medieval' chapter of our Western history.[3] In the corresponding chapter of Orthodox Christian history there was no comparable creative act, because in an earlier chapter the Orthodox Christian Society, in achieving its successful restoration of the Roman Empire, had renounced the possibility of creation in favour of the easier course of idolizing an institution which was a legacy from the past; and this natural yet disastrous aberration accounts for Orthodox Christendom's premature downfall.

In this Orthodox Christian idolization of the ghost of the Roman Empire which Leo Syrus had evoked, the subordination of the Orthodox Church to the East Roman State was the crucial act; and this act was conscious and whole-hearted. In Leo's own assertion—'Imperator sum et Sacerdos'[4]—we hear the founder of the East Roman Empire making the 'Caesaro-papistical' claim of a Constantine the Great in the imperious accents of a Justinian. We shall not be surprised to find that Leo's success in enforcing this claim throughout the greater part of his dominions[5] is the first link

[1] In the West 'la religion chrétienne, . . . cessant d'être incorporée à un seul empire, devient un lien commun entre plusieurs États, et rend le siège Rome un point de ralliement entre les nations.'—Turgot, A. R. J.: 'Esquisse d'un Plan de Géographie Politique' in *Œuvres de Turgot* (Paris 1844, Guillaumin, 2 vols.), vol. ii, p. 624.

[2] 'With the Italian city-state culture' rather than with the Italian city-state as a political institution; for this institution in itself was not a new creation, but was a ghost evoked from the life of the antecedent Hellenic Society (see the present chapter, pp. 405–6, below).

[3] See III. C (ii) (*b*), vol. iii, p. 375, footnote 2, above.

[4] The assertion is attributed to Leo in these terms by Pope Gregory II in a letter (Ep. xiii) replying to a no longer extant letter of Leo's. (See Vasiliev, A. A.: *Histoire de l'Empire Byzantin* (Paris 1932, Picard, 2 vols.), vol. i, p. 341.) Apropos of this passage Professor N. H. Baynes remarks, in a letter to the writer of this Study, that in the Orthodox Christian *Weltanschauung* 'The Emperor is *not* a priest, though his functions are closely similar. An Iconoclast emperor might in a moment of exasperation—*if* the Gregory letter is genuine—claim to be a priest, but it was said in haste. It is not the normal Byzantine view.' It does, however, seem to have been the normal Byzantine expectation that the Emperor should have the last word in ecclesiastical as well as in civil affairs; and if it be true that the Imperial Crown was usually content to leave its supremacy over the Church unasserted in theory so long as it enjoyed a free hand to exercise this supremacy in practice, then Leo's alleged assertion is illuminating. In a moment of exasperation the Emperor had let the Caesaro-papal cat out of the diplomatic bag!

[5] The test of Leo's pretensions to a 'Caesaro-papal' authority was his attempt to enforce his new-fangled policy of Iconoclasm; and this attempt was not successfully resisted anywhere in Leo's dominions except in the Ducatus Romanus and in the Ravennese Exarchate. In all Leo's other dominions, from Calabria eastwards, his Iconoclastic policy prevailed; and though his successors eventually abandoned Iconoclasm itself, they never ceased to profit by the precedent of Leo's successful insistence that the Emperor was sovereign in matters ecclesiastical as well as in politics. The

in a fatal chain of causation which ends in the breakdown of the Orthodox Christian Civilization some two centuries later.

If we study the tragedy of Orthodox Christian history, we shall observe that the destructive effect of Leo Syrus's deed of reincorporating the Church into the State declares itself in two distinct ways—one of them general and the other particular.

The general effect was to check and sterilize the tendencies towards variety and elasticity and experimentation and creativeness in Orthodox Christian life; and we can roughly measure the extent of the damage that was done to the development of the Orthodox Christian Civilization in this general way by noting some of the conspicuous achievements of the sister civilization of the West, in the corresponding stage of its growth, that have no Orthodox Christian counterparts. In the Orthodox Christian body social in its growth-phase we not only find nothing that corresponds to the Hildebrandine Papacy; we also miss the rise and spread of self-governing universities, corresponding to the new Western centres of intellectual activity at Bologna and Paris,[1] and of self-governing city-states, corresponding to the new Western centres of life in Central and Northern Italy and in Flanders.[2] And while it may

Imperial pretension which was thus successfully asserted in Orthodox Christendom did not, of course, obtain an uncontested victory, and the Orthodox Christian churchmen who opposed it showed as much spirit and resoluteness, before they succumbed to defeat, as their Western colleagues showed when they girded themselves at last for a struggle from which they were ultimately to emerge victorious over a Western revival of the Imperial idea. This abortive, but by no means feeble, resistance of the Church to the revival of 'Caesaro-papism' in the Orthodox Christian World is examined further in IV. C (iii) (*c*) 2 (β), Annex II, below.

[1] We have noticed above, on p. 345, that the University of Constantinople was founded and developed a long time in advance of any university in the West; but this Constantinopolitan school of higher studies was virtually a department of the Central Government of the East Roman Empire and was therefore *ex hypothesi* both unique and hide-bound. We miss in the Orthodox Christian World the counterparts of those intellectually adventurous universities which sprang up spontaneously in one region after another of the expanding domain of 'medieval' Western Christendom. It is significant that the South Lombard city of Salerno, which became the seat of one of the most famous and fruitful of these Western universities, had previously been under an intermittent East Roman protectorate, and under a continuous Orthodox Christian influence, from the time of Nicephorus Phocas' South Italian campaign of A.D. 885 down to the Norman conquest of the city in A.D. 1077. Yet the intellectual *floruit* of Salerno came after its reincorporation into the Western World; and the Salernitan school of medicine, which was already acquiring celebrity during the age of the city's East Roman connexion, owed its inspiration to Arabic rather than to Byzantine sources. (See Gay, J.: *L'Italie Méridionale et l'Empire Byzantin* (Paris 1904, Fontemoing), pp. 594–8, and Taylor, H. O.: *The Mediaeval Mind* (London 1911, Macmillan, 2 vols.), vol. ii, p. 251.)

[2] In this age the Orthodox Christian World not only failed to produce any city-state life of its own; it extinguished, at Cherson, the last surviving city-state of a Hellenic Society to which the Orthodox Christian Society itself was affiliated (see II. D (vi), Annex, vol. ii, p. 404, footnote 2, above); and it even blighted the development of city-state life in a portion of the Western World which was at this time temporarily under the East Roman Empire's control. There is every indication that in the eleventh century the Southern Lombards—in the East Roman province of Laghovardhía, as well as in the autonomous principalities of Benevento and Capua and Salerno—were ripe for a development of civic institutions like those which actually burst into flower in the same century in the North Lombard regions of Tuscany and the Basin of the Po. In fact,

be argued that in the development of our Western Civilization in its 'medieval' phase both the city-states and the universities were by-products of Hildebrand's work rather than monuments of separate creative acts,[1] we cannot therefore infer that all that was lacking in contemporary Orthodox Christian life was some counterpart of the Papal *Respublica Christiana*; for if we turn to the 'medieval' Western institution of Feudalism, which was independent of, and in conflict with, both the 'medieval' Western Church and the 'medieval' Western city-states, we shall find that the Orthodox Christian counterpart of Feudalism, though not non-existent, was effectively repressed, like the Orthodox Church, by the East Roman Imperial Power—with the unfortunate consequence that, like the Church, this Feudalism asserted itself belatedly and violently in Orthodox Christendom when the weakening of the Imperial Power gave it an opportunity at last.[2]

during the semi-interregnum in Southern Italy which began with Melo's revolt against the East Roman régime in 1009 and ended with the completion of the Norman conquest *circa* 1080, a number of South Lombard cities did momentarily achieve self-government (see Gay, op. cit., pp. 561–8). Yet, even in this outlying overseas dominion of the East Roman Empire, the East Roman connexion gave an impulse towards the antithesis of the city-state dispensation—that is to say, towards a centralized autocratic régime—and this impulse from an alien force was so strong and so persistent that it eventually overcame the indigenous local bent of political development. This victory of political Byzantinism in Southern Italy will appear the more remarkable when we remember that the régime under which it was finally won was not that of the East Roman Empire itself but that of its Norman 'successor-state', which merely took over the East Roman tradition at second hand. The fate of the South Lombard cities was shared by their non-Lombard neighbours. The later history of Naples, for example, who surrendered her city-state autonomy to the Normans in order to become the petty-Constantinople of the Kingdom of Sicily-beyond-the-Faro, affords a striking contrast to that of Venice, who had shared with Naples in an earlier chapter the rare distinction of never having succumbed to a Lombard conquest. From the eleventh century onwards Venice preserved for herself the political birthright that was forfeited by Naples and the economic birthright that was forfeited by Amalfi; and the secret of Venice's material success at this critical moment of Italian history is to be found in a psychological reorientation. From this time onwards Venice steadily emancipated herself from the influence of the Orthodox Christian culture and opened her arms to the culture of the West.

[1] The Western universities largely owed their stimulus and their liberty to the fact that they were under the aegis and auspices of the Papacy, instead of being under the thumb of the local temporal lord or the local bishop. The North and Central Italian city-states found the opportunity to assert their civic liberties in the breach which was made in the power of the Holy Roman Empire by Hildebrand's assault. (On this latter point see III. C (ii) (*b*), vol. iii, p. 345, above.)

[2] For the violent self-assertion of the Orthodox hierarchy against the East Roman Imperial Government from the middle of the eleventh century onwards see IV. C (iii) (*c*) 2 (β), Annex II, below. The history of Feudalism in the Orthodox Christian World is not unlike the history of the Church. In the seventh century there was a moment (see IV. C (iii) (*c*) 2 (β), Annex I, below) when it seemed as though something like Feudalism would prevail in Orthodox Christendom as Feudalism actually did prevail in Western Christendom in the early age of our Western history. In Orthodox Christendom, however, this early tendency towards Feudalism was repressed in the eighth century when Artavasdus succumbed to Leo Syrus and to Leo's son and successor Constantine V (see p. 342, above). Feudalism could not remain rampant in a world in which a ghost of the Roman Empire had been effectively resuscitated. But although in Orthodox Christendom Feudalism, like the Church, was dragooned into the service of the East Roman *Imperium Redivivum*, it proved, like the Church again, to have been merely bent without having been broken. As soon as the Imperial Government's grip began to relax, the feudal magnates of Central and Eastern Anatolia

This eventual self-assertion of both Feudalism and the Church in the Orthodox Christian World shows that, in these two spheres at any rate, the relative sterility and monotony of Orthodox Christian life in the preceding chapter of history were due not to any lack of vitality or creative power in the Orthodox Christian body social, but to the artificial and temporary repression of these faculties by *force majeure*. At the outset the social landscape in Orthodox Christendom substantially resembled the landscape in the contemporary West. Here, as well as there, the woodman had planted a goodly array of saplings in the expectation of seeing them grow up into a serried grove in the fullness of time; and in the West this reasonable expectation was duly fulfilled. It was the peculiar mishap of Orthodox Christendom that in this plantation a single tree—the 'Caesaro-papal' East Roman *Imperium Redivivum*—shot up with such abnormal speed and vigour that it completely outstripped its fellows and consequently blighted their growth by sucking all the goodness out of the soil into its own far-ramifying roots and intercepting all the light and air of heaven in order to nourish its own widespreading foliage. The excessive luxuriance of the East Roman Empire had to be paid for by the starvation of all the sister institutions within its radius. And so, instead of the grove of many tall trees which came to maturity in the West, the Orthodox Christian World produced a single giant pine ringed round by a miserable undergrowth of stunted bushes and noxious nettles, unhappy offspring of an impoverished soil and an asphyxiating shade. In contrast to the landscape in the West the landscape in Orthodox Christendom now presented a painful picture of that disharmony which is the penalty of misgrowth.

The blighting influence of the single overwhelming institution of the 'Caesaro-papal' State upon Orthodox Christian life is revealed in the perverse vitality which the Church and Feudalism displayed in Orthodox Christendom when they found their liberty at last, and it is also illustrated by some rare flashes of brilliant

raised their heads as defiantly as the Oecumenical Patriarch raised his. As we shall see below, the refractoriness of this element in the body social in this quarter of the Empire gives the measure of the strain that was imposed on Orthodox Christendom by the Romano-Bulgarian Hundred Years' War. The War of A.D. 913–27 was accompanied by the manifestly ineffective agrarian legislation of the Emperor Romanus Lecapenus, while the deadlier War of A.D. 977–1019 was punctuated by a series of open and formidable feudal revolts against the authority of the Emperor Basil II, who did not intimidate his own subjects by earning the title of 'the Bulgar-killer' (see Vasiliev, op. cit., vol. i, pp. 455–60). After the wasting of the Empire's strength by eighty years of inward decay behind a pretentious façade the feudal interest actually succeeded in capturing the Imperial Government by placing on the throne its own representative, Isaac Comnenus (*imperabat* A.D. 1057–9). It is remarkable that this should have happened already before the visible prostration of the Empire in A.D. 1071 through the double blow of the fall of Bari and the débâcle at Manzikert.

creative genius which the Orthodox Christian Society emitted at certain points in Space and Time at which it happened to be free from its almost ubiquitous Imperial incubus.

In the Space-dimension we may notice the creative achievements of those scattered and neglected outposts of Orthodox Christendom, west of Rhodope, which were never subjected to the full weight of the East Roman Imperial régime as this was felt in Thrace and Anatolia.[1]

For example, the monastic stronghold in which the Orthodox Church found its base of operations for a counter-offensive against the Imperial Power was situated in this region, on Mount Athos.[2] In all probability Macedonian Athos would have seemed no holier a mountain than Mysian Olympus in the eyes of the eleventh-century courtier-monk Michael Psellus, who repaired to the latter mountain when he made his rather perfunctory gesture of withdrawing from the World. But a holy mountain that was in sight of the Imperial City was still not holy enough; and Olympus was debarred, by its very locality, from aspiring to the eminence which Athos triumphantly attained after Psellus's day.[3]

At a still greater remove from Constantinople, on the farther side of the Adriatic, and at a moment when the East Roman Government's authority was locally in abeyance, Basilian monachism revealed a capacity for creation which it never displayed on Mount Athos and never made even a motion to display in its Anatolian homelands. In Calabria, from the latter part of the ninth to the latter part of the following century, a handful of Basilian monks, who had been expelled from their native monasteries in Sicily by the African Muslim conquerors of the island, and who found the East Roman Government as supine in protecting their Calabrian asylum as it had shown itself in defending their Sicilian home, magnificently rose to the occasion, and took upon their unaccustomed shoulders the arduous social duties which the Emperor had tacitly repudiated. These monastic pioneers relaid the founda-

[1] For the differentiation of the East Roman régime in the Cisrhodopaean and the Transrhodopaean territories of the Empire see p. 344, above. The only conspicuous creative achievement of the Cisrhodopaean torso of Orthodox Christendom during the *floruit* of the East Roman Empire was the creation of the Byzantine Greek Epic; and this is an exception which proves the rule that the East Roman Empire had a sterilizing effect on Orthodox Christian life; for the nursery of this school of 'heroic' poetry was a borderland between the East Roman Empire and the 'Abbasid Caliphate in which the writ of the East Roman Central Government at Constantinople did not run effectively (see V. C (i) (*c*) 3, vol. v, pp. 252–8, below).

[2] See IV. C (iii) (*c*) 2 (β), Annex II, pp. 620–1, below.

[3] The Greek monastic pioneers who laid the foundations of the federal community on Mount Athos in the latter part of the tenth century were afterwards emulated by the fourteenth-century Greek and Serb founders of the stylite monasteries of Metéora in Thessaly (see Miller, W.: *The Latins in the Levant* (London 1908, Murray), pp. 294–6), and by the Bulgarian founders of the monasteries on Mount Rilo. We may notice that Metéora and Rilo, like Athos itself, lay well beyond the limits of the metropolitan provinces of the East Roman Empire.

tions of Orthodox Christian social life in a derelict East Roman province which had become a no-man's-land; they reconverted a horde of vagrant and demoralized Sicilian Greek refugees into a settled and orderly community;[1] and they were able to inspire this confidence in their secular co-religionists because they knew how to charm their Muslim persecutors into showing them consideration and paying them respect.[2] Their cells became the nuclei of new Greek villages and cities on the Italian mainland; and the Latinization of the 'toe' of Italy, which had followed gradually upon the Roman conquest in the third century B.C., was now undone, after the lapse of a thousand years, by these monkish re-creators of the ancient Magna Graecia. St. Nilus and his companions also emulated the ancient Greek pioneers in the Western Mediterranean in spreading their cultural influence far beyond the bounds of their own Greek colonies. As the Chalcidian and Corinthian adventurers who founded Rhegium and Syracuse travelled on to spread the light of Hellenism in Etruria and Latium, so St. Nilus, not content with building a new Greece in Calabria, accepted a call to Rome and provided a new model for Western monasticism in his outpost-monastery of Grottaferrata.[3]

In their combination of personal adventurousness and social constructiveness these ninth- and tenth-century Basilian monks in the Far West of the Orthodox Christian World can only be compared with the sixth- and seventh-century Irish monks of the short-lived Far Western Christendom;[4] and the comparison is as instructive as it is inevitable; for the Far Western Christian êthos is at the opposite pole of the spiritual gamut from the Orthodox Christian êthos as it presents itself in those parts of Orthodox Christendom where it was burdened with the incubus of the East Roman Empire. The Irish vitality which Basilian monachism displayed in one corner of the Orthodox Christian World, when for one moment the burden was lifted, proves how crushingly heavy the incubus was and how cruelly it was deforming from its natural bent the society that was condemned to bear it.

This Irish parallel can be carried farther, for in Italy, as in Ireland, the pioneer monks had spiritual issue in a generation of scholars; and the greatest of the Irish scholars, Johannes Scotus

[1] For the work of St. Elias of Castrogiovanni and St. Nilus and the other Basilian saviours of the Orthodox Christian Society in Calabria see Gay, op. cit., pp. 254–86.

[2] At a critical moment of his hazardous career as a pioneer in the Calabrian wilderness St. Nilus was once saved from starvation by the charity of an African Muslim sea-raider (Gay, op. cit., p. 270), and he was highly esteemed by the Amīr of Palermo (Gay, op. cit., p. 282).

[3] St. Nilus established himself at Grottaferrata in A.D. 1004. For this Orthodox Christian influence upon Latin Christianity in the Ducatus Romanus at the turn of the tenth and eleventh centuries see further IV. C (iii) (*c*) 2 (β), Annex II, p. 600, below.

[4] This comparison has been made already in II. D (vii), vol. ii, p. 325, footnote 2, above.

Erigena, has a namesake and counterpart in Johannes Italus.[1] The Irish and the Lombard philosopher resemble one another in their uniqueness, each in his own time and place,[2] and in the audacious rationalism with which each of them sought to liberate philosophical speculation from the trammels of theological dogma; and they also experienced the same vicissitudes of fortune, for an audacity which seems to have passed unnoticed in the Far West created a scandal when it was carried beyond the Irish Channel or the Adriatic and was aired in the more conventional atmosphere of ninth-century Laon or eleventh-century Constantinople. Johannes Italus was a Latin convert to the Orthodox Christian culture in Southern Italy[3] who caused a flutter in the heart of the Orthodox Christian World; and he was followed—after the political transfer of Southern Italy from East Roman to Western hands as the consequence of a Norman conquest that was achieved in Johannes' own lifetime—by a Calabrian intellectual revolutionary who caused a similar flutter in Western Christendom. Joachim of Fiore (*vivebat circa* A.D. 1145–1202)[4] was a Calabrian monk who was manifestly not at home in the mental and spiritual world in which his lot had been cast by a political accident; and the impact of his genius upon this alien Western cultural environment left its mark on medieval Western religious thought in a vein of libertarian speculation that is the antithesis of what is popularly supposed to be the 'Byzantine' êthos. Some two centuries later again, in an age when the former political association of Calabria with the East Roman Empire was no longer anything more than a dim and distant memory, this long-lost outpost of Orthodox Christendom produced another *enfant terrible* in Barlaam of Seminara (*florebat circa* A.D. 1330–50), who caused an uproar in the fourteenth-century Orthodox Christian World by launching an attack on the new mystical religious movement of Hesychasm[5] in the name of a new rationalism which was the fruit of a steadily ripening Hellenic Renaissance.

[1] For the affair of Johannes Italus see Anna Comnena: *Alexias*, Book V, chaps. 8–9, and Hussey, J. M.: *Church and Learning in the Byzantine Empire, 867–1185* (Oxford 1937, University Press), chap. 5.

[2] Compare the uniqueness of Ibn Khaldūn in the cultural history of the Arabic Civilization in North-West Africa (for Ibn Khaldūn see III. C (ii) (*b*), vol. iii, pp. 321–8, above). Johannes Italus was not altogether without intellectual antecedents at Constantinople, for he was a pupil of Psellus and perhaps his master's successor in his chair of philosophy (see Hussey, op. cit., p. 71). Psellus, too, had been accused of heresy in his time, but Italus's speculations were more daring and they raised a greater storm.

[3] Anna Comnena's account (in loc. cit.) of Johannes Italus's career makes it evident that the future Hellenist and his parents had already come under the charm of the Orthodox Christian culture before the migration of the family to the eastern side of the Adriatic gave Johannes his opportunity of obtaining a first-rate Classical Greek education at Constantinople. Anna's indictment against Johannes is that this tactless barbarian convert to the Byzantine culture took the Pagan Hellenic philosophy in deadly earnest instead of *cum grano salis Byzantini*!

[4] See Grundmann, H.: *Studien über Joachim von Floris* (Leipzig 1927, Teubner).

[5] See p. 359, below.

Even more significant are those flashes of Orthodox Christian creative genius that blaze out beyond the range of the East Roman Imperial régime by eluding it in the Time-dimension. St. Nilus obtained his opportunity for performing his creative work thanks to the geographical remoteness of his field from the centre of the East Roman Empire in an age when the Empire was at its zenith. There are other creative works of the Orthodox Christian spirit which owe their liberation, not to their spatial distance from the seat of the Imperial Power,[1] but to the Time-span which separates their date from that of the East Roman Empire's apogee.

By the fourteenth century a society which, under the obsession of the Imperial idea, had extinguished the ancient civic liberties of Cherson and had blighted the promise of a new birth of civic life in Southern Italy, had been sufficiently liberated from the cramping influence of its own Imperial régime to blossom out on its own account—and this in Salonica, which at that time was the second city of a diminished Empire[2]—into an experiment in civic liberty[3] which, in its turbulent vitality, was fully a match for twelfth-century Italy or even for the Hellenic World of the fifth century B.C.[4] It was likewise the fourteenth century that saw the religious life of Orthodox Christendom renew itself in a mystical movement—known as Hesychasm—which sought to make of the Orthodox Church a spiritual ladder for bringing Man into the presence of God, after this Church had been used for some six centuries as an administrative mesh for keeping him in subjection to the State. But perhaps the most astonishing of all these fourteenth-century flashes of Orthodox Christian creativity are the mosaics in the *ci-devant* monastery church of Chora, which is now the Qahrīyeh Jāmy'sy. Here, within the enceinte of Constantinople, on the very

1 In the personality and career of a Joachim and a Barlaam we can see Time and Space working together to produce a prodigy.

2 Salonica seems to have developed and maintained a local civic êthos which was a reflexion of her geographical situation. As one of the Transrhodopaean enclaves of the East Roman Empire, she had been thrown upon her own resources and had never been subjected to the full weight of the incubus which the Imperial régime imposed upon the metropolitan provinces. By self-help Salonica had first repelled the assaults of the Slavs and Avars in the sixth and seventh centuries of the Christian Era and had eventually charmed and tamed and reconciled the barbarians who had settled down at her gates after their failure to scale her walls. The local spirit of Salonica was expressed in the worship of her tutelary saint, the warrior Demetrius.

3 See further V. C (i) (*c*) 2, vol. v, p. 107, below.

4 For this republican incident in Orthodox Christian political history see Tafrali, O.: *Thessalonique au Quatorzième Siècle* (Paris 1913, Geuthner). The Zealot régime at Salonica lasted from 1342 to 1349, with a short break in 1345. The revolution was provoked by John Cantacuzenus's usurpation of the Imperial Power in 1342—a lawless act which precipitated a long-maturing social conflict between a rich and privileged minority and the masses upon whose shoulders the whole burden of the miseries and disasters of the age had been thrust by their traditional masters. This conflict broke out all over what remained of the Empire, and first of all at Adrianople; but it was at Salonica that it went to the greatest lengths. The Zealots attempted to correct the extreme maldistribution of wealth by confiscating the revenues of the nobles and the monks, who were Cantacuzenus's partisans.

threshold of the old Iconoclast Lion's den, we can still gaze to-day at this exhibition of an Orthodox Christian art which was able to achieve in the intractable material of the Byzantine artist's choice an effect of movement and life that is scarcely surpassed by any contemporary Italian work in oil or tempera.

These fourteenth-century flashes of creative light produce an extraordinary impression as they flare out against the sombre background of a social fabric in disintegration. The fourteenth century saw the nadir of the Orthodox Christian 'Time of Troubles'. At that moment a society which had broken down at the time of the great Romano-Bulgarian War of A.D. 977–1019 was on the point of passing out of a four-hundred-years-long agony into the harsh peace of an Ottoman domination. The reason why these flashes occurred at this time can hardly be that the life of this tormented Christendom was then really growing brighter.[1] It seems more likely that the flashes proceeded from a candle, lit in ages past, which had remained hidden under a bushel[2] until the tardy destruction of that crass impediment at last allowed the light to shine for an instant before men as it was on the point of going out into the other darkness of annihilation.

If these fourteenth-century flashes were given off by the spirit of Orthodox Christendom at the moment when it was being disburdened of the leaden cope of the East Roman Empire in order to be draped in an Ottoman funeral pall, we can detect a sixteenth-century after-glow which was kindled, like the flickering Northern Lights, by a luminary whose orb had already sunk below the horizon. In Domenico Theotokópoulos 'El Greco' (*vivebat* A.D. 1541–1614)[3] the Orthodox Christian Island of Crete gave the Western

[1] If there was any increase of light at all in fourteenth-century Orthodox Christendom the illumination came from alien bodies and was a reflexion of their radiation. In that age there were two societies that were exerting a considerable influence upon Orthodox Christendom: the extinct Hellenic Society, to which the Orthodox Christian Society was 'affiliated', and the living Western Society, which was her sister and neighbour and oppressor. The influence of the Hellenic Renaissance is apparent in Barlaam's anti-Hesychast rationalism and in the Salonican Zealots' political and economic radicalism; and in both the same phenomena we may also detect the influence of the contemporary West. Barlaam, for instance, grew up in a long-since partially Westernized outpost of the Orthodox Christian World, and he was at home in Western Christendom (he gave Greek lessons to Petrarch when he was on a diplomatic mission to the Papal Court at Avignon). As for the Salonican Zealots, the dates suggest that their revolution of A.D. 1342 may have been partly inspired by the democratic revolution which had occurred in 1339 at Genoa; for, ever since the breach of A.D. 1204 between the East Roman Empire and the Venetians, the Genoese had been *personae gratae* in the East Roman ports, and in the first half of the fourteenth century there were well-established Genoese settlements, living on familiar terms with the local Greek population, at Salonica and the neighbouring town of Cassandrea (Tafrali, op. cit., pp. 125–6). These good relations continued until the Genoese reconquest of Chios and Phocaea (by the adventurer Simon Vignoso) in 1346 and the Genoese attack upon the capital of the East Roman Empire (by the colonists at Galata) in 1348.

[2] Matt. v. 15–16 = Mark iv. 21 = Luke xi. 33.

[3] See Kyrou, A. A.: *Οἱ Ἕλληνες τῆς Ἀναγεννήσεως καὶ ὁ Δομήνικος Θεοτοκόπουλος* (Athens 1938, Dhimitrákos).

World an artist whose art would appear to be the antithesis of the rigid canon of the Athoan iconists.[1] And yet, in spite of appearances, 'El Greco's' inspiration must have been derived from a native source, since it was so remote from the contemporary style of painting in the West that for more than three centuries after his own generation this changeling was regarded in the society of his adoption as an isolated and unintelligible *lusus Naturae*, until he found his disciples at last in a professedly revolutionary Western school of the present day.[2]

In 'El Greco's' blazon of a clear-edged shaft of light escaping from behind some opaque obstacle in order to pierce, with gleaming spear-head, the object which it strikes, we may perhaps discern a visual allegory of the Orthodox Christian Civilization's fate. This Cretan juggler with cross-lights would assuredly have found a congenial subject in one of those Solar eclipses in which an ashen Moon so exactly covers the orb of the true luminary, from whom she ordinarily derives her borrowed light, that we should hardly divine the hidden presence of a fiery body behind her—were it not that the veiling of the Sun's own self makes momentarily visible a mane of leaping flames which at other times is paled to nothingness by the transcendent brightness of the godlike head which wears these flaming locks. If we can imagine to ourselves this extraordinary cosmic spectacle depicted by 'El Greco's' hand, our visual simile stands out complete. The Orthodox Christian Society is the luminary under eclipse; the East Roman Empire is the leaden disk that covers it; and the streamers of astounding light that escape round the dark Moon's rim portray for us the creative work of Nilus the saint and John the philosopher and Joachim the visionary and Barlaam the rationalist and the anonymous artist of the Qahrīyeh Jamyʿsy and the famous Cretan painter to whose posthumous Byzantine genius we are ascribing our imaginary picture. The brilliance of the streamers informs us how great a light is obstructed by how grievous an impediment.[3]

[1] Just as Joachim of Fiore's theology would appear to be the antithesis of the rigid canon of Byzantine Orthodoxy (see p. 358, above).

[2] 'El Greco's' astonishing performance in being fully three centuries 'before his time' in the history of the Western art whose temple-courts he had entered as a proselyte may be compared with the similar performance of a Russian genius who likewise migrated out of Orthodox Christendom into our Western World and likewise anticipated the future march of Western history in his own line of activity. For Peter the Great's *tour de force* of anticipating Straker see III. C (ii) (*b*), vol. iii, p. 279, above.

[3] At a later point in this Study—in Part VI—we shall find that this simile of a Solar eclipse applies not only to the effect of the East Roman Empire upon the life of Orthodox Christendom, but also, not less aptly, to the effect produced upon the life of the 'apparented' Hellenic Society by the Roman Empire, of which the East Roman Empire was a ghost. The prototype, like the copy, eventually became a social incubus after having been instituted originally as a remedy for a social evil. One of the greatest living students of the social history of the Roman Empire (Rostovtzeff, M.: *The Social and Economic History of the Roman Empire* (Oxford 1926, Clarendon Press), p. 330)

The case of 'El Greco' may also remind us of another tragic feature in Orthodox Christendom's fate. Both the good and the evil that this luckless society has done have largely accrued to some other society's benefit.

Like 'El Greco' at Rome and Toledo, the Basilians in Calabria and the Lazio did their pioneer work for the future advantage of the alien Christendom of the West; and there is a more notorious example of the same involuntary altruism to the profit of the same neighbour in the fructification of the culture of the West, at the beginning of the modern chapter of Western history, through our Western discovery of the literature of the 'apparented' Hellenic Civilization among the ruins of the sister Christendom's prematurely collapsing social edifice. This fruitful Western discovery could never have been made if Orthodox Christian piety had not sedulously preserved these precious monuments of a common parent-culture through the tempests and earthquakes of the post-Hellenic interregnum in order to bring them out of its treasure-house, and furbish them up for re-use, in a Byzantine Renaissance

has described this sinister metamorphosis, and gauged its consequences, in the following terms:

'I think that the gradual decay of the vital forces of the Empire may be explained by . . . phenomena . . . connected with one prominent feature in the life of the ancient state in general—the supremacy of the interests of the state over those of the population.'

In undergoing this tragic change of role the Roman Empire did not have a peculiar history. The tragedy of the Roman Empire is the regular tragedy of the universal state, which is the species of polity to which the Roman Empire belongs (see I. C (i) (*a*), vol. i, pp. 52–3, above). In the disintegration of a broken-down civilization the universal state is the protective institution which the declining society throws up when it finds itself threatened with imminent dissolution in the culminating paroxysm of its 'Time of Troubles'. The foundation of this universal state is the society's last great constructive achievement; and the rally of its moral forces by which this achievement is accomplished wins a momentary reward in the shape of 'the Indian Summer' which visits a storm-tossed world under the universal state's aegis (for this social phenomenon see IV. C (ii) (*b*) 1, above). This beneficent guise, however, is not the ultimate aspect in which the universal state presents itself; for the moral rally of which it is the outcome is an attempt to cheat Destiny by obtaining a reprieve for a society which by this time is already under sentence of death; and therefore the reprieve which the universal state does win is only temporary and is purchased, at that, at a ruinous price. Destiny takes its revenge in a disastrous transformation of the character of a polity which is the master-institution of the declining society in this penultimate chapter of its history. The ubiquitous presence and pervasive influence of the universal state, which, in the first instance, serve so potently to conserve and revive such vital energies as the sorely stricken body social still retains, proceed thereafter, by a gradual and scarcely perceptible change of operation, to produce precisely the opposite effect—taking instead of giving, until in the end the vampire-institution sucks out the last remaining drops of the doomed society's life-blood. In Part VI, below, this plot of the tragedy of the universal state is analysed in greater detail. In the last phase of its history the universal state subjects the society upon which it has imposed itself to an eclipse which effaces, totally and forever, the moribund culture of the dominant minority; but in this eclipse likewise the darkness is relieved by streamers of light which flare out round the eclipsing body's rim. In this case the streamers come from a new creative spark which has been kindled in the dark by the Internal Proletariat, and they are the heralds of a new civilization whose faint dawn will be visible in the heavens when the eclipse is brought to an end by the break-up of the now maleficent institution which has been the cause of it.

In this tragedy of the universal state the idolization of an ephemeral institution, which is one of the alternative aberrations to which the breakdown of a civilization may be due, reasserts itself in the last act in order to prevent the disastrous consequences of the breakdown from being retrieved at the thirteenth hour.

which began in the same generation as the Carolingian Renaissance in the West and continued thereafter until the fifteenth century.[1] This preservation and resurrection of the mighty works of the Hellenic genius in the bosom of the Orthodox Christian Society ought to have brought its due reward in the fullness of time by inspiring Orthodox Christendom—as it did afterwards most effectively inspire Western Christendom—to achieve original works of its own; but in Orthodox Christian cultural history there was never any struggle for cultural emancipation from Hellenic leading-strings corresponding to that 'Battle of the Books' between the Ancients and the Moderns which was waged in the West through decade after decade of the seventeenth century until there could be no mistake about the Moderns' victory.[2] Accordingly in Orthodox Christendom the re-born Hellenic culture, like the East Roman *Imperium Redivivum*, became an incubus instead of a stimulus. It was not until its transmission to the lively mental environment of fifteenth-century Italy that this potent mental tonic was able to produce its proper stimulating effect; and thus, as it turned out, Orthodox Christendom actually performed her pious cultural labour for her Western sister's benefit. She played the thankless part of the unprofitable servant who is ordered to be cast into outer darkness because he has hidden in the earth the talent—or besant—that has been given him to work with; while the sister society, into whose possession the hoarded treasure passed, duly turned it to profitable account.

'For unto every one that hath shall be given, and he shall have

[1] For the cultural contact between civilizations in the Time-dimension which is commonly called a renaissance, see Part X, below. The renaissance of the Hellenic culture in its original Greek medium in the bosom of the Orthodox Christian Society made continuous progress from the time of its beginning in the latter part of the eighth century of the Christian Era throughout the next seven hundred years. In this persistence it showed its superiority in driving-force over the contemporary renaissance, in the West, of the same Hellenic culture in its second-hand Latin version. Like the Carolingian resuscitation of the Roman Empire, the Carolingian renaissance of the Latin culture was a flash in the pan which was followed, after another bout of mental stagnation, by a new renaissance of the Latin culture in a different region of Western Christendom. This second Western renaissance, which eventually came to birth in the North and Central Italian city-state cosmos, succeeded—in contrast to the failure of the Carolingian renaissance—because it was the expression of a new act of creation which was performed in Italy by the Western genius in this second chapter of our Western history (see IV. C (iii) (*c*) 2 (α), p. 275, footnote 2, above). Having thus succeeded in resuscitating the Hellenic culture in its Latin version, the medieval Italians crowned their achievement by enriching the Latin derivative with the Greek original, which they now went on to acquire through their contact in the Space-dimension with Orthodox Christendom. This contact between civilizations in the Space-dimension is dealt with in Part IX, below.

[2] 'The Battle of the Books' might perhaps be described not inaptly as a 'Counter-Renaissance', on the analogy of the 'Counter-Reformation'; for both movements were re-vindications of the native vein of the Western Civilization against the would-be tyranny of a ghost from the past. In the Reformation the Transalpine peoples of Western Christendom had resuscitated the Syriac germ of Western religion, as the Hellenic germ of Western intellectual life had been resuscitated by the Italians in their Renaissance.

abundance; but from him that hath not shall be taken away even that which he hath.'[1]

The notorious evil deed of the Orthodox Christian Society which redounded to the advantage of the West was the extermination of the Paulicians.

In the latest age of the history of the 'apparented' Hellenic Society, Anatolia, as we have seen,[2] had been the seed-bed of Christianity, and in fulfilling this historical function the Asiatic peninsula had produced a rich experimental variety of the cultural crop with which it had been so successfully sown. This Anatolian richness of religious life became part of the original social heritage of Orthodox Christendom when Anatolia came to be included in the nascent civilization's territorial patrimony; and one of the first-fruits of this inheritance was the Iconoclastic movement. Had Iconoclasm asserted itself before the establishment of the East Roman Empire it would perhaps have had better fortune, and it would then probably have been followed by a succession of fresh outbursts and manifestations of religious life which would have made the religious history of Orthodox Christendom as conspicuously *mouvementée* as that of the West. In the event the potentially creative force of Iconoclasm was diverted by Leo the Syrian, and again by Leo the Armenian, from its proper religious field in order to serve the extraneous political purpose of assisting the Imperial Power to assert its claim to a 'Caesaro-papal' authority;[3] and Iconoclasm played this political role so well that it missed its religious aim. When the dust of the Iconoclastic struggle (*saeviebat* A.D. 726–843) at last settled down, it became apparent that 'Caesaropapism' had triumphed in Orthodox Christendom at the Iconoclastic movement's expense. The Imperial Power was no sooner certain of its seat on a 'Caesaro-papal' throne than it showed itself content to let Iconoclasm drop; and the discarded religious movement carried away with it in its fall the whole of that rich and variegated Anatolian religious life of which Iconoclasm itself had been only one manifestation. The traditional Anatolian religious êthos, however, did not resign itself to the doom of annihilation without making a last stand in an outlying fastness.

After the suppression of Iconoclasm in the metropolitan provinces of the East Roman Empire the Anatolian religious spirit still remained incarnate in Paulicianism—a sect which appears to have been a local survival of an archaic 'Adoptionist' school of Christianity[4]—and when, at some date in the ninth century, the

[1] Matt. xxv. 29.
[2] In IV. C (iii) (*c*) 3 (α), p. 271, above.
[3] On this point see p. 352, footnote 5, above.
[4] See IV. C (iii) (*c*) 2 (β), Annex III, pp. 624–34, below.

Paulicians set up a militant republic of latter-day saints[1] in a remote and barely accessible no-man's-land between the East Roman Empire and the 'Abbasid Caliphate, on the watershed of the Halys and the Euphrates, they offered to the dissident elements in Anatolia a rallying point which was independent of the waning fortunes of Iconoclasm. If this interesting Paulician community had been suffered to survive, it might conceivably have saved the life of Orthodox Christendom by preserving for it, and eventually restoring to it, those vital elements in the Orthodox Christian social heritage which were incompatible with an East Roman 'Caesaro-papal' régime. In the Imperial capital at Constantinople and the Paulician head-quarters at Tephrice the component elements of the Orthodox Christian religious genius were polarized. But, just because the ideals for which they stood were antithetical, Constantinople and Tephrice could not leave one another in peace. The termination in A.D. 843 of the long struggle between the Iconoclasts and their Iconodule opponents for mastery in the East Roman Empire set the Imperial Government free to bend all its energies against the last remaining heretics; and the Emperor Basil I, who would not exert himself to hold Sicily against the Muslims[2] or Moravia against the Pope,[3] waged a war of extermination against the Paulician Republic[4] with all the weapons in his armoury. On the theological plane the ingenious and accommodating Oecumenical Patriarch Photius, whom his 'Caesaro-papal' master held in with so firm a hand when he was engaged in baiting the Pope,[5] was given free rein to employ his gift for heresy-hunting at the Paulicians' expense;[6] and this heresy-hunt was not carried on with

[1] The foundation of the Paulician polity at Tephrice in the ninth century may be compared with that of the Mormon polity at Salt Lake City in the nineteenth century (see II. D (vi), vol. ii, pp. 221–2, above) and with that of the Muslim polity at Medina in the seventh century (see II. D (ii), vol. ii, p. 57, footnote 3, and III. C (ii) (*b*), vol. iii, p. 278, with Annex II, above).

[2] See pp. 343–4, above.

[3] See IV. C (iii) (*c*) 2 (β), Annex II, pp. 605–10, below.

[4] It may be noted that the Emperor Basil I's own family came from the very region that produced this Emperor's Paulician adversaries. The founder of the 'Macedonian' Dynasty, like the founder of the 'Isaurian' Dynasty before him (see III. C (ii) (*b*), vol. iii, p. 274, footnote 2, above), was descended from a race of frontiersmen whose original homes were on the easternmost Asiatic borders of Orthodox Christendom, but who had been transported to the opposite extremity of the Orthodox Christian World—when their Asiatic homes became too hot to hold them—in order to guard the European bridge-head of the East Roman Empire in the Maritsa Basin against the barbarian invaders of the Balkan Peninsula. The 'Isaurian' and 'Macedonian' dynasties were themselves addicted to the policy of transportation which had been applied to their own forebears.

[5] See IV. C (iii) (*c*) 2 (β), Annex II, pp. 606–7, below.

[6] The work on the Paulicians that has been handed down under Photius's name appears, however, to be a late tenth-century paraphrase of Petrus Siculus's authentic and contemporary *Historia Manichaeorum seu Paulicianorum.* (See Grégoire, H.: 'Les Sources de l'Histoire des Pauliciens' in *Académie Royale de Belgique: Bulletin de la Classe des Lettres et des Sciences Morales et Politiques*, 5th series, vol. xxii, fasc. 4 (Brussels 1936, Palais des Académies), pp. 95–114; eundem, ibid., fascc. 6–9, pp. 224–6.)

spiritual arms alone; the military as well as the theological strength of the East Roman Empire was thrown into the conflict. In a war *à outrance* between powers so unequally matched the outcome could not be in doubt, though it might be long delayed; and, after a struggle which swayed to and fro across Anatolia and lasted from A.D. 843 to about A.D. 875, the hornet's nest at Tephrice was smoked out[1] by the master of the Imperial beehive at Constantinople.

From the East Roman Government's standpoint this was a famous victory; for the vehemence of the Empire's assault upon the Paulicians betrayed a conviction that the existence of the Paulician Republic was a menace to the Empire's security. Considering the incompatibility of principle between the two régimes, we may well believe that the official view was right; but we may also pass the private judgement that in this matter the East Roman Empire's victory was the Orthodox Christian Society's defeat. In eliminating the Paulicians[2] the East Roman Government did the same disservice to Anatolia that the Christian 'successor-states' of the Umayyad Caliphate did to the Iberian Peninsula when they expelled the Jews and the Muslims, or Louis XIV to France when he expelled the Huguenots, or the National-Socialist régime to Germany when it expelled the Jews and the Liberals. And the measure of this disservice can be taken by observing the benefits which these refugees and exiles conferred upon the countries where they eventually found asylum.

The cases of the French Huguenots and the Peninsular Sephardim have been dealt with already in this Study at an earlier point.[3] As for the Paulicians who were deported by the East Roman Government to the European frontiers of the Empire—the farthest distance that the Imperial Power could remove them from their Asiatic home[4]—they took upon their East Roman conquerors the

[1] The metaphor is apt, for Basil never captured Tephrice by force of arms. Its strength daunted him when he pushed his way to the foot of its walls in 871/2. It was not the fall of the fastness, but the death of the leader Chrysocheir, that broke the Paulicians' resistance. After Chrysocheir's death Tephrice was evacuated by his dispirited followers; and the whole of the territory of the Paulician Republic seems to have fallen into the East Roman Government's hands by about the year 875.

[2] The only monument of the Orthodox Christian Civilization in Anatolia in which any trace of a Paulician contribution can still be discerned is the Akrítas cycle of the Byzantine Greek Epic; and this is an exception that proves the rule of East Roman implacability in seeking to root Paulicianism out; for the Paulician leaders Chrysocheir and Carbeas have succeeded in finding a place in this Anatolian Orthodox Christian poem only by stealing in through a Melitenian Muslim back door. There is some irony in the fact that, while the hero himself has been invested with the name of Basil in honour of the East Roman Emperor who was the Paulicians' mortal enemy, the historical Basil's two principal Paulician opponents should have been converted by a poet's imagination into the fictitious Basil's grandfather and great-uncle respectively (see V. C (i) (*c*) 3, vol. v, pp. 255–6, below).

[3] For the Huguenots see II. D (vi), vol. ii, pp. 213 and 250; for the Peninsular Sephardim see II. D (vi), vol. ii, pp. 243–6, above.

[4] For the East Roman Government's regular practice of garrisoning the European frontiers of the Empire with settlers from the Asiatic frontiers see p. 365, footnote 4,

same revenge as was taken upon the Assyrians by the Israelites who were deported on the same grounds of policy from their Syrian home to the cities of the Medes.[1] Thanks to this harsh and high-handed measure, the dragon's-tooth seed which the victorious Power was seeking to eradicate on one flank of its empire won fresh and fairer fields for its dissemination on the opposite flank, to which it could scarcely have found its way if it had been compelled to wait in order to be wafted thither by the wind that bloweth where it listeth,[2] instead of being carried by a hostile statesman's misguidedly purposeful hand. There were Paulician troops in the army with which Nicephorus Phocas the elder carried out his South Italian campaign in A.D. 885;[3] but the destination of the majority of the Paulician deportees was probably the Bulgarian and not the Lombard frontier of the East Roman Empire;[4] for it was in the Balkan Slavinias that the religion which the Paulician exiles brought with them found its new mission-field.

On the Bulgarian frontier of the Empire, in Thrace, a batch of Asiatic Paulician deportees is known to have been planted as early as A.D. 756 (or 755)[5] by the Emperor Constantine V; and in A.D. 870, on the eve of the downfall of the Asiatic Paulician Republic of Tephrice, a project for the conversion of Bulgaria was being mooted at that distant East Anatolian head-quarters of the Paulician Church.[6] In a partial and indirect fashion this Paulician ambition was achieved; for, within less than a hundred years of the extermination of Paulicianism in its original Asiatic cradle through the

above. The earlier Asiatic colonists on the borders of the Empire in the Balkan Peninsula appear, in contrast to the Paulician deportees, to have been, not rebels against the Imperial authority, but loyalists who preferred to leave their homes rather than transfer their allegiance from the Empire to the Arab conquerors of its eastern provinces; but among these unruly frontiersmen the distinction between loyalists and rebels was perhaps not always easy to draw. In this connexion we may speculate whether the Mirdites, who at the present day are one of the leading Gegh clans of Albania, are to be traced back to those Mardaite loyalists who were evacuated from the Lebanon by the Imperial authorities as one of the conditions of the peace settlement of A.D. 688 between the Roman Empire and the Umayyad Caliphate. This similarity of names may, no doubt, be purely fortuitous; yet the present Mirdite territory would have been a natural site for the plantation of a Mardaite settlement by a seventh-century Roman statesman who wanted to cover the surviving enclave of Roman territory round Dyrrhachium against further encroachments on the part of the Slavs.

1 For the unintended and ironic outcome of the Assyrian policy of deportation in sowing the seeds of the Syriac Civilization in Iran, and thus enabling the Syriac Society, through its very misfortunes, to encircle and finally engulf the Assyrians' own Babylonic World, see I. C (i) (*b*), vol. i, pp. 79–81, and II. D (v), vol. ii, pp. 137–8, above; IV. C (iii) (*c*) 3 (α), in the present volume, p. 471, and V. C (i) (*c*) 2, vol. v, pp. 122–3, below.

2 John iii. 8.

3 See Gay, op. cit., p. 133.

4 The only deportations of Paulicians from the Asiatic to the European provinces of the Empire that appear to be directly attested are those of A.D. 756 (or 755) and of the eighth decade of the tenth century (see the next footnote and p. 368, footnote 1). For the survival of a Paulician community at Philippopolis as late as the eighteenth century of the Christian Era see IV. C (iii) (*c*) 2 (β), Annex III, p. 632, with footnote 5, below.

5 Theophanes: *Chronographia, sub anno mundi* 6247. 'The heretic Syrians' whose deportation to, and settlement in, Thrace is subsequently recorded *sub anno* 6270 = A.D. 778 were not Paulicians but were Jacobite Monophysites.

6 Petrus Siculus: *Historia Manichaeorum seu Paulicianorum*, ad init. et ad fin.

occupation of Tephrice by the East Roman forces in or about A.D. 875, the laborious weeding operations of the East Roman emperor Basil I had been more than made up for by the assiduous sowing of the Bulgarian heresiarch Bogomil. This man of destiny was a Slavophone priest of the Orthodox Church in Bulgaria who became converted to the faith of his country's new Paulician neighbours and showed his genius 'in his adaptation of this intricate Armenian religion to suit the needs of the European peasantry'.[1] This simplified—or modified—version of Paulicianism[2] spread far and wide over the Continent of Europe. The Slavonic vernacular into which the essence of the Paulician doctrine had been translated by Bogomil carried an Asiatic faith across the north-western frontier of the Bulgarian Empire into the no-man's-land between Orthodox and Western Christendom which eventually became the Kingdom of Bosnia;[3] and from this second Euro-

[1] Runciman, S.: *A History of the First Bulgarian Empire* (London 1930, Bell), p. 192. For an account of Bogomil's doctrine and work, and of the relation of the Bogomil daughter sect to its Paulician parent, see op. cit., pp. 190–6. The personal name of the founder of the sect, which became the general appellation of his followers, is a Slavonic translation of the Greek name Theophilus. The *terminus ante quem* of Bogomil's career is settled by the two recorded facts that he lived in the reign of the Bulgarian Tsar Peter (*imperabat* A.D. 927–69) and that he was anathematized by the Oecumenical Patriarch Theophylact Lecapenus, who died in A.D. 956. These dates indicate that the source of Bogomil's Paulician inspiration must have been either the Paulician community that had been domiciled in Thrace since A.D. 756 (or 755), or else some mission sent out by the Asiatic Paulicians before the East Roman Government's occupation of Tephrice *circa* A.D. 875. We have no record of a deportation of Paulicians to Thrace on the morrow of the fall of Tephrice (see p. 367, footnote 4, above), and Bogomil cannot have owed anything to the Asiatic Paulician deportees who were planted by the East Roman Emperor John Tzimisces in Eastern Bulgaria after his annexation of this territory in A.D. 972 (see p. 389, below). This latter reinforcement of the Paulician community in Europe may, however, have given an impetus to the subsequent spread of Bogomilism into the West.

[2] '[In the Balkan Peninsula the Paulicians] seem to have attempted the conversion of the Bulgars, and here also the pure doctrine of Paulicianism would appear to have become adulterated by an infiltration of Manichaeism, or at all events of ideas of a Gnostic and Dualist character; and hence arose the sect of the Bogomils. The connexion between the Paulicians and the Western Cathari is clear; but it is probable that the corrupted Paulicianism of the Bulgarians, rather than the original Paulicianism of Armenia, was the origin of Western Catharism, and that . . . the heresy travelled from Bulgaria, Bosnia and Dalmatia into Hungary and Italy.'—Turberville, A. S., in *The Cambridge Medieval History*, vol. vi (Cambridge 1929, University Press), p. 703.

[3] After the East Roman conquest of Bulgaria in A.D. 1019, Bosnia, together with Serbia and Croatia, fell under an East Roman suzerainty. Thereafter Bosnia became first a debatable zone between the East Roman Empire and Hungary, then an autonomous duchy, and finally, in 1376, an independent kingdom. The conversion of the Bosniak ruling class to Bogomilism evoked the unanimous hostility of Bosnia's Orthodox and Western Christian neighbours; and this Ishmael in Christendom was hard put to it to defend itself against a world of Christian enemies until it was rescued, in the nick of time, by the progress of the Ottoman conquests in South-Eastern Europe. The Bosniak nobility demonstrated their gratitude to their Ottoman saviours, and at the same time secured their lands against confiscation, by turning Muslim *en masse*; and from their incorporation into the Ottoman Empire in A.D. 1463 down to the Austro-Hungarian occupation in 1878 the descendants of these Bosniak converts continued to be the most loyal of the Pādishāh's European subjects. (For Sultan Selīm I's Bosniak garrison in Nubia see I. C (i) (*b*), Annex I, vol. i, p. 386, footnote 1, above; for the Bosniak Muslim school of 'heroic' poetry in the Bosniaks' native Serbo-Croat tongue see V. C (i) (*c*) 3, vol. v, pp. 327–8, below.) In 1878 the Bosniaks resisted their compulsory severance from the Pādishāh's dominions by force of arms, and, after more than half a century of Christian rule, they remain to-day as faithful as ever to the latest of their successively adopted Asiatic religions.

pean base of operations the new religion continued its advance, beyond the pale of the Orthodox Christian culture and out of hearing of the Slavonic tongue, into the heart of Western Christendom. Traversing the Croatian dependencies of Hungary and the Slovenian marches of the Holy Roman Empire, the Bogomil missionaries acquired Latin flocks in the Patarenes of Lombardy and the Albigenses of Languedoc.

In Western, as in Orthodox, Christendom the appearance of these goats among the sheep—or tares among the wheat—evoked active counter-measures; and the leaders of Western Christendom were ready enough to follow the East Roman emperor Basil I's militant policy of burning the tares[1] and separating the sheep from the goats.[2] In the crusade against the Albigenses which was authorized by Pope Innocent III[3] the vision of an Athenian tragic poet of the fifth century B.C. might have beheld an ἄγος ἀνήκεστον which could not be wiped out by Innocent's speedy attempt to undo what he had originally done against his own better feelings and sounder judgement.[4] Was this war of extermination that was levied in Christ's name by the Papacy at the height of its power the sin that doomed the master-institution of Western Christendom to meet with its tremendous downfall? Whatever may be the answer to that question,[5] it is certain that the tragedy of Albi reproduced the tragedy of Tephrice on a larger material scale; and if this had been the whole of the Western response to the Cathar challenge we should have to pronounce that the West had responded as unsatisfactorily as Orthodox Christendom; that, here too, the intrusive religion had simply been suppressed by force; and that once again the deed of violence had impoverished the spiritual life of the society which had acted the tragedy, besides demoralizing the institution which had taken the victim's blood upon its head. In Orthodox Christendom this was, indeed, the whole story; but in the West the same challenge evoked an act of creation as well as a crime.[6]

1 Matt. xiii. 30 and 40. 2 Matt. xxv. 32.

3 See further IV. C (iii) (*b*) 3 (β), pp. 559–60, below.

4 Innocent was so horrified at the evil which he had let loose that he sought to head his Crusaders off from Languedoc and push them over the Pyrenees to discharge their savagery upon the devoted heads of the Muslims in the Iberian Peninsula; but his well-meant efforts at a diversion were all in vain. The Christian wolves would not loose their fangs from their 'Manichaean' prey; and the Albigensian War, which had begun in A.D. 1208, dragged on for thirteen years after Innocent's death in 1216, to end at last, in 1229, in a peace of desolation. For Innocent's policy in this matter see further IV. C (iii) (*c*) 3 (β), pp. 559–60, below.

5 For the downfall of the medieval Papacy see further IV. C (iii) (*c*) 3 (β), pp. 512–84, below.

6 If the crime has to be debited to Pope Innocent III's account, the same Pope is at the same time entitled to the credit, not indeed for initiating, but for the perhaps hardly less important service of approving and promoting, the positive response with which the challenge of Catharism was met in the West by the saints whose work is touched upon

When the Bogomil wave swept over the valleys of the Po and the Garonne and broke against the Appennines and the Pyrenees, a Saint Dominic beyond the Pyrenees and a Saint Francis beyond the Appennines girded himself for the task of bringing this mounting Cathar flood to a halt; and in this enterprise, at the parting of the ways between a violent and a gentle course, Saint Francis wholeheartedly followed the path of Gentleness while Saint Dominic did not walk exclusively in the path of Violence. In this crisis in the history of the medieval Western Church, Dominic, as well as Francis, perceived that the Christian sheep in the Church's keeping would not have flocked so eagerly into the unfamiliar Cathar fold if they were not being grievously neglected by their own shepherds; and the spectacle of these shepherdless sheep inspired either saint with the creative compassion that had once moved his Master.

'When he saw the multitudes he was moved with compassion on them because they fainted and were scattered abroad, as sheep having no shepherd. Then saith he unto his disciples: "The harvest truly is plenteous, but the labourers are few. Pray ye therefore the Lord of the harvest that he will send forth labourers into his harvest".'[1]

The Franciscan and Dominican response to the challenge which Catharism presented to Western Christianity at the turn of the twelfth and thirteenth centuries was to put fresh life in the West into the Christian institution of monachism;[2] and the two saints did this by bringing the monks out of their rural cloisters—from which in the West they had never emerged since they had retreated into these spiritual fastnesses during the social interregnum that had followed the break-up of the Roman Empire—and sending them to carry their doctrine and their spirit among the neglected populations of the new cities that had latterly been springing up all over the expanding domain of a young and growing civilization.[3] The two orders of friars were thus given a harder task than the

in the following paragraphs. The connexion between the positive and negative sides of Innocent III's policy towards Catharism is set out further, on Grundmann's authority, in IV. C (iii) (*c*) 3 (β), Annex, below.

1 Matt. ix. 36–8 = Mark vi. 34, and Luke x. 2; cf. John iv. 35, and I Kings xxii. 17.

2 Dominic's method of coping with the heresy was 'to live the life of the heretics while teaching the doctrine of the Church' (Grundmann, H.: *Religiöse Bewegungen im Mittelalter* (Berlin 1935, Ebering), p. 102).

3 The friars of the first generation were largely drawn, like Saint Francis himself, from the class which it was their mission to convert. (For the social milieu in which the Cathars won their recruits see IV. C (iii) (*c*) 3 (β), Annex, below, following Grundmann, H., op. cit.; for the social provenance of the earliest Franciscans see Grundmann, op. cit., p. 165. They were recruited, like the heretics themselves, from the rich bourgeoisie, the nobility, and the clergy.) In making it their special task to bring a new and shepherdless urban population into a Christian fold the friars saved the medieval Western Christendom of the twelfth and thirteenth centuries from an imminent danger of breakdown from which the modern English-speaking world was saved in the eighteenth and nineteenth centuries by the Methodists.

Cluniacs or the Cistercians. These earlier reformers of monastic life in the West had set themselves to regain, or surpass, the original Benedictine standards of liturgical or intellectual or manual industry without abandoning the original environment of the Benedictine life. The Franciscans and Dominicans were required to 'let' their 'light so shine before men that they' might 'see' their 'good works and glorify' their 'Father which' was 'in Heaven';[1] and this mission demanded of them the fortitude to practise the monastic virtues without wearing the customary monastic armour against the trials and temptations of the World. The institution of these Christian Berserkers is the enduring monument which the medieval Western reaction to the Cathar propaganda has left behind; and if we look for any Orthodox Christian parallel to this we shall look in vain. In Orthodox Christendom Paulicianism was not only denied the opportunity of performing any creative act of its own; it was not permitted there even to create by proxy through calling into play the creative powers of its Orthodox opponents and destroyers.

Having now surveyed the general effect of East Roman 'Caesaro-papism' in stunting the growth and pruning out the variety of Orthodox Christian life, we may next examine the particular way in which this overwhelming institution was directly responsible for the breakdown of the Orthodox Christian Civilization.

We have already observed, in passing,[2] that the outward visible sign of this breakdown was the Great Romano-Bulgarian War of A.D. 977–1019. We may now go on to observe that while one of the belligerents in this war was that simulacrum of the Roman Empire which had been established in the nucleus of a nascent Orthodox Christian World, the other belligerent was the most important among the neighbouring barbarian communities that had been incorporated into a growing Orthodox Christian body social in the process of its expansion. In other words, the expansion and the breakdown of the Orthodox Christian Society were intimately connected with each other.

At an earlier point in this Study we have come to the conclusion, on the strength of an empirical survey, that mere expansion is not, in itself, the criterion of growth.[3] At the same time, when a society which does bear the genuine marks of being in growth is found simultaneously to be expanding in the geographical sense, we should expect *a priori* in such circumstances that the expansion would recruit the growing society's strength; and we can observe

[1] Matt. v. 16.

[2] e.g. in Part III. A, vol. iii, p. 26, and in IV. C (ii) (*b*) 1, in the present volume, p. 72, as well as in the present chapter, pp. 321 and 360, above.

[3] See III. C (i) (*a*), vol. iii, pp. 128–54, above.

empirically that this was, in fact, the effect of the contemporary expansion of the sister civilization of the West. If we ask ourselves whether the Western Christendom was strengthened or weakened, during the four centuries beginning with the reign of Pope Gregory the Great, by the successive incorporation of the English, the Bavarians, the Thuringians, the Hessians, the Frisians, the Saxons, the Scandinavians, the Poles, and the Magyars, we shall feel no doubt about the answer. These successive expansions of a growing Western Christian Civilization at the expense of a European barbarism undoubtedly strengthened Western Christendom enormously; and this is true not only in the case of the barbarians who were converted by peaceful penetration. We have seen already how the peacefully converted English and Normans and Swedes and Danes became propagators, in their turn, of the civilization which had won their voluntary allegiance. The English did this work in Germany and on 'the Celtic Fringe';[1] the Normans in the British Isles and in Calabria and Sicily;[2] the Swedes and Danes on the eastern shores of the Baltic.[3] It is more remarkable to find a constructive contribution to the life of Western Christendom being made by the Saxons, who, alone among the nine barbarian peoples enumerated above, had been converted to Western Christianity by force of arms. We have seen how Western Christendom had to pay for Charlemagne's disastrous breach with an established tradition of peaceful expansion by enduring a Scandinavian *revanche* for the Saxons' wrongs;[4] but we have also seen how the Saxons eventually threw themselves into a role which had originally been forced upon them, and took up the double burden—which had overwhelmed their Austrasian conquerors—of pushing forward the continental frontiers of Western Christendom and at the same time keeping alive a Western ghost of the Roman Empire.[5]

On this Western analogy it is surprising to find the corresponding expansion of Orthodox Christendom apparently doing nothing to enhance the expanding society's strength and vitality, but, on the contrary, precipitating its breakdown by setting the lists for an internecine struggle between the Bulgarian converts and their East Roman instructors. If we are to translate into Western terms the relations between Bulgaria and the East Roman Empire from the conversion of Bulgaria in A.D. 865 down to the outbreak of the War of 977–1019, we must equate the East Romans with the Franks and the Bulgars with the Saxons, and must then imagine

1 See II. D (vii), vol. ii, pp. 336–7, with Annex II, above.
2 See II. D (v), vol. ii, p. 201, and II. D (vii), vol. ii, p. 338, above.
3 See II. D (v), vol. ii, p. 168, above.
4 See the references on p. 322, footnote 4, above.
5 See II. D (v), vol. ii, pp. 167–8, and the present chapter, p. 338, above.

the Western Emperors of the Saxon line consuming the energies which they actually devoted to restoring order in Germany and Italy in an internecine struggle with the Crown of Lorraine or the Crown of France for possession of the title to the Holy Roman Empire. In fact, of course, this catastrophe not only did not occur in the Western World at the turn of the tenth and eleventh centuries, but could hardly be conceived as occurring in an age when the parochial states of Western Christendom had not yet acquired the sharp articulation or the clear self-consciousness which any belligerent communities must have before they can nerve themselves for a fight to the death. To find these conditions anywhere in Western Christendom outside Italy, the historical investigator must turn over the pages of the chronicle through a Time-span of at least another five hundred years. In the Age of the Ottos, the Saxons—whose pagan ancestors had opposed such a desperate resistance to the Frankish conquest a century and a half before the rise of Otto I[1]—were bone of the bone and flesh of the flesh[2] of a Western *Respublica Christiana* from which no city-state of Milan or Florence, nor Kingdom of France or England, had yet seceded in order to assert its own parochial individuality. On the other hand the contemporary Orthodox Christian Bulgars were divided from their East Roman co-religionists by a deeper moral gulf than had been fixed between the same two peoples a hundred years back, at a time when the Bulgars had still been pagans and when the gulf had therefore been religious as well as political. How are we to account for this striking difference in the respective developments of the Western and the Orthodox Christian Civilization in this age?

Before attempting to answer our question, we may cap this difference with another that is antecedent to it. By comparison with the performance of Western Christendom, Orthodox Christendom was astonishingly slow in addressing itself to the task of enlarging its own borders through the conversion of the barbarians at its European gates. While the Constantinopolitan Emperor Heraclius (*imperabat* A.D. 610–41) is reported to have emulated his older Italian contemporary Pope Gregory the Great's achievement

[1] Otto I became German King in A.D. 936 and Holy Roman Emperor in A.D. 962. The war between the pagan Saxons and Charlemagne had lasted from A.D. 772 to A.D. 802.

[2] One piece of evidence to this effect is the attitude displayed by the Lombard Bishop Liutprand of Cremona in his *Legatio*. This Lombard cleric's spontaneous aversion from everything foreign—a passion which he wears on his sleeve and makes no attempt to control—is aroused in full fury by his contact with the Orthodox Christian World, but is completely dormant when he is dealing with his Saxon masters. For Liutprand in the tenth century, Lombardy and Saxony are simply two parishes of a single Western Christian Republic, and he shows no consciousness of their ever having been divided from one another by a cultural or even a political gulf.

of converting the pagan English conquerors of Britain by arranging, for his own part, for the conversion of the pagan Serb and Croat interlopers in the Western Illyricum,[1] this spurt of missionary effort was apparently abortive.[2] The Serbs and Croats relapsed into paganism and the East Slavonic settlers in the heart of the Balkan Peninsula were left to stew in it.[3] Nor was there any immediate attempt on the Orthodox Christian side to convert the Bulgar Nomads who established a footing on the south bank of the Lower Danube in A.D. 680. The Bulgars, as well as the Slavs upon whose heels the Bulgars trod, were allowed to remain pagan for the best part of two centuries from that date. The conversion of Bulgaria to Orthodox Christianity did not take place until A.D. 865; and on the eve of that historic event the respective performances, up to date, of the two sister Christendoms in the European mission-field were strangely unequal. By that date Western Christendom had recaptured for its own part every foot of the ground that had formerly been held in this quarter of Europe by the Roman Empire; and it had pushed on beyond the ancient Roman frontiers until its own continental European bounds now extended to the line of the Elbe instead of being confined within the line of the Rhine and the Danube.[4] At the same date Orthodox Christendom was so far from winning converts beyond its own section of the Roman Empire's former European frontiers that it had not yet begun to win back the Balkan provinces from the pagan barbarism that had submerged them. The unreclaimed barbarian wilderness then still stretched almost to within range of the walls of Adrianople and Salonica and Nicopolis and Durazzo; and the Peloponnese itself was in the hands of interloping Slav tribesmen who had still to be pacified and converted.

This extreme inequality of achievement in the European mission-field appears the more extraordinary when we remember that the Orthodox Church had kept its hands free from one formidable handicap to successful missionary work which the Western Church had imposed upon itself.

In Western Christendom it was taken for granted from the outset that Latin must be the exclusive and universal liturgical lan-

[1] The report is preserved by Constantine Porphyrogenitus in his *De Imperio Administrando*, pp. 148–9 and 153. It is noteworthy that, in the story as it is told, Heraclius is said to have procured his missionaries from Rome—presumably because both the *ci-devant* Imperial Diocese and the *ci-devant* Imperial Prefecture of Illyricum were under the ecclesiastical jurisdiction of the Roman See.

[2] See Runciman, op. cit., Appendix IV.

[3] For the difference in origin between the Serbs and Croats on the one hand and the East Slavonic occupants of the heart of the Balkan Peninsula on the other see Part III. A, Annex II, vol. iii, p. 427, footnote 1, above.

[4] The weakness of the Rhine–Danube frontier of the Roman Empire lay in its inordinate length (see V. C (i) (*c*) 3, Annex I, vol. v, pp. 591–5, below).

guage not only in the former western provinces of the Roman Empire, whose inhabitants had acquired Latin as their culture-language before Christianity reached them, and had retained a Latin *patois* as their vernacular tongue, but also among the Celtic- and Teutonic- and Slavonic- and Finnish-speaking Christian progeny of the European barbarians who were successively gathered into the Western Church's fold. On this linguistic question the Western ecclesiastical authorities were intransigent. The Moravian Church which was founded by the Orthodox Christian missionaries Cyril and Methodius in A.D. 862 was broken up in A.D. 885 because its founders had endowed it with a translation of the Liturgy into the native Slavonic. On this account it earned the implacable hostility of the Western hierarchy; and this hostility was neither wiped out nor warded off by the founders' conciliatory gesture of placing their newly won converts under the authority of the Roman See.[1] Thereafter the Slavonic Liturgy, conveyed in the Glagolitic characters, was not tolerated in Western Christendom outside the bounds of certain Croatian frontier-dioceses where the Western Church had to compete with the counter-attractions of Orthodox Christianity at close quarters.[2] It is noteworthy that the Western Christian prelates who stamped out the Slavonic Liturgy in Moravia were Transalpines whose vernacular tongue was not Latin but Teutonic. In Transalpine Western Christendom an effective revolt against the liturgical dominion of the Latin language did not break out, even on the Slavonic soil of Bohemia, for another five hundred years, and on Teutonic soil it was delayed for more than a century after that. Nor was the revolt universal, even when it did come at last. Among the host of diverse linguistic groups which divide Western Christendom between them at the present day, there is hardly one which does not number among its members at least a minority that still celebrates the Catholic Liturgy in the original Latin.

In sharp contrast to this tyranny of Latin in the West, Orthodox Christendom cultivated a linguistic policy which was more liberal and indeed more 'catholic' in the non-ecclesiastical meaning of the English word. It is remarkable that in Orthodox Christendom there was no attempt to confer upon the Greek language the liturgical monopoly which Western Christendom conferred upon Latin as a matter of course. The historical nucleus of Orthodox Christendom was the Greek-speaking Christian population of Anatolia, whose forefathers had despised and rejected the Latin tongue of their Roman masters as a barbarous jargon; yet the Christian des-

[1] For the fortunes of this Moravian Slavonic Church see further IV. C (iii) (*c*) 2 (*β*), Annex II, pp. 605–10, below.

[2] See IV. C (iii) (*b*) 11, pp. 215–16, with p. 216, footnote 1, above.

cendants of those Greek-speaking subjects of the Roman Empire did not extend their forebears' disdain for Latin to the unquestionably barbarous languages of the peoples beyond the pale whom it was their own mission, not to conquer, but to convert.

The policy of translating the Orthodox Christian Liturgy into the local vernacular was applied in the earliest field of the Orthodox Christian Society's expansion, which was, as we have seen, in the Caucasus.[1] By the momentous year 862, when the Orthodox Church addressed itself at last to the task of converting the Slavs, the domain of the Oecumenical Patriarchate already extended in the opposite direction beyond the eastern limits of the Greek language in Anatolia;[2] and there, in these Iberian and Abkhasian dioceses, the Orthodox Liturgy was celebrated in the local Caucasian tongues This linguistic liberality of the Orthodox Church in the Caucasus may have been dictated originally by local considerations of policy,[3] but even if it had started as a local peculiarity it had long since been accepted as the precedent for a general rule.[4] The ninth-century Orthodox missionary Saint Cyril had prepared himself for his mission to the Slavs by reducing the Slavonic language of the hinterland of his native Salonica to literary form; and this literary labour indicates an intention to elevate Slavonic into a liturgical language and not merely to make use of it as a means of oral communication with the prospective converts. Moreover, before he found his life-work in the Slavonic mission-field, Saint Cyril had also set himself to acquire a similar mastery of the Turkish language of the Khazars in preparation for a missionary enterprise on the western fringes of the Great Eurasian Steppe.[5] It is manifest that the translation of the Liturgy into the mother tongues of barbarian converts was by this time already the Orthodox Church's established practice; and it cannot be doubted that this

[1] See I. C (i) (*b*), vol. i, p. 64, with footnote 3.

[2] In Anatolia itself the pre-Greek languages had become extinct in the last days of the Roman Empire, in the reign of Justinian I (*imperabat* A.D. 527–65).

[3] In the Caucasus the Orthodox Christianity of the Oecumenical Patriarchate had to compete with a series of rival missionary religions: in the first instance with the Monophysite Christianity of Armenia and the Zoroastrianism of Iran, and later on with the Islamic faith of the Arab founders of the Caliphate. Thus Orthodox Christendom had the same incentive towards linguistic liberality in Caucasia that Western Christendom had in Croatia.

[4] Here again we may observe a contrast between the developments of Orthodox and Western Christendom which is in Orthodox Christendom's favour; for in the West the linguistic concessions which had been made, *à contre-cœur*, to the Slavonic tongue and to the Glagolitic script were never allowed to develop from being a local curiosity into becoming a general practice. The early—and apparently easy—triumph of linguistic liberalism in the Orthodox Christian World gives us another glimpse of that native variety and elasticity of the Orthodox Christian êthos which was so cruelly repressed by the incubus of the East Roman Empire.

[5] For the career and scholarship of Saint Cyril see Dvorník, op. cit., chaps. 5–9, and Bury, J. B.: *A History of the Eastern Roman Empire from the Fall of Irene to the Accession of Basil I* (London 1912, Macmillan), chap. 12, section 3. The mission to the Khazars was abortive.

practice, in itself and *a priori*, gave Orthodox Christendom a signal advantage over Western Christendom in the field of missionary enterprise.

On this showing the *de facto* success of Western Christendom in outstripping Orthodox Christendom in the European mission-field will appear more paradoxical than ever. To resolve the paradox we must suppose that the advantage accruing to Orthodox Christendom from its linguistic liberalism was heavily outweighed by some formidable handicap; and as soon as we look for this handicap it leaps to the eye.

The missionary work of the Orthodox Church was crippled by the subjection of the Oecumenical Patriarchate to the 'Caesaro-papal' authority of the East Roman Imperial Government; for this servitude of the Orthodox Church to the East Roman State presented a painful dilemma to all prospective converts to the Orthodox Faith. If they accepted Christianity at the Oecumenical Patriarch's hands, and so came under his ecclesiastical jurisdiction, the change that they were making in their own status would not be only a change of religious belief and practice. In accepting the Patriarch's ecclesiastical jurisdiction they would be accepting implicitly, in the same act, the political sovereignty of the Patriarch's 'Caesaro-papal' master. In other words, they had really to choose between a persistence in their ancestral paganism and a conversion to Christianity which involved a forfeiture of their political independence; and, in the circumstances, it is not surprising that they should flinch from making this latter choice[1]—notwithstanding the inducement of being permitted to employ their mother tongue for the celebration of the Christian Liturgy.

This dilemma did not confront those barbarians who were invited into the Christian fold by the missionaries of the Western Church; for the acceptance of the ecclesiastical jurisdiction of the Roman See, though it involved a submission to the linguistic tyranny of the Latin language, did not carry with it the more formidable servitude of acknowledging the political sovereignty of a foreign Government. It is true that during the four centuries, beginning with the pontificate of Pope Gregory the Great, during which the Western Church achieved the conversion of the barbarians of Western Europe, the Papacy was doing its best to place itself in that position of subjection to an Imperial Power into which

[1] In pagan Bulgaria, at any rate, the Khans took positive measures to prevent the spread of Orthodox Christianity. There were persecutions of Bulgarian Christians in the reigns of Krum Khan (*regnabat circa* A.D. 808–14) and his son Omortag Khan (*regnabat* A.D. 815–31), as well as under the intervening usurpers. These persecutions are the more significant inasmuch as these same Bulgarian princes were partial to the material culture of Orthodox Christendom and had no objection to the Greek language (see p. 380, footnote 5, below).

the Oecumenical Patriarchate was thrust when Leo Syrus effectively resuscitated a ghost of the Roman Empire on Orthodox Christian ground. We have seen already[1] how the Papacy clung to the skirts of the Constantinopolitan Imperial Government until these tore away in its hands, and how it then made two successive attempts to find a substitute for a lost Constantinopolitan aegis by investing first an Austrasian and then a Saxon prince with the Imperial mantle. The Papacy, however, was prevented by a kindly Fortune from frustrating its own missionary work by these persistent endeavours to escape the political independence which had been thrust upon it.

The Papacy's first successes in the barbarian mission-field were gained in an age when the Papacy itself was politically independent of any Imperial authority *de facto*, and in regions where Roman rule had either been completely swept away, as was the case in Britain and in Cisdanubian Bavaria and in Frisia, or had never existed at all, as was the case in the Bavarian Nordgau and in Hessen and in Thuringia. In these regions in this age the barbarians were scarcely conscious of the existence of a Roman Empire; and accordingly they looked upon the Roman See, to whose initiative they owed their conversion, not as the ecclesiastical agency of a foreign Government but as a spiritual power that was not subordinate to any temporal authority. To this spiritual power a converted barbarian prince would feel inclined to submit because the priest who wielded it presented himself, not as the servant of a mundane potentate, but as the Vicar of the Prince of the Apostles of Christ; and, by the same token, it was possible for a temporal ruler to make his religious submission to the Roman See without any abdication of his own political prerogative, because the Papacy purported to be a power of a different order from his, as well as of a higher rank. Thus for barbarian converts to Western Christianity at the dawn of Western history there was no political stumbling-block; and the Vicar of the Apostle at Rome would not be held to have convicted himself of a blasphemous hypocrisy if he called upon the heathen in the words of the Apostle's Master:

> 'Take my yoke upon you and learn of me, for I am meek and lowly in heart; and ye shall find rest unto your souls. For my yoke is easy, and my burden is light.'[2]

Nor was this happy relation between the Papacy and its barbarian converts destroyed by the Papacy's eventual success in resuscitating a ghost of the Roman Empire in the West, for neither the Carolingian nor the Saxon incarnation of this Western *Imper-*

[1] See pp. 335–40, above. [2] Matt. xi. 29–30.

ium Redivivum was either universal or permanent. For example, the English remained loyal sons of the Roman Church without following Pope Leo III's example of paying political allegiance to the Imperial authority of Charlemagne; and their relations with the Holy See were thus not affected by the evocation of the Holy Roman Empire. Again, the Scandinavians and the Poles and the Magyars entered the Roman Church's spiritual fold, as the English had entered it some four hundred years earlier, 'without political prejudice'. Their acceptance of the Pope's ecclesiastical jurisdiction did not carry with it even an implicit acceptance of the political sovereignty of the Holy Roman Empire, notwithstanding the fact that at the time of their conversion this institution was once more 'a going concern'. Though the Popes who received these barbarians into the Western Church acknowledged the Saxon Emperors of the day as their own temporal lords, the actual political effect of the religious transaction was to give the *ci-devant* barbarian principalities of Hungary and Poland and Denmark and Norway and Sweden the status of Western Christian kingdoms which, like the existing Western Christian kingdoms of France and Wessex and Leon, were members of a Western *Respublica Christiana* in their own right and not in virtue of any act of political submission to the Holy Roman Empire. Thus the effect of the ecclesiastical submission of these barbarian principalities to the Roman See was not to impugn their political independence but to confirm it; and their princes took their place not as vassals but as peers of a Western Emperor who was thereby tacitly reduced, for his own part, from an oecumenical monarch to a *primus inter pares*.[1]

The expansion of Orthodox Christendom could not proceed on these happy lines because the subjection of the Patriarchal to the Imperial Power was there not an empty form but a stern reality; and the unfortunate consequences which this difference entailed were not slow to work themselves out when in A.D. 865 the East Roman Government felt itself compelled at last, by circumstances which forced its hand,[2] to secure the conversion of Bulgaria. The inherent disastrousness of 'Caesaro-papism', which disclosed itself in this emergency, is thrown into relief by the fact that, in this affair as in others, the East Roman Government displayed its customary diplomatic moderation. A disastrous institution inexorably produced its inevitable effect in spite of a statesmanlike policy.

[1] On this point see further IV. C (iii) (*c*) 3 (β), pp. 523–4, below.

[2] The circumstances were that Orthodox Christendom now found itself involved, willy-nilly, in a competition with Western Christendom for the cultural allegiance of South-Eastern Europe. For the origins and outcome of this competition see IV. C (iii) (*c*) 2 (β), Annex II, pp. 605–10, below.

To begin with, the conversion of Bulgaria to Orthodox Christianity in A.D. 865[1] was brought about by an East Roman naval and military demonstration.[2] This misuse of political power for producing a religious effect was slight by comparison with the Thirty Years' War through which a Charlemagne had imposed a Western Christianity upon the Saxons. Moreover the East Roman Government actually gilded the pill by formally ceding to Bulgaria at the same moment a large slice of the Slav-infested no-man's-land between Salonica and Durazzo.[3] Nevertheless the converted Bulgarian prince Boris reacted violently to even this tactful touch of an East Roman political whip; for, though he had been gently handled this time, Boris now saw himself exposed in perpetuity to the humiliation of being subject to an East Roman political discipline. One of the conditions of the Romano-Bulgarian treaty of A.D. 865 was that Bulgaria must accept the ecclesiastical jurisdiction of the Oecumenical Patriarchate.[4] The implied acceptance of the political suzerainty of the Patriarch's Imperial master, by whom this condition was imposed, was both manifest and intolerable; and, finding himself thus politically as well as ecclesiastically bitted and spurred, the Bulgarian colt promptly kicked against the pricks. In 866, less than twelve months after the signature of the treaty, Boris broke it by transferring the ecclesiastical allegiance of Bulgaria from the Oecumenical Patriarchate to the Roman See. This Bulgarian adherence to the Papacy was maintained from 866 to 870; and though Boris voluntarily retransferred his allegiance to the Oecumenical Patriarchate in the latter year and persisted in this policy thereafter—even when the East Roman Emperor Basil I, with his tongue in his cheek, officially awarded Bulgaria to the Papal jurisdiction in 879[5]—this first Bulgarian attempt to escape

[1] A.D. 864–5 according to Dvorník, F.: *Les Slaves, Byzance et Rome au ixe siècle* (Paris 1926, Champion), p. 187.

[2] Runciman, op. cit., pp. 103–4; Dvorník, op. cit., p. 187. Bulgaria was prostrated at the time by a famine, and she had no choice but to yield to the East Roman military demonstration—which was nominally a reprisal for a Bulgar foraging-raid into East Roman territory.

[3] Runciman, op. cit., p. 105.

[4] Runciman, op. cit., p. 106.

[5] This Bulgarian experiment in allegiance to the Roman See is discussed further in IV. C (iii) (*c*) 2 (β), Annex II, pp. 605–10, below. The reasons for the abandonment of the experiment are obscure. Perhaps the fundamental reason was because the Western Christian culture had little or no prestige in Bulgaria by comparison with the Orthodox Christian culture. Within the horizon of a contemporary West European barbarian, Latin was the only known culture-language and the Papacy the greatest known cultural institution, and this monopoly gave the Roman Church an immense moral authority in dealing with its barbarian converts in Western Europe. The Papacy had not this advantage in Bulgaria, since in Bulgarian eyes the Roman See could not compare with the East Roman Empire as an institution, while the Latin medium of culture could not compare with the Greek. Ever since the Greek citizens of Adrianople had been carried away into captivity by the Bulgar Khan Krum in A.D. 813, the princes of Bulgaria, in the last phase of their paganism, had been using the services of Greek prisoners-of-war or renegades from the East Roman Empire to introduce them to the rudiments of material culture. The palaces which Krum and his son Omortag (*regnabat* A.D. 815–31)

the political implications of allegiance to the Oecumenical Patriarchate was ominous of evils to come.

Having surmounted the danger of a permanent ecclesiastical secession of Bulgaria from the Oecumenical Patriarch's jurisdiction to the Pope's, East Roman statesmanship showed its tact again by doing everything possible to make the mansion of Orthodox Christendom to which the Bulgarian prodigal had returned an agreeable place for him to live in. One of the last acts of the Emperor Basil I (*imperabat* A.D. 867–86) was to emphasize the one obvious amenity that the Constantinopolitan ecclesiastical connexion possessed and the Roman connexion lacked. He placed at Boris' disposal the Slavophone clergy who had been expelled from Moravia in A.D. 885;[1] and the *Ausgleich* between the Khan and the Emperor which was implied in this clever gesture of Imperial courtesy seems to have been tacitly accepted by Boris on his side. During the rest of his reign Boris occupied himself in building up a Slavophone Church in Bulgaria[2] under the Oecumenical Patriarch's jurisdiction; and though this work effectively closed the door upon any return to the Roman ecclesiastical connexion, Boris does not seem to have troubled himself any longer about the East Roman Imperial suzerainty which the Patriarch's jurisdiction constitutionally carried with it. Probably Boris felt that the separate individuality of Bulgaria was sufficiently vindicated *de facto* by the ecclesiastical use of a local vernacular instead of the Greek which was the East Roman language of state; and the fact that the new liturgical language of Bulgaria was the mother tongue of the Khan's alien Slav subjects, and not that of his own Turkish-speaking kinsmen and peers the Bulgar nobility, was no doubt an additional advantage in the eyes of a Bulgarian ruler who aspired to make himself as

built for themselves were designed by Greek architects, and the work was commemorated in Greek inscriptions (see Runciman, op. cit., pp. 75–9). The city of Constantinople, too, exercised a fascination with which a dilapidated ninth-century Rome could not compete (Dvorník, op. cit., p. 255). This cultural legacy from the days of Bulgarian paganism may have been the determining factor in the ecclesiastical policy of the Christian Khan Boris in A.D. 870 and A.D. 879 (see Dvorník, op. cit., p. 264). Conversely, the attraction of an adjacent Western Christian culture may account for the anti-Methodian policy of the Moravian prince Rostislav's betrayer and supplanter Svatopluk (Dvorník, op. cit., p. 263).

[1] See IV. C (iii) (*c*) 2 (*β*), Annex II, pp. 608–9, below. These refugee clergy appear to have migrated from Constantinople to Bulgaria on their own initiative, though, of course, with the Emperor's consent (Dvorník, op. cit., pp. 311–12).

[2] In this work Boris had the help, not only of the refugee Slavophone clergy who came to Bulgaria via Constantinople, but also of another band who came direct overland from Moravia (Dvorník, op. cit., pp. 312–18). The leader of this latter band, Clement, was sent by Boris to the Far West of his dominions in the, by this date, predominantly Slavonic interior of Macedonia (Kutmičevica). Clement made his head-quarters at Ochrida; and from this base of operations he evangelized and civilized all the region round about. It will be seen that the country which Clement thus reclaimed from barbarism towards the close of the ninth century of the Christian Era was coincident with the Western Bulgaria which fought to the death against East Roman Imperialism in the Great Romano-Bulgarian War of A.D. 977–1019 (see pp. 390–1, below).

complete an autocrat in Bulgaria as the Emperor was in the East Roman Empire.[1]

By A.D. 889 Boris believed that his work was now sufficiently secure to warrant his abdicating. Four years later, when his eldest son and first successor, Vladímir, threatened to undo what he had done, Boris emerged from the cloister into which he had retired in order to save his work by deposing the betrayer of it. He seems to have made this crisis an occasion for practically completing the process of substituting the Slavonic tongue for Greek as the language of the Bulgarian Church;[2] and he did not retire into the cloister again until he had brought his third son Symeon out of it to reign in the unworthy Vladímir's stead.[3] Boris, however, was unlucky in his choices of sons to succeed him. If in Vladímir he had 'caught a Tatar' whose one idea was to reconvert Bulgaria into an ephemeral Nomad empire *in partibus agricolarum*,[4] in his monk-son Symeon he was placing on the throne of Bulgaria a *Hemiargus* or 'semi-Greek' whose megalomania was to prove still more destructive to the Slavonic Christian body politic which Boris had built up.

Symeon had been brought up at Constantinople, where he had lived, apparently, in the Imperial Palace and had received his education not only in the school of Slavonic studies that had been founded by the Patriarch Photius, but also in the Greek academy that had been founded by the Caesar Bardas.[5] When his father's intervention unexpectedly set the crown of Bulgaria upon Symeon's head, the new Khan at first attempted to find scope for his own Philhellenism, without departing from the Slavophil policy which his father had commissioned him to pursue, by promoting the translation of the Greek Classics—Pagan as well as Christian—into the new Slavonic literary medium. In the spate of translations which he churned out, Symeon at once revealed the demonic energy that was in him. This energy, however, could not find sufficient vent within the limits of a cultural field within which alone the father's narrow-verged common sense could be reconciled with the son's wider horizon and vaster ambition.[6] The education of Symeon in the Imperial Palace at Constantinople had not been only literary;

[1] There is an acute discussion of Boris' policy from A.D. 886 onwards in Runciman, op. cit., pp. 126–30.

[2] See Runciman, op. cit., p. 135.

[3] Boris' reintervention in politics in A.D. 893 is reminiscent of the régime of the series of 'Cloistered Emperors' who governed Japan behind the scenes, after a formal abdication from the throne and withdrawal into a monastery, from A.D. 1087 to A.D. 1156.

[4] For the transitoriness of the dominion of 'the Desert' over 'the Sown' see Part III. A, vol. iii, pp. 22–8, above.

[5] For this foundation see p. 345, above.

[6] In his sense for μηδὲν ἄγαν and his cult of 'the Golden Mean' the Slavophil Boris showed himself a truer Hellene in spirit than Symeon 'the semi-Greek'.

it had also been political. Besides imbibing a taste for the Greek classics, he had been captivated by 'the great idea' of a Hellenic universal state—an idea which had been raised from the dead and enshrined at Constantinople in the imposing political institution of the East Roman *Imperium Redivivum*. With the crown of Bulgaria on his head Symeon could not long avert his mind from politics, and as soon as he thought about politics he could not be content with the status—that had satisfied his father—of a Georgian or Abkhazian princeling. At the same time his father's Slavophilism and his own Philhellenism conspired to debar him from attaining the political sovereign independence upon which his heart was set by the expedient of reverting to his father's earlier policy and transferring his ecclesiastical allegiance from the Oecumenical Patriarchate to the Roman See. How, then, was Symeon to escape from the, to him, galling status of being the ecclesiastical subject of a political subject of the East Roman Emperor? Since the path to Rome was closed against him only one path remained open; and to take that path meant denouncing the tacit *modus vivendi* into which Boris had entered with Basil I and plunging Bulgaria into a war to the knife with her suzerain and neighbour; for the alternative path was the path to Constantinople. In the circumstances in which he found himself Symeon could only acquire his sovereign independence by using the throne of Bulgaria as a mounting-block for climbing on to the throne of the East Roman Empire itself. He could only escape from being the Patriarch's barbarian slave by becoming his Imperial master. Symeon's clearness of vision was matched by his audacity in choosing his course. He decided to bid for the Imperial Crown, and in taking this decision he signed the death-warrants not only of the kingdom which he possessed and of the empire which he coveted, but also of the society in which these two political institutions had their being.

This fatal ambition had probably not yet taken shape in Symeon's mind at the time when the East Roman Empire was the victim of his first war of aggression. The occasion of this war was commercial; its duration was only four years (A.D. 894–7); and in the matter of Bulgaria's frontiers with the East Roman Empire the peace settlement restored the territorial *status quo ante*. This first venture merely cost Symeon the Transdanubian half of his kingdom.[1] He might not have got off so lightly without the good offices

[1] The Bulgar Nomads were already masters of what are now the provinces of Bessarabia and Moldavia and Wallachia before they established their first footing south of the Danube, on former Roman soil, in A.D. 680. They acquired what is now Transylvania, together with the section of the Hungarian Alföld to the east of the Theiss, at the turn of the eighth and ninth centuries, when the Bulgar Khan Krum partitioned

of 'the Cloistered Emperor' his father, who was at that time still alive and still, no doubt, capable of giving sensible advice. Thereafter the death of the ex-Khan Boris in A.D. 907 removed a restraint, and the death of the East Roman Emperor Leo the Wise in 912 presented a temptation. In 913 Symeon launched his second war of aggression against the Empire; and this war, which lasted fifteen years (913–27), had far more serious consequences for both belligerents.

In the first year of these fifteen Symeon revealed his war-aim and came as near to attaining it as he was ever to come. In that campaign his offensive carried him to the walls of Constantinople; and before he withdrew he had obtained a promise that one of his own daughters should become the wife of the reigning Emperor, Constantine Porphyrogenitus. Since the Emperor was then a minor, the promise was made by the Oecumenical Patriarch Nicolaus, who was acting as regent. Apparently Symeon intended, when his daughter was installed as Augusta, to wrest the regency into his own hands and then, by an easy metamorphosis, to transform himself from regent into co-emperor.[1] But Symeon's plan miscarried; for the Patriarch's promise was promptly repudiated by the young Emperor's mother, who managed to snatch the reins of government out of the Patriarch's hands[2] almost immediately after Symeon's withdrawal to his own side of the frontier; and the opportunity, which Symeon had espied, for an unscrupulous man of action to acquire the Imperial title for himself, by way of the regency, was equally apparent to the East Roman Admiral of the Fleet, Romanus Lecapenus, who had the decisive advantage over Symeon of enjoying the freedom of the Imperial City. After taking his time and choosing his moment Romanus Lecapenus occupied the Imperial

the Avar Empire with Charlemagne. These Transdanubian possessions appear to have been retained substantially intact by Krum's successors on the Bulgarian throne till Symeon lost them as a consequence of the Romano-Bulgarian War of A.D. 894–7. The history of their loss was as follows. In 895 the East Roman Government called in the Magyar Nomads, from the Steppe beyond Bulgaria's north-eastern frontier, to attack the Bulgars in the rear; Symeon retorted by calling in, on his own side, the Pecheneg Nomads, who were treading on the Magyars' heels; the Magyars suffered a disastrous defeat under the combined Pecheneg and Bulgar attack, and were thereby driven to cross the Carpathians into the Alföld, where they acquired a new and permanent home, mainly at the expense of Moravia, but partly also at the expense of Bulgaria. Thereafter the Pechenegs distrained upon their late allies the Bulgars—who owed them handsome payment for their effective intervention against the Magyars—by occupying, for their part, the Bulgarian territories in Bessarabia, Moldavia, and Wallachia. (For the movements of the Pechenegs and the Magyars at this time see Part III. A, Annex II, vol. iii, pp. 441–3, above.) This was the end of the Bulgars' Transdanubian empire. A critical examination of the interrelation, sequence, and dates of these events in the Eurasian hinterland of Bulgaria will be found in Macartney, C. A.: *The Magyars in the Ninth Century* (Cambridge 1930, University Press), pp. 177–88.

[1] For this interpretation of Symeon's stipulations in 913 see Runciman, op. cit., p. 157, with Appendix X.

[2] For the relations between the Oecumenical Patriarch Nicolaus, the East Roman Emperor Leo the Wise, and Leo's fourth wife Zoe Carbopsina, who was Constantine Porphyrogenitus's mother, see IV. C (iii) (*c*) 2 (β), Annex II, pp. 598–601, below.

Palace in the spring of 919; and before the calendar year was out he had married the young Emperor to a daughter of his own and had acquired the Imperial title for himself, while Symeon gnashed his teeth in the outer darkness. Therewith Symeon's last hope of achieving his war-aim was extinguished,[1] but nothing would induce him to stop the war, short of his own death; and that did not overtake him till eight years later.

Meanwhile the East Roman Government baffled its formidable Bulgarian adversary by adopting the strategy which had once been pursued by the Athenians, on Pericles' advice, in the first phase of the Atheno-Peloponnesian War of 431–404 B.C. In that Hellenic struggle the Athenians had effectively won the first round by making up their minds to leave at the enemy's mercy the open country of Attica and to stand on the defensive behind the impregnable fortifications that covered Athens and linked her with the Peiraeus and with the sea, whence they could draw unfailing supplies from an overseas empire which was beyond their Peloponnesian adversaries' reach. In the Romano-Bulgarian War of A.D. 913–27 the East Roman strategy was the same, *mutatis mutandis*. The East Roman Government allowed the Bulgarian armies to range almost at will over the continental European territories of the Empire up to the walls of Constantinople and Salonica and Durazzo,[2] while the East Roman land-forces stood on the defensive behind the walls of Constantinople and their other European maritime fortresses, and the East Roman Navy kept these fortresses supplied with the necessary provisions and at the same time covered and insulated the metropolitan provinces of the Empire in Anatolia.[3]

In the open country on the European side of the Bosphorus and the Dardanelles the Imperial Government was chary of accepting battle except vicariously; but its vicarious counterstrokes were formidable. In the year 917, for instance, it unleashed against Symeon first the Pecheneg Nomads and then the Serbs: a Western Slav people who had lately been played upon by the radiation of Orthodox Christian culture at second-hand, through Bulgaria, and who were now persuaded, by East Roman diplomacy, to repay their Bulgarian benefactors with the same ingratitude that the Bulgars themselves were showing towards the Greeks. It was perhaps on this occasion that Bulgaria lost to the Pechenegs the last remnant of her Transdanubian possessions in Wallachia.[4] The entry of

[1] Runciman, op. cit., p. 163.

[2] In 916 Symeon seems to have penetrated as far as the north coast of the Gulf of Corinth (Runciman, op. cit., p. 159).

[3] The East Roman Navy also insulated Symeon from his potential overseas ally the Fāṭimid Caliph in Ifriqīyah. For the importance, in this connexion, of the recent East Roman acquisitions in Southern Italy see p. 343, footnote 3, above.

[4] Runciman, op. cit., p. 160, footnote 1.

Serbia into the lists was still more awkward for Symeon; for thenceforth he had to fight on two fronts, and although the Serbs were perpetually being defeated they were never put out of action. At the close of the campaigning season of 924 a parley between the principals[1] resulted in a truce between Bulgaria and the East Roman Empire. But even then Symeon could not bear to revert to the works of peace with which he had opened his reign. He simply diverted his military efforts from the south-eastern front to the north-western, and in 926 he succeeded, at last, in reducing Serbia to subjection; but this conquest merely tempted him in the same campaigning season to attack Serbia's sister and neighbour Croatia, and this last act of aggression brought upon the Bulgarian army an overwhelming and decisive defeat. Symeon died of it in the following year; and in the year of his death—A.D. 927—the Bulgaro-Roman truce of 924 was converted into a peace.

In this peace the East Roman Empire recovered the territorial *status quo ante* in exchange for an acquiescence in the constitutional *uti possidetis*; and this was a compromise for which the way had been prepared by Symeon himself during the last three years of his reign. Having despaired at last, in 924, of transforming himself into the Imperial master of the Oecumenical Patriarch by mounting the East Roman Throne at Constantinople, Symeon had resolved to secure his sovereign independence, as best he could, by assuming the Imperial title within the frontiers of his Bulgarian patrimony and then setting up a local Patriarch of his own. He had proclaimed himself 'Emperor of the Romans and Bulgars' in 925 and had proclaimed the Archbishop of Preslav Patriarch of the new Empire in the following year.[2] The East Roman Government had recognized neither of these acts, and had explicitly protested against the former of them; and thus at the opening of the peace negotiations of 927 the metamorphosis of the Bulgarian Khanate into a 'Romano-Bulgarian' Empire was only unilaterally a *fait accompli*. In exchange for securing the territorial integrity of the East Roman

[1] The parley took place just outside the walls of Constantinople on an extemporized pier which was run out into the Golden Horn off the Cosmidium (in the neighbourhood of the present suburb of Eyyūb). Symeon boarded this pier by land, the Emperor Romanus (with the Patriarch Nicolaus in his suite) by water. The negotiators parleyed over a wall, like Pyramus and Thisbe, or like the Emperors Napoleon and Alexander in their barge on the Thalweg of the River Niemen in A.D. 1807.

[2] This time-lag in Symeon's proclamation of a Bulgarian Patriarch is perhaps to be explained by the fact that during the greater part of the year 926 there was a Papal legate at Symeon's court. The Papacy—still hoping to secure Bulgaria's ecclesiastical allegiance—had been quick to recognize Symeon's Imperial title; and the legate had been sent to improve the occasion. Apparently the Papal Chancery had not realized that, instead of reopening the possibility of adherence to the Roman See, Symeon was closing it, once and for all, by formally laying claim to a 'Caesaro-papal' authority. The appointment of a Bulgarian Patriarch necessarily made Symeon's standpoint clear; and on this account, perhaps, the appointment was delayed until after the Papal legate's departure from Preslav (see Runciman, op. cit., pp. 173–4).

Empire in Europe the East Roman Government now consented to perfect for Symeon's son and successor Peter the title which Symeon had unlawfully assumed. In the peace settlement of 927 the Constantinopolitan Chancery accorded to the son the recognition which had been withheld from the father. They made the unprecedented concession of gazetting Peter as an Emperor[1] and the Archbishop of the Bulgarian See of Dristra as a Patriarch independent of the Oecumenical Patriarch of Constantinople and supreme over the Orthodox Church within the Emperor Peter's dominions.[2] At the same time the new Bulgarian Emperor was given the East Roman Emperor Romanus's grand-daughter, Maria Lecapena, in marriage;[3] an annual subsidy from the East Roman to the Bulgarian Treasury was arranged for under the 'face-saving' name of a paternal allowance to the Imperial bride; and the Bulgarian Ambassador at Constantinople was made, *ex officio*, the *doyen* of the diplomatic corps.[4]

The peace which was concluded on these terms lasted for forty years; yet in fact, though not in form, it was a mere prolongation of the truce of A.D. 924; for the circumstances in which it was made, and the principle on which it was based, precluded it, *a priori*, from becoming a permanent settlement. Like the tacit *Ausgleich* of A.D. 886 between the Khan Boris and the Emperor Basil I, the Romano-Bulgarian peace-treaty of A.D. 927 was a compromise—but with the fatal difference that the new compromise was not one that could work. Boris had been willing to shelve the delicate constitutional question of the relation in which he and the Emperor stood to one another in virtue of their respective relations to the Oecumenical Patriarch, while Basil on his side had been willing to let Bulgaria

1 See Runciman, op. cit., Appendix XI.

2 Apparently the East Roman Chancery refused to recognize Symeon's Patriarch Leontius of Preslav; and, since Symeon himself was dead, the East Roman Government thus avoided recognizing either of Symeon's two unilateral usurpations of title as far as the original beneficiaries were concerned. The removal of the Bulgarian Patriarchate from the political capital at Preslav to the outlying city of Dristra also promised to weaken the Bulgarian Emperor's 'Caesaro-papal' authority. Just for this reason the Bulgarian Patriarchate seems to have been re-transferred from Dristra to Preslav before long; but the Patriarchs of Preslav never obtained East Roman recognition. (See Runciman, op. cit., pp. 181–2.)

3 Since the Tsar Peter was at this time a minor under a regency, Romanus Lecapenus may have hoped in 927 to make himself master of the throne of his Bulgarian grandson-in-law, as Symeon in 913 had hoped to make himself master of the East Roman Throne by becoming the father-in-law of the young Emperor Constantine Porphyrogenitus. If so, this roundabout road to a throne proved a blind alley on this occasion as on that. The stakes on the two occasions were not, however, the same; for while it would have been an honour in itself for a Bulgarian princess to marry an East Roman Emperor, even if nothing practical came of it, the condescension involved in the marriage of an East Roman princess to a Bulgarian Tsar was so great that even the incorporation of Bulgaria into the East Roman Empire would hardly have compensated for it.

4 This status of the Bulgarian Ambassador at the Court of Constantinople gave umbrage to the Envoy of the Saxon Emperor of the West who visited Constantinople in A.D. 968 (see Liutprand of Cremona: *Relatio de Legatione Constantinopolitana*, chaps. 11 and 18).

acquire her ecclesiastical autonomy, and retain her political independence, *de facto*. In A.D. 913, however, Symeon had destroyed this good understanding by insisting upon dragging out into the open the political implications of Bulgaria's submission to the ecclesiastical jurisdiction of the Patriarch. With tactless logic he had proclaimed the undeniable truth that any one who was a sheep in the Oecumenical Patriarch's flock must, *ipso facto*, be a political subject of the Patriarch's Imperial master; and he had gone on to translate this doctrine from the realm of theory into the realm of practical politics by waging a fifteen years' war on the strength of it. By A.D. 927 it had become impossible to thrust back the formidable problem which Symeon had raised into the oblivion in which Boris and Basil had sought to bury it in 886, and equally impossible to feign blindness to the true solution. It was now demonstrated that in Orthodox Christendom the jurisdictions of the East Roman Emperor and the Oecumenical Patriarch must be geographically coextensive; and, since Symeon had failed to bring about this necessary and inevitable state of affairs by his expedient of attempting to annex the Empire politically to the Patriarch's foreign ecclesiastical province of Bulgaria, it followed that sooner or later the indispensable political unification would have to be brought about by the inverse process of annexing Bulgaria to the Empire.

The further, and fiercer, Romano-Bulgarian war which this process would entail might be delayed by the compromise of duplicating both the Imperial and the Patriarchal office, but it could not be averted by this device, since the East Roman ghost of the Roman Empire was a universal and indivisible institution in its essence. Thus Symeon's act in 913 was ἀνήκεστον; from that time onwards the two leading states in the Orthodox Christian World were doomed to continue their struggle until one or other of them succumbed to a 'knock-out blow'; and on a superficial view it might seem as though this evil was brought upon Orthodox Christendom by Symeon's personal wrong-headedness. The fundamental cause of the disaster, however, was the 'Caesaro-papal' constitution of the East Roman Empire; for it was this that drove Symeon down the wrong path in the first instance and then made the consequences of his error irretrievable. Within the bosom of a single society there was not room, in perpetuity, for more than one 'totalitarian state'.

The peace of A.D. 927 did not last longer than the lifetime of the Bulgarian Tsar's East Roman wife Maria Lecapena, who had been re-christened Irene to signify the truth that the peace settlement was incarnate in her person. She died in 965; and thereupon Tsar Peter was persuaded to insult the East Roman Emperor Nicephorus

Phocas by demanding the continuance of Maria's annual allowance on the ground that it was a 'customary tribute'. Nicephorus retorted by making war upon Bulgaria in the East Roman Government's traditional vicarious fashion; he called in a barbarian—this time the Scandinavian prince Svyatoslav of Russia—to attack Peter in the rear; Peter replied by unleashing the Pechenegs against the Russians; and therewith the situation passed out of the control of both the Imperial Governments. The Pecheneg diversion was abortive, while the Russian menace was so formidable that Nicephorus was soon almost as terrified as Peter himself of the northern monster which the arts of East Roman diplomacy had too cleverly enticed out of its lair. In 969 the two Emperors put their own quarrel behind them and sought to arrange for a joint defence of their respective European possessions against the coming Russian avalanche. In the same year, however, both Emperors were overtaken by Death, and both Empires by Svyatoslav. In an autumn campaign Preslav, the Bulgarian capital, was captured, with the Bulgarian Imperial family inside it, by the Russian invaders; the Bulgarian Empire was swept out of existence; and the heart of Bulgaria between the south bank of the Danube and the Balkan Range, where the Bulgars had found their first footing on Roman soil nearly three hundred years back, now became a battle-field for Russian and East Roman armies.

The stake for which these foreign armies fought on Bulgarian soil was the dominion of the Balkan Peninsula, and this issue was decided in A.D. 972 in a single campaigning-season—at the end of which Svyatoslav found himself compelled to purchase a free retreat across the Danube at the price of leaving all his Bulgarian conquests in the hands of his East Roman conqueror, the Emperor John Tzimisces. The spoils of victory included not only the whole eastern portion of the territory of the Bulgarian Empire, but also the person of the reigning Bulgarian Emperor. At the celebration of John Tzimisces' triumph in Constantinople the Tsar Boris solemnly abdicated from his throne in the East Roman Emperor's favour; and John's first act in his new dominion was to extinguish the Bulgarian Patriarchate. The streets of Constantinople had not witnessed such an Imperial triumph as this since the last king of the Vandals had been led through them, captive, in A.D. 534; yet the words which the unhappy King Gelimir had been heard to repeat as he went through that agonizing ordeal[1]— ' "Vanity of vanities", saith the Preacher, "Vanity of vanities; all is vanity" '[2]— were not more applicable to Gelimir's humiliation than to Jus-

[1] The incident is recorded by Procopius: *A History of the Wars of Justinian*, Book IV, chap. 9.

[2] Eccl. i. 2.

tinian's triumph, and not more applicable to the triumph of Justinian than to that of John Tzimisces. Justinian's facile conquest of the Vandal Power in Africa in A.D. 533–4 had lured him into involving himself in his exhausting sixteen years' war of A.D. 537–53 with the Ostrogothic Power in Italy.[1] By a similar operation of 'the Envy of the Gods' the East Roman Emperor John Tzimisces' facile conquest of Eastern Bulgaria in A.D. 972 involved his ward and successor, Basil II, in a war with Western Bulgaria which lasted for forty-three years—from A.D. 977 to A.D. 1019—and wore out Orthodox Christendom.[2]

The Western Bulgarians found leadership in a new dynasty, which threw down the gauntlet to the conquerors of the Eastern Bulgarians in the symbolic gesture of re-establishing a Bulgarian Patriarchate; and the West Bulgarian Prince Samuel[3] proved to be a man of the same stamp as his adversary the East Roman Emperor Basil 'the Bulgar-killer'. The struggle between these two ruthless and indomitable antagonists not only lasted nearly three times as long as the previous war between Tsar Symeon and the cautious regents of Basil's grandfather Constantine Porphyrogenitus; it was also vastly more destructive; for, while Samuel imitated Symeon's strategy of overrunning the whole interior of the Balkan Peninsula, Basil was not content to stand on the defensive; and, since Nicephorus Phocas' unfortunate Russian experiment had taught the East Roman Government to eschew the traditional policy of attacking Bulgaria by proxy, Basil's field operations were conducted, and the consequent losses were sustained, by the East Roman Imperial forces themselves.

During the first phase of the war Samuel pushed even farther afield than Symeon had penetrated before him. He not only recovered Eastern Bulgaria; he passed the Bulgarian frontiers of A.D. 927–69 and rounded off his dominions by conquering the East Roman fortresses of Larisa in Thessaly and Durazzo on the Adriatic. Like Symeon, however, he discovered that such conquests of the fringes of the enemy empire's territory could not bring the enemy to his knees nor the war to an end. The war became a war of attrition; and then Time worked inexorably in favour of the belligerent whose *potentiel de guerre* was the greater. Decade by decade Basil concentrated his strength more and more intensively upon the Bulgarian War and turned the screw tighter and tighter

[1] See III. C (i) (*b*), vol. iii, p. 162, above, and V. C (ii) (*a*), vol. vi, p. 223, below.

[2] This disastrous effect of the Romano-Bulgarian War of A.D. 977–1019 has been touched upon by anticipation in IV. C (ii) (*b*) 1, pp. 72–5, above.

[3] The Imperial title does not appear to have been assumed by Samuel so long as he believed that any legitimate representative of the previous dynasty was alive. The event is to be dated *circa* A.D. 996–7—by which date Samuel had been ruler of Bulgaria for about twenty years *de facto* (Runciman, op. cit., p. 230).

upon Samuel. Between 990 and 1000 he succeeded in stemming the tide of Bulgarian invasion; in 1001 he set himself to win back Eastern Bulgaria; in 1003 he made his first attack on Macedonia, which was the seat of Samuel's power;[1] from 1006 onwards he wore down his opponent's strength in an unbroken series of annual campaigns which were proportionately costly to himself, since he was setting his troops the task of conquering and holding a wild country in which the enemy was at home, and in which the *terrain*, and the enemy's knowledge of the *terrain*, were formidable obstacles to an invader.

In the last phase of the war Basil's operations resembled Sherman's march through Georgia in A.D. 1864 or Sulla's devastation of Samnium in the years 81–80 B.C.[2] The conqueror was now striking not merely to kill but to annihilate. He advertised the spirit in which he intended to deliver the *coup de grâce* in his gruesome treatment of the fourteen or fifteen thousand prisoners whom he took at the Battle of the Pass of Cimbalongus in 1014. Out of every two hundred eyes he put out one hundred and ninety-nine, and then sent these companies of ninety-nine blind men with one-eyed leaders to find their way back to their prince. When they reached his presence Samuel died of the sight. In 1015 Basil momentarily occupied Ochrida, the fastness in the Macedonian Lake-Country which Samuel had selected for his political and ecclesiastical capital. But even the death of Samuel and the fall of Ochrida did not bring the end; Basil had to evacuate the dead Tsar's empty lair, and it was not till 1018 that the Bulgarian resistance utterly and irretrievably collapsed. The last and remotest Bulgarian fortress—Sirmium, on the Save—did not fall till 1019. Therewith the problem which Symeon had unmasked in 913 was solved by Basil's complete attainment of an objective which was the exact inverse of Symeon's war-aim. The 'knock-out blow', which was the sole practicable means of eliminating one of two rival empire-builders, had at last been delivered; and, at the cost of a hundred years' war, the whole of Orthodox Christendom[3] now found itself duly united under one Imperial rule; but the victim of these brutal politics was not the East Roman Empire which in Symeon's schemes had been cast for that appalling role. The victim in the event was Bulgaria herself.

In A.D. 1019 it seemed on the surface as though the East Roman

[1] For the geographical coincidence between Samuel's political domain and the ninth-century mission-field of Clement of Ochrida see p. 381, footnote 2, above.

[2] See the appalling account of Samnium as Sulla left it—and as Strabo still saw it, the better part of a century later—in Strabo's *Geographica*, Book V, pp. 249–50, which is cited again in V. C (i) (*c*) 1, vol. v, p. 37, below.

[3] With the exception of Russia; but Russia had been converted only in A.D. 989 (see II. D (vii), vol. ii, pp. 352–3, above).

Empire were completely triumphant and Bulgaria completely prostrate. Bulgaria had, in fact, disappeared from the political map, while the victorious Power was attaining an undreamed-of territorial extension. There was a moment towards the middle of the eleventh century[1] when the dominions of the East Roman Government stretched not only, as before, from the Caucasus to Calabria, but from the Euphrates to the Danube and from Armenia to Croatia. The political map, however, was no index of the social situation. It was a pretentious superstructure erected on rotten foundations; and, although to contemporary eyes this eleventh-century East Roman pile was imposing, it betrays, instead of masking, the underlying rottenness to the eye of a latter-day historian who commands the advantage of being able to survey it in retrospect with a knowledge of its whole story. To the instructed eye this overgrown and top-heavy pile, so far from being a tower of strength, is an architectural enormity which proclaims the imminence of its own collapse. When the crash did come in A.D. 1071,[2] it seemed to the minds of the astonished and awe-stricken spectators to be an inexplicable act of God. Within little more than fifty years of Basil's crushing victory over Bulgaria the victims' fate had overtaken the victors! In the historian's reckoning, on the other hand, it is the length, rather than the shortness, of the interval between the Bulgarian and the East Roman collapse that is a matter for surprise; for both catastrophes, as the historian sees the picture, were consequences—and inevitable consequences—of the Great Romano-Bulgarian Hundred Years' War. It is only surprising that the East Roman victim of that jointly inflicted and jointly suffered calamity should have been able to stave off its doom for half a century longer than its Bulgarian antagonist in an internecine conflict. On this reckoning the historian is not surprised to find that, when the East Roman Empire met its fate at last, it displayed considerably less capacity than Bulgaria for recuperation.

The substantial recuperation which Bulgaria did, in truth, achieve is vouched for by a fact which we have had occasion to notice in a different context. We have seen[3] that, between the conversion of Bulgaria to Orthodox Christianity in A.D. 864–70 and the occupation of the interior of Anatolia by the Saljūq Turkish converts to Islam in A.D. 1070–5, the centre of gravity of Orthodox Christen-

[1] It would be misleading to single out any particular year as the date of the East Roman Empire's territorial zenith, since the Empire's losses in Apulia began as early as A.D. 1040, when the Norman and North Lombard mercenaries who had just returned from Maniakis' Sicilian Expedition revolted against the East Roman authorities and occupied Melfi, while at the other extremity of the Orthodox Christian World the Empire's gains in Armenia did not attain their maximum extent until A.D. 1046.

[2] The year in which Bari was captured by the Normans and the Emperor Romanus Diogenes was taken prisoner by the Saljūqs at Manzikert.

[3] In II. D (iii), vol. ii, p. 79, above.

dom—leaving its Russian offshoot out of account—perceptibly shifted from the Asiatic to the European side of the Straits. Inasmuch as Bulgaria had come to occupy the lion's share of the Orthodox Christian domain in the Balkan Peninsula while Anatolia had been the heart of the East Roman Empire as originally constituted by the work of Leo Syrus, this migration of the citadel of the Orthodox Christian Civilization from Anatolia to the Balkans in the course of those two centuries can have only one meaning. It must mean that, in spite of superficial appearances, Bulgaria really came off less badly than the East Roman Empire in the Hundred Years' War of A.D. 913–1019, and that the true victim was the official victor.

This contrast between the respective experiences of the East Roman Empire and Bulgaria, in and after their Hundred Years' War, is one example of a social 'law' which comes into play in conflicts in which the antagonists are not on an equality in their level of civilization. In such a conflict the less civilized combatant is apt to suffer egregious defeats and to show an extraordinary capacity for surviving them, while his more civilized opponent is apt to have the inverse experience of winning brilliant victories and then emerging exhausted from a struggle which, 'on points', has gone entirely in his favour. This 'law' operates because progress in civilization brings with it an enhancement of power to put material and spiritual 'drive' into any action by mobilizing and expending, at any moment and for any purpose, an ever greater proportion of the individual's or community's or society's total skill and energy and strength. In creative or constructive enterprises this gift tells, of course, wholly in its possessor's favour and thereby becomes the cause of further progress, besides being the reward of progress already achieved. But, like all great gifts of the Gods, this enhanced capacity for effective action is an edged tool which may be used at will for either good or evil by the creature in whose hands it has been placed; and its potentialities for evil are let loose as soon as it is employed on a destructive activity like War. When thus employed, the gift does not lose its potency; like some jinn that is constrained to execute blindly the behests of any mortal that happens to have power over the magic talisman, this gift of stronger driving-power, which comes with higher civilization, cannot fail, for evil or for good, to produce its inevitable effect; but when it produces this for evil it brings down an ironic punishment upon the head of the misguided mortal who has misused the gift for that illegitimate purpose. By enabling him to excel in destruction his driving-power condemns him to destroy himself; and therefore, when destruction is the order of the day, the least efficient man of action comes off the best. An ineffectiveness which may have hindered him from soaring skywards now changes from a handicap into a safeguard that checks the impetus of his fall towards the abyss.

In our own world in our own day the working of this 'law' has been illustrated by the difference in the experience of the several Powers that came out on the losing side in the General War of 1914–18; for the losers numbered among them both the most and the least highly organized of the belligerents, and their fortunes have differed in accordance with this difference in degree of *Aktionsfähigkeit.* Of all the belligerents Germany had carried the art of mobilizing social resources for military purposes to the greatest lengths; and from 1914 to 1918 it was Germany who won the signal victories, while the signal defeats were suffered by Turkey and Russia, two belligerents who were imperfectly naturalized aliens in the Western World, and who were therefore weak vessels for waging war according to Western standards. In the next chapter, however, the roles were reversed; for in 1918 Germany, who for four years had been astonishing the World by her striking-power, excited still greater astonishment by her sudden and complete collapse, while from 1919 to 1922 the Turks and the Russians, who had long since been 'counted out' by the spectators of the conflict, produced a sensation in the opposite sense by posthumously retrieving their previous reverses. At a time when Germany was utterly incapable of taking up arms again and was playing the traditional Turkish role of being 'the Sick Man of Europe', the Turks and the Russians were each doggedly fighting a 'war after the war' against the officially victorious 'Allied and Associated Powers'; and moreover they were actually getting the better of it against adversaries who were almost as highly organized for War, and therefore almost as deeply exhausted by four years of fighting, as Germany herself. If we draw an analogy between the war of 1914–18 and the war of 913–1019 and equate the East Roman Empire with Germany, and Bulgaria with Russia or Turkey, the sequel in this case will become as comprehensible as it is in the comparable case of which we ourselves have been first-hand witnesses.

While Bulgaria lived to make abortive attempts to throw off the East Roman yoke in A.D. 1040 and 1073, and a successful attempt in 1186,[1] the East Roman Empire failed to recover from the social

[1] In an impartial attempt to account for Bulgaria's recuperation after the war of A.D. 913–1019 the entire credit cannot be given to the relative simplicity of the Orthodox Christian culture in Bulgaria at the time of this ordeal. Some credit is also due to the moderation which Basil 'the Bulgar-killer' showed in taking advantage of the victory which he had won by such ruthless methods. Though Basil annexed Bulgaria to the

disorders which it had brought upon itself through its demonic pursuit of military victory. The deep derangement, in this age, of Orthodox Christian life within the East Roman frontiers revealed itself in the outbreak and progress of two maladies which interacted disastrously with one another. The first malady was an agrarian crisis;[1] the second was a bout of militarism; and both were portents, because they were complaints from which the Orthodox Christian body social had been singularly free in the days of its good health.

When the nascent Orthodox Christian Civilization had emerged from the post-Hellenic interregnum at the turn of the seventh and eighth centuries of the Christian Era, it had started life in possession of one immensely valuable social asset which it owed to the very destructiveness of the foregoing age of anarchy. The legislation of the eighth-century East Roman Emperors Leo Syrus and his son Constantine V shows that Orthodox Christendom in their day was very much freer than the contemporary West from that concentration of the ownership of land, and consequent polarization of agrarian society into a handful of magnates and a multitude of serfs, which had been one of the mortal diseases of the moribund Hellenic Civilization in the last days of the Roman Empire. The agrarian life of eighth-century Orthodox Christendom, as mirrored in these contemporary legal texts, bears no resemblance to the social landscape of the Greek-speaking provinces of the Roman Empire in the Age of Justinian. And this breach of continuity was salutary, since it was followed by a new start. The young Orthodox Christian Society that here comes into view is not a world of serfs and magnates but a world of free peasants living in village communities. This healthy agrarian foundation was doubtless one of the causes of the rapid growth which the Orthodox Christian Civilization achieved during the next two hundred years; but with

East Roman Empire outright, he refrained from attempting to assimilate his new dominions to his old dominions administratively. For example, the taxpayers in the *ci-devant* Bulgarian territories were still allowed to pay their taxes in kind, as they had paid them to Symeon and to Samuel, instead of being forced into the East Roman money economy. In the ecclesiastical sphere, again, the reigning Bulgarian Patriarch at Ochrida was simply degraded from the rank of a Patriarch to that of an Archbishop without either losing his see or being deprived of his autonomy or being compelled to abandon the Slavonic in favour of the Greek Liturgy. The acts of A.D. 886 and 926 and 927 were not undone; and under an East Roman domination which lasted for more than a century and a half the Orthodox Church in Western Bulgaria remained Slavonic in its language and exempt in its government from the ecclesiastical jurisdiction of the Oecumenical Patriarch of Constantinople. (The Oecumenical Patriarchate had to wait for Mehmed the Conqueror to invest it with that cure of West Bulgarian souls which was not entrusted to it by Basil 'the Bulgar-killer'!) In the third place the victorious Power showed its generosity towards the conquered by throwing open the East Roman public service to the Bulgarian nobility. Thus the liberality of the East Roman régime played an honourable part in keeping Bulgaria alive under an East Roman yoke. (This point has been touched upon, by anticipation, on p. 344, footnote 2, above.)

1 This has been touched upon by anticipation in IV. C (ii) (*b*) 1, pp. 72–3, above.

the outbreak of war between the East Roman Empire and Bulgaria in 913 a sinister change begins to show itself.

In the legislation dating from the reign of Tsar Symeon's East Roman contemporary Romanus Lecapenus (*imperabat* A.D. 919–44) a novel and conspicuous feature appears in a series of repeated (and therefore presumably abortive) enactments for protecting the small freeholder against the encroachments of the great proprietor. If legislation may be taken as evidence for social facts, we may infer that the evil of *latifundia* was now making its appearance in Eastern and Central Anatolia for the first time since the Roman Emperor Justinian I had legislated against the great landed proprietors of Cappadocia;[1] and it can hardly be an accident that the agrarian laws of both Justinian and Lecapenus date from a time at which the legislating Government was engaged in an exhausting foreign war. One of the commonest social effects of War upon the internal economy of a belligerent country is to produce a maldistribution of wealth or to aggravate a maldistribution that already exists. Classic examples are the effect of the Hannibalic War and its aftermath upon the agrarian economy of Roman Italy,[2] and the effect of the life-and-death struggle with the Danes upon the agrarian economy of the English Kingdom of Wessex.[3] The corresponding effect of War in an industrial society is exemplified in the social consequences of the General War of 1914–18, which stare our own generation in the face. On this showing, we may confidently make the sometimes hazardous inference *post hoc propter hoc* in guessing at the relation between the Romano-Bulgarian War of 913–27 and the agrarian legislation of Romanus Lecapenus. We may assume that the relation is one of cause and effect; and we shall be fortified in this view when we find that the longer and more exhausting war of 977–1019 was accompanied, in the internal life of the East Roman Empire, by more violent symptoms of agrarian *malaise*.

In the earlier phases of that war the Emperor Basil was repeatedly diverted from his proper business of killing Bulgars in the Balkan Peninsula through being called away to put down insurrections raised by his own East Roman magnates in Anatolia. The rebellion of Bardas Sclerus in A.D. 976–9 was followed by that of his conqueror, Bardas Phocas, in 987–9; and Bardas Sclerus, who had joined forces on this occasion with his former opponent in order to revolt for the second time, kept up a guerrilla warfare after the defeat and death of his momentary ally until Basil was constrained

[1] The record of Justinian's attack on the Cappadocian *latifundia* is preserved in Novella 30 (44), 5, edition of Zachariä von Lingenthal (Leipzig 1881, Teubner, 2 vols. + 2 appendices), vol. i, p. 268, cited by Vasiliev, op. cit., vol. i, pp. 207–8.

[2] See III. C (i) (*b*), vol. iii, pp. 170–1, above, and IV. C (iii) (*c*) 3 (β), in the present volume, pp. 507–8, below.

[3] See II. D (v), vol. ii, p. 200, above.

to purchase his capitulation at the price of an amnesty. This flagrant treachery on the part of subjects who cannot have been unaware of the gravity of the foreign war on which the Emperor was then engaged is only to be explained by supposing that, for them, the struggle in the interior of the Empire had become an issue of greater moment than the conflict with Bulgaria. These Anatolian magnates were tempted into rebellion by the prospect of being able to defeat the Imperial Government's hostile agrarian policy at a moment when the Government's strength was being strained by the task of coping with graver troubles at the opposite extremity of its dominions; and it is possible that the rebels were not only tempted into taking up arms by the Government's distress, but were also goaded into rebellion by fresh turns of the governmental screw, imprudences into which the East Roman Government may have been driven by its desperate need of raising additional supplies in order to meet the costs of the first-class war which it was waging at the time in Europe. The worst possible forebodings of the defeated rebels were assuredly fulfilled by Basil's agrarian law of A.D. 996.

Whatever may have been the precise relation between these formidable rebellions in Anatolia and the inexorable pressure of the Great Bulgarian War, the sequel proves conclusively that a Basilius Bulgaroctonus brought the East Roman Empire to disaster by emulating a gross error of statesmanship which had once been committed by a Justinianus Gothicus[1] with similarly disastrous consequences for the universal state that was the East Roman Empire's prototype. In order to achieve an ephemeral conquest of Italy Justinian remorselessly ate out the heart of Illyricum, a region which was of vastly greater value than Italy to the later Roman Empire because it was an irreplaceable recruiting-ground of the Roman Army. This Illyrian recruiting-ground suffered even more cruelly from Justinian's Great Gothic War than the Italian battlefield. The drafts required to replace the casualties on the other side of the Adriatic drained Illyricum of its manhood; and in A.D. 550 some of the last of the Illyrian reserves had to turn aside, when they were on the march to their Italian grave, in order to rap over the knuckles the importunate interloping barbarians, who were in such a hurry to fill the doomed Illyrian peasantry's place that they could not even bring themselves to linger discreetly on the farther bank of the Danube until the last of the race which they were supplanting had been drummed away to die by the perverse ambition of an unpaternal Government. The penalty which the

[1] See the present chapter, pp. 326–8 and 390, above, and V. C (ii) (*a*), vol. vi, pp. 223–5, below.

Roman Empire paid for Justinian's ephemeral reconquest of Italy was a permanent occupation of the Balkan Peninsula, from Danube to Taygetus, by the barbarian Slavs. In the history of the East Roman Empire the conquest of Bulgaria had a corresponding sequel.

In the East Roman Empire's structure the role which had been played by Illyricum in Roman history from the reign of Probus to the reign of Justinian I was played, from the reign of Leo Syrus to the reign of Basil II, by the Anatolic and Armeniac army-corps districts in Central and Eastern Anatolia. This was the region which was the recruiting-ground of the East Roman Army during the three centuries ending with the Romano-Bulgarian War of 977–1019; and here again the fate which overtook this uniquely valuable region half a century later gives the measure of the sacrifice that a barren victory exacted. As the heart of Illyricum had been occupied in the sixth century by the Slavs, so the heart of Anatolia was occupied in the eleventh century by the Turks; and in this case, as in that, the occupation was permanent. The East Roman Government never succeeded in winning this vital territory back; and the failure is not to be attributed wholly to the prowess of the Saljūq intruders. There is some evidence[1] that the Saljūqs' notable success in holding for the next two centuries the greater part of the Anatolian ground which they had won at a stroke in A.D. 1070–5 was partly due to the sympathy and support that these aliens received from the local remnants of the Anatolian peasantry. These Anatolian victims of Basil 'the Bulgar-killer's' Balkan ambitions[2] apparently found the Saljūq whips a lighter chastisement than the Imperial scorpions by which they had been tormented for some hundred and fifty years by the time of the Saljūqs' arrival. At any rate, this previously Greek-speaking Orthodox Christian peasantry turned Turk, and turned Muslim, *en masse*;[3] and their

[1] This evidence is discussed by Ramsay, Sir W. M., in op. cit. infra, pp. 23–34.

[2] The peasantry of Eastern and Central Anatolia were the victims not only of Basil II but of Leo Syrus; for it was on their shoulders that the dead weight of Leo's reconstructed Roman Empire ultimately rested. This story has repeated itself in the history of the Russian offshoot of Orthodox Christendom, where, again, the peasantry has had to bear the burden of the political structure erected by Peter the Great. In this case, as in that, an ambitious political structure, recklessly piled up upon inadequate foundations, has turned into a crushing social incubus from which the society that has been cursed with it has only been liberated by a catastrophic collapse. Thus the main incident in the tragedy of Orthodox Christian history has repeated itself with singular exactness. Yet there is no evidence that Peter's fatally successful essay in state-building was inspired by Leo's. Leo's model was the Roman Empire, while Peter borrowed his 'totalitarian state', 'Caesaro-papism' and all (see III. C (ii) (*b*), vol. iii, p. 283, footnote 2, above), from the contemporary West. For the Protestant inspiration of the Petrine institution of the Holy Synod see Masaryk, T. G.: *The Spirit of Russia* (London 1919, Allen & Unwin, 2 vols.), vol. i, pp. 61–4.

[3] For the progress, in Anatolia, of the Turkish language and the Islamic religion, at the expense of the Greek language and of Orthodox Christianity, from the eleventh century to the present day, see Wächter, A.: *Der Verfall des Griechentums in Kleinasien im xiv. Jahrhundert* (Leipzig 1903, Teubner); Ramsay, Sir W. M.: *The Intermixture of Races in Asia Minor: Some of its Causes and Effects* (Oxford 1917, University Press);

wholesale cultural and religious apostasy suggests that before ever their new Turkish masters appeared on the scene they had become spiritually alienated not only from the East Roman political régime, but also from the Orthodox Christian Civilization upon which the East Roman Empire had imposed itself as a crushing incubus.[1]

If the East Roman agrarian crisis, which was one of the two social maladies brought on by the conflict with Bulgaria, had this utterly disastrous denouement, the extremeness of the disaster is perhaps partly to be accounted for by the fact that the agrarian evil was accentuated by the accompanying malady of militarism.

As though the economic and social strain of the Great Bulgarian War upon the heart of the East Roman Empire were not enough, the East Roman Government, which had originally been drawn into the conflict in the Balkans against its own will by Symeon's megalomania, so radically changed its policy that before the first round of its life-and-death struggle with Bulgaria was over it had deliberately embarked on a course of military aggression against its Muslim neighbours on its opposite frontier.

In A.D. 926, on the morrow of the Romano-Bulgarian truce of 924—without waiting for the definite conclusion of peace, which did not follow till 927—the Emperor Romanus Lecapenus sent part of his army to win territory on the Euphrates from a foundering 'Abbasid Caliphate. The war of conquest which was thus opened on the Empire's south-eastern frontier was carried on systematically by Romanus's general John Curcuas from A.D. 926 to 944;[2]

Dawkins, R. M.: *Modern Greek in Asia Minor* (Cambridge 1916, University Press). In the present Study this problem has been touched upon, by anticipation, in IV. C (ii) (*b*) 1, in the present volume, p. 75, above.

[1] The success of the Slavs and the Bulgars in holding their own permanently in the Balkan Peninsula is perhaps likewise partly to be explained by a similar fraternization, there, between the barbarian interlopers and the local remnant of the provincials—in this case the Latinized Illyrians and Thracians whose survival is attested by the existence of their latter-day representatives, the Balkan 'Diasporà' of Romance-speaking Vlachs. That the ancestors of the Vlachs did fraternize with the Slavs and Bulgars who drifted into the depopulated tracts of the *ci-devant* Illyricum is suggested by the remarkable fact that when—some 600 years after the arrival of the Slavs, and 500 years after the arrival of the Bulgars—Basil 'the Bulgar-killer's' work was undone by the emergence of a Balkan 'successor-state' of the East Roman Empire in A.D. 1186, the foundation of this new polity was the joint achievement of the Bulgars and the Vlachs—so much so that the names of both peoples figured, side by side, in the new Balkan Empire's official style and title. This persistent importance of the Vlachs in Bulgaria raises the question whether they may not actually have given two sovereigns to the Bulgarian state in an earlier chapter of Bulgarian history. In the interval between the extinction of the House of Attila in A.D. 739 and the foundation of the Dynasty of Krum in the last years of the eighth century, two of the ephemeral occupants of the Bulgarian Throne respectively bore the names of Sabinus and Paganus. Were these Latin-speaking Illyrian renegades? Or is the Latin appearance of the two names accidental? Paganus, for example, may be an elegant version of a perfectly good Eurasian Nomad name which was borne, five centuries later, by the Mongol Bayan. Names are seldom good evidence in themselves, and yet this pair of names is intriguing. We may perhaps feel greater confidence in suggesting a Latin etymology (Cimbalongus = Campus Longus) for the name of the Macedonian battlefield of A.D. 1014 (see p. 391, above).

[2] The cultural effects of Curcuas' conquest, in A.D. 928, of the 'Abbasid Empire's Melitenian march are examined in V. C (i) (*c*) 3, vol. v, pp. 254–8, below.

and it was subsequently extended to other sectors of the Islamic front by the Emperor Nicephorus Phocas, who conquered Crete in 961,[1] Cilicia in 965, and Northern Syria in 969. John Tzimisces had no sooner dealt with the Russian peril in the Balkans than he turned his attention to the Syrian front and spent the last years (A.D. 973–6) of his short reign on Syrian campaigns. Even Basil II—who might have been expected to feel that killing Bulgars with one hand and putting down Anatolian rebels with the other was as heavy a tax as he could venture to impose upon his Empire's military strength—did not hesitate to spend still more East Roman blood and treasure on making unprofitable military demonstrations in Syria in 995 and 999. Thereafter, when the Great Bulgarian War had been ended at last—at the terrible cost that has been indicated—by the 'knock-out blow' of A.D. 1018–9, this tardy relief from one military commitment seems only to have sent the East Roman military mind of that generation in search of fresh military adventures in new quarters. One of the last acts of Basil's reign was an abortive expedition against the Muslims of Sicily in 1025; and this was followed up by a naval war against the Muslims of both Sicily and Ifriqīyah in 1032–5 and by a further attempt to conquer Sicily in 1038–40. This ambitious policy of expansion on the south-west was matched on the north-east by the annexation, between A.D. 1021 and 1046, of one after another of the Monophysite Christian 'successor-states' of the 'Abbasid Caliphate in Armenia.

Of all these offensive military operations against the Syriac World along a maritime and continental front that extended from Tunisian waters to the threshold of Azerbaijan, the only two that were perhaps justifiable on political and social grounds were the Emperor Nicephorus's conquests of Crete and Cilicia. In capturing Candia and Tarsus the East Roman conqueror was smoking out two hornets' nests from which the East Roman Empire had been systematically and persistently raided.[2] But in pressing on across the Amanus to conquer Antioch and establish an East Roman protectorate over Aleppo Nicephorus was simply adding to the liabilities of the Empire by burdening it with a new dominion which was as extensive, and as dangerously exposed to invasion from the interior of the continent, as the new dominion which Basil I and Leo the

[1] Unlike the previous conquests of John Curcuas and the other conquests of Nicephorus Phocas at the Muslims' expense, Crete was not a province of the 'Abbasid Caliphate. It was a *ci-devant* East Roman possession which had been captured in A.D. 823 by Muslim pirates from Andalusia. Before Nicephorus's successful expedition to Crete in 961 there had been an abortive attempt to reconquer the island in 949.

[2] For the regular half-yearly spring and autumn raids upon Anatolia which were carried out from a base of operations at Tarsus see II. D (vii), vol. ii, p. 368, with footnote 1. The Andalusian pirates of Candia infested the coasts and islands of the Aegean.

Wise had acquired in Southern Italy—and this without any of the political and strategic necessity which had justified that earlier forward move in that other quarter.[1] As for the Sicilian and Asiatic military adventures of Basil 'the Bulgar-killer' and his successors in the government of the East Roman Empire during the second quarter of the eleventh century, they were directly responsible for the crash of A.D. 1071. In weakening or overthrowing the Muslim 'successor-states' of the 'Abbasid Caliphate in Syria and its Monophysite 'successor-states' in Armenia, this East Roman militarism was simply filling valleys and levelling hills in order to prepare the way for the Saljūq and make straight his paths[2] towards the empty spaces that were awaiting his advent in the rotten heart of an Orthodox Christian Anatolia. Similarly, in attempting to conquer Sicily, the same militarism, with the same perversity, was creating an opportunity for the Normans to seize the East Roman provinces of Laghovardhía and Calabria, with the Muslim island into the bargain.

The forward policy which was pursued by the East Roman Government in this quarter from 1025 to 1040 was particularly wanton, because it was embarked upon after the Government had received a series of plain warnings that it had more than enough on its hands here as it was. The first warning was the resumption of African Muslim piratical raids.[3] Bari itself, after having enjoyed more than a century of immunity, was raided in 988 and again in 1003, and on the latter occasion it was only saved by the intervention of the Venetians,[4] while it required Pisan assistance to enable the East Roman fleet to defeat its Muslim adversaries off Reggio in 1006.[5] A further, and still plainer, warning was given by the abortive revolt of the Empire's Apulian Lombard subject Melo at Bari in 1009, and by the fugitive's unsuccessful incursion into Apulia in 1017–18 at the head of a band of Norman mercenaries. For though, once again, the East Roman authorities in Italy were able to repel and punish the assault to which they had been subjected, this assault would scarcely have been attempted if in this quarter the East Roman Power had not been inviting attack by its palpable weakness. Yet, heedless of these warnings, the East Roman Government embarked upon the

[1] For the considerations which were probably in the minds of the East Roman statesmen who were responsible for the forward policy in Italy at the turn of the ninth and tenth centuries, see p. 343, above.

[2] Luke iii. 4–5. See further V. C (i) (*c*) 3, vol. v, p. 247, below.

[3] This is interpreted by Gay, op. cit., p. 367, as evidence that the East Roman Empire in its South Italian extremity was already suffering from overstrain.

[4] In or after A.D. 998 Basil II appears to have officially transferred to Venice—which at that time still acknowledged the East Roman Government's suzerainty—the task of policing the Adriatic, with the commercial and political perquisites which this duty carried with it.

[5] For these naval operations see Gay, op. cit., pp. 368–9.

Sicilian expedition of 1038–40; and it was from this that its Italian disasters arose. The beginning of the end of the East Roman dominion in Apulia was the simultaneous revolt in 1040 of the Apulian subjects of the Empire who were being called upon to supply a fresh draft of conscripts for the Sicilian War,[1] and of the North Lombard and Norman mercenaries[2] who had returned from the Sicilian war-zone exasperated at the discipline to which they had been subjected there.[3]

It will be seen that the militarism which made its appearance with the launching of John Curcuas' Asiatic offensive in A.D. 926, and which went on gathering impetus till it was pulled up short, a century and a half later, by the crash of A.D. 1071, was as fatal to East Roman interests as it was foreign to East Roman tradition. How are we to account for this innovation, which involved not only a change of policy but also a change of êthos?

The mere change of policy can perhaps be accounted for sufficiently by the temptation which was offered to East Roman ambitions in the spectacle of the decrepitude of the 'Abbasid Power from the early decades of the tenth century onwards. It was the urgency and imminence of the Arab Muslim pressure that had called the East Roman Empire into existence two hundred years back.[4] Through two centuries of almost unintermittent warfare the Empire had stood the strain and, in standing it, had been the salvation of Orthodox Christendom. Now that the pressure was relaxing—now that the mighty Syriac Power which had so long overshadowed Orthodox Christendom and battered at the Empire's

1 They revolted under the leadership of Melo's Byzantinized son Argyrus, who made himself master of Bari in 1040 without repudiating his allegiance to the East Roman Empire.

2 One of the North Lombard mercenaries who were recruited for the East Roman Government's Sicilian expedition of A.D. 1038–40 was the father of the future philosopher John Italus (see p. 358, footnote 3, above).

3 The story of the quarrel, during the East Roman expedition against Sicily in A.D. 1038–40, between the East Roman commander Maniakis and the Milanese condottiere Ardwin, with the sequel in which Ardwin revenges himself by raising an Apulian revolt and bringing in the Normans to help him, is singularly reminiscent, point for point, of the Herodotean account of the quarrel, during the Achaemenian expedition against Naxos *circa* 499 B.C., between the Achaemenian commander Megabates and the Milesian despot Aristagoras, with the similar sequel in which Aristagoras likewise revenges himself by raising an Ionian revolt and procuring the help of the Athenians. (Compare Gay, op. cit., pp. 452–5, with Herodotus, Book V, chaps. 28–38.)

4 For this explanation of the genesis of the East Roman Empire see II. D (vii), pp. 368–9, above, and Part IX, below. Compare the history of the Danubian Hapsburg Monarchy, which was called into existence by the pressure of the Ottoman Power upon Western Christendom and which then momentarily expanded at the Ottoman Empire's expense as the Ottoman pressure relaxed—only to fall to pieces in the same catastrophe that carried the break-up of the Ottoman Empire to its completion (see II. D (v), vol. ii, pp. 177–88, above). Just as the Danubian Hapsburg Monarchy failed to outlive the Ottoman Power whose aggressiveness had been its *raison d'être*, so the East Roman Empire lost its social health and its moral balance as soon as the 'Abbasid Power collapsed—with the result that the East Roman Empire too became a prey for the Latin and Turkish kites who had been attracted, from west and east, by the 'Abbasid Empire's carcass.

gates was itself breaking into fragments—was the Empire to refrain from reaping the fruits of its long endurance? Was it to neglect the opportunity, which had come at last, of turning the tables? It must be admitted that the East Roman counter-offensive was what was to be expected from human nature; yet this general explanation does not altogether meet this special case; for during the two centuries beginning with the accession of Leo Syrus the East Roman Government's statesmanship had consistently shown itself superhuman—or inhuman—in its moderation. The change of policy cannot be fully comprehended unless we can also account for the implied change of êthos; and we can, in fact, account for this by observing that a new social element was brought into power at Constantinople by the new Bulgarian peril. Though the Bulgar Khan Symeon could not attain the East Roman Throne himself, he could, and did, unintentionally enable the East Roman naval officer Romanus Lecapenus to seat himself upon it. It was this crowned naval officer who initiated the militarist policy that was inaugurated by the Asiatic campaigns of A.D. 926–44, and it was a pair of crowned military officers—Nicephorus Phocas (*imperabat* A.D. 963–9) and John Tzimisces (*imperabat* A.D. 969–76)—who carried the new policy farther. Both these latter Emperors had the East Roman military tradition in their bones. The Anatolian magnate Phocas was a grandson of the Nicephorus Phocas who had conquered Southern Italy for Leo the Wise in 885, and a nephew of a Leo Phocas who had been defeated by Khan Symeon on the Achelous in 917. The Armenian soldier-of-fortune John Tzimisces was a great-nephew of John Curcuas. And Basil 'the Bulgar-killer', whose long reign immediately succeeded the successive short reigns of these two military usurpers, proved to be the one representative of his dynasty who was imbued with the military spirit.[1] Thus for sixty-two years—from 963 to 1025—the East Roman Empire was in military hands;[2] and the new penchant towards militarism, which was imparted to the Imperial policy under this régime, persisted thereafter by sheer momentum[3] until it carried the Empire into irretrievable disaster.

[1] This spirit did not reveal itself in Basil till A.D. 985, when the Emperor was twenty-seven years old and had already been officially sole master of the Empire for ten years (since the death of John Tzimisces in 976). A conspiracy which threatened his tenure of the Imperial throne in 985 appears to have had the psychological effect on Basil of transforming him from an ostensibly frivolous and idle young man into an ascetic autocrat and an untiring professional soldier.

[2] The only break in the continuity of this long military régime was the first decade of the sole reign of Basil (see the preceding footnote); but even this decade was a time of war, since the forty-three years' struggle between the East Roman Empire and the West-Bulgarian war-lord Samuel of Ochrida began in A.D. 977.

[3] The persistence of this new spirit of military adventure—alien though this was from the original genius of East Roman statesmanship—is demonstrated by the fact that it survived the crash of A.D. 1071 and reasserted itself during the Comnenian rally

The truth was that the spirit of moderation which was the original note of East Roman statesmanship had been the East Roman Empire's saving grace; and when once this spirit was lost an institution which had always been a grievous incubus upon the life of Orthodox Christendom became utterly intolerable. It was not, however, the irrational play of Chance or a malicious stroke of 'the Envy of the Gods' that transformed the original êthos of the East Roman Empire into its antithesis with this fatal consequence. The transformation was due to an inward necessity and not to an external accident; for it was natural that a growing society should expand, and inevitable, in the circumstances of Orthodox Christian social history, that such expansion should bring with it a multiplication of the incubus with which the expanding society was already saddled; and, since there was not room for more than one ghost of the Roman Empire to haunt a single house, a life-and-death struggle between the East Roman Empire and its Bulgarian double followed the conversion of Bulgaria automatically. In this internecine warfare between two idolized ghosts the Orthodox Christian Civilization went down to destruction.

We have dwelt at some length upon the idolization of the East Roman Empire and its consequences, because this tragic story throws light on something more than the nemesis that attends the idolization of an ephemeral institution; it shows up the perverse and sinful nature of idolatry itself as a transference of loyalty from the whole to the part and a transference of worship from the Creator to the creature. In Orthodox Christendom from the eighth century onwards the loyalty which should have been reserved for the Orthodox Christian Society as a whole was restricted to a single institution—the East Roman Empire—which was confined to one plane of social life and had been erected there by its worshippers' own hands. From the tenth century onwards, when the expansion of Orthodox Christendom had come to embrace the Bulgars as well as the Greeks within the Orthodox Christian fold, the unworthy object of the idolatrous society's worship was still further

until it precipitated the second crash that brought the Empire to the ground at the turn of the twelfth and thirteenth centuries. If the Comneni were to save the Empire, it was evident that they must make the most of the opportunity that was offered by the shock which the Saljūq Power in Anatolia had received from the impact of the Crusaders. The Comneni ought to have concentrated the whole of their strength upon a supreme effort to wipe the Saljūqs out and thus recover the heart of Anatolia. Instead of that, they dissipated their energies upon vain attempts to assert their suzerainty over the new Crusader principalities in Syria, and upon barren wars against distant European adversaries: the Hungarians beyond the Danube and the Normans beyond the Adriatic. The Romano-Hungarian wars of 1128–9 and 1151–5 and 1166–8 and the Romano-Norman war of 1147–58 account for the failure of the Comneni to deliver a 'knock-out blow' to the Anatolian Saljūqs in the Romano-Turkish wars of 1109–16 and 1119–20 and 1146–7 and 1160–2 and 1176–7. The defeat of the East Roman army by the Saljūqs at Myriocephalum in A.D. 1176 reduplicated and clinched the disaster of the defeat at Manzikert in 1071.

narrowed down by being multiplied from the singular into the plural and thereby ceasing to be coextensive with the society in range, even on its own superficial plane. From A.D. 927 onwards the misguided devotion of the Orthodox idolators to a political fetish was divided between one parochial empire at Constantinople and another at Preslav. Since both empires claimed an oecumenical jurisdiction by divine right, a life-and-death struggle between them was inevitable; and when the idolators' house was thus divided against itself, it is no wonder that it could not stand.[1]

If the universal nemesis of idolatry is manifested with unusual clarity in the Orthodox Christian case, it is also noticeable that this particular example has a specially close bearing upon a case which touches ourselves more nearly.

The concentration of idolatrous worship upon a political institution, and the dissipation of this political idolatry among a plurality of idolized parochial states whose relations are hostile because their pretensions are incompatible, is an aberration into which the Orthodox Christian Society has not been alone in falling. Our own Western Society has set its feet upon the same path of destruction after having made a promising start upon the path of Life.

In the *Respublica Christiana* which Hildebrand set himself to build in the West[2] in a generation when Orthodox Christendom had already broken down under the crushing weight of the *Imperium Redivivum*, our Western Society was endowed with an institution which was a new creation instead of being a ghost evoked from the Past, and which promised to become an ever more powerful stimulus to social growth instead of being an ever more cumbersome drag upon it. But this fair prospect was blighted within two hundred years of Hildebrand's time by the ὕβρις to which the Papacy succumbed in the hour of its triumph over the Hohenstaufen;[3] and, owing to this tragic failure of the master-institution which the Western Christendom had created for itself in the second chapter of its history, the institutional heirloom from this chapter that exercised the dominant and decisive influence upon the course of the next chapter was one of the subordinate institutions of medieval Western Christendom which had been an incidental product of the strife between the Papacy and the Holy Roman Empire. A role which had appeared to be the manifest destiny of the Papal *Respublica Christiana* now passed to the North Italian City-State[4]

[1] Matt. xii. 25 = Mark iii. 24 = Luke xi. 17.

[2] See the present chapter, pp. 339–40, above.

[3] For the Papal performance of the tragedy of κόρος-ὕβρις-ἄτη see IV. C (iii) (*c*) 3 (β), pp. 512–84, below.

[4] For the dominant role of the medieval Italian city-state culture in setting the tone of the third chapter of our Western history see III. C (ii) (*b*), vol. iii, p. 375, footnote 2, above.

which had found room to establish itself in the no-man's-land between the Papal and Imperial fronts.[1] And the upstart institution which thus came to the fore, after the key to the future of Western Christendom had slipped through the fingers of the Vicar of Peter, had much more in common with the baneful Orthodox Christian institution of the *Imperium Redivivum* than with the abortive Western *Respublica Christiana.*

Like the Byzantine *Imperium Redivivum*, the Italian city-state was a ghost called back to life out of the dead past of the Hellenic Society to which both the Christendoms were affiliated. While the *Imperium Redivivum* was a ghost of the universal state which the Hellenic Society had thrown up in the penultimate stage of its disintegration, the city-state was a ghost of the parochial state in which the Hellenic Society had found its master-institution in its growth-stage. The institution which held the field in Western Christendom at the transition from the second to the third chapter of our Western history was thus parochial in its essence; and when in that time of transition this Italian political invention—or political revival—propagated itself beyond the Alps and translated itself from the city-state on to the kingdom-state scale,[2] our Western World was saddled in its turn with a plurality of parochial sovereign states of the same calibre, and the same pretensions, as the East Roman and Bulgarian Empires that had confronted one another in the Orthodox Christian World after the peace settlement of A.D. 927.

In thus arriving at the state which was the ruin of the sister society, our Western Society has no doubt been successful—or fortunate—in having managed to postpone the advent of the evil day. The political efficiency which was achieved in Orthodox Christendom in the eighth century was not emulated in the West till the eleventh century, and then only within the limits of Northern Italy, and on the miniature city-state scale. The West was not burdened with an efficient state of the East Roman Empire's calibre until the Italianization of the Transalpine kingdom-states began in the fifteenth century;[3] and it was not till the sixteenth century that the tenth-century conflict between the East Roman and Bulgarian Empires in Orthodox Christendom was reproduced in the West in the rivalry between the Hapsburg Power and France. Even since then, Time has continued to be kind to us; for whereas

[1] For the genesis of the medieval Western city-state cosmos see III. C (ii) (*b*), vol. iii, pp. 344–7, above.

[2] For this change of scale see III. C (ii) (*b*), vol. iii, pp. 350–63, above.

[3] The Kingdom of the Two Sicilies is an exception which proves our rule, since this was a Western 'successor-state' of the East Roman Empire, and its talent for efficient administration on a large scale was a Byzantine legacy which came as a windfall to the Norman conquerors and their heir the Emperor Frederick II Hohenstaufen.

it took little more than a century for the two Orthodox Christian Empires to compass, in destroying one another, the destruction of the society that had borne them both, we live to bear witness that our own Western Society still survives in a generation which stands at a four-hundred-years' remove from the generation of Francis I and Charles V—the two modern Western parochial sovereigns who started that series of modern Western wars which we have not yet succeeded in bringing to an end. But can we count upon Time to prolong our reprieve to Eternity? And is it really a reprieve that Time has been granting us? Has not Time perhaps been fattening our Western body social, like a sacrificial victim, for a mightier holocaust than Orthodox Christendom was ever able to afford?[1] If we face this last question honestly and utter our opinion openly, an affirmative answer may be wrung from our lips as we stand on the threshold of the fourth chapter of our Western history and look back upon the history of a third chapter that is now complete.[2]

If we seek to sum up what this third chapter has brought to pass, our thoughts will recur to our study of the intractability of institutions,[3] and we shall be forced to remind ourselves that for four centuries our modern Western master-institution, the Parochial Sovereign State, has been steadily strengthening its ominous hold upon our Western life by taking advantage of the successive impacts of new social forces. In the impact of Italian efficiency upon Transalpine government, the impacts of Democracy and Industrialism upon War and upon Parochial Sovereignty, the impact of Democracy upon Education, and the impact of Nationalism upon the historic political map, the titanic operations of the Earth-Spirit on the roaring loom of Time—the rhythmic weaving and the glowing life that ought to have fashioned a living garment for God[4]—have been diverted to the sinister task of manufacturing a Shirt of Nessus. The spirit of Nationality, which is the bastard offspring of the impact of Democracy upon Parochial Sovereignty, confronted us with its death's-head glare at the beginning of this Study, where we defined it 'as a spirit which makes people feel and act and think about a part of any given society as though it were the whole of that society'.[5] In the same place[6] we denounced this spirit as a political counterpart of the sin of polytheistic idolatry

[1] This question has been raised already in the present chapter on p. 318, above, and it is taken up again in V. C (ii) (*b*), vol. vi, pp. 312–21, below.

[2] For the transition from the third to the fourth chapter of our Western history in the third quarter of the nineteenth century of the Christian Era see Part I. A, vol. i, p. 1, footnote 2, above.

[3] See IV. C (iii) (*b*), *passim*, above.

[4] Goethe: *Faust*, ll. 501–9, quoted in Part II. B, vol. i, p. 204, above, and in V. C (iii), vol. vi, p. 324, below.

[5] Part I. A, vol. i, p. 9, above.

[6] Vol. i, p. 9, footnote 3. See also IV. C (iii) (*c*) 3 (β), in the present volume, p. 543, below.

—the monstrous 'association' of false gods with God—which once aroused the creative indignation of the Prophet Muhammad. If that is the besetting sin of our Western Civilization in our day, as we must perforce confess it to be, then, indeed, we must lay aside every weight;[1] for we shall need the last reserve of our strength for running the race that is set before us against a doom to which our sister society has already succumbed. 'Beware, therefore, lest that come upon you which is spoken of in the Prophets.'[2]

The Pharaonic Crown.

Up to this point in our survey of the pernicious effects of the idolization of an ephemeral institution the idols which we have passed in review have all been states of some kind or other: city-states or nation-states or universal states or their ghosts. States, however, are not the only kind of institution that has attracted idolatrous worship. Similar honours have been paid, with similar consequences, to the sovereign power in a state—a 'divine' kingship or an 'omnipotent' parliament—or again to some caste or class or profession on whose skill or prowess the existence of some state has been deemed to depend.

A classic example of the idolization of a political sovereignty incarnated in a human being is offered by the Egyptiac Society in the time of 'the Old Kingdom'.[3] In another connexion we have noticed already that the acceptance, or exaction, of divine honours by the sovereigns of the Egyptiac United Kingdom was one symptom of a 'great refusal' of a call to a higher mission—a fatal failure to respond to the second challenge in Egyptiac history—which

1 Hebrews xii. 1.

2 Acts xiii. 40.

3 Examples have to be carefully chosen, for there is, of course, no truth in the vulgar Western generalization that 'every Oriental worships his sultan as a god'. This is one of the trite variations on the catchword of 'the Unchanging East' which we have criticized above (in I. C (iii) (*b*), vol. i, pp. 164–8). There have, of course, been other non-Western societies besides the Egyptiac Society in which kings have been regarded —or, at any rate, treated—as divine beings. The Andean Society, the Far Eastern Society in Japan, and the Hindu Society in its overseas extensions in Java, Camboja and Champa (see Sir C. Eliot: *Hinduism and Buddhism* (London 1921, Arnold, 3 vols.), vol. iii, p. 115), may perhaps be added to the list; but this form of idolatry has been the exception, not the rule, in the Sumeric Society, and it has not been practised in the Babylonic Society or in the Syriac or in the Indic or in the Hindu in India or in the Sinic or in the Far Eastern Society in China. Divine honours were never paid to an Achaemenian King of Kings, or to an 'Abbasid Caliph of the Prophet and Commander of the Faithful, or to a Chinese Son of Heaven. On the other hand, in the Hellenic Society, to which our own Western Society is 'affiliated', divine honours were perpetually, and in the end regularly, paid to living conquerors and autocrats from beginning to end of the Hellenic decline and fall. The earliest recorded recipient of this idolatrous worship in the Hellenic World is Lysander, the Spartan soldier and politician who delivered the 'knock-out blow' to Athens in the Atheno-Peloponnesian War of 431–404 B.C. The series continues, through Alexander the Great and the Macedonian rulers of the Hellenic 'successor-states' of the Achaemenian Empire, to Caesar and Augustus and the post-Augustan Roman Emperors. (For a fuller survey of the currency of this practice of deifying the rulers of universal states see V. C. (i) (*d*) 6 (δ), Annex, vol. v, pp. 648–57, below.)

brought the Egyptiac Civilization to the early breakdown that so tragically cut short its precocious youth.[1] The crushing incubus which this series of human idols imposed upon Egyptiac life is perfectly symbolized in the pyramids, which were erected by the forced labour of their subjects in order to render the Pyramid-Builders magically immortal and divine.

'It is not only externally that the pyramids at Memphis are the distinctive monument (*das Wahrzeichen*) of "the Old Kingdom"; they are also the expression of its inmost essence. The entire state is concentrated in the person of "the Great God"—as the Pharaoh is styled in the war-memorials of "the Old Kingdom" on the Sinai Peninsula, whereas "the Good God" is the standard later usage—and the state's highest task is to ensure to him the perpetuation of the luxury of his royal estate in death as in life, and this to all eternity. The Egyptiac religion, with its hocus-pocus of magic, knows the road by which this objective can be reached, while the progress of civilization provides the technical and material means for attaining it with the greatest possible completeness.'[2]

This king-worship had no sooner produced its disastrous effect of breaking the Egyptiac Civilization down than it evoked a moral revulsion against a religious aberration which had demanded so awful a sacrifice. The 'folk-tales' about the Fourth Dynasty, which were handed down till they came to the ears of Herodotus some two thousand five hundred years after the age in which the Pyramid-Builders lived, included a tradition that King Menkaure, the builder of the last of the three classic pyramids at Gīzah, repented him, already, of the evil which his fathers had done, and defied the will of the Divine Ennead itself by insisting upon releasing the people of Egypt from their oppression.[3] The monuments and records of the Fifth Dynasty indicate that, in 'the Silver Age' of 'the Old Kingdom', Religion was beginning to take a more moral, and *pari passu* a less regicentric, form;[4] and the change of outlook came with a rush when 'the Silver Age' passed over into a 'Time of Troubles'.[5] That age saw the triumph of a religion which came out of the bosom of the Egyptiac internal proletariat and which expressed the spiritual reaction of the Egyptian peasantry to the

[1] See III. C (i) (*d*), vol. iii, pp. 212–15, above. The first challenge in Egyptiac history had been the physical task of mastering the jungle-swamp of the Lower Nile Valley (see II. C (ii) (*b*) 2, vol. i, pp. 302–15, above). The second challenge was the question of how the ruler of the United Kingdom of Egypt was to use the enormous power over the lives of his fellow human beings which had been placed in his hands by the accomplishment of the feat of creating an Egypt out of the jungle-swamp.

[2] Meyer, E.: *Geschichte des Altertums*, vol. i, part (2), 3rd edition (Stuttgart and Berlin 1913, Cotta), pp. 181–2.

[3] See the tale of Mycerinus in Herodotus, Book II, chaps. 129–34.

[4] See Breasted, J. H.: *The Development of Religion and Thought in Ancient Egypt* (London 1912, Hodder & Stoughton), pp. 177–8.

[5] For the Egyptiac 'Time of Troubles', *circa* 2424–2070/60 B.C., see I. C. (ii), vol. i, p. 137, above, and V. C (i) (*c*) 3, vol. v, pp. 266–7, below.

oppression that had broken their back;[1] and the converse of Osiris' advance was the deified Pharaoh's retreat.

The 'endeavour', for which the pyramids stood, 'to achieve immortality by sheer physical force'[2] was, indeed, discredited during the 'Time of Troubles' by a strictly material demonstration which was conclusive in the case of so strictly material an aim as that which the Pyramid-Builders had been pursuing. Their achievement of immortality in an Other World depended, avowedly, upon their ability to furnish their sepulchres in This World with a never-ceasing service of priests whose task was to say offices and make offerings *in saecula saeculorum.* To this end the Pyramid-Builders had done, in their lifetime, everything that wealth and law and magic in league with one another could do to enslave the energies of future generations for the execution of the Pyramid-Builders' own egotistic purpose. But in the 'Time of Troubles', when 'the land' turned 'round as doth a potter's wheel',[3] all their endowments were swept away and all their dispositions were disregarded.[4]

The Bolshevik spirit in which, in that age of anarchy and violence, the common people of Egypt revolted against an incubus under which they had laboured for centuries, is mirrored in a poem—*The Admonitions of a Prophet*—in which the experiences of the breakdown were recorded in retrospect after the rally that accompanied the foundation of the Egyptiac universal state.[5]

'The door-keepers say: "Let us go and plunder." The washerman refuseth to carry his load . . .

'Nay, but poor men now possess fine things. He that once made for himself sandals now possesseth riches. . . .

'Nay, but Elephantine and Thinis [?] and the . . . of Upper Egypt [?], they pay taxes no more by reason of the unrest. . . . To what purpose is a treasury without revenues? . . .

'Nay, but the public offices are opened, and their lists are taken away. Serfs become lords of serfs.

'Nay, but the [officials?] are slain and their lists taken away. Woe is me because of the misery in such a time!

1 For the worship of Osiris see I. C (ii), vol. i, pp. 140–5, above, and V. C (i) (*c*) 2, vol. v, pp. 150–2, below.

2 Breasted, op. cit., p. 179, quoted in I. C (ii), vol. i, p. 141, above.

3 'The Admonitions of a Prophet' in Erman, A.: *The Literature of the Ancient Egyptians*, English translation (London 1927, Methuen), p. 95.

4 This did not happen until after the 'Time of Troubles' had set in, if that change is to be equated with the transition from the Fifth to the Sixth Dynasty *circa* 2424 B.C. (see I. C (ii), vol. i, p. 137, above). Our modern Western archaeologists have unearthed a decree of King Pepi II in which this Pharaoh of the Sixth Dynasty exempts from all state taxation the priesthood and endowment of the pyramid of a Pharaoh of the Third Dynasty, King Snefru (see Breasted, J. H.: *The Development of Religion and Thought in Ancient Egypt* (London 1912, Hodder & Stoughton), p. 81).

5 For the foundation of the Egyptiac universal state through the political reunification of the Egyptiac World *circa* 2070/60 B.C. see I. C (ii), vol. i, p. 139; II. D (v), vol. ii, p. 112; and IV. C (ii) (*b*) 2, in the present volume, p. 85, above, and V. C (ii) (*a*), vol. vi, p. 190, below.

'Nay, but the scribes of the sack, their writings are destroyed. That whereon Egypt liveth is a "When I come, it's brought me".

'Nay, but the laws of the judgement-hall are placed in the vestibule. Yea, men walk upon them in the streets, and the poor tear them up in the alleys.

'Nay, but the poor man hath attained to the condition of the Nine Gods. That procedure of the House of the Thirty is divulged.

'Nay, but the great judgement-hall is a "Go out, that he may come in". The poor go and come in the Great Houses.

'Nay, but the children of the magistrates are thrown on to the streets. He that hath knowledge saith: "Yea". The fool saith: "Nay". He that hath no knowledge, to him seemeth it good.

'Nay, but they that were in the Pure Place, they are cast forth upon the high ground. The secret of the embalmers, it lieth open.'[1]

This overwhelming spectacle of the mummies of godlike kings being cast out upon the face of the desert was matched by the spectacle of the desecrated and derelict pyramids, which had now become immortal monuments of their builders' failure to achieve their own immortality. The very wealth which the Pyramid-Builders had heaped up in their sepulchral chambers, or ear-marked for the service of their mortuary ritual, had produced the exact opposite of its intended effect by serving as a loadstone to the covetousness of spoilers who were not deterred by any fear of either gods or men and were not visited by either divine or human retribution.

Behold the places thereof;
Their walls are dismantled,
Their places are no more,
As if they had never been. . . .
Lo, no man taketh his goods with him.
Yea, none returneth again that is gone thither.[2]

No wonder that by the time of the foundation of the Egyptiac universal state the efficiency of the royal mortuary ritual was no longer believed in.[3]

'If thou callest burial to mind, it is sadness, it is the bringing of tears, it is making a man sorrowful, it is haling a man from his house and casting him upon the hill. Never wilt thou go forth again to behold the Sun. They that builded in granite and fashioned a hall [?] in the pyramid, that achieved what is goodly in this goodly work—when the builders are become gods, then their offering-tables are empty [and they

[1] 'The Admonitions of a Prophet' in Erman, op. cit., pp. 94–100.

[2] Song on the futility of the pyramids, dating from the time of the Eleventh Dynasty (i.e. the period of transition from the 'Time of Troubles' to the universal state), quoted by Breasted, op. cit., pp. 182–3.

[3] See I. C (ii), vol. i, pp. 142–3, above, and compare Meyer, E.: *Geschichte des Altertums*, vol. i, part (2), 3rd edition (Stuttgart and Berlin 1913, Cotta), pp. 294 and 296.

are] even as the weary ones which die upon the dyke without a survivor; the flood hath taken its end [of them] and likewise the heat of the Sun, and the fish of the river-bank hold converse with them.'[1]

These spiritual experiences of the Egyptiac 'Time of Troubles' are reflected in a new attitude towards the sovereign power which is discernible after the establishment of the Egyptiac universal state.

'Under the Twelfth Dynasty the kings . . . eventually attained to a power which was not less absolute than that which had been exercised by the Pharaohs of "the Old Kingdom." . . . But, all the same, their status is essentially different from that of Snefru and Cheops. The naïve point of view that the whole country only exists in order to serve the King and to build his giant tomb for him has not only disappeared but has actually swung round into the contrary view that the royal power exists because the prosperity of the country, and of all its inhabitants, depends upon it.'[2]

This narrowing of the gulf between the sovereign and the people during the 'Time of Troubles' seems afterwards to have proceeded a stage farther as a consequence of the peculiar sequel to the break-up of the Egyptiac universal state. We have seen[3] that the ensuing interregnum was cut short and cancelled by a restoration of the universal state within little more than a hundred years after its fall. This Mycerinus-like defiance of Fate was inspired by a fanatical hostility to the tincture of an alien civilization in the culture of the interloping barbarian Hyksos; and the 'Zealotism' which proved to be a sufficiently dynamic force to drive the Hyksos out created a spiritual bond between the rank-and-file of the Egyptiac people and the new dynasty in which they had found their leadership in their 'holy war'. Under 'the New Empire' the divinity of the sovereign was little more than titular, and the Emperor actually lived among his people, and among the other members of the Im-

[1] 'The Dispute with his Soul of One who is tired of Life' in Erman, op. cit., pp. 87–8.

[2] Meyer, E.: *Geschichte des Altertums*, vol. i, part (2), third edition (Stuttgart and Berlin 1913, Cotta), pp. 278–9. The literary evidence on which Meyer's thesis rests is examined in Breasted, op. cit., pp. 210–50. In *The Admonitions of a Prophet* the atmosphere of ruin has already given place to an atmosphere of reconstruction before we reach the point at which our sole manuscript breaks off. 'Herein . . . we may discern a great transformation. The pessimism with which the men of the early Feudal Age [i.e. the Egyptiac "Time of Troubles"—A. J. T.], as they beheld the desolated cemeteries of the Pyramid Age, or as they contemplated the hereafter, and the hopelessness with which some of them regarded the earthly life were met by a persistent counter-current in the dominant gospel of righteousness and social justice set forth in the hopeful philosophy of more optimistic thinkers' (Breasted, op. cit., p. 249). In other words, the establishment of an Egyptiac universal state, in the shape of the so-called 'Middle Empire', after the 'Time of Troubles', was the symptom of a rally on the moral as well as the material plane.

[3] In I. C (ii), vol. i, pp. 138–9 and 144–5, and in IV. C (ii) (*b*) 2, in the present volume, p. 85, above. See further Part V. A, vol. v, pp. 2–3; V. C (i) (*c*) 2, vol. v, p. 152; and V. C (i) (*c*) 4, vol. v, p. 351, below.

perial Family, not as a god but as a man.[1] The completely human family life which was led by Ikhnaton[2] within the privacy of his palace at Tell-el-Amarna may have scandalized the public opinion of his generation; yet the Imperial revolutionary was merely carrying to its logical conclusion a tendency which was already implicit in the spirit of the age.

This 'humanization' of the status of the sovereign was—significantly—accompanied by a corresponding tendency in other matters which were of almost equal importance in Egyptiac life. In the religious field, for example, an immortalization which under 'the Old Kingdom' had been the odious monopoly of a privileged minority at the expense of an exploited majority was brought within everybody's reach by the triumph of the Osirian religion.[3] In the literary field, again, the Imperial revolutionary who failed to impose his radical religious reform upon the Egyptiac Society under the restored universal state did succeed in perpetuating his equally radical literary reform of 'scrapping' the dead classical language of 'the Middle Empire'—as he had sought to 'scrap' the classical religious syncretism of his own predecessor Thothmes III[4]—and making a new literary medium out of the living vernacular language of the day.[5] This vernacular literature which burst into flower in Ikhnaton's reign (*imperabat circa* 1370–1352 B.C.) was more lively than its classical predecessor. 'Men saw the World as it is, and took a pleasure in it'[6]—as is witnessed by thc love-songs which this latter-day Egyptiac literature has bequeathed to us.[7]

It is evident that in the course of its long-drawn-out decline the Egyptiac Society made a persistent, and not altogether unsuccessful, effort to recoil from the aberration that had caused its breakdown. The contrast between an Ikhnaton and a Chephren,[8] or between an anonymous love-song of 'the New Empire' and a royal pyramid of 'the Old Kingdom', reveals the struggle for the Egyptiac soul which a spirit of humanism waged with a spirit of idolatry for two thousand years. But this humanism was not enough to conquer its formidable adversary and reverse the process of decline and

[1] On this point see Hall, H. R.: *The Ancient History of the Near East* (London 1913, Methuen), pp. 277–9.

[2] For Ikhnaton's abortive religious revolution see I. C (ii), vol. i, pp. 145–6, above, and V. C (i) (*d*) 6 (δ), Annex, vol. v, pp. 695–6, below.

[3] On this point see I. C (ii), vol. i, pp. 142–3, above, and V. C (i) (*c*) 2, vol. v, p. 151, below.

[4] See I. C (ii), vol. i, p. 145, footnote 5, above; the present chapter and volume, p. 421; V. C (i) (*d*) 6 (δ), vol. v, p. 530; and V. C (i) (*d*) 6 (δ), Annex, vol. v, pp. 653–4 and 695, below.

[5] Erman, op. cit., p. xxvi. See also the present Study, V. C (i) (*d*) 6 (γ), vol. v, p. 496, below.

[6] Erman, op. cit., loc. cit.

[7] See the specimens in Erman, op. cit., pp. 242–51.

[8] This contrast comes out not only in their recorded aims and achievements, but in the portraits of themselves—as they themselves wished to be portrayed—which they have bequeathed to posterity.

fall; and there is a poignancy of failure in its efforts which touches our own sensibilities as we contemplate to-day the vestiges of its record. The epitaph of this pathetic Egyptiac humanism is 'Too late and too trivial!' It could not prevail against the demonic energy and earnestness of the king-worship which the pyramids embody. If we balance the two contending spirits in those divine scales in which the human soul was weighed at the Osirian judgement of the dead, we shall find that the more amiable spirit lightly kicks the beam. *En fin de compte* the dominant spirit of the Egyptiac Society from the Age of the Pyramid-Builders onwards is that of a 'servile state' and not that of a *fête champêtre.*[1]

The Mother of Parliaments.

The idolization of a political sovereignty incarnated in a human being is an aberration that is not exclusively represented by the classical Egyptiac example. If we look for an analogue in our modern Western history, we can easily discern a vulgar version of a royal Son of Re in the French 'roi soleil', Louis XIV. This Western Sun-King's palace at Versailles weighed as heavily upon the Land of France as the pyramids at Gīzah weighed upon the Land of Egypt; and the French Revolution was as inevitable a consequence of the idolization of the Crown as that Egyptiac social upheaval in which 'the land' turned 'round as doth a potter's wheel'.[2] 'L'État c'est moi' might have been spoken by Cheops, and 'Après moi le déluge' by Pepi II. But perhaps the most interesting example which the modern Western World affords of the idolization of a sovereign power is one that is rather less sensational.

In the apotheosis of 'the Mother of Parliaments' at Westminster the sovereign object of idolization is not a sovereign human being but a sovereign committee; and the incurable drabness of committees has here co-operated with the obstinate conceit of matter-of-factness in the modern English social tradition to keep this idolization of Parliament within respectable limits. The English worshipper of the House of Commons is only required to cast upon the altar that perfunctory grain of incense which sufficed for the Imperial Cult of a pedestrian Claudius or a prosaic Vespasian; and an Englishman who looked abroad upon the World in the year 1938 might reasonably claim that his temperate devotion to his own political divinity was being handsomely rewarded. Was not the country which had preserved its loyalty to 'the Mother of Parliaments' in a happier case than its neighbours who had gone

[1] For the servile êthos of the Egyptiac Society in its latter days see III. C (ii) (*b*), vol. iii, p. 215, and IV. C (ii) (*b*) 2, in the present volume, p. 85, footnote 5, above.
[2] See the quotation on p. 410, above.

a whoring after other gods?[1] Had the Lost Ten Tribes of the Continent found either tranquillity or prosperity in their feverish adulation of outlandish 'Duces' and 'Führers' and 'Kommissars' and 'Corporative States' and 'Third Reichs' and 'Soviet Socialist Republics'? In 1938 the answer to this practical question was undoubtedly in favour of the Englishman who asked it; and yet it still left something to be said; for the Englishman himself would admit that the blessings which his Mother Goddess was now bringing him were conspicuous chiefly by contrast with other men's present ills; and he would also admit that the recent Continental offspring of the ancient Insular Parliament had proved, on the whole, to be a sickly brood—incompetent to bring political salvation to the non-British majority of the living generation of Mankind, and incapable of holding its own against the post-war plague of dictatorships.

Perhaps the truth is that the very features in the character and history of the Parliament at Westminster which are the secret of its hold upon an Englishman's respect and affection are so many positive stumbling-blocks in the way of making this venerable English institution into a political panacea for the World. The Englishman is proud of his Parliament because he remembers that, alone among the many institutions of its kind that had come into being in the Transalpine kingdoms of Western Christendom during the second chapter of our Western history, this English Parliament was successful, at the transition from the Medieval to the Modern Age, in withstanding the impact of the Italian city-state culture by finding a way of combining the new-fangled Italian political efficiency with the old-fashioned Transalpine political liberties.[2] Yet this unique success of the Parliament at Westminster in outlasting 'the Middle Ages' by adapting itself to the exigencies of the Modern Age perhaps makes it less likely that this antique institution can now achieve another equally creative metamorphosis in order to meet the challenge of a 'Post-Modern' Age which is knocking upon the door with new and different exigencies of its own.

If we look into the structure of Parliament, we shall find that it is essentially an assembly of the representatives of local constituencies. This essential feature is just what we should expect from the date and place of the institution's origin; for the medieval kingdom of England, like other Transalpine kingdoms in the same age, was a congeries of village communities—interspersed with boroughs as a cake is sprinkled with plums. In such a polity as that, the significant and important grouping for political purposes

[1] Judges ii. 17. Compare Exodus xxxiv. 15, and Leviticus xvii. 7.

[2] For this achievement see III. C (ii) (*b*), vol. iii, pp. 358–63, and IV. C (iii) (*b*) 8, in the present volume, pp. 198–200, above.

was that of neighbourhood. The people with whom any given subject of the King was likely to have a common political interest were the people whose homes lay within a day's walking or riding distance of his own; and in a society so constituted the proper constituencies for a representative parliamentary assembly were manifestly local constituencies of sufficiently small size to allow every voter in each of them to know something about his fellow constituents and something about his member. This social basis of the structure of Parliament remained unchanged when the impact of the Italian culture ushered in a new age, and again when this challenge was successfully met by the creative transformation of Parliament in the seventeenth century. But the very success of Parliament in weathering the political storms of the seventeenth century had the consequence of singling England out to be the laboratory for a vast economic innovation during the two centuries that followed; and this English Industrial Revolution has undermined the social foundations beneath the English Parliament's feet. The Industrial Revolution has transformed a congeries of many hundred small and mutually independent units of economic life into a single unit which is co-extensive with the whole of the United Kingdom and which is one and indivisible economically, as the Kingdom itself is politically.[1] In the new England that has been conjured into existence by the new force of Industrialism within the last 150 years, the link of locality has lost its significance for political as well as for most other social purposes. And the new English voter, if we ask him who is his neighbour, will certainly not think of all those hundreds of thousands, or even millions, of people whose homes now lie within one day's travelling-distance of his own home by railway or motor-car. Nor will his own home strike him as a natural centre to measure from; for, in his outlook, it is no longer a fixed point. Unlike the tiller of the ground, who is rooted in the soil like a tree, the urban industrial worker may be here to-day and gone to-morrow to any place to which he may have been drawn by a momentary prospect of employment. For such a voter in such a social milieu the only rational answer to the question 'Who is your neighbour?' is: 'My fellow railwayman or or my fellow miner, in every corner of the Kingdom from Land's End to John-o'-Groat's.' The true constituency has ceased to be local and has become occupational. But an occupational basis of representation is a constitutional *terra incognita* in which the Westminster Parliament could not acclimatize itself without a radical change of structure; and for that 'the Mother of Parliaments' in her venerable old age not unnaturally shows no appetite.

[1] See IV. C (iii) (*b*) 4, p. 170, above.

To all this, no doubt, a twentieth-century English admirer of Parliament as it is may justly reply with a *solvitur ambulando.* In the abstract, he may admit, a thirteenth-century system of parliamentary representation is unsuitable to a twentieth-century community; but he will point out that in twentieth-century England the theoretical misfit seems to work as a matter of fact; and he will even be able to explain how this strange thing can be. In prophesying some serious social dislocation if an old political institution is allowed to remain unadjusted to a new economic basis, we have forgotten, he will tell us, to take one pertinent factor into account. In declaring it impossible to square the circle, we have failed to reckon with the skill of an old hand in performing *tours de force.* 'We English', this Englishman will explain, 'are so thoroughly at home with the political institutions which we have built up that, in our own country and among ourselves, I believe we can make them work under any conditions.' This is not an idle boast; and it is therefore quite conceivable that the system of parliamentary representation by local constituencies may actually survive longest in the country where it was earliest put out of date by the Industrial Revolution. This is conceivable because, as our hypothetical Englishman has pointed out, the country which is the birth-place of the Industrial System happens to be the birth-place of 'the Mother of Parliaments' as well. In the circumstances it is even possible that the English may not only cling to their Parliament-worship, but may escape the usual fate of idolators and persist in their error with impunity—to their own edification, and to the amazement of the 'lesser breeds without the law'. By the same token, however, it seems probable that England will not cap her seventeenth-century feat by becoming for a second time the creator of those new political institutions which a new age requires.

In our day the need for fresh political creation is once again urgent; for the flow of the Industrial Revolution, with the fundamental change of social structure that it necessarily brings in its train, has not stopped short at the shores of the island out of whose bosom the volcano originally erupted. Industrialism has now spread far and wide over the World; and in every country where it has established itself it has turned the existing political institutic into social anachronisms. Since few countries have the English luck to possess a political constitution which they know—or think they know—how to work under all conditions, most countries will be forced to find a new constitution to fit the new circumstances of their economic life. When a new thing has to be found, there are only two ways of finding it—namely, creation and mimesis—and mimesis cannot come into play until somebody has performed a creative act for his fellows to imitate. In the fourth chapter of our Western history, which has opened in our time, who will the new political creator be? Perhaps he will be an Italian or a German, perhaps a Russian or a Chinese; but at the start of a long, and probably arduous, race it is an unprofitable exercise of the fancy to guess at the winner. At this early stage it is only possible to pick out the competitors who are apparently out of the running; and this, at least, we can do in the present case. We can predict with some confidence that the new political creator in the now dawning age will not be any English worshipper of 'the Mother of Parliaments'.

Scribes, Priests, and Janissaries.

We may close this survey of institutional idols by glancing at the idolatrous worship of castes and classes and professions; and here we already have something to go upon. In studying the social structure of the arrested civilizations[1] we have come across two societies of the kind—the Spartans and the 'Osmanlis—in which the keystone of the arch was a caste that was virtually a corporate idol or deified Leviathan.[2] If the aberration of idolizing a caste is capable of arresting a civilization's growth it will also be capable of causing its breakdown; and, if we re-examine the breakdown of the Egyptiac Society with this clue in our hands, we shall perceive that the 'Divine' Kingship was not the only idolized incubus that weighed upon the backs of the Egyptiac peasantry under 'the Old Kingdom'. They also had to bear the burden of a 'bureaucracy' of litterati; and a share in the responsibility for the breakdown must be attributed to this privileged class.

The truth is that a deified kingship presupposes an educated secretariat. Without such support it could hardly maintain its statuesque pose on its pedestal, any more than Moses could have kept his hands outstretched over the vale of Rephidim from sunrise to sunset if his arms had not been upheld by Aaron and Hur.[3] The political unification of the whole of the Lower Nile Valley, from Elephantine to the Mediterranean coast, under a single sovereign power, and the systematic exploitation of the resources of this United Kingdom for the benefit of the deified wearer of the Double Crown, were feats of co-ordinated social effort which re-

[1] In Part III. A, in vol. iii, above.

[2] If we may rightly classify the Ottoman Pādishāh's Slave-Household and the Lacedaemonian chain-gang of Spartiate 'Peers' as corporate gods, then assuredly the weaker vessels among the human cells which once composed these inhuman Leviathans must often have anticipated, in their *for intérieur*, the auto-blasphemous reflexion—'It is not all beer and skittles being a god!'—which is attributed to a well-known living god of our own generation.

[3] Exodus xvii. 8–16.

quired an elaborate administration; and an organized government on this scale is hardly conceivable without a professional civil service which not only knows how to read and write but which is literate to its finger-tips.[1]

Thus the Egyptiac litterati were the power behind the throne, and indeed, in point of time, they were also before it. This bureaucracy could boast of itself that 'before Pharaoh was, I am'. It was indispensable, and it knew it; and it took advantage of this knowledge of its power in order to 'bind heavy burdens and grievous to be borne and lay them on men's shoulders,' while the Egyptiac scribes themselves would not 'move' these same burdens 'with one of their fingers'.[2] The privileged exemption of the litteratus from the intolerable common lot of the sons of toil is the theme of the Egyptiac bureaucracy's glorification of its own order in every age of Egyptiac history. The note is struck blatantly in *The Instruction of Duauf*:[3] a work, composed during the Egyptiac 'Time of Troubles', which has been preserved to us in copies made a thousand years later, as a writing exercise, by the schoolboys of 'the New Empire'. In this 'instruction which a man named Duauf, the son of Khety, composed for his son named Pepi, when he voyaged up to the Residence, in order to put him in the School of Books, among the children of the magistrates', the gist of the ambitious father's parting exhortation to his aspiring child is:

'I have seen him that is beaten, him that is beaten: thou art to set thine heart on books. I have beheld him that is set free from forced labour: behold, nothing surpasseth books. . . .

'Would that I might make thee love books more than thy mother; would that I might bring their beauty before thy face. It is greater than any calling. . . . If he hath begun to succeed, and is yet a child, men greet him. . . .

'Every artisan that wieldeth the chisel [?], he is wearier than him that delveth. . . . In the night, when he is set free, he worketh beyond what his arms can do; in the night he burneth a light.

'The stone-mason seeketh for work [?] in all manner of hard stone. When he hath finished it, his arms are destroyed, and he is weary. When such an one sitteth down at dusk, his thighs and his back are broken. . . .

'The field-worker, his reckoning endureth for ever; . . . he, too, is wearier than can be told, and he fareth as well as one fareth among lions. . . .

[1] Professor J. L. Myres in *The Dawn of History* (London, no date, Williams & Norgate), pp. 68–70, rightly insists upon the fact that it was the prior invention of the art of writing which made it possible to establish and maintain a polity on the scale of the Egyptiac United Kingdom. Even in the Andean World, where writing, in the strict sense, seems to have been unknown from first to last, the elaborate organization of the Empire of the Incas, which was the Andean universal state (see I. C (i) (*b*), vol. i, pp. 121–2, above), depended upon the correspondingly elaborate system of knot-mnemonics or *quipus* (see V. C (i) (*d*) 6 (γ), vol. v, p. 491, below).

[2] Matt. xxiii. 4 = Luke xi. 46.

[3] Text in Erman, op. cit., pp. 67–72.

'The weaver in the workshop, he fareth more ill than any woman. His thighs are upon his belly, and he breatheth no air. . . .

'Let me tell thee, further, how it fareth with the fisherman. Is not his work upon the river, where it is mixed with the crocodiles? . . .

'Behold, there is no calling that is without a director except [that of] the scribe, and he is the director. . . .'

A thousand years later, under 'the New Empire', the same spirit breathes through the copy-book exhortations and warnings to schoolboys[1] which convey the bureaucracy's unfaltering good opinion of itself as it still bestrides the broken back of a plebs that, by this time, has collapsed under the burden. 'Do not be a husbandman'; 'Do not be a soldier'; 'Do not be a charioteer'; 'Do not be a soldier, a priest or a baker'; 'Be an official': these were the warnings with which the writing-master, in those days, still drove home into his pupils' minds his exhortation to be diligent.

In the Far Eastern World there is a familiar analogue of this Egyptiac 'litteratocracy' in the incubus of 'mandarin rule' which the Far Eastern Society has inherited from the latest age of its Sinic predecessor.[2] The Confucian litteratus used to flaunt his heartless refusal to lift a finger to lighten the load of the toiling millions by allowing his finger-nails to grow to lengths which precluded every use of the hand except the manipulation of the scribal brush, and through all the chances and changes of Far Eastern history he has emulated his Egyptiac *confrère's* tenacity in keeping his oppressive seat. Even the impact of the Western culture, which has momentarily robbed the Confucian Classics of their prestige, has not thrown the Chinese litteratus out of his saddle. Though the examinations in the Confucian Classics are now abolished and the labyrinthine rows of examination-cells lie desolate, the litteratus still wields his ancient power in the name of a modern sage,[3] and imposes upon the peasant as effectively as before by flourishing in his face a diploma from the University of Chicago or the London School of Economics and Political Science.

In the course of Egyptiac history the alleviation which a long-suffering people obtained—albeit, too late—through the gradual humanization of the sovereign power was offset by successive additions to the class-incubus. As though the burden of carrying the bureaucracy had not been enough to bring the common people to the ground, they were further saddled, under 'the New Empire',

1 Specimens in Erman, op. cit., pp. 189–98.

2 For the institution of a competitive public examination in the Confucian Classics, as the avenue of entry into the Imperial Civil Service, in 125 B.C. or 124 B.C. under the Prior Han see III. C (ii) (*b*), vol. iii, pp. 329–30, above.

3 Since the outbreak of the present Chinese Revolution in A.D. 1911 the place once occupied in Chinese hearts and minds by Confucius seems to have been taken by Dr. Sun Yat-Sen.

with the incubus of a priesthood which was organized into a puissant Pan-Egyptiac corporation, under the presidency of the Chief Priest of Amon-Re at Thebes, by the Emperor Thothmes III (*imperabat solus circa* 1480–1450 B.C.).[1] A century after its incorporation the Egyptiac priesthood proved strong enough to defeat the Imperial heresiarch Ikhnaton (*imperabat circa* 1370–1352 B.C.); and three hundred years after that, when 'the New Empire' broke up, the Chief Priest of Amon actually became the residuary legatee of the Divine Kingship itself. About the year 1075 B.C. the reigning pontiff, Hrihor, picked up the now masterless—and powerless—Imperial Crown and placed it on his own head.[2] Thenceforward the Egyptiac mandarin had a fellow rider in the shape of an Egyptiac Brahman;[3] and after that the broken-backed Egyptiac circus-horse was compelled to stumble on upon his everlasting round of the arena until the pair of riders was increased to a trio by the mounting of a *miles gloriosus* on the pillion behind the scribe and the pharisee.

The Egyptiac Society, which had been as free from militarism throughout its natural term of life as the Orthodox Christian Society was in its age of growth, had been goaded by its encounter with the Hyksos—as the East Roman Empire was goaded by its encounter with Bulgaria—into a militaristic course. Not content with driving the Hyksos out beyond the pale of the Egyptiac World, the Emperors of the Eighteenth Dynasty yielded to the temptation of passing over from self-defence into aggression and taking their revenge for the Hyksos' domination over Egypt by carving out an Egyptian Empire in Asia. This wanton military adventure was easier to embark upon than to withdraw from; and when the tide turned again in the days of Ikhnaton the strain began to tell. The Nineteenth Dynasty found itself compelled to mobilize the now fast waning strength of the Egyptiac body social in order to save a remnant of the Asiatic empire and finally to preserve the integrity

1 See I. C (ii), vol. i, p. 145, footnote 5, and the present chapter and volume, p. 413, above, and V. C (i) (*d*) 6 (δ), vol. v, p. 530, and V. C (i) (*d*) 6 (δ), Annex, vol. v, pp. 653–4 and 695, below. For the stages by which this corporation developed, during the Dark Age after the decay of 'the New Empire', into a virtually closed hereditary caste, see Meyer, E.: 'Gottesstaat, Militärherrschaft und Ständewesen in Ägypten' in *Sitzungsberichte der Preussischen Akademie der Wissenschaften, Jahrgang 1928, Philosophisch-Historische Klasse* (Berlin 1928, de Gruyter), pp. 522–3.

2 See II. D (v), vol. ii, p. 116, footnote 1, above, and the present volume, IV. C (iii) (*c*) 3 (β), pp. 515–17, below.

3 The incubus of 'Brahmanocracy' has been inherited by the Hindu Society from its Indic predecessor, as the incubus of 'litteratocracy' has been inherited from the Sinic Society by the Far Eastern. An analogy between the Brahman caste in the Indic and Hindu worlds and the privileged fraternity of 'the pure' (*W'ēb*) in the Egyptiac World is accepted by Meyer in op. cit., p. 528; but he finds a closer analogy to the social development of the Egyptiac World after the decay of 'the New Empire' in the social development of the later Roman Empire, with its barbarian soldier caste and its simultaneous tendency to make all occupations hereditary (see Meyer, op. cit., p. 529).

of Egypt herself; and under the Twentieth Dynasty the aged and tormented frame of the Egyptiac Society was smitten with a paralytic stroke as the price of its final *tour de force* of flinging back the combined hosts of European and African and Asiatic barbarians that had been hurled against the Egyptian frontiers by the impetus of the post-Minoan Völkerwanderung.[1] When the fallen body at last lay prostrate and motionless on the ground, worn out by a régime of hard labour which had been imposed without pity or reprieve for a term of more than two thousand years, the native priest and litteratus, who still sat tight in the saddle with no bones broken by the fall, were joined by the grandson of the Libyan invader, who now strolled back as a soldier of fortune into a derelict Egyptiac World from whose frontiers his grandfather had been hurled back by the final feat of native Egyptian arms.[2] The military caste, begotten of these eleventh-century Libyan mercenaries, which continued to bestride the carcass of the Egyptiac Society for a thousand years after, may have been less formidable to its opponents in the field than the Janissaries or the Spartiates, but it was doubtless just as burdensome at home to the peasantry beneath its feet.[3]

[1] See I. C (i) (*b*), vol. i, pp. 92–3 and 100–2, above, and V. C (i) (*c*) 3, vol. v, p. 267, and V. C (ii) (*a*), vol. vi, p. 207, below.

[2] The apparently peaceful process by which the descendants of these Libyan soldiers of fortune eventually supplanted their native Egyptian employers in the political mastery of the Egyptiac World is compared by Meyer (in op. cit., p. 524) with the supplanting of the Ayyūbids by their own Mamlūks in the thirteenth century of the Christian Era. On this see further V. C (i) (*c*) 4, vol. v, pp. 352–3, below.

[3] The burden upon the backs of the Egyptiac peasantry was perhaps mitigated by the fact—which seems to emerge from the imperfect evidence at our command—that they were not called upon to bear more than one of the two latter-day social incubuses in any given case. The Egyptiac World seems, in fact, to have been partitioned geographically between the intrusive Libyan military caste and the native Egyptian priesthood. The priesthood retained the monopoly of exploiting the peasantry in four temple-states which centred respectively round the shrines of Amon-Re at Thebes, Ptah at Memphis, Re at Heliopolis, and Horus at Letopolis (for these Egyptiac temple-states and their counterparts in the histories of other civilizations see Meyer, op. cit., p. 521; eundem: *Geschichte des Altertums*, vol. ii, part (1), 2nd edition (Stuttgart and Berlin 1928, Cotta), p. 511; and the present chapter, p. 312, footnote 1, above, and IV. C (iii) (*c*) 3 (α), p. 471, and IV. C (iii) (*c*) 3 (β), pp. 515–18, below). The domains of these four temple-states appear to have been free from Libyan military settlements, to judge by the list of these which is given by Herodotus in Book II, chaps. 164–6; for though Herodotus does record the presence of a Libyan garrison at Thebes, there is no trace of any military force except the local native militia in the Thebaid before the destruction of the Theban temple-state during the struggle between the Napatans, Assyrians, and Saites in the eighth and seventh centuries B.C. (Meyer in op. cit., pp. 522 and 524–6). Except for Thebes, the Libyan garrison-towns in Herodotus's list are all confined to the Delta—and this excluding the three Deltaic temple-states above mentioned. The only place in Upper Egypt where there was certainly a Libyan garrison before the posting of the garrison at Thebes was Heracleopolis; and this city was the seat of a temple-state as well as the seat of the Libyan clan which gave birth to Shoshenq, the founder of the Twenty-Second Dynasty (see Meyer in op. cit., pp. 513, 521, 524, 526). It would seem that in the Heracleopolite nome, and in this province only, the Egyptiac peasantry had to pay dues to the priests and to the Libyans simultaneously; but in this connexion it may be observed that the garrison at Heracleopolis is not mentioned by Herodotus, who does mention the garrison at Thebes. Is it possible that the later Theban garrison was identical with the old Heracleopolite garrison, and that there was never at any time more than one Libyan garrison in Upper Egypt, though this garrison was stationed at different places in differ-

With the spectacle of an Egyptiac Society borne down to the ground by this trio of idolized castes we may close our study of the nemesis that attends the idolization of an ephemeral institution. We have next to consider the idolization of an ephemeral technique.

(γ) *The Idolization of an Ephemeral Technique.*

Reptiles and Mammals.

If we now turn to consider the idolization of techniques, we shall recognize at the outset of our inquiry that certain classic examples of the extreme penalty for a flagrant commission of this sin have already come under our observation in our survey of the arrested civilizations,[1] which has also furnished us with our classic examples of the extreme penalty for a flagrant idolization of institutions.[2] In the Ottoman and the Spartan social systems the key-technique of being shepherds of human cattle, or hunters of human game, was idolized side by side with the two master-institutions of the Pādishāh's Slave-Household and the standing army of Spartiate 'Peers' who were enslaved to the impersonal despotism of the Lycurgean *agôgê*. And when we pass from the arrested civilizations evoked by human challenges to those evoked by challenges from Physical Nature, we find that the idolatrous worship of a technique comprises the whole of their tragedy. The Nomads and the Esquimaux have fallen into arrest through an excessive concentration of their energies on the technique of literally shepherding authentic cattle on the Steppes, and literally hunting non-human game on the ice or in the waters of the Arctic Seas.

In the same connexion we have taken cognizance of the at first sight paradoxical, but on second thoughts manifestly inevitable, fact that in all these cases the cultivation of a human technique into a superfine and excessively exacting art has condemned these human victims of their own human skill to a retrogression towards an animalism which is the negation of humanity; and if we now peer back into pre-human chapters in the history of Life on this planet we shall find ourselves confronted by other examples of the same paradoxical 'law'.

ent periods? The relation between the priests and the soldiers in the Egyptiac World from the time of the foundation of the Libyan Twenty-Second Dynasty onwards may be compared with the relation between the Confucian litterati and the Manchurian 'bannermen' in Intramural China under the Manchu Dynasty. The Egyptiac temple-states of that age have a living counterpart in the Lamaistic Mahayanian Buddhist temple-state called the Shiretu Khurie Banner which is situated on the western edge of the Extramural Chinese province of Jehol. This living Far Eastern temple-state is ruled by a Prince-Lama, and has a population of about 12,000 sedentary agricultural Mongols occupying a territory measuring about seventy miles by thirty (see Lattimore, O.: *The Mongols of Manchuria* (London 1935, Allen & Unwin), pp. 253–9).

[1] See Part III. A, in vol. iii, above. [2] See IV. C (iii) (*c*) 2 (β), pp. 303–423, above.

This 'law' is enunciated in the following general terms by a modern Western scholar who has made a comparative study of its operation in the non-human and the human domain:

'Life starts in the sea. There it attains to an extraordinary efficiency. The fishes give rise to types which are so successful (such, for instance, as the sharks) that they have lasted on unchanged until to-day. The path of ascending Evolution did not, however, lie in this direction. In Evolution Dr. Inge's aphorism is probably always right: "Nothing fails like success." A creature which has become perfectly adapted to its environment, an animal whose whole capacity and vital force is concentrated and expended in succeeding here and now, has nothing left over with which to respond to any radical change. Age by age it becomes more perfectly economical in the way [in which] its entire resources meet exactly its current and customary opportunities. In the end it can do all that is necessary to survive without any conscious striving or unadapted movement. It can therefore beat all competitors in the special field; but equally, on the other hand, should that field change, it must become extinct. It is this success of efficiency which seems to account for the extinction of an enormous number of species. Climatic conditions altered. They had used up all their resources of vital energy in adapting to things as they were. Like unwise virgins, they had no oil left over for further adaptations. They were committed, could not readjust, and so they vanished.'[1]

The fatally complete technical success of the fishes in adapting themselves to the physical environment of Life in the marine overture to its terrestrial history is enlarged upon by the same scholar in the same context.

'At the level when Life was confined to the sea and the fishes were developing, they threw up forms which evolved a spine and so represented the vertebrates in the highest form then evolved. From the spine there spread out on each side, to aid the head, that fan of feelers which in them became the fore-fins. In the shark—and almost all the fish—these feelers were specialized so as to become, no longer feelers, but paddles: amazingly efficient flukes for bringing the creature head-foremost on its prey. Rapid reaction was everything, patient negotiation nothing; and these flukes not only ceased to be testers, explorers, examiners: they became increasingly efficient for water-movement and for nothing else. It looks as though pre-piscan pre-vertebrate life must have lived in warm shallow pools and perhaps always have been in touch with the floor, as to-day the gurnet by its feelers keeps contact with the solid bed. Once, however, swift unpremeditated movement became everything, specialization drove the fishes out into water where they lost touch with the bottom and all solids; and water, which till then had been really no more than a bearing or lubricant to carry them over the solid surface which they were constantly exploring—water then became

[1] Heard, Gerald: *The Source of Civilization* (London 1935, Cape), pp. 66–7.

their only element. This meant [that] their power of being stimulated by new circumstances was greatly limited. . . .

'That type of fish, then, which gave rise to the next advancing order of animals must have been a creature which did not adopt this extreme specialization of the fin. For, first, it must have been a creature which kept in touch with the floor, and so remained more variously stimulated than the fishes which lost touch with a solid environment. And, secondly, it must have been a creature which for the same reason kept in touch with the shallows and kept this touch by means of forelimbs which, because they could not therefore become wholly specialized as water-driving flukes, retained a more generalized "inefficient" exploratory and tentative character. The skeleton of such a creature has been discovered—a creature whose forelimbs are, it might almost be said, rather clumsy hands than proper fins; and through these members it looks as though the transition from shallow pool to flooded shore was made, the deep sea was left behind, the land was invaded, and the amphibians arrived.'[1]

In this triumph of the fumbling and irresolute amphibians in their competition with the deft and decisive fishes, we are witnessing an early performance of a drama which has since been replayed many times over with as many different changes in the cast. In the next performance that invites our attention, we shall find the fishes' part being taken by the amphibians' formidable progeny of the reptilian tribe, while the amphibians' own part in the preceding performance is taken this time by the ancestors of those mammalian animals in which the Spirit of Man has recently become incarnate. The primitive Mammals were meek and puny creatures who unexpectedly inherited the Earth because the heritage had been left derelict by the magnificent Reptiles who were the previous lords of terrestrial creation; and the Mesozoic Reptiles—like the Pleistocene Esquimaux and Nomads[2] and 'Osmanlis and Spartans—were conquerors who forfeited their conquests by straying into the blind alley of over-specialization.

'[The] apparently abrupt ending up of the Reptiles is, beyond all question, the most striking revolution in the whole history of the Earth before the coming of Mankind. It is probably connected with the close

[1] Ibid., pp. 67–9.

[2] A suggestive double parallel between the respective downfalls of the Mesozoic Reptiles and the Nomads and between the respective triumphs of the Mammals and the peoples of Western Christendom is made by Mr. H. G. Wells in *The Outline of History* (London 1920, Cassell), p. 386:

'Just as in the Mesozoic Age, while the great Reptiles lorded it over the Earth, there were developing in odd out-of-the-way corners those hairy mammals and feathered birds who were finally to supersede that tremendous fauna altogether by another far more versatile and capable, so in the limited territories of Western Europe of the Middle Ages, while the Mongolian monarchies dominated the World from the Danube to the Pacific and from the Arctic Seas to Madras and Morocco and the Nile, the fundamental lines of a new and harder and more efficient type of human community were being laid down.'

of a vast period of equable warm conditions and the onset of a new austerer age, in which the winters were bitterer and the summers brief but hot. The Mesozoic life, animal and vegetable alike, was adapted to warm conditions and capable of little resistance to cold. The new life, on the other hand, was before all things capable of resisting great changes of temperature. . . .

'As for the Mammals competing with and ousting the less fit Reptiles, . . . there is not a scrap of evidence of any such direct competition. . . . In the later Mesozoic a number of small jaw-bones are found, entirely mammalian in character. But there is not a scrap, not a bone, to suggest that there lived any Mesozoic Mammal which could look a dinosaur in the face. The Mesozoic Mammals or mammal-like Reptiles—for we do not know clearly which they were—seem to have been all obscure little beasts of the size of mice and rats, more like a down-trodden order of Reptiles than a distinct class; probably they still laid eggs and were developing only slowly their distinctive covering of hair. They lived away from big waters, and perhaps in the desolate uplands, as marmots do now; probably they lived there beyond the pursuit of the carnivorous dinosaurs. Some perhaps went on all fours, some chiefly went on their hind legs and clambered with their forelimbs. They became fossils only so occasionally that Chance has not yet revealed a single complete skeleton in the whole vast record of the Mesozoic rocks by which to check these guesses.'[1]

The propositions put forward by Mr. Wells down to this point in his exposition appear to be generally accepted. The Reptiles were supplanted by the Mammals because the Reptiles had lost the ability to adapt themselves to changes in their environment, and not because they had suffered defeat in any direct encounter with a nascent new order of living creatures who had not yet begun to emerge out of their original weakness and obscurity by the time when the gigantic Reptiles perished from off the face of the Earth. In the post-mortem inquiry over the carcasses of these monsters the verdict of the experts seems to be unanimous. But, in a common ordeal to which the Reptiles succumbed, what was it exactly that enabled the Mammals to survive and in consequence to inherit an Earth which the Reptiles had now vacated at the summons of Death? On this supremely interesting question Mr. Wells' answer is not confirmed by the other contemporary scholar whom we have been quoting in the present context.

According to Mr. Wells the rudimentary Mammals survived because, in spite of their obvious general weakness, they happened to be strong in just that form of strength which the particular ordeal demanded.

'These little Theriomorphs, these ancestral Mammals, developed hair. Hairs, like feathers, are long and elaborately specialized scales. Hair is

[1] Wells, H. G.: *The Outline of History* (London 1920, Cassell), pp. 22–4.

perhaps the clue to the salvation of the early Mammals. Leading lives upon the margin of existence, away from the marshes and the warmth, they developed an outer covering only second in its warmth-holding (or heat-resisting) powers to the down and feathers of the Arctic sea-birds. And so they held out through the age of hardship between the Mesozoic and Cainozoic ages, to which most of the true Reptiles succumbed.'[1]

Is this the true secret of the Mammals' relative success? If it is, it merely tells us that fur is a more effective physical armour against the cold than scales or carapaces. But other, and perhaps deeper, explanations are forthcoming. Bishop Barnes puts his finger on the principle which we have embraced in this Study under the name of 'Etherialization'.[2] 'In Mammals, developments resulting in greater simplicity [by contrast with Reptiles] are noteworthy.'[3] Mr. Heard suggests that the armour which saved the Mammals' lives was not physical but psychic, and that the strength of this psychic defence lay in a physical defencelessness.

'The giant Reptiles were themselves hopelessly decadent before the rise of the Mammals. There was no hope any longer for this . . . step in Life's advance. They had begun [as] small, mobile, and lively creatures. They grew so vast that these land-ironclads could scarcely move; and many had to remain all their time awash in pools where water would bear some of their otherwise crushing weight. All their energy seems to have gone into their bodies, and their brains remained practically non-existent—in many cases the spinal column hardly enlarging when it entered the skull. Their heads were no more than periscopes, breathing-tubes and pincers.

'Meanwhile, as they slowly swelled and hardened up to their doom—until, it seems (with such a genus, for example, as Triceratops), bone-growth went on of itself; a huge degenerative accumulation of rigid tissue—there was already being fashioned that creature which was to leap the boundary and limits then set for Life, and start a new stage of energy and consciousness. And nothing could illustrate more vividly the principle that Life evolves by sensitiveness and awareness; by being exposed, not by being protected; by nakedness, not by strength; by smallness, not by size. The forerunners of the Mammals have now been discovered in the Cretaceous: the age which ends the Age of the Reptiles. These transitional types are minute rat-like creatures. In a world dominated by monsters the future is given to a creature which has to spend its time taking notice of others and giving way to others. It is undefended, given fur instead of scales. It is unspecialized, given again those sensitive feeling forelimbs and, no doubt, those antennae—the long hairs on the face and head—to give it irritating stimulation all the time. Ears and eyes are highly developed. It becomes warm-blooded, so [that] it may be constantly conscious throughout the cold, when the Reptile falls into

[1] Wells, op. cit., loc. cit. [2] In III. C (i) (*c*), vol. iii, pp. 174–92, above.

[3] Barnes, E. W.: *Scientific Theory and Religion* (Cambridge 1933, University Press), p. 472.

anaesthetic coma—kept alive in discomfort, that it may be constantly taking in and [that] its consciousness, in the end, may have to go on comparing conditions [which] it remembers enjoying with those [which] it now endures. So its consciousness is blown upon and developed. The varied continuous stimulant is reacted to with varied answer, because the creature, being unprecedented, is capable not of one but of many replies, none of which can settle the question for it.

'Here, then, we have the sensitive shoot—"the tender plant out of a dry ground"—from which we are sprung.'[1]

Manchester and Osaka.

In the tragedy of the Reptiles we are presented with a case in which the penalty for the idolization of an ephemeral technique has been not an arrest upon the threshold of life but a breakdown following the attainment of an exuberant maturity; and we can, of course, think of more familiar cases of this latter variation on the plot of the play in our own human history. Indeed, an English student of history can put his finger on a human case near home; for 'the Mother of Parliaments', whose latter-day constituents are perhaps now in danger of idolizing the great political institution created by their ancestors,[2] has her domicile in a country that has won for itself in the realm of economic technique the equally proud title of 'the Workshop of the World'; and there are certain alarming indications, in this domain as well, that England in our day is paying her penalty for the perilous honour of having been the first country to achieve the Industrial Revolution.

In our day the country that gave birth to the Industrial System of production is a by-word for its technological conservatism; and its arch-conservatives are not the surviving representatives of the pre-industrial dispensation in those rare patches of the English country-side that have contrived to resist the penetrating and pervasive influence of a latter-day English world of mines and mills. On the contrary, they are the colliers and the textile-manufacturers whose grandfathers and great-grandfathers were the pioneers in the discovery of our modern industrial technique. These pioneers led the way in the Industrial Revolution not only for England but for the World; and it is evidently just for this reason that the epigoni are now making themselves notorious for an êthos which is the exact antithesis of the adventurous, experimental, adaptable, creative spirit that made the pioneers' fortune. The epigoni cannot believe that all is not 'for the best' in a technique which gave its inventors a virtual monopoly of the world market for

[1] Heard, Gerald: *The Source of Civilization* (London 1935, Cape), pp. 71–2.
[2] See IV. C (iii) (*c*) 2 (β), pp. 414–18, above.

industrial products for the greater part of a century; and even the belief that they are still living 'in the best of all possible worlds' for British manufacturers dies singularly hard in the face of a growing array of increasingly successful foreign competitors. It is now more than half a century since Germany and the United States—relieved, by the outcome of the wars of 1861–71, from their former handicaps of geographical disunity and political pre-occupation—first entered the lists of the industrial tournament and threw down the gauntlet to Great Britain;[1] and since the war of 1914–18 the ranks of Great Britain's industrial competitors have been joined by Japan, who was an *alter orbis*, unacquainted with any form of Western technique, until 'the eighteen-sixties', and even by France, who missed her opportunity, at the turn of the eighteenth and nineteenth centuries, of making the inventions which Great Britain then invented, and winning the rewards which Great Britain duly won, because she then allowed Napoleon to recall her from a new industrial adventure to the old enterprise—already proved barren by a series of abortive essays—of establishing a political hegemony over Europe by military force.[2] Yet even this formidable and ubiquitous competition with which the *ci-devant* 'Workshop of the World' is now confronted has not led the British manufacturer to overhaul the technique by which his ancestors once made an easy conquest of a virgin world market; and *à fortiori* it has not led him to adopt the technique through which his ancestors' English monopoly has been successfully disputed by his own foreign competitors.

These German, American, and Japanese poachers upon old English industrial preserves have had to face the problem of forcing an entry into a field already occupied by the English pioneers; and they have solved it by working out new kinds of technique which the Englishman had never thought of—or needed to think of—before their intrusion upon the scene: for instance, the technique of co-ordinating under a single management all the successive economic processes from the production of the raw materials to the marketing of the manufactured product, and the technique of procuring an unprecedentedly intimate and effective co-operation between the producer and the financier and between a nationally organized industry and the national Government. Like the English pioneers in their heyday, the present foreign competitors of the English epigoni have been free from the handicap of inheriting

[1] See IV. C (iii) (*b*) 4, pp. 175–8, above.

[2] For the non-French functions of the Napoleonic Empire see V. C (i) (*d*) 6 (γ), Annex I, vol. v, pp. 619–45, below. For the stimulus given to French industry by the devastation of the principal industrial areas of France in the war of 1914–18 see II. D (iv), vol. ii, pp. 107–8, above.

an older technique with a record of past efficacity which invites its present possessors to continue to bow down and worship it; and so, like the English pioneers, they have been free to make creative inventions. It is the English epigoni—in contrast to both their English predecessors and their foreign contemporaries—who are captivated by the idolization of an ephemeral technique; and the seriousness of the handicap can be gauged by the plight in which our English industry finds itself to-day.

In this light we can see that Great Britain is suffering doubly from her success, since 1914, in avoiding both the two calamities of invasion and inflation which have overtaken France and Germany respectively.[1] It is not only that these two industrial competitors of hers have been positively strengthened by the stimulus of blows to which they have effectively responded. From the English point of view it is perhaps even more serious that Great Britain herself, in escaping these blows, has lost a golden opportunity of relieving herself from the incubus of her own industrial past. She might have faced an industrially rejuvenated France and Germany with less cause for apprehension if only the same stroke of Fortune which has reinvigorated them had at the same time shattered the British idol of an obsolete pioneer technique.

This industrial competition between an old-fashioned England and a new-fangled Germany and Japan and United States is a drama which has the same denouement as the biological competition between the Mesozoic Reptiles and the Cainozoic Mammals; but the plots differ in one important respect. The two orders of animals, as Mr. Wells points out in the passage quoted above, did not compete directly with each other, but settled the question of who was to inherit the Earth by each grappling, separately and independently, with an identic challenge from the Physical Environment. On the other hand, our latter-day human question of who is to capture the world market is being settled by a direct encounter between the competitors, *corps à corps*. The plot of this human drama might be stated, from the point of view of a living English industrialist, in the words of a living English student of one of the physical sciences: 'A step in evolution in any animal group is followed by an evolutionary advance on the part of their parasites.'[2] In fact, our present conflict of industrial techniques is not inaccurately described—in a phrase which is frequently heard to-day—as 'economic warfare'; and if we now extend our survey to the classic form of warfare in which the technique employed is not

[1] For this English immunity from French and German misfortunes see II. D (iv), vol. ii, pp. 108–9, above.

[2] Haldane, J. B. S.: *Possible Worlds* (London 1927, Chatto & Windus), p. 42.

economic but military, we shall find that, in this sinister kind of human intercourse, the 'parasite' is perpetually preying upon a 'host' who, on his side, is perpetually being betrayed by his own self-conceit into placing himself at the 'parasite's' mercy.

Goliath and David.

In our human military history the analogue of the biological competition between the tiny soft-furred Mammal and the massive armoured Reptile is the saga of the duel between David and Goliath;[1] and if we take this legendary Syriac combat as our starting-point, we shall find the same drama acted and reperformed in a continuous series of matches between new-fangled and old-fashioned military techniques which will remind us of 'The Chain of Destruction' that Mayne Reid describes in *The Boy Hunters*.

Before the fatal day on which he challenges the armies of Israel, Goliath has won such triumphant victories with his spear whose staff is like a weaver's beam and whose head weighs six hundred shekels of iron, and has found himself so completely proof against hostile weapons in his panoply of casque and corselet and target and greaves, that he can no longer conceive of any alternative armament;[2] and he believes that in this armament he is invincible. He therefore challenges the enemy of the day to choose a champion to meet him in single combat, on the assumption that, if any champion is forthcoming, he will likewise be a spearman armed *cap-à-pie*, and in the assurance that any Israelite who has the hardihood to fight the Philistine champion with his own weapons will be an easy prey for him. So hard set is Goliath's mind in these two ideas that, when he sees David running forward to meet him with no armour on his body and nothing in his hand that catches the eye except a staff, Goliath takes umbrage, instead of taking alarm, at his adversary's apparent unpreparedness, and exclaims: 'Am I a dog, that thou comest to me with staves?' Goliath does not suspect that this youth's impertinence is not a piece of boyish folly but is, on the contrary, a carefully considered manœuvre (David having actually realized, quite as clearly as Goliath himself, that

[1] See the story as it is told in 1 Samuel xvii.

[2] For the Assyrian provenance of Goliath's armament see III. C (i) (*b*), vol. iii, p. 165, footnote 1, above. In contrast to this view of the origin of the hoplite's panoply, which is that of Professor G. Glotz, greater credit is given to the native inventiveness of the peoples of the Aegean area in J. Kromayer and G. Veith's *Heerwesen und Kriegführung der Griechen und Römer* (Munich 1928, Beck), p. 21, footnote 4. 'Although', they write, 'there can be no doubt that certain isolated pieces of equipment were borrowed by the Greeks from the East, there is at the same time no ground for questioning the accuracy of our evidence that, on the banks of the Nile as well as in the army of the Great King of Assyria, the fully-armed Greek hoplite of the 8th and 7th centuries [B.C.], with his heavy but highly protective armament, made a powerful and exotic impression. The panoply of the Homeric hero is thus none the less something peculiarly Greek for having come into existence under Oriental inspiration.'

in Goliath's own accoutrements he cannot hope to be Goliath's match, and having therefore rejected, after trying on, the panoply which Saul has pressed upon him); nor does Goliath notice the sling in the hand which does not hold the staff, nor wonder what mischief may be hidden in the shepherd's bag. And so this luckless Philistine Triceratops stalks forward pompously to offer his unvisored forehead as a target for the sling-stone which is to slay him at one shot before ever his contemptible adversary comes within range of his hitherto lethal spear.

Goliath of Gath was not the first hoplite in the history of Life on Earth to court and incur this disconcerting doom; for armour far more ponderous than his had been worn by reptilian and mammalian cataphracts before ever Goliath's first human ancestor had made his appearance on the terrestrial scene.

'One seductive and ultimately always fatal path [of Evolution] has been the development of protective armour. An organism can protect itself by concealment, by swiftness in flight, by effective counter-attack, by uniting for attack and defence with other individuals of its species and also by encasing itself within bony plates and spines. The last course was adopted by the ganoid fishes of the Devonian with their shining armour. Some of the great lizards of the later Mesozoic were elaborately encased. Some Tertiary mammals, especially in South America, were immense and bizarre creatures; and one wonders how long a period of evolutionary history was needed for them thus to arm themselves. Always the experiment of armour failed. Creatures adopting it tended to become unwieldy. They had to move relatively slowly. Hence they were forced to live mainly on vegetable food; and thus in general they were at a disadvantage as compared with foes living on more rapidly "profitable" animal food. The repeated failure of protective armour shows that, even at a somewhat low evolutionary level, mind triumphed over mere matter. It is this sort of triumph which has been supremely exemplified in Man.'[1]

It is ideally exemplified in the saga of David and Goliath. Yet, while this classic tale sums up for all time a philosophic truth that is also illustrated by the slowly unfolding history of human competition in armaments, it is at the same time a matter of historical fact that the individual hoplite champion of the post-Minoan interregnum—a Goliath of Gath or a Hector of Troy—did not succumb to David's sling or Philoctetes' bow but to the Myrmidons' phalanx:[2] a veritable Leviathan in which a multitude of hoplites set shoulder to shoulder and helmet to helmet and shield to shield.[3]

[1] Barnes, E. W.: *Scientific Theory and Religion* (Cambridge 1933, University Press), pp. 474–5.

[2] For the origin and diffusion of the phalanx technique see I. C (iii) (*b*), Annex I, vol. i, p. 428, footnote 2; and III. C (i) (*b*), vol. iii, p. 165, footnote 1, above.

[3] *Iliad* xvi, ll. 211–17.

While each single phalangite in the rank-and-file was a replica of Hector or Goliath in his accoutrements, he was the antithesis of the Homeric hoplite in his spirit; for the essence of the phalanx did not consist in the equipment of its component men-at-arms, but in the discipline which had transformed a barbaric rabble of individual warriors into a military formation whose orderly evolutions could accomplish ten times as much as the unco-ordinated efforts of an equal number of equally well-armed individual champions.

This new military technique, of which we already catch some anticipatory glimpses in the *Iliad*, made its indubitable entry upon the stage of history in the shape of a Spartan phalanx which marched through the rhythm of Tyrtaeus's verses to its socially disastrous military victory in the second Messeno-Spartan War;[1] but the triumph of the Spartan phalanx was not definitive. After driving all its 'opposite numbers' off the field, it succumbed, in its turn, to new techniques; and it is significant that this discomfiture of the Spartan phalanx came to pass as soon as the Spartans were tempted to 'rest on their oars' on the strength of their victory in the Atheno-Peloponnesian War of 431–404 B.C.—a victory which seemed to complete the military supremacy of Sparta in Hellas and so to crown the victory which the same Spartan tactics had gained over the Messenians more than two hundred years before. Within thirty-three years of the Athenian débâcle of 404 B.C. the triumphant Spartan phalanx had been ignominiously put out of court: first by an Athenian swarm of peltasts[2]—a host of Davids with which the phalanx of Goliaths found itself quite unable to cope—and then by a Theban column, a tactical innovation which improved the phalanx, with decisive effect, by introducing an uneven distribution of its depth and weight and 'drive', and thereby capping the old asset of discipline with the new element of surprise. The Athenian and Theban techniques, however, were as swiftly and surely undone by their successive triumphs as the Spartan technique itself; for their respective victories over the Spartan phalanx in 390 and 371 were both cancelled at one stroke in 338 B.C. by a Macedonian formation in which a highly differentiated skirmisher and phalangite had been skilfully integrated with a heavy cavalry into a single fighting force.[3]

[1] See III. C (i) (*b*), vol. iii, p. 165, above.

[2] For the peltast technique see loc. cit.

[3] For the Macedonian combination of phalangite with skirmisher, and for the concomitant change in the phalangite's equipment, see loc. cit., above, and also IV. C (iii) (*c*) 2 (γ), Annex, p. 636, footnote 3, below.

'One of the characteristics of Alexander's battle-tactics is that the differentiation between the tasks of the different arms has advanced still farther than it had gone in the tactics of Epaminondas. Each individual arm now co-operates—for its part and in its special role—with the whole, in such a way as to give the whole the aspect of a living organism. The function of the Macedonian cavalry is to strike the decisive blow by

If the Macedonian phalanx, with its light-armed fringe and its cavalry arm, surpassed the Spartan phalanx as an instrument of war in the measure of the difference in range between the Macedonian and the Spartan conquests, then the gulf between the two techniques was great indeed, since the Spartan phalanx merely conquered Hellas, while the Macedonian army conquered both Hellas and the Achaemenian Empire. From the banks of the Cephisus and the Eurotas to the banks of the Jaxartes and the Beas, the Macedonians marched at will without meeting any opponent who was able to stand up to them. But the most impressive testimony to the prowess of the Macedonian military machine is not the long list of the military Powers that were successively defeated by Philip II and Alexander the Great; it is the avowal which was made, after the event, by the victorious enemy commander of the opposing army in a decisive battle which was fought 170 years after Philip's crushing victory at Chaeronea.

'The consul Lucius [Aemilius Paullus] had never seen a phalanx in his life until he encountered one—for the first time—in the Roman war with Perseus; and, when it was all over, he used freely to confess to his friends at home that the Macedonian phalanx was the most formidable and terrifying sight that had ever met his eyes—and this from a soldier who had not merely witnessed, but had actually participated in, a greater number of actions than any other captain of the day.'[1]

At Pydna, however, in 168 B.C. it was not Perseus' phalanx but Paullus's legions that emerged victorious; and the eulogy of the Macedonian formation which has just been quoted is at the same time a funeral oration pronounced over its dead body by the master of the Roman formation which dealt the phalanx its death-blow. The Macedonian army of the second century B.C. was as little able to cope with the Romans as the Athenian or Theban or Achaemenian fighting forces of the fourth century B.C. had been able to cope with the Macedonian army of Philip II and Alexander the Great; and the cause of this sensational περιπέτεια in Macedonian military fortunes was the senile adulation of a technique[2] which had carried all before it through five successive generations.

charging home and then wheeling round to take the enemy on the flank; the function of the Thessalian cavalry is to fight a non-committal action of sorties, retreats, about-turns and renewed onsets; the function of the phalanx is to deliver a frontal attack in heavy massed formation; the function of the light troops is to cover the army's flanks and fight at long range; and the whole set of operations is co-ordinated, and is informed with a unitary spirit.'—Kromayer, J., and Veith, G.: *Heerwesen und Kriegführung der Griechen und Römer* (Munich 1928, Beck), pp. 118–19. (Cf. pp. 144 and 246–7.)

[1] Polybius, Book XXIX, chap. 17.

[2] One symptom of this technical senility was the pathological exaggeration of the regulation length of the Macedonian phalangite's *sarisa* (see IV. C (iii) (*c*) 2 (γ), Annex, pp. 636–7, below). Another symptom was a tendency to rely more upon the phalanx and less upon the light infantry and the cavalry. As has been noted above, it was a masterly co-ordination of the use of all three arms that was the secret

Ἄνδρες Ἀλεξάνδροιο παρασπισταὶ βασιλῆος,
οἳ πάρος εὐρείης λὰξ ἐπέβητ' Ἀσίης,
εἴθ' ἤγειρα παρ' ὔμμιν αὐτήν τε πτόλεμόν τε·
εἴχετε γὰρ χάρμην, εἴχετε, θεσπεσίην.

A hard-won Macedonian victory over a diminutive Athens and Thebes had been followed by an easy Macedonian conquest of the vast Achaemenian Empire;[1] and thereafter the Macedonian soldiers 'rested on their oars' as the unchallenged masters of all but the outskirts of the Habitable World,[2] while, beyond their western horizon, the Romans were revolutionizing the art of war through an experience gained from their sufferings in their tremendous struggle with Hannibal. The immense superiority of the post-Hannibalic Roman over the post-Alexandrine Macedonian fighting-machine was conclusively demonstrated at their first encounter;[3] and the omen given by the cavalry skirmish in Illyria in 200 B.C.

of the victories of Philip and Alexander; but, if an estimate had to be made of the relative importance of the contribution of each arm to the common achievement, the verdict would be that Alexander might conceivably have conquered the Achaemenian Empire without the phalanx, but could not conceivably have succeeded if he had lacked either of the other two components of his composite fighting-force (see Hogarth, D. G.: *Philip and Alexander of Macedon* (London 1897, Murray), pp. 63–4; eundem: 'The Army of Alexander' in *The Journal of Philology*, vol. xvii (London & Cambridge 1888, Macmillan), pp. 5–17, especially pp. 5 and 8–10).

1 The conquest was easy all the way from the passage of the Dardanelles to the transit of 'the Caspian Gates'. For the very much sturdier resistance which the Macedonian arms encountered in the north-eastern marches of the Achaemenian Empire, over against the Eurasian Steppe, see II. D (v), vol. ii, p. 140, above.

2 Though the Macedonians themselves waited blindly and passively for their doom to overtake them, the future was divined on inference from the past—and this as early as the next generation after Alexander the Great—by the Athenian philosopher and statesman Demetrius of Phalerum, who governed Athens in the Macedonian interest from 317 to 307 B.C.; and after Demetrius's prophecy had been conclusively vindicated in 168 B.C. at Pydna it was quoted with admiration by the Arcadian historian Polybius:

'The fate of Macedon has often vividly recalled to my mind the words of Demetrius of Phalerum. In his work on Fortune, in which his object is to indicate unambiguously to his fellow men the mutability of this principle, Demetrius interrupts his narrative of the epoch of the overthrow of the Persian Empire by Alexander in order to make the following observations:

'"In order to realize the baffling character of Fortune there is no necessity to take account of vast periods of time extending over many generations. The past half-century provides a sufficient example. Supposing that, fifty years ago, some divinity had foretold the future to the Persians and the King of Persia or to the Macedonians and the King of Macedon, do you imagine that they would ever have believed that at the present date the very name of Persia—at that time mistress of almost the entire Habitable World—would be utterly blotted out, while the Macedonians, whose name was previously unknown, would have the World at their feet? In my belief, however, this is only one of the signs and wonders by which Fortune is perpetually demonstrating to Mankind her power, her incommensurability with human life, and her revolutionary practice of disconcerting human reason. In setting Macedon in the seat of mighty Persia, she has signified the fact that her investiture of Macedon with the insignia of empire is equally revocable and contingent upon her discretion."

'In the case of Perseus this eventuality has come to pass. The words of Demetrius have proved themselves inspired and prophetic; and, now that my own narrative has brought me to the epoch of the overthrow of the Macedonian Kingdom, I feel that, as a first-hand witness of the event, I should not be justified in passing it over without pointing the moral myself and giving his due to Demetrius. To my mind there is a supernatural prescience in his dictum. He has accurately anticipated the course of events almost a century and a half in advance' (Polybius, Book XXIX, chap. 21).

3 See the passage from Livy which has been quoted in II. D (v), vol. ii, p. 163, above.

was fulfilled in 197 B.C. at Cynoscephalae and was confirmed in 168 B.C. at Pydna.

The Roman legion triumphed over the Macedonian phalanx because it carried the integration of the light infantryman with the phalangite, which the Macedonians had begun,[1] a long step farther In the Macedonian technique this integration depended on a meticulously exact co-ordination of two arms which were at the farthest possible extreme from one another in their equipment and their training, and which were actually still segregated from one another in separate units.[2] If this vital co-ordination between the Macedonian phalanx and the Macedonian light infantry happened to break down on the battle-field, then either arm, just because of its extreme specialization, was in danger of finding itself at the mercy of a more versatile adversary. Accordingly everything depended on the precision of military evolutions in the field; and the necessary precision was obviously impossible to guarantee. Such natural *contretemps* as the fog at Cynoscephalae and the broken ground at Pydna were enough to dislocate a Macedonian army's formation with results that were disastrous when the enemy was a fighting-force with the efficiency of the post-Hannibalic Roman army.

This Roman efficiency was a thing of yesterday; for in the Central Italian penumbra of the Hellenic World an old-fashioned phalanx of the pre-Macedonian, and indeed pre-Theban, type had been seen in the field at as recent a date as the day of Cannae, when the heavy Roman infantry, embattled in an antique Spartan phalanx-formation, had been rounded up from the rear by Hannibal's Spanish and Gallic heavy cavalry, and had then been slaughtered like cattle by his African heavy infantry on either flank.[3] But in the hard school of their repeated defeats in the Hannibalic War the

[1] In the Macedonian phalanx as it was in Alexander's day 'we have . . . the best parallel to the Roman infantry' (Hogarth, 'The Army of Alexander', p. 8).

[2] Hogarth (op. cit., p. 7) gives some grounds for supposing that the phalanx itself may have been 'mixed with lighter files'. If there is anything in this conjecture, it would follow that the post-Hannibalic Roman infantry technique was virtually anticipated by Philip and Alexander.

[3] See Tarn, W. W.: *Hellenistic Military and Naval Developments* (Cambridge 1930, University Press), p. 67. According to Veith (in Kromayer and Veith, op. cit., pp. 291 and 293) the phalanx-formation in which the Roman heavy infantry fought at Cannae was not the customary Roman formation of the age but was an anachronism—perhaps by then already as much as a century out of date—into which the Romans had relapsed in a kind of psychological 'regression' set in motion by the shock of the disasters which had overtaken the up-to-date 'manipular phalanx' at the Trebia and at Trasimene. In reverting to the old-fashioned phalanx at Cannae the Romans played for safety and incurred annihilation. On this view, the old-fashioned phalanx formation and tactics had been yielding, in the Roman art of war, to the rudiments of the manipular formation and tactics ever since the time of the Romano-Samnite and Romano-Epirot wars (*circa* 343–274 B.C.). On this showing, the Roman transformation of the Spartan phalanx into the more flexible manipular phalanx was contemporaneous with the Macedonian transformation of the same Spartan phalanx into the more ponderous Macedonian phalanx (see Veith in op. cit., p. 262)—unless Hogarth (see the preceding footnote) is correct in believing that the distinctive feature of Alexander's phalanx, too, was its 'mobility and adaptability' (Hogarth, op. cit., p. 5).

Romans had taught themselves an improvement in infantry technique which transformed the Roman Army, at a stroke, from the least to the most efficient fighting-force in the Hellenic World of the day by eliminating the crucial weakness of the prevailing Macedonian system. In those creative years the Romans had invented a new type of armament and a new type of formation which made it possible for any given soldier, and any given unit, to play either the light infantryman's or the hoplite's part, and to change over from the one kind of tactics to the other at a moment's notice in the face of the enemy.[1]

The superiority of this post-Hannibalic Roman infantry technique over a Macedonian technique that had been static for more than a century before the outbreak of the second Romano-Macedonian War in 200 B.C. is lucidly explained by the contemporary Arcadian observer Polybius:

'The phalanx, with its unique and potent technique, can count, as is easily demonstrable, upon sweeping away any enemy formation that ventures to face it front to front. Its charge is irresistible. . . . What,

[1] The post-Hannibalic Roman legionary was capable of playing either the light infantryman's or the hoplite's part for the reason that he was as unlike the one as the other in his equipment. With his throwing-spear, sword, and huge convex oblong shield, he was really a reimpersonation of the Mycenaean warrior of whom we catch a last glimpse in the Homeric Epic as the hoplite supplants him. Moreover the post-Hannibalic legionary, like his Mycenaean prototype, was an individual fighter—though he had discovered the secret of combining the advantages of individualism with those of drill (see Veith in op. cit., pp. 361–2). Is it possible that, in this far corner of the Hellenic World, the Mycenaean equipment and tactics actually survived, in competition with the new-fangled phalanx, in order to come into their own again when the phalanx was played out? Be that as it may, it seems clear that it was the very old-fashionedness of the form of the Spartan phalanx, as the Romans employed it, that gave them the opportunity of developing the manipular phalanx out of it. The Roman version of the Spartan phalanx never reached the stage of homogeneity in armament between the front and rear ranks. The latter never ceased to be manned by imperfectly armed javelin-men; and all that was required in order to produce the rudiments of the manipular phalanx was to make the front and rear ranks exchange arms—handing the *pilani*'s javelins to the *hastati* and the *hastati*'s spears to the *pilani* (see Veith in op. cit., p. 278). Through this transposition the Romans (unlike the Macedonians, even with their ever lengthening *sarisas* (see IV. C (iii) (*c*) 2 (γ), Annex, pp. 636–7, below)), succeeded in solving the problem of bringing into effective action the whole of their force throughout its depth from front to rear. (For this problem see Veith in op. cit., pp. 289–90.) In the new formation the now Mycenaean-armed '*hastati*' opened the battle, while the now Spartan-armed '*pilani*', who had previously been mere makeweights, obtained an independent value of their own as a heavy reserve (the *triarii*, who were thrown into action after the '*hastati*' and the '*principes*' had successively engaged the enemy). This incidental invention of the reserve was perhaps the greatest original Roman contribution to the Art of War (Veith in op. cit., p. 3). According to Veith the lesson of Cannae caused the Romans to repent of their regression to the Spartan phalanx without making them blind to the inadequacy of the manipular phalanx which had been the lesson of the Trebia and Trasimene. They solved the problem by carrying the evolution which was inchoate in the manipular phalanx to the logical conclusion that has just been described; and by the end of the Hannibalic War the process was complete—full-fledged manipular tactics being employed on both sides at the battles of Great Plains and Zama (Veith in op. cit., pp. 293–6). The gradual supplanting of the spear by the javelin-and-sword as the principal weapon of the Roman army in the course of the fourth and third centuries B.C. may be compared with the supplanting of the pike by the musket-and-bayonet in our modern Western military technique in the course of the sixteenth and seventeenth centuries of our era.

then, is the explanation of the triumph of the Romans? And what is the catch that makes the employment of the phalanx spell defeat?

'The catch lies in the discrepancy between that element of indeterminability—both of situations and of *terrain*—which is inherent in War as a practical art, and the inelasticity of the phalanx, which in practice can only do itself justice in one particular situation and on one particular kind of *terrain*. Of course, if, whenever it was a question of a decisive engagement, the enemy were under compulsion to accept the situation and the *terrain* that happen to suit the phalanx, then presumably the employment of the phalanx would be an infallible talisman of victory. But if it is in fact always possible—and easily possible—for the enemy to decline battle on these terms, then the phalanx-formation ceases to be formidable.

'Moreover it is admitted that the phalanx requires a *terrain* which is level and clear and innocent of any such obstacles as ditches, outcrops, ravines, crags and water-courses—any of which are quite enough to throw it out of step and to dislocate its formation. It will also be admitted on all hands that the kind of *terrain* which the phalanx requires —a *terrain* innocent of obstacles over a stretch of two thousand yards and upwards—is almost impossible to find, or is at any rate exceedingly rare; and, even supposing that it has been found, it is always possible, as we have pointed out, for the enemy to decline battle . . . [or, if he does accept battle with the phalanx on level ground, the enemy can still always secure the victory by keeping part of his own force in reserve, engaging the phalanx with the rest of his force just so far as to loosen the phalanx's formation and cause it to expose its flanks, and then throwing his reserves against the flanks or rear of the phalanx when these are no longer covered by light infantry and cavalry].[1] In short, the situations that are in favour of the phalanx can be easily evaded by the enemy, whereas the phalanx cannot evade the situations that tell against it; and, if the facts as I have stated them are true, this is manifestly an enormous handicap.

'Moreover a phalanx, like any other force, has to march through all kinds of country, to encamp, to forestall the enemy in occupying key-positions, to conduct and undergo sieges, and to encounter unforeseen emergencies. All these operations—which are part and parcel of War—are apt to be influential, and are sometimes decisive, in determining the issue. And for all such operations the Macedonian military technique is clumsy, and sometimes entirely ineffective, because it does not permit the phalangite to do himself justice either in the ranks or as an individual. On the other hand the Roman military technique is effective for all these operations alike, because every Roman soldier, once under arms and on duty, is equally well adapted for dealing with every kind of *terrain* and situation and emergency; and not only so, but he is also equally in his element, and equally master of the situation, whether he is called upon to take part in a general or in a partial engagement, or to go into action by companies, or to carry on individually. It will be seen that

[1] The passage between brackets is a précis of the corresponding passage in the original.—A.J.T.

the Roman fighting-machine is enormously superior to its rivals in its efficiency in detail, and it is therefore only natural that the Romans should be enormously more successful than their adversaries in attaining their military objectives.'[1]

This versatility, which was the characteristic feature of the full-fledged Roman military genius, made the integration of the skirmisher with the hoplite complete; for the mobility of the one and the irresistibility of the other were now combined in the person of every legionary; and when the legion, after having been evoked by Hannibal and employed, with destructive effect, against the antiquated Macedonian array, had been perfected in the Roman anti-barbarian and civil wars by a series of great captains beginning with Marius and ending with Caesar, it had attained the greatest efficiency which was possible for infantry before the invention of firearms.[2] At the very moment, however, when the legionary was becoming perfect after his own kind, he received the first of a long series of defeats from a pair of mounted men-at-arms with utterly different techniques—the light horse-archer[3] and the mail-clad lancer or cataphract[4]—who between them were eventually to drive the legionary

[1] Polybius, Book XVIII, chaps. 29–32, apropos of Titus Quinctius Flamininus's victory over King Philip V at Cynoscephalae in 197 B.C. The same contrast has been described in the following terms by a modern Western scholar, Dr. Georg Veith:

'The Greek was at all times conscious of his own limitations in the sphere of military capacity; hence his tendency towards specialization, in an effort to bring to the highest perfection—even at the cost of one-sidedness—the relatively little of valuable military material that the individual Greek possessed in himself. This was the origin of the manifold distinctions of special troops within each of the arms, and of that peculiarly characteristic mark of the Greek art of war: an evolution whose line of progress was from the simple to the complex, and which pushed the specialisation of equipment to the farthest limits. (This evolution reached its highest point under Alexander the Great, which was also the moment when the whole Greek art of war was at its zenith.) Conversely, among the Romans we find—as an ideal which was thoroughly attainable and was also actually attained—the soldier in himself, who, in his soldierly capacity, has to be—and duly is—available in equal measure for every kind of special employment. The logical consequence is a development, in the Roman art of war, from a differentiation—which is to be found, here too, at the beginning—to a parity of importance as between the different arms and equipments, and thence to a principal force which is homogeneous through and through (the always indispensable special weapons sinking to the status of subsidiary weapons in the hands of foreign formations). Thus the Greek evolution from the simple to the complex finds its contrast in a Roman development from the complex to the simple; and this simple instrument attains, in virtue of its very simplification, a perfection which renders it capable of at least as great a versatility in its employment as was within the reach of the complicated Greek army of the Macedonian period and the Age of the Diadochi.'—Kromayer, J., and Veith, G.: *Heerwesen und Kriegführung der Griechen und Römer* (Munich 1928, Beck), p. 3.

[2] For this chapter in the history of the evolution of the legion see III. C (i) (*b*), vol. iii, p. 166, above.

[3] The light build of the horse-archer's (in contrast to the cataphract's) mount is conveyed in the representation on a coin struck by the Roman general Labienus (see *The Cambridge Ancient History*, Plates, vol. iv, plate facing p. 8, fig. [*o*]).

[4] The heavily armed cavalryman or cataphract, like the heavily armed infantryman or hoplite, was perhaps an Assyrian invention—the hoplite being in that case the earliest and the cataphract the latest creation of the Assyrian military genius. At any rate, our first evidence for the existence of the cataphract is the portrayal of a rudimentary representative of the type on Assyrian bas-reliefs of the 7th century B.C., where he appears side by side with the heavily armed charioteer. Since these reliefs are later in date than the irruption of the Cimmerian and Scyth Nomads into South-Western Asia (see II. D

off the field *à la débandade*. The victory of the horse-archer over the legionary at Carrhae in 53 B.C. forestalled, by five years, the classic combat of legionary against legionary in 48 B.C. at Pharsalus, a battle in which the Roman infantry technique was probably at its zenith.[1] The omen of Carrhae was confirmed, more than four centuries later, at Adrianople, where the cataphract gave the legionary his *coup de grâce* in A.D. 378.[2]

The disaster at Adrianople, which was the tragic end of an ascendancy that the legionary had retained—albeit with increasing difficulty—for nearly six hundred years, has been vividly described by a contemporary Roman officer who was also a Latin historian.[3]

On the eve of this catastrophe the confidence of the Roman high command in the traditional Roman military technique was still so overweening that the Emperor Valens, who had just succeeded in making contact with the Gothic host that was then ravaging the Roman territory of Thrace, insisted on administering immediate punishment to the refractory barbarians.[4] He would not wait for

(v), vol. ii, p. 136, above), we may conjecture that the Assyrians were inspired to take this first step towards the creation of the cataphract by their encounter with these horse-archers from the Eurasian Steppe. Assyria, like the Sinic World, probably derived the art of riding from this Eurasian source (see III. C (i) (*b*), vol. iii, p. 167, footnote 1, above), and, *a fortiori*, the art of using the bow on horseback—just as, some twelve hundred years earlier, the neighbours of Eurasia had been initiated, through a previous eruption of Nomads, into the art of chariotry (till then unknown to the sedentary societies, as was, indeed, the horse itself). The Assyrians' reaction to their encounter with the Nomads seems to have been to combine the Nomads' archery-on-horseback with the Assyrian heavy infantryman's defensive armour. In the Achaemenian Age a *cap-à-pie* suit of armour was worn on horseback by the Persian grandee Masistius at the Battle of Plataea in 479 B.C. (see Herodotus, Book IX, chap. 22). The Achaemenidae would also appear to have made a start in armouring the war-horse as well as his rider, *teste Xenophonte* (*Anabasis*, Book I, chap. 8, § 7; *Cyropaedia*, Book VI, chap. 1, §§ 50–1, and chap. 4, § 1; Book VII, chap. 1, § 2; *De Re Equestri*, chap. 12, § 8). From the Achaemenian Empire a fighting-machine which was thus perhaps of Nomadic inspiration was borrowed back—with the improvement of armouring both rider and horse—by the neighbouring Nomads on the border of the Steppe between the Pamirs and the Caspian. The Massagetae, for instance, are described by Herodotus (Book I, chap. 215) as armouring their horses in the fashion that is ascribed by Xenophon to the Achaemenian cavalry. In this Nomad incarnation the cataphract then moved back south-westwards with the Parni who founded the Parthian Empire (see II. D (vii), vol. ii, p. 371, footnote 2, and II. D (vii), Annex V, vol. ii, p. 435, footnote 1), and north-westwards with the Sarmatians, who passed the cataphract on to the Goths when the Goths trespassed upon the great gulf of the Eurasian Steppe between the Black Sea and the northern forests. It was the Parni who made it technically possible to complete a process which the Assyrians appear to have first set in motion. On the pastures of Media they bred a horse of such size, strength, and elegance that he could bear the weight of a complete suit of armour for himself as well as for his rider (see Tarn, W. W.: *Hellenistic Military and Naval Developments* (Cambridge 1930, University Press), pp. 76–83; eundem: *The Greeks in Bactria and India* (Cambridge 1938, University Press), pp. 308–10). This Parthian full-fledged cataphract is portrayed in a *graffito* at Dura (see *The Cambridge Ancient History*, Plates, vol. iv, plate facing p. 26, fig. [*c*]). The Parthian cataphract helped the Parthian horse-archer to defeat the legionary at Carrhae in 53 B.C.; the Gothic cataphract confirmed his defeat in A.D. 378 at Adrianople.

[1] The Age of Caesar marks the 'qualitativen Höhepunkt des römischen Kriegswesens' according to Kromayer and Veith, op. cit., p. 251.

[2] For the annals of the secular duel between the legionary and the cataphract see III. C (i) (*b*), vol. iii, pp. 164 and 166, above.

[3] Ammianus Marcellinus: *Res Gestae*, Book XXXI, chaps. 11–13.

[4] The Goths had been given passage across the Lower Danube by the Roman author-

the reinforcements which his nephew and colleague Gratian was bringing by forced marches from the west, though he had received dispatches announcing that Gratian's army was now on the point of joining hands with his;[1] and he would not entertain the overtures which the Goths—disconcerted at having evoked so strong a Roman military reaction—were belatedly attempting to make to their indignant Imperial adversary. Valens gave the order for his legions to march at once upon the Gothic lager; and at first sight it seemed as though his intransigent policy were justified by its effect. 'The terrifying din of [the legionaries'] clashing arms, and their aggressive drumming on their shields, so intimidated the barbarians—who were also weakened by the absence of a part of their host which was operating at a distance under the command of Alatheus and Saphrax, and had not yet had time to return, though the order was on its way to them—that they sent *parlementaires* to ask for peace.' It looked as though the legions had won their victory without having had to strike a blow; but in reality Valens' intransigence had not broken the Goths' spirit but had inspired them with the courage of despair; and the parley was a feint.

The purpose of the Gothic commander Fritigern was simply to gain time until he could take up the Roman challenge with his whole force—including the absent corps, which consisted of the heavy cavalry—and his ruse was successful; for he managed to draw the parley out—while the Romans stood to arms, without food or water, through the heat of the day—until 'the Gothic cavalry, reappearing on the scene with Alatheus and Saphrax at its head, and stiffened by a contingent of Alani,[2] burst upon the Roman

ities, at the Goths' own request, out of the *cul-de-sac* in which the great western bay of the Eurasian Steppe comes to an end between the Lower Danube and the Carpathians, and they had been allowed to settle, as *foederati* of the Empire, on Roman territory between the Danube and the Balkan Range. In intention and in principle this had been a friendly act, since the Goths, in the *cul-de-sac* which had been their previous home, were threatened with annihilation by the eruption of the Huns from the heart of the Steppe beyond the Volga and the Yaik. The arrangement between the Gothic refugees and the Roman authorities ought to have proved mutually beneficial, since the refugees, in finding an asylum on Roman soil, might have been expected to become a bulwark of the Empire against the assaults of the common Hun enemy. Unfortunately the execution of the agreement was at once followed by friction; and the blame for this was largely on the Roman side, since the minor officials of the Imperial administration seem to have regarded their Government's generous policy towards the Goths as an opportunity for fleecing and bullying the refugees on their own account. In any case, wherever the fault lay, the Goths broke with the Imperial Government and began to pillage the country-side on which they had been settled as friends and allies of the Empire. And, not unnaturally, this behaviour was hotly resented by the Roman authorities, in whose eyes it was not only flagrant treason but was also base ingratitude.

[1] Valens' impatience is put down by Ammianus to his jealousy of Gratian and his consequent determination to keep all the Gothic laurels for himself. His decision to go into action at once was taken against the advice of his *Magister Equitum* Victor: 'Sarmata, sed cunctator et cautus.'

[2] The Alani were one of the hordes of those Sarmatian Nomads upon whose pastures the Goths had intruded when they broke out of the northern forests into the great western bay of the Eurasian Steppe. The eruption of the Huns from the heart of the

army as a thunderbolt bursts against a mountain-range, charged at lightning speed, and swept away, in a whirlwind of slaughter, as many of the Roman troops as it managed to engage at close quarters'. The legionaries were thrown out of their formation and were herded together into so dense a mass that they had no longer any room to wield, or even draw, their swords; and in this helpless plight they suffered the fate which their own predecessors had once inflicted on the Macedonian phalangites. Having caught the legionaries at this irretrievable disadvantage, the cataphracts pressed home their attack without giving their discomfited opponents a chance to rally, until 'at length, under the weight and "drive" of the barbarian offensive, the Roman line gave way, and the legionaries—driven to the last resort in a desperate situation—took to their heels in a chaotic *sauve qui peut*'. The historian vouches for the fact that 'the Roman casualties amounted to about two-thirds of the effectives engaged' (the Emperor Valens himself was among the missing); and he expresses the opinion that, 'apart from the Battle of Cannae, there' was 'no record, in all the annals of Roman military history, of any other action in which the carnage was so great as this'.

In measuring Adrianople by Cannae, Ammianus gives proof of his historical insight, for it was the slaughter at Cannae, where the Roman infantry had been at the mercy of Hannibal's heavy cavalry, that had stimulated the Roman military genius into transforming a clumsy phalanx on the old-fashioned Spartan model into the mobile legion which had been victorious first at Zama and then at Cynoscephalae and Pydna. In the year of Adrianople, however, the lesson of Cannae was nearly six hundred years old; and during those six centuries the Roman legionaries had 'rested on their oars', like the Macedonian phalangites before them,[1] until they allowed themselves to be overtaken and ridden down by an Oriental heavy cavalry which was a more formidable engine of war than Hannibal's

Steppe had now blown Sarmatians and Goths, pell-mell, out of Nomads' land into the Roman Empire. It was from the Sarmatians, as we have seen (p. 439, footnote 4, above), that the Goths had acquired the technique of the cataphract.

[1] This Roman repetition of a Macedonian story of degeneration in military technique appears to have been remarkably close. The Macedonian phalangite, who had won his triumphs over his Theban adversary by combining a longer range of weapon with a superior mobility (see IV. C (iii) (*c*) 2 (γ), Annex, p. 636, footnote 3, below), had eventually succumbed to the Roman legionary because, in the meantime, he had sacrificed mobility to massiveness (see the present chapter, pp. 434–5, above). On the evidence of Arrian's Ἔκταξις κατ' Ἀλανῶν (A.D. 136), a modern Western scholar (Parker, H. M. D.: *The Roman Legions* (Oxford 1928, Clarendon Press), pp. 248–9 and 258–60) has conjectured that in the legions (as distinct from the auxilia) the Roman Army was relapsing, as early as the second century of the Christian Era, from the mobile manipular formation into the unwieldy Thebano-Spartan formation to which the Roman infantry had reverted once before with such disastrous consequences at Cannae (see p. 436, footnote 3, above). On this point see also Darkó, E.: 'Influences Turaniennes sur l'Évolution de l'Art Militaire des Grecs, des Romains et des Byzantins' in *Byzantion*, vol. x (Brussels 1935), p. 459.

European squadrons, and which could not be coped with effectively without some fresh innovation in infantry technique. The effective innovation was discovered in the end, but not for a thousand years, and then not by Roman wits. Though the Romans had received repeated warnings of the legionary's inferiority to Oriental cavalry —in Crassus's disaster of 53 B.C. and Valerian's of A.D. 260 and Julian's of A.D. 363—they had not been stimulated to make any fresh creative advance in infantry technique. They had left the legion, unreformed, to its fate; and when 'the knock-out blow' was duly delivered in the fullness of time in A.D. 378 at Adrianople, they could think of no more original remedy than to discard the defeated legionary outright and to take over the victorious cataphract at second-hand.[1] Gratian's colleague and successor, Theodosius, rewarded the barbarian horsemen for having annihilated the Roman infantry by hiring them to fill the vacant place; and, even when the Imperial Government had paid the inevitable price for the brief respite that was purchased by this short-sighted policy, and had seen the mercenary barbarian troopers partition all its western provinces into barbarian 'successor-states', the new native army,[2] which saved the Greek and Oriental provinces, at the eleventh hour, from going the same way, was armed and mounted on the barbarian pattern.[3]

[1] See III. C (i) (*b*), vol. iii, p. 164, above.

[2] For the creation of a new native army by the Roman Government at Constantinople in the course of the fifth century of the Christian Era see IV (iii) (*c*) 2 (β), pp. 324–5, above.

[3] See the description—given by Procopius of Caesarea in *A History of the Wars of Justinian*, and quoted in this Study in III. C (i) (*b*), vol. iii, p. 163, above—of the cataphracts who were Belisarius's instrument for the reconquest of Africa and Italy in the sixth century of the Christian Era. The arm already existed in the Roman Army, even before the disaster of A.D. 378 raised the cataphract's prestige to the skies and reduced the legionary's prestige to zero. At the battle of Adrianople itself, after the legions had given way, the Emperor Valens took refuge with the two heavy-cavalry regiments of Lancearii and Mattiarii, 'qui, dum multitudo tolerabatur hostilis, fixis corporibus steterant inconcussi' (Ammianus, op. cit., Book XXXI, chap. 13); and before that, in the Imperial bodyguard which had accompanied the Emperor Constantius on his state entry into the city of Rome in A.D. 356, there had been 'a sprinkling of cataphract cavalrymen, popularly known as *clibanarii*' [i.e. 'hard-ware boys' or 'men in ironmongery', from *clibanus*, which was the Greek word for an iron baker's-oven], of whose accoutrements Ammianus (op. cit., Book XVI, chap. 10) gives the following description: 'Their persons were protected by being cased in cuirasses and swathed in metal hoops which gave them the appearance of being not so much men of flesh and blood as statues brought to a fine finish by the hand of a Praxiteles. Their armour consisted of thin loops of metal plating which were adjusted to the curves of the body and which not only encircled the trunk but were also carried down all the limbs with such skill that, whatever bodily movement the trooper might require to make, his metallic integument would conform to it by adjusting itself at the joints—and this without exposing any gaps.' Evidently the Roman armourers of the fourth century of the Christian Era had borrowed from the Sarmatians the idea of a heavy cavalryman armed *cap-à-pie*, and had then translated the Sarmatian scale-armour into the hoop-armour which was already being worn, at the turn of the first and second centuries, by Trajan's legionaries (both the Roman legionary's hoop-armour and the Sarmatian cataphract's scale-armour are portrayed in the bas-reliefs on Trajan's Column). The hoop-armour of the legionary was confined to shoulder-pieces and corselet; but the more difficult art of encasing, without impeding, an arm or a leg had been worked out on the gladiatorial arena in the armament of the *secutor*. A combination of the *secutor* with the Trajanic legionary gives the fourth-

The ignominy of the legionary's end is accentuated by the strange fact that the cataphract who rode him down on the plains of Thrace in A.D. 378 was himself a degenerate. The Parthian cavalryman who had forced Crassus's legions to capitulate at Carrhae in 53 B.C. had been a horse-archer, like his native Nomad prototype; the Sarmatian and Gothic cataphracts who annihilated Valens' legions at Adrianople were mere lancers[1] who won their victory by the crude and clumsy method of charging home, in substitution for the refined technique of overwhelming their enemy—in the manner of the Suren's horse-archers at Carrhae in 53 B.C.—with a ceaseless discharge of arrows supplied by a never-failing camel commissariat.[2] Carrhae 'ought to have revolutionized the World's warfare; but in fact it produced little effect, for Surenas was put to death next year and his organization broken up'.[3] The future lay not with the light horse-archer but with the cataphract, who had been represented at Carrhae in the Parthian ranks[4] without making any notable contribution to the brilliant victory of his unarmoured comrade. And the cataphract had no sooner put on the Assyrian infantryman's armour than he had begun to discard the Nomad's bow for the hoplite's lance. The rudimentary Assyrian cataphract still remained a horse-archer; and a force of a thousand Sakas who fought for the last of the Achaemenidae at Gaugamela in 331 B.C. are described as still being equipped with bows[5] though

century *clibanarius* when the 'hard-ware boy' is mounted on a horse—as he must be if he is to move! (The *clibanarius*'s mount seems to have been as heavily armoured as his rider, to judge by another description, which carries our evidence for the existence of this type of heavy cavalryman in the Roman Army back to the time of Constantius's father Constantine the Great. 'Men and horses alike are encased in a covering of iron. The name that they go by in the Army is *clibanarii*. The men are not only armour-clad themselves; the horses, too, on which they are mounted, have their chests protected by a cuirass that reaches from their heads right down to their legs and makes them proof against the danger of being wounded without hampering their gait' (Nazarius: *Panegyricus Constantino Augusto Dictus*, chap. 22, in Baehrens, G.: *XII Panegyrici Latini* (Leipzig 1911, Teubner), p. 173).) A combination (see Darkó, op. cit., in *Byzantion*, vol. x (1935), p. 466) of the defensive armour of the *clibanarius* with the missile-weapon of the light-armed horse-archer (who was both an older and a longer-lived type of Nomad cavalryman than the heavy-armed lancer) gives the sixth-century Roman cataphract. This re-equipment of the *ci-devant* Nomad heavy cavalryman with the original Nomad weapon which the cataphract had abandoned in favour of the lance (see p. 444, above) was the last stroke of the Roman military genius—unless it was merely a Roman mimesis of a compromise between the Scythian and the Sarmatian equipment which had been worked out, five hundred years earlier, on the Cimmerian Bosphorus (see p. 445, footnote 8, below). We catch a last glimpse of this later Roman cataphract in the *Τακτικά*, attributed to the Emperor Maurice (*imperabat* A.D. 582–602), which, according to Darkó (op. cit., in *Byzantion*, vol. xii (1937), pp. 121–4), was perhaps really written by Maurice's successor Heraclius during his retirement (see III. C (ii) (*b*), vol. iii, p. 269, footnote 4, above) in the winter of A.D. 621–2. According to the same Hungarian scholar (op. cit., vol. cit., p. 128) the Roman cavalry equipment described in this treatise was modelled on that of the contemporary Avar Nomads.

1 Darkó, op. cit., in *Byzantion*, vol. xii (1937), p. 142.

2 For the munitions and the tactics that defeated the legionary at Carrhae, see Tarn, W. W.: *Hellenistic Military and Naval Developments* (Cambridge 1930, University Press), pp. 83–92, and eundem in *The Cambridge Ancient History*, vol. ix, pp. 606–11.

3 Tarn, *Developments*, p. 91.

4 See p. 439, footnote 4, above.

5 Arrian: *Alexandri Anabasis*, Book III, chap. 8, § 3.

the horses as well as the men were armoured.[1] When they went into action, however, these Saka demi-cataphracts did not shoot; they charged.[2] And the Parthian full-blown cataphract who is portrayed in the *graffito* at Dura[3] does not even carry a bow in addition to his lance. Notwithstanding the success of the light horse-archer against Crassus at Carrhae, the failure of the charging cataphract against Ventidius in the next round of this Romano-Parthian trial of strength,[4] and the renewed success of the light horse-archer against Mark Antony,[5] the Parthians opted for the cataphract;[6] and the Arsacids' example was followed by their successors the Sasanidae. It is true that Belisarius's sixth-century Roman cataphracts, as Procopius describes them,[7] were horse-archers of the Assyrian kind; but in general it was the armoured lancer, and not the armoured horse-archer, who kept the saddle for the next twelve hundred years after the light horse-archer's victory at Carrhae; and there is an extraordinary uniformity in this lancer's accoutrements over a Time-span of more than a millennium and across the length and breadth of Europe and Asia. His identity is unmistakable, whether the portrait in which he presents himself to us happens to be in some fresco, dating from the first century of the Christian Era, in a Crimean tomb;[8] or on the third- and fourth- and fifth- and sixth-century bas-reliefs of Sasanian kings in Fars; or in the clay figurines of those Far Eastern men-at-arms who were the fighting-force of the T'ang Dynasty (*imperabant* A.D. 618–907);[9] or in the eleventh-century tapestry at Bayeux which depicts the defeat of the antiquated English foot-soldiers of the day by King William the Conqueror's Norman knights.[10]

1 Arrian, op. cit., Book III, chap. 13, § 4.

2 Arrian, op. cit., loc. cit.

3 See p. 439, footnote 4, above.

4 See Tarn in *The Cambridge Ancient History*, vol. x, pp. 49–51.

5 Tarn in op. cit., vol. cit., pp. 71–5.

6 This discomfiture of the light horse-archer by the heavy-armed lancer on his native pastures is reflected in the history of the Hellenic mimesis of the Nomadic military technique. In the fourth century B.C. Alexander the Great, when he arrived at the Transoxanian fringe of the Great Eurasian Steppe, took to mixing light native horse-archers with his own Macedonian heavy cavalry; and more than four hundred years later the Roman Emperor Hadrian (*imperabat* A.D. 117–38), in his turn, introduced light horse-archers into the Roman Army (Arrian: *Τέχνη Τακτική*, chap. 44). On the other hand the Roman cavalry of the Emperor Gallienus (*imperabat* A.D. 253–68) were mostly not horse-archers but heavy lancers who were presumably the prototypes of the fourth-century *clibanarii* (see p. 443, footnote 3, above) of the Emperors Maxentius, Constantius and Valens. (For these facts see Darkó, op. cit., in *Byzantion*, vol. x (1935), pp. 452–3, 460 and 462.)

7 In the passage already quoted in this Study in III. C (i) (*b*), vol. iii, p. 163, above.

8 See Rostovtzeff, M.: *Iranians and Greeks in South Russia* (Oxford 1922, Clarendon Press), pp. 121, 129, and 169. The Bosporan knight of the first century, like the Roman man-at-arms of the sixth (see p. 443, footnote 3, above), put on the Sarmatian cataphract's armour without throwing aside the Scythian *hippotoxotes*' bow.

9 See Rostovtzeff, op. cit., pp. 203–4, or, still better, any collection of T'ang figurines.

10 The Time-interval of nearly seven centuries that separates the Battle of Hastings from the Battle of Adrianople is an illustration of the fact that in the realm of human affairs, as in the Physical Universe, it takes Time to travel through Space. The cataphract's breach of the shield-wall, which took place as early as A.D. 378 in the Thracian

If this longevity and ubiquity of the cataphract are astonishing, it is also noteworthy that he only becomes ubiquitous in a degenerate form; and, since we have observed already, at an earlier point in this Study, that sheer material range and scale are apt to be symptoms of decay, we shall not be surprised when we read the next chapter in the cataphract's history. The story may be told, again, in the words of a contemporary who in this case was also an eye-witness.

'I was in the army of the Under-Secretary when he went forth to meet the Tatars on the western side of the City of Peace [Baghdad], on the occasion of its supreme disaster in the year A.H. 656 [which began on the 8th January, A.D. 1258]. We met at Nahr Bashīr, one of the dependencies of Dujayl; and there would ride forth from amongst us to offer single combat a knight fully accoutred and mounted on an Arab horse, so that it was as though he and his steed together were [solid as] some great mountain. Then there would come forth to meet him from the Mongols a horseman mounted on a horse like a donkey, and having in his hand a spear like a spindle, wearing neither robe nor armour, so that all who saw him were moved to laughter. Yet ere the day was done the victory was theirs, and they inflicted on us a great defeat, which was the Key of Evil, and thereafter there befell us what befell us.'[1]

Thus the legendary encounter between Goliath and David at the dawn of Syriac history repeats itself at night-fall, perhaps twenty-three centuries later, as an attested historical fact; and, though on this occasion the giant and the pygmy played their parts on horse-back instead of on foot, the outcome was the same.

The invincible Tatar qāzāq who overcame the 'Irāqī cataphract and sacked Baghdad and starved the 'Abbasid Caliph to death in his treasury[2] and gave the *coup de grâce* to a Caliphate which had been a resumption of the Achaemenian Empire and a reintegration of the Syriac universal state,[3] was a light horse-archer of the genuine and persistent Nomadic type which had made itself known, and dreaded, in South-Western Asia for the first time through the Cimmerian and Scyth irruption at the turn of the eighth and seventh centuries B.C. In the heart of the Steppe, from which the Tatars were erupting in their turn in the thirteenth century of the

enclave of the Eurasian Steppe, did not take place till A.D. 1066 in Ultima Thule. In the language of Relativity we might even go so far as to say that Adrianople and Hastings are not two battles but one battle, of which our vision is here diffracted into two different Space–Time positions.

[1] Falak-ad-Dīn Muhammad b. Aydimir, quoted at first hand by Ibn-at-Tiqtaqā in *Kitāb-al-Fakhrī* (Cairo edition, p. 72), apropos of the attitude of the Persians towards the Primitive Muslim Arabs when these had invaded the Sasanian Empire some six hundred years before. The translation here quoted is taken from Browne, E. G.: *A Literary History of Persia*, vol. ii (London 1906, Fisher, Unwin), p. 462.

[2] See the story as it is told by Marco Polo in *The Book of Ser Marco Polo*, translated and edited by Sir Henry Yule, 3rd edition (London 1903, Murray, 2 vols.), vol. i, pp. 63–4.

[3] See I. C (i) (*b*), vol. i, pp. 75–7, above.

Christian Era, the ancient Nomad military technique had lived on to assert its superiority now, at the end of the chapter, over the armour-plated travesty of itself which was what the imitative sedentary societies had made of it in the course of some two thousand years of brief inventiveness and long stagnation. But if David-on-horseback duly discomfited Goliath-on-horseback at this historic moment,[1] the sequel to their encounter in this repetition of the story was also faithful to the original. We have seen[2] that the mailed champion on foot who was laid low by David's sling-stone was superseded thereafter not by David himself but by a phalanx of Goliaths in which each phalangite was equipped with Goliath's accoutrements but was taught to use them to better effect by fighting in a disciplined formation instead of indulging in the primitive sport of single combat. And now, in the Cavalry Age, discipline won its victory over individualism once more. For Hulāgū Khan's Mongol light horse who had overcome the 'Abbasid Caliph's knights under the walls of Baghdad in A.D. 1258 were subsequently defeated again and again—in A.D. 1260 and 1281 and 1299–1300 and 1303[3]—whenever they swam the Euphrates and tried conclusions with the Mamlūk masters of Syria and Egypt under whose aegis a new series of 'Abbasid Caliphs had found asylum.[4] In their accoutrements the Mamlūks were neither better nor worse equipped than their fellow Muslim knights who had been overthrown so ignominiously, a few years before, at Nahr Bashīr; but in their tactics the Mamlūks were true to their name and status[5] in obeying a discipline; and this discipline gave them the mastery over Mongol sharp-shooter and Frankish knight-errant.[6]

The knights of Saint Louis King of France had met their defeat at Mansūrah at the hands of the Egyptian Mamlūks eight years before the knights of the last 'Abbasid Caliph of Baghdad went

[1] The heavy-armed lancer who had supplanted the light-armed horse-archer in Nomadism's sedentary hinterlands had, however, gained at least one victory over the Nomad in his native war-gear when, in the tenth century of the Christian Era, the German King Henry the Fowler had defeated the Magyar horse-archers by substituting heavy lancers for his own German infantry (Darkó, op. cit., in *Byzantion*, vol. xii (1937), p. 145).

[2] On pp. 432–3, above. [3] See I. C (i) (*b*), Annex I, vol. i, p. 350, above.

[4] For the Cairene 'Abbasid Caliphate, which was the juridical basis of the Mamlūk Power in Egypt and Syria from A.D. 1261 to A.D. 1516, see I. C (i) (*b*), vol. i, p. 67, footnote 2, and pp. 70–71, above, as well as Part X, below.

[5] The name 'Mamlūk' means 'held as property', and the status of the Mamlūks was servitude. For the system, exemplified in the Egyptian Mamlūk polity, of making soldiers and administrators out of slaves—a system which was itself of Nomad origin, and which was carried to its highest perfection in the Ottoman Empire—see Part III. A, vol. iii, pp. 28–44, above.

[6] Etymologically 'knight-errant' is perhaps a contradiction in terms, since the Teutonic word 'knight', like the Arabic word 'mamlūk', means the servant of a master. In modern English usage, however, not only 'knight-errant' but 'knight' itself, *sans phrase*, connotes a warrior who is apt to obey no other master than himself. The Egyptian Mamlūks likewise eventually degenerated, as will appear, into a mob of wayward 'knights', without forfeiting a name which they had ceased to deserve.

down before the Mongols, and ten years before the Mongols in their turn received their first lesson from the Mamlūks on a Syrian battle-field.

In this invasion of Egypt, which was their first essay in that enterprise, the French did their worst to bring their defeat upon themselves by displaying an incompetence which is in significant contrast to the showing which they made upon their next appearance, five hundred and forty-eight years later, under a much less lovable but much more efficient commander. In A.D. 1250 Saint Louis fell into the initial strategic error of attempting to advance from the coast upon Cairo through the Delta, instead of keeping clear of this maze of waterways and marching along the rim of the desert. In consequence his advance was checked at the junction between the Damietta arm of the Nile and the Ashmūn canal; and when the detachment of knights which he succeeded in pushing across the canal on the night of the 7th–8th February immediately forfeited the fruits of this strategic success, by running wildly into a tactical disaster, the campaign was virtually at an end. Driven back into their previous camp, the defeated French were beleaguered by a victorious enemy, and ravaged by camp-fever, until the night of the 5th–6th April, when a desperate attempt on their part to break out and escape by water, down river, gave the defenders of Egypt an opportunity to complete the destruction of the invaders. On this retreat every Frenchman who was not killed was taken prisoner, and among the prisoners was King Louis himself.

It will be seen that the decisive action of the campaign was the battle of the 8th February, when the French first won, and then threw away, their sole chance of extricating themselves from what was by then already an untenable position. The issue hung upon the fortunes of the engagement between the French knights who had gained the farther bank of the canal and the Mamlūks who were covering the town of Mansūrah. The task which King Louis had assigned to these knights, if and when they succeeded in crossing the canal by the ford, was to occupy and hold the canal bank opposite his own camp, in order to make it possible at last for the main body of the French army to complete the causeway which they had been trying, for days, to throw across the water. The builders had laboured in vain so long as the enemy still held the bank towards which they were building, and was therefore in a position to destroy the work as fast as the French could carry it on. If the knights who had now made good their crossing had been content to execute their orders, the main body of their comrades would have been enabled to join them, and the whole French army might then have resumed its advance. But at this crucial moment the knights behaved as badly as the Mamlūks behaved well. 'The chief credit of the day belongs to the steady fighting of the Mamlūks, who bore the brunt of the battle and inflicted the chief punishment on their rash opponents.'[1] On the other hand the French knights, once across the canal, forgot their orders, and thereby lost the day for their king, in a childish impatience to engage the enemy and a still more childish competition among themselves for the place of honour in their own battle-array—though their orders were explicit on this point as well.

'On avait ordonné que le Temple ferait l'avant-garde, et que le comte d'Artois aurait la seconde bataille, après le Temple. Or advint que sitôt que le comte d'Artois eût passé le fleuve, lui et toute sa gent piquèrent aux Turcs, qui s'enfuyaient devant eux. Les Templiers lui dirent qu'il leur faisait grande vilenie d'aller devant eux quand il devait aller après, et ils le priaient de les laisser aller devant, comme il avait été accordé par le roi. Or le comte d'Artois ne leur osa répondre, à cause de monseigneur Fourcaud du Merle qui le tenait par le frein de son cheval, et ce Fourcaud du Merle, qui était très bon chevalier, n'entendait rien de ce que les Templiers disaient au comte, par ce qu'il était sourd; et il criait: "Or, sus à eux! Or, sus à eux!" Quand les Templiers le virent, ils pensaient qu'ils seraient honnis, s'ils laissaient le comte d'Artois aller devant eux; ils frappèrent des éperons à qui mieux mieux, et chassaient les Turcs qui s'enfuyaient devant eux, à travers la ville de la Massoure, jusques aux champs par devers Babylone.

'Quand ils voulurent revenir en arrière, les Turcs leur lancèrent des poutres et des pièces de bois, par les rues qui étaient étroites. Là fut tué le comte d'Artois, le sire de Coucy qu'on appelait Raoul, et tant des autres chevaliers qu'ils furent estimés à trois cents. Le Temple, comme le Maître me le dit plus tard, y perdit deux cent quatre-vingts hommes armés et tous à cheval.'[2]

This French disaster of the 8th February, 1250, and the crowning catastrophe of the 6th April which was the inevitable consequence, were manifestly the penalties of an unchastened egotism which could not be atoned for by a quixotic individual valour, while the Mamlūks' victory, both in the decisive battle and in the whole campaign, was just as manifestly the reward of a thorough discipline grafted upon a bravery which was not intrinsically inferior to that of the French. The possessors of both the two fundamental military virtues were bound to prevail over an adversary who was utterly lacking in the more important one.

By the close of the thirteenth century of the Christian Era, when

1 Lane-Poole, S.: *A History of Egypt in the Middle Ages*, 2nd edition (London 1914, Methuen), pp. 236–7.

2 Joinville, Jean Sire de: *La Vie du Saint Roi Louis* mise en nouveau langage par Henri Longnon (Paris 1928, A l'enseigne de la Cité des Livres), pp. 87–8.

the Mamlūks had established their superiority over the French on the one hand and over the Mongols on the other, they stood in a position of unchallenged military supremacy, within the bounds of their own horizon, that is comparable to the position of the Romans after the Battle of Pydna. In this eminent but enervating situation the Mamlūk, like the legionary, 'rested on his oars'; and it is a curious coincidence that he was allowed to rest on them for almost exactly the same length of time before he was taken unawares by an old adversary armed with a new technique. The Roman triumph at Pydna in 168 B.C. and disaster at Adrianople in A.D. 378 are divided by an interval of five hundred and forty-six years, while the number of years between the Mamlūk triumph at Mansūrah in A.D. 1250 and disaster at Imbābah in A.D. 1798 is five hundred and forty-eight. In the Battle of the Pyramids the enemy who exploded the Mamlūks' traditional reputation for invincibility were descendants of the Frenchmen at whose expense that reputation had been originally acquired; for, while in the life of the Mamlūks Time had been standing still, the passage of five and a half centuries had sufficed for the French to discard the blundering technique of Saint Louis's disorderly knights and to train themselves, instead, in the discipline of a uniformed infantry, equipped with fire-arms, on a new model which had been displayed to Western Christendom since the fourteenth century by the 'Osmanlis.[1] This metamorphosis of the French may serve as a reminder that the Gothic victory, and Roman débâcle, at Adrianople in A.D. 378 was likewise due to a metamorphosis which had been previously accomplished by the victors. The Gothic cataphracts who put the legions of Valens out of action were descended from North European barbarians of the same stamp as the Sueves and Gauls who had been an easy prey for the legions of Julius Caesar. It was the Goths' intensive schooling in horsemanship on the Steppes, in an age when the legionaries were standing at ease, that enabled Alatheus and Saphrax to avenge the defeats of Ariovistus and Vercingetorix.

We may further observe, without overstraining our parallel, that the warning which the Romans received, at Carrhae in 53 B.C., of the cataphract's coming ascendancy has its analogue in the three successive blows which the Mamlūks received in A.D. 1516–17, when they were routed—first at Marj Dābiq and then at Gaza and then again at Raydānīyah—by the Janissaries.

After the second disaster of the three, the Mamlūk survivors who made their way back to Cairo retailed to a panic-stricken populace

[1] For the Ottoman origin of our modern Western infantry technique see Part III. A, vol. iii, p. 38, footnote 2, above.

their terrifying experience of a new and irresistible Ottoman military technique.

'They arrived in the most pitiable state; the plunder and slaughter had been worse than before. Some of the Imperial Mamlūks came back on donkeys, some on camels—all having been deprived of uniforms, horses and arms. None survived, in fact, but a few for whom Fate had so decreed. They said that some of Ibn 'Othmān's troops were armed with hooks on their lances, with which they dragged the rider from his horse and threw him on the ground. Jān Birdī said that he was thus thrown down. . . . They also said that Ibn 'Othmān's troops were in numbers as swarms of locusts; that some of them were armed with muskets (firing a leaden bullet) and were carried in wooden carts, drawn by oxen and buffaloes, moving at the head of the advanced guard; and many other things of this nature.'[1]

The confusion and division of counsels which prevailed in the Mamlūk capital while Selīm the 'Osmanlī was advancing, unchecked, from the Taurus to the Nile, is a counterpart of the picture which Joinville paints of Saint Louis's camp in the Delta; and in this case, as in that, there is a grim inevitability about the last act—which was played in January 1517 when the Ottoman army arrived at the feeble fortifications that had been thrown up at the last moment, across the last stage of their road to Cairo, by the last Sultan of the Mamlūks.[2]

'The drums beat to battle, the chief amīrs and the whole force mounted and extended across the plain. Ibn 'Othmān's soldiers came on like locusts in multitude, and they were superior in point of numbers. The two armies met in the outskirts of Raydānīyah, and a terrible battle ensued. . . . Countless numbers of the Turks were killed, including Sinān Pasha, Ibn 'Othmān's former tutor and his chief wazīr, and a great many of his amīrs. Their bodies lay scattered from 'Allān's fountain (?) to the tomb of Amīr Yashbak, the Dawādār. Then the Turks recovered, coming up from every direction like clouds. They divided into two forces, one advancing under Jabal Ahmar and the other by the camp at Raydānīyah. The noise of their musketry was deafening, and their attack furious. In a short time countless numbers of Egyptian troops had fallen, including a great many of the chief amīrs, among whom was Azbak, the gunner. . . . In the short space of about sixty minutes the Egyptian army was defeated and in full retreat.

'Tūmān Bey stood his ground about eighty minutes after this, and fought on with a few of his armed slaves and Mamlūks, inflicting great losses on Ibn 'Othmān's men. Finally, when the Turks were too many for him, finding himself deserted by his troops, and fearing capture, he folded up the Royal Standard and ran and concealed himself.

1 Ibn Iyās, Muhammad b. Ahmad: *An Account of the Ottoman Conquest of Egypt in the Year A.H. 922* (*A.D. 1516*), translated by Salmon, W. H. = Oriental Translation Fund, New Series, vol. xxv (London 1921, Royal Asiatic Society), pp. 97–8.

2 For these ineffectual activities of Sultan Ashraf abū'l-Nasr Tūmān Bey see Ibn Iyās, op. cit., pp. 107–8.

'This was the third defeat [that] the Egyptian army had suffered.

'The Turkish force that had advanced under cover of Jabal Ahmar came down upon the tents of the Sultan, plundering everything—kit, arms, horses, camels and oxen, including the guns [that] the Sultan had put into position there, with the shields and palisading, and the vehicles on which the Sultan had spent so much time, labour and money, and from which he had reaped no advantage. Everything in the camp was plundered. Such was the decree of Fate.'[1]

Fate, however, dealt less harshly with the Mamlūks in the hour of their defeat than she dealt with the country which it had been the Mamlūks' *raison d'être* to defend against all comers. For the Mamlūks were not condemned to the extinction which was the logical penalty for their failure to perform their one and only function,[2] while Egypt, who had played a purely passive part in the Mamlūk-Ottoman conflict, and had taken it for granted that she would be the prize of the victors, was now compelled to provide an additional consolation prize for the vanquished, and found herself saddled with the double burden of having to maintain a new garrison of victorious 'Osmanlis[3] without being relieved of her old garrison of no longer victorious Mamlūks.[4] Sultan Selīm's motive in showing this generosity to his vanquished opponents at his new dominion's expense was perhaps a mixture of soldierly contempt for the Mamlūks' military ineptitude with professional sympathy for a corps which, however decadent, was still akin—in origin and constitution and êthos—to the Sultan's own Slave-Household.[5] He may have calculated that the Mamlūks, humiliated on the battle-field and reduced in the political hierarchy to a subordinate rank, would be incapable of endangering a once established Ottoman supremacy, while they might at the same time serve as an effective reinforcement to the Ottoman governor and garrison in holding down the Egyptian 'ulamā and fallāhīn, and also perhaps as an effective restraint upon these 'Osmanlis if the wealth and seclusion of the province committed to their charge should ever tempt them to betray their trust and to repudiate their allegiance to the Porte in order to enjoy the good things of Egypt for themselves.[6] Whatever the expecta-

[1] Ibn Iyās, op. cit., pp. 112–13.

[2] On this point see also IV. C (ii) (*b*) 2, p. 113, above.

[3] Six (Bosniak) Janissary ojāqs.

[4] This piling of an Ottoman on the top of the Mamlūk incubus which was already weighing upon the back of the long-suffering Egyptian beast of burden is a feature of the decadence of the Arabic Civilization which may be compared with the cumulative imposition of the litterati and the priests and the military upon the Egyptian peasantry in the decadence of the Egyptiac Civilization, some three or four thousand years back (see IV (iii) (*c*) 2 (*β*), pp. 418–23, above).

[5] For the species of Nomad institution *in partibus agricolarum* of which the Egyptian corps of Mamlūks and the Ottoman Pādishāh's Slave-Household were alike representatives, see Part III. A, vol. iii, pp. 28–44, above.

[6] This last consideration was the determining factor in Sultan Selīm's policy according to C. F. Volney: *Voyage en Syrie et en Égypte pendant les années 1783, 1784,*

tions and intentions of the Ottoman conqueror of Egypt may have been, his settlement did secure to the Ottoman Imperial Government an effective mastery over Egypt which lasted almost as long as the antecedent reign of the Mamlūks themselves.[1] In the end, however, the Ottoman garrison of Egypt allowed the military decision of A.D. 1516–17 to be reversed through a gradual and pacific revolution which came to pass because the Ottoman garrison abandoned, while the Mamlūk corps continued to observe, the fundamental common rule of the species of Nomad institution to which both these corporations belonged.

This rule was the rigid exclusion, *ex officio*, of the soldier's children from the soldier's service, and the recruitment of the military corporation, in defiance of human nature, by the purchase of slaves and not by the begetting of sons.[2] In permitting the Egyptian Mamlūks to survive, Sultan Selīm had implicitly sanctioned the perpetuation of the existing ways and means by which they reproduced their kind in accordance with the general rule of Nomads *in partibus agricolarum*. Under the Ottoman domination the Mamlūks were still free to import slave-boys from their customary sources of supply[3] in order to keep their complement up to strength, and they persevered in the practice when the Ottoman garrison in Egypt abandoned it. The Janissaries who were quartered in Egypt suffered still more severely in *moral* than their comrades in other parts of the Empire from the admission of the principle of heredity, which the corps extorted from the Imperial Government after the death of Sultan Suleyman in A.D. 1565.[4] For this abandonment of the fundamental rule of the service meant that the Janissaries, instead of remaining a people apart, became merged in the local Muslim population from which they took the wives

et 1785, 2nd edition (Paris 1787, Desenne et Volland), vol. 1, pp. 96–7. We may compare the precautions taken by Augustus, after his own conquest of Egypt, to make sure that no Roman governor of the new Imperial province should have it in his power to repeat the performance of Mark Antony.

[1] The Mamlūks had ruled Egypt for 267 years, from their succession to the heritage of the last Ayyūbid Sultan in A.D. 1250 to the overthrow of the last of their own Sultans in A.D. 1517. The Ottoman Imperial Government remained in effective control of Egypt for 229 years from Selīm's entry into Cairo in A.D. 1517 to the *pronunciamiento* of Ibrāhīm Ketkhuda in A.D. 1746.

[2] On this vital point see Part III. A, vol. iii, pp. 28–35, above.

[3] The Egyptian Mamlūks had originally made their purchases of boys, through Venetian middle-men, from the Mongol Khans of Qipchāq, who obtained their stocks by making systematic slave-raids upon all the sedentary populations round about their ranges—including the Russians and Poles in one direction and the Circassians in another (see Part III. A, vol. iii, p. 30, footnote 3, above). After the Ottoman conquest of Stamboul and Pera in A.D. 1453 and Caffa and Tana in 1475, the supply of slaves from Qipchāq (now reduced to the narrow limits of the Khanate of the Crimea) was diverted from the Egyptian to the Ottoman market (for this source of supply for the Ottoman Pādishāh's Slave-Household see Part III. A, vol. iii, p. 35, footnote 3, above). Thereafter the Egyptian Mamlūks drew their recruits from the Orthodox Christian populations of Georgian nationality in Transcaucasia (see Part III. A, vol. iii, p. 32, footnote 2, above).

[4] See Part III. A, vol. iii, pp. 44–5, above.

that bore the sons who now, in due course, stepped into their superannuated fathers' places in the ranks; and while the Janissaries of the metropolitan provinces intermarried with the Turkish-speaking Muslims of Rumelia and Anatolia, who were, and felt themselves to be, a ruling race,[1] the Janissaries of Egypt intermarried with an Arabic-speaking townsfolk and peasantry[2] who had been for centuries the *ra'īyah* of the Mamlūks.[3]

In these circumstances it is not surprising that the Mamlūks should have been rewarded for their refusal to 'go native' by obtaining over the degenerate Ottoman garrison an ascendancy which carried with it a *de facto* restoration of the Mamlūk rule over Egypt itself, since the Ottoman garrison, before becoming the Mamlūks' creatures, had already reduced to a cipher the authority of the Pasha who was the local representative of the Porte. Though the outward forms of Ottoman sovereignty were all still sedulously preserved at the time of the French observer Volney's visit to Egypt in A.D. 1783–5, the Pasha of the day, in his residence on the citadel of Cairo, was virtually a hostage in the Mamlūks' hands; and the pronouncement of the one Arabic word *Anzal* ('Descend!') from the mouth of the Mamlūks' herald was sufficient to bring this Ottoman bird of passage down from his precarious perch and send him back home to Constantinople at any moment, even before the expiry of his proper three-years' term.[4] The Porte winked at this practically complete usurpation of its authority in Egypt by a military corps which it had once permitted to exist on sufferance. It not only made no attempt to repeat the exploit of Sultan Selīm I and to reassert its authority by force of arms; it did not even think of condemning the Mamlūks to a choice between extinction and degeneracy by resorting to the economic weapon and cutting off the rebels' supply of slave-recruits at its Transcaucasian source!

Thus, by a curious turn of Fortune's wheel, the Mamlūks virtually recovered in the course of the eighteenth century of the Christian Era a dominion over Egypt which they had lost in A.D. 1517; but a comparison of Volney's picture of them with that of Ibn Iyās shows that they had 'forgotten nothing and learnt nothing'[5] during two and a half centuries of adversity and eclipse. As Volney

[1] See Part III. A, vol. iii, p. 35, above.

[2] See Gibb, H. A. R., and Bowen, H.: *Islamic Society and the West*, vol. i (London 1939, Milford), chap. 4, § 2.

[3] The part played by these native marriages of the Egyptian Janissaries in bringing about the historic reversal of the psychological, the social, and eventually the military and political relations between the Egyptian Janissaries and the Egyptian Mamlūks is noticed by Volney in op. cit., vol. 1, p. 99. The Mamlūks did not mate with Egyptian women, but with Transcaucasian fellow countrywomen, and fellow slaves, of their own (Volney, op. cit., vol. i, p. 99, footnote 1).

[4] Volney, op. cit., vol. i, pp. 348–51.

[5] See IV. C (iii) (*c*) 2 (α), p. 264, above.

saw them, when their accidental reprieve was almost at an end and their final disaster was imminent, the excellence of their weapons (they now affected English carbines) was entirely offset by the ungainliness of their costume, the clumsiness of their saddlery, the roughness of their horsemanship (which ruined a horse's mouth and legs), the childishness of their tactics, and, worst of all, by a lack of discipline which was the very antithesis of their original *esprit de corps.*[1]

'La pièce la plus singulière de cet habillement est une espèce de pantalon, dont l'ampleur est telle que dans sa hauteur il arrive au menton, et que chacune de ses jambes pourrait recevoir le corps entier: ajoutez que les Mamlouks le font de ce drap de Venise qu'on appelle *saille*, qui, quoiqu'aussi moelleux que l'elbeuf, est plus épais que la bure; et que, pour marcher plus à l'aise, ils y renferment, sous une ceinture à coulisse, toute la partie pendante des vêtements dont nous avons parlé. Ainsi emmaillotés, on conçoit que les Mamlouks ne sont pas des piétons agiles; mais ce que l'on ne conçoit qu'après avoir vu les hommes de divers pays, est qu'ils regardent leur habillement comme très-commode. En vain leur objecte-t-on qu'à pied il empêche de marcher, qu'à cheval il charge inutilement, et que tout cavalier démonté est un homme perdu; ils répondent: *C'est l'usage*, et ce mot répond à tout.'[2]

As for the childishness of the Mamlūks' tactics, it was exemplified in A.D. 1776, when they were confronted with the unfamiliar task of besieging the Syrian city of Jaffa in the course of a petty local war—let loose by the breakdown of the *Pax Ottomanica*—between a Mamlūk tyrant of Egypt and an Arab tyrant of Palestine.[3] On this occasion the Mamlūks began by pitching their camp within range of the defenders' artillery; and then, when a breach had been blown for them in the flimsy curtain-wall of the besieged city by an English soldier of fortune named Robinson, and the moment came for taking the place by assault,

'les Mamlouks voulaient qu'on le fît à cheval; mais on leur fit comprendre que cela était impossible; et, pour la première fois, ils consentirent à marcher à pied. Ce dut être un spectacle curieux de les voir avec leurs immenses culottes de *sailles* de Venise, embarrassés de leurs beniches retroussés, le sabre courbe à la main et le pistolet au côté, avancer en trébuchant parmi les décombres d'une muraille. Ils crurent avoir tout surmonté, quand ils eurent franchi cet obstacle; mais les assiégés, qui jugeaient mieux, attendirent qu'ils eussent débouché sur le terrain vide qui est entre la ville et le mur: là, ils les assaillirent, du haut

1 See Volney, op. cit., vol. i, chap. 11, 'Constitution de la Milice des Mamlouks', pp. 151–69.

2 Volney, op. cit., vol. i, pp. 155–6. The Parthian and Sasanian cataphracts wore drawers of the same unpractical kind, which immobilized them, with the same fatal results, as soon as they were out of the saddle.

3 See Volney, op. cit., vol. i, pp. 131–9.

des terrasses et des fenêtres des maisons, d'une telle grêle de balles que les Mamlouks n'eurent pas même l'envie de mettre le feu; ils se retirèrent, persuadés que cet endroit était un coupe-gorge impénétrable, puisqu'on n'y pouvait entrer à cheval.'[1]

This fantastic performance of the Mamlūks at Jaffa, in A.D. 1776, is a worthy pendant to the performance of their old French adversaries at Mansūrah in A.D. 1250. By this date the Mamlūks were incapable of taking a city, even when they had a Frankish artilleryman at their command to open the way. What a contrast to their performance in A.D. 1291, when they had besieged and taken Acre in the teeth of all the Franks in the World, who were then up in arms to defend the last Frankish foothold in the Christian Holy Land! Yet the Mamlūks' latter-day ineptitude in tactics was, if possible, less serious than the dissolution of their ancient discipline.

'Dans notre Europe, quand on parle de troupes de guerre, on se figure sur le champ une distribution d'hommes par compagnies, par bataillons, par escadrons; des uniformes de tailles et de couleurs, des formations par rangs et lignes, des combinaisons de manœuvres particulières ou d'évolutions générales; en un mot, tout un système d'opérations fondées sur des principes réfléchis. Ces idées sont justes par rapport à nous, mais, quand on les transporte aux pays dont nous traitons, elles deviennent autant d'erreurs. Les Mamlouks ne connaissent rien de notre art militaire; ils n'ont ni uniformes, ni ordonnance, ni formation, ni discipline, ni même de subordination. Leur réunion est un attroupement, leur marche est une cohue, leur combat est un duel, leur guerre est un brigandage. . . .'[2]

The strictures here passed upon the Mamlūks are applied by the same observer, in another place,[3] to all the military establishments of the day in Turkey-in-Asia.

'Les Turks, et surtout ceux de l'Asie, diffèrent encore plus des Européens par l'état militaire que par les usages et les mœurs. . . . Il ne faut pas s'imaginer ici des mouvemens combinés, tels que ceux qui, depuis cent ans, ont fait de la guerre parmi nous une science de calcul et de réflexion. Les Asiatiques n'ont pas les premiers élémens de cette conduite.'

In this last passage Volney's acute observation and luminous thought are distinguished by a touch of that historical sense which was the poorest piece in the intellectual armoury of most eighteenth-century French philosophers.[4] Yet, although Volney is dimly aware

[1] Volney, op. cit., vol. i, pp. 135–6.

[2] Volney, op. cit., vol. i, p. 163.

[3] Volney, op. cit., vol. i, pp. 113–16, apropos of the army with which 'Alī Bey, the tyrant of Egypt, invaded Syria in A.D. 1771, and the forces with which his aggression was disputed by the Pashas of Saida, Tripoli, and Aleppo. In this other passage the theme—and even the slightly rhetorical peroration—of the passage quoted just above occurs with a more general application.

[4] The brilliant exception is Turgot.

that the disciplined and scientific Western warfare of his day is something of recent date, he is apparently blind to the extraordinary and illuminating historical περιπέτεια upon which he has stumbled. In this vista his vision is already obscured by the two modern Western dogmas of 'the Incomparable West' and 'the Unchanging East', which mask his penetrating eyes like a pair of blinkers.[1] This *fin-de-siècle* Frenchman does not realize that the art of war which the West has acquired within the last century is not an original creation of the Western genius but is merely the result of an industrious and intelligent mimesis of an Ottoman *fait accompli*; and he is still farther from realizing that his satirical contrast between Western discipline and Mamlūk anarchy in the ninth decade of the eighteenth century is the precise inverse of the contrast that he would have had to draw if he had happened to be an Arabic observer making his comparison between the Mamlūks and the French at a date five hundred years back.

We may conjecture that Volney, when he wrote the brilliant book from which we have been quoting, had read neither Busbecq's *Exclamatio*[2] nor Joinville's chronicle of the Egyptian campaign of Saint Louis; but it is also tempting to conjecture that Volney's own mordant description of the general military ineptitude of the Mamlūks and 'Osmanlis, as he had observed it for himself at first hand, may have come to the notice of the author's younger contemporary Bonaparte at some date between the first publication of Volney's *Travels* in A.D. 1787 and the decision—which was taken at Bonaparte's instance by the Directory in A.D. 1798—to send a French military expedition to Egypt.[3]

The dazzling prospects which this project opened up, and which Bonaparte found irresistibly attractive, arose from the fact that, in the course of the two preceding centuries, the Governments of the Western World had acted upon the advice which had been pressed upon them so urgently and so eloquently by Busbecq—the first modern Western observer of first-rate ability who saw the Ottoman polity in its prime—in a pamphlet[4] which he published after his return in 1562 from his diplomatic mission to Constantinople as ambassador from the Court of Vienna. Busbecq's thesis

[1] For the catchword of 'the Unchanging East', and its effect of fortifying, in Western minds, 'the Egocentric Illusion', see I. C (iii) (*b*), vol. i, pp. 164–8, above.

[2] For Busbecq's *Exclamatio, sive de Re Militari contra Turcam instituenda Consilium*, see Part III. A, vol. iii, pp. 36–42.

[3] See Charles-Roux, F.: *Les Origines de l'Expédition d'Égypte* (Paris 1910, Plon-Nourrit), pp. 208–15, for the interest excited in France by the publication of Volney's *Voyage* in 1787 and of his *Considérations sur la Guerre Actuelle des Turcs* in 1788. See, further, op. cit., p. 302, for the mention of Volney's *Voyage* in Desaix's notes of a conversation which he had with Napoleon in September 1797 at Passeriano in the Veneto.

[4] *Exclamatio, sive de Re Militari contra Turcam instituenda Consilium*, republished in *A. Gislenii Busbequii omnia quae extant* (Leyden 1633, Elzevir).

was[1] that the only remaining chance of saving the sovereign Powers of the West from the imminent doom of an Ottoman conquest lay in scrapping the mobs of ragged, ill-armed, and semi-criminal vagrants that passed for armies in sixteenth-century Western Christendom, and replacing them by uniformed, disciplined forces, armed with muskets, on the model of those Janissaries by whose military prowess the sovereignty, and indeed the very existence, of all the Western states was being threatened in Busbecq's time. This course was duly followed by the princes of his own world to whom the Flemish publicist had addressed himself. Between Busbecq's day and Bonaparte's, while the Janissaries were becoming 'a nation of shopkeepers' at Constantinople and were 'going native' at Cairo, a passable imitation of the Janissary corps, as Busbecq had seen and described it, was being recruited—by the approved Ottoman methods of conscripting peasants and drilling jail-birds and kidnapping 'likely fellows'—in all the leading states of Western Europe; and by A.D. 1798 the French Janissaries were ready to repeat the exploit which had been successfully carried out by their Ottoman exemplars in A.D. 1516–17. The Mamlūks, on their part, in the year when Napoleon landed, were just what they had been in 1516, and just what Saint Louis's knights had been in 1250 (when the Mamlūks themselves had borne much more resemblance to the soldiers of Napoleon or the soldiers of the first Selīm); and a student of history who compares the records of the three campaigns in the narratives of three eyewitnesses—Joinville for 1250 and Ibn Iyās for 1516–17 and Jabartī for 1798—cannot fail to be struck by the remarkable uniformity of atmosphere, as well as of incident, that he will find in these three pictures. Here is the picture as it is painted by Jabartī.

'On Sunday the 10th of this holy month [of Muharram] messengers from Alexandria brought [to Cairo] letters containing the news that on Friday the 8th of the same month ten English ships had made their appearance in the offing and had approached close enough inshore to be visible from the beach.

'A little later, fifteen more ships came to join them.

'The townspeople were wondering what the foreigners could have come for, when a little boat stood in and landed ten persons, who proceeded to wait upon the notables of the city and upon the governor-plenipotentiary, the Sayyid Muhammad Kuraym, of whom we shall have more to say later.

'These foreigners said that they were Englishmen, and they added that they were on the look-out for some Frenchmen, who had started, with a considerable fleet, for an unknown destination. They were afraid, they said, of seeing these Frenchmen make a surprise attack on Egypt,

[1] See Part III. A, vol. iii, p. 38, footnote 2, above.

because they knew that the people of Egypt would not be able to repel the invaders or to prevent them from landing.

'The Sayyid Muhammad Kuraym supposed that the English *parlementaires* were laying a trap for him; he did not give the slightest credence to what they said, and his answer to them was forbidding. The foreigners then went on to say: "We shall be content to keep the sea with our ships, in order to defend the city and patrol the coast; we shall ask you for nothing but water and provisions, and for these we will undertake to pay." The notables of the city, however, refused, like the Governor himself, to enter into relations with the English, and said to them: "This country belongs to the Sultan, and neither the French nor any other foreigners have any business here; so be good enough to leave us." At these words the English messengers returned to their ships and went off to look for their provisions somewhere else, instead of at Alexandria, "in order that God might accomplish the work that was foreordained in his decree." . . .

'On Wednesday the 20th of the same month letters [received in Cairo] from Alexandria, Rosetta and Damanhūr brought the news that on Monday the 18th a French fleet, in great force, had arrived off Alexandria. . . . By the next morning the French had spread, like locusts, all round the city. Thereupon the people of Alexandria had joined forces with the Badu who had come from Bahīrah with the kāshif of that province, and had attacked the French; but they had found themselves unable either to repel or to resist them. . . . They were quite unprepared for the struggle; and, moreover, the arsenals contained neither arms nor munitions; so they realized that they were courting certain defeat, and accordingly sued for peace. . . .

'On the Monday it was learnt that the French had reached Damanhūr and Rosetta. . . .

'[On Sunday, the 1st Safar] Ibrāhīm Bey [one of the leading Mamlūks of the moment] went . . . to Bulāq and convened the Pasha, the 'ulamā and all the shaykhs for consultation. They . . . decided that fortifications should be thrown up along a line from Bulāq to Shubrah, and that Ibrāhīm Bey should stay at Bulāq with his troops. . . . On Monday [the 2nd Safar] Murād Bey came to Imbābah to arrange for the construction of fortifications from there to Bashtil; he personally undertook the direction of the work. . . . On the Tuesday the trumpets were sounded to summon the inhabitants to come out of the city and man the fortifications at Bulāq; so everybody went to Bulāq, and nobody was left in Cairo except the women and children and the old men who were past active work. . . .

'On Friday the 6th of the same month the French reached Kūm-al-Aswad, and on the Saturday morning they reached Umm Dīnār. . . . At midday, at the height of the heat, a party of troops, encamped on the west bank of the Nile, mounted and advanced towards Bashtil, near Imbābah, and when these Egyptian troops saw the French army they hurled themselves upon it with fury. The French received them with a continuous fusilade, and in this engagement both sides fought with ferocity. The defterdār Ayyūb Bey, the kāshif 'Abdallah Bey, other kāshifs of Muhammad Bey al-Alfī, and large numbers of Mamlūks, were killed in this battle. The survivors were pursued by about six thousand French troops under the command of General Desaix, who was afterwards governor of Upper Egypt. . . .

'Desaix pursued the Mamlūks right up to Murād Bey's fortifications. . . . The French troops who were advancing to engage Murād Bey had manœuvred, as the French do, in such a way that at a certain moment the Egyptian soldiers found themselves caught between two fires, on their front and in their rear; the drums beat, and the musketry fire doubled in intensity, and the artillery fire did the same. The wind whistled, the dust whirled, the air was darkened by the powder-smoke, the combatants' ears were deafened by the ceaseless reports of the explosions—you would have thought that it was an earthquake, or that the sky was falling.

'The engagement lasted three quarters of an hour, and the Egyptian army on the west bank was routed. Many troopers were drowned that day in the Nile, so hard were they pressed by the enemy; many others were taken prisoner. At the close the French were left masters of the battlefield and of all the fortifications. As for Murād Bey, he fled to Gīzah with all his suite, looked in at his palace, and then left for Upper Egypt within a quarter of an hour.'[1]

This first-hand account, from the pen of al-Jabartī, of the French descent upon Egypt in A.D. 1798 resembles the first-hand account of the Ottoman descent in A.D. 1516–17—which we have already quoted from the chronicle of Ibn Iyās—in conveying from the direct experience of an unsophisticated spectator of an actual event an impression which is imaginatively created by a stroke of literary art in the opening passages of Mr. H. G. Wells' fantasy *The War of the Worlds*. In this twentieth-century Western work of fiction the 'Martian' invaders suddenly appear 'out of the blue' upon the surface of a planet whose inhabitants have had no suspicion of their approaching advent and have made no preparations for contending with a war-machine which is not only quite unfamiliar and new-fangled but is also so much more potent than their own that it seems completely invincible at the first encounter. In the experience of a sixteenth-century and an eighteenth-century Egyptian observer the unheralded and unexpected impact of the Ottoman and the French infantry—with their 'Martian' uniforms and drill and fire-arms—made the same impression 'in real life', when it swept away the Mamlūks who rode out to meet their fate with that blind confidence in their own ineptitude which had been the death of Saint Louis's knights at Mansūrah in A.D. 1250.

[1] Jabartī, Shaykh 'Abd-ar-Rahmān al-: *'Ajā'ib-al-Āthār fi't-Tarājim wa'l-Ahbār* (Cairo, A.H. 1322, 4 vols.), vol. iii, *ad init.* French translation—*Merveilles Biographiques et Historiques* (Cairo 1888–96, Imprimerie Nationale; Paris 1888–96, Leroux: 9 vols.), vol. vi, *ad init.*

The history of the Egyptian Mamlūks illustrates the truth of the saying that

'One day is with the Lord as a thousand years, and a thousand years as one day. The Lord . . . is long-suffering to usward, not willing that any should perish. . . . But the day of the Lord will come as a thief in the night; in which the heavens shall pass away with a great noise, and the elements shall melt with fervent heat, the earth also and the works that are therein shall be burnt up. . . .[1] For when they shall say: "Peace and safety", then sudden destruction cometh upon them, as travail upon a woman with child; and they shall not escape.'[2]

On the occasion of their first discomfiture, when they were taken unawares by the Janissaries in A.D. 1516–17 after having vegetated in a military technique which had been obsolete by that time for some two hundred years, the Mamlūks were let off lightly. They were not only reprieved from the doom of annihilation to which they had exposed themselves, but they were also eventually reinstated, by a turn of Fortune, in the dominion over Egypt. But when they then vegetated on and allowed the same fate to overtake them for the second time, they exhausted their draft upon the long-sufferingness of their Creator; and the leniency which the Ottoman Sultan Selīm I had been moved to exercise in A.D. 1517 was not displayed by the Ottoman soldier of fortune Mehmed 'Alī, who stepped boldly and ably into the political vacuum which was left in Egypt when the French conquerors of the Mamlūks and the English adversaries of the French had cancelled one another out. The fiasco of A.D. 1798, which demonstrated conclusively that the Mamlūk corps had degenerated into an *ἄχθος ἀρούρης*, received condign punishment in the massacre of 1811.[3]

We have now traced our 'chain of destruction' from Goliath the first of the hoplites to Murād Bey the last of the cataphracts;[4] and we need not linger long over the latest links, which are exceedingly familiar to Western students of history in our generation. We need only remind ourselves that, since the moment at the turn of the seventeenth and eighteenth centuries of the Christian Era when the 'Osmanlis allowed the new infantry technique which they had

[1] 2 Peter iii. 9–10.

[2] 1 Thess. v. 3; cf. Matt. xxiv. 36–51 = Mark xiii. 32–7, and Luke xii. 35–48, xvii. 26–37, and xxi. 34–6.

[3] For the destruction of the Mamlūks by Mehmed 'Alī see Part III. A, vol. iii, p. 31, and p. 50, footnote 1, above.

[4] Not quite the last; for the 'Die-Hard' band of survivors from the catastrophe of 1811 who held out against Mehmed 'Alī thereafter in the African hinterland of Egypt on the upper reaches of the Nile (see vol. iii, p. 31, above), bequeathed their armament and technique to those mailed horsemen, in the service of the khalīfah of a Sudanese Mahdī, who went down under the fire of British infantry in 1898 at Omdurman (see V. C (ii) (*a*), vol. vi, pp. 227 and 235, below). In the year 1938 there were cataphracts still to be seen in all their glory in Northern Nigeria and in Rājputāna; but in both these countries their role had by then become merely decorative.

invented to be wrested out of their hands by their long-despised opponents in the West, this technique has neither remained static nor been held as a permanent monopoly by any single Western nation.

The French army which overthrew the Mamlūks at the Battle of the Pyramids in 1798 was already something different from the earliest version of the Western imitation of the Janissaries. It was a recent product of a French *levée en masse* which, since 1793, had succeeded in superseding, by successfully diluting, the small but superlatively well-drilled professional Western army of the eighteenth century, after this had been brought to the highest perfection of which it was capable by the pedantry of a Frederick William I and the genius of a Frederick the Great.[1] The ascendancy which had been established at Valmy—before the interlude of the Egyptian expedition—by an organized French nation-in-arms over the soldiers of the *ancien régime* was to be confirmed thereafter at Austerlitz[2] and Jena; and the overthrow of the old Prussian army at Jena was to stimulate a Prussian pleiad of military and political men of genius to outdo the French in the new *tour de force* of combining discipline with numbers—and this with such effect that the humiliations of the War of 1806–7 would be wiped out in the *Befreiungskrieg* of 1813–14.

The French so far failed to take to heart the lesson of those latter years that they brought defeat upon themselves a second time, with still more calamitous results for France, in 1870–1; but the French were happier than the Mamlūks, inasmuch as their second debâcle did not prove to be the end of their military glories. So far from that, they suffered less, in the long run, from losing the war of 1870–1 than the Germans suffered from winning it; for the Prussian General Staff was so dazzled by the brilliance of its own success in 1870 that, forty-four years later, it was still unable to think of a European war in terms of any other strategy, with the consequence that in the General War of 1914–18 the Prussian war-machine brought defeat upon Germany and her allies by evoking an unforeseen *riposte* in the shape of a siege on an unprecedented scale. In 1918 the old methods of 1870 were proved, by the sensational collapse of the previously predominant con-

[1] This ominous increase in the 'drive' of Western warfare has been touched upon in IV. C (iii) (*b*) 3, pp. 150–5, above.

[2] Napoleon's victory at Austerlitz is one of the few European events that Jabartī mentions in a chronicle which runs through the whole period of the French Revolution and the Napoleonic Wars. Even in his account of the year A.H. 1213 (A.D. 1798–9), in which the disturbances in Europe impinged, with a vengeance, upon the even tenour of Egyptian life, the traditionally minded Arabic chronicler designates, as the most important event of the year, the intermission of the annual pilgrimage to the Holy Cities of the Hijāz owing to the alarums and excursions of the Wahhābīs (Jabartī, *Merveilles Biographiques et Historiques*, vol. vi, p. 121).

tinental European military Power, to be no match for the new methods of trench warfare and economic blockade. And in the year 1938 it was again already certain that the technique which had won the war of 1914–18 would not be the last link in the chain—if Mankind were so perverse as to go on cultivating the Art of War after it had attained a degree of deadliness at which any further indulgence in belligerency seemed likely to bring with it the total destruction of Society.

In another war in the West the 'post-war' British Navy and the 'post-war' French system of semi-subterranean frontier fortifications might well prove to be nothing but mill-stones round the necks of the winners of what would then be remembered by Posterity, not as 'the war to end War', but merely as the event of 1914–18 in a military competition which the lacerated competitors had failed to bring to a timely end. In another war the French fortifications might be overleapt, and the British Grand Fleet sunk in harbour, by enemy aircraft laden with all the destructive contrivances of the twentieth-century Western chemists. 'The next war', if it ever came to wipe 'the Great Society' out of existence, might well be won—if the notion of 'victory' then still retained any meaning—by a 'post-war' professional force whose strength would lie, not in numbers, but in a discipline and training which would enable these twentieth-century Janissaries to profit to the full from an unrivalled command over an armoury of new-fangled weapons. A gang of such militarized mechanics might conquer by the same arts and virtues as the grenadiers of Frederick the Great and the musketeers of Selīm I; and if the victorious war-band of Strakers-at-arms were the German *Reichswehr*, then the wheel of European military history would have come round full circle. During the thirteen 'post-war' years that elapsed between the coming into force of the Peace Treaty of Versailles in January 1920 and the advent of Herr Hitler to power in the Reich in January 1933, it seemed possible that this destiny might have been forced upon Germany by the enemy statesmen who had imposed a long-service professional army upon her at the Peace Conference of Paris. But this ironical prospect had been superseded by one that was more ironical still by the time when the Austrian Führer of Prussia-Germany had been five years in the saddle. Herr Hitler's mission was to liquidate the *Versailler Diktat*; and he was unwilling to accept from the *ci-devant* victors even a blessing in disguise which they had perhaps conferred on Germany without ever intending to do her good. Herr Hitler's single-track aim was to get rid of every jot that had been imposed on Germany, without taking the tittles on their merits. And accordingly the brilliance of the audacity with which he duly recovered Germany's military freedom of action was matched by the strictness of the conventionality of the use which he made of this success. He set himself to demonstrate Germany's liberation from the shackles of Versailles by giving her precisely the kind of army that the treaty forbade her to possess; and this imperious psychological necessity entailed a serious technological retrogression. Under the Nazi regime the formidable professional force which had been thrust upon the Weimar Republic by hostile foreign hands was deliberately replaced by a conscript citizen army of that long since antiquated type that had been out of the French 'Ideas of Seventeen Eighty-Nine'!

Having now watched Goliath and David fight first on foot and then on horseback, we cannot leave the amphitheatre without waiting to see the arena transformed into a *naumachia* for our pair of gladiators to repeat their duel afloat. We may aptly conclude our survey of the destruction which is invited by any idolization of an ephemeral technique with an illustration that is offered by one of the curiosities of naval history. When the Romans took to the sea in the course of the first Romano-Punic War (*gerebatur* 264–241 B.C.), they had to face a Carthaginian navy which was heir to all the refinements that had been introduced successively into the art of naval warfare in the Mediterranean during the two centuries that had elapsed since the generation of Themistocles. According to the story—whether this be authentic fact or the 'philosophic truth' of legend—the Roman landlubbers nonplussed the Carthaginian masters of the naval art by cancelling two centuries of naval progress at a stroke and reducing naval warfare once again to that primitive kind of land-warfare-on-shipboard which it had been at the beginning of all things. Incapable of meeting the Carthaginians on equal terms in the skilful game of the διέκπλους and ruminating regretfully upon their own conspicuous ascendancy on shore, the Romans are said to have invented a gangway, slung from a mast and fitted with a grappling-iron, by means of which they literally came to grips with the Carthaginian warships. By this shockingly unprofessional innovation in technique[1] they seized the

[1] This alleged Roman invention of the *corax* or *corvus* in the fourth decade of the third century B.C. has one well-authenticated precedent in 'the iron hands' with which the Athenian warships grappled the enemy craft in the great battle of 413 B.C. in Syracuse harbour when the Athenian fleet made its supreme effort to break out and gain the open sea. But the circumstances in which this reactionary technique was employed by the fifth-century masters of the art of naval warfare were manifestly exceptional. The engagement was being fought, of necessity, in a confined space, and, since the number of ships engaged was large on either side, there was simply no room for manœuvring (on this point see Thucydides, Book VII, chap. 70). Moreover, the Athenian commander Nicias is represented as describing this reversion to the methods of land-warfare not as a happy idea but as a dismal necessity: ἐς τοῦτο γὰρ ἠναγκάσμεθα ὥστε πεζομαχεῖν ἀπὸ τῶν νεῶν (Thucydides, Book VII, chap. 62).

tactical initiative, inhibited their astonished and indignant opponents from employing their traditional tactics of manœuvring and ramming, and forcibly substituted the tactics of grappling and boarding, with decisive effects upon the fortunes of the war.

If there is any truth in this story, it brings out the connexion between breakdown and idolatry very clearly; for in this instance we see an intrinsically superior technique which has been idolized by its adepts being defeated by an intrinsically inferior technique which has no point in its favour except that it has not yet had time to be idolized, because it is an innovation; and this strange spectacle suggests very forcibly that it is the act of idolization that does the mischief, and not any intrinsic quality in the object. *αἰτία ἑλομένου· θεὸς ἀναίτιος*.[1]

3. *Κόρος, Ὕβρις, Ἄτη*

(α) *The Suicidalness of Militarism.*

The Strong Man Armed.

Having concluded our survey of the aberration of 'resting on one's oars' which is the passive way of succumbing to the nemesis of creativity, we may now go on to examine, by the same empirical method, the active aberration which is described in the three Greek words *κόρος, ὕβρις, ἄτη*.[2] In order to bring out the difference between these two modes of courting destruction, let us begin our survey of *κόρος-ὕβρις-ἄτη* in the military field, in which we have just brought our survey of 'resting on one's oars' to a close.

Both modes are exemplified in the behaviour of Goliath, as this is depicted in the Syriac saga. On the one hand we have seen how Goliath incurs his doom by vegetating in the once invincible military technique of the individual hoplite champion without foreseeing or forestalling the new, and superior, technique which David is bringing into action against him. At the same time we may observe that Goliath's destruction at David's hands might have been postponed, and possibly averted, if only Goliath's unenterprisingness in the matter of technique had been accompanied by a corresponding passivity of êthos. Unfortunately for Goliath, however, this *miles gloriosus*'s technological conservatism was not offset by the saving grace of 'negative self-feeling'; and he was so blind to the danger to which he was exposing himself by rusting in his obsolete panoply that he actually went out of his way to 'ask for trouble' by offering himself as a champion on behalf of the whole Philistine army, and challenging the enemy to send any man they

[1] Plato: *Respublica*, Book X, 617 E.

[2] For the distinction between 'resting on one's oars' and *κόρος-ὕβρις-ἄτη* see IV. C (iii) (*c*) 1, pp. 257–9, above.

chose to meet him in single-combat. Thus ὕβρις conspired with unenterprisingness in Goliath's soul to entice the giant to his lamentable fate; and the legendary Syriac figure whose name has become a by-word for 'unpreparedness' is also the prototype of the aggressive 'militarist': a Philip II dispatching his infantry against Holland and his armada against England, or a Napoleon III declaring war on Prussia, or a Wilhelm II invading Belgium 'in shining armour'.[1]

The blindness of the militarist is the theme of a famous parable in the New Testament:

'When a strong man armed keepeth his palace, his goods are in peace; but when a stronger than he shall come upon him and overcome him, he taketh from him all his armour wherein he trusted, and divideth his spoils.'[2]

The militarist is so confident of his own ability to look after himself in that social—or anti-social—system in which all disputes are settled *manu militari*, and not by process of law or conciliation, that he throws his sword into the scales when the issue between a régime of violence and a régime of organized peace is trembling in the balance. The sword's weight duly tips the balance in favour of the continuance of the old barbaric dispensation; and the militarist, exultant at having once more made his will prevail, now points to this latest triumph as a final proof that the sword is omnipotent. In the next chapter of the story, however, it turns out that he has failed to prove his thesis *ad hominem* in the particular case which exclusively interests him; for the next event is his own overthrow by a stronger militarist than himself. His success in prolonging the militarist régime has simply insured that he himself shall learn, at last, what it feels like to have one's throat cut. We may think of the Aztecs and the Incas, each remorselessly warring down their weaker neighbours in their own respective worlds, until they are overtaken by Spanish *conquistadores* who fall upon them from another world and strike them down with weapons for which theirs are no match. It is equally illuminating, and considerably more profitable, to think of ourselves.

In the Hellenic Mythology the doom which 'the strong man armed' invincibly insists upon bringing upon himself is portrayed in the legend of how Cronos brutally supplants his father Uranus in the lordship of the Universe, only to taste, in his turn, of Uranus's experience at the hands of the usurper's own son Zeus.[3]

[1] This rhetorical expression was used by the German Kaiser to describe the posture in which he gave Austria-Hungary his diplomatic support in the European crisis of 1908 over the Austro-Hungarian annexation of Bosnia.

[2] Luke xi. 21–2 = Matt. xii. 29 = Mark iii. 27.

[3] For the explanation, in mythological language, of how it was that Zeus, the τριακτήρ

In Zeus we have the picture of the militarist who is saved in spite of himself, thanks to the suffering of another being who is nobler, as well as wiser, than he is; and Prometheus' salvation of Zeus is a Hellenic counterpart of Jesus's salvation of Peter when Peter commits the militarist's crime at the crucial moment in the Garden of Gethsemane.

'And, behold, one of them which were with Jesus stretched out his hand and drew his sword and struck a servant of the High Priest's and smote off his ear. Then said Jesus unto him: "Put up again thy sword into his place; for all they that take the sword shall perish with the sword."'[1]

In the Old Testament the classic portrayal of the militarist's self-contrived discomfiture is given in the story of Ben-Hadad and Ahab.[2] When King Ben-Hadad of Damascus is besieging King Ahab of Israel in his city of Samaria, the aggressor sends messengers into the beleaguered city to demand of his victim the surrender of everything that he possesses, and Ahab returns the soft answer: 'My lord, O king, according to thy saying, I am thine and all that I have.' But Ben-Hadad will not forbear from humiliating his humble adversary still further; so he sends a second message to inform Ahab that the conqueror's servants will now come to search his house, and that, 'whatsoever is pleasant in' Ahab's 'eyes, they shall put it in their hand and take it away'. Thereupon Ahab replies that he still accepts the first demand but rejects the second; and, when Ben-Hadad proceeds to breathe fire and slaughter, Ahab says to the bearers of this third message: 'Tell him: "Let not him that girdeth on his harness boast himself as he that putteth it off."' Thereafter, according to Ben-Hadad's will, and against the wishes of Ahab, the issue between the two kings is decided in a pitched battle; and in this battle the aggressor brings upon himself an overwhelming defeat. The story ends with a tableau in which the servants of Ben-Hadad come out—from the city in which they and their master are now being besieged in their turn—with sackcloth on their loins and ropes on their heads, and plead with the victorious Ahab for mercy. And Ahab is not betrayed into making Ben-Hadad's mistake by the giddiness of the περιπέτεια that

(see Aeschylus: *Agamemnon*, ll. 171–2, quoted in I. B (v), vol. i, p. 48, above), contrived to avoid the fate of his two predecessors, after having imitated the behaviour of the second of them, see Part III. B, vol. iii, pp. 115–17, above.

1 Matt. xxvi. 51–2 = Mark xiv. 47 = Luke xxii. 49–51 = John xviii. 10–11. In the passage in the Gospel according to St. John the act of violence is explicitly ascribed to Peter; in the passage in the Gospel according to St. Luke Jesus is represented as also restoring the situation in a material sense by miraculously healing the injured man's wound. (This incident in the story of the Passion of Jesus is touched upon again in V. C (i) (*c*) 2, vol. v, p. 73; V. C (i) (*d*) 1, vol. v, p. 393; V. C (ii) (*a*), vol. vi, pp. 178–9, and V. C (ii) (*a*), Annex II, vol. vi, pp. 391–2 and 527–8, below.)

2 The story is told in 1 Kings xx.

has so swiftly inverted the two kings' respective positions. To the message 'Thy servant Ben-Hadad saith: "I pray thee, let me live",' Ahab answers: 'Is he yet alive? He is my brother.' And, when, on his instructions, Ben-Hadad is brought with honour into his presence, Ahab makes a treaty with his penitent opponent—on the extremely favourable terms which Ben-Hadad is in haste to offer him—and then straightway lets him go free.

Assyria.

We may next consider the case of the Assyrian militarism which cast its shadow over the Syriac World in Ahab's and Ben-Hadad's generation.[1]

The disaster in which the Assyrian military power met its end in 614–610 B.C. was even more overwhelming than those which overtook the Macedonian phalanx in 197 and 168 B.C. or the Roman legions in 53 B.C. and A.D. 378 or the Egyptian Mamlūks in A.D. 1516–17 and A.D. 1798. The disaster at Pydna cost Macedon her political independence; the disaster at Adrianople was surmounted by the Roman Empire at the price of 'scrapping' the defeated legionary and enlisting the victorious cataphract in his place; the French repetition of the original Ottoman blow was needed in order to remove the Mamlūk incubus, once for all, from the backs of an Egyptian peasantry which managed to survive the French and the Ottoman as well as the Mamlūk domination. On the other hand the disaster which was the end of the Assyrian military power capped the destruction of the Assyrian war-machine with the extinction of the Assyrian state and the extermination of the Assyrian people. In 614–610 B.C. a community which had been in existence for more than two thousand years,[2] and had been playing an ever more dominant part in South-Western Asia over a period of some two and a half centuries, was blotted out almost completely.

'The noise of a whip and the noise of the rattling of the wheels and of the pransing horses and of the jumping chariots.

'The horseman lifteth up both the bright sword and the glittering spear; and there is a multitude of slain and a great number of carcases; and there is none end of their corpses—they stumble upon their corpses. . . .

'Thy shepherds slumber, O King of Assyria; thy nobles shall dwell in

[1] In 853 B.C. Ben-Hadad and Ahab were fighting side by side against Shalmaneser III at the Battle of Qarqar (see IV. C (ii) (*b*) 1, p. 67, above; the present chapter, p. 473, footnote 3, and p. 475; and V. C (ii) (*b*), vol. vi, p. 303, below).

[2] For the appearance of the Assyrians in the 27th century B.C. upon the stage of Sumeric history in the rôle of pioneers who had been conquering a commercial empire by the arts of peaceful penetration, see I. C (i) (*b*), vol. i, p. 110, footnote 3, above.

the dust; thy people is scattered upon the mountains, and no man gathereth them.'[1]

In this instance the curse of the victim who had lived to see his oppressor's fall was fulfilled in the sequel with an extraordinary precision.[2] In 401 B.C., when Cyrus the Younger's ten thousand Greek mercenaries were retreating up the Tigris Valley from the battle-field of Cunaxa towards the Black Sea coast, they passed in succession the sites of Calah and Nineveh, and were struck with astonishment, not so much at the massiveness of the fortifications and the extent of the area which they embraced, as at the spectacle of such vast works of Man lying uninhabited. The weirdness of

[1] Nahum iii. 2–3 and 18. The burden of Nineveh is the whole theme of the book of the vision of Nahum the Elkoshite. The great event which evoked this paean of exultation from one of the victims of the vanquished Assyrian monster is described more briefly and dryly in the records of the Power which played the leading part in bringing Assyria to the ground. 'A great havoc of the people and the nobles took place; . . . they carried off the booty of the city, a quantity beyond reckoning; they turned the city into ruined mounds' is the account of the transaction that is given by the Babylonian Chronicle (quoted in *The Cambridge Ancient History*, vol. iii (Cambridge 1925, University Press), p. 127).

[2] It is instructive to compare with Nahum's exultation over the fall of Assyria a passage (Isaiah xiv. 4–12) in the same *genre* in which a later Syriac poet exults over the subsequent fall of Assyria's Babylonian 'successor-state', which had assumed Assyria's sinister role as far as the few then still surviving independent states in Syria were concerned.

'How hath the oppressor ceased! the golden city ceased!

'The Lord hath broken the staff of the wicked and the sceptre of the rulers.

'He who smote the people in wrath with a continual stroke, he that ruled the nations in anger, is persecuted, and none hindereth.

'The whole Earth is at rest and is quiet; they break forth into singing.

'Yea, the fir trees rejoice at thee, and the cedars of Lebanon, saying: "Since thou art laid down, no feller is come up against us."

'Hell from beneath is moved for thee to meet thee at thy coming: it stirreth up the dead for thee, even all the chief ones of the Earth; it hath raised up from their thrones all the kings of the nations.

'All they shall speak and say unto thee: "Art thou also become weak as we? Art thou become like unto us?"

'Thy pomp is brought down to the grave, and the noise of thy viols; the worm is spread under thee, and the worms cover thee.

'How art thou fallen from heaven, O Lucifer, son of the morning! How art thou cut down to the ground, which didst weaken the nations!'

In sheer poetic power this passage surpasses—at any rate in the seventeenth-century English version—the corresponding passages of Nahum; and in this we may discern a reflexion of the special experience of Judah; for Judah—in common with Tyre but unlike the great majority of the Syrian communities of the age—happened to suffer more cruelly at the hands of Assyria's Babylonian 'successor-state' than at the hands of Assyria herself. On the whole, however, the militarism of the Neo-Babylonian Empire, in spite of being in the Assyrian vein, was a mild affair compared with the Assyrian militarism which it replaced; and, notwithstanding the evil reputation which has been fastened upon him by his Jewish victims, Nebuchadnezzar, as well as Nabonidus, was much less addicted to the arts of war than to those of peace. In the light of this fact it is interesting to observe that this prophecy against Babylon in the Book of Isaiah was not confirmed so signally as Nahum's prophecy against Assyria was by the march of events. It is true that Babylon fell to Cyrus in 539 B.C. as Nineveh had fallen to Nabopolassar and Cyaxares in 612 B.C.; but there is no comparison between the two events. So far from being annihilated by Cyrus, the city of Babylon lived on to rise up in revolt against Darius and Xerxes, to welcome Alexander with open arms, and to enjoy an 'Indian Summer' of intellectual fraternization with Hellas before she peacefully faded out of existence—or, rather, drifted across from the banks of the Euphrates to the neighbouring banks of the Tigris, in order to become Seleucia-Ctesiphon—in the last century B.C., some five hundred years after her annihilation had been proclaimed in the Jewish poem here quoted.

these empty shells, which testified by their inanimate endurance to the vigour of a vanished life, is vividly conveyed by the literary art of a member of the Greek expeditionary force who has recounted its experiences. Yet what is still more astonishing to a modern Western reader of Xenophon's narrative[1]—acquainted, as he is, with the history of Assyria, thanks to the achievements of our modern Western archaeologists—is to find that, although Xenophon's imagination was deeply struck, and his curiosity keenly aroused, by the mystery of these deserted cities, he was unable to learn even the most elementary facts about their authentic history. Although the whole of South-Western Asia, from Jerusalem to Ararat and from Elam to Lydia, had been dominated and terrorized by the masters of these cities at a Time-distance of little more than two centuries from the date at which Xenophon passed that way, the best account that he is able to give of them—presumably on the authority of the Greek army's local guides—is more wildly fabulous than the account of the Egyptian Pyramid-Builders which has found its way into the work of Herodotus[2] after having travelled in the solvent waters of the stream of 'folk-memory'[3] for the length of little less than two and a half millennia. As Xenophon heard the story of Calah and Nineveh, these were two cities of the Medes which had been besieged by the Persians when Cyrus was wresting the empire from Astyages, and had been miraculously depopulated by divine intervention after the Persians had found themselves unable to take them by storm. Not even the bare name of Assyria was associated with the sites of her second and third capitals in the current legends, attaching to these sites, which came to the ears of the passing Greek inquirer.

'Where is the dwelling of the lions and the feedingplace of the young lions, where the lion, even the old lion, walked, and the lion's whelp, and none made them afraid?'[4]

As a matter of fact, if the Ten Thousand had happened to march up the right bank of the Tigris, instead of crossing, as they did, to the left bank at Sittace on the Babylon-Susa road, they would have passed the site of Asshur—the first and eponymous capital of the *Assyrium nomen*—and here they would have found, still squatting among the ruins,[5] a small and miserable population that had not yet forgotten its historical title to the Assyrian name.[6] Yet

[1] Xenophon: *Expeditio Cyri*, Book III, chap. iv, §§ 7–12.

[2] See III. C (i) (*d*), vol. iii, p. 214, above.

[3] The operation of 'folk-memory' is examined in V. C (ii) (*a*), Annex II, vol. vi, pp. 438–64, below.

[4] Nahum ii. 11.

[5] The city of Asshur was taken and sacked by the Medes in 614 B.C., two years before the sack of Nineveh.

[6] See *The Cambridge Ancient History*, vol. iii (Cambridge 1925, University Press), p. 130.

Xenophon's fabulous account of Calah and Nineveh is nearer to 'the philosophic truth' than our own archaeologists' discovery of the traces left by the squatters at Asshur; for in substance the catastrophe of 614–610 B.C. did wipe Assyria out; and in the Achaemenian Empire of Xenophon's day the surviving Assyrian helots were incomparably less conspicuous than the vestiges of the peoples round about, whom the Assyrian militarists had once trampled under foot and ground, as they thought, to powder. In an age when the very name and nationality of Nineveh or Calah were forgotten, Susa, which had been sacked by Asshurbanipal's army *circa* 639 B.C., was the capital of an empire whose effective dominion now extended, in almost every direction, an immense distance beyond the farthest points ever reached by Assyrian raiders. One of the subsidiary capitals of this empire was Babylon, which had been sacked by Sennacherib in 689 B.C. The Phoenician city-states, which the Assyrians had incessantly bullied and fleeced from the ninth century to the seventh, were now autonomous and contented members of a Syriac universal state;[1] and even the Syriac and Hittite communities of the interior, which had apparently been pounded into pulp by the Assyrian flail, had contrived to retain a semblance of their former statehood in the guise of hierocratically administered temple-states.[2] In fact, within two centuries of Assyria's fall it had become clear that the Assyrian militarists had done their work for the benefit of others, and for the greatest benefit of those whom they had used the most despitefully. In grinding down the highland peoples of the Zagros and the Taurus the Assyrians had opened a passage for the Cimmerian and Scythian Nomads to make their descent upon the Babylonic and Syriac worlds;[3] in deporting the broken peoples of Syria to the opposite extremity of their empire they had placed the Syriac Society in a position to encircle and eventually assimilate the Babylonic Society to which the Assyrians themselves belonged;[4]

[1] See V. C (i) (*c*) 2, vol. v, p. 123, footnote 2, below.

[2] See *The Cambridge Ancient History*, vol. iv (Cambridge 1926, University Press), pp. 187–8; Tarn, W. W.: *Hellenistic Civilisation* (London 1927, Arnold), pp. 114–16. The temple-state about which we have by far the fullest information, and which is also of unparalleled historical importance, is the one which was organized round the temple of Yahweh at Jerusalem in the fifth century B.C. But, though uniquely famous, this Judaean hierocracy was only one representative of a class. These post-Assyrian temple-states in South-Western Asia may be compared with the temple-states (Thebes, Heliopolis, Letopolis, Memphis) in the Egyptiac World which were the indigenous 'successor-states' of the Egyptian 'New Empire' (see IV. C (iii) (*c*) 2 (β), p. 422, footnote 3, above, and IV. C (iii) (*c*) 3 (β), pp. 515–17, below). There is a modern Western analogue of this in the crop of prince-bishoprics which made its appearance side by side with the secular 'successor-states' of the Holy Roman Empire after 'the Great Interregnum', and which ripened to harvest after the tribulation of the Thirty Years' War (see IV. C (iii) (*b*) 11, pp. 220–1, above).

[3] See II. D (v), vol. ii, p. 136, above.

[4] See I. C (i) (*b*), vol. i, pp. 79–81, and II. D (v), vol. ii, pp. 137–8, above, and V. C (i) (*c*) 2, vol. v, pp. 122–3, below.

in imposing a political unity upon the heart of South-Western Asia by main force they had prepared the ground for their own 'successor-states'—Media, Babylonia, Egypt, and Lydia—and for these successors' common heir, the Achaemenian Empire. Why was it that in the sequel to the long Assyrian terror the monster came off, as these comparisons and contrasts show, so very much worse than his victims?

The victims themselves, in retrospect, could only explain this tremendous περιπέτεια by invoking 'the Envy of the Gods'.

'Behold, the Assyrian was a cedar in Lebanon with fair branches and with a shadowing shroud and of an high stature; and his top was among the thick boughs. . . .

'The cedars in the garden of God could not hide him; the fir trees were not like his boughs, and the chesnut trees were not like his branches; nor any tree in the garden of God was like unto him in his beauty.

'I have made him fair by the multitude of his branches, so that all the trees of Eden, that were in the garden of God, envied him.

'Therefore thus saith the Lord God: "Because thou hast lifted up thyself in height, and he hath shot up his top among the thick boughs, and his heart is lifted up in his height—

' "I have therefore delivered him into the hand of the mighty one of the heathen; he shall surely deal with him; I have driven him out for his wickedness.

' "And strangers, the terrible of the nations, have cut him off and have left him; upon the mountains and in all the valleys his branches are fallen; and his boughs are broken by all the rivers of the land; and all the people of the Earth are gone down from his shadow and have left him." '[1]

Are we able in this instance to interpret the working of 'the Envy of the Gods' in terms of the stricken creature's own behaviour? At first sight the fate of Assyria does, indeed, seem difficult to comprehend; for her militarists cannot be convicted of the passive aberration to which we have attributed the undoing of the Macedonians and the Romans and the Mamlūks, who 'rested on their oars'. At the time when the Mamlūk and Roman and Macedonian war-machines each met with its fatal accident they were each of them long since static, hopelessly obsolete, and shockingly out of repair. On the other hand the Assyrian war-machine, which is singled out by the completeness of its final disaster, is also distinguished from these other war-machines—in what would seem to be the opposite sense—by the efficiency with which it was being perpetually overhauled and renovated and reinforced right down to the day of its destruction.[2] The fund of military genius which

[1] Ezekiel xxxi. 3 and 8–12.

[2] See Hunger, J.: *Heerwesen und Kriegführen der Assyrer auf der Höhe ihrer Macht* = *Der Alte Orient*, 12 Jahrgang, Heft 4 (Leipzig 1911, Hinrichs), p. 34.

produced the embryo of the hoplite in the fourteenth century B.C.,[1] on the eve of Assyria's first bid for predominance in South-Western Asia, and the embryo of the cataphract horse-archer in the seventh century B.C.,[2] on the eve of Assyria's own annihilation, was also productive throughout the seven intervening centuries, and never more so than in the final paroxysm of the four historic bouts in which the Assyrian militarism discharged itself upon the World.[3] The energetic inventiveness, and the restless zeal for improvements, which were the notes of the latter-day Assyrian êthos in its application to the Art of War, are attested unimpeachably by the series of bas-reliefs, found *in situ* in the royal palaces, in which the successive phases of the Assyrian military equipment and technique during the last three centuries of Assyrian history are recorded pictorially with careful precision and in minute detail.

On this evidence we can detect the following improvements between the end of the third bout, *circa* 825 B.C., and the end of the fourth bout just over two hundred years later. The mounted infantryman of Asshurnazirpal's day, who had been placed on horseback—no doubt, in imitation of the Nomads—without being relieved of the encumbrance of his infantryman's shield, has now turned into an embryonic cataphract who has discarded the shield in exchange for a flexible cuirass.[4] This equipment of the cavalry with body-armour has been made feasible by an improvement in the shape and material of the cuirass itself, which is now made of metal scales and is cut off at the waist, in substitution for the clumsy wadded or leathern kaftan, reaching from the neck to the knees, which had done duty for a cuirass in the earlier age.[5] The cavalryman's legs, which are thus left exposed, are protected in compensation by stockings reaching to the thighs and boots reaching to the calf; and the same footgear enables the infantry to operate in rough country with greater ease than in an age when

[1] See III. C (i) (*b*), vol. iii, p. 165, footnote 1, and IV. C (iii) (*c*) 2 (γ), in the present volume, p. 431, footnote 2, above.

[2] See IV. C (iii) (*c*) 2 (γ), p. 439, footnote 4, above.

[3] The first bout is signalized by the successive Assyrian offensives against the Mitannian Power in Mesopotamia and the Kassite Power in Babylonia in the fourteenth century B.C., and by Shalmaneser I's well-timed attack upon the Hittite World in the third decade of the thirteenth century, when Khatti was within an ace of breaking down under the long strain of her hundred years' war with 'the New Empire' of Egypt. The second bout is marked by Tiglath-Pileser I's momentary expansion to the Syrian coast of the Mediterranean at the turn of the twelfth and eleventh centuries. The third bout begins with Asshurnazirpal's repetition of Tiglath-Pileser I's exploit in 876 B.C., continues in Shalmaneser III's systematic and sustained attempt to complete the conquest of Syria, and gradually subsides, in the second half of the ninth century, after the check administered to Shalmaneser by the Syrian coalition at the Battle of Qarqar in 853 B.C. (see the references on p. 468, footnote 1, above). The fourth bout begins with the accession of Tiglath-Pileser III in 745 B.C. and goes on crescendo until the career of Assyria is cut short for ever in the grand finale of 614–10 B.C.

[4] Hunger, op. cit., p. 11. See also the present Study, IV. C (iii) (*c*) 2 (γ), p. 439, footnote 4, above.

[5] Hunger, op. cit., p. 17.

sandals had been the only alternative to going barefoot.[1] Within the same span of Time there have been a number of improvements in the war-chariots: for instance, an increase in the diameter of the wheels, in the height of the sides of the body, and in the number of the crew—the driver and the archer being now reinforced by a couple of shield-bearers.[2] There has also been an improvement in the shape of the wicker screens from behind which the foot-archers shoot.[3] Perhaps the greatest improvement of all, however, is one of which we are informed, not by the pictorial evidence of the bas-reliefs, but by the written word of the inscriptions; and this is the institution of a royal standing army, which was probably the work of either Tiglath-Pileser III (*regnabat* 747–727 B.C.) or Sargon (*regnabat* 722–705 B.C.). The standing army served as a nucleus, and not as a substitute, for the national militia on which the Assyrian Crown had previously depended for the recruitment of its field armies. Nevertheless the establishment of a standing army must have raised the general level of Assyrian military efficiency, and have insured that the technical improvements, mentioned above, should produce the maximum of effect.

By Asshurbanipal's time (*regnabat* 669–626 B.C.), on the eve of the great catastrophe, two centuries of steady progress in the Art of War had produced an Assyrian army which was as well prepared for every task as it was scientifically differentiated into a number of specialized arms. There were the chariotry and the demi-cataphract horse-archers; the heavy foot-archers, armoured from helmet to boots, and the light foot-archers who risked their lives in head-bands, loin-cloths, and sandals; the hoplites, armed like the heavy foot-archers, except that they carried spear and shield instead of bow and quiver; and the peltasts, likewise carrying spear and shield, but wearing, in lieu of a cuirass, a pectoral secured by crossed shoulder-straps.[4] There was probably also a corps of engineers, for there was certainly a siege-train—not, indeed, of catapults, but of battering-rams and rolling towers—and, when these engines had done their work, and the walls of the enemy fortress had been breached, the Assyrian directors of military operations knew how to cover the storming parties with volleys of arrows from massed batteries of archers. Thus fitted out, the Assyrian army was equally ready for siege operations, for mountain warfare, or for pitched battles on the plains; and its activism in the sphere of technique

[1] Hunger, op. cit., p. 11.
[2] Ibid., pp. 8–10.
[3] Ibid., p. 14.
[4] In Asshurbanipal's reign the Assyrian peltasts were further differentiated from the hoplites by being equipped with a crested helmet of an Urartian pattern akin to the Hellenic type, in lieu of the conical helmet which was the native Assyrian military headgear (*The Cambridge Ancient History*, vol. iii, p. 20).

was matched by an activism in tactics and strategy. The Assyrians were firm believers in the sovereign virtue of the offensive.[1]

'None shall be weary nor stumble among them; none shall slumber nor sleep; neither shall the girdle of their loins be loosed, nor the latchet of their shoes be broken;

'Whose arrows are sharp, and all their bows bent, their horses' hoofs shall be counted like flint, and their wheels like a whirlwind;

'Their roaring shall be like a lion, they shall roar like young lions; yea, they shall roar and lay hold of the prey, and shall carry it away safe, and none shall deliver it.'[2]

This was the spirit of the Assyrian army down to the last, as was shown by the account which it gave of itself in the Harran campaign of 610 B.C., when it was fighting for a lost cause, with the capital city of the Empire already taken by storm and blotted out. It will be apparent that the Assyrian army on the eve of its annihilation was not at all in the condition of the Macedonian and Roman and Mamlūk armies in 168 B.C. and A.D. 378 and A.D. 1798. Why, then, did it suffer a more appalling disaster than theirs? The answer is that the very activism of the Assyrian military spirit aggravated Assyria's doom when at last it closed in upon her.

In the first place the policy of the unremitting offensive, and the possession of a potent instrument for putting this policy into effect, led the Assyrian war-lords in the fourth and last bout of their militarism to extend their enterprises and commitments far beyond the limits within which their predecessors had kept. Assyria, as we have seen,[3] was subject to a perpetual prior call upon her military resources for the fulfilment of her task as warden of the marches of the Babylonic World against the barbarian highlanders in the Zagros and the Taurus on the one side and against the Aramaean pioneers of the Syriac Civilization on the other. In her three earlier bouts of militarism she had been content to pass from the defensive to the offensive on these two fronts, without pressing this offensive *à outrance* and without dissipating her forces in other directions. Even so, the third bout, which occupied the two middle quarters of the ninth century B.C., evoked in Syria the temporary coalition of Syrian states which checked the Assyrian advance at Qarqar in 853 B.C.,[4] and it was met in Armenia by the more formidable *riposte* of the foundation of the Kingdom of Urartu, an ex-barbarian military Power which now borrowed the Assyrians' culture in order to equip itself for resisting their aggression on equal terms.[5] In spite of these recent warnings, Tiglath-Pileser

[1] Hunger, op. cit., p. 34. [2] Isaiah v. 27–9. [3] In II. D (v), vol. ii, pp. 134–5, above.
[4] See IV. C (ii) (*b*) 1, vol. iv, p. 67, and the present chapter, p. 468, footnote 1, and p. 473, footnote 3, above, and V. C (ii) (*b*), vol. vi, p. 303, below.
[5] See II. D (v), vol. ii, p. 135, above.

III (*regnabat* 746–727 B.C.), when he inaugurated the last and greatest of the Assyrian offensives, allowed himself to harbour political ambitions and to aim at military objectives which brought Assyria into collision with three new adversaries—Babylonia, Elam, and Egypt—each of whom was potentially as great a military power as Assyria herself.

Tiglath-Pileser put a conflict with Egypt in store for his successors when he set himself to complete the subjugation of the petty states of Syria; for Egypt could not remain indifferent to an extension of the Assyrian Empire up to her own Asiatic frontiers, and she was in a position to frustrate or undo the Assyrian empire-builders' work unless and until they made up their minds to round it off by embarking on the more formidable enterprise of subjugating Egypt herself. Tiglath-Pileser's bold occupation of Philistia in 734 B.C. may have been a strategic master-stroke which was rewarded by the temporary submission of Samaria in 733 and the fall of Damascus in 732. But it led to Sargon's brush with the Egyptians in 720, and Sennacherib's in 700, on the Syro-Egyptian border; and these inconclusive encounters led on, in their turn, to Esarhaddon's conquest and occupation of Egypt, from the Delta to the Thebaid inclusive, in the campaigns of 675 and 674 and 671 B.C. Thereupon it became manifest that while the Assyrians were strong enough to rout Egyptian armies and occupy the land of Egypt and repeat the feat, they were not strong enough to hold Egypt down. Esarhaddon himself was once more on the march for Egypt when death overtook him in 669; and though the Egyptian insurrection which then broke out was successfully suppressed by Asshurbanipal in 667, he had to reconquer Egypt once again in 663. By this time the Assyrian Government itself seems to have realized that in Egypt it was engaged on Psyche's Task; and when Psammetichus unobtrusively expelled the Assyrian garrisons in 658–651 Asshurbanipal turned a blind eye to what was happening. In thus cutting his Egyptian losses the King of Assyria was undoubtedly wise; yet this wisdom after the event was a confession that the energies expended on five Egyptian campaigns had been wasted; and Asshurbanipal's withdrawal did not restore the *status quo ante* 675 B.C.; for the loss of Egypt in the fifth decade of the seventh century was a prelude to the loss of Syria in the next generation.

The ultimate consequences of Tiglath-Pileser's intervention in Babylonia were far graver than those of his forward policy in Syria, since they led, by a direct chain of cause-and-effect, to the catastrophe of 614–610 B.C.[1]

[1] This Assyro-Babylonian conflict has been touched upon, by anticipation, in II. D (v), vol. ii, pp. 135–6, and in IV. C (ii) (*b*) 2, in the present volume, pp. 101–2, above.

This Assyrian aggression in this quarter in 745 B.C. must have been difficult to reconcile with the treaty in which the Assyro-Babylonian frontier had been delimited by friendly agreement—and this along a line which was decidedly favourable to Assyria—in the opening decade of the eighth century B.C. Probably Tiglath-Pileser justified his action on the ground that the anarchy into which Babylonia had since fallen was spreading to the Assyrian side of the border; and, after marching in, he appears to have received some kind of mandate from the citizens of Babylon, who saw in this sovereign of a neighbouring sedentary kingdom of kindred culture a possible protector of civic life in Babylonia against the rising tide of local Aramaean and Chaldaean Nomadism. It may also be true that both Tiglath-Pileser and his successors were genuinely anxious to restrict the Assyrian commitments in Babylonia to a minimum, and to avoid annexation. Tiglath-Pileser himself in 745 left Nabopolassar, the reigning king of Babylonia, on his throne; and it was only after Nabopolassar's death eleven years later, and after the subsequent suppression of a consequent Chaldaean tribal insurrection against the Assyrian protectorate, that Tiglath-Pileser 'took the hands of Bel' in 729. This precedent was followed by Shalmaneser V; but it was not followed by Shalmaneser's successor Sargon until a second, and far more serious, Chaldaean insurrection forced Sargon, in his turn, to 'take the hands of Bel' in 710; and, even then, the Assyrian victor sought an understanding with the discomfited Chaldaean arch-insurgent Merodach-Baladan. Thereafter, when Sennacherib succeeded his father Sargon in 705, he deliberately abstained from assuming the Babylonian Crown; and, even when a fresh Chaldaean insurrection necessitated his intervention in Babylonia in 703, he conferred the Babylonian Crown first upon an Assyrianized Babylonian prince, and then upon an Assyrian prince who was not himself the heir to the Assyrian Throne. It was only after the great insurrection of 694–689 that Sennacherib formally put an end to the independence of Babylonia by installing his own son—and designated successor—Esarhaddon as Assyrian governor-general.

These facts certainly seem to testify to an Assyrian policy of moderation *vis-à-vis* Babylonia; but they afford still more conclusive evidence that the policy was a failure. Again and again the Assyrian Government's hand was forced by Chaldaean insurrections which only became more frequent and more formidable in the face of persistent Assyrian forbearance. And while the Assyrian intervention did perform the miracle of conjuring order out of a Babylonian chaos, this order, so far from being achieved under an Assyrian aegis, was the by-product of an anti-Assyrian movement which steadily grew in scope and lustily throve upon defeat.

The first stage in a process which continued for a century and culminated in a Medo-Babylonian grand alliance was the political unification of all the Chaldaean tribes of Babylonia between 731 and 721 B.C. under the leadership of the Chief of Bit Yakin, Merodach-Baladan. The next stage was an alliance between the Chaldaeans and the Kingdom of Elam, whose Government had been as seriously alarmed by Tiglath-Pileser's intervention in Babylonia as the Egyptians had been alarmed by his descent upon Philistia. Thanks to this Elamite alliance, Merodach-Baladan was able to enter the City of Babylon in 721 and to reign there as king of Babylonia for some twelve years, in spite of the fact that at this stage the citizens of the capital still felt the rule of the local Nomad more irksome than that of the foreign sedentary Power. Nor was Merodach-Baladan's career at an end when he was ejected from Babylon by the armies of Sargon in 710. After his Assyrian conqueror's death in 705 we find the indefatigable Chaldaean entering into relations with the Arabs of the Shāmīyah and the Hamād, and sending an embassy across their ranges to so distant a fellow enemy of Assyria as the King of Judah, Hezekiah. Thereafter, in 703, Merodach-Baladan succeeded in re-occupying Babylon with the aid of his Elamite allies; and although before the year was out he was ejected for the second time by force of Assyrian arms, and died a few years later as a refugee in Elam, the removal of the Chaldaean leader brought the Assyrian Government no nearer to a solution of the Chaldaean problem; for, with Elam still supporting them, the Chaldaean tribesmen successfully defied Sennacherib's efforts to put them out of action. When the Assyrian war-lord occupied and devastated their tribal lands in Babylonia proper, they took refuge among the marshes and mud-banks at the head of the Persian Gulf; and, when in 694 he built a fleet on the Tigris, manned it with Phoenician crews, and put the Assyrian army on board in order to destroy the Chaldaeans in their aquatic fastness by amphibious operations, he merely gave the Elamites the opportunity to fall upon his line of communications, enter Babylon, and carry his puppet-king of Babylonia away captive. Nor did it profit Sennacherib when he took his revenge next year by defeating the Elamites in the field and capturing, in his turn, the puppet whom they had set upon the Babylonian throne in his own puppet's place; for he failed to re-occupy Babylon; and the vacant throne was mounted by a man of character, Mushezib-Marduk, who succeeded in weaning the citizens of the capital from their pro-Assyrian policy.

This secession of the City of Babylon in 693 from the Assyrian to the Chaldaeo-Elamite camp was perhaps the decisive event in the long process of building up an anti-Assyrian front; for although the Assyrians were, as usual, victorious over the combined Chaldaean and Elamite forces, and were able in the end to teach Babylon a lesson by sacking her in 689, the lesson which she learnt was the opposite of that which her teachers intended. Through this impious outrage upon a city which was the cultural capital of their world, the Assyrians achieved a feat of political alchemy in Babylonia which the Babylonians could never have achieved for themselves. In the white heat of the common hatred which this Assyrian 'frightfulness' had now aroused among the ancient urban population as well as among the intrusive Nomads, citizens and tribesmen forgot the mutual antipathy which had hitherto divided them, and became fused together into a new Babylonian nation which could neither forget nor forgive what it had suffered at Assyrian hands, and which could never rest until it had brought its oppressor to the ground.

At this penultimate stage of the long and tragic process which Tiglath-Pileser III had unwittingly set in motion in 745 B.C., the anti-Assyrian feeling in Babylonia was so strong that it was able to dominate, and bend to its purpose, the soul of an Assyrian prince-of-the-blood who had been placed upon the Babylonian throne by *force majeure* and who was actually the brother of the reigning king of Assyria itself. *Circa* 654 B.C. Asshurbanipal found the existence of the Assyrian Empire threatened by a hostile coalition between the Babylonian Crown, the Chaldaean and Aramaean tribes of the Babylonian country-side, the Kingdom of Elam, the Northern Arabs, several South Syrian principalities, and the recently established 'successor-state' of the defunct Assyrian dominion over Egypt. This combine of anti-Assyrian forces, which was wider than any that had ever been brought together by Merodach-Baladan or by Mushezib-Marduk, was headed by Asshurbanipal's own brother, Shamash-shum-ukin; and his action will appear the more extraordinary when we consider that by that date he had been in peaceful occupation of the Babylonian Throne, with Asshurbanipal's goodwill, for some fifteen years, in execution of their father Esarhaddon's political testament. Moreover the arch-rebel's principal ally, Elam, had just received—perhaps as recently as the very year before Shamash-shum-ukin staked his fortunes on her support[1]—the heaviest defeat that had ever yet been inflicted upon her by Assyrian arms, a defeat in which the reigning king

[1] Asshurbanipal overthrew Teumman in 655 B.C.; Shamash-shum-ukin revolted against Asshurbanipal *circa* 654–653 B.C.

and his heir-apparent had been killed and both the royal cities captured. These facts give the measure of the strength of the Babylonian national movement that swept Shamash-shum-ukin off his feet.

In this crisis the Assyrian army was victorious once again. The traitor Shamash-shum-ukin escaped a worse fate by burning himself alive in his palace when Babylon was starved into surrender in 648; and *circa* 639 Elam was dealt such an annihilating blow by Assyrian arms that her derelict territory passed under the dominion of the Persian highlanders from her eastern hinterland and became the jumping-off ground from which the Achaemenidae leapt into an empty saddle when they made themselves masters of all South-Western Asia a century later. This sacrifice of the Babylonian nationalists' Assyrian and Elamite instruments in the war of 654–639 B.C. did not, however, prevent the Babylonian national movement itself from attaining its objective; for, if the Achaemenidae found the saddle empty in the sixth century, this was because the Assyrian rider had been thrown at last before the seventh century was out. Immediately after Asshurbanipal's death in 626 Babylonia revolted again under a new national leader; and this Nabopolassar completed the work which Merodach-Baladan had begun. In the new Kingdom of Media he found a more potent ally to fill the place of the defunct Kingdom of Elam; and Assyria, who had not recovered from the War of 654–639, was wiped out of existence in the war of 614–610 B.C. Even then, *in extremis*, the Assyrian army could still win victories in the field. With the help of Assyria's former vassals and present patrons the Saites, it drove the Babylonians back upon Harran in 610, at a stage in this war of annihilation when Harran itself, as well as Nineveh and Asshur, was already sacked and devastated, and when the army was fighting with its back to the Euphrates in the last unconquered corner of the Assyrian homeland; but this final victory must have been the Assyrian army's death agony, for this is the last recorded incident in the Assyrian military annals.

When we gaze back over the century and a half of ever more virulent warfare which begins with Tiglath-Pileser III's accession to the throne of Assyria in 745 B.C. and closes with a Babylonian Nebuchadnezzar's victory over an Egyptian Necho at Carchemish in 605, the historical landmarks which stand out the most prominently at first sight are the successive 'knock-out blows' by which Assyria destroyed entire communities—razing cities to the ground and carrying whole peoples away captive. We think of the sack of Damascus in 732; the sack of Samaria in 722; the sack of Musasir in 714; the sack of Babylon in 689; the sack of Sidon in 677; the sack of Memphis in 671; the sack of Thebes in 663; the sack of Susa *circa* 639. Of all the capital cities of all the states within reach of Assyria's arm, only Tyre and Jerusalem remained inviolate on the eve of the sack of Nineveh in 612. The loss and misery which Assyria inflicted on her neighbours is beyond calculation; and yet the legendary remark of the canting schoolmaster to the boy whom he is whipping—'It hurts you less than it hurts me'—would be a more pertinent critique of Assyrian military activities than the unashamedly truculent and naïvely self-complacent narratives in which the Assyrian war-lords have presented their own account of their performances for the instruction of Posterity.

The full and bombastic Assyrian record of victories abroad is significantly supplemented by rarer and briefer notices of troubles at home that give us some inkling of the price at which the victories were purchased; and, when we examine this domestic chronicle of Assyria at the height of her military power, we shall no longer find it strange that her victoriousness was eventually the death of her.

An increasing excess of military strain revenged itself in an increasing frequency of palace revolutions and peasant revolts. As early as the close of the second bout of aggression in the ninth century B.C. we find Shalmaneser III dying in 827 with his son on the war-path against him, and Nineveh, Asshur, and Arbela in rebellion. Asshur rebelled again in 763–762, Arrapka in 761–760, Gozan in 759; and in 746 the rebellion of Calah, the Assyrian capital of the day, was followed by the extermination of the ruling dynasty. Tiglath-Pileser III (*regnabat* 745–727 B.C.) was a *novus homo* who could not conceal his provenance under the borrowed cloak of an historic name; and, if he was also the Assyrian Marius, the Roman analogy suggests that the establishment of a professional standing army is to be taken as a symptom of an advanced stage of social disintegration. We know that in the Italy of Marius's day it was the ruin of a warlike peasantry, which had been uprooted from the soil by perpetual calls to military service on ever more distant campaigns, that made a standing army both possible and necessary—possible because there was now a reservoir of unemployed 'man-power' to draw upon, and necessary because these men who had lost their livelihood on the land must be provided with alternative employment if they were to be restrained from venting their unhappiness and resentment through the channel of revolution. We may discern in the establishment of the Assyrian standing army a parallel attempt to find the same military solution for the same social problem. This military solution, however, was no more successful in allaying the domestic troubles of Tiglath-

Pileser's Assyria than it was in allaying those of Marius's Italy. Tiglath-Pileser's successor Shalmaneser V (*regnabat* 727–722 B.C.) seems to have fallen foul of the City of Asshur, like Tiglath-Pileser's predecessors. Sennacherib in 681 was murdered by one of his own sons, who was apparently hand in glove with the Babylonian nationalists; and we have seen already how Asshurbanipal's throne and empire were threatened by the action of his brother Shamash-shum-ukin, King of Babylon, in 654, when this renegade Assyrian prince placed himself at the head of an anti-Assyrian coalition. Therewith the two streams of domestic *stasis* and foreign warfare merge into one; and after Asshurbanipal's death this swells into a mighty river whose rushing waters bear Assyria away to her now inevitable doom. During the last years of Assyrian history the domestic and the foreign aspect of Assyria's disintegration are hardly distinguishable.[1]

The approaching doom cast its shadow over the soul of Asshurbanipal himself in his declining years.

> 'The rules for making offerings to the dead and libations to the ghosts of the kings my ancestors, which had not been practised, I reintroduced. I did well unto god and man, to dead and living. Why have sickness, ill-health, misery and misfortune befallen me? I cannot away with the strife in my country and the dissensions in my family. Disturbing scandals oppress me alway. Misery of mind and of flesh bow me down; with cries of woe I bring my days to an end. On the day of the City-God, the day of the festival, I am wretched; Death is seizing hold on me and bears me down. With lamentation and mourning I wail day and night; I groan: "O God, grant even to one who is impious that he may see Thy light." How long, O God, wilt Thou deal thus with me? Even as one who hath not feared god and goddess am I reckoned.'[2]

This confession is remarkable in its unconventionality and moving in its sincerity and even pathetic in its bewilderment, but above all it is illuminating in its blindness. When this mood overtook him, did the last of the Assyrian war-lords never find himself silently reciting that terrible catalogue of cities sacked and peoples wiped out by Assyrian arms—a list which concluded with his own sack of Susa and annihilation of Elam? Or was the burden of this memory so intolerable that the tormented militarist thrust it from him, in desperation, whenever it threatened to overwhelm him?

[1] This ultimate fusion between the foreign wars and the domestic troubles of Assyria is an example of that transference of the field of action from the Macrocosm to the Microcosm which we have studied in III. C (i) (*d*), vol. iii, pp. 192–217, above. In detail, the transmutation of the Assyro-Babylonian conflict into a civil war between the two Assyrian brothers, King Asshurbanipal of Nineveh and King Shamash-shum-ukin of Babylon, may be compared with the transmutation of the Romano-Punic conflict over Sicily into the Sicilian slave-wars (III. C (i) (*d*), vol. iii, pp. 198–9, above).

[2] This passage from Asshurbanipal's own records is quoted in *The Cambridge Ancient History*, vol. iii, p. 127.

His successor Sin-shar-ishkun, at any rate, must have lived through a moment when these haunting recollections closed in on him and would not be denied, as the Athenians were beset by the ghosts of their misdeeds when they received the news of the Battle of Aegospotami.

'At Athens the disaster was announced by the arrival of the *Paralus*,[1] and a wail spread from the Peiraeus through the Long Walls into the city as the news passed from mouth to mouth. That night no one slept. Besides mourning for the dead they mourned far more bitterly for themselves, for they expected to suffer the fate which they had inflicted upon the Melians (who were colonists of the Lacedaemonians) when they had besieged and captured their city, and upon the Histiaeans, the Scionians, the Toronians, the Aeginetans and many other Hellenic peoples. Next morning they held an assembly in which it was decided to block up all the harbours except one, to clear the fortifications for action, to dispose troops to man them, and to put the city into a thorough state of defence for the eventuality of a siege.'[2]

As the Athenian dêmos felt and acted at this dreadful moment in 405 B.C., the last king of Assyria must have felt and acted in 612 B.C., when he received the news that his Scythian allies, who had been his last hope of worldly salvation, had gone over to the enemy and that the united forces of the hostile coalition were closing in irresistibly upon Nineveh. The rest of the story is not the same in the two cases; for the Athenian dêmos capitulated and was spared by the generosity of the victors, while King Sin-shar-ishkun in Nineveh stood a siege, held out to the bitter end, and perished with his people when the city was taken by storm at the third assault. Thus the doom which Asshurbanipal had deprecated overwhelmed his successor and was not averted either by Asshurbanipal's tardy contrition or by his partial conversion from the works of War to the arts of Peace. Asshurbanipal's learned library of Babylonic literature (an Assyrian museum of a culture which an Assyrian militarism had blighted) and his exquisite bas-reliefs (designed by living Assyrian artists, and depicting the scientific slaughter of man and beast by the Assyrian military technique) had made of Nineveh by the year 612 B.C. a treasure-house which is not altogether incomparable with the Athens of 405–404. The treasures of Nineveh were buried under her ruins to enrich a remote Posterity in the heyday of a civilization which does not reckon the Babylonic Society among its forebears. But, if Nineveh perished where Athens survived, this was because Assyria had already committed suicide before her material destruction over-

[1] The *Paralus* and the *Salaminia* were the two fastest sailers in the Athenian navy, and were used for carrying dispatches.

[2] Xenophon: *Hellenica*, Book II, chap. 2, §§ 3–4.

took her. The clearly attested progress of the Aramaic language at the expense of the native Akkadian in the Assyrian homeland during the last century and a half of Assyria's existence as a state shows that the Assyrian people was being peacefully supplanted by the captives of the Assyrian bow and spear in an age when the Assyrian military power stood at its zenith.[1] Depopulation was the price which had to be paid for militarism, and it was a price that was ultimately as ruinous for the Assyrian army as for the rest of the Assyrian body social. The indomitable warrior who stood at bay in the breach at Nineveh in 612 B.C. was 'a corpse in armour', whose frame was only held erect by the massiveness of the military accoutrements in which this *felo de se* had already smothered himself to death. When the Median and Babylonian storming party reached that stiff and menacing figure, and sent it clattering and crashing down the moraine of ruined brickwork into the fosse below, they did not suspect that their terrible adversary was no longer a living man at the moment when they struck their daring, and apparently decisive, blow.

The Burden of Nineveh.

We have sketched our portrait of the Assyrian militarism at full length because it is the prototype of so many signal examples of the same aberration. The tableau of the 'corpse in armour' conjures up a vision of the Spartan phalanx on the battlefield at Leuctra in 371 B.C.,[2] and of the Janissaries in the trenches before Vienna in A.D. 1683.[3] The ironic fate of the militarist who is so intemperate in waging wars of annihilation against his neighbours that he deals unintended destruction to himself recalls the self-inflicted doom of the Carolingians or the Timurids, who built up great empires out of the agony of their Saxon or Persian victims, only to provide rich spoils for Scandinavian or Uzbeg adventurers[4] who lived to see the empire-builders pay for their imperialism by falling from world power to impotence within the span of a single lifetime.

Another form of suicide which the Assyrian example calls to mind is the self-destruction of those militarists—be they barbarians or people of higher culture with a capacity for putting their talents to a better use—who break into, and break up, some universal

[1] See I. C (i) (*b*), vol. i, p. 79, above, and V. C (i) (*c*) 2, vol. v, p. 119, and V. C (i) (*d*) 6 (γ), vol. v, pp. 487–91 and 499, footnote, 2 below.

[2] See Part III. A, vol. iii, pp. 73–4, above.

[3] See Part III. A, vol. iii, pp. 46–7, above.

[4] For the collapse of the Carolingian Empire see II. D (v), vol. ii, p. 167; II. D (vii), vol. ii, pp. 343–5 and 368; and IV. C (iii) (*c*) 2 (β), in the present volume, pp. 322–3, above, and the present chapter, pp. 488–90, and IV. C (iii) (*c*) 3 (β), p. 523, below; for the collapse of the Timurid Empire see I. C (i) (*b*), Annex I, vol. i, pp. 368–77, and Part III. A, Annex II, vol. iii, p. 447, above.

state or other great empire that has been giving a spell of peace to the peoples and lands over which it has spread its aegis. The conquerors ruthlessly tear the imperial mantle into shreds in order to expose the millions of human beings whom it has sheltered to the terrors of darkness and the shadow of death,[1] but the shadow descends inexorably upon the criminals as well as upon their victims. Demoralized on the morrow of their victory by the splendour and the vastness of their prize, these new masters of a ravished world are apt, like the Kilkenny cats, to perform 'the friendly office' for one another until not one brigand in the band is left alive to feast upon the plunder.[2]

We may watch how the Macedonians, when they have overrun the Achaemenian Empire, and have pressed on beyond its farther frontiers into India, within the eleven years following Alexander's passage of the Hellespont, next turn their arms with equal ferocity against one another during the forty-two years intervening between Alexander's death in 323 B.C. and the overthrow of Lysimachus at Corupedium in 281 B.C. The grim performance was repeated a thousand years later in another passage of Syriac history, when the Primitive Muslim Arabs emulated—and thereby undid—the Hellenic Macedonians' work by overrunning in twelve years the Roman and Sasanian dominions in South-Western Asia over almost as wide a sweep of territory as had once been conquered in eleven years by Alexander from the Achaemenidae.[3] In this Arab case the twelve years of conquest were followed by the twenty-four years of fratricidal strife which began with the assassination of the Caliph 'Uthmān in A.D. 656 and culminated in the martyrdom of the Prophet's grandson Husayn in A.D. 680. Once again the conquerors of South-Western Asia fell on one another's swords; and the glory and profit of rebuilding a Syriac universal state[4] which Alexander had overthrown was left to the usurping Umayyads and to the interloping 'Abbasids, instead of falling to those

[1] Luke i. 79.

[2] The proneness of the victorious barbarian war-bands to exterminate one another has been noticed already in I. C (i) (*a*), vol. i, pp. 58–9, above; see further V. C (i) (*c*) 3, vol. v, pp. 221–2, below.

[3] For the Primitive Muslim Arabs' feat of conquering the Oriental provinces of the Roman Empire with one hand and the whole of the Sasanian Empire with the other hand simultaneously, between A.D. 632 and A.D. 643, see I. C (i) (*b*), vol. i, p. 73, above. In these twelve years of conquest the Arabs emulated the achievement of the Macedonians in 334–323 B.C. without quite equalling it. While the larger part of the area conquered was the same, the Arabs fell short of their Macedonian predecessors both on the north-west and on the north-east. On the north-west they did not win any permanent foothold in the Anatolian Peninsula; on the north-east they did not begin the conquest of the Oxus-Jaxartes Basin until more than half a century, or complete it until more than a century, had passed since their occupation of the north-eastern frontier fortresses of the Sasanian Empire in A.D. 643–51 (see II. D (vii), vol. ii, pp. 375–84, above).

[4] For the Arab Caliphate as a 'reintegration' or 'resumption' of the Achaemenian Empire, which had been the first essay in a Syriac universal state, see I. C (i) (*b*), vol. i, pp. 75–7, above.

companions and descendants of the Prophet whose lightning conquests had prepared the way. The same spectacle is presented in the New World when the Aztecs and the Incas go down before the Spaniards. The Spanish *conquistadores* of the Mexic and the Andean universal state overran two continents—from Florida to the Isthmus, and from the Isthmus to Chile—only to fight over the spoils as ferociously as the companions of Muhammad or the companions of Alexander; and the Macedonian war-lord in his grave was not so powerless to maintain discipline among the troops that had once followed him in the field[1] as was a living sovereign at Madrid to impose the king's peace upon the adventurers who paid him a nominal allegiance on the other side of the Atlantic. The same suicidal Assyrian vein of militarism was displayed by the barbarians who overran the derelict provinces of a decadent Roman Empire. The Visigoths were overthrown by the Franks and the Arabs; the smaller fry among the English 'successor-states' in Britain were devoured by Mercia and Wessex; the Merovingians were brushed aside by the Carolingians, and the Umayyads by the 'Abbasids.[2] And this suicidal ending of our classic example of a 'heroic age' is characteristic, in some degree, of the latter end of all the Völkerwanderungen that have overrun the domains of other decrepit universal states.

There is another variety of militaristic aberration of which we shall also find the prototype in the Assyrian militarism when we envisage Assyria not as an artificially isolated entity in herself, but in her proper setting as an integral part of a larger body social which we have called the Babylonic Society.[3] In this Babylonic World Assyria was invested, as we have seen, with the special function of serving as a march whose primary duty was to defend not only herself, but also the rest of the society in which she lived and had her being, against the predatory barbarian highlanders from the east and the north and the aggressive Aramaean pioneers of the Syriac Civilization from the opposite quarters of the compass.[4] In articulating a march of this Assyrian kind out of a previously undifferentiated social fabric, a society stands to benefit in all its members; for while the march itself is stimulated in so far as it responds successfully to the challenge—which it has now taken upon itself—of resisting external pressures,[5] the interior—which

[1] In the fratricidal wars between the diadochi of Alexander the royal secretary, Eumenes of Cardia, was able to make good the prestige which he forfeited in the eyes of the Macedonian Argyraspides on account of his own non-Macedonian birth by continuing to pitch the royal tent as though Alexander were still alive and in the army's midst. (See Plutarch's *Life of Eumenes*, chap. 13.)

[2] See I. C (i) (*a*), vol. i, p. 58, above.

[3] For the sense in which the term is used in this Study see I. C (i) (*b*), vol. i, pp. 115–19, above.

[4] See II. D (v), vol. ii, pp. 133–7, above.

[5] For the stimulus of pressures see II. D (v), *passim*, in vol. ii, above.

the march now shields—is relieved of pressure in a corresponding degree, and is thereby set free to face other challenges and accomplish other tasks. This division of labour is salutary so long as the march continues to direct its specialized military prowess exclusively to its appointed task of repelling the external enemy. So long as they are used for this socially legitimate purpose, the military virtues need not be socially destructive—even though the necessity of bringing them into play at all may be a lamentable testimony to the imperfection of human nature in those generations of men who have been setting their feet upon the lower rungs of the ladder of Civilization during these last six thousand years. But these virtues, such as they are, become fatally transformed into the vice of Militarism, in the sinister sense, if ever the frontiersmen turn the arms which they have learnt to use in warfare with the outsider beyond the pale against the members of their own society whom it is their proper task to defend and not to attack.

The evil of this aberration is not so much that it exposes the society as a whole to the assaults of the external enemy whom the frontiersmen have hitherto kept at bay; for the frontiersmen seldom turn against their own kith and kin until they have established so great an ascendancy over their proper adversaries that their hands are free for other mischief and their ambitions fired for aiming at greater objectives. Indeed, when a march turns and rends the interior of its own society, it usually manages to hold the external enemy off with its left hand while it is waging a fratricidal war with its right. The deadly harm of this misdirection of military energies lies not so much in the opening of the gates to an alien invader—though this is sometimes one of the incidental consequences in the end—as in the betrayal of a trust and in the precipitation of an internecine conflict between two parties whose natural relation with each other is to dwell in unity.[1] When a march turns against its own interior, it is taking the offensive in what is really a civil war; and it is notorious that civil wars are waged with greater bitterness and ferocity than any others. This explains the momentousness of the consequences that ultimately followed from the action of Tiglath-Pileser III in 745 B.C., when he turned his Assyrian arms against Babylonia instead of continuing to exercise them exclusively against Nairi and Aram, which were their legitimate field; and we shall see, from a survey of other instances which this Assyrian prototype calls to mind, that the denouement of the ensuing Assyro-Babylonian hundred years' war, catastrophic as it was,

[1] 'Behold, how good and how pleasant it is for brethren to dwell together in unity' (Psalm cxxxiii. 1) is even more eminently true of the relations between communities than of those between individuals in a human society.

was not peculiar to this particular case. The aberration of the march which turns against the interior is, in its very nature, disastrous for the society as a whole; and it is destructive, above all, to the party which commits the original act of ὕβρις. When a sheep-dog who has been bred and trained to be the shepherd's partner lapses into the êthos and behaviour of the wolves whom it is his duty to chevy away, and betrays his trust by harrying the sheep on his own account, he works far worse havoc than any genuine wolf could work so long as a loyal sheep-dog was snapping at his flanks; but at the same time it is not the flock that suffers the most heavily from the catastrophe which follows the sheep-dog's treachery. The flock is decimated but survives; the dog is destroyed by his outraged master; and the frontiersman who turns against his own society is dooming himself to inexorable destruction because he is striking at the source from which his own life springs. He is like a sword-arm that plunges the blade which it wields into the body of which it is a member; or like a woodman who saws off the branch on which he is sitting, and so comes crashing down with it to the ground while the mutilated tree-trunk remains still standing.

Charlemagne.

It was perhaps an intuitive sense of the perversity of this misdirection of energies that moved the Austrasians to protest so vehemently in A.D. 754 against their war-lord Pepin's decision to respond to Pope Stephen's call to arms against their brethren the Lombards. The Papacy had turned its eyes towards this Transalpine Power, and had whetted Pepin's ambition by anointing him king in 749[1] and crowning him on the eve of the projected Italian expedition, because Austrasia in Pepin's generation had distinguished herself by her prowess in serving as a march of Western Christendom on two fronts: against the pagan Saxon barbarians who were pushing their way towards the Rhine from the no-man's-land of Northern Europe,[2] and against the Muslim Arab conquerors of North-West Africa and the Iberian Peninsula who were pressing on across the Pyrenees.[3] In 754 the Austrasians were invited to divert their energies from the fields in which they had just been finding their true mission, and to inflict

[1] The ceremony on this occasion was performed by the Englishman Boniface, the apostle of the Papacy in Transalpine Europe. The subsequent crowning of Pepin in A.D. 754 was performed by the Pope in person at St. Denis.

[2] See II. D (v), vol. ii, pp. 167–8, above.

[3] See II. D (v), vol. ii, pp. 203–4; II. D (vii), vol. ii, pp. 361–2 and 378–81; and II. D (vii), Annex IV, vol. ii, pp. 427–33, above; and V. C (i) (c) 3, vol. v, pp. 221–2, below.

upon the Lombards in Italy the fate which Austrasian arms had prevented the Arabs and the Saxons from inflicting upon the Franks themselves in Gaul. The misgivings of the Austrasian rank-and-file over this Italian adventure were proved by the event to be better justified than their leader's appetite for it; for in overriding the objections of his henchmen King Pepin forged the first link in a chain of military and political commitments which bound Austrasia to Italy ever more tightly. Pepin's Italian campaigns against Aistulf in 755 and 756 led on to Charlemagne's Italian campaign against Desiderius in 773–4—notwithstanding the effort of Charlemagne's mother and Pepin's widow Queen Bertrade to heal a breach between Frank and Lombard which King Pepin had opened against his people's will. When Bertrade arranged a marriage between her own and Pepin's son, who had now succeeded his father, and the daughter of Aistulf's successor Desiderius, Charlemagne repudiated his Lombard wife Desiderata and fulfilled his own father's ambitions by conquering his wife's father's kingdom outright. But Charlemagne's seizure of the Lombard Crown did not dispose of the Italian question or relieve the Transalpine Power of its ultramontane anxieties. In extinguishing the independence of the Lombard Kingdom Charlemagne saddled his own house irrevocably with the burden of defending and controlling the Papacy; and his protectorate over the Ducatus Romanus involved him in more distant complications with Lombard principalities and East Roman outposts in the South of Italy. Even when, on the fourth of the expeditions which he was compelled to make to Rome, he attained the apogee of his outward success in being crowned by the Pope, and acclaimed by the Roman people, as Augustus, the honour cost him the annoyance of a diplomatic conflict with the Court of Constantinople which dragged on for more than ten years.[1]

The true verdict on Charlemagne's Italian policy is given by the chronological table of the acts of his reign, which shows how these ultramontane commitments repeatedly diverted him—and this often at critical moments—from his major military task of prosecuting the Great Saxon War. After throwing down the gauntlet to the Saxons by marching into the heart of their country, and hewing down the Irminsul, in 772, Charlemagne disappeared beyond the Alps during 773 and 774, and so left the way open for the Saxons in the latter year to take reprisals on Hessen. Thereafter the would-be 'knock-out blow' of 775–6 had to be suspended in the spring of the latter year while the smiter of the Saxons went off on a second ultramontane expedition to put down a rebellion raised by

[1] See IV. C (iii) (*c*) 2 (*β*), p. 328, footnote 3, above.

Hrodgaud, the Lombard Duke of Friuli. In the middle of the next and most formidable phase of the war, in which the Saxons were led for eight years (777–85) by Widukind—a captain whose strategy was the offensive defensive—Charlemagne had to pay the third visit to Italy, and second to Rome, of his reign; and the lull in the Saxon War which followed the submission of Widukind in 785 gave no rest to Austrasian arms, for the year 787 saw Charlemagne pay his third visit to Rome, lead an inconclusive expedition against the South Lombard Duchy of Benevento, and impose his authority by a military demonstration upon the Lombards' old friends, and his own restive vassals, the Bavarians. The fourth and last phase of the Saxon War, in which the conquered but uncowed barbarians made a desperate and long-drawn-out effort to throw off the Austrasian yoke with the aid of the Frisians (*nitebantur* A.D. 792–804), was in progress during Charlemagne's fourth visit to Rome, and fifth to Italy, in 800–1.

We have already had occasion to notice how grievously this war of attrition against the Saxons exhausted the Carolingian Power.[1] The exhaustion declared itself in the break-up of the Carolingian Empire on the morrow of Charlemagne's death, and in the Scandinavian *revanche* for the Saxons' sufferings—a counter-attack which was opened even before the Austrasian conqueror of the Saxons had departed this life. It must also be remembered that the Saxon front beyond the Rhine was not the only frontier of Western Christendom for which Austrasia was responsible; she was likewise the warden of the Arab frontier beyond the Pyrenees; and, when Charlemagne overthrew the Lombard Kingdom and reduced the Bavarians to obedience, he inherited from his vanquished adversaries the wardenship of a third frontier, the Avar front beyond the Styrian Alps. It may have been inevitable that in the second year of his deadly duel with Widukind Charlemagne should have been drawn away into the Transpyrenaean expedition which ended so unfortunately at Roncesvalles; but with a Transpyrenaean as well as a Transrhenane front to hold, and with disaffection always smouldering in Aquitaine, it is evident that Charlemagne could not afford in any case to enter into new commitments on the Italian side of the Alps; and his Italian policy became suicidal when it was combined, as it was, with an ambitious forward movement on both the Transalpine fronts which the great Austrasian militarist had inherited from his forebears. It was the wantonly imposed burden of Charlemagne's five Italian expeditions that aggravated to breaking-point the load which weighed upon Austrasia's back.

[1] See the references on p. 484, footnote 4, above.

Timur Lenk.

If Charlemagne broke Austrasia's back by turning her arms against the Lombard and Bavarian interior of a nascent Western Christendom when the whole of her strength was required for her terrific struggle with the Saxons beyond her Rhenish pale, Timur, in like fashion, broke the back of his own Transoxania by squandering in aimless expeditions into Iran and 'Irāq and India and Anatolia and Syria the slender reserves of Transoxanian strength which ought to have been concentrated upon Timur's proper mission of imposing his peace on the Eurasian Nomads.

We have seen in an earlier part of this Study[1] how Timur acquitted himself of that mission. In the course of nineteen years (A.D. 1362–80) of strenuous campaigning he had repulsed the attempts of the Chaghatāy Nomads to reconquer the Transoxanian oases; assumed the offensive in his turn against the foiled invaders on their native ranges in 'Mughalistan'; and rounded off his own dominions in the Eurasian march of the Iranic World by liberating the oases of Khwārizm on the Lower Oxus from the Nomads of Jūjī's appanage. Upon the completion of this great task in A.D. 1380 Timur had a greater prize within his reach—no less a prize than the succession to the Eurasian Empire of Chingis Khan—for in Timur's generation the Eurasian Nomads were in retreat on all sectors of the long frontier between the Desert and the Sown.[2] While Timur was winning his victory over the hordes of 'Mughalistan' and Qipchāq on the sector between the Pamirs and the Caspian, the Moldavians and Lithuanians[3] and Cossacks[4] were cutting short the appanage of Jūjī at its opposite extremity in the great western bay of the Steppe between the Iron Gates of the Danube and the Cataracts of the Dniepr; the Muscovites were shaking off the yoke of the Qipchāq horde; and the Chinese were driving out the Mongol Khāqāns—the senior branch of Chingis Khan's house, and the nominal overlords of all the Chingisid appanages—from Qubilay's capital at Peking[5] into a no-man's-land beyond the outer face of the Great Wall from which these barbarian intruders had originally come. In every quarter the Nomads were on the run, and the next chapter in the history of Eurasia[6] was to be a race between the

[1] Part II. D (v), vol. ii, pp. 146–8, above.

[2] See Part III. A, Annex II, vol. iii, p. 439, above.

[3] See II. D (v), vol. ii, p. 172, above. [4] See II. D (v), vol. ii, p. 155, above.

[5] See II. D (v), vol. ii, p. 121, above, and V. C (i) (*c*) 4, vol. v, p. 351, and V. C (ii) (*a*), vol. vi, p. 193, below.

[6] The word is used in this Study to designate the area covered by the Eurasian Steppe together with the ring of sedentary countries round its fringes that are subject to the Steppe's influence. The region thus defined has a much more genuine climatic, social, and historical individuality than the European and Asiatic continents which loom so large in the text-books of geography; for the Ural River—which every schoolboy knows by name as the boundary between Asia and Europe—is not a frontier in any

resurgent sedentary peoples round about for the prize of Chingis' heritage. In this competition the Moldavians and Lithuanians were too remote to be in the running; the Muscovites were wedded to their forests and the Chinese to their fields; the Cossacks and the Transoxanians were the only competitors who had succeeded in making themselves at home on the Steppes without uprooting the sedentary foundations of their own way of life.[1] Each in their own way, they had acquired something of the strength of Nomadism and had combined this with the strength of a sedentary civilization. To a sharp-eyed observer in A.D. 1380 it might have seemed as though the victory in the race for the dominion of Eurasia must lie between these two runners; and at that moment the Transoxanian competitor had, to all appearance, by far the better chance, for, besides being stronger in himself and nearer to the heart of the Steppe, he was also the first in the field, while, as the recognized champion of the Sunnah, he had potential partisans among the sedentary Muslim communities who were the outposts of Islam on the opposite coasts of the Steppe: in Qāzān and Krim on the one hand, and in Kansu and Shensi on the other.

For an instant Timur appeared to appreciate his opportunity and to grasp at it with determination. The civil war between rival sections of the Qipchāq horde, which had permitted Timur to conquer Khwārizm and the Muscovites to assert their independence, was duly taken advantage of by Timur for a more ambitious purpose than the mere acquisition of a single border province. He intervened in the internal affairs of Qipchāq by giving his support to one of the rival pretenders, Toqatmysh; it was thanks to Timur's aid that Toqatmysh was able in the course of the years 1378–82 to unite the whole of Jūjī's appanage under his own leadership, reduce the Muscovites to obedience again by taking and burning Moscow itself, and inflict a heavy defeat upon the Lithuanians.[2] All this was done by Toqatmysh as Timur's vassal, and the effect was to make Timur master, directly or indirectly, of the whole western half of the Eurasian Steppe with its surrounding sedentary dependencies, from the Irtish to the Dniepr and from the Pamirs to the Urals. At this juncture, however, the Transoxanian conqueror of the Eurasian no-man's-land suddenly turned right-about, directed his arms towards the interior of the Iranic World, and devoted the remaining twenty-four years of his life to a series of barren and destructive campaigns in this quarter. Even when

significant sense. The genuine frontiers that divide the Eurasian Steppe from China, South-Western Asia, Western Europe, and Russia are described in Part III. A, Annex II, vol. iii, pp. 399–402, above.

[1] For the Cossack way of life see II. D (v), vol. ii, pp. 155–7, above.

[2] For these events see II. D (v), vol. ii, p. 147, above.

Toqatmysh, emboldened by seeing his suzerain fly off at a tangent, unintentionally drew him back into his proper field through an act of audacious aggression, Timur obstinately resumed his new course as soon as he had disposed of the nuisance in Qipchāq in a winter campaign across the Steppes which was the most brilliant and characteristic *tour de force* in the Transoxanian captain's whole history.[1]

A brief exposition of the annals of the last twenty-four years of Timur's life will show how persistently, throughout that span of nearly a quarter of a century, he rejected an opportunity which he had held in the hollow of his hand at the moment of transition from the first to the second phase of his career.

Timur spent the seven years 1381–7 in conquering Iran and Transcaucasia, save for a single punitive expedition in 1383–4 against a still recalcitrant Chaghatāy Khan in 'Mughalistan'. He did not even take warning from a brush between his own troops and Toqatmysh's which occurred in 1385 in Azerbaijan; and at the beginning of 1388 he was in Fars, on the point of rounding off his conquest of the Iranian Plateau, when he was urgently recalled to Samarqand by Toqatmysh's invasion of Khwārizm and Transoxania. His crushing victory over Toqatmysh at Urtapa, on the opposite coast of the Qipchāq Steppe, in 1391 replaced in Timur's hands the opportunity which he had held in 1380 and had neglected since 1381. This time it was in his power to make himself the direct master of Qipchāq and all its dependencies. Moreover, after his triumphal return to Samarqand from Qipchāq at the beginning of 1392, he was able to stamp out the last embers of revolt in 'Mughalistan' and to establish his suzerainty definitively over the Chaghatāy horde. Eurasia now lay at his feet; but instead of stooping to pick up the prize he rode off again, that summer, in the opposite direction, made straight for Fars—that is to say, for the point on his course at which he had been compelled to desist from the conquest of South-Western Asia in 1388—and proceeded systematically with the subjugation of 'Irāq and Armenia and Georgia. In the course of this famous 'Five Years' Campaign' (July 1392–July 1396) Timur once again was drawn, in spite of himself, out of his intended course by a fresh incursion of Toqatmysh into Transcaucasia in the spring of 1395. Timur's counter-stroke carried him across the Caucasus and the Terek and the Steppes into Muscovy;[2]

[1] For this campaign of A.D. 1391 see loc. cit.

[2] Timur's incursion into Muscovy on this occasion does not appear to have been carried to the point of occupying the city of Moscow itself, *pace* Sharaf-ad Dīn 'Alī Yazdī, the Persian historian who recorded Timur's career in the generation following Timur's own (see the *Zafar-Nāmah* (Calcutta 1887–8, *Bibliotheca Indica* series, 2 vols.), vol. i, p. 761). For Sharaf-ad-Din's tutorship over Yunus Khān Chaghatāy of 'Mughalistan' see II. D (v), vol. ii, p. 149, above.

but in 1396 he retraced his steps from Qipchāq to South-Western Asia, and returned to Samarqand across Iran.

From the summer of 1396 to the spring of 1398 Timur rested at Samarqand from his devastating labours; but this pause was not followed by a consolidation or extension of his hold upon Eurasia. Having now completed the pulverization of the heart of the Iranic World (of which he was himself a child), he set himself next to harry, in turn, its south-eastern and north-western extremities, where the Taghlāqī princes of Hindustan and the 'Osmanlī princes of Rūm were at that time extending the Iranic domain at the expense of the Hindu World and Orthodox Christendom respectively. Timur's amīrs objected to crossing the Hindu Kush and attacking their own Turkish kinsmen and co-religionists in India[1] as strongly as the henchmen of Pepin had once objected, in similar circumstances, to crossing the Alps and attacking their Lombard kinsmen in Italy;[2] but Timur, like Pepin, made his own will prevail.[3] The Indian campaign kept him occupied from the spring of 1398 to the spring of 1399; and by the autumn of the latter year he was off again on what was destined to be the most famous, though it was not really the most brilliant, chapter of his military career: a second five years' campaign which included his encounter with the Maghribī philosopher Ibn Khaldūn at Damascus in 1401[4] and his defeat and capture of the Ottoman Sultan Bāyezīd Yilderim in 1402.[5]

Returning to Samarqand in the July of 1404, Timur was on the war-path again by November; and now at last, for the first time in twenty-three years, his face was deliberately set in an auspicious direction; for his objective, this time, was China; and although it may be doubted, in the light of his record in South-Western Asia, whether he would have repeated the Mongols' feat of conquering China outright—a task which it had taken even the Mongols seventy years (A.D. 1207–77) to complete—nevertheless this latest enterprise of Timur's, had he lived to carry it out, might have had enduring consequences of historical importance; for even a passing raid on China might have left Timur in permanent possession of the eastern sectors of the southern border of the Eurasian Steppe from the Tarim Basin to Manchuria; and that would have placed the whole of the Steppe in his power. At this point, however, we pass into the realm of conjecture; for even a militarist who was

1 See Lane-Poole, S.: *Medieval India* (London 1903, Fisher Unwin), p. 155.

2 See p. 488, above.

3 Timur was doubtless tempted by the anarchy into which the Taghlāqī Power had fallen since the death of Fīrūz Shah in A.D. 1388. (For Fīrūz Shah's Slave-household see Part III. A, vol. iii, p. 31, footnote 1, above. For the onset, after Fīrūz Shah's death, of the second bout of a 'Time of Troubles' in the Hindu World see V. C (ii) (*b*), vol. vi, p. 301, below.)

4 See III. C (ii) (*b*), vol. iii, p. 327, footnote 3, above.

5 See II. D (iv), vol. ii, p. 102, and II. D (v), vol. ii, p. 148, above.

favoured with Timur's lucky star could not throw away twenty-three years with impunity. On his China campaign he had marched no farther eastward than Utrār before Death overtook him.

Timur's self-stultification is a supreme example of the suicidalness of Militarism, as will appear from a comparison between his fiasco and Charlemagne's.

In both cases the attempt of the march to conquer the interior was ephemeral—and indeed it is seldom that a relatively backward community does succeed in assimilating to itself by the crude expedient of military conquest another community which is in advance of it on the same path of civilization. Like the Transoxanian domination which Timur imposed by force of arms upon Iran and 'Irāq, the Austrasian domination which Charlemagne imposed upon Lombardy and Bavaria faded away after the conqueror's death. Yet the effects of Charlemagne's militarism were not altogether transient; for his empire held together in some fashion for three-quarters of a century after his own hand was removed; and the destinies of its several parts were permanently modified through their union into a single body social which lived on, in the shape of a *Respublica Christiana*, long after the evaporation of the military force by which the union had originally been brought about. By contrast, Timur's empire was not only shorter-lived than Charlemagne's but was also without any social after-effects of a positive kind. West of the Caspian Gates it dissolved in A.D. 1405 upon the news of Timur's death; in Khurāsān and Transoxania it broke up into weak and warring fragments after Shah Rukh's death in A.D. 1446;[1] and the only traceable after-effect is wholly negative. In sweeping away everything that it found in its path, in order to rush headlong to its own destruction, Timur's imperialism simply created a political and social vacuum in South-Western Asia; and this vacuum eventually drew the 'Osmanlis and the Safawis into a collision which dealt the stricken Iranic Society its death-blow.

Again, Charlemagne's diversion of Austrasian military energies from the frontiers of Western Christendom to the interior was fatal to Austrasia herself without proving equally fatal to the society of which Austrasia was a part. The expansion of the Western Christendom at the expense of the continental European barbarians was eventually taken up and carried on, from the line at which Charlemagne had come to a halt, by the descendants of Charlemagne's Saxon victims, and her expansion at the expense of the Syriac World in the Iberian Peninsula by a number of local Western Christian principalities, several of which were direct 'successor-states' of the Carolingian Empire. On both these fronts

[1] See I. C (i) (*b*), Annex I, vol. i, p. 369, above.

the price that the Western Christendom had to pay for Charlemagne's militarism was a pause which lasted for rather less than two centuries, and which was then followed by three centuries (*circa* A.D. 975–1275) of further advance.[1] On the other hand Timur's militarism deprived the Iranic Society for ever of its Promised Land in Eurasia.

The Iranic Society's forfeiture of the heritage of the Nomad World declared itself first on the plane of religion. Throughout the four centuries ending in Timur's generation Islam had been progressively establishing its hold over the sedentary peoples round the coasts of the Eurasian Steppe and had been captivating the Nomads themselves whenever they trespassed out of the Desert on to the Sown. In the tenth century of the Christian Era, when the military and political power of the Muslim sovereigns of the 'Abbasid Caliphate was in dissolution, their religion was conquering the sedentary Turkish peoples on the Middle Volga[2] and in the oases of the Tarim Basin and the Nomad Turkish followers of the Saljūq and the Ilek Khans on the Transoxanian fringe of the Steppe between the Sea of Aral and Lake Balkash. Even in the last and greatest eruption of the post-'Abbasid Völkerwanderung, when the Steppe was convulsed to its depths and discharged upon Dār-al-Islām a horde of Nomads who had never been touched by the radiation of the Islamic culture and who were prejudiced against Islam, when they encountered it, by their tincture of Nestorian Christianity,[3] the injury which Islam sustained from the spasmodic persecution to which it was subjected by the early Mongol Khāqāns was more than counterbalanced by the unintentional service which it received from the Mongols' policy of deliberately intermixing the peoples and cultures of their vast and heterogeneous empire. It was thanks to these pagan Nomad war-lords that Islam was propagated into China—and this not only into the north-western provinces adjoining the older Islamic domain in the Tarim Basin, but also into the new province of Yunnan in the far south-west, which was carved out of a barbarian no-man's-land and added to China by Mongol arms. Thereafter, when at the turn of the thirteenth and fourteenth centuries of the Christian Era the three western appanages of the Mongol Empire—the house of Hulāgū in Iran and the house of Jūjī on the Qipchāq Steppe and the house of Chaghatāy in Transoxania and Zungaria—were converted to Islam one after another, it looked as though nothing could now prevent Islam from becoming the religion of all Eurasia; and by the

[1] See I. B (iv), vol. i, p. 38, and II. D (v), vol. ii, pp. 167–9 and 204, above.

[2] The White Bulgars, who were presumably the ancestors of the present Tatars of Qāzān.

[3] See II. D (vii), Annex VIII, in vol. ii, especially pp. 449–52, above.

time when Timur arose as the champion of the Sunnah in Transoxania, a Muslim 'Diasporà' which had seeded itself round the western and southern coasts of the Steppe had prepared the ground—as we have noticed already[1]—for him to reap the harvest of a Pan-Eurasian Islamic empire. It is the more significant that the propagation of Islam in Eurasia, which had made such headway down to Timur's time, came to a dead halt thereafter. The only subsequent gain that Islam made in this quarter was the conversion of the Turkish Khanate of Western Siberia at some date shortly before the Cossack conquest in A.D. 1582;[2] and this success in one remote and backward corner was little for Islam to boast of in a generation which saw another of the 'higher religions' captivate all the rest of the Eurasian Nomads who had hitherto remained in their primitive paganism.

The outstanding religious event in Eurasia at the turn of the sixteenth and seventeenth centuries of the Christian Era was the conversion of the Mongols (in A.D. 1576–7) and their westerly kinsmen the Calmucks (*circa* A.D. 1620) to the Lamaistic form of Maḥayanian Buddhism;[3] and this astonishing triumph of a fossilized relic of the religious life of the long extinct Indic culture gives some measure of the extent to which the prestige of Islam had fallen in the estimation of the Eurasian Nomads during the two centuries that had elapsed since Timur's day.[4]

On the political plane the Iranic culture which Timur had first championed and then betrayed proved equally bankrupt. The sedentary societies which did, in the end, perform the feat of taming the Eurasian Nomadism politically were the Russian branch of the Orthodox Christian Society and the Chinese branch of the Far Eastern; and the sentence of servitude which Fate had pronounced upon the Nomads when Timur made his winter-passage across the Steppe and overthrew Toqatmysh at Urtapa in A.D. 1391 was never executed by Transoxanian hands. It was confirmed when, in the middle of the seventeenth century, the Cossack servants of

[1] See p. 496, above.

[2] This, and not 1586 (the date given in II. D (v), vol. ii, p. 157, above), appears to be the true date of Yermak's crossing of the watershed between the Volga and the Ob.

[3] See Part III. A, Annex II, vol. iii, p. 451, above (following Courant, M.: *L'Asie Centrale aux xviie et xviiie Siècles: Empire Kalmouk ou Empire Mantchou?* (Lyon 1912, Rey), pp. 12–14 and 17), and V. C (i) (*c*) 2, vol. v, p. 137, and V. C (i) (*c*) 3, vol. v, pp. 309–10, below.

[4] For the Lamaistic form of the Mahāyāna as a fossil of the Indic culture see I. B (iii), vol. i, p. 35, and I. C (i) (*b*), vol. i, pp. 90–2, above. For the role of Tibet as the fastness in which this fossil has survived, see II. D (vi), Annex, vol. ii, p. 405, footnote 1, above. The radiation of a religious influence from Tibet over the eastern half of the Eurasian Steppe in the sixteenth and seventeenth centuries of the Christian Era will appear the more extraordinary when we consider that at this date the pagan Mongol and Calmuck Nomads were insulated from Lhasa geographically by a continuous belt of Muslim population which extended from west to east, through the oases of the Tarim Basin, into the Chinese provinces of Kansu and Shensi.

Muscovy and the Manchu masters of China ran into each other as they were feeling their way in opposite directions round the northern edge of the Steppe, and fought their first battle for dominion over Eurasia in the neighbourhood of Chingis Khan's ancestral pastures in the upper basin of the Amur.[1] The partition of Eurasia and the subjugation of its ancient Nomad occupants by the same pair of competitors was completed a century later when the Emperor Ch'ien Lung (*imperabat* A.D. 1735–96) broke the power of the Zungar Calmucks in A.D. 1755 and gave asylum to the already broken Torgut Calmuck refugees from the dominions of the Tsar in A.D. 1771.[2] Therewith the latest tidal wave of the Eurasian Nomadism was spent;[3] and when the Muscovite and the Manchu Power had divided the allegiance of the Qāzāqs[4]—the flotsam and jetsam of the latest wave but one, who were now drifting sluggishly over the eastern portion of the Qipchāq Steppe, between the Irtish and the Yaik—the whole of Eurasia, up to the northern outskirts of the Transoxanian oases, found itself under either Russian or Chinese control.

Nor did the injury inflicted by Timur's militarism upon the Iranic World, including the conqueror's own Transoxanian homeland, stop short at the loss of a potential field for expansion across and around the Eurasian Steppe. The conclusive condemnation of the destructive militarism which possessed Timur during the last twenty-four years of his career is to be found in the fact that, besides being barren in itself, it actually led in the fullness of Time—as its consequences worked themselves out in the third and fourth generation—to the undoing of the constructive work to which Timur had devoted himself for nineteen years before he ran amok in A.D. 1381. The liberator of the nascent Iranic Society in Transoxania spent the rest of his life in so recklessly wearing out the energies which he had first mobilized against a Nomad intruder that the world which he had made safe against the hordes of Chaghatāy and Jūjī found itself exposed, within little more than a hundred years after the death of the liberator-turned-militarist, to a recurrence of the Nomad peril in the shape of the Uzbegs;[5] and in this emergency the epigoni of Timur's house were impotent—heirs, as they were, to the debilitating social legacy of Timur's mili-

[1] See Part III. A, vol. iii, p. 19, above, and V. C (i) (*c*) 3, vol. v, pp. 315–6, below.

[2] For this backward ebb, into the heart of the Steppe, of a Calmuck tide which had poured out of it in all directions a century and a half before, see the reference to De Quincey in Part III. A, vol. iii, p. 19, footnote 3, above, and V. C (i) (*c*) 3, vol. v, p. 315, below.

[3] For a discussion of Nomad eruptions in general, and of the Calmuck eruption in particular, see Part III. A, Annex II, in vol. iii, above.

[4] Incorrectly spelt 'Kazaks' in vol. iii, pp. 18–19, 418, 422, 423 and 521, above. For the etymology of the Turkish word see V. C (i) (*c*) 3, vol. v, p. 282, footnote 1, below.

[5] On this point see Part III. A, Annex II, vol. iii, p. 447, above.

tary excesses—to repeat their ancestor's original feat. The Uzbeg 'drive' at the heart of the Iranic World was eventually arrested, not by any Timurid prince of Farghānā or Khurāsān, but by the new Safawī Power of Shah Ismā'īl; and even Shah Ismā'īl's arms, which did effectively bar the Uzbegs' farther progress, were unable to drive the intruders right back into the Eurasian no-man's-land out of which they had issued. With his relatively distant base of operations in Azerbaijan and with his grandiose ambitions on the west—ambitions which involved him in an unequal contest with the 'Osmanlis—his power to play the liberator on the eastern front was limited; and after expelling the Uzbegs once for all from Khurāsān he was compelled in the end to leave them in permanent possession of Transoxania.[1]

Thus, a century and a half after the year in which Timur had girded himself to liberate his country from the dominion of the Chaghatāy horde, Transoxania fell under the yoke of another swarm of Nomads, from the back-of-beyond, who were even more barbarous than the hateful and contemptible 'Jātah'; and under this yoke the former Eurasian march of the Iranic World, which had once spread her terror as puissantly as Assyria, was destined to lie prostrate and passive for the next three hundred and fifty years, until, in the third quarter of the nineteenth century of the Christian Era, the long-ground-down peasantry of the Transoxanian oases obtained at last the alleviation of exchanging an Uzbeg for a Russian master.

It is a curious reflection that, if Timur had not turned his back on Eurasia and his arms against Iran in A.D. 1381, the present relations between Transoxania and Russia might have been the inverse of what they actually are. In those hypothetical circumstances Russia to-day might have found herself included in an empire of much the same extent as the area of the Soviet Union but with quite a different centre of gravity—an Iranic Empire in which Samarqand would be ruling Moscow instead of Moscow ruling Samarqand. This imaginary picture of an alternative course of Iranic history may appear outlandish because the actual course has been taking an altogether different direction for the last four hundred years and more. At least as strange a picture will unfold itself before our mind's eye if we plot out an alternative course of Western history in which the consequences of Charlemagne's militarism for our world are imagined to have been as utterly disastrous as those of Timur's militarism actually were for his. On this analogy we shall have to picture Austrasia being submerged

[1] For these transactions in South-Western Asia in the early years of the sixteenth century of the Christian Era see I. C (i) (*b*), Annex I, in vol. i, above.

by the Magyars and Neustria by the Vikings in the tenth century, and the heart of the Carolingian Empire remaining thereafter under this barbarian domination until in the fourteenth century the 'Osmanlis step in to impose the lesser evil of an alien civilization upon these derelict marches of Western Christendom.

Thus, besides forfeiting a Promised Land, Timur undid his own work of liberating his native country; but the greatest of all his acts of destruction was committed against himself. He has succeeded in making his name immortal at the price of erasing from the minds of Posterity all memory of the deeds for which he might have been remembered for good. To how many people in either Christendom or Dār-al-Islām to-day does Timur's name call up the image of a champion of Civilization against Barbarism, who led the clergy and people of his country to a hard-won victory at the end of a nineteen-years-long struggle for independence? To the vast majority of those to whom the name of Timur Lenk or Tamerlane means anything at all, it commemorates a militarist who perpetrated as many horrors in the span of twenty-four years as had been perpetrated in a century by a succession of Assyrian kings from Tiglath-Pileser III to Asshurbanipal inclusive. We think of the monster who razed Isfarā'in to the ground in 1381; built two thousand prisoners into a living mound, and then bricked them over, at Sabzawār in 1383; piled 5,000 human heads into minarets at Zirih in the same year; cast his Lūrī prisoners alive over precipices in 1386; massacred 70,000 people, and piled the heads of the slain into minarets, at Isfahān in 1387; massacred the garrison of Takrit, and piled their heads into minarets, in 1393; massacred 100,000 prisoners at Delhi in 1398; buried alive the 4,000 Christian soldiers of the garrison of Sivas after their capitulation in 1400; built twenty towers of skulls in Syria in 1400 and 1401; and dealt with Baghdad in 1401 as he had dealt fourteen years earlier with Isfahān. In minds which know him only through such deeds, Timur has caused himself to be confounded with the ogres of the Steppe—a Chingis and an Attila and the like—against whom he had spent the better half of his life in waging a Holy War. The crack-brained megalomania of the homicidal madman whose one idea is to impress the imagination of Mankind with a sense of his military power by a hideous abuse of it is brilliantly conveyed in the hyperboles which the English poet Marlowe has placed in the mouth of his Tamburlaine:

> I hold the Fates bound fast in yron chaines,
> And with my hand turne Fortune's wheel about,
> And sooner shall the Sun fall from his Speare,
> Than Tamburlaine be slaine or overcome. . . .

The God of war resignes his roume to me,
Meaning to make me Generall of the world;
Jove, viewing me in armes, lookes pale and wan,
Fearing my power should pull him from his throne.
Where ere I come the fatall sisters sweat,
And griesly death by running to and fro,
To doo their ceassles homag to my sword. . . .
Millions of soules sit on the bankes of Styx,
Waiting the back returne of Charon's boat,
Hell and Elysian swarme with ghosts of men,
That I have sent from sundry foughten fields,
To spread my fame through hell and up to heaven. . . .
Nor am I made Arch-monark of the world,
Crown'd and invested by the hand of Jove,
For deeds of bounty or nobility;
But since I exercise a greater name,
The Scourge of God and terrour of the world,
I must apply my selfe to fit those tearmes,
In war, in blood, in death, in crueltie. . . .
I will persist a terrour to the world,
Making the Meteors, that like armèd men
Are seene to march upon the towers of heaven,
Run tilting round about the firmament,
And breake their burning Lances in the aire,
For honor of my woondrous victories.[1]

The Margrave turned Moss-trooper.

In analysing the careers of Timur and Charlemagne and the kings of Assyria from Tiglath-Pileser III to Asshurbanipal, we have observed the same phenomenon in all three cases. The military prowess which a society develops among its frontiersmen for its defence against external enemies undergoes a sinister transformation into the moral malady of Militarism when it is diverted from its proper field in the no-man's-land beyond the pale and is turned against the frontiersmen's own brethren in the interior of a world which it is their mission to protect and not to devastate. A number of other examples of this destructive social evil will readily occur to our minds.

We shall think of Mercia turning against the other English 'successor-states' of the Roman Empire in Britain the arms which she had sharpened in the performance of her original function as the English march against Wales;[2] of the Plantagenet Kingdom of England attempting in the Hundred Years' War to conquer the sister Kingdom of France instead of attending to her proper business

[1] Marlowe, Christopher: *Tamburlaine the Great*, ll. 369–72; 2232–8; 2245–9; 3824–30; 3875–80.
[2] See II. D (v), vol. ii, pp. 195–6, above.

of enlarging the bounds of their common mother, Latin Christendom, at the expense of 'the Celtic Fringe'; and of the Norman King Roger of Sicily turning his military energies to the extension of his dominions in Central Italy—at the expense of the South Lombard duchies and the Holy Roman Empire and the States of the Church —instead of devoting himself to carrying on his forebears' work of enlarging the bounds of Western Christendom in the Mediterranean at the expense of Orthodox Christendom and Dār-al-Islām. In the Mexic World we see the Aztecs warring down the Toltecs, to whom they owed their own initiation into the Mexic culture, instead of confining themselves to their proper task of guarding the northern march against the unconverted Chichimecs of the wilderness; in the Andean World we see the Incas bending their energies to the subjugation of their lowland neighbours in the coastlands and their highland neighbours in Ecuador, who were co-heirs with them in the heritage of the Andean Civilization, while they made little headway against the dangerous savages of Amazonia or the valiant barbarians of Southern Chile and the Pampas, whom it was their mission to keep at bay.[1] In like fashion the Mycenaean outposts of the Minoan Civilization on the European mainland misused the prowess which they had acquired in holding their own against the continental barbarians, in order to turn and rend their mother Crete;[2] and the Macedonians and the Romans, whose function in the Hellenic World was to serve as wardens of the marches against the same barbarians, committed in their turn the same crime as the Mycenaeans when they contended with their neighbours, and finally with each other, for the illegitimate prize of a Pan-Hellenic hegemony.[3] In the Sinic World the part of Rome was played by Ts'in, the western march against the barbarian highlanders of Shensi and Shansi and against the Nomads of the Eurasian Steppe, when her princes stepped into an arena which had formed itself in the interior and there eventually delivered the 'knock-out blow' in the struggle between the contending states.[4]

In the Egyptiac World the classic Southern March in the section of the Nile Valley immediately below the First Cataract trained itself in arms, in the execution of its duty of damming back the Nubian barbarians up-river, only to turn right-about, direct its arms down-river against the Egyptiac communities in the interior, and take advantage of its military superiority in order to establish by brute force the United Kingdom of the Two Crowns.[5] This act

[1] See II. D (v), vol. ii, pp. 206–8, above. [2] See II. D (v), vol. ii, pp. 159–60, above.
[3] See II. D (v), vol. ii, pp. 160–4, above.
[4] See I. C (i) (*b*), vol. i, p. 89, and III. C (i) (*b*), vol. iii, p. 167, above, and V. C (ii) (*b*), vol. vi, pp. 291–5, below.
[5] See II. D (v), vol. ii, pp. 112 and 114–15, above.

of Militarism, which was at once the making and the marring of the Egyptiac Civilization, has been depicted by its perpetrator, with all the frankness of self-complacency, in one of the earliest of the Egyptiac records that have come into the hands of our modern Western archaeologists. The palette of Narmer portrays the triumphant return of the Upper Egyptian war-lord from the conquest of Lower Egypt. Swollen to a superhuman stature, the royal conqueror marches behind a strutting file of standard-bearers towards a double row of decapitated enemy corpses, while below, in the image of a bull, he tramples upon a fallen adversary and batters down the walls of a fortified town. The accompanying script is believed to enumerate a booty of 120,000 human captives, 400,000 oxen, and 1,422,000 sheep and goats.[1]

In this gruesome work of an archaic Egyptiac art we have the whole tragedy of Militarism as it has been acted over and over again since Narmer's time by the Sennacheribs and Tamerlanes and Charlemagnes of twenty different civilizations down to our own militarists in the Western World of to-day. Perhaps the most poignant of all the performances of this tragedy during its run of some six thousand years up to date is that of which Athens was guilty when she transformed herself from a 'liberator of Hellas'[2] into a 'tyrant city'[3] by misusing for the oppression of her Hellenic allies and protégées the naval power with which she had armed herself so short a time before in order to save herself—and rescue all Hellas in the act—from the aggression of the Achaemenidae. This Athenian aberration brought upon the whole of Hellas, as well as upon Athens herself, the never-retrieved disaster of 431–404 B.C. And, if an Athens under arms succumbed to so gross a sin, with such fatal consequences, can any of those military and naval Powers of our modern Western World who surpass Athens in arms as signally as they fall short of her in the arts, feel sure of preserving their own moral integrity?

In all the examples of which we have just been reminding ourselves in a cursory review, the suicidalness of Militarism is as evident as it is in the three classic cases with which we have dealt

[1] A photograph of the palette will be found in Rostovtzeff, M.: *A History of the Ancient World* (Oxford 1926, University Press, 2 vols.), vol. i, Plate IV, opposite p. 30; and in *The Cambridge Ancient History*, Plates, vol. i (Cambridge 1927, University Press), plate facing p. 78, fig. [*c*]. For the statistics of the spoil see Dawson, C.: *The Age of the Gods* (reissue: London 1933, Sheed and Ward), p. 153.

[2] See the judgement which Herodotus goes out of his way to record in Book VII, chap. 139. The conviction with which this sceptical-minded observer expresses his opinion on the point is made all the more striking by the apologetic tone in which he delivers himself—writing, as he was, at a time when any praise of Athens had been made invidious by the odious misbehaviour of Athens herself.

[3] The description of the Athenian Empire which is placed in the mouth of the Athenian politician Cleon by the historian Thucydides (Book III, chap. 37) in his version of a public speech which was delivered by Cleon in 427 B.C.

at greater length; and it comes out most strikingly of all where the fatal change of front has not been exclusively devastating in its effects, but has also been incidentally constructive. The diversion of Athenian and Macedonian arms from the external frontier towards the interior of the Hellenic World was disastrous for Hellas even though the Athenian and Macedonian militarists were doing something to provide the Hellenic Society with the political world order of which it then stood in need.[1] The corresponding changes of front which were made by Rome and Ts'in and the Incas were likewise disastrous to their respective societies in spite of the fact that in each of these cases the militarist community did succeed, through the triumph of its militarism, in providing its society with a universal state. And Narmer's change of front from up-stream to down-stream in the Nile Valley had a sinister effect upon the subsequent course of Egyptiac history even though it resulted in the establishment of the United Kingdom. In the palette of Narmer we have the first evidence of that brutal vein in the Egyptiac êthos which so soon arrested the growth of the Egyptiac Civilization. The descendants of the Lower Egyptian peasants whom Narmer had slaughtered or enslaved were those unfortunate human beings who were converted into 'man-power' by the Pyramid-Builders.[2]

The military field which we have been surveying in this chapter is illuminating for the study of the fatal chain of *κόρος-ὕβρις-ἄτη* because military skill and prowess are edged tools which are apt to inflict fatal injuries upon those who venture to wield them if there is even the slightest clumsiness or misjudgement in their use. When an individual or a government or a community that has command of military power mistakes the limits of the field within which this power can be used with effect, or misconceives the nature of the objectives which it is possible to attain by means of it, the disastrousness of this aberration can hardly fail to make itself conspicuous through the seriousness of the practical consequences. But what is palpably true of military action is also true of other human activities in less hazardous fields where the train of gunpowder that leads from *κόρος* through *ὕβρις* to *ἄτη* is not so explosive. Whatever the human faculty, or the sphere of its exercise, may be, the presumption that because a faculty has proved equal to the accomplishment of a limited task within its proper field it may therefore be counted upon to produce some inordinate effect in a different set of circumstances is never anything but an intellectual and a moral aberration and never leads to anything but certain disaster.

[1] See IV. C (iii) (*b*) 10, pp. 210–13; IV. C (iii) (*c*) 2 (α), p. 265; and IV. C (iii) (*c*) 2 (β), pp. 305–6, above.

[2] See III. C (i) (*d*), vol. iii, pp. 212–15, above.

(β) *The Intoxication of Victory.*

The Roman Republic.

One of the more general forms in which the tragedy of κόρος-ὕβρις-ἄτη presents itself is the intoxication of victory—whether the struggle in which the fatal prize is won be a war of arms or a conflict of spiritual forces. Both variants of this drama may be illustrated from the history of Rome: the intoxication of a military victory from the breakdown of the Republic in the second century B.C., the intoxication of a spiritual victory from the breakdown of the Papacy in the thirteenth century of the Christian Era.

The demoralization to which the governing class in the Roman Republic succumbed at the close of half a century of titanic warfare (220–168 B.C.) which had begun with the terrible ordeal of the Hannibalic War and had ended in the conquest of the World, is caustically described by a contemporary Greek observer who happened to be one of the victims.

'The first result of the friendship between Polybius and Scipio Aemilianus[1] was a dynamic enthusiasm for higher things which took possession of them both and which inspired them with the ambition to win moral distinction and to compete victoriously in this field with their contemporaries. The great prize on which they had thus set their hearts would have been difficult to attain in ordinary circumstances; but unhappily in the Rome of that generation the standard of the competition was lowered by the general demoralization of Society. Some were "all out" for women, others for unnatural vice, and many for "shows" and drink and all the extravagance for which "shows" and drink gave occasion. These were all vices for which the Greeks had a weakness, and the Romans had caught this infirmity from them instantaneously during the third Romano-Macedonian War. So violent and so uncontrolled was the passion for these vices that had overcome the younger generation of Romans that it was quite a common thing to buy a boy-favourite for a talent and a jar of caviare for three hundred drachmae—behaviour which drew from Marcus Cato in a public speech the indignant exclamation that the demoralization of Roman Society was glaringly exposed in the mere fact of handsome boys fetching a higher price than land, and jars of caviare than live-stock. If it is asked why this social malady "lighted up" at this particular time, two reasons can be given in answer. The first reason was that, with the overthrow of the Kingdom of Macedon, the Romans felt that there was no Power now left in the World that could challenge their own supremacy.[2] The second reason was that the

[1] This friendship started at the time when Polybius was a political deportee, interned in Italy, after the victory of Rome in the third Romano-Macedonian War (*gerebatur* 172–168 B.C.). For the circumstances see III. C (ii) (*b*), in vol. iii, p. 315, above.—A.J.T.

[2] The demoralizing release of Roman souls from the salutary fear of a formidable

material display, both private and public, of life in Rome had been enormously enhanced by the removal to Rome of properties (χορηγίων) from Macedonia.'[1]

This was the moral pass to which the Roman governing class had been brought by the overwhelming victory which had descended upon the Republic after years of agony in which she had been tottering on the verge of an abyss. The first reaction of a generation which had lived through this bewildering experience was a blind presumption that a victor's irresistible material power was the key to a solution of all human problems, and that the only conceivable end of Man was an unbridled enjoyment of the grossest pleasures which this power could place within his grasp.[2] The victors did not realize that this very state of mind bore witness to the moral defeat which a militarily vanquished Hannibal had succeeded in inflicting upon them.[3] They did not perceive that the world in which they passed for victors was a world in ruins, and that their own ostensibly victorious Roman Republic was the most sorely stricken[4] of all the prostrate states of which this ruined world was made up. In this moral aberration they wandered in the wilderness for more than a hundred years; and in this awful century they inflicted one calamity after another upon a world which their victory had placed at their mercy, and the greatest calamities of all upon themselves.

Even in the military coin which was their own chosen currency their bankruptcy soon became manifest. The hard-won Roman triumphs over a Hannibal and a Perseus were followed by a series of humiliating Roman reverses at the hands of antagonists who were utterly outmatched by Rome in military strength: the broken, disarmed, and almost defenceless Carthage upon whom the Roman

foreign foe is traced by Saint Augustine (*De Civitate Dei*, Book I, chap. 30) to the overthrow, not of Macedon in the Third Romano-Macedonian War, but of Carthage in the Third Romano-Punic War. 'Deleta quippe Carthagine, magno scilicet terrore Romanae rei publicae depulso et exstincto, tanta de rebus prosperis orta mala continuo subsecuta sunt ut . . .'—A.J.T.

[1] Polybius: *An Oecumenical History*, Book XXXI, chap. 25. The effect that Polybius here ascribes to Paullus's victory in Greece in 168 B.C. is ascribed to Sulla's campaigns in Asia in the second decade of the last century B.C. by Sallust: 'Ibi primum insuevit exercitus Populi Romani amare potare, signa tabulas pictas vasa caelata mirari, ea privatim et publice rapere, delubra spoliare, sacra profanaque omnia polluere' (*Bellum Catilinae*, chap. 11).

[2] 'Qui labores, pericula, dubias asperasque res facile toleraverant, eis otium divitiae, optanda alias, oneri miseriaeque fuere. igitur primo imperi, pecuniae deinde cupido crevit; ea quasi materies omnium malorum fuere.'—Sallust, op. cit., chap. 10.

[3] 'Quippe secundae res sapientium animos fatigant: ne illi corruptis moribus victoriae temperarent.'—Sallust, op. cit., chap. 11. 'Tunc iam Roma subiugaverat Africam, subiugaverat Graeciam, lateque etiam aliis partibus orbis imperans tanquam se ipsa non valens ferre sua se quodammodo magnitudine fregerat' (Augustine: *De Civitate Dei*, Book XVIII, chap. 45, perhaps unconsciously reproducing Horace's 'Suis et ipsa Roma viribus ruit' (Epode xvi, l. 2, quoted in V. C (i) (*d*) 3, vol. v, p. 406, below)).

[4] 'Similior victo fuerit ille qui vicit.'—Augustine: *De Civitate Dei*, Book III, chap. 19, apropos of the outcome of the Hannibalic War.

Government passed a cold-blooded sentence of annihilation in 149 B.C.; the barbarian Numantines who defied all Roman efforts to subjugate them from 153 to 133; the enslaved and expatriated Orientals who broke out of their ergastula on the Sicilian plantations in 135 and 104;[1] the mutinous gladiators at whose head Spartacus ranged as freely over Italy from 73 to 71[2] as Hannibal himself had ranged from 218 to 211; the 'Citizens of the Sun' who put their faith in Aristonicus of Pergamum and held out against the power of Rome for three years (132–130) in the strength of their belief in the coming of a new dispensation;[3] and the rebellious native princes—a Jugurtha[4] and a Mithradates[5]—who repudiated their allegiance and taxed their outraged suzerain's strength to the uttermost before she succeeded in bringing them to book.

The reason why Rome thus covered herself with military dishonour on the morrow of a military triumph was because during this century her officers were leading soldiers who had no longer anything to gain by victory against an enemy who, on his side, had no longer anything to hope for from laying down his arms.[6] Both the mobilization of the Italian peasantry and the subjugation of the barbarians and the Orientals were now being exploited heartlessly for the pecuniary profit of the Roman governing class. The provinces were being drained of their inanimate wealth and their human inhabitants in order to provide lucrative contracts for Roman business men and cheap man-power for Roman senators' cattle-ranches and plantations; and the land which was being stocked with this alien slave-labour in order to multiply the fortunes of a small class of already rich men was Italian land which was being placed at the disposition of these capitalists by the impoverishment and eviction of the former peasant proprietors. The nucleus of the latifundia which 'ruined Italy'[7] was the devastated area in the South which became public property as a result of the Hannibalic War, partly in punishment for the defection of the original owners to the invader's camp, and partly because the original owners had simply disappeared. Thereafter the new class of post-war 'planters' and 'ranchers' was able to add field to field by buying up the freeholds which were thrown upon the market when their owners were mobilized and kept under arms for years

1 See II. D (vi), vol. ii, p. 214, and III. C (i) (*d*), vol. iii, pp. 198–9, above; and V. C (i) (*c*) 2, vol. v, pp. 69–70, below.

2 See V. C (i) (*c*) 2, vol. v, p. 70, below.

3 See V. C (i) (*c*) 2, vol. v, pp. 69 and 179–80; V. C (i) (*d*) 6 (δ), Annex, vol. v, p. 692, footnote 2; and V. C (i) (*d*) 11, Annex I, vol. vi, p. 351, below.

4 See V. C (i) (*c*) 3, vol. v, p. 218, and V. C (ii) (*a*), vol. vi, p. 234, below.

5 See V. C (i) (*c*) 2, vol. v, p. 69, below.

6 'Ei milites, postquam victoriam adepti sunt, nihil reliqui victis fecere.'—Sallust, op. cit., chap. 11.

7 C. Plinius Secundus: *Historia Naturalis*, Book XVIII, chap. 6.

on end in some distant theatre of chronic frontier-warfare—on the western borders of the two provinces in Spain, or on the northern borders of the province of Macedonia.[1]

In this age the subjects and the citizens of the Roman Republic were fellow victims of a *ci-devant* Roman governing class which had been transmuted by the intoxication of victory into a band of robbers.[2] In 104 B.C., when the whole Hellenic World was overshadowed by the common menace of a barbarian avalanche from Northern Europe, the King of Bithynia, which was officially a friendly state under Rome's protectorate, could reply with biting irony, when the highest representative of the Roman Government served him with a requisition for a contingent of troops, 'that most of his subjects had been kidnapped by the [Roman] tax-farmers and were now living in slavery in territories under Roman administration'.[3] And in 133 B.C. a high-minded young Roman aristocrat who attempted to carry out a social reform, and thereby precipitated a revolution,[4] could declare without contradiction:

> 'The wild animals that range over Italy have a hole, and each of them has its lair and nest, but the men who fight and die for Italy have no part or lot in anything but the air and the sunlight. . . . It is for the sake of other men's wealth and luxury that these go to the wars and give their lives. They are called the lords of the World, and they have not a single clod of earth to call their own.'[5]

The militant refusal of Tiberius Gracchus's peers to support him in seeking a remedy for the Roman peasantry's wrongs evoked a revolution which festered into a civil war; and the self-destructive violence which was let loose within the bosom of the Roman Commonwealth by the murder of the would-be reformer in 133 B.C. was brought under control again only by the establishment of the *Pax Augusta* in 31 B.C. after the Battle of Actium.

To a Roman poet, reviewing the tragedy in retrospect, it seemed evident that in this century of self-inflicted agony the Roman people were being punished for their sins.

[1] For the spread of the slave-plantation system in Southern Italy after the Hannibalic War see III. C (i) (*b*), vol. iii, pp. 170–1, above.

[2] 'Ex divitiis iuventutem luxuria atque avaritia cum superbia invasere: rapere consumere, sua parvi pendere aliena cupere, pudorem pudicitiam, divina atque humana promiscua, nihil pensi neque moderati habere.'—Sallust, op. cit., chap. 12. 'Ut Romani illi qui vita integriore mala metuebant ab hostibus, perdita integritate vitae crudeliora paterentur a civibus; eaque ipsa libido dominandi, quae inter alia vitia generis humani meracior inerat universo populo Romano, posteaquam in paucis potentioribus vicit, obtritos fatigatosque ceteros etiam iugo servitutis oppressit.'—Augustine: *De Civitate Dei*, Book I, chap. 30.

[3] Diodorus of Agyrium: *A Library of Universal History*, Book XXXVI, chap. .

[4] See V. C (i) (*c*) 2, vol. v, p. 78; V. C (i) (*d*) 1, vol. v, pp. 388–9; V. C (i) (*d*) 8 (α), vol. vi, pp. 52–3; V. C (i) (*d*) 8 (ε), vol. vi, p. 94; and V. C (ii) (*a*), vol. vi, pp. 219–20, below.

[5] Tiberius Gracchus, quoted by Plutarch: *Lives of the Gracchi*, chap. 9. See, further, V. C (i) (*c*) 2, vol. v, pp. 70–1; V. C (i) (*c*) 1, Annex, vol. v, pp. 573–4; and V. C (ii) (*a*), Annex II, vol. vi, p. 381, with Table VIII, logion (α), p. 414, below.

Ergo inter sese paribus concurrere telis
Romanas acies iterum videre Philippi,
nec fuit indignum superis bis sanguine nostro
Emathiam et latos Haemi pinguescere campos.[1]

And even then, when the blood-price had been paid twice over, Virgil was tormented by a fear that Augustus himself might not be granted grace to lift the curse.

Di patrii, Indigetes, et Romule, Vestaque mater
quae Tuscum Tiberim et Romana palatia servas,
hunc saltem everso iuvenem succurrere saeclo
ne prohibete. satis iam pridem sanguine nostro
Laomedonteae luimus periuria Troiae.[2]

On this note of prayer[3] the poem ends, without presuming to anticipate the answer; and in ending thus the poet's intuition was right; for the *Pax Augusta*, as we have seen,[4] inaugurated no 'Golden Age', but only an 'Indian Summer'.[5] By the time when Virgil wrote those lines the injury which Roman ὕβρις had already inflicted upon Rome herself, and upon the whole of the Hellenic Society, was quite past repair. The most that the gods of the dominant minority were able to grant to the last of their favourites was a respite which was not a reprieve; and even this respite was to redound to the benefit, not of the bankrupt gods' own people, but of a *nova progenies*:[6] a 'coming race' whose eyes were set upon a distant horizon and whose faith was founded on the power of a different saviour.[7] The irreparable event which had occurred in the Hellenic World between the generation of Polybius and the generation of Virgil was the Secession of the Proletariat;[8] and the inexorable event which was to follow between the generation of Virgil and that of Marcus Aurelius was the budding, within the bosom of this Proletariat, of the germ of a new social order.

The material grievance which Gracchus had sought to remedy by political action was eventually redressed in a perversely anti-social way when the descendants of such Italian peasants as had succeeded in still clinging to the land were ruthlessly evicted by a succession of revolutionary war-lords, from Sulla to Augustus himself, in order to provide allotments for the descendants of their

[1] Virgil: *Georgicon* Book I, ll. 489–92. [2] Ibid., ll. 498–502.

[3] For the sense of sin to which the prayer testifies see V. C (i) (*d*) 5, vol. v, pp. 435–6, below.

[4] In IV. C (ii) (*b*) 1, pp. 58–63, above.

[5] In the view of Saint Augustine (*De Civitate Dei*, Book III, chap. 21) Augustus 'videtur . . . quasi morbida vetustate collapsam veluti instaurasse ac renovasse rem publicam'.

[6] Virgil: *Eclogue* iv, l. 7.

[7] The diverse conceptions of the Saviour that take shape in the minds of the children of a disintegrating civilization are examined in V. C (ii) (*a*), *passim*, in vol. vi, below.

[8] See I. B (iv), vol. i, p. 41, and I. C (i) (*a*), vol. i, pp. 53–6, above, and V. C (i) (*c*), *passim*, vol. v, below.

uprooted brothers who had long since become incapable of effectively 'going back to the land' after having been forced for years on end to make the camp their home and the sword their means of livelihood.

> Impius haec tam culta novalia miles habebit,
> barbarus has segetes.[1]

This travesty of the Gracchan remedy was even worse than the disease of an uprooted and militarized citizen-proletariat. It dealt the final blow to Italian agriculture.[2] But, at a moment when the social problems of Italy were utterly defeating all the manœuvres of Roman statesmanship, the parable of the wild things' 'holes' and 'nests', which Tiberius Gracchus had once employed in a political speech as a figurative search-light to show up a social wrong, was being applied to illustrate a different and a deeper truth by a prophet in Syria[3] who made no impression on the minds of the Roman authorities of the day (not even when, in the course of their administrative routine, they had occasion to put him to death). When Jesus took upon himself the sufferings of a Galilaean peasantry who had been despoiled by the same predatory hand as the peasants of the Ager Mantuanus, and when he said to the scribe 'the foxes have holes and the birds of the air have nests but the Son of Man hath not where to lay his head',[4] he was using the Gracchan image in order to make the Proletariat understand that the wrongful and violent spoliation of their material goods was not a ground for revolutionary reprisals, or even perhaps for political reforms, but was actually a blessing in disguise because it was an unsuspected source of spiritual wealth.

'Blessed are the meek, for they shall inherit the Earth. . . .

'Blessed are they which are persecuted for righteousness' sake, for theirs is the Kingdom of Heaven.'[5]

In a lesser degree this intoxication of victory, which carried the Roman governing class to perdition after their conquest of the Hellenic World in the half-century ending in the Battle of Pydna, was likewise the ruin of the Spaniards and the Portuguese after their conquest of the New World at the beginning of the Modern Age of our Western history, and again the ruin of the British after their conquest of Bengal and Canada in the Seven Years' War.

[1] Virgil, *Eclogue* i, ll. 70–1.

[2] For the restoration of Italian agriculture, some five or six centuries later, as an incidental economic consequence of the spiritual movement which was started by Benedict of Nursia, see III. C (ii) (*b*), vol. iii, p. 266, and IV. C (iii) (*b*) 4, in the present volume, p. 49, above.

[3] For the attribution of the same saying both to Tiberius Gracchus and to Jesus see V. C (ii) (*a*), Annex II, vol. vi, p. 381, with Table VIII, logion (α), p. 414, below.

[4] Matt. viii. 20 = Luke ix. 57–8 = 'Q'. For the literary relation between the Christian and the pagan version of this λόγιον see V. C (ii) (*a*), Annex II, Table VIII, vol. vi, p. 414, below.

[5] Matt. v. 5 and 10.

The Spaniards and Portuguese, who in A.D. 1493 had obtained from the Pope an arbitral award,[1] partitioning between them the whole of the Overseas World as though no other claimants were in the field, saw their monopoly broken within less than a century when the Dutch and the English and the French made free with the Spanish preserves in America and the Portuguese preserves in Africa and India, and both the Iberian Powers' preserves in the Far East, after the defeat of the Spanish Armada. And the intoxication of the Iberian pioneers with their original achievement—their overweening pride in the knowledge that

We were the first that ever burst
into that silent sea[2]—

was the gaping joint in their armour through which their lynx-eyed and nimble-handed European competitors directed their disabling thrusts at the turn of the sixteenth and seventeenth centuries.

As for the English, they were temporarily shaken out of the moderation which they have studiously practised both before and since by the extraordinary lavishness of Fortune when she showered Canada upon them with one hand and Bengal, simultaneously, with the other. In 1763 it seemed 'the manifest destiny' of the British Empire to swallow up the whole of North America as well as the whole of India. Yet twenty years later Great Britain had lost the better half of one of the two sub-continents and was in imminent danger of losing the whole of the other. It is true that the verdict of History has now acquitted British statesmanship of exclusive responsibility for the break-up of the First British Empire. American historians have latterly done much to show that in the fratricidal war of 1775–83 the war-guilt was divided; and the name of Warren Hastings no longer sounds so sinister as it was made to sound a century and a half ago. Nevertheless the fact remains that the Thirteen Colonies would never have been lost to the British Crown if from 1763 to 1775 it had shown towards them the same tact and consideration as it has repeatedly shown towards Canada from 1774 onwards. Nor would Bengal have been retained —nor, *a fortiori*, enlarged into an empire embracing all India—if the predatory practices of the Company's servants in the East, from Clive and Warren Hastings downwards, during the twenty-six years following the intoxicating victory of Plassey had not been discouraged by the abortive India Bill of 1783 and the effective India Bill of 1784 and the long-drawn-out state trial of 1786–95.

1 Embodied in Pope Alexander VI's three successive bulls of the 3rd May, the 4th May, and the 25th September, 1493, which were taken as the basis for the Spanish-Portuguese Agreement of the 7th June, 1494.

2 Coleridge, S. T.: *The Ancient Mariner*.

However sincerely Clive may have 'marvelled at' his 'own moderation', his economy of virtue would assuredly soon have cost his countrymen the loss of an Oriental dominion which his excess of unscrupulousness had suddenly won for them, if they had not exerted themselves to improve upon Clive's moral standards under the sobering influence of their American disaster.

The Roman See.

Perhaps the most signal of all public examples of the disastrous consequences of the intoxication of victory is afforded by one of the chapters in the long, and still living and lengthening, history of the Papacy.

The chapter in the history of this greatest of all Western institutions which began on the 20th December, 1046, with the opening of the Synod of Sutri by the Emperor Henry III,[1] and which closed on the 20th September, 1870, with the occupation of Rome by the troops of King Victor Emmanuel, displays certain broad correspondences with a chapter of almost equal length in the history of the Roman Republic which began with the *Clades Alliensis* of the 18th July, 390 B.C., and closed with the occupation of Rome by Alaric on the 24th August, A.D. 410. In both these dramas the wheel comes round full circle. In the historical tragedy of Papal Rome the ecclesiastical head of Western Christendom was compelled twice over to capitulate in his own See to a secular sovereign, as in the tragedy of pagan Rome the city which was the warden of the continental European marches of the Hellenic World[2] was likewise compelled twice over to admit a barbarian trespasser within her walls. In both these chapters of history the period of more than eight hundred years which the wheel of Fortune took to revolve was occupied by an extraordinary feat and an extraordinary fall. And in both chapters Rome brought her fall upon herself.

Without elaborating our parallel too fancifully, we may notice how these two versions of the Roman tragedy resemble one another act by act.

Just as the *Clades Alliensis* evoked among the citizens of the Roman Republic the mood in which, half a century later, they contended with the Samnites for the hegemony of Italy and won the prize through their victory in a fifty years' war (343–290 B.C.),[3] so the blow dealt to the Papacy by the Emperor Henry III at the Synod of Sutri reverberated in the soul of Hildebrand[4] for thirty

[1] For the preceding chapter in the history of the Papacy, which the Synod of Sutri brought to a close, see IV. C (iii) (*c*) 2 (*β*), pp. 335–40, above.

[2] For this role of Rome in the life of the Hellenic Society see II. D (v), vol. ii, pp. 161–4, above.

[3] See II. D (iv), vol. ii, pp. 101–2, above.

[4] While the proceedings at the Synod of Sutri shook Hildebrand and the other

years until he threw down the gauntlet to the Emperor Henry IV and launched the Papacy on its fifty years' contest with the Empire over the question of Investiture (A.D. 1075–1122). And if the conflict between the Papacy and the Salian Dynasty is comparable to the warfare between Rome and Samnium, the more violent, bitter, and devastating conflict between the Papacy and the Hohenstaufen Dynasty is still more strikingly reminiscent of the warfare between Rome and Carthage. In either case the duel between Rome and her arch-enemy took three rounds to fight itself out; and each successive round was fought with greater savagery than its predecessor. If the struggles between Pope Alexander III and the Emperor Frederick I, and between Pope Gregory IX and the Emperor Frederick II, may be regarded as the respective analogues of the First and Second Romano-Punic wars, the spirit in which the Romans made the Third Romano-Punic War, with the deliberate purpose of annihilating in cold blood an enemy who was already prostrate, was unmistakably revived in the Catonian implacability with which an Innocent IV and an Urban IV kept up their feud with the Emperor Frederick II after their great enemy's death, and insisted upon converting it from a quarrel with a single individual into a vendetta which could not be appeased by any lesser retribution than the complete ruin and annihilation of the whole of the offender's house.

In this Hohenstaufen-Punic act of the twice-performed Roman play the resemblances even extend to details. For example, the strategy of Frederick Barbarossa after his acknowledgement, in the peace-treaties of Venice (A.D. 1177) and Constance (A.D. 1183), of his failure to reassert the Imperial authority in Lombardy may be compared with Hamilcar Barca's strategy after the cession of the old Carthaginian dominion in Sicily in the peace settlement of 241 B.C. As Hamilcar set himself to conquer for Carthage a new and more valuable empire in the Iberian Peninsula, so Frederick secured for the House of Hohenstaufen the reversion of the Kingdom of Sicily. In either case a Power which had just been foiled in one trial of strength with its Roman adversary proceeded to occupy a new coign of vantage from which it could attack Rome on a second front with fresh supplies of men and money. In either case the consequence of this masterly stroke on the part of Rome's opponent was a second trial of strength on a greater scale which

Curial champions of reform into militancy, neither Hildebrand himself nor Saint Peter Damian nor Cardinal Humbert appears to have shown any personal animus against the Emperor Henry III—who had, after all, been seeking to serve the cause of reform in his high-handed use, or abuse, of his Imperial prerogative (see the evidence presented by Carlyle, R. W. and A. J.: *A History of Mediaeval Political Theory in the West*, vol. iv (Edinburgh and London 1922, Blackwood), pp. 20–1).

ended in confirming Rome's victory, but which brought her, first, so near to defeat, and left the victor's heart so morbidly obsessed by fear and hatred of the vanquished, that Rome could not rest until she had returned to the attack and had dealt her already beaten and stricken enemy 'the knock-out blow'.

In the next act a victorious Rome collapses ignominiously under the weight of a vindictiveness which has led her to pursue her adversary's destruction to her own undoing. The century of humiliation (A.D. 1303–1418) which was the nemesis of the Papacy's relentless pursuit of its vendetta against the Hohenstaufen has its analogue in the century of suffering with which the Roman Republic had to pay for the cold-blooded destruction of Carthage.[1] The desecration of the Pope's personal sacrosanctity through the brutal handling of Boniface VIII by Guillaume Nogaret and Sciarra Colonna may be compared with the pricking of the bubble of Roman military prestige by the ignominy of Mancinus's capitulation to the Numantines. In the sequel 'the Babylonish captivity' of the Papacy may be compared with the bout of revolution into which the Republic fell in 133 B.C.,[2] and 'the Great Schism' with the civil war out of which the Empire emerged in 31 B.C.

In either version, again, the last act is a melancholy and tedious anti-climax in which the play drags on for some four centuries longer before the curtain descends. If we fix our attention upon the abortive rallies by which the gloom of this twilight age is partially relieved, we may discern a dim resemblance between the pontificate of Martin V and the principate of Augustus and between 'the Counter-Reformation' and 'the Indian Summer' of the Antonines.[3] And as we watch the last scene of all we may detect in Pope Pius IX, who became 'the prisoner in the Vatican' as soon as the French garrison withdrew from Rome and the Italian army marched in, an historical counterpart of the Emperor Honorius, who became 'the refugee in Ravenna' when Rome was left at Alaric's mercy by the removal of Stilicho's protecting hand.

It will be apparent that our analogy with a chapter in the history of the Roman Commonwealth can give us some insight into the history of the Roman See between A.D. 1046 and A.D. 1870. Yet on a further analysis both the rise and the fall of the Papacy in this extraordinary passage of its career will be found to display features

1 See the present chapter, pp. 505–10, above.

2 One striking feature that the Papal régime during the period of 'the Babylonish Captivity' at Avignon has in common with the Republican régime in the Post-Gracchan Age is the development, on the grand scale, of an efficient but parasitic system of finance. A fiscal agent of the Papal Curia in the fourteenth century of the Christian Era and a Roman *publicanus* of the second century B.C. would have recognized one another as birds of a feather; and the affinity between them is not fortuitous; for either of these two Roman systems of finance was the Dead Sea fruit of a devastating war.

3 For this 'Indian Summer' see IV. C (ii) (*b*) 1, pp. 58–63, above.

which it would be difficult to illuminate by any historical parallels. In one aspect after another the Papal *Respublica Christiana* seems to defy classification and to reveal itself as something unique.

Perhaps the closest counterpart of the institution which was founded at Rome by the genius of Hildebrand in the eleventh century of the Christian Era is the régime which was inaugurated at Thebes by Hrihor, the Chief Priest of Amon-Re, in the eleventh century B.C.[1] The Rome of Hildebrand's day, like the Thebes of Hrihor's, was a holy city whose holiness was the legacy of an extinct political power.[2] In either city the place once filled by the emperor of a universal state was now occupied by the guardian and ministrant of the shrine of the city's tutelary divinity or saint; and this civic ecclesiastical dignitary had become the acknowledged shepherd, not only of the city itself, but of an oecumenical flock whose forebears had looked to Rome or Thebes, not for religious guidance, but for political leadership. In either case, again, the

[1] See II. D (v), vol. ii, p. 116, footnote 1, and IV. C (iii) (*c*) 2 (*β*), in the present volume, p. 421, above.

[2] Amon of Thebes became the paramount god, and the Chief Priest of Amon-Re the principal ecclesiastical dignitary, in the Egyptiac World in consequence of the fact that Thebes was the capital city of the Egyptiac universal state. If this universal state had not been founded by a dynasty from the Thebaid in the twenty-first century B.C. and restored by a dynasty from the Thebaid in the sixteenth century, it is certain that in the fifteenth century the Chief Priest of Amon-Re would not have been invested, as he was in the actual event, with the presidency of the Pan-Egyptiac corporation into which all the priests of all the gods in all the 'nomes' were organized by the Emperor Thothmes III (for this event, see I. C (ii), vol. i, p. 145, footnote 5, and IV. C (iii) (*c*) 2 (*β*), in the present volume, p. 421, above, and V. C (i) (*d*) 6 (*δ*), vol. v, p. 530, below). On the same showing, we may be sure that Rome would never have come to be the seat of the Papacy if in an earlier chapter of her history she had not been the nucleus and the capital of the Hellenic universal state. If the role of Rome in Hellenic history had been played, as it might have been played, by Athens (see IV. C (iii) (*c*) 2 (*α*), p. 264, and IV. C (iii) (*c*) 2 (*β*), pp. 306 and 314, above), or by Olynthus (see III. C (ii) (*b*), Annex IV, in vol. iii, above), then in a later age the Holy See would have been established on Attic or Chalcidian ground and not in the Ager Vaticanus. It is true that the Popes who laid claim to the loyalty and allegiance of Western Christendom from the eighth century onwards did not base their claim upon the former political supremacy of Pagan Rome. The name of power in which they spoke was not the name of Romulus or Caesar or Augustus, and not even the name of Constantine, but the name of Peter; and their text was not *Tu regere imperio populos, Romane, memento* but 'Upon this rock I will build my church', while the insignia in which they depicted the nature of their authority were the keys and not the *fasces*. At the same time it is certain that Peter would never have become connected with Rome (and this is equally certain, whether we regard the connexion as historical or as legendary) if Rome had not already played her historic part in secular history before the beginning of the Christian Era. The association of 'the Prince of the Apostles' with the *caput mundi* was inevitable; and their union would have been consummated without fail even if the capital of the world into which the Christian Church was born had happened to lie elsewhere—in Olynthus or in Athens or wherever it might have been. We may therefore affirm that the fortune of 'the Eternal City' would not have been made for the second time by Saint Peter if it had not been made in the first instance by the statesmen and generals who were the architects of the Roman Empire. It was the Scipios and the Gallios who unwittingly secured for Rome the priceless boon of becoming the Apostle's resting-place. How astonished these patriots would have been if the Delphic Apollo had informed them that their mundane labours were to result in turning their Rome into the holy city of an Oriental religion, and that no other benefit which they could conceivably confer upon her could be so great as this unwitting and involuntary gift. (For the legacy of Pagan Rome to Christian Rome see Schneider, F.: *Rom und Romgedanke im Mittelalter* (Munich 1926, Drei Masken Verlag).)

exercise of this wider authority by a local ecclesiastical functionary was rendered possible by the presence, in every part of the area over which this arch-priest claimed jurisdiction, of a clergy which was recruited, trained, and disciplined on a more or less uniform plan, was united by a potent *esprit de corps*, and was of one mind in looking to the shepherd of souls in the *ci-devant* political capital as the divinely appointed head and centre of a Church Universal. These points of resemblance between Hildebrand's *Respublica Christiana* and Hrihor's *Respublica Ammoniaca* are striking; but behind them all there is one essential difference between the two institutions. Hrihor simply assumed the secular crown[1] which had been worn by the lay rulers of 'the Middle Empire' and 'the New Empire' (the original and the resuscitated Egyptiac universal state) from the era of the Eleventh Dynasty down to the reign of the last *fainéant* Ramsid whom Hrihor himself had brushed aside; but this mere transference of a traditional secular authority from the hands of an effete lay dynasty into those of a capable and powerful ecclesiastical functionary was neither a political nor a religious success. The assumption of an alien office taxed the resources and drew upon the prestige of the Chief Priest of Amon-Re without bringing back to life the defunct authority of the Pharaoh whom the priest was impersonating.[2] The ecclesiastical usurper quickly became as impotent as the secular sovereign whom he had replaced; and, although his descendants prudently forbore from following Hrihor's example in assuming the Pharaonic style and title,[3] they were compelled in the tenth century B.C. to yield up their hereditary Chief Priesthood of Amon-Re, together with the *de facto* government of the Thebaid, with which this ecclesiastical office was now bound up, to the descendants of the intrusive Libyan war-lords who had carved up other portions of the derelict domain

[1] Hrihor gives himself the full Pharaonic style and title in his inscriptions (Meyer, E.: 'Gottesstaat, Militärherrschaft und Ständewesen in Ägypten (zur Geschichte der 21. und 22. Dynastie)' in *Sitzungsberichte der Preussischen Akademie der Wissenschaften, Jahrgang 1928, Philosophisch-Historische Klasse* (Berlin 1928, de Gruyter), pp. 495–532).

[2] Hrihor attempted to bolster up his political authority by entering into an *Ausgleich* with a secular Pharaoh, Smendes of Tanis, who was the *de facto* ruler of the Delta. This Deltaic partner was a pillar of strength for the priest-king of the Thebaid, since the political centre of gravity of the Egyptiac World had passed from the Thebaid to the Delta as far back as the thirteenth century B.C. (see II. D (v), vol. ii, pp. 112–18, above). Conversely, the traditional religious prestige of the Theban deity no doubt made it well worth while for Smendes to enter into partnership with Hrihor. Either partner seems to have assumed, with the other partner's acquiescence, a plenitude of the Pharaonic power within his own *de facto* domain; and their relation must have been not unlike that which subsisted between the co-emperors who held the Roman Imperial office in commission at various times from the generation of Diocletian to that of Zeno. The Pharaonic crowns of Tanis and Thebes were united on the head of Pinozem I, who was Hrihor's grandson and at the same time son-in-law of Smendes' son and successor Psusennes (Psibkhenno) I. When, however, Pinozem I actually entered into his Tanitic secular heritage, he abdicated from his Theban Chief Priesthood and conferred this upon one of his sons (Meyer, op. cit., pp. 496–8).

[3] Meyer, op. cit., p. 497.

two or three centuries ending in 480 B.C.,[1] by the priesthood of the Delphic Apollo. Like the Apostle at Rome, the god at Delphi advised and reprimanded the Governments of the local states of the world over which he presided, besides dealing with private individuals. In particular, the activities of an Urban II or an Innocent III or a Gregory VIII or a Gregory X in evoking and directing the Crusades find their parallel in the activities of the Delphic Oracle in promoting and guiding an equally militant expansion of the Hellenic Society round the coasts of the Mediterranean in the eighth and seventh and sixth centuries B.C. But this analogy between the tutelary functions of Peter in Western Christendom and Apollo in Hellas is imperfect, like the other analogies which we have already suggested; and, here once more, the difference behind the likeness is fundamental. While the Apostle's authority was to some extent active and jussive, the god's seems to have been almost entirely passive and permissive. The Apostle sometimes took the initiative in issuing commands and prohibitions which were most unwelcome to the Governments or individuals concerned and which would certainly never have been solicited, even if they had to be obeyed when once they had been promulgated by the importunity of a pontiff who had not waited to be asked. On the other hand the god left it to his votaries to approach him or not as they chose, and if, when they did seek his advice, they elected to disregard it, they were free to flout his oracle at their peril. The god took no responsibility upon himself for guiding an inquirer's 'feet into the way of peace'.[2] A docile inquirer would have to congratulate himself, rather than give thanks to the Lord Apollo, if he were able to testify that 'by the word of thy lips I have kept me from the paths of the destroyer';[3] and when an inquirer proved unteachable the god waited sardonically to see his own divine wisdom vindicated in the fullness of time by the human fool's catastrophe. Between Delphi and the rest of Hellas, as between Papal Rome and the rest of Western Christendom, there was a constant coming and going of messengers on sacred errands; but the most significant travellers on the roads which converged upon Delphi were the private inquirers or public *θεωροί*[4] from the city-

[1] The prestige of Delphi never recovered from the devastating effects of the supreme error—of the heart as well as of the head—which the Delphic priesthood made in ranging itself on the side of the big battalions on the eve of Xerxes' invasion of European Greece. The damage was not repaired by the sedulous propagation of the legend of the god's miraculous intervention in defence of his shrine; and the blow was fatal—coming, as it did, at a moment when the authority of the oracle was bound in any case to be challenged in the light of the intellectual *Aufklärung* which was setting in in the generation of Aeschylus.

[2] Luke i. 79.

[3] Psalm xvii. 4.

[4] For the technical meaning of the Greek word *θεωρός* see III. C (ii) (*b*), vol. iii, p. 253, footnote 1, above.

states of Hellas, while the most significant travellers on the roads which radiated from Rome were perhaps the Papal *legati a latere* to the *mulūk-aṭ-ṭawā'if* in the provinces of Peter's spiritual empire. This difference in the direction of the more important traffic[1] points to a difference between the god's relation to his votaries and the Apostle's relation to his flock.

Of course the traffic between Papal Rome and her ecclesiastical provinces was not all outward-bound; for every road must also lead to a city from which every road radiates, and the outgoing traffic of legates and tax-gatherers was crossed by an incoming traffic of pilgrims, petitioners, and litigants. These visitors to Rome did not come merely to obtain in person the Apostle's judgements; they came to worship at his shrine and venerate his relics—acts of piety which could not be performed anywhere outside Saint Peter's Church *in Agro Vaticano*. This fact reminds us that the power of the Papacy in medieval Western Christendom was derived from yet one other thing besides the character and ability of the Pope himself and his Curia, the status and organization of the clergy throughout the domain of the Roman Patriarchate, the prestige which Christian Rome derived from her pagan predecessor, and the still greater prestige with which her bishop was invested in his capacity of successor to 'the Prince of the Apostles' who had honoured Pagan Rome by taking her for his see. The other thing, in addition to all these, which contributed to the Papacy's strength—and perhaps had more effect than anything else upon the imagination and emotion of the masses—was the possession of a unique talisman in the shape of the tomb which was reputed to contain the Apostle's mortal remains.[2] And this aspect of Papal

[1] Mr. Geoffrey Barraclough, who kindly read this chapter before publication, observes, in a letter to the writer: 'In spite of the beginning of the next paragraph, the active, directive side of Roman action seems to me to be overstressed—the element of passive reaction to the calls of private inquirers and private interests made too incidental. The latter was characteristic of Papal government more than the former; or at any rate it was the latter which accounted for the real centralization of the Church in the 13th and 14th centuries.' Fuller expositions of Mr. Barraclough's view on this point will be found in his *Papal Provisions* (Oxford 1935, Blackwell), ch. 12; in *Public Notaries and the Papal Curia* (London 1934, Macmillan), pp. 130–1; and in *The English Historical Review*, vol. xlix, pp. 214–16. On Mr. Barraclough's showing, the analogy between the medieval Papacy and the Delphic Oracle *prae* 480 B.C. is closer than had been supposed by the writer of this Study.

[2] It was this loadstone that drew the Vicar of Peter back to Rome in the fifteenth century after his migration to Avignon in the fourteenth. There was everything to be said for the migration from the standpoints of administrative convenience and social amenity. Rome—the decayed capital of an extinct Hellenic universal state—was situated in what was now a remote, backward, and turbulent province on the extreme south-eastern edge of the Western Christendom; and her situation had not been appreciably altered by the superficial Westernization of the Orthodox Christian domain in Southern Italy and Sicily as a result of the Norman Conquest in the eleventh century. On the other hand Avignon was an orderly, civilized place near the heart of the medieval Western World. It lay in the middle sector of Lothaire's portion of Charlemagne's heritage (see I. B (iv), vol. i, pp. 37–40, above), on the border-line between the Holy Roman Empire and France, in the valley of the Rhône (which, in spite of the growth of

Rome has a number of analogues in other holy cities: in Jerusalem with its Holy Sepulchre, in Medina with its tomb of the Prophet, in Najaf with its tomb of the Caliph and Martyr 'Alī, in Karbalā with its tomb of the Martyr Husayn, and in Canterbury with its tomb of the Prelate and Martyr Thomas Becket.[1] The Rome that contained the tombs of Saint Peter and Saint Paul resembled all these other sepulchre-cities in being a focus of emotion and a lode-star of pilgrimage; but this analogy breaks down like all the rest; for what sepulchre-city save Rome alone has ever succeeded in transmuting a focus of emotion into a seat of authority, and in exerting her magic influence over her pilgrims, not merely at the moment when they are standing, rapt and awe-stricken, on the threshold of the Holy of Holies, but throughout their working lives, in the humdrum environment of their homes?

It will be seen that there is a vein of uniqueness in the Papal *Respublica Christiana* which baffles our attempts to describe its character by the method of analogy. It can be better described, in negative terms, as an exact inversion of the 'Caesaro-papal' régime[2] against which it was a social reaction and a spiritual protest; and this description perhaps gives, better than any other, the measure of Hildebrand's achievement.

When the Tuscan Hildebrand took up his abode in Rome, as a stranger within her gates, in the second quarter of the eleventh century, he found himself in a derelict outpost of the East Roman Empire which was occupied by a degenerate offshoot of the Byzantine Society. For three centuries past, the natives of the Ducatus Romanus had shown themselves incapable not only of defending their own borders against their Lombard neighbours in Gregory's own Tuscany and in the Basin of the Po, but even of keeping order among themselves when a Transalpine Power stepped in to hold

the traffic over the Brenner, was still the main highway between the Cisalpine and the Transalpine portion of the domain of the Roman Patriarchate). Situated as it was, Avignon was well on the way from the traditional ecclesiastical headquarters of Western Christendom on the lower Tiber to its genuine headquarters of that day in the upper valley of the Saône—at the junction of the routes between the basins of the Rhône, the Rhine, and the Seine—in a Burgundy which embraced Luxeuil (see II. D (vii), vol. ii, p. 330, above) and Cluny and Cîteaux. The fact that, notwithstanding these overwhelming material advantages, Avignon was unable to hold its own against Rome as an alternative residence for the Holy See, gives the measure of the importance of the Tomb *in Agro Vaticano* as a source of Papal prestige and power.

[1] The sagacious Ptolemy Sôtêr sought to head this list of sepulchre-cities with the name of Alexandria when he took possession of the founder's body and built a tomb for it in the most famous of the cities that had been called after Alexander in his life-time. Ptolemy grasped the importance of the prestige which it was possible for a city to derive from the possession of the relics of an historic personality. In the event, however, it was not as the site of Alexander's sepulchre, but as the political capital of Ptolemy's Empire and as the workshop of the Hellenic World, that the Egyptian Alexandria grew to greatness.

[2] For a definition and discussion of 'Caesaro-papism', apropos of the idolization, in Orthodox Christendom, of a resuscitated ghost of the Roman Empire, see IV. C (iii) (*c*) 2 (*β*), pp. 347–8, above.

the Lombards at arm's length. And these latter-day Romans were financially and spiritually bankrupt besides being militarily weak and socially turbulent The overseas portion of the Patrimonia Petri or Papal estates, which had still supplied Gregory the Great with resources for keeping alive the population of a *ci-devant* capital city,[1] had subsequently gone the way of the estates on the Italian mainland during the four centuries that had elapsed between the death of the first Gregory and the birth of his seventh Papal namesake; and in the eleventh century the Papacy no longer possessed any assured or regular sources of income.[2] As for the moral bankruptcy of the Ducatus Romanus in that age, it is revealed not merely in the sordid annals of its social history but in the necessity in which the Romans now found themselves of looking abroad for spiritual light and leading. To raise the local standard of monastic life the Romans had to turn for help and guidance to Calabria[3] and to Cluny; and the first attempts to regenerate the Papacy took the form of passing over Roman candidates and appointing Transalpines. The precedent was set by the appointment of the Saxon Emperor Otto III's former tutor, the French scholar Gerbert of Aurillac, who mounted the Papal throne as Sylvester II (*pontificali munere fungebatur* A.D. 999–1003); and, after a reversion to Popes of Roman birth which ended in the humiliation of A.D. 1046, the Chair of St. Peter was not occupied by a Roman again until the election of Innocent II in A.D. 1130. Of the fourteen Popes who reigned in the interval, eight were Transalpines,[4] two were Tuscan Lombards, two were South Italians, and two were Romagnols. This shows how low the reputation of the Roman people stood in the eyes of a Western World which was now to be brought under the spell of the Roman See by the work of Hildebrand and his successors.[5] The

[1] See III. C (ii) (*b*), vol. iii, p. 269, above. [2] See p. 536, footnote 2, below.

[3] See IV. C (iii) (*c*) 2 (β), p. 357, above.

[4] The Tyrolese Poppo of Brixen, who became Pope Damasus II in A.D. 1048, may be reckoned among the Transalpines for sociological purposes, in spite of the physiographical fact that Brixen lies on the southern side of the watershed between the Adige and the Inn.

[5] What the Lombards thought of the Romans before Rome was restored to glory by the Tuscan Lombard Hildebrand is revealed in the following passage from the works of Liutprand of Cremona, who was Hildebrand's senior by about a hundred years. The passage occurs in the twelfth chapter of Liutprand's report on his mission to Constantinople in A.D. 968. He is describing the high words that passed between himself and the East Roman Emperor Nicephorus Phocas during a dinner-party that the Emperor was giving in his honour.

'When I was on the point', writes Liutprand, 'of answering him back . . . he would not let me, but added, by way of insulting me: "You are not Romans, but Lombards!" He wanted to say more, and signed to me with his hand to keep quiet, but I lost my temper and burst out. "That fratricide Romulus," I said, "after whom the Romans are named, was a son of a whore—born, I mean, in adultery—as every schoolboy knows. What he did was to set up an alsatia in which debtors, fugitive slaves, murderers, and other criminals whose lives were forfeit received asylum until their numbers mounted up to a mob of undesirables whom their host dubbed Romans. This is the noble origin of the people whom you style the Lords of the World (*kosmocratores, id est imperatores*). And these are also the people whom we—and by 'us' I mean us Lombards, Saxons,

only special asset which the Ducatus Romanus possessed was a certain precocity in the art of administration which it displayed in common with the main body of the Byzantine World.[1] This was the unpromising site on which Hildebrand laid the foundations of his *Respublica Christiana.*

In this despised and alien Rome Hildebrand and his successors succeeded in creating the master-institution of Western Christendom. They won for Papal Rome an empire which had a greater hold than the Empire of the Antonines upon human hearts, and which on the mere material plane embraced vast tracts of Western Europe, beyond the Rhine and Danube, where the legions of Augustus and Marcus Aurelius had never even set foot, not to speak of establishing a permanent occupation. Indeed, this Papal dominion was wider than Charlemagne's, who had succeeded—though at ruinous cost[2]—in advancing his frontier from the Rhine to the Elbe and thereby achieving a feat which had proved to be beyond the strength of Augustus; for even Charlemagne never pushed his conquests beyond the Channel or the Baltic, while the medieval Papacy had inherited a spiritual dominion over England from the pontificate of Gregory the Great, two hundred years before Charlemagne's time, and had gone on to make a spiritual conquest of Scandinavia some two hundred years after Charlemagne's death.

These Papal conquests were partly due to the constitution of the Christian Republic whose frontiers the Popes were enlarging; for it was a constitution which inspired confidence and affection instead of evoking hostility and resistance.[3] The Papal *Respublica Christiana* was based on a combination of ecclesiastical centralism and uniformity with political diversity and devolution; and, since the superiority of the spiritual over the temporal power was a cardinal point of constitutional doctrine, this combination made the note of unity predominant, without depriving the adolescent Western Society of those elements of liberty and elasticity which are indispensable conditions for growth. Indeed, the acceptance of the social unity of Western Christendom, which was implicit in a common recognition of the spiritual authority of the Pope, carried with it a certain guarantee for the political independence of any local

Franks, Lorrainers, Bavarians, Swabians, and Burgundians—despise so utterly that, when we lose our temper with our enemies and want to insult them, we pronounce the single word 'Roman!'—conveying, in the use of this pregnant appellation, all the baseness and cowardice and avarice and effeminacy and mendacity of which human nature is capable."'

[1] For this gift and its fatal consequences in Orthodox Christendom see IV. C (iii) (*c*) 2 (β), pp. 320–408, above.

[2] See II. D (v), vol. ii, p. 167; II. D (vii), vol. ii, p. 345; IV. C (iii) (*c*) 2 (β), in the present volume, pp. 322–3; and IV. C (iii) (*c*) 3 (α), pp. 488–90, above.

[3] On this point see IV. C (iii) (*c*) 2 (β), in the present volume, pp. 377–9, above.

community that took upon itself the Papal yoke—a burden which, in the eleventh century, was still apostolically light. It was by entering into direct relations with the Holy See, and thereby becoming acknowledged members of the Western Christian Society in their own right, that the newly converted barbarian kingdoms of Hungary and Poland exorcised the danger of being conquered and annexed by the *Regnum Teutonicum* as the Saxons, in their day, had been forcibly 'Westernized' by Charlemagne, and as the Irish and the Prussians in a later century were to be subjected, respectively, by the English Crown and by the Teutonic Order.[1] Thanks to the Holy See the Hungarians and the Poles were able, like the English, to enjoy the social and cultural benefits of membership in the society of Western Christendom without having to pay the price of forfeiting their political independence. It was also thanks, in large measure, to an alliance or community of interests with the Holy See that the city-states of Lombardy were able to vindicate their political autonomy against the Emperor Frederick I and to maintain it against the Emperor Frederick II.[2]

Nor was the medieval Papacy illiberal in its attitude towards aspirations after local self-government, even in those Central Italian territories over which it claimed secular as well as ecclesiastical authority in virtue of the successive donations of Pepin and Charlemagne and Matilda. It appears to have accepted the situation without protest when the movement which was turning cities into city-states spread from Lombardy, where it had first asserted itself, into Romagna and the Marches and Umbria. In Tuscany in A.D. 1198 Pope Innocent III gave his recognition to the newly formed league of city-states, and urged Pisa to join it; and this benevolence extended to the Ducatus Romanus itself, which was the Papacy's metropolitan province. The Papal influence was here exerted to protect the nascent civic liberties of Tivoli and Tusculum and Viterbo against the aggressiveness of the citizens of Rome; and the Holy See was quick to make peace with the civic movement in Rome itself when it broke out there, in 1143, in a militant and revolutionary form. The Roman revolution of 1143 was followed by the settlement of 1145 between the new republic and Pope

[1] The subjugation of Ireland by the English Crown was sanctioned in advance by an incumbent of the Papal office who was perhaps unable to forget that, before he became Pope Hadrian IV, he had been the Englishman Nicholas Breakspear (for the Bull *Laudabiliter* see II. D (vii), vol. ii, p. 337, footnote 1, above); but this case seems to be exceptional. Indeed, it is the only notable instance in which the medieval Papacy lent its authority to promote the conquest of a small and weak community within the bosom of Western Christendom by a large and strong one. The part played by the Papacy in helping Hungary and Poland to escape the heavy yoke of the Holy Roman Empire, and the city-states of Lombardy to throw it off, is more characteristic of the Papal policy towards the political system of medieval Western Christendom.

[2] See III. C (ii) (*b*), vol. iii, pp. 345–6, above.

Eugenius III; and this settlement was revised and renewed in 1188 during the pontificate of Clement III.

At the turn of the twelfth and thirteenth centuries, when the civic movement was in full flood in Italy and when the Papal authority stood at its zenith over Western Christendom, a Welsh poet was 'pointing out . . . how strange it was that the Pope's censure, which in Rome could not move trifles, was elsewhere making the sceptres of kings tremble; and that he to whom in Rome a poorly kept garden would not yield was striving to bend kingdoms to his nod'.[1] Giraldus Cambrensis fancied that he was here exposing a paradox which was a theme for satire; but if this was one of the subjects which he discussed with Pope Innocent III in an interview which the Pope once granted him in a leisure hour,[2] we may conjecture that the Pontifical statesman found little difficulty in convincing the Welsh man-of-letters of his error. The very reason why in this age a majority of the princes and city-states of Western Christendom accepted the Papal supremacy with little demur was because the Pope was not then under suspicion of attempting to trespass upon the domain of the secular power.[3] So far from claiming a monopoly of territorial sovereignty, like the contemporary emperors at Constantinople, or a primacy *inter pares*, like the Holy Roman Emperors in the West from Otto the Great onwards in their relations with the independent kings of France or England or Leon, the Holy See in this age was not concerned in the competition for territorial rulership.[4] It was exercising on an oecu-

[1] Mann, the Right Reverend Monsignor H. K.: *The Lives of the Popes in the Middle Ages* (London 1910–29, Kegan Paul, 15 vols.), vol. xi, p. 72. The original Latin of Giraldus's verses runs as follows:

> Mirum quae Romæ modicos sententia papae
> non movet, hic regum sceptra movere potest.
> quae minimos minime censura coercet in urbe
> saevit in orbe fremens celsaque colla premens.
> cui male sublatus Romae non cederet hortus
> nititur ad nutum flectere regna suum.

Giraldi Cambrensis Opera, edited by Brewer, J. S., vol. i (London 1861, Longmans Green), p. 377 (with another version on p. 374).

[2] See Mann, op. cit., vol. xi, p. 68.

[3] Evidence, drawn from Innocent III's own letters, that he 'did not, as Pope, claim supreme temporal power', is presented in Carlyle, R. W. and A. J.: *A History of Mediaeval Political Theory in the West*, vol. v (Edinburgh and London 1928, Blackwood), p. 158.

[4] There was, however, in Hildebrand's day—and presumably under Hildebrand's inspiration—a movement in the Papal Curia to secure a recognition of the Holy See's feudal overlordship over Western Christian kingdoms which lay outside the limits of the Holy Roman Empire. The Norman principalities in Southern Italy accepted this status of vasseldom to the Holy See in A.D. 1059, Aragon in 1063, Dalmatia in 1076, Provence in 1081, Tarragona in 1091, Portugal *circa* 1140. On the other hand, England rejected a proposal that she should enter into this status *circa* 1079, and France *circa* 1081 (Dufourcq, A.: *L'Avenir du Christianisme: Première Partie: Histoire Moderne de l'Église*, vol. vi, fourth edition (Paris 1924, Plon), p. 167). After his accession to the Papacy, Hildebrand made similar proposals to the Kings of Hungary and Denmark, to the Corsicans, and even to a Russian prince (see Carlyle, R. W. and A. J.: *A History of Mediaeval Political Theory in the West*, vol. iv (Edinburgh and London 1922, Blackwood), Part I, ch. 4.

menical scale an authority of a spiritual character which was on a different plane from any territorial prerogative, and which, so long as it remained on this plane, did not become a danger to local political liberties.[1] The proof positive of the Pope's intention to stand above the territorial battle, and of his unwillingness to descend into the arena, was his acquiescence in his own practical exclusion from participation in the civil government of the city which was his episcopal see; and in this light the contrast between the Pope's impotence in Rome and his power in Western Christendom at large is seen to be no paradox at all, but a necessary consequence of the constitution of the *Respublica Christiana*. It is not too much to say that throughout the history of the Papacy down to the present day the oecumenical religious authority of the Popes and their local territorial power have regularly varied in inverse ratio with one another.

This statesmanlike aloofness from territorial ambitions was combined, in the Papal hierocracy at its zenith, with an energetic and enterprising use of the administrative gift which was the Byzantine dowry of Papal Rome. While in Orthodox Christendom this gift had been fatally applied to the *tour de force* of putting substance into a resuscitated ghost of the Roman Empire, and thereby crushing an adolescent Orthodox Christian Society under the incubus of an institution which was too heavy for it to bear,[2] the Roman architects of the *Respublica Christiana* turned their administrative resources to better account for building a lighter structure, on a new plan, upon broader foundations. The gossamer filaments of the Papal spider's web, as it was originally woven, drew medieval Western Christendom together into an unconstrained unity which was equally beneficial to the parts and to the whole. It was only later, when the fabric coarsened and hardened in the stress of conflict, that the silken threads changed into iron bands, and that these

[1] On this passage the writer has received the following comment from Mr. G. Barraclough:

'"Authority of a spiritual character" is good theory; but such authority has to exercise itself on material things, and there is no guarantee that the boundaries, distinct enough in most spheres, will not become blurred in others. That is, e.g., the difficulty in England. Henry II, Edward I, and Henry IV all grant up mere *spiritualia* to the Pope—or, better, cannot conceive themselves as having any interest in them. But they take a different attitude regarding *causae spirituali annexae* or *causae mixtae*. Thus, in regard to the benefice, is it the *officium* which counts, and is any dispute therefore "spiritual"? This in regard to the one point of jurisdiction. It can be agreed that the Pope did not then "attempt to trespass": neither did the Kings—but there was a "no-man's-land". They tried to settle the problems that this raised impartially (cf. Mollat, G.: 'L'Application du Droit de Régale Spirituel en France' in the *Revue d'Histoire Ecclésiastique*, 1929, for the Parliament of Paris; Barraclough, *Papal Provisions*, p. 85, for the Roman Rota) and not to make capital out of them; but it was not always easy to do so even in fact, and certainly not in theory. Thus you get the position implied in the phrase: "Dñs Papa scit et tolerat!" On the major scale of politics, what of Innocent III's interventions all over the medieval world? From his point of view, he was justified in regarding it as an exercise of spiritual authority, but it was natural that others did not.'

[2] See IV. C (iii) (*c*) 2 (*β*), pp. 320–408, above.

came to weigh so heavily upon the local princes and peoples, and so grievously to restrict their movements and cramp their growth, that at last they burst their bonds in a temper in which they hardly cared if, in severally liberating themselves, they were destroying that oecumenical unity which the Papacy had established and preserved.[1]

In that Papal work of creation it was not, of course, either a capacity for administration or an avoidance of the snare of territorial ambitions that was the vital creative force. The fundamental reason why the Roman See was able in this age to conjure into existence a Christian Republic under a Papal aegis was because, at this stage, the Papacy threw itself without hesitations or reservations into the task of giving leadership and expression and organization to an adolescent Western Civilization's awakening desires for a higher life and a larger growth. The Hildebrandine Papacy identified its own purpose and *raison d'être* with aspirations which were dimly and dumbly stirring in the hearts and minds of the *Plebs Christiana*; it gave these aspirations form and fame, and thereby transformed them from the day-dreams of isolated individuals or scattered minorities into common causes which carried the conviction that they were supremely worth fighting for, and which swept men off their feet when they heard these causes preached by Popes who were staking upon them the fortunes of the Holy See and perhaps their own lives as well. The victory of the Christian Republic was won in the Papal campaigns for the purification of the clergy from the two moral plagues of sexual incontinence and financial corruption, for the liberation of the life of the Church from the interference of secular powers, and for the rescue of the Oriental Christians and the Holy Land from the clutches of the Turkish champions of Islam; but this was not the whole of the Hildebrandine Papacy's work; for the great Popes under whose leadership these 'holy wars' were fought on those diverse fronts were not entirely engrossed in the struggles of the Church Militant. Even in the times of greatest stress they had a margin of thought and will to spare for works of peace in which the Church was displaying her finest self and was exercising her most creative activity. Pope Alexander III (*fungebatur* A.D. 1159–81) was fostering the nascent universities of the West at a time when he was a penniless refugee, with an Emperor lunging at him from one flank and an Antipope snapping at him from the other. And the series of movements in which a torpid monasticism was first reawakened at Cluny and Cîteaux and then transformed into a new thing by Saint Dominic and Saint Francis, were each in

[1] See IV. C (iii) (*b*) 11, vol. iv, pp. 214–22, above.

turn observed, approved, supported, and propagated by the Holy See, though it was the exception and not the rule for the Pope himself to be a member of a religious order.

This genius for descrying the seeds of noble things and for bringing the crop to harvest was the crowning virtue of the Papacy in the days of its Hildebrandine greatness; and this genius was not displayed only in a fruitful patronage of promising institutions like the universities or the religious orders; besides being an august patron of institutions the Papacy was an apostolic fisher of men;[1] and its greatest triumph was its enlistment of the purest souls and ablest wits and strongest characters of Western Christendom in the service of the Holy See—a service which was embraced with enthusiasm by eminent men and women because it offered them scope for living lives and doing deeds for which there was no opportunity in the secular world. These valiant and faithful servants of the Holy See were drawn from every country of Western Christendom and from every class of society and from every type of character. There were mystics and intellectuals and men of action; monks and kings and peasants and lawyers; Lombards and Burgundians and Frenchmen and Germans and Romans—for the very *faex Romana* which an Otto III and a Henry III had justly judged unworthy, in their day, to supply a Roman candidate for the Roman See, gave birth in the following century to that noble Lotario de' Conti di Segni who was to ascend, as Innocent III, a throne which had been disgraced by the Theophylacts and Crescenzi.

In this goodly company of *servientes servo servorum Dei* there were some, like Hugh of Cluny and Bernard of Clairvaux and Matilda of Tuscany and Louis IX of France, who performed their service in the provinces or *outre mer*, while others were called from the ends of the Earth to do their work in the Curia and there perhaps to rise, through the Cardinalate, to the highest position attainable by any citizen of the medieval Western Republic.

The first name on the roll of eminent servants of the Holy See in the Hildebrandine Age who completed their service in the Papal chair is that of Hildebrand himself: the greatest man of action in the history of our Western Society hitherto, if greatness is to be measured by the nature of the aim as well as by the extent of the performance.[2] Ildebrando Aldobrandeschi was the child of a Tuscan peasant who was sent to Rome to be educated; was taken into

[1] Matt. iv. 19.

[2] 'His was that rarest and grandest of gifts: an intellectual courage and power of imaginative belief which, when it has convinced itself of aught, accepts it fully with all its consequences and shrinks not from acting at once upon it.'—Bryce, James: *The Holy Roman Empire*, chap. 10.

the Papal Curia by his schoolmaster when Giovanni Graziano became Pope Gregory VI; and served the Holy See thereafter for 28 years (A.D. 1045–73) before he himself became Pope Gregory VII (*fungebatur* A.D. 1073–85).

The second of the six predecessors of Pope Gregory VII who leaned in turn upon the deacon Hildebrand, and never found him a broken reed, was Bruno of Egisheim, the son of an Alsatian nobleman who was a first cousin of the Saxon Emperor Conrad II. Educated for the Church, Bruno qualified himself for the highest office in it by serving a twenty-three years' apprenticeship in his native Lotharingia. Nominated for the Papacy by the Emperor Henry III in response to a request from the Romans themselves for an Imperial nominee, Bruno only accepted the nomination on condition that it was confirmed in Rome, upon his arrival there, by a free election; and it was on this understanding that Hildebrand, on his part, accepted Bruno's pressing invitation to go to Rome with him as his right-hand man.[1] The noble friendship and potent collaboration of the Alsatian and the Tuscan during Bruno's pontificate as Leo IX (*fungebatur* A.D. 1049–54) launched the Hildebrandine movement on its historic course with a momentum which continued to carry it onward for more than two hundred years.

Among Hildebrand's successors, Odo of Châtillon-sur-Marne was a knight's son who became a monk of Cluny and then served the Curia as Cardinal of Ostia before he became Pope Urban II (*fungebatur* A.D. 1088–99) and translated into action one of Hildebrand's cherished projects when he launched the First Crusade.[2]

The Romagnol Rainer of Blera was another monk of Cluny who became Pope Paschal II (*fungebatur* A.D. 1099–1118) and all but succeeded in settling with the Emperor Henry V the formidable question—over which Henry IV and Hildebrand had joined battle —of where the line was to be drawn between the respective jurisdictions of Church and State.[3]

Guy de Vienne was a Burgundian prince who was Archbishop of his own city before he became Pope Calixtus II (*fungebatur* A.D. 1119–24) and brought to terms, by hard fighting and shrewd

[1] Hildebrand had left Rome in 1047 in order to accompany his first master, Pope Gregory VI, in his Transalpine exile; and, after travelling with him to Cologne, he had travelled on, after the exiled Pope's death, to Cluny. From Cluny he had come, like Bruno, to Worms in order to attend the conference which was convened there by the Emperor Henry III for taking action on the Roman request. When Bruno, after his nomination, invited Hildebrand to go to Rome with him, Hildebrand consented against his own desire, as a matter of ecclesiastical obedience.

[2] See V. C (i) 3, vol. v, pp. 242–4, below, for the origin and range of a movement of Western expansion in which the First Crusade was not quite the first step.

[3] On the difficulties of this problem—which is still a cause of perplexity and strife in the latter-day Western World of our own generation—see Mr. G. Barraclough's observations on p. 526, footnote 1, above.

compromise, the Emperor who had got the better of the less worldly-wise Pope Paschal II.

Bernardo Paganelli was a Tuscan nobleman—a son of the lord of Montemagno in the Lucchese—who became a monk of Clairvaux and was sent by St. Bernard to serve Pope Innocent II in Rome—a service in which he rose to be Pope Eugenius III (*fungebatur* A.D. 1145–53), the negotiator of the settlement of A.D. 1145 between the Holy See and the revolutionary Roman Republic.

Rolando Rainucci, or Bandinelli, was a Sienese canonist who learnt his law at Bologna, was brought to Rome and made a cardinal by Pope Eug nius III, and justified his master's opinion of him by the indomitable courage with which he held out victoriously against the Emperor Frederick I and three successive Antipopes as Pope Alexander III (*fungebatur* A.D. 1159–81).[1]

Ubaldo Allucingoli was a canonist from Lucca who, as Pope Lucius III (*fungebatur* A.D. 1181–5), knew how to hold the ground which Alexander III had won from the Emperor Frederick.

Umberto Crivelli was the son of Milanese parents—belonging to the prosperous bourgeoisie—who became a canon of Bourges, and afterwards Archbishop of his native city, before he failed, for all his fulminations, as Pope Urban III (*fungebatur* A.D. 1185–7), to prevent the marriage of Frederick's son Henry with Constance of Sicily.

Alberto di Morra was a Beneventan monk of the Premonstratensian monastery of Saint Martin at Laon who served the Holy See as Papal Chancellor before, as Pope Gregory VIII (*fungebatur* A.D. 1187), he became a peacemaker—first between the Holy See itself and the Holy Roman Empire, and then between Pisa and Genoa—in the cause of the Crusades.

Lotario de' Conti di Segni was a nobleman of the Ducatus Romanus who studied in the universities of Paris and Bologna before he was called, at the early age of 37, to preside over the Hildebrandine Church, in its hour of noonday splendour, as Pope Innocent III (*fungebatur* A.D. 1198–1216).

Cencio Savelli was a member of another noble Roman house who served the Curia as *Auditor* (judge) and *Camerarius* (treasurer) before he ascended the Papal throne as Pope Honorius III (*fungebatur* A.D. 1216–27) and attempted to cope with a plausibly evasive Frederick II.

Ugolino de' Conti di Segni was a great-nephew of Pope Innocent III who, as Cardinal of Saint Eustachius, half appreciated and half patronized Saint Francis of Assisi, and who ventured, as Pope

[1] In Mr. Barraclough's judgement (*Papal Provisions*, p. 1) it was Alexander III who translated Gregory VII's claims into accomplished facts.

Gregory IX (*fungebatur* A.D. 1227–41), to try conclusions, in the strength of his worldly wisdom, with 'the Wonder of the World' who had baffled Pope Honorius III.

Sinibaldo Fieschi, son of Ugo Count of Lavagna, was a Genoese canonist who served as Papal *Auditor* and Vice-Chancellor and Rector of the Marche before, as Pope Innocent IV (*fungebatur* A.D. 1243–54), he threw himself—'impiger, iracundus, inexorabilis, acer'[1]—into the festering war between the Holy See and the Emperor Frederick II, and waged it *ad internecionem*.

Rainaldo de' Conti di Segni was a nephew of Pope Gregory IX who carried on the Papal struggle against the Hohenstaufen as Pope Alexander IV (*fungebatur* A.D. 1254–61) without departing from his predecessor's policy in this respect, but who at the same time tried to save the Church herself from the evil effects of the political conflict by revoking many of Innocent IV's ruinous acts,[2] following in regard to the Friars the more generous policy of his own kinsman and predecessor Gregory IX, and preparing the way for Gregory X's valiant strivings to bring about a spiritual rally.

Jacques Pantaléon was the son of a tradesman in Troyes who studied in the University of Paris, became a canonist, served Pope Innocent IV as his legate militant in Germany, and eventually dealt 'the knock-out blow' to the House of Hohenstaufen with his own hand when, as Pope Urban IV (*fungebatur* A.D. 1261–4), he induced the relentless Charles of Anjou to accept the crown of Sicily.

Guy Fulcodi was the son of a nobleman of St. Gilles in Languedoc who had served the Counts of Toulouse as a legal adviser. Guy himself performed the same service for King Louis IX of France till he was made a cardinal by Pope Urban IV and then became Pope himself as Clement IV (*fungebatur* A.D. 1265–8). In passing over from the Law to the Church, and rising from the Cardinalate to the Papal Throne, Fulcodi never won his manumission from the service of a royal master; he merely exchanged a Louis for a Charles; and the exchange was unfortunate; for, if Louis was a saint whose service was perfect freedom, Charles was a hard man, reaping where he had not sown and gathering where he had not strawed.[3] For all his uprightness, Pope Clement sank from being Charles' patron to becoming his accomplice, and from being his accomplice to becoming his tool, while the cold-blooded Angevin dealt with the brood of Frederick II as Jehu had dealt with the House of Ahab.[4]

[1] Horace: *Ars Poetica*, l. 121.

[2] See the criticism of Innocent IV by Alexander IV that is quoted on p. 539, footnote 4, below.

[3] Matt. xxv. 24.

[4] 2 Kings x. 1–11.

Tibaldo Visconti of Piacenza was a student of the University of Paris and Archdeacon of Liége whose heart was in the Crusades. In this cause he laboured single-mindedly as Pope Gregory X (*fungebatur* A.D. 1271–6) at the Council of Lyon in A.D. 1274 to bring to an end 'the Great Interregnum' which had been inflicted upon the Holy Roman Empire by Pope Innocent IV, as well as to heal the schism between the Western and the Orthodox Church. The crusade which he had worked for was in sight when Death overtook him.

Pietro di Morrone was the eleventh son of an Abruzzese peasant who lived as a hermit in the wilderness before the Conclave elected him to be Pope Celestine V (*fungebatur* A.D. 1294), and who abdicated, less than four months after his consecration, from an office which was a torment to him.

Benedetto Gaetani was a nobleman of Anagni who studied the civil as well as the canon law, became a Papal notary and a cardinal, and put his worldly wisdom at the service of Pope Celestine V in order to smooth the path for his unworldly master's 'Great Refusal'[1] and for his own eager but unfortunate acceptance, as Pope Boniface VIII (*fungebatur* A.D. 1294–1303), of the tiara whose weight the hermit could not endure.

This bare list of famous names[2] is enough to show that the medieval Papacy, like the modern English governing class and the Ottoman Pādishāh's Slave-Household, had the power of attracting into its service all the talents of the society in which it was the master-institution.[3] The first impression which the list will make on our minds is that of the extraordinary variety of the aptitudes and experiences which the Hildebrandine Church knew how to use in a cause which was so much vaster and so much grander than the *raison d'être* of any national state or multi-national empire. A closer scrutiny will show that these diverse types of eminence were not all equally apt for doing the precise and special work of controlling the destinies of the Christian Republic through the instrumentality of the Roman Curia. The fortunes of a Gregory VI or a Paschal II—not to speak of Celestine V—suggest that a man who was eminent as an unworldly saint would perhaps find himself at a disadvantage on the Papal throne, where he might be hindered by his office from exercising his gifts and be hampered by his gifts

[1] Dante: *La Divina Commedia*: 'Inferno', Book III, l. 60.

[2] If we read the roll-call aloud, it is the Lombard names, with their sonorous Italian setting and their intractable Teutonic core, that engrave themselves most deeply on the memory—calling up, as they do, the incisive characters of the great men of action who bore them. A similar impression is made by the South Slavonic names in the roll of the Ottoman vezīrs.

[3] The kinship of the Roman Church with the Ottoman Slave-Household in this respect is pointed out by the American scholar Dr. A. H. Lybyer in a passage which has been quoted in this Study in Part III. A, vol. iii, p. 33, above.

from fulfilling his office. When we compare the respective results of a Paschal II's and a Calixtus II's dealings with a Henry V, we may be inclined to think that the virtues of a saint were a less valuable endowment than the family tradition of a sovereign count[1] for a Pope who was called upon to live up to the Hildebrandine faith that God had

> 'made him lord of his house and ruler of all his substance,
> 'To bind his princes at his pleasure and teach his senators wisdom.'[2]

A count in Pope's clothing, like Calixtus II or Eugenius III, might be the most effective vicegerent of God for calling to order a prince like the aggressive Emperor Henry V or a senator like the turbulent revolutionary Arnold of Brescia. If the capable and commanding nobleman were, as Eugenius was, a monk and a saint besides, so much greater the edification; but, for the service of the Holy See, the nobleman's qualities were perhaps more important; and, to judge by the prowess of Alexander III in fighting his desperate battle with Frederick I, the qualities of the lawyer were even more valuable than those of the nobleman for waging the warfare of the Church Militant. It was perhaps better still to combine the lawyer's cutting edge with the nobleman's robust self-assurance; for this was the combination of worldly gifts which triumphed, in an Innocent IV and a Clement IV, over the demonic energies of Frederick II and his offspring. If we follow our argument as far as this, however, we shall find ourselves in deep waters; for Boniface VIII was a nobly born lawyer likewise; and it was Boniface's infatuation that brought down the whole magnificent structure of the Papal *Respublica Christiana* with a crash, to lie in ruins side by side with that Holy Roman Empire which had been shattered, less than half a century back, by an Innocent's implacability. These two stiff-necked and self-confident men of the world, with their aristocratic imperiousness and their legal exactingness, did far more than the soft-hearted and incompetent Abruzzese peasant's son to destroy all that had been built up by Pope after Pope for two centuries on end upon the Hildebrandine foundations.[3]

[1] Calixtus II's father was the Sovereign Count of Burgundy.

[2] Ps. cv. 21–2.

[3] 'I should not agree with the remarks about Boniface VIII. It is the old Creighton view; but compare, in criticism, Powicke's Creighton lecture, published in *History*, vol. xviii, pp. 307–29. My view would be modified by taking deeper account of the Franco-Angevin policy: i.e. I should look further back in this connexion and in others.'—Mr. G. Barraclough in a letter to the writer. Mr. Barraclough's own view of the pontificate of Innocent IV will be found in *The English Historical Review*, vol. xlix, p. 212. While the writer of this Study would be making himself ridiculous if he ventured to contest either Mr. Barraclough's or Professor Powicke's judgement in this domain, he does venture to submit that his own acceptance—for what it may be worth—of an antique judgement is perhaps not altogether unjustified on the criterion which he himself is following. The ἄτη incurred by Pope Boniface VIII was not, of course, the end of all things in the history of the Papacy. In administrative efficiency, for example, the Papal Curia may not

If Hildebrand himself on his death-bed could have confronted, with foreknowledge of the event, the long array of his coming successors, he would assuredly have cried out, in his Master's words, 'verily I say unto you that one of you shall betray me';[1] and the only plea that could have been offered in self-defence by a then unborn Benedetto Gaetani or Sinibaldo Fieschi would have been that his future betrayal of Hildebrand was already predetermined by Hildebrand's own betrayal of himself. Our catalogue of great Popes, from Gregory VII to Boniface VIII inclusive, proclaims that the elements of greatness which created the Papal *Respublica Christiana* were also the elements that destroyed it, and that these seeds of destruction were being sown from the outset.

The fall of the Hildebrandine Church is as extraordinary a spectacle as its rise; for all the virtues that had carried it to its zenith seem to change, as it sinks to its nadir, into their own exact antitheses. The divine institution which had been fighting and winning a battle for spiritual freedom against material force was now infected with the very evil which it had set itself to cast out from the body social of Western Christendom. The Holy See which had taken the lead in the struggle against simony now required the clergy throughout the Western World to pay their dues at a Roman receipt of custom for those ecclesiastical preferments which Rome herself had forbidden them to purchase from any local secular power.[2] The Roman Curia which had been the head and front of moral and intellectual progress—a tower of strength for the saints who were raising the monastic life to new heights, and for the schoolmen who were creating the universities—now turned itself into a fastness of spiritual conservatism. The ecclesiastical sovereign power in the Christian Republic now suffered itself to be deprived by its local secular underlings—the princes of the rising parochial states of Western Christendom—of the lion's share of the product of financial and administrative instruments which the Papacy itself had skilfully devised in order to make its authority effective;[3] and this forfeiture of a share in the product was followed by a forfeiture

have reached its apogee until after the migration to Avignon, and the autocratic authority of the Papacy over the Church was only established in and after the pontificate of Martin V (see the present chapter, pp. 573–6, below). On the other hand the moral authority of the Papacy did, surely, never recover from the shock which it had sustained in the days of Innocent IV and Boniface VIII.

1 Matt. xxvi. 21.

2 Fees for investiture with ecclesiastical offices had, of course, always been paid to some one—i.e. to the local ordinary and his officials—before ever the controversy over Investiture arose; and, moreover, the payment of a fee upon appointment was not the same thing as the purchase of an office. Yet the essence of the evil which Hildebrand was attacking was the subjection of the life of the spirit to the power of the purse; and this was an evil in which the Papal Curia itself became deeply implicated when its budget was swollen by the portentous cost of the internecine conflict with the Emperor Frederick II.

3 On this point see further pp. 539–40, below.

of the means of production as well when in England a King Henry VIII took over the Papal machinery within the frontiers of his own realm and thenceforward worked the machine with his own hands for his own profit exclusively. In the face of this final act of spoliation the Holy See found itself helpless. And as the local prince of a Papal principality the Sovereign Pontiff eventually had to content himself—like Napoleon on Elba—with the paltry consolation-prize of sovereignty over one of the least of the 'successor-states' of his own lost empire.[1] Has any other institution ever given so great occasion as this to the enemies of the Lord to blaspheme?[2] The downfall of the Hildebrandine Papacy is a more extreme case of περιπέτεια than any that we have yet encountered in our study of the nemesis of creativity. How did it happen, and why?

How it happened is foreshadowed in the first recorded transaction in Hildebrand's public career.

The creative spirits in the Roman Church who set themselves in the eleventh century to rescue our Western World from a feudal anarchy by establishing a Christian Republic then found themselves in the same dilemma as their spiritual heirs who are attempting in our day to replace an international anarchy by a political world order. The essence of their aim was to substitute a reign of spiritual authority for the reign of physical force, and in their struggle against violence the spiritual sword was the weapon with which their supreme victories were won. No physical force was exerted in Hildebrand's act of deposing and excommunicating the Emperor Henry IV; yet the moral effect of the Pope's winged words upon the hearts of the Emperor's Transalpine subjects was so intense that within a few months it brought Henry to Canossa. There were, however, other occasions on which it seemed as though the established régime of physical force was in a position to defy the strokes of the spiritual sword with impunity; and it was in such situations that the Roman Church Militant was challenged to give its answer to the Riddle of the Sphinx. Was the soldier of God to deny himself the use of any but his own spiritual arms, at the risk of seeing his advance brought to a standstill? Or was he to fight God's battle against the Devil with the adversary's own weapons, if the only practicable way of ejecting the adversary from his entrenchments was to hoist him with his own petard? Which was the true Christian act of faith? To eschew all weapons but God's, and trust in God to make David's sling prevail against Goliath's

[1] The comparison, of course, is imperfect in one vital point; for after losing his administrative and financial empire over the Western World the Pope still retained an infinitely more important spiritual empire of a kind which a Napoleon could never acquire and which even an Innocent IV could never completely destroy.

[2] 2 Sam. xii. 14.

panoply? Or to remind himself that the Devil and his armoury, like everything else in the Universe, were the Creator's creatures, and to believe that no created thing could remain unhallowed if it were used in the Creator's service? 'What God hath cleansed, that call not thou common'[1] was a text which might appear to support the second of these two alternative answers, and it was also a text which might seem to have been directly addressed to the Vicar of Peter.

The question presented itself in an urgent practical form to the would-be reformer Pope Gregory VI when he assumed the burden of the Papal office in A.D. 1045. In order to serve as the instrument of reform, the Holy See must be efficiently organized; to be organized, it must have money; and the necessary supplies of this material means to a spiritual end were not forthcoming; for, while the old Papal revenues from the Patrimonia Petri had disappeared with the Patrimonia themselves, the new revenues arising from the offerings of the pilgrims were being stolen from the very altar of Saint Peter's own church by the brigand-nobles of the Ducatus Romanus[2]—the one place in Western Christendom where the Prince of the Apostles had no honour, just because it was the country which he had made his own. No one would dispute that this sacrilegious robbery was as wicked in itself as it was damaging to the interests of the Papacy and the Christian Republic; and there was no prospect of the criminals becoming amenable to spiritual appeals or spiritual censures. The physical force which they themselves were employing was the only human agency to which they would yield. Was it justifiable to meet force with force in this flagrant case? The question was answered when the gentle Giovanni Graziano ascended the Papal throne as Gregory VI and appointed Hildebrand to be his *capellanus*; for the guardianship of Saint Peter's

[1] Acts x. 15.

[2] The scanty evidence in regard to the Papal finances in this age is marshalled by K. Jordan: 'Zur päpstlichen Finanzgeschichte im 11. und 12. Jahrhundert' in *Quellen und Forschungen herausgegeben vom Preussischen Historischen Institut in Rom*, vol. xxv (Rome 1933–4, Regenberg), pp. 61–104. Between the date of the Lombard irruption into Italy in A.D. 568 and that of Pope Stephen III's journey to Frankland in A.D. 753–5 the Papal Patrimonia in the form of landed estates scattered far and wide over the vast domain of the Roman Patriarchate had all been lost save for the remnant contained in the Ducatus Romanus itself; and the temporary financial relief which the Papacy had obtained in the latter part of the eighth century thanks to the donations of Pepin and Charlemagne had been more than offset, between the end of the ninth century and the middle of the eleventh, by the onset of a feudal anarchy which had diverted into alien hands the revenues of estates of which the Papacy was still nominally the owner (Jordan, op. cit., pp. 62–4). The moment of Pope Gregory VI's accession seems to have coincided with the nadir of the Papacy's finances (Jordan, op. cit., pp. 64–5). It is true that, in compensation for the lost revenues from the Papacy's own landed property, the Papal treasury was by this time already beginning to receive revenues of a new kind—dues from monasteries under Papal patronage, and Peter's Pence and tribute from kingdoms on the fringe of Western Christendom which recognized some kind of Papal overlordship (see IV. C (iii) (*c*) 2 (β), vol. iv, pp. 378–9, and the present chapter and volume, p. 525, footnote 4, above)—but these new sources of revenue do not appear to have yielded appreciable sums until the twelfth century (Jordan, op. cit., pp. 70–80).

altar, with the gifts that were heaped upon it, was the *capellanus*'s principal duty;[1] and Hildebrand promptly fulfilled it by raising an armed force and routing the brigands *manu militari*.

In taking this first momentous step in his career the Papal *capellanus* was making Muhammad's response to a challenge that had confronted the Arabian prophet in his native city of Mecca. Like Muhammad in Mecca in the seventh century of the Christian Era, Hildebrand in Rome in the eleventh century had to cope with the problem of performing a spiritual task in a political vacuum;[2] and, in support of a solution in which he was unwittingly following an Islamic precedent, Hildebrand could have quoted Christian Scripture for his purpose. He could have quoted to the brigands 'my house shall be called the house of prayer, but ye have made it a den of thieves';[3] and quoted to the Pope 'the zeal of thine house hath eaten me up'.[4] But which of the scenes in the mystery play was Hildebrand really acting? Was he playing the part of Jesus when he 'made a scourge of small cords'[5] and 'went into the Temple of God and cast out all them that sold and bought in the Temple and overthrew the tables of the moneychangers'?[6] Or was he doing in fact what Jesus had been falsely accused of doing when the Pharisees said 'this fellow doth not cast out devils but by Beelzebub the prince of the devils'?[7]

At the moment when Hildebrand took action the inward moral character of his act was difficult indeed to divine. At his last hour, forty years after, the answer to the riddle was already less obscure; for in A.D. 1085, when he was dying as a Pope in exile at Salerno, the more venerable city that was his see lay prostrate under the weight of an overwhelming calamity which her bishop's policy had brought upon her only the year before. In 1085 Rome had just been looted and burnt by the Normans—more ferocious brigands than any native Roman breed—whom the Pope had called in to assist him in a military struggle which had gradually spread from the steps of Saint Peter's altar, where it had started forty years before, until it had engulfed the whole of Western Christendom. The climax of the physical conflict between Hildebrand and Henry IV gave a foretaste of the deadlier and more devastating struggle which was to be fought out *à outrance* between Innocent IV and Frederick II; and by the time when we come to the pontificate of Innocent IV

[1] A general control over the Papal finances seems to have been one of the functions of the office of 'Archdeacon of the Roman Church' to which Hildebrand was subsequently appointed in A.D. 1059 (Jordan, op. cit., p. 66).

[2] See III. C (ii) (*b*), Annex II, vol. iii, especially pp. 470–2, above.

[3] Matt. xxi. 13 = Mark xi. 17 = Luke xix. 46 (see V. C (ii) (*a*), Annex II, vol. vi, pp. 425–6, below).

[4] John ii. 17.

[5] John ii. 15.

[6] Matt. xxi. 12.

[7] Matt. xii. 24.

our doubts will be at an end. Sinibaldo Fieschi bears witness against Ildebrando Aldobrandeschi that, in choosing the alternative of meeting force by force, Hildebrand was setting the Hildebrandine Church upon a course which was to end in the victory of his adversaries the World, the Flesh, and the Devil over the City of God which he was seeking to bring down to Earth.

No Politick admitteth nor did ever admit
the teacher into confidence: nay ev'n the Church,
with hierarchy in conclave compassing to install
Saint Peter in Caesar's chair, and thereby win for men
the promises for which they had loved and worship'd Christ,
relax'd his heavenly code to stretch her temporal rule.[1]

If we have succeeded in explaining how the Papacy became possessed by the demon of physical violence which it was attempting to exorcize, we have found the explanation of the other changes of Papal virtues into their opposing vices; for the substitution of the material for the spiritual sword is the fatal and fundamental change of which all the rest are corollaries.

How was it, for example, that a Holy See whose main concern with the finances of the Western clergy had been in the eleventh century the eradication of simony, should have become so deeply engaged, by the thirteenth century in allocating for the benefit of its nominees, and by the fourteenth century in taxing for its own benefit, those ecclesiastical revenues which it had once redeemed from the scandal of prostitution to secular powers for the purchase of ecclesiastical preferment? The unhappy transformation of the Papal Curia's financial role in Western Christendom was manifestly due to the ever increasing demands upon the Papal Exchequer which were being made by the perpetually recurring warfare between the Papacy and the Empire. On this point the dates speak for themselves.[2] A financial screw which had been given one turn when Alexander III had been at war with Frederick I, was turned again—and this time without mercy—when Gregory IX and Innocent IV were waging their more desperate warfare against Frederick II. It was the clergy of France and England who were chiefly distrained upon; for in Germany the Emperor's authority was still so far effective that it could hinder the clergy of that country from

[1] Bridges, Robert: *The Testament of Beauty* (Oxford 1929, Clarendon Press), Book IV, ll. 259–64.

[2] In at least one important department of Papal administration and finance, however, the apparent testimony of the dates proves to be deceptive. The institution of Papal 'provisions' grew up between the middle of the twelfth and the middle of the thirteenth century—that is to say, contemporaneously with the fighting out of the hundred years' war between the Papacy and the Hohenstaufen. Yet this development turns out neither to have taken place on the Curia's initiative nor to have worked, at this stage, to the Curia's financial profit. (On this point see Barraclough, G.: *Papal Provisions* (Oxford 1935, Blackwell), pp. 153–5.)

contributing to the war-chest of the Emperor's Papal antagonist; and in Italy—though she was the richest country in thirteenth-century Europe—the Pope found it as difficult to extract subsidies from the Italian clergy as to wring blood from a stone. In England by the middle of the thirteenth century it was being asserted that the revenue flowing out of the country to the Pope, and to the other foreign ecclesiastics who had been 'provided for' by the Pope out of English ecclesiastical resources,[1] was considerably larger than the revenue that was reaching the treasury of the King of England himself.[2] Both in England and in France this financial exploitation excited a resentment and provoked a restiveness which found voice in energetic protests;[3] but, although Innocent IV was enough of a statesman to realize that he was placing an intolerable strain upon an invaluable loyalty, he was too hard pressed by the financial exigencies of his war to the knife with the Hohenstaufen to be able to relax his own pressure upon England and France appreciably.[4]

For this remorseless turning of the financial screw upon the provincial clergy the Roman Curia was forced in the end to pay an ironical penalty.[5] It was compelled to surrender a share—and eventually the lion's share—of its provincial spoils to the local secular princes. While the clergy writhed under the Papal exactions and lamented the invention of the fiscal machinery through which they were put into execution, the princes merely resented the fact that this new-fangled taxing-machine, which was showing itself so admirably effective, was not at their disposal; and they set themselves, not to destroy it, but to capture it for their own benefit. The transfer of the Papal taxing-machine from the Pope's to the

[1] While the English Crown and clergy may have lost financially through Innocent IV's 'provisions' out of English ecclesiastical resources, these did not, at this date, bring the Curia any appreciable financial gain (*see* p. 538, footnote 2, above). The advantages derived by Innocent IV from his 'provisions' were not financial but political. They were a means of installing his own supporters in, and excluding his adversary's supporters from, a number of key-positions on the ecclesiastical map of Western Christendom. On the other hand the Papal drafts upon the revenues of the provincial churches that were levied on other accounts came in the course of the thirteenth century to play so important a part in the financial life of the Western World that firms of international bankers were formed to collect and remit them.

[2] Mann, op. cit., vol. xiii, pp. 353–4.

[3] For the protests of the English clergy to Innocent IV see Mann, op. cit., vol. xiv, pp. 233–66.

[4] 'Innocentius Papa . . ., nimia duri temporis tunc eum importunitate cogente, plura, quamquam forte invitus, fecisse dinoscitur quae ipsemet proponebat succedente opportunitate utiliter immutare.'—Pope Alexander IV, in a letter dated the 18th August, 1255 (quoted by Mann, op. cit., vol. xiv, p. 299). Coming from Innocent's own successor on the morrow of Innocent's death, this discreetly expressed criticism of Innocent's policy is impressive. It has, however, to be discounted to some extent in the light of the relations between the two pontiffs here in question (see p. 531, above). In a letter to the writer of this Study Mr. G. Barraclough recalls that 'Alexander was a firm opponent of Innocent, and had been virtually "retired" during his predecessor's pontificate'. In Mr. Barraclough's judgement Alexander was moved by animus 'to attribute to Innocent many things that were more far-reaching'.

[5] See pp. 534–5, above.

princes' hands began with the occasional concession, by the Pope to some prince, of a royalty on the Pope's own takings from the clergy in that prince's dominions—either as an inducement to the prince to facilitate the collection of the balance by the Papal agents, or in consideration of the prince's undertaking to spend his royalty, when he received it, on a crusade against the Muslims or the Hohenstaufen. As early as A.D. 1252 Pope Innocent IV and King Henry III of England were suspected of being engaged in this kind of collusion;[1] and in 1254 the Pope actually authorized the King to divert, for the conquest of the Kingdom of Sicily from the Hohenstaufen, the proceeds of a tithe which the King had been collecting from the ecclesiastical revenues of England since 1250, on the Pope's authority, for the purpose of a Crusade to the Holy Land![2]

The Kings of England and France and the other countries of Western Christendom beyond the pale of the Holy Roman Empire were wiser in their generation than 'the Wonder of the World' when they turned a deaf ear to Frederick II's appeals to his peers to make common cause with him in resisting the aggression of the Papal Power against himself and his house.[3] Frederick tried to frighten them into coming to his help by warning them that, if and when the Papacy did succeed in crushing the greatest of all the secular Powers in the Western body social, the monster would then have the smaller fry at its mercy and would proceed to mete the same measure to them as to the Hohenstaufen Emperor-King. The unwillingness of Frederick's brother princes to respond to his call—notwithstanding their manifest lack of enthusiasm for the cause of Frederick's Papal adversary—seems to show that they did not take the Emperor's warning very seriously[4] and that they had a shrewder idea than Frederick professed to have, or than Gregory IX and Innocent IV can have had in fact, of what the actual consequences of this 'Punic War' between the Empire and the Papacy would be.

[1] Mann, op. cit., vol. xiv, p. 258. [2] Ibid., p. 271.

[3] Frederick made a general appeal to the other princes of Western Christendom in 1227, after his excommunication by Gregory IX, and again in 1239 after his excommunication by the same Pope for the second time (Mann, op. cit., vol. xiii, pp. 217–19 and 286–7).

[4] An advocate of Frederick's thesis would have been able to adduce some historical evidence of recent date in support of it. He could have pointed out that the war of 1159–77 between Pope Alexander III and the Emperor Frederick I had been matched, in England, by the contemporary struggle—from 1162 to 1174—between Archbishop Thomas Becket and King Henry II. In this provincial conflict between Church and State, however, the ecclesiastical combatant had proved more formidable after his martyrdom in A.D. 1170 than before it. In his lifetime Becket had not found it easy to enlist on his side either the clergy of England or the Roman Curia in a quarrel with King Henry II on what was largely a personal issue. The Pope at the time had his hands full elsewhere, and he had no desire to incur the King of England's hostility. On the other hand the Curia did not miss its opportunity of taking advantage of the crime by which the King in the end put himself hopelessly in the wrong.

The outcome was, of course, the usual outcome of a great war which is fought out to the bitter end. The nominal victor succeeded in dealing the death-blow to his authentic victim at the cost of sustaining fatal injuries himself; and the real victors over both the belligerents were the neutral *tertii gaudentes*. When Pope Boniface VIII acted as though Frederick's forecast had been correct, and hurled against the King of France the pontifical thunderbolt with which the Emperor had been blasted by Boniface's predecessor Innocent IV, the sequel demonstrated that, as a result of the deadly struggle of A.D. 1227–68, the Papacy had sunk to the level of weakness to which it had reduced the Empire, while the Kingdom of France had become as strong as either the Papacy or the Empire had been before they had destroyed each other. In a trial of strength in which King Philip emerged unscathed by the Papal thunderbolt's blast, Pope Boniface was shown to be defenceless against the sacrilegious buffetings of a Guillaume Nogaret and a Sciarra Colonna; and Boniface's successors learnt this cruel lesson so well that they meekly came to Avignon to sit on the door-step of a new secular master who was quite as imperious as the Henrys and the Fredericks, without possessing the shadow of an Emperor's traditional title to exercise secular jurisdiction over a Pope.

The events of A.D. 1303–5 made it certain that the local secular princes would inherit, sooner or later, within their respective territories, the whole of the administrative and financial power and organization which the Papacy had been gradually establishing for itself all over Western Christendom. The process of transfer was only a matter of time. We may notice, as landmarks on the road, the passage in England of the Statute of Provisors in 1351 and the Statute of Praemunire in 1353; the concessions which the Curia was compelled to make, a century later, to the secular powers in France and Germany as the price of the abandonment of their support of the Council of Basel;[1] the Franco-Papal concordat negotiated at Bologna in 1516, in which the Roman See made an unequal division, with the French Crown, of existing Papal prerogatives in French territory, at the expense of the Gallican Church and the University of Paris; and the passage in England of the Act of Supremacy in 1534. This series of landmarks may remind us that the transfer of the medieval Papacy's prerogatives to the local secular Governments had begun, all over Western Christendom, some two hundred years before the Reformation, and that it worked itself out to its conclusion in the states which remained Catholic as well as in those which became Protestant. In both groups of states alike the sixteenth century saw the process completed; and it is,

[1] See IV. C (iii) (*b*) 11, pp. 217–18, above.

of course, no accident that the same century also saw the laying of the foundations upon which the 'totalitarian' parochial states of the modern Western World have been built up in the course of the last four centuries.

In earlier parts of this Study[1] we have traced the genesis of these modern parochial sovereign states of the kingdom-state calibre back to the city-states of medieval Italy. We can now see that the impact of Italian Civic Efficiency upon Transalpine Government is not the only clash of historical forces out of which our latter-day juggernauts have taken their formidable shape. A second, and perhaps equally prolific, source of the plenitude of power which these parochial sovereign states have now acquired has been the impact of their parochialism upon the Papal *Respublica Christiana*.[2] When the Papacy exhausted its strength in its deadly conflict with the Holy Roman Empire, it placed itself at the mercy of the parochial secular states; and it was then promptly despoiled by them of the panoply with which it had equipped itself for fighting its medieval battle. The oecumenical administrative and financial machinery through which the medieval Curia governed and taxed the provincial churches survives to-day in the corresponding apparatus of each of the parochial states of the modern Western World.[3] The oecumenical system of representative councils—from the First General Council of the Lateran (A.D. 1123) to the Council of Basel (A.D. 1431–49)—through which the members and the head of the Hildebrandine body ecclesiastic periodically adjusted their relations with one another, has a counterpart, if not a relic, to-day in our parochial secular parliaments.[4] Above all, the devotion which the provincial clergy, throughout medieval Western Christendom, once learnt to give to the Pope, as the living human head of an oecumenical society which was a mundane embodiment of the *Civitas Dei*, now

[1] See III. C (ii) (*b*), vol. iii, pp. 350–63, and IV. C (iii) (*b*) 8, in the present volume, pp. 198–200, above.

[2] See IV. C (iii) (*b*) 11, pp. 214–22, above.

[3] For the financial machinery of the medieval Papacy see Barraclough, G.: *Papal Provisions* (Oxford 1935, Blackwell); Lunt, W. E.: 'The Financial System of the Medieval Papacy' in *The Quarterly Journal of Economics*, vol. xxiii, pp. 251 seqq. (Boston 1909, Ellis); eundem: *Papal Revenues in the Middle Ages* (London 1934, Milford); Samaran, C., and Mollat, G.: *La Fiscalité Pontificale en France au xive siècle* (Paris 1905, Fontemoing); Mollat, G.: *Les Papes d'Avignon* (Paris 1912, Lecoffre).

[4] The general councils of the medieval Western Church were a Western revival of the oecumenical councils of the Catholic Church in the fourth and fifth centuries. Some of the earliest of the Western parochial secular parliaments—e.g. the parliaments convened in England in 1246 and in Apulia in 1256 and the Estates General convened in France in 1302—were summoned for the purpose of resisting an extension of the Papal prerogative. Were these parochial parliaments—in which the local clergy were at least as well represented as the local laity—inspired by the example of the general councils of the Church, on the principle of fighting the Holy See with its own weapons? The verdict of the experts appears, at the moment, to be that the main principles of conciliar and parliamentary organization and procedure are so different as to make it difficult to imagine that the ecclesiastical institution can have served as the model for the secular.

survives in the loyalty which the parochial secular 'successor-states' of the medieval Christian Republic receive to-day from their subjects without much distinction between laymen and clerics.

This hold upon human hearts is the most precious of all the spoils which the 'successor-states' have taken from the greater and nobler institution which they have plundered; for it is by commanding loyalty, far more than by raising and spending revenues or maintaining and employing armies, that these 'successor-states' have succeeded in keeping themselves alive. At the same time this spiritual heritage from the Hildebrandine Church is the element in the constitution of our modern parochial states which has turned these once harmless and useful institutions into a grave menace to the welfare of our civilization. For the spirit of devotion which was a beneficent creative power in Western Christendom when it was directed through the gates of a *Civitas Dei* towards God himself, has degenerated into a maleficent destructive force in the process of being diverted from its original divine object and being offered instead to an idol made by human hands.[1] Parochial states, as our medieval forebears knew, are man-made institutions, useful and even necessary in their place, which deserve from us that conscientious but unenthusiastic performance of a minor social duty which we render, in our time, to our municipalities and county councils. To idolize these pieces of social machinery, which have nothing divine about them, is to court a spiritual disaster; and this is the disaster towards which our modern Western World is heading to-day[2] as an ultimate consequence of the spiritual spoliation of the Holy See by the secular principalities which were once kept in their place by the Papacy's moral authority.

The sole, and paltry, compensation which the Papacy received from its despoilers was a tiny share in the territorial sovereignty which the local secular princes were forging for themselves out of their Papal spoils. The effective establishment of the Pope's territorial sovereignty proceeded *pari passu* with his virtual eviction from the moral presidency of an oecumenical Christian Commonwealth. In the great age of the Hildebrandine Church the Popes, as we have seen,[3] were content—notwithstanding the donations of Pepin and Charlemagne and Matilda—to forgo the practical exercise of territorial sovereignty even in Rome itself. The first piece of territory over which any Pope exercised full powers of civil government *de facto* as well as *de jure* was the Venaissin—a fragment of the Burgundian portion of the heritage of the Counts of Toulouse which was ceded to Pope Gregory X by King Philip III

[1] See IV. C (iii) (*c*) 2 (β), p. 303, above.

[2] See IV. C (iii) (*c*) 2 (β), pp. 318–20 and 405–8, above.

[3] See pp. 523–6, above.

of France in 1274, while the Council of Lyon was in session. Ostensibly this Council—at which Rudolf of Hapsburg sought and obtained the recognition of his election as King of the Romans, and the Greeks sought and obtained their restoration to communion with Rome, on the Pope's own terms[1]—was a Papal triumph which placed the coping-stone upon the Hildebrandine edifice. Actually, however, the foundations of the mighty structure had been fatally undermined before its upper-works were finished off; and the collapse of A.D. 1303–5 occurred before the Pope's territorial dominions received their next extension through the purchase of the city of Avignon by Pope Clement VI in 1348. Thereafter, between 1353 and 1367, when the republican movement in Rome had been discredited—after two centuries of licence—by the antics of Rienzi, and when civic liberties were on the wane all over Central and Northern Italy, a Spanish soldier, Cardinal Albornoz, made an effective conquest of the greater part of the Donation of Charlemagne on behalf of a Papal master who was then still hugging the golden chains of a humiliating 'Babylonish Captivity'; and at the turn of the fourteenth and fifteenth centuries, at the height of the Great Schism, Albornoz's work was repeated and confirmed by Pope Boniface IX with one hand, while with the other hand he was contending with his rival Benedict of Avignon. In the course of the next hundred years these Italian possessions of the Papacy became securely welded together into one of the ten despotically governed principalities into which the sixty or seventy medieval city-states of Central and Northern Italy were consolidated during the transition from the Medieval to the Modern Age.[2] In this one field the Papacy achieved, in its decline, a success which had never come its way in the period of its Hildebrandine greatness; and the achievement was not undone, or even interrupted, by a series of unprecedented disasters: the 'Babylonish Captivity' of 1309–76,[3] the Great Schism of 1378–1417, the Reformation, and the Sack of Rome in 1527. The reason was that the erection of the Papal principality was an almost automatic consequence of the establishment of a new international order—or anarchy—in the Western World; and in yielding to this new dispensation, which was an utter reversal of the Hildebrandine régime, the Papacy was simply allowing itself to drift on an irresistible tide which was not, this

[1] See IV. C (iii) (*c*) 2 (β), Annex II, p. 616, below.

[2] For this process of consolidation see III. C (ii) (*b*), vol. iii, pp. 354–7, above.

[3] The disaster lay in the 'capture' of the Papacy by the French Crown, and not in the scene of the 'captivity'; for the metaphorical Babylon on the banks of the Rhône was much better placed than the metaphorical Zion on the banks of the Tiber for serving the fourteenth-century Papal Curia as a centre for the administration of an ecclesiastical empire which extended at the time from Sicily to Ireland and from Portugal to Finland. (On this point see p. 520, footnote 2, above.)

time, of the Papacy's own raising. The modern Papal State was one of the Machiavellian secular 'successor-states' into which the Hildebrandine ecclesiastical commonwealth was partitioned; and it lasted as long as the rest of the territorial system of which it was part and parcel—maintaining itself on the Rhône till A.D. 1791 and on the Tiber till A.D. 1870.

The consciousness that it was now drifting with the tide, and that it had lost control over its own destinies, was no doubt the psychological cause of the conservatism to which the Papacy abandoned itself from the time when it received the shock of the Protestant Reformation until the time when it began to recover from the later shock which was administered to it by the Italian *Risorgimento*. Realizing that it was now at the mercy of wind and wave, the Papacy came to see its safety in stagnation.

'When thou wast young, thou girdedst thyself and walkedst whither thou wouldest; but when thou shalt be old thou shalt stretch forth thy hands, and another shall gird thee and carry thee whither thou wouldest not.'[1]

For a person or institution that has come to this pass, any change is formidable, because it will not be a change that is voluntary, and may be a change for the worse. It was in this spirit that the Papacy set its face, not only against the hierarchical and theological innovations of the Protestant Reformation, which were deliberately antagonistic to the Hildebrandine order of society, but also against some of the new discoveries of modern Western Physical Science and new ideas of modern Western Social Philosophy.

We have now perhaps found some answer to the question how the Papacy came to suffer its extraordinary περιπέτεια; but in describing the process we have not explained the cause. We may be justified in our thesis that the downfall of the Papacy in every sphere can be traced back to its abandonment of the spiritual in favour of the material sword, and that this fatal change can be traced, in its turn, to Hildebrand's choice in the first act of his public life. Yet, even if it were demonstrable that Hildebrand's decision in A.D. 1045 to parry force with force was the ruin of the Hildebrandine enterprise as a matter of fact, this would not prove that what did happen was bound to happen *a priori*. The single example of the Hildebrandine tragedy, impressive though it may be, can prove no more, in itself, than the truism that the use of material means towards a spiritual end is always a dangerous game. To live dangerously, however, is the inevitable condition of being alive at all; and there is no decisive evidence for the operation of a moral Gresham's Law to make it certain that, whenever

[1] John xxi. 18.

force is employed in a spiritual cause, this dangerous manœuvre will always incur defeat. There may be cases in which the same manœuvre can be resorted to with a chance of success, and some cases, perhaps, among these, in which no other line of action holds out any prospect of victory, so that there the choice will lie between risking defeat in a hazardous move and accepting defeat without a struggle. In fact, notwithstanding the experience of the Hildebrandine Church, this Riddle of the Sphinx remains inscrutable still. And in our own later generation, when we find ourselves confronted once more by Hildebrand's dilemma, with the advocates of an uncompromising pacifism arrayed *ancipiti Marte* against the advocates of enforcing peace, we cannot pronounce that Hildebrand's choice was intrinsically the wrong one simply because it resulted in a disaster in Hildebrand's case. It is therefore not enough to show how this disaster occurred; we have also to answer, if we can, the question why.

Why was it that the medieval Papacy became the slave of its own tools, and allowed itself to be betrayed, by its use of material means, into being diverted from the spiritual ends to which those means had been intended to minister? In the history of the Roman See, as in that of the Roman Republic, the explanation of an ultimate defeat is to be found (so it would seem) in the untoward effects of an initial victory. The dangerous game of fighting force with force had in these cases fatal results because, to begin with, it succeeded only too well. Intoxicated by the successes which their hazardous manœuvre obtained for them in the earlier stages of their struggle with the Holy Roman Empire, Pope Gregory VII and his successors persisted in the use of force, and carried it to extremes, until it defeated the users' purpose by becoming an end in itself. While Gregory VII fought the Empire with the object of removing an Imperial obstacle to a reform of the Church, Innocent IV fought the Empire two hundred years later with the object of breaking the Imperial Power. The downfall of the Hildebrandine Papacy was a supremely tragic performance of the drama of κόρος-ὕβρις-ἄτη.

We can verify the working out of this *Leitmotiv* in two ways. We can discern it in a contrast between some earlier and some later scene in the play; and we can detect it by an analysis of the plot.

The first pair of outwardly similar but inwardly diverse scenes is one in which three rival claimants to the Papacy are summoned before the judgement-seat of a council of the Church under the presidency of a Holy Roman Emperor, with the result that two of them are declared illegitimate, the third is permitted to avoid deposition by abdicating, and the Holy See thus rendered vacant is filled in due course by the election of a new candidate. In A.D. 1046 it was Pope Gregory VI who was compelled by the Emperor Henry III to abdicate, at the Synod of Sutri, in order to make way for Suidger of Bamberg to ascend the Papal throne as Clement II; in A.D. 1415 it was Pope John XXIII who was compelled to abdicate by the Fathers of the Council of Constance, under the auspices of the Emperor Sigismund, in order that Oddone Colonna might become Pope Martin V. Externally the two scenes might seem almost indistinguishable, but there is a difference in êthos between the two protagonists which gives some measure of the moral disaster to which the Papacy had succumbed in the course of the four intervening centuries. Pope Gregory VI was an unworldly saint who had rendered himself technically guilty of the offence of Simony by purchasing the Papal office, with money legitimately acquired, in order to rescue it from the hands of his unworthy god-son, Pope Benedict IX. The offence had been so strictly formal, and the motive so plainly pure, that John Gratian's action had been acclaimed by Peter Damian as the salvation of the Church, while Hildebrand showed his opinion of it by taking service under his old schoolmaster as his *capellanus* and assuming this master's pontifical name when his own turn came, long afterwards, to ascend the Papal throne as Gregory VII. The condemnation of Gregory VI was a travesty of justice which aroused indignation all over Western Christendom and inspired Hildebrand[1] to devote his life to fighting for the liberation of the Church from an arbitrary 'Caesaro-papism'. Yet the victim of this judicial act of injustice accepted and endorsed the sentence without a murmur. Not so the condottiere Baldassare Cossa, 'the most profligate of Mankind',[2] whom the Council of Constance had to deal with as Pope John XXIII. 'He fled, and was brought back a prisoner; the most scandalous charges were suppressed; the Vicar of Christ was only accused of piracy, murder, rape, sodomy, and incest; and, after subscribing his own condemnation, he expiated in prison the imprudence of trusting his person to a free city beyond the Alps.'[3] The poison of worldliness had worked potently in the course of less than four hundred years to produce the contrast between this scene and that.

There is another pair of scenes in which a Pope invades Southern Italy with an armed force, meets with an ignominious defeat from

[1] See pp. 512–13, above.

[2] Gibbon, E.: *The History of the Decline and Fall of the Roman Empire*, ch. lxx.

[3] Gibbon, op. cit., cap. cit. Since the date at which Gibbon wrote these demurely deadly sentences, a substantial summary of the evidence against John XXIII has come to light (see Waugh, W. T., in *The Cambridge Medieval History*, vol. viii (Cambridge 1936, University Press), p. 7, footnote 2). The reason why 'the most scandalous charges were suppressed' is still, however, unknown (op. cit., p. 8, footnote 1).

the Power whom he is attacking, and dies of chagrin. In the first scene it is Pope Leo IX who is defeated in 1053 by the Normans;[1] in the second scene it is Pope Innocent IV who is defeated in 1254 by Manfred. Outwardly the *ci-devant* Bruno of Egisheim was more deeply humiliated than the *ci-devant* Sinibaldo Fieschi; for he led his army in person, was taken prisoner on the battle-field, and died in virtual captivity, while his more prudent successor two hundred years later assigned the command of his army to his nephew and died a free man. The difference, however, is all the other way when we take account of motives and states of mind. Pope Leo was attempting, in co-operation with the secular arm of the Emperors of both East and West, to carry out a police operation against a band of brigands whom their victims spoke of not as Normans but as Hagarenes, to signify that they were the truceless enemies of Church and State. Yet, even in so good a cause, this nobleman's son who had been brought up among men of war was filled with compunction at the thought that he had lent the countenance of his Papal office to the shedding of blood;[2] and what broke his heart was the slaughter of his followers and not his own defeat and capture by the outlaws whom he had hoped to subdue. Innocent, on the other hand, was on the war-path against the son of a dead and defeated enemy against whom he nursed such an implacable hatred[3] that he must needs pursue his vendetta into the second and the third generation. The chagrin that killed him was his rage at being foiled in an attempt to carry the war into the enemy's country and to chevy out of his father's ancestral kingdom a prince who had abandoned his father's aggressive ambitions and who was only anxious to be left in peace.[4] Militarily, Innocent's and Leo's Apulian expeditions ended in much the same way, but morally there is no comparison between them; and this moral gulf gives the measure of the Papacy's spiritual degeneration during the intervening span of two hundred years.

Yet another pair of scenes whose likeness and difference tell the same tale of a moral decline and fall is a pair which offers the outwardly identic spectacle of a Pope being kidnapped and brutally handled by men of violence with the cold-blooded intention of

[1] See IV. C (iii) (*c*) 2 (β), Annex II, pp. 611–12, below.

[2] Herein Bruno's temperament presents an instructive contrast to that of his adviser, and eventual successor, Hildebrand.

[3] In substitution for the words 'implacable hatred' Mr. G. Barraclough suggests the phrase 'consistent policy based on a conviction of the impossibility of co-operation with the Hohenstaufen, and of the danger of their presence in Italy'.

[4] This statement of Manfred's attitude and intentions is, in Mr. Barraclough's submission, 'beside the point from Innocent's point of view, just as Hitlerian protestations of goodwill and peacefulness are beside the point for France to-day'. In the opinion of the writer of this Study Mr. Barraclough's striking parallel damns Poincaré-la-Guerre without exculpating Sinibaldo Fieschi.

breaking his nerve and so bringing him to make a great concession which he would never have conceded on its merits. In the first of these two scenes we see Pope Paschal II being seized in A.D. 1111 by the Emperor Henry V at the high altar of St. Peter's and carried away captive into the Campagna; in the second we see Pope Boniface VIII being assaulted at Anagni in A.D. 1303 by Guillaume Nogaret and Sciarra Colonna. The purpose of Henry V was to extort from Pope Paschal an acknowledgement of the Emperor's right to confer Investiture; the purpose of Guillaume Nogaret was to extort from Pope Boniface a retractation of certain bulls which the Pope had promulgated against Nogaret's royal master. To this extent the two scenes are in conformity; it is when we consider the respective antecedents of this pair of outrages against the Pope's sacrosanctity that the moral difference comes to light. Behind Nogaret's brutal assault upon Boniface there was no treachery and much provocation. For nearly two years past the Pope had been conducting against the King of France an ever more violent war of words, with the evident intention of coercing the King into a public submission and thereby leading him in triumph as a royal captive of the pontifical bow and spear. The first shots had been fired in *Clericis laicos* and *Ineffabilis amoris. Salvator mundi* and *Ausculta fili* had been followed up by *Unam sanctam*—a bull which roundly asserted the supremacy of the pontifical over the secular sword—and *Unam sanctam* by *Super Petri solio*, a bull in which the King was excommunicated. In raising the question of swords, Boniface had been 'asking for trouble'; and, when he gets it, we cannot feel that the coin of violence in which Nogaret pays him is very different from the Pope's own mintage. On the other hand the antecedents of Henry's brutal assault upon Paschal were such as to leave the Emperor altogether without excuse. On that very morning, and in those very precincts, he had just concluded with his victim a concordat[1] in which he had renounced the very claim which he now compelled the Pope to concede under physical duress; and he had renounced it in exchange for a renunciation of equal magnitude on Paschal's part. The agreement was that, in consideration of Henry's abandonment of a claim to confer Investiture upon ecclesiastics, the Church should surrender all the *regalia*—the powers and rights and revenues of a secular order—which it had acquired in the course of ages, and should content itself with the proceeds of its tithes and free-will offerings. If this agreement had been ratified and carried out, it would have achieved a radical settlement of

[1] Henry's assent does, it is true, appear to have been given subject to the condition that the agreement should be ratified 'firma et autentica ratione, consilio quoque vel concordia totius ecclesiae ac regni principum assensu' (Carlyle, op. cit., vol. iv, p. 116, quoting Ekkehard's Chronicle *sub* A.D. 1111).

the question over which the Empire and the Papacy were then at issue; and Henry's failure to ratify was not Pope Paschal's fault. Henry failed because he could not carry with him the bishops of Germany, who did not care to obtain their liberation from Lay Investiture if the sacrifice of their *regalia* was to be the price; and, having failed, he not only went back upon his bargain but determined to extort a recognition of his previous claim by committing an act of the grossest treachery and violence. If Boniface largely deserved what he got, Pope Paschal assuredly did not.

Finally we may contrast the spectacle of Pope Celestine V making his 'Great Refusal' in A.D. 1294 with the spectacle of that other 'harmless old man' who 'was left in a solitary castle to excommunicate twice each day the rebel kingdoms which had deserted his cause',[1] and who persisted in this exercise from his deposition in 1417 until his death in 1422/3. If the approach of moral decay is foreshadowed in Celestine's pathological flight from responsibility,[2] its advent is proclaimed in Benedict's pathological clinging to power. In either gesture there is that note of exaggeration which is one of the surest symptoms of moral as well as physical misgrowth.[3] The exaggeration runs to the length of caricature; and in either case it is the caricature of an element which is to be found in the character of other Popes of very different spiritual stature. In the soul of each of those spiritual giants the conflicting impulses to which a Celestine and a Benedict respectively gave way had both been perpetually present, and therefore perpetually at war, without ever overriding a will which was able to keep them both in order because it was stronger than either of them. A Gregory VII or a Gregory I had been tormented by the burden of the Papal office because he had all the time been aware of an Other World from which the cares of This World were keeping him in exile; yet he had carried the burden indomitably to his journey's end because he had divined that his duty lay in This World so long as he was a sojourner in it, and that only 'he that endureth to the end shall be saved'.[4] This ceaseless struggle between conflicting impulses under a higher control—this inward spiritual warfare which wrings from the titan's breast the cry 'O wretched man that I am!'[5]—is the well-spring of Hildebrandine lives and achievements. When we pass from a Hildebrand to a Celestine and a Benedict, and see in them the same creative impulses deprived of all their virtue

1 Gibbon, op. cit., cap. cit.

2 'A historian might argue that his renunciation was the only sensible thing that Morrone did as Pope—it was not the "flight from responsibility" that was questionable, but the weakness of will that led to its acceptance, and the stupidity of the policy of the cardinals who made the election.'—Mr. G. Barraclough, in a letter to the writer.

3 On this point see IV. C (iii) (*c*) 2 (γ), Annex, below.

4 Matt. x. 22.

5 Rom. vii. 24.

by a fatal divorce from one another and an equally fatal breakage of their bond of spiritual discipline, we perceive that the end of the Hildebrandine order is at hand.

The operation of *κόρος-ὕβρις-ἄτη* which we have detected in these comparisons of successive pairs of scenes is revealed still more clearly when we take the play as a whole and analyse the plot.

The first act opens in A.D. 1046 with a challenge to the Roman See which is taken to heart by Hildebrand.

In Hildebrand's generation the Western Christendom was passing out of the first into the second chapter of its history—out of a defensive state of mind in which the height of ambition was to keep alive, as the Abbé Siéyès boasted in a later age that he had lived through the French Revolution, into an adventurous state of mind in which this vegetative life for life's sake began to seem hardly worth living unless it could now be transcended, on the Aristotelian scheme of social growth,[1] in an effort to make life a stepping-stone towards attaining the true end of Man. This troubling of the waters of Western life in the eleventh century of the Christian Era revealed itself most powerfully in a mighty movement for reforming the conduct of the Church,[2] which in that age was another name for the Western Society itself; and this movement presented a challenge to the Roman See because, in the relations between the Papacy and the Western body social, it made it impossible for the *status quo ante* to persist. It was only in a society that was numb with misery—as Western Christendom had been from the twilight of Charlemagne's generation to the dawn of Otto the Great's—that the prerogative of moral leadership could be left, even nominally, in the hands of an institution which was disgracing itself as the Roman See disgraced itself during that profligate passage in its history. From the moment when the Western World as a whole began to shake off its moral torpor and aspire to a better life, the Roman See was confronted with the alternative of leaping at one bound from the lowest to the highest rung of the moral ladder as it stood in that age, or else being pilloried in its actual state of degradation and seeing its kingdom numbered and finished and divided and given to the Medes and Persians.[3] There was a danger-signal for discerning eyes in the Lateran in the tremor of indignation which ran through Western Christendom—

[1] Aristotle: *Politics*, Book I, chap. 2, § 8 (p. 1252 B): τέλειος πόλις . . . γινομένη μὲν οὖν τοῦ ζῆν ἕνεκεν, οὖσα δὲ τοῦ εὖ ζῆν.

[2] In the eleventh century 'la renaissance de la richesse, l'essor des nations, la vigueur des états permet à l'Église d'abandonner les tâches dont la défaillance de l'Empire Romain l'a peu à peu chargée, et de se consacrer toute à sa mission spirituelle, à son œuvre édificatrice.'—Dufourcq, A., op. cit., vol. vi, 4th edition, p. 2. Compare Carlyle, op. cit., vol. iv, pp. 49–51 and 58–60.

[3] Dan. v. 25–8.

and with particular vehemence in the Transalpine parts—when it was reported in 1024 that the Greeks were in negotiation with the Papacy for the purchase of Papal acquiescence in the Patriarch of Constantinople's long-maintained and long-contested pretension to the title of 'Oecumenical'.[1] This explosion of anger at an only too credible rumour that the Pope was selling his birthright for a mess of pottage showed that the profligacy of the Roman See was notorious and odious to the Western *Plebs Christiana.* And when, a score of years later, the Papal *capellanus* Hildebrand, in whose own soul the spirit of the age was working, saw an Emperor conduct the trial and procure the condemnation of a Pope on a charge of Simony, he read the meaning of this writing on the wall and went into action. In that hour Hildebrand set himself the tremendous task of reversing the judgement upon the Roman See which had just been pronounced at Sutri; and in thirty years of titanic labour he succeeded in achieving the impossible. By 1075 the double battle against the sexual and the financial corruption of the clergy had been won throughout the Western World, and the victory had been gained by the moral prowess of a Roman See whose profligacy had been the greatest of all the scandals of the Western Church in the preceding century. This victory had been Hildebrand's personal work. He had fought for it beyond the Alps and behind the Papal Throne until the fight had carried him at last into the office which he had raised from the dust; and he had fought with every weapon, spiritual or material, that had come to his hand. It was at the moment of triumph, in the third year of his reign as Pope Gregory VII, that Hildebrand took a step which his champions can plausibly represent as having been almost inevitable[2] and his critics—no less plausibly—as having been almost inevitably disastrous.[3] In that year Hildebrand extended his field of battle from the sure ground of Concubinage and Simony to the debatable ground of Investiture.

Logically, perhaps, the conflict over Investiture might be justified as an inevitable sequel to the conflicts over Concubinage and

[1] For the controversy over this title see IV. C (iii) (*c*) 2 (β), p. 333, above.

[2] 'Inevitable' has to be qualified by 'almost', considering that in the view of the leaders of the Cluniac movement the domestic moral reform of the Church by her own efforts, which Cluny had initiated, was *not* impossible to carry through without undertaking the second and still more formidable task of recovering the Church's freedom from external control by liberating her from lay influence. In the Cluniac view the two issues were *not* inseparable, and therefore Cluny parted company with the Roman Curia when the battle over Investiture was engaged by Hildebrand.

[3] Hildebrand possesses in common with another militantly idealistic religious innovator, Ikhnaton, an apparently perennial capacity for arousing passionate feelings, whether of devotion or of hostility, in the hearts of all who cross his path *in saecula saeculorum.* The controversy that rages over the characters and careers of these two great men among the scholars of our own generation is conducted with at least a touch of the animus which was displayed by Hildebrand's and Ikhnaton's own respective contemporaries.

Simony if all three struggles were looked upon as aspects of one single struggle for the liberation of the Church. To a Hildebrand at this critical point in his career it might almost seem labour lost to have freed the Church from her servitude to Venus and to Mammon, if he were to leave her still fettered by her political subjection to the Secular Power. So long as this third shackle lay heavy upon her, would she not still be debarred from doing her divinely appointed work for the regeneration of Mankind? This argument on the lips of the apologists for Hildebrand's new departure in the year 1075 begs a question which Hildebrand's critics are entitled to ask, even if they fail to prove conclusively that the answer to it is in their own favour. In A.D. 1075, were the circumstances such that any clear-sighted and strong-minded occupant of the Papal throne was bound to judge that there was no longer any possibility of sincere and fruitful co-operation between the reforming party in the Western Church, as represented by the Roman Curia, and the Secular Power in the Western Christian Commonwealth, as represented by the Holy Roman Empire? On this question the onus of proof lies with the Hildebrandines on at least two accounts.

In the first place neither Hildebrand himself nor his partisans ever sought—either before or after the promulgation of Hildebrand's decree prohibiting Lay Investiture in 1075—to deny that the secular authorities had a legitimate role to play in the procedure for the election of the clerical officers of the Church from the Pope himself downwards.[1] In the second place, within the thirty years ending in 1075 the Roman See had been working hand in hand with the Holy Roman Empire in the older conflict over the issues of Concubinage and Simony. Indeed, their co-operation had become so sincere and so cordial that the Emperor Henry III, who had forced Pope Gregory VI out of office and into exile in 1046, chose Pope Victor II ten years later, when the Emperor was on his deathbed, to be the guardian of his six-years-old son.[2] It is true that, in the domain of the Empire, if not in the Western World as a whole, Henry III's premature death in A.D. 1056 had been followed by a moral relapse—especially in the matter of Simony—which had begun during the minority of Henry III's namesake and son and successor Henry IV and had not ceased when the young prince had taken over the reins of government himself in A.D. 1069.[3] In fact, 'behind any particular occasions of difference there lay a more general cause, and this was the fact that after the death of Henry III

[1] On this point see Carlyle, op. cit., vol. iv, Part I, chs. 2 and 3, and Part II, *passim*, especially ch. 2.

[2] For the friendliness of the Emperor Henry III's relations with the reform party in the Curia after, as well as before, A.D. 1046 see p. 512, footnote 4, above.

[3] See Carlyle, op. cit., vol. iv, pp. 55, 61–2, and 170–1.

the temporal authority was no longer co-operating with the spiritual in the attempt at reform, but seemed rather to be responsible for the continuance of grave evils, such as Simony and the secularization of the clergy. It was under these circumstances that the Papacy began to develop the policy of limiting or prohibiting the intervention of the secular authority in ecclesiastical appointments. This may have been justifiable and even necessary, but it must be admitted that it was a step of an almost revolutionary character';[1] and if, in spite of all justifications and provocations, Hildebrand had foreborne to throw down the gauntlet in A.D. 1075, it is conceivable that the relations of the Emperor Henry IV with Pope Gregory might have ended in being not less happy than his father's relations with Pope Victor.

To raise the new issue of Investiture with a militancy which was bound to set Empire and Papacy at variance was the more hazardous inasmuch as this third issue happened to be far less clear than those others on which the two authorities in Western Christendom had, not so long since, seen eye to eye.

One source of ambiguity arose from the fact that, by Hildebrand's day, it had become established that the appointment of a clerical officer of episcopal rank required, in order to make it valid, the concurrence of several different parties in taking action of several different kinds. It was one of the primeval rules of ecclesiastical discipline that a bishop must be elected by the clergy and people of his see and must be consecrated by a quorum of the validly consecrated bishops of the province. And the secular power had never at any time—since the issue had been raised by the conversion of Constantine—attempted to usurp the ritual prerogative of the bishops or to challenge, at any rate in theory, the electoral rights of the clergy and people. The role which the secular authorities had exercised *de facto*—without prejudice to the question of what the situation might be *de jure*—was that of nominating candidates and wielding a power of veto over elections; and this power, which was grounded in Roman Imperial practice, had been successfully reasserted in the West by the Holy Roman Emperors Charlemagne and Otto I, in anticipation of Henry III, against the Papacy itself, which was the highest ecclesiastical office in the Western World. There may be some uncertainty about the scope of the powers which, on the morrow of the Synod of Sutri, were conferred upon Henry as *patricius* by the Roman clergy and people; but it is certain that the first step in the making of a Pope Leo IX out of a Bruno Bishop of Toul, and of a Pope Victor II out of a Gebhard Bishop of Eichstett, was the despatch of a diplomatic

[1] Carlyle, op. cit., vol. iv, p. 66.

mission across the Alps from Rome to the Emperor to ask for an Imperial nomination; and in the second of these instances the Roman mission came with Hildebrand at its head. Even as late as the year 1059, after Henry's death, Hildebrand took care to obtain the assent of the Empress Regent before he gave his own support to the candidature of Gerard Bishop of Florence; and at the famous Lateran Council which was held in the same year by Hildebrand's candidate after he had been duly elected to be Pope Nicholas II, when the Fathers laid down a procedure for Papal elections in the future, the Emperor's rights in the matter were once again formally acknowledged, even though they were left undefined. If the traditional role of the Secular Power in the appointment of the highest ecclesiastical dignitary in the West was as substantial as this, the case for the exercise of a corresponding lay influence over the appointment of ordinary bishops and abbots might almost be taken as proven *a fortiori*, and it is not certain that the legitimacy of this influence, within its traditional limits, was disputed by Hildebrand even after the promulgation of the decree of 1075.[1]

This uncertainty arises out of a second ambiguity which is of a verbal order and which 'runs through the whole literature of the subject'.[2] The word 'Investiture' is ambiguous in itself. It may be used in the general meaning of appointment, or in the technical meaning of the bestowal of the pastoral staff and ring. And an opponent of Lay Investiture may be opposing the practice in this narrow technical sense without necessarily at the same time seeking to exclude the secular authorities from influencing appointments to clerical offices in the traditional ways.

By the eleventh century the traditional case for the exercise of some degree of secular control over clerical appointments had been reinforced by a new consideration of a practical kind which likewise applied to the lower ranks as well as to the apex of the Western hierarchy and which introduced yet a third ambiguity into an already complicated problem. This third ambiguity lay in the matter of the clergy's functions. The 'Caesaro-papistical' thesis[3] manifestly gains in strength if the clergy over whom the secular power claims to exercise control become possessed, on their part, of secular as well as ecclesiastical emoluments and authority; and this had actually been happening all over Western Christendom during the three centuries ending in the reign of the Emperor Henry III. The donations of Pepin and Charlemagne to the Papacy

[1] For the evidence on this head see Carlyle, op. cit., vol. iv, pp. 69–72.
[2] Carlyle, op. cit., vol. iv, p. 74.
[3] For the nature of 'Caesaro-papism' see IV. C (iii) (*c*) 2 (β), pp. 346–53, above.

were merely the classical examples of a wide-spread transfer, into clerical hands, of the civil power's *regalia*; and this oecumenical secular movement had been at no time so active as during the two centuries between the death of Charlemagne and the birth of Hildebrand. By the year 1075, when Hildebrand launched his campaign against the Lay Investiture of clerics, a very large part of the civil administration of Western Christendom was in the hands of clerics who held it as of feudal right, so that the exemption of the clergy from Lay Investiture in the broader sense would now carry with it an abrogation of the Secular Power's authority over large tracts of its own proper field and a transformation of the Church into a civil as well as an ecclesiastical *imperium in imperio*.[1] To demand this—if Hildebrand did unequivocally demand so much—was to declare war; and, if we ask ourselves what can have led so great a man as Hildebrand to take so grave a step, the most convincing answer will be that his judgement was clouded on this critical occasion by the intoxicating consciousness of his previous triumphs.[2] 'All things are possible to him that believeth'[3] is a dangerous text for a human being to act upon, even when the man is a Gregory VII.

The gravity of Hildebrand's action in 1075 is revealed by the dimensions of the catastrophe which was its sequel. On this issue

[1] It will be seen that this awkward logical consequence (on one interpretation of the term 'Investiture') of Hildebrand's declaration of war upon Lay Investiture in A.D. 1075 was the inverse of the equally awkward logical consequence of the Orthodox Church's conversion of the Khan of Bulgaria in A.D. 864–5. Under the then prevailing East Roman régime of 'Caesaro-papism' the Khan of Bulgaria was, as we have seen (in IV. C (iii) (*c*) 2 (*β*), pp. 379–81, above), implicitly placing himself under the secular sovereignty of the East Roman Emperor in the act of submitting himself to the ecclesiastical authority of the East Roman Emperor's civil servant the Oecumenical Patriarch. Conversely, Hildebrand in 1075 was implicitly claiming, for the Pope and other prelates of the Western Church, a secular independence of, in addition to an ecclesiastical authority over, the Holy Roman Emperor and other secular princes of Western Christendom. In the West in the eleventh century a new idea was colliding with old facts, whereas in Orthodox Christendom in the ninth century an old idea had collided with new facts. But, notwithstanding these antitheses, the two collisions had the identical effect of precipitating a disastrous conflict.

[2] A hostile critic might perhaps prefer to vindicate Hildebrand's judgement, at the expense of his character, by suggesting that he had never forgiven the Emperor Henry III for having humiliated the Papacy in the person of Hildebrand's own revered master Gregory VI; that in 1075 he at last took a revenge to which he had been looking forward for thirty years; and that he had waited to spring until his redoubtable enemy had been succeeded by an inexperienced son, and until the young man had his hands full with the insurrection that had broken out in Saxony in 1073 almost at the moment of Hildebrand's own accession to the Papacy. No doubt Henry IV's Saxon troubles did influence Hildebrand's choice of his moment for striking; for so great a man of action as Hildebrand was could not be blind to such considerations, and the Saxons did in fact become his close allies in the struggle against a common enemy. Yet a Machiavellian picture of Hildebrand is unconvincing. If he was really nursing his revenge throughout those thirty years, why did he not induce one of his three predecessors on the Papal throne, who were all under his influence, to strike at the Salian Dynasty before Henry IV came of age? He did not think of it because his mind was set in a larger mould and was intent on nobler things than paying off old scores. Canossa was not just a *riposte* to Sutri in Hildebrand's mind, though to smaller minds than his it might assume that appearance in historical perspective.

[3] Mark ix. 23.

of Investiture Hildebrand staked the whole of the moral prestige which he had won for the Papacy in thirty years; and his hold upon the consciences of the *Plebs Christiana* in Henry IV's Transalpine dominions was strong enough, in conjunction with the strength of Saxon arms, to bring the Emperor to Canossa. Yet, although Canossa may have dealt the Imperial dignity a blow from which it perhaps never quite recovered,[1] the sequel to that moral triumph was not an end, but a resumption, of the struggle which Hildebrand had let loose two years before. The end was not brought even by Paschal II's fundamental but abortive settlement with Henry IV's son and namesake in 1111, nor again by Calixtus II's successful but superficial settlement with the same Emperor in 1122; for, although the question of Investiture was officially disposed of by the Concordat of Worms, those fifty years of conflict had produced a rift between the Papacy and the Empire which might perhaps be precariously bridged but which was now too wide to be closed and too deep to be filled. When a Frederick I succeeded to the heritage of the Henrys and was armed, by Bolognese doctors of the disinterred *Corpus Juris*, with a Justinianean conception of the Imperial prerogative to match the Hildebrandine conception of the Apostolic power, the unhealed wound in the Western body social broke open again, and the new Justinian's battle with an ineffective Hadrian IV and an indomitable Alexander III reproduced the battle that had been fought by his predecessor Henry V with a saintly Paschal and a masterful Calixtus. The fire which Hildebrand had kindled in 1075 was still burning fiercely a hundred years later.

The second act in the tragedy opens with a respite which coincided in time with the pontificate of Pope Innocent III (*fungebatur* A.D. 1198–1216).

This precious breathing-space had not been secured by the labours of the young man who ascended the Papal throne in 1198 at the age of thirty-seven. In so far as it was due to statesmanship, the credit belonged to Innocent's predecessors Alexander III and Lucius III, the respective Papal negotiators of the Peace of Venice (1177) and the Peace of Constance (1183). Statesmanship, however, had done less for Innocent than the Chance which had drowned Barbarossa in Calycadnus in 1190 and had then carried off his formidable son and successor Henry VI only seven years later, in the very year before Innocent's own accession. These two premature deaths in rapid sequence left the House of Hohenstaufen

[1] 'Had all other humiliation been spared, that one scene in the yard of Matilda's castle . . . was enough to mark a decisive change and inflict an irretrievable disgrace on the crown so abased. Its wearer could no more, with the same lofty confidence, claim to be the highest power on Earth, created by and answerable to God alone. Gregory had extorted the recognition of that absolute superiority of the spiritual dominion which he was wont to assert so sternly.'—Bryce, James: *The Holy Roman Empire*, ch. 10.

without a competent grown man to defend its interests; and the double accident might seem providentially designed to nullify the effects of the Hannibal-stroke by which Henry VI in 1194 had reaped the fruits of a political marriage which his father had arranged, and had offset the loss of Lombardy by the acquisition of Sicily. In 1198 the two crowns—Sicilian and Imperial—which Henry VI had succeeded in uniting were once again on different heads; and although both the wearers were still Hohenstaufen they were in no position to act together against the Holy See because they were both of them politically paralysed: the King of Sicily, Henry's son Frederick II, by his tender age, and the Emperor, Henry's brother Philip, by the rivalry of a *Gegenkaiser* belonging to the rival German house of Welf. With Germany torn in two by civil war, and with the child-king of Sicily under Innocent's own guardianship, the young Pope had his hands free to play the part of President of the Christian Republic as Hildebrand had conceived it; and Innocent III did duly become the Solomon or Suleymān the Magnificent or Hārūn-ar-Rashīd of the Hildebrandine Papacy.[1]

This was a brilliant role, and it was impressively sustained by a noble figure; but, if there is any substance in the analogies by which we have just described it, Innocent's pontificate was not so triumphant in reality as it appeared to be on the surface. The three secular potentates with whom we have compared this prince of the Roman Church were all of them spoilt children of Fortune who had entered into other men's labours—Solomon into David's, Suleymān into Selīm's, and Harūn into As-Saffāh's—and all of them, again, were lordly spendthrifts who ran through their own inheritance and left a reckoning to be paid by their successors. This is the company to which Innocent III belongs. As a man of action—and it is as this that he stands or falls—he is unquestionably noble; yet this nobility is tarnished by a touch of ὕβρις and baulked by a grain of obtuseness.

The fallibility of Innocent's judgement is revealed in his handling of the weapon of the crusade; in his dealings with the Empire and the Hohenstaufen; and in his attitude towards the greatest man of his generation, Saint Francis.[2]

His first act after his accession was to preach a crusade for the rescue of the remnants of the Frankish principalities in Syria from the clutches of the Ayyubid Power; and this enterprise went grievously awry. Though the outposts of Western Christendom

1 For the Solomons on the thrones of universal states who sun themselves in the fleeting warmth of 'Indian Summers', see V. C (ii) (*a*), vol. vi, pp. 191–6, below.

2 For the connexion between the first and the third of these three points see IV. C (iii) (*c*) 3 (β), Annex, below.

past; he actually selected for his candidate, among the members of the Hohenstaufen House, a boy who already wore the Sicilian Crown, and who would therefore be in a position to execute his father Henry's design of taking the Roman See between two fires if Innocent's assistance enabled him to win the Imperial Crown as well. Innocent's estimate of Frederick II's character and intentions seems to have been as wide of the mark as his estimate of Otto's had been a few years before. No doubt Frederick was anxious to take his revenge upon Otto for having overrun the Sicilian dominions on the Italian mainland, but Innocent had no evidence that the boy was either grateful to Innocent himself for having intervened on his behalf, or well-disposed to the Papacy as an institution. At the interview between the fifty-two-years-old Pope and the eighteen-years-old king in A.D. 1212 Innocent was completely taken in by Frederick's precocious plausibility.

'One of the first acts of Frederick was to renew to the Pope in person the homage he had already paid to his deputy for the Kingdom of Sicily. Innocent, charmed with the youth's courage and docility, espoused his cause with vigour. By letter he called upon the communes of North Italy and the people of Germany to cast in their lot with Frederick; he poured money into the youth's purse, procured for him a Genoese fleet to conduct him to their city, and sent a cardinal-legate with him to win for him greater obedience.'[1]

Thanks to Innocent's support Frederick was crowned King of the Romans at Mainz before the year was out, and Otto's star duly sank as Frederick's rose towards its zenith. Yet, when Innocent was thus exerting all his powers in order to make his protégé master of Germany, he does not seem to have taken the precaution of exacting from him in advance a pledge that he would surrender his Sicilian Kingdom if he were successful in his Transalpine enterprise.[2] It was not till the year 1216, when Innocent was on his death-bed, that Frederick issued a bull engaging himself, as soon as he should have received the Imperial Crown, to hand on the Sicilian Crown to his son, 'in order to preclude the suspicion of anything in the nature of a union between the Kingdom and the Empire . . . to the possible detriment of the Apostolic See and of our own heirs'.[3] The declaration, when it came, was specious, like most of Frederick's acts; but from Innocent's point of view it

[1] Mann, op. cit., vol. xi, pp. 214–15. The authorities are cited in Carlyle, op. cit., vol. v, pp. 230–1.

[2] Perhaps Innocent was counting on the fact that Frederick, before assuming the Imperial title and leaving Sicily for Rome *en route* for Germany, had not only sworn fealty to the Pope and accepted a concordat on Innocent's terms, but had had his infant son Henry crowned as King of Sicily.

[3] Latin text quoted in Mann, op. cit., vol. xi, p. 220, footnote 3, and in Carlyle, op. cit., vol. v, p. 237, footnote 3.

came too late; for by 1216 Frederick, though he had still to be crowned Emperor in Rome, was already in the saddle in Germany without having yet evacuated his seat on the Sicilian Throne. In these circumstances the execution of his promise rested in his hands alone. Meanwhile, he held the Roman See in a vice, as his father had momentarily held it in the years 1194–7; and thus Innocent left the great institution which had been placed in his keeping in so prosperous a political condition eighteen years before, at the mercy of a son of Henry VI and a grandson of Frederick Barbarossa.

This lack of intuition in divining character, which Innocent showed when he lent his support to an Otto against a Philip and to a Frederick against an Otto, is more flagrantly apparent in his attitude towards Saint Francis. This shepherd of souls who was unduly soft and credulous in accepting at their face value the specious protestations of princes, showed himself unduly cold and cautious when he had to appraise the sainthood that shone like the Sun through Francis' countenance; and here it is difficult to draw the line between obtuseness and ὕβρις. Was Innocent unaware of Francis' greatness or indifferent to it? Did his aloofness from the deepest spiritual movement of his age reflect the pre-occupation of a man of affairs or the superciliousness of an aristocrat?[1] Even if we give Innocent the benefit of the doubt and acquit him, as Francis himself would have hastened to acquit him, of ὕβρις on Francis' account, at any rate we must count it for righteousness to Innocent's great-nephew Ugolino de' Conti that the future Pope Gregory IX was more sensitive than his relative and predecessor to Francis' sainthood, though he too was an aristocrat and a man of the world. And there is another count against Innocent III on which the charge of ὕβρις cannot be rebutted. A Pope whose predecessors had been content to style themselves 'Vicar of Peter' assumed the style of 'Vicar of Christ'.[2] This was an ominous

[1] For the relations between Innocent and Francis see Sabatier, P.: *Vie de Saint François d'Assise*, chap. 6, and Grundmann, H.: *Religiöse Bewegungen im Mittelalter* (Berlin 1935, Ebering), pp. 128–51. For the relations between Innocent and the religious movement of which Saint Francis was the pioneer within the bounds of the Church see Grundmann, op. cit., *passim*, but especially, perhaps, the passages quoted in the present study in IV. C (iii) (*c*) 3 (*β*), Annex, below.

[2] 'Soon after he ascended the Papal Throne, Innocent III began to use the phrase "Vicar of Christ" in connexion with his office. It had not been used before his time; and the implication that the successors of Peter were not his deputies, but received their commission, as he did, immediately from Christ, is significant of the conviction upon which the policy of Innocent was founded. . . . The assertions of Innocent III went far to establish the Papacy in the possession of semi-divine honours.'—Thompson, A. H., in *The Cambridge Medieval History*, vol. vi (Cambridge 1929, University Press), p. 644. On p. 43 of the same volume Professor E. F. Jacob quotes an illuminating passage (which is also quoted from Migne, *Patrologia Latina*, vol. ccxvii, col. 665 A and B, in Carlyle, op. cit., vol. v, p. 153, footnote 2) from a sermon (III) which was preached by Innocent III himself on one of the anniversaries of his consecration:

'Nam caeteri vocati sunt in partem sollicitudinis, solus autem Petrus assumptus est

departure from the humility of a Gregory the Great, who had taken the title of *Servus Servorum Dei* when his colleague John the Faster at Constantinople had proclaimed himself 'Oecumenical' Patriarch. In the year of Innocent's death John's 'Oecumenical' successor was a refugee at Nicaea from a Patriarchal See that was under the heel of Innocent's truant crusaders. The omen was unfavourable to the successors of the first Roman 'Vicar of Christ'. 'Woe unto you when all men shall speak well of you'[1] is Innocent's epitaph.

Innocent's failure of judgement can be measured best, like Hildebrand's, by marking its sequel; for the breathing-space which had opened with Innocent's accession did not outlast his death. It was followed by a battle between the Papacy and the Emperor Frederick II which surpassed in fury the battles of earlier Popes with the first Hohenstaufen Frederick and with the last two Franconian Henrys. Up to a certain point history repeated itself. In the first round of the struggle the gentle role of a Paschal II or a Hadrian IV was played by the unwarlike and undecided Pope Honorius III,[2] while in the next round the harder and more worldly Pope Gregory IX played the militant role of a Calixtus II or an Alexander III. This time, however, it took more than one militant pontificate to wear down the strength of the Papacy's Imperial antagonist; and the worldly-wise Ugolino de' Conti, who had patronized as well as appreciated Saint Francis, and who excommunicated Frederick in 1227 in the mood of a realist who means to stand no nonsense, died fourteen years later *re infecta*. It needed Sinibaldo Fieschi's two-handed sword to shear through the Saracenic armour that had turned the edge of an Ugolino's razor-blade; and that terrible weapon in those implacable hands made havoc of everything in its path as it swung to and fro across the face of Europe in pursuit of its elusive prey.

'In those days wickedness prevailed; the people of God were without

in plenitudinem potestatis. In signum spiritualium contulit mihi mitram, in signum temporalium dedit mihi coronam; mitram pro sacerdotio, coronam pro regno, illius me constituens vicarium qui habet in vestimento et in femore suo scriptum: "Rex regum et dominus dominantium; sacerdos in aeternum, secundum ordinem Melchisedech".'

Even this is not the highest flight of Innocent's ὕβρις. In another sermon (II) on the same subject (quoted from Migne, op. cit., vol. cit., cols. 657–8, in Carlyle, op. cit., vol. cit., p. cit., footnote 1) Innocent follows up a sentence which is identical with the first sentence of the passage quoted above, with the almost blasphemous assertions:

'Iam ergo videtis quis iste servus qui super familiam constituitur: profecto vicarius Iesu Christi, successor Petri, christus Domini, deus Pharaonis; inter Deum et hominem medius constitutus, citra Deum, sed ultra hominem; minor Deo, sed maior homine; qui de omnibus iudicat, et a nemine iudicatur; Apostoli voce pronuntians: "qui me iudicat, Dominus est".'

Could ὕβρις call down judgement upon itself more vociferously than this?

[1] Luke vi. 26.

[2] Honorius's statement of policy after his election in A.D. 1216 was that 'he wished to proceed by clemency rather than by vigour' (*Epistulae Honorii*, i, 30, quoted by Mann, op. cit., vol. xiii, p. 209).

a ruler; Rome lay desolate; the glory of the clergy departed; and the people of God were divided. Some followed the Church, and these took the Cross [against Frederick], while others followed Frederick the *ci-devant* Emperor, and these insulted the Divine Religion. . . . Mercy and Truth and Justice were no longer to be found on Earth.'[1]

Germany had not seen such a war since Charlemagne's attrition of the Saxons, and Italy not since the extermination of the Ostrogoths by Belisarius and Narses. In Italy, in this fifth decade of the thirteenth century,

'Men could neither plough nor sow nor reap nor cultivate the vine nor gather the vintage nor live on the farms—especially in the territories of Parma, Reggio, Modena, and Cremona. Close to the cities themselves, however, men tilled the ground under the guard of the city militia, who were divided into quarters corresponding to the city gates. Armed soldiers guarded the labourers all day, and the country people carried on their agricultural work under these conditions. This was necessary on account of the highwaymen, thieves and robbers who had multiplied exceedingly and who kidnapped people and carried them off to dungeons to be ransomed for money. They also lifted the cattle, and ate or sold them. If their prisoners did not raise a ransom, they hanged them by the feet or the hands and pulled out their teeth and put paddocks and toads (*buffones sive ruspos*) in their mouths to hurry them up in producing the ransom money; and these tortures were more bitter and abominable to them than any form of death. The brigands were more cruel than demons; and in those times one human being was about as glad to meet another human being on the road as he would have been to meet the Devil himself; for everyone was living in perpetual suspicion of everyone else—suspecting his neighbour of intending to kidnap him and throw him into a dungeon, in order that "the ransom of a man's life" might be "his riches" (Proverbs xiii. 8). So the land was reduced to a desert, empty of both husbandman and wayfarer. For in the days of Frederick—and especially after his deposition from the Imperial office, and after Parma had rebelled against him and had lifted her heel—"the highways were unoccupied, and the travellers walked through byways" (Judges v. 6). And evils multiplied on the Earth. Wild birds and wild animals multiplied quite beyond measure—pheasants, partridges and quails, hares, roebuck and fallow-deer, buffaloes, wild-boars and ravening wolves. These wild beasts no longer found creatures—lambs or sheep—to eat, as they had been used to finding them, on the farms, because the farms had been burnt to ashes. And so the wolves used to gather in packs round the moat (?) of a city (*circa foveas alicuius civitatis*)

[1] 'Eodem tempore prevaluit iniquitas, et populus Dei sine rectore fuit et Roma in desolatione, et decor clericalis periit, et divisus est populus Dei—partim sequebantur Ecclesiam, et hii signati sunt, partim favebant Fridrico quondam imperatori, et hii insultabant Divine Religioni . . . Et Misericordia et Veritas et Judicium de Terra sublata sunt.'—*Annales Scheftlarienses Majores*, sub anno 1246, apud *Monumenta Germaniae Historica*, ed. by Pertz, S. H., vol. xix of the whole series = vol. xvii of the Scriptores (Hanover 1861, Hahn), p. 342. (The Monastery of Schäftlarn stands on the banks of the River Isar, above Munich, in the diocese of Freising.)

and howl aloud under the extreme torment of their hunger. And they used to creep into the cities by night and devour people—women and children among them—who were sleeping under porches or in waggons. Sometimes they even burrowed through the house walls and strangled the babies in their cradles. No one who had not seen them—as I saw them—could believe the horrors which were committed at that time, not only by men, but by beasts of various kinds.'[1]

This was the darkness that descended upon Western Christendom after the brief noon-day of Innocent III's pontificate. And it was not for nothing that Sinibaldo Fieschi chose Lotario de' Conti's pontifical name when his own turn came to ascend the Papal throne. Notwithstanding the sharpness of the contrast between the characters of the Roman nobleman and the Genoese, the pontificate of the fourth Innocent followed that of the third as inevitably as night follows day.

The third and culminating act of the tragedy opens on the 13th December, 1250, which is the date of Frederick II's sudden and premature death. Would Pope Innocent IV accept this heaven-sent opportunity of restoring peace to Western Christendom, or would he pursue his vendetta against Frederick's house to the bitter end? Peace was not only demanded by the misery and devastation which this latter-day Hannibalic War had spread; it was cried out for by the conscience of the *Plebs Christiana*, which found its spokesman in Saint Louis. The King of France was as unwilling to place his sword at Innocent's service for the destruction of Frederick as he was to make common cause with the Emperor against the Pope. His single-minded aim was to bring to an end this impious civil war in the bosom of Western Christendom in order to release and unite her forces for a fresh crusade. Saint Louis made vain attempts at mediation in 1245, and again in 1246, and his anxiety was well warranted; for in the latter year Innocent actually forbade the preaching of the crusade *d'outre mer* within the boundaries of the Holy Roman Empire, and ordered that certain moneys which had been raised in the Empire for the conduct of the war against the Muslims should be diverted to the coffers of the Pope's own puppet *Gegenkaiser*, William of Holland. The Frisian crusaders who had already enlisted under Louis's banner were allowed, and perhaps encouraged, to commute their vows and acquire their merit by fighting, instead, for William against

[1] Salimbene's *Chronicle*, first edition (Parma 1857, Fiaccadorii), pp. 70–71, *sub anno* 1247. The last touch in this grim picture recalls to the writer of this Study a vision of Western Anatolia as he saw it, during the Graeco-Turkish war-after-the-war, in 1921, when the only plough-marks on the surface of a desolate country-side were the rootings of the wild boars who had entered into the heritage of the vanished human inhabitants. The picture as a whole will recall to the minds of readers of our generation the aspect of China as it has come to be since the outbreak of the Revolution in A.D. 1911.

Frederick. The utmost concession that Innocent would make to Louis's protests was that the crusade *d'outre mer* should be preached in five Lotharingian dioceses on the fringe of the Empire along the French border.[1] In 1248, when Louis *en route* for his Mediterranean port of embarkation had his last interview with Innocent at Lyon and sought to mediate between Pope and Emperor—once more in vain—the royal saint is reported to have told the Papal sinner that the sin would be on his head if the Egyptian expedition failed;[2] and by the date of Frederick's death this curse was in operation; for, eight months before Frederick died in Apulia, Louis had been taken prisoner in the Delta.[3] Now that Frederick was dead, would Innocent lift the curse by making peace with Frederick's children? Innocent's answer was in the negative; and this negative answer—which assuredly[4] was no mere error of judgement but was a moral aberration as well—spelt the suicide of the Hildebrandine Papacy.

The death of his arch-enemy did not move Innocent from the stand which he had taken three years before, when he had declared his determination never to make peace so long as either Frederick himself or any of his sons remained king or emperor.[5] In this declaration Frederick's brood was deliberately included in a ban which had been confined, in an earlier Papal anathema,[6] to Frederick's own person; and Innocent did not now abate one jot or tittle of the war-aims to which he had committed himself. His rejoinder to the news of Frederick's death was to command the notables of Sicily to place the kingdom at his own disposition. When Frederick's son Conrad took up his father's Sicilian heritage, Innocent renewed the excommunication against him and ransacked Christendom to find a Papal nominee to the Sicilian Throne who could and would take the kingdom from Frederick's heirs by force of arms. When Conrad, dying only four years after his father at

1 Mann, op. cit., vol. xiv, p. 169. The five dioceses in question were Liége, Cambrai, Toul, Metz, and Verdun. It is interesting to observe that these were all French-speaking districts. In the Papal permission accorded to these French-speaking Lotharingians to march with the King of France can we see a first glimmer of our latter-day Western linguistic nationalism?

2 Mann, op. cit., vol. xiv, p. 170, on the authority of Matthew Paris (*Chronica Maiora*, Luard's edition in the Rolls Series, vol. v, p. 175). The story may, of course, have been *ben trovato*, either for the political purpose of deepening Innocent's infamy or for the artistic purpose of heightening the tragic pathos of the subsequent fortunes of Louis's ill-starred enterprise; yet there is no positive ground for assuming that the incident is fabulous; and it is in entire conformity with the character of both parties.

3 See IV. C (iii) (*c*) 2 (γ), pp. 447–9, above.

4 *Pace* the plea of a distinguished modern Western historian which has been quoted on p. 548, footnote 3, above.

5 'Promittimus . . . nec etiam pacem aliquatenus cum praefato Frederico reformabimus ita quod ipse vel aliquis filiorum suorum rex aut imperator existat.'—Innocent IV, letter of the 4th May, 1247, quoted by Mann in op. cit., vol. xiv, p. 97, footnote 1.

6 In a letter of the 28th January, 1247, the formula had been promulgated with reference to Frederick alone (see Mann, op. cit., vol. xiv, p. 96).

the age of 26, commended his infant son Conradin to the protection of the Holy See, the Pope rejected the bequest and announced his intention, pending the child's coming of age, to take over the government of the kingdom himself. This was the policy which Innocent bequeathed to his successors; and it duly ended in the extinction of Frederick's line through Manfred's death in battle in 1265 and Conradin's on the scaffold in 1268.

Their executioner was Charles of Anjou—a most unsaintly brother of Saint Louis—yet it is significant that even this hard and covetous secular prince should have hesitated for nearly eleven years before he accepted in 1264, at the hands of Pope Urban IV, an offer of the Kingdom of Sicily that had been made to him by Pope Innocent IV as early as 1253. To what considerations in Charles' mind was this extraordinary hesitation due? It was not that he was unambitious, for the passion of his life was to acquire a kingdom as great as that which his brother had inherited; and when once he was launched upon his Sicilian enterprise his lustful vision overshot the Straits of Otranto, as well as the Straits of Messina, and embraced the Empire of Romania. Nor was it that Charles doubted the Pope's ability to 'deliver the goods'; for the Kingdom of Sicily was a fief of the Holy See which was legally at the overlord's disposal if the tenure could be shown to have fallen vacant or forfeit; and in 1246 Innocent had actually enabled Charles to acquire the County of Provence, though this Imperial fief had not been Innocent's to bestow. The consideration which moved Charles' counsellors to oppose his acceptance of Innocent's offer in 1253,[1] and led Charles himself to leave the question in abeyance for ten years after that, was the consciousness that this Papal invitation to do a terrier's work and exterminate Frederick's brood in the hole where they had gone to earth was an invitation to commit an enormity which would cry aloud for vengeance. When Charles eventually succumbed to the temptation which was dangled before his eyes by Innocent and his successors, the enormity was indeed committed and the vengeance duly followed. Manfred and Conradin were avenged upon Charles in the Sicilian Vespers, which paralysed Charles' power and blighted his ambitions three years before his death. They were avenged upon the Papacy when Innocent IV's thirteenth successor, Boniface VIII, picked his quarrel with the second successor of Saint Louis, Philip the Fair,

[1] When this opposition was raised, Innocent 'suggested to his legate a way out of the difficulty which did much more credit to him as a lawyer and a diplomat than as a Pope. Albert was to promise in his name to agree to such recommendations on the disputed points as should be made to him by two prelates and a knight nominated by Charles. But the Count was previously to give the legate an undertaking in writing that the said promise was to be without real effect. But the advisers of Charles were not satisfied.'—Mann, op. cit., vol. xiv, p. 135.

'Woe to that man by whom the offence cometh!'[1] The Papacy's Angevin agent escaped with the loss of half his ill-gotten kingdom; the Papacy itself was punished with the loss of the whole of its Hildebrandine heritage; and it was condemned, in addition, to execute this sentence with its own hands.

If an Athenian tragic poet of the fifth century B.C. could have been given the story of the Hildebrandine Papacy as the theme for a trilogy, he would probably have impersonated *κόρος* in Gregory VII and *ὕβρις* in Innocent IV, and in that case he would certainly have cast Boniface VIII for the role of *ἄτη*; for in the pontificate of Boniface the Papacy, now distraught by the blood-guiltiness which Innocent had fastened upon her, strode over the edge of a precipice with eyes that were open yet unseeing.

The note of *ὕβρις* which Innocent III had struck when he proclaimed himself 'the Vicar of Christ,' and Innocent IV when he included Frederick's children in the remorseless vow which he had taken against Frederick himself, was sounded for the third time by Boniface VIII when he seized the occasion of the turn of the century to inaugurate the institution of the Papal Jubilee. It was the enthusiasm of the response to his call and the multitude of the pilgrims who flocked to Rome in the Holy Year 1300 from all quarters of Western Christendom that fostered in the Pope's imagination his fatally delusive belief in his own terrestrial omnipotence. The fervour was genuine, and the heads could be counted; but this pilgrimage to the Apostle's shrine was an act of homage to the idea of the Papacy as Hildebrand had impressed it upon Western minds, and not to the reality as it had been shaped by the coarser hands of Hildebrand's successors. Boniface saw the pilgrims but not their neighbours who had stayed at home; he heard the acclamations around him, and these agreeable voices drowned, in his ears, the murmurs of a provincial clergy who were still being called upon to pay the Papal war-taxes a generation after the Papal Punic Wars had been brought to their dreadful termination. He did not understand that neither the clergy nor the *Plebs Christiana* would be willing to risk life and fortune in order to support a Papal against a secular tyranny; he assumed that they would rise at his call as they had risen at Hildebrand's. In this delusion he provoked the King of France into drawing his sword, and then ran straight upon the extended sword-point, in confidence that any secular weapon must crumple under the drum-fire of his own ecclesiastical artillery.

The sequel to this suicidal act was the outrage at Anagni and 'the Babylonish Captivity' at Avignon and the Great Schism which

[1] Matt. xviii. 7.

rent Western Christendom in two; and each of these calamities might have been foreseen and feared and averted by Boniface himself if his vision and judgement and action had not been confounded by the ἄτη that was incarnate in him.

A *coup de force* against the Pope's own person was the first counter-attack that any Pope had to expect from a secular prince upon whom he had declared war. Had Boniface forgotten in 1303 how Paschal II had been kidnapped by Henry V in 1111, and Hildebrand himself by Cencio on Christmas Day 1075? If a Henry IV could find a Cencio to do his dirty work, why should not a Philip the Fair find a Sciarra Colonna?

Again, the attraction of the Papacy into the orbit of the French Crown did not begin in 1305 when the Gascon Bertrand de Goth was elected, by grace of King Philip, to be Pope Clement V, and obediently came to be crowned at Lyon and lodged at Avignon on his secular master's threshold. Long before that, Pope after Pope had sought asylum in France from the moment when the struggle between the Papacy and the Empire began. Urban II had come to Auvergne to preach the First Crusade; Paschal II had been safe from outrage when he was negotiating with Henry V at Châlons-sur-Marne; Gelasius II had died out of Henry's reach at Cluny; Calixtus II had fought the same Emperor from a French base of operations until his ascendancy over his adversary was sufficiently well established to enable him to set foot in Rome; Innocent II had fled to France before the face of the Jewish antipope Pietro Pierleone; Alexander III had withdrawn into a French citadel when Frederick I, at the zenith of his power, had made Italy too hot for him; and Innocent IV had followed Alexander's tactics at the height of his own struggle with Frederick II. Even when the destruction of the Hohenstaufen and the Great Interregnum in the Empire had relieved the Papacy from all danger of being attacked by an emperor in Italy, Pope Gregory X looked beyond the north-western bounds of the Italian Peninsula and fixed his choice upon the French-speaking city of Lyon, on the last stage of the road leading out of the Holy Roman Empire into the French Kingdom, as the trysting-place for a council which was to deal with three matters of such capital importance for the whole of Western Christendom as the reconstruction of the Empire and the reconciliation of the Greeks[1] and the resumption of the Crusades. Could not Boniface feel it in his bones that the pull of France had become the greatest danger by which the Holy See was threatened now that the threat from Germany had been removed? And could not he understand that the surest way of making this pull irresis-

[1] See IV. C (iii) (*c*) 2 (β), Annex II, p. 616, below.

tible was to challenge the King of France, who now held the Papacy in the hollow of his hand, to a trial of strength?

As for the Great Schism, it had been already foreshadowed by the time of Boniface's pontificate in the series of interregna which had been interrupting the Hildebrandine succession for some fifty years past. A twenty-seven months' interregnum had preceded the election of Boniface's own immediate predecessor Celestine V in 1294; there had been a thirty-three months' interregnum before the election of Gregory X in 1271; and a nineteen months' interregnum before the election of Innocent IV in 1243. The inability of the cardinals to agree upon a successor to Gregory IX at the supreme crisis of the struggle between the Papacy and Frederick II, when Hannibal was thundering at the gates, was proof in itself that the electoral machinery which had been installed on Hildebrand's initiative in 1059 was badly out of gear. The Hildebrandine provision for regular and orderly and peaceable elections to an office which was apt to fall vacant at short intervals was one of the essential foundation-stones of the whole Hildebrandine edifice, just as, conversely, the turbulence and corruption of the Papal elections during the preceding century and a half had been one of the principal causes of the Papacy's abasement in that unhappy period. If the Hildebrandine conclave which had then exorcized the Marozian pandemonium of violence and intrigue were now to beget interregna, the last state of the Papacy might be worse than the first. A corrupt election or a contested election might be less disastrous than a failure to make any election at all. The evil was borne in upon Pope Gregory X by the antecedents of his own election; and three years later, in 1274, the Council of Lyon, sitting under his presidency, passed, in the teeth of the College of Cardinals, the constitution *Ubi periculum* for expediting Papal elections in the future. This constitution, however, was promptly abrogated by Pope John XXI in 1276; a fresh interregnum between the death of Nicholas IV and the election of Celestine V was the consequence; and Boniface VIII, who had been a member of the conclave that stuck in the mud on that unseemly occasion, knew well enough that the eventual choice of the shy Abruzzese hermit had not been an inspiration of the Holy Spirit, or even a sop to public opinion, but had been a counsel of despair. This despair had been justified in the event by the 'Great Refusal' which had opened the way for Benedetto Caetani himself to mount the Papal throne.[1] No living man had had better opportunities than his of apprehending the seriousness of the heart-disease which was the Papacy's legacy from the terrible overstrain of its struggle with Frederick II.

[1] See p. 550, footnote 2, above.

A heart which was subject to such protracted stoppages as these might fail altogether if the patient were exposed to another great exertion or great shock. That Boniface, of all men, knowing what he knew, should have challenged the King of France when the Papacy was in this parlous state would be inexplicable in a man who was altogether in his right senses.

The fourth and last act in the Hildebrandine tragedy opens after the turn of the fourteenth and fifteenth centuries with the advent of the Conciliar Movement.

The scandal of the Great Schism[1] moved the children of the Papacy—a provincial clergy whom a Hildebrand had once rescued from the heavy hand of the secular power, and universities whom an Alexander III had nursed through their infancy—to come to the rescue of the most venerable institution in Western Christendom. Their misgivings at the rancour and rapacity of an Innocent IV and their resentment at their own sufferings from the growing fiscal and administrative tyranny of the Curia were now reinforced by two further considerations: a concern for the life of the Western body social, which might sustain a fatal injury through the self-destruction of its most vital organ; and a compunction towards an institution whose Hildebrandine virtues were once again remembered, side by side with its Innocentian vices, now that Hildebrand's work was in mortal danger of being utterly undone. Accordingly a Holy See which had commanded devotion in the days of a Hildebrand and an Alexander III, and had then bred disillusionment in the days of an Innocent IV and a Boniface VIII, came to inspire a different emotion again when the house divided against itself was on the verge of collapse. This new attitude, of which the Conciliar Movement was the outcome, combined a filial piety with a moral reprobation. The reformers were anxious to save the Papacy from suicide, but their anxiety was for the sake of the Christian Republic as well as for the sake of the Papacy itself. They were determined to reconstruct the falling house, but not on the former plan. Whatever Hildebrand's original design may have been, his building, as it had grown under his successors'

1 The Great Schism evidently made a far more painful impression upon the fourteenth-century Western conscience than 'the Babylonish Captivity'. The migration of the Curia to Avignon might be the Romans' funeral; but for the Western *Plebs Christiana* at large, who regarded the Papacy as their common possession, it did not much matter where the Pope took up his abode as long as he remained somewhere within the borders of the Western Commonwealth; and Avignon (see p. 520, footnote 2, above) stood only second to Lyon (see p. 569, above) in respect of its geographical convenience as a centre for the ecclesiastical administration of the Western Patriarchate. On the other hand the Great Schism, which the Romans did not much mind so long as one of the rival Popes again made Rome his headquarters, filled the rest of Western Christendom with dismay because it was destructive of the unity of the *Respublica Christiana*. On this account the Papal schism evoked a much more vigorous reaction than the Papal sojourn at Avignon in the Western World as a whole.

hands, had become top-heavy. The ancient primacy of the Roman See among the thousand bishoprics of Western Christendom had towered up into a modern centralized autocracy; the Papal aegis that had been stretched over the devoted heads of the *Plebs Christiana* had turned into a cope of lead. This increasing top-heaviness was the fault in the pontifical architecture which was bringing the building down in ruin. It would be folly to re-erect the house on the old lines and so invite a repetition of the catastrophe. The reconstructed pyramid must have a lower apex and a broader base.

It will be seen that in the programme of the Conciliar Movement the Papacy was being offered a chance of retrieving its position, but that the offer was conditional—as any offer of salvation must be if it comes at the thirteenth hour when it is already too late to restore the *status quo ante*. In this act the former relations between the Roman See and the provinces of the Western Ecclesiastical Commonwealth were inverted. It was the provinces, now, that were taking the initiative and coming to the rescue; and a rescuer has an intrinsic right to exercise a certain control over the conduct of the party that is receiving his aid, while, conversely, he who has to accept the help of others because he has failed to help himself has an intrinsic duty to yield to his helpers' guidance. The condition to which the Papacy was asked to assent as the price—and guarantee—of its rehabilitation was the introduction of a parliamentary element into the constitution of the Western body ecclesiastic. In the ecclesiastical field this idea was nothing new. In the history of the Church, Oecumenical Councils were an older institution than Patriarchs; and we have seen above[1] how the Hildebrandine Papacy deliberately revived the Conciliar system in the West in the twelfth century in order to fortify itself against the Empire, and how in the following centuries the Kings of England and France—perhaps herein taking a leaf out of their Papal adversary's book—took care to fortify themselves with parliamentary support when they summoned up their courage to resist the Papal pretensions. In the fifteenth century the Papacy was asked to carry one stage farther in the ecclesiastical field the development of an institution which had been re-introduced into that field by Pope Calixtus II and had since been adopted in the field of parochial secular affairs by King Edward I of England and King Philip IV of France. Would the Papacy be willing to atone for its past and assure its future by bowing, in this matter, to the will of Western Christendom? Once again a Pope had to take a decision which was momentous for the fate of the Western World as well as for that of the Roman See; and, once again, the answer was in

[1] See p. 542, above.

the negative. The Papacy rejected the parliamentary principle and opted for an unrestricted sovereignty in a restricted field as the alternative to accepting a limited constitutional authority over a loyal and undivided Christian Commonwealth.

The decision was taken at the Council of Constance (*sedebat* A.D. 1414–18) in the crucial year 1417. After the Council had performed its negative task of ridding the Western Church of the three unworthy pretenders who had been contending for the title to the Papal office, two further tasks lay before it: the reform of the government of the Christian Commonwealth in both principle and practice; and the election of a worthy incumbent for its highest magistracy. In what order were these tasks to be taken? The Conciliar Party desired that the Council should first decide upon the reforms and then elect a Pope who would be bound in advance to govern in accordance with the new constitution; the Curial Party desired that the Pope should be elected first, in order that the proposed reforms might be worked out under Papal auspices. In this dispute over procedure the question of substance was at stake; and the Conciliar Party accepted defeat when the Emperor Sigismund agreed on their behalf that the new Pope should be elected first. When once this crucial point had been conceded, it was in vain that Sigismund stipulated for the postponement of the new Pope's coronation until after the reforms had been promulgated; in vain that the Council hastened to pass the decree *Frequens*,[1] which provided for the Council's own re-assembly at stated regular intervals; and in vain that, when the conclave was formed, the twenty-three cardinals were reinforced by thirty non-Curial electors representing the five nations into which the Council was articulated. The first act of Cardinal Oddone Colonna, after his election to be Pope Martin V,[2] was to confirm the rules of the Papal Chancery which had been issued by Pope John XXIII; and this was an ominous act; for John was the most disreputable of Martin's three rival predecessors, and his rules embodied abuses which the Council had marked down for reform, as well as non-contentious standing orders which had to be legally in force if the wheels of Papal administration were to be kept running. Thereafter Pope Martin made proposals for reform on his own part; but he evaded the crucial point of defining the causes for which a Pope might be admonished or deposed; the statutes which were passed under his auspices[3] covered only a few

[1] On the 9th October, 1417.

[2] On the 11th November, 1417.

[3] On the 21st March, 1418, seven reformatory decrees were approved and accepted by the Council in fulfilment of a decree of the 30th October, 1417, which had provided, among other things, that, before the dissolution of the Council, the new Pope (who at that date had still to be elected) was, with the Council's assistance, to reform the Church in eighteen specified matters.

of the questions which the Council had placed on the agenda; and the rest were left over for the Pope to deal with in separate concordats which he was to negotiate with the several nations of the Western Commonwealth.[1] By the time when the Council adjourned and the Pope left Constance for Rome, the course of the next chapter of Western history had been determined; for the outcome of the Council of Constance was confirmed by the heavier defeat which the Conciliar Movement sustained at the subsequent Council of Basel (*sedebat* A.D. 1431–49) in the pontificate of Eugenius IV.

'The same year and almost the same day were marked by the deposition of Eugenius at Basel and, at Florence, by his reunion of the Greeks and Latins. In the former synod (which he styled, indeed, an assembly of demons) the Pope was branded with the guilt of simony, perjury, tyranny, heresy and schism and declared to be incorrigible in his vices, unworthy of any title, and incapable of holding any ecclesiastical office. In the latter he was revered as the true and holy Vicar of Christ, who, after a separation of six hundred years, had reconciled the Catholics of the East and West in one fold and under one shepherd. The act of union was subscribed by the Pope, the [East Roman] Emperor, and the principal members of both churches. . . . A clamour was artfully propagated against the remnant of a schism in Switzerland and Savoy which alone impeded the harmony of the Christian World. The vigour of opposition was succeeded by the lassitude of despair; the Council of Basel was silently dissolved; . . . all ideas of reformation subsided; the Popes continued to exercise and abuse their ecclesiastical despotism.'[2]

This outcome of the rival councils of Basel and Florence might seem to have reinstated the Papacy in the triumphant position which it had occupied at the close of the Council of Lyon in the pontificate of Gregory X, and to have wiped out all the humiliations through which this extraordinary institution had passed during the intervening chapter of its history which had begun at Anagni with the outrage upon Boniface VIII and had closed at Constance with the election of Martin V. In reality that chapter could not be expunged from the pontifical records as though it were an accidental misfortune without any causal relation to its historical antecedents and therefore without any practical significance.[3] Actually,

[1] These concordats were duly negotiated, and their terms were registered on the 15th April, 1418; but they were only concluded for a term of five years and they were nowhere properly put into effect (see *The Cambridge Medieval History*, vol. viii, p. 18).

[2] Gibbon, E.: *The History of the Decline and Fall of the Roman Empire*, ch. lxvi.

[3] 'Point after point of the charges brought forward at the Council of Constance against the Papal administration of the preceding thirty years is equally apposite to the conditions obtaining eighty years later. The misdemeanours which were a chronic disease of the Curia in and after the second half of the fifteenth century are in the fullest sense a legacy from the time of the Schism.'—Hofmann, W. von.: *Forschungen zur Geschichte der Kurialen Behörden vom Schisma bis zur Reformation* (Rome 1914, Loescher, 2 vols.), vol. i, p. 1.

as we have seen, the fall of A.D. 1303 had followed hard upon the heels of the triumph of A.D. 1274 because the triumph had masked a perilous state of exhaustion and weakness, and in masking it had blinded the Papacy to the urgent need in which it stood of minding its steps and mending its ways. To ignore the lesson of the humiliations of 1303–1417 in an hour when the Papacy was at last triumphant once again was to court a fresh disaster; and this was the mistake which was made by the Curia in the critical years between the election of Pope Martin V in 1417 and the dissolution of the Council of Basel in 1449. Popes Martin V (*fungebatur* A.D. 1417–31) and Eugenius IV (*fungebatur* A.D. 1431–47) were not indeed hostile to reform in principle; so far from that, the former, at any rate, did seriously attempt to carry out many of the measures which the Council of Constance had demanded.[1] But these Papal efforts at reform were stultified by the fatal weakness of their not being the Papacy's paramount aim or interest. During these critical pontificates the Pope's overriding concern was to assert his own pretension to exercise an autocratic authority; and in this frame of mind he was less inclined to welcome the Conciliar Movement as a potent reinforcement to the cause of reform than he was to turn against that cause for fear that its promotion by the Conciliar method might produce, as a by-product, a limitation of the Papal prerogative. This Papal impulse to subordinate the reform of the Church to the aggrandisement of the Papacy was perhaps responsible, more than any other factor, for that misunderstanding between the Papacy and the Conciliar Movement which came to an open breach in the quarrel between Pope Eugenius IV and the Council of Basel. And in the intoxication of its victory over the Conciliar Movement in this naked trial of strength the Papacy abandoned itself once more to the lust for power[2] which had been its besetting sin since the days of Hildebrand. With one hand it clung to the despotic ecclesiastical power over the provinces of the

[1] 'In face of the attitude of the Pope (which was indeed only the attitude that was to be expected)—and especially after the decree promulgating the Chancery rules [see the present chapter, p. 573, above—A.J.T.] which reaffirmed in traditional fashion all the reservations, including those to which exception had been taken, without regard to the negotiations [at the Council of Constance]—no very energetic measures on the part of the new Pope [Martin V] were to be looked for. A considerable time was, in fact, to pass before the appearance of anything like a thorough-going reform bull. Unobtrusively, however, one individual measure after another was taken for bringing some provisional order into the situation in the individual offices [of the Curia], tightening the control over the existing arrangements, and thus preparing the way for a general reform. . . . There was hardly any motion that the Reform Movement had made which was destined to be left unconsidered in the further course of [Martin V's] pontificate. . . . [And] yet the activity of Martin V's endeavours in this field did not bear fruit in any corresponding success.'—Hofmann, op. cit., vol. i, pp. 11–12.

[2] For the encroachment of a capricious Papal absolutism upon the Curia's traditional regard for legality and regularity during the interval between the failure of the Conciliar Movement and the outbreak of the Reformation see Hofmann, op. cit., vol. i, pp. 323–6.

Western Church which it had been unexpectedly successful in retaining; with the other hand it continued to build up its secular territorial power in Central Italy, and, in playing their part as fifteenth-century Italian despots, the Popes became steeped in that pride of life which was the dominant note of the medieval Italian culture in its fifteenth-century over-ripeness. In this generation and this mood a Rodrigo Borgia on the Papal throne out-heroded a Baldassare Cossa;[1] and, once again, the fox was caught.[2] Within less than a hundred years after the dissolution of the Council of Basel in 1449 the Papacy was in even worse case than it had been in when the Council of Constance had opened in 1414.[3] The Pope had defeated the Conciliar Movement to his own undoing. 'He made a pit and digged it, and is fallen into the ditch which he made.'[4]

After the turn of the fifteenth and sixteenth centuries the power which the Papacy had refused to share constitutionally with a parliament of the Christian Commonwealth was lawlessly snatched out of its hands by the parochial secular princes, who might have been kept within bounds by the oecumenical authority of a Pope in Council, but who now found an easy prey in a Pope who alienated and disillusioned the *Plebs Christiana* by recklessly setting his own will to power against the people's yearning for reform and relief. The Papacy had rebuffed the Conciliar Movement as Rehoboam once rebuffed the congregation of Israel, and the same consequences followed.

'The king answered the people roughly, and . . . spake to them . . . . . . saying: "My father made your yoke heavy, and I will add to your yoke; my father also chastised you with whips, but I will chastise you with scorpions." . . . So when all Israel saw that the king hearkened not unto them, the people answered the king saying: "What portion have we

[1] Cossa reigned as Pope John XXIII from 1410 to 1415; Borgia, as Pope Alexander VI, from 1492 to 1503. Mr. Barraclough objects that 'this moral judgement completely ignores the administrative (and other) capacities of the Borgia'; but *respice finem*.

[2] 'A hole to catch foxes in' was Pope John XXIII's exclamation when, on his disconsolate journey to Constance, he caught his first sight of the city lying in a hollow of the hills.

[3] 'Far from preparing the way for a lasting improvement, the restoration period of the Papacy played its part in leading on to the subsequent situation. Its merit lay in its success in overcoming a number of defects and getting rid of a number of abuses. But this improvement was only a rally; it was not a cure. This comes out in the fact that from this time onwards the same measures had to be renewed again and again at relatively short intervals in regard to the same points. In spite of the warning lessons of the Schism, which had been thoroughly taken to heart at the Council of Constance, the task of striking at the root of the evil—i.e. combating the causes of the increasing deterioration of discipline—was perpetually being put off; and there was a long persistence in the mistaken idea that all defects and misdevelopments could be got rid of merely by issuing ordinances, without at the same time taking severer measures to ensure that such ordinances should be strictly carried out. There was not a total blindness to this inner contradiction; in the later reforms the appropriate means were often proposed, but they were never applied.'—Hofmann, op. cit., vol. i, p. 16.

[4] Psalm vii. 15.

in David? Neither have we inheritance in the son of Jesse. To your tents, O Israel. Now see to thine own house, David". So Israel departed unto their tents'[1]—

and in every tent they found some Henry Tudor who was eagerly waiting for his opportunity to play Jeroboam's part. It was by licence of the disillusionment of a popular feeling which had tried and failed to rally round the Papacy in the Conciliar Movement that the parochial princes could venture with impunity, a century later, to rise up against the Papacy and despoil it.[2]

The losses of power that were inflicted on the Papacy in the sixteenth century were staggering.

As an Italian territorial sovereign the Pope now saw himself dwarfed, as hopelessly as his peers the Grand Duke of Tuscany and the Signoria of Venice, by the rising Transalpine and Transmarine Powers.[3] It was in vain that he had welded Tivoli and Viterbo onto Rome, and Umbria and the Marches onto the Agro Romano, and the Legations onto the Marches. A Papal principality which had extended itself from the Tyrrhene Sea to the Adriatic and from the Garigliano to the Po might be a Great Power in Italy, but it was a pygmy in a new world which contained the France of Louis XI and the England of Henry VII and the Spain of Ferdinand and Isabella.[4] After attempting to strut in arms on this giant's stage, and exposing itself to such humiliating experiences as its war of A.D. 1556–7 with King Philip II of Spain, the Papacy learned the lesson which Athens learned in the Chremonidean War,[5] and withdrew as far as possible from active participation in an international war-game which it had found too boisterous.[6] But this tardy Papal recognition of the drawbacks of territorial sovereignty did not save Pope Innocent XI from being bullied by Louis XIV or Pope Pius VII from being dragged at the chariot-wheels of Napoleon.

While the Pope suffered this fate as an Italian secular prince, he suffered still more grievous misfortunes as the oecumenical sovereign of the Western Church. In this latter capacity he saw the

[1] 1 Kings xii. 13–16.

[2] 'It is the lack of feeling on *either* side—and notably on the royal side—which is the startling thing about Henry Tudor's "reformation". Indifference not only where indifference was to be expected, but where indifference should not have been—that is the key-note, and that is the failure of the Papacy (before Trent): that it produced, not feeling—even hostile feeling—but indifference'.—Mr. G. Barraclough in a letter to the writer.

[3] For this dwarfing of the Italian states by the Italianized Powers of an outer circle see III. C (ii) (*b*), vol. iii, pp. 299–305, above.

[4] On this point see III. C (ii) (*b*), vol. iii, pp. 356–7, above.

[5] See III. C (ii) (*b*), vol. iii, pp. 338 and 340, above.

[6] The withdrawal of the Papal principality into a position of persistent neutrality in the seventeenth century was an anticipation of the policy which was adopted in the nineteenth century by the surviving small states of Western Europe: Switzerland, Belgium, Holland, and the Scandinavian Kingdoms.

whole of his power reft away from him in the states that turned Protestant, and four-fifths of it in those that professedly remained Catholic—for their Catholic Majesties were not less rapacious than their Protestant Majesties in robbing the Papacy of its powers for their own benefit; the only difference in their policy was that they left the Papacy in possession of that fraction of its powers which, in the countries that turned Protestant, was abandoned by the prince to his subjects as a prison-yard exercise-ground for the individual conscience.

These sixteenth-century blows were the nemesis of the Papacy's fifteenth-century relapse into ὕβρις; but they were also the stimulus of a sixteenth-century revival.[1] In this extremity the Catholic Church was snatched from the jaws of destruction by the very present help[2] of a band of saints who utterly eclipsed the respectable but prosaic fathers of Constance and Basel, and whose like had not been seen in Western Christendom since Saint Louis had died in 1270 on the last crusade and Saint Thomas in 1274 on his way to the Council of Lyon. Saint Ignatius Loyola (*vivebat* A.D. 1495–1556)[3] captured the intellectual prowess of Italy, which had ministered to a Papal pride of life when a Giovanni de' Medici was reigning as Pope Leo X,[4] and bent it to the service of reform by yoking it with a Janissarian discipline.[5] Saint Teresa (*vivebat* A.D. 1515–82) and Saint John of the Cross (*vivebat* A.D. 1542–91) restored the lapsed austerities of the Carmelite Order and found their way through this door into a new world of mystical illumination. Saint Philip Neri (*vivebat* A.D. 1515–95) set a new standard of loving-kindness towards the poor and the sick, and a new standard of devotion for the ministry of secular priests. Saint Charles Borromeo (*vivebat* A.D. 1538–84) wholly succeeded, where Pope Innocent III had half failed,[6] in performing the exacting task of an ecclesiastical administrator. Saint Francis de Sales (*vivebat* A.D. 1567–1622) was as intrepid a missionary of the Catholic Faith in the Protestant lion's den at Geneva as Saint Francis Xavier (*vivebat* 1506–52) was among the heathen in the Indies. These super-human men and women worked a work in our Western World which is still operative to-day and which has perhaps not

[1] For the stimulus of blows see II. D (iv), vol. ii, above.
[2] Psalm xlvi. 2.
[3] For Saint Ignatius Loyola's life as an illustration of the movement of Withdrawal-and-Return see III. C (ii) (*b*), vol. iii, p. 270, above.
[4] *Papa Leo X munere fungebatur* A.D. 1513–21.
[5] The first General of the Society of Jesus, when he organized his spiritual army, anticipated the secular princes of the West by more than a century in rivalling the discipline of the Ottoman Pādishāh's Slave-Household. A contemporary 'Osmanlī might have described the Jesuits as the *qullar* of the Patriarch of Rome.
[6] See the present chapter, pp. 557–63, above, and IV. C (iii) (*c*) 3 (β), Annex, pp. 652–6, below.

yet begun to bear its richest fruits. In their own age, however, (if it is not sheer nonsense for historians to pin down saints within temporal bounds), the dead weight of the Papal tradition brought the sixteenth-century saints' impetuous advance to a premature halt. They liberated the Papacy from the pride of life, but its lust for power proved too strong for them; and so the sixteenth-century rally failed, after all, to save the day. In the seventeenth century the Roman Church relapsed into a spiritual torpor which awoke into a counter-revolutionary activity—both political and intellectual—when it was stirred by the impact of an eighteenth-century Philosophy and a nineteenth-century Physical Science; and by the three hundredth anniversary of Saint Ignatius's death a Papacy which had once been the heart of the Western body social seemed to have become an atrophied member, in which the blood no longer coursed and the life no longer throbbed. The pontificate of Pius IX (*fungebatur* A.D. 1846–78), who saw the territorial sovereignty of the Papacy extinguished when the armed forces of the Kingdom of Italy entered Rome in 1870, marked as abysmal a fall in the fortunes of the Holy See as the pontificate of Clement VII (*fungebatur* A.D. 1523–34), who saw Rome sacked in 1527 by the Protestant mercenaries of the Emperor Charles V, or the pontificate of John XXIII (*fungebatur* A.D. 1410–15), who was brought to book at Constance.

As we read this tale of rout and rally and relapse which brought so great an institution so low in the course of some six hundred years, we shall be struck by a series of signal failures to learn from experience. Hildebrand himself, who had obtained his opportunity because the Emperor Henry III had overplayed a strong hand in 1046, made precisely Henry III's mistake when, thirty years later, he overplayed his own strong hand in dealing with Henry IV. Innocent III, as we have seen, was not deterred by the deplorable outcome of the Fourth Crusade from launching his crusade against the Albigenses with equally deplorable consequences; and the exposure of his credulity towards Otto Welf did not put him on his guard against Frederick II. Innocent IV did not perceive that the Holy See would be as much at the mercy of a King of Sicily who was brother to the King of France as it had been at the mercy of a King of Sicily who was himself the King of Germany—though the essential danger lay in being taken between two fires, without its making any substantial difference whether the Transalpine fire was German or French. Boniface VIII did not apprehend that if an insistence upon legal pretensions insufficiently supported by material power had been fatal to the Emperor Frederick I in his dealings with the Lombard communes, it would be equally fatal to

Pope Boniface in dealing with the Kingdom of France. A Martin V and a Eugenius IV, when they set themselves to frustrate the Conciliar Movement, did not remind themselves that King Philip IV of France and King Edward III of England had deliberately fortified themselves with parliamentary support before their successful defiance of the Papacy in the fourteenth century, and therefore did not draw the statesman-like inference that an oecumenical parliament of the Western Ecclesiastical Commonwealth, so far from being a menace to the Pope's authority, was likely to be a tower of strength to him in a coming struggle with the parochial secular princes. A Julius II did not reflect that a pagan virtuosity in arts and arms, which had not saved from destruction the Papacy's arch-enemy Frederick II, was unlikely to bring salvation to the power by which Frederick had been conquered. And, in general, the experience of the Papacy in the fifteenth and sixteenth centuries in its encounters with the Renaissance and the Reformation did not make it any the more expert in dealing, in the eighteenth and nineteenth centuries, with the new forces of Democracy and Physical Science which had been generated by a fresh eruption of the Western social volcano.

As we contemplate this record of flood-lit truths unheeded and golden opportunities untaken, we cease to wonder at the unparalleled series of calamities by which the Hildebrandine Papacy has been afflicted in the long agony of its decline and fall: 'the Babylonish Captivity,' the Great Schism, the Protestant Reformation, the Italian *Risorgimento*. Are these the final fruits of the tree which Hildebrand planted? If so, the nemesis of creativity surpasses itself when it takes the form of the intoxication of victory.

The tragedy of the Hildebrandine Papacy is the tragedy of Periclean Athens. Athens became the oppressor of her sister city-states whom she had liberated from the oppression of the Achaemenidae; the Roman See became the oppressor of her sister churches whom she had liberated from the oppression of the Secular Power in Western Christendom. In both tragedies the protagonist inverts his role; in both, the change is the outward visible sign of an inward spiritual débâcle; and, in both, this mortal sin is visited with a condign punishment. In the Hellenic drama the devastation which the sin and the punishment deal does not stop short at the affliction of the victims and the abasement of the villain of the piece; it takes its course until it brings about the breakdown of the whole civilization in whose life the actors are playing their parts. In our Western drama, in which we ourselves are actors as well as spectators, are the sin and punishment of the Hildebrandine

Papacy destined to bring the history of Western Christendom to the same tragic ending?

As we gaze round our spiritually devastated world in our generation, we can take the measure of the evil which has been brought upon us by the Hildebrandine failure now that its consequences have had nearly seven centuries to work themselves out since Innocent IV fought his Hannibalic War. And in the light of this latter-day knowledge we can see that the Hildebrandine Papacy's greatest crime against our Western Society has been, not its extermination of the Hohenstaufen or its assassination of the Conciliar Movement, but its felony against itself. In committing those crimes the Papacy did its best to commit suicide; and in dealing itself this prostrating blow it has left the house vacant for the entry of seven—and seventy times seven—other spirits who are all more wicked than the supplanted householder.[1] In the four hundred years that have now been added to the tale of Western history since the outbreak of the Reformation the sins of Jeroboam have far surpassed the sins of the degenerate scion of David's house who gave the usurper his chance to seize nine-tenths of the Kingdom.

'And Jeroboam said in his heart: "Now shall the kingdom return to the house of David. If this people go up to do sacrifice in the house of the Lord at Jerusalem, then shall the heart of this people turn again unto their lord, even unto Rehoboam King of Judah; and they shall kill me and go again to Rehoboam king of Judah." Whereupon the king took counsel and made two calves of gold, and said unto them: "It is too much for you to go up to Jerusalem; behold thy gods, O Israel, which brought thee up out of the Land of Egypt." And he set the one in Bethel, and the other put he in Dan. And this thing became a sin. . . .'[2]

The golden calves which our latter-day Jeroboams have set up in our Western World are called 'totalitarian states'; and these are the gods which they invite—nay, command—us to worship in place of the God of Benedict and the God of Gregory and the God of Hildebrand and the God of Francis. To-day these false prophets of an odious idolatry[3] sit in Hildebrand's seat. But their

[1] Matt. xii. 45 = Luke xi. 26.

[2] 1 Kings xii. 26–30.

[3] The disastrousness of the sequel to the breakdown of our medieval Western Papal hierocracy is underlined by Auguste Comte in his *Considerations on the Spiritual Power* (reprinted from his *Système de Politique Positive*, vol. iv (1854), Appendix, in *Early Essays on Social Philosophy*, translated from the French of Auguste Comte by H. D. Hutton, second edition (London, no date, Routledge)):

'Of all the revolutionary prejudices which have sprung up during the last three centuries owing to the decline of the old social system, the most ancient, the most deeply rooted, the most generally accepted, the one that lies at the root of all the rest, is the principle which proclaims that no spiritual power should exist in Society, or, what comes to the same thing, that this power should be entirely subordinated to the Temporal Power' (op. cit., p. 283).

Comte goes on to point out (op. cit., pp. 285–7) that in international relations the

mandate is not inexhaustible, and, by the same token, our own doom is not sealed.

The cup of these usurpers' iniquities has run over in a generation which has seen the Papacy drink its own cup of humiliation to the dregs. On the 20th September, 1870, the wheel of Destiny completed its Great Year by coming round, full circle, to the pre-Hildebrandine situation of the 20th December, 1046. In the long flood of adversity the ὕβρις that was the Holy See's undoing has perhaps at last been washed away, and already history has begun to repeat itself. When the blow which was dealt to the Roman Church by a militant Italian nationalism in 1870 was immediately followed in a militantly nationalist Germany by the launching of the *Kulturkampf*, it almost seemed as though the last hour had struck for the Catholic Faith; yet that bloodless war of attrition on German soil ended in the first victory which the Church had gained for three hundred years—and this in a conflict with Bismarck, the most redoubtable Jeroboam of the age. Nor was the Catholic Church defeated in the struggle with state-worship in France which broke out in 1904. So far from that, it was becoming apparent in the fourth decade of the twentieth century that in France the future lay, not with the anti-religious ideas in the Ideology of 1789, but with the spiritual influence of the lives of a nineteenth-century band of saints whom the challenge of the French Revolution had called into action in France and Piedmont, as the sixteenth-century saints had been called into action in Spain and Italy and Savoy by the challenge of the Reformation.[1] In Saint Jean-Baptiste Vianney, the curé d'Ars (*vivebat* A.D. 1786–1857), there was an epiphany of sainthood in the life of a parish priest; in Don Giovanni Bosco (*vivebat* A.D. 1815–88) there was an epiphany in the life of a 'social worker'; in Saint Bernadette Soubirous of Lourdes (*vivebat* A.D. 1844–79) there was an epiphany in the life of a child of the Proletariat; in Saint Thérèse Martin, 'the Little Flower' (*vivebat* A.D. 1873–97), there was an epiphany in the life of a child of the Bourgeoisie. This outburst of sainthood in the continental strongholds of a nineteenth-century secularism was the movement

Papal authority has been replaced by nothing but a Balance of Power between parochial secular governments, and (op. cit., pp. 288–95) that, within the bosom of each parochial community, the fruits have been a mental anarchy, a lack of public morality, a social materialism, and a corrupt bureaucracy. He damns the Holy Alliance with faint praise (op. cit., p. 328, footnote 1) as a *pis aller*, which is not quite so bad as the Balance of Power, in a society that has not succeeded either in preserving the Spiritual Power or in restoring it.

For Comte's advocacy of the separation of the two powers see further Caird, E.: *The Social Philosophy and Religion of Comte* (Glasgow 1885, MacLehose), pp. 47–8 and 210–11. Comte saw clearly (Caird, op. cit., pp. 44 and 51) that the Spiritual Power could only exercise its own proper function on condition of resisting all temptations to resort to direct action in the temporal sphere.

1 See p. 578, above.

from the depths which was reflected on the surface of life in the successful resistance of the Church, as an institution, to the assaults of the German state *post* 1871 and of the French state *post* 1904. In the year 1938 it looked as though the victor in those preliminary skirmishes were now going into action in a pitched battle in which the whole strength of either side might be engaged; and in this conflict, if it was indeed at hand, the fate of Western Christendom would once more be in the balance.

At this hour of decision it is meet and right that all men and women in the Western World who 'have been baptized into Christ' as 'heirs according to the promise'[1]—and, with us, all the Gentiles who have become 'partakers of' the 'promise' and 'fellow heirs of the same body'[2] through the adoption of our Western way of life —should call upon the Vicar of Christ to vindicate the tremendous title which Pope Innocent III has bequeathed to subsequent successors of Saint Peter. Did not Peter's Master say to Peter himself that 'unto whomsoever much is given, of him shall be much required, and to whom men have committed much, of him they will ask the more'?[3] To the Apostle at Rome our forefathers committed the destiny of Western Christendom, which was the whole of their treasure; and when 'that servant, which knew his Lord's will', 'prepared not himself, neither did according to his will,' and was beaten, in just retribution, 'with many stripes',[4] those blows fell with equal weight upon the bodies of 'the menservants and maidens'[5] whose souls had been entrusted to the keeping of the *Servus Servorum Dei.*

> Quidquid delirant reges plectuntur Achivi.
> Seditione, dolis, scelere atque libidine et ira
> Iliacos intra muros peccatur et extra.[6]

The punishment for the ὕβρις of the servant who has said in his heart 'My lord delayeth his coming'[7] has been visited upon us; and it is for him who has brought us to this pass to deliver us from it, whosoever we may be: Catholics or Protestants; Christians or men of other faiths; believers or unbelievers; bond or free.

> 'They were scattered because there is no shepherd, and they became meat to all the beasts of the field when they were scattered.'[8]

David has no defence against Eliab's taunt.[9] Yet who but this very David, who has once deserted his flock, has the strength and hardihood to beard and smite and slay the lion and the bear and to deliver the lamb out of his mouth?[10] Will our truant David once

[1] Gal. iii. 27 and 29. [2] Eph. iii. 6. [3] Luke xii. 48.
[4] Luke xii. 47. [5] Luke xii. 45.
[6] Horace: *Epistulae,* Book I, Ep. ii, ll. 14–16. [7] Luke xii. 45.
[8] Ezekiel xxxiv. 5. [9] 1 Samuel xvii. 28. [10] 1 Samuel xvii. 35.

more take the field, to gather what Rehoboam has scattered and unite what Jeroboam has divided? And if, at a zero hour when all is sin and shame, a second Hildebrand does come to the fight and the rescue, will our deliverer this time be fore-armed, by the wisdom that is born of suffering,[1] against that fatal intoxication of victory which has ruined the great work of Pope Gregory VII?

[1] πάθει μάθος—Aeschylus: *Agamemnon*, ll. 177–8, quoted in this Study in I. C (iii) (*b*), vol. i, p. 169, footnote 1; II. C (ii) (*b*) 1, vol. i, p. 298; and IV. C (iii) (*b*) 11, in the present volume, p. 218, above; and in V. C (i) (*c*) 2, vol. v, p. 78; V. C (i) (*d*) 4, vol. v, p. 416, footnote 3; and V. C (ii) (*a*), vol. vi, p. 275, below.

ANNEX TO IV. C (i)

WHICH ARE THE TRUE CATASTROPHES: THE BREAKDOWNS OF CIVILIZATIONS OR THEIR BIRTHS?

IN the passages of Plato that we have quoted in the chapter to which this Annex attaches, there is a noteworthy discrepancy between the *Laws* and the *Timaeus* on the one hand and the *Politicus* on the other.

The passage from the *Politicus* agrees with the passages from the *Laws* and the *Timaeus* in the assumption that the fortunes of Mankind are bound up with the vicissitudes of Physical Nature and that these two co-ordinated series of physical and human events move in a cyclic alternation of prosperity and adversity. It differs from them, however, in its philosophy of human history. According to the *Laws* and the *Timaeus*, the prosperous phases of human history are those which, in this Study, we have called the growth-phases of civilizations, and it is these growths of civilizations (which are conceived as desirable) that are disastrously cut short by the periodic cataclysms. According to the *Politicus*, on the other hand, the prosperous phases of human history correspond to what, in this Study, we have called the static Yin-state of primitive societies[1]—idealized into an ἐπὶ Κρόνου βίος.

'When God was shepherd, there was no state and no ownership of women and children.... All the historical conditions of life were absent, while on the other hand they enjoyed fruits in abundance from trees and other plants, which were not the product of cultivation but were raised spontaneously by the Earth herself. For the most part they camped in the open without clothes or bedding, the climate having been tempered so as to do them no injury, and they found soft couches in the grass which was produced by the Earth in abundance.'[2]

According to the *Politicus*, moreover, it was this state of Nature—which was likewise a state of Grace—that was brought to an end by the abrupt reversal of direction in the rotatory motion of the Cosmos at the moment when the divine helmsman let go his rudder;[3] and the sinister change in human fortunes which was involved in this cosmic catastrophe was not the change from the growth of a civilization to its breakdown but was the antecedent transition to the genesis of a civilization from the static condition of a primitive society in its Yin-state. In other words, the recurrent

[1] See Part II. B, vol. i, pp. 192–5, above.
[2] Plato: *Politicus*, 271B 5–272A. Compare the *Tao Te King*, chap. 80.
[3] See IV. C (i), pp. 26–7, above.

calamity that overtakes Mankind is not the breakdown of civilizations but their outbreak.

Consistently with this philosophy of history the births and growths of civilizations are explained in the *Politicus* as the response of Mankind to the challenge of the abandonment of the Cosmos by God.

'When Mankind had been deprived of the care of the Spirit who had been our shepherd, the majority of wild beasts that were fierce by nature turned savage, while Man himself became weak and defenceless. In consequence he was harried by the wild beasts, and in this first phase he was destitute of all equipment and resources, since his spontaneous food-supply had failed before he had been taught, by the stress of necessity, to provide for himself. For all these reasons Man found himself in the direst straits, and this is the origin of those legendary Gifts of the Gods with which we have been presented, together with the instruction and training necessary for the use of them—fire from Prometheus, the arts and crafts from Hephaestus and his consort, and seeds and plants from other benefactors. Every stone in the foundations of human life has been hewn from this quarry. The watch (aforementioned) which had been kept over Man by the Gods had now suddenly failed, and Man was forced to live by his own efforts and to keep watch over himself, exactly like the Cosmos as a whole, with which we are ever partakers in its imitation and following of God through all the alternating phases of our own life and growth.'[1]

According to the philosophy of the *Politicus* this heroic achievement of Human Civilization, in response to the challenge of Man's desertion by God, is—and can be—nothing but a forlorn hope. 'What God abandoned, these defended'; but the human defences are doomed to fall, because the Cosmos 'always performs its functions best during the phase least far removed from its release', while, 'as time goes on, the . . . original disharmony begins to gain the upper hand, until in the final phase it breaks out openly'.[2] Ultimately Mankind is saved, not by Man's own efforts, but by a fresh intervention of God—an intervention which is as abrupt and as arbitrary as His original withdrawal. And God saves Man by winding the painful attempt at Civilization up and bringing Human Society back to the blissful primitive level.

On this showing, the attempt at Civilization is not the quest of an attainable and desirable goal, but is at best a creditable *pis aller*. On the other hand in the *Laws* (in the immediate sequel to the passage quoted on p. 24, above) and in the *Timaeus* (in the passage above-quoted on pp. 24–5) the births and growths of

1 Plato: *Politicus*, 274 B–D.

2 The passage of the *Politicus* in which these sentences occur has been quoted in the present volume, on p. 27, above, in the chapter to which this Annex attaches.

civilizations, though they are described in much the same terms, are placed in a radically different setting. Instead of being represented as responses to the challenges of cosmic catastrophes, they are represented as following these catastrophes only after vast intervals of time, when the survivors of the catastrophes begin at last to recover from their prostration and stupefaction. Instead of being represented as a *pis aller* and a forlorn hope, these eventual new stirrings of life are assumed to be both admirable and promising endeavours. And instead of being cut short, when they have reached the brink of a disaster, by a beneficent intervention of God which makes all things new by making all things primitive again, these promising endeavours are cut short, when they are on the verge of achievement, by a cruel cataclysm which sweeps away the cumulative results of social progress and brings Man down again to a primitive level which is regarded, in these dialogues, as a state of Nature which is not a state of Grace but a state of Savagery. The difference between the two philosophies may be summed up by saying that the human disaster which the cosmic catastrophe entails is the destruction of civilizations according to the *Laws* and the *Timaeus*, and the perpetration of civilizations according to the *Politicus*. The attempt at Civilization, which is the one philosophy's good, is the other philosophy's evil.

It will be seen that the philosophy of the *Politicus* is identical (apart from the cyclic element) with that of the Syriac myth of the Fall of Man as this is presented in the Book of Genesis, where the state of Nature in the Garden of Eden is regarded as a state of Grace, while Man's response to the challenge of expulsion from the Garden—the response in which he builds up a civilization in the sweat of his brow—is regarded as the working out of a perpetual sentence of penal servitude: a sentence imposed upon Man as the penalty for the sin of disobedience on account of which he has been expelled from the Earthly Paradise.

It will also be seen that it is the Plato of the *Politicus* rather than the Plato of the *Laws* and the *Timaeus* whom Virgil follows in the Fourth Eclogue, when he represents the whole history of the Hellenic Civilization as a criminal aberration from which a long-tormented Humanity is now to be released at last through a return to an idealized state of Primitive Nature:

> Te duce, si qua manent sceleris vestigia nostri,
> irrita perpetua solvent formidine terras . . .
> ipsae lacte domum referent distenta capellae
> ubera, nec magnos metuent armenta leones . . .
> molli paulatim flavescet campus arista,
> incultisque rubens pendebit sentibus uva,

et durae quercus sudabunt roscida mella . . .
cedet et ipse marì vector, nec nautica pinus
mutabit merces: omnis feret omnia tellus.
non rastros patietur humus, non vinea falcem;
robustus quoque iam tauris iuga solvet arator.[1]

So much for the contradiction in the minds of the philosophers and poets of the Hellenic breakdown and disintegration. But we, in our world and our generation, assuredly cannot be content simply to take note of this contradiction and to leave it unresolved; for it raises a problem which concerns us to-day as deeply as it once concerned a Plato and a Virgil. We shall return to this problem at a later point.[2]

[1] Virgil: *Eclogue* IV, ll. 13–14, 21–2, 28–30, 38–41.

[2] In Part VII, below.

ANNEX I TO IV. C (iii) (*c*) 2 (β)

THE TRANSADRIATIC EXPEDITION OF THE EMPEROR CONSTANS II AND ITS ANTECEDENTS IN HELLENIC HISTORY

As the memories of childhood reawaken in old age in the consciousness of a human being, so, in the life of a human society, there is sometimes a repetition, in the last chapter of its decline and fall, of some situation which has occurred in its history once already in an earlier chapter. With this clue to guide us we may detect a parallelism between the Emperor Constans II's expedition in the seventh decade of the seventh century of the Christian Era from the latter-day capital of a moribund Hellenic universal state[1] to the remnant of its Transadriatic dominions and a previous series of expeditions from the homelands of the Hellenic Society to its Transadriatic colonial annexes which were undertaken successively by Timoleon of Corinth in 344 B.C.[2] and King Archidâmus of Sparta in 342 and King Alexander of Epirus in 333 and Prince Cleonymus of Sparta in 303 and King Pyrrhus of Epirus in 280–274.[3]

This ancient series of Greek military expeditions from east to west of the Adriatic had an object which, *mutatis mutandis*, was identical with Constans' object a thousand years later. Constans set out to rescue the Province of Sicily, and the other relics of the Exarchates of Italy and Africa, from the doom with which they were threatened by the simultaneous aggression of the Arabs in Africa and the Lombards in Italy; the Corinthian and Spartan and Epirot knight-errants who led the Hellenic 'crusaders' of the fourth and third centuries B.C. came to defend the colonial Greek communities in Sicily and Magna Graecia against a similar attack on two fronts: a Carthaginian attack in Sicily and an Oscan attack in Italy which was delivered in successive Bruttian and Lucanian and Samnite and Roman waves.[4] On the earlier occasion the enterprise failed irretrievably after five attempts; and we may suppose

[1] The transference of the centre of gravity of the Roman Empire from Rome to Constantinople in the course of the fourth and fifth centuries of the Christian Era is an instance of the general 'law' that the governing power in a universal state first arises on the periphery of the world which the universal state embraces, and then gravitates towards the centre as time goes on. This 'law' is illustrated and discussed in Part VI, below.

[2] See V. C (ii) (*a*), vol. vi, pp. 248 and 251, below.

[3] All these earlier Hellenic knight-errants in the west except Timoleon made their first landing, like the Emperor Constans, at Tarentum.

[4] For this South Italian front of Hellenism and its elimination see further V. C (i) (*c*) 2, vol. v, pp. 213–4, below. The analogy between the Beneventan Lombards and the Samnites is drawn in Gay, J.: *L'Italie Méridionale et l'Empire Byzantin, 867–1071* (Paris 1904, Fontemoing), p. x.

that it would have failed ultimately likewise upon its repetition a thousand years later—even if Constans had lived out his life to its natural term and found successors to carry on his policy—since the factors which were the manifest causes of the failure in the fourth and third centuries B.C., when the experiment was tried out to the bitter end, were also in operation in the seventh century of the Christian Era, when the repetition of the experiment was cut short after a trial of no longer than six years' duration.

On the earlier occasion the enterprise failed for four distinct reasons. In the first place the Western Greeks were heavily outmatched by their assailants; in the second place their champions from the Greek homelands were unable to bring over with them large enough forces to redress the balance; in the third place the effectiveness of the reinforcements, such as they were, was diminished by a lamentable lack of cordiality in the co-operation between the knight-errants and their protégés; in the fourth place the relieving forces were distracted and dissipated by being called upon to intervene on two different fronts simultaneously. All these adverse factors reappear in the local situation as it stood in the seventh century of the Christian Era. For example, Constans found himself just not strong enough to subjugate the Lombard principality of Benevento, as Alexander of Epirus had once failed, by a comparably narrow margin, to subjugate the Samnite Confederacy; and Constans, had he lived, would assuredly have quarrelled with his principal Italian protégée the Papacy,[1] as Alexander of Epirus did live to quarrel with his principal Italian protégée the city-state of Tarentum.

On the earlier occasion perhaps the most potent of all the factors that militated against success was the sheer inferiority of the Western Greeks to their ring of assailants in weight of numbers and extent of territory. The Greek communities in Sicily were so far alive to the danger to which they were exposed by this numerical weakness that, time and again, they submitted to the surrender of their parochial autonomy and their civic liberty for the sake of pooling their resources.[2] Yet, although they distinguished themselves by this readiness—which was a rare virtue in the Hellenic World—to pay the necessary price for the benefits of solidarity, the strength which the Sicilian Greeks found in their unity under the successive despotisms of the Deinomenidae and the Dionysii and Agathocles and Hiero was still not enough to save them in the end

[1] The protracted martyrdom which had been inflicted by Constans upon Pope Martin from A.D. 653 to A.D. 655 must have been perpetually in the mind of Martin's successor, Pope Vitalian, during the Emperor's twelve days' visit to Rome in A.D. 663.

[2] For this recurrent and characteristic feature of Sicilian Greek history see III. C (ii) (b), vol. iii, p. 357, footnote 1, above, and V. C (ii) (a), vol. vi, p. 183, below.

from being trampled under foot when their island became the battleground of the Carthaginians and the Romans. In this final struggle for supremacy in the Western Mediterranean, in which the victor's prize was the privilege—and burden—of becoming the founder of a Hellenic universal state,[1] the Sicilian Greeks were not in the running.[2] On this showing we may conjecture that, even if Constans had lived on long enough in Sicily to repeat the performance of those ancient Sicilian Greek empire-builders, his building could not have withstood for long the shock of successive Arab and Berber and Lombard and Frankish assaults. In the seventh century of the Christian Era Syracuse had really no more chance of supplanting Constantinople as the last capital of the Hellenic universal state than she had had of becoming its first capital, instead of Rome, in the third century B.C. From the beginning to the end of Hellenic history Sicily was never at any time capable of providing the basis for a Hellenic world power.

In fine, we may conclude that if either Constans or his grandfather Heraclius had succeeded in carrying out their plan they would have erased, once for all, the last faint shadow of an Imperial Government at Constantinople, but this without succeeding in replacing it by any substantial or enduring Imperial Government at Carthage or Syracuse or Ravenna.

[1] Omnia cum belli trepido concussa tumultu
horrida contremuere sub altis aetheris oris,
in dubioque fuere utrorum ad regna cadendum
omnibus humanis esset terraque marique . . .

Lucretius: *De Rerum Natura*, Book III, ll. 834–7.

[2] In the third century B.C. the Sicilian Greek Power of Hiero and Hieronymus was as utterly outclassed by Carthage and Rome as in the sixteenth century of the Christian Era Venice and Milan were outclassed by France and Spain and the Danubian Hapsburg Monarchy (see III. C (ii) (*b*), vol. iii, p. 357, above).

ANNEX II TO IV. C (iii) (*c*) 2 (β)

THE ABORTIVE RESISTANCE OF THE CHURCH TO THE REVIVAL OF 'CAESARO-PAPISM' IN ORTHODOX CHRISTENDOM

In the chapter to which this Annex attaches, we have noted that in Western Christendom the Church eventually asserted its supremacy over the Temporal Power, and that, in successfully enforcing this pretension in the second chapter of our Western history, the Papacy performed a creative act which enabled our Western Civilization to proceed a stage farther in its growth.[1] In the same connexion we have seen that in Orthodox Christendom the Church succumbed to a pretension on the part of the Temporal Power to possess and exercise the 'Caesaro-papal' authority which had once been wielded in a Christian Roman Empire by a Constantine the Great and a Justinian,[2] and that this defeat of the Orthodox Church by the East Roman Government is to be regarded, in the history of the society in which both these institutions lived and moved and had their being, as a social aberration which was demonstrably responsible for this Orthodox Christian Society's premature breakdown. For an observer, in retrospect, of these accomplished facts it is a tempting exercise of his historical judgement to summon the Orthodox and the Western Church before his mental judgement-seat, hold a summary inquiry into their respective records in these two historic transactions, and render a comparative verdict eulogizing the Western Church in the measure of its *de facto* success and conversely censuring the Orthodox Church in the measure of its *de facto* failure. Such a verdict would be as injudicious as it is facile, and we must be vigilantly on our guard against being seduced into accepting it.

To put ourselves on our guard we may remind ourselves of the simple fact that the generation of Hildebrand is separated by a Time-span of not much less than six hundred years from the generation of Odovacer, and that, throughout this long period which intervened between the *de facto* break-up of the Roman Empire in the West and the initiation of a deliberate endeavour to establish a Papal *Respublica Christiana*, the persistent policy of the Papacy was to replace itself under an Imperial tutelage from which it had been liberated against its will by *force majeure*.[3] At first the Papacy had clung forlornly to the skirts of a still surviving Imperial Government at Constantinople, and then—when the rotten fringe

[1] See IV. C (iii) (*c*) 2 (β), pp. 339 and 405, above.
[2] See *cap. cit.*, pp. 346–53, above.
[3] See *cap. cit.*, pp. 335–9, above.

of the worn-out Byzantine *scaramangium* tore away in the Papal suppliant's desperately clutching hands—a Pope Stephen II (III) had gone in search of a substitute-protector beyond the Alps, and a Pope Leo III had invested this barbarian *deus ex machina* with a robe of office which was fondly expected to wear better because it was a counterfeit, woven of coarser stuff than the genuine Imperial silk. This chapter in the history of the Papacy is neither inspiring in itself nor prophetic of the magnificently creative chapter which actually followed. And our observation of this vein of unexpectedness in the course of our Western ecclesiastical history should warn us, when we come to pass judgement on the Orthodox Church, against hastily jumping to the conclusion that, just because the Orthodox Church succumbed to the Temporal Power, it must have brought this fate upon itself by offering its neck poor-spiritedly to the yoke. As a matter of fact we shall find, upon examination, that the Church which was defeated by a Leo Syrus and a Leo Sapiens fought as good a fight as the Church which was victorious over a Henry IV and a Frederick Barbarossa.

The Orthodox Church which was challenged to prove its mettle by a revival of 'Caesaro-papism' in the eighth century had inherited from the Primitive Christian past as fine a tradition of resistance to the Imperial Power as any of which the West could boast. During the struggle of the Primitive Church with the Pagan Empire the Christian martyrs in the Greek and Oriental provinces had been as numerous and as valiant as in the Latin;[1] and in the ensuing Post-Constantinian Age, when the Church had been almost lulled to sleep on the Empire's bosom[2] and had not yet experienced the rude awakening which was destined to overtake her upon the Empire's imminent death and dissolution, the rather rare examples of clerics who went into opposition against the Christian Imperial Power include Greeks and Orientals[3] as well as 'Hesperians'. The

[1] In absolute numbers the Greek and Oriental martyrs were far more numerous, no doubt; but these absolute numbers, if we knew them, would have to be reduced to the percentage which they represented of the total Christian community in the different regions, and down to the generation of Constantine, at any rate, the Christian community in the Latin provinces was in itself a smaller portion of a smaller total population than the Christian community was in the other two-thirds of the Empire. Even on this proportional basis, however, there is reason to believe that the toll of martyrdoms in the Greek and Oriental provinces was at least as heavy as in the Latin provinces, relatively to the difference in the respective absolute numbers of possible candidates for martyrdom in the different regions.

[2] See IV. C (iii) (c) 2 (β), pp. 349–50, above.

[3] In the Oriental provinces of the Roman Empire the fifth century saw the Nestorian and Monophysite mass-movements against the 'Melchite' adherents of the Imperial Catholic Church. These movements, however, were endeavours, not so much to free the Church from the domination of the Temporal Power, as to free the still submerged portion of the Syriac World from the Hellenic ascendancy to which it had been subject since the days of Alexander the Great. (For this aspect of Nestorianism and Monophysitism see I. C (i) (b), vol. i, p. 91; II. D (vi), vol. ii, p. 236; and II. D (vii), vol. ii, pp. 286–7, above, and V. C (i) (c) 2, vol. v, p. 127, below.)

insistence of Ambrose that Theodosius the Great should do public penance for the sin of the Salonica Massacre was certainly a magnificent display of clerical courage which happened to be crowned with success. Yet the Bishop of Milan's successfully courageous act in calling Theodosius to account is not more worthy of admiration than the unsuccessful bravery of a justly famous Patriarch of Constantinople in publicly protesting against the misdemeanours of Theodosius's son and successor Arcadius. Indeed, we may be inclined to appraise John Chrysostom's defeat at a higher moral value than Ambrose's victory when we bear in mind the difference in the temperaments, endowments, and antecedents of the two saints. Ambrose—the son of a Praetorian Prefect, and himself already launched upon a promising career in the Imperial service before the people of Milan commandeered him for their bishop by main force—was a man of action of the same mettle as Theodosius himself; John Chrysostom was a scholar who would have led the sheltered life of a professor of literature if the dedication of his eloquence to the cause of Religion had not moved his conscience to go into action in the field of public life and inspired him with the faith to endure the pains of defeat in what was for him a strange and formidable arena. We may also remind ourselves that Saint John's see of Constantinople was not merely an Imperial capital but was essentially that and nothing else; for an interregnum of more than a hundred years' length effectively insulated the traditions of the New Rome founded by Constantine the Great in A.D. 330 from those of the ancient Greek city-state of Byzantium which had been devastated, and deprived of its statehood, by Septimius Severus in A.D. 196. On the other hand Saint Ambrose's see of Milan was a *ci-devant* city-state which had preserved its sense of continuity with its own past in spite of being used as an Imperial capital temporarily and provisionally. It is clear that Saint Ambrose would be fortified by his social environment in his resistance to the Imperial Power, while Saint John, on the contrary, would be weakened by his.

If we leap the interregnum which follows the break-up of the Roman Empire, and proceed to examine the respective records of the Orthodox and the Western Church in the critical period that begins with the launching of the Iconoclastic policy of the East Roman Emperor Leo Syrus, we shall find that every famous Western champion of the rights of the Church has his counterpart and peer in Orthodox Christendom.

Pope Gregory II and his successors in St. Peter's Chair were not more stalwart in their opposition to Leo's Iconoclastic decree of A.D. 726 than the Oecumenical Patriarch Germanus, who held out under the Emperor's nose until at the end of four years the Emperor could find no better means of countering this formidable intransigence than the *ultima ratio* of throwing the Patriarch out of office. If the Papal opponents of Iconoclasm were able to indulge in the same intransigence without incurring the same fate, this was simply because the rehabilitated Government at Constantinople had made up its mind that it could not afford to take energetic action so far afield as Italy beyond the bounds of Calabria.[1] In retaliating against the Papacy Leo therefore contented himself with the forcible withdrawal, from the Pope's ecclesiastical jurisdiction, of all the eastern part of his former ecclesiastical domain from Calabria and Sicily to Crete and Salonica inclusive;[2] and these territories were transferred to the jurisdiction of the successors of Germanus at Constantinople, whom the Emperor expected to find more amenable to his will now that they had Germanus's fate before their eyes as a warning example of the penalty of clerical opposition to the 'Caesar-Pope' in the Imperial capital. Nevertheless, when Iconoclasm—repealed for a season by the Empress Irene (*imperabat* A.D. 780–90 and 797–802)[3]—was reinstituted by the Syrian Leo's Armenian namesake Leo V (*imperabat* A.D. 813–20), the indomitable Iconodule Patriarch Germanus found a worthy successor in the reigning Patriarch Nicephorus, who opposed Iconoclasm no less stalwartly, held out no less intransigently, and had likewise to be put out of the way by an eventual recourse to the *ultima ratio* of deposition. Nor was Nicephorus the only famous cleric of his generation in Orthodox Christendom who had the courage to suffer for opposing the Emperor Leo V's religious policy. He had good companions in Theodore of Studium (*vivebat* A.D. 759–826)[4] and in Theodore's uncle Abbot Plato.

Thus the Oecumenical Patriarchate was at least as fearless as the Papacy in opposing an Iconoclast Imperial Government in act and deed, and this at a much greater material risk; and *a fortiori* the Orthodox Church outstripped the Western Church in fighting the same battle in the field of theological controversy, in which the

1 For this East Roman policy of conserving energy and avoiding a dispersal of force see IV. C (iii) (*c*) 2 (β), pp. 342–4, above.

2 See IV. C (iii) (*c*) 2 (β), pp. 337 and 346, footnote 2, above.

3 During her first term Irene was acting as regent for her son the Emperor Constantine VI; during her second term she was reigning as his supplanter. The date of the first repeal of Iconoclasm was 787.

4 Theodore of Studium appealed from the successor of Constantine to the successor of Peter. His policy was to find in the Papacy a rallying-point and a leadership for all the Iconodule forces in the East Roman dominions; and this policy was reasonable, since the Pope was the most powerful of the Iconodule Catholic Patriarchs who were not at the East Roman Government's mercy. Unhappily Theodore found the Papacy a broken reed; and this was perhaps inevitable, since the Papacy in Theodore's day was anxious, not to assert itself against the Temporal Power, but to take shelter under its wing (see IV. (iii) (*c*) 2 (β), pp. 335–9, above).

Latins were notoriously tiros and the Greeks past-masters. This war of ink and paper against Imperial Iconoclasm had, of course, to be conducted by a scholar in some tranquil retreat where he was beyond the reach of the East Roman Emperor's arm; but the historic *malleus iconoclastarum* was not a Latin doctor wielding his pen under the aegis of an Iconodule King of the Franks, but a Greek controversialist, John Damascene, whose patron and protector was a Muslim Umayyad Caliph.[1]

After the resistance of Popes Gregory II (*fungebatur* A.D. 715–31) and Gregory III (*fungebatur* A.D. 731–41) to the Iconoclastic policy of the Emperor Leo Syrus the next signal occasion on which a Pope set himself in opposition to an Emperor was when Pope Nicholas I (*fungebatur* A.D. 858–67) refused to countenance the offence of King Lothaire II of Lorraine in repudiating his lawful wife in favour of another woman, and persisted in this refusal even when the Emperor Lewis II took up his kinsman's cause and sought to coerce the Pope by making a military demonstration against Rome. This is the earliest prominent example of one of the most honourable, as well as courageous, ways in which the Papacy, in its prime, was to assert its authority against temporal princes. Pope Nicholas I's bold motion to curb and castigate the licentiousness of Lothaire of Lorraine was rewarded, after a long struggle, by the capitulation of the royal culprit; and this passage of arms inaugurated a long series of victorious Papal assaults upon the matrimonial misdemeanours of princes—a series which was only brought to an end by Pope Clement VII's unlucky experience with King Henry VIII of England some seven centuries later. This long-sustained Papal *tour de force* of 'lion-taming' was, of course, a magnificent performance; for the Pope was utterly outmatched in physical force by the temporal rulers whom he so resolutely called to order; and yet, time and again, these wild beasts quailed under the spiritual coercion of an unarmed priest—snarling and lashing their tails at the first crack of the Papal whip, yet creeping up for pardon in the end with ears laid back and tails between their legs.[2] The forcefulness—and artfulness—of these Papal tamers of princes is admirable; and the performance is perhaps the

[1] It is perhaps worth noting that the three men—the Emperor Leo Syrus (*imperabat* A.D. 717–40), the Pope Gregory III (*fungebatur* A.D. 731–41), and the theologian John Damascene, *alias* Mansūr ash-Shāmī (*vivebat prae* A.D. 700 – *prae* 754)—who between them did so much to produce the schism between Orthodox Christendom and Western Christendom, were, all three of them, either Syrians or of Syrian origin, though Syria lay outside the domains of both the nascent civilizations whose destinies these three men were deciding. This trivial fact is a small but pointed nail in the coffin of the racial explanation of the histories of civilizations.

[2] The secret of the Papacy's apparently miraculous power of bringing temporal rulers to heel was, no doubt, the sensitiveness of public feeling and public opinion throughout the Western *Respublica Christiana* in responding to Papal pronouncements and Papal acts. The temporal subjects of a local prince were all of them at the same time the

supreme demonstration of the medieval Papacy's moral and intellectual power. Yet we may observe that in exercising this moral censorship over the princes of Western Christendom, as in opposing the ritual and doctrinal innovations of the Iconoclast Emperors of Constantinople, the Papacy, while risking much, was not staking its very existence. The limitations of the risk involved were brought out in the final encounter in which one royal lion at last broke this Papal spell, and broke it for ever, by truculently refusing to obey. The militant contumacy of King Henry VIII cost the Papacy the allegiance of England, and this was certainly a serious blow; yet the wound thereby inflicted on the Holy See was patently very far from being a mortal one, for it was manifest, from first to last, that the Patriarchate of Western Christendom was not in danger of bleeding to death in consequence of the amputation of a couple of outlying archbishoprics.

We may now observe that the censorship of princely morals, which was exercised by the Papacy from Pope Nicholas I's time onwards in the tradition of Saint Ambrose, was likewise exercised —with equal fearlessness but, again, at a far greater risk—by the Oecumenical Patriarchate in the same age.

For example, Pope Nicholas I himself was moved to support his contemporary the Patriarch Ignatius, who had been deposed in A.D. 858 for his public protests against the evil living of the Caesar Bardas—the virtual master of the East Roman Empire at the time. Ignatius's stand against Bardas cannot be accounted less courageous or less admirable than Nicholas' stand against Lothaire simply because the East Roman Emperor Basil I managed to use Ignatius (without Ignatius's intention or connivance) as a pawn in his political game, whereas Nicholas managed to get the better of the clumsy and impotent Western Emperor Lewis II. In view of the

spiritual subjects of the Pope; and if their temporal ruler was rash enough to risk a conflict of allegiances he was likely to find that his subjects' allegiance to the Pope had the stronger moral hold upon them, so that the contumacious prince was threatened with a loss of his own local authority, as well as with the moral disapproval of all the rest of Western Christendom. These were forces against which no medieval Western princeling could permanently contend. But the ability of the Papacy to mobilize these formidable moral forces in the Papal cause on any given occasion clearly depended upon the maintenance of a moral prestige which was overwhelmingly superior to that of any temporal ruler. This essential superiority of prestige was possessed in the ninth century by Pope Nicholas I as against Charlemagne's unimpressive diadochi and epigoni; and it was possessed again in still greater measure by a sufficient number of Popes in a series that opened with Hildebrand and closed with Innocent III. From the middle of the eleventh to the middle of the thirteenth century the Papacy could feel confident of emerging victorious in the long run from any conflict with any Western temporal ruler. Thereafter the moral prestige on which this Papal potency depended was ruined by the Papacy itself in its hybristic self-idolization. Yet the accumulated prestige of the master-institution of the medieval West was so immense that it took centuries of folly and misconduct to dissipate it. 'The Babylonish Captivity' had to be followed by the Great Schism, and the Great Schism by the Conciliar Movement, before a Henry VIII could defy the Papal censorship of royal morals with impunity (see IV. C (iii) (*c*) 3 (β), pp. 512–84, above).

political circumstances, Basil's restoration of Ignatius to his Patriarchal chair in A.D. 867 cannot, perhaps, be regarded as a moral victory for the Patriarch over the Imperial Power; indeed, the true situation was made cruelly apparent ten years later when, upon Ignatius's death in 877, Basil promptly appointed to succeed him his erstwhile supplanter, the pliant worldling Photius. Yet this rather ignominious sequel to Ignatius's bearding of Bardas did not deter a more famous and forceful Patriarch in the next generation from discharging in his turn this formidable Patriarchal duty of calling the ruling personality in the East Roman Empire to account.

When the Emperor Basil I's son and successor, the Emperor Leo the Wise, set his heart in A.D. 905 upon marrying for the fourth time, and requested the reigning Oecumenical Patriarch Nicolaus Mysticus[1] to give his blessing to this Imperial project, the Patriarch refused to countenance an act which would be a flagrant breach of canon law—without allowing himself to be influenced by the fact that the Emperor was his personal friend and that he held his office by the Emperor's appointment. The farthest that he would go was to baptize and recognize the son who had just been born to the Emperor, out of wedlock, by the lady with whom the Emperor now desired to regularize his relations; and the Patriarch went thus far only on the understanding that the lady herself should be dismissed from the Imperial Court. When Leo accepted these terms and then broke them—three days after the Patriarch had performed his stipulated part—by having the marriage ceremony celebrated for him by another hand and then crowning this fourth wife as his Augusta, Nicolaus became intransigent; and on Christmas Day 906, when nearly twelve months had passed, he gave publicity to his attitude by a gesture which was worthy of Saint Ambrose himself. On Christmas Day 906 the Patriarch closed the doors of Saint Sophia in the Emperor's face; and this time the contest was not ended by the Emperor's retort—which was, no doubt, a foregone conclusion—of arresting and deporting and deposing the intransigent holder of the Patriarchal office and appointing a more pliant personality to replace him. Nicolaus lived to be restored to the Patriarchate by Leo's brother and successor Alexander after Leo's death in 912,[2] when Leo's unlawful fourth wife was also duly compelled, after all, to retire from

[1] The surname meant, not mystic, but confidential secretary or *Geheimrat* (Hussey, J. M.: *Church and Learning in the Byzantine Empire, 867–1185* (Oxford 1937, University Press), p. 136, footnote 3).

[2] Leo himself appears to have repented on his death-bed and to have given orders for the Patriarch Nicolaus's reinstatement (*The Cambridge Medieval History*, vol. iv (Cambridge 1923, University Press), p. 257).

the palace to a convent. Nicolaus then lived on to become, after Alexander's death, the President of a Regency Council which took over the government of the Empire on behalf of Leo's—and his fourth wife's—son Constantine Porphyrogenitus; and he still retained his Patriarchate when he lost his political position in A.D. 913, after a four months' tenure, through the return of the young Emperor's exiled mother to power. He remained in office long enough to see the guardianship of the boy-Emperor, and the mastership of the Empire which this guardianship carried with it, wrested out of the hands of the Empress-Dowager in A.D. 919 by the Admiral Romanus Lecapenus;[1] and under this new régime the Patriarch had the satisfaction of formally registering his own complete official victory in the struggle upon which he had entered some fifteen years before. In A.D. 920 the Patriarch Nicolaus, then in undisputed occupation of his Patriarchal Chair, was able to bring to an end, on his own terms, the schism between his own supporters and those of his temporary supplanter the Anti-Patriarch Euthymius. In an 'Act of Union',[2] which received the signatures of both parties, fourth marriages were condemned categorically, though in general terms.

Since the ultimate issue in the conflict between the Patriarch Nicolaus and the Emperor Leo the Wise had been not the particular question of fourth marriages but the general question of whether in Orthodox Christendom the Imperial office was subject to Patriarchal censorship, it might seem as though the signature of 'the Act of Union' signified a victory of the Church over the State of the same stamp as Pope Nicholas I's victory over the Emperor Lewis II. Indeed, a disinterested observer, had he been called upon to estimate the relative prospects of the Oecumenical Patriarchate and the Papacy in that year 920, would almost certainly have prophesied that the Patriarchate would have both the greater and the nobler future.[3] In A.D. 920 the Papacy—bereaved of Imperial protection through the deliberate abstention of the East Roman Government and the lamentable débâcle of the Carolingians—was in the disgraceful plight of being used as a political tool by a gang of parochial Roman adventurers. From 904 to 966 the Papacy was in the hands of the 'family' of Theophylact the Vestiarius, as represented by the lovers and the sons and the grandsons of this gangster's wife and daughters. As late as 974 his grandson

[1] The political aspect of these events in the domestic history of the East Roman Empire has been dealt with already, in its relation to the Romano-Bulgarian War of A.D. 913–27, in IV. C (iii) (*c*) 2 (β), pp. 384–5, above.

[2] Ὁ Τόμος τῆς Ἑνώσεως.

[3] It is significant that throughout the struggle between the Patriarch Nicolaus and the Emperor Leo VI it was the Emperor and not the Patriarch that enjoyed the countenance and support of the Papacy (*The Cambridge Medieval History*, vol. iv (Cambridge 1923, University Press), pp. 256–8).

Cencius was able to depose and murder a Pope and install a pretender; and when this Antipope had to evacuate Rome he took refuge at Constantinople and was restored in 984 by an East Roman expeditionary force—to such good effect that he died in possession of St. Peter's Chair.[1] Thereafter, in 997, the anti-German faction in the Ducatus Romanus chose a Greek for their Antipope after they had driven out Otto III's Pope Bruno. Nor was it only for material assistance that Rome in this age addressed herself to Orthodox Christendom. At the turn of the tenth and eleventh centuries such spiritual life as was to be found in Rome at the time was inspired by Basilian monks who had been drawn to Rome from Calabria by the crying need for filling a spiritual void.[2] On the eve of Hildebrand's birth there was nothing whatever in the Roman scene to suggest the imminence of the Hildebrandine revival. Even beyond the Alps the Cluniac movement, though now well under way, had not yet revealed its potentialities.[3] In fact, for a full century after the Oecumenical Patriarch Nicolaus's triumph in A.D. 920 a disinterested observer might reasonably have pronounced that the spiritual citadel of Christianity was neither Rome nor Cluny but Constantinople. Yet any such pronouncement would have been promptly confuted by the sequel. Our hypothetical observer would not only have been astonished to see Marozia's grandson Pope John XII succeeded by Hildebrand within ninety years; he would have been perhaps even more surprised to see the Oecumenical Patriarch Nicolaus Mysticus succeeded by—nobody!

The truth seems to be that though Nicolaus was a much stronger character, as well as a much abler man, than his predecessor Ignatius, he was nevertheless outmanœuvred by the upstart Emperor Romanus Lecapenus in 919 in much the same way as Ignatius had been manipulated by the upstart Basil I in 867. In any case the Patriarch Nicolaus's ostensible victory did not accrue to the advantage of the Oecumenical Patriarchate—and this in spite of the fact that it could not have come at a more opportune moment for enabling the Patriarchate to recover the position which it had occupied, three hundred years before, in the time of the Patriarch Sergius. From the death of Leo the Wise in A.D. 912 till the end of Basil II's minority in A.D. 985 the legitimate occupants of the Imperial Throne were all the time either minors or political nonentities. Here was an unparalleled opportunity for some other power or institution in the body of the Orthodox Christian Society

[1] For this incident see IV. C (iii) (c) 2 (β), p. 338, footnote 1, above.

[2] See IV. C (iii) (c) 2 (β), p. 357, above.

[3] Indeed, since about A.D. 940 the Cluniac and other monastic reformers of France and Lotharingia had been coming for inspiration to the Basilian monastic settlements on Monte Gargano (see Gay, J.: *L'Italie Méridionale et l'Empire Byzantin* (Paris 1904, Fontemoing), p. 385).

to assert itself at the expense of the Imperial Crown and thus do Society the service of putting an end to that unhealthy predominance of one single institution which had prevailed for the past two hundred years. The power marked out for playing this role was the Oecumenical Patriarchate, which had just won a great moral victory over the Imperial Crown on the eve of the Crown's eclipse. Yet the Patriarchate failed to seize the opportunity that was offered to it. The Patriarch Nicolaus's regency in the year 913 did not create a precedent. Perhaps the deciding factor was the perilousness of the position in which the East Roman Empire found itself at this moment *vis-à-vis* Bulgaria; and this peril, as we have seen,[1] was part of the nemesis to which the Orthodox Christian Society had exposed itself through having subordinated the Church to the State during the eighth and ninth centuries. Whatever the explanation may be, the historical fact is that the regency of the East Roman Empire was not now secured by the Oecumenical Patriarchate as a permanent constitutional prerogative, but was usurped from 919 onwards until 976 by a series of military adventurers, beginning with Romanus Lecapenus and his sons and ending with Nicephorus Phocas and John Tzimisces. This military regency was a vigorous but a violent régime; and it met the foreign peril that had brought it into power by a grandiose policy of conquest which was a new and, as it proved, a disastrous departure in East Roman statesmanship.[2] It was after the East Roman Empire's fifty-seven years of military dictatorship that the Orthodox Christian Civilization broke down; and the breakdown and the dictatorship are demonstrably related to one another in the relation of effect and cause. If, during those critical years in the middle of the tenth century, the unhealthily predominant role of the East Roman Imperial Government in the life of Orthodox Christendom had been moderated by a touch of clericalism instead of being accentuated, as it actually was, by a bout of militarism, it seems probable that the disaster might have been staved off, and possible that it might have been averted.[3]

If we now glance back, from this point, over the history of the Orthodox Christian Civilization during its prematurely interrupted

[1] In IV. C (iii) (*c*) 2 (β), pp. 377–91, above.

[2] For this latter-day East Roman militarism see IV. C (iii) (*c*) 2 (β), pp. 399–403, above.

[3] More than a century after the time of the Patriarch Nicolaus Mysticus, his successor Michael Cerularius (*fungebatur* A.D. 1043–58) took advantage of the weakness which had overtaken the Imperial Power, after the death of the Emperor Basil II in 1025, in order to grasp at the prize which Nicolaus had missed. Cerularius seems to have come rather near to success in his dealings with the Emperors Michael VI Stratioticus and Isaac Comnenus; but even if his success had been complete it would have come too late, since the breakdown of the Orthodox Christian Civilization had by then already taken place. (The episode of Cerularius's Patriarchate is discussed in Hussey, J.M.: *Church and Learning in the Byzantine Empire, 867–1185* (Oxford 1937, University Press), pp. 152–7.)

growth-phase, we can perceive both the extent and the limits of the State's ascendancy over the Church.

In the course of the two centuries that elapsed between the accession of Leo Syrus and the beginning of the regency of Romanus Lecapenus the East Roman State did effectively reduce the hierarchy of the Orthodox Church in its dominions to the status of a public service which had to be as amenable as any other branch of the Imperial administration to the will of a Government which was an absolute autocracy. When a Germanus came into collision with a Leo Syrus, or a Nicephorus with a Leo Armenius, or an Ignatius with a Caesar Bardas, or a Nicolaus with a Leo Sapiens, it was always the Emperor, and never the Patriarch, whose will prevailed; and this 'law' of East Roman history was illustrated just as pointedly when Ignatius was reinstated by Basil I or Nicolaus by Basil's son Alexander. On the other hand the Imperial Crown discovered that it could only carry off this cherished assertion of its sovereign authority over the Oecumenical Patriarchate by constituting itself the unimpeachable guardian and the zealous exponent of an Orthodoxy of which it could not at the same time constitute itself the judge. If the precious political precedent that had been set by Leo's drastic treatment of Germanus was to be harvested by Leo's successors on the Imperial Throne, then they must pay for this political advantage in religious coin by accepting Germanus's views, instead of Leo's, on the subject of the proper place of icons in Christian worship; and, on the same principle, if the Admiral Romanus Lecapenus was to make quite certain that the regency of the Empire, which he had usurped for himself, should not revert to the Patriarch Nicolaus, then, again, he must pay in the same religious coin for the same political commodity by accepting Nicolaus's views on the subject of the unlawfulness of fourth marriages. From the Crown's standpoint the vital necessity, on every occasion of encounter, was to put the Patriarchate in its place: that is, to advertise the fact that the Emperor and not the Patriarch was the master. If this fundamental proposition of East Roman political theory was effectively demonstrated in consequence of an Emperor's decision to purge Christian worship of icons or to contract a fourth marriage, then, when once the demonstration had been made, the Crown could afford to abandon Iconoclasm and to admit that fourth marriages were unlawful—and, henceforth, woe betide the Patriarch who dared to preach or practise what the Emperor had now renounced! So long as he was acknowledged to be master the Emperor was willing to be Orthodox; and so long as he was allowed to assert his mastery by his own tests he was willing to leave the definition of Orthodoxy to his clerical servants.

If this is a correct account of the relations between Church and State in the Orthodox Christian Society during its growth-phase, it will not be found applicable to the 'Time of Troubles' which set in after the breakdown in the tenth century. In the course of this later and more calamitous age we shall notice a considerable shift in the Balance of Power between the two leading institutions of the Orthodox Christian social system, and we shall observe that the change is in the Church's favour. The discomfiture of the State by the Church in this chapter of Orthodox Christian history is proved on the touchstone of the burning question of the age.

As the Orthodox Christian Society disintegrated it grew steadily weaker by comparison with its neighbours—the coeval sister society of Western Christendom on the one side and the nascent Iranic successor of the moribund Syriac Society on the other—and, as this happened, there was a change of emphasis in the field of religious controversy. The icon question, which had long ago been settled by compromise,[1] was now no longer a living issue; the question of ecclesiastical censorship over Imperial morals was in abeyance; the burning question now was that of the relation between the Orthodox and the Western Church. This question, of course, had its doctrinal aspect—the omission or insertion of the *Filioque* in the Creed—and its hierarchical aspect—the ecclesiastical independence of the Eastern Patriarchates or their subordination to the Roman See—but at bottom it was a question of politics. If the two churches could compose their differences, then Orthodox Christendom might hope to secure Western help against Turkish aggression. Conversely, if these differences were to rankle into a permanent and acknowledged schism, then Orthodox Christendom had to fear that the Franks might anticipate the Turks in making her their prey. This political issue was manifestly crucial; the fate of the East Roman Empire, and of the Orthodox Christian Society itself, was in the balance; and once again, as in the eighth and ninth centuries, the Orthodox Church and the East Roman Government were ranged on opposite sides—but this time under new conditions and with a different result.

This time it was not possible to arrive at a compromise on the previously accepted lines of tacitly separating the political and ecclesiastical aspects of the conflict from one another; for the political issue, now, was not simply the question whether the Church should admit the superior authority of the Imperial will on the unwritten and even unspoken understanding that the Constantinopolitan 'Caesar-Pope' should exercise the Papal functions of his 'totalitarian' authority in accordance with ecclesiastical rulings.

[1] See V. C (i) (*d*) 9 (β), vol. vi, p. 117, below.

The answer to the political question in the present controversy depended neither upon the Orthodox Church nor upon the East Roman Imperial Government, but upon an alien power: the other, and now far stronger, Christendom in the West. This alien power now had the fate of Orthodox Christendom in its hands; it had the choice of either saving Orthodox Christendom or destroying her; and it would not choose the political course that meant her salvation unless the hierarchical and doctrinal issues were first of all settled to its satisfaction. In these circumstances East Roman statesmanship was bound to exert itself to the utmost in order to satisfy the Western Christians' ecclesiastical demands; and therefore, this time, it was not open to the East Roman Government to achieve its political aim by the time-honoured expedient of leaving the definition of Orthodoxy to the clerics. This time the ecclesiastical question and the political question hung together indissolubly; and the Emperor therefore had to insist *à outrance* upon a definition of Orthodoxy that would make his policy possible. He found, however, that the limits of his authority in the ecclesiastical sphere were unaltered and inelastic. In the definition of Orthodoxy the Church still had the last word; and now that the East Roman Imperial authority was perceptibly on the wane the Imperial statesmanship could not induce the Church to relinquish a prerogative to which it had clung, in the teeth of the Imperial Government, when the Empire had been at its zenith. On the questions of the *Filioque* and the Papal supremacy, as on those of icons and fourth marriages, the Church had its way; and the East Roman Government had to resign itself to the inevitable political consequences, though these were nothing less than the annihilation of the last vestige of the East Roman Empire and the forcible political unification of a long-distracted Orthodox Christian World under the pall of a *Pax Ottomanica.*[1]

In this connexion it is noteworthy that the attitude of the East Roman Government on the questions of the Papal supremacy and the *Filioque* was from first to last conciliatory towards the Papacy by comparison with the attitude of the hierarchy of the Orthodox Church.[2]

[1] For the role of the Ottoman Empire in Orthodox Christian history as the Orthodox Christian universal state see Part III. A, vol. iii, pp. 26–7, above, and V. C (ii) (*a*), vol. vi, pp. 190–1, and V. C (ii) (*b*), vol. vi, pp. 298–300, below.

[2] The Orthodox hierarchy was never ready to acknowledge the Papal supremacy in matters of discipline or of doctrine—even when it was in desperate need of support against the East Roman Imperial Power. In the last resort the Orthodox hierarchy preferred the political yoke of an Emperor to the ecclesiastical yoke of a Pope if it was driven to make a choice between the two servitudes. On the other hand the Basilian monks, who had no hierarchical considerations to deter them, did not hesitate to place themselves under the banner of the Pope in their struggle against the Iconoclast East Roman Emperors.

This difference became apparent during the first crisis in the relations between Orthodox and Western Christendom—a crisis which began with Pope Nicholas I's championship of the *ci-devant* Oecumenical Patriarch Ignatius after his deposition in A.D. 858,[1] and which died away after the second deposition of Ignatius's supplanter Photius in A.D. 886.[2] The crisis was a dangerous one because the original conflict over a question of ecclesiastical discipline was enlarged and envenomed, not only by the introduction of a question of doctrine, but also by a competition for the ecclesiastical allegiance of the whole interior of South Eastern Europe from the Adriatic to the Carpathians and from the head-waters of the Maritsa to those of the Elbe.[3] In this formidable transaction

[1] For the collision between the Patriarch Ignatius and the Caesar Bardas see pp. 597–8, above.

[2] The formal healing of the schism appears to have been accomplished in the years A.D. 898–900 (*The Cambridge Medieval History*, vol. iv (Cambridge 1923, University Press), pp. 255–6, and Hussey, J.M.: *Church and Learning in the Byzantine Empire, 867–1185* (Oxford 1937, University Press), p. 135).

[3] This competition was a consequence of the removal of certain obstacles which had latterly insulated the two Christendoms from one another on the landward side. Under the Roman Empire within the Continental European frontiers that had been secured for it by Augustus (see V. C (i) (*c*) 3, Annex 1, vol. v, pp. 591–5, below) there had, of course, been direct communication overland, round the head of the Adriatic, between the Balkan and Asiatic provinces of the Empire on the one side and the West European provinces on the other; but Narses' march from a Balkan base of operations to an Italian theatre of war in A.D. 552 was the last recorded use of this overland route in the Empire's history. The overland communications between Constantinople and Milan, or Constantinople and Cologne, were severed by the Nomad pseudo-Avars' occupation of the Hungarian Alföld in A.D. 567 and the Nomad Bulgars' occupation of the southern as well as the northern half of the Lower Danube Basin in A.D. 680 in the wake of the Slav infiltrations of the sixth century. (See Part III. A, Annex II, vol. iii, pp. 425 and 427, above.) By the middle of the ninth century, however, the insulation which had resulted from the combined effect of these barbarian intrusions had been overcome, partly through Charlemagne's extirpation of the incurably barbarous Avars in A.D. 791, and partly through the peaceful radiation of both the two adjoining Christian cultures into Bulgaria and the Slavinias. In the seventh decade of the ninth century the pull of the two Christendoms upon the barbarians of South Eastern Europe became strong enough to make the barbarians themselves feel that they could no longer hold their own in the new homes which their immigrant forefathers had bequeathed to them unless they came to terms with one or other of the formidable, and at the same time fascinating, cultures that were exerting an ever-increasing influence upon these barbarians' lives; and, having all come more or less simultaneously to this conclusion, they severally decided that the adventure in civilization on which they had now determined to embark would be less hazardous if they chose the more distant, rather than the nearer, of the two Christendoms to be their god-parent. Accordingly we find Rostislav (or Rastislav), the barbarian prince of the Slavonic principality of Moravia, whose dominions lay close up against the expanding eastern frontier of the Carolingian Empire, applying to the East Roman Government at Constantinople for missionaries to instruct his subjects in the Christian Faith (Dvorník, F.: *Les Slaves, Byzance et Rome au ixe Siècle* (Paris 1926, Champion), pp. 147 and 157–9), while Boris, the contemporary Khan of Bulgaria, whose dominions lay in an equally uncomfortable proximity to the Thracian frontier of the East Roman Empire, retorted to the East Roman Government's prompt dispatch to Moravia of the missionaries Cyril and Methodius—a move which threatened him with encirclement—by allying himself, in the same year, with the Western Emperor Lewis II (Dvorník, op. cit., p. 186). This Bulgarian move led the East Roman Government, in its turn, to hustle Bulgaria in 865 into an acceptance of Christianity from Orthodox Christian hands by the adroit combination of a military demonstration (see IV. C (iii) (*c*) 2 (β), p. 380, above) and a territorial *douceur* (see the same chapter, p. 343, footnote 2, above). Boris, thus outmanœuvred by East Roman statesmanship in 865, sought to safeguard a Christian Bulgaria against the overwhelming pressure of the Orthodox Christian Power which was her immediate neighbour by the clever stroke of placing Bulgaria under Papal jurisdiction in 866—a counter-move which promised to neutralize

the East Roman Government limited itself to two moderate aims and contented itself with achieving these and these only. The first aim was to make it unmistakably clear that the Emperor and not the Pope was the Oecumenical Patriarch's master; the second aim was to prevent the Pope from recovering his ancient ecclesiastical jurisdiction over Illyricum, of which he had been deprived in A.D. 732 by the Emperor Leo Syrus.[1] The aims of the Patriarch Photius were more ambitious and more aggressive. He wanted to discredit once for all the Papacy's claim to ecclesiastical supremacy over the other Patriarchates, and in order to compass this aim he was ready to open a doctrinal as well as a disciplinary breach between the Churches by convicting the Pope of heresy. The East Roman Government, however, was careful not to extend its support of its servant the Oecumenical Patriarch any farther than the Imperial policy required.

When Pope Nicholas I insisted upon the restoration of Illyricum, Calabria, and Sicily to his own jurisdiction, as a condition of his recognizing the legitimacy of Photius's investiture, the Imperial Government gave Photius its support. But after Photius, in 867, had gone so far as to denounce the Pope publicly for his concurrence in the Western heresy of adding the *Filioque* to the Nicene Creed, the newly enthroned Emperor Basil I deposed the over-militant Photius and restored Ignatius (whose act of *lèse-majesté* had not been committed against Basil personally, and whose spirit had been chastened in the meanwhile by some nine years of languishing in the wilderness). Thereupon the Emperor wrote to the Pope 'to ask him to send legates to a council at which the past should be forgotten, the Roman precedence stated and supremacy hinted, and no one should mention the word *Filioque*'.[2] At this Constantinopolitan Oecumenical Council of A.D. 869–70 Basil was, indeed, concerned with other things—to wit, the two fundamental aims of the Imperial policy—and he took the Papal legates by surprise in displaying an efficiency in the pursuit of his own interests which contrasted strongly with his indifference to the interests of his Patriarch. The Emperor saw to it that the procedure for the ex-Patriarch's trial should be arranged to the Emperor's own liking and not to the legates' liking; and when a Bulgarian embassy applied to the Council for a judgement as to whether the ecclesiastical allegiance of Bulgaria was owing to Rome or to Constan-

the East Roman success of the preceding year. It will be seen that the action taken by a barbarian Rostislav and a barbarian Boris in the years 862–6 raised the whole question of the ultimate ecclesiastical and cultural allegiance of South Eastern Europe. There is an illuminating discussion of this question in Dvorník, op. cit., chs. 5–9.

[1] See IV. C (iii) (*c*) 2 (β), p. 337 and p. 346, footnote 2, and the present Annex, p. 595, above.

[2] Runciman, S.: *A History of the First Bulgarian Empire* (London 1930, Bell), p. 112.

tinople, the Emperor saw to it, again, that the representatives of the four Eastern Patriarchates should all pronounce in favour of Constantinople over the Papal legates' heads.[1]

When, after this, the Papacy continued to make obstinate efforts to entice Bulgaria back to that ecclesiastical allegiance to the Roman See which she had acknowledged during the five years ending in 870,[2] Basil took the opportunity of Ignatius's death in 877 to re-appoint Photius to the Patriarchal Chair, with instructions, this time, to solicit the Pope's approval for his appointment and to accept the condition, which the Pope proceeded to lay down, that the ecclesiastical jurisdiction over Bulgaria must be retroceded to the Papacy by the Patriarchate. This Photian *volte face* by Imperial command induced the Pope to send legates to a new council which met at Constantinople in 879; and here the Papal legates were persuaded to concur in referring the question of Bulgaria's ecclesiastical allegiance to the decision of the East Roman Emperor. Presumably they were given to understand in advance that if the Emperor's title to make the award were recognized he would render the award in their Pontifical master's favour. In any case the Emperor did actually decide in this sense; and the transaction is characteristic of the Imperial policy. What the Imperial Government really had at heart was to obtain a public acknowledgement that on the question of the ecclesiastical allegiance of Bulgaria the last word lay neither with the Patriarchate nor yet with the Papacy but with the Imperial Government itself; and for the sake of securing this victory in principle the Imperial Government was not unwilling to make a provisional concession on a point of practice.

As a matter of fact this award in the Papacy's favour cost the East Roman Empire nothing; for the Bulgarians (disillusioned by their short experience of Papal jurisdiction)[3] annulled the Imperial

[1] On the historical merits of the case the Eastern Patriarchs were substantially in the right; for both the contemporary Bulgarian capital of Pliska, and the subsequent capital of Preslav, which was substituted for Pliska in the reign of Symeon (*imperabat* A.D. 893–927), lay within the former bounds of the *ci-devant* Roman Province of Moesia Secunda, which belonged to the Imperial Diocese of Thrace, which, in turn, was under the ecclesiastical jurisdiction of the Patriarchate of Constantinople. At the same time it is true that the ninth-century acquisitions of Bulgaria in the interior of the Balkan Peninsula, from Sardica south-westwards, lay within the former bounds of the *ci-devant* Roman Prefecture of Illyricum, which had originally fallen within the jurisdiction of the Roman See. As for Transdanubian Bulgaria, which lay within the bounds of the original Roman Province of Dacia, this was an ecclesiastical no-man's-land to which neither the Roman nor the Constantinopolitan Patriarchate could lay claim, since Dacia had been re-abandoned to the barbarians by Aurelian in the third century before the ecclesiastical geography of the Christian Roman Empire had been worked out.

[2] For this passing incident in Bulgarian ecclesiastical history see IV. C (iii) (*c*) 2 (β), pp. 380–1, and the present Annex, p. 605, footnote 3, above.

[3] In his reply to Boris' original overtures to the Roman See in A.D. 866 Pope Nicholas I had returned a non-committal answer to the Bulgarian Khan's request that he should be allowed to have a Patriarch of his own (Dvorník, op. cit., p. 192). Thereafter the

award *de facto* by a policy of 'masterly inactivity'; and no doubt the Emperor had informed himself that this would be the sequel before he entered into his understanding with the Papal legates.[1] Thus the Emperor managed to deprive the Papacy of any plausible ground for convicting him of injustice, or even of unfriendliness, in his dealings with the Roman See, while at the same time he effectively secured that the whole of the interior of the Balkan Peninsula—both the *ci-devant* Diocese of Thrace and the *ci-devant* Prefecture of Illyricum—should be incorporated into the body social of Orthodox Christendom instead of gravitating towards the now alien and rival Christendom of the West.

In pursuing this policy of gaining the gist of what he wanted without goading the Papacy into making a breach with him Basil was also careful not to push his cultural imperialism in South Eastern Europe farther afield than seemed strictly necessary for the East Roman Empire's political security. So long as he could make sure of Bulgaria, which lay at his gates, he was content to let the distant Moravia go; and in this Moravian field the tactics of our modern Western imperialism—'first the missionary, then the consul, then the soldier'[2]—were not pursued by the cautious ninth-century East Roman statesman. Basil appears to have borne no grudge against the Photian missionaries, Cyril and Methodius, for their early decision[3]—which they took on common-sense geographical grounds—to place their new Moravian Church under the Papal jurisdiction.[4] And when, after the death of Cyril's sur-

same Pope had recalled from Bulgaria his legate Bishop Formosus of Porto because he suspected him of pandering to Boris' ambition to obtain ecclesiastical autonomy (Dvorník, op. cit., pp. 193–4). The last stroke that alienated Boris from Rome was the intransigence of the Curia in refusing to appoint as Bishop of Bulgaria the candidate on whom Boris had set his heart (Dvorník, op. cit., p. 195).

[1] In fact, on the question of the ecclesiastical allegiance of Bulgaria the Papal legates were the victims of a trick, and they also succumbed to two other pieces of East Roman diplomatic sharp practice. Without realizing, apparently, what they were doing, they subscribed to an anathema against anybody who added anything to the Nicene Creed (that is, an anathema against the Pope for accepting the *Filioque*); and they also subscribed to a conciliar resolution rejecting the Pope's proposal to prohibit the nomination of laymen to the Episcopate (i.e. rejecting the Pope's manœuvre for disqualifying Photius).

[2] This description of our modern Western method of encroachment upon the lives of non-Western societies is attributed to the Emperor Theodore of Abyssinia, who duly met his end at the hands of a Western expeditionary force.

'Je connais, avait-il dit, la tactique des gouvernements européens quand ils veulent prendre un état d'Orient. On lance des missionnaires d'abord, puis des consuls pour appuyer les missionnaires, puis des bataillons pour soutenir les consuls. Je ne suis pas un rajah de l'Indoustan pour être berné de la sorte: j'aime mieux avoir affaire aux bataillons tout de suite.'—Lejean, G. (ancien vice-consul de France à Massaoua): *Théodore II, le Nouvel Empire d'Abyssinie, et les Intérêts Français dans le Sud de la Mer Rouge* (Paris 1865, Amyot), p. 160.

[3] This decision seems to have been taken not later than A.D. 867, for the Pope to whom the two Photian missionaries made their application was Nicholas I, who died on the 13th November of that year.

[4] The persistence of the friendship between the Imperial Court and the Photian missionaries in Moravia is proved by the fact that, *circa* A.D. 881, Methodius received and accepted an invitation from the Emperor Basil I to pay him a visit at Constantinople,

vivor Methodius in 885, the fledgeling Methodian Church was forcibly broken up, with the Papacy's connivance, by German missionaries of the Latin rite,[1] Basil appears again to have refrained from protesting against a high-handed act which implied the unqualified and definitive incorporation of the Moravian half of the South-East European no-man's-land into the body social of Western Christendom. The East Roman Government contented itself with rescuing the survivors of the Moravian clergy of the Slavonic rite and placing their services at the disposal of the Bulgarians,[2] who had revealed their intention to throw in their lot with Orthodox Christendom by tactfully ignoring the Emperor's own award of the year 879.[3]

This display of moderation and humanity was a master-stroke of East Roman diplomacy; for it served three purposes simultaneously. It gave the Bulgarians a concrete proof of East Roman goodwill and good faith; it emphasized the advantages of allegiance to a Church which tolerated and encouraged the ecclesiastical use of the local vernacular, by contrast with the irksomeness of the Western Church's oppressive imposition of an alien Latin; and in the third place it widened the gulf between a Bulgaria which took kindly to the Slavonic Liturgy and a Roman Church which would presumably be unwilling ever to concede to Bulgaria an indulgence which it had revoked so quickly, and so ruthlessly, in Moravia.[4] Thus Basil anchored Bulgaria to the Orthodox allegiance; and his son and successor Leo the Wise clinched Basil's work by calling in the Nomad Magyars,[5] with the result that these pagan barbarians

and also acceded to the Emperor's request to him to leave behind him a priest and a deacon of his party, with Slavonic books (Dvorník, op. cit., p. 278).

[1] After the death of Cyril during the two brothers' visit to Rome, Methodius had succeeded, with some difficulty, in persuading Pope Nicholas I's successor, Pope Hadrian II, to give the Moravian Church a *quid pro quo*, in exchange for its acceptance of the Papal jurisdiction, in the shape of a Papal authorization to employ a Slavonic Liturgy (see IV. C (iii) (*b*) 11, p. 216, footnote 1, above). This insistence of Methodius upon the use of the local vernacular, combined with his refusal to follow the Papacy in introducing the *Filioque*, were the offences which drew down destruction upon the Moravian Church after the death of the second of its two great founders (see IV. C (iii) (*c*) 2 (*β*), p. 381, above).

[2] Runciman, op. cit., pp. 124–6; Dvorník, op. cit., pp. 298–9; see also the present Study, IV. C (iii) (*c*) 2 (*β*), p. 381, above.

[3] See pp. 607–8, above.

[4] It is an intriguing, though perhaps an unanswerable, question whether there was any continuity of tradition between the short-lived Cyrillo-Methodian Slavonic Church of Moravia, which was founded in A.D. 862 and was suppressed by violence in A.D. 885, and the likewise ephemeral Hussite Slavonic Church which arose in the Bohemian part of Rostislav's Moravian principality some five centuries later. Both these 'Czecho-Slovak' religious movements were distinguished by a passionate attachment to the mother tongue, a deep hostility to Germanism, and an unwillingness to accept the supremacy of the Roman See except on their own terms. Are these remarkable resemblances simply the outcome of a fortuitous similarity of circumstances? Or was there in fourteenth-century Bohemia a subterranean 'folk-memory' of the Cyrillo-Methodian Church which was brought to the surface by the attraction of the kindred ideas of a latter-day English Wyclif?

[5] For the circumstances see Part III. A, Annex II, vol. iii, p. 442, above.

occupied the Hungarian Alföld and thereby insulated the Cisdanubian remnant of an Orthodox Christian Bulgaria from the Transdanubian remnant of a Western Christian Moravia.[1] No doubt the East Roman Government was relieved to see the problems that had been raised in A.D. 862, by the establishment of contact between the two Christendoms overland, disposed of in A.D. 895 by the reintroduction of that wedge of insulating paganism which had been provided by the Avars before their annihilation in A.D. 791.[2]

The East Roman Emperor Basil I showed equal tact in handling the delicate relations between the East Roman Government and the Papacy that were involved in the expansion of the East Roman Empire's political dominions in Southern Italy.[3] In A.D. 732 Basil's predecessor Leo Syrus had transferred from the ecclesiastical jurisdiction of the Papacy to that of the Oecumenical Patriarchate[4] the East Roman territory of Calabria, which in Leo's day was confined to the 'toe' of Italy (from the basin of the River Crati, inclusive, southwards) together with the enclave of Gallipoli in the 'heel'.[5] Between 876 and 915 this modest overseas holding of the East Roman Empire on Continental Italian ground was expanded into an imposing dominion which included the whole of Southern Italy up to Gaeta on the one coast and the Gargano Peninsula on the other; and all the territory between the new frontier of 915 and the old frontier of 876[6] was, at the time of the East Roman conquest,

[1] The Magyars evicted the Moravians and the Bulgars from their respective possessions in the Alföld; the Pechenegs, treading on the Magyars' heels, evicted the Bulgars from their remaining Transdanubian possessions in the territories now known as Moldavia, Wallachia, and Transylvania (see IV. C (iii) (*c*) 2 (β), p. 383, footnote 1, above).

[2] There is an unmistakable conformity between the respective variations of the ecclesiastical relations between the Orthodox and Western churches and the geographical relations between the Orthodox and Western Christian worlds. The ecclesiastical relations became bad at the time of the first re-establishment of geographical contact overland in A.D. 862; this first ecclesiastical crisis passed off about the time when this geographical contact was broken by the Magyar occupation of the Alföld *circa* A.D. 895; a fresh crisis in ecclesiastical relations broke out after the second re-establishment of contact overland through the conversion of the Magyars to Western Christianity at the turn of the tenth and eleventh centuries. This time the re-establishment of geographical contact was permanent, and—conformably—the ecclesiastical schism was definitive.

[3] For the history and motives of this East Roman expansion in Southern Italy—which began with the occupation of Bari in 876, was consummated in the campaign of Basil's general Nicephorus Phocas the elder in 885, and was confirmed by the extirpation of the nest of African Muslim pirates on the Garigliano in 915—see IV. C (iii) (*c*) 2 (β), pp. 343–4, above.

[4] See IV. C (iii) (*c*) 2 (β), pp. 337 and 346, footnote 2, and the present Annex, p. 595, above.

[5] The rest of the 'heel' had been conquered by the Lombard principality of Benevento between A.D. 671 and A.D. 687, after the death of the Roman Emperor Constans II. For Constans' previous attack on Benevento see IV. C (iii) (*c*) 2 (β), Annex I, above.

[6] This territory falls into three categories: first the *ci-devant* possessions of the Lombard Duchy of Benevento in Apulia which had been conquered from the Lombards by Muslim raiders from Ifriqīyah in A.D. 840–5, wrested from these African conquerors by the East Roman Government in 876, and annexed to the East Roman Empire out-

under the ecclesiastical jurisdiction of the Papacy. It would have been logical for the Emperor Basil to extend the ecclesiastical jurisdiction of his Patriarch, at the expense of the Pope, *pari passu* with the extension of his own political sovereignty at the expense of the previous political masters of Southern Italy; but a step that would have been logical would also have been highly impolitic, and Basil was careful to refrain from taking it. It has been conjectured that his son and successor Leo the Wise had a tacit understanding with the Roman See over the ecclesiastical allegiance of the South Italian bishoprics on the borderline.[1] In any case the three dioceses of Taranto, Oria, and Brindisi remained under the Papal jurisdiction and continued to use Latin as their liturgical language;[2] and the only new diocese of Greek language and Constantinopolitan allegiance that was created in Southern Italy at this time was that of Santa Severina in old Calabrian territory which had been under East Roman rule all along.[3]

This statesmanlike moderation of Basil and Leo remained the norm of East Roman ecclesiastical policy in Southern Italy so long as the East Roman dominion lasted—with a single exception, which proves the rule, during the reign of the military dictator Nicephorus Phocas the younger (*imperabat* A.D. 963–9).[4] Having quarrelled with the Western Emperor Otto I over the political possession of Southern Italy, the East Roman Emperor Nicephorus revenged himself on the Papacy—which had called Otto in and had taken shelter under his aegis[5]—by setting himself to detach from the Roman allegiance a number of bishoprics in the East Roman provinces of Laghovardhía and Vasilicata—a move to which the Papacy replied by strengthening its own ecclesiastical organization in the East Roman protectorates of Benevento and Salerno.[6] This change in East Roman ecclesiastical policy may have been one of the causes of the revolt of the Empire's Apulian Lombard subjects against the Imperial Government in A.D. 1009;[7] but the strain imposed upon the relations between that Government and the Papacy was not so serious as to prevent these two Powers from taking concerted military action in A.D. 1053 against the Norman adventurers

right; second the surviving 'successor-states' of the Lombard Duchy of Benevento—the Duchies of Benevento, Capua, and Salerno—which were compelled to accept an East Roman protectorate in 885; third the three city-states of Amalfi, Naples, and Gaeta which had never been conquered by the Lombards and which paid to the East Roman Empire of Leo Syrus and Basil I the allegiance which they had never ceased to pay to the Roman Empire of Justinian and Heraclius.

1 Gay, J.: *L'Italie Méridionale et l'Empire Byzantin* (Paris 1904, Fontemoing), p. 188.

2 Gay, op. cit., p. 191.

3 Gay, op. cit., p. 190.

4 The Emperor Nicephorus was the grandson, as well as the namesake, of the general who rounded off the East Roman domain in Southern Italy in the campaign of A.D. 885.

5 See IV. C (iii) (c) 2 (β), p. 338, above.

6 An account of this struggle will be found in Gay, op. cit., pp. 347–64.

7 See IV. C (iii) (c) 2 (β), p. 401, above.

who were at that time threatening to sweep away the whole political *status quo* in Southern and Central Italy.[1]

From the foregoing survey it will be apparent that one of the uses to which the East Roman Government put its 'Caesaro-papal' authority over the Orthodox Christian Church—at any rate, from the reign of Basil I onwards—was to prevent the ecclesiastical rivalry between the Oecumenical Patriarchate and the Papacy from leading to an irremediable rupture. And this use of the monopoly of power which Leo Syrus had concentrated in the East Roman Government's hands was good as far as it went. The monopoly itself, however, was a social evil of such intrinsic maleficence that, as we have seen,[2] it involved not only the East Roman Empire, but the entire Orthodox Christian body social, in a premature breakdown. And as soon as this breakdown produced one of its inevitable fruits, in a weakening of the East Roman Government's power, the Orthodox Church took its revenge upon an oppressively 'totalitarian' political institution by casting off these galling political chains and trampling vindictively upon the tyrant who now lay prostrate. This belated revolt of the Orthodox Church against the East Roman Imperial Government[3] in the days of the Orthodox Christian Society's decline was natural, but it was also suicidal; for the point on which the tardily emancipated Orthodox Church chiefly delighted to oppose and frustrate the East Roman Government's policy was in the matter of the Empire's good understanding with the Papacy; and when this indispensable column in the architectural design of East Roman statesmanship was pulled down, *furore Sampsonico*, by a subversive-minded Church Militant, the whole edifice of Orthodox Christian Society collapsed.

This disastrous consequence of a rather abrupt change in the Balance of Power between the Orthodox Church and the East Roman State was demonstrated by the success of the Oecumenical Patriarch Michael Cerularius (*fungebatur* A.D. 1043–58) in deliberately producing a schism between the Orthodox Church and the Western Church in defiance of the unanimous wishes of the East Roman Government and the Papacy and at the very time of the military alliance of these two Powers against the Normans which has been mentioned above. At this delicate moment, when the existence of the East Roman dominion in Southern Italy was at stake and when

1 The joint Papal and East Roman operations of A.D. 1053 were, of course, a fiasco. The East Roman expeditionary force (commanded by Argyrus, the Byzantinized son of the Apulian Lombard rebel Melo) was driven off the field, while Pope Leo IX's German troops failed to save their master from being taken prisoner. (Pope Leo IX's military expedition against the Normans is touched upon in IV. C (iii) (*c*) 3 (*β*), p. 548, above.)

2 In IV. C (iii) (*c*) 2 (*β*), pp. 352–404, above.

3 This ecclesiastical insurrection against the incubus of the East Roman Empire was part of a wider movement—extending over most of the non-political field of social life—which has been touched upon in IV. C (iii) (*c*) 2 (*β*), pp. 353–64, above.

friendly relations with the Papacy were therefore more than ever desirable from the East Roman Government's standpoint, Cerularius opened a bombardment of the Roman Church from those latterly silent theological batteries which had first been mounted by his predecessor Photius. On the occasion of Photius's attempt to play this dangerous game his mischievous activities had been promptly and severely quashed by the Emperors Basil I and Leo the Wise; and, when Cerularius assumed the Photian role, an attempt to repress the Patriarch in the traditional Imperial manner was duly made by Constantine IX Monomachus, the Emperor of the day; but, instead of accommodating himself to the Imperial policy like his pliant predecessor, Cerularius proved recalcitrant and unmanageable.

Imperial pressure did, indeed, so far avail as to conscript Cerularius's ungracious co-operation in an attempt to preserve those correct official relations between the Imperial Government and the Papacy that had subsisted, for the most part, since the healing of the Photian schism in A.D. 898–900; and the Imperial diplomacy was able to insist that the first move in these ecclesiastical negotiations should be made by a cleric who was perhaps rather less out of sympathy with the Imperial policy than the Patriarch himself.[1] The negotiations were started by a letter from the autocephalous Archbishop of Ochrida (an Orthodox prelate whose see lay in the West Bulgarian territories of the East Roman Crown, which were outside the Oecumenical Patriarch's jurisdiction)[2] to the Archbishop of Trani (the most Byzantinophil of the Latin prelates in Southern Italy, by contrast with his neighbour and rival of Bari, who was the protagonist in the anti-Byzantine party).[3] This attempt at an ecclesiastical *rapprochement* had the warm approval and support of Argyrus, the Byzantinized son of the Apulian Lombard rebel Melo,[4] who had been sent out to Italy by the East Roman Government in 1051 on the mission of restoring the Imperial authority after it had been shaken by the double blow of the Norman invasion and the treason of the previous East Roman Governor Maniakis. In fact, it is possible that Argyrus—by origin a Lombard of the Latin rite—was the actual author of the policy, for at the time of his appointment we find him protesting against Cerularius's idea of weaning from the Latin rite the Empire's Latin

1 Archbishop Leo of Ochrida cannot have struck the Latins as being conspicuously sympathetic to their cause, or he would not have been included, as he was, in the anathema which was pronounced against the Patriarch by the Papal legates in 1054 after the deposit of their bull of excommunication (see p. 614, below).

2 For the preservation of the ecclesiastical autonomy of this *ci-devant* West Bulgarian Patriarchate after the annexation of the West Bulgarian Empire to the East Roman Empire in A.D. 1019 see IV. C (iii) (*c*) 2 (β), p. 394, footnote 1, above.

3 For this first stage of the negotiations see Gay, op. cit., pp. 491–5.

4 See p. 612, footnote 1, above.

subjects in Italy.[1] Cerularius, on his part, may have feared that the policy promoted by Argyrus might work together with the contemporary increase in the prestige and power of the Papacy[2] to checkmate the Oecumenical Patriarchate's South Italian ambitions and perhaps even to eliminate its authority altogether in the regions west of the Adriatic.[3] Cerularius was determined to prevent the Imperial Government and the Papacy from securing their respective interests in Southern Italy by a bargain at the Oecumenical Patriarchate's expense; and so he displayed an intransigence and an aggressiveness that were calculated to provoke, and did provoke, a rupture.

In 1053 Cerularius forcibly closed the churches of the Latin rite in Constantinople; and when three Papal legates arrived in Constantinople in the spring of 1054 the Patriarch refused to meet them. The representatives of the Pope were hospitably entertained by the Emperor and were cordially received at the monastery of Studium with its philo-Roman tradition; but the courtesy of the Imperial Government and the monks could neither overcome nor outweigh the Patriarch's studied hostility; and finally, on the 16th July, 1054, the Papal legates deposited on the altar of St. Sophia a document declaring Cerularius excommunicated in the name of their master. The Emperor not only failed in an effort at the thirteenth hour to repair the breach; he was actually compelled by the pressure of public opinion to write the Patriarch an open letter apologizing for his own complacency towards the Roman See and throwing the blame upon Argyrus. Thereafter, with the Emperor's reluctant assent, the Patriarch convened a council of the prelates within his jurisdiction, and on the 20th July, 1054, this Council formally condemned the Papal bull. Thus the East Roman Government's attempt to secure an ecclesiastical *rapprochement* ended unhappily in producing the opposite result of a formal and open schism which was the Patriarchate's tardy but telling revenge upon the Imperial Government for three centuries of humiliation.

This ecclesiastical breach did not break the *entente* between the Papacy and the East Roman Government, but in alienating the sympathies of the East Roman Empire's Latin subjects it played into the hands of the Normans,[4] and it must therefore be regarded as one of the factors responsible for the extinction of East Roman rule in Italy in the course of the next twenty-five years. In-

[1] Gay, op. cit., p. 471.

[2] Pope Leo IX (*fungebatur* A.D. 1049–54) was a capable and strong-minded Transalpine cleric who had realized the need for reform and had taken the most effective step possible towards setting a reform movement in motion when he had chosen Ildebrando Aldobrandeschi the Tuscan to be his right-hand man (see IV. C (iii) (c) 3 (β), p. 529, above).

[3] Gay, op. cit., p. 497.

[4] See IV. C (iii) (c) 2 (β), pp. 401–2, above.

cidentally the conquest of the East Roman dominion in Southern Italy by the Normans carried with it the retransference of all the conquered territories—including Calabria and Sicily—from the ecclesiastical jurisdiction of Constantinople to that of Rome. But the Orthodox Christian hierarchy did not draw the obvious inference. Its Italian losses simply exasperated it into an obstinate determination to make sure that the schism of A.D. 1054 should never be closed except—*quod erat absurdum*—through a complete and uncompromising acceptance of the Orthodox Church's terms; and the permanent alienation from one another of the two Christendoms, which was the result of this ecclesiastical intransigence, was a far graver consequence—not only for the East Roman Empire, but for Orthodox Christendom as a whole—than the loss of a Transadriatic outpost.

The policy of keeping on good terms with the Papacy, which had been bequeathed by the Emperor Basil I to his successors on the East Roman Imperial throne, was maintained, with momentary lapses, by the East Roman Government so long as the East Roman Empire continued to exist; but the later Emperors were as unsuccessful as Constantine Monomachus in their attempts to put the policy into effect in the teeth of the Orthodox hierarchy's resistance; and this resistance became all the more fanatical as the disintegration of the Orthodox Christian Society demonstrated, at each further stage of its disastrous course, that the Government and not the hierarchy was in the right.

From the morrow of the restoration of a shadow of the East Roman Empire at Constantinople in A.D. 1261,[1] after the disastrous interlude of a Western usurpation, down to the moment of its final obliteration through the Ottoman Conquest in A.D. 1453, the line of Emperors which began with the re-conqueror of Constantinople, Michael VIII Palaeologus (*imperabat* A.D. 1259–82), and which ended with his descendant Constantine XI Dhraghasis (*imperabat* A.D. 1448–53), made repeated efforts to close the breach that had been opened in A.D. 1054; and these latter-day East Roman statesmen displayed the traditional East Roman sense of political realities. They faced the fact that the Balance of Power between the two Christendoms had now turned overwhelmingly in favour of the West, and they conformed their policy to this change of circumstance by consenting now to come, both literally and metaphorically, on to Western ground. Michael Palaeologus himself was so far from being dazzled by his personal success in recovering the

[1] For the work of the Greek principality of Nicaea in expelling the Western usurpers who had seized Constantinople and Greece in A.D. 1204, under pretext of conducting a 'Fourth Crusade', see Part III. A, vol. iii, p. 27, above.

Imperial City that he lived in dread of seeing this audacious vindication of an historic right bring down upon him the Western *revanche* of another 'crusade' with the Greek 'schismatics' for its victims instead of the Muslim 'unbelievers'; and this prudent anxiety led him, in A.D. 1274, to attend an oecumenical council, convened by Pope Gregory X in the Transalpine city of Lyon,[1] where the schism was officially closed by the Emperor's acceptance of the Papal supremacy and the *Filioque*. As early as 1282, however, Michael's weaker successor Andronicus II was compelled to denounce the Union of Lyon under Orthodox ecclesiastical pressure; and the same fate overtook the Emperor John Palaeologus's repetition of Michael's act in 1439 during the Council of Ferrara and Florence. Once again the articles of capitulation to which an East Roman Emperor had given a facile assent in a Western council-chamber were repudiated by his clergy and people at home; and though, this time, the Imperial Government avoided the additional humiliation of being compelled by its own subjects to denounce a compact with an alien Power which was humiliating enough in itself, this last assertion of the Imperial will profited the Empire nothing.

The last of the Palaeologi, the heroic Constantine Dhraghasis, whose fate it was to play Hector's role in the *excidium* of the Third Troy, was still in communion with Rome when he stood in the breach, awaiting the Janissaries' irresistible assault, on the 29th May, 1453; but he had been basely betrayed by the Western allies whose bounden duty it was to succour their beleaguered co-religionist. Giustiniani and his like no more availed to save the devoted city from its doom than Rhesus had availed to bring effective relief to the Byzantine Hector's Homeric prototype. The same day saw the fall of the Imperial City and of the Imperial namesake of Constantine the Great; and, if we may venture to sum up the common cause of their ruin in a single sentence, we may say that this tragedy occurred in the fifteenth century of the Christian Era because the 'Caesaro-papism' of the Roman Emperor Constantine had been first successfully revived in the eighth century by the East Roman Emperor Leo Syrus and then successfully defied in the eleventh century by the Oecumenical Patriarch Michael Cerularius.

If we probe somewhat deeper into the causes of the shift in the Balance of Power between the East Roman Government and the Orthodox hierarchy during the four centuries, ending in the year 1453, which witnessed the Empire's extinction, we shall probably come to the conclusion that the change is not fully explained by the progressive weakening of the Imperial Power. This negative

[1] See IV. C (iii) (c) 3 (β), pp. 532 and 544, above.

factor would hardly have operated with such potent effect if it had not been reinforced by a positive increase in the strength of the Church; and if we inquire, in turn, into the causes of this advance in ecclesiastical authority, we shall discover two: one of them external to the life of the Church, and the other intrinsic to its development in this age.

The external factor which strengthened the hands of the Orthodox hierarchy in its successful opposition to the Imperial Government's policy of reconciliation with the Papacy was the force of feeling and opinion in the Orthodox Christian World, which became increasingly hostile to the West and therefore increasingly ready to allow the Church to mobilize it against the Imperial Government on behalf of an anti-Western policy.

From the moment when the two Christendoms first re-encountered one another upon the recovery of the Western World from the post-Carolingian interregnum,[1] they each displayed an instantaneous antipathy for the other. On the Western side this feeling declares itself with a ludicrous violence in almost every line of the report on his diplomatic mission to Constantinople in A.D. 968 which the North Lombard bishop Liutprand of Cremona wrote for his Saxon master the Western Emperor Otto I.[2] On the Orthodox Christian side the learned Imperial authoress Anna Comnena (*vivebat* A.D. 1083–*post* 1148), in her *Alexiad* or history of the life and times of her father the East Roman Emperor Alexius I (*imperabat* A.D. 1081–1118), displays a dislike for the Westerners and all their works which is not less intense for being less vulgarly expressed than Liutprand's animus against Anna's world.[3] From

[1] For this interregnum see IV. C (iii) (*c*) 2 (β), pp. 322–3, above.

[2] See the *Legatio, passim*, in *Liutprandi Episcopi Cremonensis Opera* (ed. by Becker, J.: Hanover and Leipzig 1915, Hahn). It may be noted that this was Liutprand's second visit to Constantinople, and that, in his account of his first visit, which is also extant (see the *Antapodosis*, Book VI, in ed. cit., pp. 151–8), the emotional colour is by no means hostile. How are we to account for this change in Liutprand's feelings towards Orthodox Christendom during the comparatively short interval of nineteen years between A.D. 949 and A.D. 968? Is it simply a personal change which is to be explained by the fact that on his second visit he was in the service of a prince who at that moment was on bad terms with the Constantinopolitan Government? Or are we to detect in Liutprand's change of tone the reflexion of a general change for the worse in public feeling towards Orthodox Christendom throughout the Western World? In this connexion we may observe that Liutprand's Anti-Byzantinism, as he displayed it in A.D. 968, was not shared by all Liutprand's Western contemporaries. His own kinsmen, the Southern Lombards, continued to take kindly to Byzantine culture for at least another hundred years; and this was true *a fortiori* of those Italian communities—an Amalfi and a Naples and a Gaeta and a Ducatus Romanus—which had never fallen under Lombard rule. We have already noticed, in IV. C (iii) (*c*) 2 (β), p. 357, and in the present Annex, p. 600, above, the influence of Basilian monachism upon the religious life of the Ducatus Romanus of the tenth and eleventh centuries. The secular masters of Rome in the same age—the family of the Vestiarius Theophylact and their descendants the Crescentii and the Counts of Tusculum—were manifestly more 'Byzantine' than 'Transalpine' in their culture and their êthos. And even the Transalpine conquerors of Southern Italy came under the Byzantine spell from Otto II and Otto III to Frederick II inclusive.

[3] See, for example, Anna's account of the Western invention of the cross-bow, which

that time onwards until the latter part of the seventeenth century this antipathy persisted on both sides; but, as often happens, the weaker of the two parties to the relation made up for its physical impotence by the vehemence of its feelings.

Within less than a hundred years of Anna's day these feelings had risen to such a pitch of intensity on the Orthodox Christian side that, when the people secured an accomplice on the Imperial throne in the person of the disreputable Comnenus Andronicus I (*imperabat* A.D. 1182–85), they instantly indulged in a general massacre of all the Western residents in the East Roman dominions.[1] The feelings which had prompted this atrocity were naturally not assuaged by the prompt and savage reprisals that were taken by the Sicilian Normans and the Venetians; and the detestation of Western Christendom in the Orthodox Christian World was burnt into the souls of all later generations when Venetian diplomacy diverted 'the Fourth Crusade' from Palestine to Constantinople, with the result that in A.D. 1204 the Imperial City was captured and sacked, and the East Roman Empire itself partitioned, by a piratical gang of Latin military adventurers.

Thereafter a rabid Anti-Westernism became the master-passion of the Orthodox Christian Society; and this was the one field in which the otherwise discordant nations of Orthodox Christendom, who had wrecked their common civilization by their internecine strife,[2] could bring themselves to make common cause. The Latin conquerors of the East Roman Empire found, to their dismay and their undoing, that the Bulgars—who, after 167 years of political servitude, had successfully thrown off the East Roman yoke in A.D. 1186, only eighteen years before the Latin conquest of Constantinople—were as implacably hostile to the Western interlopers as were their Greek co-religionists. This spirit in Orthodox Christendom not only frustrated the efforts of East Roman statesmanship to achieve a *rapprochement* with the West during the two centuries that followed the Greek reoccupation of Constantinople in 1261; in the

has been cited in III. C (iii), vol. iii, pp. 385–6, above. In dealing with Western people, as distinct from Western things, Anna reserves the cream of her invective for bespattering the Normans, who had, of course, surpassed all other Westerners up to date in the amount of injury that they had inflicted upon the East Roman Empire (and who, for that matter, were hated just as intensely, and with just as good reason, by their own fellow Westerners, and Anna's fellow victims, the Southern Lombards and the English). At the same time Anna arraigns all Westerners, without distinction, for their egotism, self-conceit, loquacity, impulsiveness, inconstancy, and boorishness (see the *Alexiad*, *passim.*). Anna's contempt for the Western culture is vindicated by an *argumentum ad hominem* in her anecdote of the fighting priest (*Alexiad*, Book X, chap. 8).

1 This Near Eastern atrocity of the year 1182 of the Christian Era may be compared with the general massacre of all the Roman residents in Asia Minor in the year 88 B.C.: a similar act of popular fury which was likewise committed under the aegis of a political adventurer who in that episode was King Mithradates Eupator of Pontic Cappadocia (see V. C (i) (c) 2, vol. v, p. 69, below).

2 See IV. C (ii) (b) 2, p. 82, footnote 3, and IV. C (iii) (c) 2 (β), pp. 320–408, above.

same measure, it assisted the contemporary efforts of Ottoman statesmanship to impose the boon of political unification upon Orthodox Christendom by force. After a long and intimate and painful experience of both the two neighbouring societies the Orthodox Christians found the Ottoman version of Islam less unpalatable than the Latin version of Christianity; and when, in the end, they were forced to make the choice between Latin patronage and Ottoman domination, they did not hesitate to choose the latter as the lesser evil. The Greek grandee who declared in A.D. 1453, when Mehmed the Conqueror's hand was already raised above Constantinople to deliver the *coup de grâce*, that 'the turban of the Prophet' was preferable to 'the tiara of the Pope',[1] was accurately expressing in his mordant epigram the sentiments of all his co-religionists—Bulgars and Serbs and Rumans, as well as Greeks—who were now in the act of being united with each other, and divorced from the Christians of the West, through the triumph of a non-Christian Power.

Thus, from the eleventh century onwards, popular feeling fought potently on the side of the Orthodox Church in its contest with the East Roman Imperial Government over the capital question of Orthodox Christian relations with the West; but the Church's eventual victory over the East Roman State was not solely due to the support of this external ally in this part of the battle-field. The Church eventually established its ascendancy over the State not only in the matter of relations with the West but along the whole front on a battle-field that extended over almost every province of life; and this general change to the Church's advantage in the Balance of Power between Church and State must be ascribed to an intrinsic strengthening of the Church—both in organization and in *moral*—which began in the twelfth century[2] and continued thereafter.

When the Comnenian Dynasty (*imperabant* A.D. 1081–1185)[3] temporarily rallied the East Roman Empire[4] from the shock which

[1] Gibbon, Edward: *The History of the Decline and Fall of the Roman Empire*, ch. lxviii, quoted already in I. B (iii), vol. i, p. 29, and in IV. C (ii) (*b*) 1, in the present volume, p. 71, above.

[2] At the turn of the eleventh and twelfth centuries the moral standing of the Orthodox Church had been low—the feebleness of the secular clergy being matched by the immorality of the regulars (for a careful yet vivid picture, see Oeconómos, L.: *La Vie Religieuse dans l'Empire Byzantin au Temps des Comnènes et des Anges* (Paris 1918, Leroux), chs. 6–9). The subsequent rally was heralded by the careers of Saint Christódhoulos and Bishop Eustathius.

[3] These are the dates of the continuous rule of the Comneni as East Roman Emperors at Constantinople. They do not include the reign of the forerunner Isaac Comnenus (*imperabat* A.D. 1057–9), who stands to his Comnenian successors as the Holy Roman Emperor Rudolf of Hapsburg stands to the later Hapsburg wearers of the Western Imperial Crown. Again, these dates do not include the reigns of those scions of the Comnenian House who ruled at Trebizond over a local 'successor-state' of the East Roman Empire from A.D. 1204 to A.D. 1462.

[4] For this rally see further V. C (ii) (*b*), vol. vi, p. 298, below.

it had received in the middle of the eleventh century through the simultaneous assaults of the Normans and the Saljūqs, they duly re-asserted the Imperial Government's 'Caesaro-papal' pretensions;[1] but this was not the leading note of the relations between State and Church in the new age. The forerunner of the new dynasty, Isaac Comnenus, had recompensed the Patriarch Michael Cerularius for his good offices in hoisting Isaac on to the Imperial Throne by transferring to the Patriarchate in perpetuity certain important rights of patronage and administration in ecclesiastical affairs which had hitherto been retained in the Imperial Government's hands. The *Restitutor Imperii*, Alexius I, himself made a momentous new departure, tantamount to an abandonment of 'Caesaro-papism' in principle, when he conceded civil as well as ecclesiastical autonomy to the Basilian monastic communities on the peninsula of Athos[2] and the island of Patmos;[3] and at Athos this concession in principle obtained its full practical effect when the supervisory control over the monastic federal republic, which Alexius I Comnenus had retained in his own Imperial hands, was transferred to the hands of the Oecumenical Patriarch[4] by the Emperor Andronicus II Palaeologus (*imperabat* A.D. 1282–1328).

The effect of Alexius's and Andronicus's generosity upon the fortunes of the Orthodox Church is comparable to the advantage which the Papacy secured in the West through the donations of Pepin and Charlemagne. 'The Holy Mountain', like 'the Holy See', became an inexpugnable stronghold from which the Church could confidently take the offensive against the Secular Power, in the knowledge that its opponent could never retaliate by cancelling the gift that it had irrevocably made. With Athos as their base of operations, a new party of 'Zealots' arose in the Orthodox Church in the course of the twelfth century, to do battle with the Photian-

[1] See Vasiliev, A. A.: *Histoire de l'Empire Byzantin* (Paris 1932, Picard, 2 vols.), vol. ii, pp. 121–2, and Oeconómos, L.: *La Vie Religieuse dans l'Empire Byzantin au Temps des Comnènes et des Anges* (Paris 1918, Leroux), chs. 4 and 6. The latter author gives chapter and verse for the view that 'les empereurs du xiie siècle ne furent pas à l'égard de leurs patriarches plus tolérants que leurs prédécesseurs. Bien au contraire, le chef de l'Église byzantine est alors subordonné au basileus plus complètement que jamais' (p. 104).

[2] The monastery of the Great Laura, which was the nucleus of the cluster of monasteries on the Athos Peninsula, had been founded by St. Athanasius, the spiritual director of Nicephorus Phocas the younger, in A.D. 961, when the peninsula had once more become a safe place for monks to inhabit thanks to Nicephorus's success in destroying the nest of Andalusian pirates in Crete.

[3] Vasiliev, op. cit., vol. ii, p. 124. For details of Alexius's act of cession of the island of Patmos to the would-be reformer of Basilian monachism, Saint Christódhoulos, see Oeconómos, op. cit., pp. 147–9, following the documents printed in Miklosich, F., and Müller, J.: *Acta et Diplomata Graeca Medii Aevi Sacra et Profana* (Vienna 1860–90, Gerold, 6 vols.), vol. vi, pp. 44–8.

[4] Saint Christódhoulos' abortive monastic republic on the island of Patmos had been expressly exempted from the Oecumenical Patriarch's control by the terms of the Emperor Alexius I's charter (Oeconómos, op. cit., p. 149). For the history of the Patmian experiment see also Hussey, op. cit., pp. 190–3.

minded 'politicals'.[1] And the outcome of the Emperor Andronicus's act of placing Athos under the authority of the Oecumenical Patriarchate *de jure* was to enable the Mountain and 'the Zealots' to capture the Patriarchate *de facto* and to retain their control over it in perpetuity.[2] This *union sacrée* between the prelates and the monks of the Orthodox Church against the East Roman Imperial Government and the Papacy was both a consequence and a cause of the Imperial Power's decay. It could hardly have been achieved if the hierarchy had not ceased to be subservient to the Emperors or if the monks, on their part, had not ceased to need the support of the Papacy in order to set the Emperors at defiance. At the same time this alliance of the prelates and the monks, under the leadership of the latter, notably increased the fighting power of the Orthodox Church Militant,[3] and proportionately decreased the Imperial Government's chances of carrying out a philo-Papal policy against the Orthodox Church's will.

Moreover, by that time the Patriarchate had at last established the right—for which it had fought so courageously against a Caesar Bardas and a Leo the Wise[4]—of censoring an Emperor's morals. In A.D. 1262 Andronicus II's predecessor on the Imperial throne, the redoubtable re-conqueror of Constantinople Michael Palaeologus, had been excommunicated by the Patriarch Arsenius in punishment for his crime of blinding his political victim the ex-Emperor John Lascaris; and, when Michael made the traditional Imperial retort of proclaiming the presumptuous cleric's deposition, Arsenius refused to consider himself deposed. From his place of exile at Proconnesus he exerted a greater spiritual influence over the Emperor's Orthodox subjects than he had wielded when he was in material possession of the Patriarchal Throne at Nicaea and Constantinople; and his moral victory was commemorated in the name of the Arsenites: a new party in the Church, who stood for ecclesiastical independence of the Imperial authority in spiritual things. A similar independence of mind was displayed, in a different cause, by John Vekkos, a cleric who was Arsenius's younger contemporary and who first made himself prominent as an opponent of Michael Palaeologus's project for the Union of the Churches. On this account Vekkos was imprisoned by the Emperor; and although he became a convert to the Unionist cause and was promoted by

[1] Vasiliev, op. cit., vol. ii, pp. 354 seqq. A Western student who thinks in terms of his own history will be reminded of the controversy in France, some four hundred years later, between the Catholic League and the *Politiques*.

[2] Vasiliev, op. cit., vol. ii, p. 360.

[3] 'In matters of individual spiritual development, Emperor and secular clergy could only stand aside and share, or envy, the reverence which rich and poor alike gave to those monks whom they could recognize as holy men.'—Hussey, op. cit., p. 119.

[4] See pp. 597–9, above.

Michael to the Patriarchate in 1275, after the Union of Lyon, he proved the sincerity of his conversion when, in 1282, the Emperor Andronicus II revoked the Act of Union in deference to the prevailing current of feeling in Orthodox ecclesiastical circles. On this occasion Vekkos refused to abandon a cause which he had deliberately, and profitably, embraced, now that it had turned out to be unpopular; and he remained faithful to his Unionism until his death, thirteen years later, in prison.

In entrenching itself on Athos, and asserting itself in Constantinople, during the second, and culminating, phase of the Orthodox Christian 'Time of Troubles',[1] the Orthodox Church was equipping itself—no doubt unconsciously and unintentionally—for the task which was assigned to it by the great Ottoman statesman Mehmed the Conqueror. The ruthless Ottoman slayer and supplanter of the last of the East Roman Emperors not only gave a gracious investiture to a new Oecumenical Patriarch,[2] but proceeded to confer upon his creature Gennadius[3] a jurisdiction to which no incumbent of the Oecumenical Patriarchate would ever have dreamed of aspiring so long as an East Roman Emperor or a Bulgarian Tsar or a Serbian Despot still retained his throne.[4] The Pādishāh Mehmed made the Patriarch Gennadius his *millet-bāshȳ* for the *Millet-i-Rūm*, which, being interpreted,[5] means that he made him the deputy-shepherd of all the Pādishāh's *ra'īyeh* of the Orthodox Christian Faith throughout the Pādishāh's dominions. Thus, when the Ottoman Empire attained its widest extent during the century that opened with Mehmed II's reign, the Greek Patriarch of Constantinople found himself—no doubt to his own bewilderment—reinstated over his former Greek flock, given authority over them in civil and temporal affairs, and empowered to exercise the same authority over his Greek subjects' Bulgar and Serb and Ruman and Greek and Arab co-religionists in the ecclesiastical domains of his own peers: the Patriarchs of Alexandria and Jerusalem and Antioch, the President of the Autocephalous Church of the Greek island of Cyprus, the Patriarch of Bulgaria, and the autonomous archbishops of Ochrida and Peč.[6] At this moment of simultaneous

[1] For this relapse see V. C (ii) (b), vol. vi, pp. 298–9, below.

[2] See V. C (ii) (a), vol. vi, p. 203, footnote 4, below.

[3] Gennadius was at this time the leader of the Anti-Unionist party in the Orthodox Church. Before taking his monastic vows he had been prominent, under his secular name of George Scholarius, as the private secretary of the Emperor John VIII Palaeologus and a supporter of the Union. He had been converted to the Anti-Unionist persuasion by Mark of Ephesus, who had been the leading 'Die-Hard' at Ferrara and Florence.

[4] This point has been touched upon by anticipation in IV. C (iii) (c) 2 (β), p. 346, footnote 2, above.

[5] For the Ottoman social and political system see Part III. A, vol. iii, pp. 22–50, above.

[6] For the restoration of the 'autocephaly' of Peč (*Turcicè* Ipek) by Sultan Suleymān's Serb-born Grand Vizier, Mehmed Sököllü, in A.D. 1557, see Part III. A, vol. iii,

exaltation and abasement the Patriarchate of Constantinople at last justified the title of 'Oecumenical', which it had assumed nearly a thousand years before,[1] by effectively exercising at least a civil jurisdiction over the Orthodox Church throughout the World.[2]

It will be seen that, in a sense, the fortunes of the Oecumenical Patriarchate were made by the Ottoman conquest of the main body of Orthodox Christendom in the fourteenth and fifteenth centuries, somewhat as the fortunes of the Papacy had been made, a thousand years earlier, by the barbarian conquest of the Latin provinces of the Roman Empire in the fourth and fifth centuries of the Christian Era. During the intervening millennium the Papacy had first slowly built up an oecumenical dominion over Western Christendom and had then slowly lost the pre-eminent position that it had previously gained.[3] It is curious to observe that the Oecumenical Patriarchate's belated rise approximately coincides, stage by stage, with the Papacy's decline and fall. The Oecumenical Patriarch Arsenius (*fungebatur* A.D. 1255–67), who brought the East Roman Emperor Michael VIII Palaeologus to a moral Canossa, was not far from being the contemporary of Pope Boniface VIII (*fungebatur* A.D. 1294–1303), at whose expense the spell of Papal invincibility was so brutally broken by Philip the Fair of France. The rise of 'the Zealots', and of Athos, was contemporaneous with 'the Babylonish Captivity' and the Great Schism; and the triumph of the secular power of the 'Osmanlis, who brought the whole of the Orthodox Christian World under the Oecumenical Patriarch's authority, was quickly followed in the West by the establishment of those modern parochial sovereign Powers that have now broken the Papal *Respublica Christiana* into fragments

p. 40, footnote 1, above. The Greek imperialism of the Phanariots (see II. D (vi), vol. ii, pp. 222–8, above) procured the abolition of Sököllü's Serb Patriarchate of Peč in A.D. 1766; and in 1767 this Greek ecclesiastical triumph was crowned by the abolition of the West Bulgarian Archbishopric of Ochrida (Gibb, H. A. R., and Bowen, H.: *Islamic Society and the West*, vol. i (Oxford 1939, University Press), ch. 14). The Arabophone Orthodox community had long since felt the weight of a Greek ecclesiastical tyranny that was backed by the irresistible force of the Ottoman Government's political and military power. After the conquest of the metropolitan provinces of the Arabic World by Sultan Selīm I (see I. C (i) (*b*), Annex I, vol. i, pp. 387–8, and IV. C (iii) (*c*) 3 (α), in the present volume, pp. 450–2, above) the first Orthodox Patriarch of Jerusalem who was a Modern Greek in nationality, Germanos II (*accessit* A.D. 1518: see Bertram, Sir A., and Luke, H. C.: *Report of the Commission appointed by the Government of Palestine to inquire into the Affairs of the Orthodox Patriarchate of Jerusalem* (London 1921, Milford), p. 23), prohibited the acceptance of Arabophone postulants in Orthodox monasteries and thereby excluded the Arabophones from all possibility of ever becoming bishops, since by this time it was one of the established conventions of the Orthodox Church that its bishops should be taken from the ranks of the regular clergy exclusively (Gibb and Bowen, op. cit., cap. cit.).

[1] See IV. C (iii) (*c*) 2 (β), p. 333, above.

[2] The whole of the Russian Church remained under the ecclesiastical jurisdiction of the Oecumenical Patriarchate from the conversion of Russia to Orthodox Christianity at the close of the tenth century (see II. D (vii), vol. ii, pp. 352–3, above) down to the establishment of the autonomous Patriarchate of Moscow in A.D. 1582–9.

[3] See IV. C (iii) (*c*) 3 (β), pp. 512–84, above.

ANNEX III TO IV. C (iii) (*c*) 2 (β)

PAULICIANS, BOGOMILS, CATHARS

Any religious community which has been branded as 'heretical' has suffered, *ex hypothesi*, the misfortune that has overtaken the Boeotians and the Philistines.[1] Its reputation has come to be at the mercy of victorious adversaries whose victory has been so complete that it has enabled them not only to stamp out, or keep under, the discomfited sect, but also to make sure that its features shall be known to Posterity through no other picture than the victors' own hostile and malevolent caricature. This was the fate of the Paulicians, until an authentic and original, though mutilated, liturgical book of the Paulician Church—*The Key of Truth*—was discovered[2] in 1891, and published in 1898, by an English scholar.[3] Dr. Conybeare's edition of this text has thrown a wholly new light upon the character and history of a movement which both fascinated and puzzled Gibbon;[4] and his introduction is a monument of scholarship and a mine of erudition—though it is unfortunately marred by an *odium theologicum* against the 'Incarnationist' (i.e. 'Conceptionist') persecutors of this 'Adoptionist' Church.[5]

From Dr. Conybeare's researches it would appear that the Paulician community was a piece of jetsam that had been deposited in the folds of the Taurus and Anti-Taurus Ranges[6] by an archaic 'Adoptionist' wave of Christianity which preceded the 'Conceptionist' wave in spreading outwards from a common centre of dispersion in Syria[7] but which was overtaken and obliterated by the pursuing wave on every sector of their common circular field of expansion except for one or two points where the jetsam cast up by the earlier wave was preserved high and dry in some mountain

[1] See II. D (ii), vol. ii, p. 50, above.

[2] The manuscript of *The Key of Truth* had been lodged in 1837 in the archives of the Holy Synod of the Gregorian Monophysite Armenian Church at Echmiadzin, after having been confiscated from a group of Paulician Armenians who had migrated from the Ottoman to the Russian side of the Russo-Turkish frontier in Transcaucasia after the Russo-Turkish War of 1828–9.

[3] Conybeare, F. C.: *The Key of Truth: A Manual of the Paulician Church of Armenia*: the Armenian text edited and translated with illustrative documents and introduction (Oxford 1898, Clarendon Press).

[4] See Gibbon, Edward: *The History of the Decline and Fall of the Roman Empire*, ch. liv.

[5] In places, Dr. Conybeare's animus almost equals that which was once displayed by this latter-day Western scholar's 'Incarnationist' *bêtes noires* against their ancient 'Adoptionist' victims whom he has so chivalrously taken under his wing and so romantically idealized.

[6] For other religious survivals in these secluded highlands see II. D (vi), vol. ii, pp. 257–8, above.

[7] For this primitive 'Adoptionist' version of Christianity see Meyer, E.: *Ursprung und Anfänge des Christentums*, vol. iii (Stuttgart and Berlin 1923, Cotta), pp. 236–8.

fastness.[1] On the opposite edge of the field, 'Adoptionism' found another fastness in the mountains of Asturia, in the remote north-west of the Iberian Peninsula.[2] Dr. Conybeare hazards the speculation that another relic of 'Adoptionist' Christianity may be found in the Far Western Church of 'the Celtic Fringe', and that the irreconcilability of an 'Adoptionist' with a 'Conceptionist' Christology may have been the real stumbling-block in the way of a good understanding between the Church of St. Columba and the Church of Rome.[3]

The essence of the 'Adoptionist', as opposed to the 'Conceptionist', faith is a belief that Jesus was not born divine, but that in virtue of his human spiritual achievements and merits he was designated by God as the Son of God when, at the moment of his baptism, he was taken possession of by the Holy Spirit as a human vehicle for its divine activity.[4] This 'Adoptionist' Christology has been nobly formulated by the statesman-theologian Paul of Samosata, who was Patriarch of Antioch from A.D. 260 to A.D. 272 and from whom the Paulicians appear to have derived their name.[5]

'In fixity and resoluteness of character he likened himself to God, and, having kept himself free from sin, was united to God, and was empowered to grasp, as it were, the power and authority of wonders. By these he was shown to possess, over and above the will, one and the same activity [with God], and won the title of Redeemer and Saviour of our Race. . . .

'We do not award praise to beings which submit merely in virtue of their nature, but we do award high praise to beings which submit because their attitude is one of love—and, so submitting, because their inspiring motive is one and the same, they are confirmed and strengthened by one and the same indwelling power, of which the force ever grows, so

[1] For the phenomena of concentric waves of dispersion and fossils in fastnesses see II. D (vi), vol. ii, pp. 255–9, with Annex; and II. D (vii), vol. ii, pp. 361–93, above.

[2] For this Asturian 'Adoptionism' see Conybeare, op. cit., pp. clxx–clxxix. It was in the Iberian Peninsula that this form of Christianity assumed this name. For Asturia's historic role of serving as a fastness see II. D (vii), vol. ii, p. 362, footnote 4, and II. D (vii), Annex VIII, vol. ii, pp. 446–7, above, and V. C (i) (*c*) 3, vol. v, pp. 205–6, below.

[3] Conybeare, op. cit., pp. clxxix–clxxx. To a layman the evidence which Dr. Conybeare cites for this view may seem rather lacking in substance. Indeed, Dr. Conybeare is manifestly prone to espy suppressed and persecuted 'Adoptionists' everywhere. For the Far Western Church see II. D (vii), vol. ii, pp. 322–40, with Annexes II, III, and IV, above.

[4] The Christology which Dr. Conybeare calls 'Incarnationist' ought properly to be called 'Conceptionist', since it holds no monopoly of the fundamental Christian belief that God has been incarnate in the human personality of Jesus on Earth. The reality of the Incarnation is not denied by the 'Adoptionists'. The point on which these differ from the 'Conceptionists' is in regard to the moment in the human life of Jesus at which the Incarnation took place. According to Mark it took place, not at the moment of Jesus's conception in his mother's womb, but at the moment of his baptism by John in Jordan. This 'Adoptionist' Marcan Christology still shimmers through the 'Conceptionist' veneer with which it has been overlaid in the Gospels according to Saint Matthew and Saint Luke, and it is not contradicted in the Gospel according to Saint John (see further V. C (ii) (*a*), vol. vi, pp. 267–75, below).

[5] See p. 627, below.

that it never ceases to stir. It was in virtue of this love that the Saviour coalesced with God, so as to admit of no divorce from him, but for all ages to retain one and the same activity with him—an activity perpetually at work in the manifestation of good.'[1]

Holding this belief about the means by which a human Jesus became a Christ the Son of God, the 'Adoptionists' were led into the further belief that a human follower of Jesus who went through the same spiritual struggle under the inspiration of the same love might win the same guerdon if he were admitted to the same rite of baptism at the same age. The eighth-century 'Adoptionists' of Asturia were said to say 'Et ille Christus, et nos Christi';[2] and the dogma is elaborated in the *symbolum fidei* of their leader Elipandus: 'Si conformes sunt omnes sancti huic filio Dei secundum gratiam, profecto et cum adoptivo adoptivi, et cum advocato advocati, et cum Christo Christi'.[3] In the first half of the ninth century the great Paulician missionary in the East Roman Empire, Sergius, appears to identify himself with Christ in a passage from an alleged epistle of his which is quoted by the Greek Orthodox controversialists of the age.[4] One of the Paulician *émigrés* from Ottoman to Russian territory in 1837[5] deposed, in a recantation made to the authorities of the Gregorian Church, that he had heard a certain Gregory of Kalzwan, who was one of the Paulician adepts, say: 'Behold, I am the Cross; light your tapers on my two hands, and give worship. I am able to give you salvation, just as much as the Cross and the Saints.'[6]

This 'Adoptionist' version of Christianity was not only pre-'Conceptionist'; it was also pre-iconic, pre-hierarchical and pre-monastic. Arianism was a sophisticated version of it, Nestorianism a partial reversion to it, Iconoclasm an excerpt from it—an excerpt which was so ample in the Hyper-Iconoclasm of the Emperor Constantine V that Conybeare claims him as a Paulician in all but name.[7]

The name 'Paulician' proves, on philological analysis, to have been given to the sect by their opponents in an Armenian-speaking social milieu; for 'Paulician' is an Armenian adjectival form denot-

1 Passages quoted, from the surviving fragments of Paul of Samosata's *Discourses to Sabinus*, by F. C. Conybeare in *The Encyclopaedia Britannica*, eleventh edition, s.v. 'Paul of Samosata'.

2 Just as the adepts in the worship of Osiris became Osirides (see I. C (ii), vol. i, p. 143, above) and the Bacchanals Bacchi. This notion is less repugnant to the Orthodox than it is to the Western branch of the Catholic Church. For deification (θέωσις) as the goal of Orthodox Christian mysticism see Hussey, J. M.: *Church and Learning in the Byzantine Empire, 867–1185* (Oxford 1937, University Press), chap. ii.

3 These passages are quoted by Conybeare, in op. cit., pp. clxxiii and clxxv, from the *Epistula Heterii et Sancti Beati ad Elipandum*, a Catholic attack on the heretic which was composed in A.D. 785.

4 Conybeare, op. cit., pp. li–lii.

5 See p. 624, footnote 2, above.

6 Conybeare, op. cit., pp. xxvii and lii.

7 Ibid., pp. xlii and cxvi–cxvii.

ing association with 'Paulik'; and 'Paulik' is a derogatory Armenian diminutive of 'Paul'. This depreciatory element in the formation of the word shows, further, that the Paul with whom the sect was thus insultingly associated cannot have been St. Paul the Apostle; and there is, in fact, positive evidence that they were named after Paul of Samosata. The derivation of their tenets from this third-century heresiarch is expressly asserted by the Byzantinized Armenian Gregory Magister[1] who persecuted the Paulicians of Armenia, on the East Roman Government's account, in the sixth decade of the eleventh century; and this testimony is borne out by a comparison of *The Key of Truth* with the authentic fragments of Paul of Samosata's doctrine that have survived. In short, the Paulicians were the spiritual descendants of the 'Pauliani' who were condemned by the Council of Nicaea in A.D. 325.[2]

One seventh-century Paulician missionary, however, seems to have been so little aware of the origin of the faith which he held and propagated that he accepted the abusive *sobriquet* which the sect had received from its enemies and proceeded to identify the Paul, to whom the sect was referred, with the Apostle himself. This Pauline Paulician was the Constantine who came from the North-East Armenian district of Mananalis (next door to the present village of Chaurm, which was the home of the Paulician *émigrés* of A.D. 1837)[3] and who founded a new branch of the Paulician Church in the Greek-speaking territory of the East Roman Empire in North-Eastern Anatolia, west of the Euphrates, in A.D. 660. This Constantine took the Pauline name of 'Silvanus', and he called his new church 'Macedonia'. His successors followed his example—four of them taking, respectively, the names of 'Titus', 'Timotheus', 'Epaphroditus', and 'Tychicus', and calling their new foundations 'Achaia', 'Philippi', 'Laodicea', 'Ephesus', and 'Colossae'.[4] This group of Paulician churches on East Roman ground is the best known part of the Paulician Church, because it was this group that came into collision with the East Roman Government in the ninth century and that propagated the faith in Europe. But this Pauline conceit appears to have been peculiar to them, and to have been unknown in the earlier home of the Paulician Church in the Armenian territories on the other side of the Euphrates.[5]

There is no other evidence that the Paulicians were especially devoted to the Apostle Paul, and there is no evidence at all that this alleged attachment to Paul led them (as their enemies averred)

[1] See the extracts from Gregory Magister's letters in Conybeare, op. cit., Appendix III.

[2] Conybeare, op. cit., pp. cv–cvi. [3] Ibid., pp. lxix–lxx.

[4] See J. B. Bury's *editio minor* of Gibbon's *The History of the Decline and Fall of the Roman Empire*, vol. vi, 2nd edition (London 1902, pp. Methuen), 112–13.

[5] Conybeare, op. cit., p. cxxix.

into displaying a hostility towards Peter. *The Key of Truth* merely declares that the Church rests on all the Twelve Apostles, and not on Peter alone;[1] and in the Paulician liturgy for the ordination of the elect, which is preserved in this book, the candidate appears actually to receive the ritual name of Peter at the hands of the officiant, as a sign that he has become, like his Apostolic namesake, a rock on which the Church is built and an authority empowered to bind and to loose.[2]

Again, the Paulicians were neither Marcionites (as certain modern scholars have conjectured) nor Manichaeans (as their contemporary Catholic opponents persistently asserted in order to defame them with an odious name).[3] Both the Greek and the Armenian Anti-Paulician controversialists testify that this sect, which they sought to brand as Manichaean, actually anathematized Mani;[4] and one of these Armenian theologians, the Gregorian Catholicus Nerses Shnorhali (*fungebatur* A.D. 1165–73), who attacks his Paulician contemporaries, also testifies to the existence, in his day, of genuine Manichees in Armenia who were quite separate from the Paulicians, and whom the Catholicus deals with in a different context.[5] The Paulician and the Manichaean Church resembled one another in being divided into two orders, and two only, of the *catechumeni* or *auditores* on the one hand and the *electi* or *perfecti* on the other, and also in making the *electus* an object of ritual adoration. But these common features are also to be found in other religions—e.g. the Orphic Faith—which may have been their common source; and the differences that they display are more striking: for example, the Manichaean *electi* were celibate, vegetarian ascetics of an Indic type, whereas the Paulician *electi* had to be married and to bring up children and to earn their own living, like other men.[6] The Paulicians were not only pre-monastic but were also anti-monastic; and we may reasonably trace to them the anti-monastic vein in the Iconoclasm of Leo III and Constantine V. The only evidence that the Paulicians—or the Bogomils or the Cathars—were Manichaeans, in the sense of holding dualistic views of a Zoroastrian type, comes from the mouth of their enemies;[7] and this evidence must be heavily discounted, since these enemies, having once branded them with the Manichaean name, would very readily attribute to them, *a priori*, all the tenets which the authentic Manichaeans were recorded to have held.[8] As a matter of fact, in the crucial field of

1 Conybeare, op. cit., p. cxxx. 2 Ibid., pp. xxxvii, xxxix, and cxliii–cxliv.

3 Ibid., p. cxxx. 4 Ibid., pp. xlv and cxxxi.

5 See Conybeare, op. cit., p. cxxxii, with the quotations from Nerses in Appendix V.

6 Conybeare, op. cit., pp. cxxiii and cxxxi. 7 Ibid., pp. xlv–xlvi.

8 'Orthodox Christians often used the word "Manichaean" to describe heretics whose doctrines were imperfectly understood but seemed to impugn the goodness of God or the salvability of the human body. The Bogomils of Bulgaria, the "Cathari" and

Christology the authentic Manichees stood much nearer to the Catholics than to the Paulicians, as appears from *The Acts of Archelaus*, a controversial theological dialogue purporting to have been held in the eighth decade of the third century between Mani and a certain Archelaus who is described as being the Bishop of Kashkar in Lower 'Irāq. In this dialogue the 'Conceptionist' position is maintained by the founder of the Manichaean Faith, while his Christian opponent maintains the 'Adoptionist' position which was afterwards the cardinal tenet of the Paulicians.[1]

Finally, we can discard the conjecture that either the seventh-century 'Adoptionism' of the Armenian Constantine of Mananalis or the eighth-century 'Adoptionism' of the Spaniard Elipandus of Toledo was a direct and deliberate reaction of the local Christian Church to the impact of Islam. On this view 'Adoptionism' was a post-Muhammadan movement which was designed to keep the

"Patarenes" of Lombardy, and above all the Albigensians, have often been called Manichees in ancient and modern times. It is likely that fragments of their teaching were really derived from Manichaean sources. But, now that we have so much more exact knowledge of what the Religion of the Manichees really was, I think it misleading to call these sects, even the Albigensians, by the name of Manichees. In any case it is hazardous to use Albigensian material to illustrate the religion we are studying.'—Burkitt, F. C.: *The Religion of the Manichees* (Cambridge 1925, University Press), pp. 11–12.

'Catholic writers, convinced that the Albigenses were Manichaeans, were content to go to the works of Saint Augustine against the Manichaeans and to attribute indiscriminately to the Albigenses all the errors enumerated in those pages. Such a procedure, not necessarily adopted in any spirit of conscious unfairness, was so obviously unscientific that it makes it difficult to use the evidence of these writers with any confidence.'—Turberville, A. S., in *The Cambridge Medieval History*, vol. vi (Cambridge 1929, University Press), p. 699.

'After the close of the twelfth century the Catholic polemics against the heresy laid their principal emphasis upon . . . the heretics' dualistic speculations and upon the outgrowth of these—the more eagerly because in these questions Catharism was least able to justify itself by [its favourite argument of] appealing to the New Testament. This exercised such a persistent influence on subsequent views about the heresy that, ever afterwards, this dualism was assumed to be the heresy's kernel and foundation, and all the other tenets were disposed of as mere corollaries of this one. In reality, however, down to the end of the twelfth century, it is not the speculative problems of dualism, but invariably the questions of the religious life and of the Church that are at the heart of the controversy between Heresy and Catholicism. At the first appearance of the heresy in the West, in the first half of the eleventh century, its tenets include, so far as we know, no dualistic doctrines whatsoever. Nevertheless the Catholic literature on the subject styles the heretics "Manichaeans" from the outset. And this practice has often seduced the ecclesiastical polemists into looking up, in the works of Augustine, what the teaching of the Manichaeans was, and then simply ascribing this teaching to the heretics of the writers' own time. [In a footnote the author cites examples of this practice—A.J.T.] Where this is not the case—where, that is to say, we can be certain, beyond possibility of mistake, that our source is reproducing the genuine convictions and teaching of the contemporary heresy—and more especially in all official ecclesiastical documents dealing with the heresy question, there is either no trace at all of dualistic speculations, or else these speculations retire quite into the background.'—Grundmann, H.: *Religiöse Bewegungen im Mittelalter* (Berlin 1935, Ebering), pp. 24–5. Cf. p. 17.

[1] For *The Acts of Archelaus* see Conybeare, op. cit., pp. xcvii–civ. There seems to be some uncertainty about the location of the bishopric that is attributed to Archelaus in this work. If it is the city and district in Lower 'Irāq which are known as Kashkar in Syriac and as Kaskar in Arabic, then the scene of the dialogue has been laid next door to Mani's home-country, Mesene. If, on the other hand, Archelaus's see is, as Conybeare suggests, to be found, not in Lower 'Irāq, but in Middle Kurdistan, at Kharkar (not Kashkar), this would be not so far from Paul of Samosata's see of Antioch.

Christian flock within the fold by revising certain features of the Christian Faith which were particularly vulnerable under a Muslim attack. The theory, however, is decisively refuted by two facts. In the first place the 'Adoptionist' Christology, so far from being post-Muhammadan, is, as we have seen, pre-Nicene, and it can be detected in so early a Christian document as *The Shepherd of Hermas*. In the second place the Primitive Muslim Arab conquerors were not concerned to convert their Christian subjects and neighbours outside the limits of Arabia itself. In their non-Arabian dominions they preferred to keep the non-Muslim 'People of the Book' as supertax-payers, rather than convert them at the expense of the public revenues of the Caliphate.[1] Hence the pastors of the Christian flock in or near the Arab Empire were under no pressure at that time to forestall a threatened secession of Christians to Islam by revising their Christology in an Islamic direction. So far as there is any resemblance between the Islamic and the Paulician Christology, this is to be traced to the influence, upon Islam, of Nestorianism; for Nestorianism was a partial reversion to the 'Adoptionist' position which the Paulicians had never abandoned. In so far as Islam did influence the fortunes of the surviving remnant of the 'Adoptionist' Church, this influence was unintentional and indirect.

In both its Armenian and its Spanish fastness this archaic form of Christianity was stirred into fresh activity and dragged out into the light in the eighth century of the Christian Era through the accident that in that age both these fastnesses were violated. The highlands of the Taurus and Anti-Taurus now became a debatable borderland between the Arab Caliphate and the East Roman Empire,[2] while the highlands of Asturia came to play a similar role between the Caliphate and the Austrasian Frankish Power.[3] Therewith, two regions which had both hitherto lain secluded and ignored, far off from the main thoroughfares of the life of the World, rather suddenly acquired an unprecedented importance and notoriety as crucial war-zones and vital marches between contending empires;[4] and both the two resuscitated ghosts of the Roman Empire were thereby compelled to adopt a definite attitude towards the ancient form of their religion which they each now rediscovered on their respective Syriac frontiers. In these parallel circumstances the Austrasian and East Roman statesmen took opposite lines—Charlemagne lending his authority to an attempt to suppress the Asturian 'Adoptionist' Elipandus, while Leo Syrus—whose family came

1 See IV. C (iii) (*b*) 12, p. 226, above, and V. C (i) (*d*) 6 (δ), Annex, vol. v, pp. 674–7, below.
2 See IV. C (iii) (*c*) 2 (β), p. 365, footnote 4, above.
3 See II. D (vii), Annex VIII, in vol. ii, above.
4 For the literary consequences see V. C (i) (*c*) 3, vol. v, pp. 252–61, below.

from Germanicea,[1] next door to the birthplace of Paul of Samosata —apparently drew inspiration from the remnant of the 'Adoptionist' Church in the Anti-Taurus for launching a new religious movement of his own which he attempted to impose by force upon Orthodox Christendom.

The outcome of this encounter between Paulicianism and Orthodoxy, which began with the opening of Leo's iconoclastic campaign in A.D. 726 and ended with the collapse of the Paulician Republic of Tephrice between A.D. 871 and 875, has been touched upon already in the present volume.[2] In this Annex it only remains to support the statement, which has been made in the same place,[3] that the Cathars of Lombardy and Languedoc, as well as the Bogomils of Bulgaria and Bosnia, were direct offshoots of the Asiatic Paulician Church.

The substantial identity of the Paulician, the Bogomil, and the Cathar faith is not in doubt. The common features are too similar and too numerous to be explained away as fortuitous,[4] and it is clear that we are in the presence of a single religion masquerading under different names in different places. The only question at issue is whether the Bogomils and the Cathars were European converts of the Paulicians—which would mean that they only became 'Adoptionists' in an age posterior to the transplantation of Paulician *émigrés* from the regions of Malatīyah and Erzerum to Thrace in A.D. 756 (or 755)[5]—or whether they were respectively descended from local 'Adoptionists', which would mean that their 'Adoptionism' was as ancient as that of the Paulicians themselves and that they were separate and independent relics of the same archaic pre-Nicene wave of Christian propaganda.

This second view is advocated by Dr. Conybeare;[6] and the opinion of a scholar who is a past-master in this subject is evidently entitled to the greatest respect. Yet a layman may perhaps hazard the opinion that on this point Dr. Conybeare's scholarship has been

1 See III. C (ii) (*b*), vol. iii, p. 274, footnote 2, above.

2 See IV. C (iii) (*c*) 2 (β), pp. 364–6, above.

3 In IV. C (iii) (*c*) 2 (β), pp. 366–9, above.

4 For example, the Albigenses and their contemporary co-religionists in the Rhineland not only made the *electus* an object of ritual adoration (see Conybeare, op. cit., pp. lv–lvii and cxxxiv–cxxxv); they also conferred the ritual name of Peter upon the recipient of their rite of *consolamentum* (see Conybeare, op. cit., pp. cxliii and clxv).

5 Theophanes, who reports this transplantation *sub anno mundi* 6247 (= A.D. 756 or 755), observes that it resulted in a diffusion of the Paulician heresy. It was, indeed, to be expected that these *émigrés* would include a considerable number of Paulicians, since the migration was evidently *en masse*, while the regions from which the settlers came all lay within the triangle between Samosata (the home of Paul), Manalalis (the home of Constantine-Silvanus), and Colonea (the field of Constantine-Silvanus's missionary labours). Theophanes does not tell us whether there were any Paulicians as well as Monophysites among 'the heretic Syrians' whose deportation to, and settlement in, Thrace he records *sub anno mundi* 6270 (= A.D. 778) (see IV. C (iii) (*c*) 2, p. 367, footnote 5, above).

6 Conybeare, op. cit., pp. cxlvi–cl and cxcvi.

biased by his *odium theologicum*. He has formed a mental picture of the 'Incarnationist' (i.e. 'Conceptionist') Catholic Church as an oppressive institution with a precarious tenure—holding down, temporarily and by force, an older 'Adoptionist' Christianity which has not only been the first in the field everywhere but has also managed everywhere to hold its ground and to reassert itself against its oppressor in the fullness of time. This picture shows up the Catholic Church as a usurper without legitimate title, and reveals the latent 'Adoptionist' Church as the true heir of the Primitive Church Universal.[1] The undisguised pleasure which Dr. Conybeare takes in this view of the history of Christianity gives his readers cause to suspect that he may have unconsciously pushed the evidence in support of it rather farther than it will really go. A case in point is his attempt to claim the Celtic Church[2] as a part of his ubiquitous 'Adoptionist' Church; and the *reductio ad absurdum* of the view is the suggestion[3] that the Bogomils of Bulgaria may have been descended from the local 'Adoptionists' of the Balkan Peninsula, instead of being converts of the Asiatic Paulicians[4] who are known to have been planted on the Bulgarian frontier of the East Roman Empire in A.D. 756 (or 755) by Constantine V, to have been reinforced in the eighth decade of the tenth century by John Tzimisces, and to have survived at Philippopolis—where John Tzimisces had planted them—till the eighteenth century.[5] On the eve of the collapse of the Paulician Republic of Tephrice, its indomitable citizens were planning to enter into competition with the Church of Constantinople and the Church of Rome for the spiritual conquest of Bulgaria—according to the testimony of a Greek witness, Petrus Siculus, who spent nine months at Tephrice in A.D. 870[6]—and we can hardly doubt that

1 'The Adoptionist Church remained one and undivided, and was unaffected by the scission of East and West. . . . Thenceforward the only real union of East and West was a union of heresy or heresies, and the only bond between the great persecuting churches was their common hatred of the persecuted sects. There continued after the fourth century the same unrestricted intercourse between the Adoptionists of the West and those of the East as there had been up to that age' (Conybeare, op. cit., p. 126). Here, surely, we can see the critical scholar changing, before our eyes, into the pious composer of an edifying legend.

2 See p. 625, above.

3 In op. cit., p. cxcvi.

4 For the relation between the Asiatic Paulicians and the Bogomils see IV. C (iii) (c) 2 (β), pp. 367–8, above.

5 For the survival of Paulicians (not Bogomils) at Philippopolis Dr. Conybeare himself (op. cit., pp. cxxxviii–cxxxix) cites a letter of Lady Mary Wortley Montague's, dated Adrianople, 1st April, 1717. The Emperor Alexius I Comnenus (*imperabat* A.D. 1081–1118) had found the descendants of John Tzimisces' Paulician deportees ensconced in Philippopolis cheek-by-jowl with a community of Bogomils and another community of Armenian Monophysite Christians (possibly descended from the deportees of A.D. 778); and he had made a determined attempt to convert them to Orthodox Christianity—but this without success, though he had resorted to force when argument had proved of no avail (Anna Comnena: *Alexias*, Book XIV, chs. 8–9). The same emperor was equally unsuccessful in a subsequent attempt to convert the Bogomils (Anna Comnena, op. cit., Book XV, chs. 9–10).

6 See Petrus Siculus: *Historia Manichaeorum seu Paulicianorum*, ad init. et ad fin. (cited in IV. C (iii) (c) 2 (β), p. 367, footnote 6, above).

the Bogomil Church is a monument of the successful execution of this project, which the Paulicians who were already established in Thrace were doubtless able to expedite. The debatable case is that of the Albigenses; for, even if there is no evidence for the existence of a primitive 'Adoptionist' Church in Gaul, the existence of 'Adoptionism' in the North of Spain in the latter part of the eighth century is well attested; and on *a priori* geographical grounds it would, no doubt, seem more credible that the twelfth-century 'Adoptionism' of Languedoc should be derived from eighth-century Spain than that it should have to be traced all the way across Europe and Asia Minor to eighth-century Armenia. Nevertheless there are certain pieces of evidence—and these are placed in our hands by the conscientious scholarship of Dr. Conybeare himself—which do suggest that the more remote derivation is the true one.

For instance, we find some German representatives of a school of heretics who, 'having taken their rise in Gascony, from some unknown author, had multiplied like the sand of the sea in France, Spain, Italy and Germany', being convicted at Oxford in A.D. 1160 under the name of *Publicani*; in 1179, again, the *Publicani* are condemned, by name, by the Third Lateran Council, and are expressly identified with the Albigenses, Cathari, and Patarini; and this word *Publicani* is simply a Latinization of *Pauliciani* in its contemporary Greek pronunciation.[1] Now the name 'Paulicians' does not seem to have attached to the eighth-century Spanish 'Adoptionists', or even to the Armenian Paulicians east of the Euphrates, who are called Thonraketzi (i.e. inhabitants of the district of Thonrak) by their Gregorian compatriots. The name only attaches with certainty to the North-East Anatolian followers of Constantine of Mananalis; and we may fairly infer that, if the name of this Anatolian 'Adoptionist' community is borne, five centuries after Constantine's time, by the twelfth-century 'Adoptionist' Church in Languedoc, then the 'Adoptionist' Faith itself, as well as its Asiatic title, must have come to the valley of the Garonne from the valley of the Euphrates.

There is also a piece of etymological evidence for the passage of the Cathar Faith from Tephrice to Albi via the valley of the Maritsa; for in medieval France the popular term of abuse for the Cathars

[1] Conybeare, op. cit., pp. cxxxix–cxl. Dr. Conybeare suggests (op. cit., p. cxlvii) that in the latter part of the twelfth century the Paulician name was learnedly applied to indigenous Gallic 'Adoptionists' by Western Catholic divines who had already come across the Paulicians in the Levant in consequence of the Crusades and who perceived that the two sects were identical in their beliefs. Such a discovery, however, is more in the line of a twentieth-century student of 'comparative religion' than in that of a twelfth-century inquisitor, and in fact the medieval Western adversaries of the Albigenses betray in their own polemics the haziness of their knowledge of the tenets which they were endeavouring to refute. (On this point see the present Annex, p. 628, footnote 8, above.)

—and, by analogy, for heretics in general—was *Bougres* (i.e. Bulgars).[1] And, apart from this presumptive evidence, we find a connexion between the Cathars of the West and the Bogomils of the Slavinias explicitly attested by contemporary Western observers. It is recorded, for example, that there were delegates from Bulgaria at a General Council which was held by the Cathars in the neighbourhood of Toulouse in A.D. 1167.[2] And this statement is reinforced by further evidence which dates from the thirteenth century, when, owing to the work of the Inquisition, the beliefs and practices and affiliations of the Cathars had come to be rather better known than they had been in the latter part of the twelfth century, when the existence of the sect in the West had first begun to attract attention. *Sub anno* 1223 Matthew Paris chronicles a report that the Albigenses paid allegiance to a Pope who lived on the confines of Bulgaria, Croatia, and Dalmatia;[3] and another Western writer, whose *floruit* was in the middle of the thirteenth century, states that the various Cathar churches of Europe—of which he gives a list ranging from Northern and Southern France and Northern and Central Italy to Slavonia and Constantinople—are all derived from the two parent churches of Bulgaria and 'Dugranicia' (? po-Granica, Krain, Carniola).[4] Conybeare seeks to explain this twelfth-century association by the hypothesis that by this time the ancient 'Adoptionist' churches of Western and South-Eastern Europe, having now each emerged from their respective lurking-places, had recognized and joined hands with one another. But this hypothesis does not explain how it was that the West European Cathars had come, not only to admit their kinship with their brethren in the Balkans, but also to concede to the latter a primacy in the Faith. The natural explanation of this fact is that which is given by the contemporary Western authorities for it, who explain it by telling us that the Catharism of the Balkans was the *fons et origo* of Catharism in the West. We may therefore allow ourselves to believe, *pace* Dr. Conybeare, that the Western *Publicani* were really spiritual descendants of the Anatolian Paulicians through the Balkan Bogomils.

1 Turberville, A. S., in *The Cambridge Medieval History*, vol. vi (Cambridge 1929, University Press), p. 702.

2 Turberville, loc. cit.

3 Conybeare, op. cit., p. cxlvii.

4 Ibid., p. cxlviii.

ANNEX TO IV. C (iii) (*c*) 2 (γ)

IDOLATRY AND PATHOLOGICAL EXAGGERATION.[1]

It is a commonplace that idolatry, in the narrower technical sense, runs to pathological exaggerations of which the legendary sacrifice of Iphigenia in Aulis—*tantum religio potuit suadere malorum*[2]—and the authentic ritual of human sacrifice in Mexico[3] and procession of Juggernaut's car in Bengal are three classic examples. The same tendency can be observed in a number of other manifestations of idolatry in the broader sense in which the term is used in this Study; and this wider range of the same phenomenon is worth glancing at, because idolatry is one of those things whose essence is illuminated, and not obscured, by caricature.

As our point of departure, we may take a passage from the pen of Monsieur Bergson:

'Is Primitive Humanity accurately mirrored in the "primitives" who are under our observation to-day? That seems improbable, since among them, as among ourselves, Nature is covered by a thick layer of habits which have been preserved by the social milieu and which are deposited by it in each individual. There is reason, however, to believe that this layer is here not so thick as it is in Civilized Man, and that it allows Nature to show through more transparently. The multiplication of habits in the course of centuries must, indeed, have operated among the primitives in a different way—operated, that is, on the surface, by a passage from analogue to analogue, and under the influence of accidental circumstances, in contrast to the progress of technique or of knowledge or, in short, of civilization—a progress which continues in some one single direction over quite long periods, and which is not superficial but cumulative, inasmuch as it is produced by variations which are superposed upon, or dovetailed into, one another, and which accordingly result in profound transformations and not just in superficial elaborations. . . .

'It must not be forgotten that the primitives of to-day or yesterday have lived through just as many centuries as we have, and that they have thus had plenty of time to exaggerate—or, as one might put it, to exacerbate—whatever irrational elements there may have been in primitive tendencies which, in themselves, were natural enough. The true primitives were almost certainly more sensible, if [we may assume that] they kept within the limits of the tendency and of its immediate effects. [But] everything is subject to change, and, as we have stated above, the change will take place on the surface if it cannot work down into the depths.

1 This Annex has a bearing on IV. C (iii) (*b*) 1, above, as well as on the chapter to which it has been attached.

2 Lucretius, *De Rerum Natura*, Book I, l. 101.

3 See the ghastly description in Frazer, J. G.: *The Golden Bough*, 3rd edition, part vi: *The Scapegoat* (London 1913, Macmillan), ch. 7.

There are societies which progress . . . and the change here takes the form of an increase in intensity: its direction is relatively constant, and the movement is towards an ever higher degree of efficiency. On the other side there are societies which [just] keep their level— and this, necessarily, a low one. Since these societies [likewise] change all the same, there occurs in them something which is no longer the intensification implied in qualitative progress, but is a multiplication or exaggeration of what has been there to start with. In this domain, invention—if the word is still applicable—no longer demands effort. A belief which once responded to a need leads to a new belief which bears an external resemblance to its predecessor and accentuates some one of its superficial characteristics, but which no longer serves any purpose. Thenceforward the society marks time, adding and amplifying incessantly. Through the twofold operation of repetition and exaggeration, irrationality turns into absurdity, and oddness into monstrosity.'[1]

The pathological exaggeration which is here presented to us by a modern Western philosopher as the characteristic penalty of an infatuation with a particular phase of human social life, displays itself in general in two variant forms. The simpler form is a sheer augmentation of size; the slightly more sophisticated form is an unhealthy exaggeration of characteristic features. The augmentation of size may take place in either one or two or three dimensions.

A hideous illustration of the one-dimensional augmentation is the immoderate growth of a rat's tooth upon the loss of the corresponding tooth, in the opposite jaw, which normally grinds, and is ground by, it. If this natural check is removed, the tooth that no longer has an 'opposite number' to keep it within bounds will proceed to grow *ad infinitum* until it has tortured its wretched owner to death by first making it impossible for him to close his mouth and then, if it is a lower-jaw tooth, transfixing his palate and piercing his brain.

The human analogue of this super-toothed rat is the Macedonian phalangite, whose pike (*sarisa*), like the rat's tooth,[2] ran incontinently to length as soon as it was left without any 'opposite number' to keep its elongation within reasonable limits. The virtue of this Macedonian pike lay in its outranging the Theban or Spartan spear without outweighing this advantage by simultaneously reducing the mobility of the pikeman;[3] and for this purpose the mini-

[1] Bergson, H.: *Les Deux Sources de la Morale et de la Religion* (Paris 1932, Alcan), pp. 133 and 143; cf. pp. 171 and 182.

[2] For the conception of human tools as detachable limbs, or of animal limbs as undetachable tools, see Part III. A, vol. iii, pp. 79–88, and III. C (i) (c), vol. iii, p. 177, above.

[3] The Spartan hoplite's spear was the longest weapon that could be manipulated with one hand, and used for stabbing, over the rim of the large round shield with which the hoplite's other hand was occupied. The Macedonian phalangite was able to manipulate a pike that outranged this Spartan spear because he gave both hands to it at the price of diminishing his defensive equipment by contenting himself with a small round target

classic example is the difference which we observe between the diverse peoples and castes of India. We admire the Gurkhas more than the Kashmiris, and the Rājputs more than the Bengalis; and this is not just a prejudice which can be accounted for by our peculiar relation to our Indian fellow subjects; for, by the same token, we admire Colonel Newcome more than Jos. Sedley. There is, indeed, an old-fashioned type of English military or naval officer—nice in his sense of honour, considerate to his fellow human beings, and kind to animals (though he enjoys killing them for sport!)—who has been regarded, for at least two centuries past, as one of the finest English products of our Western Christian Civilization. Nor can this admiration be dismissed with contempt as being naïve or snobbish. If we look into it seriously and with no *parti pris*, we shall assuredly be confirmed in our belief that it is deserved. For 'the military virtues' are not in a class apart; they are virtues which are virtues in every walk of life. Courage, which is the most prominent of them, is a cardinal virtue in every action to which a human being can set his hand—or hers; and the other virtues which we have ascribed to our legendary colonel or commodore are also patently legal tender in civil as well as in military life. Colonel Newcome and the Chevalier Bayard; Cœur-de-Lion and Roland; Olaf Tryggvason and Siegfried; Regulus and Leonidas; Partāp Singh and Prithīrāj; Jalāl-ad-Dīn Mankobirnī and 'Abdallah al-Battāl; Yoshitsune Minamoto and Kuang Yü: what a goodly company they are, and how large a place they fill in the historical landscape of these last five or six thousand years within which Mankind has embarked upon the enterprise of Civilization!

What are we to make of the vein in our social tradition which till yesterday was still inspiring heroes such as these and which to-day still moves the rest of us to admire them? If we wish to understand either the value of 'the military virtues' or the sincerity of the admiration which they win, we must take care to look at them in their native social setting; and one feature of this which is pertinent to our present inquiry leaps readily to the eye. 'The military virtues' are cultivated and admired in a milieu in which social forces are not sharply distinguished in people's minds from the non-human natural forces, and in which it is at the same time taken for granted that natural forces are not amenable to human control.

'Down to modern times, War was almost universally regarded as something which in itself required no justification. Its drawbacks and horrors were, indeed, recognised, but at worst it was considered an inevitable evil, a calamity, a scourge sent by God, of the same unavoidable nature as the plague.[1] To a community threatened by Vikings, or other aggressive neighbours, this was the obvious way to regard it. From the victim's point of view there *was* no distinction in principle between the sudden incursions of such people and those of a horde of locusts or a cloud of disease germs. But this made it all the more natural to admire and honour the prowess of an Alfred or a Charlemagne, who could protect his people from disaster in such circumstances. Down to modern times, though the justification for a particular war might be questioned, and its hardship realized, fighting was all in the day's work, an incident of human existence the abolition of which was hardly an imaginable possibility. In these circumstances, while few may have praised war, everyone valued the warrior, and submitted willingly to his leadership and control. Down to the nineteenth century the army was regarded as almost the only profession open to a gentleman, and a gentleman is "armiger".'[2]

The gentleman and scholar who has communicated these observations to the writer of this Study goes on, in the course of the same letter, to make an illuminating comparison between War and 'Sport'.

'In prehistoric times, before the domestication of animals, the hunter discharged a very necessary function in providing food. Surrounded by raiding barbarians, the soldier equally served to make life more tolerable and justice more capable of attainment. The finest men attached themselves to these pursuits, and their achievements were rightly honoured, and the same type of man tends to inherit their instincts with their qualities. This is why we prefer Colonel Newcomes to Jos. Sedleys. But their functions have become less necessary; in the case of the hunter, perhaps, entirely useless.'

The comparison is illuminating because, in the case of hunting, we see a pursuit which, at a primitive level of life, has been socially valuable and even vitally necessary becoming unquestionably superfluous at an early, and a frequently attained, stage of economic advance. At this stage the practice of hunting for a livelihood becomes transformed, perhaps usually by a gradual process of change, into an economically otiose 'sport'. On this analogy, can we posit a stage of social progress at which the practice of War in sheer self-defence against uncontrollable hostile forces becomes comparably transformed into a socially otiose 'Militarism'? On this analogy the sinister 'Militarism' which we can distinguish empirically from the innocent prowess of the happy warrior might perhaps be defined as a practice of War for War's sake when the

[1] 'Choose thee either three years' famine; or three months to be destroyed before thy foes, while that the sword of thine enemies overtaketh thee; or else three days the sword of the Lord, even the pestilence' (1 Chron. xxi. 11–12; cf. 2 Samuel xxiv. 12–13).

[2] Mr. G. M. Gathorne-Hardy in a letter to the present writer.

institution has ceased both to be, and to be regarded as being, a social necessity.

In our Western World in the so-called 'modern' chapter of its history we have seen War placed on the same shelf as hunting during an eighteenth-century 'lull' when War was only in vogue as 'the sport of kings'.[1] The bad name of 'militarist', which glances off the armour of a Cœur-de-Lion or a Bayard, is a Devil's cockade which sticks fast in the *tricorne* of a Charles XII or a Frederick the Great. The kings who took their sport on the Western battle-fields of that age were 'militarists' beyond question. Yet, in the light of our later experience, it has to be said in their favour that Frederick and his kind were not the most pernicious exponents of 'Militarism' that were to afflict our modern Western Society. Frederick, for example, would never have dreamed of glorifying War as it has been glorified in a classic passage from the pen of a later Prussian militarist, Hellmuth von Moltke.

> 'Perpetual Peace is a dream—and not even a beautiful dream—and War is an integral part (*ein Glied*) of God's ordering of the Universe (*Weltordnung*). In War, Man's noblest virtues come into play (*entfalten sich*): courage and renunciation, fidelity to duty and a readiness for sacrifice that does not stop short of offering up Life itself. Without War the World would become swamped in materialism.'[2]

In this extravagant eulogy of War there is a note of passion, of anxiety and of rancour which is a far cry from the urbane and philosophic scepticism of a Frederick the Great. So profound a change of tone is presumably the echo of comparably profound changes of temper and circumstance which had come over the Western World within the period of less than a hundred years that had elapsed between Frederick's death in A.D. 1786 and the year in which von Moltke wrote this letter to Bluntschli. We can observe two such changes which are of this magnitude.

By the time when our nineteenth-century Prussian militarist was an old man, the eighteenth-century cultivation of War as 'the sport of kings' had, in fact, evoked two reactions which were not only distinct but were antithetical. Both reactions proceeded from the common postulate that to fight for fun was shocking; but, while

[1] For War as 'the sport of kings' see IV. C (iii) (*b*) 3, pp. 143–9, above. For the 'lull' in the eighteenth century see V. C (ii) (*b*), vol. vi, pp. 315–16, below. The intimacy of the association between the two forms of 'Sport' with which our eighteenth-century Western kings amused themselves is commemorated in the name *chasseurs* or *Jäger* which is still borne by a number of regiments in the historic Continental European armies. The name is a reminder of the fact that, in the eighteenth century, the same footmen were employed as huntsmen and as soldiers, turn and turn about, to suit the convenience or the caprice of their royal masters.

[2] Letter, dated the 11th December, 1880, from Hellmuth von Moltke to Johann Kaspar Bluntschli, published in Bluntschli's *Gesammelte Kleine Schriften* (Nördlingen 1879–81, Beck, 2 vols.), vol. ii, p. 271.

one school of reformers took the line that an evil which had been turned into a sport both could and should be abolished altogether,[1] the other took the line that the evil could not be borne if it were not to be endured for a serious purpose. Thus, when the royal sportsmanship of the eighteenth century fell into a unanimous discredit, the nineteenth-century 'pacifists' found themselves confronted by a nineteenth-century brood of 'militarists' of von Moltke's type who were far more formidable than their frivolous eighteenth-century predecessors.

This quarrel over the reform of an eighteenth-century abuse between two opposing parties of nineteenth-century 'progressives' perhaps accounts for von Moltke's tone in the passage that we have quoted. In this *extravaganza* he is bidding defiance to contemporary 'pacifists'.

'It is when an institution no longer appears necessary, that fantastic reasons are sought or invented for satisfying the instinctive prejudice in its favour, which its long persistence has created. It is just the same with the sport of the hunter; you will find its most elaborate defence in very recent literature, precisely because what is now challenged was at an earlier period taken for granted.'[2]

In this contest between the 'pacifist' who seeks to abolish 'the sport of kings' and the 'militarist' who seeks to re-convert it into a serious business of the peoples, what are the omens to-day? We can hardly forbear to ask a question which may be the riddle of our Society's destiny; but the omens, as far as we can read them, are not at present reassuring. In our own day we see von Moltke's provocative thesis being adopted as one of the fundamental articles of their creed by the prophets of Fascism[3] and National-Socialism, and being accepted with enthusiasm by the masses whom these prophets have succeeded in converting to their faith. This so-called 'heroic' attitude towards life is being welcomed with open arms, and taken in deadly earnest, at this moment by millions of young men, and the reason why it appeals to them is manifest. They are greedy for the virtues in the form of 'the military virtues' because they have been starved of other kinds of spiritual bread, like the Prodigal Son who, when starved of human food, 'would

[1] For the tardiness of the development of this movement for the abolition of War see IV. C (iii) (*b*) 3, pp. 152–3, above.

[2] Mr. G. M. Gathorne-Hardy, in the letter quoted above.

[3] 'We are becoming—and shall become so increasingly, because this is our desire—a military nation. A militaristic nation, I will add, since we are not afraid of words. To complete this picture: warlike—that is to say, endowed ever to a higher degree with the virtues of obedience, sacrifice, and dedication to country' (Signor Mussolini, in a speech delivered on the 24th August, 1934, at the close of the Italian army manœuvres of that summer). 'War alone brings all human energies to their highest tension and sets a seal of nobility on the peoples who have the virtue to face it' (Mussolini: 'The Doctrine of Fascism' in the *Enciclopedia Italiana*, vol. xiv, no date [*circa* 1934]).

fain have filled his belly with the husks that the swine did eat'.[1] Moreover we know what these prodigals' spiritual sustenance used to be, and when their starvation began. These latter-day Western worshippers of 'the military virtues' are the epigoni of generations which were nurtured in 'the Christian virtues'; and they began to be starved of the traditional Christian morality, upon which their forebears had been brought up, when, at the turn of the eighteenth and nineteenth centuries, the unbelief of a cultivated minority in the Western World began to infect the less sophisticated masses.

The truth is that the spirit of Man abhors a spiritual vacuum; and, if a human being, or a human society, has the tragic misfortune to lose a sublime inspiration by which it has once been possessed, then, sooner or later, it will seize upon any other spiritual food that it can find—however coarse and unsatisfying this new fodder may be—rather than remain without any spiritual sustenance at all. In the light of this truth the recent spiritual history of our Western Society can be told—and the glorification of War can be explained—as follows: Owing to the breakdown of the Hildebrandine Papacy, which was the master-institution of our medieval Western Christendom, our Western *Plebs Christiana* received such a grievous moral shock that the Christian way of life, in which our forebears had been brought up, very largely lost its hold upon us;[2] and, finding ourselves, at the end of a series of calamities and disillusionments, with our house swept and garnished[3] by an intellectual *Aufklärung*, but untenanted by the Christian spirit that had formerly dwelt in it,[4] we cast about for other tenants to fill an agonizing spiritual void. In this search we addressed ourselves to the alternatives that lay nearest to our hand. Our Western culture had three sources—namely, the internal proletariat and the external proletariat and the dominant minority of the Hellenic Society to which our Western Society was 'affiliated'[5]—and when Christianity, which was the religious legacy of the Hellenic internal proletariat, appeared to fail us we turned hungrily to the religions of the Hellenic external proletariat and the Hellenic dominant minority. As it happened, these two religions were virtually the same; they were, both of them, variants of the primitive idolatrous worship of the tribe or state;[6] and therefore the

[1] Luke xv. 16. [2] On this point see IV. C (iii) (*c*) 3 (β), pp. 580–1, above.

[3] Matt. xii. 44 = Luke xi. 25.

[4] See V. C (i) (*d*) 6 (δ), Annex, vol. v, pp. 669–72, below.

[5] See I. C (i) (*a*), vol. i, pp. 52–62, above.

[6] It is strange that the creators of the Hellenic Civilization should have remained on the same religious level as the Teutonic barbarians in the no-man's-land beyond the northern frontiers of the Roman Empire; but we have seen (in I. C (i) (*b*), vol. i, pp. 95–100, above) that the Hellenes derived their religion, not from the Minoans who had created the culture to which Hellenism was 'affiliated', but from the Achaean barbarians who had eventually overrun a derelict Minoan World; and we have also seen (in II. D

modern Western apostate from Christianity, in his search after a new god, found the same idol awaiting his adoration in whichever of the two alternative directions he cast his eyes. Machiavelli consulting his Livy and Rousseau his Plutarch and De Gobineau his Sturlason and Hitler his Wagner were each led, by his respective literary or musical oracle, to the altar-steps of the same Abomination of Desolation: the Totalitarian Parochial State. In this pagan worship of the parochial community—be it Hellenic or Gothic or Scandinavian in its inspiration—the cult of 'the military virtues' is an obligatory practice, and the glorification of War a fundamental article of faith. And we can now understand why von Moltke exclaims, with a passion which is assuredly sincere, that 'Perpetual Peace is not even a beautiful dream,' and why he deprecates the abolition of War in a fear, which is manifestly genuine, lest the realization of the 'pacifist's' dream may simply plunge our neo-pagan world back again into a spiritual vacuum.

In fact, we may be driven to admit that von Moltke is right in taking this stand if he is right in his underlying assumption that modern Western Man is confined to a choice between two, and only two, alternatives. If we have really lost the power or the will to practise the virtues of Gethsemane, then it is certainly better to practise those of Sparta or Valhalla than to practise none at all. And in a *ci-devant*[1] Christian society this conclusion is no longer academic; for, in turning our conditional clause into the simple indicative, von Moltke is now being followed by the masses; and his disciples in our generation can claim, without fear of contradiction, that they have the big battalions on their side. The latter-day Western cult of 'the military virtues' as the Ten Commandments of a Totalitarian Parochial State is fast becoming the prevalent religion of the age; and this faith, archaistically[2] barbaric though it be, will never be overcome by the Mephistophelian spirit of sheer negation[3] against which it is itself a victorious protest. Societies are apt to get the religions, as well as the governments, that they deserve; and, if we have become unworthy of our Christian birthright, then we have condemned ourselves to worship the resuscitated ghost of an Odin or an Ares. This barbaric faith is better than none at all; in the deaths of a Leonidas and an Olaf Tryggvason the heroism which 'Militarism' inculcates has risen to

(vii), vol. ii, pp. 315–22, and in II. D (vii), Annex V, vol. ii, pp. 434–7, above) that these Achaean barbarians were the cultural kinsfolk of the Teuton barbarians who overran a derelict Hellenic World some eighteen centuries later.

[1] See I. B (iii), vol. i, p. 39, above.

[2] The expedient of Archaism, which is one of several alternative attempts to find a satisfactory response to the challenge of social disintegration, is examined in IV. C (i) (*d*) 8, vol. vi, pp. 49–97, below.

[3] 'Ich bin der Geist, der stets verneint!'—*Faust*, l. 1338, quoted already in II. C (ii) (*b*) 1, vol. i, p. 277, above.

the height of sublimity; but this is not the sublimity of the saints, and not a heroism which leads anywhere except to suicide. Witness the fates of the abortive Scandinavian Civilization and the arrested Spartan Civilization, which we have surveyed elsewhere.[1] And such will likewise be the fate of our Western Civilization if von Moltke is right in his underlying assumption of fact, as well as in his moral deduction from it. It remains to be seen whether this assumption is correct, or whether on the other hand Christianity, so far from being out of the running, has still the power to release the soul of *Homo Occidentalis* from the grip of a hideous and destructive paganism by offering him, once more, a higher positive alternative. Can Hildebrand arise again in his might to heal the wounds inflicted upon the souls of his flock by the sins of a Rodrigo Borgia and a Sinibaldo Fieschi?[2] This is the greatest of all the questions that have to be answered in our Western World in this twentieth century.

In following the clue that has been given us by von Moltke, and examining the hold which the worship of 'the military virtues' has been reacquiring over our Western souls in these latter days, we may find that we have made some progress towards solving our problem of whether the institution of War is intrinsically and irredeemably evil in itself. We have discovered, in effect, that the problem has been wrongly propounded. Perhaps the truth is that no created thing can ever be evil intrinsically and irredeemably, because no created thing is incapable of serving as a vehicle for the virtues that flow from the Creator. 'The military virtues' are virtues none the less for being jewels set in blood and iron; but the value lies in the jewels themselves and not in their horrible setting; and it is flying in the face of all experience to jump to the conclusion that the only place where we can ever hope to find these precious things is the slaughterhouse where they have happened to make their first epiphany to human eyes. The diamond that is secreted in the clay does not remain there, but finds a fitter setting in the crown of a king; and when once the diamond-mine has yielded up its treasure it ceases to be anything but a death-trap for the miner who cannot now tear himself away from the scene of his habitual toil and his accidental trove. What is true of the dross in which the diamond has lain buried is likewise true of the ephemeral institution of War in which an eternal principle of goodness has glimmered darkly for a season, in the guise of 'the military virtues', in order that it may shine out brightly hereafter in the perfect physical peace of the City of God. It is the divine

[1] In II. D (vii), vol. ii, pp. 340–60, and in Part III. A, vol. iii, pp. 50–79, above.
[2] See IV. C (iii) (c) 3 (β), pp. 583–4, above.

virtue—unchanging in itself, but always changing its temporal abode—that casts the reflexion of its own inner light upon each of its successive dwelling-places; and each of these dwelling-places assumes a derelict ugliness as soon as the temporarily indwelling spirit has ceased to lighten its darkness.

'There is hardly any occurrence or phenomenon about which we need always be of the same mind if we trace it back through the ages. That is, no evil was originally an evil, but only became so.... Many ... instances of things originally good, but which have outlived their purpose, could be quoted; and among them perhaps we might include War. Like everything which has life, War never remains stationary, but is always developing. Animals did not wage war, but human beings did, and our descendants—the "supermen", as Goethe and Nietzsche call them—will cease to do so.... The [institution of] War, with which history has acquainted us, was once born; it was young and now is old. But, just as the love of a maid seems to us lovely and that of an old woman repulsive, even so it is with War: we cannot and must not judge alike two things which from their very nature and meaning are wholly different. There is nothing whatever in common between Achilles' eternal Song of Hate and Lissauer's Hymn of Hate to England; and similarly there is the profoundest difference between the battles in the Scamander Valley and the fighting between the Meuse and the Moselle.'[1]

If we have persisted in the worship of War when the goodness which once found a genuine though inadequate expression in 'the military virtues' has been given an incomparably higher sphere for its exercise in the Christian life, then we have been guilty of that idolization of an ephemeral institution which is one form of the nemesis of creativity.[2] And our sin is aggravated if, after centuries spent in attempting the impossible feat of serving two masters, we have latterly held to the lower and despised the higher[3]—relapsing altogether into the service of Odin and Ares, and repudiating even that half-hearted service which was rendered to Christ by our forebears. This last state of paganism is vastly worse than the first;[4] for the deliberate and self-conscious perversity of von Moltke's and Mussolini's archaistic 'Militarism' is as different from the innocently archaic 'military virtues' of the Chevalier Bayard and Colonel Newcome as the dusk of evening is different from the gleam of dawn. The innocence which the Colonel inherited from the Chevalier can never be recaptured in our Western World by the heirs of Frederick's and Napoleon's cynicism. Colonel Newcome's own author was well aware, when he created this lovable character in the middle of the nineteenth century, that his creature's charm

[1] Nicolai, G. F.: *The Biology of War*, English translation (London 1919, Dent), pp. 420–1.

[2] See IV. C (iii) (c) 2 (β), pp. 303–423, above.

[3] Matt. vi. 24 = Luke xvi. 13.

[4] Matt. xii. 45 = Luke xi, 26.

and tragedy both owed something to the fact of his being already an anachronism. The devotees of a Mussolinian Mars Redivivus will not be Newcomes or Bayards; they will be Robots and Martians. This process of perversion, which is the Dead Sea fruit of an Idolatry mated with Archaism, is the exact reverse of that process of 'etherialization', and that progressive transference of the field of action from the Macrocosm to the Microcosm, in which, at an earlier point in this Study, we have discovered our criterion of growth.[1] If this criterion is the true one, it informs us *a priori* that the institution of War cannot be morally static. Granting that this gruesome institution has provided a field for the exercise of 'the military virtues' yesterday, we may be sure that to-morrow the 'chivalrous' kind of War will either rankle into a 'Militarism' without a vestige of virtue or beauty or else will be transfigured into a *militia Christi* in which the physical warfare of one man against another will have been translated into a spiritual warfare of all men united in the service of God against the powers of evil.

If our present apostasy proves only to be the last convulsion of a paganism *in articulo mortis*, and if this supreme crisis in the long-drawn-out struggle between paganism and Christianity is to end in paganism being driven completely off the field, we may dream of an age to come in which Physical War will have passed out of our life and faded out of our memory until the very word 'war' loses currency—as the kindred word 'sacrifice' has lost it already —except in a meaning which was originally a metaphor. In those days, when men speak of 'war', they will be referring to the war of the spirit; and if they are ever reminded of the physical warfare which was the constant scourge of their predecessors for some six or seven thousand years, they will think of it in the category of one of those cruel initiation rites to which *Homo Catechumenus* used to submit himself in order to win his way at last into a Communion of Saints in which the theatre of War has been transferred from an outward to an inward battlefield. The warfare of that perfect *Respublica Christiana* has been depicted with a poetic wealth of military imagery,[2] and has been described with the prophetic vision of sainthood,[3] by one of its citizens who came to proclaim the advent of the *Civitas Dei* many hundreds or thousands of years in advance. Saint Paul was delivering his message to the citizens of the war-stricken cities of a Hellenic universal state in an age of Hellenic history when the gleam of 'the military virtues' could still catch and captivate the eye from beneath the tarnish deposited by the 'Militarism' of a 'Time of Troubles'; and the Apostle seizes

[1] See III. C (i) (c) and (d), vol. iii, pp. 174–217, above.

[2] Eph. vi. 10–17.

[3] 2 Cor. x. 3–5.

upon all the noble and glorious connotations of War that still survive in his converts' minds in order to convey to them, in a chain of military metaphors, the more etherial glory and nobility of the Christian life.

'Though we walk in the flesh, we do not war after the flesh (for the weapons of our warfare are not carnal, but mighty through God to the pulling down of strong holds): casting down imaginations, and every high thing that exalteth itself against the knowledge of God, and bringing into captivity every thought to the obedience of Christ.'[1]

Additional Note

Perhaps the considerations set out above may partially meet the following criticism of an earlier part of this Study which the author has received from Mr. G. F. Hudson of All Souls College, Oxford:

'What troubled me in my reading of the chapters on "Challengc-and-Response" was the fear that too much emphasis on the role of hard conditions in producing Civilization may work in favour of the "heroic" Nazi idea, which I am sure is the last thing you would wish! The advocates of unrestricted economic competition and of *Machtpolitik* have always urged that their kind of world makes for progress and high achievement, while a humanitarian social and international order would lead to stagnation and futility. It seems to me essential to distinguish between the *value* of different kinds of responses and to differentiate a type of challenge presented by power and wealth from that presented by hardship and oppression. Challenges of the latter kind bring responses that are primarily economic and military, and along with great achievement in these fields goes an outlook which tends to be harsh, brutal and "uncivilized" by the finer standards of Civilization (cf. in various ways

[1] The following comment on this passage from the Second Epistle of Saint Paul to the Corinthians has been communicated to the writer of this Study by Mr. G. M. Gathorne-Hardy:

'Saint Paul's great picture of the Christian in Ephesians is rendered attractive by being dressed in all the panoply of War; and herein, to my mind, lies the true significance of the passage of 2 Corinthians which you quote at the end of this section. The stress is by no means on the renunciation of fleshly warfare, but on the substitution of something more terribly effective. This is how it runs in Moffatt's translation:

'"My mind is made up to tackle certain people who have made up their minds that I move on the low level of the flesh. I do live in the flesh, but I do not make war *as the flesh does*; the weapons of my warfare are not weapons of the flesh, but divinely strong to demolish fortresses—I demolish theories and any rampart thrown up to resist the knowledge of God, I take every project prisoner to make it obey Christ, I am prepared to court-martial any one who remains insubordinate, once your submission is complete."

'The striking thing here is the sustained use of a military metaphor, as calculated to appeal to man's noblest instincts. Had St. Paul shared the views of the modern "pacifist" with regard to war, or had his hearers done so, the metaphor would sound absurd. It is easy to test this. "The poison with which I seek my ends is not carnal", or "I do not use an earthly 'jemmy' to crack the heavenly crib!" The meaning would be the same, but the argument would lose its appeal. No, St. Paul's constant use of military metaphor signifies that in his day warfare was regarded as a noble and glorious occupation.'

At the same time this use of military metaphor in the Epistles of Saint Paul is the first step—and a long step—towards a transfiguration of the word 'War' from a physical to a spiritual meaning.

Rome, Prussia and the North British, Yankee Puritan, Industrial response). But success in the economic and military responses inevitably brings wealth and power: i.e. it eliminates the conditions which gave rise to the civilization; and the challenge now to be met is that of success itself. If such success must bring degeneration, the only remedy is to retain the adverse conditions, or some discipline equivalent to them, artificially. But this introduces a contradiction into human effort, for every response to a challenge is a genuine effort to overcome that challenge. The response to the challenge of the American wilderness was Chicago, but the success of the response eliminates the wilderness. Thus the problems of modern America are of quite a different kind from those of the Frontier Age, and the idea of some Americans (expressed in a film *The World Changes*, which you may have seen) that Industrialism has been all a mistake, and that America can only save her soul by getting back to subsistence-farming, is in fact a counsel of despair, for logically it implies that all Man's effort to conquer Nature and increase wealth is self-defeating. The answer, however, appears to be given by the histories of two places which you quote as examples—Athens and Venice. In both cases a community not favoured by Nature compensates itself and grows great by trade. But in both cases it is only *after* the economic problems have been solved, and the hardships of living on the "thin soil of Attica" or the Lido mudflats have long been forgotten, that the cities make their great contributions to Civilisation in the higher sense. Athens and Venice were "sitting on the top of the World" and no longer grappling with "hard countries" when they produced Sophocles and Plato, Giorgione and Titian. It is, I contend, harder to live well in Capua than to cross the Alps; and to suggest that Capua represents the absence of challenge, and emphasize material hardship as a spur to creation, is to weigh down the scales against the finer intellectual and aesthetic and "Epicurean" development of Civilization in favour of Spartans, Puritans, "strong men", "go-getters", "militarists", Cato and Herr von Papen (who have quite enough of the game already!).'

ANNEX TO IV. C (iii) (*c*) 3 (β)

INNOCENT III'S RESPONSE TO THE CHALLENGE OF CATHARISM

AT two points in this Part of the present Study[1] we have touched upon the connexion between Pope Innocent III's proclamation of a martial crusade against the Albigensian Cathars and his approval of the spiritual movements that were being initiated in Western Christendom at the time by Saints Dominic and Francis. Innocent's approval of the spiritual revival within the bosom of the Church was as lukewarm as his recourse to the sword against the heretics was half-hearted; and this lukewarmness in a good cause will perhaps more than offset the half-heartedness in a bad cause when we are appraising Lotario de' Conti's spiritual worth as a human being. If, however, we mercifully allow that great Pope the easier option of being judged, not as a man, but merely as a statesman, we shall find evidence of statesmanship of an exceedingly high order in the dual policy which Innocent worked out and applied as his solution for the problem of Catharism. The nature of this policy has been clarified in an illuminating work from the pen of a modern Western scholar.[2]

The problem of Catharism was even graver than that of the relations between the Spiritual and the Temporal Power which confronted the Western Church in the same age. The two problems had both presented themselves in the course of the eleventh century, and their common root was the corruption of the Western Church in general, and the Papacy in particular, in the immediately preceding period of Western history.[3] This scandal provoked the simultaneous attacks which the Western Church sustained at the hands of the heretics and of the secular powers respectively. Both attacks were formidable, but the heretics' onslaught was the more dangerous of the two because it had a longer reach. While the secular powers did not look beyond one or other of the alternative aims of exploiting the Church or reforming it, the Cathars threatened to destroy it by proclaiming principles which shook the Church's existing structure to the foundations.

The crucial issue between these converts to an Oriental heresy and the authorities of a Western Church against which they were

[1] In IV. C (iii) (*c*) 2 (β), pp. 369–71, and IV. C (iii) (*c*) 3 (β), pp. 558–60 and 562, above.

[2] Grundmann, H.: *Religiöse Bewegungen im Mittelalter* (Berlin 1935, Ebering).

[3] For this corruption see IV. C (iii) (*c*) 2 (β), pp. 370–1, and IV. C (iii) (*c*) 3 (β), pp. 521–3 and 551–2, above.

in revolt was not the Christological dispute between a Paulician 'Adoptionism' and an Orthodox 'Conceptionism'.[1] Still less was it the more general theological issue between a Manichaean dualism which was attributed to the heretics by the Catholics *a priori*[2] and a monism which the Catholics professed in theory without always managing to avoid the pitfall of dualism in their own theological speculations when they were off their guard. The principles over which the medieval Western battle between orthodoxy and heresy was fought were not matters of theology at all, but were matters of practical life.

'The notion of Christian poverty and of living the Apostolic life of the itinerant preacher is the essential content of the heresy [which made its appearance in Western Christendom in the eleventh century]. This is so at Cologne as well as in the South of France; and this notion always continued in fact to be the principal *motif* of the heresy, among Cathars and Waldensians alike, down to the beginning of the thirteenth century. To lead the life of the Apostles and to be their true successors is the gist of the heretics' claim; and it was this claim that brought about their breach with the Church. . . . [Theological] speculations retire quite into the background in face of what was really the principal question—the question whether the true Church of Christ is to be found among those who claim for themselves the Apostolic Succession and, with it, the exclusive and effective authority to confer all ecclesiastical orders, or whether, on the contrary, it is to be found among those who live as the Apostles lived and as the Gospel demands.'[3]

These two evangelical ideals of the Apostolic life and a voluntary poverty made a powerful appeal to the *Plebs Christiana* of the Western World in the second chapter of Western history: in the first place because at this time and place these ideals had the charm of novelty;[4] in the second place because they shone out so dazzlingly against the dark foil of current conduct in the life of the Established Church; and in the third place because the advocates of this new evangelicalism were impressive practisers of what they were preaching. The Cathars were not disgruntled proletarians[5] who, under a show of piety, were seeking—even if only half-consciously—to reduce their more prosperous neighbours to a level of poverty above which they themselves had no hope of rising. Catharism was not a protest against the experience of poverty; it was a revulsion from the experience of wealth.[6] Waldes, for

1 For the distinction between an 'Adoptionist' and a 'Conceptionist' version of Christianity see IV. C (iii) (c) 2 (β), Annex III, above, and V. C (ii) (a), in vol. vi, pp. 267–75, below.

2 See the passage quoted from Grundmann in IV. C (iii) (c) 2 (β), Annex III, p. 628, footnote 8 (on p. 629), above.

3 Grundmann, op. cit., pp. 21 and 25–6.

4 Ibid., p. 15.

5 Ibid., pp. 29 and 157.

6 Ibid., pp. 58–9, 168–9, and 194–5.

example, the eponymous founder of the Waldenses, was a rich man who had made his fortune by usury.[1] And, while some of the heretics were uneducated (*rusticani*),[2] the cultivated and well-to-do element predominated.[3] Clerics and nobles, but never proletarians, are expressly mentioned as joining their ranks, and the legal profession was well represented among them.[4] It was the self-imposed rules of these religious communities, and not any involuntary circumstances in the previous state of life of their members, that debarred them from retaining wealth and from accumulating it;[5] and, if their preachers acquired the name of weavers, this was because they were preachers-turned-weavers (on the model of Saint Paul), not weavers-turned-preachers.[6]

When the rich and noble thus embraced an evangelical poverty for Christ's sake, this was a sure sign of the genuineness of their religious conviction.[7] The potency of their preaching was proportionate to the degree of their own personal sacrifice. This was a movement which the medieval Western Established Church could not afford either to flout or to ignore. Yet the first reaction of the Church to Catharism was aridly negative. When the ecclesiastical authorities found that they could not snuff Catharism out by giving it the bad name of Manichaeism, they denounced the Cathars on the better substantiated grounds that they were setting up a Counter-Church and that their programme of going back to the Gospels involved the abandonment of a number of vital Catholic institutions.[8] Even when the authorities did not set themselves to suppress the heresy by force, they refused the heretics permission to put their evangelical ideals into practice. For instance, when in A.D. 1179 the Waldenses petitioned the Roman Curia for licence to live their Apostolic life, they were refused the right to preach after being put through a mere travesty of an examination.[9] Such levity and lack of vision in high places, of course, merely confirmed, instead of refuting, the heretics' indictment of the Church, and accelerated the progress of the heresy instead of retarding it.

This was the state of affairs as Innocent III found it on his accession; and the policy that he devised for dealing with it is his chief title to be regarded as a great pontiff.

'The decisive turn in the relations between the hierarchical Church and the religious movement was taken during the pontificate of Innocent III. Until then the religious movement had grown, through its own native forces, outside the Church and in increasing opposition to it—

1 Grundmann, op. cit., p. 161.
2 Ibid., p. 29.
3 Ibid., p. 167.
4 Ibid., pp. 34–5, 159–61, 162, 165–6.
5 Ibid., pp. 159–61.
6 Ibid., pp. 32–4.
7 Ibid., op. cit., p. 38.
8 Ibid., pp. 23–4.
9 Ibid., pp. 59–61.

while the Curia had neglected (apart from the relatively trivial attempts at the beginning of the twelfth century) to look for ways of creating a field of activity inside the Church for the new forms of religious life: voluntary poverty and itinerant preaching. All efforts to secure ecclesiastical recognition for these forms of life had been answered by the Church with a veto and with an instruction that any transgression of this veto was to be punished as heresy. But at the same time the Church lacked both the means and the energy to enforce this veto in practice and to suppress the religious movement effectively.

'This was the strained situation which Innocent III found when he mounted the Papal Throne at the beginning of 1198. In this situation he did not immediately intervene with a definite comprehensive programme; and in fact he never attempted to transform the situation on uniform and radical lines by taking systematic creative measures. On the other hand, from the beginning of his pontificate until his death, in all the measures which the Curia felt itself obliged to take *vis-à-vis* the religious movement and the heresy, Innocent steadfastly and unwaveringly maintained a position, and pursued aims, which betokened a fundamental departure from the policy of his predecessors. He sought to bridge the gulf between the religious movement and the hierarchical Church by conceding to the demands for Apostolic itinerant preaching and for evangelical poverty a possibility of finding scope for action inside the Church—but this only on condition that the orthodox doctrine was not tampered with and that the Papal and hierarchical authority received an unqualified recognition. By this policy he compelled the devotees of the evangelical life, voluntary poverty and Apostolic preaching to make the choice between the Church and heresy—without maintaining the previous ruling that allegiance to the Roman Church should imply a renunciation of the ideals of the religious movement. On the other side he showed an uncompromising severity, and brought into action all the forces and the means at his command, in combating heresy in so far as it refused to accept, in consideration of these concessions, its own reincorporation into the ecclesiastical order. And finally he enlisted for this struggle against heresy precisely those circles which shared with the heretics their participation in the religious movement but which had duly consented to be incorporated into the society of the Catholic Church. This policy resulted on the one hand in the formation of a series of communities, congregations and orders (the mendicant orders, above all) in which the movement for religious poverty found its ecclesiastically recognized orthodox expressions, while on the other hand it produced the new ways of combating heresy: the Albigensian War and later the Inquisition. This does not mean that Innocent either created or even willed these new structures and new methods. The living forces that led to them had not proceeded from him, and he had no part or lot in them. His policy was not the expression of a religious conversion of the governing element in the Church; it sprang from a clear insight into the Church's tasks *vis-à-vis* the religious movement of the age—a movement that could never be mastered by mere vetos and condemnations without any constructive work on the Church's part. Innocent III did not experience in himself the religious forces of his time, but he did recognize their existence; and he has to his credit the important achievement of having known how to incorporate these forces into the hierarchical Church and having exercised the cleverness and the tact, the foresight and the energy, that were requisite for this task. Thereby he not only averted the danger that the hierarchical Church might irretrievably cut itself off from the living religious forces of that age; he also smoothed the path and pointed the way for the reformation of the Christian life in the Catholic Church of the thirteenth century. His policy decided that the formless fermentation of the religious movement should succeed in bringing forth the great new orders and ordinances.'[1]

If Innocent had not adopted this policy in his Roman Curia, Francis in his Umbrian city-state might have been driven out of the Church's fold into the Cathars' wilderness. Both Francis himself and Bernard of Quintavalle came from just the same social milieu as Waldes;[2] the first generation of Franciscans, like their Cathar contemporaries, were mainly drawn from the well-to-do bourgeoisie and the nobility and the clergy;[3] and they were mistaken for heretics on their first appearance in France.[4] This affinity between Franciscanism and Catharism in respect of their common virtue of unworldliness enabled the spirit of Saint Francis to prevail over the spirit of Waldes and Bogomil-Theophilus and Constantine-Silvanus and Paul of Samosata when the Western Church had signally failed to quell this alien spirit by calumny and obstructiveness and violence. And on this showing we must conclude that, while Francis might never have been given the scope for doing his work within the bosom of the Church if it had not been for Innocent, it is equally improbable that Innocent's dual policy would have been blessed with success if it had not been for Saint Francis and Saint Dominic. If this is our conclusion, we shall be more than ever at a loss to understand the apparent superciliousness of Innocent's bearing towards Francis at his first encounter with this heaven-sent executant of the worldly will of a hard-pressed ecclesiastical statesman.

1 Grundmann, op. cit., pp. 70–2. Compare pp. 10–11.
2 Ibid., p. 164.
3 Ibid., p. 165.
4 Ibid., p. 154.